AMERICAN WATER
RESOURCES ADMINISTRATION

YANG-CH'ENG SHIH

Volume II

BOOKMAN ASSOCIATES, INC.
New York

CONTENTS

VOLUME II

Man belongs not only to his family, his
profession, his community, his province
and his country, but also to the world.

CHAPTER 3

STATE ADMINISTRATION

Article 1   Regulation

Section 1   Navigation Improvement

(a) Protection of navigation channels---In Rhode Island,
the Division of Harbors and Rivers of the Department of Public Works (originally the Board of Harbor Commissioners) has
the authority "to prosecute for, and to cause to be removed,
all unauthorized obstructions and encroachments" in navigable
waters, and to "regulate the depositing of mud, dirt or other
substances" therein (General Laws of Rhode Island, ch. 112,
secs. 9 and 10: Laws 1876, ch. 556, sec. 3; rewritten as L.
1877, ch. 611 secs. 1 and 2; not since amended). Similar statutory provisions are found in a few other states; but in
these provisions the main form of obstruction is the dam built
across a navigable waterway. They will be discussed in Section 5 of this Article below.

(b) Regulation of water terminals---This exists in thirteen states, and is separable into two types as follows:

First type: Licenses or permits for the construction of
            water terminals are required (permissive)---
            Pennsylvania, New Jersey, Connecticut (for
            Bridgeport only),(1907), Montana (1914) (par-
            tial), Minnesota, (1939), Kentucky, New York
            (1928).
Second type: In addition to the permissive licensing regu-
            tion, the state marks out harbor lines (direc-
            tive) --- Rhode Island, Illinois, Alabama,
            Washington (disguised as a measure of the
            state enterprise of land management), Iowa
            (1927), Massachusetts (1872).

First-type States

(1) Pennsylvania (for the Delaware River System only)---Li-
censes of the commissioners of navigation for the Delaware
River system are required for the construction, extension or
alteration of wharves or piers, bridges or other harbor structures (Statutes, tit. 55, sec. 6: P. L. 496 of 1907, sec. 7;
as last amended by P. L. 1960 of 1937, no. 385, sec. 4).
no. 385, sec. 4).

(2) New Jersey---Plans for the construction or alteration of
docks, wharves, piers, bulkheads, bridges, pipe lines, cables
or other similar or dissimilar water-front developments upon
navigable rivers or streams must be approved by the state department of conservation and economic development (Revised

Statutes of New Jersey, tit. 12, ch. 5, sec. 3: Laws 1914, ch.
125, sec. 4). It may be noted that each such approval is a
permit.

(3) Connecticut (for Bridgeport only)---Anyone intending to
build in the port and harbor of Bridgeport "any bridge, wharf,
pier or dam, or the filling in of any flats, or the driving
of any piles below high-water mark shall, before beginning
such work, give written notice to "the harbor master of said
port (a state officer). "No such wharf shall be commenced
until the plan and the mode of performing the same is approved
. . . by the harbor master . . . . All such works shall be
executed under the supervision of said harbor master" (General
Statutes of Connecticut, sec. 4748, subsec. (b), enacted 1939).

(4) Montana (partial licensing)---The law gives a general
license to all owners of lands riparian upon navigable waters
to construct docks and wharves over, across and upon submerged lands, which are state property. Such license, however,
conveys no title to such submerged lands, and "may be revoked
by the State of Montana at any time." The authority of the
state in this matter is exercised by the state railroad commission (Laws 1909, ch. 38). The administrative licensing
authority is partial and incomplete in that the responsible
administrative agency does not issue, but merely revokes, the
licenses. It may also be noted that non-riparian parties are
not licensed by law to build wharves and docks on navigable
waters.

(5) Minnesota---"The commissioner (of conservation), subject
to the approval of the county board, shall have power to grant
permit . . . to establish, construct, maintain and control
wharves, docks, piers, levees, breakwaters, basins, canals and
hangers in or adjacent to public waters of the state, except
within the corporate limits of cities or villages" (Minnesota
Statutes, sec. 105.42, 2nd para.: Laws 1947, ch. 142, sec. 6,
2nd para.).

(6) New York---The construction, reconstruction or maintenance
of docks, piers, wharves and other landing places must be approved by an order of the superintendent of public works. But
this regulation does not apply to facilities maintained by the
department of docks, if any, in a city of over 175,000 population. He may also order the repair of a structure when it is
found in an unsafe condition (Conservation Law, sec. 948: Laws
1928, ch. 242; as amended by L. 1940, ch. 651).

Second-type States

(1) Massachusetts---The department of public works may prescribe harbor lines after a hearing in any harbor in the state,
but they are effective only when approved by the state legislature (General Court) (General Laws of Massachusetts, ch. 91,

sec. 34: Acts 1866, ch. 149, sec. 3; as last amended by Acts
1930, ch. 99, sec. 2). Within such lines, the said department may license the construction or extension of wharves,
piers, seawalls, roads, bridges, pipelines, conduits, dams
and other structures. Pipelines and conduits, when entirely
built underground, may extend beyond the harbor lines (ibid.,
sec. 14: Acts 1872, ch. 236, secs. 1; 2; as last amended by
Acts 1931, ch. 426, sec. 206).

(2) Rhode Island---The division of harbors and rivers of the
state department of public works marks, and the governor,
with the consent of the senate, approves, harbor lines "to be
established in any of the public tide waters of the state.
Except authorized by statute, no one can build in such waters
any bridge, wharf, pier or other structure until authority
is given and plans are approved by the said division. (General
Laws, ch. 112, secs. 8 and 11: Acts 1876, ch. 556; as last
amended by Acts 1918, ch. 1665).

(3) Illinois---(1) The Department of Public Works and Buildings lays out and fix "shore or harbor lines" in all watercourses (Revised Statutes, ch. 19, sec. 71, para. 2: L. 1911,
p. 115, sec. 24; as last amended by L. 1919, p. 972).[2] (2)
The said Department, with the approval of the Governor, issues
permits for the construction of all terminal facilities in
the channels of navigable watercourses and their tributaries,
and may abate unauthorized structures at the expense of their
owners or operators or order the latter to make necessary modifications or repairs (ibid., sec. 65: L. 1911, p. 115, sec.
18; as last amended by L. 1945, p. 380).

(4) Alabama---The state department of state docks and terminals "may establish harbor lines, exterior and interior, when
not in conflict with similar lines established by the United
States. The department is hereby empowered to grant licenses
in the name of the state to any riparian owner (emphasis added)
for the construction of wharves, booms and other aids to navigation when such wharves, booms or aids are appurtenant to
his upland" (Code of Alabama, tit. 38, sec. 39: Acts 1927, p.1).

(5) Washington (disguised)---In Washington, there is no administrative regulation over the construction of wharves and
docks, but such regulation exists at the levels of counties
and municipalities. However, as a measure of the state enterprise of land management, the state board of land commissioners
locates and establishes "harbor lines beyond which the state
shall never sell or lease any rights whatever", and determines
"the width of the harbor area between such harbor lines and
the line of ordinary high tide, which shall be forever reserved for landings, wharves, streets and other conveniences of
navigation and commerce" (Revised Code of Washington, sec. 43.-
65.040: L. 1927, ch. 255, secs. 11 and 105). Thus the establishment of harbor lines by the state land board is at once an

enterprise and a regulation measure. A <u>lease</u> of submerged
lands by the said board is, technically speaking, an enterprise activity pure and simple. However, the procedure and
conditions of a lease is such that in a practical sense it
amounts to a license.[3]

(6) <u>Iowa</u>---The state conservation commission, under an act
of 1927 (ch. 40), (a) may grant permits for the construction
of "any pier, wharf, sluice, piling, wall, fence, obstruction,
building or erection of any kind upon or over any state-owned
land or water"; and (b) may "prohibit, restrict or order the
removal thereof, when in the judgment of said commission it
will be for the best interest of the public." Should the
owner or operator of the structure refuse or fail to remove
it upon the order of the commission, it may be removed by the
commission at his cost. Under this law, the conservation
commission merely issues permits, but does not mark harbor
lines. However, the provision for the removal of structures
serves the same purpose as do the harbor lines.

Section 2 Flood Control and Drainage

    In most if not all of the states, it would seem, the gov-
ernor has the authority of declaring flood emergency and taking necessary measures to save lives and property of citizens.
For example, on 21 November 1950 the governor of California
"declared the existence of a state of emergency in the Sacramento and San Joaquin Valleys as nine days of heavy rains and
melting snows continued to overtax streams and put thousands
of California residents to flight" and "ordered all state
facilities placed at the disposal of stricken areas while ref-
ugees, evacuated by National Guardsmen and local authorities,
poured into Red Cross emergency headquarters."[4] During the
flood of May-June 1953, which was the greatest flood recorded
in the northern part of the state, the governor of Montana
declared a state of emergency in fourteen counties of north-
western Montana.[5] In at least one state, namely, Oregon, this
authority of the governor is expressly provided in statute.
As provided in an act of 5 May 1950 (ch. 574), the governor
of Oregon, when a certain area is endangered by floods, earth-
quakes and other disasters, may declare such area to be an
"emergency disaster area" for a period to be designated by
him. In such area, he is further authorized, among other
things, "to close all roads and highways . . . to traffic or
by his order to limit the travel on such roads to such extent
as he shall deem necessary and expedient", and "to require the
aid and assistance of any state or other public or quasi-public
agencies in the performance of the duties and work attendant
upon the emergency conditions in such area."

    Flood-plain zoning is a very desirable regulatory measure
which can be taken by the states toward the elimination of
flood damages.[6] The Flood Control Zoning Act of the state of

Washington (Revised Code, ch. 86.16: Laws 1935, ch. 159; as
amended by L. 1939, ch. 85) is an outstanding example of such
regulation. According to the provisions of this act, the
state supervisor of flood control, after notice and hearing,
may establish flood-control zones in areas subject to flood
damages and issue permits for the construction and operation
of all works and structures affecting flood waters in these
zones. As of March 1954, sixteen flood-control zones had
been established and three hundred and thirteen permits issued. ". . . Once a zone is established its existence is permanent;" and "a large portion of the permits are issued in
perpetuity for permanent structures."[7]

In Iowa a law was enacted in 1949 (ch. 203) establishing
the Iowa Natural Resources Council. It authorizes the said
Council to establish, by order and after hearing, "a floodway as a Council Floodway and alter, change, or revoke and
terminate the same. In the order, . . . the Council shall
fix the length thereof at any practical distance, and fix the
width or the landside limits thereof so as to include portions
of the flood plains adjoining the channel, which, with the
channel, are reasonably required to efficiently carry and discharge the flood waters or flood flow of such river or stream."
"The Council shall avoid to the greatest possible degree the
evacuation of persons residing the area of any floodway and
the removal of any residential structures occupied by such
persons in the area of floodway." This provision, it would
seem, is a measure of flood-plain zoning, as the Council floodways are in effect flood-control zones. As of January 1954,
this provision "has not been invoked . . . . There are definite engineering, legal, and administrative problems which
must be resolved before a satisfactory method of floodway determination can be made."[8]

Another regulatory measure is the regulation of flood-
control works. The laws of Indiana and Iowa are typical examples. In Indiana:

> . . . No individual, partnership, association, corp-
> oration or political subdivision of this State shall
> construct or install or undertake any work of any
> nature whatever which is designed to regulate or
> control the streams or other waters of this State
> for the purpose of preventing floods caused by ex-
> cessive precipitation or otherwise, unless such
> plans shall first have been submitted to and approv-
> ed by the Department of Conservation and are found
> to be feasible and such as will ultimately consti-
> tute a part of an integrated plan for the entire
> state or any designated watershed thereof, and
> which will not prove disadvantageous to any other
> section or sections of this State . . . (Statutes,
> sec. 60-736: Acts 1937, ch. 230, sec. 1).

In sec. 31 of the above-mentioned 1949 act of Iowa, it is also
provided that "all works of any nature for flood control in
this state, which are hereafter established and constructed,
shall be coordinated in design, according to sound and accepted engineering practice so as to effect the best flood control obtainable throughout the state", and that all such
works, to be installed and constructed either by a private
or by a public party, must be approved by the above-mentioned
Natural Resources Council after hearing, whether such works
function in the sole interest of flood control or merely serve
this purpose collaterally with or incidentally to other purpose or purposes. Similar measures have also been found in
Kansas, Kentucky and Minnesota. In Kansas, an act of 1931
(ch. 184, sec. 1)9 provides that permission of the Division
of Water Resources of the State Board of Agriculture must be
obtained before any landowner constructs a levee or a dike
to protect his lands against floods, except when the said
levee or dike is built on his own lands. In Kentucky, under
the provisions of an act of 1948 (ch. 229, sec. 2), plans and
specifications for the construction of "any levee, dike, bridge,
fill, embankment or other obstruction across or along any
stream" must be approved by the Flood Control and Water Usage
Board of the Department of Conservation, whether such works
are built by a private person or by a local governmental unit.
In Minnesota, under the above-mentioned law of 1937, as amended, permits of the Department of Conservation are required for
the construction of levees and other flood-control works.

In Wisconsin laws, there is an interesting provision which
is designed to preserve the flood-carrying capacity of a watercourse (which is also its navigable capacity if it is navigable), which reads:

> It shall be unlawful to deposit any material or to
> place any structure upon the bed of any navigable
> water where no shore line has established or beyond
> such shore line where the same has been established,
> provided, however, that the Public Service Commis-
> sion may grant to any riparian owner the right to
> build a structure, or to maintain a structure al-
> ready built and now existing, for his own use, if
> the same does not materially obstruct navigation,
> or reduce the effective flood flow capacity of the
> stream or is not detrimental to public interest
> (Statutes, sec. 30.02(1)(b), 1st sent.: Laws 1905,
> ch. 270, sec. 2; as last amended by L. 1951, ch.
> 712, sec. 1).

This provision is supplemented by another provision, which requires "all slash, which during the process of cutting timber
or taking out other forest products, falls into or is deposited in any lake or stream" to be "immediately removed therefrom by the timber owner or cutting operator conducting the

operations when in the opinion of the (Conservation) Commission such removal is in the public interest. If such slash is not removed within thirty days, the Commission may do the work and the landowner, timber owner or cutting operator responsible for such slash shall be liable to the state jointly, severally or individually for the cost of such work. . ." (Statutes, sec. 26.12(6)(d): L. 1931, ch. 128; as last amended by L. 1951, ch. 77).

Under the laws of Illinois, it is the duty of the Department of Public Works and Buildings "to prevent the carrying capacity of streams to be limited and impaired by fills, deposits, obstructions, encroachments therein . . . to an extent where the same cannot safely dispose of the flood waters which may naturally, lawfully and properly be discharged therein . . ." No persons or agencies can make any fill, deposit or encroachment in or on a watercourse until plans and specifications therefor are approved and permits are issued by the said Department. The said Department is also authorized to order the removal of any deposit or structure in or on a watercourse that is found impairing or endangering its flood-carrying capacity, and the operation of dams in the light of the disposal of flood waters (Revised Statutes, ch. 19, sec. 70: L. 1911, p. 115, sec. 23; as last amended by L. 1941, p. 282).

Akin to the Illinois regulation is the provision in sec. 19 of the above-discussed Iowa law of 1949, which authorizes the Natural Resources Council "to remove or eliminate any structure, dam, obstruction, deposit or excavation in any floodway (i.e., a watercourse with special reference to its flood-carrying function) which adversely affects the efficiency of or unduly restricts the capacity of the floodway, by an action in condemnation, and in assessing the damages in such proceeding . . ." The person responsible for any such obstruction, though not required to do so, may request the said Council to make an order determining the effect of such obstruction upon the flood situation and permitting or prohibiting the same accordingly (para. 3). This measure virtually amounts to a permit system operated on what may be called a voluntary or an automatic basis. Its effectiveness seems to lie midway between the ordinary compulsory permit system and prohibitive administration.

An interesting type of flood-control regulation, which is administered by courts rather than regular administrative agencies, is found in the following provision in the laws of Washington:[10]

> Ten or more owners of real property abutting on a meandered lake (but not on a stream or river) may petition the superior court of the county in which the lake is situated, for an order to provide

for the regulation of the outflow of the lake in
order to maintain a certain water level therein in
the interests of flood control, and the court,
after hearing, is authorized to make an order fix-
ing the water level thereof and directing the supervisor (of water resources, State Department of Conservation and Development) to regulate the outflow
therefrom for the purpose of maintaining the water
level so fixed: Provided, That this section shall
not apply to any meandered lake or reservoir used
for the storage of water for irrigation or other
beneficial purposes, or to lakes navigable from
the sea (Revised Code, sec. 90.24.010: Laws 1939,
ch. 107, sec. 2).

The purpose of this regulation seems to be the utilization of
a meandered lake as a flood-control reservoir serving, in particular, to protect the riparian lands.

In the field of drainage, a New York statute of 1918 (as
amended:) provides that all drainage works must be approved
by the Department of Conservation. In none of the other
states is there any state regulation on drainage.[11]

Section 3 Water Supply and Water Conservation

Subsection 1 Water Supply

The most common and the most important measure of state
water-supply regulation is the issuance of permits for or the
approval of plans of the construction of all public and private water-supply systems or works. The following states issue
such permits:

Kansas (1907)---General Statutes, sec. 65-163 (Laws 1907, ch.
            382, sec. 3; as last amended by L. 1943, ch.
            219, sec. 1).
Michigan(1913)--Compiled Laws, sec. 325.203 (Acts 1913, No.98,
            sec. 5)
Virginia(1916)--Code, sec. 62-50 (Acts 1916, ch. 360, sec. 5).
Oklahoma(1917)--Statutes, tit. 63, sec. 613 (L. 1917, ch. 166,
            sec. 3).
Alabama(1919)---Code, tit. 22, sec. 136 (Acts 1919, No. 658,
            sec. 15, subdiv. 4).
Missouri(1919)--Statutes, sec. 199.200 (L. 1919, p. 371, sec.
            3).
Pennsylvania
  (1923)---------Statutes, tit. 32, sec. 593 (L. 1923, No. 294,
            sec. 3).
North Dakota
  (1937)---------Revised Code, sec. 61-0221 (L. 1937, ch. 255,
            sec. 9; as last amended by L. 1953, ch. 256,
            sec. 2).

California------Health and Safety Code, sec. 4010 et seq.
(1947)   (Stats. 1947, ch. 992, sec. 1; as last amend-
                ed by Stats. 1949, ch. 1550, sec. 6).

In the following states, plans of construction should be approved by the state before the commencement of construction:

New York(1905)--Conservation Law, sec. 521 (L. 1905, ch. 723,
                sec. 2; as last amended by L. 1928, ch. 242,
                sec. 31).
New Jersey(1909)Statutes, sec. 58:11-2 (L. 1909, ch. 253, sec.
                2), sec. 58:11-3 (ibid., sec. 3) and sec. 26:
                1A-37, subdivi.(i) (L. 1947, ch. 177, sec.37).
Connecticut-----General Statutes, sec. 4016 (Acts 1915, ch.
(1915)   306; as amended in 1935).
Wisconsin(1919)-Statutes, sec. 144.04 (L. 1919, ch. 447, sec.
                2; as last amended by L. 1949, ch. 529).
Wyoming(1923)---Compiled Statutes, sec. 63-204 (L. 1923, ch.
                92, sec. 4).
Massachusetts---General Laws, ch. 40, sec. 39C (Acts 1938, ch.
(1938)   172, sec. 3).
Tennessee(1945)-Code, sec. 5826.2 (Acts 1945, ch. 52, sec. 2).
Texas (1945)----Revised Civil Statutes, art. 4477-1 (L. 1945,
                ch. 178), sec. 12(a).
Indiana(1949)---Statutes, sec. 35-2903: Acts 1949, ch. 157,
                sec. 1752).
Illinois(1951)--Revised Statutes, ch. 111.5, sec. 121a et seq.
                (L. 1951, p. 2091).

The state agency in charge of this permissive measure is
the "State Health Department" (generic) in all these states
except:

1. New Jersey, where the responsible agency is the Divi-
    sion of Water Policy and Supply of the Department of
    Conservation (not the said Department acting through
    the said Division);
2. New York, the Water and Power Commission of the Depart-
    ment of Conservation (not the said Department through
    the said Commission);
3. North Dakota, the State Water Conservation and the
    State Department of Health jointly; and
4. Pennsylvania, the Water and Power Resources Board of
    the Department of Forests and Waters (not the said De-
    partment through the said Board).

Among the auxiliary regulatory measures, one is the requirement of periodic examination of water-samples by the "State
Health Department."[12] In Tennessee (Code, sec. 5826.5: Acts
1945, ch. 52, sec. 5) and Illinois (Revised Statutes, ch. 111.5,
sec. 121j), the said Department may order correction of defects
in the operation of the works. In Texas and New Jersey, persons in charge of the operation of the works should hold a li-

cense from the said Department.[13]

In the laws of Texas, it is provided that "no physical connection between the distribution system of a public drinking water supply and that of any other water supply shall be permitted unless such other water is of a safe sanitary quality and the interconnection is approved by the State Department of Health" (Revised Civil Statutes, art. 4477-1, op. cit., sec. 11(d), 1st sent.).[14] In New Jersey, an Act of 25 March 1942 (ch. 24) authorized the then State Water Policy Commission to order interconnection between any two or more water-supply systems during the Second World War.

Under the laws of New York, the diversion of water from the Delaware River or any of its tributaries for domestic and municipal uses either within or without the Delaware River Basin must be approved by the Water and Power Commission of the Department of Conservation (Conservation Law, sec. 503: L. 1943, ch. 709, sec. 1). New Jersey enacted a law on 11 May in 1905 (ch. 238) which prohibited transportation of water in lakes and streams of that state outside state boundaries. This law was upheld by the United States Supreme Court on 6 April 1908.[15] Similar laws were subsequently enacted in California in 1911 (ch. 104), in Idaho in 1915 (ch. 111, sec. 8, as amended by L. 1925, ch. 3, sec. 1), in Colorado in 1917 (ch. 151) and in New Mexico in 1953 (ch. 64, sec. 2, but applicable to underground waters only).

Subsection 2 Water Conservation

(a) Underground Waters---Underground waters have received greater attention of the state government than surface waters in water-conservation regulation. In most of the states having this regulation, the regulation is concerned with artesian wells only. The simplest form of this regulation (i.e., that of artesian wells) is a blank prohibition against waste of water (purely criminal), coupled in some states with the requirement of capping and casing (e.g. California and Colorado) or a definition of "waste" (California, for example). The laws of Colorado (Statutes, ch. 11, secs. 2 and 3: L. 1887, p. 52, secs. 1 and 2) and California (Water Code, Division 1, ch. 1: Stats. 1907, ch. 101, as amended) contain provisions of this kind. A more progressive form of the regulation of artesian wells with view to preventing waste of water consists in the attachment of administrative action to the prohibitive regulation. This is found in Texas, Minnesota, Idaho, North Dakota, Nevada and Florida. For the sake of brevity, the relevant statutory provisions of these states are cited below:[16]

Texas------"Any artesian well which is not tightly cased, capped and furnished with such mechanical appliances as will readily and effectively arrest and prevent the flow from the well through the strata through

which it passes is hereby declared a <u>public nuis-</u>
<u>ance</u> and subject to be <u>abated</u> as such, <u>upon the</u>
<u>order</u> of the (state) board (of water engineers)."
--L. 1917, ch. 88, sec. 91.

Minnesota--". . .<u>The Commissioner (of Conservation)</u> is authorized to require the owners to control artesian
wells to prevent waste." -- L. 1939, ch. 327, sec.
5; as amended by L. 1947, ch. 142, sec. 15.

Idaho------"Any artesian well, which is not capped, equipped
or furnished with such mechanical appliance as
will readily control the flow of water from such
well, is hereby declared to be common nuisance;
and any artesian well, which is capped, equipped
or furnished with a mechanical appliance for arresting and preventing the flow of water therefrom,
which cap, equipment or mechanical appliance has
not been <u>approved by the commissioner of reclama-</u>
<u>tion</u>, is hereby declared to be a common nuisance
. . ." Every owner, occupant or tenant of the
land upon which an artesian well is situated "shall
apply to the commissioner of reclamation for the
<u>approval</u> of any installed or proposed mechanical
device for controlling the flow of water from such
artesian well; . . . and shall change, alter or
install only such equipment as shall be <u>approved</u>
by the commissioner of reclamation." -- L. 1921,
ch. 196.

North
Dakota----Artesian wells should be equipped with a valve or
valves to control the flow of water. The <u>state</u>
geologist is authorized to <u>enforce</u> this provision.
And, "the state geologist, the state engineer, and
the county superintendent of schools of any county
in which an artesian well is located may make such
additional reasonable <u>rules and regulations</u> governing such well as a majority shall determine. . ."--
L. 1921, ch. 17, as amended by L. 1925, ch. 89.

Nevada-----"No person controlling an artesian well shall suffer the waters therefrom to flow to waste . . . .
The owner of any artesian well from which water is
unnecessarily wasted shall be deemed guilty of a
misdemeanor, and, if upon fifteen days' written
notice . . . the owner fails to abate or refuses
to abate such waste, the <u>state engineer</u> . . . may...
take such steps as may be necessary to <u>abate such</u>
<u>waste</u> . . . . The cost thereof . . . shall con-
stitute a valid lien against the interest of such
owner or owners in default . . ." -- L. 1939, ch.
178, sec. 8. (For the definition of "waste", see
ibid., sec. 2).

Florida----All artesian wells must be provided with valves
for controlling water-flow. In case of default on
the part of the person or persons having control

thereof, the <u>state geologist</u> or the sheriff concerned may install the same at the expense of the
former. -- L. 1953, ch. 28253.

A stronger form of state regulation over <u>artesian wells</u>
is the imposition of certain limitations on the use of the
water taken from such wells. There are limitations as to the
kinds, amounts and time of the use of water. In the above-
mentioned law of California, the beneficial use of artesian
water is limited to one-tenth of the miner's inch per acre on
a yearly basis in case of irrigation. In Colorado, a law of
1935 (ch. 8) limits the use of artesian water to domestic and
manufacturing purposes, in the hilly areas of that state.
Washington laws have declared a kind of "closed season" on the
use of artesian water, and prohibit the "escape" of water from
an artesian well, except for domestic and stock uses, between
15 October of each year and 15 March of the ensuing year, in
areas where artesian water is customarily used for irrigation
(<u>Revised Code</u>, ch. 90.36: L. 1901, ch. 121; as amended by L.
1929, ch. 138). Under the laws of South Dakota (<u>Code</u>, ch. 61.-
04: L. 1891, ch. 80, sec. 42 et seq.; as last amended by L.
1941, ch. 369, sec. 1), artesian wells may be bored only for
domestic, manufacturing or irrigation purposes, and with respect to wells constructed subsequent to 9 March 1891, no
more water can be withdrawn for such uses than is actually
needed. The State Engineer is authorized to re-locate an artesian well if he, upon the complaint of any party affected,
should find it interferes with other wells.

The regulation of <u>artesian water</u> in New Mexico (L. 1935,
ch. 43) is even more comprehensive and far-reaching. Not only
the drilling but also the repair, plugging or abandonment of
an artesian well is to be approved by the state engineer. The
wasting of water of an active artesian well is declared a public nuisance, which the owner is required to abate. In the
default of the latter, the State Engineer or the artesian conservancy district concerned may summarily abate it at his cost.
The right to use the waters of an artesian well abandoned for
more than four years is forfeited to the state; and if any
water is found being wasted, the same officer or district may
summarily stop it. A loss of more than 20 percent during delivery in canals, ditches and so forth is considered a waste.
Earthen ditches are limited to a length of 1.5 miles and concrete-lined or other impervious ones to 2 miles if built prior
to 6 September 1912. Artesian waters can be stored only for
the purposes of irrigation, and no storage reservoir can be
built with a greater capacity than is necessary to store a
continuous flow for 48 hours (or 96 hours when the maximum discharge is less than 300 gallons per minute).

In New York, Utah, Wisconsin, Indiana, New Jersey and Arizona, there is state regulation of <u>all underground waters</u>,
both artesian and non-artesian. New York laws require the ap-

proval by the Division of Water Power and Control of the Department of Conservation of the installation or operation by any person of a well or wells in the Counties of Kings, Queens, Nassau and Suffolk when the total capacity of all old and new wells on any one property withdraw water in a rate exceeding forty-five gallons per minute (Conservation Law, sec. 521-a: L. 1933, ch. 563, sec. 3; as last amended by L. 1954, ch. 135). Under Utah laws, the State Engineer may at any time order the owner, lessee or person in charge to repair or install caps, valves or casings on any well or tunnel or to plug or fill it in order to prevent waste or contamination of underground water (Code, sec. 73-5-9: L. 1935, ch. 105, sec. 2). In Wisconsin, no wells may be constructed, installed or operated where any such wells singly or collectively discharge more than 100,000 gallons of water a day, without the approval of the State Board of Health (Statutes, sec. 144.03, subdivs. (7) and (8): L. 1945, ch. 303).

In Arizona, the Ground Water Law of 1945[17] stipulates that all old irrigation or drainage wells in existence prior to 3 October 1945 must be registered with the State Land Department, and that prior notice of intention to drill a new well must be submitted to the same agency before construction is started. This law was augmented by the Ground Water Law of 1948, which provides that the said Department, either in its own motion or upon the petition of twenty-five persons using underground water primarily for irrigation purposes or of one-fourth of all the underground-water users of a certain underground-water basin or aquifer, may declare and designate such basin or aquifer as a critical ground-water area, after a public hearing. In such area, no irrigation well may be drilled without first obtaining a permit from the State Land Commissioner; and "no permit shall be issued for the construction of an irrigation well within any critical area for irrigation of lands which were not irrigated at the effective date of the Ground Water Code of 1948 (i.e., 24 June 1948)" or of lands not under cultivation between 24 June 1943 and 24 June 1948. In addition, "the Commissioner may require any person making a groundwater withdrawal in a critical groundwater area to furnish reasonable factual information regarding the use and quantity of such withdrawals, . . . whether the withdrawal be by means of irrigation wells, domestic wells, industrial wells, or in some other manner"; and, "to prevent waste, all flowing wells must be capped or equipped with valves ..."[18] In 1953, a law was passed (ch. 42) which designated certain areas in Central Arizona as "restricted areas," in which the drilling of irrigation wells was prohibited until 31 March 1954. The same law also introduced two kinds of new permits. First, permits of the said Commissioner are required for the replacement or deepening of an existing irrigation well. Secondly, a permit must be obtained from the same officer to complete an irrigation well the construction of which is already commenced.[19] Such permit expires at the end of three months from the date of its issuance, and the well concerned may not irrigate more than 320 acres of land.

New Jersey statue (Statutes, tit. 54, ch. 4A: L. 1947, ch. 376; as amended by L. 1951, ch. 193, sec. 1) directs that "the Division of Water Policy and Supply of the State Department of Conservation shall delineate from time to time such areas of the state where diversion of subsurface and percolating waters exceeds or threatens to exceed, or otherwise threatens or impairs, the natural replenishment of such waters." In such areas, no diversion more than 100,000 gallons a day may be made without a permit from the said Division. However, valid diversions existing at the time of the passage of the Ground Water Act of 1947 (ch. 376, op. cit.) are exempted from this law. In 1951, a law was enacted (ch. 193, op. cit., sec. 2 et seq.) which requires owners of abandoned wells to seal these wells. "A well not in operation for three or more years or improperly maintained to prevent contamination may be deemed to have been abandoned."

Under an Act of 1951 (ch. 29), the Department of Conservation of Indiana has the authority to designate areas where the withdrawal of underground waters exceeds their natural replenishment as restricted use areas. In such areas, permits of the said Department are required for new withdrawals of underground water (that is, withdrawals in addition to those existing at the time of the designation of a restricted use area, which may be zero) in an amount (for each withdrawal) of more than 100,000 gallons a day. It may be noted that this regulatory measure does not affect the right to the use of water in a manner other than the limitation of the quantity of water to be used, and that for this reason it is not to be regarded as a measure of water-use regulation (which means the regulation of the right to the use of water). This is made the more explicit by the provision that permits are issued only to the owners or tenants of the overlying lands. To further help conserve the underground waters, the said Department may require the water used to return, as far as possible, to the ground, and order owners of artesian wells to install control devices. These measures, too, are operative only in restricted use areas so designated by the said Department.

As will be discussed in the following Section, in the several Western states, some or all of the underground waters are subject to state water-use regulation through the issuance of water-use permits. So far as underground water is concerned, such permits carry as a necessary incident the permission of the state for the construction and operation of wells. A number of states have laws providing for the licensing of the profession of well-drilling.[20] Such licensing supplements state regulation of underground waters; for its objective is apparently to insure that all wells are so constructed as to secure best conservation of underground waters.

656   AMERICAN WATER RESOURCES ADMINISTRATION

(b) <u>Surface Waters</u>---Under the laws of Illinois, it is the duty of the Department of Public Works and Buildings "to establish by regulations water levels below which water cannot be drawn down behind dams from any stream or river, . . . in order to retain enough water in such streams to preserve the fish and other aquative life in the stream, and to safeguard the health of the community . . ." (L. 1941, p. 282, by way of further amendment to L. 1911, p. 115, sec. 23: <u>Revised Statutes</u>, ch. 19, sec. 70). This regulation measure is evidently designed to conserve waters in the watercourses of the state for the purposes of fishery and wildlife, water sanitation and water supply.

Similar measures are found in North Dakota (certain areas), Minnesota and Vermont. In Minnesota, any public body or any two or more riparian owners concerned may establish and maintain the levels of any public watercourse of the state, but they can do this only with the approval of the Commissioner of Conservation (L. 1947, ch. 142, sec. 7). The Water Conservation Board of Vermont has the general authority to "make and promulgate rules and regulations governing surface levels of natural lakes and ponds (but not rivers) which are public waters of Vermont" (a provision in Acts 1947, No. 83, sec. 5, as amended by Acts 1949, No. 147, sec. 2). By an Act of 1951 (Acts 1951, No. 197), the State Public Service Commission is authorized to establish the natural maximum and minimum levels of Lake Seymour at its outlet.

In North Dakota, the State Engineer may "take such action as may be necessary to conserve the water levels and rehabilitate the streams and brooks in the Turtle Mountain region of North Dakota lying in Bottineau and Rolette Basins . . ." (<u>Revised Code</u>, sec. 61-1509: L. 1931, ch. 72, sec. 1). It would seem that the State Engineer may accomplish the purposes of this provision either by enterprise or by regulation.[21]

Attachment: Interstate Apportionment of Water

(a) <u>Compulsory apportionment by decrees of the United States Supreme Court</u>---Water-diversions from interstate waters (whether navigable or not) have often resulted in controversies between riparian states. Some of the controversies have been settled in the United States Supreme Court. Others have been settled through the conclusion of interstate compacts. There are of course controversies which have continued without settlement. In passing upon its judgments on these controversies, the United States Supreme Court has taken the following attitude:[22]

> The decision of suits between states, Federal, state and international law is considered and applied by this Court as the exigencies of the particular case may require. The determination of the

relative rights of contending states in respect of
the use of streams flowing through them does not
depend upon the same considerations and is not
governed by the same rules of law that are applied
in such states for the solution of similar questions of private rights (at 670).

Upon a consideration of the pertinent laws of
the contending states and all other relevant facts,
this Court will determine what is an equitable
apportionment of the use of such waters (at 670-
671).

All decisions on these controversies have been and are to be
made in accordance with rules of Equity instead of those of
written law.[23] There are even no fixed rules of Equity as
to what is generally an equitable apportionment. All decisions have been made on a case-to-case basis.

The first interstate water suit was the Kansas v. Colorado,
206 U. S. 46 (1907), which was brought to the Supreme Court
of the United States in 1901. In this case the state of
Kansas petitioned for an injunction against the diversion by
the state of Colorado of water from the Arkansas River. The
petition of Kansas was dismissed on the ground that Kansas,
having adopted the riparian doctrine of water rights for water
appropriations within Kansas, could not "complain if the same
rule is administered between herself and a sister state" (at
104-105), that as a matter of fact, Colorado diversion did not
constitute "a source of serious detriment to the Kansas counties along the Arkansas river" (at 113), and that equality
of right and equity between the two states forbids any interference with the present withdrawal of water in Colorado for
purposes of irrigation" (at 113-114). However, the Court
made the following reservation: "If the depletion of the waters of the river by Colorado continues to increase, there
will come a time when Kansas may justly say there is no longer
an equitable division of benefits, and may rightfully call for
relief against the action of Colorado, its corporations and
citizens, in appropriating the waters of the Arkansas for irrigation purposes" (at 117). Subsequently the two states
again brought their suit to the Court, with Kansas alleging
that Colorado had increased her use of water for irrigation
resulting in actual damages to Kansas.[24] The Court took notice of the fact that "despite Colorado's alleged increased
depletion, the acreage under irrigation in western Kansas
through existing ditches has steadily increased, over the
period 1895-1939, from approximately 15,000 acres to approximately 56,000 acres. Moreover, the arid lands in western Kansas are underlaid at shallow depths with great quantities of
ground water available for irrigation by pumping at low initial and maintenance cost" (320 U. S. 383, 399). The suit
was again dismissed without making an apportionment of water.

The second case was <u>Wyoming v. Colorado</u>, 259 U. S. 419
(1922), which was instituted in 1911 and in which Wyoming
prayed for an injunction against the state of Colorado and
two Colorado corporations against a proposed diversion of
waters from the Laramie river. In this case, as distinguished
from the above case where Kansas adopts riparian doctrine of
appropriation while Colorado adopted the doctrine of prior
appropriation, both Wyoming and Colorado are states in which
the doctrine of prior appropriation prevails. In cognizance
of this fact, the Court was of the opinion that "the doctrine of appropriation (i.e. prior appropriation -- the author)
. . . furnishes the only basis which is consonant with the
principles of right and equity applicable to such a controversy as this is" (at 470). "As the available supply is 288,000
acre-feet, and the amount covered by senior appropriations in
Wyoming is 272,000 acre-feet, there remain 15,500 acre-feet
which are subject to this junior appropriation in Colorado."
Accordingly, the Court decreed that not more than 15,500 acre-
feet of water could be taken each year by Colorado (at 496).
In this case, the Court also collaterally sustained trans-
watershed diversion of water on the ground that "diversions
from one watershed to another are commonly made in both states,
and the practice is recognized by the decisions of their
courts" (at 466).

The next case was the <u>Wisconsin v. Illinois</u>; <u>Michigan v.
Illinois</u> and <u>New York v. Illinois</u> (combined), 278 U. S. 367
(1929). The states of Wisconsin, Minnesota, Michigan, Ohio,
Pennsylvania and New York sought an injunction against the
state of Illinois and the sanitary district of Chicago to
withdraw 8,500 cubic feet per second of water from Lake Michigan at Chicago. The said district was originally permitted
by the Secretary of War to divert 4,167 cubic feet per second,
which was increased, on 3 March 1925, also with the permission
of the Secretary of War, to 8,500 cubic feet per second. The
states of Missouri, Kentucky, Tennessee, and Louisiana inter-
vened and joined the district in maintaining that the diversion by the district aided in the navigation of the Mississippi
River. The Court went into the nature and history of the diversion. The following facts were noticed: Originally the
district applied for permission to divert 10,000 second-feet
of water for the purpose of discharging the sewage, and this
application was successively denied by the Department of War.
In 1908, a suit was brought by the United States to enjoin a
diversion beyond 4,167 second-feet. Pending the suit, the sanitary district disobeyed the restriction imposed by the Secretary of War and increased its diversion to 8,500 second-feet.
Subsequently a temporary permit was issued by the Secretary to
the district for the 8,500-second-feet diversion, with the
condition that the district undertook other plans for sewage
disposal (at 417-418). On the basis of this observation, the
Court dicided that the district's increased diversion was illegal, and compelled it to return to the original rate of di-

version in order "to restore the navigable capacity of Lake
Michigan to its proper level" (at 420). In this case the
paramount purpose of navigation (i.e. water supply in the interest of navigation) prevailed over an inferior purpose of
sewage disposal (i.e. water supply in the interest of sewage
disposal); and at the same time a national purpose (navigation)
took precedence over a local purpose (sanitation in Chicago).
Such rules of priority, it would seem, are bound to govern
all similar cases. Apportionment was not at issue in this
case, inasmuch as the problem of water supply concerned is
one of water supply for non-consumptive uses.

Three interstate water supply cases were decided in 1931;
namely, Connecticut v. Massachusetts, 282 U. S. 660; New Jersey v. New York, 283 U. S. 336; and Arizona v. California,
283 U. S. 425. In the first case, a number of conflicting
uses of water were considered. In denying the request of
Connecticut for an injunction against Massachusetts' diversion of water from two small tributaries of the Connecticut
river which lie wholly within Massachusetts (at 673), the
Court noticed that the Boston area was in serious need of
water (at 664-665), that "the diversion will not perceptibly
or materially interfere with navigation" (at 666) nor will
it disturb hydroelectric power generation in Connecticut (at
667), and that drinking and domestic uses are the highest
uses of water (at 673). However, Connecticut was given a
"right to maintain a suit against Massachusetts whenever it
shall appear that substantial interests of Connecticut are being injured through a material increase of the amount of the
waters of the Ware and Swift diverted by or under the authority of Massachusetts over and above the quantitites authorized
by the Acts of 1926 and 1927 (of Massachusetts) as heretofore
limited by the War Department" (at 674). The second case
deals with the proposed diversion of water of about 400 million
gallons per day from certain tributaries of the Delaware river
by the city of New York to the watershed of the Hudson river
in order to augment the water supply of that city. Against
this diversion New Jersey prayed for an injunction, joined by
Pennsylvania. The petitioning state insisted "on a strict
application of the rules of the common law of private riparian
proprietors" (at 342). The Court repudiated any fixed formula
in apportioning interstate waters (at 343) and rendered its
decision in favor of the city of New York (and the state of
New York) on the ground that the proposed diversion would not
impair the navigable capacity of the Delaware river, subject
to the following reservations: (1) New Jersey was entitled to
an injunction suit whenever New York diversion exceeded 400
million gallons per day; (2) before diversion the city of New
York should construct a sewage disposal plant at Port Jervis,
New York; (3) in no event should the flow of the Delaware river be so impaired by the diversion as to fall below 0.5 c.s.m.
at Port Jervis, New York or Trenton, New Jersey; and (4) "the
diversion . . . shall not constitute a prior appropriation and

shall not give the State of New York and City of New York any
superiority over the State of New Jersey and Commonwealth of
Pennsylvania in the enjoyment and use of the Delaware river
and its tributaries" (at 346-348). In both these cases, the
Court refused to grant relief to possible or potential impairment of water supply of one by the use of water of another
state. This rule was more expressly elucidated in Arizona v.
California, 283 U. S. 425, in which Arizona attempted to stop
the construction of the Boulder Canyon project in a suit instituted against the United States and all other Colorado-
River-Basin states. The injunction was dismissed for "it is
not based on any actual or threatened impairment of Arizona's
rights but upon assumed potential invasions" (at 462). However, "if by operations of the dam any perfected right of
Arizona, or of those claiming under it, should hereafter be
interfered with, appropriate remedies will be available" (at
463).

    In Washington v. Oregon, 297 U. S. 517 (1936), and in
Nebraska v. Wyoming, 325 U. S. 589 (1945),[25] the Supreme Court
was called upon to make actual apportionment of certain interstate streams, all of the states involved in these two cases
being states of prior appropriation. In the former case, the
Court refused to apportion the waters of the Walla Walla river
system as requested by Washington because of "uncertain evidence of prior right and still more uncertain evidence of damage" (at 529). In the latter case a very complicated method
of apportionment of the North Platte river was decreed (at
665-672) and permission was given states concerned to apply
for the modification thereof within ten or five years (at 655).
The decree was generally based on private appropriative rights
of both Nebraska and Wyoming (see 627). The apportionment
does not, however, affect domestic and municipal uses of water,
which are not restricted thereby (at 656).[26] Although the
doctrine of prior appropriation was the guiding principle of the
court in apportioning the waters of the North Platte river, the
following dictum is worthy of notice:

> Apportionment calls for the exercise of an informed
> judgment on a consideration of many factors. Prior-
> ity of appropriation is the guiding principle. But
> physical and climatic conditions, the consumptive
> use of water in the several sections of the river,
> the character and rate of return flows, the extent
> of established uses, the availability of storage
> water, the practical effect of wasteful uses on
> downstream areas, the damage to upstream areas as
> compared to the benefits to downstream areas if a
> limitation is imposed on the former -- these are all
> relevant factors. They are merely an illustrative,
> not an exhaustive catalogue (at 618).

This was the first time that definite and objective standards

were listed by the Supreme Court for an equitable apportionment of interstate waters.

(b) Contractual apportionment by interstate compacts---
This method of apportioning interstate waters was fully sustained by the Supreme Court of the United States in Hinder-
lider v. LaPlata Cherry Creek Ditch Co., 304 U. S. 92 (1938)
in the following dicta:

> The extent of the existing equitable right of
> Colorado and of New Mexico in the La Plata River
> could obviously have been determined by a suit
> in this Court . . . . But resort to the judicial
> remedy is never essential to the adjustment of in-
> terstate controversies unless the states are unable
> to agree upon the terms of a compact, or Congress
> refuses its consent (104-105).
>
> Whether the apportionment of the water of an
> interstate stream be made by compact between the
> upper and lower states with the consent of Congress
> or by a decree of this Court, the apportionment is
> binding upon the citizens of each state and all
> water claimants, even where the state had granted
> the water rights before it entered into the com-
> pact (106).

In fact, the Supreme Court has preferred apportioning by interstate compacts:

> The reason for judicial caution in adjusting
> the relative rights of states in such cases is that,
> while we have jurisdiction of such disputes, they
> involve the interests of quasi-sovereigns, present
> complicated and delicate questions, and, due to the
> possibility of future change of conditions, necessi-
> tate expert administration rather than judicial im-
> position of a hard and fast rule. Such controver-
> sies may appropriately be composed by negotiation
> and agreement, pursuant to the compact clause of
> the Federal constitution . . . . Such mutual accom-
> modation and agreement should, if possible, be the
> medium of settlement, instead of invocation of our
> adjudicatory power. -- Colorado v. Kansas, 320 U.S.
> 383, 392 (1943).

As in the case of judicial apportionment, there is no general rule of apportioning or regulating interstate waters by
interstate compacts. In the Rio Grande Compact of 17 June
1930, it is expressly provided (art. 13) that "the physical
and other conditions characteristic of the Rio Grande and peculiar to the territory drained and served thereby, and to the
development thereof, have actuated this compact, and none of
the signatory states admits that any provision herein contained

establishes any general principle or precedent applicable to other interstate streams" (46 Stat. 767, 772).[27] Similar provision has been embodied in the Republican River Compact of 26 May 1943 (art. 1: 57 Stat. 86, 87), the Belle Fourche River Compact of 26 February 1944 (art. 1, B: 58 Stat. 94, 95), the Costilla Creek Compact of 11 June 1946 (art. 1, second para.: 60 Stat. 246, 247), and the Yellowstone River Compact of 30 October 1951 (art. 14: 65 Stat. 663, 669).

Actual apportionments made by the various interstate compacts have varied greatly. The Sabine River Compact of 10 August 1954 between Louisiana and Texas (68 Stat. 690) simply provides that the waters of the Sabine River above the Sabine Lake which forms the interstate boundary line between the two signatory states which are not stored in reservoirs (other than domestic and stock water reservoirs) "shall be equally divided between the two states . . .", that waters stored in reservoirs (other than domestic and stock water reservoirs) built on this reach of the Sabine River "shall be shared by each state in proportion to its contribution to the cost of storage",[28] and that a minimum flow of 36 cubic feet per second shall be maintained at the head of this reach (Art. V). The La Plata River Compact of 29 January 1925 (art. 2) divides the waters of the La Plata river between the states of Colorado and New Mexico in the following manner:

> (1) At all times between the first day of December and the 15th day of the succeeding February, each state shall have the unrestricted right to the use of all water which may flow within its boundaries.
> (2) Between the 15th day of February and the first day of December -- (a) Each state shall have the unrestricted right to use all the waters within its boundaries on each day when the mean daily flow at the interstate station is one hundred (100) cubic feet per second or more. (b) On all other days the state of Colorado shall deliver at the interstate station a quantity of water equivalent to one-half of the mean flow at the Hesperus station for the preceding day, but not to exceed one hundred (100) cubic feet per second.
> (3) Whenever the flow of the river is so low that in the judgment of the state engineers of the states the greatest beneficial use of its waters may be secured by distributing all of its waters successively to the lands in each state in alternating periods, -- the use of the waters may be so rotated between the two states in such manner, for such periods, and to continue for such time as the state engineers may jointly determine.

The Colorado River Compact, signed 24 November 1922, effective

25 June 1929 (46 Stat. 3000), after dividing the Colorado-River-Basin states into two groups, the Upper-Basin states, consisting of Colorado, New Mexico, Utah, and Wyoming, and the Lower-Basin states, comprising Arizona, California and Nevada, provides that (art. 3) each group is entitled to exclusive beneficial consumptive use of 7,500,000 acre-feet of water per year and that the lower-basin group may have an additional 1,000,000 acre-feet per year if possible. The Republican River Compact apportions to Colorado, Kansas and Nebraska respectively 54,100 acre-feet, 190,300 acre-feet and 234,000 acre-feet per year from certain designated streams. Besides, Kansas is entitled to "entire water supply originating in the Basin downstream from the lowest crossing of the river at Nebraska-Kansas state line;" and Colorado is permitted the exclusive right to divert waters from the Pioneer Irrigation Canal.

Some apportionments are rather delicate. For example, the Pecos River Compact of 9 June 1949 (art 3) makes the following apportionment:

> (a) New Mexico shall not deplete by man's activities the flow of the Pecos River at the New Mexico-Texas state line below an amount which will give to Texas a quantity of water equivalent to that available to Texas under the 1947 condition.
> (b) The beneficial consumptive use of the waters of the Delaware River is hereby apportioned to Texas, and the quantity of such beneficial consumptive use shall be included in determining waters received under provisions of paragraph (a).
> (c) The beneficial consumptive use of water salvaged in New Mexico through the consumption and operation of a project or projects by the United States or by joint undertaking of Texas and New Mexico, is hereby apportioned 43 percent to Texas and 57 percent to New Mexico.
> (d) The beneficial consumptive use of water which shall be non-beneficially consumed, and which is received, is hereby apportioned to New Mexico, but not to have the effect of diminishing the quantity of water available to Texas under the 1947 condition.
> (e) Any water salvaged in Texas is hereby apportioned to Texas.
> (f) Beneficial consumptive use of unapportioned flood waters is hereby apportioned 50 percent to Texas and 50 percent to New Mexico.

A very complicated system of apportionment is also adopted by the Costilla Creek Compact of 11 June 1946 (art. 4). Hardly any two compact bear any similarity in their apportionment arrangements. However, it is natural that standards set forth

in Nebraska v. Wyoming, 325 U. S. 589, 618 may serve as guides
to all interstate water compacts.[29]

Normally, all waters of a certain river system or stream
group covered by an interstate water compact are apportion-
able irrespective of the fact that some part thereof may
traverse public lands of the Federal Government. However,
there is recently a tendency to exempt from apportionment
waters which are within the boundaries of national parks
seemingly with view to preserving natural conditions of these
areas. In the Snake River Compact of 21 March 1950 it is
expressly provided (art. 14) that nothing in that compact
"shall be deemed . . . to apply to any waters within the
Yellowstone National Park or Grand Teton National Park." The
Yellowstone River Compact of 30 October 1951 defines the waters subject to apportionment as those belonging to the Yellowstone River system "other than waters within or waters
which contribute to the flow of streams within the Yellowstone National Park" (preamble).

The last-mentioned two compact also contain provisions
regarding trans-watershed diversion of water. The Snake
River Compact in article 4 provides that "no water of the
Snake River shall be diverted in Wyoming for use outside the
drainage area of the Snake River except with the approval of
Idaho; and no water of any tributary of the Snake River heading Idaho for use outside the drainage area of said tributary
except with the approval of Wyoming." In the Yellowstone
River Compact it is stipulated that "no water shall be diverted from the Yellowstone River without the unanimous consent
of the signatory states" (art. 10).

Some compacts contain provisions which aim at removing
regidity of the apportionment arrangements. In the Republican River (art. 6), Belle Fourche River (art. 6), Snake River
(art. 8) and Yellowstone River (art. 8) Compacts, right is
given a state to apply to another state for permits for the
construction or participation in the construction of projects
utilizing waters allocated to the latter. The Yellowstone
River Compact further provides (art. 5, F) that "from time to
time the (Yellowstone River Compact) Commission shall re-
examine the allocations herein made and upon unanimous agreement may recommend modifications therein as are fair, just,
and equitable. . ." The Canadian River Compact of 17 May
1952, in article 6, authorized the Canadian River Compact
Commission to permit New Mexico and Texas to impound, for periods not exceeding 12 months, more water than respectively
apportioned them by the compact, if such action does not affect beneficial use of water in the other state.

Section 4   Use of Water (Water Rights)

Rights of private persons to the use of natural bodies of
water were originally possessed exclusively by the riparian

landowners and were not regulated otherwise than by rules of
the customary common law. Under these rules, persons who are
not riparian landowners to a certain body of water have no
right whatever to the use of that body of water, even though
they may be in great need of it. To meet these defects of
the common-law system, practices first evolved and laws have
subsequently been enacted in a number of states which modify
this system and in many instances place the appropriation of
water by private persons under administrative instead of judicial regulation. These laws are of two general types:
Those which completely detach rights to the use of water from
riparian land-ownership and make them entirely dependent upon
actual needs of water;[30] and those which restrict the common-
law privilege of riparian landowners but which do not extend
the right to the use of water to non-riparian landowners or
the landless. The former category of laws prevails in the
West and the latter in the East.[31] The legal principle underlying the first category of regulatory laws is commonly known
as "the doctrine of prior appropriation." The principle governing the common-law system of water rights, whether with or
without administrative regulation, may be termed "doctrine of
riparian appropriation", or simply "riparian doctrine."[32]
Regulation under the doctrine of prior appropriation exists
in all 17 Western States. But regulation under the riparian
doctrine is found only in a few Eastern States, while in the
majority of the Eastern States the common-law rule of riparian
appropriation is in its unregulated state.

     (a) Regulation in Western States---Throughout the history
of its development, the doctrine of prior appropriation has
received the endorsement of the United States Supreme Court.
There are two stages in the development of the doctrine, identifiable by two distinct theories in support thereof, namely,
(1) the California doctrine and (2) the Colorado doctrine.
Both doctrines or theories have been approved by the Supreme
Court of the United States. In the early rulings of the courts
of California,[33] the doctrine of prior appropriation was conceived to be based on the proprietory right of the Federal
Government over the public domain, and therefore applicable
only to waters on the unappropriated vacant lands of the public domain. Prior appropriation consisted simply of the splitting of the general riparian right of the Federal Government
into rights of prior appropriation of persons who settled on
the domain before receiving title or patent to any part thereof. For lands not in Federal ownership, riparian doctrine
still prevailed. This is the so-called the California doctrine.
In 1872, the Territorial Supreme Court of Colorado enlarged
the scope of prior appropriation to cover both public and private lands. This attitude was adhered to by the Supreme Court
of the State of Colorado after the admission of Colorado into
the Union, and became known as the Colorado doctrine. For a
considerable period of time the California doctrine was followed by the states of Washington, Oregon, North Dakota, South

Dakota, Nebraska, Kansas, Oklahoma, and Texas; and the Colorado doctrine was adopted by the states of Montana, Idaho, Wyoming, Nevada, Utah, Arizona, and New Mexico.[34]

The California doctrine was first confirmed by the United States Supreme Court in Atchison v. Peterson, 20 Wall. 507 (1874) and later recognized in Basey v. Gallagher, 20 Wall. 670 (1875), Jennison v. Kirk, 98 U. S. 453 (1879), Broder v. Water Co., 101 U. S. 274 (1879), and Sturr v. Beck, 133 U. S. 541 (1890).[35] The ruling in Atchison's case was as follows:

> This equality of right (under the common law -- the author) among all the proprietors on the same stream would have been incompatible with any extended diversion of the water by one proprietor, and its conveyance for mining purposes to points from which it could not be restored to the stream. But the government being the sole proprietor of all the public lands, whether bordering on streams or otherwise, there was no occasion for the application of the common law doctrine of riparian proprietorship with respect to the waters of those streams. The government, by its silent acquiescence, assented to the general occupation of the public lands for mining, and to encourage their free and unlimited use for that purpose, reserved such lands as were mineral from sale and the acquisition of title by settlement. And he who first connects his own labor with property thus situated and open to general exploitation, does, in natural justice, acquire a better right to its use and enjoyment than others who have not given such labor (22 L. ed. 416).

In U. S. v. Rio Grande Dam and Irrigation Co., 174 U. S. 690 (1899), the Court switched itself to the new Colorado doctrine. It disregarded the proprietory rights of the United States over public lands as having any bearing upon the right of a non-riparian appropriator of water, and recognized the authority of the states to change common-law rules. This attitude has been retained by the Court in all subsequent cases.[36] Since the California doctrine has been discarded by the Federal Courts the Colorado doctrine is now the only valid legal rule or theory regarding state regulation of water rights in the West.

At first, the rights of prior appropriation (i.e. the rights of persons to appropriate water for beneficial uses according to actual need of water and under the rule that he who first appropriates water in time is first in right) were acquired by self-assertion. This was done either by posting a notice to that effect or by making a registration with the local courts. If it met with contending claims, a court de-

cision confirming the self-asserted right would be necessitated.[37] This method of water appropriation has been replaced
by administrative appropriation, in which a right to the use
of water is granted by the state after application therefor.
This new method first appeared in Wyoming in the constitution of 1890,[38] and is now in force in all Western states except Montana, where the old method still prevails.

As a basis for the state regulation of water rights, the
laws of all Western states except Kansas and Montana have
declared waters subject to appropriation to be public property; in Kansas and Montana, these waters are declared to be
for "the use of the people" and for "public use", respectively.[39] Such declarations are embodied in state constitutions
in Colorado, Idaho, Nebraska, Nevada, New Mexico and Wyoming
and in statutes in all other Western states. In all of the
seventeen Western states, waters in all surface watercourses
are subject to appropriation.[40] The laws of the several Western states differ as to the appropriation of underground waters, which will be discussed later.

In Arizona, Colorado, Idaho, Montana, Nevada, New Mexico,
Oregon, Utah and Wyoming, the riparian doctrine has been entirely abrogated, and in these states no new riparian rights
can be obtained.[41] In California, Kansas, Nebraska, North
Dakota, South Dakota, Texas and Washington, and to a lesser
extent also in Oklahoma, the riparian doctrine exists side by
side with the doctrine of prior appropriation and the right
of a riparian landowner to appropriate water of a watercourse
flowing through his riparian land in reasonable quantities
for domestic and irrigation uses solely by virtue of his riparian ownership is still recognized.[42]

In some states, certain waters are specifically exempted
from statutory appropriation. In South Dakota, for example,
navigable waters are not subject to such appropriation (Code,
sec. 61.0101: Code of 1919, sec. 348 and Laws 1907, ch. 180,
sec.; as amended by L. 1927, ch. 221). To these waters, only
the riparian rule applies.[43] A 1931 enactment of Texas (Acts
1931, ch. 128, sec. 6) provides that water-appropriation laws
of that state do not apply to "any stream which constitutes
or defines the international border or boundary between the
United States of America and the Republic of Mexico."[44] In
Oregon, certain watercourses are withdrawn from prior appropriation by special laws.[45] A more flexible provision is in
force in Utah, whereby the state engineer may recommend to
the governor to withdraw for any period of time certain water
source from appropriation (Code, secs. 73-6-1 and 73-6-2: Laws
1917, ch. 73; as last amended by L. 1939, ch. 111).[46]

It is an interesting problem whether waters on Federally-
owned lands and the water in Federally-owned reservoirs are
appropriable by state authorities. With respect to lands in

national forests, it is provided in sec. 1 of an Act of 4
June 1897 that

> All waters within the boundaries of national for-
> ests may be used for domestic, mining, milling, or
> irrigation purposes, under the laws of the state
> wherein such national forests are situated, or
> under the laws of the United States and the rules
> and regulations established thereunder (30 Stat.
> 36; 16 U. S. C. 481).

According to this provision, waters in national forests are
subject to state administrative appropriation in the absence
of conflicting Federal legislation. For waters made available by Federal irrigation projects, the Reclamation Act of
17 June 1902 expressly stipulates that they are governed exclusively by state water laws (sec. 8: 32 Stat. 388, 390).
This stipulation was recently sustained by the United States
Supreme Court in U. S. v. Gerlach Live Stock Co., 339 U. S.
725 (1950), in which the Court made the following comment:

> By directing the Secretary (of the Interior) to
> proceed under the Reclamation Act of 1902, Con-
> gress elected (emphasis added) not "to . . . in-
> terfere with the laws of any state . . . . relat-
> ing to the control, appropriation, use or distri-
> bution of water used in irrigation, or any vested
> right acquired thereunder" (at 739).

It is worth notice that the said stipulation is a self-imposed
limitation on the part of the Federal Government. To other
Federal areas, state jurisdiction over water-appropriation
would not extend except by special Congressional authorization or administrative agreement.[47]

It is needless to mention that state water-use regulation
over navigable waters is always subject to the paramount Federal authority over navigation. As regards non-navigable
waters, if they are tributaries to navigable waters, their
diversion and appropriation should not be so made as to endanger or impair the navigable capacity of the latter.[48]
State regulatory authority over the use of water must further
be restricted by the water-apportioning decrees of the United
States Supreme Court or interstate compacts.[49] For Montana,
it is again limited by Article VI of the American-British
Boundary Water Treaty signed 11 January 1909 and proclaimed
effective 13 May 1910 (36 Stat. 2448, 2451), which provides
that the waters of the St. Mary and Milk Rivers and their
tributaries, which are located in the State of Montana and
the Provinces of Alberta and Saskatchewan, should be equally
apportioned between the United States and Canada for the purposes of irrigation and power, and that during the irrigation
season, i.e., between 1 April and 31 October in each year, the

United States and Canada are respectively entitled to a prior
appropriation of 500 cubic feet per second or three-fourths
of the natural flows of the Milk and the St. Mary Rivers. For
the State of Texas, in the appropriation of the waters of the
Rio Grande system, the state authority is limited by Article
4 of the American-Mexican Water Treaty signed 3 February 1944
and effective 8 November 1945 (Treaty Series 994; 59 Stat.
1219, 1225-1228) which apportions the waters of the Rio Grande
system below Fort Quitman, Texas, between the United States
and Mexico, under which the United States are entitled only
to (1) all of the waters reaching the main channel of the Rio
Grande from the Pecos and Devils Rivers, Goodenough Spring,
and Alamito, Terlingna, San Felipe and Pinto Creeks, (2) one-
half of the flow of the main channel of the Rio Grande below
the lowest major international storage dam, (3) one-third
of the flow reaching the main channel from the Conchos, San
Diego, San Rodrigo, Escondido and Salado Rivers and the Las
Vacas Arroyo, and (4) one-half of all other flows both in
the main channel and in the tributaries, which should in no
case be less than 350,000 acre-feet a year in each five-year
period. Article 10 of the same Treaty (at 1237-1238) guaran-
tees Mexico a quantity of from 1,500,000 to 1,700,000 acre-
feet each year of the waters of the Colorado River. But this
provision seems to impose no direct limitation on the water-
appropriation laws of the Colorado-River-Basin states, which
are directly restricted by the interstate compact for the
waters of the Colorado River system.

The water-appropriation administration in the Western
States consists, in general, of three phases or parts; namely,
(1) Appropriation, (2) Adjudication, and (3) Distribution.
These are separately discussed below.

(1) Appropriation: In most states, this phase or part
is further split into two stages. First, a permit or license
is granted to an water-appropriation applicant which authorizes
him to construct works for the diversion of water. Then, after these works are completed, he is given a certificate which
establishes his water-right. Such a process is based on the
so-called "doctrine of relation", under which the right to
the use of water is initiated at the time of the construction
of the diversion works, but is incomplete or imperfect until
the water has actually been diverted to where it is to be beneficially used. This doctrine, as has been held by some students of water rights, serves to protect relatively big water
appropriators.50

In Washington, prospective water appropriators should
first apply to the supervisor of water resources of the state
department of conservation and development for a permit to
construct the diversion works and to appropriate water therewith. Then, after the diversion works are constructed or installed, "upon a showing satisfactory to the state supervisor

of water resources that any appropriation has been perfected
. . . it shall be the duty of such state supervisor of water
resources to issue to the applicant a certificate . . ."
(Revised Code, sec. 90.20.100: Laws 1917, ch. 117, sec. 34,
as amended by Laws 1929, ch. 122, sec. 5). Secondary permits
are required for the construction of reservoirs (ibid., sec.
90.28.080; Laws 1917, ch. 117, sec. 38). Exactly the same
procedure prevails in Arizona (Laws 1919, ch. 164, as amended
by Laws 1921, ch. 64) and Nevada (Code, secs. 7944, 7957 and
7962, enacted 1913, as last amended by Stats. 1951, ch. 110).
Wyoming system is similar, in which permits for appropriation
of water are first issued and after completion of diversion
certificates of priority are granted (Laws 1890-91, ch. 8,
sec. 34; as amended by Laws 1945, ch. 88), and in which special permits are required for the construction of reservoirs
"to store or impound, for beneficial uses, any of the unappropriated waters of the State of Wyoming" (Laws 1903, ch. 69,
sec. 1; as amended by Laws 1941, ch. 24, sec. 1). The two-
stage practice also prevails in the California (permit-license)
(Water Code, secs. 1250, 1252, 1255, 1380, 1605, 1610 and
1611), Kansas (permit-certificate of appropriation) (Laws 1945
ch. 390), Nebraska (permit-certificate) (Laws 1919, ch. 190,
secs. 16 and 20), New Mexico (permit-certificate of construction) (Laws 1907, ch. 49, secs. 24 to 30, inclusive), North
Dakota (permit-certificate of construction) (Code, secs. 61-
0403, 61-0406, 61-0407, 61-0409 and 61-0410, enacted 1905 and
amended 1913), Oklahoma (permit-certificate of completion)
(Oklahoma Statutes Annotated, tit. 82, ch. 1: Laws 1905, ch.
21; as amended by Laws 1925, ch. 76).

Oregon (permit-certificate of water right Laws 1909, ch.
216, secs. 45 and 53) and South Dakota (permit-certificate of
completion Code, secs. 61.0126, 61.0129, and 61.0131: Laws
1907, ch. 180, secs. 23, 26 and 29). But in these states special permits are not required for the construction of reservoirs. In Idaho a three-stage process obtains. Applicants
for appropriation are required to apply to the State Reclamation Engineer for a permit to appropriate water; and after the
construction of the diversion works is completed the said
officer issues him a certificate certifying to the completion
of the said works. Finally upon proof of actual application
of water to beneficial use, a license is issued which carries
the right to the use of water (Water Code, secs. 41-202 to
41-214). Besides, in the construction of "any dam or dike,
for the purpose of storing or appropriating or diverting any
of the waters of this state, when the same is to be more ten
feet in height or having a storage capacity of more than one
hundred acre-feet", plans and specifications thereof should be
approved by the Department of Reclamation before the start of
such construction (Ibid., sec. 41-1507). Utah adopts the two-
stage procedure; but in the first stage, that of the application for and approval of the appropriation of water by the construction of necessary storage and diversion works, no permit

or license is issued. The only document issued by the State
Engineer to a water-right applicant is the final certificate
of appropriation (Laws 1919, ch. 67; as last amended by Laws
1953, ch. 131).

Texas is the only state in which the appropriation procedure consists of only one stage. Under Acts 1917, ch. 88;
the laws of that state (Revised Civil Statutes, art. 7470 et
sec: as last amended by Acts 1953, chs. 352, 355, 357 and
358). Prospective water users should apply to the State Board
of Water Engineers for permits which shall authorize them to
construct water-diversion works and at the same time grant
them title to the water diverted upon completion of these
works.51 Special permits are required for diversions of water
from one watershed within the state to another watershed.

In Colorado, the appropriation of water in a manner other
than by virtue of ownership of riparian land is partly administrative and partly judicial. Prospective appropriators
(non-riparian) file their applications with the State Engineer,
but it is the court that gives them the right to the use of
water (Laws 1917, p. 641, sec. 1). In Montana there is no
administrative regulation at all over water appropriation.
All that an appropriator is required to do is to post his claim
at the place where he intends to make a diversion of water,
and his water right is established if the diversion is actually
made within 40 days after this and a notice of this fact is
filed with the county clerk within twenty (20) days after the
diversion. Montana is only state in which the old method of
obtaining water rights through priority of use is still in
operation.52

In 1953, an interesting act (ch. 355, sec. 1) was added
in Texas (Revised Civil Statutes, art. 7467 c), which provides
for the issuance by the Board of Water Engineers of (1) sea-
sonal permits of appropriation, and (2) temporary permits not
exceeding three months. This is an administrative novelty in
that water appropriation permits (when reinforced by water
right certificates) are generally permanent in nature.

In a few states, legislative action is required for certain kinds of water appropriation. In Arizona, applications
to appropriate water for hydroelectric power development must
be approved by an act of the state legislature if the energy
to be developed exceeds 25,000 horsepower (Laws of 1919, ch.
164, sec. 7, as last amended by Laws of 1927, ch. 109, sec.1).
In Montana, "None of the waters . . . shall ever be appropriated, deverted, impounded, or otherwise restrained or controlled within the state for use outside the boundaries thereof, except pursuant to a petition to and an act of the legislative assembly of the state of Montana permitting such action
. . ." as in California, (Revised Codes, sec. 89-846: Laws
1921, ch. 220, sec. 1).

In Washington and Idaho, trans-state diversions of water do not require legislative action, but are made on a reciprocal basis.[53] Sometimes special laws are passed authorizing special water appropriations. For example, in Oregon a special law was passed in 1925 which (1) granted exclusive right to the City of Medford to appropriate, subject to the then existing water rights, waters of the Big Butte Creek and its tributaries for municipal purposes, and (2) permitted the Eagle Point Irrigation District to appropriate up to 100 cubic feet per second of water of the Big Butte Creek for power development provided not less than 10 cubic feet per second remains to flow over the diversion point.

In South Dakota, there is also appropriation or rather apportionment of water among riparian landowners. The laws make it a "duty of the State Engineer upon the request of five or more landowners having riparian rights on any definite stream immediately to apportion such waters among them in such a manner as will permit all persons to receive the benefits of such stream" (Laws of 1935, ch. 214, sec. 2). This is an interesting provision, and merits consideration by other states in which the common law riparian doctrine is still active.[54]

In regard to the grant of water rights of prior appropriation, a time limit is usually prescribed after the expiration of which the right becomes void if found not in actual use. This is an important point of departure of the doctrine of prior appropriation from the doctrine of riparian appropriation. The time limits now adopted in the various Western states are as follows:[55]

Five years----Arizona, Idaho, Nevada, Oregon, Utah and
              Wyoming
Four years----New Mexico
Three years---California, Kansas (laws 1945, ch. 390, sec.
              17), Nebraska, North Dakota, South Dakota
              and Texas.
Two years-----Oklahoma
Not specified-Colorado, Montana (failure to use water
              beneficially means abandonment of the right)
              and Washington

(2) Adjudication (of existing water rights): With regard to the determination or adjudication of existing water rights, practices of the 17 Western states are divisible into three general groups to be discussed below.

Group (A)---In Wyoming (Wyo. Compiled Statutes Annotated, sec. 71-205 et seq.: Laws 1890-1891, ch. 8, sec. 20 et seq., as amended), Nevada (Nevada Compiled Laws, sec. 7905 et seq.: act of 20 Feb. 1909, sec. 18 et seq., as amended), Oregon (Revised Statutes, ch. 539: Laws 1909, ch. 216, sec. 11 et seq., as last amended by L. 1947, ch. 88, sec. 2), Texas (Laws 1917, ch. 88, sec. 105 et seq.), Arizona (Arizona Code Annotated, sec. 75-114 et seq.: Laws 1919, ch. 164, sec. 16 et seq., as amended), Nebraska (Revised Statutes of Nebraska, sec. 46-227 et seq.: Laws 1919, ch. 190, tit. 7, art. 5, division 2, sec. 8 et seq.), South Dakota (South Dakota Code, sec. 61.0105: Laws 1935, ch. 214, sec. 2), California (Water Code of 1943, secs. 2500 to 2768) and Kansas (General Statutes of Kansas, sec. 82a-704: Laws 1945, ch. 390, sec. 4), existing water rights are determined by administrative action, with court affirmation in case of complaint or appeal, or as required by the statute.[56] In Oregon, Texas, Arizona and Nevada, administrative action is taken only upon petition of one or more water users and in South Dakota upon petition of five (riparian) water users.[57]

Group (B)---This includes Idaho (Idaho Code, sec. 42-1401: Laws 1903, p. 223, March 11, sec. 37, as amended by Laws 1905, p. 357, March 9, sec. 4) and Colorado (Colorado Statutes Annotated, ch. 90, sec. 189: Laws 1943, ch. 190), where water rights are determined by the courts with technical assistance of the administrative agency concerned.[58]

Group (C)---In all other states of the West, water rights are adjudicated by courts in special proceedings which are instituted by the responsible water agencies. In Washington (Revised Code of Washington, ch. 90.12: Laws 1917, ch. 117, sec. 14 et seq.), Utah (Utah Code Annotated, sec. 73-4-1 et seq.: Laws 1919, ch. 67, sec. 20 et seq., as amended) and Montana (Revised Codes of Montana, sec. 89-848: Laws 1939, ch. 185, sec. 2), court action is directly instituted by the state water agency; but in North Dakota (North Dakota Revised Code, sec. 61-0315 et seq.: Laws 1905, ch. 34, sec. 14 et seq.), Oklahoma (Oklahoma Statutes Annotated, tit. 82, sec. 11 et seq.: Laws 1905, p. 276ff) and New Mexico (New Mexico Statutes Annotated, sec. 77-402 et seq.: Laws 1907, ch. 49, sec. 19 et seq.), it is brought by the state water agency through the state attorney-general. In Washington and Utah, petition of water users[59] is required before the institution of court action.[60]

In Nebraska, the adjudication seems to be made on an individual basis. In Kansas it seems that all existing water rights in the entire state are determined in a single action. In Colorado each determination covers a water district. In New Mexico and California it covers a stream system, i.e., a stream and its tributaries. In Montana and Nevada, it covers either a stream or a stream system. In Oklahoma and North Dakota, adjudication is made for each stream system or each source of water supply. In Arizona, Texas and Utah each stream or water source (in Utah either surface or ground) is the unit of adjudication. In all other states the stream is the unit of adjudication. The general practice of settling

water-right disputes collectively is worth our attention.[61]
It is also to be noted that not in a single state are the
water rights adjudicated by judicial action alone, which
proves the general inadequacy of the ordinary courts in handling matters which are purely or primarily technical in nature.

(3) Distribution of Water: The majority of the Western
states have divided the state into water districts and other
sub-divisions which are coterminous with natural watersheds
for which water commissioners or masters are appointed, with
or without petition of the water users, whose duty it is to
make water surveys and examinations and to supervise or direct
the actual diversion, apportionment and distribution of water.
Laws of Kansas, Montana and the two Dakotas do not provde for
the establishment of water districts. In Kansas, administrative supervision and help in the diversion and distribution
of water is required (Laws of 1945, ch. 390, sec. 20). In
South Dakota, water commissioner may be appointed annually
to do the same kind of work for any stream system or source
of water if necessary (Code, sec. 61.0121, first sentence,
1939). In Montana, the laws provides that upon petition of
at least ten percent of the water users of a ditch, the district court may appoint a water commissioner "to divide, apportion and distribute the waters of said ditch." (Revised
Codes, sec. 89-1023: Laws 1919, ch. 181, sec. 7)

A common provision found in the water laws of most Western
states, which is characteristic of the doctrine of prior appropriation, is that the right to the use of water is based
on and commensurate with beneficial uses of water.[62] Among
these uses, "drinking and other domestic purposes are the
highest uses of water."[63] The other beneficial purposes, are
throughout the history of the law of prior appropriation,
mining and irrigation. At first, mining prevailed over irrigation. Gradually the courts of the states (under the leadership of California) adopted the so-called "rule of impartial-
ity", which made mining and irrigation equal purposes. After
the stoppage of hydraulic mining in the early eighties, irrigation began to enjoy priority over irrigation.[64] At the present time, the general order of priority among the basic beneficial uses of water in the West is as follows: First, domestic and municial; second, irrigation or agricultural; and
third, industrial (including mining). All other purposes are
inferior purposes.[65] In a few states, more delicate or different order has been adopted. For example, in Kansas, "where
appropriations of water for different purposes conflict they
shall take precedence in the following order, namely: Domestic,
municipal, irrigation, industrial, recreational, and water
power uses" (Laws of 1945, ch. 390, sec. 7). Texas sets the
order as follows: domestic and municipal, including livestock
uses; irrigation; mining; hydroelectric power; navigation;
recreation.[66] In the Pacific Northwest, fishery is one of

most important economic activities, and for this reason special provisions have been embodied in their water laws giving
minimum protection to fishery interests, although fishery is
an inferior to many other purposes. As mentioned above, Oregon and Idaho have chosen to close certain waters to appropriation. In Washington, all applications for permits of appropriation must be reviewed by the Director of Fisheries and
the Director of Game and will not be approved if found by
them that water-diversion may endanger the life of game or
commercial fish (Laws of 1949, ch. 112, sec. 46).

The very basic characteristic of the doctrine and law of
prior appropriation is "first in time, first in service", provided the water rights concerned belong to the same order of
priority. Senior rights always prevail over junior rights.
However, in many states municipalities have been given general preferences over private persons.[67] So a water-right
of a municipality is higher in order to one held by a private
person or association, even though the former is later in
time.[68]

All of the above discussion about the administration of
water-appropriation laws holds true with respect to all surface watercourses. In the following states, the same laws
apply to all underground waters:

Idaho,   according to the Ground Water Act of 1951 (Laws
                1951, ch. 200), as amended in 1953 (L. 1953, ch.
                182). As a matter of fact, since the case of Le-
                Quime v. Chambers, 98 P. 415, 15 Idaho 405 (1908),
                all underground waters have been held by the Idaho
                courts as subject to appropriation under the prior-
                ity rule. -- Bower v. Moorman, 147 P. 496, 27 Idaho
                162 (1915). This decision was based on an interpre-
                tation of the water-appropriation act of 11 March
                1903, sec. 1. In Silkey v. Tiegs, 5 P. 2d 1049
                (1931), it was held that underground waters may be
                appropriated either by the statutory permit or by
                actual diversion and application to a beneficial
                use. This is recognized and reiterated by sec. 4
                of the Ground Water Act of 1951.

Kansas,   according to the Ground Water Act of 1945 (L. 1945,
                ch. 390, sec. 7, subsec.(a)). Under the old water-
                appropriation law, "waters flowing in well-defined
                subterranean sheets or lakes, shall be subject to
                appropriation with the same effect as the water of
                superficial channels" (L. 1891, ch. 133, sec. 5).
                In State ex rel. Peterson et al. v. Kansas State
                Board of Agriculture et al., 158 Kan. 614, 149 P.
                2d 605 (1944), it was held that underground waters
                were not subject to prior appropriation.

Nevada,   according to the Ground Water Act of 1939 (Stats.

1939, ch. 131), as last amended by Stats. 1953, ch. 162. This Act amended the original Ground Water Act of 1915 (Stats. 1915, ch. 210), which made all underground streams appropriable. It may be noted that no permits are required for "the development and use of underground water for domestic purposes where the draught does not exceed two gallons per minute and where the water developed is not from an artesian well" (sec. 3).

New Mexico, according to the Ground Water Act of 1931 (L. 1931, ch. 64), as last amended in 1953 (L. 1953, chs. 60 and 64). It should be noted that "no permit or license to appropriate underground waters shall be required except in basins declared by the state engineer to have reasonably ascertainable boundaries" (L. 1953, ch. 64, sec. 3) (for the background of this section, see 31 Dicta 41, 44-45, February 1954, by Charles D. Harris), but that all artesian waters are to be appropriated by permits. In the case of the use of underground waters in an amount not exceeding three acre-feet and for a period not exceeding one year in connection with prospecting, mining or drilling operations, a permit is issued for each operation.

Oklahoma, according to the Ground Water Act of 1949 (L. 1949, p. 641).

Oregon, for counties lying east of the summit of the Cascade Mountains only, according to the Ground Water Act of 1927 (L. 1927, ch. 410), as amended in 1933 (L. 1933, ch. 263) and 1953 (Oregon Revised Statutes of 1953, sec. 537.510 et seq.).

Utah, according to Wrathal v. Johnson et al., 40 P. 2d 755, 86 U. 50 (1935), through a most liberal interpretation of the Water Appropriation Act of 1919; and also according to the new Water Appropriation Act of 1935 (L. 1935, ch. 105). It should be mentioned that under the law of 1919 (but not under the law of 1903), underground streams were appropriable. The State Engineer may also divide the waters of an aquifer among their several claimants (L. 1935, ch. 105, sec. 1; as amended by L. 1941, ch. 96, sec. 1) (para. 2).

Washington, according to the Ground Water Act of 1945 (L. 1945, ch. 263). However, permits are not required for withdrawals of underground waters for stock-watering, or for the watering of garden or lawn not exceeding one-half acre in area, or for domestic or industrial uses below 5,000 gallons a day. Prior to 1945, underground streams were appropriable. -- Evans v. Seattle, 47 P. 2d 984, 182.

The laws of North Dakota declare that "all waters within the limits of the state from all sources of water supply belong to the public and are subject to appropriation for beneficial use" (North Dakota Code, sec. 61-0101: Laws 1905, ch. 34, sec. 1; as amended by Laws 1939, ch. 255, sec. 1). This is in effect identical to the corresponding declarations made in the laws of Oregon (Laws 1909, ch. 221, sec. 1) and Washington (Revised Code of Washington, sec. 90.04.020, second sentence: Laws 1917, ch. 117, sec. 1). The latter provisions have been expressly explained by the respective state legislatures, in the respective Ground Water Acts above-mentioned, as applicable only to surface waters.[69] By analogy, the North Dakota declaration would cover surface waters only. There have been no court decisions touching the applicability of North Dakota water-appropriation laws to the underground waters or certain kinds thereof.

Underground waters are not appropriable under administrative permits in Wyoming. However, rights to the use of underground waters (all kinds of underground waters) acquired under the doctrine of prior appropriation is expressly recognized in the Ground Water Act of 1947 (ch. 107), as amended in 1949 (Laws 1949, ch. 22). The same act also authorizes the State Engineer to determine the capacities of all ground-water aquifers of the state as a basis for the adjudication of ground-water rights, which are acquired solely by actual diversion and application to beneficial uses, and, besides, it authorizes the State Board of Control (of which the State Engineer is chairman) to adjudicate ground-water rights. Rights for domestic or stock uses and for the watering of lawn or garden not exceeding four acres in area are exempted from the jurisdiction of the State Engineer and the State Board of Control.

In all other states, not all but only some underground waters are subject to appropriation by permits. In Arizona,[70] California,[71] Colorado,[72] Montana,[73] Oregon (west of the summit of the Cascade Mountains),[74] South Dakota,[75] and Texas,[76] the so-called "underground streams" are subject to administrative appropriation. The term underground streams is best defined in the following passage:[77]

> Underground streams of water, having defined banks, spoken of by the textbooks and decisions, refer mainly to streams of water in the arid regions, which flow partly on and partly beneath the surface, but always in a well-defined channel, and within well-defined banks.

However, underground streams are not necessarily tributary to any surface stream.[78]

It has been statutorily provided in Arizona (Arizona Code Annotated, sec. 75-101, op. cit.), Colorado (Laws 1917, ch. 152, a special act), Montana (Revised Code of Montana, sec. 89-801: Laws 1885, p. 130, sec. 1; as last amended by Laws 1901,

p. 152, sec. 1; Laws 1921, ch. 228, sec. 1: "springs" being
included by the 1901 amendment, Oregon (Laws 1893, p. 150, H.
B. 99, sec. 1) and South Dakota (South Dakota Code, sec. 61.-
0101, op. cit.) that springs are subject to appropriation under administrative permits. In California, springs are appropriable or not according as whether they are connected with
appropriable waters (i.e. surface waters and underground
streams) or with inappropriable water (i.e., percolating
ground waters).[79] But in Texas springs cannot be administratively appropriated, for they are the exclusive property of
the land-owner.[80]

With respect to other kinds or forms of underground water,
it has been held by courts in California that water flowing
from artesian wells on the public domain is subject to appropriation for irrigation purposes.[81] However, in South Dakota,
artesian water is held to be the property of the landowner
and is exempt from appropriation.[82] Colorado courts have
held that underground waters supplying or tributary to surface watercourses are part of the latter and are therefore
appropriable.[83] Such waters may be either underground streams
or percolating ground waters. This rule is not found in other
states.

It may thus be noted that in Arizona, California, Montana,
Oregon (West of the Cascades), South Dakota, Texas and probably also North Dakota, all percolating ground waters (i.e.,
underground waters other than underground streams), and in
Colorado all percolating waters other than those supplying
or tributary to surface watercourses are not subject to appropriation under the doctrine of prior appropriation, but are
property of the owner or owners of overlying lands. However,
this does not mean that these waters are not subject to administrative and or judicial regulation and control, as is the
case under the common law in Britain.[84] The ownership and enjoyment of the proprietary right to the percolating ground waters in the United States is governed by the so-called doctrine
of "correlative rights." Under this doctrine, commonly refer-
ed to as the "American rule" with respect to percolating waters,
as distinguished from the British rule of absolute ownership,
a landowner has no absolute right to the use of the percolating water beneath his or her land, but only a relative right
to it which is (a) conditioned by similar rights of the neighboring landowners drawing upon the same ground-water aquifer
and (b) limited to reasonable beneficial uses. This rule was
first clearly announced in California in Katz v. Walkinshaw,
141 Cal. 116, 74 P. 766 (28 November 1903), and has been recognized and reaffirmed in practically all subsequent cases touching this problem both in California[85] and in other states.[86]

(b) Regulation In Eastern States---Under the laws of Iowa,
no water can be taken out of any navigable or non-navigable
river or stream in the state for industrial uses unless a per-

mit for such taking has been obtained from the Iowa natural
resources council (Iowa Code, sec. 469.1, enacted in 1924
by Senate File Bill 186, as amended by Acts 1949, ch. 203,
sec. 21).

Wisconsin laws provide for administrative permits for the
diversion of water from natural watercourses (Wisconsin Statutes, sec. 31.14: L. 1935, ch. 287, as amended by L. 1943,
375, sec. 5). A distinction made between the surplus water,
that is water "not being beneficially used", and non-surplus
waters should be approved by the Public Service Commission.
The Commission's approval is given in the form of permits.
In the case of non-surplus (or riparian) water, diversion is
permitted only after the consent of the riparian landowners
affected. Surplus or flood waters of a watercourse may be
diverted only for purpose temporarily of maintaining the normal flow or level of some other watercourse; but non-surplus
or riparian waters may be diverted for irrigation. Such regulation is almost in principle the same as that in force in
some Western States.[87] An interesting problem arises as to
whether there is an order of priority among the permit-holders
using water from the same source. The official opinion of the
State of Wisconsin on this problem is as follows:[88]

> Nothing in the statute requires the Commission to
> revise its allocation of water under prior permits
> when another permit is granted on the same stream.
> Such a procedure is unnecessary where there is
> still sufficient surplus of water in the stream or
> where the necessary consents are obtained. The
> desirability of making reallocation on prior per-
> mits where there is insufficient water for all who
> apply is a matter for the decision of the Commis-
> sion in its exercise of its informed judgment.
> Such a permit may be withdrawn or amended by the
> Commission at any time, as no rights are vested in
> an applicant by its issue, the matter being one of
> privilege under the continuing control of the Com-
> mission.

In answer to the question raised by the Public Service Commission. "Can the Commission give a permit to a non-riparian
owner?", the Attorney-General of the State of Wisconsin thinks
"Since the statute says nothing in respect to the issuance of
permits to non-riparian owners it must be assumed that the common law applies" However, it would seem that as the riparian
landowners have rights under common law to the riparian or
non-surplus water of a watercourse, which are recognized by
the Laws of 1935 and 1943 above discussed in their provision
for the riparian landowners' consent to diversions of such
water, permits for the diversion thereof must necessarily be
issued to persons who are not landowners riparian to that watercourse. As for permits for the diversion of surplus waters,

they may be given to both riparian landowners, who are other-wise not entitled to the use thereof, and other persons.

On 24 June 1939, an act was enacted by Pennsylvania adopt-ing two measures for the regulation of water rights of public water supply agencies but not those of individual water users. In the first place, a public water supply agency, whether a municipality or a private corporation, must actually make use of its claim to any water right. If within one year after the passage of the said act (i.e., by 24 June 1940) public water supply agencies did not take water under their claims to water rights, such claims or rights were ipso facto for-feited. But all active claims continued to be effective, and were to be recorded by the Water and Power Resources Board of the Department of Forests and Waters, the record to be known as "Water Acquisition Record." All new water rights are to be acquired only by permits to be issued by the said Board upon application. All permits may be revoked by the Board.

The water-use regulation in Illinois and Minnesota bears a close resemblance to that in the West. In Illinois, the Department of Public Works and Buildings has been authorized to issue permits to non-riparian parties for the appropriation and use of waters of public watercourses for industrial, manu-facturing, water-supply, hydroelectric power and other public-utility purposes without interfering with navigation, for re-newable terms of not more than forty years, with the concurr-ence of the municipal authorities concerned if the water is taken from a watercourse located in or adjoining a municipal-ity (Revised Statutes, ch. 19, sec. 65, para. 2, added by Laws 1945, p. 381). Besides, the statute expressly limits the right to the use of water "to such water as shall be rea-sonably required for the beneficial use to be served." A State Water Resources and Flood Control Board has been creat-ed, one of the functions of which is "to arbitrate and provide ways and means for the equitable reconciliation and adjustment of the various claims and rights to water by users or uses" (ibid., ch. 127, sec. 200.1 et seq.: L. 1945, p. 383).

In Minnesota, there is actually a Water Code (Laws 1937, ch. 468; as last amended by Laws 1947, ch. 142). Among other things, it provides that

> It shall be unlawful for the state, any person, partnership or association, private or public corp-oration, county, municipality, or other political subdivision of the state to appropriate or use any waters of the state, surface or underground, with-out the written permit of the commissioner (of conservation). . . . Nothing in this section shall be construed to apply to the use of water for do-mestic purposes serving at any time less than 25

persons, or to the use of water for any purpose
originating within the geographical limits of any
municipality, nor to any beneficial uses and rights
in existence prior to July 1, 1937 (emphasis added).

The permit issued by the Commissioner of Conservation are,
like water appropriation permits in the West, permanent in
nature but subject to revocation at any time. A permit automatically becomes invalid if actual appropriation of water
does not take place within five years after the issuance of
the permit. In 1949, another law was passed (ch. 599) by the
legislature of Minnesota, introducing a special kind of water
appropriation permit for mining purposes. Under this law,
permits may be granted by the Commissioner of Conservation
for drainage, diversion, control or use for the mining of iron
ore or taconite, for terms only long enough to cover a mining
operation. These permits, however, are irrevocable. A statute less extensive in scope was enacted by North Carolina
legislature on 14 April 1951, which requires a permit from
the Department of Conservation and Development for the taking
of water from a surface watercourse for the purpose of irrigation with view to preserving the normal volume of flow of the
watercourse.

Louisiana, in 1910 (Acts of 1910, no. 258), declared the
waters and beds of all navigable streams and of all bayous,
lagoons, lakes and bogs to be property of the state. Arkansas,
in an act of 1941 (Laws of 1941, ch. 84), proclaimed that "in
the event it becomes necessary for the commissioner to determine the relative values to the public of proposed uses of
water, wildlife uses (including fish) shall be deemed to be
inferior to domestic and municipal uses, irrigation and stock
watering uses, and water power and mining uses" (sec. 1, last
sentence). Both of these provisions embody some feature of
the Western law of prior appropriation. The two states, however, have not transplanted other features of the Western water right system to their respective jurisdictions.[89]

Upon recommendation of the Technical Advisory Committee on
Quantity of Water of the Interstate Commission on the Delaware
River Basin, which is made up of representatives of the States
of New Jersey, New York and Pennsylvania, these three states
in 1943 and 1944 enacted identical laws (Laws of Pennsylvania
of 1943, Act no. 193; Laws of 1943 of New York, ch. 709; laws
of New Jersey of 1944, ch. 121) providing for the regulation
of diversions of water from the Delaware River and its tributaries. Any such diversion by any person, corporation or entity in any of these states should be approved by the state
water agency.[90] After a hearing at which representatives of
the water agencies of the other two states are to be invited
to participate. In these identical laws, there are common
standards guiding the respective state water agencies in their

approval of water diversions, which aim at the conservation
of the waters of the Delaware River System for domestic and
municipal supply.[91] The decisions of the water agencies are
subject to those of the United States Supreme Court.

Some states have laws providing for the appropriation of
ground waters, but not that of surface waters. A law of Maryland requires licenses from the Department of Geology, Mines
and Water Resources for the appropriation and use of ground
waters, and provides that ground waters can be used only for
domestic and agricultural purposes.[92] An act of 1 July 1947
of New Jersey directed the Department of Conservation to delineate, from time to time, areas of the state where the diversion of subsurface or percolating waters exceeds or threatens to exceed the natural replenishment thereof. In such
areas, the act provides, "no person, corporation or agency
of the public shall hereafter divert or obtain water from
subsurface or percolating sources in excess of 100,000 gallons per day for any purpose "without a permit of the said
Department.

Section 5   Dams and Other Works of Water Control and Utiliza-
            tion

The regulation of dams and other works of water control
and utilization (such as dikes and revetments) is generally
directed at the physical attributes and effects of these
structures merely as structures, and is not concerned with their
functions as instruments of water-resources management. That
is to say, it is not a "purpose regulation," such as the regulation of navigation, or of flood control, or of water supply. The objectives of this regulation are, in general, (1)
to protect public interests (in any purpose or purposes of
water-resources management as well as in other matters) from
possible adverse effects of the structure, or, briefly, public interest; and (2) to protect life and property against
structural failure, or, briefly, public safety. As of the
end of 1953, this regulation was existent in the following
states:

Maine------Revised Statutes, ch. 166, sec. 32, proviso (Laws
           1925, ch. 202), and secs. 45 and 46 (L. 1879, ch.
           169; as amended by L. 1897, ch. 277).
Connecticut-General Statutes, ch. 240 (Enacted 1878; as last
           amended in 1939).
Colorado---General Statutes, ch. 90, sec. 83 et seq. (L. 1899,
           ch. 126; as amended by L. 1925, ch. 122).
Montana----Revised Codes, sec. 89-702(Revised Code of 1907,
           ch. sec. 2139; as amended by L. 1917, ch. 168,
           sec. 1).
Oregon-----Revised Statutes, secs. 540.350 and 540.360 (L.1909,
           ch. 216, secs. 56 and 57; as last amended by L.
           1929, ch. 312, secs. 1 and 2).

Rhode
  Island----General Laws, ch. 638, secs. 4 and 5 (Acts 1909,
          ch. 407; as amended by Acts 1935, ch. 2250, sec.
          64).
New Jersey-Statutes, tit. 58, ch. 4 (L. 1912, ch. 243; as
          last amended by L. 1919, ch. 44, sec. 1).
Massachusetts---General Laws, ch. 91, sec. 12 (Acts 1914,
          ch. 717, secs. 3 and 4; as last amended by Acts
          1931, ch. 394, sec. 61) and sec. 12A (Acts 1939,
          ch. 513, sec. 6).
Wisconsin--Statutes, sec. 31.05 et seq. (L. 1915, ch. 380;
          as last amended by L. 1947, ch. 124).
Washington-Revised Code, sec. 90.28.060 (L. 1917, ch. 117,
          sec. 36; as amended by L. 1939, ch. 107, sec. 1).
Utah-------Code, sec. 73-5-5 et seq. (L. 1919, ch. 67, secs.
          73 to 75; as last amended by L. 1953, ch. 131,
          sec. 1).
Iowa-------Code, ch. 469 (Enacted in the Code of 1924; as
          amended by Acts 1949, ch. 203, sec. 21 et seq.).
New York---Conservation Law, sec. 948 (L. 1928, ch. 242; as
          amended by L. 1940, ch. 651).
California-Water Code, sec. 6075 et seq. (Stats. 1929, ch.
          766; as amended by Stats. 1941, ch. 557, sec. 9).
Kansas-----General Statutes, sec. 82a-301 et seq. (L. 1929,
          ch. 203, sec. 1; as amended by L. 1933, ch. 330,
          sec. 1).
Vermont----Statutes, sec. 9397 et seq. (L. 1929, No. 80; as
          last amended by L. 1947, No. 202, sec. 9528 et
          seq.).
West Virginia---Code, sec. 5988, 2nd sentence (Enacted 1 Jan-
          uary 1931).
Minnesota--Statutes, sec. 105.43 et seq. (L. 1937, ch. 468,
          sec. 5 et seq.; as amended by L. 1947, ch. 142,
          sec. 6 et seq.).
New Hampshire---Revised Laws, ch. 267, sec. 15 et seq. (L. 1937,
          ch. 133).
North Dakota---Revised Code, sec. 61-0220 (L. 1937, ch. 255,
          sec. 9; as amended by L. 1939, ch. 256, sec. 9).
Ohio-------Revised Code, sec. 1521.06 (L. 1949, p. 96).
Nevada-----Stats. 1951, ch. 110, sec. 12 (added to Stats. 1913,
          ch. 140, as sec. 77.5 thereof.
Kentucky---Acts 1948, ch. 229, sec. 2 (See p. 647, above).

   In Maine, Rhode Island, New Jersey, Wisconsin, Utah, Iowa[93]
New York,[94] California, Vermont, New Hampshire, North Dakota,
Ohio and Nevada, only dams are under regulation. In all other
states listed above, not only dams but also dikes or other
structures are brought under regulation. The regulation has
its emphasis on the construction, and only a relatively few
states have undertaken to regulate the operation of the structures. These two phases of the regulation are separately discussed below.

(1) Regulation over construction---This again may be divided

into the following two phases:

(a) <u>Enabling or authorization of the structures and the construction work</u>---This prevails in all of the above-listed states with the exception of Montana.[95] In strict analysis, there is distinction between the enabling or authorization of the <u>structures</u> and that of <u>construction</u>. In the former case, which may be designated as <u>strong</u> enabling or authorization, the state grants both the <u>right</u> to construct the structure and its assent to the <u>plan</u> of construction. In the latter case, which may be called <u>weak</u> enabling or authorization, the right to construct the structure is presupposed, but the plan of construction is given state approval so that the exercise of this right does not physically conflict with public rights and interests.[96] The strong system exists in Connecticut, Wisconsin, Iowa, Kansas, Minnesota,[97] Massachusetts,[98] Maine, New York, Vermont, West Virginia and North Dakota.[99] The weak system obtains in Colorado, Oregon, Rhode Island, New Jersey, Washington, California, New Hampshire, Kentucky, Ohio and Nevada, where the right to construct the structures seems to be unquestionable but the "plans and specifications" of the structures must be approved by the state.

The enabling or authorization regulation is expressly declared to be for both public interest and public safety in Wisconsin, Iowa and Minnesota, for public interest alone in Vermont and Ohio, and for public safety alone in Connecticut, Oregon, New Jersey, Washington, Utah, New York, California, West Virginia, New Hampshire and North Dakota. In Colorado, Rhode Island, Massachusetts, Maine, Kansas, Kentucky and Nevada, the laws are silent as to the objectives of this regulation, which may be both public interest and public safety or either.[100] While public safety always refers to the loss of life and damage to property, the definition of public interest fits with no common pattern. In Ohio, the law provides that plans and specifications of the structures are to be examined "only with respect to overall use of the water resources in the immediate area affected and in the state as a whole." In Minnesota, "public welfare" or "public interest" is not defined. In Vermont, the public interest, or, in the terminology of the statute, "public good", is

> defined to mean that which shall be for the greatest benefit of the people of the state of Vermont. In determining whether the public good shall be served thereby, the (state public service) commission shall give due consideration, among other things, to the quantity, kind, and extent of cultivated agricultural land that may be flooded or rendered unfit for use by such proposed project . . . In determining such question of public good it shall give further due consideration to the affect of such proposed project upon scenic and recreation-

al values, upon fish and wild life, upon town
grand lists and revenues, upon forests and forest
programs, upon the natural flow of the water in
the stream below the dam and upon any hazards to
navigation, fishing, bathing and other public uses.
The commission shall likewise, in determining the
question of public good, investigate the question
whether the cutting clean and removal of all timber and tree growth from all or any part of the
flowage area is reasonably required for the public
good . . . The commission shall likewise, in determining the question of public good, consider
the public benefits resulting from such proposed
development . . .(Statutes, sec. 9400).

Such definition is comprehensive almost to the point of dis-
couraging the construction of any dam or reservoir.

The enabling regulation applies to all navigable and non-
navigable rivers and streams in all the states which have
adopted it, with the exception of Massachusetts and Maine.
In Massachusetts, it concerns only (1) the Connecticut River
and certain portions of the Westfield and Merrimack Rivers
and (2) all rivers and streams "within the commonwealth with
respect to which expenditures from federal, state or municipal
funds[101] have been made for stream clearance, channel improvement or any form of flood control or prevention work." The
coverage of the Maine statute is even narrower: only those
rivers and streams are under regulation whose waters ultimately reach the ocean at a point outside the territorial limits
of the United States (law of 1925). Except for the Connecticut and non-tidal portions of the Merrimack River of Massachusetts, where licenses are granted for terms of five years,
the duration period of the enabling is not specified in the
laws of any of the states concerned.

Small dams and structures are exempted from the enabling
requirement in the following states:

Colorado---dams of less than 10 feet in height or impounding
          less than 1,000 acre-feet of water.
Oregon-----dams of less than 10 feet in height or impounding
          less than 3 million gallons of water; splash dams
          for driving logs; farm dikes constructed on owners'
          own land; and ditches of less than 5 second-feet in
          capacity.
New Jersey-dams raising water above mean low water by not more
          than 5 feet; dams the drainage area of which is
          less than 0.5 square mile, for both construction and
          repair, For repair only, dams with reservoirs of
          less than 10 acres in surface area and raising wa-
          ter by less than 8 feet, in absence of complaint.
Washington-reservoirs of not more than 10 acre-feet in capaci-

ty.

Utah-------reservoirs of not more than 20 acre-feet in capa-
            city.
New York---dams having drainage areas not exceeding one
            square mile and a height of not more than 10 feet.
Kansa------dams built on private streams for non-agricultural
            purposes (see Laws 1939, ch. 354) which are under
            10 feet in height and impounds not more than 15
            acre-feet of water; properly placed jetties or
            revetments to stabilize caving banks.
Vermont----dams impounding not more than 500,000 cubic feet
            of water
West Virginia---dams of not more than 10 feet in height.
North Dakota----dams of not more than 10 feet in height or
            impounding not more than 30 acre-feet of water.
Nevada-----dams of not more than 10 feet in height or im-
            pounding not more than 10 acre-feet of water.

In Ohio, "works relating to municipal water supply, temporary
industrial use, or domestic use, or for farm purposes" are
exempted. In the remaining states, no such or other exemptions have been made.

"Construction" is expressly stipulated to cover reconstruction in Rhode Island, New Jersey, Massachusetts, Wisconsin, New York, California, Kansas, Vermont, Minnesota, New
Hampshire and Nevada. It would seem that this should also be
the rule in other states although their laws are not explicit
on it. The laws of New Jersey and California further bring
repair of structures under the enabling regulation. It may
be incidentally remarked that repair may be short of reconstruction. In Wisconsin, Iowa, New York and California, administrative authorization is required of the operation and
maintenance of existing structures. In Wisconsin, however,
only dams on navigable waters are under this additional regulation. In Connecticut, California, Minnesota and Wisconsin
(for dams on the Wisconsin River only)[102] the same requirement
is imposed on the removal of dams and other structures, too.
Under the laws of New Jersey, the owner of a dam has the un-
abridged right to abandon or remove the dam within twenty
years after its construction; but beyond this period this
should be done with state approval if a majority of nearby
landowners petition the state for the continued operation of
the dam.

In general, the enabling regulation applies to all private
parties and incorporated local governmental units. In New
York, the law speaks of "any private person or corporation"
and "any public authority." The latter term is likely to include the state, any state agency and an unincorporated local
governmental unit. In Minnesota it is expressly provided that
the state and all local governmental units are subject to this
regulation. Vermont has made the unique attempt of bringing

the Federal Government under this regulation, which surely
will result in highly complicated constitutional controversies.

(b) <u>Supervision over construction work</u>---Resident supervision is authorized or permissible in Connecticut, Colorado,
New Jersey, Utah and Vermont, to insure compliance with the
terms of the authorization or enabling regulation. By "resident supervision", it is meant supervision of construction
by an engineer specially appointed for this purpose. In
Utah the resident engineer has the re-inforced authority to
order necessary changes and alterations of the engineering
design or plan in order to safeguard life and property. In
New Hampshire, North Dakota and Nevada the laws allow the
state administrative agency concerned to make inspections of
the construction work, which is a milder form of supervision
than resident supervision. In North Dakota, the state agency,
as a result of the inspection, may further order necessary
changes or alterations for the sake of safety.

(2) <u>Regulation over operation</u>---There are two aspects of
this regulation, to wit:

(a) <u>Supervision of operation</u>---This is as a rule ancillary to construction-enabling or authorization. Inspections
of operation can always be presupposed;[103] for any violation
of or non-compliance with the terms of enabling can only be
detected by inspection.

However, such inspection, which is necessarily routine
in nature, can hardly be classified as an independent measure
of operation-regulation. With regard to independent operation-regulation meausres, the laws of California have authorized the state administrative agency to require owners of
structures to keep records of operation and to issue necessary
rules and regulations for their operation and maintenance to
safeguard life and property. Under the laws of Iowa, the
plan of operation of any dam must be approved by the state
administrative agency. In the laws of Colorado, it is provided that "the State Engineer shall annually determine the
amount of water which it is safe to impound for the several
reservoirs within this state and it shall be unlawful for the
owners of any reservoir to store in said reservoir water in
excess of the amount so determined by the State Engineer."
Similar authority is enjoyed by the Public Service Commission
of Wisconsin.[104] All these measures deal with the engineering or physical operation of the structures only. In Iowa
laws a peculiar provision is found whereby the state is given
authority to confiscate dams owned or controlled by unlawful
trusts or capital-combinations and hydroelectric power dams
involved in monopolistic practices.

(b) <u>Emergency measure against structure failure</u>---This is provided in the laws of the following fifteen states:

Maine---"The governor with the advice and consent of the council shall annually appoint a competent practical engineer, .
. . who shall, upon petition of ten resident taxpayers of any
town or several towns, the selectmen of any town, or the county commissioners of any county, inspect any dam or reservoir
located in such town or county, . . . and after personal examination and hearing, . . . shall forthwith report to the
governor his opinion of the safety and sufficiency thereof"
(Revised Statutes, ch. 166, sec. 45; Laws 1877, ch. 169; as
amended by L. 1897, ch. 277). "If . . . the engineer reports
that such dam or reservoir is unsafe, . . . then the owners,
occupants or lessees thereof shall immediately make such alterations, repairs and additions to said dam or reservoir as
such engineer recommends; and in default thereof, . . . the
said owners, occupants or lessees shall be enjoined (by supreme or superior court) from the use of such dam or reservoir
. . . and the water contained in said dam or reservoir may be
discharged therefrom by order said engineer . . ."

Connecticut---"The (Stream Control) Board shall make or cause
to be made such periodic inspections of all such structures
as may be necessary to reasonably insure that they are maintained in a safe condition. Any person, firm or corporation
which would suffer loss of life or property by the breaking
away of any such structure may petition the board . . . for
an inspection . . . If after any inspection . . . the board
finds any such structure to be in an unsafe condition, it shall
order the person, firm or corporation owning or having control
thereof to place it in a safe condition or to remove it. . ."
(General Statutes, sec. 4730, second part).

Colorado---Upon complaint by three or more persons concerned
and after examination, the State Engineer shall cause water
behind an unsafe dam to be withdrawn to a safe level.

Montana---Upon complaint by three or more persons concerned
and after examination, the state engineer may ask the county
attorney to abate the danger inherent in an unsafe dam or dike.

Oregon---The State Engineer, either upon complaint by any person concerned or in his own initiative, may inspect an unsafe
dam or other hydraulic structure and order its owner to make
corrective modifications thereof. In case of default, he may
order the owner to release the stored water and to cease the
use of the structure. Further neglect of the order will render the structure a nuisance subject to judicial action.

Rhode Island---The chief of the Division of Harbors and Rivers
of the Department of Public Works may, either in his own motion
or upon complaint by a person or a local governmental unit concerned, may examine an unsafe dam. In case the danger is im-

minent, he may order the owner of the dam to empty the reservoir in whole or in part and to make necessary repairs.

New Jersey---Exactly the same as Rhode Island.

Utah---When a dam is found to be unsafe after an inspection made either in his own motion or upon the complaint of any person interested, the State Engineer "may order the release of all or any part of the water impounded and . . . regulate future storage or forbid it entirely until the dam is repaired or reconstructed . . ." He may also order necessary repairs of unsafe ditches and other diverting works.

New York---"The Superintendent of Public Works shall have power, whenever in his judgment public safety shall so require, to make and serve an order . . . directing any person, corporation, officer or board constructing, maintaining or using any structure . . . either to remove said structure or to repair or reconstruct the same . . ." In case of default, he may perform the work at the cost of the delinquent party, in addition to the imposition of a fine.

California---Whenever, any dam is the condition of imminent danger, or whenever it is threatened by floods, the Department of Public Works (through the State Engineer) may either lower the water level of the reservoir or completely empty it, or take other necessary steps to safeguard life and property.

Vermont---When a dam is found unsafe after an investigation and a hearing made upon the petition of ten taxpayers or by the authorities of any town, the Public Service Commission may order the repair, reconstruction or removal of said dam.

Minnesota---"Upon complaint or upon his own initiative, the Commissioner (of Conservation) is authorized to examine any reservoir, dam or waterway obstruction. If the Commissioner determines that such reservoir, dam or waterway is unsafe or needs repair, he shall notify the owner thereof to repair or remove the same as the exigencies may require."

New Hampshire---The Water Control Commission, after an inspection, may order the repair or reconstruction of an unsafe dam.

Nevada---Substantially the same as California.

Wisconsin---The Public Service Commission may order the emergency repair of dams built on the Wisconsin River (Statutes, sec. 31.18(1), op. cit.).

Section 6 Hydroelectric Power Development (Licensing)

In the several Western states except Oregon, hydroelectric power development constitutes but one of the various beneficial

uses of water, and, in general, is governed by the water-appropriation laws in the same way as other beneficial uses. Only
in South Dakota and Washington are there special provisions
in such laws regarding power development. Under South Dakota
water-appropriation laws, "no appropriation of water, in excess of 25 horsepower, for power purposes, made after the
first day of July 1913, shall be for a longer period than 50
years . . ." (Code, sec. 61.0152: Laws 1913, ch. 365). In
Washington, special annual "license fee" is required of permits of appropriation for the purpose of power development.
In states where there is state regulation of dams, such regulation may or may not cover power dams. In this Section
only the regulation (primarily licensing) of hydroelectric
power projects as such will be discussed. As of the end of
1953, such regulation is found in the following states: (1)
New Jersey---The plans and specifications of the construction
of any hydroelectric power dam must be approved by the Division of Water Policy and Supply of the Department of Conservation. If a dam is built on a navigable watercourse, the said
Division may require the construction of necessary canals,
locks, or like structures to safeguard the interest of navigation. No power dam can be allowed to raise the waters in
the watercourse above the dam to a height of more than ten
feet above low-water mark (Statutes, sec. 48:14-11; being L.
1897, ch. 195, sec. 2, as amended by L. 1922, ch. 33, sec. 1).
(2) Wisconsin---Regulation is contained in the Wisconsin
Statutes, ch. 31, commonly known as the "water power law"
(L. 1915, ch. 380, as amended). It applies primarily to power
dams constructed over navigable waters. Permits of the Public Service Commission are required for (1) the construction
or operation and maintenance of both new and old dams and (2)
the raising or enlarging of old dams, over navigable watercourses (L. 1915, ch. 380, sec. 3; as amended by L. 1917, ch.
474, secs. 6, 8, 13). All such permits should contain regulations of power rates (L. 1929, ch. 327). The said Commission also issues certificates of public convenience and necessity for the acquisition of existing power dams on navigable
watercourses.[105] It is also vested with the authority and
duty to examine, at least once a year, all power dams of a
generating capacity of more than 750 horsepower, and inspect
any dam or reservoir upon complaint of the government of any
city, town or village concerned, whether the dam or dams are
located on navigable or non-navigable watercourses. In addition, it may order necessary repairs or releases of water as
a measure of securing public safety L. 1915, ch. 380, sec. 3;
as amended by L. 1917, ch. 474, sec. 19).
(3) New York---The Water and Power Control Commission of the
state Department of Conservation issues licenses for maximum
terms of fifty years for the construction of hydroelectric
power projects on waters in which the state has a proprietary
right or interest. It also issues preliminary permits for
such projects. But licenses issued by the said commission
shall not become effective unless they are approved by the

governor (Conservation Law, art. 14: L. 1921, ch. 579; as last amended by L. 1943, ch. 46).

(4) Pennsylvania---The Water and Power Resources Board of the Department of Forests and Waters issues permits for all hydroelectric power developments, whether they fall within Federal jurisdiction or not. The permits are issued for a maximum term of fifty years, but at the end of the period they may be renewed or extended. However, after one term, the said Board may compulsorily purchase the project of a permittee or let it be sold to another permittee. For those projects which are within Federal jurisdiction, state permits shall be null and void if within a specified period no Federal permits have been issued on the same projects. In case certain Federal rights over such projects are waived by the Federal Government, the same rights may be exercised by the state. Potential regulation is contemplated of the construction and operation of "dams or changes in streams to supply water for steam power within the jurisdiction of the United States"; and the above regulatory measures would automatically apply to such works if and when the same should be regulated by the Federal Power Commission (Act No. 704 of 1923; as amended by Act No. 255 of 1953).

(5) Virginia---The State Corporation Commission issues permits of a maximum term of fifty years for hydroelectric power developments on all state waters, both navigable and non-navigable (Code of Virginia, tit. 62, ch. 5; Acts 1928, ch. 424).

(6) Oregon---The Hydroelectric Commission issues permits for maximum terms of fifty years and preliminary permits for maximum terms of two years for all hydroelectric power developments in the state (Laws 1931, ch. 67).

(7) Iowa---A certificate of convenience and necessity from the State Executive Council (composed of the governor, the secretary of the state, the state auditor, the state treasurer and the secretary of agriculture) is required for any hydroelectric power project constructed or operated in the state (Laws 1947, ch. 246, sec. 1).

(8) Vermont---An act of 1949 (Act No. 223) provides that hydroelectric power dams are to be approved by the state Water Conservation Board instead of the Public Service Commission as in the case of other dams. It seems that prior to the enactment of this act the regulation of hydroelectric power developments was governed by the same laws which regulate the construction and operation of dams in general, and that since then this practice has been continued, except for this change in the regulating agencies.

Another aspect of state licensing of hydroelectric power projects, which is akin to the issuance of "presidential per-

mits" in Federal regulation, is the permission for the exportation of hydroelectric energy out of the state. In New Hampshire, such exportation should be approved by the Public Service Commission (Laws 1926, ch. 240, sec. 33), and in Maine
by the state legislature (Revised Statutes, ch. 46, sec. 1:
Laws 1909, ch. 244, sec. 1). Regulation of such exportation
also exists in Wisconsin, West Virginia, Vermont, Indiana
and Maryland.106 In Idaho, the exportation of electric energy generated from the waters of the Pend d'Oreille, the Clark
Fork of the Columbia River, the Spokane River and their tributaries is prohibited (Idaho Code, sec. 42-408: Laws 1915,
ch. 111, sec. 8; as amended by L. 1925, ch. 3, sec. 1).

Section 7 Water Sanitation

Subsection 1 Water Pollution Control

    (a) Special Water Pollution Control

    (1) Control of pollution impairing special uses of water
---There are the following two types of this control:

    (i) Against pollution of waters used as domestic water
supplies. This is found in most states. In some states, the
control is implemented by non-administrative, criminal regulation, as, for example, in Oregon (Laws 1889, p. 89, sec. 1;
as last amended by L. 1945, ch. 276, sec. 1---prohibition of
pollution of waters used for domestic and stock purposes) and
Tennessee (Code of Tennessee, sec. 10878: Acts 1903, ch. 310,
sec. 2). In other states, administrative regulation (that
is, regulation involving some action on the part of a state
administrative agency) is provided. Some representative examples may be cited. In Mississippi, for example, the statute
prohibits the pollution of streams which threatens fish life
or renders them unfit for domestic use. To private persons,
this prohibition is absolute, and therefore partakes of the
nature of criminal regulation. But the State Board of Health
may, on certain conditions, permit cities and villages to
pollute the streams through the discharge of sewage. When
the pollution is excessive, the Board may order correction
(Mississippi Code, sec. 2414: Laws 1898, ch. 89; as amended
by L. 1932, ch. 239). Under the laws of Ohio, any local governmental unit or public institution, or fifty electros of
the state may complain to the Director of the Department of
Health of the discharge of sewage and other wastes into a
watercourse by any person, institution, corporation, city or
village. If the said Director, after investigation, finds
the complaint to be true, he may, after a hearing, order the
responsible party to install treatment works (Ohio Revised
Code of 1953, sec. 6111.09 et seq.: Laws 1908, p. 74; as last
amended by L. 1945, p. 409).

    In Rhode Island, the Director of Health may determine

standards of purity for any stream, lake, well or any other
body of water used as a source of municipal water supply.
In such waters, bathing, washing or any other form of pollution is prohibited (General Laws, ch. 635: Acts 1911, ch. 683;
as amended by Acts 1935, ch. 2250). Under the laws of California, the state Department of Health or a local health officer may issue peremptory order for the abatement of contamination of surface or underground waters threatening public health
through poisoning or the spread of disease (Health and Safety
Code, sec. 5410 et seq.: Stats. 1935, ch. 649; as amended by
Stats. 1949, ch. 1550).

But all these are merely special administrative measures.
It should be pointed out that in most states the state health
department issues permits or licenses and (or) approves plans
for the construction of sewage systems. The main purpose of
this regulation is to prevent the pollution of municipal and
domestic water supply at its source.

One of the pollution-control measures worthy of special
attention is the regulation designed to protect watersheds of
streams used as sources of municipal and domestic water supply,
which is found in a few states. In New Jersey, a law was
passed in 1909 (ch. 141; slightly amended by L. 1921, ch. 58),
which authorized the State Health Department to designate
(upon request of the city concerned) the watershed of a city
from which it obtains its water supply, and to prohibit railroad trains and steam bots to discharge wastes from water-
closets and urinals within the territorial limits of such
watershed. In 1921, another laws came into force (ch. 280)
which requires written permits of the said Department for
the establishment of factories on any watershed above the
point where any public supply of water is taken.

In the laws of Wyoming, there is the following provision:[107]

> No municipal or other public or private corpor-
> ation and no company or person shall hereafter con-
> struct, build, establish or operate any railroad,
> logging road, logging camp, electric plant, manu-
> facturing or industrial plant of any kind, upon or
> over any watershed of any public water supply sys-
> tem, unless such corporation, company or person
> shall protect said water supply from pollution by
> such sanitary precautions as shall be approved by
> the state board of health, and any such corporation,
> company or person intending to construct, build,
> or establish or operate any railroad, logging road,
> logging camp, electric plant, manufacturing or in-
> dustrial plant of any kind upon the watershed of
> any public water supply system, shall furnish the
> state board of health with detailed plans and spe-
> cifications of the sanitary precautions to be taken,

which must be approved by said board (Compiled
Statutes, sec. 63-206: Laws 1923, ch. 92, sec. 6).

In Nevada, an act of 29 March 1946 provides for special
regulatory protection for the Lake Tahoe Watershed. Written
permits from the State Department of Health are required for
the construction of dwellings, buildings, waterworks, and
sewerage systems within the watershed. Besides, the "direct
discharge of sewage or other wastes into Lake Tahoe or within
100 feet of the established high water rim of Lake Tahoe, or
within 100 feet of a stream, reservoir, spring, well or other
water supply in the Lake Tahoe watershed is prohibited; excepting in that instance where disposal of sewage or other waste
by reason of property characteristics, topography, or other
limitations cannot be provided other than with 100 feet of
Lake Tahoe, then the State Health Department shall issue the
required permit subject to installation and operation of such
sewage works as may be necessary to provide protection to the
Lake Tahoe water and watershed."

(11) Pollution control for the protection of fish and
other aquatic life. Absolute criminal regulation against
water pollution endangering fish life is provided in such
states as Colorado (Statutes, ch. 73, sec. 158: Laws 1899,
p. 213, sec. 7), Oklahoma (Statutes, tit. 29, sec. 273; L.
1909, p. 305; as amended by L. 1915, ch. 185, sec. 11), Oregon (L. 1921, ch. 153, sec. 70; as amended by L. 1931, ch.
370, sec. 51), Utah (Code, sec. 23-3-4: L. 1923, ch. 36, sec.
12; as amended by L. 1953, ch. 39, sec. 2), Florida (Statutes,
sec. 372.75: L. 1929, ch. 13644, sec. 29), Tennessee (Code,
sec. 5176.75: Acts 1937, ch. 84, sec. 82, replacing previous
provision) and Kentucky (Revised Statutes, sec. 150.460: Acts
1942, ch. 68, sec. 47). In Louisiana, the criminal prohibition is qualified by the permission to pollute during an
"open season" beginning 1 October and ending 31 December of
each year. And the regulation is for the protection of waters
used both for fishery and irrigation (Acts 1952, No. 203).

In some other states, administrative regulation is provided. The regulation in Mississippi was just discussed, and
need not be repeated. In Massachusetts, the Department of
Health, upon initiation of the state fish authorities, may
regulate and prohibit the discharge into coastal and inland
waters substances injurious to fish life (Acts 1941, ch. 599;
as amended by Acts 1952, ch. 501). The Department of Fish
and Game of California, whenever it determines that a continuing and chronic pollution of fishery waters exists, "shall
report such condition to the appropriate regional water pollution control board and shall cooperate with and act through
such board in obtaining correction in accordance with any laws
administered by such board" (Fish and Game Code, sec. 481.5:
Stats. 1949, ch. 1553, sec. 1).108 In the laws of New York,
it is provided that

> No person shall erect or maintain any privy, pig-
> sty, inclosure for poultry, barn or barnyard, or
> drain from any building, whence drainage or refuse
> may find its way into water used by any state fish
> hatchery. Every such privy, pigsty, inclosure,
> barn, barnyard and drain is hereby declared to be
> a public nuisance and may be summarily abated by
> the department (of conservation). -- Conservation
> Law, sec. 213, last para. (Laws 1938, ch. 40, sec.
> 1; as last amended by L. 1952, ch. 760).

It may be noted that New York regulation covers only a certain feature of fishery.

(2) Control of special sources of pollution---The following two types of pollution are under this control:

(1) Pollution by oil and gas. Regulation of this type
of pollution aims primarily at the protection of underground
waters. It is purely criminal in nature in such states as
Oklahoma (Oklahoma Statutes, tit. 52, sec. 296: Laws 1909, p.
432; and ibid., tit. 82, sec. 901: Laws 1927, ch. 38, sec. 1),
Texas (Revised Civil Statutes of Texas, art. 4444: Laws 1913,
p. 90; as last amended by L. 1923, p. 177),[109] and Maryland
(Laws 1949, ch. 239). In Texas and Maryland, enforcement
(in the form of inspection and prosecution) by administrative
agencies is provided for. There is express provision of this
kind in Oklahoma, but as a matter of fact the Division of
Water Resources of the Oklahoma Planning and Resources Board
has assumed regulation behind the shield of the criminal regulation in preventing and controlling water pollution by oil
mining.[110]

Administrative regulation is also found in a number of
states. In Iowa, the driller, owners or operators of oil and
gas wells are required to take measures to prevent the pollution of underground waters, and to file reports with the state
geologist (Code, sec. 84.1: Acts 1939, ch. 63, sec. 1). The
Oil and Gas Conservation Commission of Nevada has authority
to regulate the disposal of salt water in oil fields and to
require, if necessary, the drilling, casing and plugging of
oil and gas wells, in order to prevent the pollution or contamination of underground water sources (Stats. 1953, ch. 202,
sec. 4, subsec. 4, in part).

Regulation in Kansas, which consists of both criminal
and administrative measures, is perhaps the most extensive
and delicate of its kind (General Statutes, ch. 55 and part
of ch. 65. Mention will be made only of measures of administrative regulation. In the first place, the State Corporations
for the plugging of oil or gas-prospecting wells after their
use is finished, in order to prevent the pollution of surface
or underground waters suitable for domestic use and irrigation

(ibid., sec. 55-128: Laws 1913, ch. 201, sec. 1; as amended
by L. 1935, ch. 208, sec. 1) (1st sent.). Written authority
from the said Commission is required for the disposition of
salt water produced in oil and gas mining operations (ibid.,
sec. 65-171d: Laws 1933, ch. 85, sec. 1; as amended by L.
1953, ch. 284, sec. 1) (3rd proviso). The plans of disposition should be approved by both the said Commission and the
State Board of Health (ibid., sec. 55-1003: Laws 1945, ch.
234, sec. 2). Moreover, "it shall be unlawful for any person
having possession, control or the use of any oil field waste
disposal well wherein salt water, mineralized brine, oil or
refuse produced from any oil well is disposed below the surface of the earth to inject such salt water, mineralized brine,
oil or refuse from any oil well therein at a pressure in excess of the maximum pressure established by the Kansas state
board of health and contained in the permit issued by the
Kansas corporation commission" (Laws 1953, ch. 270 sec. 1,
1st sent.). The corporation commission may also adopt rules
and regulations the surface cementing of the oil and gas wells
and the driving of pipes (General Statutes of Kansas, secs.
55-136 to 55-138: Laws 1947, ch. 311). Whenever the storage
of salt water or mineral brines in ponds is found to be likely
to cause pollution of water, the State Board of Health shall
order the parties concerned to stop the use of such ponds until they are made impervious to salt water or mineral brines
(ibid., sec. 65-171d, provisoes: Laws 1933, sp. sess., ch. 85,
sec. 1; as last amended by L. 1953, ch. 284, sec. 1). In addition to these statutory measures, the State Board of Health,
under its general authority in regulating water pollution (to
be discussed later), has issued administrative regulation for
the Kansas and the Walnut River Basins which provide, with regard to oil-pollution, (1) that all oil storage tanks shall
be surrounded by an earth dike with a free board of 1.5 feet,
(2) that all brine ponds and waste oil ponds shall have a
free board of 2.5 feet, (3) that, for the Kansas River Basin,
after 1 July 1951, no brines may continue to be stored in
ponds, or discharged in any manner into a surface of underground
watercourse and (4) that, for the Walnut River Basin, "oil re-
finery wastes should be substantially free of toxic substances
. . . before they are discharged to a watercourse."

There are no statutory provisions regarding the regulation
of pollution of water sources by oil and gas industries in
Mississippi and Louisiana. However, the Stream Control Commission, of Louisiana under its general sub-legislative authority (contained in Revised Statutes, sec. 1435), has adopted
detailed administrative rules governing the disposition of
"waste oil, oil field brine, and all other materials resulting
from the drilling for production of, or transportation of oil,
gas or sulphur."[111] Administrative regulation over the pollution of oil field wastes in Mississippi is incorporated in article III of the "rules and regulatinns for pollution control,"
adopted 5 November 1946 by Mississippi Game and Fish Commission

under its general water-pollution regulatory authority (Laws 1946, ch. 381).

In a few other states, there is administrative regulation on the underground storage of oil and gas products. For example, on 21 June 1951, an act was passed by Illinois which requires an order of approval of the State Commerce Commission for any underground storage of gas. ". . . No such order shall be issued by the commission unless it shall contain and be based on findings that the proposed storage will be confined to geological stratum or strata lying more than 500 feet below the surface of the soil; that the proposed storage will not injure any water resources . . ." (sec. 2).[112] Similar regulation was adopted by Minnesota in an act of 1953 (ch.512). As provided in this act, permits of the Department of Conservation are required for the displacement of any underground waters by the underground storage of gas or liquid under pressure. These permits must contain the same conditions as are imposed on underground storage of gas in Illinois.

(ii) Pollution by mining and other specified wastes. In contrast to (i), this regulation principally serves to protect surface waters. In 1913, an act was passed by Pennsylvania which forbids, to a qualified extent, "any person, partnership or corporation to place or discharge . . . in or into any of the running streams, . . . any anthracite coal, anthracite culm, or refuse from any anthracite coal-mine; or to deposit any such coal, or culm, or refuse upon the banks of such streams . . ." In California, a law of 1941 (Stats. 1941, ch. 1215) obligates all hydraulic placer mining operators (1) to construct settling ponds to clarify the water effluents used in the mining processes before they are discharged into the streams and (2) to mix the said effluents with aluminum sulphate and lime or otherwise clarify them. But regulation in both Pennsylvania and California is purely criminal and non-administrative.

The laws of West Virginia stipulate that coal washery should be kept free of pollution, and that in case of violation the State Department of Health may prevent such washery from draining or being discharged into any watercourse (Code, sec. 2458: Laws 1915, 2nd ex. sess., ch. 5; as last amended by L. 1929, ch. 13, sec. 69). In Idaho, in a law of 1953 (ch. 183), it is provided, among other things, that "before any person may conduct a dredge mining operation on lands and beds of streams, . . . he shall file with the inspector of mines of the state of Idaho an application for a permit . . ." (sec. 6-(a), 1st sent.). When the mine washery shall flow into a watercourse, the permit should contain a requirement to the effect that where reasonable the mine operator "shall construct settling ponds through which the water may pass before entering the stream so as to prevent . . . the flow of sediment or silt into the stream" (sec. 4).

The various regulatory measures as discussed above merely
regulate the _wastes_ of the mining operations, but not the mining operations themselves. In California, there is a law
which makes it unlawful, from 1 July to 30 November of each
year, in the Trinity and Klamath River Fish and Game District,
to conduct any mining operation and otherwise to pollute the
waters, apparently with view to protecting fish life (Fish
and Game Code, sec. 482: Stats. 1931, ch. 760, sec. 1; as last
amended by Stats. 1939, ch. 760, sec. 1).

In Maine, permits of the Water Improvement Commission
must be obtained for the discharge or deposit of any oil or
of sawduct and other wastes of lumber industries into any
watercourse or upon its banks (Revised Statutes, ch. 72, sec.
6: Laws 1947, ch. 266, sec. 3; as last amended by L. 1953, ch.
403, sec. 4). The Department of Public Health of Rhode Island, under the law authorizing general pollution control may
regulate the discharge of oils into streams from vessels. The
purposes of both these regulatory measures are not explicitly
indicated, though it may be understood that their primary objective is to protect fishes.

(b) General Water Pollution Control---By general water
pollution control it is meant that the each measure of regulation covers all polluting substances[113] and takes into consideration all prominent uses of waters likely to be affected
by water pollution.[114] Each regulatory measure is comprehensive in scope and multiple-purpose in nature. Normally, general water pollution control embraces all cases that are under
special water pollution control with respect to special uses
of water. Therefore, in states which have adopted general
control, either special control measures with respect to special uses of waters are unnecessary, or they are alternative
or supplemental or even additional to general control measures.
As a matter of fact, there is in most states a limited co-
jurisdiction between the state health department and the state
general water pollution agency [115] in cases dealing with the
pollution of sources of municipal and domestic supply by municipal and domestic sewage.[116] It may be noted that general
pollution control does not ordinarily handle special types of
pollution such as pollution by oil and gas or by mining operations, although in a few states the authority for the latter is placed in the general water pollution agency. As of
the end of 1953, general water pollution control regulation,
which is essentially administrative and usually does not include any purely criminal measures, was adopted in the following states:

Kansas---General Statutes of Kansas, sec. 65-164 (Laws 1907,
          ch. 382, sec. 4, as amended by L. 1909, ch. 226, sec.
          2), which dealt with municipal and domestic water
          supply only; extended to cover the protection of ani-
          mal and aquatic life by ibid., sec. 65-171a (L.1927,

ch. 239, sec. 1). Augmented by administrative regulations adopted in 1950 and 1953, for the Kansas
and Walnut River Basins respectively, under the authority of ibid., sec. 65-171d (L. 1933, sp. sess.,
ch. 85, sec. 1; as last amended by L. 1953, ch. 284,
sec. 1).

Wisconsin---Wisconsin Statutes, sec. 144.05(1) (Laws 1917,
ch. 430; as last amended by L. 1949, ch. 435); sec.
144.51(4) (L. 1927, ch. 264, sec. 2; as amended by
L. 1949, ch. 603); sec. 144.53 (same origin); and
sec. 144.537 (L. 1949, ch. 603).

Rhode Island---General Laws of Rhode Island, ch. 634 (Laws
1920, ch. 1914; as last amended by L. 1935, ch.2250).

Iowa-----Iowa Code, sec. 135.18 et seq. (Acts 1923, ch. 37;
as last amended by Acts 1949, ch. 79).

Connecticut---General Statutes of Connecticut, sec. 4043 et
seq. (Acts 1925, ch. 143; as last amended by Acts
1953, No. 203).

Michigan---Compiled Laws of Michigan, sec. 323.1 et seq.
(Acts 1929, No. 245, as amended by Acts 1949, No.
117).

West Virginia---West Virginia Code, ch. 16, art. 11 (Acts
1929, ch. 14; as last amended by Acts 1953, ch. 145).

South Dakota---South Dakota Code, sec. 61.0106 et seq. (Laws
1935, ch. 174; as amended by L. 1947, ch. 416).

North Dakota---North Dakota Revised Code, sec. 61-0221 (Laws
1937, ch. 255, sec. 9; as last amended by L. 1953,
ch. 256, sec. 2).

Pennsylvania---Pennsylvania Statutes Annotated, tit. 35, sec.
691.1 et seq. (Acts of 22 June 1937 and 8 May 1945).

Oregon---Oregon Revised Statutes of 1953, sec. 449.005 et seq.
(Laws 1939, ch. 3; as amended by L. 1943, ch. 25)
(1943) amendment, however, affects organization only).

Louisiana---Louisiana Revised Statutes, sec. 1441 (Acts 1940,
No. 367, sec. 9); augmented by an administrative regulation adopted 1 August 1951 under the authority of
ibid., sec. 1435 (Acts 1940, No. 367, sec. 3; as
amended by Acts 1942, No. 199, sec. 1).

Mississippi---Mississippi Code, sec. 5929-01 et seq. (Laws
1942, ch. 252; as amended by L. 1946, ch. 381); augmented by "Rules and Regulations for Pollution Control", adopted 5 November 1946.

Indiana---Acts 1943, ch. 214; as amended by Acts 1945, ch.132.

Vermont---Vermont Statutes, sec. 6305 (Acts 1943, No. 109, sec.
2; as last amended by Acts 1951, No. 131) and sec.
6307 (Acts 1943, No. 109, sec. 5).

Maine---Revised Statutes of Maine, ch. 72 (Laws 1945, ch. 345;
as last amended by L. 1953, ch. 403).

Minnesota---Minnesota Statutes, sec. 144.371 et seq. (Laws
1945, ch. 395).

North Carolina---Laws 1945, ch. 1010; as last amended by L.
1951, ch. 606).

Tennessee---Code of Tennessee, ch. 31 (Acts 1945, ch. 399; as
amended by Acts 1951, ch. 228).

Washington---<u>Revised Code of Washington</u>, ch. 90.48 (Laws 1945,
        ch. 216).
Virginia---<u>Code of Virginia</u>, tit. 62, ch. 2 (Acts 1946, ch.
        399; as amended by Acts 1952, ch. 702).
Maryland---Laws 1947, ch. 697; as last amended by L. 1953,
        ch. 155. Augmented by regulation no. 4 (effective
        1 August 1948 and revised 26 January 1951) and reg-
        ulation no. 5 (effective 1 June 1952).
New Hampshire---<u>Revised Laws of New Hampshire</u>, ch. 166-A
        (Laws 1947, ch. 183; as last amended by L. 1951,
        ch. 1).
Alabama---Acts 1949, No. 460.
Arkansas---Acts 1949, No. 472.
California---<u>Water Code</u>, sec. 13000 et seq. (Stats. 1949,
        ch. 1549).
Delaware---Laws 1949, ch. 324; augmented by general orders
        nos. 1 and 2, effective 26 May 1951.
New York---Laws 1949, ch. 666; as amended by L. 1952, ch.818.
        (Under Laws 1903, ch. 468, sec. 1, as last amended
        by L. 1928, ch. 395, sec. 4, the department of health
        may issue permits for the discharge of sewage and
        wastes into streams. Under L. 1921, ch. 510, sec.
        4, as amended by L. 1928, ch. 395, sec. 3, the said
        department may, with the approval of the governor
        and the attorney general, order the abatement of
        water pollution. These provisions were repealed by
        the 1949 law).
Kentucky---Acts 1950, ch. 69.
South Carolina---Acts 1950, No. 873.
Illinois---An act of 12 July 1951 (Laws 1951, p. 1461).
Ohio---<u>Ohio Revised Code of 1953</u>, sec. 6111.01 et seq. (act
        of 27 September 1951).
Utah---Laws 1953, ch. 41.

        Regulation in Louisiana is concerned with industrial
wastes only. In Wisconsin and Pennsylvania there are separate
though similar regulatory measures (at the statutory level)
for sewage and industrial and other wastes. Strictly speaking, therefore, regulation in these three states cannot be
regarded as belonging to <u>general</u> water pollution control in
its full sense. But partly because it envisages all ordinary
uses of water and partly because it is administered (except
in Kansas) by an ad-hoc water pollution control agency, it
is included in this discussion. In all other states, the
regulation is one of general water pollution control without
qualification.

        In the sixteen states of Kansas, Pennsylvania, North Car-
olina, Washington, Virginia, Maryland, Alabama, Arkansas, California, Delaware, New York, Kentucky, South Carolina, Illinois,
Ohio and Utah, the statute expressly declares that the regulation is applicable to both surface and underground waters.
Despite this declaration, all the general pollution measures

adopted in each of the above-listed states in actuality only
apply to surface waters.[117]

General water pollution regulation is, in general, made
up of the following three regulatory measures (exclusive of
purely criminal measures, which are omitted):

(A) The abatement of water pollution, which means either
the stoppage of the discharge of polluting substances (that
is, municipal and domestic sewage and industrial and other
wastes) or the necessary treatment thereof. In all of the
states having adopted general pollution regulation, with the
exception of North Dakota, Washington and New Hampshire, the
general water pollution regulatory agency has the authority
to issue orders to parties responsible for the pollution for
the abatement of pollution.[118] In New Hampshire, acts of
classification of streams (enacted upon recommendation of
the water pollution commission) serve as general orders of
pollution abatement, non-compliance with which (within a
period of time to be specified by the commission) automatically
exposes them to judicial action. In Washington, abatement
of pollution can only be effected through cumbersome and uncertain judicial procedure.

(B) With the exception of Rhode Island, Oregon, North
Dakota, Indiana, and Washington, permission of the state
pollution control agency is required for the discharge of
new sources of additional amounts of polluting substances.
In Maryland, Delaware and Mississippi such requirement is
adopted by administrative rules and regulations, but in all
the remaining states it is adopted by statute. In Louisiana,
Maryland, Delaware and Mississippi, it applies to industrial
wastes only; in the other states, it applies to both industrial wastes and sewage. In Louisiana, Maryland, Delaware
and Michigan, an order of approval is needed; in Maine the
state issues "licenses" and in Virginia "certificates"; but
in all other states, "permits" are issued. In Wisconsin,
only temporary permits can be issued. In Kansas the State
Board of Health issues the permits after consideration by the
governor, the Attorney General and the Secretary of the State
Board of Health; but in all other states, the authority of
the state pollution control agency in this respect is full
and unchecked. In Connecticut, not only the direct discharge
of polluting substances into streams requires a permit, but
also the discharge on their shores within a distance of fifty
feet from the high water marks. In Maine, with regard to
Class-A waters, "there shall be no discharge of sewage or
other wastes into water of this classification and no deposits of such material on the banks of such waters in such a
manner that transfer of the material into the waters is likely." This places the banks of Class-A waters, but not those
of other waters, under the care of the state water improvement commission. At the other extreme, exemptions from the

requirement are allowed in South Dakota (class-B waters), Alabama ("industrial streams")[119] and Ohio.[120]

(C) With the exception of Kansas, Rhode Island, Iowa, Connecticut, Michigan, South Dakota, Vermont, Maine, Tennessee, New Hampshire, Alabama and California, permission of the state is required for the construction of works for the treatment of polluting substances. In Wisconsin, Louisiana and Maryland, this requirement applies only to industrial wastes, but in other states it applies to both industrial wastes and sewage. In Maryland, it is adopted through administrative action; in all other states it is a statutory measure.[121] In Wisconsin, Pennsylvania, North Dakota, Oregon, Louisiana, Indiana, Minnesota, Washington and Maryland all that is required is the approval of plans of construction. In Virginia, "certificates" of approval are issued. In the remaining states, "permits" are issued. Wisconsin, where the requirement is waived in cities of less than 45,000 population, is the only state where the requirement operates on a conditional basis. In Kansas, the two administrative rules for the Kansas and Walnut River Basins require all cities and industries located in these two basins to construct works for the treatment of sewage and industrial wastes in a fixed schedule. The same order has also been adopted by Mississippi Game and Fish Commission. The action taken by Kansas and Mississippi is positive and thoroughgoing, and is much more effective than the mere requirement of state permission for the construction of treatment works.

With respect to measure (A), in a number of states it is reinforced by the stipulation that if complaint is made by parties concerned, the general pollution agency is obliged to investigate into the alleged act of pollution and to issue an order requiring abatement if it is verified. The parties allowed to make such complaint are as follows:

Pennsylvania---any responsible person.
Rhode Island---any party concerned.
Kansas---------a local governmental unit.
Wisconsin------six persons.
Iowa-----------a local governmental unit; or 25 residents of
               the state; or any state agency or agencies.
South Dakota---a local governmental unit; or 100 electors of
               the state.
Oregon---------any person, group of persons, or municipality.
(No provision for complaint in the other states).

The general water pollution control aims at "clean and pure water." As no water can be made absolutely clean and pure for ordinary beneficial uses, some standards must be adopted to delimit and guide the actual application of the various regulatory measures. In general, the same standards of purity and cleanness apply to all waters of the state.

However, in a few states, a graded system of purity standards
is adopted. Under this system, the waters of the state are
classified into several groups, each to have a separate set
of standards. In Pennsylvania, all waters free from pollution
at the time of the passage of the law providing for the regulation (i.e., 22 June 1937) are designated as "clean waters",
into which only "completed treated" polluting substances can
be discharged. In New Hampshire, the state legislature classifies the waters of the state by statute, upon recommendation
of the Water Pollution Commission.[122] In South Dakota, Maine,
New York and South Carolina, the waters are classified administratively under statutory criteria. In Alabama, the
1949 law designated certain waters as "industrial streams"
to be exempted from discharge-permit requirement, and the
Water Improvement Advisory Commission may designate additional
ones. Criteria for classification and number of classes are
provided in law in Vermont, and certain waters are directly
classified as Class A and Class B waters in the same law.
However, the Water Conservstion Board is authorized to change
the classification of Class B waters and to designate Class
C and Class D waters. Minnesota laws have vested in the Water
Pollution Commission full authority "to make such classification of the waters of the state as it may deem advisable."
It may be remarked that the system of water-classification
is an important modification of the general pollution control regulation and is apparently a compromise made by the
state to cities and industries.

Subsection 2 Mosquito Control

     Administrative regulation of water impoundments with view
to preventing the breeding and spread of mosquitoes is in operation in a number of states. It is authorized in some states
by special statutory enactments and in others by administrative regulations made under the broad authority of the state
health agencies.[123]

     (1) By statutes---A law of Tennessee (Acts 1945, ch. 41)
provides for the issuance of permits by the Department of
Health for the impounding of waters by any person, corporation
or public agency. The said Department has also the authority
to inspect, from time to time, impounded areas, and, upon
finding conditions conducive to mosquito-breeding, to order
the owners or operators concenred to make necessary corrections. In Connecticut, the control of mosquitoes falls within the jurisdiction of two agencies, namely, the Health Department and the Board of Mosquito Control. "When it shall
have been brought to the attention of a health officer or
board of health that rain water barrels, tin cans, bottles or
other receptacles or pools (emphasis added) near human habita-
tions are breeding mosquitoes, such health officer or board of
health shall investigate and cause any such breeding places to
be abolished, screened, or treated in such manner as to prevent

the breeding of mosquitoes . . ." (General Statutes, sec. 3857: Acts 1913, ch. 143). The principal function of the Board of Mosquito Control is concerned with the drainage of swamps. This, however, is an enterprise activity and will be discussed later. Under the laws of Texas, "all persons, firms, corporations and governmental agencies that impound any body of water for public use shall cooperate with the state and local departments of health in the control of disease-bearing mosquitoes on the impounded area" (Revised Civil Statutes, art. 4477-1: Laws 1945, ch. 178).

(2) By administrative regulations---Mosquito-prevention regulations have been adopted by the health departments of many southern states. Virginia, which adopted them in 1922, seems to be the first of these states in the adoption of such regulations. Alabama, South Carolina and Georgia fol-lowes suit in 1923, 1924 and 1925, respectively. Tennessee adopted them in 1936 and Mississippi and North Carolina in 1937. Alabama regulations of 1923, as amended in 1927, and South Carolina regulations of 1924, as amended in 1950, may be taken as representative of similar regulations in other southern states, as the same pattern of regulation has been followed in all southern states.[124]

In Alabama, two regulatory measures are provided, symbol-ized by two kinds of permits: the preliminary permit and the final permit. Sec. 1 of the 1927 regulation (now still in force) stipulates:

> Any person, firm, corporation, county, or mu-nicipality desiring to impound water, or who pro-poses to raise the level of a previously existing pond by the elevation of the point of overflow of a dam, shall, prior to the initiation of any con-struction activities, make application to the State Board of Health for, and obtain from it, pre-liminary permit for the impounding of such water. Provided, That this section shall not be construed to apply to ponds of less than one-tenth acre for watering stock or other domestic purposes, nor to impound water so located that no portion of them lies within one mile of any permanent human habi-tation, congregation, or place of business, other than that of the owner.

The preliminary permit is granted upon compliance of the ap-plicant with the following conditions: (1) removal of marginal vegetation, (2) cutting of brush, trees and undergrowth to a minimum of one foot below the level of the impounded water, (3) shore clearance, (4) construction of ponds for the propa-gation of minnows, and (5) connection of depression with the reservoir. After the preliminary permit is granted, the im-poundment may be proceeded under the personal supervision of

an inspector of the state board of health. When the impound-
ment is completed , the board then issues the final permit for
the maintenance thereof, the validity of which is contingent
upon the taking of certain post-impoundment measures, including the removal of floating debris and the prevention of the
growth of mosquito-supporting aquatic plants. "A bottom
drain at the low point of the dam is essential for the control of grasses and weeds. A permit will not be issued unless there is a bottom drain large enough to drain the area
within a maximum time of seven days" (explanation of sec. 5
by the State Board of Health). The permit-holders are further pursuaded (but not required) to make water-level fluc-
tuations and to apply larvicides at regular intervals during
mosquito-breeding seasons, among other mosquito-prevention
measures.[125]

The regulation of South Carolina provides for the issuance
of (1) construction permits and (2) maintenance permits. The
former are issued on the condition that applicants cut and
remove brush and undergrowth and construct ditches to connect
the reservoir with surrounding depressions. The latter are
issued only when applicants comply with the following requirements: removal of flotage and debris, shore-line clearance,
and prevention of weed growth   These regulatory measures are
essentially the same as those provided in the Alabama regulations.

In a number of states (e.g., South Dakota, Minnesota, Kentucky, New Mexico, Arizona, Wisconsin, New York, Wisconsin
and Mississippi), the state health department (in New York,
the governor) may by administrative order remove "nuisances",
which may include both mosquitoes and water-polluting substances. The ordinary procedure is that the said department issues
an order to the landowner concerned to remove or abate a nuisance, and that in case of default the said department is
either authorized to abate it at the cost of the defiant landowner (with Wisconsin as example), or authorized to institute
judicial action against him (with Arizona as example).[126] But
in some state this is a local regulatory or a purely judicial
measure.[127]

Section 8 Public Utilities

Public utilities refer to those commercial undertak ings
which serve the essential needs of the public and which are
inherently monopolistic or tend to be monopolistic. They include companies and firms engaged in air, water or land transportation (aircraft, steamers, railroads, motor vehicles,
street cars, etc.), communication (radio, telegraphy, tele-
phones, etc.), the generation or manufacture and transmission
or delivery of electricity, water, gas, oil, etc., sewerage.
the operation of canals and water terminal facilities (wharf-
fingers), and activities of similar economic nature. Some pub-

lic utilities involve the conservation, development, utilization or control of water resources. However, these utilities are regulated by the states, as by the Federal Government and municipalities, not directly as projects of water-resources conservation, development, utilization or control but as monopolistic or potentially monopolistic business activities.

Public utilities are regulated by the state government in all of the forty-eight states, although the number and kinds of public utilities under such regulation vary from one state to another.[128] In all of the forty-eight states except Minnesota, Mississippi, South Dakota and Texas, one or more water-resources utilities are under state regulation.[129] The types of water-resources utilities under state regulation are as follows:[130]

(i) <u>Electric utilities (generation or transmission)</u> (both hydro and fuel)---Alabama, Arizona, Arkansas, California, Colorado, Connecticut, Delaware, Florida, Georgia, Idaho, Illinois, Indiana, Iowa, Kansas, Kentucky, Louisiana, Maine, Maryland, Massachusetts, Michigan, Missouri, Montana, Nebraska, Nevada, New Hampshire, New Jersey, New Mexico, New York, North Carolina, North Dakota, Ohio, Oklahoma, Oregon, Pennsylvania, Rhode Island, South Carolina, Tennessee, Utah, Vermont, Virginia, Washington, West Virginia, Wisconsin, Wyoming.

(ii) <u>Water-supply utilities</u>---Alabama, Arizona, Arkansas, California, Colorado, Connecticut, Delaware, Georgia, Idaho, Indiana, Kansas, Kentucky, Maine, Maryland, Massachusetts, Michigan, Missouri, Montana, Nevada, New Hampshire, New Jersey, New Mexico, New York, North Carolina, North Dakota, Ohio, Oklahoma, Oregon, Pennsylvania, Rhode Island, South Carolina, Tennessee, Utah, Vermont, Virginia, Washington, West Virginia, Wisconsin, Wyoming.

(iii) <u>Water-terminal utilities or wharfingers</u>---Alabama, Georgia, Idaho, Illinois, Iowa, Maine, Pennsylvania, West Virginia.

(iv) <u>Sewerage utilities</u>---Montana, Nevada, New Jersey, Pennsylvania, Virginia, West Virginia.

(v) <u>Canal companies</u>---Alabama, New Jersey, Pennsylvania, South Carolina, Virginia.

(vi) <u>Irrigation companies</u>---Nebraska, Nevada, Kansas.

(vii) <u>Drainage companies</u>---Nevada.

(viii) <u>Livestock companies</u>---North Dakota.

(ix) <u>Private dams and reservoirs for flood control and hydroelectric power development</u> (regulated not as dams and reservoirs but as utilities)---Vermont.

Pennsylvania (electricity, water supply, water terminals, sewerage, canals), Virginia (electricity, water supply, sewerage, canals), and West Virginia (electricity, water supply, water terminals, sewerage) have the greatest numbers of water-resources utilities under state regulation, while in Florida and Louisiana there is only one such utility regulated by the state government, e.g., electricity. The water-resources utilities regulated at the state level in Georgia and Nebraska are respectively electricity and water terminals and electricity and irrigation companies. It should be noted that in most states electricity and water supply are the only water-resources utilities subject to state regulation.

Public utilities are regulated by the government on account of their economic impacts upon the public. So far as state regulation is concerned, it is pillared on the following main aspects: (1) the establishment of an utility, (2) its service, (3) its rates or charges and (4) its business behavior. These are to be discussed separately.[131]

(1) Establishment---This usually refers to the establishment of a public utility or rather its business in a certain community or locality, generally a city or town. What is concerned here is not the right (constitutional, statutory, or sub-statutory) to undertake the enterprise of a public utility, but one to start its business. The former consists of a license or permit granted by the Federal agency and (or) the state agency concerned and, so far as the conduct of business in a particular city or town is concerned, a franchise granted by that city or town. The right to start business is one which enables a public utility to actually exercise the right to undertake enterprise which it has already obtained in a particular locality or community. This right is usually granted in the form of a "certificate of public convenience" by the state commission having jurisdiction over public utilities (hereinafter to be designated generically as the "state public service commission").

"The general impression has been that competition was supposed to be a legitimate and proper means of protecting the interests of the public and promoting the general welfare of the people in respect to service by public utility corporations; but history and experience has clearly demonstrated that public convenience and necessities of the community do not require the construction and maintenance of several plants or systems of the same character to supply a city or the same locality, but that public convenience and necessity require only the maintenance of a sufficient number of such instrumentalities to meet public demands. If more than one instrumentality is to be sustained when one is amply sufficient, the actual cost of the public served is not only necessarily greater than it would be under one system, but also less convenient."[132] Thus the purpose of the certificate of public convenience and necessity (or a certificate or declaration of similar terminology or function) is to secure the minimum number of public utilities of the same kind in any given locality or area and thereby to assure the maximum efficiency of the service to be rendered.

In the following states (with respect to the water-resources utilities specified) a certificate of public convenience and necessity is required for the construction or extension of any facilities or equipment by any public utility in any locality or area where it has already been granted the right to undertake its enterprise:[133]

> Alabama (electricity, water, canals, wharfingers)
> Arizona, California, Colorado, Delaware, Idaho, Kansas, Kentucky, Maryland, Missouri, New Hampshire, New Mexico, New York, North Carolina, Tennessee, Utah, Virginia, and Wyoming (electricity, water).
> Iowa (wharfingers)
> Kansas (electricity, water, irrigation companies).
> Nevada (electricity, water, sewerage, irrigation, drainage).
> New Jersey (electricity, water, sewerage, canals).
> North Dakota (electricity, water, livestock)
> Pennsylvania (electricity, water, wharfingers, sewerage, canals).
> South Carolina (electricity).
> Vermont (electricity, water, flood-control and power dams and reservoirs).
> West Virginia (electricity, water, wharfingers, sewerage).
> Kansas (electricity, water, irrigation companies).

In North Dakota, certificates of public convenience and necessity are not required for: "1. an extension within any municipality or district which it has lawfully commenced operations; 2. an extension within or to territory already served by it necessary in the ordinary course of its business; or 3. an extension into territory contiguous to that already occupied by it and not receiving similar service from another utility, if no certificate of public convenience and necessity has been issued to any other public utility." Similar exceptions are found in Arizona, Arkansas, Colorado, Idaho, Maryland, Nevada, New Mexico and Utah.

In the following states, certificates of public convenience and necessity are required only for the opening of business of an utility in areas which are already served by one or more other utilities rendering the same service:[134]

> Indiana, Michigan, Oregon (in cities of more than 2,000 population only), and Wisconsin (electricity, water).
> Louisiana and Rhode Island (electricity).

In Connecticut, Iowa (in rual areas only), Massachusetts(
for lines extending from one city or town to another) and
Nebraska (approval required of lines having a voltage of 700
volts or more only), the state public service commission approves and supervises the construction of electric transmission lines. In Connecticut the approval of the state public
service commission is required for the sale of electricity;
in Nevada, for the sale in wholesale of electricity produced
as a by-product; and in Massachusetts, for the sale in wholesale of electricity by an electric utility. These regulatory
measures are, like the grant of certificates of public convenience and necessity, also concerned with the establishment
of public utilities.

(2) _Service_---In the following states, the public service commission, may, either upon complaint or in its own
initiative, order public utilities to make repairs, improvements, changes and extensions in their physical plants and
facilities:

> Alabama (wharfingers, canals).
> Arizona, Colorado, Missouri, New York, North Caro-
>   lina, Ohio, Rhode Island, Utah and Washington
>   (electricity, water).
> Florida (electricity).
> Idaho (electricity, water, wharfingers).
> Illinois (electricity, wharfingers).
> Nevada (electricity, water, sewerage, irrigation,
>   drainage).
> Virginia (water, sewerage).
> West Virginia (electricity, water, wharfingers,
>   sewerage).

The commissions of the following states may only order extensions of physical plants:

> Connecticut (electricity) (extended to unserved
>   areas having a density of population of two
>   subscribers per mile of transmission line).
> Delaware, Oregon and Virginia (electricity, water).
> Louisiana and South Carolina (electricity)
> Virginia (electricity, water, sewerage) (extensions
>   to rural territory upon petition of five per-
>   sons concerned).

In the following states, the commissions may enact administrative rules and regulations concerning the rendering of services
of public utilities:

> Arizona, Arkansas, California, Delaware, Kansas,
>   Maryland, New Hampshire, New Mexico, Oklahoma,
>   South Carolina, Tennessee, Wisconsin and Wyo-
>   ming (electricity, water).

> Georgia (electricity)
> Maine (electricity, water, wharfingers).
> Montana and Virginia (electricity, water, sewerage).
> New Jersey (electricity, water, sewerage, canals).
> North Dakota (electricity, water, livestock).
> Pennsylvania (electricity, water, wharfingers,
>   sewerage, canals).
> Vermont (electricity, water, flood-control and
>   power dams and reservoirs).

In the following states, the state public commission may order joint use of facilities and equipment (i.e., pooling) by two or more utilities of the same kind:

> Arizona, Colorado, Kentucky, Oregon and Utah (elec-
>   tricity, water)
> Idaho and Maine (electricity, water, wharfingers).

In the following states, the commission may order the install-ment of safety devices:

> Colorado, Kentucky, Rhode Island, and Utah (elec-
>   tricity, water)
> Idaho (electricity, water, wharfingers).
> Illinois (electricity, wharfingers).
> Nevada (electricity, water, sewerage, irrigation,
>   drainage).
> Oregon and Wisconsin (electricity).
> West Virginia (electricity, water, wharfingers,
>   sewerage).

The commissions of the following states may order the perma-nent or temporary abandonment of contraction of service of a public utility: New Hampshire (electricity, water), South Car-olina (electricity), and Tennessee (electricity, water). On the other hand, in the following it is provided that a public utility cannot abandon or contract its business without the approval of the commission:

> Alabama (electricity, water, canals) (certificates
>   of public convenience and necessity required)
> Alabama (wharfingers) (permits required).
> Maine (electricity, water, wharfingers).
> Pennsylvania (electricity, water, wharfingers, sew-
>   erage, canals).
> South Carolina (electricity).
> Wisconsin (electricity, water).

In 1952, an act was enacted in Virginia which created a new, unique measure of regulation relating to the services of public utilities (Acts 1952, ch. 696: Code, sec. 56-509 et seq.). It provides that in "an imminent threat of substan-tial curtailment, interruption or suspension in the operation"

of a (transportation, communication,) water-supply or electric utility, the governor may take possession of the plant
facilities of the said utility, in whole or in part, and operate them for the benefit of the people, until the utility
is in a position to resume operations and render its normal
service.

(3) Rates[135]---A distinction may perhaps be made between
that may be called the positive and the negative aspects of
state regulation of the rates or charges of the services or
products of public utilities.

(a) Positive regulation. In the following states, new
schedules of rates of public utilities must be submitted to
and approved by the state public service commission before
they become effective:

> Florida and Michigan (electricity)
> New Hampshire, Ohio (effective for a maximum per-
>   iod of two years), Oklahoma, Tennessee, Wis-
>   consin (for increases of rates only) and Wyo-
>   ming (electricity, water)
> Georgia (electricity, water, wharfingers)
> Nebraska (irrigation companies)

In the following states, new rates need not be approved by
the commission, but they must be submitted to it and become
effective after the lapse of a certain period of time from
the date of submission:

> 2 months:
>   Pennsylvania (electricity, water, wharfingers,
>   sewerage, canals).
> 1.5 months:
>   Massachusetts (electricity)
> 1 month:
>   Alabama (electricity, water, wharfingers,
>   canals) (For dules submitted to it prior to
>   the effective date thereof.)
>   Arizona, Arkansas, California, Colorado, Con-
>   conticut, Delaware, Indiana, Kansas, New Hamp-
>   shire, New Mexico, New York, North Carolina,
>   Oregon, Rhode Island, South Carolina, Utah
>   and Washington (electricity, water).
>   Idaho and Maine (electricity, water, wharfin-
>   gers).
>   Montana and Virginia (electricity, water,
>   sewerage).
>   Iowa (wharfingers)
>   Nevada (electricity, water, sewerage, irriga-
>   tion, drainage)
>   North Dakota (electricity, water, livestock).
>   Vermont (electricity, water, flood-control and

            power dams and reservoirs).
            West Virginia (electricity, water, wharfingers,
            sewerage).
      20 days:
            Kentucky (electric, water).
      10 days:
            Wisconsin (electricity, water) (for reductions
            only).

The period specified may as a rule be shortened by the commission by special orders.

    In Maryland (electricity, water), Missouri (electricity,
water, flood-control and power dams and reservoirs, if new
rates amount to a reduction in old rates), new rates need
only be submitted to the commission and are effective immediately thereupon.

    The laws of Alabama, Kansas, Kentucky and New Mexico allow
the rates of electric and water-supply utilities to be determined by contract between the municipalities and the utilities companies concerned (i.e., prescribed by municipal franchises), but such contracts must be approved by the state public service commission.[136] In Alabama and New Mexico, a maximum term of thirty and twenty-five years respectively is set
for such contracts. Through the approval of such contracts,
the state commission indirectly regulates the rates of public
utilities.

    (b) **Negative regulation**. In all of the states mentioned
in subsection (a) above, the state public service commission
has the authority to correct, either in its own initiative
or upon complaint by affected parties, after investigation
and hearing, prevailing rates of public utilities found to
be unjust and unreasonable or otherwise illegal.[137] The challenged rates will be invalidated, and new rates prescribed
by the commission in lieu thereof. In New York, the new rates
prescribed by the commission in lieu thereof. In New York,
the new rates so fixed are effective for a maximum period of
three years. In the other states, they continue in effect
until they are changed by the utilities according to the procedure described in subsection (a) above.

    In most of these states, the commission may, during the
process of investigation and hearing, suspend the operation
of the rates under investigation for a certain period of
time, which is:[138]

    One year---New Hampshire, South Carolina (for electric
                but not water utilities) (but under ordinary
                conditions, three months)
    Ten months---Massachusetts and Washington.
    Ten months (but ordinarily two months)---Virginia

Nine months (but ordinarily six months)---Oregon, Penn-
        sylvania and Rhode Island.
Eight months (but ordinarily three months)---Maine.
Eight months (but ordinarily four months)---Kentucky.
Six months (but ordinarily four months)---Arizona.
Six months (but ordinarily three months)---Arkansas, New
        Jersey, and North Carolina.
Five months (but ordinarily four months)---Iowa.
Four months---Connecticut, Illinois, Maryland, Missouri,
        New York, North Dakota, West Virginia and Wis-
        consin (in Wisconsin, for reductions only).
Three months---New Mexico and Wyoming.
Two months---Alabama, and South Carolina (for water but
        not electric utilities).
Two months (but ordinarily one month)---Nevada.

In Alabama (canals, wharfingers), Arizona (electricity,
water), New Hampshire (electricity, water) and North Dakota
(electricity, water, livestock), public utilities charging
excessive rates may be required to repay to the customers
the amount paid above the rates finally fixed by the state
public service commissions in the procedure discussed above,
plus interest.

(4) Business---The most important measure of regulating
the business behavior of public utilities is perhaps the requirement of approval of the public service commission for
the issuance of securities. In the following states, such
approval is required for the issuance of stocks and that of
bonds and other evidences of indebtedness payable in periods
more than one year:

Kansas (electricity, water, irrigation companies).
Arizona, Arkansas, California, Delaware, Indiana, Mary-
        land, Missouri, New Hampshire, New York, Ohio,
        Oregon, Rhode Island, Tennessee, and Washington
        (electricity, water).
Florida, Idaho, Massachusetts, and South Carolina (elec-
        tricity) (In Massachusetts, it is further pro-
        vided that preferred stocks should at no time ex-
        ceed twice the amount of general or common stocks).
Georgia (electricity, wharfingers)
Maine (electricity, water, wharfingers).
New Jersey and Virginia (electricity, water, sewerage,
        canals).
Pennsylvania (electricity, water, wharfingers, sewerage,
        canals).
Vermont (electricity, water, flood-control and power dams
        and reservoirs).

In New Mexico (electricity, water) and Wyoming (electricity),
such approval is required for the issuance of all stocks and
bonds and other evidences payable in periods more than eight-

een months (1.5 years); in Alabama (electricity, water, wharfingers; in an aggregate amount equivalent to at least five
percent of the tangible fixed capital), Kentucky (electricity,
water) and North Carolina (electricity, water), of all stocks
and bonds and other evidences of indebtedness payable in periods more than two years; in Georgia (water), Illinois (electricity, wharfingers), Michigan (electricity, water),[139] and
North Dakota (electricity, water, livestock), of all stocks
and bonds and other evidences of indebtedness; in South Carolina (water), of all bonds and other evidences of indebtedness. In many of these states, the purposes for which securities may be issued are statutorily specified; in others
these purposes are to be specified by the commission. In all
cases, the commission passes upon the amount of securities
to be issued.

In the following states, the sale, lease, transfer, assignment, mortgaging, or like disposition of tangible and intangi-
ble properties and rights (including franchises) must be approved by the commission:

Alabama and Maine (electricity, water, wharfingers)
Arizona, Arkansas, California, Delaware, Indiana, Mary-
        land, Missouri, New Hampshire, New Mexico (for
        sale or lease of facilities only), New York, Ohio,
        Oregon, Rhode Island and Washington (electricity,
        water).
Idaho, Massachusetts (on a minimum amount of $35,000),
        and South Carolina (electricity).
Kansas (electricity, water, irrigation companies)
New Jersey and Virginia (electricity, water, sewerage,
        canals).
North Dakota (electricity, water, livestock).
South Carolina (water, for mortgaging only).
Vermont (electricity, water, flood-control and power dams
        and reservoir; for sale and lease, in a minimum
        amount equal to 10 percent of entire property with-
        in the state in any year).
West Virginia (electricity, water, wharfingers, sewerage).

In Indiana, Kansas, Maryland, Missouri, New Hampshire,
New York, Oregon and Utah, the acquisition by an electric
or water utility of both stocks and bonds, and in Arizona,
Arkansas, California, Maine, Massachusetts, New Mexico, North
Dakota, Ohio, Pennsylvania (in a minimum amount equal to five
percent of the capital stock of another other utility), Rhode
Island, Vermont, Virginia and West Virginia, the acquisition
by an electric or water utility[140] of the stocks, of other
utilities rendering the same service[141] must be approved by
the commission.

In the following states, the full or partial merger or
consolidation of two or more utilities must be approved by the

commission:

> Arkansas, California, Delaware, Indiana, Missouri, New
>> Mexico, Oregon, Rhode Island, Utah and Washington
>> (electricity, water).
> Illinois (electricity, wharfingers).
> Maine (electricity, water, wharfingers).
> New Jersey (electricity, water, sewerage, canals).
> North Dakota (electricity, water, livestock).
> South Carolina (electricity).
> Vermont (electricity, water, flood-control and power dams
>> and reservoirs).
> West Virginia (electricity, water, wharfingers, sewerage).

In the following states, approval of the commission is required of contracts or dealings with affiliates:[142]

> Maine (electricity, water, wharfingers).
> Massachusetts (electricity, only for contracts having a
>> longer term than one year).
> Massachusetts (water).
> New Hampshire, Rhode Island, Washington and Wisconsin
>> (electricity, water).
> Pennsylvania (electricity, water, wharfingers, sewerage,
>> canals).
> Virginia (electricity, water, sewerage, canals)
> West Virginia (electricity, water, wharfingers, sewerage).

Other regulatory measures on the business behavior of
public utilities involving the approval of the public service
commission are listed below:

> Arkansas (electricity, water)---organization and re-organ-
>> ization.
> Delaware (electricity, water)---guaranty, endoresement or
>> assumption of liabilities of securities of other
>> utilities which mature more than one year.
> Massachusetts (electricity)---making of loans; purchase
>> of electricity for more than one year.
> Massachusetts (water)---acquisition of real estate in ex-
>> cess of legally limited amount
> Nevada---purchase of electricity for re-sale.
> New Hampshire (electricity)---transmission out of state.
> New Jersey (electricity, water, sewerage canals)---sale
>> of stocks to other utilities; contracts for pay-
>> ment in excess of $25,000; investment of deprecia-
>> tion funds in securities of any kind.
> New Mexico (electricity, water)---purchase of plant.
> New York (electricity, water)---transfer of stocks to
>> other utilities.
> Oregon (electricity, water)---purchase of electricity or
>> water from an enterprise which produces it as a by-
>> product.

Utah (electricity, water)---all contracts of expenditures
　　and purchases.
West Virginia (electricity, water, wharfingers, sewerage)
　　---acquisition of properties or franchises of
　　other utilities.

The state regulatory authority extends to all private,
profit-making public-utility companies and firms. Since the
cooperatives are organized for non-profit purposes, they are
generally exempt from state public-utility regulation. Municipally owned and operated public utilities, though operated
for profit, may be exempt from state regulation on account
of their public nature.[143] In most states, the public utility law has expressly excluded municipalities from its application. Public utilities which are owned by municipalities
but which are operated by private parties are probably regarded as private utilities.[144] State public-utility regulation is applicable to municipalities, in whole or in part,
only in the following states:[145]

Alabama (electric and water utilities only).
Arkansas (only one measure---the approval of extension of
　　service to suburban areas).
Iowa (water-terminals only).
Maine
Maryland (electric utilities only) (and only one measure
　　---the approval and authorization of construction
　　or operation of generation or transmission facili-
　　ties) (City of Baltimore excepted).
Montana
Nevada
New Hampshire (when operating beyond corporate limits).
New York (electric utilities only).
North Dakota (only two measures---certificates of public
　　convenience and necessity, and regulation of bus-
　　iness).
Pennsylvania (only one measure---certificates of public
　　convenience for extension of service beyond corp-
　　orate limits).
South Carolina (electric utilities only) (only with re-
　　spect to services rendered outside corporate lim-
　　its) (issuance of securities not under regulation).
Vermont
Washington (only one measure---regulation of business).
West Virginia
Wisconsin
Wyoming

In New Mexico, the state public-utility regulation is not
by itself applicable to municipalities, but a municipality
may, after a referendum, voluntarily subject itself thereto.

In general, the public service commission, in regulating

public utilities, may prescribe standards of service, test
devices of measurement, assess the value of properties, require the submission of reports, issues rules and forms for
the keeping of accounts and for other purposes and examines
books and records. But these are not independent regulatory
measures, but merely instrumentalities of regulation.

Section 9 Fish and Wildlife

(a) Regulation of game fish and wildlife---To provide a
basis for the regulation of fish and wildlife resources, particularly game fish and wildlife, many states have, by constitutional or statutory enactments, declared public ownership of these resources. The following examples are representative of the prevailing practice:

Iowa:

> The title and ownership of all fish, mussels, clams, and
> frogs, in any of the public waters of the state, and in
> all ponds, sloughs, bayous, or other land and waters ad-
> jacent to any public waters stocked with fish by overflow
> of public waters, and of all wild game, animals, and
> birds, including their nests and eggs, and all other wild-
> life, found in the state, whether game or non-game, native
> or migratory, except deer in parks and in public and pri-
> vate reserves, the ownership of which was acquired prior
> to April 19, 1911, are hereby declared to be in the state,
> except as otherwise in this Act provided (Iowa Code, sec.
> 109.2: Acts 1911, ch. 118, sec. 1; as last amended by Acts
> 1939, ch. 77, sec. 14).

Minnesota:

> The ownership of wild animals and all wildlife and other
> aquatic vegetation growing in the public waters of the
> state, insofar as they are capable of ownership, is in
> the state in its sovereign capacity for the benefit of
> all people (Laws 1919, ch. 400, sec. 3; as last amended
> by L. 1945, ch. 248, sec. 1).

New York:

> The State of New York owns and has title to all fish,
> birds, and quadrupeds in the state except those legally
> acquired and held by private ownership. Any person who
> kills, takes or possesses such fish, birds, and quadrupeds
> thereby consents that title thereto shall remain in the
> state for the purpose of regulating and controlling the
> use and disposition of the same (Conservation Law, sec.
> 150: Laws 1938, ch. 40, sec. 1).

Washington:

The wild animals and wild birds in the State of Washington and the game fish in the waters thereof are the property of the State of Washington. (Revised Code, sec. 77.12.010: Laws 1947, ch. 275, sec. 11) (1st sent.).

Such declaration, like similar declaration of public ownership of water, does not make the fish and wildlife resources the property of the state in the same sense as other properties of the state, which the state owns in its capacity of a juridical person not materially different from that of a private person and which it can dispose of in a manner in which private persons dispose of their property. Such declaration is made solely for the purpose of regulation. This is expressly stated in the laws of such states as New York (above cited) and Alabama (Code, tit. 8, sec. 59, being Acts 1933, p. 67; and tit. 8, sec. 82, being Acts 1935, p. 813). Otherwise, the state regulation of fish and wildlife, as well as that over water uses, would have been a state enterprise.

It may also be remarked that with respect to public ownership, there is distinction between wildlife (wild animals and birds) and game fish. The former, whether they are on public or private land or water, are public property in all states. As regards fish, they are state property only when they habitate in public waters in states such as Iowa and Minnesota. In other states, such as New York and Washington, all game fish belong to the state whether they are found in public or in private waters.

The general purpose of state administration over fish and wildlife is the maintenance of a proper population balance for each species of fish or wildlife to the best interest of the public. So far as regulation is concerned, this is effected through licensing, prescription of open and closed seasons and of limits of fishing and hunting (including trapping), stipulation as to the manner and methods of fishing and hunting, and supplementary measures.[146]

Hunters and fishermen are required to buy annual licenses from the fish and game agency of the state in which hunting and fishing is to take place, fees for non-residents being invariably higher than those for residents. A person may buy as many fishing or hunting licenses as the number of states in which he plans to fish or hunt. A certain number of free licenses are generally given by a state fish and game agency as a token of courtesy to the President of the United States, governors and fish and game officials of all other states, and other specified groups of persons. The available data showing state hunting, fishing and trapping licenses are given in the following tables:

It is to be noted that fishing or hunting licenses are licenses to fish or hunt only. They do not entitle or authorize

Hunting Licenses Issued By the Several States
Since Fiscal Year 1919

Fiscal year	Resident	Non-resident	Total	Revenue($)
1919	?	?	3,598,268	?
1920-22	?	?	?	?
1923	4,307,066	34,432	4,341,498	5,385,489
1924	4,357,410	37,628	4,395,038	5,594,982
1925	4,862,889	42,851	4,904,740	6,190,864
1926	5,287,194	45,181	5,332,375	7,130,101
1927	5,949,247	48,913	5,998,160	8,194,673
1928	6,413,454	49,101	6,462,555	9,338,174
1929	6,376,699	52,062	6,428,761	9,391,412
1930	6,842,381	58,553	6,900,934	10,017,564
1931	6,320,262	47,252	6,367,514	9,899,195
1932	5,739,688	36,946	5,776,634	9,122,699
1933	5,701,061	36,947	5,741,965	8,754,827
1934	5,876,083	41,962	5,918,045	9,068,882
1935	5,939,849	48,215	5,988,064	9,256,759
1936	6,604,745	53,413	6,658,158	10,466,237
1937	6,806,291	53,719	6,860,010	11,348,006
1938	6,849,047	54,353	6,903,400	11,498,413
1939	7,453,814	57,485	7,511,299	12,494,877
1940	7,580,125	66,068	7,646,193	12,998,168
1941	7,847,922	76,830	7,924,822	14,464,478
1942	8,441,560	90,794	8,532,354	13,921,974
1943	7,999,770	91,417	8,091,187	13,598,423
1944	7,383,731	107,411	7,491,142	13,530,313
1945	8,036,538	154,363	8,190,901	15,512,252
1946	9,597,978	256,335	9,854,313	19,805,443
1947	11,673,215	393,548	12,066,763	28,558,447
1948	11,210,858	180,952	11,391,810	29,814,327
1949	12,534,456	224,242	12,758,698	34,966,687
1950	12,441,145	195,656	12,637,801	37,641,734
1951	12,448,739	212,254	12,660,993	38,138,738
1952	13,618,925	283,503	13,902,428	36,993,668
1953	14,488,216	344,563	14,832,779	40,551,316

Fishing Licenses Issued By the Several States
Since Fiscal Year 1933

Fis. year	Resident	Non-Resident	Total	Revenue ($)
1933	4,553,441	304,617	4,858,058	6,775,370
1934	4,602,446	253,499	4,855,945	6,586,810
1935	4,710,771	410,549	5,121,320	7,009,009
1936	5,277,431	555,017	5,832,448	8,002,887
1937	6,254,478	667,109	6,901,587	9,309,949
1938	6,751,811	684,366	7,436,177	10,220,788
1939	7,111,545	746,730	7,858,275	10,837,168
1940(Est.)	7,131,649	799,505	7,931,154	11,227,504
1941	7,151,754	852,280	8,004,034	11,617,841
1942	7,501,688	921,530	8,423,218	10,731,040
1943	7,283,777	744,897	8,028,674	10,024,329
1944	7,208,569	621,908	7,830,477	9,840,073
1945	7,522,373	757,859	8,280,232	10,580,311
1946	9,975,618	1,093,099	11,068,717	15,003,796
1947	11,155,766	1,464,698	12,620,464	22,667,301
1948	12,479,123	1,598,838	14,077,961	27,324,644
1949	13,587,224	1,891,346	15,478,570	32,657,940
1950	13,308,667	2,029,091	15,337,758	34,018,009
1951	13,871,278	2,155,421	16,026,699	35,554,285
1952	14,819,671	2,308,225	17,127,896	33,609,539
1953	15,134,182	2,518,396	17,652,478	35,602,903

Trapping Licenses Issued By the Several States
Since Fiscal Year 1948

Fiscal Year	Resident	Non-Resident	Total	Revenue($)
1948	354,415	3,046	357,461	832,951
1949	533,174	737	533,911	903,891
1950	?	?	?	?
1951	359,145	1,016	360,161	707,883

The sources of the above three tables consist of
materials made available to the author through the
courtesy of Mr. Lansing A. Parker, Chief, Branch of
Federal Aid, U. S. Fish and Wildlife Service on 30
December 1953 and in February 1954.

the license-holders to enter public or private lands without
the permission of the owners thereof. For the privilege of
entry into their lands, the latter may legally impose additional charges on the former, as if the game belonged to
them.[147] In some states, public lands have been declared free
to anglers and hunters. In these states, licenses practically
(though not technically) cover both the privilege to fish or
hunt and the right to enter public lands for the purpose of
fishing or hunting. For example, Oregon laws provide that:

> Navigable rivers, sloughs, or streams between the
> lines of ordinary high water thereof, of the state
> of Oregon, and all rivers, sloughs and streams
> flowing through any public lands of the state,
> shall hereafter be public highways for the purpose
> of angling, hunting or trapping thereon, and any
> rights or title to such streams, or the land be-
> tween the high water flowliness or within the
> meander lines of navigable streams, shall be sub-
> ject to the right of any person owning an angler's,
> hunter's or trapper's license of this state who
> desires to angle, hunt or trap therein or along
> the banks to go upon same for such purpose. --
> Laws 1921, ch. 153, sec. 35; as last amended by
> L. 1929, ch. 474, sec. 6.

In California, it is provided in the state constitution
(art. 1, sec. 25, in 1910) that

> the people shall have the right to fish upon and
> from the public lands of the state and in the wa-
> ters thereof, excepting upon lands set aside for
> fish hatcheries, and no land owned by the state
> shall ever be sold or transferred without reserv-
> ing in the people the absolute right to fish there-
> upon; and no law shall ever be passed making it a
> crime for the people to enter upon the public lands
> within this state for the purpose of fishing in
> any water containing fish that have been planted
> therein by the state . . .

Washington laws provide that "all state lands hereafter leased
for grazing purposes shall be open and available to the public
for purposes of hunting and fishing unless closed to public
entry because of fire hazard or unless lawfully posted by
lesses to prohibit hunting and fishing thereon" (ch. 171 of
Sess. Laws of 1947, second para., first sentence). California
constitutional provision is of special interest in that it
places a permanent servitude of fishing and hunting on private
lands that were acquired from the state. In most states, arrangements are made by the state game agencies with owners of
private and public lands for the establishment upon these lands
of "public fishing or hunting areas or grounds" on which li-

censed anglers and hunters may fish and hunt freely. This
will be discussed later.

No license is required to kill game animals or birds when
they are doing damages to property or injuries to human lives.
Certain animals and birds may be designated as "unprotected",
and may be killed without license. These are usually predatory species, and their game value is belittled by their
harmfulness.

The days of the year when fishing or hunting is allowed
is called the "open season" for fishing or hunting; the number of fish each angler is allowed to take per day the "creel
limit" and that of game "bag limit". All these are established
by the state fish and game agencies in a democratic process
in which views of the various interested groups are fully
heard. However, there are certain general principles governing these. For example, "it would be unreasonable to expect
open seasons on game birds and animals that inhabit cultivated
fields, during the time when tramping through unharvested areas
would damage crops. Likewise, to hunt big game during the
time that the exact territory they occupy is carrying a heavy
concentration of domestic livestock could not be considered
wise management". "Furthermore, it is probably not a wise
practice to have fishing seasons open during the time that
fish are engaged in spawning, unless there is an actual surplus of fish in the particular waters and it is considered
desirable to decrease the populations."[148]

Bag and creel limits are governed in general by population
census. Both open seasons and bag and creel limits are generally tending to be short, under the philosophy of fishing
or hunting for fun and not for food. However, with respect
to deer and elk, there is a general tendency toward longer
seasons and greater bag limits because of overpopulation of
these two big game species.[149]

Regulation of the manner and methods of fishing and hunting has the general objective of preventing the taking of
fish and game in a commercial amount. As fishing and hunting
is taken as a game, it is supposed to be done in a leisurely
and natural way and to be shared by as many people as possible.
For these reasons presumably, the use of explosives, mechanical and commercially used devices are generally forbidden.
There is also a general prohibition against the sale of fish
and game taken under non-commercial or game fishing and hunting licenses or keeping game alive in captivity. Other regulatory measures include the licensing of fur-animal trapping,
game or fur farming, taxidermy, fish propagation, etc., tag-
ging for informational purposes, and regulation on transportation of game.[150] As a safety measure for children, an act of
Washington (laws 1947, ch. 275, in sec. 38) authorized the
State Game Commission to set aside, by administrative rules

and regulations, certain watercourses for exclusive fishing by minors. An Oregon law of 1949 (ch. 290, in sec. 1) in a similar manner, designated the Mill Creek in Marion County to be for the sole use of persons under 18 years of age. Such streams would also serve as training grounds for young anglers and possess high educational values.[151]

Worthy of special notice is a tendency toward greater administrative authority in the field of fish and game regulation. In the past, open seasons and bag and creel limits were in every state all fixed by statute and were too rigid to be practicable. Recently laws of most states have been revised to provide determination of these by administrative action.[152] For example, a Wisconsin law of 1933 (Laws 1933, ch. 152: Wisconsin Statutes, sec. 29.174) authorized the Conservation Commission to establish open and close seasons, bag limits,[153] size limits, rest days, and other conditions governing fishing and hunting. Under a 1937 enactment (Laws 1937, p. 583, sec. 7), Colorado Game and Fish Commission has authority, among other things, (i) to fix and alter open seasons and bag limits, (ii) to close and re-open lakes and streams or parts thereof to fishing, (iii) to prescribe the means of taking fish or game, (iv) to regulate the transportation and storage of all game fish, birds or animals or parts thereof, etc. In Alabama, "the Director of Conservation is empowered: To formulate a state wild life policy; to fix open seasons during which game birds, game and fur-bearing animals may be taken; to fix daily and season bag limits on game birds, and game animals; to designate by name what species of fish shall be game fish; to fix daily creel limits one game fishes; to regulate the manner, means, and devices for catching, or taking game fishes, game birds, game and fur-bearing animals, and the manner, means, and devices for catching or taking all other species of fish not designated as game fish; to close the season of any species of game in any county or area, when upon a survey by the department it is found necessary to the conservation and perpetuation of such species, and re-open such closed season when it is deemed advisable; to designate by name what animals shall be classified as game, or fur-bearing animals, and the time, manner, means and devices for taking same . . ." (Code, tit. 8, sec. 17: Acts 1939, No. 163, sec. 3). All rules and regulations promulgated by the director "shall have the effect of law" (Code, tit. 8, sec. 21: Acts 1943, no. 531). In Washington, according to a law of 1947 (Laws 1947, ch. 275), the state game commission establishes open seasons, bag limits and closed areas of both hunting and game-fishing (sec. 24). These may be changed by the director of game with the approval of the commission (sec. 25). The commission also classifies wild animals and birds (but not fish) (secs. 10 and 12) and regulates the propagation and preservation, importation and transportation and sale within the state of wild animal and birds and game fish (sec. 13). In California the fish and game commission has been authorized

by acts of 1947 and 1949 (Stats. 1947, ch. 109 and Stats.
1949, ch. 914) to establish or change or alter open seasons,
bag and possession limits and size limits (size limits for
fish only), and the territorial limits of fishing or hunting,
and to prescribe the manner and means of fishing and hunting.
In Arkansas, by a constitutional amendment no. 35, adopted
7 November 1944 and effective 1 July 1945, the fish and game
commission is given "exclusive . . . authority to issue licenses and permits, to regulate bag limits and the manner of
taking game and fish and fur-bearing animals", and also "the
authority to divide the state into zones, and regulate seasons and manner of taking game, and fish and fur-bearing therein, and fix penalties for violations . . ." The fish and game
commission of Utah, under the Fish and Game Code (Laws 1953,
ch. 39), has very extensive authority with respect to the establishment of open and close seasons, bag limits, closure
of areas to fishing or hunting, the establishment of game refuges, etc. (sec. 23-2-12). It may be taken as representative of the last phase of the expansion of administrative
authority in state fish and wildlife regulation, with administrative establishment of game refuges as the climax of this
movement.

In some states, administrative authority on these matters
is limited. In North Dakota, for example, the open seasons
are determined by statutes, but the governor acting upon the
recommendation of the commissioner of game and fish may vary
them by orders or proclamations (Revised Code, sec. 20-0801:
Laws 1927, ch. 141, as amended). In Connecticut, the state
board of fisheries and game is authorized to extend or curtail open seasons or permit additional hunting, fishing or
trapping, only when the general assembly is not in session
(General Statutes, sec. 4850, enacted in 1935 and last amended in 1947). Besides, the governor may proclaim closed season on fishing and hunting when there is forest fire hazard
for any period of time and may extend the open season for an
equal period of time (ibid., sec. 4851: Acts 1923, ch. 259,
sec. 23; as last amended in 1937. In Pennsylvania, the act
of 3 June 1937, as amended 24 June 1939 and 2 May 1949, authorizes the state game commission to prescribe open seasons
and bag limits for the hunting of game birds and animals, but
at the same time it sets up the seasons and limits; and provision is included that the statutory seasons and limits are
to operate when the commission fails to establish such seasons or limits. In addition, as provided in an act of 12
May 1925, the governor has authority, among other things, "(a)
to close for a period not to exceed one season at one time
any county or counties or any section of any county . . . to
either hunting or fishing"; and "(b) to close for any period
any stream or part of any stream to fishing." In Arizona,
before the enactment of Laws 1945, ch. 52, which gave full
authority to the game and fish commission with respect to
open seasons and bag limits, the said commission, under Laws

1929, ch. 84, has only authority to modify or dispense with the statutorily established open and close seasons and bag and creel limits.

Another remark should be made on the regulation of migratory birds, which are under Federal-state co-jurisdiction. Since Federal statutes and treaties constitute the supreme law of the land, no state can impose regulation on migratory birds in a manner inconsistent with the Migratory Bird Treaties, the Migratory Bird Treaty Act, and regulations made in pursuance thereof. This has been recognized by most states in their game laws. In the State of Washington, for example, seasons for the hunting of migratory birds established by the United States Fish and Wildlife Service are "adopted" by the state game commission.[154] In Missouri, it is expressly provided in the Wildlife and Forestry Code (sec. 28) that "migratory game birds may be pursued, taken, possessed, transported, or used during such time, and in such manner and numbers, as may be prescribed under the provisions of the Federal Migratory Bird Treaty Act." In an act of 21 July 1947, the state of Illinois made a similar concession. In Alabama, "all regulations promulgated and enforced by the Department of Conservation relative to migratory birds conform with (emphasis added) the Migratory Bird Regulations as enacted by the United States Department of the Interior, Fish and Wildlife Service."[155] Some states, however, have shown recalcitrance of varying degree toward the Federal jurisdiction over the migratory birds. Oregon laws, for example, provide that "in no instance . . . will the federal laws be construed so as to provide an open season during a period closed by state statute or game commission order, or to provide a larger bag limit than is allowed under the state law or game commission order" (Game Code of 1950, sec. 57). The state of Georgia once openly defied Federal authority and set its own open seasons, but finally "the state authorities have reversed themselves."[156] This proves the impracticability of complete defiance of Federal migratory-bird regulation (which, from a broader point of view, is part of international regulation).

(b) Regulation of non-game fishery and wildlife---The regulation of non-game or commercial fishery is similar to that of game fishery, and, like the latter, displays a high degree of uniformity among the several states. Licenses from state fishery agencies are usually required of (1) each fisherman, (2) each fishing vessel, (3) certain special kinds of fishing gear and devices, (4) fish propagation, (5) manufacturing and processing and (6) sale. Open seasons and areas open to fishing are specified either by statute or by administrative regulation, as well as the minimum sizes and maximum amounts of fish to be taken and the gear to be used. Fishing by destructive methods and fishing for other than food and research purposes are generally prohibited.

Non-game wildlife are chiefly predators and fur-bearing animals. Administration with respect to predatory birds and animals is non-regulatory and is performed by only a small number of states. Fur-bearing animals are under regulation by the state in almost all states. Usually a license is required for trapping, the conduct of fur business, artificial propagation and transportation. Open seasons, number limits of trapping and the location, kinds and sizes of traps are usually regulated. In some states landowners do not need license to trap on their own premises, particularly when the animals are damaging property. Special protection is given beaver and beaver dams, and in some states the state game agency has the exclusive or preferred right to remove them.[157]

(c) <u>Territorial application of state fish and wildlife laws</u>---An interesting fact in regard to the state fish and wildlife laws is that they have been extended to areas under Federal jurisdiction. The following Federal regulation concerns fishing in certain areas of the National Park System (hunting being forbidden in the System):

> Any person fishing in the waters of the Yosemite, Sequoia, Kings Canyon, Lassen Volcanic, Grand Canyon, Rocky Mountain, Grand Teton, Acadia, Wind Cave, Great Smoky Mountains, Shenandoah, and Zion National Parks, the Lake Mead Recreational Area, and the monuments under the jurisdiction of the National Park Service, must secure a sporting fishing license as required by the laws of the state or states in which such park or monument is situated. All fishing in such parks and monuments must be done in conformity with the laws of the state regarding open seasons, size of fish, and the limits of catch, except as otherwise provided in paragraphs (b) to (m) of this section, which are applicable to all parks and monuments.--36CFR 1.4 (a)

As for Federal wildlife refuges, it is provided in sec. 4 of the act of 10 March 1934 (48 Stat. 401, 402) that Federal rules and regulations governing the administration of wildlife conservation areas are not to be inconsistent with state laws. By an administrative regulation (50 CFR 21.42; 21.32). state fish and game laws are made applicable to Federal wildlife refuges. Finally, "state regulations as to licenses, seasons, and bag limits apply to national-forest lands."[158]

The application of state fish and game laws to interstate boundary waters is another interesting problem. Some states have by interstate compacts provided for fish and game laws on such waters or some other measure of coordination between fish and game regulation of one boundary state and that of another. On 24 January 1907, Congress approved (34 Stat. 858) the interstate compact between New Jersey and Delaware respecting their fishing rights on the Delaware River. Art. 4 of this compact provided for the legislation by the two states of "uniform laws to regulate the catching and taking of fish in the Delaware River and Bay between the said states", which "shall constitute the sole laws for the regulation of the taking and catching of fish in the said river and bay" . . . (at 860). A less strong means of coordination is found in the interstate compact between Oregon and Washington, approved by Congress on 8 April 1918. It provides (first para.):

> All laws and regulations now existing, or which may be necessary for regulating, protecting, or preserving fish in the waters of the Columbia River, over which the States of Oregon and Washington have concurrent jurisdiction, or any other waters within either of said states, which would affect said concurrent jurisdiction, shall be made, changed, altered, and amended in whole or in part, only with the mutual consent and approbation of both states (40 Stat. 515).

Some states have declared their willingness to enforce laws of neighboring states upon a reciprocal basis. In an act of 2 May 1925 (Statutes, tit. 30, sec. 145), the Pennsylvania declared concurrent jurisdiction over the Delaware River below Trenton Falls with New Jersey, and promised common enforcement of fish and game laws of the two states over the waters and shores thereof. A law of Connecticut of 1941 provides, that

> If and when the state of Rhode Island, the state of Massachusetts or the state of New York shall enact a similar law for arrest and punishment for violation of the fish and game laws of this state, or of the state of Rhode Island, the state of Massachusetts, or the state of New York, committed or attempted to be committed by any person or persons fishing in that portion of any waters lying between such states and this state, any game protector, fish and game warden or other person of either state who is authorized to make arrests for such violations of the fish and game laws of any such other state or this state shall have authority to make arrests on any part of any such waters lying between such states . . .(Gen. Stats., sec. 4863, enacted in 1941).

Laws of similar nature have also been enacted in New York (Laws 1942, ch. 116) (anticipating action of Vermont, New Jersey, Pennsylvania, Connecticut and Rhode Island), Maine (Inland Fish and Game Laws, 8th biennial revision, 21 July 1945, sec. 17) (relating to waters bordering on New Hampshire), New Hamp-

shire (Laws 1945, ch. 16) (relating to waters bordering on
Massachusetts and Maine) and Rhode Island (Acts 1945, ch.
1611) (anticipating action of New York, Connecticut and Massachusetts). An Idaho law of 1935 (Laws 1935, ch. 115, sec.
1) differs from the laws of all these Eastern states in that
it prohibits fishing or on those parts of the Snake River
which form the boundary lines between that state and the
states of Oregon and Washington in a manner and by methods
outlawed by either the laws of Idaho or those of Oregon or
Washington (as the case may be), with anticipating reciprocal
action from Oregon or Washington. It should be noted that in
none of these cases is there any provision for common or concerted regulation on the part of the neighboring states, but
that the laws of all of them are in force over boundary waters and their shores.   In Wisconsin, "the conservation commission is (hereby) authorized to regulate hunting and fishing on and in all interstate boundary waters . . ." (Statutes,
sec. 29.085: Laws 1933, ch. 242, as amended Laws 1937, ch.
366) without even a mention of reciprocal law enforcement.
Under these circumstances, conflicts between the neighboring
states in fish and wildlife regulation are unavoidable. As
a measure of compromise, the following statute of Oregon deserves notice:

> The right to take fish and game from the waters of
> the Snake river or the islands of the Snake river,
> where the same forms the boundary line between the
> state of Idaho and the state of Oregon, by a hol-
> der of either an Idaho or an Oregon license in ac-
> cordance with the fish and game laws of the respec-
> tive states hereby is recognized and made lawful,
> and it shall be the duty of law enforcement offi-
> cers to honor the license of either state and the
> right of the holder thereof, to take fish and game
> from said waters and said islands in accordance
> with the laws of the state issuing said license
> (Laws 1941, ch. 88, para. 1)

This compromise was made without reciprocity, and is commendable. The following New Hampshire statute (Rev. Laws, ch.245,
sec. 32-a: Laws 1949, ch. 69) requires reciprocal action on
the part of the neighboring state or states, but it also stipulates interstate coordination in regulation:

> If, in the case of a lake or pond (but not a river
> or stream--the author) situated partly in this
> state and partly in another state, the laws of such
> other state permit fishing (but not hunting--the
> author) in that part thereof lying within such
> other states by persons licensed or otherwise en-
> titled under the laws of this state to fish in
> that part of such lake or pond lying within this
> state, persons licensed or otherwise entitled under

the laws of such other state to fish in the part
of such lake or pond lying within such other state
shall be permitted to fish in that part thereof
lying within this state, and, <u>as to such lake or
pond, the operation of the laws of this state relative to open and closed seasons, limits of catch,
minimum sizes of fish caught and methods of fishing shall be suspended upon the adoption and during the continuance in force of rules and regulations relative to these subjects and affecting
that part of such lake or pond within this state,
which rules and regulations the director (of fish
and game department) is hereby authorized to make,
and from time to time add to, alter and repeal.
Before making, adding, to, altering or repealing
such rules and regulations, said director shall
confer with the officer or board having like duties
in such other state, in order to secure uniformity
of law, rules and regulations as to the whole of
such lake or pond, if practicable</u> . . . (Emphasis
added)

So far as the avoidance of conflicts of administration between
the neighboring states is concerned, this provision is in advance of the above-cited Oregon law of 1941, although in the
latter the reciprocity requirement is waived. However, in
regard to the general problem of state fish and wildlife regulation over interstate boundary waters, an interstate compact or agreement stipulating permanent combined or coordinated action seems to be a necessity. Such interstate instrument may even provide for interstate regulation to be administered by an interstate agency.

   (d) <u>Regulation of water projects with view to protecting
fish resources</u>. The laws of a great number of states, require
the owners or operators of dams or diversion structures to
construct fish ladders or fishways to facilitate the passage
of fish over the dams and fish screens to prevent fish from
running of the natural watercourses, the construction of fish
screens being required only in Western States, where irrigation projects are constructed. For example, Idaho Code provides (sec. 36-1103 et seq., enacted 1893, as amended) that
fishways should be constructed in any dam or obstruction on
a stream, and in case of default the State Fish and Game Department may construct them at the expense of the person or
firm concerned. Colorado Game and Fish Laws contains the
same requirement which, however, does not apply "to a point
in a stream at which the whole volume of water is taken out
and lawfully applied, without unnecessary waste, to a beneficial use" (sec. 154: <u>Laws</u> 1909, p. 212, sec. 3). Before
the construction of a dam or other obstructive structure, the
owner should give a notice to the Commissioner of Game and
Fish, who may give reasonable directions on the construction

and maintenance of the fishway (sec. 155: Laws 1899, p. 213, sec. 4). The fishway should be constructed and maintained by the owner or operator of the dam or other obstruction, and in his default the Commissioner may do this at the expense of the said owner or operator (sec. 156: Laws 1899, p. 213, sec. 5). Pennsylvania has similar statutory provisions. But Pennsylvania statutes further provide that in case the construction of fishways is impossible, the owner or operator of the dam should pay to the State Board of Fish Commissioners 4.5 percent annually on the estimated cost of construction of the fishway to be expended for fish stocking in the pool above the dam (act of 2 May 1925). Maryland statute (Laws 1929, ch. 47, sec. 13) requires the construction and maintenance of at least one fish ladder at each dam, but it contains no enforcement procedure. It further allows the Department of Game and Inland Fisheries to enter into agreement with the owner of the dam for the annual payment of 4.5 percent of the estimated cost of constructing fish ladders for use in stocking fish. In states such as Maine and Michigan, fishways are to be constructed only when necessary, and the state fish agency will build them at the expense of the owner of the dam in the latter's default (8th Biennial Revision of Inland Fish and Game Laws of Maine, effective 21 July 1945, sec. 10; and Michigan Act no. 123, 1929). In Kentucky, fish ladders or roads, where required and practicable, are to be erected and maintained only during April, May and June of each year (Acts 1942, ch. 68, sec. 49). In Missouri, the Wildlife and Forestry Act of 6 April 1946 (sec. 21) requires the construction at any dam of a fishway or other fish-protection device of the kind to be approved by the Conservation Commission; but if the construction of this is impossible, the Commission may require the owner or operator of the dam to build a fish hatchery instead. In Wisconsin, the Public Service Commission, in connection with its issuance of permits for the construction of dams, may, when necessary, require the construction of fishways, as discussed above. In states such Wyoming (Compiled Stats., sec. 47-509: Laws 1941, ch. 81, sec. 1) and Massachusetts (act of 1 January 1942: (General Laws, sec. 32) it is the state that constructs fishways on dams when necessary. When fishways are constructed by the state, it is state enterprise and not state regulation. In a few states, e.g., Arkansas, the owners of dams are required to construct fishways, but the requirement is enforced entirely by courts and carries no administration (Statutes, sec. 47-512, enacted 1879). Fish screens are required to be constructed on water-diversion works by such Western States as Oregon (Laws 1945, ch. 442, 3rd para.) and Washington (Laws 1947, ch. 275, sec. 61, with respect to game fish and Laws 1949, ch. 112, sec. 45, with respect to commercial fish). The laws of Utah, besides requiring the construction of fish screens at diversion works, also provided that fish screens should be constructed at both the intake and the outlet of a private pond "so as to effectually prevent any fish from entering or leaving such pond . . ." (Fish and Game Code, or Laws 1953, ch. 39, sec. 23-3--9, emphasis added).

Aside from the requirements for the construction of fishways and that of fish screens, there is a third type of state regulation for the protection of fishlife. Colorado Game and Fish Laws, in sec. 102 (Laws 1899, p. 198, sec. 13), Provide:[159]

> No person owning or controlling any reservoir, lake, or body of water into which public waters flow and which furnishes the water supply in whole or in part to any stream containing fish, shall divert or lessen such water inflow or supply to an extent detrimental to the fish in such stream or body of water.

Such provision aims at the maintenance of definite amount of water flow in a watercourse in the special interest of fishlife. This provision, however, is purely criminal in nature and involves no administrative action. In the laws of New Hampshire, it is provided that when any person shall withdrawn or lower the water in any stream or in any public lake or pond to a degree which will endanger fish life therein, he should notify the department of fish and game in advance of his intention of so doing "so that the department may take out the fish in the waters so drawn down or lowered" (Laws 1949, ch. 91). Similar provision is found in the laws of Utah (L. 1953, ch. 39, sec. 1).

In 1947 a law was enacted in Maine (L. 1947, ch. 184) which provides that "no person shall build any dam for purposes of holding a head of water for use in driving lumber, ties or pulpwood without first filing written notice with the commissioner of inland fisheries and game." This law was probably designed to protect the spawning grounds of fishes from the effects of such dams.

A very interesting provision is found in the statutes of Washington, which reads (L. 1949, ch. 99, 1st sent.):

> In the event that any person, firm, corporation or government agency desires to construct any form of hydraulic project or other project that will use, divert, obstruct or change the natural flow or bed of any river or stream or that will utilize any of the waters of the state or materials from the stream beds, such person, firm, corporation or government agency shall submit to the Department of Fisheries and the Department of Game full plans and specifications of their proposed construction or work, complete plans and specifications for the proper protection of fish life in connection therewith, . . .

> shall secure the written approval of the Director
> of Fisheries and the Director of same as to the
> adequacy of the means outlined for the protection
> of fish life in connection therewith and as to the
> propriety of the proposed construction or work
> and time thereof in relation to fish life, before
> commencing construction of work thereon.

Under this provision, which is most comprehensive in
scope, consideration will be made not only of the need of
fishways or fish screens and of the impact of water manipulation upon fish life, but also of possible interference with
fish spawning and general environments of fish life. It
should be regarded as one of the latest developments in the
administration of fish resources.

Section 10 Forestry

Forestry regulation at the state level exists in a relative small number of states in varying degrees.[160] In general,
it covers the following three aspects or features, by order
of popularity of each: forest-fire prevention, regulation of
timber cutting and pest control, of which regulation of timber-cutting is positive and the remaining two features are
negative in nature.

(a) Forest-fire prevention---This is the most common
feature of state regulation on forestry, as nearly a third
of the forest land of the nation is too low in productivity
to warrant other protective measures.[161] This regulation,
in its broad connotation, is found in all forty-eight states.
However, the forest-fire regulatory laws of the fifteen states
of Alabama, Arizona, Arkansas, Delaware, Georgia, Iowa, Kansas, Missouri, Nebraska, North Dakota, Oklahoma, South Dakota,
Tennessee, Texas and Virginia are purely criminal in nature
and do not involve administrative action (as of the end of
1953).[162] Forest-fire regulation in its narrower sense exists therefore only in 33 states. Among these, Colorado and
Wyoming have only county and no state regulation. Thus state
forest-fire regulation is found in only 31 states.[163]

This administration is directed at the following groups
of persons: (1) owners (including tenant, occupants or other
persons having charge or control) of forest and wood lands,
(2) timber operators or persons harvesting timber and other
forest products (who in most cases are owners of forest or
wood lands),[164] (3) users of forest and wood lands, particularly railroads, campers, hunters and fishermen, and (4) the
general public. Criminal regulation being omitted, the administrative measures adopted by the 31 states may be roughly
classified, according to their comprehensiveness,[165] into the
following ten groups:

Group 1: All four groups of objects above-mentioned
          (Washington, Oregon and New Hampshire)
Group 2: General public (including general users), owners
          and operators (Idaho, New Jersey and Montana)
Group 3: General public (including general users), oper-
          ators and railroads (Connecticut, Maine, Wis-
          consin and Louisiana)
Group 4: General public (including general users) and
          operators (Massachusetts, Minnesota and Rhode
          Island).
Group 5: General public (including general users) and
          railroads (New York, Pennsylvania, Ohio and
          Maryland).
Group 6: General public and owners (West Virginia and
          Utah).
Group 7: General public and general users (California,
          Vermont, North Carolina and Indiana).
Group 8: General public (Michigan, Nevada, South Carolina,
          Illinois and Mississippi).
Group 9: Owners (Florida and Kentucky).
Group 10: Users (New Mexico).

A few examples will be given. The regulation of Washington
consists of:

(A) General regulation

(i) Against owners---Except for eastern part of the state,
where adequate fire-protection facilities have been installed
by the Federal Government, every owner must provide forest-
fire protective measures satisfactory to the supervisor of
forestry of the department of conservation and development
(hereinafter abbreviated as supervisor). In case of default,
the latter will take over the responsibility at the former's
cost, which, however, shall not exceed seven cents per acre
per year on lands of western and five cents per acre per year
on lands of eastern part of the state. "The owner, operator,
or person in possession of land, on which a fire exists, or
from which it may have spread, . . . shall make every reasonable effort to control and extinguish such fire immediately
after receiving written notice to do so from the supervisor,
or a warden or ranger;" and in his default the latter "shall
summarily abate the nuisance thus constituted by controlling
or extinguishing the fire, and the cost thereof may be recovered from" him.

(ii) Against operators---In the first place, "snags must
be felled currently with the logging". Timber-product manu-
factureres, in burning wood waste material at or near any mill
situated within a quarter of a mile of any forest material,
must properly confine the place of burning and take caution
to prevent forest fire; and suitable spark-arresting devices
should be installed at any burner, destructor, chimney or the

like. To clarify the responsibility of the operators, they
may apply to the supervisor for certificates of clearance as
conclusive evidences of their full or partial compliance with
these requirements. It is to be noted that the administrative
action involved in this regulatory measure is not compulsory
but is to be initiated by its objects. It is not strictly an
administrative measure, but merely a potentially administrative measure.

(iii) General users---"Everyone clearing right-of-way
for railroad, public highway, private road, ditch, dike, pipe,
or wire line, or for any other transmission or transportation
utility right-of-way, shall pile and burn on the right-of-way
all refuse timber, brush, and debris as rapidly as clearing
or cutting progresses, or at such other times as the supervisor may specify . . ." "When during an open season for the
hunting of any kind of game, it appears to the director (of
conservation and development) that by reason of extreme drought,
the use of firearms or fire by hunters is liable to cause forest fires, he may by proclamation suspend the open season and
make it a closed season for the shooting of wild birds or animals of any kind, for such time as he may designate . . ."

(B) Special regulation

(a) Closed seasons

(1) General closed season---The general closed season of
the year for the purposes of forest-fire regulation is from
15 April to 15 October. During this period: (1) "No one shall
burn any inflammable material . . . unless a different date .
. . is fixed by order of the supervisor of forestry, without
first obtaining permission in writing from the supervisor, or
a warden, or ranger, and afterwards complying with the terms
of said permit. However, if such fire is contained in a
suitable device sufficient . . . to prevent the fire from
spreading, said written permission will not be necessary."
For this measure, the closed season is from 15 March to 16
October for the western part of the state (against the general
public). (2) The operation of timber production within one-
eighth mile must be conducted under specified conditions (here
omitted); and the closed season may be extended by the supervisor (against operators). (3) The operation within one-
eighth mile of any spark-emitting railroad logging locomotives,
common-carrier railroad trains, railroad speeders, steam logging engines, etc., is prohibited unless they are equipped
with fire-prevention devices; and the closed season for this
measure may be extended by the supervisor (against railroads
and operators). (4) Permits must be obtained from the supervisor for the disposition by burning of refuse or waste
material on forest lands. "The supervisor, or any warden, or
ranger, may require the cutting of such dry snags, stumps and
dead trees within the area to be burned as . . . constitute a

menace or are likely to further the spread of fire." ". . .
The warden may furnish him with a man to supervise and control the burning, who . . . shall have the authority of a
warden while in such service, including the right to revoke
the permit if . . . the burning authorized would endanger any
valuable timber or other property". "In times and localities
of unusual fire danger, the director (of conservation and development) may suspend any or all burning permits and may
prohibit the use of fire in the area affected." (against operators).

(ii) Special closed seasons---(1) "It shall be unlawful
to use fire for blasting on any area of logging slash or area
of actual logging operation for the period of June 15th to
October 15th. This period may be extended by the supervisor
if hazardous weather conditions warrant." But "upon the issuance of a written permit by the supervisor or warden or
ranger, fuse may be used during the closed season under the
conditions specified in the permit" (against operators). (2)
"When in the opinion of the supervisor, weather conditions
arise which present an extreme fire hazard, . . . he may issue
an order closing all logging, land clearing, or other industrial operations which may cause a forest fire to start, and
such closure shall be for the periods and regions designated
in the order (against operators and general users).

(b) Closed areas---In general, "when in the opinion of
the director (of conservation and development), any forest
region is particularly exposed to fire danger, he may designate such region . . . as a region of extra fire hazard, and
he shall promulgate rules and regulations for the protection
thereof. For the forests in the Olympic Pennisula in particular, "it shall be unlawful for any person to do any act
which shall expose any of the forests or timber upon such
land to the hazard of fire". This regulatory measure is likely to affect owners, operators, users and the general public
alike. It may also be noted that special closed seasons as
discussed in (ii) (2) above are acoompanied by special closed
areas.

The regulation of Idaho is as follows:

(A) General regulation

(1) Against owners and the general public---Any person
responsible for the starting or the existence of a forest
fire should have it under control or should extinguish it when
it is out of his control. If he fails or refuses to do this,
the state forester may summarily do the same at the cost of
the former, who shall also pay a fine equivalent to ten percent of such cost.

(2) Against operators---All persons engaged in the cut-

ting of timber or timber products should enter into an agreement with the state forester for the disposal of slash. In
case of non-compliance with this requirement, the state forester may enjoin the timber-cutting operations through proper
court proceedings. When in further defiance of the order of
the state forester timber or timber products are removed without proper slash-disposal, the state forester may dispose of
the slash at the expense of the defiant owner of the timber
or timber products removed (L. 1925, ch. 150, secs. 5 and 7;
as amended by L. 1949, ch. 273, secs. 1 and 2). All slash
left in the vicinity of railroads, highways, etc., must be
piled and burned by the operator concerned, or by the state
forester at the latter's expense in case of default.

(B) Special regulation during the closed season---The
closed season normally begins on 1 June and ends on 30 September each year. But it may be advanced or extended by the
governor upon the recommendation of the state forester. During this period:

(1) Against the general public---Permits from the state
forester must be obtained for the setting of all fires in
any forest land or field. Every fire permitted must be kept
under control; and no permit can be issued when a fire cannot
be controlled because of weather, winds or shortage of men
or equipment. The governor, with the advice of the state forester, may close to entry forest lands in any section of the
state, in which no one can travel without a permit of the
state forester.

(2) Against owners---The state board of forestry may
make reasonable rules and regulations setting forth standards
of forest fire protection to be followed by owners or tenants
of forest lands or persons in control of timber thereon. If
these rules or regulations are neglected, the state forester
shall provide patrol and protection at their cost.

In New Jersey there is regulation:

(a) Against the general public---(1) "In any district
for which firewardens have been appointed, . . . no person
shall set fire to or cause to be burned waste, fallows, stumps,
logs, brush, dry grass, fallen timber or anything that may
cause a forest fire, without first obtaining the written permission of the fire warden, or a division, section or district
fire-warden", when the burning is within 200 feet of any forest or brush land, salt marsh, or field containing dry grass
or other inflammable material. (2) ". . .Whenever, by reason of drought, the forests of the state are in danger of
fires, the governor shall have authority to forbid . . . any
person or persons except those authorized by such proclamation, from entering forests, woodlands or open lands in such
parts of the state as he deems the public interest requires,

and may . . . suspend or curtail any open season for taking fish, game birds, game animals and fur-bearing animals, or any of them, therein".

(b) Against owners and operators---(1) "The owner or lessee of any woodlands, any contractor or employees with the authority of the owner, or any person doing public work in or upon, such woodlands, who shall permit or suffer the accumulation of brush or tree tops, or any litter from felled trees, to lie or be upon such woodlands to such an extent or in such manner as to facilitate either the origin or spread of forest fires, or who shall establish or permit any dump or area for the disposal of waste, rubbish, or debris of any nature, the maintenance, use or disposal of which will facilitate either the origin or spread of forest fires, shall be deemed thereby to have created an extraordinary fire hazard, and to have made and maintained a public nuisance". "On complaint of a firewarden or any citizen, the board shall cause an investigation to be made . . . If, in his judgement, a situation endangering the security of adjacent property . . . exists, it shall require the responsible party to remove such menace . . . ." (2) "The board, when satisfied that existing conditions tend to the origin of forest fires in any locality, shall provide for the maintenance of patrolmen to watch for and extinguish fire in such places and for so long as the danger exists". The cost of this compulsory service is to be collected from the parties responsible for the conditions (1931, last amended 1948).

In New York, (1) During serious fire hazards, the Department of Conservation may close state-owned lands to the general public or restrict the activities of the general public on such lands. This measure may be extended to privately owned lands with the consent of the owners thereof. It may be noted that this measure is at once an enterprise (management of state forest lands) and a regulation (control of forest fires). (2) The Governor may close all forest and woodlands (both public and private) to entry by the general public, and may suspend fishing, hunting and trapping therein. (3) Permits of the Department of Conservation are required for the burning of trees, brush, stumps, slash, grass, sawdust or logs in any of the fire towns (general public). (3) "No device for generating power which burns wood, coke, lignite or coal shall be operated in, through or near forest land, unless the escape of sparks, cinders or coals shall be prevented in such manner as may be required by the department (of conservation)." (users and operators) (4) "All railroads shall, on such parts of their right of way as are operated through forest lands, maintain from April 1st to November 15th of each year a sufficient number of competent fire patrolmen unless relieved by the department." (5) "The right of way of all railroads which are operated through forest lands shall be kept cleared of all inflammable material when-

ever required by the department." (5) "No <u>locomotive</u> shall
be operated unless equipped with fire protective devices . .
. approved by the department."[167]

The regulation of Michigan consists of the following two
measures:

(1) When the ground is not covered with snow, permits
must be obtained from the Director of the **Department** of Conservation for the starting of an open fire. When the fire
is started by a railroad company or a road contractor, it
must be further under the control of some competent person.
(2) The Governor may prohibit or restrict the use of fire
in forest areas during drought.

As for criminal regulation, it ordinarily involves no
administrative action. However, in many states, the state
forestry agency is vested with the authority of <u>enforcing</u>
such regulation. The enforcement provisions generally fall
under two categories. In the first category of states, such
as California, Michigan and Florida, the enforcement is solely or primarily the duty of the state forestry agency. For
example, California statute provides that "it shall be the
duty of the state forester or his duly authorized agent to
enforce the state fire laws . . ." In Michigan it is the
Department of Conservation that is authorized to enforce forest fire laws. Florida statute provides that the Governor
may appoint not more than 20 special officers to enforce the
criminal provisions of forest-fire laws. In these states,
"enforcement" exercised by the state forestry agency seems to
imply <u>both</u> the prosecution of offenses before the courts <u>and</u>
the promulgation of necessary supplementing or implementing
administrative rules and regulations, and thus imparts to the
criminal regulation some color of administrative action.

In the other category of states, the enforcement duties
of the state forestry agency or its employees are not more
than and not different from those of prosecuting attorney or
a peace officer. For example, the state forest officers of
Delaware are invested with the authority of forest fire wardens and "police powers similar to sheriffs, constables and
other police officers". The <u>Code of Alabama</u> provides that
"all employees of the department of conservation shall have
the powers of peace officers in the enforcement of the fire
and forest laws of the state of Alabama" (1st sent. of sec.
209 of tit. 8, enacted 1939). It is evident that under these
provisions, enforcement stops at judicial prosecution.

(b) <u>Timber cutting</u>---State regulation of the cutting of
timber and the removal of other timber products exists only
in a small number of states.[168] It is separable into the
following different patterns:

(A) Criminal or non-administrative regulation---Nevada and Louisiana. (Prohibitive)

(B) Enforcement of statutory standards of timber-cutting by administrative agencies through inspections or otherwise---Idaho, New Mexico, Mississippi and Virginia (Directive)

(C) Determination of standards by administrative agencies---Arkansas, Maryland and California (Directive)

(D) Approval of plans of timber-cutting by administrative agencies---Utah, Massachusetts and Virginia (Permissive)

(E) Issuance of permits for timber-cutting by administrative agencies---Oregon, Washington and Rhode Island (Permissive)

Pattern (A) Regulation

(1) Nevada---An act of 16 March 1903 (ch. 93) adopted a prohibitive measure which makes it a misdeanor "to sell or offer for sale any live or growing wood obtained from any common, white, yellow, or any fir, tamarack, spruce or flat-leaved cedar tree less than one foot in diameter two feet from the ground." This remains the only regulatory measure in effect today.

(2) Louisiana---It is provided in sec. 15 of Act No. 90 of 1922, as amended by sec. 2 of Act No. 153 of 1926, that "the owners of forest lands which hereafter be severed, or bled for turpentine, or those who sever or bleed for turpentine forest lands belonging to another, shall leave standing and unbled an average of two seed trees per acre for every ten-acre plot. The seed tree is defined as a healthy tree of the variety being cut or bled not less than ten inches in diameter, four and a half feet from the ground." But this law applies only to the taking of turpentine and does not extend to the removal of other timber products or the cutting of timber.169

Pattern (B) Regulation

(1) Idaho---Laws of 1937, ch. 140 designated the various forest protective districts of the state, which were established by Laws of 1925, ch. 150 (sec. 2), as "Cooperative Sustained Yield Districts." It is also provided in this act that in the harvesting of pine forests, all yellow pine trees of 16 inches or less in diameter and all white pine trees of less than 12 inches in diameter should be left uncut. Where immature stands are removed in specialized harvesting operations, there should be left as growing stock not less than 200 thrifty yellow or 300 thrifty white pine trees of sapling and pole size or larger per acre of land under operation. In areas where reproduction is not likely to occur, a certain number of mature trees per acre must be saved from cutting

(secs. 6 and 7). There are also certain rules regarding the
technique of cutting. Upon the state forester is imposed the
duty to examine and inspect the logging operations to determine whether or not these statutory rules have been complied
with.[170]

(2) New Mexico---Laws of 1939, ch. 141 (not amended) requires,
among other things, "any person, firm, association, or corporation cutting saw timber from lands within the state of New
Mexico" to "take all reasonable precaution in felling trees,
skidding and transporting logs to protect young trees on the
area being cut and to reserve uncut sufficient trees of seed-
bearing size on the land being cut over to insure natural
reforestation", by reserving and leaving uncut, in commercial
timber-cutting operations, "all measuring 12 inches or less
in diameter outside bark, at a point 4.5 feet from the ground
and in addition" leaving "not less than two live, wind firm
seed trees per acre measuring 17 inches or more in diameter
outside bark, at a point 4.5 feet from the ground; provided.
. . that in the event no live, wind firm trees measuring 17
inches or more in diameter . . . on said area at the time of
cutting then the largest live wind firm trees available on
said area shall be left for seed trees . . ." The Commissioner
of Public Lands is authorized to go upon all forest lands to
inspect logging operations.

(3) Mississippi---In the Mississippi Forest Harvesting Act
of 1944 (ch. 240), specific standards of timber-cutting are
stipulated. For example, naval-stores trees shall not be cut
unless they attain certain inches in diameter and unless there
are left unfaced on each acre of forest land 100 trees of four
inches in diameter or four seed trees of ten inches in diameter. Pine trees shall not be cut unless there are left standing on each acre of land four trees of ten inches in diameter.
In cutting pine trees under ten inches in diameter, there
should be left uncut on each acre of land 100 trees of four
inches in diameter or four trees of ten inches in diameter.
Comparable standards are applicable to the cutting of hardwood
and mixed hardwood and pine trees. In all events seed trees
must be saved from cutting. The state forestry commission is
authorized to make inspections and institute court proceedings
to insure the enforcement of these standards.

(4) Virginia---In harvest or commercial cutting of pine trees
there must be left uncut at least four conebearing loblolly
or shortleaf pine trees 14 inches or larger in diameter on each
acre of land so cut. When this is impracticable, "there shall
be left uncut and unimpaired in place of each conebearing loblolly or shortleaf pine tree of this required diameter class
not present two such conebearing trees of the largest diameter
less than 14 inches in diameter. Such pine trees shall be for
the purpose of reseeding the land . . ." All trees reserved
uncut for reseeding purposes "shall not be cut until at least

ten years have elapsed after the cutting of the timber on such
lands." However, the above requirement does not apply to
lands on each acre of which "there are present at the time
of final cutting of the timber as many as 500 or more loblolly
or shortleaf pine singly or together, 6 feet or more in height,
or 300 seedlings 10 feet or more in height." There is no regulation on the cutting of timber of trees other than loblolly
or shortleaf pines (Acts 1940, ch. 326; as last amended by
Acts 1948, ch. 498). Although this stipulation is essentially non-administrative or criminal in nature, "the state forester shall distribute notices calling attention to the provisions of this Act to forest wardens for posting in conspic-
uous places on all counties where loblolly or shortleaf pine
timber grows in appreciative quantities, and may cause such
notices to be published in newspapers of general circulation
in such counties". Such action of the state forester may be
said as a weak form of administrative enforcement (other than
prosecution). It is to be remarked that (1) this act "shall
not apply in any county unless the board of supervisors of
such county has . . . declared it to be effective in such
county; . . ." and that (2) this measure may be replaced by
Pattern (D) regulation.

Pattern (C) Regulation

(1) <u>Arkansas</u>---Under sec. 9 of Acts of 1933, No. 13, the
Division of Forestry and Parks of the Arkansas Resources and
Development Commission has the duty and authority to impose
regulations, restrictions and limitations in conformity with
the accepted custom and usage of good forestry and conditions
of the tract of forest land to be cut. But this provision is
inapplicable to incorporate parties.

(2) <u>Maryland</u>---Maryland regulation of forestry practice is
partially regionalized. The laws direct the State Forests
and Parks Commission to divide the state into a number of
districts and to appoint a district forestry board of not
less than five members representative of interested parties
as well as a district forester. The various district forestry boards, aside from giving advice and assistance to forest
and wood land owners, should adopt work plans for timber cutting, and rules of forest practice after public hearing, which
rules, when approved by the State Forests and Parks Commission,
have the force of law. Besides, the latter issues licenses
to all <u>persons engaged in forest products business</u>.[174] As
conditions of the licenses, all licensees are required to foster conditions for regrowth, leave young growth from cutting,
to arrange for restocking after cutting, to make application
for inspection, and so forth (Laws 1943, ch. 722, sec. 53 et
seq.).

(3) <u>California</u>---Under the Forest Practices Act of 1945 (Stats.
1945, ch. 85), as amended (Stats. 1947, ch. 983), the whole

state is divided into four districts, for each of which the
Governor appoints a forest practices committee of five members for an indefinite tenure.[172] Such district forest practices committees, in addition to their duties in fire prevention, pest control and reforestation, draft for their respective districts forest practices rules with the consent of
timber owners of two-thirds of the total forest land acreage
of each district, which, when finally approved by the State
Board of Forestry, have the force of law. The Director of
Natural Resources, through the State Forester, may make inspections in the enforcement of such rules.

Pattern (D) States

(1) Utah---Any person intending to cut timber from publicly
owned forest lands should submit a written plan of cutting to
the Chief Forester-Fire Warden, and no timber should be cut
unless the said plan has been approved by the said officer
(Code, sec. 19-7-17; Laws 1937, ch. 24, sec. 13; as added by
Laws 1941, 2nd sp. sess., ch. 1, sec. 2). It may be observed
that this law is not applicable to privately owned lands.

(2) Massachusetts---The cutting of commercial timber and timber products in an amount of not less than 25,000 board feet
and fifty cords on any parcel of forest land must be conducted
under rules formulated by a four-member state forestry committee and approved by the Commissioner of Natural Resources.
Each forest owner or timber operator, before the starting of
any cutting operation, must notify the Division of Forestry
of the Department of Natural Resources of his intention of
cutting. Thereupon the said Division shall examine the forest land concerned and prepare on behalf of the former a plan
of operation setting forth proper methods of cutting and the
minimum number of trees to remain standing for reforestation
purposes. The said Division is also required to inspect the
operation to make sure that the plan of operation is faith-
fully complied with (Laws of 1943, ch. 539; as amended by
Laws 1952, ch. 427).

(3) Virginia---According to the 1948 amendment of the above-
mentioned Acts of 1940, ch. 326 (as amended by Acts 1942, ch.
413), the statutory standards may be dispensed with in cases
where a cutting or management plan has been voluntarily submitted to the State Forester by the operator and approved by
the said officer prior to any timber-cutting operation.

Pattern (E) States[173]

(1) Oregon---Timber cutting was first under state regulation
as a result of the enactment of the General Forestation Act
in 1929 (ch. 138). Sec. 9 of this act declared it "unlawful
for any person to harvest or cause to be harvested any forest
crop, or to remove or cause to be removed any forest growth,

from privately owned lands which have theretofore been classified as reforestation lands[174] without first having obtained
a written permit so to do from the board (of forestry), which
said board shall set forth the unit value, by units of proper
measurement, of the respective kinds of forest crops on said
premises; said unit value . . . to be the true unit marked
value of such respective products, immediately prior to harvesting . . ." But this provision was merely a companion to
forest land tax reform. On 8 March 1941, the Oregon Forest
Conservation Act was passed, which specifically regulates
timber-cutting. While the above-mentioned provision of 1929
was seemingly still effective, the law of 1941, in sec. 4,
provided that

> Any person, firm or corporation cutting live tim-
> ber for commercial use from lands within the state
> of Oregon, shall . . . leave reserve trees of com-
> mercial species deemed adequate under normal con-
> ditions to maintain continuous forest growth and/
> or provide satisfactory restocking to insure fu-
> ture forest growth. In the conduct of logging op-
> erations and prior to and during slash disposal by
> burning,. . . proper precaution shall be taken and
> every reasonable effort made by the operator to
> protect residual stands and/or trees left uncut as
> a source of seed by fire or unnecessary damages
> resulting from logging operations.

Standards for the fulfillment of this requirement applicable
to the eastern and western parts of the state are specified
respectively in secs. 5 and 6. Administrative action was required on two occasions. In the first place:

> In the event that any operator shall desire to
> adopt other practical methods than those contained
> in secs. 5 and 6 hereof for providing for future
> forest growth, . . . including but not limited to
> artificial restocking or partial or selective cut-
> ting of the entire stand, said methods may be sub-
> mitted in lieu of the provisions of secs. 5 and 6
> hereof if, 30 days prior to the commencement of
> operations, said operator shall have submitted in
> writing to the state forester such substitute plan,
> and unless, prior to the commencement of said op-
> erations, the state forester shall have disapproved
> the same (sec. 7).

Secondly, the state forester should annually examine all harvested forest areas, and see whether the cutting have been
made in compliance with the above-mentioned requirements. If
satisfied, he shall issue to the operator a release from penalties. Otherwise, he should notify him of the delinquencies
and order him to make necessary corrections. In case of de-

fault, the state forester may take action at the cost of the
operator (secs. 10 and 11).

On 27 February 1943, this act was amended (ch. 142) with
a substantial increase of administrative authority. Before
this amendment, the State Forester approves rules of cutting
only when the operator chose not to abide by the provisions
of sec. 5 or sec. 6 of the act. Now all cuttings are to be
made in accordance with "such rules and regulations as may
be promulgated by the state forester and approved by the
state board of forestry" (sec. 4 amended), and secs. 5 and 6,
continued without substantial amendment, would seemd to be
the guides of action for the state forester instead of directives to the operators. By a further amendment adopted 28
March 1947 (ch. 294), the regulatory permit system was introduced, which replaced the permit system embodied in sec.
9 of the above-mentioned act of 1929, which was a concomitant
of forest tax reform. Sec. 4 of the Forest Conservation Act,
as now amended, reads as follows:

> The state forester hereby is authorized to issue
> permits for the harvesting for commercial purposes
> of timber or other forest products, and on and
> after January 1 of any year , or during any part
> of said year, it shall be unlawful for any person
> to harvest or cause to be harvested any timber or
> other forest tree products for commercial purposes
> from lands within the state of Oregon without first
> having obtained a written permit for said year so
> to do (emphasis added) from the state forester,
> which permit shall provide: 1. That both the
> state forester and landowner shall comply with
> such rules and regulations as may be promulgated
> by the state forester and approved by the state
> board of forestry, within the limits of the stated
> requirements of secs. 5 and 6, ch. 237, Oregon
> Laws 1941, as amended, and shall in any event either
> leave trees of commercial species deemed adequate
> by the state board of forestry under normal condi-
> tions to maintain continuous forest growth or pro-
> vide adequate restocking to insure future forest
> growth . . . 2. That in the conduct of logging
> operations and prior to and during slask disposal
> by burning, . . . it shall be the duty of every
> operator and landowner to protect residual stands
> and trees left uncut as a source of seed supply.

The standards set forth in secs. 5 and 6 of the original act
of 1941 are still valid, but they are operative only when
adopted by the State Forester in the regulations promulgated
by him.[175]

(2) Washington---The regulation of forest practices and tim-

ber cutting is provided in the Forest Practices Act of 1945 (ch. 193, effective 1 January 1946).[176] It applies not only to private forest lands but also to public forest lands in the state.[177] Under this act, harvest-cutting is distinguished from non-harvest-cutting. For the former, renewable annual permits from the state supervisor of forestry are required. "It shall be the duty of every permittee to provide that during the process of logging adequate precautions shall be taken to leave reserve trees of commercial species deemed adequate under normal conditions to maintain continuous forest growth, or provide adequate restocking to insure future forest production" (sec. 4, as amended by Laws 1947, ch. 218, sec. 3, 1st sent.). Standards are given (in secs 5 and 6) for "adequate precautions", which are as follows:

> Sec. 5 The provisions of this act shall be deemed to have been complied with in the areas east of the summit of the Cascade mountains within the State of Washington if at the time of issuance of a certificate of clearance by the Forester (i.e. the Supervisor of Forestry) in accordance with chapter 140, Laws of 1941, there shall have been reserved and left uncut all immature Ponderosa pine trees sixteen inches or less in diameter breast high outside the bark. Where compliance with the above provisions of this section would not leave at least four Ponderosa pine seed trees per acre at least twelve inches in diameter breast high outside the bark and well distributed over the area cut, there shall be left additional seed trees of commercial species predominant in the stand, including but not limited to Ponderosa pine, sixteen inches in diameter or larger breast high outside the bark in a quantity sufficient to aggregate four thrifty seed trees per acre well distributed over the area cut.
>
> On areas of second growth and prior cut timber, where poles, piling, mine timbers or other special products are being harvested or where stand improvement cutting is practiced, not over one-half the trees between twelve inches and eighteen inches diameter breast high outside the bark shall be cut in any ten-year period beginning on the date of initial cutting, and the remaining trees shall be evenly distributed over the area. In stands which are predominantly lodge-pole pine, there shall be reserved and left uncut five percent of each forty-acre subdivision well stocked with trees of seed bearing size (as amended by Law 1947, ch. 218, sec. 4).
>
> Sec. 6 The provisions of this act shall be deemed to have been complied with in the area west of

the summit of the Cascade mountains, if at time
of issuance of a certificate of clearance by the
supervisor there have been reserved and left uncut not less than five percent of each quarter
section, or lesser subdivision, well stocked with
commercial coniferous trees not less than sixteen
inches in diameter breast high outside the bark
until such time as the area is adequately stocked
by natural means. On areas that support stands
where the average tree is less than sixteen inches
in diameter the designated seed area left uncut
shall be not less than five percent of each quarter
section or lesser subdivision and shall be left
untouched unless the entire subdivision is being
cut on the basis of thinning for stand improvement.
The foregoing may be accomplished by leaving marginal long corners of timber between logged areas,
or strips of timber across valleys, or along rid-
ges and natural fire breaks, or by leaving staggered strips and uncut settings (as amended by Laws
1947, ch. 218, sec. 5 and subsequently further
amended by Laws 1953, ch. 44, sec. 2).

It seems to be clear that forest land owners or operators may
choose not to adopt exactly these standards. In such cases,
it would be the right and duty of the state supervisor of
forestry to approve any modifications or alternatives which
they may suggest.

To insure compliance by forest land owners and operators
with the standards discussed above or approved by the Supervisor of Forestry, the latter may employ a sufficient number
of inspectors for purposes of inspection. In case of default
the Supervisor may order the discontinuance of the timber-
cutting operations concerned pending compliance with the standards. If still no action is taken by the forest land owner
or operator within five years after the order of the Supervisor, the latter shall thereupon restock the cut-over area
within two years thereafter, the cost of which, which shall
not exceed $16 per acre, are to be borne by the delinquent
owner or operator. In enforcing this phase of the regulation,
"the supervisor shall also have power to prevent any new operation or operations in this state by the delinquent operator" (all above, sec. 8, as amended 1953, ch. 44, sec. 3).

(3) Rhode Island---The statute merely provides the annual
registration with, and the issuance of certificates of registration by, the division of forests and parks of the department of agriculture and conservation before the starting of
any timber-cutting operations (General Laws ch. 223, sec. 8:
Laws 1932, ch. 1928). No standards of cutting or management
are provided for, nor is the authority of the said division
in imposing conditions on the registrants. Such a measure is

rather a weak form of permissive regulation on timber-cutting.

In the following states, there is indirect state regulation of the cutting of timber in the forest land tax reform programs, regulation being imposed on timber owners as a condition for tax reduction. It is not regular regulation in that it operates on a contractual and not on a compulsory basis.[178]

(1) _Michigan_---(a) For farm woodlots: Public Acts of 1911, ch.135, provided that private farm land owners, who own not more than 160 acres of land, at least one-half of which is cultivated, may apply to the county treasurer for setting up a forest reservation not exceeding one-eighth of the total area of land in his ownership, the application forms to be prepared and furnished by the State Board of Agriculture. In such reservations there should be planted at least 170 trees per acre. Such reservations are exempt from the ordinary property tax, but in lieu thereof there is to be levied against the forest trees a severance tax (called "fee") of five percent of the cash value of the stumpage. Owners of the reservation, to whom the benefits of this tax reform accrue, had the following obligations with regard to the management of the reservations: (1) no grazing can be allowed; (2) re-planting whenever trees are removed or die; and (3) timber removed is limited to one-fifth of the total number of trees growing in any one year and is to be made in accordance with regulations of the State Board of Agriculture. In 1917, the act was amended (Public Acts 1917, ch. 86), so that at least 1,-200 trees should be planted in each forest reservation, with spacing of 6 by 6 feet on open areas. The obligations of the landowners have been modified as follows: (1) No grazing is allowable until 90 percent of the trees are 2 inches in diameter and unless it is practiced under regulations of the State Board of Agriculture; (2) the reservations should be fully stocked at all times under regulations of the said Board; and (3) whenever trees are removed there should be complete restocking under regulations of the said Board.

(b) For commercial forest lands: Under Public Acts of 1925, ch. 94, the owners of commercial forest lands may apply to the Department of Conservation for the designation of his forest lands as "commercial forest reserves", which must be used exclusively for growing merchantable timber and must be under good management. The reserves are exempt from the general property tax, in place of which are to be imposed an annual specific tax of five cents per acre and a yield or stumpage tax of rates varying from 2 to 10 percent of the total stumpage value depending on the length of time between the establishment of the reserve and timber cutting. Before the cutting of timber, permits must be obtained from the Department of Conservation. If the management of any reserve is found to be contrary to the purposes of their establishment, the Depart-

ment may de-classify such reserve. The landowners may also
voluntarily withdraw the forest reserves. But upon withdrawal they should pay to the state in addition to the above-
mentioned stumpage tax "a fee of three cents per acre for
each and every year the land has been registered as a commercial forest reserve, but not to exceed the first 20 years."

(2) Indiana---Owners of forest lands may apply to State Forester to classify their lands as "forest plantations" or as
"native forest lands", the characteristics of both of which
are specified in the statute in a detailed manner. These
lands may be withdrawn by the owners at any time. They may
also be cancelled by the state upon violation of the terms
of the agreement. These classified forest lands are to be
taxed at the annual rate of $1 per acre, and the standing
timber is exempt from tax assessment. But upon the withdrawal or cancellation of the lands from the above classification,
an "increment tax" is to be taxed which is the difference between the last and the first assessments, less any increase
in the last appraisement occasioned solely by the construction of ditches or levees. When the lands remain in the classification, no grazing can be allowed, and special permits of
the state forester are required for uses thereof or of the timber which are not inconsistent with the classification. There
is also implied regulation in the very definitions of the
lands (Statutes, tit. 32, ch. 3 (Acts 1921, ch. 210; as last
amended by Acts 1947, ch. 185).

(3) Louisiana---The State Forestry Commission may enter into
a contract with a forest land owner for a maximum period of
40 years, and obligate the latter to certain forestry practices. At the time of contract the lands are assessed for
the purposes of taxation, and the assessed value is not to be
changed throughout the period of the contract. "If at any
time within the contract period the owner or owners of the
said land (i.e., forest land) shall fail to maintain it in
all respects according to the written agreement entered into
by the owner and upon which the said land was given a fixed
assessment value for a fixed number of years, said contract
shall be subject to cancellation for such default and the
said land and any timber thereon shall be restored to the
assessment rolls and thereafter shall be taxed the same as
other similar lands and timber; and in addition thereto the
owner or owners shall pay the state and parishes a sum equivalent to the difference between the taxes actually paid and
the taxes which would have been levied . . . had it not been
assessed under the provisions of this section, plus interest
at 6 percent from the dates upon which such taxes would have
become due" (General Statutes, tit. 24, sec. 3330: Act No. 90
of 1922, sec. 11; as last amended by Act No. 362 of 1946, sec.
1).

(4) Wisconsin---(a) For any tract of forest crop lands of

not less than 40 acres situated within a forest protection
district: The owner may enter into a contract with the Conservation Commission for a renewable period of 50 years under
which he promises to pay (1) to the town or towns concerned
annually an "acreage share" of 10 cents per acre[179] and (2)
a severance tax to the Conservation Commission, at the time
of cutting wood products, of 10 percent of the stumpage value. The Commission may limit the amount of the wood products
to be removed. If this amount is exceeded, severance taxes
should be doubled. The contract may be terminated either by
the Commission or by the owner. In either case, the tax reductions are to be repaid to the state, plus an interest of
5 percent. Grazing may be allowed on such lands (Statutes,
secs. 77.01-77.14: Laws 1927, ch. 454; as last amended by
Laws 1947, ch. 109).

(b) For any tract of forest crop lands of not less than
40 acres which is not situated within a forest protection
district: The same law applies except that (1) no severance
tax is to be levied, (2) that the acreage share shall be 20
cents per acre per year, and that (3) grazing or any other
use than forestry is not allowed (Ibid., sec. 77.15: Laws
1949, ch. 362).

(c) For tracts of farm woodlands of less than 40 acres:
The contract period is ten years, subject to renewal. The
owner or operator undertakes to promote the growth of trees
and to prohibit grazing and burning; and the Commission agrees
to assist in preparing a management plan. A "woodland tax"
of 20 cents per acre is to be levied on such lands. The Commission may cancel the contract upon non-compliance therewith on the part of the owner or operator; but the latter has
no right to withdraw. When the contract is cancelled, the
taxes reduced are not to be recovered (Ibid., sec. 77.16 Laws
1953, ch. 384).

(5) Delaware---Owners of forest lands may make an application
to the State Forestry Commission for the establishment and designation of his forest lands as commercial forest plantation,
which must be no less than five acres in contiguous area.
Such plantation is exempted from taxes for a period of 30
years. But the owner must agree to maintain and development
thereon a commercial forest stand. Live trees cannot be cut
until they "have been marked for removal with the approval
and under the supervision of the state forestry department."
The State Forester is directed to make periodic inspections
of all such plantations, and report his findings to the state
forestry commission. If an owner is remiss of his duties,
the Commission, upon the recommendation of the State Forester,
may cancel the plantation. In this case, as well as in case
of voluntary withdrawal of the lands by the owner himself,
the taxes exempted must be repaid in full, but there is no
penalty for the default (Code, tit. 7, ch. 35: L. 1931, ch. 72,

sec. 2).

(6) <u>Missouri</u>---The Conservation Commission, upon application
by any owner of forest lands, may create "forest crop lands",
which shall be used exclusively for growing wood and timber.
Each unit of such lands must be at least 40 acres in area,
valued not more than $10 per acre. "During the time any such
lands are classified as forest crop lands . . . they shall be
assessed for general taxation purposes at $1 per acre and
taxed at the local rates of the county wherein the lands are
so located." In addition, a graduated "yield tax" is to be
levied. The rates of this tax are as follows: from one to
ten years after designation of the lands as forest crop lands,
four percent; from eleven to twenty years, five percent; from
twenty-one to twenty-five years, six percent. The losses in
revenue due to the general tax reduction suffered by the counties are to be annually reimbursed by the Conservation Commission out of the receipts of the yield tax. The owner must
develop a plan of management to be approved by the Commission.
The owner may voluntarily withdraw his lands from the classification, in which case he repays the state all tax reductions,
plus a penalty equivalent to five percent interest thereon.
The Commission may also cancel the classification for violation of the terms of agreement. Thereupon, all tax reductions
should be repaid by the owner, plus an additional levy of two
cents per acre per year (covering the entire period of tax reduction) (L. 1945, pp. 672-680, H. B. 1006).

(7) <u>New Hampshire</u>---The system of New Hampshire is peculiar
in that the tax reform itself is absolute and is not contingent upon any contractual arrangement between the state forestry agency and the landowners. However, a special reduction in taxes is allowed to reward those owners who have carried out forestry practices approved by such agency. All
growing commercial wood and timber are released from the general property tax and the school tax, but the <u>lands</u> on which
wood and timber grow are still subject to such taxes. A yield
tax amounting to 10 percent of stumpage value is collected at
the time of timber cutting. This is the tax reform. As an
encouragement to the adoption of scientific forestry practices,
an owner may voluntarily accept standards of cutting as recommended by the district forest advisory board concerned and
approved by the State Forester with the advice and consent of
the State Forestry and Recreation Commission. This entitles
him to a reduction in the yield tax in the amount of 3 percent
of the stumpage value. Another peculiarity of the New Hampshire program is the following provision: "Whenever it shall
appear to the assessing officials that a town or city is un-
reasonably deprived of revenue because of the failure of an
owner to cut standing wood or timber when it shall have arrived
at the degree of maturity most suitable for its use, such standing wood or timber shall be taxed in the same manner as general
property and be subject to the same rights of appeal, the intent

being to prevent the holding of standing wood or timber indefinitely without the payment of any taxes." Provision is
also made of the raising by the issuance of bonds and notes
of a reimbursement fund of $300,000, which is to be annually
distributed by the state treasurer to the various cities and
towns on application to compensate for the loss in tax revenues they have suffered as a result of the reform (Revised
Laws, ch. 79-A: L. 1949, ch. 295; as last amended by L. 1953,
ch. 256).

(8) Ohio---Upon application of an owner, the Chief of the
Division of Forestry of the Department of Natural Resources
may set aside any forest-bearing lands as "forest lands",
which shall be taxed annually at 50 percent of the local tax
rate upon its value. The said Chief is authorized to make
rules and regulations for the management of these lands.
These lands may be withdrawn by the owner, or they may be
cancelled by the said Division for violation of the rules
and regulations of management (Code, sec. 5554-1 et seq.: Act
of 1 September 1951).

Indirect regulation of timber-cutting may also be found
in cases where private forest lands are designated as state
forests or auxiliary state forests or the like. Here the
regulation is imposed in exchange for services performed or
privileges granted by the state to the owners of such forest
lands. Minnesota is an outstanding example of this practice.
In Minnesota, the cutting of timber in auxiliary forests may
be done under the instructions and inspection of the Department of Conservation. If timber is cut in defiance of such
instructions, the Department may cancel the contract creating
the auxiliary forest (L. 1927, ch. 247, sec. 7; as last amended by L. 1953, ch. 246). In Alabama, North Carolina and Pennsylvania, Minnesota practice is mixed with tax exemption, and
state regulation of timber cutting is made as a price for
both tax exemption and the rendering of services.

(c) Pest Control---There are two sets of pest-control
measures: (1) control of insect and disease pests of all
plants, i.e., forest trees, fruit trees, shrubs and other
plants, both cultivated and wild; and (2) control of insect
and disease pests of forestry trees only. The former exists
practically in every state, and is administered by the department of agriculture (usually through the state entomologist)
or an independent state entomologist or an ad-hoc agency.[180]
The latter is found in a limited number of states, and is under the jurisdiction of the state forestry agency (except in
Virginia, where it is the duty of the state entomologist).

State pest regulation of the first type generally consists
of (1) inspection of plants infested with insects or infected
with diseases; (2) summary extermination of these plants in
case of the failure of owners in exterminating them; and (3)

quarantine against areas of infestation or infection, both
within the state and in a neighboring state. These central
measures are supplemented by inspection of nurseries, control
over shipment of plants, and other related measures. Regulation of the second type, that is, regulation applicable to
forestry trees only, in its general pattern, includes only
(2) of the above-listed central measures, and quarantine is
provided for in New York only. It may be noted that the
second-type regulation essentially duplicates, only that partially, the first-type regulation. Summary extermination of
insect infested and disease-infected trees and other plants
is the core of both types of regulation. This measure was
upheld by the United States Supreme Court in _Miller and
Schoene_, 276 U. S. 272 (1928).

Regulation of the second type is an immediate measure of
forestry administration. By 1953, it had been adopted in
Rhode Island (Laws 1909, ch. 242; and Laws 1917, ch. 1540),
Virginia (Acts 1914, ch. 36; as last amended by Acts 1936,
ch. 19), New Hampshire (Laws 1917, ch. 195), New York (Laws
1917, ch. 283, as last amended by L. 1930, ch. 23; and Laws
1923, ch. 54, as last amended by L. 1949, ch. 191), Oregon
(Laws 1921, ch. 198; as last amended by _Revised Statutes of
1953_, sec. 527.310 et seq.), Minnesota (Laws 1929, ch. 218),
California (Stats. 1923, ch. 82; as last amended by Stats.
1953, ch. 1135), Idaho (Laws 1947, ch. 139), Maine (Laws 1949,
ch.124), Washington (Laws 1951, ch. 233), Massachusetts (Acts
1952, ch. 480), Montana (Laws 1953, ch. 25) and North Carolina (Laws 1953, ch. 910). In Oregon, California, Idaho, Maine,
Washington, Montana and North Carolina, the regulation applies
to all kinds of forest insect and disease pests; but in the
remaining states, it is applicable to certain specified pests
only. The objects of regulation in these states are as follows:

Rhode Island---Gypsy and brown-tail moths (L. 1909);
      white-pine blister rust (L. 1917).
Virginia---Cedar rust.
New Hampshire---White-pine blister rust.
New York---White-pine blister rust (L. 1917); gypsy moths
      and other forest insects (L. 1923).
Minnesota---White-pine blister rust.
Massachusetts---White-pine blister rust.

Except in New York where both summary pest-eradication and
quarantine are provided for, the only regulatory measure prevailing in all states having special forest pest regulation
is the summary eradication of the pests which, in the case of
insect pests, means the killing of the insects and, in the
case of forest diseases, may mean the destruction of forest
trees and the medium plants. The summary measure is taken
generally when owners of forest lands concerned fail to take
action. The cost of removing the diseased plants is borne by

the delinquent owners in Virginia, New York and Oregon. In Washington, 25 percent of the costs are recoverable from the owners of premises. But in all other states, the costs are to be paid by the state. The cost of spraying and otherwise treating insect-infested trees seems to be a state expense in all states. In the control of white-pine blister rust, the laws of Rhode Island provide for the paying by the state to owners concerned compensation for any species of the genus Ribes destroyed, if demand therefor is made to the state within 24 hours after the notification of the work by the state. In Massachusetts, compensation must be made by the state for the destruction of cultivated berry-bearing shrubbery in white-pine blister rust control operations.

Section 11   Miscellaneous

In some states, there is state regulation of artificial rain-making. In an Act of 1951 (ch. 131), the State of Wyoming "claims its sovereign right to the use and for its residents and best interests the moisture contained in the clouds and atmosphere within its sovereign state boundaries" The State Engineer is authorized to issue revocable permits, upon the recommendation of the Weather Modification Board, for the conduct of weather-modification activities (sec. 4). Similar laws have been enacted in Colorado (L. 1951, ch. 295), California (Stats. 1951, ch. 1677) and South Dakota (L. 1953, ch. 321). Laws for the regulation of artificial rain-making have also been found in Nevada (Stats. 1953, ch. 113) and Wisconsin (L. 1953, ch. 14), but they are milder in tenor. Nevada law only requires rain-makers to notify the State Engineer of their operations; and registration is all that is required under Wisconsin law. The bill passed by the legislature of New York in 1953 was vetoed by the Governor, who remarked that[181]

> The subject is one which requires thorough study and the taking into account of the interstate nature of the problem. Artificial precipitation of rain does not stop at state boundaries. Frequently the induction of rain is accomplished in one state through activities in another state. Consequently a control program should contain provisions for reciprocity of regulation and enforcement. The possibility of Federal regulation should also be taken into consideration.

In Vermont, there is state regulation of water resources in the primary interest of recreation. Under an Act of 1951 (No. 166), the State Board of Forests and Forest Parks may designate and establish restricted areas of water to be used exclusively for swimming and bathing, and adopt rules and regulations for their administration or management. In pursuance of this act, restricted swimming areas have been designated

in Sand Bar, Branbury, Elmore, St. Albans Bay, Maidstone and
Crystal Lake.[182] It should be pointed out that all these
areas are, as a matter of fact, part of state parks. The
designation of specific swimming areas in these places may
be regarded as a measure of state park administration, which
is an enterprise and not a regulatory act. But when such
areas are located on private and other non-state lands, the
measure is regulatory.

Article 2 Enterprise

Section 1 Navigation

    (a) Canals---". . .Many of the more ambitious early canal
projects were built by the states rather than by the Federal
Government."[183] As early as 1785, Virginia subscribed to the
stock of a company which constructed a lateral canal around
the falls in the James River.[184] "The first important canal
in the United States, the Erie Canal,[185] was completed in
1825 from Troy on the Hudson to Buffalo on Lake Erie, opening
route to the growing west with far-flung natural waterway
connection. Its early effect was to divert business from the
Mississippi River route and from the ports of Philadelphia
and Baltimore, laying the foundations for the commercial
greatness of New York. Following the success of this enterprise other states undertook the construction of canal systems,
and private corporations supplied a number of similar works,
especially for the anthracite coal trade."[186] By 1838, a
total of $60,201,551 was incurred by the states in indebted-
ness financing the construction of canals. Only in a few
states, notably New Jersey and Delaware, were canals construt-
ed by private enterprise.[187]

    The New York State Barge Canal appears to be the only state
canal now in operation. This canal is an expansion of the
above-mentioned Erie Canal, and was constructed without Federal aid. "As early as 1792 private capital undertook initial
steps to develop a canal system . . . But success was not
in sight until 1817 when the State took over its construction.
On October 26, 1825 the Erie Canal was opened to traffic...."[188]
The canal, costing $7 million, was then regarded as the larg-
est piece of engineering work.[189] "The original Erie Canal
was but 40 feet wide at the water line, with a four-foot channel and a bottom width of 28 feet. Several stages of enlargement ensued, the last of which was authorized in 1895 and abandoned four years later. Expansion of the Canal to its present
status was implemented in 1903 when by popular vote a bond
issue for $101,000,000 was authorized for that purpose. This
provided for improvement of the Erie, Oswego and Champlain
canals. In 1909 another bond issue for $7,000,000 was voted
for improvements to the Seneca and Cayuga Canals and two years
later a third bond issue for $19,800,000 was authorized for
development of proper terminals and facilities for Canal traf-

fic."190 This improvement was completed in 1918, and secured
a channel depth of 12 feet maintained by electrically operated locks.191 In 1935 a project designated as "Great Lakes
--Hudson River Waterway" was adopted by the Federal Government under the authority of the Emergency Relief Appropriation Act of 8 April 1935 (49 Stat. 115). This project, re-
authorized by the River and Harbor Act of 30 August 1935 (49
Stat. 1028, 1030) and modified by the River and Harbor Act of
2 March 1945 (59 Stat. 10, 13), is nothing but a further improvement of the New York State Barge Canal system at the expense of the Federal treasury. "The improvement provides for
a depth of 13 feet below normal pool level through all locks
between Waterford and Oswego, deepening between locks to 14
feet below normal pool levels, widening at bends and elsewhere and increasing the overhead clearance to 20 feet at
maximum navigable stage at bridges and other overhead structures. The widths of the channel to be provided under the
project are 100 feet in earth cuts, 120 feet in rock cuts, 200
feet in river sections, with widening at bends and elsewhere
as may be necessary. The length of the waterway . . . is
about 184 miles of which 160 miles are in the Erie Canal from
Waterford to Three Rivers Point and 24 miles are in the Oswego
Canal from Three Rivers Point to Oswego." Total cost of improvement amounts to more than $31 million, according to 1951
estimates. The Waterway is to be maintained by the State of
New York at its own expense. The improvement work was commenced in September 1935 and by 30 June 1951 was substantially
completed.192

The New York State Barge Canal System carried a freight
of 4,513,817 tons during 1938 and a freight of 3,949,739 tons
during 1949.193 "A by-product in the operation of the fixed
dams of the Erie Canal at Crescent and Vischer Ferry is the
electric power which is generated by utilizing surplus canal
waters that would otherwise be wasted. The generation and
sale of such power is authorized by Chapter 488 of the Laws
of 1925, as amended. The revenue obtained for the period
from January 1, 1949 to December 1949 amounted to $300,847."
"The extension and modernization of these plants is recommended. . ."194 By 1882, the year when tolls on the canal were
abolished, the canal enterprise was more than self-paying;
and the total gross revenues ($121,461,871) far exceeded total
costs of construction and maintenance ($78,862,153).195 At
the present time, the operation and maintenance of the system
is dependent principally upon the sales of hydro-electric
energy and the services rendered at the State Grain Elevator
at Oswego.196

The state canal which is next both in importance and in
the length of the time of operation was the Illinois and Michigan Canal. "An act of Congress in 1822 (30 March: 3 Stat.
659) granted to the State of Illinois right-of-way for a canal
from Chicago to La Salle. In 1827 Congress granted the State,

for aid in raising funds for construction of the canal, land
amounting to about 284,000 acres. The improvement became
known as the Illinois and Michigan Canal."[197] Construction
began 4 July 1836, with borrowed money, and was completed 10
April 1848.[198] "As completed, the Canal was 96 miles long,
60 feet wide at the surface, 36 feet wide at the bottom, and
6 feet deep. Its sixteen locks admitted vessels of 105-foot
length and 17.5-foot beam."[199] The Illinois and Michigan Canal
belonged to the so-called "summit canals". It "crossed the
continental divide between Chicago and Des Plaines rivers,
on a summit level eight miles above the lake, and then par-
alleled the Des Plaines river the Upper Illinois river to La
Salle, Illinois, where it entered the latter stream. The
summit of the canal was supplied with water by pumps located
in a plant on the Chicago river. Originally, only enough
water was pumped to answer the needs of navigation in the
canal, but thereafter, in 1861, the legislature provided for
improvement in the canal by excavation and a larger flow of
water from Lake Michigan."[200] "Final cost of the canal, including bond and loan interest, was about $9,500,000, which
was paid entirely out of receipts for the sale of canal lands
of the 1827 grant and from earnings of the canal itself. The
entire account was cleared in 1853, five years after the canal
opened." "During the first ten years of its operation, it
carried over ten million tons of commerce and thousands of
passengers. Traffic rose steadily to a peak in 1882, but
from then on it slowly declined." The canal failed in its
competition with the railroads, and finally went out of operation in October 1914.[201]

Among minor state canals, one example is the Inner Harbor
Navigation Canal of the State of Louisiana, popularly known
as the Industrial Canal. It was built by the state through
the Board of Commissioners of the Port of New Orleans (a state
agency) in 1918-1923. Connecting the Mississippi River with
Lake Pontchartrain through a lock, the canal "is some 5.5 miles
in length with a depth of 30 feet, and is being dredged from
time to time to a channel width of about 500 feet. This canal
is now a link in the Intracoastal Canal System, the lock, the
forebay, and a portion of the canal being under lease to the
United States Government, which lease provides for the operation of the lock on a 24-hour basis, with toll-free passage
through it for all vessels . . . "[202] In 1950, an act (No.
124) authorized the Department of Public Works to purchase
the Southwestern Louisiana Canal, commonly known as the East-
West Canal, at a price of $75,000, and maintain and operate
it without charge of tolls. The State of Louisiana also operates the Meyers Canal and the Doullut Canal, which were built
by private interests, for the movement of seed and market oysters on a toll-free basis.[203]

In New Jersey, the Department of Conservation (now the department of conservation and economic development) constructed

the Manasquan-Bayhead Canal,[204]which will be discussed later.
In Michigan, lands were granted to the state by the Federal
Government in 1852 for the construction of a canal at the
falls of the St. Marys River. The construction of the canal
was started by the state the next year, and was completed in
1855. However, in 1881 it was transferred to the Federal
Government in conformity with the River and Harbor Act of 14
June 1880. The canal was a short lateral canal.[205]

(b) Improvement of navigable waters---There has been record of a number of instances in which the states have constructed and maintained open-channel and canalization navigation
projects. Most of these state projects dated prior to 1920.
In 1784, the State of South Carolina appropriated funds for
the improvement of the Great Pedes River, and "additional
funds were made later. In 1873 the United States Government
assumed control of the improvement . . ."[206] The improvement
of the Hudson River has alternated between the State of New
York and the Federal Government. The work is limited to the
stretch of the river between the head of navigation at Troy
and New Baltimore, which is about 20 miles long and which was
one time obstructed by bars and shoals.[207] In the period
1797-1819, the state of New York spent a total of $185,708.40
in the construction of jetties and wing-dams, which, however,
did no more good than harm.[208] This work was continued until
1831, when the improvement work was taken over by the Federal
Government, which supplemented it with dredging.[209] Work
since 1831 is best described in the following passage:[210]

> The principle of improvement adopted by the United
> States . . . was this, namely, to control the chan-
> nels by means of longitudinal dikes, intended to
> aid in scouring away the bars and shoals and to
> help this action by dredging. Under this principle
> the United States Government, in 1835-1837, con-
> structed several dikes in the Hudson . . .
>
> Then followed a long interval of time in which
> nothing was done by the United States. But in 1863
> the State of New York took the matter up, and be-
> tween that period and 1867, besides repairing the
> old dikes, it built new ones as follows (six in all,
> names and localities omitted):
>
> In 1864 the General Government again took up the
> subject . . . .

The Illinois River is another river on which commendable
improvement was accomplished by the State authorities before
the Federal Government assumed responsibilities. After the
Illinois and Michigan Canal was completed in 1948, "the State
of Illinois continued the improvement down the Illinois River
and to that end constructed locks and dams at Henry and at
Copperas Creek." These two structures were, however, directed

by the state legislature in an act of 1919 to be transferred
to the Federal Government, which accepted the offer in River
and Harbor Act of 21 January 1927. The transfer was executed
on 28 March 1928.[211] On the lower reaches of the Illinois
River, the State of Illinois canalized the river for a distance of more than 100 miles to a depth of 7 feet at low water
by means of the Kampsville and La Grange Dams, which were
located 31.5 and 77.5 miles above the mouth of the river and
were completed in 1893 and 1889, respectively.[212] Also as
authorized by the River and Harbor Act of 1927, the United
States took possession of these dams and locks on 1 July 1928
and maintained them until 1939, when they were removed and
in their place two new dams were constructed.[213] For the
upper portion of the river, the State of Illinois in an act
of 17 June 1919 adopted a plan of improvement which called
for the construction of five dams and locks at Lockport, Bran-
don Road, Dresden Island, Marseilles, and Starved Rock, and
dredging of some 638,000 cubic yards of earth and 29,500 cubic
yards of rock. Permit for this project was given by the Department of War on 7 May 1920 and the construction work was
started in 1921. The project was designed to provide a minimum depth of 8 feet and a minimum width of 150 feet from the
upper end of the Federal project on the Illinois River to
Lockport, a distance of 60 miles. It was financed by a $20-
million bond issue authorized through an amendment to the state
constitution in 1908, twelve years before the construction of
the project was authorized by the Federal Government. Like
the previous improvements, this project was also transferred
to the Federal Government, the transfer being authorized by
River and Harbor Act of 3 July 1930. On that date, $15 mil-
lion was spent by the state and the project was well near completion.[214]

Earlier projects of comparable magnitude have also been
reported in other states. In 1857 and 1858 the State of Texas
undertook the improvement of the Brazos River from Washington
to its mouth, a distance of 255 miles, and $60,000 was appro-
priated for this purpose. "The kind of improvement cannot be
ascertained, but there was general complaint of its insuffic-
iency."[215] "Sabine River, Texas, was improved in 1873 by the
State of Texas at an expense of $51,455."[216] In 1834 the State
of Kentucky began the canalization of the Green and Barren Rivers, which was completed in 1841. "It included four locks in
Green River and one lock in Barren River, giving continuous
navigation for a draft of 4 feet from the Ohio River to Bowl-
ing Green, except at time of low water below Lock No. 1, Green
River." As the state failed to maintain the works in good
repair, they were sold to the Federal Government in 1888 for
$135,000, the transaction being authorized by the River and
Harbor Act of 11 August 1888.[217] The State of Kentucky also
constructed, in the 1870's(?), five locks and dams on the lower
96 miles of the Kentucky River. These structures were reported in a state of dilapilation in 1879.[218] Between 1837 and

1841, the State of Ohio was engaged in the improvement of the Muskingum River, which incurred an expenditure of $1,500,000. The project consisted of ten dams, eleven locks and five lateral canals totalling 3.67 miles. These works, too, became the property of the United States. The transfer, which was authorized by the River and Harbor Act of 5 August 1886, took place on 7 April 1887, when they were in a very bad condition.[219]

The New Jersey State Inland Waterway project was adopted by the state legislature in 1908 (ch. 83), and was completed in 1916. It began at the Cold Spring Inlet (Cape May) and ended at Bayhead, covering a distance of 114.7 miles, with projected depth of 6 feet but controlling depth of 4 feet and a minimum width of 100 feet. The waterway for most of its length utilized existing natural streams and bays, and actual dredging work was conducted over a length of only 31.-25 miles. In 1911, the extension of the waterway from Bayhead to Manasquan River, a distance of 2.5 miles, was authorized (ch. 213), which consisted in the construction of a canal through fast land, and which was completed on 26 February 1926. As discussed, the entire waterway became a part of the Atlantic section of the Intracoastal Waterway of the Federal Government in pursuance of provisions of the River and Harbor Act of 2 March 1945, which authorized further dredging thereof to a depth of 12 feet.[220]

Among the smaller state navigation-improvement projects, a number of examples may be given. "Between 1822 and 1829, before improvement of the rivers was started by the Federal Government, the State of North Carolina spent about $70,000 in improving the portion of the (Cape Fear) River between Wilmington and Big Island by jetties and dredging."[221] During the same period the same state also dredged the Taylors Creek near its terminals.[222] "During the years 1870 and 1871, the State of Louisiana cleared and dredged Bayou Teche from St. Martinsville to Port Barre to an extent sufficient to provide navigation over the route during the periods of high water."[223] In 1873, the State of New York spent $5,000 to dredge the channel of the Peconic River from Mud Creek to Merritts Bay to a depth of from five to six feet. On the same stream, "state appropriations of $10,000 and $25,000 made in 1888 and 1913, respectively, were expended for dredging a channel 6 feet deep and 60 feet wide from Flanders Bay to the public wharf at the foot of McDermott Avenue, 1,500 feet below the head of navigation."[224] For the Indian River, the State of Michigan in 1875 ordered a survey of the inland route of the river, and later a sum of $20,000 was appropriated to open the rivers and connected lakes for navigation from Lake Huron at Cheboygan to Crooked Lake. Improvements of the channels to provide a depth of 5.5 feet was started in 1876 and continued to 1879, and the state improvement was supplemented by dredging undertaken by the interested logging companies.[225]

In 1902, the State of Massachusetts was reported as being engaged in the construction of timber jetties for the protection and improvement of the mouth of the Bass River at a cost of about $22,000.[226] For the Weymouth Fore River, the same state in 1903 and 1904 dredged a channel of 15 feet deep and 100 feet wide at mean low water for 2,000 feet downstream from the Weymouth Fore River Bridge, at a total cost of $10,-235.87.[237] "The Commonwealth of Massachusetts has expended $514,026.75 for improvements in the Mystic River (a tidal stream of 7 miles long." The work consisted entirely of dredging.[228] After the completion of the State Inland Waterway, the state legislature of New Jersey in an act of 1927 (ch. 172) authorized the improvement of "Metedeconk river, Toms river, Parker run, or either one or all of them, as well as such other streams, creeks, rivers or inlets as connect with or are tributaries to the Inland Waterway System of this state or that connect with or flow through any of the tidal waters bordering or adjacent to the Atlantic ocean . . . by deepening or widening the same," the said streams to be part of the Inland Waterway System. In the same year the improvement of the Shrewsbury river was authorized (ch. 213). In the last twenty years or so, the State of New Jersey has also undertaken a number of small projects consisting of the construction of turning basins and the improvement of harbor channels.[229]

"Previous to the adoption of the Indian River Inlet project by the Federal Government (River and Harbor Act of 26 August 1937), the State of Delaware spent about $230,000, over a period of 15 years, mainly for dredging and jetty construction in attempting to stabilize the inlet channel. These efforts were unsuccessful."[230] In the San Joaquin River, the State of California has made three cut-offs to facilitate navigation.[231]

S ome state navigation-improvement works are constructed by state highway agencies in order to protect the highways. For example, in 1931 the State Roads Commission of Maryland widened the channel of the Northeast Branch of the Anacostia River from a point 150 feet above the Baltimore Avenue Bridge to the junction with the Northwest Branch and the channel of the combined streams was widened from this junction to a point approximately 500 feet below the Bladensburg Bridge.[232] In the Grand Marais Harbor, "the Minnesota State Highway Department has expended over $33,000 in the construction and maintenance of shore revetments to protect the highway from wave action inside the harbor."[233] Similar works have been constructed by Oregon State Highway Department on the Willamette River system.[234] In Louisiana, the legislature in 1950 appropriated (Act No. 375, general session, and Act No. 28, second extraordinary session) $300,000 out of highway funds to the Department of Public Works for the construction of a seawall jetty or other structures to protect a highway situated on Grand Isle, Parish of Jefferson. These works are essentially

part of the highway systems, and their function of improving
navigation is incidental.

At the present time, state enterprise of navigation improvement is kept on an active basis only in Louisiana, Massachusetts, New Jersey, New York, and perhaps a few other
states. In Louisiana a sum of $75,000 was appropriated in
1952 to the Department of Public Works to improve Bayou Cas-
tine in the vicinity of Mandeville by dredging or otherwise,
and to construct, erect, and repair necessary bulkheads in
the mouth of this stream (Act No. 623). In the same year,
Massachusetts legislature authorized and directed (ch. 561)
the Department of Public Works to construct sea walls at the
head of Cohasset harbor, subject to local construction. These
and other state projects, if any, are necessarily small in
size, compared with Federal projects in the field.

(c) Water terminals---The construction and operation of
water terminal facilities by state agencies constitute a state
enterprise when these facilities are open for the public.
State agencies may construct and operate water terminal facilities for their own use. For example, "the Connecticut State
Shellfish Commission operates a wharf (in Milford Harbor) not
open to the public."[235] Such cases are not within the scope
of the present discussion, for they do not constitute an independent state administrative service. Water-terminal enterprise has been undertaken by the state government in a number
of states, primarily as an auxiliary to private, municipal and
other local enterprises in the same field. Some examples may
be given.

"The State of New York provided terminal and transfer facilities at all important points along the Erie and Oswego Canals, and at Buffalo, Troy, Albany, and New York Harbor. The
freight-handling equipment, as well as the storage and dock
facilities, is governed by the requirements of particular locality. The State-owned terminal at Oswego is equipped with
a grain elevator of 1,000,000 bushels capacity."[236] The state
barge canal terminal at Whitehall is equipped with a 15-ton,
hand-operated derrick and storehouse.[237] In New York Harbor,
the state has constructed seven barge canal terminals, "all
of which are equipped with transit sheds and have some unloading equipment. Three of these terminals are still in operation as terminals for barge traffic, the largest of which is
in Gowanus Bay and has facilities for berthing barge steam-
ships. The other four terminals are used as tie-up facilities
for barges and canal boats."[238] The state barge canal terminal at Troy "consists of a concrete bulkhead 950 feet long,
with 12 feet of water alongside at lowest low water. Although
designed primarily for handling canal freight, the terminal
can be used for handling other cargo."[239]

The State of Louisiana owns sizable terminal facilities

in Ports of New Orleans and Lake Charles, which are managed
by special boards for the two ports on behalf of the state
government. In New Orleans, the state terminal system "includes 39 deep water wharves having a total frontage of about
6.4 miles mainly on the left bank of the (Mississippi) river
and, in addition, several wharves and landings on the Industrial Canal. The deep water wharves include those serving
the public cotton warehouses, the public grain elevator, and
the Foreign Trade Zone."[240] One wharf (Charbonnet St.) is
operated by the Gulf Atlantic Warehouse Co. and one (St. Mau-
rice Ave.) by the Federal Barge Lines.[241] The remaining
wharves are operated by the Board of Commissioners of the
Port of New Orleans, and are open to the public. 5.5 miles
of the total 7 miles of the state wharf properties in the
port are covered with modern steel sheds. Among the accessor-
ies of the wharves, there are "a terminal grain elevator, having a storage capacity of 2,600,000 bushels; a public commodity warehouse, having a storage capacity of 461,856 high density bales of cotton, and now utilized not only for the storage of cotton but also of general commodities; two banana-un-
loading wharves, equipped with 12 mechanical banana unloaders,
having a total unloading capacity of 26,400 tons per hour; a
two-story green coffee warehouse, having a storage capacity
of approximately 285, --- bags of coffee; as well as many
subsidiary and auxiliary facilities."[242] Besides, "the Board
of Commissioners has a ten-million-dollar expansion program
under way. The program includes the construction of one wharf
and the extension of three others. Six other wharves will be
rehabilitated by laying new foundations and rebuilding the
floors. Already completed are the new wharf (cost $1,500,000)
and two of the three wharves scheduled for enlargement."[243]
In the Port of Lake Charles, state-owned terminal facilities
consist of two wharves of 1,600 feet each, with five sheds
totalling 437,780 square feet and rail tracks totalling 47,300
feet (8.96 miles), together with a great number of storage,
handling and hoisting facilities and mechanisms.[244]

In San Francisco, California, and Boston, Massachusetts,
the biggest sea-ports on the Pacific and Atlantic Coasts, there
are also state-owned terminals. Of the 96 terminals in San
Francisco, 70 are owned by the State of California through
the Board of State Harbor Commissioners for the Port of San
Francisco. However, only 15 state terminals are directly operated by the state (through the said board). Of these 15, a
few are under the joint operation of the said board and some
other party. State piers wharves are used either for general
cargo or for special loading and landing purposes. "The general cargo piers provide 11.4 miles of berthing space with
35-foot depths alongside for deep-draft vessels . . . . All
these piers are equipped with transit sheds having an aggregate inclosed floor space of more than 102 acres . . ." "The
single facility at the port equipped to handle bulk and sacked
grain, moved by water carrier, is owned by the State of Calif-

ornia,[245] operated by the Islais Creek Grain Terminal Corporation." In addition, "the Board of State Harbor Commissioners has provided a row of ten skidways for use at a nominal
charge by fishing boats.[246] The grain elevator was placed
in operation in 1949, and it has a capacity of 500,000 bushels. The Board of State Harbor Commissioners also owns a
refrigeration terminal with 650,800 cubic feet of storage
space, and special terminals for copra and bananas. Since
1948, it has operated a foreign trade zone.[247]

The state of Massachusetts, prior to 1945, controlled,
through its Department of Public Works (Division of Waterways), the following terminals in Boston: (1) Commonwealth Pier No. 1, which is operated by the U. S. Navy; (2)
Metropolitan Sewer Wharf (for receipt of fuel coal), which
is operated by the Metropolitan District Commission; (3) Com-
monwelath Docks, Outer Wharf, operated by the Downes Lumber
Co.; (4) Commonwealth Docks, Inner Wharf, operated by the
same company; (5) Commonwealth Pier No. 5, operated by the
Port of Boston Authority for general cargo and passengers;
(6) Commonwealth Pier No. 6, operated by the Boston Fish Market Corporation; and (7) Parker Harbor or Graselli Wharf, operated by Thomas T. Parker, Inc., for securing, repair and
storage of pleasure craft.[248] It is worthy of notice that
none of these terminals was under the direct operation of the
department of public works. In addition, the state owns the
Logan Airport, which, unlike the above-mentioned facilities,
was maintained and operated by the said department.[249] In
1945, the Port of Boston Authority was created to administer
the state-owned terminal facilities in the Port of Boston,
and to develop additional facilities. For the latter purpose,
$9,700,000 were appropriated by the state legislature, and in
1947 a master plan was prepared outlining the projects to be
undertaken. Under this master plan, the following works have
been accomplished or planned:[250]

1. Hoosac Cargo and Grain Terminal, completed August
   1950, a three-berth terminal with a grain elevator
   of 1-million-bushel storage capacity, replacing the
   former Hoosac Piers.
2. Mystic Pier No. 1, completed July 1952, with a berthing space for three ships, replacing the former Mystic Piers.
3. East Boston Pier No. 1, including modernization of
   grain facilities on Pier No. 4, completed December
   1951.
4. The Castle Island Terminal rehabilitation, to be commenced July 1953.
5. The Northern Avenue Project, comprising three general
   cargo terminals, two industrial centers, a vehicular
   ramp, and open storage, scheduled to be started in
   1955.
6. East Boston Pier No. 3 modernization project, to be

started upon completion of the adjacent proposed Pier
No. 1.

In Charleston, South Carolina, another seaport, "the
South Carolina State Ports Authority owns and operates the
Union Pier and the Columbus Street Terminal Wharf and under
sub-lease operates two-thirds of the former Port of Embarkation terminal at North Charleston, now owned by the City of
Charleston and leased to the West Virginia Pulp and Paper
Company. The Union Pier can accommodate one cargo vessel at
its face . . . The North Charleston Terminal is the only one
of the general cargo facilities owned by the State Ports Authority at which there is fixed hoisting equipment."[251] Besides,
the Authority "operates the belt-line railway serving all
wharves and warehouses (of all kinds of ownership), and connecting with trunk lines entering the city."[252]

The State of Maine has a special agency for the administration of water terminals, the Maine Port Authority. This
agency operates the Maine State Pier at Portland, which was
constructed in 1923 and which is the only state-owned terminal
property.[253] This wharf has a berthing capacity for three
deep-sea ships, and is 1,000 feet long with varying widths.
Cargo-handling facilities consist of a covered transit shed
built of concrete decks and steel frame, open storage for
about fifty carloads, tracks and paved area connecting railroads and highways. The Authority does not operate a grain
elevator, but in May 1949 it initiated a grain-inspection service.[254]

North Carolina, like South Carolina, has a state terminals
agency called the State Ports Authority, which manages the
state-owned terminal facilities located in Wilmington and
Morehead City. In December 1949, the Authority obtained a
fifty-year lease from the United States Maritime Administration of the northern end of the shipyard property as the site
for the development of a state pier at Wilmington. In the
same time (but formally on 1 April 1951), the Authority purchased the terminal facilities of the Morehead City, the operation of which was then in a condition of insolvency. In 1949,
the state legislature authorized a $7,500,000 bond issue to
finance the construction and rehabilitation of terminal facilities in these cities. The Wilmington and Morehead City projects were launched respectively in June and August 1950; and
both projects were completed in 1952. The Morehead City Ocean
Terminal project consists in the construction of a steel sheet
pile bulkhead and timber relieving platform approximately 1,-
200 feet long, one large fire-proof transit shed of approximately 60,000 square feet, two storage warehouses of 35,640
and 51,840 square feet respectively, harbor dredging, and other
minor items of work. The old City dock is 1,350 feet long and
has one transit shed. Reconstruction of the old structure was
scheduled to be started in 1953. The two new warehouses have

been leased to the United States Navy, while other facilities are directly operated by the Authority. Facilities at Wilmington include a marginal concrete-piling wharf of 1.510 by 200 feet, with a berthing capacity for three ocean ships, two transit sheds of 79,000 square feet each built on concrete deck, a storage warehouse of 98,000 square feet, a fumigating plant and a scale house. It may be noted that the state is only owner of terminal facilities available to the general public at Morehead City, where there are no private terminals except a small dock owned and used by an oil company.[255]

In Mobile, Alabama, most of the terminal facilities are owned and operated by the state. The state-controlled facilities consist of piers capable of accommodating as many as 30 deep-craft ships, general-cargo transit sheds having a total space of as much as 1,530,779 square feet, and 472,264 square feet of dry and 531,000 cubic feet of cold storage space.[256]

The State of Georgia has constructed and placed under its own operation a wharf at Savannah Harbor. In another port, Brunswick Harbor, "plans are being prepared (on 30 June 1952) for the construction of a State Port Terminal to be located in Brunswick River 2.7 miles below the center of the city."[257]

In Chicago, the State of Illinois owns the Island Fish Company Wharf, which is used by the said company for mooring fish boats, a barge terminal leased to a private company, and a 1,500-bushel grain elevator.[258] The State of Ohio owns a wharf at Toledo, which is leased to the United States Navy,[259] and a dock at Sandusky, which is used to moor state fish patrol boats and is not open to the public.[260] In Baudette Harbor, the State of Minnesota does not own or operate a pier or wharf, but it has constructed a boathouse and a warehouse adjoining the public wharf owned by the village of Baudette.[261]

In New Jersey, the State Highway Department may construct piers and wharves in counties of sixth class and operate them as a state enterprise (Statutes, sec. 27:7-49: Laws 1930, ch. 253, sec. 1). The Department of Highways and Public Works of the State of Tennessee possesses a similar authority, under which it may construct and operate "any public facilities . . . for the loading and landing of cargo whenever state highways intersect or parallel any navigable waters within or bounding the State of Tennessee . . ." (Code, sec. 3260.1: Acts 1935, ch. 36, sec. 1). No terminal facilities had been constructed by the Tennessee Department of Highways and Public Works as of March 1954,[262] nor had been any constructed by the New Jersey Department of Highway as of May 1954.[263]

Section 2   Flood Control

The state governments of some states have undertaken the

construction and the operation and maintenance of flood-control projects. As early as 1847, the State of Arkansas built a levee on the east side of Fourche Island in the Arkansas River and a small channel dam placed in the upper outlet branch of Fourche Bayou at the head of the island. "The dam was designed to prevent the backwaters of the Arkansas River from entering Fourche Bayou. With the exception of 2 miles, all of this early levee system was destroyed by caving banks. The dam was destroyed in 1907 by a freshet from Fourche Bayou."[264] In the City of Beardstown, Illinois, the state of Illinois repaired a numicipal-built levee following the 1922 flood, and again in 1927-1928 constructed the existing concrete floodwall at a cost of $313,000 which extends some 3,-200 feet along the river front of Beardstown, and additional levees connecting with each end of the floodwall.[265]

In 1921 the State of Minnesota advanced a plan for the control of the floods of the Minnesota River, which called for the construction of three reservoirs. Two of these reservoirs were actually constructed in 1935 with Federal relief funds. The Lac Qui Parle Reservoir was impounded by a dam constructed on the Minnesota River below the mouth of the Lac Qui Parle River. This project also includes an earth diversion dam and other control works in the Chippewa River, "diversion channel through Watson Sag to divert Chippewa River floodwaters into the reservoir and channel improvements in the Minnesota River below the mouth of the Chippewa River to provide bank-full discharge capacity of 4,000 cubic feet per second." The reservoir will cover the Lac Qui Parle Lake. The other project constructed by the State of Minnesota is the Big Stone Reservoir project. It consists of "an excavated channel with levees to divert Whetstone River directly into Big Stone Lake; a low earth dam and control works at the foot of the lake; and enlargement of the Minnesota River channel below the dam to provide bank-full discharge capacity of 400 cubic feet per second."[266]

In Idaho, a law of 1919 (ch. 29; last amended by L. 1933, ch. 84) authorized the construction under an ad-hoc commission of levees, jetties, dams or other works to rectify the channel of the Snake River. Similar works were authorized to be constructed in the same manner on the Boise River by a law of 1937 (ch. 27). "The work was levees and revetments and was a part of a larger effort under the joint sponsorship of the counties, the state and Federal relief agencies." However, "the sponsoring counties have never assumed responsibility for maintaining the work and neither has the state although some individuals have tried to maintain enough of the structures to protect their own farm land."[267] It is apparent that these local flood-protection works have contributed very little to the purposes to which they were devoted.

In the laws of Vermont, it is provided that the State Pub-

lic Service Commission "shall have authority to order removal
from streams sandbars, debris or other obstructions which, in
the opinion of a competent engineer to be appointed by the
governor, may be a menace in time of flood, or endanger property or life below, or the property or riparian owners.
When approved by the governor the expense of investigation
and removal of the obstruction shall be paid by the state
funds . . ." (Public Laws, sec. 6129: Acts 1929, No. 80, sec.
8). This law was passed after the 1927 flood, and has seemingly become obsolete; and no actual work has been recorded.[268]

In Wisconsin, any twenty-five land-owners in the drainage
basin of any watercourse may petition the State Public Service
Commission to construct necessary flood-control works. The
Commission may approve the construction of such works after
hearings and surveys. Thereupon the Governor appoints a Flood
Control Board composed of one member of the board of supervisors of the county in which the major part of the improvement
is located, one member of the board of supervisors of the
county in which the larger amount of the property to be benefited is located, and one person residing in the drainage basin concerned. In this Board is invested the responsibility
of constructing the works as and operating and maintaining
them. Construction costs are raised by special benefit assessments, and the costs of operation and maintenance are paid
each year by the cities, towns and villages concerned (Statutes, ch. 87: L. 1931, ch. 481; as last amended by L. 1945,
ch. 511).

Pennsylvania has recorded outstanding achievements in
flood control enterprise. "Subsequent to the flood of May
1942, the Pennsylvania Department of Forests and Waters has
expended approximately $325,000 in state funds in clearing
and otherwise improving the channel of Lackwaxen River in the
town of Honesdale and in various reaches upstream to points
above Prompton. The work included restoring a privately owned
dam at Seelyville, removing a privately owned low dam that was
located approximately 230 feet upstream from the mouth of Dyberry Creek in Honesdale, cutting back the right bank from the
dam site to a point approximately 250 feet downstream from the
confluence with Dyberry Creek, thus easing the turn in the
Lackwaxen. This work has undoubtedly improved the hydraulic
characteristics of the channel for flows up to bank-full
stage."[269] During the biennium beginning 1 June 1948, the
same Department constructed a number of flood-control projects
consisting of dams and reservoirs, levees, and channel-improvement works. It also completed 62 dredging and snagging projects at the request of local government agencies and with their
financial cooperation.[270]

On the Winooski River in Vermont, "in June 1933, following
the organization of the Civilian Conservation Corps, construction was undertaken with Civilian Conservation Corps personnel

on two earth-fill dams at East Barre and Wrightsville. As
originally planned in the 308 report on the Winooski River,
these reservoirs were to be operated jointly in the interest
of flood control and power development. As constructed, the
dams were built somewhat smaller than originally proposed,
being restricted to flood-detention purposes entirely, without any storage being reserved for conservation use." " The
dams were completed in the fall of 1935, and shortly thereafter were officially turned over to the State of Vermont."[271]

State flood-control projects are also found in Illinois,
Iowa and Louisiana, and perhaps a few other states. In 1949,
$25,000 were appropriated the Division of Waterways of Illinois
Department of Public Works and Buildings, "for the purpose of
completing certain improvements on the Fox River, in the City
of Aurora, in Kane County." In the same year, appropriation
were also made to the same Division for the construction of
flood-control works in the City of Rosiclare and in Addison
Creek in Cook County. However, these works may be constructed
by the said Division either in cooperation with the Federal
Government or with local agencies, and therefore may not actually be state projects. During the fiscal year 1950, Iowa
Conservation Commission made repairs to a low dam in Beavers
Meadows, Butler County, and revetments to streams in the Butler and Polk Counties.[272] In 1950, an act was passed by Louisiana state legislature appropriating $20,000 to the state
department of public works "to divert the waters of the Amite
River in the vicinity of Amite Baptist Church Cemetery, Parish
of Livingston, and to install revetments or other bank protection with view of protecting said Cemetery from the waters
of said River."

Some flood-control works are constructed by state government as an incident to the states' activities to other fields
than flood control, most commonly in connection with state
highway administration. For example, a steel piling wall,[273]
has been constructed by the New York State Department of Highways along the east bank of Dodge Creek in Portville.[274] The
same Department, with the cooperation of the highway departments of several counties, has also "done minor amounts of
cleaning and bank protection work on tributaries of Dyke Creek
where structures were endangered."[275] "In Jackson Hole, Wyoming, the Wyoming Highway Department has built numerous dikes
and groins to protect the approaches and left abutment of the
Jackson-Wilson Highway Bridge over Snake River."[276] "The Idaho
Bureau of Highways also has constructed some bank-protection
works in the vicinity of the Lorenzo Highway Bridge, in order
to protect the bridge abutments."[277] In the State of Washington, "there was a change of course of the Lewis River done by
the State Highway Commission in 1942."[278] Occasionally other
agencies have also built local flood-protection works. For
example, "in the late fall of 1941, the Gary Park Commission
rebuilt the leaves along the Little Calumet River in Gleason

Park that had washed out during the flood of June 1941."279
In North Dakota, "during the years of 1938 and 1939, the State
Training School constructed a levee to protect its property
from inundation by the Heart River. This levee follows the
right bank of the Heart River from the Northern Pacific Railroad bridge at the west edge of Nandan to the bluffs near the
southeast corner of the State Training School grounds. This
levee was overtopped by the March 1943 flood and most of the
levee was destroyed." But it was rebuilt by the Corps of
Engineers with state funds.280 Oregon State Hospital constructed a levee on the Umatilla River at a cost of $20,000
to protect its property.281 All these works are constructed
to protect the states' own properties. Strictly speaking,
they do not form a part of state flood-control enterprise.

Another phase of state flood-control enterprise is in connection with the maintenance of local flood protection works
constructed by the Federal Government. Ordinarily, these
Federal works are maintained and operated by local governmental units, including special districts. However, in exceptional cases, it is the duty of the state government. For instance,
in California, the State Department of Public Works assumes
this duty when no local agency is willing to perform it (Stats.
1949, ch. 641).282 In Washington, under Laws 1941, ch. 204,
the state subsidizes local units in this maintenance work.

In the following provision of the laws of Washington (Revised Code, ch. 90. 24: Laws 1939, ch. 107, as amended), another interesting but unique measure of flood control is found:

> Section 90.24.010 Ten or more owners of real pro-
> perty abutting on a meandered lake may petition
> the superior court of the county in which the lake
> is situated, for an order to provide for the regu-
> lation of the outflow of the lake in order to main-
> tain a certain water level therein, in the inter-
> ests of flood control, and the court, after hear-
> ing, is authorized to make an order fixing the wa-
> ter level thereof and directing the supervisor (i.
> e., supervisor of water resources of the department
> of conservation and development) to regulate the
> outflow therefrom for the purpose of maintaining
> the water level so fixed: Provided, That this sec-
> tion shall not apply to any meandered lake or res-
> ervoir used for the storage of water for irrigation
> or other beneficial purposes, or to lakes navigable
> from the sea.

During the biennium of 1 October 1950 to 30 September 1952,
for example, orders were issued by the courts setting forth
the maximum levels of Star Lake and Lake Sawyer in King County
Loon Lake in Stevens County and Liberty Lake in Spokane County.
Controlled outlets were installed which are operated by the

Division of Water Resources of the State Department of Conservation and Development.[283]

Section 3 Reclamation

1. _Irrigation_---Under sec. 4 of the Sundry Civil Appropriation Act of 18 August 1894, commonly referred to as the Carey Act (28 Stat. 372, 422), it is possible for the several states (Western) to construct and operate irrigation works to irrigate Federal lands that are to be granted to them as a result of such enterprise. However, Wyoming appears to be the only state which has availed itself of this act.[284] "This first segregation granted to Wyoming was approved by the Department of the Interior on January 28, 1896. This was for Segregation List No. 1, and embraced approximately 15,000 acres to be reclaimed by the Bench Canal from waters of the Greybull River. The first arid land patent granted to this State by the General Land Office was filed on January 21, 1900, and conveyed 3,855.25 acres of land under the Cody Canal. Irrigation development under the Carey Act progressed rather rapidly until about the year 1912 when it became difficult to dispose of irrigation securities. After the passage of the Carey Act, the Carey Act Department secured the segregation of 1,453,758 acres of land under 55 projects. Approximately $8,000,000.00 has been spent in the construction of irrigation projects under the supervision of the Carey Act Department in the office of the Commissioner of Public Lands, State of Wyoming . . . . This would represent a much larger amount if placed in terms of present day costs. There has been patented to the state 227,251.85 acres under 30 completed systems. Settlers have been placed on 187,295.73 acres of Carey Act lands, and 181,311.41 acres have been patented to them. The total acreage under irrigation under Carey Act would be approximately 187,000 acres."[285]

It is needless to say that state irrigation enterprise can also be initiated independently of the Carey Act. In Utah a law was passed in 1909 which authorized the State Land Board to construct and operate irrigation projects to irrigate state and private lands with funds derived from the sale of half a million acres of Federal lands granted to the state (Laws 1909, ch. 116; as amended by L. 1921, ch. 125, sec. 1: _Code of 1953_, tit. 65, ch. 4). It would seem that under this law, an irrigation project was constructed by the state in Piute, Sevier and Sanpete Counties and was known as the Piute Irrigation project. However, a law passed in 1919 directed that this project be sold by the state (1919, last amended). There is no information as to the purchaser of this project and the date of the transaction, nor is it known whether this was the only irrigation project ever constructed by the State of Utah. In all events, as of 30 April 1954, "there are no lands being irrigated by any state projects under the control of the Land Board . . ."[286]

Montana seems to be the only state which has now an active state irrigation enterprise in dependent of the Carey Act. In 1934, the Montana state legislature created the Montana Water Conservation Board whose principal duty has been to construct or rehabilitate and operate irrigation projects.[287] "The water conservation (i.e., irrigation) projects constructed or rehabilitated by this agency total 173, of which 44 are major projects and 129 are small projects most of which were built in conjunction with Works Progress Administration (Federal) and which are located principally in southeastern Montana counties. The Board's projects store 410,705 acre-feet of water, and 218,972 acre-feet of water can be furnished by direct diversion of stream flow making a total of 629,677 acre-feet available from the projects. Water supply for new lands under the projects is made available to 133,294 acres and 252,920 acres can be served with a supplemental supply. There are 662 miles of canals, and 78.5 miles of laterals." "The Board has contracts for sale of water with 2,051 separate water users." "The total cost of these projects has been $16,820,584.26, of which amount the Board received in cash grants $3,483,898.07 and material and labor grants $3,-326,751.57, . . . principally from agencies of the Federal Government. The state through the 'conservation fund' provided $5,756,434.62 of the construction cost and $4,303,500.00 was received through the sale of water conservation revenue bonds."[288] The Upper Musselshell Project furnishes normal irrigation water to 6,000 acres of new land and supplemental irrigation water to 29,000 acres of land already under irrigation; the Lower Musselshell Canals full irrigation water supply for 13,000 acres and supplemental supply for 1,500 acres; the Broadwater-Missouri Project full supply to 5,000 acres and supplemental supply to 10,000 acres; the Deadman's Basin Project full supply to 4,000 acres and supplemental supply to 11,500 acres.[289] These are among the largest of the state irrigation projects under the jurisdiction of the said Board.

2. Drainage---The laws of Massachusetts provide for the drainage of wetlands by a special agency called the State Reclamation Board. The drainage work is initiated by the Board upon the petition of land proprietors concerned and is carried out in "reclamation districts" created by the board, each district being in charge of 3, 5 or 7 commissioners appointed by the Board. The cost of work done in each district is to be paid by the land owners in that district, but part of the cost may be paid by the state (General Laws, ch. 252, secs. 1-10: Acts 1702, ch. 11; as last amended by Acts 1929, ch. 288).[290] "The first drainage district (i. e. reclamation district) was initiated in 1921. Following this original district were: 4 in 1922; 1 in 1923; 2 in 1924; 2 in 1925; and 1 in 1930, making a total of eleven districts. At the present time, improvement of agricultural lands is carried on by soil conservation districts . . . . Improvement of lands for industrial sites now

represents investment ventures by private capital."291

In Florida, a law of 1905 designated the governor, the comptroller, the state treasurer, the attorney general and the commissioner of agriculture to constitute the State Board of Drainage Commissioners (Statutes, sec. 298.69). The duty of this Board was to construct and maintain drainage works (L. 1905, ch. 5377, sec. 1, which does not appear in the Florida Statutes). The drainage work was to be done in drainage districts (not corporate bodies) established by the board, and was to be financed by a special acreage tax (L. 1905, ch. 5377, sec. 2, not appearing in the Statutes). By an act of 1913 (L. 1913, ch. 6454, sec. 1: Statutes, sec. 298.70), the Board was further authorized to incur debts to finance its works. However, an act passed in the same year provided for the creation of incorporated special drainage districts as an alternative to if not a substitute for the state drainage enterprise (as amended: Statutes, secs. 298.01 to 298.68). Under this new law, the State Drainage Board, in addition to undertaking drainage enterprise by itself, may also initiate the incorporation of special drainage districts in the same way as private land owners; but if any lands controlled by the board are drained this way, the drainage work is not a state enterprise. It has been reported that the said board was once engaged in the drainage of the Everglades area.292 But there is no information whether there are now any active state drainage project or projects in Florida.

Louisiana is another state which has a state drainage enterprise on statute at least. In 1944, an act was enacted (Act No. 58) under which "the department of public works may, on its own initiative and at its own expense, with any money appropriated by the state for these purposes, drain and reclaim, or cause to be drained and reclaimed, the undrained or partially drained marsh, swamp and overflow lands in the state, with the view of controlling floods and causing settlement and cultivation of the lands." The work may be performed by the said Department either independently or in cooperation with the Federal Government (sec. 1) or with local governmental units or drainage or levee districts. In accordance with this act, a total of $10 million has been appropriated by the state legislature (Act No. 204 of 1948 and Act No. 614 of 1952). Actual work done is, however, unknown to the author. It is possible that the funds appropriated have been used to subsidize local drainage projects.

In Minnesota, state drainage enterprise was authorized by an act of 1907 (Laws 1907, ch. 470, as amended), but it was terminated by an act of 1947 (Laws 1947, ch. 142, sec. 20). Nevertheless, under a law of 1949 (Laws 1949, ch. 498, sec. 6), as amended (Laws 1953, ch. 654), the Department of Conservation "may undertake projects for the drainage of any state-owned lands within any game preserve, conservation area, or

other area subject to the provisions hereof so far as he shall
determine that such lands will be benefited thereby in fur-
therance of the purposes for which the area was established,
and may pay the cost thereof out of any funds appropriated
and available therefor." It is evident that such drainage is
only part of the management of a game preserve, a conservation area, etc., and does not constitute an independent drainage enterprise.

The laws of New York have not provided for a state drainage enterprise as such. However, the Department of Conservation, acting through the Water Power and Control Commission,
has under its operation four drainage projects which in 1950
covered an aggregate area of 28,245 acres.[293] The nature of
these project is not clear.

Drainage may be achieved incidentally in the operation of
other state enterprises. The 1950 agricultural census shows
three drainage projects undertaken by the State of Illinois,
which benefited a total of 3,091 acres. These three projects
are all on state institutional farms.[294] State highways are
generally provided with drainage works. These works may incidentally serve the nearby non-highway lands.[295]

Section 4 Forestry

1. _Fire protection_[296]---In general, the several states
have authority to provide fire protection to state-owned forest and other wild lands. With the exception of a few states
(e.g., Arizona and Kansas), the several states have actually
performed this work. However, state fire protection services
on forest and other wild lands owned by private persons and
local governmental units are provided in most states under
special statutory authorizations.[297] These statutory authorizations come under two categories: (1) enforcement measures
(compulsory) in state forest-fire regulation, and (2) independent enterprise measures (contractual). Fire-protection
or control measure in both categories may be generally divided
into (primarily for the sake of convenience of discussion):
(a) fire-fighting, (b) fire patrol, (c) the construction of
fire lines or fire-breaks as a measure of fire-prevention but
not as a part of fire-fighting, and (c) the construction and
installation of lookout towers and communication systems (tel-
ephones and radios). As enforcement measures, these measures
are generally taken by the state in the default of landowners.

(a) _Enterprise incidental to state regulation_---(1) Fire-
fighting is provided in Idaho and Utah. (2) Fire patrol is
provided in Oregon, New Hampshire, New Jersey, Idaho, West
Virginia, Kentucky. (3) General fire protection and prevention, which implies primarily the construction of lookout towers and communication systems, but may also include the construction prevention fire-breaks and the maintenance of fire

patrol, is provided in Washington and Montana.

(b) <u>Independent enterprise</u>---(1) Fire-fighting is authorized in the following states:

Connecticut---<u>General Statutes</u>, sec. 3476 (Acts 1905, ch. 238;
               as last amended by Acts 1927, ch. 149, sec. 1);
               sec. 3477 (<u>ibid</u>., as last amended in 1947) and
               sec. 3495 (enacted in 1943).
Washington--- <u>Revised Code</u>, sec. 76.04.070 (Laws 1905, ch. 164,
               sec. 4; as last amended by L. 1933, ch. 68, sec.
               1).
New Hampshire-<u>Revised Laws</u>, ch. 233, sec. 31 (Laws 1909, ch.
               128, sec. 10; as last amended by L. 1953, ch.
               187).
Colorado------<u>Statutes</u>, ch. 134, sec. 139 (Laws 1911, ch. 138,
               sec. 7).
Virginia------<u>Code</u>, sec. 10-57, 1st para. (Acts 1914, ch. 195;
               as last amended by Acts 1944, ch. 104).
North Carolina-<u>General Statutes</u>, sec. 113-55 (Laws 1915, ch.
               243, sec. 6; as last amended by L. 1951, ch.
               575).
Texas---------<u>Revised Civil Statutes</u>, art. 2613, sec. 10 (Laws
1915, ch. 141; as amended by L. 1951, ch. 201).
California----<u>Public Resources Code</u>, sec. 4007 (Stats. 1919,
               ch. 176, sec. 2; as amended by Stats. 1941, ch.
               1154, sec. 1).
Tennessee-----<u>Code</u>, sec. 550 (Acts 1921, ch. 156, sec. 3; as
               amended by Acts 1923, ch. 7, secs. 29; 30).
Rhode Island--<u>General Laws</u>, ch. 224, sec. 2 (Laws 1923, ch.
               281, sec. 2).
Wisconsin-----<u>Statutes</u>, sec. 23.09, subsec. (7), heading (9),
               enacted by Laws 1927, ch. 426.
New Jersey----<u>Revised Statutes</u>, tit. 13, ch. 9 (Laws 1931, ch.
               350; as amended by L. 1932, ch. 111, sec. 1).
Arkansas------<u>Statutes</u>, sec. 41-513 (Acts 1935, No. 85, sec.
               7).
Florida-------<u>Statutes</u>, sec. 590.02(1), (b) and (c) (Laws
               1935, ch. 17029, sec. 14; as amended by L. 1951,
               ch. 26915, sec. 1).
Georgia-------<u>Code</u>, sec. 43-249 (Acts 1937, No. 103, sec. 9).
Alabama-------<u>Code of Alabama</u>, tit. 8, sec. 206 (Acts 1939,
               No. 492, sec. 3).
Nevada--------Stats. 1945, ch. 149, sec. 4; as amended by
               Stats. 1949, ch. 248.
Kentucky------<u>Revised Statutes</u>, sec. 149.160 (Acts 1946, ch.
               204, sec. 3).
Indiana-------Acts 1951, ch. 136.

It may be noted that in practically every state which has
a state forest agency the statute permits the said agency to
draft and impress labor compulsorily to fight and suppress
forest fires anywhere in the state under its supervision and

direction. This is indirect authorization of forest-fire
fighting, and is found in most states.

(2) State forest-fire control is specifically authorized
in the following states:

Washington----Revised Code, sec. 76.04.070 (Laws 1905, ch.
              164, sec. 4; as last amended by L. 1933, ch.
              68, sec. 1).
Vermont-------Statutes, sec. 7070 (Laws 1910, No. 20, sec. 4;
              as last amended by L. 1921, No. 17, sec. 3).
Minnesota-----Statutes, sec. 88.08 (Laws 1911, ch. 125, sec.
              10; as amended by L. 1925, ch. 470, sec. 14).
North Carolina-General Statutes, sec. 113-54 (Laws 1915, ch.
              243, sec. 4; as last amended by L. 1951, ch.
              575).
Rhode Island--General Laws, ch. 224, sec. 6, last para., 3rd
              sent. (Laws 1920, ch. 1887; as last amended by
              L. 1933, ch. 2033).
Ohio----------Ohio Code, sec. 1177-10 (Laws 1921, p. 89; as
              last amended by L. 1949, p. 84).
Tennessee-----Code, sec. 550 (Acts 1921, ch. 156, sec. 3; as
              amended by Acts 1923, ch. 7, secs. 29; 30).
Massachusetts-General Laws, sec. 28A (Acts 1929, ch. 284; as
              last amended by Acts 1953, ch. 496).
West Virginia-Code, sec. 2230 (Laws 1929, ch. 13, sec. 107;
              as last amended by L. 1945, ch. 67).
New Jersey----Revised Statutes, sec. 13: 9-45 (Laws 1931, ch.
              350, sec. 11).
Florida-------Statutes, sec. 590.04 (Laws 1935, ch. 17029,
              sec. 3). For Everglades Fire Control District,
              also Laws 1939, ch. 19274, sec. 9.
Texas---------Revised Civil Statutes, art. 2613, sec. 10a (Laws
              1941, ch. 530, sec. 1).
Nevada--------Stats. 1945, ch. 149, sec. 4; as amended by
              Stats. 1949, ch. 248.

(3) Special authorization for the construction of pre-
suppression fire-breaks is found in:

Minnesota-----Statutes, sec. 88.04 (Laws 1911, ch. 125, sec.
              7) and sec. 88.09 (Laws 1927, ch. 329, secs. 1
              and 2; as last amended by L. 1953, ch. 148, sec.
              1).
New York------Conservation Law, sec. 50, subsec. 19 (Laws
              1916, ch. 451; as last amended by L. 1928, ch.
              242, sec. 5).
Michigan------Compiled Laws, sec. 320.2 (Acts 1923, No. 143;
              as amended by Acts 1929, No. 139).
New Jersey----Revised Statutes of New Jersey, sec. 13:9-2 (Laws
              1931, ch. 350, sec. 1).
Florida-------Florida Statutes, sec. 590.04 (Laws 1935, ch.
              17029, sec. 3).

(4) Special authority for the construction of lookout towers (with necessary communication systems) and forest roads is given the state forest agencies by laws of the following states:302

Maine---------(a) For Maine Forestry District, Revised Statutes, ch. 32, secs. 72; 73; 80; 81; 83; 86 (Laws 1909, ch. 193, secs. 1; 2; 7; 8; 10; as last amended by L. 1939, ch. 224). (b) For other areas, ibid., secs. 72-A to 72F (Laws 1949, ch. 355).

North Carolina-General Statutes, sec. 113-54 (Laws 1915, ch. 243, sec 4; as last amended by L. 1951, ch. 575).

Pennsylvania--Statutes, sec. 1311 (Act of 3 June 1915, art. 1 sec. 102(j); as amended by an act of 26 April 1923).

New York------Conservation Law, sec. 50, subsecs. 17 and 19 (Laws 1916, ch. 451; as last amended by L. 1928, ch. 242, sec. 5).

Rhode Island--General Laws, ch. 224, sec. 5 (Laws 1917, ch. 1545; as last amended by L. 1928, ch. 1166).

Ohio----------Ohio Code, sec. 1177-10j (Laws 1921, p. 89; as last amended by L. 1949, p. 84).

Minnesota-----Statutes, sec. 88.09 (Laws 1927, ch. 329, secs. 1 and 2; as last amended by L. 1953, ch. 148, sec. 1).

West Virginia-Code, sec. 2230 (Laws 1929, ch. 13, sec. 107; as last amended by L. 1945, ch. 67).

California----Public Resources Code, sec. 4301 (Stats. 1931, ch 952, sec. 1; re-enacted in 1939).

Florida-------Statutes, sec. 590.04 (Laws 1935, ch. 17029, sec. 3). For Everglades Fire Control District, also Laws 1939, ch. 19274, sec. 9.

Connecticut---(fire roads)---"When 75 percent of the owners of land abutting on a closed or legally discontinued highway, which passes through woodland, shall petition the state forest fire warden to maintain such highway for the purpose of forest fire prevention, said warden, upon written agreement with such land owners and written agreement with the selectmen of such town or towns as may be affected by the same, may . . . improve and maintain such highway for the purpose of fire prevention . . ." (General Statutes, sec. 3494, enacted in 1937).

Among the various specific measures of forest fire control discussed above, the construction and (or) maintenance of forest roads are supplemental to fire-fighting, for these roads are principally used to move fire-fighting trucks. The construction of pre-suppression fire-breaks is a preventive measure, although fire-breaks constructed during actual fires

are, like the setting of back fires, means of fire-fighting.
Both fire patrol and the construction of lookout towers are
used for fire detection.

Two more remarks should be made. (1) Forest roads may
be used as fire-breaks. This is expressly provided in the
laws of Minnesota, which declare all highways, roads, and
trails within forest areas to be established fire-breaks (Statutes, sec. 88.05: Laws 1933, ch. 320, sec. 1: also Laws 1937,
ch. 113, sec. 1). In New Jersey, fire-breaks are nothing but
access roads. (2) As a measure of fire direction, lookouts
are more effective and economical than, and therefore tend to
replace, foot patrols. However, airplane patrol is more efficient than lookouts, and is likely to force the latter into
desuetude.[299] In some states, the maintenance of a foot patrol service is now not considered necessary, as its use is
greatly overshadowed by lookouts. As a matter of fact, the
laws of Ohio expressly provide that patrolmen are to be appointed only in cases where lookouts are insufficient to take care
of the unusual fire hazards.

Aside from the above-mentioned special authorizations, general authority of the state forest agencies in fire protection
and control is provided in the following states:

(1) General authority only, without any of the above-mentioned special authorizations.[300]

Delaware------Code, tit. 7, sec. 2908 (Laws 1927, ch. 50, sec.
              6).
Iowa----------Code, sec. 107.24 (Acts 1931, ch. 26, sec. 7;
              as last amended by Acts 1945, ch. 92, sec. 1).

Illinois------Laws 1933, p. 1077.

Montana-------Laws 1939, ch. 128, sec. 5.

Oregon--------Laws 1939, ch. 525, sec. 1; as amended by L.
              1945, ch. 109, sec. 1.

Utah----------Code, sec. 24-1-11 (Laws 1941, 2nd spe. sess.,
              ch.1, sec. 2; as amended by L. 1945, ch. 33,
              sec. 1)

Louisiana-----Revised Statutes, tit. 56, sec. 1524 (Acts 1944,
              No. 179, sec. 4).

Mississippi---Code-sec. 6046-01 et seq. (Laws 1944, ch. 238).

Missouri------Laws 1945, p. 677, sec. 21.

South Carolina---Acts 1945, No. 106.

South Dakota--Code, sec. 25.1310 (Laws 1945, ch. 90, sec. 9).

Idaho---------Laws 1945, ch. 74, sec.

New Mexico----Laws 1951, ch. 150.

This general authority covers all of the various specific
control measures in New Mexico; but they are undertaken not
by the state directly, but by the United States Forest Service
in trust of the state. For the remaining states, (1) fire-
fighting is provided in all of them except Iowa; (2) fire patrol is provided in all of them except Iowa and South Dakota,
and also except Mississippi, where detection of fires by lookouts is considered adequate; (3) pre-suppression fire-breaks
have been constructed in Utah and Louisiana;[301] and (4) lookout towers (with communication systems) have been constructed
in all of them except Iowa and Utah. These services are performed on both state and private lands. It may be noted that
Iowa conservation commission has constructed fire roads, trails
breaks and ponds on state-owned lands.

(2) General authority is also provided in the laws of the
following states to reinforce special authorizations:[302]

Rhode Island--General Laws, ch. 224, sec. 24 (Laws 1928, ch.
                1166), in addition to fire-fighting, fire pa-
                trol and the construction of lookouts. This
                authority is not utilized.
North Carolina---General Statutes, sec. 113-29 (Laws 1939, ch.
                317, sec. 1), in addition to fire-fighting, fire
                patrol and the construction of lookouts. Under
                this general authority, pre-suppression fire-
                breaks have been constructed on private lands.
New Jersey----Revised Statutes, sec. 13:9-3 (Laws 1931, ch.
                350, sec. 2), in addition to fire-fighting,
                fire patrol and the construction of pre-suppres-
                sion fire-breaks. Under this general authority,
                lookouts have been constructed.
Washington----Revised Code, sec. 76.04.020 (Laws 1905, ch.
                164, sec. 2; as amended by L. 1911, ch. 125,
                sec. 2), in addition to fire-fighting and fire
                patrol. Under this general authority, pre-sup-
                pression fire-breaks, lookouts and fire roads
                have been constructed.
Texas---------Revised Civil Statutes, art. 2613, sec. 10 (Laws
                1915, ch. 141; as amended by L. 1951, ch. 201),
                in addition to fire-fighting and fire patrol.
                Under this general authority, the same work has
                been done as in Washington.
Tennessee-----Code, sec. 550, op. cit., in addition to fire-
                fighting and fire patrol. Under this general
                authority, lookouts have been constructed.
Nevada--------Stats. 1945, ch. 149, sec. 5, in addition to
                fire-fighting and fire patrol. Under this gen-
                eral authority, lookouts have been constructed.

California----Public Resources Code, sec. 4007 (Stats. 1919,
              ch . 176, sec. 2; as amended by Stats. 1941,
              ch . 1154, sec. 1), in addition to fire-fight-
              ing and the construction of lookouts. Under
              this general authority, the state has provided
              both foot and aerial patrol and constructed
              lookouts.

Connecticut---General Statutes, secs. 3476; 3477 (Acts 1905,
              ch . 238; as last amended in 1947), in addition
              to the construction of lookouts. Under this
              general authority, the state may extinguish for-
              est fires, and has constructed lookout towers.

Georgia-------Code, sec. 43-206 (Acts 1925, No. 217, sec. 3).
              in addition to fire-fighting. Under this gen-
              eral authority, the state has provided both
              aerial and motor patrol, and has constructed
              pre-suppression fire-breaks on private lands
              and lookout towers.

Wisconsin-----Statutes, sec. 26.11 (1) (Laws 1927, ch. 29,
              secs. 1 and 3; as last amended by L. 1951, ch.
              488), in addition to fire-fighting. Under this
              general authority, the state maintains fire pa-
              trol, constructs pre-suppression fire- breaks
              lookout towers and forest roads, on both state
              and non-state lands.

Colorado------Statutes, ch. 134, sec. 131(9) et seq. (Laws
              1943, ch. 150), in addition to fire-fighting.

Kentucky------Revised Statutes, sec. 149.140 et seq. (Acts
              1946, ch. 204; as amended by Acts 1948, ch.
              202), in addition to fire-fighting. Under
              this general authority, the state has provided
              fire patrol and constructed lookouts.

Indiana-------Acts 1951, ch. 136, in addition to fire-fight-
              ing. Under this general authority, lookout
              towers have been constructed.

There is neither general nor special authorization for
forest-fire control and prevention in Arizona, Kansas, Nebraska, North Dakota, Oklahoma, South Dakota and Wyoming. However, the State of Oklahoma maintains and operates lookout
towers and occasionally airplanes for fire detection, and
maintains some 600 miles of fire trails. For the other five
states, there is no state forest-fire-control enterprise, at
least on private and other non-state lands.

Georgia probably stands foremost in this enterprise. As
of the end of 1952, Georgia Forestry Commission owned 298
lookout towers with a two-way radio communication system.
Many miles of firebreaks are plowed each year at the request
of land owners. It maintain both aerial and motorized fire
patrol services. Airplanes used includes those owned by the
commission and those leased from private companies.[303] Florida Board of Forestry owned, as of 30 June 1952, two airplanes

and 150 lookout towers, and had plowed thousands of miles of pre-suppression firebreaks on private lands.[304] As of March 1954, the State of Oregon owned one airplane and 141 lookout towers, and had constructed 3,973 forest roads and installed 1,973 miles of telephone lines and 833 radio units. Besides, it annually expends $100,000 to maintain roads originally constructed by private parties for fire-control purposes. More than 300 trucks and vehicles are operated by the state board of forestry. The department of conservation and development, as of March 1954, maintained a fire-fighting service on about 15,515,000 acres of privately owned timberland, which were located in 78 of the state's 100 countries. It operated about 200 vehicles and 122 lookout towers, most of which are steel structures of a height varying from 15 to 120 feet. It has installed about 600 miles of telephone lines and 375 radio sets, of which 75 were fixed stations in lookout towers and the rest were mobile units. These are but a few examples, but they represent the general pattern of this enterprise found in other states, though in varying degrees.

Modern trends in state forest and wild fire control enterprise seem to point to: (1) the maintenance of a sufficient number of motorized fire-fighting units dispersed in the various parts of the state; (2) the construction of certain number of "primary" or "base" lookout towers (steel or masonry) for fire detection; (3) the use of airplanes for both fire detection and fire-fighting; (4) the construction and maintenance of forest roads for the multiple purpose of serving as pre-suppression firebreaks, moving fire-fighting trucks and helping in timber harvesting; and (5) the use of radio as a means of communication. The State of South Carolina has for the last few years maintained forest-fire danger measurement stations in the several counties, to record weather changes and indicate "burning indexes". These indexes are undoubtedly very helpful in fire prevention[305]

The state supervisor of forestry of Washington may, with the approval of the director of conservation and development, "appoint within any region or district. . . where there is timber requiring protection, one or more said supervisor deems that forest fire danger exists" (Revised Code, sec. 76.04.060: Laws 1905, ch. 164, sec. 2; as last amended by L. 1937, ch. 97, sec. 1). Among other duties, these wardens are required to "patrol their districts; visit all parts of roads and trails, and frequented places and camps as far as possible; . . . . extinguish small or smoldering fires; summon, impress or employ help to stop conflagration . . . ." (ibid., sec. 76.04.070: L. 1905, ch. 164, sec. 4; as last amended by L. 1933, ch. 68, sec. 1). Under the laws of Virginia, "when any forest warden sees or there is reported to him a forest fire, he shall repair immediately to the scene of the fire and employ such persons and means as in his judgment are expedient and necessary to extinguish the fire . . . ." (Code of 1950, sec. 10-57, 1st para.: Acts 1914, ch. 195, as amend-

ed by Acts 1944, ch. 104). "Whenever possible, the state forester shall collect the costs of fire fighting done . . .
from the person responsible for the origin of the fire . . ."
(ibid., sec. 10-58). In Wisconsin the state conservation
commission has under its administration a system of intensive
forest fire protection, which includes 16,115,000 acres of
forest lands. "This system is divided into the Northwest,
Northern, Northeast and Central areas, covering all or parts
of thirty-five counties in the northern and central parts of
the state. Each area unit is composed of either two or three
protection districts for a total of ten."[306]

"In earlier days forest fire fighters relied mainly on
axes, shovels, and other hand tools. Although there is still
need for some handwork on nearly every fire, most of the States
are rapidly converting to mechanized equipment. More extensive use of fire-line plows in the Southern and Lake States
and of bulldozers in the Lake States and in the heavily timbered Western States, has stepped up the efficiency of fire
suppression . . . . Four-wheel-drive jeeps and trucks equipped with water tanks and power pumps are proving their worth.
The construction of new lookout towers means better area coverage for quick detection of fires. Many of the States now
use air patrol to aid in detection when visibility from sta-
tionary lookouts is poor. A few States own airplanes, but
most find it cheaper to contract for their use as needed."
As "rapid communication is essential in forest fire control",
"most States now have two-way radio installations on their
automobiles and trucks, so key suppression men can at all
times be in contact with headquarters, dispatches, and primary lookout towers."[307] In some states, as for example Alabama, there are both mobile and fixed radio stations for use
in forest fire control.[308] As of 1950, "the forty-three states
with organized fire control organizations now own 3,500 radios, 2,201 transportation trucks, 1,619 tanker trucks, 503
plows 720 power pumpers 584 tractors, and 115 bulldozers.
Primarily fire detection is provided by 2,575 lookout towers.
The states maintain more than 38,000 miles of telephone lines[309]

It has been estimated that approximately 439 million acres
of non-Federal forest lands need public fire protection service. "During 1948 about 80 percent of the lands needing public aid in fire control was given protection by the states
and agencies cooperating with them. Protection is being extended to the remaining 20 percent, or roughly 100 million
acres of unprotected lands. . ." "State fire protection agencies in 1948 confined the area burned to 0.58 percent of the
area protected, whereas on unprotected areas it is estimated
that wild fires burned about 14 percent." "Although many
states have been carrying on forest fire control activities
for a quarter of a century or more, outstanding progress has
taken place during the last four or five years."[310]

In areas of high forest fire hazards, special measures of
fire protection may be warrantable. For example, a law of
Washington of 1953 (ch. 74) designated the Yacht burn situated
in Clark, Skamania and Cowlitz Counties of that state as a
"high hazard forest area", requiring special measures of "rehabilitation". The Division of Forestry of the Department
of Conservation and Development is authorized to "map, survey,
fell snags, build firebreaks and access roads, increase forest protection activities, and do other work deemed necessary
to protect forest land from fire in the rehabilitation zone."
Initial costs for the construction of firebreaks will be
bonned by landowners (including the state itself and its local units), but legislation is anticipated authorizing partial reimbursement by the state. It should be noted that
other works than the construction of firebreaks are to be
financed entirely by the state.

2. Reforestation---This work includes (1) the planting
of forest trees on state and private lands, and (2) the distribution of seedlings or young trees to private land owners
and local governmental units, generally through sale at low
prices. The division of forestry of Washington department
of conservation and development, by November 1952, had planted a total of 21,465,051 trees on a total of 35,391 acres of
lands located in 17 counties.[311] In the period 1907-1952,
Vermont Forest Service planted 31,687,736 trees on private
and municipal lands, plus 3,927,427 trees in state forests.[312]
The foresters and forest fire wardens of the State of Idaho,
at a conference in May 1952, planted some 16,000 ponderosa
pine seedlings, although "over half plantation failed . . .
because of . . . inexperience of the planters."[312] It seems
that very few states have reforested this way any lands other
than state forests. In a practical sense, state reforestation
enterprise may be identified with the distribution of seedlings and transplants.

The latter work is aimed principally at private lands
which require reforestation, which it is reported to aggregate
about 62 million acres.[314] It is done with Federal financial
aid provided in sec. 4 of the Clarke-McNary Act of 7 June 1924
(43 Stat. 653, 654), as amended 26 October 1949 (63 Stat. 909).
As of 30 June 1951, all but five states conducted tree-distri-
buting programs with Federal cooperation and assistance. "One
of these five states conducts a program without Federal cooperation. Two of the states are served to some extent by adjoining states. Four states operate no nurseries but distribute trees which they buy from private and Federal nurseries.
Eighty-three nurseries, in all, are operated by the states
and territories. A number of these nurseries are being enlarged and several new ones are planned." The production of
trees in these states nurseries are 84 million in 1947, 157
million in 1948, 239 million in 1949, 350 million in 1950 and
400 million in 1951 Federal fiscal years. "Prior to fiscal

year 1951, trees produced under the Federal-State cooperative
program could be distributed only to farmers." Beginning
with 1951 fiscal year, as a result of the 1949 amendment of
the Clarke-McNary Act, benefits have been extended to non-
farm people."[315]

A brief review may be made of the accomplishments of the
several states in tree-distribution. In 1951 approximately
1,300,000 and in 1952 more than 1,500,000 seedlings were sold
by the Washington Department of Conservation and Development,
largely to private farmers. A small part were sold to Washington State College for redistribution.[316] Since the beginning of the program in 1923 to 30 June 1947, the Department of Conservation of New Jersey distributed a total of
31,247,000 young trees to farmers, civic organizations, industries, state institutions and local governmental units.[317]
During 1951, Wisconsin Conservation Commission distributed
23.5 million seedlings and transplants to farmers, state and
county forests, civic groups, etc. Of this amount, 22 million were produced at the nurseries and 1.5 million obtained
from Federal nurseries.[318] In the 1951-52 fiscal year, California Department of Natural Resources sold and distributed
232,462,000 trees produced at the two state nurseries for a
total sum of $12,786.[319] The production and distribution of
seedlings in the four nurseries maintained by Georgia Forestry Commission during the 1951-52 and 1952-53 planting seasons totalled more than 92,000,000, sufficient to reforest
102,000 acres.[320] The Forestry Commission of South Carolina
began tree distribution in the year 1947-48. By 1951-52, a
total of 114,929,035 seedlings were distributed. Each land
owner is given the right to receive 3,000 seedling trees
free of charge at the nursery.[321] In Mississippi, "there
are 5,000 seedlings available for each qualified landowner
under the Free Seedling Law; additional seedlings are sold
at the cost of production."[322] In Ohio, the department of
natural resources has adopted the practice of distributing
free trees to 4-H Club members and vocational agriculture
students, although quantities of planting stock so distributed are exceedingly small.[323]

Missouri Conservation Commission distributes both forest
and shrub seedlings. In the spring of 1952, 2,687,234 forest seedlings and 3,951,192 shrub seedlings were distributed
by the commission. The latter were distributed to farmers
for plantation in wildlife restoration projects. It may also
be noted that of the 2,687,234 forest seedlings, 1,490,979,
or more than one-half, were delivered to the United States
Forest Service.[324]

In 1951-1952, the conservation commission of West Virginia distributed 2,685,173 tree seedlings, of which 2,541,000
were produced at the state forest tree nursery, 52,000 were
obtained from the United States Forest Service and 92,000 from

a Pennsylvania state nursery.[325] The State of South Dakota
does not maintain any state forest tree nursery. The trees
needed in the distribution program "are bought under contract
from commercial nurseries in the state and from a Federal
nursery in Nebraska. They are sold at or slightly above cost
prices and made available to farmers and ranchers and other
landowners . . . . In addition to farm sales, this stock is
a source of supply to county extension agents, soil conservation districts, and the Wildlife Cover Development Program.
. . Rural school districts and cemetery associations and
similar public organizations are also eligible to purchase
these trees for windbreak plantsings."[326] During the fiscal
year 1953, 2,116,950 seedlings were procured. Of this amount,
2,081,425 were actually distributed for plantation. Of this
number, 1,368,400 were planted as wildlife cover (1,294,550
hardwood trees and 73,850 conifer trees, but none of shrub
species); and 333,000 were distributed to farmers (271,875
hardwood trees), 299,875 to soil conservation districts
(221,900 hardwood trees) and 80,150 to state parks (22,100
hardwood trees) for plantation for commercial timber.[237]

3. Pest Control---The state regulation on forest pests
as discussed before may also be regarded as a state enterprise. It differs from ordinary state enterprises in that
it is compulsory, particularly in connection with the control
of forest diseases. In the control of forest insects, the
compulsory nature of state regulation may well be counter-
balanced by the material benefits which owners of trees receive through the spraying of the trees. In such cases, the
action of the state is in fact more in the nature of enterprise than of regulation. Besides enterprise which is incidental to regulation, independent state enterprise in forest
pest control is possible (1) by special statutory authorization, and (2) under the general authority of the state forest administrative agencies in the protection and preservation of forest resources. In an enactment of 1937, the Department of Conservation of Minnesota is authorized to cooperate with the State Entomologist and

> to use the equipment for the spraying of trees on
> privately-owned lands for the purpose of checking
> or controlling insect epidemic outbreaks which may
> be injurious to private property, and may make
> such charges as shall be necessary to cover all
> or part of the cost of such operation . . .(Stat-
> utes, sec. 89.13: Laws 1937, ch. 398, sec. 2).

This may be taken as an example of special statutory authorization for pest-control enterprise.

An examination may be made of the actual work done by the
several state in controlling forest insect and disease pests.
For about four decades, the gypsy moths have infested the
vast areas of forest lands in the northeastern part of the

country. The work of controlling this insect pest has been
undertaken by the Federal Government for the entire region
except the southern part of the State of New York and certain
small spots on Long Island of the same state. In the latter
areas, the work has been assumed by the Department of Conservation of the State of New York ever since 1923. Recently,
the said Department has used two airplanes in spraying the
infested trees. The State of New Jersey, in 1935, scouted
gypsy moths in three townships, but this work was only temporary.[328]

The spruce budworm is a defoliating insect that has in
recent years done considerable damage to forests throughout
the West. "Control by aerial spraying DDT has been conducted
over 2,793,000 acres of Douglas fir in Oregon during the period 1949-1952."[329] "The project was conducted by the State
Board of Forestry. On the national-forest lands involved,
the Federal Government paid full costs. On private lands
the general cost-sharing pattern was one-half by the State
and the other half spread equally between the Federal Government and the private owners."[330] In the State of Washington,
the major part of the control work is done by the United
States Forest Service. But the division of forestry of the
department of Conservation and Development of the State of
Washington since 1951 has been responsible for the prosecution of the Icicle Creek Control Project. In 1951 the division sprayed a total of 9,420 acres with a total cost of $11,-
861, of which $8,842 was granted by the Federal Government,
$2,139 borne by the state and $880 contributed by private owners.[331]

The Conservation Commission of Wisconsin initiated the
work of forest pest control in 1950 by the appointment of a
forester-entomologist. "In 1952, two more forester-entomolo-
gists were employed." "In 1951 direct control measures were
used against the pine tussock moth in Douglas county which
was attacking jack pine . . . Approximately 3,000 acres were
sprayed with the use of planes." "Direct control was also
used against the Saratoga spittle bug in Oconto, Marinette and
Florence counties. Approximately 2,600 acres were sprayed
from the air using DDT. In addition, numerous small plantations were sprayed with knapsack sprayers and portable mist
blower to control the red-headed pine sawfly. In 1952 approximately 1,600 acres were sprayed from the air in Oconto and
Marinette counties for the Saratoga spittle bug, and 500 acres
were covered in Vilas county to control the same insect. In
Sank and Richland counties operations were carried out against
Swaine's jack pine sawfly and the redheaded pine sawfly, 420
acres were sprayed in all. An additional 1,100 acres was
sprayed on the ground with knapsack sprayers. These acres
were small plantations and control work was for the red-headed
pine sawfly."[332]

The Division of Forestry of the Department of Natural Resources of California, from 1945 to 1953, undertook as many as 33 forest insect control projects. During this period, the State Legislature appropriated $210,000, of which $85,000 was actually expended. A like sum was contributed by the land owners concerned.[333]

4. The State Forests---"In the early days there was generally more interest in getting publicly owned lands into private ownership for exploitation than in the reverse of this process. A positive State forestry program, and especially a program of State ownership of forest land, often did not develop until a State had more or less gone 'through the wringer' of forest depletion."[334] "In 1885, New York began the acquisition of extensive forest land for the Adirondack and Catskill Forest Reserves. Other state forests organized at early dates were the Mont Alto in Pennsylvania in 1891, the Pillsbury in Minnesota in 1899, the Clark County in Indiana in 1903, and the Higgins Lake and Houghton Lake in Michigan in 1903."[335] In 1909, the eleven states of Connecticut, Indiana, Maryland, Massachusetts, Michigan, Minnesota, New Hampshire, New Jersey, New York, Pennsylvania and Wisconsin has a total of 2,827,605 acres in their forest reserves or preserves.[336] The state forests in 1950 are shown in the following table:[337]

STATE FORESTS

	No. Units	Acreage
Alabama	101	17,041
California	8	70,500
Colorado	1	70,980
Connecticut	25	109,828
Delaware	5	4,200
Florida	3	24,971
Georgia	2	2,000
Illinois	3	10,278
Indiana	14	68,512
Iowa	10	13,452
Kansas	1	4,000
Kentucky	1	3,624
Louisiana	2	8,800
Maine	1	21,000
Maryland	8	76,697
Massachusetts	70	170,000
Michigan	22	3,750,000
Minnesota	32	2,011,270
Mississippi	1	1,760
Missouri	7	121,000
Montana	7	235,876
New Hampshire	99	20,219
New Jersey	9	56,628
New York	337	501,195

Ohio	14	82,381
Oregon	25	523,000
Pennsylvania	23	1,675,211
Rhode Island	3	3,407
South Carolina	4	17,744
South Dakota	4	84,000
Tennessee	9	71,272
Texas	5	6,510
Vermont	24	68,936
Virginia	6	7,010
Washington	2	290,000
West Virginia	7	61,800
Wisconsin	8	269,556
Total	903	10,514,658

The acreages will be greater if the gross areas within exterior boundaries are referred to instead of state-owned acreages. For example, the gross total acreage of the 22 state
forests of Michigan was 6,098,324 as of 30 June 1950 while on
the same date net state-owned acreage was 3,685,244, or about
60 percent of the former.[338]

"State forests have been established in a number of States
by means of purchase programs."[339] An outstanding example is
New York. "Since 1923, the New York State College of Agriculture, in cooperation with other state agencies, has been study-
ing and classifying farm areas in New York State with reference
to their suitability for agricultural purpose. As a result of
these studies, certain farm areas have been designated as suitable only for recreation and forestry, and in 1931 the State
authorized a program of purchase to bring submarginal farm
land, much of which has been abandoned, into public ownership
for forestry and recreational uses. The 20-year program an-
ticipates State acquisition of land at an average rate of
100,000 acres per year until 4,200,000 acres have been acquired."[340] Some states have acquired substantial areas of
cut-over and burned-over land through tax delinquency.[341] It
is estimated that "tax-delinquent lands comprise about 31 percent of total acreage of all state forests. These lands are
principally in Minnesota, Michigan, New York and Washington.[342]
"Programs of the Federal Government also have resulted in some
lands going into State forests. One of these was the former
Resettlement Administration program of buying tracts of submarginal farm land and retiring it from agricultural use.
Many of these old farm lands are now reforested, and although
federally owned are leased to the States and generally managed
as a part of the State forest system."[343]

State forests have been managed both for the production of
timber and timber products and for the protection of watersheds.
However, since state forests consist mostly of immature stands,
the production and sale of timber and timber products is lim-

ited in scope. "The largest returns have come from the mature forests of the Western states: Washington reported an
annual income of $736,000, Montana, $455,000, and Idaho,
$97,000. East of the Mississippi, only Pennsylvania, Ohio,
Michigan, New York and Florida reported a production of forest products whose value exceeded $50,000 annually." Manage-
ment for the protection of watersheds, too, is found principally in the Western states.[344] In Connecticut, which may
be representative of some other states, the state owns and
operates charcoal kilns and sawmills, the producing power of
which seems to be very small.[345]

A number of states have recognized the importance of the
principle of sustained yield in the management of the state
forests. For example, in Colorado the statute expressly provides that state forests hall be administered as units of
sustained yield (ch. 134, sec. 131(6): Laws 1937, ch. 211,
sec. 6, as amended Laws 1941, ch. 179, sec. 1). Sustained
yield involves both improvement in cutting (negative) and rehabilitation and development (positive). As for cutting, it
was reported in 1946 that cutting practices conducive to
sustained yield were found in only 23 percent of all state and
local forests of commercial value.[346] A commendable start of
the work of rehabilitation and development was made by Oregon
on 2 March 1949, when the Oregon Forest Rehabilitation Act was
passed (Laws 1949, ch. 102). The act makes it incumbent upon
the State Forester, under the direction of the State Board of
Forestry," to rehabilitate, reforest and develop state owned
forest lands so as to secure the highest permanent usefulness
of the whole people of the state of Oregon." An "Oregon Forest Rehabilitation Fund" was created to be raised by bond
sales as well as receipts from the state forests themselves,
the bonds to be repaid by forestry taxes, the rates of which
are to be adjusted to the amount of bonds issued. By April 1953,
nearly $3 million of bonds had been sold. With the Oregon
Forest Rehabilitation Fund, "over 43,000 acres have been seed-
ed by helicopter; 13,300 acres had planted; 42 miles of fire-
breaks constructed and 110 miles of access roads. Most of the
work has been accomplished on the Tillamook burn, greatest
single fire catastrophe in Oregon, destroying some 12.5 billion board feet of finest virgin timber in the western United
States. This former paradise has been 34 percent restored
(March 1953)."[347] Seemingly under the stimulus of this Oregon achievement, the law of Washington providing for the forest development fund was amended in 1951, which allowed the
use of part of this fund "to carry on activities on state forest lands" (Revised Code, sec. 76.12.110: Laws 1923, ch. 154,
sec. 6; as last amended by laws 1953, ch. 118, sec. 2; Laws
1951, ch. 149, sec. 1). But for the whole country, it seems
that much remains to be done in the scientific management of
state forests.

Section 5 Fish and Wildlife

State fish and wildlife enterprise is focussed on three themes: (1) protection of fish and wildlife resources against unnecessary and undesired depletion, (2) artificial propagation of species which are subject to over-hunting or taking,[348] and (3) control of populations. All these tasks aim at the proper balance of fish and wildlife resources as against man and nature.

1. Protection

(a) Protection of Wildlife---As a state enterprise, this is done through(1) the establishment of wildlife refuges, and (2) habitat improvement, which is a newer approach, and which coupled with regulation tends to replace (1).[349]

(1) Wildlife refuges: Wildlife refuges are essentially sanctuaries for certain species of wildlife where they are protected from hunting and trapping. This conception of the sanctuary is, by itself, wholly unrelated to enterprise, but is rather substantiated by the prohibition of hunting, which may be achieved by regulation. Except for state ownership of the areas, the establishment of wildlife refuges would not be designated as an enterprise. They were established because it was thought that only by public ownership of the area could the prohibition against hunting be effectively executed.

On 18 March 1870, the State of California established the Lake Merritt Refuge (now maintained and operated by the City of Oakland), which was the first state wildlife refuge of the country. On 28 March 1878, the same state established the Mount Diablo Refuge. In 1903, Indiana became the second state to creat a wildlife refuge, and was followed by Pennsylvania in 1905, Alabama in 1907, Massachusetts in 1908, Idaho in 1909 and Louisiana in 1911. Between 1913 and 1925 state wildlife refuges were established in twenty-four states.[350] By 1950, forty-six states had created wildlife refuges which totalled 50 million acres in gross area.[351] As of April 1953, forty states and two territories operated some 1,500 wildlife refuges covering an aggregate of some 5.6 million acres in state ownership, as given in the table:[352]

State or Territory	Number of refuges	Total acreage (a)
Alabama	3	71,960
Arizona	14	68,971(b)
Arkansas	2	(Leased Federal lands)
California	3	7,429
Colorado	46	51,078
Connecticut	None	---
Delaware	3	4,000
Florida	64	115,000
Georgia	12	(Leased lands)
Idaho	6	8,130
Illinois	13	31,000

Indiana	6	19,967
Iowa	99	29,559
Kansas	3	25,222
Kentucky	260(c)	8,950(d)
Louisiana	19	548,000
Maine	42	200,000
Maryland	21	10,947
Massachusetts	17	13,928
Michigan	7(e)	8,385
Minnesota	?	662,365
Mississippi	13	67,880
Missouri	None	---
Montana	None	---
Nebraska	3	60,000
Nevada	None	---
New Hampshire	14	12,469
New Jersey	None	---
New Mexico	206	77,404
New York	?	99,985
North Carolina	24(f)	?
North Dakota	11	12,990
Ohio	None	---
Oregon	28	2,535,845
Oklahoma	6	67,946
Pennsylvania	185	49,034
Rhode Island	3	14,100
South Carolina	3	75,000
South Dakota	125	(Leased land)
Tennessee	2	?
Texas	5	65,991
Utah	24	54,600
Vermont	3	1,500
Virginia	7	38,000
Washington	None	---
West Virginia	7	26,112
Wisconsin	145	25,000
Wyoming	None	---
Alaska	None	---
Hawaii	5	261,477
Puerto Rico	3	97,619
Virgin Islands	None	---
Total	1,463, more than	5,527,843, more than

Notes---(a) Net state or territorial ownership only. (b) For ten refuges only. (c) 15 for big game and balance for small game. (d) In addition, 320,000 acres under lease. (e) Including one State Park and Game Area of 500 acres. (f) 8 on state land, 2 on private land and 14 on Federal land. The 24 refuges total 153,229 acres.

The authority of establishing wildlife refuges was at first vested exclusively in the state legislatures. In recent decades, however, administrative agencies in many states have been given this authority.[353] The change from legislative to administrative action in the establishment of state wildlife refuges represents a change in the conception of the wildlife refuges. "At the present time the value and desirability of large, inviolate big-game refuges in modern game management programs has changed entirely. Most of the western states have succeeded in having their inviolate refuges abolished, or in enacting laws which permit the game departments to open, . . . the refuges to hunting when such action is found to be desirable."[354] The temporary nature of the refuges necessitates their establishment and abolition or modification in a sub-statutory manner.

At the present time, the very need of establishing wild-life refuges is under challenge in many states. The creation of wildlife refuges, which are supposed to be more or less permanent in character and to be owned or controlled by the state government, is being replaced by the regulatory action of the game agencies of closing land areas or streams to hunting or fishing for certain periods of time, together with the enterprise activity of habitat improvement.[355]

(2) Habitat improvement: Being of relatively recent origin, the enterprise of wildlife habitat improvement has grown under the conception that _wildlife_ can be _raised_ and _harvested_ like agricultural crops for human consumption and recreation on the basis of sustained yield. It consists of the artificial manipulation of the ways and environments of living of wild animals and birds short of **domestication**. This state enterprise was initiated under the impetus, and has been undertaken, with the aid provided successively in the Federal Civilian Conservation Corps programs and the Federal Wildlife Restoration Act of 2 September 1937 (50 Stat. 917), as amended 18 August 1941 (55 Stat. 632), 24 July 1946 (60 Stat. 656) and 7 August 1946 (60 Stat. 867). The enterprise, as officially defined in this act, consists in "the selection, restoration, rehabilitation and improvement of areas of land or water adaptable as feeding, resting or breeding places for wildlife . . ." (sec. 2).

Habitat improvement programs are under way in the several states for the benefit of either small game or big game or waterfowl. In general, "the West is primarily interested in deer, elk, and antelopes; but game birds, fur animals and desert species also receive their proper share of attention in development, land-acquisition and research projects. The Midwestern and Lake States, being principally agricultural in character, have programs stressing beneficial practices for farmland wildlife, including pheasants, quails, rabbits and small fur animals. In the South, bob-whites attract considerable attention, but wild turkeys, white-tailed deer and fur animals also receive attention. In the Northeastern States,

where forest wildlife is abundant and subject to great hunting pressure but where farmland species also are important,
projects are concerned with deer, ruffed grouse, pheasants,
rabbits and fur animals. Projects to benefit waterfowl are
not of a regional nature and are interspersed throughout the
States."356

    The following is a summary of work accomplished by the
several states by 30 June 1952:357

        To assure adequate habitat for quail, phea-
    sant, rabbits, and other species in the face of
    increasing hunting pressure and intensified farm-
    ing, 36 states made tree, shrub, and herbaceous
    plantings on private farmlands. Cooperative agree-
    ments were executed with landowners to protect
    these investments. Field borders of lespedeza and
    living fences of multiflora rose were emphasized
    in the Southern and Central States. To the north-
    ward and westward, tree and shrub planting on erod-
    ed and nonarable areas and on sites set aside for
    windbreaks was stressed . . . .
        On state owned or controlled refuges and pub-
    lic shooting grounds, habitat was improved for up-
    land game by planting food patches, by thinning
    and clearing, and by prescribed burning in timber
    stands unproductive of wildlife. Forty-one states
    constructed roads, trails, firebreaks, bridges,
    and storage buildings to facilitate management op-
    erations.
        Thirty-eight states sought to remedy the in-
    roads of agricultural drainage on waterfowl habi-
    tat by restoring and creating marshes. New York's
    outstanding success with its small-marsh program
    has prompted other states to follow suit. The
    Empire State has built 92 marshes totaling 346
    acres. Mississippi, Tennessee, Kentucky, and Ala-
    bama improved food conditions on large water res-
    ervoirs by farming and share-cropping draw-down
    areas. Nesting boxes were erected in seven states
    where an absence of tree cavities was limiting
    wood-duck protection . . . .
        Overuse of western range lands has resulted
    in big-game starvation in many localities. In
    addition to reducing herds to the range-carrying
    capacity, seven Western states are employing new-
    ly developed range-revegetation techniques. Ari-
    zona, California, and New Mexico continue to build
    guzzlers and other devices to improve arid game
    ranges. By distributing salt at proper time and
    place, it is possible to attract game onto the
    summer range at an early date, thereby easing the
    pressure on critical winter ranges. Montana alone

distributed 143,000 pounds of salt for this purpose (for fiscal year 1952?).

Twenty-seven states restocked vacant game
ranges by trapping and transplanting from areas of
surplus. Deer, turkey, beaver, antelope, and rac-
coons were the major species relocated. Texas not
only supplied its own needs, but also furnished
white-tailed deer to several southern states.
South Dakota and Wyoming wild-turkey plantings
have increased to the point where the original releases are being trapped for stocking other suitable locations.

California probably stands foremost among the several
states in wildlife habitat improvement. In 1947, the legislature of California authorized a comprehensive, state-wide
Wildlife Conservation program (Stats. 1947, ch. 1325), and
appropriated $9 million to be spent in three years for carry-
ing it out. The program aims "to acquire and restore to the
highest possible level, and maintain in a state of high productivity those areas (in the state) that can be most successfully used to sustain wildlife and which will provide adequate
and suitable recreation" (sec. 1 of Stats. 1947, ch. 1325),
and is said to have "never been attempted in this or any other
state."[358] An additional $3 million was appropriated by an
act of 1951 (Stats. 1951, ch. 1401), to be available for three
more years. By 30 June 1952, 78 projects of fish and wildlife
conservation had been authorized, involving a total cost of
$9,525,150. Of these, four projects involving a total cost
of $441,077 were for upland game habitat improvement and ele-
ven projects involving a total expenditure of $3,806,310 for
waterfowl habitat management.[359]

(b) Protection of fish---Several enterprise measures have
been adopted by the several states, especially Western states,
where many streams are shallow and where irrigation is widely
practiced, in the protection of their fish resources. One of
these is stream clearance, in which natural and artificial
barriers in the streams are removed to facilitate fish passage.
For example, California department of fish and game, as a part
of its fish habitat improvement program, has employed crews to
"remove old dams, log barriers, rock and debris, piles, and
any obstructions that might slow up the flow of water or prevent fish from going upstream to lay their eggs."[360] The same
work is performed by the State of Washington, perhaps in a
even larger scale. During the fiscal year 1950, log jams and
log splash dams were removed in many streams, and "stepped
pools were blasted in the Skookumchuck River falls area above
Vale . . ."[361] In April 1950 work was started on the 38,000-
dollar project of clearing 400 miles of streams in the Cowlitz
watershed, and by February 1951 a total of 78 streams had been
so treated.[362] In July 1950, it was reported that "the channel at the mouth of the Clallam River, seriously blocked with
debris, gravel and sand, was recently opened through the coop-

erative efforts of the departments of game and fisheries."363
By the end of 1952, clearance projects had been completed on
20 rivers and streams, opening approximately 350 miles of
spawning and rearing area to salmon runs. This work was done
largely by the personnel of the Department of Fisheries, but
in a few cases it was performed by contract.364

It has already been mentioned above, that as a regulatory
measure many states require the installation of fish ladders
and screens at water manipulation projects. A few states
have adopted this as an enterprise measure too. In Wyoming,
for example, the statute provides that the Game and Fish Commission may erect fishways or fish ladders on any dam or other
structure if necessary (Compiled Statutes, sec. 47-509: Laws
1941, ch. 81, sec. 1). Similar statutory provision is found
in Massachusetts (General Laws, sec. 32, effective 1 January
1942). Colorado laws have authorized the state Game and Fish
Commission to construct and maintain fish screens "at the intake of any and all ditches taking water from streams of the
state where young trout have been placed at the expense of
the state, said streams of not over eight feet in width or at
an altitude of 8,500 feet or over" (Laws 1913, p. 283, sec. 1).
Unconditioned authority in installing fish screens on all
ditches and canals has been given Oregon State Game Commission
by an act of 1945 (Laws 1945, ch. 442).

On the side of actual accomplishment, the State of Washington, during the fiscal year 1950, built two fish ladders
in the lower Columbia river basin, one on the Abernathy Creek
and the other on the Mill Creek.365 The Fish and Game Commission of California, in the biennium 1948-1950, maintained
some existing fishways and plans were drawn up for the construction of three new fishways.366 In the field of fish-
screening, the State of Washington has done a very successful
work. It was started in 1939 and has been conducted jointly
the Department of Game and the Department of Fisheries. By
the end of 1952, nearly 250 fish installations had been constructed, which had "effectively sealed off all irrigation
systems with rotary screens."367

Fish-rescue is another type of fish-protective work. In
California rescue is given fish "that are trapped in lakes
or streams which are drying up. These fish would die quickly
for lack of food and oxygen in the water even before the lake
or stream became completely dry. The fish are caught in nets
and taken to other streams that have plenty of water. The
Department (of Fish and Game) often rescues a million fish a
year this way."368 In Kansas great numbers of fish locked in
ice during severe winter months have been rescued each year369
Iowa has two Mississippi rescue stations at Lansing and Sabu-
la.370 It would seem that the rescue work is directed at fish
stranded in chutes and sloughs fed with Mississippi flood waters after the subsidence of the floods.

Perhaps the most important fish-protective work is what may be termed fish habitat improvement. In California, for example, the Fish and Game Department has been engaged in the construction of dams for the maintenance and stabilization of water levels of watercourses. During the biennium ending 30 June 1952, seven flow maintenance rock and masonry dams were constructed at the outlets of seven lakes at a total cost of $14,670. The work was done by a five-man crew of the said Department.[371] In Louisiana, an act was passed in 1950 which appropriated $20,000 to the Departments of Public Works and of Wildlife and Fisheries to construct one or more weirs in the State Canal in St. Landry Parish "for the purpose of maintaining in said State Canal and in the streams emptying therein sufficient water to sustain fish life and to promote both commercial and recreational fishing at low water stages." The State of Michigan has been engaged in the improvement of fish streams through the blasting or rock bottoms, the improvement of spawning areas, bank revetments, and the construction of dams, delectors and brush shelters.[372] The State of Pennsylvania had, by April 1954, constructed as many as 150 deflectors in fish streams.[373] It may be noted that the above-discussed stream-clearance projects are part of the fish-habitat improvement enterprise in the broad sense of this term.

2. Propagation

(a) Propagation of wildlife: Game Farms---Game farms for artificial propagation of wildlife were first established in about 1905 in such states as Illinois, Indiana and Pennsylvania.[374] The first state-operated game farm was established in 1906 in Illinois.[375] The state enterprise of artificial propagation of wildlife has grown to such a size that it is now the largest source of artificially raised game for release.[376] Theoretically, artificial propagation of wildlife is justifiable for the following purposes: (1) to stock areas with new species which are more adaptable to such areas than native species, (2) to stock areas with species threatened with extermination, (3) to stock areas which are improved for increased capacity to sustain wildlife, (4) to remedy distortions in sex balance, and (5) to provide a "hunting buffer" for the protection of native species.[377] As a matter of fact, the production of most state farms is limited to ring-necked pheasant and the bobwhite quail, two of the favorite species of the American hunters.[378] It seems that they are produced without consideration of any of the above-mentioned reasons.

The operation of state game farms is very costly.[379] As a matter of fact, "state game farms are rapidly becoming less important in modern game management programs. They are passing out of existence in various parts of the country. In some instances states maintain farms chiefly because of their public relations value, not the additional game they provide

for the hunter's bag."[380] As of April 1953, the number of
state- and territory-operated game farms are listed below:[381]

(a) States (13) and territories (3) which do not operate game
        farms---Alabama, Arizona, Connecticut, Delaware,
        Indiana, Mississippi, Missouri, Nevada, North Car-
        olina, Rhode Island, South Dakota, Texas, Vermont,
        Hawaii, Puerto Rico, Virgin Islands.
(b) States (17) which operate only one game farm---Arkansas,
        Colorado, Florida, Georgia, Iowa, Kentucky, Maine,
        Michigan, Nebraska, New Hampshire, New Mexico,
        North Dakota, South Carolina, Tennessee, Virginia,
        Wisconsin, Wyoming.
(c) States (5) which operate two game farms---Idaho, Minne-
        sota, Ohio, Utah, West Virginia.
(d) States (7) which operate three game farms---Illinois,
        Kansas, Louisiana, Montana, New Jersey, Oregon,
        Oklahoma.
(e) States (3) which operate four game farms---Maryland, Mass-
        achusetts, Pennsylvania.
(f) States (3) which operate a greater number of game farms-
        --California (six), New York (six), Washington
        (ten).

(b) Propagation of fish: fish hatcheries---As of March
1949, all 48 states except Delaware and Mississippi operated
fish hatcheries for artificial propagation of fish, mostly
game fish. The numbers of state-owned fish hatcheries and
rearing stations in the 46 states are listed below:[382]

State	Number of Hatcheries	Number of rearing stations
Alabama	3	---
Arizona	3	1
Arkansas	3	---
California	25	---
Colorado	12	12
Connecticut	8	---
Florida	3	---
Georgia	5	---
Idaho	16	---
Illinois	7	---
Indiana	13	---
Iowa	22	---
Kansas	2	---
Kentucky	2	5
Louisiana	3	---
Maine	11	12
Maryland	5	2
Massachusetts	8	---
Michigan	14	9
Minnesota	19	18
Missouri	8	---

Montana	11	---
Nebraska	4	---
Nevada	1	---
New Hampshire	4	4
New Jersey	2	---
New Mexico	5	---
New York	20	---
North Carolina	8	---
North Dakota	1	---
Ohio	7	2
Oklahoma	6	---
Oregon	38	---
Pennsylvania	9	---
Rhode Island	2	---
South Carolina	10	---
Tennessee	3	---
Texas	10	---
Utah	12	1
Vermont	4	8
Virginia	3	1
Washington	37	---
West Virginia	4	---
Wisconsin	26	3
Wyoming	7	1
Total	305	79

(Besides, Montana has 10, Oregon 6, Wyoming 5
and Washington 1 egg-taking stations).

Annual production of the state hatcheries, based on 1947-1949
data, for 44 states (all 48 states except Delaware, Louisiana,
Mississippi and Tennessee) is as follows:[383]

Fry.	1,650,900,304
Fingerlings.	170,179,628
6 inches and bigger.	32,672,038
Total	1,853,751,970

The expense in the operation of fish hatcheries is also
high. Studies made by the New York State Conservation Department have shown that the cost of producing one pound of trout
is 87.7 cents, which is broken down as follows:[384]

Personnel service	36.39 cents
Fish food	35.67
Hatchery maintenance and operation.	10.53
Investment and interest	5.15

Hatchery-reared fishes are usually stocked in lakes and
streams that are open to public recreational fishing, and in
exceptional cases are also available for stocking in private
waters.[385] Special mention seems to be unnecessary of the
more or less established practice of stocking watercourses

whose original fishery resources are subject to a heavy fishing drain. In recent years a new practice has developed in which artificially reared fishes are stocked in lakes unproductive of fish life. This practice seems to be limited to the West. Most of lakes in this category are situated on high mountains. "Primarily of glacial origin, most of them were originally barren of trout and also other fishes because of their origin and because of waterfalls in their outlets, which prevented the natural ascent of fishes."[386] Except for artificial stocking (of fishes either naturally or artificially reared) there will not be any fishes in these lakes. In at least some of the Western states, great efforts have been made in planting fish in these waters. "There are between seven hundred and one thousand lakes locked in the Cascade and Wallowa Mountains of Oregon which cannot be reached by road. A majority of these lakes have been stocked with trout by the Oregon State Game Commission." "Roughly, three hundred of these 'back country lakes' are stocked each year with eastern brook and rainbow trout. The lakes most heavily fished are stocked annually, while some of the more isolated lakes are planted only every two or three years. Stocking is done by packstrings and airplanes."[387] In California, "thousands of lakes . . . have been stocked with fingerling trout packed in with horses or on the backs of employees of the Fish and Game Commission. In the future many of these lakes will be restocked by airplane."[388] Some lakes in low areas also need fish-stocking. Fox example, "in the lowland lakes of western Washington, practically no spawning areas exist. In order to provide fishing in these lakes, it is necessary to stock heavily year after year."[389]

Besides the artificial hatching of fresh-water fishes, some states are also engaged in the artificial propagation of shellfish. For example, an act of the state of Washington of 1949 (ch. 112) set up a number of state "oyster reserves" and authorized the Department of Fisheries to plant in these reserves oysters to be sold to shellfish growers, processors and beach oyster farmers on a self-liquidating basis. In Alabama, the Department of Conservation has regularly planted oyster shells on reefs depleted with that fish resources.[390]

(a) Public hunting and fishing area---The creation and establishment of public hunting and fishing areas or grounds is a measure of control because it supplements the state regulation of hunting and fishing. The hunting or fishing license issued by state game agencies carries with it merely the statutory right to hunt or fish; but no game or fish can be taken without some place where to hunt or fish. Hunting is practiced mostly on land areas. Lands are either publicly or privately owned. Not only privately owned lands are protected against trespass by hunters, but also public lands are closed to hunting unless it is so expressly permitted by the agencies controlling them. Fishing involves the use of both the waterflow and the banks of watercourses. For navigable watercourses, the waterflow is by common law generally open to fishing, but the banks are in many states in the possession of the riparian landowners. The banks of all non-navigable watercourses are, under common law, the property of the riparian landowners. Their waterflow bears the same legal characteristics, except in the Western States, where it is declared to be public property for the purposes of water appropriation. It may be remarked that as fishing does not involve the appropriation or taking out of water from the watercourse, public ownership of the waterflow of a non-navigable watercourse in the Western States does not open it to public fishing. To solve this legal problem of land-ownership, the legislatures of many states have authorized the state game and fish agencies to establish public hunting and public fishing areas or grounds.391 Primarily, this consists of the acquisition of fee-simple to lands and watercourses and the management thereof for the sole or primary purpose of facilitating public hunting and fishing, or of the acquisition of easements to lands and watercourses (for navigable watercourses, to banks thereof) for public hunting and fishing. This work may be augmented or supplemented by (1) the installation of facilities for use and convenience of hunters and fishermen (such as parking lots, sanitary facilities, roads, etc.), and (2) measures (such as habitat improvement and artificial stocking) to insure a dependable stock of game and fish available for hunting and fishing.392

Many public hunting and fishing areas or grounds are created on state lands. For example, an act of 1943 of Oregon (Laws 1943, ch. 203) authorized the State Land Board to convey to the State Game Commission 3,000-8,000 acres of lands constituting the bed of Summer Lake in Lake County and waters over the same, upon payment by the latter of $2.50 per acre, for shooting grounds and other purposes. A law of Utah of 1947 (Laws 1947, ch. 45) authorized the State Fish and Game Commission to use certain designated unsurveyed state-owned lands for the purpose of establishing public shooting grounds and fishing waters and for some other purposes. In an act of 1945 of Washington (Laws 1945, ch. 179), certain owned tidelands in Skagit and Snohomish Counties were declared to be public shooting grounds. Under Idaho law, all public navigable waters and waters flowing through state lands have been declared "highways for the purpose of angling or fishing thereon" (Code, sec. 36-901: Laws 1919, ch. 65); and a certain number of streams have been declared as public navigable waters for the purpose of fishing (ibid., sec. 36-907: Laws 1917, ch. 56; as last amended by L. 1935, ch. 96, sec. 15). In many cases public hunting grounds are nothing but habitat-improvement areas discussed above and game refuges partly or conditionally opened to hunting. As a matter of fact, the present tendency in game management is to combine the three concepts of game refuge, habitat improvement and public hunting in a single enterprise.

Some public hunting and fishing grounds, particularly hunting grounds, are established on Federal lands. In these areas, what is emphasized is not so much the right to hunt as the installment of proper improvements. As mentioned before, many states have entered into agreements with the United States Forest Service whereby parts of national forests have become state public hunting grounds. "For all practical purposes cooperative programs now operate in all states where there are one or more national forests." The total area of public hunting grounds thus established within the national forests amounts to about five percent of the total area of national-forest lands.[393] In these special areas of the national forests, the United States Forest Service is generally responsible for the maintenance and improvement of habitat, and for determinin g the degree to which national forests may be used for fishing and hunting, while the state fish and game agencies controls public fishing and hunting. Hunters and anglers are usually required to purchase permits in addition to hunting and fishing licenses from the state game and fish agencies, and receipts are shared between them and the Forest Service.[394] Similar arrangements have recently been made between state game agencies and the United States Fish and Wildlife Service with respect to certain national waterfowl refuges in Missouri, California, Wisconsin and certain other states.[395] With respect to the grazing districts administered by the United States Bureau of Land Management, it is provided, in a similar manner, in sec. 9 of the Taylor Grazing Act of 28 June 1934 (48 Stat. 1269, 1273) that "the Secretary of the Interior shall provide, by suitable rules and regulations, for cooperation with . . . official state agencies engaged in conservation or propagation of wildlife interested in the use of the grazing districts . . ."[396] Although the term "public fishing grounds" is not used and special agreements of the kind discussed above are not required, all national parks, national forests and many other Federal areas are open to public fishing, under regulations prescribed by the Federal agencies concerned. They are not called state public fishing areas because the public fishing comes not as a result of state efforts.

Besides outright land-acquisition, special arrangements may be made by state game and fish agencies to obtain hunting and fishing easements or servitudes on private lands. For example, the Pennsylvania Game Commission in 1936 initiated a cooperative farm-game program, in which owners of farm lands agree to open their lands to public hunting, except areas set apart as refuges or safety zones. By the end of the calendar year 1949, the program included 153 projects comprising more than 6,700 farms with a total area of more than 670,000 acres.[397] In Virginia, laws were enacted in 1930 which provided that owners of private forest or wooded lands may offer such lands to the State Department of Conservation and Development to be used as a forest, game, fish and recreation reserve.

Upon acceptance of such offer by the said department, the
state automatically enjoys exclusive hunting and fishing privileges over and on such lands and may sell such privileges
to the public (Code, sec. 10-22 et seq.). Under Connecticut
laws, the State Board of Fisheries and Game may by agreement
obtain fishing, hunting, trapping, or shooting rights or privileges on any land or water within the state (General Statutes, sec. 4855). In California, under an act of 1947 (Fish
and Game Code, sec. 1159), the Department of Fish and Game
may enter into agreements with private land owners for the
establishment of cooperative hunting areas, each of which
must be at least 5,000 acres in size and may consist of adjoining lands of one or more owners. These areas are open
to public hunting, but "the owners or owner or lessees or
lessee of a cooperative hunting area may collect a daily fee
not to exceed two dollars per day per area from each permit
hunter."

Hunting and fishing easements may even be established on
state-owned lands not otherwise open to public hunting and
fishing. For example, in about 1949, the State of Connecticut
established a public shooting area in the Wooster Mountain
State Park.[398] Washington laws provide that "all state lands
. . . leased for grazing purposes shall be open and avilable
for the public for purposes of hunting and fishing unless
closed to public entry because of fire hazard or unless lawfully posted by lessee to prohibit hunting and fishing thereon.

Some examples may be given of state enterprise of the establishment and operation of public hunting and fishing grounds.
In Nevada, there are approximately 8,300 acres in public hunting areas acquired by the state, and approximately 800,000
acres in hunting areas leased or withdrawn by the state.[399]
Minnesota owns 1,211,730 acres in public hunting grounds.[400]
In Washington, eight areas of big-game hunting grounds covering a total of 154,261 acres, eleven waterfowl projects covering 136 acres and about 400,000 acres of pheasant area were
open to public hunting as of March 1954. As of the same time,
the Department of Game owned 168 public fishing areas, of
which 104 areas "have been improved for parking and have sanitary facilities" and eight areas are artificial dam-impound-
ments.[401] In Massachusetts, the Department of Conservation
had, as of the end of 1951, acquired easement to a total of
eighty miles of stream banks for public fishing.[402] As of
1950, Michigan had 480 public fishing sites totalling more
than 45,000 acres and including over a million feet of water
frontage, of which 320 sites were on lakes and 160 on streams.[403]
In Wisconsin, there were 100 state public hunting grounds aggregating about 283,483 acres as of 30 June 1950, of which
about 233,316 acres (82.3 percent) were leased.[404]

The following remarks should perhaps be made on state

public hunting and fishing areas or grounds: (1) At the present time, it would seem that public hunting and fishing
areas or grounds, officially called by such names, are established only at the state level. (2) Owners of wild lands not
included in public hunting and fishing grounds may voluntarily open their lands to hunting and (or) fishing. The national forests (areas not included in public hunting grounds),
state forests and locally owned forests other than those
maintained as watersheds of municipal water supplies are ordinarily open to hunting and fishing; and national parks and
state and local parks are normally admissible to fishermen.
(3) In a practical sense, the establishment of public hunting and fishing grounds is a recreational measure not different from the establishment of parks rather than a measure of
fish and game administration.

(b) Control of undesirable species---The following classes of such species are subject to state control: (1) predators (2) rough fish, and (3) harmful birds and animals.

(1) Control of predators: In a majority of states, the
laws rely on private persons to control predatory animals
and birds, who are encouraged to do so under state or county
bounty laws. The bounty system has three defects: (1) With
the exception of the crow, predators are not easily identifiable by amateur hunters and ordinary men claiming bounties.[405]
This results in the wasteful killing of non-predatory species.
(2) As a matter of fact, few persons take predatory animals
and birds because of the bounties, but in most cases they are
taken quite accidentally; and (3) in many cases predators
were caught in one state and fraudulently brought to another
where bounties (or higher bounties) were paid.[406] For these
reasons, the bounty system has been considerably discredited
in recent decades. In the following states, it has been abolished, and instead special personnel are employed by the state
game agencies to eliminate predators:

    Arizona---Code, sec. 57-105, para. 2 (Laws 1929, ch. 84,
            as amended)
    Florida---Statutes, sec. 372.17 (Laws 1929, ch. 13644,
            sec. 5)
    Mississippi---Code, sec. 5849 (Laws 1932, ch. 123).
    Montana----Revised Codes, sec. 26-104(6) (Laws 1921, ch.
            193, as amended).
    New Mexico---Laws 1931, ch. 117, sec. 2.

In California (Fish and Game Code, sec. 29) and Washington
(Laws 1947, ch. 275, sec. 76; laws 1949, ch. 112, sec. 44,
1st sent.) direct state control exists side by side with bounty system. In Pennsylvania, the bounty system prevails except
in auxiliary state game refuges, where the personnel of the
state game commission used to remove foxes, weasels, opposums,
hawks, owls and other predators.[411] There are no state-boun-
ty laws in New Jersey (only county-bounty laws), but special

personnel have been employed by the Department of Conservation to exterminate predatory animals and birds. A total
of 4,270 vermin were so taken by that agency during the fiscal year ending 30 June 1952.[408]

The sea-lamprey may be regarded as a fish predator for
practical purposes, though it belongs to the category of par-
asites. In Wisconsin, the Conservation Commission has been
engaged in a program of controlling sea-lamprey, with consists in the trapping of the lamprey on their way to the
spawning grounds and the destruction thereof before they spawn.
"Sea lamprey traps were operated in six locations during the
spawning run in the spring of 1950 in streams tributary to
Lake Michigan. A total of 16,410 sea lamprey were taken in
these traps during the spring of 1950 as compared to about 6,-
000 destroyed in 1949."[409]

(2) Control of rough fishes: "It is generally assumed
that such 'coarse' or 'rough' fishes as suckers, mullets,
buffalo, carp, bull-heads, catfishes and sheephead (to list
those more or less common in some Michigan lakes) are lacking
in game quality or are of little food value (because of taste,
boniness or mere prejudice) and that they in some way limit
or adversely affect the production of game fish. They are
often alleged to eat the eggs or young of the desired species,
or to compete for food with either the adults or the young of
the game fishes, or to ruin the fish environment. It is a
common practice, therefore, to attempt the removal of coarse
fish from game-fish waters. . ."[410] "The undesirable rough
fish were probably introduced into the lakes (and streams)
by anglers using the fingerling for bait; some of these es-
caped off the hook and survived, or at the end of the day's
fishing the angler dumped his can of bait into the lake (or
stream), this establishing the species. Fishing intensity
for the desirable game fish increased through the years rapidly, and the desirable game fish were reduced to such an extent that they no longer could compete against the huge food
demand of the rough fish, resulting in a non-productive body
of water for the angler."[411]

Permanent rough fish traps may be used as in Iowa, to remove rough fish from game fish waters.[412] Another method of
rough-fish removal is to drain off the water of a lake completely and catch all the rough fishes. Then the lake is
filled again with water and stocked with game fish.[413] However, it seems that water poisoning is the method most widely
used in this country. In the process of poisoning, all fishes in the lake, both rough and game fishes, are poisoned and
killed and their carcasses serve as fertilizers of the water,
which is afterwards restocked with new game fishes. Rough
fish elimination is conducted mostly on lakes, but occasionally it is also practiced on streams.[414]

It has been reported that the chemicals used in lake poisoning are very expensive. They cost about $10-$50 per surface acre per season.[415] Besides, "there is no justification for playing up the fighting qualities of a seven-inch trout and belittling the fighting qualities of such species as carp, channel catfish, and mudfish (bowfin). Some of these so-called undesirables are quite willing and able to resist capture." "Creating a demand for the so-called less desirable species is good conservation."[416] With regard to the contention that rough fishes, as fish food, are not so palatable as game fish, it is largely a matter of prejudice.[417] The luxurious undertaking of rough fish removal is worth revaluation.

"Rough fish control" is sometimes used synonymously with "lake rehabilitation." But these two terms need be distinguished. It seems that the latter term should be used to mean that each lake should contain only fishes most adaptable to the natural conditions of the lake (or stream), and that in right quantities. All fish species which are not quite adaptable to the conditions of one watercourse should be removed to watercourses to which they are most adaptable; and new species may be introduced into it which by nature are its proper inhabitants. In cases where a watercourse is overpopulated with fish of natural species, which are thus "stunted" so to speak, then as a measure of rehabilitation the stunted fish, in spite of the fact that they belong to desirable species, may be removed and new, healthy species planted.[418] While the justification of rough fish control as such may be doubtful, the principle underlying fish-water rehabilitation is absolutely sound, provided it is economically feasible.

The State of Washington is reported to be the leading state in the field of fish-water rehabilitation. As of March 1953, "the state of Washington has rehabilitated 22,500 acres of water . . . . Of this amount we have brought 17,783 acres into actual production as of the fishing season of 1953." "The state that is next in lake rehabilitation is New Hampshire with 3,425 acres; Oregon is third with 1,690; Michigan 980; Arizona 911; Colorado 518. Of all the lakes rehabilitated to the present time the state of Washington has done over 70 percent."[419]

(3) Control of harmful birds and animals: Many states have undertaken to control animals and birds which damage crops and property. For example, it is provided in sec. 19 of the Colorado Game and Fish Laws that whenever wild animals are found detrimental or harmful to life, health, crops, timber, property or cultivation of lands, the game and fish commission may kill or cause or permit to be killed such animals, "provided . . . that in the case of elk only old elk bulls shall be killed, and such killing shall be done only by game wardens or regular deputy game wardens" (Laws 1933, p. 504,

sec. 1). Under sec. 126(4) of the same Laws, the same Commission may kill and pelt beaver on private lands upon request of the owners thereof, when they damage property (Laws 1941, p. 440, sec. 4). In Washington, under a law of 1947 (ch. 275, sec. 33), the Director of Game "may remove or kill any wild animal, game fish or wild bird that in his judgment is destroying or injuring property . . ." Under the same law (secs. 64-67), as amended or augmented by a law of 1951 (ch. 262, sec. 1), "if beavers or other burrowing animals are damaging or endangering any land, the owner or occupant of such land may notify the state game commission of such danger, and the commission shall cause such animals to be trapped or killed by state trappers . . ." "If the commission fails to act within 14 days after receipt of notice, any such owner or occupant may trap or kill such animals, but if he does so such person must notify the commission regarding the number of such animals disposed of and when possible surrender the pelts thereof to the commission." Beaver-control laws have also been enacted in Minnesota (Laws 1953, ch. 633) and Nevada (L. 1953, ch. 358). Nevada law is similar to Washington law, and like the latter the initiative rests with the landowners. In Minnesota the initiative is in the county authorities; and, where private property is affected, the consent of the landowner is required for either the removal of beaver or the destruction of beaver dams. The Kansas Forestry, Fish and Game Commission regularly bombs crows which are destructive of farm crops, and removes beaver from areas where they do the same harm.[420] In Oregon, the State Game Commission has been engaged in the work of protecting crop lands from damages of big game, though without express statutory authorization. It "has hired herders in a number of instances to patrol croplands through the night and drive the animals off. Unfortunately, attempts to drive habitual offenders away from farmlands are seldom successful, and permits authorizing complainants to kill offending animals are commonly used when small numbers of big game animals take residence within a major agricultural area where they are not hunted and where they are a continuous source of damage."[421]

Certain wild animals and birds may be specially protected by a state, which it is under no circumstances to kill. In Colorado, when such wild animals are damaging property, they are not to be killed, but instead the state compensates the owner of the property for the damage he suffers (Fish and Game Laws, sec. 42: Laws 1931, p. 401 sec. 1). This represents another aspect of the state enterprise of the control of harmful wildlife.

Section 6 Recreation

The several states, like the national government, own parks and many other kinds of recreational areas. The numbers and acreages of these various kinds of state-owned recreation-

al areas. The numbers and acreages of these various kinds of
state-owned recreational areas of each state are shown in the
following tables:

1. STATE PARKS (All kinds)
(Including state beaches)

State	Number	Acreage
Alabama(1)	15	34,493
Arizona	1	950
Arkansas	6	14,580
California(2)	86	580,666
Colorado(3)	1	975
Connecticut(4)	47	17,782
Delaware	1	2
Florida	21	67,859
Georgia(5)	17	34,057
Idaho(6)	4	8,189
Illinois	36	21,804
Indiana(7)	16	43,364
Iowa(8)	19	15,540
Kansas	22	16,629
Kentucky	13	10,906
Louisiana(9)	9	11,288
Maine	11	159,851
Maryland(10)	10	4,970
Massachusetts(11)	11	7,467
Michigan	51	92,331
Minnesota(12)	34	82,611
Mississippi	9	9,615
Missouri(13)	23	57,984
Montana	12	18,265
Nebraska	7	2,390
Nevada	5	11,489
New Hampshire	24	24,981
New Jersey	20	18,380
New Mexico	3	2,700
New York(14)	62	2,346,005
North Carolina	11	34,141
North Dakota	3	1,931
Ohio(15)	18	23,784
Oklahoma	8	48,280
Oregon(16)	105	41,490
Pennsylvania	43	105,521
Rhode Island(17)	11	2,124
South Carolina(18)	19	44,599
South Dakota	8	72,658
Tennessee	15	71,373
Texas	42	58,092
Utah	0	0
Vermont(19)	20	6,142
Virginia	10	26,791
Washington(20)	43	55,214

West Virginia	16	35,973
Wisconsin(21)	28	16,630
Wyoming	2	42
TOTAL, 48 States	998	4,061,838

Notes:

(1) Including one "wayside park".
(2) Including 3 "memorial state parks".
(3) Called "memorial park".
(4) Including one "memorial state park".
(5) Including 3 "memorial state parks".
(6) Including one "memorial state park".
(7) Including one "memorial state park".
(8) Including one "memorial state park". The Mcgregor Areas, consisting of three state parks and certain other areas, are here regarded as a single park.
(9) Including one "memorial state park".
(10) Maryland has no munuments, but it has a "Washington Monument State Park".
(11) Including one "memorial state park", one "state forest park" and one "state beach".
(12) Including 5 "state memorial parks".
(13) Including one "memorial state park.
(14) Including 2 "memorial state parks'.
(15) Including one "state beach park".
(16) Including one "wayside park" and 5 "memorial state parks".
(17) Including 2 "memorial state parks".
(18) Including one "memorial state park".
(19) Called "state forest parks".
(20) Including 2 "memorial state parks".
(21) Including one "memorial state park" and 7 "roadside state parks".

---

2. STATE WAYSIDES[1]

(Excluding those maintained by state highway departments)

State	Number	Acreage
Iowa	5	128
Louisiana(2)	1	13
Minnesota	15	685
New Hampshire	5	2,758
Ohio	5	135
Oregon	36	14,816
South Carolina	6	224
TOTAL, seven states	73	18,759

(1) The seven roadside state parks of Wisconsin, totalling

1,228 acres, are included within "state parks".
(2) Called "wayside park" in Louisiana.

3.   STATE MONUMENTS

State	Number	Acreage
Alabama	2	338
California	19	1,047
Colorado	2	52
Connecticut	8	20
Illinois	8	39
Iowa	13	690
Kentucky	2	39
Louisiana	3	141
Minnesota(1)	9	6
New Mexico	9	154
Rhode Island	3	?
Texas	1	1-
Utah	4	85(upward of)
TOTAL, 13 states	83	2,623(except R.I.)

(1)   Called "park monuments" in Minnesota

4.   STATE HISTORIC SITES

State	Number	Acreage
Alabama	3	171
Arizona	1	11
Georgia(1)	6	1
Maryland	1	1
Massachusetts	1	2
New Hampshire	3	176
New Jersey	17	25
New York	28	506
North Carolina	2	38
North Dakota	37	545
Pennsylvania(2)	14	484
Rhode Island	7	126(upward of)
Texas	2	14
Washington	8	495
TOTAL, 14 states	130	2,595(upward of)

(1)   Called "marker sites" in Georgia.
(2)   Called "historic properties" in Pennsylvania.

5.   STATE MEMORIALS

State	Number	Acreage
Florida	16	2,138

Illinois	16	87
Indiana	10	684
Maine	12	349
Ohio	50	4,203
Oklahoma	4	129
Rhode Island(1)	3	142
TOTAL, seven states	90	7,732

(1) Called "memorial fields" in Rhode Island.

6. STATE SHRINES

State	Number	Acreage
Kentucky	6	312
Texas	2	17
TOTAL, two states	8	329

7. STATE RESERVES, RESERVATIONS AND LIKE AREAS

State	Number	Acreage
Iowa(1)	30	7,003
Massachusetts	10	14,750
Minnesota	4	787(upward of)
New Hampshire	1	6,232
New York	6	1,677(upward of)
Ohio	10	2,915
Rhode Island	14	4,405
TOTAL, seven states	75	37,769(upward of)

(1) Excluding "lake reserves" in Iowa.

8. STATE RECREATION AREAS

State	Number	Acreage
Maryland	1	1,802
Michigan(1)	15	56,014
Nebraska	51	7,765
North Carolina	1	1,000
North Dakota	7	414
Rhode Island	4	12,852
South Dakota(2)	25	3,439
Virginia(3)	3	?
Washington	5	156
TOTAL, nine states	112	83,442(except Virginia

(1) Called "recreation grounds" in Nebraska.

(2) Including 8 "recreation areas" and 17 "recreational de-
     velopment areas".
(3) Located in state forests.

9. STATE PARKWAYS

State	Number	Acreage
Illinois	2	3,092
Iowa	1	350
New York	18	16,354
Rhode Island	4	191
TOTAL, four states	25	19,987

10. STATE RECREATIONAL WATER AREAS
(Excluding public fishing grounds)

State	Designation	Number	Acreage
Iowa	Lake reserves	17	703
Ohio	State lakes	5	30,000
Ohio	State lake reserves	18	6,297
Ohio	State reservoir lakes	2	14,678
Ohio	State canalways	2	140
TOTAL, two states		44	51,812

(The above list is not complete. For example, Alabama Department of Conservation created three State Public Lakes in the
summer of 1950; five in the summer of 1951 and two in the summer of 1952. These lakes were built with funds of the game,
fish and seafood division, and are administered by the division of parks, monuments and historical sites, of the said
department. -- Alabama Department of Conservation, Annual Report 1 October 1950 to 30 September 1951, p. 129. A law of
Idaho of 1925 made the waters and beaches of the Big Payette
Lake available for public recreation. -- Idaho Code, sec. 67-
4301: Laws 1925, ch. 83. Similar arrangement was made in
1927 for the Priest, Pend d'Oreille and Coeur d'Alene Lakes.--
Ibid., sec. 67-4304 and 67-4305: Laws 1927, ch. 2.)

11. MISCELLANEOUS STATE RECREATIONAL AREAS
(Excluding public hunting and fishing grounds,
museums and aboretums)

State	Designation	Number	Acreage
Michigan	Group camps	2	?
Montana	Camp	1	?
New York	Battlefield	1	6
North Carolina	Group camp	1	1,000
North Dakota	International Peace Garden	1	888

Oregon	Various (1)	4	1,576
TOTAL, 6 states		10	3,470

(1) Emigrant Hill Overlook, Lincoln County Wood Supply Tract, Van Duzer Forest Corridor, and Yachats Ocean Road.

-----All above tables are based on information contained in National Park Service, <u>State Parks: Area, Acreages and Accommodations</u>, 31 December 1950 (mimeo.).

The distribution of the various kinds of state recreational areas among the 48 states is shown in the following summary table. Rhode Island has the greatest variety of such areas, with Iowa coming next. It may be noted, however, that good recreation administration does not necessarily call for the use of a great number of designations. The general designations "parks", "monuments" and "historic sites" may perhaps cover all kinds of existing state recreational establishments.

DISTRIBUTION OF THE VARIOUS KINDS OF STATE RECREATIONAL AREAS BY STATES

State	1	2	3	4	5	6	7	8	9	10	11
Alabama	x		x	x							
Arizona	x			x							
Arkansas	x										
California	x		x								
Colorado	x		x								
Connecticut	x		x								
Delaware	x										
Florida	x				x						
Georgia	x			x							
Idaho	x										
Illinois	x		x		x				x		
Indiana	x				x						
Iowa	x	x	x				x		x	x	
Kansas	x										
Kentucky	x		x			x					
Louisiana	x	x	x								
Maine	x				x						
Maryland	x			x				x			
Massachusetts	x			x			x				
Michigan	x							x			x
Minnesota	x	x	x				x				
Mississippi	x										
Missouri	x										
Montana	x										x
Nebraska	x							x			
Nevada	x										
New Hampshire	x	x		x			x				

New Jersey	x		x					
New Mexico	x	x						
New York	x		x		x		x	x
North Carolina	x		x			x		x
North Dakota	x		x			x		x
Ohio	x	x		x	x		x	
Oklahoma	x			x				
Oregon	x	x						x
Pennsylvania	x		x					
Rhode Island	x	x	x	x	x	x	x	
South Carolina	x	x						
South Dakota	x					x		
Tennessee	x							
Texas	x		x	x	x			
Utah		x						
Vermont	x							
Virginia	x					x		
Washington	x		x			x		
West Virginia	x							
Wisconsin	x							
Wyoming	x							

California is the state which established the first state park. "Even before the establishment of Yellowstone National Park, the Congress had recognized the desirability of preserving scenic areas for public use. In 1864, it had enacted legislation granting Yosemite Valley and the Mariposa Tree Grove to the State of California, with the proviso that they 'be held for public use, resort, and recreation.'" However, "in 1905, the State legislature authorized return of these areas to Federal jurisdiction, for inclusion in Yosemite National Park."[422] The state parks average about 4,100 acres and are about one-thirty-first (1/31) of the average area of the national parks. Although relatively small in area, the state parks, it seems, contain much higher percentage of water areas than the national parks. Many state parks are famous for their natural or artificial lakes, lagoons, waterfalls or beaches. It seems that only in a few instances are state parks noted for natural wonders other than these as the national parks.[423]

Many of the nation's noted beaches are included within the state park systems. "Some of the eastern seaboard states . . . were the first to recognize the need for public recreational developments along the ocean front. New York's Coney Island has long been famous and its more recent Jones Beach State Park is an outstanding example of a water recreation development near a large population center. Other splendid examples are to be found in . . . Hunting Island State Park in South Carolina . . ." "Oregon has been notably successful in acquiring Pacific Coast shoreline for the development of state park areas." "Outstanding examples of water develop-

ments for recreation on the shores of the Great Lakes are In-
diana Dunes, Grand Haven, and Illinois Beach State parks on
Lake Michigan; Pennsylvania State Park on Lake Erie; and Fair
Haven Beach State Park on Lake Ontario."[424] Among the state
parks of Washington, the Deception Pass, Illahee, Saltwater,
Sequim Bay, Twanoh and Twin Harbors State Parks are beach
areas.[425] The Goose Bay, Yellow Bay, Big Arm, Bitterroot
Lake, Hell Creek and Rock Creek State Parks of Montana; the
Hugh Taylor Birch, Gold Head Branch, Fort Clinch, Little Tal-
bot Island and Desoto State Parks of Florida; the Aroostook,
Lake St. George, Mt. Blue, Reid and Sebago State Parks of
Maine; and the Elmore, Sandbar, St. Albans Bay, Crystal Lake,
Brandbury and St. Catherine state forest parks of Vermont al-
so contain beaches.[426] The use of tidelands and beaches for
state parks is specially promoted by statute in California
(Stats 1941, ch. 113), Michigan (Laws 1941, Nos. 307 and 308)
and Texas (Laws 1941, ch. 7). Many state parks are designated as a state beach park or are called by similar names.
These are listed below:[427]

> Massachusetts---Edgartown-Oak Bluffs State Beach
> Ohio---Painsville State Beach Park
> Alabama---Romar Beach Wayside Park
> California---Alamitos Beach State Park, Avila Beach State
>   Park, and 35 other similar parks.
> Illinois---Illinois Beach State Park
> Michigan---Orchard Beach State Park
> Minnesota---McCarthy Beach State Park
> New York---Verona Beach State Park and 6 other similar
>   parks.
> Oregon---Harris Beach State Park, Short Sand Beach State
>   Park and South Beach Wayside
> Rhode Island---Nausauket Beach State Park and Scarborough
>   Beach State Park
> South Carolina---Edisto Beach State Park and Myrthle
>   Beach State Park
> South Dakota---Hartford Beach State Park
> Wisconsin---Big Foot Beach State Park

Among state-owned or state-controlled recreational areas
other than state parks may be mentioned state waysides, which
"are small recreational areas developed as an adjunct to the
modern highway. In most of the states they are developed as
an integral part of the highway system. They provide the
motorist convenient places where he may stop for a scenic
view, a short period of rest and relaxation or a picnic lunch.
Twenty-five states reported 1,570 wayside areas, with a total
acreage of 5,357."[428] In fact, the state highways may by
themselves be regarded as recreational areas for the special
purpose of pleasure-driving, in the same manner as natural
and artificial watercourses and waterways are used for plea-
sure-boating. In some states, laws have been enacted authorizing state highway departments to make landscape improve-

ments of state highways by planting trees and shrubs and otherwise.[429] These improvements may of course include way-side development, but their overall purpose is to beautify the entire highway system of the state so as to make them attractive to tourists and pleasure-seekers. However, the highways are not built for the primary purpose of recreation. In 1934, the Department of Conservation of New Jersey rehabil-itated the 60-mile-long Delaware and Raritan Canal, which ceased operation in 1934, by rebuilding locks and control structures, dredging and walling, for the twofold purpose of carrying and selling water supply to industries at New Bruns-wick and of providing canoeing, fishing and swimming possi-bilities.[430] Of more interest is the State Riding and Hiking Trail of California. As of 31 August 1950, the state of Cal-ifornia had acquired rights of way over 608 miles of trails, which are located in the twelve counties. The entire Trail, if completed, is 877.5 miles.[431]

Facilities that are commonly provided in state parks are picknicking, camping and cabin-lodging, fishing, swimming, bathing, boating, hiking and sight-seeing. In some state parks, such as Aroostook, Bradbury Mt., and Camden State Park of Maine, Diamond Hill Recreational Area of Rhode Island and Rib Mountain State Park of Wisconsin, ski trails have been constructed.[432] Some state parks contain underground caves or caverns which attract great numbers of visitors each year. The Lewis and Clark Caverns State Park, 2,770 acres in area, as its name indicates, has 3.2 miles of caverns which consti-tute its principal recreational features.[433] In the Florida Caverns State Park of Florida, there is "a surprising net-work of underground passageways festooned with fantastic for-mations."[434] As many as six state parks (Alley Spring, Arrow Rock, Lake of the Ozarks, Meramec, Roaring River, and Wash-ington) of Missouri contain caves.[435] However, state parks generally lack other geologic and natural wonders comparable to those found in national parks.

The administration of state park systems (including parks and other recreational units) is discussed below under three headings, namely, (1) acquisition of the area, (2) improve-ment of the area, and (3) park management.

(1) Acquisition---Nearly all states have by statute vest-ed in the state park agencies the authority of acquiring lands for parks or other recreational areas. It is estimated that between 73,000 and 154,000 acres were acquired by the state park agencies each year from 1943 to 1948. In most cases the acquisition is effected through purchases; in other cases lands were acquired by donation, transfer from the Federal Government or from other state agencies, tax delinquency and lease. Purchase of Federal lands has been facilitated by an amendment of the Surplus Property Act passed 10 June 1948, sec. 1 (62 Stat. 350), under which Federal surplus lands may

be sold to states and local units for public parks for 50
percent of the fair value thereof.[436]

The authority of acquisition implies that of establishing
the park. In 1952 a Virginia act was passed (ch. 416) whereby "the Governor is also . . . authorized and empowered to
direct the discontinuance of the operation of any or all
state parks when in his judgement the public interest so requires." Such legislation completes the trend of establishing and abolishing special-use land areas by administrative
action.

The acquisition and also development of waysides are especially facilitated by the incorporation of this work in
the Federal-Aid State Highway Program. In the memorandum of
the Deputy Commissioner, Bureau of Public Roads, U. S. Department of Commerce, to the various division engineers of
the Bureau dated 22 March 1946, it is ruled that "plans, specifications, and estimates for highway projects on the Federal-
Aid highway system to be carried out under the Federal-Aid
Highway Act of 1944, including projects in urban areas, and
more particularly portions of the Federal-Aid highway system
included in the national system of interstate highways, should
include provision", among other things, for the "conservation
and protection of major landscape features such as desirable
trees, strips of woodland, weathered rock outcrops, springs,
shorelines, and natural sites for wayside development." It
would thus seem that the acquisition and development of waysides by state highway agencies are covered by the said Federal aid.

(2) Improvement---Much more emphasis has been placed on
water areas by state park agencies than by the National Park
Service in the development of parks under their respective
jurisdictions. In states destitute of natural lakes, artificial
lakes or reservoirs have been created by the construction of
dams or otherwise as an integral part of state park improvement program. For example, Virginia has built a reservoir of
141 acres in surface area on the Smith River (a tributary to
the Roanoke River) in Fairystone State Park.[437] When the Kansas Forestry Fish and Game Commission which also administers
state parks, in 1925 found that there is only one natural lake,
Lake Inman, in the entire state the said Commission initiated
a program of the construction of artificial lakes in the various state parks. It was reported in 1950 that lake-side pic-
nics, rides and drives existed in twenty-two state parks.[438]
During the biennium ending 30 June 1950, the Conservation Commission of Iowa constructed two recreational reservoirs of 400
and 70 acres each in surface area.[439] In Indiana, "legislative
action in the 1947 session provided the Department (of Conservation) with a million-dollar construction fund, the main projects being dams to create lakes in Versailles State Park and
in the Whitewater Memorial State Park. . ."[440] In states such

as Maine with abundance of natural lakes, the construction
of artificial lakes is of course unnecessary.[441]

The states have also paid due attention to the protection
of beaches, which is another point of park administration
that is not found with the National Park System. For example,
by an act of 1940 (ch. 52), as amended in 1950 (Laws 1951,
ch. 31), the Department of Conservation of New Jersey is authorized "to repair, reconstruct, or construct bulkheads, seawalls, break-waters, groins or jetties, beach-fills or dunes,
on any and every beach front along the Atlantic ocean, in the
state of New Jersey, or any beach front along the Delaware bay
and Delaware river, Raritan bay, and Sandy Hook bay, or at
any inlet or estuary or any inland waters adjacent to any inlet or estuary along the shores of the state of New Jersey,
to repair damages caused by erosion and storm, or to prevent
erosion of the beaches and to stabilize the inlets or estu-
aries." In Idaho, an act of 1950 (Laws 1950, E. S., ch. 61)
authorized the State Reclamation Engineer to construct outlet control works "to be located in Priest Lake . . . at a
level which will preserve for the use of the people, the beach,
boating and other recreational facilities which are now located on said lake." In 1952, the legislature of South Carolina
appropriated $200,000 to the State Highway Department for the
construction of groins and other structures to protect the
coastal beaches of that state (Acts 1952, No. 718, sec. 68,
inter. alia). The State Highway Department of Delaware has
been given similar authority by a number of special acts (L.
1943, chs. 27, 28; L. 1945, ch. 29; L. 1949, chs. 305, 311,
709).

These measures, it may be observed, are not limited to
state parks.[442] Examples may be also given of beach protection and beach construction that is wholly within the limits of state parks. One of these examples is the development
of the Endicott Rock State Park undertaken by the New Hampshire
State Forestry and Recreation Commission. The work was stim-
ulated by the project of the U. S. Corps of Engineers for the
dredging of the channel between Lake Winnipesaukee and Paugus
Bay. The State Planning and Development Commission "detailed
plans for construction of a rock fill jetty extending out from
the historic Endicott Rock. Arrangements were made with the
U. S. Army Engineers to dump the dredged sand inside the jetty
to improve and extend the existing beach. The Forestry and
Recreation Commission carried out the job of jetty construction
at a cost of $5,000. The result was an estimated $20,000 worth
of improvement accomplished for one-quarter of that cost."[443]
A similar work has been found with the Doheny Beach State Park
of California. "A project for the dredging of the basin at
the mouth of San Juan Creek, handled . . . by the Division of
Water Resources, was nearing completion by June 30, 1950.
Dredgings from the creek basin were deposited along the ocean
beach at the north side of the creek."[444] In both these in-

stances, however, the effect of beach protection was achieved
as an incident of the improvement of some watercourse. In
South Carolina, "two groins of creosoted timbers were constructed in the negro area at Hunting Island State Park. The
State Highway Department supervised the Construction as they
are in charge of all groin work . . . . These groins have
stabilized an excellent beach front and bathing use has mounted several fold."[445] In New Jersey, there was project at
Swartswood Park of constructing an artificial beach, which
"includes 300 feet of sand beach, safety float lines and a
large float complete with four ladders, life guard stand and
two spring boards." On 30 June 1947 the project was about
80 percent complete, and it should have been completed by
1950.[446] The same state in 1943 "constructed a timber groin,
250 feet in length, as part of its program for beach protection along the southerly shore of Sandy Hook Bay."[447]

During the fiscal year ending 30 June 1952, the Department of Natural Resources of Ohio, through the Division of
Shore Erosion, completed the construction of beach protection
works in Avon Lake Village, Lakeview and Century Parks. The
works built at Avon Lake Village Park consist of groins in
front of its lake front. "Each of the groins is approximately
100 feet in length and spaced 100 feet on centers. About 500
feet of beach is being protected by this construction. In
addition to the groin construction, the bank was armored a-
gainst wave attack with a precast concrete slab pavement.
The Project cost $47,578.24, with the village paying one-
third of this amount." "The work at Lakeview Park consisted
of constructing a stone block groin near the west property
line, placing stone tees across lake ends of the groins and
making repairs to existing groins. At Century Park tees were
placed across the lakeward ends of groins and repairs made
to existing groins." Total cost for these two improvements
amounted to $111,683.30, one-third of which was contributed
by the City of Lorain.[448] For the biennium ending 30 June
1952, the same Department, through the Division of Parks,
constructed five beaches and acquired five miles of beach and
shore line on Lake Erie for public use.[449]

A peculiar type of state park improvement work has been
conducted by the State of Ohio through the Department of
Natural Resources. This is the regular dredging of lakes in
the state park system, which is done by the personnel and
with the equipment of the Department.[450]

The construction of access roads is, as with the administration of the National Park System, an important aspect of
state park administration. However, no statistics is available as to the achievements of the several states in this
particular matter.

(3) Service management: Ordinarily it is the state that

builds and operates picknic areas, campsites, cabins, bath-
houses and swimming and boating facilities in state parks,
but hotel, cafeteria, cafe and similar services are as a rule
operated by concessionaires.[451]

Section 7   Hydroelectric Power Development

Single-purpose enterprise of hydroelectric power development exists in law or in fact only in New York, Arizona, Washington and Oklahoma.   In New York, a law of 1931 (Laws 1931,
ch. 772: Public Authorities Law, art. 5, tit. 1) created the
Power Authority of the State of New York, whose duty it is
to improve the navigation and develop hydroelectric power of
the International Rapids of the St. Lawrence River in cooperation with the Federal Government and Canada.   As will be discussed later, since the work of navigation improvement is to
be assumed by the Federal Government and Canada, the Authority
can only engage itself in single-purpose power development.
On 15 July 1953 the said Authority was granted a license for
this enterprise by the Federal Power Commission (Project No.
2000), and on 4 November 1953 additional permission was given
by Executive Order 10500 (18 F. R. 7005).   The construction
of this enterprise, the cost of which was estimated to be
about $600 million, was started on 10 August 1954, simultan-
eously with its counterpart in Canada, and will be placed in
operation in 1958.[452]

The **Arizona** Power Authority was established in 1944 (Laws
1944, 2nd sp. sess., ch. 32: Code, ch. 75, art. 19).   Although
by law the Authority may generate electric energy by itself, actually it only purchases power from the Bureau of Reclamation
of the Federal Government.   It has also leased the necessary
transmission facilities from the same Bureau, though it has
the statutory authority to construct is own transmission facilities.   Power is sold at wholesale.   For the fiscal year
ending 30 June 1953, a total of 1,051,813,910 kilowatt-hours
of energy was sold by the Authority.   Of this amount, about
43.3 percent was sold to private utilities, and the remainder
to municipalities, power and irrigation districts and non-
profit cooperatives.[453]

In Washington, a law of 1953 (ch. 281) created the State
Power Commission and charged it with the functions of generating and selling hydraulic and fuel electric energy and, in
case of hydro-electric energy, of maintaining and operating
incidental navigation, flood control, reclamation and fish-
protection facilities, if any of these facilities are provided
by the Commission.   The Commission may choose not to generate
electric energy itself, but only to sell energy produced by
the Federal Government or by a city or public utility district.
However, should it elect to construct hydroelectric power generation projects, it has priority over the cities and utility
districts.   It is interesting to note that in case the Commis-

sion decides on power generation by itself, the construction and operation work need not be directly undertaken by the commission. "Any two or more cities or (public utility) districts may with the consent of the commission form an operating agency of the state power commission for the purpose of acquiring, constructing, operating and owning plants, systems and other facilities and extensions thereof for generation and (or) transmission of electric energy." Revenue bonds may be issued by the Commission to finance the construction work.

The Oklahoma Planning and Resources Board has, under statute, authority to develop hydroelectric power when private development is inadequate or unsatisfactory (Statutes, tit. 82, sec. 482, subsec. (7): Laws 1927, ch. 70, sec. 3). It would seem that this authority has not as yet been invoked.

Section 8 Water Supply and Water Conservation

1. Water Supply---State water-supply enterprise has been found in Louisiana only.[454] On 1 July 1952 an act Act No. 191) was passed which authorized the Atchafalaya Basin and Lafourche Basin Levee Districts each to contribute $250,000 toward the construction of a pumping plant at the head of Bayou Lafourche, in the vicinity of Donaldsonville, with which to convey fresh water from the Mississippi River to Bayou Lafourche, and thus to relieve the said districts of existing and future obligations imposed upon them by state laws to maintain a fresh-water supply in Bayou Lafourche. This act, however, did not designate the agency which was to construct the said pumping plant. On 10 July 1952, another act was passed (Act No. 566) authorizing the Department of Public Works to construct such a pumping plant and appropriating $400,000 for the fiscal years 1952-1954 for this purpose. Thus the construction of this pumping plant became a state enterprise. Construction was subsequently started, and was scheduled to be completed by "the fall of 1954 if additional funds are provided and unforseen difficulties do not arise to delay its completion." When completed, the pumping plant "will be turned over to the Board of Commissioners of the Bayou Lafourche District for operation and maintenance."[455]

In 1948, an act was passed by the Louisiana legislature which authorized the Department of Public Works to construct dams and other works within the boundaries of the Anacoco Prairie State Game and Fish Refuge partly to serve the purposes of the Refuge and partly to "create and impound an industrial water supply . . ." In 1950, authorization was made and moneys were appropriated for the construction of dams in Grand and Vernon Parishes (Acts Nos. 243 and 259 of 1950).[456] The exact nature and progress of these dams have not been ascertained by the author.

In South Dakota a law was passed in 1935 (Laws 1935, ch.

213: <u>Code</u>, ch. 61.05) which gave the State Geologist the
authority to drill or acquire, with the approval of the Governor, one or more artesian wells in the various areas of
the state and to lease, also with the approval of the Governor, the water so developed to persons, firms, corporations
or associations for irrigation, stock-watering and other uses.
"It was contemplated that these wells would be used as centers for watering stock, primarily." However, ". . .no such
well was ever drilled . . ." "The artesian fever that apparently hit the state when this water supply was new has died
down since it has been discovered that the supplies are limited and the artesian head is lowering rather rapidly."[457]

2. <u>Water Conservation</u>---In 1881, the State of New York
constructed the Old Forge (0.9 billion cubic feet) and Sixth
Lake (0.3 billion cubic feet) Reservoirs on the Middle Branch
of the Moose River (a tributary of the Black River) "in part
compensation to the water powers of the Black River for water
diverted from the river at Forestport to the Erie Canal."
But in 1920 the operation of these two reservoirs was turned
over by the State Conservation Commission to the Black River
Regulating District.[458]

"During the period from 1930 through 1941, the States of
Minnesota and North Dakota constructed, with financial aid
from various unemployment agencies, a large number of water-
conservation projects consisting chiefly of lake outlet-con-
trol structures in Minnesota and detention dams on tributary
streams in North Dakota. In general, the dams are low-head
concrete or masonry structures of standard design. Those in
North Dakota total approximately 95 and are primarily designed
to retain low flows for conservation and municipal water supply. In contrast, the average low dam in the Minnesota portion of the basin (Red River of the North) includes one or
more stop log bays permitting regulation of lake levels, varying from 2 to 5 feet. Approximately 50 dams of this type
were constructed under the supervision of the State of Minnesota . . ."[459]

In Louisiana a sum of $25,000 was appropriated in 1948
to the Department of Public Works to repair a dam on Iatt
Lake in Grant Parish or to construct a new dam in place thereof, in order "to conserve and retain waters in said lake."
In 1950, $100,000 was appropriated to the same Department
(Act No. 126) for the construction and improvement of Lake
Martin in St. Martin Parish and Lake Charlo in St. Martin
and Lafayette Parishes. The Water Resources Board of New
Hampshire has the authority to repair dams to undertake
stream clearance and channel improvement with view to regulating the levels of lakes, ponds and streams in the state (<u>Re-
vised Laws of New Hampshire</u>, ch. 266, sec. 22 et seq.: Laws
1951, ch. 235, sec. 1). Small sums of money have been appropriated for this work (Laws 1951, ch. 235, sec. 2: L. 1953,
ch. 287).

As for underground water conservation, the legislature of Idaho in 1939 appropriated $1,500 to the Department of Reclamation to cap the flowing wild wells in Oneida (Laws 1939, ch. 258). Under a law of 1945 (Laws 1945, ch. 136), the State Engineer of Utah may plug, repair or otherwise control artessian wells on both state and private lands which are wasting public waters.[460] In 1935, the Oklahoma Planning and Resources Board was authorized and directed "to begin the capture and impounding of flowing streams as near as practicable at the head of the stream sought to be captured, and shall construct canals, pipes, conduits, etc., to conduct such conserved waters to the uplands, and there impound and (or) distribute the same into the soil, if not otherwise utilized, to the end that the greatest restoration of the ground water and water supply be availed . . ." (Statutes, tit. 82, sec. 488: Laws 1935, ch. 70, art. 3, sec. 11).

In an act of 1952 (No. 554) the legislature of Louisiana appropriated $100,000 for the fiscal years 1952 and 1953 to the Department of Wildlife and Fisheries for the removal of water hyacinth and alligator grasses from the waters of the state. A like sum of money was appropriated by the legislature of New Mexico in an act of 1953 (Laws 1953, ch. 164) to the State Engineer for the biennium ending 30 June 1955 to eliminate water-consuming plants in the Rio Grande. This is another type of water-conservation work.[461]

Water may be incidentally conserved in state (and of course local) highway construction. An Ohio law of 11 August 1949 provides that the State Highway Department (and also a city or county), in constructing highways, may construct dams and reservoirs for water conservation upon the request of the Division of Water of the Department of Natural Resources. A similar law was enacted in Virginia in 1952 (Acts 1952, ch. 499). It is provided that "whenever any highway is being constructed and the highway is to pass over any stream or low land the obstruction of which is necessary to such construction, or if the present highway construction can be utilized to provide a suitable dam for a fish pond or water storage area, then upon application of the adjacent property owner. . . the state highway commission may permit such use, provided that . . . any additional cost incurred thereby shall be borned by such property owner."

Section 9 Water Sanitation

1. Water Pollution Control---In Kansas, the State Conservation Commission, upon complaint of any party concerned, may plug an ownerless abandoned oil or gas well found to cause or to be likely to cause the pollution of underground water supplies (General Statutes, secs. 55-139 and 55-140: Laws 1949, ch. 308, secs. 1 and 2; as amended by L. 1953, ch. 284, sec. 2). In Texas a law was enacted in 1953 (Laws 1953, ch.

141) which directed the State Board of Water Engineers "to
forthwith cap or plug any and all improperly plugged oil wells
now flowing salt water into the Frio River and contaminating
the fresh water supply of Frio River which is being used as
a water supply for the city of Caaliham and other domestic
uses . . ." Both these measures are directed at underground
water sources.

Iowa seems to be the only state in which there has been
state enterprise for the control of pollution of surface waters. In 1939, the State of Iowa sponsored a Federal Works
Progress Administration project called the "Iowa Great Lakes
Sewage Disposal System", located in Dickinson County. It
consists of a sewage treatment plant and a number of intercepting sewers, and serves the towns of Spirit Lake, Okoboji
and Arnolds Park. The project was completed on 4 October
1939, and had since been operated by the State Conservation
Commission until 1 May 1952, when it was transferred to the
Great Lakes Sanitary District under sec. 4 of ch. 13 of Acts
1951. At the time of this transfer, the project was capable
of disposing of about 200,000 gallons of sewage per month.
The costs incurred by the State of Iowa in the operation of
this project totalled $200,639.44. In 1953, the state legis-
lature appropriated a sum of $25,000 for the treatment or elim-
ination of blue-green algae in Storm Lake in Buena Vista County (Acts 1953, ch. 16). Blue-green algae reportedly contam-
inate the waters for domestic uses, and their elimination is
therefore a measure of water-pollution control.[462]

2. _Mosquito Control_---In 1933, mosquito-control work was
carried on by the State of New Jersey in two counties, with
labor provided by the Civilian Conservation Corps of the Federal Government.[463] The State of Rhode Island, through its
Department of Agriculture and Conservation, has since 1945
constructed and maintained mosquito-control ditches and carried
on mosquito-spraying work on small areas of state-owned lands[464]
In Connecticut, the statute provides that the Board of Mosquito
Control "may enter upon any swamp, marsh or other land to ascertain if mosquitoes breed thereon, or to survey, drain, fill
or otherwise treat, or make any excavation or structures necessary to eliminate mosquitoes breeding on such lands", and that
"whenever any swamp, marsh or other land shall have been drained to the approval of the board of mosquito control, said
board shall keep the same in repair and free from obstruction
and construct or repair tide gates or otherwise treat such
areas so as to make such work effective" (_General Statutes_,
secs. 3859 and 3860: Acts 1915, ch. 264; as last amended in
1939). The State Highway Department of Delaware, under a law
of 1945, may enter upon public or private property to eliminate mosquitoes as nuisances (_Code_, tit. 16, ch. 19: Laws 1945,
ch. 271) (in sec. 2).

By an act of 1929 (Acts 1929, ch. 288), the Reclamation

Board of Massachusetts was authorized to undertake mosquito-
control enterprise under the provisions of the above-discussed state drainage laws. Initial operations conducted under
the authority of this act consisted in the installtion of
3,500 miles of ditches on 265 square miles of salt marsh.
Other mosquito-control works have been performed on fres-
water or ordinary wetlands in the following projects:[465]

Year	Project	Area
1930	Cape Cod project	All of Barnstable County.
1945	Berkshire project	All of Berksire County.
1945	East Middlesex project	130 square miles in Middesex County.
1953	South Shore project	140 square miles in Norfold and Plymouth Counties.

Section 10 Land and Soil Management

        The states own both real-estate and sovereign lands.
The former consist of (1) state public domain, (2) lands
granted and sold to the several states by the Federal Government, and (3) lands acquired from private persons, including
the tax-delinquent lands. In their sovereign capacity, the
states own the so-called "submerged lands", which include
beaches of coastal and inland waters and banks and beds of
inland waters. (1) and (2) of state real-estate lands are
mutually exclusive. The thirteen original states and Texas
and Kentucky have (1), but not (2).[466] With respect to category (2) lands, most of them have been sold out by the several states for purposes designated by the Federal Government
at the time of transfer. Only a few states now own these
lands in considerable acreages.[467] In 1945, California owned
about 800,000 acres;[468] in 1951, Alabama owned about 139,450
acres.[469] Tax-delinquent lands are lands owned by private
persons which passed into government ownership as a result of
non-payment of property taxes. Tax-delinquency began from
the time of the First World War and continued with increased
severity through the depression of the 1930's.[470] It was
accompanied by mass migration of farm labor to the urban areas.
The owners of cut-over land, mostly land speculators, finding
no settlers to buy the land, failed to pay the taxes thereon,
thus forcing the state and local governments to assume ownership thereto.[471] "This 'new public domain' becomes state
property in 19 states, county property in 23, and in the six
New England States it reverts to the towns. There is no
accurate record of the area owned by these units of government because of tax delinquency, but it probably amounts to
50 million acres."[472] Tax-delinquency still continues, but
at a reduced rate. In Michigan, for example, in 1939-1950,
a total of 2,671,153.52 acres of land reverted to the Department of Conservation because of tax delinquency, of which 2,-
208,975.00 acres were abandoned in 1939.[473]

The acreages of submerged lands and the uses to which they are devoted in the several states are shown in the following table:[474]

Approximate areas and present uses of submerged lands within State boundaries

[Expressed in acres]

State	Inland waters [1]	Great Lakes [2]	Marginal sea [2]	Present uses and revenues include—
Alabama	239,840		101,760	Sand, gravel, shell, oysters, oil and gas leases.
Arizona	240,560			Sand and gravel.
Arkansas	241,280			84,641 acres under oil and gas lease; sand and gravel.
California	1,508,600		2,540,860	Oil, gas, sand, gravel, kelp, and shell.
Colorado	179,200			Sand, gravel, and gold.
Connecticut	70,400		281,000	50,000 acres of marginal sea under lease; shell fish, sand, gravel, oysters, clams, mussels.
Delaware	70,560		53,760	Oyster bed leases, sand, gravel.
Florida	2,750,720		4,697,600	903,000 acres of Gulf of Mexico under lease. 2,748,000 acres of land under inland waters and under lease; oil, gas, sand, gravel, sponges, oysters.
Georgia	229,120		192,000	Sand and shell, approximately 1,000 acres of land in marginal sea leased.
Idaho	479,360			Sand and gravel. 1,302.96 acres under lease for gold and gravel.
Illinois	280,920	976,640		Sand, gravel, coal, and clay.
Indiana	55,040	145,920		Sand, gravel, coal, oil, mussel shells, peat, and marl. The revenue during 1918-19 included: sand and gravel, $50,565.68; oil, $101,413.51; coal, $4,455.56.
Iowa	188,160			Sand and gravel, coal, stone, ice, shell.
Kansas	104,320			Sand, gravel, oil, and gas. 6,944.96 acres of submerged lands under mineral leases.
Kentucky	185,040			Fish, mussel, shells, coal, gas, oil, sand and gravel.
Louisiana	2,141,440		2,668,160	Sand, gravel, oysters, and other marine products. 2,191,179 acres under lease in coastal waters.
Maine	1,392,600		759,680	Kelp, clams, lobsters, mussels, fish. Total income of $14,000,000.
Maryland	441,600		59,520	Oil and gas leases on entire marginal sea. Receive $20,557 annual rentals.
Massachusetts	224,600		368,640	Clams, lobsters, mussels, sand, rock.
Michigan	764,160	21,645,760		Leases cover oil and gas, sand and gravel.
Minnesota	2,597,760	1,415,680		Sand, gravel, clay.
Mississippi	189,440		136,320	Sand, gravel, oyster shell.
Missouri	258,560			Sand and gravel.
Montana	526,080			Do.
Nebraska	373,760			Do.
Nevada	475,520			Do.
New Hampshire	179,200		8,960	Kelp leases, sand and shell.
New Jersey	200,960		249,600	$55,000,000 improvements below high-water mark, including Atlantic City piers.
New Mexico	99,200			Sand and gravel.
New York	1,054,080	2,321,280	243,840	Recreation beaches, surf; removal of sand and earth. Millions of improvements on filled-in lands.
North Carolina	2,284,800		577,920	Oysters, shellfish, clams, sand, seaweed, shrimp.
North Dakota	301,040			Sodium sulphate, good prospects for oil, sand and gravel. Revenues dedicated to school fund.
Ohio	64,000	2,212,480		Sand and gravel.
Oklahoma	470,040			Mineral leases, sand and gravel.
Oregon	408,840		568,320	Sand and gravel, oil, gas, kelp.
Pennsylvania	184,320	470,400		Oil sands, clays, and coals.
Rhode Island	99,840		76,800	Sand, gravel, oysters.
South Carolina	295,040		359,040	Sand and gravel. All lands leased for oil and gas explorations.
South Dakota	327,040			Sand and gravel. Possibility of oil under submerged lands.
Tennessee	182,400			Sand and gravel.
Texas	2,364,800		2,466,560	Sand, gravel, oysters, shell, shrimp, sulfur, oil, and gas.
Utah	1,644,800			Mineral leases for salt; sodium sulphate, oil and gas.
Vermont	211,840			Sand, gravel, and quarries.
Virginia	886,240		215,040	Sand, gravel, oysters.
Washington	777,600		300,800	Placer gold, gold, copper, lead, silver, zinc, coal, limestone, marl, peat and salines, sand and gravel, and rentals on 130 oil and gas leases; 1 producing oil well in the tidelands area.
West Virginia	88,240			Sand and gravel, and prospecting for coal, oil and gas.
Wisconsin	920,960	6,439,680		Sand, gravel and marl.
Wyoming	261,120			Sand and gravel.
Total (expressed in acres)	28,060,640	38,595,840	17,029,120	

[1] Areas of the United States, 1940, Sixteenth Census of the United States (Government Printing Office, 1942), p. 2 et seq. The figures are very approximate but are absolute minimums.

[2] World Almanac and Book of Facts for 1947, published by the New York World-Telegram (1947), p. 138; serial No. 22, Department of Commerce, U. S. Coast and Geodetic Survey, November 1945. In figuring marginal sea area, only original State boundaries have been used. These coincide with the 3-mile limit for all States except Texas, Louisiana, and Florida Gulf coast. In the latter cases, the 3-league limit as established before or at the time of entry into the Union has been used.

It has already mentioned that the title of the state to submerged land may be transferred to private riparian owners. There can be no doubt that it, too, can be transferred to counties and cities, which are but political subdivisions of the state.[475]

The disposition of state lands which were transferred
from the Federal Government is subject to the Federal laws
making such transfer, which usually containing provisions
stipulating the manner (public auction, invariably) and sometimes minimum prices of sale and the terms of lease, sale
and lease for revenue being the only means of disposition
allowable.[476] These provisions are in general incorporated
in state constitutions. Some tax-delinquent lands have also
been sold as homesteads and leased for grazing purposes. But
it seems that the major part of these lands are reserved by
the states as state forests, state parks and state wildlife
refuges and management areas; for there are very few people
willing to buy lands abandoned by others.[477] Submerged sovereign lands are usually leased for sand, gravel, clay, oil
and gas and shellfish collection or production, as shown in
the above table. In some instances, as in Tennessee and
Washington submerged lands were sold or are subject to sale,
in the same way as real-estate lands. It would seem that
this is an exception rather than a rule.[478]

State soil conservation projects are of piecemeal nature,
except that the acquisition of tax-delinquent lands for non-
agricultural uses as discussed above may be regarded as large-
scale program of submarginal land retirement. But the effect
of soil conservation obtained in this manner is entirely incidental. A regular and planned program of submarginal land
retirement program was initiated by New York in 1931. This
was already mentioned before and will not be repeated. A
few states have paid due attention to watershed management.
In Utah,for example, the State Land Board may acquire watersheds which are being made barren by over-utilization and promote revegetation thereof (Code, sec. 65-1-75: Laws 1925, ch.
31, sec. 1) (4th sentence). Iowa Conservation Commission has
constructed many protective works, including detention reservoirs and terraces, on state-owned lands in a number of watersheds, with necessary cooperation of the owners of nearby private lands. Some of the detention dams and reservoirs were
built with labor provided by the Civilian Conservation Corps
of the Federal Government in the 1930's.[477] With funds granted by the Federal Government for the improvement of fish habitat, "Wisconsin has under way a project to enhance stream fish
habitat by improving land-use practices in the watersheds of
12 streams . . . . This project should make a significant
contribution to one aspect of the broad soil-conservation problem."[480]

Section 11 Multiple-Purpose Projects and River-Basin Develop-
           ment

It seems that no state has constructed an independent multiple-purpose project.[481] With respect to state river-basin

development, there is only one example. It is the enterprise
of the South Carolina Public Service Authority. A number of
other river-basin-development programs, which are substantially similar to this enterprise, technically do not belong
to the state, but are enterprises of special districts, which
will be discussed later.

The activities of the South Carolina Public Service Authority centers around the Santee-Cooper power and navigation
project, which is a multiple-purpose project. The navigation
phase of this project dates back to 1771, when the Province
of South Carolina mapped a canal connecting the Santee and
Cooper Rivers. In 1786 the Company for the Inland Navigation
from Santee to Cooper River was chartered by the state legislature. Work was started in 1793, and the canal was completed in July 1800 at a cost of $750,000. "It was 22 miles long,
35 feet wide, at the surface of the water, and had a minimum
depth of 4 feet. There were ten locks, all built of brick or
stone. For more than 50 years the Santee Canal served as an
important transportation route but development and competition of railroads finally forced its abandonment. Rebuilding
to conform to modern needs was considered frequently, but
nothing concrete materialized until conception of a plan to
combine hydro-electric power development with the navigation
feature. A general investigation was made in 1951 by Maj.
Thomas B. Lee, who declared a navigation and hydro-electric
project was feasible and practical. In 1926 the Columbia
Railway and Navigation Co. secured a license and permit from
the Federal Power Commission to generate electricity by water
power in the Santee-Cooper basin. The subsequent national
depression prevented carrying out the plan. In 1933 a movement was begun in Charleston to have the Santee-Cooper project built and operated under public control. This culminated
in the passage by the state legislature in 1934 of the act
setting up the South Carolina Public Service Authority to
direct the construction and operations (act 887 of 1934: Code
of Laws, ch. 163-B)."482

Besides the principal duties of navigation improvement
and hydro-electric power development, the Authority is invested with the authority "to reclaim and drain swampy and flood-
ed lands", "to reforest the water sheds of the Cooper, Santee
and Congaree Rivers to prevent soil erosion and floods" and
"to investigate, study and consider all undeveloped power sites
and navigation projects in the State . . . (on) the Congaree
River and its tributaries below . . .Camden . . ." It is evident that the work of the Authority is the multiple-purpose
development of three interconnected river-basins. The Santee-
Cooper Navigation and Power Project is the principal multiple-
purpose project of this program. With the financial assistance
of the Works Progress Administration of the Federal Government,
construction of this project was commenced in September 1935.
By an act of 1939, the acquisition by the Authority of the Fed-

eral Power Commission license of the Columbia Railway and
Navigation Co. was approved. The project involves the construction of three dams, namely, the West Pinopolis Dam, the
East Pinopolis Dam and the Santee Dam and some 30 miles of
dikes, which impound two reservoirs, namely, Lake Moultrie
and Lake Marion. These two reservoirs have a total gross capacity of 2,460,000 acre-feet, of which 1,630,000 acre-feet
are active. The original power house and the lock are built
on the Pinopolis Dam. The former accommodates five 40,000
horse-power and one 13,300 horse-power turbines which drive
four 34,000 kilovolt-ampere and one 11,350 kilovolt-ampere
generators. The lock is 1,010 feet in height with a lift of
75 feet, and is the highest navigation lock in the world.[483]
"In September 1949, South Carolina Public Service Authority
filed an application for amendment of license for its Santee-
Cooper project to authorize the construction as a part of the
project of a power plant at the spillway of the Santee Dam.
Although the proposed construction is not of special importance as to size, it is of interest because it will utilize
the water required by the license to be released continuously
down the Santee River in the interest of navigation which
other wise would be wasted without generating any power."[484]
Amendment of the license was authorized on June 20, 1950."[484]
Besides the two hydro plants, the Authority has also constructed a steam power plant of a capacity of 96,000 kilowatts, which
was scheduled to be completed by the summer of 1953.[485]

As a part of its river-basin program, the Authority have
provided shooting, fishing and other recreational services on
the water and land areas under its control, established an
extensive reforestation program, and carried out an active
program of mosquito-control.[486]

Article 3   Assistance to Private Persons

State assistance to private persons is generally non-
financial. One of the most significant fields in which state
assistance is available is forestry extension work, undertaken, in general, under the stimulus of and with financial
assistance provided by sec. 5 of an Act (Clarke-McNary of 7
June 1924 (43 Stat. 653, 654), as amended. The work is carried by the state agricultural extension service (which is
the state university or state college) in each state, and consists of the dissemination of necessary information through
all available means of mass education regarding the management
of farm forests and woodlots, particularly tree-planting,
which is performed by a extension forester with the help of
county extension agents and local community organizations.
As of 30 June 1952, 45 states and the Territory of Puerto Rico
each employed one or more extension foresters to carry out
this program.[487]

In some states, laws have been passed authorizing state

forestry agencies (and not extension services) to render actual technical services and advices (and not merely educational
work) to owners of forests and farm-woodlots (and not merely
farmers). For example, the Department of Forests and Parks
of Maryland, by an act of 1941, was authorized to give advice
to tenants or property owners in the vicinity of wooded areas
in Hartford County "as to the means and methods of safely
conducting fires in the open air for the purpose of burning
grass, weeds, leaves, brush, stumps, logs, fallen timber,
slash, debris, rubbish or other inflammable material" In
New York, the Department of Conservation may furnish technical
services to private forest land owners in forest operation,
including timber marketing, reforestation, etc., provided
that the latter agree to comply with forestry practices to
be prescribed by the district forest practice board concerned
(there being 20 districts in the state), as approved by the
State Forest Practice Board and the Commissioner of Conservation (Laws 1946, ch. 52; as last amended by L. 1949, ch. 148).
An act was passed in Virginia in 1946 which authorized the
State Forester to provide technical services with respect to
the cutting and marketing of timber and other forest products
to forest land owners, at a charge equivalent to 10 percent
of the sales of the products removed (Code, tit. 9, ch. 4,
art. 3: Forestry Practice Act of 1946). This Virginia act
was reproduced in North Carolina and Arkansas in 1947, with
a change to the effect that the charge of the state services
is 5 instead of 10 percent of the timber sales. In Arkansas,
services performed on lands not more than 80 acres in area
are free of charge.[488] Similar state services to be performed at cost are also available in Indiana (Acts 1919, ch. 60),
Kentucky (Acts 1948, ch. 204) and South Dakota (Laws 1953,
ch. 115). Under an act of 1952, the State of Virginia undertakes to give technical assistance to forest land owners for
the control of forest pests (Code, sec. 10-90.5: Acts 1952,
ch. 657).

In other states, the availability of state technical assistance in forestry is based on general statutory authority, or
is implied. It is on this basis that the district foresters
of Michigan give advice to forest land owners on management
methods, and assist them in the marking and sale of mature
trees and in reforestation.[489] Similar assistance is provided
by Wisconsin, Connecticut, Missouri and many other states.[490]

Many states provide assistance to private persons in activities in fish and wildlife conservation and recreation.
One form of assistance is the provision of materials for the
fencing of agricultural lands against damages by big game
animals. In Washington, for example, "the twenty-eighth Regular Session of the State Legislature passed a bill authorizing the State Game Commission to enter into cooperative agreements with land owners for the fencing of agricultural and
horticultural lands where deer and elk could not be controlled

by seasons. The Thirtieth Session of the Legislature appropriated $70,000 for the prevention of deer and elk damage."491
". . . The Game Department furnishes the materials and the
land owners do the actual building."492   Similar work has
been performed by the Game and Fish Department of Colorado in
many areas in the western part of the state.493   In Pennsylvania the provision of this kind of material assistance is
provided for in the state game law (secs. 1301 and 1302),
which also provides for state payment of damages done by
bears on lands open to public hunting (sec. 1303).   Under
the state fencing assistance program of Oregon, which was
initiated in 1949, the State Game Commission "agrees to reimburse cooperative landowners at the rate of $2.50 per rod
of fence completed according to specifications. The present
cost of fencing materials, exclusive of posts, averages approximately $2.00 per rod. The landowner pays for the cost of
posts above the remaining fifty cents and furnishes all labor."494   Here financial assistance is provided in lieu of
material assistance.

Another type of state assistance to private persons in
connection with game administration is related to habitat improvement projects. For game habitat on the private land in
the pheasant range of southern Michigan. The project operates
under a simple agreement between the landowner and the Department (of Conservation) in which the Department furnishes technical assistance, planting stock, and materials, and the farmer does the planting and agrees to protect the improvement
for a specified period."495

State assistance available to private fishery program may
be explained by the following quotation from the Annual Report
1951-1952 of the Missouri Conservation Commission (at p. 35):496

> Seventy-five service calls were made during
> the current fiscally year. And, in addition, a
> number of local calls were made to ponds and lakes
> in Boone County, Callaway County, and Cole County.
> Moreover, on-the-spot advice was given to many pond
> owners when scheduled service calls were being made.
>   Service calls have included the following types
> of services:
>
> 1.   Advice on minnow hatchery construction and
>   development. 2
> 2.   Advice on development of trout management
>   area .4
> 3.   Advice on construction of fishing lakes. . .4
> 4.   Aquatic vegetation problems. 5
> 5.   Partial renovation 3
> 6.   Complete renovation. 5
> 7.   Investigation of fish kills. 3
> 8.   Investigation of parasitized or diseased
>   fish .2

An interesting program was initiated by the Department of
Conservation of Michigan in July 1950 for the improvement of
the Rifle River watershed in the interest of trout fishing.
Appropriations have been made available for four years in the
amount of $50,000 a year. Actual work of improvement is done
by private farmers, but the State Department of Conservation
furnishes technical aid and assistance, labor, heavy machinery,
planting stock and other paterials needed, and also makes
recommendations to the various classes of land owners in the
watershed area.[497]

State assistance to private agencies and institutions
concerned with public recreation consists in the giving of
advice in the planning of recreation activities, which has,
however, an indirect bearing on water resources management.[498]

Some states provide general engineering services to private persons and organizations, in connection with their activities in the management of water resources. In Nevada, for
example, in accordance with an act of 1947, the owners of water rights may ask the State Engineer to remove beaver dams
which interfere with their water rights. The furs of the beaver killed in such removal are to be disposed of by the state
engineer, but the proceeds paid to the owners. In Kansas,
as provided in an act of 1941 (Laws 1941, ch. 5: General Statutes, secs. 82a-411 et seq.), the Division of Water Resources
of the State Board of Agriculture, upon the request of any
landowner, may make surveys and prepare plans and specifications for the construction of dams and reservoirs capable of
impounding water to a depth of at least ten feet. In attempt
to control private wells, a law was passed by the Utah State
Legislature in 1945 (ch. 136) "which provided the State Engineer with funds for the purchase of necessary equipment and
authority on behalf of the State to enter into cooperative
agreements with the well owners (for well-sealing). The work
under this agreement has been designated as State Engineer's
Project 100-48-10. The State Engineer's Office has furnished
the equipment and the 'know how', while the well owner has
furnished the materials and other labor necessary."[499] A peculiar engineering service is performed by the State Water Conservation Board of Montana. As of 1952, it had furnished engineering service to 19 rural electrification cooperatives in
the construction of 10,108 miles or rural electrification
transmission lines, and had "engineered and supervised the
building of structures and other work for many districts and
private irrigation companies in the state".[500] ". . .This
work was done as far as possible on a cost basis" while instances are not lacking in which the state suffered a net
loss.[501]

As already mentioned at the beginning of this Article, the states generally are not in a position to furnish financial assistance to private persons. However, exceptions may occasionally be found. For example, the Lyman Water Company built the Lyman Dam in 1911. "About the year 1920, due to heavy floods down the Little Colorado River, upon which the reservoir is located, the dam failed. The water company was not financially able to rebuild the dam, but the State Legislature of Arizona came to the rescue by loaning the company $600,000, and taking a mortgage on all the lands, at that time supposed to be 15,000 acres to be irrigated from the reservoir. It was subsequently found that the water supply was sufficient for only about 4,000 acres, and that is the land now served by the reservoir. Naturally, the landowners were not able to discharge the debt to the State, and the mortgage on these lands were subsequently written off." So the loan became a grant.502

In Wyoming, a law of 1953 (Laws 1953, ch. 187) authorized the Natural Resources Board to make loans to local governmental units and private persons to finance water resources development projects, particularly small projects costing not more than $100,000. In Utah, an enactment of 1909 (amended 1921) authorized the State Land Board to make loans out of the "reservoir grant fund" to private irrigation corporations and associations for the construction of irrigation projects (Laws 1909, ch. 116, sec. 2; as amended by L. 1921, ch. 125, sec. 1: Code, of 1953, sec. 65-4-2). Under this law, loans were extended to two private irrigation companies. As these loans were never repaid, the irrigation loan law was repealed by the state legislature.503 In New Mexico, the State Department of Health may make money grants to mutual domestic water consumers' associations (organized in rural areas only) for the construction of domestic water-supply projects (Statutes, sec. 14-4557 et seq.: Laws 1947, ch. 206; as last amended by L. 1951, ch. 52). A total of sixty grants had been made by the end of October 1954, aggregating about $490,000. The grantees are in general required to provide certain amount of funds to match the state grants.504 The state grants, it may be noted, cover only costs of construction of the storage or diversion works but not those of works of distribution, for their primary purpose is to replace unsafe water supplies with safe supplies.505

NOTES

1. For Kentucky see p. 647, below.

2. The authority of the department in establishing harbor lines is alternative to similar authority of a city or a village.

3. See Revised Code of Washington, secs. 79.16.030, 79.16.040 and 79.16.050 (L. 1927, ch. 255, secs. 127, 128 and 129).

4. The New York Times, 22 November 1950.

5. Rpt. Chief of E. 1953, p. 9.

6. See President's Water Resources Policy Commission, Report, vol. II, pp. 127-128; 239-240; 321-322, etc.

7. Letter to the author from Mr. Gregory M. Hastings, Deputy Supervisor, Division of Flood Control, Washington Department of Conservation and Development, dated 10 March 1954.

8. Letter to the author from Mr. Robert L. Smith, Director, Iowa Natural Resources Council, dated 5 January 1954.

9. General Statutes, sec. 24-105. This act amended L. 1911, ch. 175, sec. 1, as amended by L. 1917, ch. 176, sec. 1, which did not provide for administrative action.

10. The action of the Superior Court is administrative and not judicial.

11. It may be noted that while in other states drainage is a state or local as well as private enterprise, in New York it is solely a private enterprise.

12. See Code of Alabama, tit. 22, sec. 118 (Acts 1919, No. 658, sec. 15, subdiv. 2; as amended by Acts 1943, No. 426); New Jersey Statutes, sec. 58:11-4 (L. 1909, ch. 253, sec. 4; as amended by L. 1915, ch. 378, sec. 1); Revised Civil Statutes of Texas, art. 4477-1, op. cit., sec. 11 (c); Revised Statutes of Illinois, ch. 111.5, sec. 121h.

13. Revised Civil Statutes of Texas, art. 4477-1, op. cit., sec. 11 (a); New Jersey Statutes, sec. 58:11-14 (L. 1918, ch. 23, sec. 2).

14. "Any other water supply" seems to refer to irrigation or stock-water supply.

15. Hudson County Water Co. v. Roberts H. McCarter, 209 U.S. 349.

16. Emphasis is supplied by the present author in all citations. It may be pointed out that the Idaho laws cited herein are not affected by L. 1951, ch. 200, as amended by L. 1953, ch. 182, which provides for the appropriation of underground waters under the priority rule. The cited Nevada provision belongs to the law providing for the priority appropriation of underground waters, but this provision is not part of the water-use regulation. The same law provides for the capping and casing of wells (both artesian and non-artesian). This latter provisions is also considered as a part of the water-use regulation, as it is imposed on the water-use permittees and not on the owners of the wells as such. The cited Texas provision, too, is part of the law governing administrative water-appropriation, although that provision is not part of the water-use regulation.

17. In Arizona, certain underground waters are subject to priority appropriation, but this appropriation is <u>not</u> governed by the Ground Water Laws of 1945, 1948 and 1953.

18. Arizona State Land Department, <u>Ground Water Manual</u>, April 1949, p. 7.

19. Cf. Laws of 1952, ch. 49.

20. See Laws of Utah of 1937, ch. 130, sec. 2 (as amended by L. 1941, ch. 96, sec. 1); Laws of Maryland of 1945, ch. 325, sec. 18; Laws of New Jersey of 1947, ch. 377 (as amended by L. 1951, ch. 261); Laws of New Mexico of 1949, ch. 178, sec. 1, etc.

21. There is no regulation for the conservation of surface waters in other states (as of the end of 1953).

22. <u>Connecticut v. Massachusetts</u>, 282 U. S. 660 (1931).

23. In fact, there is no written law on this subject.

24. <u>Colorado v. Kansas</u>, 320 U. S. 383 (1943). Also see, under the title, 316 U. S. 645; 319 U. S. 729; 320 U. S. 717; 321 U. S. 803; and 322 U. S. 708.

25. Leave of the Court for the filing of the suit was granted to Nebraska in <u>Nebraska v. Wyoming</u>, 293 U. S. 523 (1934); Wyoming's petition for the dismissal of Nebraska's equity bill was denied in <u>Nebraska v. Wyoming</u>, 295 U. S. 40 (1935); Colorado was impeached as a defendant in 296 U. S. 553; the United States was granted leave to intervene in 304 U. S. 545.

26. In dissenting, Justices Roberts, Frankfurter and Rutledge "think the decision constitutes a departure from principles long established and observed by the court in litigations between the states of the Union . . . . Without proof of actual damage in the past, or of any threat of substantial damage in the near future, the court now undertakes to assume jurisdiction over three quasi-sovereign states and to supervise uses of an interstate stream on the basis of past use . . ." (at 657).

27. But this compact did not provide for an apportionment of the waters of the Rio Grande.

28. Neither state shall construct a storage reservoir on this reach of the Sabine River without the consent of the other.

29. These compacts <u>must</u> conform to these standards, for in the last analysis they are all reviewable by the United States Supreme Court.

30. These laws evolved out the customs of the early miners in California which were voluntarily observed and enforced by the mining camps before they were recognized by the state courts and later by Federal courts. --- S. T. Harding, "Background of California Water and Power Problems", 38 <u>California Law Review</u> 551 (October 1950).

31. See <u>Clark v. Nash</u>, 198 U. S. 361, 370 (1905).

32. Some writers have abbreviated the term "prior appropriation" to "appropriation", which seems to be unwarranted. "Appropriation" is the taking or appropriation of water. "Prior appropriation" means appropriation of water in accordance with priority in making the appropriation, and "riparian appropriation" implies that appropriation of water is limited to riparian landowners.

33. Beginning with <u>Irwin v. Phillips</u>, 5 Cal. 140 (1855).

34. S. C. Wiel, "Fifty Years of Water Law", 50 Harvard Law Review 252-259 (December 1936).

35. S. C. Wiel, Water Rights in the Western States, 3rd ed., 1911, pp. 146-147.

36. Clark v. Nash, 198 U. S. 361 (1905); Kansas v. Colorado, 206 U. S. 46 (1907); Connecticut v. Massachusetts, 282 U. S. 660 (1931); California-Oregon Power Co. v. Beaver Portland Cement Co., 295 U. S. 142 (1935).

37. Elwood Mead, Irrigation Institutions, 1903, pp. 68-81.

38. Buam, Federal Power Commission and State Utility Regulation, 1942, p. 4.

39. See President's Water Resources Policy Commission, Report, vol. III, pp. 711-777.

40. In Idaho, lakes of a surface area of less than five acres are appurtenant to land and are not subject to appropriation. -- Idaho Code, sec. 41-206; Jones v. McIntire, 91 p.2d 373, 60 Idaho 338 (1939). In Texas, water-appropriation permits are not required for the impounding of not more than 200 acre-feet of water for domestic uses or for watering livestock. -- Texas Revised Statutes, art. 7500a: Acts 1925, ch. 136, sec. 5; as amended by Acts 1953, ch. 235; for background of this, see Ibid., art. 7492: Acts 1917, ch. 88, sec. 15. At the other extreme, permits are required in Oklahoma to appropriate even the seepage water from works constructed for the diversion and utilization of water appropriated from natural sources, in addition to the payment of reasonable charges therefor to the owner of the works. -- Oklahoma Statutes Annotated, tit. 82, sec. 102: Laws 1905, ch. 21, sec. 45.

41. But riparian rights obtained prior to the enactment of the prior appropriation laws continue to be valid.

42. For all above, see W. A. Hutchins, Selected Problems in the Laws of Water Rights in the West, 1942, p. 30.

43. See St. Germain Irrigation Co. v. Hawthorn Ditch Co. et al., 34 S. D. 260, 143 N. W. 124 (1913). Cf. North Dakota Laws of 1905, ch. 34, sec. 1, as amended by L. 1939, ch. 255, sec. 1.

44. See United States-Mexico Water Treaty of 1944 (Treaty Series No. 944), art. 4.

45. Laws 1915, ch. 36, sec. 1, as amended by L. 1953, ch. 48 (some 23 waterfalls near the Columbia River Highway from Sandy River to Hood River exempted, presumably in the interest of recreation); L. 1935, ch. 242, sec. 1 (Hackett Creek and its tributaries exempted, in the interest of fishery); L. 1935, ch. 273, sec. 1, as amended by L. 1953, ch. 221 (Johnson Creek reserved for fish protection); L. 1949, ch. 545, sec. 1, as amended by L. 1953, ch. 222 (six rivers and their tributaries reserved for fishery). Laws 1949, ch. 232, withdrew the lower portions of the Rogue River from appropriation for other uses than domestic and municipal water supply, stock watering and irrigation.

46. A complete list of gubernatorial proclamations making such withdrawals appears in the Report of the State Engineer of Utah For the Biennium 1948-1950, p. 20ff.

47. In Henry Winters v. U. S., 207 U. S. 564 (1908), the Supreme Court declared that the authority of the Federal Government to reserve

the waters of an Indian Reservation and exempt them from appropriation under the state laws "is not denied, and could not be" (at 577). If the Federal Government can withhold waters in Indian lands, over which it has only fiduciary rights, from the operation of state water-right laws, there would seem doubtless that the same reservation can be made by the Federal Government of the waters in lands owned by the Federal Government in fee simple.

48. U. S. v. Rio Grande Dam and Irrigation Co., 174 U. S. 690, 708 (1899).

49. The discussion of these is omitted in this book.

50. Elwood Mead, Irrigation Institutions, 1903, pp. 65-66. It may incidentally be noted that administrative appropriation of water is primarily concerned with water for irrigation. Consult Revised Code of Washington, sec. 90.20.110 (Laws 1917, ch. 117, sec. 35).

51. Letter to the author from Mr. H. A. Beckwith, Chairman, Board of Water Engineers of the State of Texas, dated 7 September 1951.

52. In Montana, "the right to conduct water from and over the land of another for any beneficial use includes the right to raise any water by means of dams, reservoirs, or embankments to a sufficient height to make the same available for the use intended . . ." (Revised Codes of Montana sec. 89-820: Civil Code of 1895, sec. 1894)

53. U. S. Corps of Engineers, North Pacific Division, Review Report on Columbia River and Tributaries, 1 October 1948, p. 11-52; California Water Code (Stats. 1943, ch. 368), sec. 1230 (first enacted, Stats. 1917, ch. 195, sec. 1).

54. Cf. City of Canton v. Shock et al., 66 Ohio 19; 63 N. E. 600, 602-603 (25 February 1902)

55. See Hutchins, op. cit., pp. 392-393.

56. Court confirmation is statutorily required in Oregon, Arizona and California. Texas laws provide that in case suit is brought in a court by the water users directly, the court may transfer it to the State Board of Water Engineers to be determined administratively.

57. In South Dakota only riparian water rights are subject to adjudication.

58. In California and Utah the state engineer may be asked by the courts to appoint referees. This is another form of assistance.

59. In Washington, by one or more water right claimants; in Utah, by five or more of majority of water users.

60. In Utah, water rights can also be settled through arbitration of the State Engineer, subject to the unanimous consent of all persons interested and the confirmation by a court decree. -- Code, sec. 73-2-16 (L. 1941, ch. 96, sec. 2).

61. For the raison d'etre of this practice, see Pacific Live Stock Co. v. Oregon State Water Board, 241 U. S. 440, 449(1916); Cowell v. Armstrong, 290 p. 1036, 210 Cal. 218 (1930) and Senate Hearings on S.18, 1951, p. 90.

62. Hutchins, op. cit., p. 316.

63. Connecticut v. Massachusetts, 282 U. S. 660, 673 (1931).

64. S. C. Wiel, op. cit., p. 324.

65. Hutchins, op. cit., pp. 337-345.

66. Ibid., p. 343.

67. Ibid., pp. 351-352. For example, see Calif. Water Code, sec. 1460.

68. Ibid.

69. Sec. 5 of the Oregon Ground Water Act; sec. 1 of the Washington Ground Water Act. Similar provision is found in an act of 1907 of South Dakota, which read: "All the waters within the limits of the state from all sources of water supply belong to the public and, except as to navigable waters, are subject to appropriation for beneficial use." That this provision did not include the underground water is made evident by the amendment thereof in 1927, which, after substantially repeating the original provision of 1907, declared that percolating waters other than underground streams are property of the landowner and are thus exempt from appropriation by the public.

70. Arizona Code Annotated, sec. 75-101 (Laws 1919, ch. 164, sec.1; as amended by Laws 1921, ch. 64, sec. 1).

71. Cross v. Kitts, 10 P. 409, 69 Cal. 217 (1886); Los Angeles v. Pomeroy, 57 P. 585, 124 Cal. 597 (1899); Water Code of 1943, sec. 1200 (Stats. 1913, ch. 586, sec. 42; as amended by Stats. 1933, ch. 357, sec. 1) (not amended since 1943).

72. Medano Ditch Co. v. Adams, 29 Colo. 317, 68 P. 431 (1902).

73. Smith v. Duff, 102 P. 984, 39 Mont. 382 (1909).

74. Taylor v. Welch, 6 Oregon 198 (1876); Hayes v. Adams, 218 p. 933, 109 Or. 51 (1923); Bull v. Siegrist, 126 p. 2d 832, 169 Or. 180 (1942).

75. South Dakota Code, sec. 61.0101, op. cit.

76. Revised Civil Statutes, art. 7467(Acts 1921, ch. 124, sec. 2): "underflows" are appropriable. Underflows probably refer to underground streams: see Farb v. Theis, 250 S. W. 290 (1923).

77. Deadwood Central R. R. v. Barker, 14 S. D. 558, 86 N. W. 619, 622 (1901).

78. Ryan v. Quinlan, 124 p. 512, 45 Mont. 521 (1912).

79. Ely v. Ferguson, 91 Cal. 187, 27 P. 587(1891); Southern Pacific R. Co. v. Dufour, 95 Cal. 615, 30 P. 783(1892); Prather v. Hoberg, 24 Cal. 2d 549, 150 P. 2d 405 (1943).

80. Texas Co. v. Burkett, 296 S. W. 273, 117 Tex. 16 (1927).

81. Wolfskill v. Smith, 5 Cal. App. 175, 89 P. 1001 (1907).

82. St. Germain Irrigation Co. v. Hawthorn Ditch Co., 143 N. W. 124, 32 S. D. 260 (1913).

83. Faden et al. v. Hubbell et al., 28 P. 2d 247, 251 (1933); DeHaas v. Benesch, 116 Colo. 344, 181 P. 2d 453 (1947).

84. For British common-rule on percolating waters, see Coulson and Forbes, The Law of Waters, 6th edition by S. Reginald Hobday, 1952, pp. 220-221.

85. City of San Bernardino v. City of Riverside, 198 P. 784, 186 Cal. 7 (1921); Ravis v. I. S. Chapman and Co., 19 P. 2d 511, 130 Cal. App. 109 (1933); Orchard v. Cecil F. White Ranches, 217 P. 2d 143 (1950).

86. Ryan v. Quinlan et al., 45 Mont. 521, 124 P. 512(1912); Patrick v. Smith, 134 P. 1076, 75 Wash. 407 (1913) (now obsolete); Canada v. City of Shawnee, 64 P. 2d 694, 179 Okl. 53 (1937) (now obsolete); Binning v. Miller, 102 P. 2d 54, 55 Wyo. 451 (1940); Cantwell v. Zinser, 208 S. W. 2d 577 (Texas, 1948); Bristor v. Cheatham, 255 P. 2d 173, 75 Ariz. 227 (1953).

87. A comparison may be made with the water law of California. "California water law recognizes two distinct types of water: riparian flow and flood water. Riparian water is allocated to land owners adjacent to the stream upon the basis of acreage and the history of beneficial usage. Under State law, riparian water may not be dammed, but must be used from day to day in proportion to stream flow. The other type of water, flood water, is allocated by the State water resources division after requests are filed and hearings are held. This water can be allocated to users who may not be adjacent to the stream, and the important factor of flood water is that it may be impounded and used during dry periods." -- 98 Cong. Rec. 5128 (12 May 1952). It should be noted that in Wisconsin even the riparian waters are appropriable, only with the consent of the riparian land-owners. Wisconsin system is practically the same as that of Texas: see Acts of Texas of 1917, General Laws, ch. 88, secs. 2 and 3.

88. Memorandum of the Attorney-General of the State of Wisconsin to Wisconsin Public Service Commission, dated 12 December 1950.

89. A prohibitory measure has been allowed by the United States Supreme Court. In Hudson County Water Co. v. McCarter, 209 U. S. 349, 356(1908), the Court held that riparian landowners cannot appropriate waters outside of state limits, if so prohibited by state laws. For Lousiana regulation of use of water by irrigation companies, see Louisiana Revised Statutes, title 45, sec. 62 (Acts 1920, No. 43, sec. 2).

90. In Pennsylvania, the Water, Power and Resources Board of the Department of Forests and Waters; in New York, the Water Power and Control Commission of the Department of Conservation; in New Jersey, the Division of Water Policy and Supply of the Department of Conservation of Economic Development (prior to February 1945, the State Water Policy Commission; from February 1945 to October 1948, the Division of Water Policy and Supply of the Department of Conservation, which was the successor of the former; in October 1948 the Department of Conservation was combined with the Department of Economic Development to become the Department of Conservation and Economic Development.)

91. These standards are merely guides to administration and do not constitute administration by themselves. For this reason, the regulation embodied in these identical laws (concurrent legislation) is not interstate administration but state administration. Compare p. 1015, below.

92. The Book of The States, 1950-51, p. 415.

93. For the regulation over appropriation of water, which is a "purpose" or functional regulation, see pp. 678-679, above.

94. For the regulation of terminals, also a "purpose" of functional

regulation, see. p. 643 , above.

95. In Montana such regulation is vested in the county government.

96. It may be noted that under the strong enabling system a structure, even if it is feasible and beneficial, may not be authorized.

97. In these five states permits are required. In Connecticut, in
addition to permits for the structures, there are certificates for construction, which are issued after the construction work is completed.

98. Licenses.

99. Decree (Maine) or order (the remaining states) of approval.

100. In another provision, the laws of Kansas provide for the approval of plans for the construction of dams (and bridges) across navigable
rivers by the Corporation Commission (or by the Highway Commission where
a dam or bridge forms part of the state highway system). It is stipulated that "no plans for the construction of any such dam shall be approved
. . . unless it contain flood gates or openings that can be opened in
times of highwater, so as to prevent the overflow of lands in the vicinity of said dam." -- General Statutes, sec. 68-1051 et seq.

101. This is perhaps taken as representative of public interest.

102. Wisconsin Statutes, sec. 31.18(1): Laws 1849, ch. 62, secs. 1;
2 and 12; last amended by L. 1951, ch. 712, sec. 3).

103. This is expressly provided in the laws of Connecticut and California.

104. The said commission regulates water levels of any reservoir.

105. "Certificates of public convenience and necessity" is a term
in public-utility regulation (that is, the regulation of a power or other
public-utility company as a business); but here the term means simply
a sort of permits.

106. The administration in these five states (probably more) is non-
statutory. See Hugh L. Elbree, Interstate Transmission of Electric Power,
1931, pp. 16-18.

107. Cf. General Statutes of North Carolina, sec. 14-383 (Laws 1913,
ch. 56).

108. The regional water pollution control boards are charged with
general water pollution control to be discussed below. For purely criminal regulation, see Ibid., sec. 481.

109. In this state, the main pollution problem "is in dealing with
the disposal of oil field brines." -- Letter to the author from Mr. D.
F. Snallhorst, Chairman, Texas State Water Pollution Advisory Council,
dated 15 January 1954.

110. See Annual Report of 1952 of the said division.

111. A copy of these rules may be obtained from the said Commission.

112. For annual permits for the drilling of oil and gas wells and
other regulatory measures, see act of 29 July 1941, as amended by an act
of 12 July 1951.

113. Generally classified under (1) municipal and domestic sewage, and (2) industrial and other wastes.

114. Generally, domestic, stock and fishery uses.

115. In some states, the general pollution control agency is the state health department.

116. It may incidentally be pointed out that Wisconsin and West Virginia are the only states which has provided for administrative coordination (that is, coordination effected through administrative procedure) between the state health department and the state general pollution control agency. For West Virginia it is statutorily provided that permits for the discharge of sewage and for the construction of sewage treatment works are issued by the state water commission after application therefor are approved by both the commission and the state health department. Administrative coordination in Wisconsin, which, unlike that in West Virginia, does not constitute a part of the general water pollution control regulation itself, is contained in Wisconsin Statutes, sec. 144.535 (Laws 1949, ch. 603) and sec. 144.565 (L. 1945, ch. 94). The regulation exercised by the state department of health to which the above provisions are applicable is provided for in ibid., sec. 144.03(3) (Laws 1945, ch. 303) and sec. 144.04 (Laws 1913, ch. 568, sec. 1; as last amended by L. 1927, ch. 264). Although administrative coordination is found only in West Virginia and Wisconsin, organizational coordination has been adopted in most states. For one thing, the state general pollution agency is as a rule a plural body, in which the state health department is always represented. Furthermore, the executive officer of the former agency is usually an officer of the latter agency. It is needless to mention the fact that in a number of states the general water pollution control agency is nothing but a subordinate agency of the state health department.

117. It may incidentally be pointed out that of the general water pollution regulatory agencies of the several states, only Mississippi Game and Fish Commission and Louisiana Stream Control Commission had, by the end of 1953, assumed jurisdiction over underground waters. It may further be noted that the regulation in these two states which affects or protects underground waters is the regulation over oil-field wastes and does not belong to general pollution control, and that in the laws of these states, there is no special reference to underground waters.

118. In Iowa, with the approval of the Natural Resources Council.

119. Industrial streams are designated in the statute providing for the regulation, and additional industrial streams may be designated from time to time by the water improvement commission.

120. Four or five cases, all of minor importance. In practice, the water pollution control board, from 27 September 1952 to the end of 1952, "exempted 300 villages with a total population of only 115,000, who do not have water works. After investigation, the board also exempted 29 other villages as not having significant water pollution problems at this time. In the cases of municipalities whose sewerage systems are tributary to the sewers of other communities -- mostly suburbs of large cities -- permits are not required." -- Ohio Water Pollution Control Board, Annual Report for 1952, 2nd page. However, it is not known whether the same practice prevails in any other state or states.

121. In North Dakota, a Rule or Regulation was adopted by the State Water Conservation Commission on 19 July 1943 (which is the only Rule or Regulation ever adopted by the said Commission), which substantially repeats the anabling statutory provision. Assistance of Mr. Vernon S.

Cooper, Assistant Secretary, North Dakota State Water Conservation Commission, in his letter to the author dated 4 August 1954, is gratefully acknowledged.

122. Up to the end of 1953, the following acts of classification had been enacted: Laws 1949, chs. 199; 247; L. 1951, chs. 32; 41; 42; 43; 44; 45; 62; 210; L. 1953, chs. 37; 38; 59; 60; 61.

123. Mosquitoes can also be controlled as an incident to the regulation of dams.

124. Letters to the author from Messrs. Arthur N. Beck, Chief Engineer and Director, Bureau of Sanitation, Alabama Department of Public Health, dated 5 October 1951, and F. E. Gartell, Assistant Director of Health, Tennessee Valley Authority, dated 24 October 1951. South Carolina regulations appear in the Code of Laws of South Carolina, vol. 7, at pp. 618-620.

125. See "Suggested Methods of Mosquito Control Measures on Small Artificially Created Lakes", distributed by Alabama State Public Health Department.

126. See Wisconsin Statutes, sec. 146.14 (Revised Statutes of 1849, ch. 26, secs. 5-8; as last amended by L. 1949, chs. 262 and 265); Kentucky Revised Statutes, sec. 211.210 (Acts 1954, ch. 157, sec. 15); Arizona Code, sec. 68-112a (Laws 1954, ch. 140, sec. 8); Mississippi Code, sec. 7037 (Codes of 1892, sec. 2277; as amended by L. 1922, ch. 234).

127. By local governmental units: Ohio, West Virginia, etc.; entirely judicial: Washington, etc.

128. Railroads are the only public utility that is regulated by the state government in each of the forty-eight states.

129. Code of Alabama, tit. 48, chs. 1 (first enacted 1915) and 4 (first enacted 1920); Arizona Code, ch. 69, art. 2 (first enacted 1912), and Arizona Constitution, art. 15; Arkansas Statutes, tit. 73(1935); California Constitution, art. 12, sec. 22, and California Public Utilities Code (based on a 1915 law); Colorado Statutes Annotated, ch. 137 (first enacted 1913); General Statutes of Connecticut, chs. 258 (first enacted 1911) and 264 (first enacted 1915); Delaware Code Annotated, tit. 26 (first enacted 1949); Florida Statutes, ch. 366 (1951); Georgia Code Annotated, sec. 93-414 et seq. (first enacted 1907); Idaho Code, tit. 61 (first enacted 1913); Illinois Revised Statutes, ch. 111-2/3 (first enacted 1921); Indiana Statutes, tit. 54 (first enacted 1913); Iowa Code, sec. 384.4 (Acts 1913, ch. 74, sec. 5; as amended by Acts 1937, ch. 205, sec. 1); General Statutes of Kansas, ch. 66, art. 1 (first enacted 1911); Kentucky Revised Statutes, ch. 278 (first enacted 1934); Louisiana Revised Statutes, tit. 45, ch. 3 (first enacted 1926); Revised Statutes of Maine, ch. 40 (first enacted 1913); Annotated Code of Maryland, art. 78 (first enacted 1910); Annotated Laws of Massachusetts, chs. 164 (first enacted 1885); 165 (first enacted 1933) and 166 (first enacted 1911); Compiled Laws of Michigan, ch. 460 (for Acts Nos. 106 and 144 of 1909 and Act No. 69 of 1929); Annotated Missouri Statutes, ch. 393 (1913); Revised Codes of Montana, tit. 70, ch. 1 (first enacted 1913); Revised Statutes of Nebraska, sec. 46-275 et seq. (1919) and sec. 310 et seq. (1915); Nevada Compiled Laws, sec. 6100 et seq. (first enacted 1919); Revised Laws of New Hampshire, tit. 25 (first enacted 1911); New Jersey Statutes, tit. 48, ch. 2 (first enacted 1911); New Mexico Statutes, sec. 72-501 et seq. (first enacted 1941); New York Public Service Law (first enacted 1910); General Statutes of North Carolina, ch. 62, art. 4 (first enacted 1933); North Dakota Revised Code, tit. 49 (first enacted 1919); Ohio Revised Code, tit. 49 (first enacted 1906); Oklahoma Statutes, tit. 17,

ch. 8 (first enacted 1913); Oregon Revised Statutes, ch. 757 (first enacted 1911); Pennsylvania Statutes, tit. 66, ch. 7 (first enacted 1913);
General Laws of Rhode Island, ch. 122 (first enacted 1912); Code of Laws
of South Carolina, tit. 58, ch. 3 (first enacted 1910); Code of Tennessee,
sec. 5447 et seq. (first enacted 1919); Vermont Statutes, sec. 9359 et
seq. (first enacted 1908); Code of Virginia, tit. 56 (first enacted 1904);
Revised Code of Washington, tit. 80 (first enacted 1911); West Virginia
Code, ch. 24 (first enacted 1913); Wisconsin Statutes, ch. 196 (first
enacted 1907); Wyoming Compiled Statutes, ch. 64 (first enacted 1915).

130. Montana laws provide for the regulation of wharfingers by the
State Railroad Commission (now Public Service Commission in this respect)
(Revised Codes, sec. 89-605; L. 1909, ch. 38, sec. 5). However, this
regulation has never been exercised. -- Letter to the author from Mr.
James B. Patten, Secretary-Counsel, Montana Board of Railroad Commission-
ers, ex-officio Public Service Commission, dated 3 September 1954. For
the authority of the Kansas Corporation over irrigation companies, see
General Statutes, sec. 42-355 et seq. (L. 1891, ch. 133, art. 6).

131. It should be remarked that these four different measures in
many cases do not apply to the same utilities.

132. Idaho Power and Light Co. v. State Public Utilities Commission,
141 P. 1083, 26 Idaho 222 (1914).

133. In Maryland, mere "permission and approval" of the public service commission; in New Hampshire, mere "approval" (considering "public
convenience" and "public interests"); in Tennessee, certificates of "public convenience"; in Vermont, "general good".

134. In Wisconsin, a certificate is not to be granted where an electric (but not water) cooperative association is about to start business.

135. It has been held by many jurists that "the function of rate
making is purely legislative in character . . ." (43 Am. Jur. 83). In
as much as all state administrative measures and the functions and duties
of all state administrative agencies are created or granted by the state
legislatures (in pursuance of general and special constitutional authorizations), it is without any practical significance to designate any
particular measure or set of measures or the functions and duties of any
particular administrative agency as purely or partially "legislative".
Some scholars have also endeavored to make a distinction between the so-
called "rate-making" and "order-making". In this connection, it may be
noted that the determination of rates is one of the many subjects of the
making of administrative orders and that procedurally an order carrying
a decision on the rates of a public utility does not differ from other
orders (all orders are generally issued after due notice and a hearing
of the parties affected or concerned).

136. Consult 43 Am. Jur. 89. In Kansas, also irrigation compan ies.

137. In the public utilities laws of the several states, there is
usually a criminal provision or provisions which outlaw unjust, unreasonable and discriminatory rates.

138. The commissions of the following states do not have this auth-
ority: California, Colorado, Delaware, Florida, Georgia, Idaho, Indiana,
Kansas, Michigan, Montana, Nebraska, Ohio, Oklahoma, Tennessee, Utah,
Vermont, and (for increases in rates only) Wisconsin.

139. A minimum amount equivalent to 40 percent at par value of the
outstanding capital stock is set for securities maturing less than one
year.

140. In Massachusetts, electric utilities only; in Maine, also
wharfingers; in North Dakota, also livestock companies; in Pennsylvania,
also sewerage, water-terminal and canal companies; in Vermont, also
flood-control and power dams and reservoirs; in Virginia, also sewerage
and canal companies; in West Virginia, also water-terminal and sewerage
companies.

141. For Indiana, also other utilities located in the same area.

142. For definitions of "affiliates", see the public utilities laws
of the several states listed.

143. Springfield Gas and Electric Co. v. City of Springfield, 257
U. S. 66, 70 (1921).

144. It is so specifically ruled in the laws of North Carolina.
Also consult the laws of Washington.

145. For legality in extending state public-utility regulation to
municipalities, see 43 Am. Jur. 97. In Alabama, regulation with respect
to water-terminal and canal utilities are not applicable to municipalities, but they are applicable to state enterprises. Assistance of Messrs.
Clayton W. Coleman, Secretary, Louisiana Public Service Commission,
Thomas A. Johnson, General Counsel, Missouri Public Service Commission,
and E. T. Drew, Secretary, New Jersey Department of Public Utilities,
in their letters dated respectively 24 June, 24 June and 8 July 1954,
is gratefully acknowledged.

146. For a brief history of these measures, see I. N. Gabrielson,
Wildlife Management,1951, pp. 56-57; 60-74; E. H. Graham, The Land and
Wildlife, 1947, pp. 29-30; 33; and 23 State Government 135 (1950, by R.
R. Renne).

147. "In European countries game belongs to the man who owns the
land. To hunt one must be the guest of an owner of an estate or purchase hunting or fishing privileges at a price beyond the reach of a
working man." -- California Department of Natural Resources. (by Harold
C. Bryant). Fish and Game Laws and The Reasons for Them, undated, p. 3.

148. "Think It Over, Mr. Sportman", Colorado Conservation Comments
(by Colorado Game and Fish Commission), vol. 10, no. 2 (June 1947) p. 4.

149. Washington State Game Commission, "Deer Management Program of
the State of Washington" (mimeo). 29 June 1948; and Washington State
Game Dept., Game Bulletin, vol. 2, no. 3 (July 1950), p. 1.

150. For details, study the fish and game laws and regulations of
any one or two states, which will be quite enough for general academic
purposes. Also consult Gabrielson, Wildlife Management, 1951, ch. 4,
pp. 56-80.

151. Washington State Game Department, Game Bulletin, vol. 3, no. 1
(Jan. 1951), pp. 3; 5.

152. Senate of the State of Cal., Cal.'s Fish and Game Program, 15
May 1950, p. 31.

153. In a broader sense, the term "bag limit" covers both bag and
creel limits.

154. Washington State Game Department, Game Bulletin, vol. 2, no.
3, (July 1950), p. 1. But the Game Code is silent on migratory birds.

155. Alabama Laws and Regulations Relating to Game, Fish, Etc.,
Season 1950-1951, p. 145.

156. Colorado Game Fish Commission, Colorado Conservation Comments,
Vol. 10, no. 8, (December 1948), p. 15.

157. For details on state regulation of commercial or food fishery
and fur-bearing animals, consult relevant laws and regulations of any
two or more states.

158. U. S. Department of Agriculture, Our National Forests, 1951,
p. 15.

159. Consult pp. 674-675, above.

160. A narrow meaning of state regulation is used here. It excludes
purely prohibitive or non-administrative (i.e. purely judicial) regulation. Furthermore, state assistance to private persons, participation
of private persons in state administration, etc., are not state regulation.

161. J. R. Whitaker and R. A. Ackerman, American Resources: Their
Management and Conservation, 1951, p. 213.

162. In the Black Hills Forest Fire Protection District of South
Dakota, there is Federal trust regulation.

163. In these 31 states, there are both administrative regulation
and criminal (judicial) regulation.

164. It may be noted that forest-fire regulation directed at timber
operators may also be provided, either statutorily or sub-statutorily,
as a part of state regulation of timber cutting and general forestry
practices.

165. The comprehensiveness of the laws of any state does not necessarily represent their merits, which are measured by their adequacy as
against the actual forest fire situation and the position of forest resources in the general economy in the state.

166. It may be noted that the period when the ground is not covered
by snow is practically a closed season.

167. All above: Conservation Law of New York, sec. 54 (1916, last
amended).

168. It should be remarked that forestry practices laws of some
states do not provide for regulation.

169. It is to be noted that Act No. 90 of 1922 also provided for
forest tax reform, but that sec. 15 of this act is not contingent upon
such reform. The reform provisions have been amended by subsequent acts.

170. Sec. 10 of this act provides for the exemption of taxes on
young and seed trees, which, however, is independent of timber-cutting
regulation.

171. These licenses are not permits for cutting timber.

172. Two members shall be private timber-owner-operators, one member a commercial timber owner, one member a farm woodland owner, and one
member either a member of the state board of forestry or an employee of
the division of forestry of the state department of natural resources.

173. The authority of the states to require permits or licenses for the cutting of timber and other forest products was sustained by the United States Supreme Court in Avery Dexter v. State of Washington, 338 U. S. 863 (1949).

174. The same act directed the state board of forestry to classify and designate such lands after public hearing, and each year to reclassify and designate the same lands. The initiative is entirely in the state and no consent of the private owners is necessary.

175. Secs. 10 and 11 of the act were also amended in 1943 and 1947, but the changes are insubstantial. Sec. 4 of the act was further amended by an act of 1953 (Laws 1953, ch. 195, sec. 1), by the addition of a stipulation to the effect that the state forester should hold the issuance of a permit upon being notified by the state tax commission or county collector of the delinquency in the payment of taxes.

176. This act and the 1947 amendment of the Oregon Forest Conservation Act of 1941 were derived from the Blue Eagle Lumber Code authorized by the National Industrial Recovery Act of 1933, and have been strictly enforced. -- William B. Greeley, Forests and Men, 1951, p. 192.

177. **West Norman Timber Inc. v. The State of Washington, 137 Wash. 437, 449 (1950).**

178. It should be noted that not all forest tax reform laws provide for such regulations as a price to be paid for the benefits of such reforms.

179. Of the tax receipts, the town retains 40 percent, and delivers 20 percent to the county and 40 percent to the school districts.

180. For example, Agriculture and Market Law of New York, sec. 161 et seq. (Laws 1887, ch. 403; as last amended by L. 1927, ch. 212, sec.2); Code of Georgia Annotated, sec. 5-701 et seq. (Acts 1898, No. 78; as last amended by Acts 1937, No. 332); Delaware Code Annotated, tit. 3, sec.110 et seq. (Laws 1899, ch. 216, not amended); Vermont Statutes, secs. 4582 and 4583 (Laws 1906, No. 223, secs. 1 and 2; as last amended by L. 1941, No. 78, sec. 2); Agricultural Code of California, sec. 100 et seq. (Stats. 1907, ch. 437; as last amended by Stats. 1953, ch. 1243); Arkansas Statutes, sec. 77-101 et seq. (Acts 1917, No. 414; as last amended by Acts 1939, No. 203, sec. 1 -- subsequent amendments affecting administrative organization only); Annotated Missouri Statutes, sec. 263.010 et seq. (Laws 1925, p. 112; as last amended by L. 1939, p. 204); Code of Alabama, tit. 2, sec. 456 et seq. (1927 Agricultural Code, sec 296 et seq.), Revised Code of Washington, ch. 17.24 (Laws 1927, ch. 292; as last amended by L. 1947, ch. 156); Revised Civil Statutes of Texas, article 135a-1 (Laws 1929, 2nd C. S., ch 15).

181. Second paragraph of the governor's veto message dated 16 April 1953.

182. Vermont State Forest Service, Biennial Report for 1951-1952, p. 9.

183. House Document 159, 79th Congress, September 1944, p. 326.

184. Ibid., p. 325.

185. Construction of the canal was commenced in 1817.--President's Water Resources Policy Commission, Report, vol. III, p. 87.

186. National Resources Planning Board, _Transportation and National Policy_, May 1942, p. 21.

187. _Encyclopaedia of Social Sciences_, vol. XV, p. 378.

188. New York Department of Public Works, _Official Map Showing State Canals and Waterways_, 1951.

189. F. P. Kimball, _New York--The Canal State_, 1937, p. 9.

190. _Official Map_, op. cit.

191. F. P. Kimbal, _op. cit._, p. 38. To supplement the water supply of the Barge Canal, seven storage reservoirs have been constructed and operated by the State on the headwaters of the Black River above Forestport. -- Black River Regulating District of New York. _The Facts About Panther Mountain Reservoir_, 3rd ed., January 1953, p. 29.

192. _Rpt. Chief of E. 1951_, pp. 211-214. The improvement work was suspended 1942-1946. -- _Official Map_, op. cit.

193. N. Y. Dpt. of P. W., _Rpt. for 1949_, p. 121.

194. _Ibid._, pp. 130-131.

195. F. P. Kimball. _op. cit._, p. 29.

196. N. Y. Dpt. of P. W., _Rpt. for 1949_, p. 132.

197. House Document 669, 76th Congress, 1940, p. 22.

198. Ill. Dpt. of Public Works and Buildings, Division of Waterways, _Highlights in the History of the Illinois and Michigan Canal_ (mimeo.), 22 April 1948, p. 14.

199. _Ibid._, p. 15.

200. _Wisconsin v. Illinois_, 278 U. S. 309, 401-402 (1929).

201. _Highlights in the History_, Etc., op. cit., p. 15. A portion of the canal was already abandoned as a result of the construction of the Sanitary and Ship Canal by the Sanitary District of Chicago and that of five navigation locks and dams in the Illinois and Des Plaines Rivers between Starved Rock and Lockport by the Illinois Department of Public Works and Buildings. -- House Document 669, 76th Cong., 1940, p. 22. An act of 9 July permitted the City of Ottawa to use the canal as an outlet of storm water runoff.

202. Quotation from a pamphlet published in 1950 by the Port of New Orleans, sent to the author by Mr. R. E. Hunter, Chief of Technical Information Branch, New Orleasns District Engineer's Office, U. S. Corps of Engineers, on 11 March 1952.

203. House Document 697, 79th Cong., 2nd sess., 1946, p. 7.

204. Letter to the author from Mr. W. T. Vanderlipp, Acting Commissioner, New Jersey Department of Conservation and Economic Development, dated 28 August 1951.

205. _Scranton v. Wheeler_, 179 US 141, 142-143 (1900).

206. House Document 1162, 60th Cong., 2nd sess., 1908, p. 2.

207. Rpt. Chief of E. 1887, p. 650.

208. Rpt. Chief of E. 1885, p. 682.

209. Ibid., p. 677.

210. Ibid., p. 678.

211. Senate Document 126, 71st Cong., 2nd sess., 1930, p. 26.

212. Rpt. Chief of E. 1927, pp. 1309; 1403.

213. Rpt. Chief of E. 1931, p. 1280; Rpt. 1940, pp. 1221; 1455.

214. House Document 686, 77th Cong., 2nd sess., 1942, p. 12; Rpt. Chief of E. 1952, p. 1770; Senate Document 126, 71st Cong., 2nd sess., 1930, pp. 2; 5; 40-42.

215. Rpt. Chief of E. 1902, p. 2602.

216. Ibid., p. 2600.

217. Rpt. Chief of E. 1931, pp. 1400; 1402.

218. Rpt. Chief of E. 1879, p. 1398.

219. Rpt. Chief of E. 1887, p. 240.

220. House Document 727, 65th Cong., 2nd sess., 1918, p. 6; House Document 133, 76th Cong., 1st sess., 1939, p. 3; 9; 32; and letter to the author from Mr. Peter J. Gannon, Chief of the Bureau of Navigation, New Jersey Dept. of Conservation and Economic Development dated 30 January 1953.

221. House Document 87, 81st Cong., 1st sess., 1949, p. 16.

222. House Document 111, 81st Cong., 1st sess., 1949, p. 13.

223. Senate Document 93, 77th Cong., 1st sess., 1941, p. 17.

224. House Document 237, 76th Cong., 1st sess., 1939, p. 7.

225. House Document 142, 82nd Cong., 1st sess., 1951, p. 17.

226. Rpt. Chief of E. 1902, p. 2575.

227. House Document 555, 82nd Cong., 2nd sess., 1952, p. 3.

228. House Document 645, 80th Cong., 2nd sess., 1948, p. 9.

229. See Laws 1937, ch. 68; Laws 1940, chs. 88 and 89, etc.; and House Document 358, 79th Cong., 1st sess., 1945, p. 9.

230. House Document 304, 81st Cong., 1st sess., 1949, p. 11.

231. House Document 752, 80th Cong., 2nd sess., 1948, p. 20.

232. House Document 202, 81st Cong., 1st sess., 1949, p. 36.

233. House Document 187, 81st Cong., 1st sess., 1949, p. 9.

234. House Document 531, 81st Cong., 2nd sess., 1952, p. 1703.

235. Rpt. Chief of E. 1949, p. 117. Other examples: Massachusetts State Bureau of Marine Fisheries owns a pier in Boston which is leased to the U. S. Navy. -- U. S. Corps of Engrs. and U. S. Maritime Administration, Port Series No. 3 (mimio.), revised 1946, p. 46. Virginia State Department of Highways owns and operates three wharves in Norfolk, one wharf in Newport News and one wharf in Old Point Comfort. -- Port Series No. 11 (mimio.), revised 1948, pp. 33-34; 223; 263.

236. Rpt. Chief of E. 1951, p. 212.

237. Ibid., p. 216.

238. U. S. Corps of E., Port and Terminal Facilities At The Port of New York (mimio.), 1942, part 1, p. 60.

239. U. S. Corps of E., Port and Terminal Facilities At The Ports on the Upper Hudson River, 1941, p. 36.

240. U. S. Corps of E. and U. S. Mari. Admin., Port Series No. 20 (mimeo.), revised 1947, p. 22.

241. Ibid., p. 25.

242. Letter to the author from R. E. Hunter, Chief of Technical Information Branch, New Orleans District Office, U. S. Corps of Engineers, dated 11 March 1952.

243. Office of the Chief of Engineers, U. S. Dpt. of the Army, Civil Works News Bulletin, July 1951, p. 3.

244. Letter to the author from Mrs. B. A. Thorson, Secretary, Lake Charles Harbor and Terminal District, dated 20 March 1952.

245. U. S. Corps of E. and U. S. Mari. Admin., Port Series No. 30, revised 1951, pp. 13-68. Robert H. Wylie, "The Port of San Francisco", 33 The Dock and Harbor Authority (British) 291 (February 1953). The latter reference also contains a brief history of the port of San Francisco.

246. Ibid.

247. Ibid.

248. U. S. Corps of Engineers and U. S. Maritime Administration, Port Series No. 3 (mimeo.), revised 1946, pp. 43; 58; 93; 98; 99.

249. Ibid., p. 158.

250. George L. Way, "The Port of Boston, U. S. A.", 33 The Dock and Harbour Authority (British) 323 (March 1953).

251. U. S. Corps of Engineers and U. S. Maritime Administration, Port Series No. 13 (mimeo.), revised 1950, pp. 13-14.

252. Rpt. Chief of E. 1951, p. 530.

253. Letter to the author from Mr. Harold E. Kimball, Executive Secretary, Maine Port Authority, dated 6 January 1954.

254. Maine Port Authority, The Port of Portland, 1953, pp. 10; 20-21; 94.

255. Informational material, mostly mimeographed and undated, kindly supplied by Fr. Frank C. Adams, Public Relations Director, North Carolina

State Ports Authority, on 6 January 1954.

256. U. S. Corps of Engineers and U. S. Maritime Administration, Port Series No. 18 (mimeo.), revised 1949, pp. 12-13.

257. U. S. Corps of Engineers and U. S. Maritime Administration, Port Series No. 14 (mimeo.), revised 1946, p. 116; Rpt. Chief of E. 1952, p. 535.

258. U. S. Corps of Engineers, Lake Series No. 7 (mimeo.), revised 1951, pp. 75; 78; Rpt. Chief of E. 1952, p. 1771.

259. U. S. Corps of Engineers, Lake Series No. 5 (mimeo.), revised 1950, p. 41.

260. U. S. Corps of Engineers, Lake Series No. 4 (mimeo.), revised 1950, p. 95.

261. Rpt. Chief of E. 1951, p. 1724.

262. Letter to the author from Mr. O. L. Peeler, Right-Of-Way Engineer-Attorney, Tennessee State Department of Highways and Public Works, dated 16 March 1954.

263. Letter to the author from Mr. John W. Aymar, Supervising Engineer, Appraisals and Negotiations, New Jersey State Highway Department, dated 26 May 1954.

264. House Document 718, 76th Cong., 3rd sess., 1940, p. 24.

265. House Document 332, 81st Cong., 1st sess., 1949, p. 17.

266. House Document 230, 74th Cong., 1st sess., 1935, pp. 9-10.

267. Letter to the author from Mr. Mark R. Kulp, State Reclamation Engineer, Boise, Idaho, dated 26 February 1953.

268. Letter to the author from Mr. Oscar L. Shepard, Chairman, Vermont Public Service Commission, dated 4 February 1954.

269. House Document 113, 80th Cong., 1st sess., 1947, pp. 20-21.

270. Pennsylvania Department of Forests and Waters, Biennial Report for the said biennium, pp. 41-46.

271. House Document 656, 76th Cong., 3rd sess., 1940, pp. 9-10.

272. Iowa Conservation Commission, Report for 1950, p. 37.

273. That is, retaining walls.

274. Senate Document 245, 79th Cong., 2nd sess., 1946, p. 19.

275. House Document 232, 81st Cong., 1st sess., 1949, p. 19.

276. House Document 531, 81st Cong., 2nd sess., 1952, p. 1165.

277. Ibid., p. 1166.

278. Letter to the author from Mr. Earle F. Bryant, Mayor, Town of Woodland, Washington, dated 19 September, 1953.

279. House Document 153, 82nd Cong., 1st sess., 1951, p. 25.

280. House Document 294, 79th Cong., 1st sess., 1945, p. 36.

281. House Document 531, 81st Cong., 2nd sess., 1952, p. 2354.

282. For each project, a maintenance area is to be established by the state reclamation board, which may be divided into a number of zones according to the extent of benefit received. If a local agency decides to maintain and operate it, it may request the dissolution of the maintenance area.

283. Washington Department of Conservation and Development, Biennial Report, for the biennium 1 October 1950 to 30 September 1952, p. 21.

284. Wyoming was the home state of Senator Joseph Carey, sponsor of the Carey Act. -- R. M. Robbins, Our Landed Heritages, 1942, p. 329. A certain source of information refers to the State of Idaho as another state which has built irrigation works under the Carey Act. But Mr. E. N. Humphrey, Deputy State Reclamation Engineer of the State of Idaho, in his letter to the author dated 3 November 1951, stated: "I believe there must be some misunderstanding regarding the State of Idaho having undertaken an irrigation enterprise at the state level . . . I do not recall a single case in which the state has attempted to construct and administer an irrigation project."

285. Letter to the author from Mr. L. C. Bishop. Wyoming State Engineer, dated 24 October 1951. For details, see the latest biennial report of the Commissioner of Public Lands of the State of Wyoming.

286. Letter to the author from Mr. Robert H. Ruggeri, Title Examiner, Utah State Land Board, dated 30 April 1954.

287. ". . . This Board did not acquire any lands under its projects from the Federal Government through the terms of the Carey Act or other methods." -- Letter to the author from Mr. R. J. Kelly, Assistant Secretary, Montana State Water Conservation Board, dated 23 January 1953.

288. Montana Reclamation Association, Irrigation Pays (pamphlet), 1952, pp. 2-3.

289. Ibid., pp. 15; 18; 20; 26.

290. These districts are not incorporated special districts, but merely field units of state administration.

291. Letter to the author from Mr. Bertran I. Gerry, Secretary, Massachusetts State Reclamation Board, dated 27 April 1954.

292. R. A. Gray and F. Tryon, The Government of Florida, 1941, p.64.

293. U. S. Bureau of the Census, Preliminary Release of the 1950 Census of Agriculture, Drainage of Agricultural Lands, 30 October 1951; and letter to the author from Mr. Ray Hurley, Chief, Agricultural Division, U. S. Bureau of the Census, dated 3 January 1952.

294. Ibid. However, in his letter of 6 January 1954, Mr. George H. Iftner, Assistant Director of Illinois State Department of Agriculture, informed the author that "the only drainage enterprises on the institutional farms are two tile systems." Mr. Iftner did not indicate the area of lands benefited, which in his mind is probably not very large.

295. See North Dakota Laws of 1951, ch. 338, sec. 2. Also consult Delaware Laws of 1937, ch. 238, sec. 3.

296. Unless otherwise indicated, all facts embodied in this sub-
section are based on letters to the author from Messrs. William S. Taber,
Delaware State Forester, Robert E. Rutherford, Information and Education
Assistant, Georgia Forestry Commission, and James W. Craig, Mississippi
State Forester, dated 15 March 1954; J. Whitney Floyd, Utah Chief Fores-
ter-Firewarden, and P. W. Tillman, Assistant State Forester, North Caro-
lina Department of Conservation and Development, dated 16 March 1954; W.
F. Schreeder, Connecticut State Forester, and George O. White, Missouri
State Forester, dated 17 March 1954; William G. Hughes, Protection Assis-
tant, Oregon State Board of Forestry, dated 18 March 1954; H. B. Newland,
Director of the Division of Forestry, Kentucky Department of Conservation,
and Ralph F. Wilcox, Indiana State Forester, dated 19 March 1954; Ralph
T. Wall, Chief, Forest Information, Louisiana Forestry Commission, dated
23 March 1954; William O. Jordan, Attorney, Legal Division, New Mexico
State Land Office, dated 24 March 1954; Don Lee Fraser, Deputy Supervisor, Division of Forestry, Washington Department of Conservation and Development, dated 26 March 1954; Neil LeMay, Chief Ranger, Wisconsin Conservation Commission, and Carl I. Peterson, Tennessee State Forester,
dated 29 March 1954; E. E. Nuuttila, Illinois State Forester, and Louis
C. Duncan, Office Manager, Arizona State Land Department, dated 1 April
1954; Robert L. Guernsey, Idaho State Forester, dated 2 April 1954;
Louis D. Ferrari, Nevada State Forester Firewarden, William H. Fairbank,
Jr., Deputy State Forester, California Department of Natural Resources,
A. D. Folweiler, Director, Texas Forest Service, and Harry R. Woodward,
South Dakota State Forester, dated 5 April 1954; O. A. Alderman, Chief,
Division of Forestry, Ohio Department of Natural Resources, dated 6
April 1954; Donald E. Stauffer, Director, Division of Forestry, Oklahoma
Planning and Resources Board, dated 9 April 1954; Duane L. Green, Farm
Forester, North Dakota School of Forestry, and E. A. Amderson, Assistant
State Forester, State of Montana Board of Land Commissioners, dated 9
April 1954; Harold G. Gallaher, Extension Specialist, Kansas Agricultural
Extension Service, dated 12 April 1954; William J. Seidel, State Fire-
warden, New Jersey Department of Conservation and Economic Development,
dated 13 April 1954; and M. A. Ellerhoff, Superintendent of Forestry,
Iowa State Conservation Commission, dated 15 April 1954.

297. Federally owned lands are as a rule taken care of by the Federal Government itself, except in special cases in which fire protection
on Federal lands is under state trust administration.

298. In Vermont, there is no special statutory provision for the
construction of look towers by the state. However, the statute permits
the state forester to appoint and employ watchmen in private lookout
towers (Vermont Statutes, sec. 7072: Laws 1910, No. 20, sec. 6).

299. Vermont Forest Service, Biennial Report, 1951-1952, p. 38;
Florida State Board of Forestry, Biennial Report, 1950-1952, 9th page;
Assembly of California, Third Progress Report of the Assembly Interim
Committee on Agriculture, 1953, p. 53.

300. Utah laws provide that "it shall be the duty of the state land
borad to cooperate with the sheriffs of the various counties in extinguishing and preventing fires on watershed lands, and for such purposes
it may employ men to patrol watershed lands" (Utah Code Annotated, sec.
65-1-75: Laws 1925, ch. 31, sec. 1) (3rd sentence). But the state land
board is not the forestry agency of Utah.

301. State forest agencies of Delaware and Mississippi used to construct fire-breaks on private lands as a preventive measure, but this
practice has been discontinued. Probably this is also the case with
South Carolina.

302. Florida has all of the special authorizations. Still Florida

statute provides for general fire-control authority (Statutes, sec. 590.-
02(1), sub-heading (b): Laws 1935, ch. 17029, sec. 14; as amended by L.
1951, ch. 26915, sec. 1).

303. Georgia Forestry Commission, Biennial Report of Progress,
1951-1952, pp. 12; 16.

304. Florida Board of Forestry, Biennial Report, 1950-1952, 8th,
10th and 11th pages.

305. South Carolina State Commission of Forestry, Annual Report for
1952, pp. 39-40. It may be noted that forest roads may also be used for
pleasure driving or hiking, and that lookout towers, if properly built,
may possess recreational value too.

306. Wisconsin Conservation Commission, Biennial Report for the fiscal years ending 30 June 1949 and 30 June 1950, p. 67.

307. Report of the Chief of Forest Service for 1950, p. 7.

308. Alabama Department of Conservation, Annual Report for the year
1 October 1948 to 30 September 1949, pp. 85-86.

309. The Book of the States, 1950-51, p. 420.

310. Ibid., p. 419.

311. Washington Department of Conservation and Development, Division
of Forestry, Combined 47th and 48th Annual Reports, p. 34.

312. Vermont State Forest Service, Biennial Report 1951-1952, p. 25.

313. Biennial Report of the State Forester of Idaho, 1951-1952, p.16.

314. The Book of the States, 1950-51, p. 420.

315. Rpt. Chief of Forest Service 1951, p. 56.

316. Washington Department of Conservation and Development, Division
of Forestry, Combined 47th and 48th Annual Reports, p. 38.

317. New Jersey Department of Conservation, Second Annual Report,
1946-47, pp. 55-56.

318. Wisconsin Conservation Commission, Twenty-third Biennial Report,
pp. 32-34.

319. Assembly of California, Third Progress Report of the Assembly
Interim Committee On Agriculture, 1953, p. 115.

320. Georgia Forestry Commission, Biennial Report of Progress, 1951-
1952, p. 25.

321. South Carolina State Commission of Forestry, Annual Report
1950-1951, pp. 43-44; Annual Report 1951-1952, pp. 54-55.

322. Mississippi Forest Service, Biennial Report, 1949-1951, p. 1I.

323. Ohio Department of Natural Resources, Report 1951-1952, pp.20-
21.

324. Missouri Conservation Commission, Annual Report, 1951-1952,
p. 58.

325. West Virginia Conservation Commission, Annual Report 1951-1952, p. 18. The distribution was as follows: 1,127,690 to 596 individuals; 530,000 to the Soil Conservation Service; 1,015,808 to the Division of Game Management of the Commission; and 11,675 to the Division of Education and Publicity of the Commission.

326. South Dakota Department of Game, Fish and Parks, Annual Report, 1952-1953, pp. 87-88.

327. South Dakota Department of Game, Fish and Parks, Annual Report, 1952-1953, pp. 87-88.

328. Annual Report of the Bureau of Entomology, U. S. Dpt. of Agri., 1924, p. 7; Report of the same, 1925, p. 9; Annual Report of the Chief of the Bureau of Entomology and Plant Quarantine, 1935, pp. 25; 29; Report of the same, 1936, p. 22; Report of the same, 1949, p. 12.

329. Assembly of California, Progress Report of Assembly Interim Committee on Agriculture, 1953, p. 100.

330. Rpt. Chief of Forest Service 1950, p. 11.

331. Washington State Department of Conservation and Development, Division of Forestry, Combined 47th and 48th Annual Reports, p. 36.

332. Wisconsin Conservation Commission, 23rd Biennial Report, pp. 20-21.

333. Third Progress Report of Assembly Interim Committee on Agriculture, op. cit., p. 85.

334. Rpt. Chief of Forest Service 1950, p. 25.

335. Standley G. Fontanna, "State Forests", Yearbook of Agriculture, 1949, p. 390.

336. Fifty Years of Forestry in U. S. A., p. 228 (by Joseph S. Illick).

337. 44 Recreation 129 (June 1950).

338. Michigan Department of Conservation, Biennial Report, 1949-1950, p. 135.

339. Rpt. Chief of Forest Service 1950, p. 25.

340. U. S. Dpt. of Agri., State Legislation For Better Land Use, April 1941, p. 91. Consult N. Y. Conservation Law, sec. 60-a.

341. Rpt. Chief of Forest Service 1950, p. 25.

342. Yearbook of Agriculture, 1949, p. 391 (by S. G. Fontanna).

343. Rpt. Chief of Forest Service 1950, p. 25.

344. Yearbook of Agriculture, 1949, p. 393 (by S. G. Fontanna).

345. Armstead, State Services of Connecticut, 1946, p. 259; Digest of Connecticut Administrative Reports to the Governor, 1949-1950, p. 654.

346. U. S. Department of Agriculture, The Management Status of Forest Lands in the United States (mimeo.), 1946, p. 13, table 6. Also consult p. 14, table 7.

347. Letter to the author from Mr. Homer G. Lyon, Jr., Reforestation Director, Oregon State Board of Forestry, dated 3 April 1953.

348. Theoretically, artificial propagation may be made of species that are threatened with elimination (by natural causes), too. However, it has not been practised to any appreciable extent in this country.

349. E. H. Graham, The Land and Wildlife, 1947, pp. 46-47; I. N. Gabrielson, Wildlife Management, 1951, pp. 108-111; California Fish and Game Code, Secs. 39.1 and 39.2 (Statutes 1951, chs. 1610 and 1323).

350. I. N. Gabrielson, Wildlife Refuges, 1943, pp. 7-8; 205; 211; 224.

351. R. R. Renne, 23 State Government 137 (1950); E. H. Graham, op. cit., p. 46.

352. Based on direct communication with game agencies of all states and territories except Alaska in April-May 1953. Alaska does not have a game agency (territorial).

353. See, for example, Code of Alabama, tit. 8, sec. 27 Acts 1935, No.240); Arkansas Acts 1927, No. 95; Arizona Code, sec. 57-103, para. 5, last sentence (Laws 1929, ch. 84, sec. 3; as amended by L. 1945, ch. 52, sec. 2); Colorado Fish and Game Laws, sec. 241 (2) (L. 1937, ch. 153); General Statutes of Connecticut, sec. 4922 (Acts 1923, ch. 259, sec. 54; as amended in 1947); General Laws of Massachusetts, ch. 131, sec. 90, 1st sent. (L. 1941, ch. 599, sec. 2), Oregon Laws 1949, ch. 242, sec. 4; and Revised Code of Washington, sec. 77.12.040 (L. 1947, ch. 275, sec. 14). In Alabama the approval of the governor is required.

354. Senate of the State of California, Report of the Wildlife Conservation Board, 15 May 1950, p. 192. A comparison between the "Official Map of Florida Wildlife Refuges As Of January 1950" and a map showing "Wildlife Management Areas in Florida", both published November 1952, reveals that parts of some refuges has been included within wildlife management areas and were open to hunting. (These maps were made available to the author through the courtesy of Mr. E. B. Chamberlain, Jr., of the Florida Game and Fresh Water Fish Commission on 4 May 1953).

355. Report of the Wildlife Conservation Board, op. cit., p. 222. Also consult Gabrielson, Wildlife Refuges, op. cit., p. 206.

356. Rpt. Sec. Inter. 1941, p. 379.

357. Rpt. Sec. Inter. 1952, pp. 341-342.

358. Senate of California, California's Fish and Game Program, 15 May 1950, Forward.

359. California Department of Fish and Game, Forty-Second Biennial Report, January 1953, p. 18.

360. California Department of Fish and Game, "Inland Game Fish Conservation" (mimeo.), Student Bulletin M-1.

361. Washington Department of Fisheries, 1950 Annual Report, pp. 19-20.

362. Ibid., p. 25.

363. Washington State Game Department, Game Bulletin, vol. 2, no. 3 (July 1950), p. 8.

364. Washington State Department of Fisheries, 62nd Annual Report, February 1953, pp. 17-20.

365. Washington State Department of Fisheries, Annual Report 1950, p. 25.

366. California Fish and Game Commission, 41st Biennial Report, p. 83.

367. Washington State Department of Fisheries, Annual Report 1950, p. 21; 62nd Annual Report, op. cit., p. 23.

368. California Department of Fish and Game, "Inland Game Fish Conservation", op. cit.

369. Kansas Forestry, Fish and Game Commission, 13th Biennial Report, 30 June 1950, p. 18

370. A. V. Tunison et al., "Survey of Fish Culture in the United States", The Progressive Fish Culture, January 1949, p. 35.

371. California Department of Fish and Game, Forty-Second Biennial Report, January 1953, p. 35.

372. Michigan Department of Conservation, Biennial Report, 1949-1950, pp. 75-82.

373. Letter to the author from Mr. Gordon L. Trembley, Chief Aquatic Biologist, Pennsylvania Fish Commission, dated 2 April 1954.

374. E. H. Graham, The Land and Wildlife, 1947, pp. 33-34.

375. I. N. Gabrielson, Wildlife Management, 1951, p. 130.

376. Ibid., p. 125.

377. Transactions of the 13th North American Wildlife Conference, 1948, pp. 207-208 (by Allen T. Studhome).

378. Gabrielson, op. cit., p. 130.

379. E. H. Graham, op. cit., p. 191.

380. Senate of California, California's Fish and Game Program, 15 May 1950, p. 121.

381. Based on direct communication with the game agencies of all states and territories except Alaska in April-May 1953. There is no game agency in the Territorial Government of Alaska. In Connecticut, however, an act was passed in 1953 (Act No. 391) which authorized the State Prison to raise, in cooperation with the state board of the fisheries and game, not more than 30,000 pheasants a year in the prison farm, with money paid out of the state game fund, for the purpose of stocking state public shooting areas. For practical purposes, Connecticut may be listed as having one state game farm.

382. U. S. Fish and Wildlife Service, Fishery Leaflet 41 (mimeo.), March 1949. In this publication, the names and addresses of all state-owned fish hatcheries and rearing stations are listed.

383. The Progressive Fish Culturist, October 1949, p. 257 and ibid., January 1949, pp. 47-57. The total production figure is only slightly higher than that of the Federal fish hatcheries.

384. Transactions of the 80th annual meeting of the American Fisheries Society, 1950, p. 152 (by Oliver R. Kingsbury).

385. See Jack Simson, "Fish Distribution in Colorado", Colorado Conservation Comments, vol. 10, no. 14 (July 1950), pp. 9-10, and Calif. Dpt. of Fish and Game, Forty-Second Biennial Report, January 1953, p. 53.

386. California Department of Fish and Game, Forty-Second Biennial Report, January 1953, p. 95.

387. Oregon State Game Commission, Oregon Back Country Lakes (undated pamphlet), first page.

388. Senate of California, California's Fish and Game Program, op. cit., p. 34.

389. Washington State Game Department, "Game Fish of Washington" (undated mimeo. pamphlet), p. 11.

390. Alabama Department of Conservation, Annual Report for the fiscal year 1 October 1948-30 September 1949, p. 41; Annual Report for the fiscal year 1 October 1950-30 September 1951; pp. 119-120.

391. See, for example, Washington Game Code, 1951, sec. 29; California Fish and Game Code, 1951, ch. 1323); Oregon Game Code, sec. 29 (Laws 1941, ch. 275, sec. 16); Acts of Vermont of 1951, No. 134.

392. The foregoing paragraph is based on the reading of a great number of annual and biennial reports of state game and fish agencies.

393. Letter to the author from Mr. Lloyd W. Swift, Chief, Division of Wildlife, U. S. Forest Service, dated 16 July 1952. Such areas may cover non-Federal lands either within or outside of the exterior boundaries of the national forests. See House Hearings on Conservation of Wildlife, 79th Cong., 2nd sess., Nov. 1945 and June 1946, pp.160-161.

394. L. W. Swift, "Management of National Forest Lands For Wildlife" (mimeo.), 17 September 1948.

395. See Rpt. Sec. Inter. 1951, p. 308.

396. See pp. 416-417, above.

397. J. L. Carey, Game Conservation in Pennsylvania, 2nd ed., 1950, pp. 52-56. The project lands aren't however, designated as "auxiliary game refuges".

398. Digest of Connecticut Administrative Reports to the Governor, 1949-1950, p.653.

399. Information provided the author through the courtesy of Nevada Fish and Game Commission on 4 April 1953.

400. Letter to the author from Mr. Frank D. Blair, Director, Division of Game and Fish, Minnesota Department of Conservation, dated 7 April 1953.

401. Letter to the author from Mr. Clarence F. Pautzke, Chief, Division of Fishery Management, Washington State Department of Game, dated 15 April 1954.

402. Massachusetts Department of Conservation, Division of Fisheries and Game, Annual Report 1950-1951 (mimeo.), p. 7.

403. Michigan Department of Conservation, Biennial Report, 1949-1950, p. 73.

404. Wisconsin Conservation Commission, Biennial Report 1948-1950, p. 20.

405. Wallace B. Grange, The Way to Game Abundance, 1949, pp. 319-320.

406. Walter Nerlbrech, "Predator Control Versus Nature's Balance", Washington State Game Bulletin, vol. 3, No. 1 (January 1951), p. 6.

407. See Pennsylvania Game News, November 1950, p. 102.

408. Division of Fish and Game, N. J. Dpt. of Cons. and Econ. Deve., Annual Report for the fiscal year ending 30 June 1952, p. 29.

409. Wisconsin Conservation Commission, Biennial Report for biennium ending 30 June 1950, pp. 15-16.

410. Michigan Institute for Fisheries Research (by C. L. Hubbs and R. W. Eschmeyer), Improvement of Lakes for Fishing, May 1938, pp.162-163.

411. Washington State Game Commission, Fisheries Biological Progress Report, April 1946-April 1947, p. 7.

412. Iowa State Conservation Commission, Biennial Report for the biennium ending 30 June 1950, p. 208.

413. New Mexico Department of Game and Fish, Annual Report 1953, page 11.

414. See Transactions of the 75th annual meeting (1945) of the American Fisheries Society, 1948, p. 36 (by Robert C. Ball); Oklahoma Game and Fish News, January 1952, p. 6; California Department of Fish and Game, 42nd Biennial Report, op. cit., p. 36; Washington State Game Commission, 8th Annual Report, 1947-1948, p. 4ff; Oregon State Game Commission, Biennial Report, 1949-1950, under the heading "Lake Rehabilitation."

415. Ray H. Hess, "Warm Fishing in Colorado", Colorado Conservation Comments, vol. 10, no. 9 (March 1949), p. 11.

416. Transactions of the 14th North American Wildlife Conference, 1949, pp. 217, 218 (by R. W. Eschmeyer).

417. See California Department of Natural Resources, Division of Fish and Game, Commercial Fish Catch of California (Fish Bulletin No.57), 1949, pp. 57-59.

418. Improvement of Lakes for Fishing, op. cit., pp. 161-162; letter to the author from Mr. W. A. Hunter, Chief, Education and Information, Wash. State Dpt. of Game, dated 17 January 1952. Of course desirable fish may also be stunted because of the existence of rough fish.

419. Letter to the author from Mr. Clarence F. Pautzke, Chief, Fishery Management Division, Washington State Department of Game, dated 15 March 1954. It is not clear whether the actual work of rehabilitation performed is in any manner different from the control of rough fish. So far as Washington is concerned, the result of this work is that "we have added approximately 7,500,000 trout to the fishermen's basket that were not there before we started this lake rehabilitation program" (ibid.). This appears to be a measure of rough fish control.

420. Kansas Forestry, Fish and Game Commission, 13th Biennial Report, 30 June 1950, pp. 41-42.

421. Oregon State Game Commn., Bienn. Rpt. 1949-1950, op. cit. The issuance of permits is authorized by Laws 1921, ch. 153, sec. 23; as last amended by L. 1935, ch. 429, sec. 1 (Rev. Stats. sec. 498.575).

422. U. S. Dpt. of the Interior, A Century of Conservation, 1849-1949, p. 11.

423. The impression of the author is based on a reading of the annual or biennial reports of the state parks agencies of a number of states.

424. Federal Inter-Agency Committee on Recreation, Report on the Conservation and Development of Outdoor Recreation Resources (mimeo.), July 1950, pp. A-38 and A-39.

425. Conference with Mr. William S. Pond, supervisor, recreation division, Washington State Parks and Recreation Commission, on 14 December 1951.

426. Maine State Park Commission, Public Parks in Maine (undated pamphlet) and Preliminary Report on State Park and Related Recreational Planning, January 1952; Montana State Park Commission, "Existing and Potential Recreation Areas and Facilities" (mimeo. sheet), November 1952; Florida Board of Parks and Historic Memorials, Florida Parks Invite You (a folder) and A Report to the People of Florida, 1953; Vermont State Forest Service, Vermont State Forests and Forest Parks (a folder). This enumeration is not intended to be exhaustive.

427. National Park Service, State Parks: Areas, Acreages and Accommodations (mimeo.). 31 December 1950.

428. Report on the Conservation and Development of Outdoor Recreational Resources, op. cit., p. A-16.

429. For example, Rhode Island Laws, ch. 1557; Washington Laws 1937, ch. 53, sec. 88 (Revised Code sec. 47.40.010); Ohio Code, secs. 1178-6 and 1179-3 (enacted 11 October 1945).

430. New Jersey Department of Conservation, Annual Report, 1 July 1946 to 30 June 1947, pp. 88-92.

431. California State Park Commission, Annual Report, 1949-1950 (mimeo.), p. 6.

432. Maine State Park Commission, Public Parks in Maine (undated pamphlet); Rhode Island Dpt. of Agriculture and Conservation, 17th Annual Report, 1951, p. 40; Wisconsin Conservation Commission, 23rd Biennial Report for fiscal years ending 30 June 1951 and 30 June 1952, p. 43.

433. Montana State Park Commission, "Existing and Potential Recreation Facilities", op. cit. and Montana State Highway Commission, 1953 Montana Highway Map.

434. Florida's Parks Invite You, op. cit.

435. Missouri State Park Board, Missouri's State Parks (undated folder).

436. The Book of the States, 1950-1951, p. 425.

437. House Document 650, 78th Cong., 2nd sess., 1944, p. 19. Consult Virginia Conservation Commission, Major Storage Reservoirs of Virginia, 1948, table 2.

438. Kansas Forestry, Fish and Game Commission, Thirteenth Biennial Report, 30 June 1950, p. 25.

439. Iowa Conservation Commission, Biennial Report, pp. 29-30.

440. Indiana Yearbook for 1947, p. 644.

441. Letter to the author from Mr. Harold J. Dyer, Director of State Parks, State Park Commission of the state of Maine, dated 10 December 1951.

442. Despite this fact, the enterprise of beach erosion control is part of recreation enterprise, since the primary use of the beach is recreation.

443. New Hampshire State Planning and Development Commission, Eighth Biennial Report, February 1951, p. 19.

444. California State Park Commission, Annual Report 1949-1950 (mimeo.), p. 79.

445. South Carolina State Commission of Forestry, Report for the fiscal year ending 30 June 1952, p. 77.

446. New Jersey Conservation Department, Second Annual Report, for the fiscal year ending 30 June 1947, p. 51.

447. House Document 89, 82nd Cong., 1st sess., 1951, p. 13.

448. Ohio Department of Natural Resources, Annual Report for fiscal year ending 30 June 1952, pp. 142-143.

449. Ibid., p. 13.

450. Ibid., p. 128.

451. Based on a reading of annual or biennial reports and or other publications of a great number of state park agencies. For the construction of fishing piers in particular, see South Carolina State Commission of Forestry, Annual Report 1951, p. 52; Tennessee Department of Conservation, Biennial Report 1951-1952, p. 29.

452. Seattle Times, 10 August 1954 (Associated Press).

453. Letter to the author from Mr. K. S. Wingfield, Administrator, Arizona Power Authority, dated 19 August 1953.

454. For the rehabilitation of the Delaware and Raritan Canal of New Jersey for the primary purpose of supplying industrial water to New Brunswick, see p. 813, above.

455. Letter to the author from Mr. Roy T. Sessums, Director, Louisiana Department of Public Works, dated 29 October 1953.

456. Additional appropriation was made by Act No. 235 of 1952.

457. Letter to the author from Mr. E. P. Rothrock, State Geologist of South Dakota, dated 28 December 1953.

458. Black River Regulating District, N. Y., The Facts About Panther Mountain Reservoir, 3rd ed., January 1953, p. 21.

459. House Document 185, 81st Cong., 1949, pp. 41-42.

460. For similar law in South Dakota, see South Dakota Code, sec. 61.0412, which was, however, repealed by Laws 1941, ch. 369, sec. 1.

461. As mentioned before, the State Engineer of North Dakota may undertake water-conservation works in the Turtle Mountain region. Information is not available regarding the actual work done.

462. Letter to the author from Mr. Wilbur A. Rush, Chief, Division of Lands and Waters, Iowa State Conservation Commission, dated 27 April 1954.

463. Engineering News-Record, 12 March 1936, p. 393.

464. See Rhode Island Department of Agriculture and Conservation, Annual Report 1945, p. 35; Annual Report 1946, p. 17; Annual Report 1949, p. 35; Annual Report 1950, p. 15. Also see Laws of Delaware of 1947, ch. 1881, sec. 4.

465. Letter from Mr. Bertram I. Gerry, op. cit.

466. Texas Board of Water Engineers,19th Biennial Report, November 1950, p. 1; B. H. Hibbard, A History of Public Land Policies, 1924, p.10.

467. Marion Clawson, "Public Land Management in the United States" (mimeo.), October 1951, p. 8.

468. Crouch and McHenry, California Government, 1945, p. 239. The figure covers school lands only.

469. Alabama Department of Conservation, Annual Report 1951, p. 135.

470. U. S. Department of Agriculture, Proceedings of Conference on Land Utilization, May 1932, p. 81; State Legislation For Better Land Use, April 1941, p. 75.

471. Richard T. Ely and George Wehrweim, Land Economics, 1940, p. 186; Proceedings of Conference on Land Utilization, op. cit., p. 81.

472. Yearbook of Agriculture, 1938, p. 232 (by Earle H. Clapp).

473. Michigan Department of Conservation, Biennial Report, 1949-1950, p. 201.

474. 97 Cong. Rec. 8915-8916 (24 July 1951).

475. For example, by an act of 1925 (ch. 155, sec. 1: Revised Civil Statutes Art. 7467a), "the State of Texas (hereby) relinquishes, quit-claims and grant unto all incorporated cities and towns that have a population of 40,000 inhabitants or more . . . all of the beds and channels, and also all of the abandoned beds and channels, of all rivers, streams and other channels that are now or that may hereafter be within the present or future coporate limits of such cities or towns, in so far as the beds and channels and such abandoned channels, of such rivers, streams and other channels may be owned or claimed as the property of said State."

476. For references to these laws, see pp. 400-414, above (main body of these laws).

477. State Legislation For Better Land Use, op. cit., pp. 99-108.

478. In art. XV, sec. 3 of the Constitution of California of 1849, as revised 1879, it is provided that "all tidelands within two miles of any incorporated city or town in this state, and fronting on the waters of any harbor, estuary, bay, or inlet used for the purposes of navigation, shall be withheld from grant or sale to private persons, partnerships, or corporations."

479. Iowa Conservation Commission, Report for the biennium ending 30 June 1950, pp. 32-34; Report for the biennium ending 30 June 1953, pp. 31-32. "The policy of the State Conservation Commission at present is only to furnish technical assistance and to some extent equipment for the construction of erosion control units and watershed treatment. The State has done considerable work on the contributing watersheds to the artificial lakes when money was directly appropriated by the legislature for this purpose. At the present time funds have been exhausted. . ." — - Letter to the author from Mr. J. A. Wymore, Assistant Engineer, Iowa State Conservation Commission, dated 4 May 1954.

480. Rpt. Sec. Inter. 1952, p. 340.

481. "Multiple-purpose project" is here defined as a dam and reservoir project built primarily for the generation of hydro-electric power (not necessarily at the dam-site), but nominally devoted to navigation improvement, flood control, irrigation and water conservation or any one or combination of such purposes.

482. South Carolina Public Service Authority, Santee-Cooper Power and Navigation Project (undated folder).

483. Doug Powell, "How South Carolina Made Waste Go To Work for the State," Southern Engineer, vol. 13, no. 3 (February 1951).

484. Rpt. Fed. Power Commission 1950, p. 48.

485. From an undated, untitled sheet of the S. C. Public Service Authority.

486. Doug Powell, op. cit.

487. Report of the Chief of Forest Service for 1925, pp. 10-11; Rpt. 1930, p. 12; Rpt. 1952, p. 39, etc.

488. Laws of North Carolina of 1947, ch. 384; Acts of Arkansas of 1947, No. 163.

489. Michigan Department of Conservation, Michigan Department of Conservation: Its Organization and Functions, March 1948, p. 15.

490. Wisconsin Conservation Commission, Biennial Report for fiscal years ending 30 June 1949 and 30 June 1950, p. 77; Connecticut Park and Forest Commission, Annual Report 1951-1952, p. 4; Missouri Conservation Commission, Annual Report 1951-1952, pp. 59-65; Washington Department of Conservation and Development, Division of Forestry, Combined 47th and 48th Annual Reports, p. 31; Ohio Department of Natural Resources, Report 1951-1953, p. 31; West Virginia Conservation Commission, Annual Report 1951-52, pp. 14-15; South Carolina State Commission of Forestry, Report 1952, pp. 51-53; Rhode Island Department of Agriculture and Conservation, Division of Forests, Report 1953, pp. 7-8; Florida Board of Forestry, 12th Biennial Report, 15th and following pages; etc. To all above-mentioned state forestry activities, Federal grants are avilable under the Cooperative Forest Management Act of 1950.

491. Washington State Game Commission, *Biennial Report, 1946-1948*, p. 63.

492. *Ibid.*, pictorial illustrations opposite p. 63.

493. Jack Culbreath, "Colorado's 1949 Big Game Winter Feeding By Air", *Colorado Conservation Comments*, vol. 10, no. 9 (March 1949), p. 30.

494. Oregon State Game Commission, *Biennial Report 1949-1950* (unpage-numbered.

495. Michigan Department of Conservation, *Biennial Report, 1949-1950*, p. 166.

496. Compar Alabama Department of Conservation, *Annual Report* for the fiscal year 1 October 1950-30 September 1951, p. 93.

497. See Wayne H. Tody and O. H. Clark, "Michigan's Rifle River Watershed Program", *Transactions* of the 16th North American Wildlife Conference, 1951, pp. 234-243; and Mich. Dpt. of Conser. *Biennial Rpt.* 1949-1950, pp. 75-77.

498. For the nature and extent of such assistance in the several states, see Federal Inter-Agency Committee on Recreation, "Summary of Recreation Services of State Agencies To Communities and to Rural Areas" (mimeo. bulletin), 12 July 1950.

499. *Report of the State Engineer (Utah)* for the biennium 1 July 1948-30 June 1950, pp. 33-34.

500. Montana Reclamation Association, *Irrigation Pays* (a pamphlet), 1952, pp. 3; 31.'

501. Letter to the author from Mr. R. J. Kelly, assistant secretary, Montana State Water Conservation Board, dated 23 January 1953.

502. Letter to the author from Mr. C. H. W. Smith, Engineer, Water Division, Arizona State Land Department, dated 6 June 1953.

503. Letter to the author from Mr. Robert H. Ruggeri, Title Examiner, Utah State Land Board, dated 30 April 1954.

504. Letter to the author from Mr. Charles G. Caldwell, Chief, Environmental Sanitation Services, New Mexico Department of Public Health, dated 25 October 1954.

505. New Mexico Department of Public Health, 17 *New Mexico Health Officer* 9 (April 1949).

CHAPTER 4

ADMINISTRATION IN OTHER JURISDICTIONS

Article 1   County Administration

Section 1   Regulation

1. <u>Rural zoning</u>---The only type of governmental regulation in the field of water resources administration that exclusively belongs to counties is rural zoning.[1] As distinguished from city zoning, which may be not more than a measure of public safety and health, rural zoning is a measure
aiming at the regulation of land use.[2] It can also be used
as a measure of flood control, when it applies to flood
plains of watercourses.[3] Rural zoning has only a history of
a quarter of a century.[4] "The power to zone the land outside incorporated places was granted to all counties in Wisconsin through a State Enabling Act in 1923. County zoning
under this act was for the purpose of controlling suburban
land and setting up residential, commercial, and industrial
districts adjacent to cities; but an amendment to the Enabling Act, in 1929, inaugurated rural zoning by permitting
the zoning of land for agriculture, forestry, and recreation.
The Michigan Enabling Act of 1935 added soil conservation
and water conservation, thus broadening the land-use control
feature as given in the Wisconsin act."[5] Up to 1952, county
zoning enabling laws had been enacted in the following states[6]

Alabama---Acts 1947, no. 344; as amended by Acts 1947, no.
            649; Acts 1949, no. 422; Acts 1951, no. 634;
            applicable only to counties of 400,000 popula-
            tion or more.
Colorado--<u>Statutes</u>, ch. 45A (Laws 1939, ch. 92).
Delaware--No general enabling legislation. However, un-
            der the <u>Revised Code</u>, ch. 168 (Laws 1931, ch.
            88; as amended Laws 1941, ch. 266), the New
            Castle County has zoning authority. Laws 1949,
            ch. 323 embodied a proposal for amending art.
            2, sec. 25 of the state constitution to extend
            zoning authority to all counties. But as fin-
            ally adopted (Laws 1951, ch. 79) on 11 May 1951,
            the proposed amendment only extends the zoning
            authority to New Castle County.
Florida---Laws 1937, ch. 17833; as amended by Laws 1941,
            20759; Laws 1945, ch. 22808; Laws 1947, chs.
            24266 and 24267; Laws 1949, ch. 25510; applying
            to counties of 180,000 population or over. Laws
            1951, ch. 27254: applying to counties of a pop-
            ulation of 60,000-80,000.

Georgia---Laws 1937-1938, no. 133 (10 January 1938), as
         amended by Laws 1949, no. 442: for counties of
         a population of 7,000-75,000. Laws 1939, no.
         281; for counties having a population of 75,000-
         100,000. Laws 1941, no. 213: for counties
         with 20,120-20,130 population. Laws 1947, no.
         15: for counties of 81,000-82,000 in population.
Illinois--Revised Statutes, ch. 34, sec. 1521 et seq.
         (Laws 1935, p. 689, 28 June 1935).
Iowa------Acts 1947, ch. 184, applicable to counties of
         60,000 residents or more.
Kansas----(1) General Statutes, sec. 19-2901 et seq.
         (Laws 1939, ch. 165; as amended Laws 1941, ch.
         196; Laws 1945, ch. 171; Laws 1947, ch. 201;
         Laws 1949, ch. 206): for all counties bordering
         upon another state having a population of 30,-
         000-100,000. (2) Laws 1951, ch. 239: for all
         counties of 100,000 population or more and all
         counties of 25,000-28,000 population having an
         assessed tangible valuation of at least $54-58
         million.
Maryland--Code, art. 66B (Laws 1933, ch. 599; as amended
         Laws 1941, ch. 523; Laws 1945, ch. 808; Laws
         1947, chs. 609 and 760).
Michigan--Compiled Laws, sec. 125.201 et seq. (Acts 1943,
         no. 183; as amended Acts 1952, no. 42).
Minnesota-Statutes, sec. 394.06 et seq. (Laws 1941, ch.
         210; as amended Laws 1945, ch. 551; Laws 1947,
         ch. 361).
Missouri--Laws 1941, pp. 481-489: applicable only to
         counties of 400,000-600,000. Laws 1945, pp.
         1327-1332: applying to counties of first
         classes. Laws 1951, pp. 406-417: for counties
         of second and third classes.
Nevada----Compiled Laws, sec. 5063 et seq. (act of 28
         March 1941; as amended by Statutes 1947, ch.
         267).
New York--Laws 1950, ch. 692.
Oklahoma--Laws 1923, ch. 182 provided, among other things,
         for the establishment of regional planning com-
         missions by cities and counties jointly. But
         the regional planning commissions are engaged
         in urban zoning only. Laws 1949, title 19, ch.
         21, as amended Laws 1951, tit. 19, ch. 19A,
         zoning authority is given all counties of 100,-
         000-244,000 population.
Pennsylvania---Statutes, sec. 510.1 et seq. (P.L. 2129,
         25 June 1937).
Rhode Island---No general enabling legislation. Acts
         1935, ch. 2233, as amended by Acts 1950-1951, ch.
         3010, invests the Town of Johnston with zoning
         authority; Acts 1948, ch. 2079 extended the
         authority to Town of North Kingstown; Acts 1949,

         ch. 2252, extended the authority to the Town of
         South Kingstown (as amended by Acts 1950, ch.
         2490).

South Carolina---Acts 1942, no. 681: applicable to coun-
         ties containing a city with a population of at
         least 70,000. Acts 1951, no. 69: applicable
         to all counties "in which there is a sudden in-
         flux of large numbers of prospective inhabi-
         tants".

South Dakota---Laws 1941, ch. 216.

Tennessee---Code, sec. 10268.1 et seq. (Acts 1935, ch.
         33; as amended Acts 1941, ch. 86).

Virginia---Code, ch. 24, art. 2, sec. 15-844 et seq. Acts
         1938, ch. 415; as amended by Acts 1948, ch. 501),
         for counties generally. Ibid., ch. 24, art. 3,
         sec. 15-855 et seq. (Acts 1927, ch. 15; as
         amended by Acts 1936, ch. 355 and Acts 1948,
         chs. 119 and 226), for certain counties.

Washington---Revised Code, ch. 35.63 (Laws 1935, ch. 44).

Wisconsin---Statutes, sec. 59.97 (Laws 1923, ch. 388; as
         last amended by L. 1949, ch. 639, sec. 12).

Under enabling state statutes, the counties may enact
zoning ordinances, which usually divide the county into a
number of districts and which provide for the permissible or
conforming and prohibited or non-conforming uses of land for
each district. Such ordinances are as a rule drafted by the
county planning commission (or equivalent agency), the establishment of which is provided in the enabling state legislation, in accordance with a master plan, and are adopted
after public hearings. All zoning ordinances are non-retro-
active, that is to say, existing non-conforming uses are not
prohibited, unless they are discontinued for a certain period
of time. This rule gravely restricts the effectiveness and
significance of rural zoning regulation.

    2. The regulation of dams and other structures of water
control and utilization---This county regulation is found in
the following states:

North Carolina---General Statutes, sec. 77-3 (L. 1787,
         ch. 272, sec. 1), sec. 77-4 (L. 1859, ch. 26,
         sec. 1) and sec. 77-6 (ibid., sec. 3).

Michigan---Statutes, sec. 110.09 (L. 1861, ch. 50, secs.
         1, 2, 5, as amended).

Massachusetts---Acts 1875, ch. 178, sec. 1; as amended
         by Acts 1924, ch. 178, sec. 1).

Florida---Statutes, secs. 347.01, 347.02 and 347.06 (L.
         1881, ch. 3300, secs. 1, 2).

Kentucky---Revised Statutes, secs. 182-170 to 182.240
         (Acts 1893, ch. 168).

Montana---Revised Codes, sec. 89-711 (Code of 1895, Po-
         litical, sec. 3450).

Colorado---Statutes, ch. 90, secs. 93 to 97 (L. 1903, ch. 122).

The regulation applies to dams (and reservoirs they impound) only in all of the above-listed states except Florida, where it is applicable to both dams and other structures of water control and utilization. In Colorado, it is concerned only with irrigation dams and reservoirs capable of irrigating at least ten acres of land.

In Michigan, Florida and Kentucky, the regulation consists entirely in licensing. In Massachusetts, county authorities approve the plans and specifications of construction, and inspect the construction work during its progress. The North Carolina measure combines regulation with planning. Only three-fourths of the bed of a watercourse as laid off by special commissioners can be used for the erection of dams by the riparian owners, and one-fourth, including the deepest part, must be left open for the passage of fish. County authorities approve plans for the construction of necessary gates and slopes. In Colorado, the county surveyor approves the site of the dam, and supervises its construction. Upon completion, the dam and all appurtenant structures must be approved by the county commissioners. In Montana, counties regulate dams only when they are built in an unsafe manner, and that only upon the complaint of some party concerned. The regulation consists in the issuance of a certificate of safety signed by a majority of three experts appointed by the county board to inspect the structure.

3. Regulation of terminal facilities---In California, the board of supervisors of a county may, with the approval of the State Railroad Commission, grant license to any person to construct wharves, piers or chutes on navigable watercourses within or bordering upon the county, which license carries with it the right of utilization of the navigable watercourse up to 150 feet from the high-water mark on each side of the structure (Harbors and Navigation Code, secs. 4000 and 4008: Stats. 1858, ch. 160, secs. 1, 4, as amended; and Government Code, sec. 26000: Stats. 1891, ch. 216, sec. 25, as last amended by Stats. 1947, ch. 424, sec. 1). Under Washington statute, the county commissioners of a county may grant a person the right, for a maximum period of twenty years, to erect a wharf at the terminus of a public highway or at any accustomed landing place, with priority given riparian owners (Revised Code, sec. 88.24.020: L. 1893, ch. 49, sec. 1).

The laws of Wisconsin have authorized counties of a population of not more than 300,000 to mark out and establish, with the approval of the State Public Service Commission, both shore and dock or pier lines for any navigable watercourse (Statutes, sec. 30.03(1): L. 1905, ch. 270, sec. 2; as last amended by L. 1949, ch. 335). County regulation in Kentucky is negative in nature: "If the county court (governing body) of the county in which a wharf, pier or bulkhead is located, believes that the wharf, pier or bulkhead obstructs navigation or encroaches on any public landing, the court may abate it" (Revised Statutes, sec. 182.020: Acts 1914, ch. 80, sec. 37, revised in wording).

4. Miscellaneous---In California, approval of the county authorities is required for any person to alter, divert or deflect the course of a navigable stream in connection with surface mining dredging operations (Water Code, sec. 7047: Stats. 1941, ch. 722, sec. 1). In Kansas, permits of the county artesian well supervisor must be obtained for the construction or repair of artesian wells. Owners of the artesian wells have the duty to stop waste of water, and in case of their default the said supervisor may install necessary devices or make necessary repairs at their expense (General Statutes, sec. 42-401 et seq.: L. 1911, ch. 210).

Oregon statute provides for county zoning in the special interest of forest fire control. The county board of commissioners of each county shall, in cooperation with the State Board of Forestry, establish two general zones: namely, Zone 1, which is composed of forest lands intermingled with agricultural lands; and Zone 2, which includes all other rural lands. Fire-protection requirements for the former are to be determined by the county commissioners, the State Board of Forestry and the State Fire Marshall jointly; but those of the latter by the county court or by the county commissioners (L. 1941, ch. 360; as amended by an Act in 1945). In Wyoming, the county commissioners may request the county sheriff to appoint one or more policemen for any city or town which is unincorporated to act as fire wardens. These officers are authorized to order any forest land owner to remove dangerous and inflammable materials from his premises (Compiled Statutes, secs. 45-201 and 45-204: Compiled Laws of 1876, ch. 54, secs. 1, 4).

Colorado counties may order railroads to plow fire guards or fire breaks in specified localities between 16 July and 1 November of each year (Statutes, ch. 139, sec. 75: L. 1874, p. 224, sec. 1; as last amended by L. 1883, p. 198, sec. 1). Similar authority is possessed by New Mexico counties, except that it is not limited to a particular period of the year, and that in case of default the county authorities may perform the work at the costs of the defiant railroads (Statutes, sec. 74-326 et seq.: L. 1884, ch. 34). Under the laws of Maryland, the county commissioners of each county may adopt a county fire prevention code to provide for the protection of lands and other properties against fires and removal of fire hazards, the appointment of inspectors for the enforcement of the code, and penalties for the violation of the pro-

visions of the code and other county ordinances regarding
fire prevention (Code, art. 25, sec. 2D: L. 1948, Extra.
Sess., ch. 38). This regulation applies to both forest and
other fires. Similar regulation is also found in a few other
states.

Arkansas seems to be the only state in which counties
undertake to regulate timber-cutting. The laws of that state
require any person who harvest timber and other forest products to request the county surveyor to survey the lands on
which timber-cutting operation is to be conducted, and to
mark and plainly establish by metes and bounds the forest
areas to be harvested (Statutes, sec. 54-201: Acts 1885, No.
45, sec. 1).[7]

In Nevada, the county authorities may appoint inspectors
to examine damages by rodents, and may order land owners concerned to exterminate them after such examination. In case
of default, the board of county commissioners may have the
work done at the landowners' expenses (Compiled Laws, secs.
372 and 373: Stats. 1909, ch. 110). Similar regulation
exists in South Dakota (Code, sec. 12.2803 et seq.: Laws
1921, ch. 354). But in the latter state, the financial burden of the land owners is fixed at a maximum rate of $15 for
each 160 acres and a minimum rate of $1 for any tract of
land in any one year. The counties of New Jersey, through
the county board of health, may abate any mosquito hazard
within limits specified by the State Department of Health
(Revised Statutes, secs. 26:2-43 and 26:2-44, being Laws 1894,
ch. 330). Moreover, the state Experiment Station, either in
its own initiative or upon the request of a county mosquito
control commission or of a local board of health, may make
surveys of all swamp and overflowed lands. If during such
surveys any mosquito-breeding places are found, the county
mosquito commission or the local board of health concerned
shall order the land owners concerned to abate such places,
and shall abate them at the cost of the latter when they neglect their duty (ibid.,sec. 26:9-2 et seq.: Laws 1905, ch. 80;
as last amended by L. 1927, ch. 143). In Virginia and Indiana, the counties have limited regulatory authority over water
pollution (Code of Virginia, sec. 15-8(3): Joint Resolution
of 10 March 1916; and Indiana Acts of 1953, ch. 94).

Under the laws of Oklahoma, the county government, in the
absence of state action, may order land owners to take measures to prevent soil erosion and drifting when such measures
are necessary (Oklahoma Statutes, tit. 82, sec. 521: Laws
1935, p. 345, sec. 9). A special aspect of soil conservation
and land management, namely the control and eradication of
noxious weeds, is placed under county regulation in the following states:

Illinois---Illinois Revised Statutes, ch. 18: Laws 1872,

p. 210; as amended by L. 1931, p. 204).

South Dakota---<u>Code</u>, sec. 62.0301 et seq.: Laws 1890, ch.
116; as last amended by L. 1917, ch. 319.

Idaho-----<u>Code</u>, sec. 22-2406 et seq.: Laws 1911, ch. 120;
as last amended by L. 1949, ch. 116, sec. 1).

Iowa------<u>Code</u>, ch. 317: Acts 1913, ch. 128; as last
amended by Acts 1951, ch. 108.

Minnesota-<u>Statutes</u>, ch. 20 (Laws 1923, ch. 318; as last
amended by L. 1951, ch. 466).

Oregon----<u>Revised Statutes</u>, sec. 570.505 et seq.: Laws
1923, ch. 265; as last amended by L. 1939, ch.
313, sec. 1.

Virginia--<u>Code</u>, sec. 15-15: Acts 1946, ch. 365. For
counties having of density of population in excess of 400 inhabitants per square mile only.

Except in Virginia, the general pattern of regulation is that
the county government first order land owners to eradicate
noxious weeds and that in their default the county government
performs the works at their cost. In Virginia, the county
government may <u>either</u> order the land owners to do the work,
<u>or, alternatively,</u> have it done by itself and charge the cost
to the land owners.

Section 2 Enterprise

1. <u>Navigation improvement</u>---(1) With respect to canals
and similar works, Michigan laws authorize the counties to
purchase canals after a referendum (<u>Compiled Laws</u>, secs. 485.-
21 and 485.22: Acts 1785, p. 287, secs. 21 and 22; as amended
by Act No. 216 of 1879). The government of any county in New
Jersey may dig out or construct "a permanent inlet or waterway through which any river or creek running in or through
such county may be connected with the ocean . . ." (<u>Statutes</u>,
sec. 40:14-10, being Laws 1897, ch. 43, sec. 1). In Ohio,
the county government may construct and improve canals and
waterways and issue bonds for that purpose (an act of 10 August 1927). (2) With respect to the removal of obstructions,
the county boards of the several counties of Illinois have
been authorized to removal "driftwood and other obstructions
from natural watercourses. . ." (<u>Revised Statutes</u>, ch. 34,
sec. 111: Laws 1877, p. 68). North Carolina counties have
authority to open or clear any inland river or stream that
runs through or border upon the respective counties (<u>General
Statutes</u>, sec. 77-1: Laws 1887).

(3) With respect to harbor improvement, it is provided
in Ohio statute that "the board of county commissioners of
any county bordering on Lake Erie may construct, open, enlarge,
excavate, improve, deepen, straighten, or extend any harbor
located in whole or in part within such county, and within the
corporate limits of a municipal corporation having an aggregate tax duplicate of less than $500,000,000 . . ." (<u>Revised</u>

<u>Code 1953</u>, sec. 307.65: Laws 1902, p. 644, sec. 1; as last
amended by L. 1931, p. 599). Under the laws of California,
"any county may improve, develop, protect, and maintain one
or more or all of the harbors within its boundaries" (<u>Harbors
and Navigation Code</u>, sec. 4131: Stats. 1945, ch. 1500, sec.
1). The statute has authorized Nassau County to "provide for
the widening, deepening or dredging of any bay, harbor, inlet or channel within the boundaries of the county and for
the construction of dikes, bulkheads, seawalls, jetties or
other similar devices necessary or appropriate to increase
the navigability of any such bay, harbor, inlet or channel.
. . " (Laws 1939, ch. 272; as amended by L. 1953, ch. 822,
in sec. 12-21.0).

Legislation in some states covers all of the three above-
mentioned and other aspects of county navigation-improvement
enterprise. In Massachusetts, "a county or town may appropriate money for the improvement of tidal and non-tidal rivers and streams, harbors, tide waters, foreshores and shores
along a public beach . . ." (<u>General Laws</u>, ch. 91, sec. 29:
Acts 1909, ch. 481, sec. 3; as last amended by Acts 1905,
ch. 524). Counties of New Jersey (as well as cities) "may
by ordinance open or keep open any inlet, stream, canal, basin
or other public waterway . . ." (<u>Statutes</u>, sec. 40:14-1, being Laws 1910, ch. 230, sec. 1).[8] Parishes as wells as municipalities of Louisiana have been authorized to undertake
such works of public improvement as "the constructing, deepening, widening, improving and maintaining of navigation canals,
and navigation channels, and the deepening, widening, improving and maintaining of existing streams, lakes and other watercourses" (<u>Revised Statutes</u>, tit. 34, secs. 361 and 362:
Acts 1921, Ex. Sess., No. 68; as last amended by Acts 1950,
No. 398, sec. 1). The statute of Florida declares it "to be
a legitimate county or municipal purpose for any county or
incorporated city or town . . . to improve and beautify waterways, including lakes, rivers, streams, ditches and canals,
. . . by opening such waterways and by clearing them of logs
and other obstructions, including water hyacinths and other
disagreeable and obnoxious vegetation . . ." (<u>Statutes</u>, sec.
342.03: Laws 1931, ch. 14651, sec. 1). Counties of Minnesota
may make any kind of improvement on any watercourse within
their respective jurisdictions for which a permit has been obtained from the State Department of Conservation (<u>Statutes</u>,
sec. 110.121: Laws 1947, ch. 123, sec. 1).

As for actual examples of county navigation-improvement
enterprise, ". . . the large resident taxpayers of Lake Charles
got together in 1921 and agreed to bond themselves and other
taxpayers of the City of Lake Charles and Calcasieu Parish
(Louisiana) to raise funds to construct a community-owned ship
channel." The work consisted in straightening and deepening
the channel of the Calcasieu River between Lake Charles and
the Intracoastal Waterway, and in enlarging the section of the

waterway from the Calcasieu to the Sabine to a 30-foot depth
and 125-foot bottom width. "The project was completed and
opened to commerce in 1926." "The planning, financing, engineering, construction and maintenance of the channel that
made Lake Charles a deepwater port were assumed in their en-
tirety by the City of Lake Charles and Calcasieu Parish."[9]

The Gulf County Canal in Florida was originally a county
enterprise. This canal extends for about 6 miles from the
St. Josephs Bay, near Port St. Joe, Florida, to a point on
the Intracoastal Waterway 37 miles southeast of Panama City
and 24 miles northeast of Apalachicola. "It was completed
in October 1938, at a total cost of $200,000, for which a
bond issue was floated by Gulf County, Florida. This canal
has a depth of 9 feet and a minimum bottom width of 70 feet,
although at its St. Josephs Bay end the width is substantially
100 feet."[10] This canal was taken over by the Federal Government under the authority of a special act of 17 June 1943 (57
Stat. 156).

For the Peconic River, New York, the County of Suffolk
in 1936 dredged it to a depth of 4 feet for some distance,
at a cost of $2,500.[11] Dixie County of Florida has provided
a sea wall in front of the Village of Horseshoe at a cost of
about $8,000.[12] In Galveston Harbor, Texas, "following the
disastrous storm of September 1900, . . . a sea wall, 17,593
feet long, was constructed by Galveston County . . . . The
sea wall was completed in July 1904, at a cost to Galveston
County of $1,581,673.30." In June 1927, an extension of this
sea wall covering a distance of 2,800 feet was completed by
the same county at a cost of $535,951.67. The cost of main-
tenance of this sea wall was $718,419.83 to 31 July 1929.[13]
In the Biloxi Bay, Mississippi, "the harbor for small craft
was constructed by Harrison County in 1943; it consists of a
pier 50 feet wide extending 330 feet into the sound, with an
ell 11 feet wide extending 325 feet east. The basin thus inclosed was dredged to a depth of 9 feet and is about 100 feet
north and shoreward of the Biloxi Harbor channel. The cost
of the harbor for small craft was $73,368.55."[14]

In the following states, there is state legislation enabling the counties to establish docks, piers, wharves and
public landings:

    North Carolina---General Statutes, sec. 77-11 (Laws 1784,
               ch. 206; as last amended by L. 1919, ch. 68).
    Maryland---Code, art. 25, sec. 162 (Laws 1823, ch. sec.
               146 (L. 1853, ch. 220, sec. 4).
    Montana---Revised Codes, sec. 16-1116 (Laws 1909, ch. 33,
               sec. 1)
    Louisiana-Acts 1921, Ex. sess., Nos. 70 and 80; as last
               amended by Acts 1946, No. 218, sec. 1 (Revised
               Statutes, tit. 33, secs. 4161 and 4162).

The pier in the above-mentioned works of Harrison County
of Mississippi is a county terminal enterprise. In 1937,
the County of Suffold of New York constructed a wharf on the
Peconic River.[15] St. Louis County of Minnesota owns a dock
on Lake Superior which has been leased to a private fishing
company.[16] One timber wharf at Manteo Bay, North Carolina,
"is owned and operated by Dare County, N. C."[17] The County
of San Luis Obispo, California, owns and operates a wharf of
280 feet long and 60 feet wide having a berthing space of 560
feet, which is used as a landing for fishing and pleasure
boats.[18] Wayne County, Michigan, owns and operates a public
wharf at Detroit,[19] and Douglas County, Wisconsin, owns the
Whitney Dock at the port of Dulluth-Superior, Minnesota and
Wisconsin, which is, however, not in operation.[20] Richmond
County, Virginia, has built two public landings on the
Totuskey Creek, just below the Totuskey Bridge, one on each
side of the stream, at a total cost of $4,000.[21]

    2. Flood control---The various measures of navigation
improvement (excluding terminal facilities) discussed in
foregoing subsection may incidentally serve the purposes of
flood control. Indeed, in many states, these measures may be
applied to both navigable and non-navigable watercourses. When
they are applied to non-navigable watercourses, they are primarily if not purely flood-control measures. In addition, general enabling legislation for county flood-control enterprise
as such had, by the end of 1953, been enacted in the following
states:[22]

     Louisiana---Revised Statutes, tit. 33, sec. 2741 (Acts
            1847, 106, sec. 8), in 2nd para.
     Tennessee---Code, sec. 4193 (Acts 1871, ch. 131).
     Nebraska---(1) Revised Statutes, sec. 23-308 (Laws 1885,
            ch. 38, sec. 1): County board may construct
            dams, dikes or embankments to protect from floods
            any tract of 320 acres or more, upon petition
            of 20 freeholders in the precinct concerned. (2)
            Ibid., sec. 23-309 et seq. (Laws 1921, ch. 269).
            (3) Laws 1951, ch. 95: Counties having a popula-
            tion of 200,000 or more may clear watercourses
            of debris, silt, snags and other obstructions
            with view to preventing floods, upon petition of
            five riparian land owners.
     Texas-----Revised Civil Statutes, art. 6830 (Laws 1901,
            1st S. S., p. 23, sec. 1; as last amended by L.
            1925, ch. 96, sec. 1).
     Arizona---Code, sec. 17-355 (Laws 1905, ch. 44, secs. 1 to
            3).
     North Dakota---Revised Code, ch. 61-12 (Laws 1919, ch. 116).
     New Mexico---Statutes Annotated, sec. 15-4701 et seq. (Laws
            1921, ch. 163).
     Washington---Revised Code, sec. 36.32.280 (Laws 1921, ch.
            30, sec. 1).

Ohio------Revised Code of 1953, sec. 6131.03 et seq. (Laws
            1923, p. 161; and L. 1937, p. 490).
California---Government Code, sec. 25680, or Water Code,
            sec. 8100 (Stats. 1929, ch. 755, sec. 7; as
            last amended by Stats. 1947, ch. 424, sec. 1).
            For non-navigable streams only, Water Code, sec.
            8126 (enacted by Stats. 1943, ch. 369, sec. 1).
            The latter provision, however, seems superfluous.
Kansas----General Statutes, sec. 82a-307 (Laws 1929, ch.
            143, sec. 2; as last amended by L. 1951, ch.
            527, sec. 1).
Pennsylvania---Statutes, tit. 16, sec. 461 (an act of 2
            May 1929, art. V, sec. 461). This provision
            was made inapplicable to counties of second
            class by an act of 28 July 1953.
Indiana---Statutes, sec. 48-4748 (Acts 1943, ch. 258,
            sec. 1). Only counties having a city of first
            class.
West Virginia---Code, sec. 591 (1400) (Acts 1951, ch.
            141).

In Nebraska (1921 law), New Mexico, Washington, Ohio,
California, Pennsylvania and West Virginia, the counties are
authorized, explicitly or by implication, to construct all
kinds of flood-control works, such as dams, levees, floodways
and channel improvements. Counties of Louisiana, Tennessee
and Indiana can only construct levees and dikes. County
flood-control works are limited to "levees, dikes and other
works" in Arizona; levees, dikes, revetments and channel improvements in Nebraska; levees, dikes and floodways in Texas;
dams and floodways in North Dakota and channel improvements
in Kansas. It may be noted that when all works other than
dams are mostly local in nature and need not be constructed
beyond county limits, but that dams, particularly storage
dams, may have to be constructed outside the territorial boundaries of the county. This is expressly permitted by the
Pennsylvania law. In New Mexico and Washington, another expedient is provided for which consists in the authorization
for joint enterprise by two or more counties, which, is desirable not only with regard to the construction of dams but
also in connection with other flood-control works (except
perhaps protective levees).

In North Dakota, the authority of the county in flood-
control enterprise is limited to non-navigable watercourses
only. So also is the case of California counties under the
law of 1943. But in all other cases county flood-control enterprise covers both navigable and non-navigable watercourses.

In North Dakota, Nebraska, Ohio and Kansas, county flood-
control projects are initiated by petition of private individuals. The number of individuals required to present the petition in each of these four states is as follows:

North Dakota---six freeholders.
Nebraska-------Owners of a major portion of the land area
        affected.
Ohio---any landowner.
Kansas---any fifty taxpayers.

In Nebraska and Ohio, in addition to the petition requirement,
the flood-control works to be constructed must furthermore be
approved by state authorities. In New Mexico, flood-control
works in each county are to be constructed under the supervision of the county flood commissioner, who is appointed by
the Governor for the county government. In all other states,
the counties have a relatively free hand in flood-control enterprise.

In addition to county flood-control enterprise as discussed
above, flood-control works may also be constructed to protect
or to facilitate the construction of county roads and highways,
as a part of the administration of the latter. This is expressly permitted in the laws of Ohio and Nebraska. The laws of
Ohio provide, on this point, that "when in its opinion it is
necessary or advisable, in order to provide protection or a
proper location for a proposed bridge or road, the board of
county commissioners may divert, alter, straighten, or clean
out a river, creek, or other watercourse . . ." (Revised Code
of 1953, sec. 6151.01: Laws 1875, p. 64). Nebraska counties,
in protecting county roads and bridges from flood damage, may
widen, straighten or alter the course of any watercourse, and
build dams, dikes, embankments and other necessary structures
thereon (Revised Statutes, sec. 39-260: Laws 1907, ch. 113,
sec. 1).

County flood-control enterprise has been successful in
several instances. Before the passage of the first National
Flood Control Act on 22 June 1936, considerable flood-control
construction and maintenance work was done on the Nooksack,
Skagit, Stilaguamish, Snohomish, Green, Puyallup, Chehalis,
Walla Walla, Yakima dn other rivers in the State of Washington.
"Practically all of the work was done by the counties in which
the particular stream was located, often with some help from
the Army Engineers."[23]   On the Lewis River, for example, "there
were two small jobs of revetment work done by Cowlitz County
during the early 1920's, . . . about 1,000 feet put on the
bank at Robinson bend and about 1,500 feet at the Kerns bend."[24]
In California, San Bernardino County constructed a levee of
4,100 feet long connecting the afore-discussed levee built by
the Corps of Engineers on behalf of the Army Air Corps.[25]   In
Wyoming, "Teton County and private interests have built numerous levees and dikes, especially on the right bank of the
Snake River, . . . in an attempt to reduce bank erosion and
prevent Snake River from cutting into Fish Creek and destroying
the town of Wilson and other property. Teton County has (also)
carried out protective work on Buffalo Fork . . ."[26]

A few examples of county flood control enterprise have been found in Ohio. "In the period 1917 to 1920, by joint action of Perry, Fairfield, and Hocking Counties, a portion of Rush Creek and Little Rush Creek was dredged to provide protection from floods of moderate stages . . . . Failure of assessed property owners in Hocking County to meet the assessments forced the county to assume the cost of the improvement in the county. The maor part of the entire project has become impaired as a result of the failure to keep the dredged channel in repair and free from growths and obstructions . . . ." "The section of Hocking River from Hookers downstream through Lancaster, a distance of about 6 miles, was widened, straightened, and leveed by Fairfield County during 1914. . . . The same channel was re-dredged in 1937, . . . and more recently smaller tributary streams which flow through the town (of Lancaster) have been dredged."[27] "Jefferson County, Ohio, . . . has improved to a limited extent, short reaches of the channels of Short Creek and Piney Fork in Dillonvale and of Short Creek and Flag Run in Adena . . . . The work consisted primarily of dredging and removing obstructions in the channels. Excavated material was placed on the adjacent banks in the form of dikes." "Improvements were only of a temporary nature, and subsequent high waters have returned a considerable part of the dredged material to the channel."[28]

As in the case of state highway systems, county flood protection works may also be provided as an incident of or an adjunct to county highway construction. For example, "the embankment of a new road constructed at Elkport in about 1936 by the Clayton County highway department (Iowa) was planned to serve as a protective dike against floodwaters of Elk Creek and Turkey River. In connection with the construction of the embankment, the channel of Elk Creek was straightened for about one-half mile above its mouth."[29] In 1938, Tillamook County of Oregon started work on about 1,500 feet of the channel change of the Hehalem River in the vicinity of mile 9 "in an attempt to prevent further bank erosion where the highway (built by the said county) and Southern Pacific Company roadbeds were being endangered."[30] These flood-control projects may not be regarded as constituting part of the independent county flood-control enterprise.

3. <u>Drainage</u>---County drainage enterprise is active in the following states, where there is a general enabling law for such enterprise:

Maryland---(<u>Code</u>, Article 25, sec. 39 et seq.: Laws 1858, ch. 271; as last amended by L. 1949, ch. 271).
Nebraska---<u>Revised Statutes</u>, ch. 31, art. 1; Laws 1881, ch. 51; as last amended by L. 1911, ch. 140).
Kansas----(<u>General Statutes</u>, sec. 24-301 et seq.: L. 1886, ch. 161, as augmented by L. 1920, ch. 42, sec. 1).
Minnesota---<u>Statutes</u>, sec. 106.1 et seq.: L. 1887, ch. 97;

as last amended by L. 1953, ch. 407)

Florida---(Statutes, ch. 156: L. 1893, ch. 4178; and
ibid., ch. 157: L. 1901, ch. 5035; as last
amended by L. 1917, ch. 7307).

North Dakota---(Revised Code, ch. 61-21: L. 1895, ch.
51; as last amended by L. 1925, ch. 131).

Michigan---(Compiled Laws, chs. 261-277: Act No. 316 of
1923, entitled "General Drainage Law", which is
based on Act No. 254 of 1897, as amended)

Missouri--(Revised Statutes of 1899, sec. 8278 et seq.;
as last amended by L. 1921, p. 303, the 1899
enactment being effected by its adoption in the
Revised Statutes of 1899 and not by a session
law)

South Dakota (Code, ch. 61.10: L. 1905, ch. 98; as last
amended by L. 1949, ch. 436, sec. 1).

Oklahoma---(Statutes, tit. 82, ch. 3: L. 1910-11, ch.
132).

Kentucky---(Revised Statutes, ch. 267: Acts 1912, ch.132;
as last amended by Acts 1952, ch. 84, sec. 63).

Ohio------(Code, sec. 6443 et seq.: L. 1923, p. 161; as
amended by L. 1937, p. 490).

Indiana---(Statutes, tit. 27: Acts 1933, ch. 264; as augmented by Acts 1953, ch. 243).

North Carolina---(General Statutes, sec. 156-139 et seq.:
L. 1943, ch. 553).

New Jersey---(Statutes, sec. 40: 30-18 et seq.: L. 1945,
ch. 112).

Louisiana---(Act No. 160 of 1946).

In New York, there is no statute specifically authorizing the
counties to undertake the construction and operation of drainage works. However, it is provided in the Optional County
Government Law (enacted 1937) that in counties operating under
plans A, B and C there should be a department of public works
whose duty it shall be "the construction and maintenance of
county roads and bridges, county drains, county sewers, and
all other county public works . . ." (sec. 404, 2nd para.).
There is no county enterprise in Delaware. But the county
treasurer, under an act of 1941 (L. 1941, ch. 219), collects
ditch taxes due to drainage companies.[31] It may also be mentioned that in states where counties had the authority to
construct drains in the past, counties may continue to maintain and operate the drains which they built when the county
drainage laws were not repealed. Such authority of the county
government is expressly provided in the law of Arkansas (Statutes, sec. 21-401: Acts 1907, No. 314, sec. 1).

In all of the above-listed states, drainage projects are
authorized by the county governing body, except: (1) in Minnesota, where the county governing body authorizes those drainage works which are situated within a single county and the
district courts authorize those extending over two or more

counties; (2) In Indiana, where both the county governing
body and the local circuit or superior court may authorize
county drains; (3) in Michigan, where the authority of establishing county drains is exercised by a drainage commissioner,
who is popularly elected at each biennial election; and (4)
in North Dakota, where the same authority is vested in a board
of drainage commissioners, which is composed of six members
appointed by the board of county commissioners for a tenure
of three years. Actual construction is invariably done by
contract, which is let by the authority establishing the
drains. It is usually supervised by some special agency or
officer. For example, in Michigan and North Dakota, the county drains are constructed under the supervision of the above-
mentioned drainage commissioner and board of drainage commissioners. In Kentucky, the construction work is in charge of
a board of drainage commissioners composed of one member annually elected by the taxpayers in each of the drainage districts established by the county governing body for this
purpose. Under Maryland laws, the supervisory authority is
placed in a board of three drainage managers, who are elected
by the taxpayers by weighted voting. Indiana laws place the
supervisory authority in the county surveyor and Nebraska laws
intrust it with a surveyor or engineer appointed by the county
board. In North Carolina, the construction of county drains
is "under the supervision and jurisdiction of the health department, or any sanitary committee, or other governmental
agency or department . . ."

In all these states except North Carolina, Louisiana and
New Jersey,[32] county drains are authorized after petition by
a certain number of landowners affected, followed by a public
hearing and in some states by an investigation and a public
hearing and in some states by an investigation and a public
hearing. In South Dakota, county drains are approved by both
the county governing body and the state engineer. At the
public hearing, the boundaries of the area to be drained are
designated. Such area is officially called a "drainage district" in Kentucky, Michigan, Missouri, Oklahoma and South
Dakota. But these "drainage districts" are not regular drainage districts having corporate status and the quality of a
governmental unit,[33] but they are merely administrative field
area. It may be further noted that as in these states it is
always the lands affected with which a county drainage project
is concerned and against which assessments are levied, it
does not matter whether these lands are designated as a "drainage district" or not.

The number of interested landowners required to sign a
petition for county drainage works varies in a wide range
among the various states. For the sake of convenience, the
different requirements are listed below:

Michigan---two-thirds of owners.

Minnesota and Florida---either majority of owners or
          owner or owners of majority of land area to be
          drained.
South Dakota---majority of owners.
Maryland---either one-third of owners of owners of one-
          third of land area to be drained.
Kentucky---25 percent (one-fourth) of owners.
Indiana---10 percent of owners (but for lands situated
          on public highways, petition by county commis-
          sioners; for lands within limits of a city or
          town, petition by the governing body of said
          city or town)
North Dakota---six owners.
Oklahoma---five owners (but when feasibility of a project
          is dubious, either petition by fifty percent of
          owners or petition by owner or owners of fifty
          percent of land area affected).
Nebraska, Kansas, Missouri and Ohio---one owner.

It may be noted that although petition is not required in
North Carolina, the authority of the county commissioners in
drainage works is limited in that they can do so only when
the collection of special benefit assessments is inadvisable.
In Minnesota, in addition to the petition requirement, county
drainage enterprise is further subject to the restriction
that no meandered lakes can be drained except upon the determination by the state conservation department that they are
not public waters or that if they are public waters drainage
can be undertaken only when so permitted by the said department.

It has been reported that "New Madrid County, Missouri,
has constructed a network of drainage ditches in that county
that have their outlets in the Little River drainage district
ditches. This county has expended about $4,400,000 for their
drainage improvements to date (30 October 1947). Extensive
drainage improvements have also been constructed by Pemiscot,
Dunklin, Stoddard, and Scott Counties in Missouri, and in
Mississippi, Poinsett, Clay, Greene, Craighead, Crittenden,
Cross, St. Francis, and Lee Counties in Arkansas."[34] In
Louisiana, a total of 34 parishes has undertaken drainage enterprise by October 1953, with drainage works aggregating
$16,819,082 in capital outlay.[35] The channels of natural
watercourses improved and new canals and ditches dug totalled
5,261 miles as of June 1953.[36] As of 1950 data of county
drainage in 17 states were as follows:[37]

State	Acreage
Delaware	352,547
Indiana	11,017,709
Iowa	6,734,863
Kansas	2,500
Kentucky	957,892

Louisiana	9,461,809
Michigan	10,194,439
Minnesota	11,269,962
Nebraska	131,973
North Carolina	91,590
North Dakota	1,565,055
Ohio	8,923,362
Oklahoma	298,853
South Dakota	706,973
Virginia	15,721
Washington	5,570
Wisconsin	141,585
Total	61,874,403

Parks---The first county in the United States which establishes a county park system is Essex County, New York. In 1895 its authorities created a park commission, and by the end of the 19th century a total of eight parks had been acquired by the commission. Orange County, New York, acquired a 160-acre park in 1900 and Ventura County, California, acquired several parks through donation in 1906. But until about 1920, only a few counties acquired and improved parks.[38] Minnesota seems to be the first state having a general enabling law for the establishment of county parks. As of 1953, similar legislation existed in the following states:

Minnesota---Statutes, sec. 371.18, subdiv. 12 (Laws 1901, ch. 71; as last amended by L 1951, ch 82, sec. 1).

Michigan---Acts 1913, No. 90.

Texas---Laws 1915, ch. 53; Laws 1931, ch. 148.

Wyoming---Compiled Statutes, sec. 26-801 (Laws 1915, ch. 54; as last amended by L. 1951, ch. 150, sec. 1).

Pennsylvania---Statutes, tit. 53, sec. 1611 (Acts 1919, No. 322; as last amended by Acts 1927, No. 38).

Utah---Code, sec. 11-2-1 et seq. (Laws 1923, ch. 100; as amended by L. 1949, ch. 70, sec. 1).

Louisiana---Revised Statutes, tit. 33, ch. 11, sec. 4552 (Acts 1924, No. 200, sec. 2; as amended by Acts 1952, No. 512, ch. 35).

Virginia---Code, sec. 15-697 et seq. (Acts 1924, ch. 35).

Wisconsin---Statutes, sec. 27.065 (Laws 1925, ch. 442, sec. 2; as last amended by L. 1943, ch. 73).

North Carolina---General Statutes, sec. 153-77(g) (Laws 1927, ch. 81, sec. 8(g), not affected by amendments).

Kansas---General Statutes, 1937, 19-2801 (Laws 1929, ch. 158, sec. 1; as amended by L. 1935, ch. 137, sec. 1); 19-2814 (L. 1935, ch. 142, sec. 1; as last amended by L. 1949, ch. 205, sec. 1); 19-2819 (L. 1935, ch. 143, sec. 1); 19-2824 (L. 1937, ch. 194, sec. 1); 19-2834 (L. 1937, ch. 193, sec. 1) and

19-2841 (L. 1937, ch. 192, sec. 1).

Montana---Revised Codes, sec. 62-101 (Laws 1929, ch. 51; as amended by L. 1947, ch. 251 sec. 1).

Colorado---Colorado Statutes, ch. 136, sec. 1 (Laws 1935, ch. 222, sec. 1; as amended by L. 1937, ch. 251, sec. 1).

North Dakota---Code, ch. 11-28 (Laws 1935, ch. 117; as amended by L. 1953, ch. 116).

Ohio---Ohio Revised Code 1953, sec. 301.26 (Laws 1935, p. 132, sec. 7). Cf. L. 1921, p. 609.

Oregon---Revised Statutes 1953, sec. 275.320 (Laws 1935, ch. 217, sec. 1; as last amended by L. 1947, ch. 165, sec. 1).

South Carolina---Acts 1935, No. 92.

South Dakota---Code, sec. 12.2401 (Laws 1935, ch. 76).

Arizona---Code, sec. 16-1502 (Laws 1939, ch. 78, sec. 2).

Tennessee---Code, sec. 5201.9 et seq. (Acts 1939, ch. 219). Fishing lakes only, but not other recreational areas.

Mississippi---Code, sec. 5979 (Laws 1940, ch. 271).

New Jersey---Laws 1940, ch. 33. Also see Laws 1935, ch. 251, sec. 2.

Nevada---Compiled Laws, sec. 2049.11 (Stats. 1945, ch. 206, sec. 1). Only counties having a population of more than 10,000.

Georgia---Code, sec. 69-601 (Laws 1946, No. 622).

Arkansas---Acts 1949, No. 333.

Illinois---Revised Statutes, sec. 25.09 (enacted 4 August 1949; as last amended 20 June 1951).

Washington---Laws 1949, ch. 94.

California---Statutes 1951, ch. 24.

West Virginia---Acts 1951, ch. 52.

Kentucky---Acts 1952, ch. 54.

New York---Laws 1952, ch. 834.

Alabama---Acts 1953, No. 455. Only counties having more than 400,000 population.

Florida---Laws 1953, ch. 28340.

Indiana counties have the authority to acquire lands for the use of public parks; but such lands must be conveyed and transferred to the state for the establishment of state parks (Statutes, sec. 26-1512 et seq.: Acts 1927, ch. 174; as amended by Acts 1945, ch. 233; and ibid., sec. 26-1536 et seq.: Acts 1947, ch. 159). The only authority of Indiana counties in park enterprise is contained in sec. 26-1535 of the Statutes (Acts 1943, ch. 231, sec. 1), which provides that the county authorities of a county not having a city of the first or second class may, upon petition by 200 landowners, appropriate funds and levy additional taxes to defray a part of the costs of maintenance of a city park. Maryland laws provide for the establishment of county forests but not county parks (Code, of Maryland, art. 66C, sec. 347: Laws 1906, ch. 294; as amended by L. 1910, ch. 161). In as much as there is no distinction between state parks and state forests in that state, it would seem that county forests in Maryland are likewise at the same time county parks.

As of 1950, 113 counties in 27 states owned 732 parks aggregating 174,884 acres, as shown in the following table:[39]

State	Number of counties	Number of parks	Total acreage
Arizona	4	19	32,849
Arkansas	1	1	40
California	12	196	6,348
Colorado	1	2	162
Florida	6	59	5,305
Georgia	2	40	1,565
Illinois	3	47	40,703
Indiana	3	4	405
Kansas	2	2	693
Kentucky	4	7	88
Louisiana	1	10	1,003
Maryland	4	16	2,740
Michigan	17	90	8,274
New Hampshire	1	1	850
New Jersey	5	61	11,146
New York	6	29	23,451
North Dakota	1	2	200
Ohio	3	16	11,600
Oregon	1	8	535
Pennsylvania	5	16	6,274
Texas	1	2	3,465
Utah	2	7	558
Virginia	1	17	153
Washington	3	33	447
West Virginia	3	6	1,157
Wisconsin	20	139	12,173
Wyoming	1	2	3,000
Total	113	732	174,884

The counties having the largest acreages of county parks are (1) Cook County, Illinois, 38,420 acres; (2) Pima County, Arizona, 30,002 acres; and (3) Westchester County, New York, 17,000 acres.[40] As in the case of state parks, artificial lakes or reservoirs may be found in county parks as a part of the park improvement. The Marion County Lake project of Marion County, Kansas, on the Woolford Creek, a minor tributary of the Cottonwood River, is a good example. "The project was constructed by the Civilian Conservation Corps as a recreational park improvement for Marion County. The dam, a rolled earth-fill structure, has a crest length of 1,150 feet, and a maximum height of 54 feet." "The reservoir has a surface area of 160 acres and a capacity of 2,76a acre-feet."[41]

5. _Forestry_---In the following states, general enabling
legislation has been enacted for the establishment and administration of county forests:[42]

Maryland---_Code_, art. 66C, sec. 347, (Laws 1906, ch. 294;
    as amended by L. 1910, ch. 161 and L. 1914, ch.
    823) (Implied).

Illinois---Laws 1923, p. 304; as amended by L. 1951, p.
    1717 (_Revised Statutes_, ch. 34, sec. 24, paras.
    9 and 12).

Indiana---_Statutes_, sec. 32-101 et seq. (Acts 1929, ch.
    17; as amended by Acts 1935, ch. 35); and _Ibid._,
    sec. 32-601 et seq. (Acts 1943, ch. 272).

New York---_Conservation Law_, sec. 219 (Laws 1929, ch.
    194; as last amended by L. 1938, ch. 571). Also
    see _Ibid._, sec. 60 (Laws 1916, ch. 451; as last
    amended by L. 1943, ch. 710, part 1, sec. 201).

Michigan---_Compiled Laws_, secs. 320.201 to 320.210 (Acts
    1931, No. 217).

Pennsylvania---_Statutes_, tit. 32, sec. 171 et seq. (an
    act of 13 April 1933).

Ohio---_Revised Code_, sec. 301.26 (Laws 1935, p. 132, sec.
    7). Also see _Ibid._, sec. 5707.08 (Laws 1921, p.
    322).

Virginia---_Code_,-sec. 10-48 (Acts 1940, ch. 40, sec. 1).

Florida---_Statutes_, sec. 591.18 (Laws 1941, ch. 20902,
    sec. 4).

Oregon---Laws 1941, ch. 38; as amended by L. 1947, ch.
    165, sec. 1 _Revised Statutes_, sec. 275.320).

Montana---_Revised Codes_, sec. 28-501 (Laws 1945, ch. 70,
    sec. 1).

Minnesota---Laws 1945, ch. 347, sec. 1(_Statutes_, sec. 459.-
    06).

Wisconsin---_Statutes_, sec. 28.10 (Laws 1947, ch. 109; as
    amended by L. 1949, ch. 474.)

In all of these states, with the exception of Pennsylvania, Montana and Minnesota, the county government has the
authority (explicit or implied) to establish county forests
by purchase, gift or tax deed (which may be said as a kind of
forced purchase). In Montana, county forests are to be created only on lands acquired through tax deed and remaining
unsold at public land auctions, though these lands may be
exchanged for other lands. In Minnesota, only tax-forfeited
lands or donated lands may be used as county forests. County
forest lands in Pennsylvania are state lands left unsold at
public land auctions and not needed by the state for state
forests or game-management areas.

As reported in 1950, county forests were found in Wisconsin, Illinois, New York, New Jersey, Michigan and Pennsylvania, with Wisconsin having the largest area.[43] As of 30 June
1952, 28 counties of Wisconsin had established county forests

totalling 2,142,372 acres. They are administered in each
county by a special committee of the county board with the
assistance of the district forester concerned of the State
Conservation Commission.[44]

   In a few states, the county government has general authority over the conservation of forest resources. The above-
cited statutory provision of Maryland, which contains an implied authorization for county forests, authorizes the county
commissioners of each county "to levy and appropriate money
for purposes of tree planting and care of trees, and for forest protection, improvement, management and purchase." Under
this provision, not only the establishment of county forests
is permissible, but the county government may take measures
to develop and conserve forest resources on other public
lands and on private lands. In Montana, "the board of county
commissioners of any county may provide money for the purposes
of forest protection, improvement and management" (Revised
Codes, sec. 10-1104: Laws 1909, ch. 147, sec. 105), In Alabama, an act was passed in 1951 (Acts 1951, No. 663), which
directed every county having a population between 27,150 and
28,800 to divide the county into as many forest protection
districts as there are members of the county governing body,
each district to have a district forest warden. The chairman
of the county governing body is authorized to administer "all
laws relating to conservation, development and protection of
forests", to supervise the activities of the several district
forest wardens, and to "plan and provide for a general program for the protection of forests within the county."

   In some states, authority has been given the several
counties to undertake the work of forest-fire prevention and
control, or some phase of this work. In South Dakota, "in
counties containing areas not embraced in any civil township,
fireguards . . . may be constructed under the supervision of
county commissioners, and the cost thereof met by special
levy upon the real property, including railroads, within the
area embraced by such fireguards (i.e., fire-breaks)" (Code,
sec. 58.1003: Laws 1893, ch. 91, sec. 3; as amended by L.
1905, ch. 111). The county government in North Dakota may
also construct fire-breaks, but only upon the petition of at
least ten percent of the qualified voters of the county (Revised Code, sec. 18-0701, being derived from the Revised Code
of 1895, sec. 1664, as last amended by Laws 1899, ch. 122,
sec. 1). There seems to be no special authority for any of
the counties, or the counties generally, of South Carolina to
construct fire-breaks on private lands. However, as reported
in 1951, "Horry County continued to construct firebreaks with
county-owned equipment. This unit constructed a total of 557
miles of pre-suppression breaks for landowners and was also
used for fire suppression plowing throughout the county."[45]

   In Colorado, the county sheriff, in his capacity as the

county fire warden, is the only agency responsible for fire-
prevention on both public and private lands, a job ordinarily performed by the state forestry agency in most other
states (Statutes, ch. 45, sec. 102: Laws 1903, ch. 83, sec.
1). In discharging this duty, the county sheriffs may organize fire-fighting and fire-patrol forces, and construct pre-
suppression fire-breaks, lookout stations, and other necessary
structures.[46] The counties of Minnesota, upon petition by two
or more land owners, may remove trees, brush, stumps, and
other inflammable materials likely to cause forest fires, and
construct fire-prevention works, with funds to be raised by
special benefit assessments (Statutes, secs. 88.28 to 88.41:
Laws 1925, ch. 263, secs. 1 to 14). In Nevada, the county
authorities of each county may, during periods of fire hazard, employ one or more fire wardens to patrol forest lands
and to suppress any forest fires that may be found started
(Laws 1927, ch. 45, sec. 2). Similar provision is found in
the laws of North Dakota, where the county commissioners of
each county having at least 25 percent of its total area in
woods and forests shall appoint two or more fire wardens for
each unorganized township within the county to perform the
same duties as those of Nevada fire wardens (Code, sec. 18-
0202: Laws 1909, ch. 125, sec. 1).

Michigan counties, in addition to the authority of establishing county forests, have the discretion to plant
shade, nut-bearing and ornamental trees along public highways (Compiled Laws, sec. 247.232, Acts 1919, No. 36, sec. 2).
Under the laws of New York, the county board of supervisors
of any county may engage itself in the suppression or control of white-pine blister rust under the technical direction of the state conservation department (County Law, sec.
225, subsec. 1, para.(e): Laws 1939, ch. 86). In many states,
the county governmental authorities may control plant insect
and disease pests.[47] As in most cases such authority is expressly limited to agricultural and horticultural lands, it
is not clear whether it can be invoked as a statutory basis
for the control of forest pests.

6. Fish and Wildlife---As reported in 1941, there was
one county game refuge (which was the only reported local
game refuge as of that year), which was the Trexler-Lehigh
Wildlife Refuge in Pennsylvania, having an area of 1,700
acres.[48] The laws of Louisiana permit the several parishes
to establish, maintain and operate both game and fish preserves. When necessary, "the governing authority of a parish may build dykes or dams, dig canals, or excavate lake
or stream beds . . ." These areas are open to public fishing and hunting, though they do not assume the name of public fishing and hunting grounds, and fees are charged for
such uses (Revised Statutes, tit. 56, sec. 721 et seq.:
Acts 1926, No. 259). Information is not available as to the
number and location of parish game and fish preserves estab-

lished, if any.

The laws of California (<u>Fish and Game Code</u>, sec. 27:
Stats. 1907, ch. 415) and Wisconsin (<u>Statutes</u>, sec. 59.08(7m):
Laws 1927, ch. 257) have authorized counties to operate fish
hatcheries. Nevada counties have a peculiar position in fish
and game administration. While in all other states such administration has become the monopoly of the state, in Nevada,
under a law of 1947 (Stats. 1947, ch. 101), the enterprise
activities of this administration are shared by the state and
the counties, although county administration is under state
supervision. Thus Nevada counties may not only establish
and operate fish hatcheries, but take all measures "for the
preservation and propagation of fish and game." As of 1949,
the counties of that state, viz., Elko County and Washoe
County, had each built a fish hatchery.[49] For several years
California counties have been engaged in fish-water improvement, and by 1952 some 300 small dams had been constructed.[50]
Under the County Government Act of 31 March 1874, as last
amended 22 April 1949, counties of Illinois may embark upon
projects for the conservation, preservation and propagation
of insectivorous birds, though actual performance is unknown.

The rodent-control work which the counties of Nevada and
South Dakota may undertake as a means to enforce rodent-control regulation as discussed before is in itself an enterprise. As for pure and independent enterprise of rodent control at the county level, it is found in Colorado (<u>Statutes</u>,
ch. 45, sec. 38(1): Laws 1903, ch. 84, sec.1; as last amended by L. 1937, ch. 229, secs. 1 and 2), Montana (<u>Revised Codes</u>,
sec. 16-1143: Laws 1917, ch. 96; as amended by L. 1919, ch.
153, sec. 1) and Minnesota (<u>Statutes</u>, sec. 18.14 et seq.: Laws
1935, ch. 29).

The counties of Colorado have also been authorized to control coyotes and other predatory animals (<u>Statutes</u>, ch. 45,
sec. 38(2): Laws 1947, ch. 164, secs. 1 and 2). The same
authority is possessed by the counties of Kansas (<u>General
Statutes</u>, sec. 19-2317 et seq.: Laws 1949, ch. 203).

7. <u>Water and soil conservation</u>---In Michigan, the counties, under the following different laws, may construct dams
and dikes along the shores or at the outlets of inland navigable lakes so as to maintain as far as possible, their natural high-water marks throughout all seasons of the year:[51]

(1) Compiled Laws of Michigan, sec. 281.1 et seq. (Act
     202 of 1911, as amended by Act 377 of 1921).
(2) <u>Ibid</u>., sec. 281.51 et seq. (Act 39 of 1937).
(3) <u>Ibid</u>., sec. 281.01 et seq. (Act 194 of 1939).
(4) <u>Ibid</u>., sec. 281.201 et seq. (Act 276 of 1945).

The same authority is vested in the counties of Minnesota

having a population of under 18,000 (Statutes, sec. 110.12:
Laws 1917, ch. 338). The authority of Michigan counties, under the present act of 1945, extends to non-navigable inland
lakes upon the petition of a majority of the recorded private
owners and also the recorded owners of a majority of the littoral frontage of any such lake.

During the drought of 1936, some 380 ponds and 444 wells
were constructed in Kansas with Federal relief aid under the
sponsorship of many counties. In this program, a number of
low dams were built.[52] In Ohio, the statute required the
State Highway Department, as well as county and city governments, when so required by the Division of Water of the State
Department of Natural Resources, "to create reservoirs, ponds,
water parks, basins, lakes or other incidental works to conserve the water supply of the state" in connection with the
construction of highways, bridges, viaducts and culverts (Revised Code of 1953, sec. 1523.14 (Laws 1933, p. 383).

Many counties in southern California have undertaken projects for artificial recharge of underground aquifers.[53]
Similar work has been performed by Nassau County of New York,
where eleven seepage basins ranging in area from one to nine
acres with a combined area of 40 acres have been constructed
and operated by the county department of water works in recharge underground water supplies with sewer effluents.[54]

In Kansas and Oklahoma, counties may take measures to
control and prevent "wind erosion" (that is, the blowing up
of top-soil by winds), which consist primarily in the planting of soil-holding crops of grasses. The work is initiated
only upon the petition of the landowners concerned in Oklahoma, and only after the county authorities confer with land
owners concerned in Kansas.[55]

As mentioned before, there are both the county enterprise
and county regulation of weed eradication in Virginia, and in
Illinois, South Dakota, Idaho, Minnesota and Oregon, county
regulation in this same field is enforced by direct county
enterprise. In Montana, such work is entirely a county enterprise, and is done on district basis. The districts are established by the county authorities as field units of this enterprise upon petition of 25 percent of free-holders of the
respective prospective districts (Revised Codes, tit. 16, ch.
17: Laws 1939, ch. 195; as last amended by L. 1951, ch. 59).

8. Water sanitation ---The enterprise of sewage disposal
generally belongs to cities and special districts. But in
exceptional cases, it can also be undertaken by counties. For
example, Ohio counties may construct sewerage plants but only
when so ordered by the State Board of Health (Laws 1904, p.
533, sec. 1). In Pennsylvania, counties other than those of
second class may construct sewers upon approval by a grand

jury and the court of quarter sessions (Statutes, sec. 16-
1001: Acts of 2 May 1929 and 28 July 1953). In Wisconsin,
only counties of 250,000 inhabitants or more (actually only
Milwaukee County) may construct sewerage works (Statutes,
sec. 59.08(13): Laws 1929, ch. 314). Under the laws of Minnesota, a county may establish sewers only when so petitioned
by 51 percent of the freeholders in an area of more than 5,-
000 square miles and having an assessed valuation of more
than $200 million (Statutes, sec. 380.01: Laws 1937, ch. 214,
sec. 1). In Virginia, county sewers are permitted only in
(1) counties having a population in excess of 750 inhabitants
(ibid., sec. 15-761.1: Acts 1948, ch. 153). As provided in
an act of 1951 (Acts 1951, ch. 17), Michigan counties are
authorized to pass sewage in county drains only under specified conditions and in accordance with specified procedure.
In New York, Onondaga County was authorized to establish sewage works by a special act of 1933 (Laws 1933, ch. 568). In
1953, special laws were enacted in North Carolina which authorized Wake, Columbia and Durham Counties to construct water
and sewer lines (Laws 1953, chs. 154, 814 and 1128).

In the following named states and counties, there has
been report of county enterprise of mosquito control, though
general statutory authorization for this is found only in
Pennsylvania (Statutes, tit. 16, sec. 451 et seq.: Act of
10 July 1935, as amended by act of 21 May 1943) and Florida
(Statutes, sec. 381.72: Laws 1949, ch. 25442):[56]

California---Monterey County.
Florida---Alabama, Leon, East Lake, and Brevard Counties.
Massachusetts---Berkshire, Middlesex and Nantucket Count-
    ies (There might be possible confusion with state
    enterprise).
New Jersey---Atlantic, Bergen, Burlington, Cape May, Es-
    sex, Hudson, Mercer, Middlesex, Monmouth, Morris,
    Ocean, Passaic, Somerset, Sussex and Union Counties.
New Mexico---Dona Ana County.
New York---Suffolk and Nassau Counties.
Oregon---Umatilla and Lane Counties.
Pennsylvania---Delaware and Blair Counties.
Virginia---Warwick County.
Washington---Skamania, Clark, Cowlitz and Grant Counties.

The mosquito-control work of Nassau County of New York,
which has a history of some forty years, is an outstanding
example of county mosquito-control enterprise. More than
200 miles of fresh-water streams as well as large numbers of
ponds, swamps, pools, swamps, pools and other wet areas in
that county are regularly checked, and more than 20,000 acres
of salt marsh patrolled. A total of some 5 million feet of
drainage ditches have been constructed and maintained as part
of the county mosquito-control program. About 25,000 catch
basins or street drains are treated every three weeks in the

period from April to October each year. In addition, there
are artificial underground water recharge basins and drainage
channels to take care of storm water.[57]

Dade County, Florida, is reported to have been engaged in
a program of preventing the intrusion of salt water into the
coastal underground water aquifers by means of locks and other
control works constructed at the the mouths of existing drainage canals.[58] It is not known whether similar work is done
at the county level anywhere else in this country.

9. Miscellaneous---Under the laws listed below, several
kinds of county enterprises are permitted:

   Wisconsin---Statutes, sec. 30.05(Laws 1905, ch. 293; as
       last amended by L. 1949, ch. 494): Counties, cities,
       towns and villages, either separately or jointly,
       may construct and maintain breakwaters and protection
       piers along the shores, and dams across the outlets
       or channels, of lakes and streams adjoining or with-
       in their respective jurisdictions.
   Nevada---Compiled Laws, sec. 1997 (Stats. 1913, ch. 13,
       sec. 1): Counties to drill artesian wells on tracts
       of land not less than 40 acres. Consult Stats. 1905,
       ch. 151.
   Idaho---Code, tit. 42, ch. 28 (Laws 1921, ch. 222): Upon
       petition by 100 or 25 percent of land owners, and
       after popular authorization of a bond issue by a
       two-thirds vote, county commissioners to undertake
       irrigation or drainage projects.
   Texas---Revised Civil Statutes, art. 803 et seq. (Laws
       1923, ch. 128): Under a procedure similar to that
       mentioned above for Idaho counties, counties to con-
       struct works for irrigation, drainage, or flood con-
       trol, or for any two or all of these purposes.
   Kansas---General Statutes, sec. 68-1501 (Laws 1913, ch.
       260, sec. 1): Counties (as well as cities) to con-
       struct works of bank protection, irrigation, hydro-
       electric power development, etc.
   Virginia---Code, sec. 15-609 (Acts 1940, ch. 386): Count-
       ies to construct any public-works project with Fed-
       eral aid, after a referendum.
   Tennessee---Code, sec. 4406.129 (Acts 1945, ch. 184, sec.
       3): Counties to construct any public-works project
       with Federal aid.
   Mississippi---Code, sec. 8499 (Laws 1924, ch. 319; as
       amended by L. 1928, ch. 18): Counties to construct
       seawalls to protect streets, roads and highways.

However, actual performances under these laws are not known.

Greenwood County of South Carolina and Crisp County of
Georgia have each constructed a hydroelectric power project

(single-purpose). They were the only counties in the United States which had a hydroelectric enterprise as of 1948.[59] The relevant data concerning these two county power projects are given below.[60]

Facts	Crisp County	Greenwood County
Height of the dam (feet)	55	80
Capacity of reservoir (ac.-ft.)	150,000	275,000
Low-pressure conduit (miles)	Zero	3.25
Stream concerned	Flint River	Saluda River
Nearby city	Warwick, Georgia	Greenwood, S. C.
Surcharge storage (ac.-ft.)	80,000	115,000
Construction started	August 1929	Spring 1935
Construction completed	August 1932	December 1940
Capacity (hydro) (kws.)	14,000	18,750
Capacity (steam) (kws.)	Zero	20,000
Transmission lines (miles)	18	162
Number of substations	8	15

Salt Lake County, Utah, was once engaged in irrigation enterprise, but it was unsuccessful and was subsequently turned over to private irrigation companies.[61]

Article 2   Municipal Administration.[62]

Section 1   Enterprise

1.   General improvement of watercourses---In the following states there are general laws which enable municipal governments to clear, deepen, straighten, revet, alter, change or otherwise improve the channels of watercourses within their respective jurisdictions:[63]

Kansas---(1) Cities of 1st class, General Statutes, sec. 13-428 (Laws 1867, ch. 70, sec. 1; as last amended by L. 1903, ch. 122, sec. 48). (2) Cities of 2nd class, ibid., sec. 14-701 (L. 1867, ch. 86, art. 3, sec. 2; as last amended by L. 1935, ch. 121, sec. 1). Authority extends to within five miles from city limits. (3) Cities of 3rd class, ibid., sec. 15-430 (L. 1867, ch. 26, sec. 29; as amended by L. 1871, ch. 60, sec. 58).
Illinois---Cities and villages, Revised Statutes, ch. 24, sec. 23-40 (Laws 1872, pp. 229, 230; as amended by L. 1941, vol. 2, p. 173).
Colorado---Cities and towns, Statutes, ch. 163, sec. 10, (An act of 4 April 1877, sec. 14), in subd. 11.
Missouri---(1) Cities of 1st class, Statutes, sec. 73.110,

subd. (1) (Laws 1909, p. 138; as last amended by
L. 1929, p. 278), within or without corporate
limits. (2) Cities of 2nd class, ibid., sec. 75.-
110, subd. (29) (Laws 1877, pp. 104, 153; as last
amended by L. 1939, p. 523). (3) Cities of 3rd
class, ibid., sec. 77.140 (Laws 1893, p. 65). (4)
Cities of 4th class, ibid., sec. 79.390 (Laws 1895,
p. 65).

New Mexico---Cities, towns and villages, Statutes, sec.
14-1809 (Laws 1884, ch. 39, sec. 14(11)).

Oklahoma---Statutes, tit. 11, sec. 663 (first appearing
in Statutes of 1890, sec. 614).

Washington----(1) Cities of 1st class, Revised Code, sec.
35.22.280 (Laws 1890, p. 218, sec. 5), in subd.
(26). (2) Cities of 2nd class, ibid., sec. 35.-
23.440 (L. 1907, ch. 241, sec. 29), in subd. (37),
for non-navigable watercourses only. (3) Cities
of 3rd class, ibid., sec. 35.24.290 (L. 1915, ch.
184, sec. 14), in subd. (8). (4) Towns, ibid.,
sec. 35.27.370 (L. 1890, p. 201, sec. 154; as last
amended by L. 1949, ch. 151, sec. 1), in subd. (10).

Idaho---Code, sec. 50-1112 (Laws 1893, ch. 97, sec. 69;
as last amended by L. 1915, ch. 97, sec. 2).

Pennsylvania---(1) All municipal corporations may, inter
alia, change the channels of watercourses. --
Statutes, tit. 53, sec. 391 (an act of 16 May 1891,
sec. 1; as amended by an act of 12 June 1893, sec.
1). Boroughs excepted by an act of 4 June 1901,
sec. 42. (2) All cities and towns may vacate,
change, alter or relocate the channels of non-navigable watercourses. -- ibid., sec. 1161 (an act
of 28 April 1899, sec. 1). Boroughs excepted by
an act of 14 May 1915, ch. 13, art. 1, sec. 1.
(3) All municipal corporations may "establish and
change the channels of watercourses and (to) wall
and cover them over . . ." -- ibid., sec. 9667
(an act of 7 March 1901, art. 19, sec. 3, clause
30). (4) "Cities may by ordinance, after the consent of the Water and Power Resources Board (of
the state department of forests and waters) and of
the Federal Government, where required, has first
been obtained, establish the lines, change and
vacate the channels, beds and mouths of watercourses through lands, marshes or waters in or adjacent to the city; crib, wall, confine, pave or
completely inclose, and prevent and remove obstructions therefrom at the expense of those causing the
same . . ." -- Ibid., sec. 12198-3401 (an act of
23 June 1931, art. 34, sec. 3401; as amended by an
act of 28 June 1951, sec. 34).

Arizona---Common-council towns, Code, sec. 16-207 (Revised
Statutes of 1901, sec. 545; as last amended by L.
1949, ch. 111, sec. 1), in subd. 5.

Nebraska---(1) Primary cities, Revised Statutes, sec. 15-
    224 (laws 1901, ch. 16, sec. 129). (2) Cities of
    1st class, ibid., sec. 16-221 (L. 1901, ch. 18,
    sec. 48; as amended by L. 1907, ch. 13, sec. 1).
    (3) Cities of 2nd class and villages, ibid., sec.
    17-529 (L. 1879, ch. 15, sec. 69; as last amended
    by L. 1947, ch. 35).
Indiana---All cities and towns, Statutes, secs. 48-502
    and 48-503 (Acts 1905, ch. 129, secs. 266 and
    267).
Alabama---All cities and towns, Code, tit. 37, sec. 470
    (Acts 1907, No. 797, sec. 93; as amended by Acts
    1939, No. 37).
Nevada---Compiled Laws, sec. 1128 (Stats. 1907, ch. 124
    sec. 28), in subd. 40.
Ohio---Revised Code, sec. 715.15 (Laws 1908, p. 8, sec.
    7s).
Massachusetts---Laws, ch. 91, sec. 29 (Acts 1909, ch.
    481, sec. 3; as last amended by Acts 1950, ch.
    524).
New Jersey---Statutes, sec. 40:56-1 (Laws 1917, ch. 152,
    art. 20, sec. 1; as last amended by L. 1951, ch.
    175, sec. 1), in paras. m, n and o.
Montana---Cities and towns, Revised Codes, sec. 11-917
    (Revised Code of 1921, sec. 5039, subd. 15; as
    last amended by L. 1927, ch. 20, sec. 1).
Michigan---Compiled Laws, sec. 117.4h (Acts 1929, No.
    126; as amended by Acts 1931, No. 295).
Florida---Cities and towns, Statutes, sec. 342.03 (Laws
    1931, ch. 14651, sec. 1).
South Dakota---Code, sec. 45.2007 (Laws 1931, ch. 189,
    sec. 8).
North Dakota---Cities adopting city-council and commission
    forms of government, Revised Code, sec. 40-0502
    (Laws 1933, ch. 175, sec. 1), in subd. 18.
Minnesota---All cities, villages and boroughs, Statutes,
    sec. 110.121 et seq. (Laws 1947, ch. 123).
Mississippi---Code, sec. 3374-122 (Laws 1950, ch. 491,
    sec. 122). A referendum is required if the cost
    of any improvement project exceeds one-fourth of
    the taxes levied in the preceding year for general
    revenue purposes.

These improvements serve not only the purposes of navigation and flood control and but also, so far as municipalities
are concerned, sewage disposal and area beautification. The
purpose of navigation will be served only when the watercourse
under improvement is navigable or will be navigable after the
improvement.

2. Navigation improvement---In the following states, municipal governments may construct and maintain navigation canals:

Illinois---Cities and villages, Revised Statutes, ch. 24,
    sec. 23-41 (Laws 1872, p. 230; as amended by L.
    1941, vol. 2, p. 173).
Florida---Statutes, sec. 167.09 (Laws 1879, ch. 3164,
    sec. 3; as last amended by L. 1949, ch. 25094,
    sec. 1), inter alia.
Ohio---Revised Code, sec. 715.15 (Laws 1908, p. 8, sec.
    7s), inter alia.
Arizona---Code, sec. 16-2301 (Laws 1912, ch. 55, sec. 2;
    as last amended by L. 1925, ch. 3, sec. 1), inter
    alia.
California---Government Code, sec. 39901 (Stats. 1917, ch.
    64, sec. 1; as amended by Stats. 1949, ch. 79, sec.
    1), in subd.(b), inter alia.
Nevada---Compiled Laws, sec. 1128 (Stats. 1907, ch. 124,
    sec. 28), in subd. 41, inter alia.
Louisiana---Revised Statutes, tit. 34, secs. 361 and 362
    (Acts 1921, Ex. Sess., No. 68, secs. 1-2; as last
    amended by Acts 1950, No. 398, sec. 1), inter alia.
    Canals may be built either within or without corp-
    orate limits.

The general authority to improve navigable watercourses
and harbors is possessed by the municipal corporations of the
following states:

Massachusetts---Towns, General Laws, ch. 91, sec. 29 (Acts
    1909, ch. 481, sec. 3; as last amended by Acts
    1950, ch. 524).
Indiana---Cities and towns, Statutes, sec. 48-5211 (Acts
    1915, ch. 188, sec. 1).
California---Government Code, sec. 39901, subd.(b), op.
    cit.
Louisiana---Revised Statutes, tit. 34, secs. 361 and 362,
    op. cit.
New Jersey---Statutes, sec. 40:14-1 (Laws 1910, ch. 230,
    sec. 1).

The cities, towns and villages of Mississippi, under an enabling enactment of 1892 (Code, sec. 3428; being Code of 1892,
sec. 2953), may (inter alia) improve harbors. The same authority (inter alia) was given cities of New Hampshire by a law
of 1935 (Revised Laws, ch. 54 (Laws 1935, ch. 113). Under the
laws of New York, whenever a municipal corporation diverts
water from a tributary of a tidal creek or estuary which, before such diversion, was navigable to vessels of twenty or
more tons, it shall be the duty of such municipal corporation
to deepen such tidal creek or estuary to a depth of at least
three feet at low water mark (Navigation Law, sec. 80: Laws
1898, ch. 469, sec. 1; as amended by L. 1901, ch. 201, sec. 1).
This seems to be the only instance in which navigation improvement is a municipal duty.

In the following paragraphs, some examples of municipal navigation-improvement enterprise are given, while complete statistics and data for the whole country are not available.

"An act of the General Assembly of Virginia on December 8, 1924, authorized the incorporation of a company for the purpose of improving Appomattox River for navigation 'from Pocahontas to Broadway.' This action was later confirmed by an act of Congress on March 3, 1825. The section covered extended from Petersburg to a point about 7 miles downstream. Pursuant to these acts, the Lower Appomattox Company, a joint stock organization, which in reality was an agency of the City of Petersburg, was formed. Improvement was commenced during the year 1825, and carried on until 1852, when the city requested aid from the Federal Government. A Federal commission was appointed, which made an investigation and submitted a report on November 26, 1852. However, no Federal aid was forthcoming until 1871, when the existing project (Federal) was adopted. Up to 1874, the city of Petersburg, through its operating company, had expended $402,900 for the improvement of the river. The work done . . . had provided a depth to Petersburg sufficient to accommodate sailing vessels, but frequent and severe freshets had caused heavy shoals to form, which required costly maintenance. The city began the excavation of Puddledock Cut in 1871, to eliminate the 'Old North' channel, which had required the heavier maintenance. This cut was nearly completed by the time the Federal Government began improvement early in 1872. A report in 1874 states that the city imposed a heavy tax to provide funds for acquiring two dredges and to continue the work in conjunction with the Federal Government. In 1884, the city acquired another dredge, which was used by both the city and the Government in the work of improvement. Between 1886 and 1912, the city of Petersburg expended $1,578,620 for dredging and the construction of regulation works, in the upper 7.5 miles of the river. The city reports (in 1938) that since 1912 it has expended $24,498 . . ."[64]

The City of Providence, Rhode Island, dredged a channel in the Providence River and Harbor during the latter half of the nineteenth century, and a total of some $507,310 was expended by the city in this work.[65] From 1840 to 1916, $2,253,165 were spent by the City of St. Louis, Missouri, in building dikes and bank protection works on the Mississippi River.[66] In about 1847, "the citizens of Augusta and thereabouts undertook to dredge out a channel above Sheppards Point, and they improved it in some localities. The place referred to is on the Kennebec River, a short distance below Hallowell."[67] In improving the Appoquinimink River, Delaware, the citizens of Odessa, Delaware, made three cut-offs in 1879, with $1,700 raised by subscription. "In 1899 and 1901 the citizens of Milford, Delaware, and vicinity, at their expense, dredged the channel at the mouth of the Mispillion River."[68]

"In the Passaic River at Newark, the city removes shoals deposited at the mouths of sewers."[69] The cities of Stockton, California; Philadelphia, Pennsylvania; Salisbury, Maryland; etc., also have records of navigation improvement works that were undertaken in the late nineteenth century.[70] "In 1913-14 the city of Houston (Texas) dredged the light-draft section of the Houston Ship Channel to a depth of 8 feet and a width of 40 feet at a cost of approximately $45,000."[71] "Gardeners Basin originally was a shallow tidal lagoon connected with Clam Creek. In 1890 private interests converted the lagoon to a basin by dredging and constructing bulkheads on the outline. In 1918 the Atlantic City (New Jersey) municipality dredged approximately 15,000 cubic yards from the basin, and again in 1935 the city dredged approximately 8,000 cubic yards to obtain 9-foot depth of water in the entrance to the basin." "In 1919 Atlantic City was expended, bringing Clam Creek into the municipality. In the same year the city widened and deepened the creek by dredging approximately 688,000 cubic yards of material, and constructed a bulkhead wharf at the head, or southwest end, of the creek, ... In 1923, the city again dredged the creek, removing approximately 214,000 cubic yards."[72] As mentioned above, the city of Lake Charles, in collaboration with Calcasieu Parish, undertook to improve the Calcasieu River in 1921.

"Under War Department permits dated April 30, 1924, and November 10, 1925, the city of Miami (Florida) dredged the yacht anchorage basin along Bay Front Park, and a channel about 150 feet wide and 18 feet deep along the westerly side of the basin to join with the municipal turning basin. A channel 18 to 25 feet deep dredged along the northerly side of Fisher Island now replaces about 4,000 feet of old Florida East Coast channel."[73] In the Shoal Harbor and Compton Creek New Jersey, "local interests constructed certain works at Fishers Point at the mouth of Compton Creek for the protection of the harbor. In 1925 a stone jetty, about 350 feet in length, was constructed at this point by the township of Middleton at a cost of about $5,000. During the period 1937-39, the township constructed 440 lineal feet of timber bulkhead and a 100-foot timber groin at a cost of about $10,000 to augment the previous work."[74] In 1937 and 1938, the Borough of Keansburg, New Jersey, did some improvement work at the mouth of the Way Cake Creek, which consisted of the reconstruction of about 425 linear feet of bulkhead, the replacement of the jetty with sunken barges and dredging, at a total cost of $57,000.[75] "The city of Sioux City, Iowa, has been issued a War Department permit for the construction of a series of pile dikes for erosion control along the left bank of the Missouri River from mile 809.0 to the present mouth of the Big Sioux River. This project (as of 1946) is about 40 percent completed. Work is now suspended because of current material shortage, but is to be resumed as soon as possible."[76] "The city of Port Arthur (Texas) reports expenditure of $710,000

for revetment and a concrete sea wall along the city side of
the Sabine-Neches Canal, which it claims reduces the amount
of maintenance dredging by reducing erosion."[77]

Occasionally navigation improvement is achieved incidentally in the construction of other municipal works. For example, "the city of New York has dredged the easterly portion
of the south channel in Jamaica Bay upstream from Mott Basin,
to provide fill for Idlewild Airport, now under construction.
Some of this dredging is beneficial to navigation."[78] There
can be no doubt that revetments can be made when public roads
or highways are constructed on the shores of a navigable watercourse.[79]

Another aspect of municipal enterprise of navigation improvement is the construction and operation of water terminal
facilities. In some instances the authority of cities and
towns in constructing and maintaining docks and wharves was
given by city charters, as with the city of Portland, Oregon;
the city of Norfolk, Virginia; and the city of Houston, Texas.[80]
Occasionally, this authority is contained in speci l acts of
the state, as is the case of the city of Tampa, Florida (Laws
1913, ch. 6782; as amended by L. 1915, ch. 7247) and the city
of Milwaukee, Wisconsin (Laws 1923, ch. 285; also L. 1929,
ch. 151). In the following states, general laws have been
enacted enabling cities and other local governmental units to
undertake the construction and operation of docks and wharves:

Florida---Statutes, sec. 167.21 (Laws 1869, ch. 1699, sec.
    15).
Louisiana---Cities, towns and villages, Civil Code, art.
    863 (Civil Code of 1789, art. 863; as amended by
    Acts 1932, No. 129).
Illinois---Cities and villages, Revised Statutes, ch. 24,
    sec. 23-42 (Laws 1872, p. 228; as amended by L.
    1941, vol. 2, p. 173).
Arkansas---Statutes, sec. 19-2313 (Acts 1875, No. 1, sec.
    18). Also see ibid., sec. 19-2720 et seq. (Acts
    1947, No. 167).
Missouri---Cities of first class, Missouri, sec. 73.110,
    subd.(1) (Laws 1909, p. 138; as last amended by L.
    1929, p. 278), inter alia. Cities of second class,
    ibid., sec. 75.110, subd. (11) (Laws 1877, p. 104;
    as last amended by L. 1939, p. 523), inter alia.
    Towns and villages, ibid., sec. 80.090, subd.(18)
    (Act of 18 June 1808; as last amended by L. 1874,
    p. 191).
Washington---Cities of first class, Revised Code, sec.
    35.22.280 (Laws 1890, p. 218, sec. 5), in subd.
    (7). Cities of second class, ibid., sec. 35.23.
    440 (Laws 1907, ch. 241, sec. 29), in subd. (28).
    Cities of third class, ibid., sec. 35.24.290 (Laws
    1915, ch. 184, sec. 14), in subd.(8).

Mississippi---Cities, towns and villages, Code, sec. 3427
(Code of 1892, sec. 2953).

Michigan---Compiled Laws, sec. 97.1, enacted 1897 (Compiled Laws 1897, sec. 3143).

Pennsylvania---Cities of first class, Statutes, tit. 53,
sec. 4312 (Act of 8 June 1907, sec. 15; as last
amended by an act of 29 May 1913, sec. 3). Cities
of second class, ibid., sec. 8681 (act of 7 March
1901, art. 4, sec. 1; as amended by an act of 1
July 1937, sec. 1). Cities of third class, ibid.,
sec. 12198-3901 (Act of 23 June 1931, art. 39,
sec. 3901; as last amended by an act of 28 June
1951, sec. 39). Towns of first class, ibid., sec.
19092-1901 (act of 24 July 1931, art. 19, sec.
1901; as last amended by an act of 27 May 1953,
sec. 3).

Iowa---Code, sec. 372.1 et seq. (Acts 1902, ch. 210; as
last amended by Acts 1941, ch. 207, sec. 1), applicable only to cities of the first class acting
under the general incorporation laws, cities of
the second class having a population in excess of
7,000, and cities acting under the commission form
of government.

Indiana---Statutes, sec. 48-1407 (Acts 1905, ch. 129, sec.
53).

Alabama---Cities and towns, Code, tit. 37, sec. 470 (Acts
1907, No. 797, sec. 93; as amended by Acts 1939,
No. 37).

Massachusetts---Cities and towns, General Laws, ch. 88,
sec. 14 (Acts 1908, ch. 606, secs. 1, 4; as amended by Acts 1930, ch. 164).

Ohio---Revised Code, sec. 715.19 (Laws 1908, p. 7, sec.
7r). Also ibid., sec. 717.01, subd.(E) (Laws 1911,
p. 154; as last amended by L. 1945, pp. 263 and
265).

South Carolina---Code, sec. 7554 (Acts 1909, No. 109; as
amended by Acts 1920, No. 498), for cities of 50,-
000 or more inhabitants only.

South Dakota---Code, sec. 45.2008 (Laws 1911, ch. 94, revised in 1939 in wording), inter alia.

Connecticut---Cities, towns and boroughs, General Statutes,
sec. 619 (Acts 1913, ch. 154; as last amended in
1943).

New York---General City Law, art. 2-A, sec. 20, subd. 8
(Laws 1913, ch. 247).

Texas---Revised Civil Statutes, art. 1184 (Laws 1913, ch.
25, sec. 1, second part).

California---Government Code, sec. 39901 (Stats. 1917, ch.
64, sec. 1; as amended by Stats. 1949, ch. 79, sec.
1).

New Jersey---Revised Statutes, tit. 40, ch. 68, art. 1
(Laws 1917, ch. 152, arts. 27 and 28; as amended
by L. 1920, chs. 119 and 205).

North Carolina---General Statutes, sec. 160-204 (Laws
    1917, ch. 136, sub-ch. 4, sec. 1; as amended by L.
    1919, ch. 262).
Kentucky---Revised Statutes, sec. 182.120 (Acts 1920, ch.
    98), for cities situated along the Cumberland River
    only.
Tennessee---Code, sec. 3528, subd.(15), (Acts 1921, ch.
    173, art. 3, sec. 1), for cities under city mana-
    ger plan only.
Minnesota---Statutes, sec. 458.03 (Laws 1927, ch. 152,
    sec. 2).
Kansas---General Statutes, sec. 12-672 (Laws 1929, ch.
    115, sec. 1).
West Virginia---Code, sec. 510(1) et seq. (Laws 1935, ch.
    68; as last amended by L. 1951, ch. 136).
Nebraska---All cities and villages, Revised Statutes, sec.
    18-701 et seq. (Laws 1937, ch. 37; as amended by
    L. 1951, ch. 20).

In New Hampshire, municipal terminals are constructed only
as a kind of "emergency public works" (Revised Laws, ch. 54:
Laws 1935, ch. 113). In Wisconsin, cities construct docks
and wharves only as an enforcement measure of municpal regulation.

All of the terminal facilities discussed in this Section
and elsewhere in this Book are facilities of water navigation.
Michigan has the unique law which authorizes home-rule cities
to construct and operate facilities "for the docking of . . .
hydroplanes . . ." (Compiled Laws, sec. 117.4h: Acts 1929,
No. 126; as amended by Acts 1931, No. 295).[81]

Municipal water terminals are located either along inland
waterways or on the ocean coasts. In the Columbia and Willamette Rivers, municipal water terminals exist in the cities
of Portland and Astoria of Oregon and Vancouver and Kalama of
Washington. The City of Portland has constructed and acquired
four terminals. Of these, however, Terminals Nos. 2 and 3
have been disposed of,[82] and therefore only Terminals Nos. 1
and 4 are now operated by the city. Terminal No. 1 include
three units of quay dock, Piers A and B, a lumber dock, warehouse no. 1 and a gear locker, and has a berthing space for
six vessels at general cargo docks and three vessels at the
lumber dock. Terminal No. 4 include Pier No. 1 and its extension and Piers Nos. 2 and 5, which have an aggregate shed
area of 58y,369 square feet and open area of 211,140 square
feet, serving both general cargoes and bulk commodities of
grain, coal, ores, vegetable oils, tallow, etc. In Terminal
No. 4 there are also a bunkers and bulk storage plant and a
bulk oil and storage plant, which are owned by the city; and
a fruit warehouse, a cold storage plant and a bulk grain elevator, which are leased by the city. In May 1952, a contract
for the construction of a 164,000-dollar transit warehouse at

Terminal No. 1 was let; and on 4 November 1952 an amendment
to the city charter was passed enabling the city to construct
a new, large and modern grain elevator and (or) to enlarge
and modernize the present grain elevator at Terminal No. 4.[83]
"At Astoria, Oregon, there is a large municipal terminal with
grain elevator and flour mill, and facilities for receiving
oil products by tankers." "At Kalama, Washington, there is
a municipal wharf for shipment of lumber and a heavy lift of
100-ton capacity."[84]

The following are lists of cities, towns and villages
located on some inland watercourses which own and operate
water terminal facilities:[85]

Upper Mississippi River---Minneapolis, St. Paul, Red Wing,
    Winoa, Minnesota; La Crosse, Wisconsin; Burlington,
    Iowa; St. Louis, Cape Giradeau, Missouri (As of
    October 1951).
Lower Mississippi---River Memphis, Tennessee; Helena,
    Arkansas; Vicksburg, Mississippi; Baton Rouge,
    New Orleans, Louisiana (As of March 1953).
Ohio River---Augusta, Newport, Covington, Warsaw, Carroll-
    ton, Milton, Louisville, Hawesville, Lewisport,
    Owensboro, Henderson, Uniontown, Smithland, Paducah,
    Kentucky; New Richmond, Cincinnati, Ohio; Aurora,
    Rising Sun, Vevay, Madison, Jeffersonville, New
    Albany, Cannelton, Tell City, Rockport, Evansville,
    Mt. Vernon, Indiana; Shawneetown, Cave-in-Rock,
    Elisabethtown, Rosiclare, Carrsville, Golconda,
    Brookport, Metropolis, Cairo, Illinois (As of 30
    June 1952).
Tennessee River---Paducah, Kentucky; Sheffield, Florence,
    Alabama; Chattanooga, Tennessee (As of 30 June
    1952).
Cumberland River---Nashville, Tennessee (As of February
    1952).
The Great Lakes---Buffalo, New York; Erie, Pennsylvania;
    Conneault, Ashtubula, Cleveland, Lorain, Sandusky,
    Toledo, Ohio; Detroit, Essexville, Bay City, Sagi-
    naw, Muckegon, Escanaba, Michigan; Chicago, Illi-
    nois; Milwaukee, Superior, Marinette, Wisconsin;
    Duluth, Warroad, Baudette, Minnesota.
Delaware River---Philadelphia, Wilmington, New Castle,
    Pennsylvania; Camden, Burlington, New Jersey;
    Bristol, Delaware.

Among other cities located on inland waterways which own
water terminals may be mentioned Portland, Oregon (Columbia
River), New York, New York (Hudson River), Beaumont, Texas
(Neches River), Orange, Texas (Sabine River), Jacksonville,
Florida (St. Johns River) and so forth.[86] Water terminals
are also operated by some cities situated on the coast without significant inland waterway linkage. Examples are Balti-

more, Maryland; Savannah, Georgia; and Los Angeles, Long Beach, Redwood City, San Diego, Oakland and Richmond, California.[87]

In general, the size of the terminal enterprise varies with the size of the city. At the Port of New York, "the city of New York is the largest owner of water front property, its holdings including most of the Manhattan water front, a considerable section of Staten Island, and certain isolated piers in Brooklyn. Most of the city-owned piers are leased to private individuals . . ."[88] The city of Philadelphia owns twenty terminals, some of which are operated by the city for general cargo purposes, but most of which are leased to private concerns, usually for ten-year periods.[89] The terminal facilities of the city of Milwaukee consist of a car-ferry terminal, two docks for bulk commodities, a oil tanker pier, a small boat pier, a fire-boat pier, an airtrip, a mooring basin, and other smaller properties.[90] Terminals maintained by small cities, towns and villages are usually small public landings.

In the great majority of states, municipalities are generally permitted to operate ferries across natural watercourses. There can be no question that terminal facilities must be constructed for the ferry service. However, these facilities are not open to public navigation use, but are strictly a part of the municipal ferry, which is not a purpose of water resources administration. Some municipal terminals are exclusively devoted to municipal uses such as the docking of city fire-boats and are closed to public landing of boats and vessels. These terminals are not different in nature from municipal ferry terminals and should not be considered as a part of independent terminal enterprise.

3. Flood control---It has already been mentioned that one of the purposes of the enterprise of stream improvements as discussed in Subsection 1, above, is flood control. In addition to this, in the following states, specific authority has been given to municipalities in general to undertake single-purpose works of flood control:

Kansas---(1) General Statutes, sec. 13-428 (Laws 1867, ch. 70, sec. 1; as last amended by L. 1903, ch. 122, sec. 48): Cities of first class may construct levees (inter alia). (2) Ibid., sec. 14-701 (L. 1867, ch. 87, art. 3, sec. 2; as last amended by L. 1935, ch. 121, sec. 1): Cities of second class may build levees within city limits or within five miles therefrom (inter alia). (3) Ibid., sec. 12-635 et seq. (L. 1917, ch. 87; as last amended by L. 1953, ch. 51, sec. 1): Any city may construct any flood control work.

Pennsylvania---Statutes, sec. 9666 (act of 7 March 1901,

art. 19, sec. 3, ch. 29): Any municipal corporation
may construct levees (inter alia).

Iowa---Code, sec. 395.1 (Acts 1904, ch. 33, sec. 1; as
last amended by Acts 1925, ch. 152, sec. 1): Cities and towns may construct levees and floodways.

Indiana---(1) Statutes, tit. 48, ch. 46 (Acts 1905, ch.
129; as last amended by Acts 1953, ch. 242, sec. 1):
Cities of 2nd, 3rd, 4th and 5th classes may construct levees. (2) Ibid., ch. 47 (Acts 1933, ch.
26; as last amended by Acts 1943, ch. 258, sec.
1): Cities of first class may construct flood-
control-works. (3) Ibid., ch. 48 (Acts 1915, ch.
74): Cities of first class having a population of
between 100,000 and 300,000 may construct flood-
control works. (4) Ibid., ch. 49 (Acts 1915, ch.
115; as amended): Cities of 2nd-5th classes and
towns may construct flood-control works.

Missouri---(1) Statutes, sec. 70.340 (Laws 1911, p. 334):
A city having a population of 100,000 or more may,
with the approval of the adjoining state concerned,
levee, shorten, divert or otherwise improve a watercourse which drains such city and an adjoining
state. (2) Ibid., sec. 77.150 (L. 1933, Ex. Sess.,
p. 102): Cities of third class may acquire property
within such cities or within one mile thereof for
the construction of dams and flood-protection systems.

Ohio---Revised Code, sec. 717.01 (Laws 1911, pp. 154-155;
as last amended by L. 1945, pp. 263 and 265): Each
municipality may "construct and improve levees,
dams, wasteways, waterfronts, and embankments and
improve any watercourse passing through the municipal corporation" (in subd. Q).

South Dakota---Code, sec. 45.2008 (L. 1911, ch. 94): Each
municipality may construct levees (inter alia).

Washington---Revised Code, sec. 35.21.090 (Laws 1911, ch.
98, sec. 4): Cities and towns may construct any
flood-control work.

Arizona---Code, sec. 16-2301 (Laws 1912, ch. 55, sec. 2;
as last amended by L. 1925, ch. 3, sec. 1): Cities
may construct levees and floodwalls and probably
also floodways.

New York---General City Law, sec. 20 (Laws 1913, ch. 247;
as last amended by L. 1936, ch. 425): " . . .
Every city is empowered . . . to acquire by condemnation real property within or without the limits of the city for the construction, maintenance
and operation of drainage channels and structures
for the purpose of flood control, when plans for
such purpose have been approved by the state department of public works . . ."

Alabama---Code, tit. 37, sec. 513 (Acts 1911, No. 273;
as amended by Acts 1927, No. 639): Each city and

town may construct seawalls, dikes, levees, embankments within its territorial limits for the
protection against marine and inland floods.

Texas---Revised Civil Statutes, art. 1180a, sec. 1 (Laws
1931, ch. 345, sec. 1): "Any city having a population in excess of 150,000 people and less than
240,000 people,. . . shall have and exercise the
power and right to straighten, widen, levee, re-
strian or otherwise control or improve any river,
creek, bayou, stream or other body of water, and
to grade or fill land and otherwise protect life
and property within the boundaries of such city,
meaning hereby to confer the power to amend or
abate any harmful excess of water, either constant
or periodic . . ."

California---Water Code, secs. 8000 to 8061 (enacted by
Stats. 1943, ch. 369, sec. 1): Cities may construct flood-control projects after authority is
obtained at a referendum for the issuance of bonds
for this purpose.

Nebraska---Revised Statutes, sec. 17-529, subd.(d), and
sec. 17-529.01, both enacted by Laws 1947, ch. 35:
Second-class cities and villages may construct
dikes and ditches for flood control within their
limits or within two miles thereof.

In Vermont, although there is no general enabling law for
municipal flood-control enterprise, towns are authorized to
change or widen the channel of a watercourse in order to protect a public highway from flood damages, at the time of the
construction or repair of such public highway (Statutes, sec.
5127: Laws 1862, No. 12, secs. 1 to 6; as amended by L. 1925,
No. 66). Similar provision is not found in other states.
However, it would seem that such provision may not be necessary, and that flood-protection as well as drainage works are
understood to be part of highway construction programs.

Some examples of actual accomplishments of American cities
in the flood-control enterprise are given below. On the Illinois River, "the city of Beardstown (Illinois) constructed
small and inadequate river-front and flank levees during the
period 1849-1922."[91] As mentioned above, these works were
later repaired by the State of Illinois. "About 1870, the
city of Macon (Georgia) built the first city levee along the
west bank of the (Altamaha) river to protect the present recreational grounds south of Fifth Street . . . . The city
levee extends about 4.25 miles from a point about 600 feet
below the crossing of the Central of Georgia Railroad and
about 1,100 feet below Fifth Street, Macon, to about mile
200.5."[92] With view to controlling the floods of the Willow
Creek (in Rio Grande Basin), "the town of Creede (Colorado)
with state aid has constructed a timber flume with an overall
length of about 3,500 feet." "The flume is 16 feet wide and

averages about 5 feet in depth. The initial section of the flume was constructed in 1895 . . ."[93]

Prior to the adoption by the Flood Control Act of 1936 of the Federal flood-control project for the Southern New York, the city of Corning, New York, built levees on the Monkey Run Creek to protect the city from the floods. These levees were of low grades and no provision was made to dispose of interior drainage. The city also stabilized the banks of this stream with wood piling, stone masonry, and concrete, and paved the bottom in some places. A section of the channel was enlarged, and devices were installed to catch sediment and debris.[94] Miles City, Montana, used to build levees against floods of 1929 record. In 1913 the same city, in cooperation with the Milwaukee Railroad, improved the Tongue River by cut-offs so as to increase its capacity of carrying flood waters.[95] The city of Portsmouth, Ohio, has built a floodwall which may protect the city against 62-foot river stage. The first section of the floodwall, from Chillicothe westward along the Ohio River to the Scioto River, which is 4,500 feet in length, was completed in 1908. The second section, from Chillicothe eastward, 3,800 feet in length, was completed in 1916; and the third section, 7,000 feet long, in 1929. Interior drainage is provided by four pumping plants [96] "Following completion of the sea wall (by Galveston County and the Federal Government, in 1927) the city of Galveston (Texas) undertook extensive grade raising of the city behind the sea wall to protect the city from inundation by storm tides. This work was started in 1903 and continued through 1931." Most of the city "has been filled." This is a unique method of flood control.[97]

"In 1919, the city of Olean (New York) completed an extensive system of dikes along the Allegheny River, Olean Creek, Kings Brook, and Twomile Creek." "The flood of July 1942 breached the dike system at several points. The city thereupon issued bonds in the amount of $200,000 for a program of dike reconstruction and general stream-channel improvements." Dikes were also provided by the Village of Portville, New York, along the Dodge Creek in 1919, and repairs were made in 1940. In 1942, Portville dikes were extended, and the channel of the stream was dredged.[98] The city of San Antonio, Texas, completed a flood-control reservoir on the San Antonio River in 1926, which has a capacity of 15,500 acre-feet.[99] In 1930, the city of Stockton, California, constructed the Hogan Dam on the Calaveras River at a cost of $1,750,000, which impounds about 76,000 acre-feet for the sole purpose of flood control.[100]

"The town and village of Andover (New York) have straightened and cleaned the channel of Dyke Creek within their respective boundaries at a cost since 1935 of approximately $10,000 each." "The village and town of Wellsville have spent

about $20,000 in a joint effort to remove shoals and keep the
channel of Dyke Creek clean. The village has built check
dams along the Madison Brook . . . . Parts of the river channel have been cleaned by the village and the state at various
times."[101] For the Genesee River in New York, "the city of
Rochester has provided for a flood flow of about 55,000 cubic
feet per second through the city, below the Genesee Valley
Park section, by the construction of retaining walls, by rebuilding dams, and by deepening the river channel, at a cost
of about $1,750,000. The construction of small dams at the
outlets of Hemlock and Canadice Lakes has added to the city
water supply and provided partial flood control by storage of
water from that portion of the watercourse."[102] In the city
of Tucson, Arizona, "local interests have constructed a closed
concrete conduit along the Tucson Arroyo . . . for a total
length of about 5,700 feet . . . . Most of the conduit is a
double box with a minimum size of 10 by 8 feet for each box.
The capacity of this conduit was insufficient for the floods
of 1940 and 1943 partly because of obstructions in the channel. Since September 1943 these obstructions were removed
by the city of Tucson."[103]

It may be noted that most if not all of the municipal
flood-control projects discussed above were built prior to
the passage of the first National Flood Control Act in 1936.
Since 1936, the Federal Government has committed itself to
the construction of both regional and local flood-control works,
and the responsibility of cities as well as other local governmental units in flood control has been primarily to maintain and operate local flood-control works constructed by the
Federal Government.

4. Drainage and irrigation---Non-agricultural drainage
by cities is found in the laws of all states, and is one of
the basic duties of the municipal government. Typical of the
state statutory provisions enabling the cities to undertake
this kind of drainage enterprise is the law of Illinois, which
provides that "the corporate authorities of cities and villages have the power, for drainage purposes, to lay out, establish, construct, and maintain drains, ditches, levees, dykes,
pumping works, and machinery . . ." (Revised Statutes, ch.
24, sec. 35-1: Act of 15 August 1941, art. 35, sec. 1). With
respect to agricultural drainage, however, only a few states
have permitted cities to engage themselves in it. The law of
New Hampshire may be cited as an example. It provides that
the selectmen of a town, "upon petition, may cause any low or
swamp lands within their town to be drained or filled when the
public health or good, or the advancement of agriculture, requires it . . ." (Revised Laws, ch. 167, enacted 1883, and
amended 1897).

The enterprise of agricultural irrigation is authorized
in four states. New Mexico laws permit cities and towns to

construct "irrigating or mining ditches and feeders" (Statutes, sec. 14-1839; Laws 1884, ch. 39, sec. 14). The cities and towns of Wyoming have been authorized "to establish, construct, purchase, extend, maintain and regulate a system of ditches, aqueducts and reservoirs for supplying water to its inhabitants and for its streets, parks and public grounds for irrigation purposes" (Compiled Statutes, sec. 29-2301: Laws 1890, ch. 52, sec. 1; as last amended by L. 1931, ch. 73, sec. 21) (in subd. 4). In Nevada, cities have the authority "to construct, purchase or lease, and maintain, canals, ditches, flumes, artesian wells and reservoirs, and to purchase or lease springs, streams or sources of water supply for the purpose of providing water for irrigation, domestic or other purposes . . ." (Compiled Laws, sec. 1128: Stats. 1907, ch. 124, sec. 28) (in subd. 41). Cities of Washington, other than cities of the first class, may embark upon irrigation enterprise when irrigation water is otherwise unobtainable (Revised Code, sec. 80.40.220: Laws 1915, ch. 112, sec. 1). However, the actual operation of these statutory provisions is unknown.

Elsewhere in the country, municipal irrigation enterprise is not statutorily authorized, but some actual instances of such enterprise have been recorded. In Fresno, California, and Antonio, Texas, for example, farms are irrigated with water passing from municipal sewage disposal systems.[104] The municipal water supply system of the City and County of Denver, Colorado, besides supplying water for municipal and domestic purposes, also supplies irrigation water.[105] At the beginning of the twentieth century, it was reported that the town councils of many towns in the West controlled a number of irrigation canals.[106] It is not known whether these irrigation canals are still under municipal control.

5. Water supply---This is by far the most important municipal enterprise in the field of water resources administration. It is also the only public water-resources enterprise that is almost exclusively intrusted to municipal governments. "The first United States water works for supplying a town or community were built in Boston in 1652 and served to bring water to the community by gravity from some springs not far away. In the United States during these early days there were few communitieis of any size so that problem of water supply was relatively simple. Wide use was made of springs, streams, wells and cisterns. It was more than a hundred years later that machinery was first used for pumping water and to make use of force mains (sic). At Bethlehem, Pennsylvania, a pump of lignum vitae was used to pump water from a spring through hemlock log pipes into a wooden reservoir as early as 1754. It is generally believed the next works of a mechanical nature were constructed at Providence, Rhode Island, in 1772 followed by the works constructed at Morriston, New Jersey, in 1791. Progress in the use of machinery was slow and it was not un-

til 1800 in Philadelphia that a steam engine was successfully
used for pumping. Several years later, in 1804 steam was applied to New York City's water system which had been inaugurated in 1799. Although several other water works were constructed during this time, there were only 16 or 17 works in
use by 1800."[107]

Of all water works, which number about 15,400, and which
supply water to urban people, about 80 percent was owned by
cities or other municipal corporations or districts, and 20
percent by private companies, as of 1950, which was the reverse of the situation 100 years ago.[108] Municipal water
works obtain their water either from surface or from ground
water sources, the relative importance of which is indicated
in the following table (1950 data):[109]

Population (thousands)	Ground Water		Surface Water	
	Number of cities	population	Number of cities	population
Over 100	22	3,085,455	144	30,382,555
50 to 100	20	1,481,810	61	4,880,250
25 to 50	67	2,406,860	115	4,594,185
10 to 25	268	3,953,690	284	4,709,565
5 to 10	543	3,581,070	323	2,569,715
1 to 5	3,526	6,995,830	1,193	3,581,315
Total	4,446	21,504,715	2,120	50,717,315

It may be noted that ground water sources are not necessarily resorted to because there is a scarcity of surface
water. In Florida, for example, where annual precipitation
ranges from 30 to 85 inches, ground water is utilized by 92
percent of the municipal water works of the state.[110]

The municipal water supply systems of Chicago, Illinois;
Saint Louis, Missouri; Cincinnati, Ohio; and Portland, Oregon may be discussed as examples of municipal water supply
systems making use of surface waters. Chicago water supply
system was first constructed in 1852, and by the end of 1950
it supplied water to 3,625,000 people within the city of Chicago plus 522,000 people in the suburban communities. Water
is taken from Lake Michigan by gravity through some 64 miles
of tunnels to pumping stations, which pump the water into the
distributing mains.[111] The city of St. Louis began to construct its water works in 1829, which became operative in
1829. "The present water supply of St. Louis is obtained
from the Mississippi River at the Chain of Rocks and from the
Missouri River at Howard Bend." From the intakes at these
places the water flows by pressure or gravity through tunnels,
reservoirs and purification plants to the distributing mains.[112]
Cincinnati water works was first constructed in 1817 by private interests and was transferred to the city in 1839. "The
water is taken from the Ohio River, near the Kentucky side,

opposite the former Village of California, into the Intake
Pier, through the Intake Tunnel to the River Pumping Station
on the Ohio side. Here the water is elevated to the large
settling basins, from which it flows to the coagulating basins,
receiving enroute the proper quantities of lime and iron sulphate, and driving the water turbines for generating electric
current. Leaving these basins, it flows to and through the
filters and is collected in the Clear-Water Reservoir before
its long trip to the City through the Gravity Tunnel to the
Main Pumping Station on Eastern Avenue. Here all water is
again pumped and distributed through the mains and services
to the consumers."113 "The City of Portland obtains its water
supply from the Bull Run River at a point 30 miles east of
the city." "The waters of the Bull Run River come from in-
numerable springs, small creeks and lakes fed by melting snow
and rainfall . . . ." "The Bull Run Storage Project was constructed on the Bull Run River at a point five miles above
the Headworks. A concrete dam 200 ft. in height and 950 ft.
in crest length was completed in 1929 at a cost of approximately $3,000,000 . . . . The storage reservoir extends 3.5
miles along the river. The Headworks is located five miles
down the river from the storage dam. At this point a gravity
dam 40 ft. in height diverts the water into three steel conduits, which carry it 24 miles to Reservoirs Nos. 1 and 5 on
Mt. Tabor at elevation 411.6 . . . . Four distribution reservoirs are located on Mt. Taber and two in Washington Park."
From the latter the water is distributed to the city consumers
and, in addition, to 60 water districts and companies outside
the city limits.114

    Memphis, Tennessee; Spokane, Washington; etc., are out-
standing examples of cities which obtain their water supply
from ground sources. The city of Memphis takes its water
supply from two sand strata. About 80 percent of the supply
is taken from a stratum approximately 500 feet deep and about
20 percent from one at the 1,400-foot depth. Thirty-one
wells have been drilled in the first stratum and nine in the
second. Water in these wells delivered through compressed air
devices to and is collected in a big underground reservoir,
where it is aerated and treated and is then pumped to the
city.115 "Spokane is one of the few large cities which obtain their water supply entirely from wells. The quality of
the water is unexcelled, as it is cold, clean, and sterile,
and has a hardness of only eight grains per gallon." "The
City of Spokane now has 11 wells sunk into a large underground
stream flowing through the glacial gravel of the Spokane Valley. The source of this underground water is apparently the
watersheds of the rivers and lakes of Northern Idaho and Western Montana." Water in these wells is pumped directly to
the distributing works.116 The source of water supply of the
Town of Wilton, Shelby County, Alabama, is a natural spring,
which has a minimum daily flow of 150,000 gallons. Water of this
spring is pumped to a storage tank built atop of hill, where by

gravity it is distributed to consumers.[117]

A special form of ground water is the so-called "underflows" of surface rivers and streams, which is the source of municipal water supply in a number of cities. For example, many municipalities in southern New Jersey get their source of water supply from the Raritan Magothy ground water, which is the underflows of the Delaware River.[118] But the most famous examples of municipal water supply systems that rely on underflows are those of Harrisburg, Virginia and Des Moines, Iowa. In Harrisburg a so-called "underground dam" was constructed in the valley of the Dry River, an ephemeral stream. The underground dam, which is a re-inforced concrete wall, is built across the valley and pentrates down to the bed of the sandstone formation. "The total length of this wall is 913 feet, depth varies from 10 feet to 22 feet. At the west end of the wall a collecting gallery was built from which the water is led by a 14-inch C. I. pipe to the transmission lines to the City which is twelve miles to the east." "Along the upstream side of the submerged dam or wall a perforated cement pipe 18 inches in diameter was laid leading to the collecting gallery." "The underground dam was constructed in 1932, at a cost of $34,000.00. The construction was done by city forces under the direction of the writer." "All flow is by gravity, the intake being 18 feet higher than the overflow of the service reservoirs in the city." "In extreme drought the city has an auxiliary supply from a spring with a flow of about 5,000 gallon per minute, this supply has to be pumped." "The water from both supplies is not filtered only chlorinated."[119]

The source of water supply of Des Moines is the underflows of the Raccoon River, which is a perennial stream. In the sand and gravel formations of the valley of the Raccoon River, "as shown by the accompanying sketch, have been placed the infiltration galleries, which consist of plain-end reinforced concrete rings two feet long, four and five feet inside diameter. These rings are smooth on one end and on the other have four one-quarter-inch lugs so constructed that when the rings are placed horizontally end to end on a wooden cradle in the bottom of a trench there is left an opening between each ring to permit the entrance of water from the surrounding sands and gravels. The gallery is constructed in one continuous line runing parallel with the river and from 150 to 300 feet back from the main river channel. At the present time the gallery is approximately three miles in length. The gallery serves the double purpose of collecting the water and carrying it by gravity to the pumping station where it is discharged into a low-lift suction well. The water is pumped from the low-lift suction well into a mixing chamber, from which it flows into the settling basins and then through the filter plant and into the clear well. From this clear well the water runs by gravity into the high-lift suction well, from which it is pumped into the distribution systems." "At

times of low water in the
river, and low ground water
plane in the area surrounding the gallery system, the
infiltration directly from
the river bed toward the gallery is insufficient to maintain a proper water stage
in the gallery system. It
is then possible to augment
the supply by either or both
of two methods. First, water may be pumped into irrigation or flooding basins."

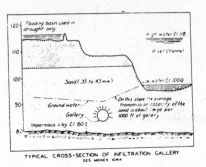

TYPICAL CROSS-SECTION OF INFILTRATION GALLERY
DES MOINES IOWA

"Second, the necessary quantity
of Racoon river water may be admitted directly into the tunnel and mixed with the gallery water."[120]

In some cities, such as St. Paul, Minnesota, and Tacoma,
Washington, municipal water is supplied by surface waters,
with ground water in reserve. In St. Paul, water is taken
from the Mississippi River, and is stored in the Vadnais Lake.
"Two artesian well fields are held in reserve. One located
along the shores of Centerville Lake has 28 wells which average 400 feet in depth and with an available capacity of from
7 to 10 million gallons a day. A second field, located at
McCarron Station, has 6 wells from 700 to 1,000 feet in depth,
with a capacity of 6 million gallons per day."[121] In Tacoma,
"water is taken from Green River by means of a concrete diversion dam 17 feet in maximum height and 152.4 feet long."
Before this source was resorted to, the city took its water
from the South Tacoma wells, which are now kept as a standby
supply for use in times of water shortage or when the Green
River becomes muddy during floods. The capacity of the Green
River supply is 70-93 million gallons per day and that of the
wells 32-55 million gallons per day.[122]

6. Hydroelectric power development, including multiple-
purpose projects---Hydroelectric electric energy is generated,
in either single-purpose or multiple-purpose projects, in the
following cities (1949 data):[123]

Alaska
        Sitka: 448 kilowatts
        Anchorage: 260 kilowatts
        Ketchikan: 7,900 kilowatts (as of 30 June 1951)
            (ultimate: 1,027 kilowatts)
        Town of Petersburg: 925 kilowatts (as of 30 June
            1951) (ultimate: 1,385 kilowatts)
        Town of Seward: 3,357 kilowatts
California
        Los Angeles: 108,543 kilowatts (1951).
        Pasadena: 2,536 kilowatts (1951)

San Francisco: 74,600 kilowatts (Ultimate: 186,500 kilowatts)

Colorado

Colorado Springs: 6,000 kilowatts (plus 25,000 kilowatts steam power)

Town of Creede: 30 kilowatts (plus 75 kilowatts of internal combustion power) (tailrace water used for municipal water supply) (See Senate Document 104, 78th Cong., 1st sess., 1943, p. 16.)

Glenwood Springs: 1,518 kilowatts

Longmont: 1,200 kilowatts (plus 3,887 kilowatts internal combustion power)

Loveland; 900 kilowatts (plus 600 kilowatts internal combustion power)

Meeker: 200 kilowatts (1939)

Connecticut

Norwich: 1,600 kilowatts (plus 14,250 kilowatts steam power)

Idaho

Idaho Falls: 2,600 kilowatts (1941)

Village of Bonners Ferry: 224 kilowatts (1951)

Sandpoint: 1,044 kilowatts (1951)

Soda Springs: 150 kilowatts (1939)

Illinois

Lockport: 12,000 kilowatts (1939)

Indiana

Fort Wayne: 425 kilowatts (plus 37,500 kilowatts steam power) (operated by Fort Wayne Water Works)

Iowa

Cedar Falls: 1,200 kilowatts (plus 4,500 steam power and 1,375 internal combustion power)

Ottumwa: 3,000 kilowatts

Maine

Kennebank: 150 kilowatts

Lubec: 96 kilowatts (plus 390 kilowatts internal combustion power)

Madison: 450 kilowatts

Michigan

Hart: 300 kilowatts (plus 2,000 kilowatts internal combustion power)

L'Anse: ---

Lansing: 1,200 kilowatts (plus 111,500 kilowatts steam power)

Lowell: 710 kilowatts (plus 4,380 kilowatts internal combustion power)

Marguette: 4,900 kilowatts (plus 3,820 kilowatts internal combustion power)

Marshall: 473 kilowatts (plus 345 kilowatts internal combustion power)

Niles: 460 kilowatts

Portland: 375 kilowatts (plus 5,350 kilowatts internal combustion power)

St. Louis: 360 kilowatts (plus 1,585 kilowatts in-

ternal combustion power)
Sturgis: 1,100 kilowatts (plus 5,350 kilowatts internal combustion power)
Traverse City: 1,280 kilowatts (plus 4,250 kilowatts steam power)
Union City: 418 kilowatts (plus 600 kilowatts internal combustion power)
Allegan: 2,240 kilowatts

Minnesota
Granite Falls: 470 kilowatts
Redwood Falls: 500 kilowatts (plus 400 kilowatts steam power and 1,320 internal combustion power)
Rochester: 2,000 kilowatts (1940)

Nebraska
Cozad: ----

New Hampshire
Littleton: 300 kilowatts
Woodsville: 400 kilowatts

New York
Boonville: 596 kilowatts
Lake Pacid: 332 kilowatts
Watertown: 6,750 kilowatts

North Carolina
Highlands: 224 kilowatts (as of 30 June 1951) (Ultimate: 448 kilowatts)
High Point: 21,000 kilowatts (1939)

Oregon
Bandon: 200 kilowatts
Eugene: 14,000 kilowatts (plus 13,500 kilowatts steam power)
Cascade Locks: 280 kilowatts
McMinnville: 200 kilowatts (plus 2,740 kilowatts internal combustion power)
Milton: 1,000 kilowatts (plus 760 kilowatts internal combustion power)

South Carolina
Abbeville: 2,000 kilowatts (1939)

Tennessee
Cookeville: 1,500 kilowatts
Lawrenceburg: 400 kilowatts

Texas
San Antonio: 1,100 kilowatts (All of this power is leased to Lower Colorado River Authority) (plus 173,500 kilowatts steam power, of which 60,000 kilowatts is leased to Lower Colorado River Authority).

Utah
Heber (three cities): 1,400 kilowatts
Logan: 1,400 kilowatts (plus 7,060 kilowatts internal combustion power)
Murray: 1,250 kilowatts (plus 3,315 kilowatts internal combustion power)
Nephi: 300 kilowatts
Monroe City: 107 kilowatts (1951)

Manti City: 395 kilowatts (1951)
Beaver City: 560 kilowatts (1951)
Ephraim: 188 kilowatts (1951)
Hyrum: 448 kilowatts (1951)
Parowan City: 370 kilowatts (1951)
Brigham City: 1,120 kilowatts (1939)

Vermont

Barton: 1,400 kilowatts
Erosburg Falls: 1,640 kilowatts
Hardwick: 1,160 kilowatts
Morrisville: 3,100 kilowatts
Swanton: 2,225 kilowatts

Virginia

Danville: 10,125 kilowatts
Harrisburg: 780 kilowatts
Martinsville: 1,300 kilowatts (1951)
Radford: 800 kilowatts
Richmond: 3,149 kilowatts

Washington

Centralia: 4,000 kilowatts
Ellensburg: 2,000 kilowatts
Seattle: 452,000 kilowatts (as of May 1953) (Ultimate: 675,000 kilowatts) (plus 61,000 kilowatts
steam power)
Tacoma: 238,000 kilowatts (as of May 1953) (Ultimate: 698,000 kilowatts) (plus 37,000 kilowatts
steam power)
Spokane: 3,900 kilowatts (1939)

Wisconsin

Barron: 208 kilowatts (plus 2,431 kilowatts intern-
al combustion power)
Black River Falls: 920 kilowatts (plus 1,781 kilo-
watts internal combustion power)
Brodhead: 262 kilowatts
Elkhorn: ----
Kaukauna: 3,581 kilowatts (as of 30 June 1951) (Ul-
timate: 5,968 kilowatts) (plus 7,400 kilowatts
leased from others)
River Falls: 375 kilowatts (plus 2,202 kilowatts
internal combustion power)
Spooner: 110 kilowatts
Stoughton: 726 kilowatts

As of July 1951, there were in all 172 hydroelectric
plants operated by municipalities in the United States, which
had an aggregate generating capacity of 777,625 kilowatts.
The ten largest of these plants (also July 1951) are:[124]

Diablo	120,000 kw.	Seattle, Washington
Gorge	74,000 kw.	Seattle, Washington
Moccasin	70,000 kw.	San Francisco, California
La Grande	64,000 kw.	Tacoma, Washington
Plant No. 1	58,000 kw.	Los Angeles, California

Cushman	54,000 kw.	Tacoma, Washington
Alder	50,000 kw.	Tacoma, Washington
Plant No. 2	42,000 kw.	Los Angeles, California
Cushman No. 1	36,000 kw.	Tacoma, Washington
Cedar Falls	22,800 kw.	Seattle, Washington

Following is a discussion of some examples of municipal hydroelectric enterprise, in both single-purpose and multiple-purpose projects. The municipal hydroelectric enterprises of the cities of Seattle and Tacoma, Washington, are the two largest such enterprises in this country. Both have the single purpose of generating commercial electric energy. Seattle's enterprise consists of the following projects:[125]

(a) Cedar River hydroelectric power development: This is made at the Cedar Falls, which is 37 miles southeast of the city. The project was adopted in a popular approval of a bond issue of $590,000 in 1902. Construction of a timber crib dam across the Cedar River at Cedar Falls and of a power plant was started the next year, which went into operation in 1904, with a generating capacity of 2,400 kilowatts. This was increased to 10,400 kilowatts in 1907 and 30,000 kilowatts in 1929, which is its present capacity.[126]

(b) Lake Union steam plant: In 1912, a hydroelectric plant was built at the site of this plant utilizing the overflow of the Volunteer Park Reservoir of the municipal water supply system. This plant was abandoned in 1917. However, in 1914, the present steam plant was constructed. This plant has a capacity of 40,000 kilowatts.

(c) Skagit River development: This involves the construction of one diversion dam, namely, the Gorge Dam, and two storage dams, namely, the Diablo and Ross Dams. The entire Skagit development was initiated in 1918, when a temporary 2,000-kilowatt hydroelectric plant was built at Newhalem, near the site of the Gorge Dam, to generate power needed for the construction of the latter. This plant was in operation in 1921, and has been preserved to the present time. The Gorge Dam, located about 50 miles above the mouth of the Skagit, was first completed in 1924 as a temporary timber crib structure, together with a 11,000-foot tunnel (20.5 feet in diameter) and the power house with two 20,000-kilowatt generators. In 1929, a third generator of the same capacity was installed; and in August 1950, another generator of 60,000 kilovolt-ampere rating was added. In 1948 the work was started of replacing the original timber crib dam with a concrete dam (still a diversion dam), and was completed in 1950. The Diablo Dam is a structure of 389 feet in height, and impounds a reservoir of 90,000 acre-feet. The construction of the dam and the power house was begun in 1927, and was completed in 1927. In 1936 and 1937, two generators of 64,500 kilowatts were installed, largest generators in the world at that time. In 1951-1952, the entire project went through the work of rehabilitation.

The Ross Dam is the largest of the three Skagit dams, and is
4 miles upstream of the Diable Dam, which is about 70 miles
upstream of the Gorge Dam. The construction of the dam was
commenced in 1937. By March 1940 it was completed to a
height of 305 feet. It attained the present height of 540
feet on 18 August 1949. At this height, it impounds a reservoir of 1,400,000 acre-feet in volume and of 22 miles in
length, extending across the Canadian boundary. The dam will
be ultimately raised to a height of 650 feet. One 100,000-
kilovolt-ampere generator was installed at the Ross Dam in
October 1952, and began in operation in December 1952; and
another of the same rating was installed on 28 April 1953.
However, the power plant was then still under construction,
and was scheduled to be completed by December 1954. The generating capacities of the various hydroelectric power plants
on the Skagit River are given below:

UNIT	AS OF MAY 1953	ULTIMATE
Newhalem (may be regarded part of Gorge)	2,000 kw.	2,000 kw.
Gorge	108,000 kw.	151,000 kw.
Diablo	132,000 kw.	132,000 kw.
Ross	180,000 kw.	360,000 kw.
Total	422,000 kw.	645,000 kw.

(d) Georgetown steam plant: This plant, having a generating capacity of 21,000 kilowatts, was acquired on 14 March
1950 from the Puget Sound Power and Light Company, which built
it in 1907.

The combined generating capacity of all of the above developments was 452,000 kilowatts of hydro and 61,000 kilowatts
of steam generated electric power, as of May 1953. Principal
transmission facilities of the city included, as of the same
time, 115 substations and 100.12 circuit-miles of 110,000-
volt, 115.73 circuit-miles of 55,000-volt, and 788.80 circuit
miles of 23,000-volt transmission lines. The total value of
all generating and transmitting facilities was estimated, as
of the same time, to be $202,208,338.

The hydroelectric power development of the City of Tacoma,
Washington, is next in size to that of Seattle. It is located
on three streams none of which is in the city area.[127]

(a) On the Nisqually River, a diversion dam was built in
1910 at La Grande site and was completed in 1912. The dam
is 215 feet in height, and water is delivered through a 6,500-
foot tunnel to the first hydroelectric plant, which was also
completed in 1912, and which has a capacity of 24,000 kilowatts. In 1942, a storage dam, called the Alder Dam was con-

structed 2 miles upstream of the La Grande Dam. It is 330 feet high and impounds a reservoir of 210,800 acre-feet. At the same time a power plant was constructed at this dam having capacity of 50,000 kilowatts and another plant was added to the La Grande site utilizing the increased river flow, which has a capacity of 40,000 kilowatts. The Alder Dam and power plant were completed in 1945 and the new plant at La Grande was completed in 1944. The total power output from the Nisqually river is 114,000 kilowatts.

(b) On the North Fork of the Skokomish River, there were built in 1924 and 1929 respectively Cushman Dams Nos. 1 and 2, both with power plants, which were completed in May 1926 and December 1930, respectively. The power plant at Cushman Dam No. 1 generates 43,000 kilowatts and that at Cushman Dam No. 2 generates 81,000 kilowatts. The total power generated from the North Fork of the Skokomish River is 124,000 kilowatts.

(3) On 28 November 1951, the City of Tacoma was granted by the Federal Power Commission a 50-year license for the development of hydroelectric power on the Cowlitz River, a tributary of the Lower Columbia River. "The proposed project, which has attracted widespread public interest because of the controversy over its fish passage facilities, will include two dams. One, to be built near Mossyrock, Washington, will be about 510 feet high and 1,300 feet long at the crest. A reservoir will extend about 21 miles upstream. A power house, at the toe of the dam, will contain three 75,000-kilowatt units, making a total capacity of 225,000 kilowatts, with provision for a fourth 75,000-kilowatt unit. The other dam, near Mayfield, Washington, will be 240 feet high and have a crest length of 850 feet. The dam would form a reservoir extending about 13.5 miles upstream to the Mossyrock Dam. The power house will have an initial installation of three 40,-000-kilowatt units with provision for a fourth of equal capacity. "Estimated cost (1951 figure) of the project is approximately $135,000,000, plus an additional $7,000,000 which the City plans to spend for the special fish passage facilities."[128] As of May 1953 no construction work had been commenced, although preliminary surveys had been made.

In addition, the city has two steam power plants. One was built in May 1922 and completed in September of the same year. It has a capacity of 12,000 kilowatts. The other plant, with 25,000-kilowatt capacity, was built in 1930 and completed in July 1931.[129] The two steam plants generate a total of 37,000 kilowatts. Transmission facilities of the city consist of 45 unattended and 9 attended substations, and 31.35 miles of 110-kilovolt single circuit and 98.20 miles of 110-kilovolt double circuit transmission lines. The total properties of the city devoted to the production of hydro and steam power was $59,935,714 as of May 1953.

The hydroelectric power enterprise of the Town of Martinsville, Virginia, may be cited as an example of the smaller
single-purpose municipal enterprises. "The Town of Martinsville, with a population of 4,200 in 1905, decided to provide
itself with electric service." "The Town purchased the Hairs-
ton Mill site on the north bank of Smith River and the R. J.
Reynolds Mill site on the south bank, and replaced the old
wood dam with one of stone. The Town then built a race-way
approximately 1,000 feet in length and erected a sheet metal
power house on a stone foundation. The generators consisted
of two 150-KW three-phase, 4,000-volt machines belted to
horizontal S. Morgan Smith water wheels operating on a 22-
foot head." "The Hydro Plant began operation June 26, 1906,
and continued with no change until 1910, when the dam was
raised six feet to a 28-foot head, and the two 150-KW generators were replaced with two 250-KW units belted to the same
water wheels. An additional water wheel was belted to a new
300-KW unit." "In January 1932 the Martinsville Hydro-electric Plant was shut down for reconstruction work on the dam."
"The renovated plant consisted of two vertical units operating on a 32-foot head. They were placed in operation May 5,
1932." They generate 1,000 kw. and 300 kw., respectively.
The municipal power house is still operating with these two
units, although it is insufficient for the needs of the growing city, which has to purchase from 5,000 to 6,000 kw. from
the Appalachian Electric Power Company.[130]

In 1909, the Heber City, Midway Town and Charleston Town,
Utah, jointly established the Heber Light and Power Plant,
an hydroelectric power enterprise. The capital stock of the
Plant was $100,000, of which Heber City owns three-fourths
and the Towns of Midway and Charleston each own one-eighth.
The enterprise is governed by a power board consisting of
the mayor of Heber City, two councilmen of Heber City chosen
by the mayor and presidents of the town boards of the Towns
of Midway and Charleston. As of September 1951, "we have
two power plants with a total capacity of 1,400 kw.; thirteen
miles of 12 kv. transmission lines and seventy miles of distribution lines. The peak load for 1950 was 1,900 kw. Utah
Power and Light Company furnishes what we are unable to generate. They also buy our surplus power." Earnings of the
plant are proportionately distributed among the three municipalities.[131]

There is a tendency to utilize single-purpose municipal
power dams for consistent but incidental recreation and fish
and wildlife conservation purposes. For example, in Tacoma,
Washington, fishing and boating facilities are provided by
concessionaries in Lake Cushman and the Alder Lake.[132] In
issuing a preliminary permit to the City of Eugene, Oregon,
for a hydroelectric development in Lim and Lane Counties, the
Federal Power Commission ordered that the city should cooperate with the state fish and game agencies and the U. S.

Fish and Wildlife Service in considering the protection of
fish and wildlife resources of the affected area.[133]

Of the multiple-purpose enterprises, which in general
provide electric energy and municipal water supply, the two
primary needs of a city, that of the City and County of San
Francisco is the largest. San Francisco program is commonly
known as the "Hetch Hetchy Project", which is part of a comprehensive river-basin-development program for the Tuolumne
River Basin, the remaining part of the program being undertaken by the Modesto and Turlock Irrigation Districts.[134]
Under the water law of California, the two irrigation have
acquired rights (senior) to the normal flows of the Tuolumne
River and its tributaries, while the City and County of San
Francisco has obtained rights (junior) to their floodwaters.[135]
By an Act of Congress of 19 December 1913 (38 Stat. 242, commonly called the "Raker Act"), the latter was granted rights-
of-way in, over and through the Yosemite National Park, Stanislaus National Forest and other public lands in California
in Tuolumne, Stanislaus, San Joaquin and Alameda counties
necessary for the construction of water supply and hydroelectric power development works, and also lands needed in the
construction of reservoirs in the Hetch Hetchy Valley Lake,
Eleanor Basin and Cherry Valley and of power houses. The
plan of San Francisco in the Hetch Hetchy project involves
the construction of (1) three storage reservoirs for the
storage of the floodwaters to which it has right of appropriation, namely Hetch Hetchy (on main stem of the Tuolumne
River), Eleanor (on Eleanor Creek, a tributary of the Cherry
River, which is a tributary of the Tuolumne River) and Cherry
Valley (on the Cherry River), (2) water delivery works, consisting of a mountain aqueduct taking water released by the
three storage reservoirs at the junction of the Tuolumne and
Cherry Rivers, a number of relay reservoirs, and water-dis-
tribution works, and (3) power houses (three) utilizing
drops of water in its course of flow through the rivers and
the water-delivery system. It is to be noted that the direct
function of the three storage reservoirs is solely to regulate
the flows of the Tuolumne and Cherry Rivers. The direct benefit of this regulation is water supply, to which hydroelectric power development is incidental. There is no direct diversion of water from the three storage reservoirs, unless
the Tuolumne and Cherry Rivers themselves, for the purposes
of the project, are regarded as "natural" water-delivery aqueducts; nor is there power development at their impounding
dams. The basic objective of the Hetch Hetchy Project is to
provide the City and County of San Francisco and the neighboring area which it serves a water supply of 400 million
gallons a day, which necessitates an ultimate aggregate capacity of 1,400,000 acre-feet of the three storage reservoirs.

Construction work was begun in 1914. On 6 May 1918, the
Early Intake Power House, which is located at the intake of

the Mountain Aqueduct, i.e., the junction of the Tuolumne
and Cherry Rivers, was placed in operation. On 23 June 1918
the Lake Eleanor Dam was completed and the Lake Eleanor Reservoir began in operation. Lake Eleanor was originally a
natural lake. With the construction of the Lake Eleanor Dam,
it was raised by 35 feet and its total capacity increased to
27,000 acre-feet. The O'Shaughnessy Dam, which impounds the
Hetch Hetchy Reservoir, was completed on 6 April 1923 to a
height of 344.5 feet. On 1 July 1938 it was raised to its
present height of 430 feet, at which the Hetch Hetchy Reservoir has a capacity of 360,000 acre-feet. On 14 August 1925
the Moccasin Power Plant, which is situated at the end of
the Mountain Aqueduct, was completed and placed in operation.
It was as late as 24 October 1934 that the Hetch Hetchy project water began to flow into the Crystal Springs Reservoir
(one of the relay reservoirs) and thence through the distribution system to San Francisco. The supply is sufficient for
the present needs of the metropolis, which amount to about
100 million gallons a day. Construction of the Cherry Dam
and Reservoir was initiated in 1951, at a total estimated cost
of $13 million, of which $9 million was contributed by the
Federal Government under provisions of the Flood Control Act
of 22 December 1944, and was scheduled to be completed by the
winter of 1954. The Cherry Valley Dam, about 320 feet high,
will impound 274,000 acre-feet of water, of which 80,000 acre-feet will be reserved for flood control and 194,000 acre-feet will be available for municipal water supply and incidental power development. The Cherry Reservoir will store
not only the flood waters of the Cherry River, but also all
of the flow from the Eleanor Reservoir, which will be diverted
to the former reservoir through a 6,400-foot tunnel.[136] A power house with 54,000-kilowatt generating will be built at
some later date about six miles south of the Cherry Valley
Dam, together with the necessary tunnel.

Since the total water supply ultimately needed by the
City and County of San Francisco is 1,400,000 acre-feet, and
since after the completion of the Cherry Valley Reservoir the
total active primary storage of the enterprise will be only
194,000 plus 360,000 or 554,000 acre-feet, there is a net
shortage of 846,000 acre-feet. To meet this shortage, the
city and county of San Francisco has entered into an agreement with the Modesto and Turlock Irrigation Districts to
raise the Don Petro Dam, which is jointly owned by these two
districts, to a height sufficient to increase the capacity of
the Don Petro Reservoir (now 290,000 acre-feet) to between
1,200,000 and 1,800,000 acre-feet, of which from 340,000 to
500,000 acre-feet will be reserved for flood detention. The
city will probably start this work sometime in 1961.

So far as the power feature is concerned, the present
Moccasin and Early intake power houses have a combined generating capacity of 74,600 kilowatts. With the completion of

the Cherry Reservoir, this will be increased to 132,500 kilowatts. With the construction of the third power house on the
Cherry River, the total output of hydroelectric energy of
the enterprise will be 186,500 kilowatts.

The water-electricity enterprise of the City of Ephraim
(Ephraim City Corporation), Utah, represents municipal multiple-purpose enterprises of small scale. The city has two
hydroelectric plants, both of which are located on the New
Canyon. The first plant, Cottonwood Plant, was built in 1905,
and started operation in May 1906. Which source of water ran
this plant, or even whether it was a hydro-plant at all, is
not known. However "we built the New Canyon ditch which
brings the New Canyon water over into the intake of the Cottonwood power canal in 1911." "The capacity of the generator
is 200 KVA at 4,000 volts. We can generate this amount for
about seven months during the summer and fall. The Forest
(Service) permit no. 1735 gives us the right to bring about
one second-foot of spring water from East slope of our mountains through the Ephraim irrigation tunnel to use for power
during the winter months only. This does not increase our
capacity but does increase the amount we are able to generate
in the winter. In 1927 we built hydro plant no. 2 one and
one-fourth miles further up the canyon. This plant is run by
spring water only and operates under a head of 1,410 feet.
The penstock or pipe line is 8,000 feet long. This plant has
a capacity of 262 KVA . . . in the summer and fall months.
. . . In 1936 we installed about 8,000 feet of steel pipe
from the tail race of No. 2 plant down to Cottonwood plant
and there installed another wheel on the shaft of the Cottonwood plant . . . . This does not increase the generator
capacity but does increase the amount we are able to generate
in the winter, which is 135 KVA. The spring water that goes
through both plants is discharged into a cement box and carried to the head house just above town, through 8,000 feet
of steel pipe, and supplies the people of Ephraim with plenty
of good spring water . . . " In 1940, a steel pipe of 8,800
feet long was put directly into the springs so that water is
hidden from human sight. In 1951, the two hydro plants were
augmented by the construction of diesel electric plant with
two generators having a combined capacity of 550 KVA.[137] In
this enterprise, it may be observed, there are no water-storage or diversion dams, but only water-delivery works.

The water-power system of the city of Augusta, Georgia,
is unique in that the city has constructed and operated all
of the structures of the system except the hydroelectric power
generating plants, which are built and operated by private
industrial interests. The system consists of a small diversion dam on the Savannah River at about mile 208, and a power
canal of seven miles in length and at present two hundred feet
in width with an average depth of twelve feet. The dam and
canal were built in 1836-1840, and the canal was enlarged to

its present dimensions in 1870. The city uses part of the
water power (mechanical) so created to pump water for the
city, but does not produce electric energy. The remaining
water power is leased to a number of textile plants, iron
works, flour mills, electric plants, lumber mills, etc., for
the generation of hydroelectric power, the aggregate capacity
of which is 9,026 horsepower. The canal provides a maximum
water head on the lower end of thirty-two feet. As the heads
are low, no power is produced during flood periods. And,
when the river stages are low, power production is interrupt-
ed too. The total cost of construction of the dam and the
canal is not available, but their present replacement value
is estimated to be some $4 million.[138]

Besides generating hydroelectric power by themselves, or
constructing and operating hydroelectric power generation
works, municipalities, like the states, counties and special
districts, may distribute hydroelectric power generated by the
Federal Government. Of the total of 47.43 billion kilowatt-
hours of electric energy generated and disposed of by the Federal Government during the fiscal year 1950, 10.17 billion
kilowatt-hours, or 21.44 percent, were distributed by municipalities (which, however, may include some counties and special districts).[139]

7. Water sanitation---All states have laws which authorize cities and towns to construct, or acquire and maintain
and operate a municipal sewage-disposal or sewerage system.
Municipal sewerage system may be combined with municipal drainage system,[140] in which case the same works serve the dual
purposes of drainage and sewerage. But the disposal of sewage
as such, though a sanitary measure involving the use of water,
is not a measure of water sanitation. On the contrary, municipal sewage disposed of without treatment is the very source
of water pollution. It is therefore the treatment of sewage
that is directly concerned with water sanitation. Although
the cost of sewage treatment (about $3 to $25 per capita) is
much less than that of sewage disposal (about $27 to $125 per
capita),[141] not all cities and towns have sewage-treatment
facilities.[142]

Municipal drainage enterprise incidentally reduces if not
completely removes the danger of mosquito-breeding. When
drainage enterprise is undertaken with the primary purpose of
promoting public health,[143] such enterprise may be a single-
purpose mosquito-control enterprise. But in certain states,
there are specific laws which enable cities and towns to undertake mosquito-control projects as such. Under the laws of
Rhode Island (General Laws, ch. 214: Laws 1934, ch. 2126; as
amended by L. 1947, ch. 1881), a number of cities and towns
of that state have, first with Federal labor aid and then with
the technical assistance of the state, constructed ditches for
the purpose of controlling and exterminating mosquitoes and put

into practice other measures of mosquito-control.[144] In New
York cities have been authorized to remove and abate mosquito-
breeding places, the costs of which are to be shared by the
city and the landowners concerned, and the work is to be performed by a commission of six members of which three are appointed by the city health board and three by the county court
(Laws 1906, ch. 583, as amended). Under Virginia laws, cities, individually or by joint action, may create mosquito districts to undertake works for controlling mosquitoes (Acts
1940, ch. 98; as extended by Acts 1950, ch. 72). In Minnesota,
any city, borough, town or village, upon petition by five percent or 250 freeholders and after approval by a referendum,
may adopt mosquito-abatement projects, which are to be undertaken by an abatement board consisting of three freeholders
appointed by the governing body of the city, borough, town or
village concerned with the assistance of state agencies (Statutes, sec. 145,34 et seq.: Laws 1949, ch. 404).

    The mosquito-control work launched by the City of New
York best illustrates the size and scale which municipal mosquito-control enterprise may readh. As reported in 1936, a
total of 3,200 miles of drainage ditches had been built by
the city department of health over the salt marshes that constituted about one-ninth of the city's total area, in addition
to a regular ten-day program of spraying more than 60,000
catch-basins, the principal mosquito-breeding places in the
apartment-house districts, as well as ponds and swamps in
the city, which was performed by 26 specially designed trucks.[145]
In Portland, Oregon, the work of clearing brush in mosquito-
infesting areas was done with Federal aid. In 1944 the Bureau of Insect Control was created within the municipal government as the responsible agency of this work. In 1947 a
program was initiated of spraying DDT by airplanes over the
Columbia and Willamette Rivers, and all reservoirs, ponds and
vicinity, which had the entire Multnomah County and its vicinity, which had an aggregate area of 150 square miles. In this
work, two airplanes were employed, as well as a number of tank
trucks holding the larvicides.[146] Mosquito-control by spraying has also been recorded in many cities in Wyoming, -- by
airplane in Douglas, Saratoga, Evanston, Thermopolis, Basin
and Greybull; by hand in Torrington, Lander, Riverton, Shoshone
and Worland, and also in Saratoga, Evanston and Thermopolis.
All water areas, ponds, rivers, marshes, irrigated lands, etc.,
are subject to this treatment.[147] Similar work has been reported in eight towns of Maryland;[148] and many cities and towns
in California (one), Florida (one), Massachusetts (thirteen),
Michigan (two), Montana (three), Nebraska (two), New York (two),
North Dakota (three), Pennsylvania (thirteen), Rhode Island
(Seventeen), Utah (one), Virginia (eight), Washington (four)
and Wisconsin (two).[149]

    8. Forestry---Cities and towns may acquire, own and main-
tain forests on watersheds of watercourses from which they ob-

tain their municipal water supply. This is an auxiliary measure of municipal water supply enterprise, instead of an independent forestry measure. But cities and towns may also
establish and manage municipal forests as an independent forestry measure. Authority for this enterprise may be derived
from the city charter, or from some special state law. It is
also possible that municipalities just happen to own forest
lands and choose to manage them for timber production and
other municipal purposes. In the states listed below general
enabling laws were in force in 1953 which permit the acquisition, establishment and administration of municipal forests:

New Jersey---*Statutes*, sec. 40:58-1 (Laws 1906, ch. 136,
    sec. 1).
Pennsylvania---*Statutes*, tit. 53, sec. 1651 (act of 22
    April 1909, sec. 1). Boroughs excepted by an act of
    14 May 1915, ch. 13, art. 1, sec. 1; and townships ex-
    cepted by an act of 14 July 1917, sec. 1500.
New York---Cities, towns and villages, *Conservation Law*,
    sec. 60 (Laws 1916, ch. 451; as last amended by L.
    1943, ch. 710, part 1, sec. 201).
Massachusetts---Towns, *General Laws*, ch. 132, sec. 35
    (Acts 1920, ch. 604, sec. 5; as amended by Acts 1924,
    ch. 24).
Ohio---*Revised Code*, sec. 5707.08 (Laws 1921, p. 322).
Indiana---All cities and incorporated towns, *Statutes*,
    sec. 32-101 (Acts 1929, ch. 17, sec. 1). For cities
    of 4th class, earlier authorized by *ibid*., sec. 48-
    5705 (Acts 1919, ch. 121, sec. 1) (by donation or de-
    vise only).
Rhode Island---Towns, *General Laws*, ch. 329, sec. 34 (Laws
    1929, ch. 1389; as amended by L. 1930, ch. 1617).
Michigan---All cities, townships, and villages (and also
    school districts), *Compiled Laws*, secs. 320.201 to
    320.210 (Acts 1931, No. 217).
Connecticut---*General Statutes*, sec. 647, enacted 1939.
Virginia---Cities and towns, *Code*, sec. 10-48 (Acts 1940,
    ch. 40, sec. 1).
Florida---Cities and towns (and also school districts),
    Statutes, sec. 591.18 (Laws 1941, ch. 20902, sec. 4).
Minnesota---Cities, towns and villages, *Statutes*, sec.
    459.06 (Laws 1913, ch. 211, sec. 1) (Counties added
    by L. 1945, ch. 347).
Illinois---*Revised Statutes*, ch. 24, sec. 69.1-1 (Laws
    1947, p. 408. Referendum required, *ibid*., sec. 69.1-2.

In 1946, there were 9,581 acres of forest land in the
State of New Hampshire which were held by cities for the protection of the watersheds of their water supplies.[150] The
small town of Newington of that state is said to have the old-
est community forest in the United States. Established in
1710, this forest of 112 acres has helped to build a church,
a town hall, a school, a parsonage, and a library; provided

part of the funds for the village water supply system; helped
pay the minister's salary, and supplied building and fuel wood
to the community.[151] Another New Hampshire town, Danville,
established two small town forests as early as 1790.[152] The
New England states have led the nation in the establishment
of municipal forests outside of this region. But "by 1938,
incomplete reports showed that about 1,500 community forests
had been established in the United States, comprising about
3,000,000 acres. In 1949, the number had risen to 3,125 and
the aggregate area to just under 4,500,000 acres. Only five
states still have no community forests, although 22 states
have less than 10 each. At the top end of the scale are Wisconsin with 321 tracts covering almost 2,400,000 acres, Michigan with 846 covering 165,000 acres, and New York with 658
tracts and 150,000 acres."[153] It is estimated that about
fifty percent of the municipal forests in the country which
embrace 80 percent of the total acreage thereof have been acquired and developed primarily for the purpose of protecting
sources of municipal water supplies, i.e., municipal watersheds.[154]

Municipal forests vary greatly in size. That of Seattle,
Washington, which is 66,380 acres in area (1952), is perhaps
the largest. For the purpose of exemplification, the areas
of forests of a number other cities are given as follows:
Newark, N. J., 35,000 acres (1944); Waynesville, N. C., 8,200
acres (1952), Manchester, N. H., 5,200 acres (1949); Springfield, Ill., 4,300 acres (1949); Kingsport, Tenn., 1,200
acres (1952); Newington, H. H., 111 acres (1952).[155] "The
average size of municipal forests for the country as a whole
is less than 600 acres."[156]

In cities which own watershed forests, special emphasis
is placed on the management of these forests to secure a
pure and clean water supply.[157] "One of the best known of
these municipal watershed forests, by virtue of its large
size and profitable management, is the Cedar Creek watershed
owned by the city of Seattle."[158] The acquisition of forest
lands was started by the city shortly after municipal water
was delivered from the Cedar River in 1901. The acquisition
was accelerated in the period 1910-1914. With the present
acreage in city ownership, there are only less than 4,300
acres left in private ownership. With the completion of an
land exchange with the U. S. Forest Service, the city will
ultimately be the sole owner of the entire watershed (91,500
acres, or 143 square miles). A comprehensive management program was put into operation by the city in 1924, with a professional forester in charge. For fire-protection two lookouts have been constructed on mountain peaks, and a fire-
suppression camp is maintained at Walsh Lake, where the city
also operates a tree nursery. An extensive system of access
roads has been constructed, and some 5,068 acres of burnt-
over areas had been reforested as of 1949. For financial
reasons, the city has followed a policy of acquiring timbered

lands in which previous owners have retained title to timber but agreed to manage it in accordance with municipal regulations. All of the land except some 8,000 acres near the Cedar Lake were acquired in this manner. In 1945 an agreement was reached between the city and four principal timber owners which provides for sustained-yield harvesting of the remaining virgin timber over a period of forty years, limiting the annual cut to 35 million board feet, subject to revision at the end of each ten years, and which applies to the entire watershed, including timber lands owned by the city, private parties and U. S. Forest Service.[159]

In the watershed owned by the city of New York, there is a force of some 150 armed guards employed by the city government to patrol the watershed in some two dozen jeep station wagons.[160] This represents the other aspect of watershed protection, namely, the prevention of trespassing and spoiling.

Municipalities usually maintain a fire department, which, besides serving urban areas, may no doubt suppress forest fires. In addition to this general municipal fire service, special municipal enterprise in the prevention and control of forest fires has been authorized in Massachusetts and Minnesota. In Massachusetts, cities and towns are required to appoint annually a forest warden with the approval of the state forester (General Laws, ch. 48, sec. 8: Acts 1886, ch. 296, sec. 2; as last amended by Acts 1941, ch. 490, sec. 10). "If a fire occurs in woodland the forest warden of the town or of a town containing woodland endangered by such fire . . . may set back fires and take necessary precautions to prevent its spread" (ibid., sec. 9: Acts 1874, ch. 228; as last amended by Acts 1920, ch. 2). Town forest wardens may also patrol forest lands during times of forest fire danger (ibid., sec. 28B: Acts 1930, ch. 309). As another forest fire prevention measure, each town may, in cooperation with other towns or with the state forester, construct lookout towers (ibid., sec. 23: Acts 1919, ch. 120). Under the laws of Minnesota, all cities, towns and villages may construct and maintain pre-suppression fire-breaks for the prevention of forest fires (Statutes, secs. 88.42 to 88.46: Laws 1925, ch. 263, secs. 15-21). Similar authority is possessed by the townships of South Dakota (Code, ch. 58.10: Laws 1893, ch. 91; as amended by L. 1905, ch. 111 and L. 1913, ch. 232) and Kansas (General Statutes, sec. 31-118 et seq.: Laws 1899, ch.99). These special statutory provisions apply to both municipally owned and private forest (or prairie) lands. There is no need to mention that municipalities owning municipal forests may protect these municipal properties from fire without specific authorization therefor.

Municipalities of Vermont (Statutes, sec. 3788: Laws 1898, No. 156, sec. 1; as last amended by L. 1933, No. 157, sec. 3467; and ibid., sec. 3781: L. 1904, No. 76, sec. 4; as last amended by L. 1943, No. 42, sec. 1), Idaho (<u>Code</u>, sec. 50-1147: Laws 1913, ch. 90; as amended by L. 1923, ch. 140, sec. 1) and Connecticut (<u>General Statutes</u>, sec. 650, 1943) have the authority to control and exterminate all forest insect and disease pests.[161] In Massachusetts (<u>General Laws</u>, ch. 132, sec. 11: Acts 1905, ch. 381, secs. 1 and 3; as last amended by Acts 1948, ch. 660, sec. 6) and Rhode Island (<u>General Laws</u>, ch. 228, sec. 6: Laws 1909, ch. 242, sec. 6), cities and towns have been specially authorized to control and exterminate gypsy and brown-tail moths. As discussed above, the municipalities as well as the state and county governments may contribute funds to the Federal Government to control white-pine blister rust pest.[162] However, such monetary contributions do not constitue a municipal enterprise.

9. Recreation---Municipal parks may be authorized by municipal charters, special state laws and general state enabling laws. As of 1953, the states listed below had general enabling law for municipal parks:

Connecticut---<u>General Statutes</u>, sec. 644 (enacted 1857, as amended by Acts 1907, ch. 121), sec. 645 (Acts 1911, ch. 72) and sec. 619 (Acts 1913, ch. 154; as last amended in 1943).

Illinois---<u>Revised Statutes</u>, ch. 24, secs. 52-1 to 52-9 (Laws 1872, p. 228; as last amended by L. 1947, pp. 622-624).

Colorado---<u>Statutes</u>, ch. 163, sec. 10 (an act of 4 April 1877, sec. 14) (in subd. 7).

Florida---<u>Statutes</u>, sec. 167.09 (Laws 1879, ch. 3164, sec. 3; as last amended by L. 1949, ch. 25094, sec. 1).

Missouri---<u>Statutes</u>, sec. 90.010 (Laws 1879, p. 45; as last amended by L. 1919, p. 608).

Vermont---Towns, <u>Statutes</u>, sec. 3647 (Laws 1880, No. 130) (upon petition by a fifth or fifty of the freeholders). For parks within the limits of highways <u>ibid</u>., sec. 5182 (L. 1880, No. 130; as amended by L. 1894, No. 83, sec. 1) (at the request of ten or more citizens).

Iowa---<u>Code</u>, sec. 370.1 (Acts 1884, ch. 151, sec. 1; as last amended by Acts 1943, ch. 176, sec. 1) and sec. 370.11 (Acts 1884, ch. 151, sec. 2; as last amended by Acts 1909, ch. 56, sec. 2).

New Mexico---<u>Statutes</u>, sec. 14-1805 (Laws 1884, ch. 34, sec. 14, subd. 7).

Utah---<u>Code</u>, sec. 10-8-8 (<u>Compiled Laws of 1888</u>, sec. 1755, subd. 8; as last amended by L. 1919, ch. 11, sec. 1).

Kansas---Townships, <u>General Statutes</u>, sec. 80-901 et seq. (Laws 1887, ch. 235; as amended by L. 1923, ch. 240). Cities, <u>ibid</u>., sec. 12-1301 (Laws 1903, ch. 135, sec. 1; as last amended by L. 1947, ch. 121, sec. 1).

New Jersey---<u>Statutes</u>, sec. 40:175-2 (Laws 1888, ch. 19,

sec. 1), for all cities except cities of the first
class.

North Dakota---Revised Code, sec. 40-5901 (Laws 1890, ch.
99, sec. 1).

Washington---Cities of the first class, Revised Code, sec.
35.22.280 (Laws 1890, p. 218, sec. 5) (in subd. 7).
Cities of the second, third and fourth classes,
ibid., sec. 35.23.170 (L. 1907, ch. 228, sec. 2;
as amended by L. 1925, ex. s., ch. 121, sec. 1).
Any city or town, ibid., sec. 35.43.040 (L. 1911,
ch. 98) (in subd. 9).

Mississippi---Code, sec. 3421 (Code of 1892, sec. 2947).

Kentucky---Cities of the first class, Revised Statutes,
sec. 97.250 et seq. (Acts 1893, ch. 244; as amended by Acts 1942, ch. 34). Cities of the second
class, ibid., sec. 97.400 et seq. (Acts 1906, ch.
15; as last amended by Acts 1942, ch. 53). Cities
of the third class, ibid., sec. 97.530 (Acts 1922,
ch. 86). Cities of the fourth class, ibid., sec.
97.550 (Acts 1928, ch. 90). Cities of any class,
ibid., sec. 97.060 (Acts 1940, ch. 140). (Assistance of State Legislative Research Commission acknowledged.)

Michigan---Compiled Laws, sec. 100.1 (Acts 1895, No. 215,
ch. 20, sec. 1), for cities. Constitution of Michigan of 1908, art. VIII, sec. 22, for cities and
villages.

Pennsylvania---Statutes, tit. 53, sec. 1558 (act of 26
June 1895; as last amended by an act of 13 May
1927), made inapplicable to third-class cities by
an act of 23 June 1931, art. 47, sec. 4701.

Arizona---Code, sec. 16-601 (an act of 18 March 1897, sec.
1) (in subd. 1).

Nebraska---Cities of the first and second classes, Revised
Statutes, sec. 19-101 (Laws 1899, ch. 15, sec. 1).
Primary cities, ibid., sec. 15-210 (L. 1901, ch.16,
sec. 129, subd. 11; as amended by L. 1911, ch. 11,
sec. 2).

Oregon---Revised Statutes, sec. 226.320 (based on L. 1899,
p. 67, as amended).

Ohio---Revised Code, sec. 719.01, subd. (B) (Laws 1903,
p. 26; as last amended by L. 1945, p. 253). Also
ibid., sec. 717.01, subd. (N) (L. 1911, p. 154;
as last amended by L. 1945, pp. 263 and 265).

Georgia---Code, sec. 69-504 et seq. (Acts 1905, No. 329),
by donation only.

Indiana---Acts 1905, ch. 129, sec. 144 (for cities of
third, fourth and fifth classes).

Oklahoma---Statutes, tit. 11, sec. 1211 et seq. (Laws
1905, p. 133; as amended by L. 1910, p. 77).

Nevada---Compiled Laws, sec. 1128 (Stats. 1907, ch. 124,
sec. 28) (in subd. 12).

Maine---Revised Statutes, ch. 84, sec. 3 (Laws 1909, ch.

183): Towns may establish town parks on donated
lands, or on town lands appropriated for this purpose by a referendum. Ibid., sec. 4 (L. 1909, ch.
183): Villages may establish parks on donated lands.

South Dakota---Code, sec. 45.2510 (Laws 1909, ch. 272,
sec. 6; as last amended by L. 1925, ch. 237, sec.
9).

Wyoming---Cities and towns, Compiled Statutes, sec. 29-
332 (Laws 1909, ch. 51, sec. 33).

Louisiana---Revised Statutes, tit. 33, sec. 531 (Acts
1910, No. 302, secs. 4 and 5; as last amended by
Acts 1944, No. 237, sec. 1). Also ibid., sec. 730
(Acts 1918, No. 160, sec. 67).

Minnesota---Statutes, sec. 430.01 (Laws 1911, ch. 185, sec.
1; as last amended by L. 1945, ch. 470, sec. 2).

New York---General City Law, sec. 20, subd. 7 (Laws 1913,
ch. 247; as last amended by L. 1943, ch. 710, part
1, sec. 703).

Rhode Island---Cities and towns, General Laws, ch. 333,
sec. 25 (Laws 1913, ch. 950).

North Carolina---Cities and towns, General Statutes, sec.
160-200, subd. 12 (Laws 1917, ch. 136, sub.-ch. 5,
sec. 1; as last amended by L. 1949, ch. 594, sec.
2). Also ibid., sec. 160-155 et seq. (L. 1945,
ch. 1052).

Texas---Revised Civil Statutes, art. 6080 (Laws 1917, p.
149).

Tennessee---Cities under city-manager and commission
plans, Code, sec. 3528 (Acts 1921, ch. 173, art.
2, sec. 2) (in subd. 15). All cities, ibid., sec.
3394 (added by Code of 1932, sec. 3394).

South Carolina---Codes of Laws, sec. 51-151 (Acts 1927,
No. 141), for cities having a population of 7,200-
7,500, 1920 census. Ibid., sec. 51-171 (Acts 1933,
No. 234), for cities of over 50,000 inhabitants
at the most recent census.

Wisconsin---Statutes, sec. 27.08 (Statutes of 1931, secs.
27.08 and 27.09)(4); as last amended by Laws 1943,
ch. 193).

Arkansas---Statutes, sec. 19-3610 (Acts 1947, No. 348,
sec. 5).

Municipal parks, like state and county parks, may contain beaches and artificial lakes formed by dams. Municipalities may also improve and protect beaches which are located
within municipal parks. Specific, express authority of municipalities for the construction of recreational dams is provided for in the laws of Iowa only (Code, sec. 469.31: Acts
1927, ch. 162, sec. 2). Special authority for municipal
beach improvement or protection (not necessarily within the
boundaries of municipal parks) is found in the laws of the
following states:

Wisconsin---Statutes, sec. 30.05 (Laws 1905, ch. 293; as
    last amended by L. 1949, ch. 494).

Massachusetts---Towns, General Laws, ch. 91, sec. 29 (Acts
    1909, ch. 481, sec. 3; as last amended by Acts
    1950, ch. 524). Also ibid., ch. 40, sec. 5, subd.
    25A (Acts 1946, ch. 358, sec. 7; as amended by Acts
    1948, ch. 89).

New Jersey---Boroughs, Statutes, sec. 49:92-9 (Laws 1915,
    ch. 12, sec. 1). Any municipality, ibid., sec. 40:
    56-1 (Laws 1917, ch. 152, art. XX, sec. 1; as last
    amended by L. 1951, ch. 175, sec. 1); also Laws
    1914, ch. 261.

Iowa---Cities of 50,000 or more inhabitants under the
    commission plan, Code, sec. 416.135 (Acts 1917,
    ch. 194, sec. 1; as last amended by Acts 1947, ch.
    220, sec. 1).

Indiana---Cities and towns situated on Lake Michigan, Stat-
    utes, sec. 48-5208 (Acts 1931, ch. 16, sec. 1).

Illinois---Cities and villages, Revised Statutes, ch. 24,
    sec. 23-101 (Laws 1945, p. 484).

In the following three states, municipalities are specifically authorized to construct and operate docks and piers on
public navigable waters for recreational boating craft:

Mississippi---Cities and towns, Code, sec. 3437 (Laws 1928,
    ch. 189).

Illinois---Cities and villages, Revised Statutes, ch. 24,
    sec. 23-101, op. cit.

Oklahoma---Statutes, tit. 11, sec. 1385.1 et seq. (Laws
    1949, p. 768).

These recreational docks and piers need not be situated within municipal parks. But if such facilities are to be constructed within municipal parks, it would seem that municipal
authorities may construct them without special authorization.

"Municipal parks in the United States date from the year
1565, when provision was made for open spaces for public enjoyment in St. Augustine, Florida. In New England, town
commons, originally established for pasturage and other public uses, were later devoted exclusively to park purposes."[163]
However, it was in 1852 that the first American city, the City
of New York, acquired land for park purposes. By 1902, some
800 cities had made preparations for the establishment of
municipal parks. In 1905, the 100 largest cities owned a
total of 59,729 acres of land in their parks.[164] In 1904,
Los Angeles established the Public Playground and Recreation
Commission, which was the first municipal park agency in the
country.[165] The numbers of cities (and other municipalities)
which had parks, the numbers of such parks and their acreages
in each state as of 1950 are shown in the following table:[166]

State	Number of cities	Number of parks	Total acreage
Alabama	17	148	2,731
Arizona	5	37	19,506
Arkansas	4	23	1,505
California	90	1,000	28,625
Colorado	12	232	25,457
Connecticut	31	371	11,334
Delaware	2	45	899
District of C.	1	130	1,210
Florida	30	670	6,312
Georgia	20	264	3,653
Idaho	8	38	578
Illinois	40	487	7,464
Indiana	33	341	12,113
Iowa	29	257	5,686
Kansas	21	124	5,073
Kentucky	16	150	3,439
Louisiana	7	142	2,748
Maine	12	68	757
Maryland	7	266	5,495
Massachusetts	65	1,070	19,787
Michigan	58	739	15,246
Minnesota	61	661	19,128
Mississippi	5	33	921
Missouri	18	226	10,286
Montana	4	16	107
Nebraska	13	144	5,561
Nevada	1	23	144
New Hampshire	13	106	1,599
New Jersey	60	424	2,350
New Mexico	5	79	853
New York	117	1,947	39,429
North Carolina	34	328	5,626
North Dakota	5	29	1,494
Ohio	46	718	16,306
Oklahoma	11	110	6,342
Oregon	19	205	7,209
Pennsylvania	87	725	20,923
Rhode Island	9	67	703
South Carolina	11	94	692
South Dakota	14	68	1,535
Tennessee	12	217	7,402
Texas	28	758	2,901
Utah	6	63	2,870
Vermont	20	50	373
Virginia	20	241	4,154
Washington	19	367	6,924
West Virginia	16	98	2,588
Wisconsin	46	581	8,156
Wyoming	4	11	797
Total	1,252	14,995	347,173

"Many municipalities own and administer recreation areas
outside their boundaries and many of the municipal recreation
departments operate under laws specifically giving them authority to acquire and administer lands for recreation purposes
both within and without the boundaries of their respective
cities."[167] The following are five cities which have the
largest acreages of municipal parks:[168]

Cities	Acreages
Washington, D. C.	33,837
New York, N. Y.	26,530
Phoenix, Arizona	19,211
Denver, Colo.	15,132
Los Angeles, Calif.	10,350

Considerable portions of the parks of Phoenix and Denver lie
outside city limits. The average size of city parks in the
United States is 38 acres.[169] Not all cities have public
parks. "Studies conducted in 1940 showed that . . . of the
1,465 communities reporting, there were 339 or about one-fifth
that had no parks."[170]

A number of city parks contain beaches. For example,
"two large beaches, Golden Gardens and Alki, are operated by
the City of Seattle Park Department. It is reported that
during the 1949 bathing season 127,063 people used these
beaches."[171] The Town of Palm Beach, Florida, owns a public
beach with a shore line of 520 feet, which, however, is not
included in a city park.[172] Many cities have been engaged
in the protection of public beaches, whether they are in city
parks or not. Some examples may be given. "As specified in
an ordinance adopted by the Palm Beach Town Council February
3, 1932, the town department of public works prepared in August 1935 an over-all plan of existing and future shore protection structures. In general, since 1935, protective structures have been erected in conformity with the official plan
for bulkhead and groin locations."[173] "Most of groins abut
the bulkheads at their inshore ends. Others extend out from
the high ground where no bulkheads exist." "Most of the
groins are of steel piling, but some are of timber, stone, concrete, or combinations of these materials."[174] From 1926
through 1946, the town expended a total of $789,700 in the
construction and maintenance of the beach protection works,
of which $24,200 was expended for maintenance.[175] "Prior to
the construction of the shore arm of the west breakwater at
Conneaut Harbor (Lake Erie), the city of Conneaut (Ohio)
built three stone-filled timber crib groins and a concrete
groin in an effort to maintain the beach and bluffs at Lake
View Park. The westerly groin has been incorporated in the
construction of the city dock. The concrete groin which was
built in 1925 is in good condition. Since the construction
of the west breakwater shore arm, the groin system has been

ineffective due to the lack of littoral drift within the harbor area."[176] The village of Huron Harbor, Ohio, "constructed, in 1929, 450 feet of rubble-mound breakwater parallel to
the shore to protect the shore line of Huron Park and attempted to build a beach for bathing purposes."[177]

In New Jersey, a state law was enacted in 1944 (ch. 93)
providing for state financial aid to cities which undertake
beach protection works. It is reported that during the fiscal year ending 30 June 1947 eleven projects were in force in
ten municipalities incurring a total cost of nearly $4 mil-
lion. The principal works are beach filling, dune building
and the construction of jetties. The material used in the
construction of jetties was first creosoted timber, later
timber and steel and recently quarry stone.[178] In Virginia,
a law was passed in 1952, which created the Virginia Beach
Erosion Commission for the city of Virginia Beach, and vested
it with the authority to construct beach protection works in
the city. Although the commission is appointed by the Governor and is thus technically a state agency, it is the city
that is required to provide for the construction funds, and
therefore the project is practically a city enterprise. The
progress of the work is unknown.

There is at least one instance in which a city built artificial lakes for recreational use. In 1911, the City of
Dallas, Texas, constructed a reservoir on the White Rock Creek,
called the White Rock Lake, with a capacity of 18,158 acre-
feet, for recreation purpose.[179] As for recreational facilities provided in municipal parks and beaches, they are usually
picknicking, swimming, boating, bathing and athletic sports.

Dams and reservoirs may be constructed by municipalities
in connection with such enterprises as water supply and hydroelectric power development. These structures, under specified
conditions, may be made available for recreation. This is expressly permitted in Oklahoma in a law of 1917 (Statutes, tit.
11, sec. 321 et seq.: Laws 1917, ch. 114; as amended by Laws
1935, p. 129), although such state legislation would seem to
be unnecessary. As a matter of fact, this Oklahoma Law not
only authorizes the use for fishing and hunting (and also fish-
propagation) of city-owned reservoirs, but also streams, lakes
and ponds (natural) from which cities, towns and villages take
their water supplies. Boating and swimming are usually undesirable on water-supply reservoirs, but permissible on power-
development reservoirs. It is needless to say that municipal
forests are also abundant in recreational potentialities.
The recreational development of all municipally owned or controlled land and water areas is an aspect of municipal recreation enterprise that is of equal importance to the establishment of municipal parks.

10. Territorial limits of municipal enterprises---Munici-

palities are small areas. To be efficient in their operation,
many municipal enterprises are bound to neglect municipal
boundaries. The water-supply and hydroelectric power enterprises are best examples. Oftentimes the sources of a municipal water supply and the power-heads of a municipal hydroelectric system are located in great distances from the municipal limits. In undertaking these enterprises, municipalities usually are permitted to acquire lands and other properties outside of their boundaries. Not only lands may be acquired in other jurisdictions, but the water or electricity
itself may be sold to areas beyond the municipal limits. This
extraterritoriality in municipal administration is also seen
in other enterprises. For example, in Oregon the municipal
parks, in Michigan the municipal parks and municipal forests,
in Arizona the municipal parks and in Ohio the municipal forests may extend "without the corporate limits" of the municipality. In some cases the municipal extraterritoriality is
limited to a certain distance from the municipal limits. For
example, one mile is the extraterritorial distance statutorily
prescribed for municipal flood control enterprise of the cities of the third class in Missouri, and municipal parks in
first of second-class cities of Nebraska and in all cities in
Missouri. A distance of five miles is set for stream improvement in second-class cities of Kansas, municipal water terminals in Louisiana, all municipal parks in North Dakota and
municipal parks of cities of over 50,000 inhabitants in South
Carolina. The jurisdiction of the City of Baltimore, Maryland, with respect to water terminal facilities, extends to
the entire Patapsco River and its tributaries.[180] An extraterritoriality of six miles is allowed by Indiana statutes to
any municipally owned and operated public utility (such as
electric power generation or transmission, or water) (_Statutes,_
sec. 54-607: Acts 1913, ch. 76, sec. 103; as last amended by
Acts 1935, ch. 293, sec. 1) (3rd para.).

    Administrative extraterritoriality also exists to a lim-
ited extent at the county level, but its relative insignifi-
cance does not warrant special discussion.

Section 2 Regulation

    1. Public utilities---The public utilities which belong
to the general field of water resources that are commonly
regulated by the municipal governments are those utilities
which are engaged in the generation or transmission of hydroelectric power, water supply and sewerage. Commercial canal,
irrigation and water-terminal (wharfinger) companies and
firms are potentially also under municipal public-utility regulation.[182] Theorectically, public utilities (privately owned or operated) may be regulated by municipalities either under the "police power" of the state delegated to them by
state constitution or statute or through the device of the
grant of franchises.[181] The latter is, however, the method

that actually prevails in each of the 48 states.[183]

Technically speaking, franchises are easements or servitudes over public streets and grounds of the municipalities, and constitute a measure of municipal enterprise of land management. In practice, however, the grant of franchises may be regarded as a measure of municipal regulation or, more safely, indirect municipal regulation.[184] In concrete terms, a municipal franchise is a contract (although a forced one) between a municipality and a public utility which contains the revocable permit of the former for the use and occupancy by the latter of the streets, roads and other public places within the municipal limits, for a specified period of time (which is usually not more than fifty years), in connection with the construction, installation, operation and maintenance of its facilities and equipment. The permit is generally accompanied by a number of conditions imposed by the grantor municipality, the most important of which is that concerned with the charges or rates and the adequacy and quality of the services to be rendered by the grantee utility company or firm. Ordinarily, municipal franchises are issued on a long-term basis, and their effectiveness as a means of regulation or indirect regulation of public utilities is questionable. Prior to about 1900, municipalities were the principal authority and municipal franchise was the chief source of public control over private-owned public utilities, particularly electric and water utilities. Since that time, its importance has been overshadowed by the rising state "police power" regulation (which is _direct_ though perhaps equally ineffective regulation) which, since 1920, has in turn been overrun, so far as hydroelectric power utilities are concerned,[185] by the Federal "commerce power" regulation.[186]

Municipal franchises[187] are now regularized by state statutory laws in most states. Under these laws, municipal franchises are generally issued by the legislative or governing body of the municipality by ordinance, that is, through the so-called "legislative" procedure. This indicates the technical importance of municipal franchises. As a matter of fact the franchise is not merely a grant of easement over the municipal properties but furthermore the execution of a municipal trust to private persons, since each of the public utilities is a public service which the municipal government is expected to perform by itself. In certain states, such as Michigan (State Constitution of 1850, art. IV, sec. 38; State Constitution of 1908, art. VIII, sec. 25), Arizona(_Code_, sec. 16-1001: Laws 1903, ch. 81, sec. 1), Montana (_Revised Codes_, sec. 11-1207: Laws 1903, ch. 85, sec. 1) and Texas (_Revised Civil Statutes_, art. 1181: Laws 1913, p. 307), municipal franchises are granted by popular referenda. Texas laws further require that franchise proposals should be initiated by 500 bona fide qualified voters; and Michigan constitution makes the franchise referendum effective by a majority of three-fifths. The pur-

pose of these special provisions is no doubt to awaken the
municipal government to its lawful duties and responsibilities
and to discourage the practice of delegating fundamental municipal services to private persons.

2. Protection of watercourses---The cities and towns of
Indiana may establish the lines and limits of watercourses
(Statutes, sec. 48-503: Acts 1905, ch. 125, sec. 267). This
may serve to protect the banks of a watercourse from unlawful
encroachments. The cities are further authorized "to prohibit or regulate the dumping of material upon the bank of or
in any river, and to prevent the obstruction of any stream .
. ." (ibid., sec. 48-1407: Acts 1905, ch. 129, sec. 53). In
Georgia, all cities and towns shall protect navigable watercourses within their respective jurisdictions by prohibiting
the throwing or depositing therein of substances which may endanger navigation or injure vessels (Code, sec. 80-126: Acts
1945, No. 336, sec. 26). Under the laws of Ohio, municipalities have the authority to prohibit the subsidence, washing,
falling or depositing in navigable watercourses and canals of
earth and other material from the abutting land and may require the landowners concerned to construct necessary retaining walls to prevent such subsidence, washing, falling or depositing of such material. In case of default, the city or
village authorities may construct them at the expense of the
delinquent landowners (Revised Code, secs. 729.21 and 729.22:
Laws 1910, p. 148, secs. 1 and 2). The cities and towns of
Iowa have the authority "to require the owner or lessee of
any lot or tract of ground within their limits, extending into, across or bordering upon any hollow or ravine which constitutes a drain for surface water, or a watercourse of any
kind, who shall, by grading or filling such lot or tract of
ground, obstruct the flow of water through such watercourse,
to construct through such lot or land a sufficient drain or
passageway for water, within such time as the council may designate . . . Upon the failure of such owner or lessee to
construct such drain or passageway within the time so fixed,
the city or town may construct the same and assess the costs
thereof on such lot or tract of ground . . ." (Code, sec.
368.15: Acts 1876, ch. 116, sec. 18). In Michigan, the highway commissioners of townships are authorized to issue permits
to private parties as well as other municipalities for the alteration, widening or deepening of the channels of watercourses (Compiled Laws, sec. 254.25: Acts 1925, No. 354, sec. 25).

The purpose of this regulation is to preserve the navigable and (or) flood-carrying capacity of the watercourses.

3. Water terminals---(1) Permissive. Under the laws of
Maine, when any person wishes to build or extend a wharf, fish
weir or trap in navigable waters within the limits of city or
town, he should obtain a license to do so from the city or
town government testifying that such structure will not obstruct

navigation (Revised Statutes, ch. 86, sec. 7: Laws 1876, ch. 78; as last amended by L. 1943, ch. 105) (in 1st para.).[188] In Washington, "whenever a person desires to erect a wharf at the terminus of a street of a city or town, he may apply to the governing body, which, if it is satisfied that the public convenience requires the wharf, may authorize it to be erected and kept in repair for any length of time not exceeding ten years" (Revised Code, sec. 88.24.030: Code of 1881, sec. 3273). By an act of 1944, all the cities of Michigan which border on a navigable watercourse are authorized to license the construction and operation of private piers, wharves, docks and other landings on such watercourse (Compiled Laws, sec. 123.501: Acts 1944, No. 66, sec. 2). Wisconsin cities both establishes dock lines and issues permits for the construction or improvement of all terminal facilities, including wharves and warehouses.[189]

(2) Directive---In North Carolina, incorporated towns are required and authorized to regulate the lines on deep water of any navigable watercourse to which wharves may be built (General Statutes, sec. 146-6: Laws 1854-55, ch. 21; as last amended by L. 1901, ch. 364). In Oregon, "the owner of any land lying upon any navigable stream or other like water and within the corporate limits of any incorporated town may construct a wharf or wharves upon the same . . ."; but the corporate authorities of the town wherein the wharf is proposed to be constructed may prescribe the mode and extent of the wharf-construction beyond the line of low-water mark so that the wharf will not obstruct navigation (Revised Statutes, secs. 780.040 and 780.050: Act of 17 October 1862, secs. 1 and 2, revised in wording). The cities of California (Government Code, sec. 39931: Stats. 1913, ch. 272, sec. 1; as amended by Stats. 1949, ch. 79, sec. 1) and the cities and villages of Illinois (Revised Statutes, ch. 24, sec. 41-14: Date of enactment not clear) have the authority to establish harbor lines beyond which no wharf can extend. Wisconsin cities may require riparian land owners to build docks for the protection of the banks of navigable waters, and may build them at the expense of the former in case of default (Statutes, sec. 30.03(7): Laws 1905, ch. 270, sec. 2; as last amended by L. 1949, ch. 335).

Under the laws of Ohio, cities may "regulate public landings, public wharves, public docks, public piers and public basins . . ." (Revised Code, sec. 715.31: Laws 1908, p. 7, sec. 7r). Oklahoma towns, too, may "regulate . . . the banks, shores and wharves" of navigable waters, but with the consent of the majority of the owners thereof (Statutes, tit. 11, sec. 1014: Act of 25 December 1890, sec. 687). The general provisions will include the establishment of harbor lines.

4. Water sanitation---In some states, the cities have

the general authority to abate nuisances, which should cover
both water pollution and mosquitoes. Orders of abatement are
first given landowners, and if they fail or refuse to obey
such orders, city authorities may take the abatement action
at the cost of the delinquent land owners.190

For specific regulation of water pollution, it is provided in the laws of New Mexico that cities, towns and villages may "provide for the cleaning and purification of waters, watercourses and canals . . ." (Statutes, sec. 14-
1810: Laws 1884, ch. 39, sec. 14, subdiv. 12). Similar authority has been vested in the cities of Michigan (Compiled
Laws, sec. 97.4: Acts 1895, No. 125, ch. 17, sec. 1). Indiana (Statutes, sec. 48-1407: Acts 1905, ch. 129, sec. 53,
subdiv. 9) and Montana (Revised Codes, sec. 11-917: Revised
Code of 1921, sec. 5039; as last amended by Laws 1927, ch.
20, sec. 1).191 The authority of Michigan and Indiana cities is more concrete in that they are further authorized to
prevent and regulate the depositing of polluting materials
in watercourses. This type of authorization is also found
in the laws of Ohio, for both cities and villages (Revised
Code, sec. 743.25: Laws 1869, p. 209; as amended by L. 1904,
p. 135). Virginia laws simply authorize cities to "prevent
the pollution of water" (Code, sec. 15-715: Acts 1908, ch.
249).192 A more interesting measure is found in a law of
1951 of Connecticut, which provides that licenses from the
town health officer are required for the discharge of filthy
water, garbage, etc., upon the watershed of any stream or
reservoir (Acts 1951, No. 176).

Specific authorizations for municipal mosquito-control
regulation are also available in some states. Iowa law provides that cities and towns "shall have power to cause any
lot of land within their limits, on which water at any time
becomes stagnant, to be filled up or drained . . . . On
failure of such owner to comply with such directions within
the time fixed, it may be done by said city or town and the
costs and expenses thereof assessed against said lot . . ."
(Code, sec. 368.14: Acts 1868, ch. 111). The cities, towns
and villages of New Mexico, too, may "provide for . . .
the draining or filling of ponds on private property whenever necessary to prevent or abate nuisances" (Statutes,
sec. 14-1810, op. cit.). In New York, municipal boards of
health may order land owners to abate mosquito-breeding
places, and may abate them in case of default, at the expense of the land owners (Public Health Law, sec. 27 et seq.:
Laws 1906, ch. 583, sec. 1; as amended by L. 1913, ch. 599,
sec. 12). More positive approach is found in the laws of
Alabama, which provides that "all cities and towns . . .
shall have the power . . . to compel the screening of all
wells, cisterns and other places in the city or town, in
which water is collected, where mosquitoes or other insects
of like kind are apt to propagate; to compel the proper set-

ting of gutters so as to prevent water stagnant therein, and
to require weeds to be cut or other things or conditions favorable to the harboring of such insects to be abated, or to
do such work at the expense of the owner . . ." (Code, tit.
37, sec. 501: Acts 1907, No. 797, sec. 146).

5. Miscellaneous---Municipalities generally have the
authority of zoning. Under the municipal-zoning enabling
laws of New Hampshire, cities and towns have the authority
to adopt zoning regulations "in accordance with a comprehensive plan and designed to lessen conjection in the streets;
to secure safety from fire, panic, and other dangers (emphasis supplied); to promote health and the general welfare; to
provide adequate light and air; to prevent the overcrowding
of the land; to avoid undue concentration of population; to
facilitate the adequate provision of transportation, water,
sewerage, schools, parks, and other public requirements" (Revised Laws, ch. 51, sec. 51 et seq.: Laws 1925, ch. 92; as
last amended by L. 1941, ch. 2). In pursuance of this law,
the City of Keene enacted an ordinance effective 3 January
1927 requiring a permit of a board of adjustment for the construction of buildings and houses in certain areas. A permit
would not be issued in areas subject to periodic floods, with
view to securing safety from dangers. Under the challenge of
a land owner, this ordinance was upheld by the Federal district and circuit courts as a proper exercise of the state's
"police power" as manifested in municipal zoning.[193] The
ruling of the circuit court (for the first circuit) in this
case has not since been questioned. A rule in constitutional
law has probably been established that municipalities may by
ordinance provide for flood-control zoning. There is no information, however, as to the actual number of states or
municipalities in which such municipal regulation exists.

Connecticut seems to be the only state in which there is
municipal flood-control regulation as such. This regulation
consists of two parts. First, the legislative body of a city,
town or borough may order any private party to remove from
any watercourse within its jurisdictional limits any debris,
wreckage or other material which may prevent the free discharge of flood waters, and may remove it in case of default
at the cost of the responsible party (General Statutes, sec.
705, enacted 1945). Secondly, "any town, city or borough
shall have authority . . . to establish . . . lines along
any part of any waterway beyond which . . . no permanent obstruction or encroachment shall be placed by any private person or any firm or corporation, unless permission is granted
. . . by the legislative body . . ." (ibid., sec. 708, enacted 1945). The second measure is in effect flood-plain zoning.

In the field of fish and wildlife administration, Arkansas laws have authorized the cities and incorporated towns to regulate, by ordinance, the propagation, protection, catching and removing of fish in ponds and lakes (Statutes, sec. 19-2332: Acts 1933, No. 95, sec. 1). In Massachusetts, coastal cities and towns may (1) grant permission for a maximum duration of five years for the construction of fish weirs, pound nets or fish traps in tidal waters or in locations where no harbor lines exist or beyond established harbor lines (General Laws, ch. 130, sec. 29: Acts 1941, ch. 508, sec. 1); and (2) regulate the taking of all kinds of shellfish (ibid., sec. 52: Acts 1941, ch. 598, sec. 1). Oregon laws designate certain areas in which the hunting of wild animals and birds is prohibited; but within the limits of a city or town, this prohibition may be lifted by ordinance of the city or town (Revised Statutes, sec. 498.115: Laws 1921, ch. 153, sec. 18; as last amended by L. 1953, ch. 178, sec. 1).

In a few states municipalities may provide for the extermination of noxious weeds.[194] This has some bearing on water resources administration when the weeds are taken away from wild lands.

Article 3   Special Districts[195]

Special districts are public corporations and governmental units which are formed for the purpose of performing some specific public service, for which the regular local governmental units (counties, towns, townships, cities, villages, boroughs) and incompetent or inadequate for physical, financial, technical, geographical or other reasons, but most commonly for financial reason alone. Many types of special districts have appeared for the conduct of certain purpose or purposes of water resources administration. These will be discussed separately.

1.   Navigation districts---There are two general sub-types of navigation districts: navigation improvement districts and port districts. The former are created for the purpose of improving harbors and watercourses; and the latter for the construction or acquisition and operation of water terminal facilities. A third type is a district with combined functions of navigation-improvement and water-terminal-operation.

Among the examples of navigation-improvement districts may be mentioned the river districts of Illinois, whose function it is to improve and straighten river channels. A river district is formed by order of the county court upon petition of a majority of landowners concerned, and is governed by a commission of three commissioners appointed by the said court who elect a chairman and a secretary. All improvement works are financed by special benefit assessments (Revised Statutes, sec. 160, enacted 1905). Washington laws provide for two kinds of navigation improvement districts; namely, (1) commercial waterways districts (Revised Code, ch. 91.04: Laws 1911, ch. 11; as last amended by L. 1947, ch. 227) and (2) river and harbor improvement assessment districts (ibid., ch. 88.32: L. 1907, ch. 236; as last amended by L. 1951, ch. 33). But the latter are assessment districts for the financing of costs needed for contribution towards Federal projects, and are therefore not regular special districts, which have their own enterprises. Commercial waterways districts, which are the only kind of regular navigation-improvement districts in Washington, are established by popular vote at a referendum called by the county board upon petition of a majority of landowners concerned, and are governed by a board of three commissioners popularly elected for overlapping terms of three years. Projects are financed by special benefit assessments against lands benefitted. Bonds may be issued in anticipation of assessments.

There are no special districts in California dedicated to the improvement of inland waterways, presumably because there are no navigable waterways there that should become the concern of a special district. But California laws have authorized the establishment of harbor improvement districts, joint harbor improvement districts, harbor districts, and recreational harbor districts (Stats. 1925, ch. 395, as amended in 1937). They are formed in a similar manner as commercial waterways and river improvement districts of Washington, but are governed by the county authorities. Besides their own earnings, they have the authority to levy special taxes (i.e., sur-taxes on general property tax) and to issue bonds.

The Inland Navigation District of Florida, which comprises eleven counties, was organized by a special state act (Acts 1927, ch. 12026; as amended by Acts 1931, ch. 14723 and Acts 1951, ch. 27275). The District is temporary in nature: its sole function is not to improve any river or stream by itself, but to purchase a navigable waterway or waterways along or through the District between the City of Jacksonville and the City of Miami and then to convey the same to the Federal Government. In discharging this function, the District, through its board of 11 commissioners,[197] is authorized to levy a special tax (not exceeding half a mill on the dollar) and to issue bonds.

Since navigation improvement is now largely a Federal responsibility, port districts are of much greater importance than navigation-improvement districts. New York is the first state having enabling legislation for the establishment of port districts (Town Law, art. 12: Laws 1901, ch. 348, as amended), under which the town board, upon petition of the owners of at least one-half of the assessed value of all real property concerned, may establish a public dock district within the town. The district does not perform any enterprise at all, but it is the town board that contracts for the construction of a public dock (which may be sold or leased). It is purely

an assessment district created for the sole purpose of raising revenue, and as such it has authority to collect special
benefit assessments to defray both construction and maintenance
costs. Washington port districts appear in Laws 1911, ch. 92,
as last amended by Laws 1953, ch. 171 (Revised Code, ch. 92).
They are formed by popular vote at special elections called
by the county boards either in their own initiative or upon
the petition of ten percent of the county voters. A board of
three commissioners, popularly elected for overlapping terms
of six years, is the district's governing body. Not more than
one-half of the costs involved in any construction undertaking
are to be borne by a port district, which are defrayed by district's operating revenues and special tax levy, the balance
to be paid out of the general fund. Port districts construct
terminal facilities as well as harbor improvement works, and
also airports, as specifically authorized in 1945. Under California laws (Stats. 1925, ch. 395, as amended in 1937), there
are municipal port districts, port districts and river port
districts. A municipal port district may comprise one or more
municipalities, and are created by ordinance of each city concerned followed by a special election. The board of port commissioners, which are appointed by the constituent cities, is
its governing authority. The board elects its own president
and vice-president, and employes a clerk, an auditor, a treasurer, a general manager, a chief engineer and an attorney.
It may issue bonds in anticipation of operating revenues and
special tax levies. The port district is formed out of one
city together with any contiguous unincorporated territory
that may be included, and is established at a special election
called by the county board upon petition of five percent of
voters resident in the proposed district. The city council appoints a board of five port commissioners as its governing
body, serving a term of four years. River port districts cover
the territory of one or more counties. Its creation and administrative organization is the same as those of the port district, except that the place of the city is taken by the principal county. Port districts and river port districts have the
same financing power as the municipal port districts. Other
states which have enacted general enabling laws permitting the
organization of port districts are Michigan (Acts 1925, no.
234; as amended by Acts 1953, No. 32) and Idaho (Laws 1931, ch.
201).[198]

Three Washington port districts are discussed below as examples of port districts in general.[199] The Port of Seattle
is a seaport without inland waterway connection. It was formed in 1911 and is coterminous with King County. It owns ten
piers out of eighty odd piers and terminals operated along the
Seattle waterfront, together with the huge, $11-million Seattle-
Tacoma International Airport at Bow Lake and the Salmon Bay
Fishing Terminal. The piers of the Port District of Seattle
are equipped with sheds and tracks. Of the ten District-owned
piers, two, Piers 38 and 39, are leased and operated by the

Seattle Port of Embarkation. Berthing space in the remaining eight piers is shown below.

Stacy-Lander Terminal: Piers 29-30	1,618 feet
Bell Street Terminal: Pier 66	1,580 feet
Lenora Street Terminal: Piers 64-65	785 feet
Spokane Street Terminal: Pier 24	1,329 feet
Hanford Street Terminal: Pier 25	1,435 feet
Pier 42 (Alaska gateway)	1,019 feet
Total	7,766 feet

At the Hanford Street Terminal, there is a grain elevator having a capacity of 2,800,000 bushels. The District also has warehouses located in the following terminals: (a) At Stacy-Lander, a four-story concrete warehouse with a floor area of 99,216 square feet; (b) at Bell Street, a concrete warehouse of 41,100-square-foot floor area, and a cold storage warehouse with a capacity of 503,346 cubic feet; (c) at Spokane Street, a warehouse of 151,117-square-foot capacity, a cold storage warehouse of 2,143,922-cubic-foot capacity, and a fresh fish storage warehouse with a capacity of 280,861 cubic feet. The Salmon Bay fishing terminal, under renovation in a million-dollar program as of 1951, would have a capacity for 1,000 fishing vessels when completed. For other terminals, a twenty-million expansion and modernization program has also been underway.[200]

The Ports (Port Districts) of Vancouver and Longview, established respectively in 1912 and 1921, are located on the Columbia River. The Port of Vancouver owns two ocean-shipping terminals, Terminals Nos. 1 and 2, and a small-boat harbor. The latter is leased to private interests but the District operates the two terminals by itself. Terminal No. 1 was constructed by the City of Vancouver and was acquired by the District in 1926. With a pier length of 1,326 feet and an open storage of 450,000 square feet, it is used principally as a lumber terminal. Terminal No. 2 was completed in 1936 with a pier length of 862 feet. It is used for handling general cargo and there is a warehouse in the terminal area. Terminal facilities of the Port of Longview, all of which were constructed by the District, consist of docks, four warehouses, a grain elevator of 1,750,000 bushels capacity, and ancillary facilities and properties, which total $2,808,606.46 in value (1952 figure).[201]

Port districts can also be established by special state laws. The Port of Portland of Oregon, the Albany Port District of New York, the South Jersey Port District of New Jersey, and the Broward County Port Authority (Port Everglades) of Florida are outstanding examples. The Port of Portland, Oregon, was created by a special act of the state legislature of 18 February 1891 (as last amended by Laws 1935, ch. 104: Revised Statutes, secs. 778.010 to 778.100). It is a municipal corpora-

tion, and comprises "that part of Multinomah County lying
west of the east boundary line of range two east of the Willamette meridian." It was authorized to construct and operate a dry dock and other terminal facilities. Its governing body is a board of nine commissioners appointed for overlapping terms of four years by the Governor of Oregon with
the consent of two-thirds of the entire membership of the
State Senate. The commission annually elects a president, a
vice-president, a treasurer and a secretary, and may employ
engineers and other officers. The Port of Portland Commission now owns and operates a drydock and a ship repair basin
at Swan Island and two drydocks at St. Johns, and the Portland Airport.[202] The Albany Port District of New York was
created by State Laws of 1925, ch. 192, and includes the cities of Albany and Rensselaer. It is governed by the Albany
Port District Commission of five members, of whom four are
residents of Albany and one a resident of Rensselaer, and who
are appointed for three years by the Governor of New York
upon nomination of the mayors of the respective cities. The
commission elects a chairman and appoints a secretary and
treasurer. It operates the original municipal terminal facilities and constructs and operates new facilities. Loans may
be incurred and bonds issued for the purpose of constructing
or acquiring the facilities, but total indebtedness of the
district shall not exceed five percent of the property valuation in the district. A special annual property tax may be
levied which shall not exceed 0.3 percent of all assessed
property valuation in the district to defray expenses other
than the payment of debt principal or interest. Terminal facilities of the Albany Port District included 4,195 feet of
completed dock wall, 1,300 feet undeveloped frontage, 400,000
square feet of covered storage, a grain elevator (world's largest single unit), a feed mill, an asphalt mixing plant, mo-
lasses storage tanks and scrap yard on the westerly or Albany
side and the lumber terminal on the Easterly or Rensselaer
side consisting of 1,205 feet of completed dock and 1,300
feet of undeveloped frontage, 30 acres of open storage and
25,000 square feet of covered storage, with rail connections
on both sides.[203]

The South Jersey Port District of New Jersey was created
by a law of 1926, comprising the Counties of Mercer, Burlington, Camden, Gloucester, Salem, Cumberland and Cape May. It
is governed by a commission of seven members elected by the
state legislature for overlapping terms of seven years, which
elects its own chairman and appoints a secretary, a treasurer
and an attorney. It owns (a) Beckett Street Terminal, which
is operated by the Port for handling general cargo; (b) American Dredging Company repair pier, which is operated by the
said company and (c) American Dredging Company pier, also operated by the said company. In addition, the Port operates
the Camden Marine Terminals under an agreement with the City
of Camden dated 6 June 1928.[204] The Broward County Port Dis-

tricts and Authority of Florida was established by an act of
6 June 1927 of the Florida state legislature (Laws 1927, ch.
12562, as amended 1929, 1931, 1943, 1945, 1947 and 1951).
The Port Authority consists of three commissioners elected by
the District voters at large for four years. The commission
elects a chairman and a vice-chairman, and elects or appoints
a secretary and a treasurer, or a secretary-treasurer. It may
also appoint a port manager to serve at its pleasure, who may
himself be a commissioner. As of 1953, the Port owned and operated Piers Nos. 1, 2, 4 and 5, with Pier No. 6 in planning.[205]

The incorporated "ports" of Oregon (Laws 1909, ch. 39) and
the "navigation districts" of Texas represent the third type
of navigation districts, i.e., districts for combined enterprises of navigation improvement (excluding harbor improvement) and terminal facilities. The latter deserves our special attention. They are to include territory of not more than
two counties or parts thereof, and are established in a procedure of petition and special election. Three navigation commissioners constitute the governing body of a navigation district, who are biennially appointed by the county commissioners, or by the State Navigation Board. The District may levy
special property tax, and issue bonds for initial capital. In
a district containing a city of 100,000 population, it is to
be governed by five navigation commissioners, of whom two are
appointed by the city council of the said city and two by
county commissioners and the remaining one, also chairman of
the commission, by the city council and county commissioners
jointly. The Harris County-Houston Ship Canal District is one
of such navigation districts. It was formed in 1922. As of 1
October 1952, the District owned and operated the following
terminal facilities: (1) 16 general and special cargo purposes
wharves, with a total berthing space of 8,982 feet available
for 19 vessels and with a total of 1,177,918 square feet of
covered area, one of which has 45,264 cubic feet of cold storage; (2) warehouse distribution; (3) cotton shed; (4) grain
elevator, a 20-storied building with a capacity of 3,500,000
bushels and (5) Port Terminal Railroad.[206] As for navigation-
improvement work of the District, "a $24,000,000 bond issue
for the construction of a dam and fresh water reservoir on the
San Jacinto River was voted in September 1950. The dam would
be located about 1 mile above the junction of the San Jacinto
River with the Houston Ship Channel. Construction of this
dam will tend to improve navigation in the Ship Channel by reducing currents at Lynchburg during flood periods. The Port's
major interest in this project is the availability of industrial fresh water for the growing Ship Channel industrial
area."[207]

2. Flood control districts---There are two kinds of flood
control districts, namely, levee districts, whose function is
the construction and maintenance of levees and dikes,[208] and
flood control districts, which envisage the use of all kinds

of flood control devices and not merely that of levees and
dikes. Almost all of the state laws (general and special)
providing for the organization of levee districts were originally enacted prior to 1930. But flood control districts
have come into existence since 1930, when the nation abandoned
the "levee only" policy in flood control enterprises.

(a) Levee districts:

The states in the Lower Mississippi Valley are credited
with having the first levee districts in the country. In 1850,
a law was passed in Mississippi (ch. 125) which authorized the
County of Bolivar to build levees along the Mississippi River,
which were to be financed by a special tax not exceeding ten
cents per acre on all county lands.[209] The levee was to be
divided into a number of districts. Although this was strictly a county enterprise, it was the embryo of levee districts.
A law of 1857 (ch. 24) extended this act to the County of
Issaquena. On 2 December 1858, the first levee district in
Mississippi was created covering the entire Yazoo-Mississippi
Delta, commonly called the "1858 Levee District". Although
the board was directly responsible to the State Legislature,
it would seem that it was not a state agency but a de facto
municipal corporation. Before the work of the 1858 District
was suspended by the Civil War, the District had surveyed over
1,600 miles of levees, and built 142.3 miles of new levees at
a cost of $1,296,377.33. But the levees were severely damaged
by the war, and District was not revived at the end of the
Civil War.[210] On 27 November 1865, a new levee district was
created by a special act of the State Legislature, which incorporated the counties of Bolivar, Washington and Issaquena
to form a levee district. The county board of supervisors of
each of these counties elected a levee commissioner for the
district, and the district was authorized to levy an annual
tax of 1 cent per pound on lint cotton and an annual tax of
ten cents per acre on all district land. By an act of 1872 (ch.
54), the board was authorized to levy an additional uniform
ad valorem tax on each acre of land not exceeding 3 percent
per annum. In 1877 (Laws 1877, ch. 45), the District was enlarged to include the whole of Sharkey County. The taxes imposed by the act of 1865 were continued, but they were reduced
to be 0.25 percent per pound of lint cotton and 2.5 cents per
acre of land. In addition, special tax levies of 0.5 per cent
per pound per annum on lint cotton and 5 cents per 100 pounds
of cotton seeds were authorized. The terms of the levee commissioners were set at two years. A law of 1884 (ch. 169)
changed the terms of the levee commissioners to four years
(over-lapping). An interesting provision in this law was that
". . . in no event shall the tax be reduced below one eighth
of one cent per pound per annum on lint cotton, a proportionate
amount on seed cotton, and a two mills ad valorem tax, until
all the bonds and accrued interest which have and hereafter
may be issued . . . shall have been fully paid off . . ."

In 1884, a special state act created the Yazoo-Mississippi Delta Levee District, a public corporation comprising all of the Counties of Tunica, Coshoma, Quitman, and Sunflower and parts of the Counties of DeSoto, Tallahatchie, Leflore and Yazoo. The Governor of Mississippi appointed two resident freeholders from each of the Counties of Tunica and Coahoma and one from each of the Counties of DeSoto, Quitman, Tallahatchie, Sunflower, Leflore and Yazoo and a stockholder of the Memphis and Vicksburg Railroad to constitute a board of levee commissioners serving a two-year term. Levees were to be financed by initial bond issues, which were to be redeemed by special tax levies of 13 mills per dollar on properties in the waterfront area and of 9 mills per dollar on properties landward from the former. This district, it may be pointed out, was the revival of the 1858 District. These two levee districts of the state of Mississippi have continued in existence up to the present day, but they ceased to build and repair levees in 1917, when the work was taken over by the Federal Government. They built and maintained levees entirely with their own funds until 1882, when the Federal Government began to make grants. Up to 1951, a total expenditure of about $33,185,896.01 was incurred by the Mississippi Levee District and a total of approximately $32 million by the Yazoo-Mississippi Levee District.[211] Federal expenditures in these two districts by the same time (including grants to the districts prior to 1917, and direct expenditures since 1917) were $33,-447,000 and $21,000,000 respectively.[212]

The Mississippi and Yazoo-Mississippi Levee Districts were the only two levee districts in Mississippi that were authorized prior to 1930.[213] In 1930, a law was passed by the Mississippi State Legislature (ch. 124) which authorized the organization of levee districts in backwater areas on the tributaries of the Mississippi River. Levees are defined as including ditches, sluiceways, floodgates, and other flood control works, and the levee districts may also build dams. A levee district is created by the county board of supervisors if it is located in a single county, and, if it covers two or more counties, by the chancery court of any of these counties, upon petition of 25 percent of electros and property owners in the proposed district. The district is governed by a board of three commissioners serving terms of four years. The first commissioners are appointed by the county board of supervisors or the chancery court establishing the district, but their successors are popularly elected. Flood-control works are financed by bond issues, which are to be paid off by an annual tax levy not exceeding 3 mills per dollar on assessed property.

Louisiana Legislature passed a general levee district act in 1878 (Act No. 5, as amended by Acts 1879, No. 33), which divided the state into six levee districts each governed by a board of levee commissioners to be composed of one member from each parish included in the district appointed by the governor for two years. Each district might levy a special surtax of 5

mills per dollar to the general land tax. However, this act
has been replaced by existing special acts, under which twenty-
one levee districts have come into existence.[214] The latter
have constructed levees and dikes as well as revetments.[215]
New Orleans Levee District, for example, has constructed more
than 100 miles of levees.[216] In 1902, the Louisiana State
Legislature even authorized (act no. 84) the Atchafalaya Basin and Lafourche Levee Districts to place a temporary dam
at the head of Bayou Lafourche, then to dredge the said bayou
and build additional locks and dams, and in the interim period
to maintain a channel of 6 feet deep by 60 feet wide throughout the bayou by supply of river water at Donaldsonville and/
or by lake connection.[217] With the exception of two districts,
all levee districts are governed by a board of levee commissioners who are appointed by the governor of the state to serve
at his pleasure or for a term of four years. The seven levee
commissioners of the Atchafalaya and Bayou De Glaise Levee District are elected by the district voters for two years, and
the Buras Back Levee District has a board of three commissioners of whom one is appointed by the Governor and two are appointed by the police jury of the Parish of Plaquemines, all
for terms of four years. In levee districts whose boards of
commissioners are entirely appointed by the Governor, the State
Department of Public Works may usually send a representative
to participate in the meetings of the boards. The financial
powers of the several districts fall under certain different
patterns. The Atchafalaya and Bayou De Glaise Levee District
levies contributions on all lands protected not exceeding 25
cents per acre for cleared and ten cents for wooded lands.
Atchcalaya Basin District collects a special tax of 5 mills
per dollar of property valuation. The Buras Back District
"may levy a special assessment, or forced contribution, not
to exceed 25 cents per bale of cotton, 5 cents per barrel of
rough rice or its equivalent quantity, 3 cents on each barrel
of vegetables or fruits, except oranges, or its equivalent, 3
cents on each box of oranges or its equivalent, produced upon
lands in the district . . ." Many districts have been subsidized by the state through the grant of state-owned lands.
Very few districts obtained from their original organic acts
the power to borrow money and to issue bonds. But a general
act of 1914 granted the power to issue bonds to all levee
districts. But all these financial provisions were principally designed to meet situations prior to 1917, when the districts themselves instead of the Federal Government actually
built the levees and other flood control works. In 1917, an
act (no. 42) was passed which authorized all levee districts
to raise funds by taxes or otherwise to be expended under the
direction of the Mississippi River Commission of the Federal
Government in accordance with the Act of Congress of 1 March
1917. An act of 1922 (no. 72) supplemented this act by further authorizing the districts to borrow money and to issue
bonds for the maintenance of Federally-built works.[218]

As of 31 December 1951, "there are 21 regularly incorporated

levee districts in Louisiana and one in Southeast Arkansas
which contain levees that protect Louisiana from overflow
and are considered by law a responsibility of the State of
Louisiana." "The Department of Public Works is the branch
of the State executive organization that performs the engineering work of the levee districts of the State, except the
Orleans Levee District which maintains its own engineering
staff."[219] Levees have been constructed in 16 of these 21
levee districts, which totalled as much as 1,452.3 miles as
of the end of 1951, averaging about 91 miles per district.[220]
It is not quite clear, however, whether these levees have
been constructed entirely by the districts themselves, or
partly by the districts and partly by the Federal Government,
or even largely by the Federal Government.

Arkansas levee districts have been created under both
general and special state laws. General state legislation
on the creation and organization of levee districts is embodied in Act No. 78 of 1879, as last amended by Act No. 75 of
1929 (Statutes, sec. 21-601 et seq.). Under this legislation,
the county court of any county may divide the county into one
or more levee districts. After each levee district is designated, the county court shall call a special election for the
election of three directors of levees and three assessors of
lands, who serve for overlapping terms of three years. A
construction plan and a tax levy schedule should be adopted
at a meeting of land-owners benefited. "Whenever . . . there
shall be lands in two or more counties subject to overflow
from the same crevasses or direction, . . . the directors of
the several levee districts . . . may by the consent of the
county courts . . . consolidate their several districts into
one district . . ." It is not known how many levee districts
have been formed under this legislation. There have been a
number of special state laws creating levee districts and
regulating their organization and work on a case-to-case basis.[221] These special acts usually name the first directors
(serving for terms of six years), who were to be succeeded
by elective directors.

Tennessee is the last state in the Lower Mississippi Valley that passed general law providing for the establishment
of levee districts (Laws 1909, ch. 185). Levee districts in
Tennessee are established by the county court of each county
upon petition of a majority of landowners concerned and after
examination by an engineer and hearings.

Laws providing for the creation of levee districts have
also been enacted in states in the Middle Mississippi and
Lower Missouri Valleys.[222]

In the Columbia River Basin, laws have been enacted in
Oregon (1895, last amended 1953) and Washington (1895, last
amended 1953) providing for the organization of "diking dis-

tricts", which are the same as levee districts in other
states.

Elsewhere in the country, the organization of levee districts has been statutorily authorized in Texas (Laws 1909,
ch. 85; as amended by Laws 1915, ch. 146; 1918, ch. 25 and
1925, ch. 21); Delaware (Revised Code, sec. 2129: Laws 1915),
West Virginia (Code, sec. 2153 et seq.: Laws 1917, ch. 26)
and Virginia (Code, sec. 21-292: Acts 1910, ch. 312; as last
amended by Acts 1926, ch. 339). In Texas there were as of
31 August 1936 a total of 98 levee districts, which had built
a total of 699.57 miles of levees and improved a total of
169.47 miles of river channels.[223]

(b) Flood control districts:

Flood control districts are distinguished from the levee
districts in three ways. (1) While levee districts were
originally organized to build levees by themselves, most
flood control districts have the predominant function of assisting the Federal Government in the construction of levees
and other local flood protection works through the provision
and contribution of rights of way and maintaining and operating these works after their completion. (2) When flood control district build their own flood control works, they build
both dams and reservoirs and levees, revetments and the like,
but it is not the practice of levee districts to construct
flood detention reservoirs. (3) The organization of levee
districts is in general controlled by county authorities or
local courts, but that of flood control districts is in most
cases controlled by state authorities.

Like the levee districts, flood control districts are au-
thorized either by general state laws or by special state laws.
The states which by 1953 had enacted general enabling laws are
Connecticut (General Laws, Act 9178, enacted 1931), Idaho (Wa-
ter Laws, ch. 27: Laws 1937, ch. 215), Washington (Revised
Code, chs. 86.04 and 86.08: Laws 1935, ch. 160, as amended by
Laws 1953, ch. 20; and Laws 1937, ch. 72), Mississippi (Code,
tit. 19, ch. 9, art. 3, sec. 4769 et seq.: Laws 1936, ch. 188),
Florida (Statutes, ch. 378: Laws 1949, ch. 25209) and Kentuc-
ky (Revised Statutes, sec. 104.450 et seq.: Acts 1950, ch.).[224]
These laws are summarized below.

Connecticut---A flood control district is formed by order of
the county board of supervisors upon petition of owners of
lands representing 25 percent of the appraised value of the
total land area to be included in the district. Its governing body is a board of five trustees, who are appointed by
the county board of supervisors for five years. The district
construct its own dams and levees, which are financed by special benefit assessments and bond issues.

Idaho---A flood district is created by order of the State Commissioner of Reclamation upon petition of owners of at least

one-third of the total taxable area in the proposed district,
and is governed by a board of 3-9 commissioners appointed by
the said Commissioner for staggering terms of three years,
each commissioner representing a division of the district.
The board elects a chairman and appoints a secretary (who may
be a commissioner) and a treasurer. Both construction and
maintenance costs are raised by special benefit assessments,
but assessments for the latter purpose shall not exceed 3 mills
for each dollar of assessed value of all real property. Flood
districts may cooperate with the Federal Government. Besides
constructing and operating flood control works, they may also
develop and dispose of hydroelectric power and sell surplus
water.

Washington---(1) Districts that construct their own works of
flood control are governed by the act of 1935. They are created by popular vote at a special election called by the State
Department of Conservation and Development upon petition of
10 percent of landowners. The governing body of the mother
county, city or town is ex officio the board of directors of
the district, which elects its chairman annually. Works constructed are financed by a special annual tax levy not exceeding two mills per dollar of property, and by bond issues. (2)
Districts that are created solely to maintain and operate Federal flood control works are governed by the act of 1937.
Their establishment is the same as that of the districts of
the other type, except that the petition is made by 50 percent
instead of 10 percent of landowners. They are governed by a
board of three directors popularly elected for three years.
Their financial support consists of special benefit assessments
and bond issues.

Mississippi---Flood control districts are established for the
purposes of maintaining and operating Federal flood control
works, assisting the Federal Government in the construction of
the same and constructing small flood control works by the
chancery court of the county in which the proposed district
or a major portion thereof is located, upon petition of the
county authorities of the county or counties concerned and
after investigation by an engineer. The governing body of a
flood control district is a board of at least three commissioners appointed by the chancery court for four years. The
number of commissioners is three if the district includes whole
or parts of not more than three counties. If more than three
counties are involved, the number of commissioners should equal
the number of counties. The districts may levy an annual ad-
valorem tax not more than 2 mills per dollar for preliminary
expense and an annual ad-valorem tax not exceeding 3 mills per
dollar for repair and maintenance. They may also borrow money.

Florida---Flood control districts are created by circuit court
upon petition by State Board of Conservation joined by owners
of 51 percent of total acreage of land in the district, for

the sole purpose of furnishing assistance and cooperation to
the Federal Government. Five members appointed by the Governor of the State with Senate consent for overlapping terms of
three years constitute the governing body of a district, which
elects a chairman and a secretary. The district is financed
by special benefit assessments, with authority to borrow money
and to issue bonds, but the issue of bonds must be approved
by a majority of freeholders.

Kentucky---"A flood control district may be established for
the purpose of maintaining and operating any flood control
works heretofore or hereafter constructed in any city or
county of the state. The boundaries of such a flood control
district shall be the floodwall or levee and the contour line
on the land back of the floodwall or levee of the same elevation as the elevation of the top of the floodwall or levee."
The establishment is effected by order of the State Commissioner of Conservation upon petition of 70 percent of freeholders in the district. The board of five directors is the
governing body of a district. They are appointed by counties
and/or cities concerned for overlapping terms of four years.
The board elects a president and selects a secretary, who is
the ex-officio treasurer. Flood control districts are financed by an annual tax levy not exceeding 15 cents per one
hundred dollars of assessed property value. No flood control
districts have been formed in Oregon up to May 1953.[225] Two
flood control districts have been formed in Idaho, which were
formed respectively in 1946 and 1952. Both of them are engaged in cooperating with the Federal Government, and have not
constructed flood control works by themselves.[226] In Washington, five flood control districts have been established under
the law of 1935 and four under the law of 1937.[227] The Mill
Creek Flood Control District of Walla Walla County is considered one of the most important. It was established on 31
December 1935. However, the activities of this district consist primarily in the maintenance of a number of concrete retaining walls built by local interest prior to 1935, and works
constructed by the Federal Government (Works Progress Administration and Corps of Engineers) after 1935, and in the provision of lands and easements in connection with Federal construction work.[228]

Flood control districts may also be created by special
state legislation. The Los Angeles County Flood Control District of California is probably the first flood control district organized in this way. It was created by Statutes of
1915, ch. 755, which has been subsequently amended on several
occasions.[229] The district comprises the major portion of
Los Angeles County, and is governed by a board of supervisors
the membership of which are the supervisors of the county of
Los Angeles County serving in an ex-officio status. Although
county other county officials also serve ex-officio as district
officials, the district may employ engineers. The functions
of the district are limited by the original act to flood con-

trol and incidental water conservation. In 1927 the district
was authorized (Stats. 1927, ch. 332) to undertake ground-
water spreading work. For construction work, bonds may be
issued when so authorized by the district electorate at a
special election, and are redeemed by annual special property tax levies. Separate annual special property tax may be
levied for the purposes of maintenance and operation. The
district is also authorized to cooperate with the Federal Government in flood control work. By the time the Federal Government undertook the flood control work in Los Angeles area
under the authority of the Flood Control Act of 1936, the
Los Angeles County Flood Control District had completed the
construction of 12 flood-control dams, 2 flood-control and
debris storage basins, one diversion dam, a number of spreading grounds and debris basins, together with some channel-improvement work. Total expenditure incurred by the district
up to 1 December 1939 was $68,800,000, of which $11,000,000
were spent for operation and maintenance.[230] In 1934, a law
was passed in New Jersey creating the Passaic Valley Flood
Control District (ch. 157). The District comprises the Counties of Passaic, Essex, Union, Morris and Bergen, Somerset,
and Hudson. Its primary purpose is to receive and expend $12
million of Federal grant for the construction of flood control works. It is governed by a commission of five members,
which are appointed by the governor with senate consent for
one-year terms, and which elects a president, a vice-president and a secretary.[231]

     In the State of Texas, a number of flood control districts
have been formed through special legislation. An act of 1935
(ch. 319) established the Lower Rio Grande Flood Control District covering Cameron, Hidalgo and Willacy Counties, whose
function is to cooperate with the Federal Government. The
District is under the management of a board of five directors
with a tenure of two years, of whom two are appointed by the
commissioners court of Cameron County and two by that of Hidalgo County and the fifth is selected by these four members.
The finance of district is equally shared by Cameron and Hidalgo Counties. The Dallas County Flood Control District was
created by an act of 1945 (ch. 355). Its governing body is
board of three directors appointed by the governor with senate
consent for overlapping terms of six years. The board selects
a secretary-treasurer and a general manager. In 1947, four
flood control districts (Lavaca County, Colorado County, Fay-
ette County and Jackson County Flood Control Districts) were
established, all by special acts (chs. 183, 184, 185 and 186).
The commissioners courts of the respective counties concerned
serve ex officio as the governing bodies of these districts,
which appoint a flood control manager as the executive officer. All districts are authorized to levy taxes (not specified) and to issue bonds. It seems evident that these districts were created entirely for financial reasons.

The West Tennessee Flood Control and Soil Conservation District of the State of Tennessee was created for the primary purpose of giving cooperation to the Federal Government (Public Acts 1949, ch. 247, as amended by Public Acts 1951, ch. 46). It comprehends all of the state lying between Tennessee and Mississippi Rivers. Its administering authority is a board of three commissioners, who are appointed by the Governor for overlapping terms of six years. It elects a president and employs a secretary. Expenses of the district are financed by special benefit assessments, which shall not exceed 50 cents per acre a year. The district is also authorized to borrow money. The Central and Southern Florida Flood Control District of Florida, created by a special law of 1949 (ch. 25214), is of similar nature.[232] Its sole function is to furnish cooperation to the Federal Government in the construction of the Central and Southern Florida flood control project authorized by the Flood Control Act of 30 June 1948.[233] The act delineates the boundaries of the district but does not establish a special governing agency other than provided in the general flood control district act enacted in the same year. A preliminary property tax at the rate of three mills per dollar was authorized for 1949, and for subsequent years, an annual property tax not exceeding one mill on the dollar was authorized. It is worthy of notice that the Central and Southern Florida Flood Control District has no authority to issue bonds, which is a deviation from the general practice of flood control and other special districts.

3. _Irrigation districts_---The first state law providing for the creation of irrigation districts was the Wright Act of the State of California of 1887 (Stats. 1887, ch. 34), which was, however, based on the irrigation-district law of the Territory of Utah enacted in 1865. The Wright Act was viewed by the Federal circuit court as violating the 14th Amendment of the Federal Constitution, but on appeal it was upheld by the Supreme Court of the United States in 1896 as a legitimate exercise of public authority in the public interest (_Fallbrook Irrigation District v. Bradley_, 164 U. S. 112, 164).[234] Today, laws permitting the creation of irrigation districts are found all of the 17 Western states and Louisiana.[235] The sequence of enactment of the first irrigation district law in each of these states is as follows:

1887	California
1890	Washington
1891	Kansas
1895	Oregon, Nebraska
1903	Idaho
1905	Colorado
1909	Montana
1915	Oklahoma
1917	North Dakota, South Dakota

1918	Texas
1919	Nevada, New Mexico, Utah
1920	Wyoming
1921	Arizona
1926	Louisiana

Some of these states have two or more kinds of irrigation districts. Thus, in Colorado, there are (1) irrigation districts under the provisions of the law of 1905, (2) irrigation districts governed by the law of 1921, and (3) "public irrigation districts" under an act of 1935. Arizona has (1) irrigation districts (under law of 1921) and (2) "irrigation water delivery districts" (under law of 1933). Kansas recognizes both irrigation districts organized under the law of 1891 and irrigation districts organized under a law of 1941. In Nebraska, irrigation districts derive their authority from the law of 1895, whereas "reclamation districts" owe their existence to an act of 1947. In California, besides the irrigation districts (Stats. 1897, ch. 189, as amended: <u>Water Code</u>, division 11), there are "water districts" (Stats. 1913, p. 815, as amended), "water storage districts" (Stats. 1921, p. 1727, as amended) and "water storage and conservation districts" (Stats. 1941, ch. 1253), all of which are organized for the single purpose of irrigation. Only "irrigation districts" will be discussed here. All irrigation districts may legally either build and operate their own irrigation works, or else operate and maintain works constructed by the Federal Government in accordance with Federal Reclamation Laws. An irrigation district, when authorized to build irrigation works, may build either water-storage or water-delivery works. However, the "irrigation water delivery districts" of Arizona do not construct water-storage works. Since most of the irrigation works are constructed or rehabilitated by the Federal Government, it would seem that a substantial proportion of existing irrigation districts are instrumentalities of Federal irrigation enterprise instead of local enterprise. As will be discussed later, the construction of Federal projects is in many cases made contingent upon the organization of a local irrigation district.

In most states, irrigation districts are engaged in single-purpose irrigation enterprise. But in some states, activities other than irrigation are permitted. For example, the water improvement districts of Texas may "furnish water for domestic, power and commercial purposes", "when operating under section 59 of article 16 of the Constitution" (<u>Revised Statutes</u>, art. 7622). By sec. 15 of Laws 1931, ch. 91 (<u>Revised Statutes</u>, sec. 46-315), Nebraska irrigation districts are authorized to generate hydroelectric power. In 1943, California irrigation districts were authorized to furnish water for any beneficial purpose, including fire protection, and to generate and sell electric power or purchase or lease it (Stats. 1943, ch. 372,

sec. 1). By a law of 1951 (ch. 49), Nevada irrigation districts were enabled to generate and sell electric energy.

The irrigation districts are established in a number of
ways, but always with the petition of landowners, which is
always followed by a hearing. The procedures prevailing in
the various states concerned may be analyzed below.

(a) Establishment by popular vote at a special election:

(1) Petition addressed to and election called by the
county administrative authorities of the county in which the
proposed irrigation district or the major portion thereof lies.
Again, there are differences as to the numbers and qualifications of the petitioners. (i) In Washington, Oklahoma and
Utah, the petition is made by either fifty or a majority of
landowners or freeholders. In Utah, the Governor may also
make the petition upon recommendation of the State Engineer.
(ii) For irrigation districts of Nebraska which are governed
by Laws 1895, ch. 70, as amended by Laws 1937, ch. 103, and
irrigation districts of Arizona which are governed by Laws
1921, it is the majority of land owners that petition the county board. (iii) In Colorado ("irrigation districts" but not
"public irrigation districts"), New Mexico, Nevada and South
Dakota, petition should be signed by a majority of landowners
who also represent a majority of the total land acreage of
the proposed district.

(2) Petition addressed to and election called by the county court or State Engineer (or equivalent officer or agency).
In Oregon, fifty or majority of land owners petition the county court.236 In North Dakota, a majority of landowners owning in the aggregate a majority of total land acreage of the
proposed district petition the State Engineer. Texas water
improvement districts are in general established by order of
the county commissioners' court without special election.
However, when the proposed district lies in two or more counties, the procedure consists of petition to the State Board
of Water Engineers by fifty property owners or owners of a
majority of the entire land area and a special election called
by the said Board.

(b) Establishment without special election, but by order
or decree

(1) Of the county administrative authorities upon petition, in Arizona with respect to the irrigation water delivery
districts, by owners of a majority of total land acreage of
the proposed district; in Texas, of a majority of land owners
who own a majority of the total land area (provided the district lies within a single county); in Kansas, for irrigation
districts governed by the older laws, of three-fourths of
land owners; in Idaho, of fifty or a majority of land owners

who own at least one-fourth of the total land area of the
district (also with examination by the State Department of
Reclamation); in Louisiana, of twenty percent of property
tax payers.

(2) In Wyoming, of the district court of the county,
upon petition of a majority of landowners; in Montana, of
the district court, upon petition of sixty percent of landowners representing sixty percent of total land area of the
district; in Kansas, for irrigation districts governed by
Laws 1941, ch. 262, of the Chief Engineer of the Division
of Water Resources of the State Board of Agriculture (equivalent to state engineer) upon petition of 70 percent of landowners, of 3 or more persons owning 60 or more acres; in Nebraska, for irrigation districts governed by the act of 11
June 1947, of the State Department of Roads and Irrigation
(equivalent to state engineer) upon petition of owners of
thirty percent of the lands to be irrigated; in Colorado, for
"public irrigation districts" as provided in Laws 1935, ch.
146, of the State Conservation Board, an ad-hoc agency composed of the Governor, the Attorney-General and the State Engineer, upon petition of a majority of landowners who own in
the aggregate a majority of lands included in the proposed
district.

Irrigation districts are as a rule governed by a board
of directors or a board of commissioners which is in most
cases popularly elected. In Arizona (for irrigation districts
organized under Laws 1921, ch. 149), North Dakota, South
Dakota, Washington, Oregon and Idaho, the board of directors
is elected for overlapping terms of three years, and the
board of directors of California irrigation districts is elected for overlapping terms of four years. As for the number of
directors, it is three in North Dakota, Oregon and Washington
(under existing law), multiples of three in Arizona, five in
California, and three or five or seven in Idaho and South
Dakota. Directors are elected by precincts or divisions in
Washington, Oregon, Arizona and California, but in Washington and Oregon they may also be elected at large. In Idaho,
each director represents a division of the district, but he
is elected at large. Louisiana irrigation are governed by
a board of five commissioners appointed by the police jury or
juries of the parish or parishes concerned for four years.
In Wyoming there is a board of three or five commissioners
for each irrigation district, who are appointed by the district court of the county concerned for two years. A mixed
or middle-of-the-road method of selecting the governing board
is that the first membership are appointed but that their
successors are elected. This prevails in Kansas and Montana,
and also in Colorado with respect to public irrigation districts organized under Laws 1935, ch. 146 and in Arizona with
respect to irrigation water delivery districts. In the latter
case, the first membership of the board of directors, whose

number ranges from five to twenty-five, are appointed by the
Governor, and their successors are popularly elected, for
overlapping terms of six years. The officers of the Kansas
irrigation districts "shall be a board of irrigation commissioners, consisting of a president, secretary and treasurer,
and shall hold their offices for a period of one year. They
shall be elected at an annual election. . . The board of
county commissioners shall have power to appoint the first
officers . . ." (General Statutes, sec. 42-363). The governing board of Montana irrigation districts consists of
three or five or seven commissioners serving a term of two
years, each representing a division of the district. The
first commissioners are appointed by the district court and
their successors are elected. The irrigation water delivery
districts of Arizona are governed by a board of three trustees
with terms of two years. The first trustees are appointed by
the county board of supervisors and their successors popularly elected. The governing board commonly elects a president
and appoints a secretary, who may be a member of the board.

All irrigation districts, with the single exception of the
public irrigation districts of Colorado, have the power of
taxation. All irrigation districts, with the single exception
of the irrigation delivery districts of Arizona, have the
power to issue bonds, in some cases after popular vote. There
are three methods of taxation, namely, (1) special benefit
assessments, which are levies on lands proportionate to the
benefits received from irrigation; (2) special tax levy, which
is uniform, ad valorem tax on all lands included in the district and which is in the nature of a surtax to the general
property tax; and (3) acreage tax, a uniform tax on all lands
collected on the basis of area instead of valuation. The
rate of (1) is in general flexible, but that of (3) is usually
fixed. There is also usually a millage limit (i.e., number
of mills on the dollar) in the case of (2). The methods of
taxation adopted in the various states for their irrigation
districts are listed below.

(1) Special benefit assessment---Kansas (under act of
     1941), Nevada, North Dakota and South Dakota.
(2) Special tax levy---Arizona, California, Colorado,
     Kansas (under act of 1891), Nebraska, New Mexico,
     Oklahoma, South Dakota (for payment of bond interests
     only), Texas and Utah.
(3) Acreage tax---Louisiana (50 cents per acre per year
     for construction and 10 cents per acre per year for
     maintenance) (for a period of forty years), Montana
     ($4.00 per acre per year for all costs and expenses)
     and Oregon (at a rate sufficient to defray all costs).
     In Oregon, special tax levy may be used to raise funds
     for cooperation with the Federal Government.

All irrigation district laws analyzed above are general

laws. In exceptional cases, irrigation districts may be created by special state laws. In such cases, petition is of
course unnecessary, although actual initiative may still be
taken by special local interests concerned. To cite an example, the legislature of North Dakota passed a law on 19
March 1949 (ch. 347) creating the Missouri-Souris Conservancy
and Reclamation District, whose function it is to operate the
Missouri-Souris Unit of the Missouri River Basin Project of
the United States Bureau of Reclamation. Fifteen counties
are designated for inclusion in the District, and permission
is given neighboring counties to join. The District is governed by a board of directors composed of one director appointed by each component county, which elects a chairman, a vice-
chairman, a secretary and a treasurer. The board may levy an
annual tax on property not exceeding one mill on the dollar
of taxable valuation, but it has no authority to borrow money.

The numbers of active irrigation districts and total
acreages irrigated thereby in the eighteen states in which irrigation districts may be organized are shown in the following table: 237

State	Number of Districts	Total acreage irrigated	Date of data
Arizona	22	89,877 (a)	1949-50
California	104 (b)	21,332,321 (c)	1950
Colorado	20	155,216	1950
Idaho	56	1,105,523 (d)	1952
Kansas	2	68,489	May 1953
Louisiana	None	None	May 1953
Montana	43(e)	395,851 (f)	January 1949
Nebraska	41	1,150,000	May 1953
Nevada	5	Unknown	May 1953
New Mexico	65	374,203	May 1953
North Dakota	6	45,000	May 1953
Oklahoma	1	52,000	June 1953
Oregon	53	470,163	July 1952
South Dakota	3	Unknown	October 1953
Texas	58	Unknown	1948
Utah	None	None	March 1954
Washington	81	533,311 (g)	June 1953
Wyoming	31	560,863	June 1953

(a) For 11 districts only. (b) Of this number, four
are water storage districts. (c) Of this acreage, 2,-
172,701 belong to irrigation districts (incomplete), and
159,620 acres are in three water storage districts. (d)
For 53 districts only. (e) Incomplete. (f) For 40
districts only. (g) This was the acreage irrigated by
75 irrigation districts as of 31 December 1952.

By way of illustration, the works constructed by some of
the irrigation districts are described below.

(1) Turlock and Modesto Irrigation Districts, California
---Turlock and Modesto Irrigation Districts were respectively
established in May and July, 1887, the same year when the
Wright Act (the first state irrigation district law) was passed. The two districts have ever since the beginning of
their activities joined each other in their irrigation enterprise. The common source of water supply of the two districts
is the Tuolumne River, from which water is diverted to the
two districts at the La Grande Dam, which the two districts
jointly constructed in 1891-1894. About 181,000 acres (about
90 percent of all lands in the district) are irrigated in the
Turlock and about 70,000 acres in the Modesto District. But
the two districts separately own and operate water distribution works. The Turlock District, which is the major partner,
"operates 250 miles of main canal and laterals and 1,660 miles
of community ditches. The community ditches are owned by the
irrigators and several hundred of them operate as Improvement
Districts under the main District." In addition, it operates
168 pumps whose function it is to control ground water, and
which pump into the irrigation system about 200,000 acre-
feet of water of which 150,000 acre-feet occurs during the
irrigation season (Figures of 1 May 1953). In the Modesto
District, there are 162.7 miles of main canal and laterals,
57.2 miles of drainage canals, 71.5 miles of concrete-lined
canals and laterals and 83 drainage and 21 irrigation pumps
(figures of 1 January 1952). Irrigation began in 1904. In
1911-1913 the Dallas Warner Foothill Reservoir (30,000 acre-
feet) was built by the two districts jointly, and in 1912-1914
the Owens Reservoir (50,000 acre-feet) was built by the Turlock District. They are both storage reservoirs and serve to
extend the irrigation season by approximately one month, or
to July or August depending upon the flow conditions of the
Tuolumne River, but they do not increase the area irrigated.
In 1921 the two districts started to build the Don Pedro Dam
and Reservoir for hydroelectric power development, flood control and river regulation in the interest of irrigation, with
the last-mentioned function as its principal function. It
was completed on 8 August 1923. The dam is 284 feet above the
river-bed and the reservoir has a gross capacity of 290,000
acre-feet, of which 100,000 acre-feet are devoted to flood
control. The Don Pedro Reservoir has further prolonged the
irrigation season to October 15th of each year. The power
house at the end of the Don Pedro Dam, which began in operation in November 1923, generates 37,500 kilowatts of electric
power. [238]

(2) Imperial Irrigation District, California---This is
the largest irrigation district in the United States, having
a gross area of 893,545 acres. Organized on 25 July 1911,
it is located entirely in Imperial County, and includes all
of the cultivated lands in the Imperial Valley, [239] which is
the delta of the Colorado River formed of sand dunes lying
274 feet below the sea level and which is a dry desert as a

result of evaporation of water.[240] The District obtains its
water supply from the Colorado River. Irrigation works constructed by the District consist of 1,700 miles of distribution canals bringing water to 500,000 acres of land, and 1,-
400 miles of drainage canals or open drains that serve over
95 percent of all irrigated lands of the District, together
with tile drains which serve some 125,000 acres. It also operates the All-American Canal constructed by the Federal Government to transport water of the Colorado River to the Imperial and Coachella Valleys.[241] According to the provisions
in sec. 7 of the Boulder Canyon Act of 21 December 1928 (45
Stat. 1057, 1062), the Imperial Irrigation District and the
Coachella Valley County Water District have obtained the statutory right (Federal) to develop hydroelectric power on the
All-American Canal. But the part of this right which is enjoyed by the Coachella Valley County Water District was in
1934 leased to the Imperial Irrigation District for a period
of 99 years. Two hydroelectric plants have been built and
operated by the Imperial Irrigation District on the All-American Canal with a total capacity of 24,400 kilowatts. These
two plants are supplemented by a Diesel power plant of a capacity of 12,000 kilowatts which the District built prior to
the construction of the two hydro plants and a steam power
plant of 20,000-kilowatt capacity which the District acquired
from the California Electric Power Company in 1943 together
with other properties of the Company. "From May, 1936, when
the District's power operations first commenced, until February, 1941, all of the power for the District's system was
supplied by the Diesel plant at Brawley. On the latter date,
the two hydro plants . . . began generating power." The electric power of the District is sold at retail to some 26,000
customers in Imperial County and Coachella Valley in River-
side County and to Lower California of Mexico in wholesale.[242]

    (3) Talent Irrigation District, Oregon----It was formed
in May, 1916, and "comprises 10,400 acres of irrigated land
located in the upper valley of Bear Creek, a tributary of
Rogue River, surrounding the towns of Ashland and Talent. It
has constructed two dams and reservoirs and a number of canals
and laterals. The Hyatt Prairie Reservoir, 14 miles east of
Ashland, impounded by a dam built in 1922 on Keene Creek (a
tributary of Klamath River) and with a capacity of 16,200
acre-feet, stores water to be released down stream, which is
diverted several miles away from the dam by canal across the
Cascade Divide into the Emigrant Creek (a tributary of the
Bear River). It is a storage reservoir used to regulate the
flow of the Keene Creek in the interest of irrigation, but
not a storage reservoir used directly for the purpose of irrigation. On the Emigrant Creek, there is the Emigrant Creek
Dam and Reservoir (8,300 acre-feet) built in 1924, which is
a storage reservoir directly used for the purpose of irrigation. "Canals from Emigrant Reservoir distribute water along
both sides of Upper Bear Creek Valley. These canals traverse
some rather rough country and cross several small canyons

through siphons and flumes. There is also one siphon crossing Emigrant Creek and two crossing Bear Creek." In addition, there are diversions by canals from Bear, McDonald,
Greeley, Wagner and Neil Creeks and other minor sources. The
District owns eight main canals and laterals totaling 75.8
miles. Sub-laterals are constructed and maintained by landowners with rights of way provided by the District.243

(4) El Cajon Valley Irrigation District, California---
Formed on 17 November 1950, it has a gross area of 5,900
acres, of which 1,000 acres are irrigated. Water supply
comes from more than 300 wells, most of which are small in
capacity and shallow in depth.244

4. Drainage districts---Drainage districts are organized
for the drainage of either overflowed lands or naturally wet,
swamp or marshy lands. The drainage of overflowed lands is
generally conducted for agricultural purposes, as lands subject to overflow of flood waters are mostly of high agricultural value. The drainage of wet, swamp or marshy lands is
undertaken either for agricultural or for sanitary purposes.
The means and devices used in the drainage of overflowed
lands are levees and channel improvement works as well as
drains and ditches, while drains and ditches constitute the
principal means of draining the natural wet-lands. In substance, the drainage of overflowed lands is nothing different from flood control.245

Drainage districts are created either by general or by
special state laws. The states (34 in all) having general
legislation permitting the establishment of drainage districts
and the dates of such legislation (the dates of amendments
and supplements are omitted) are listed below.246

     1868---California (ch. 415, sec. 30 et seq.).
     1879---Illinois (p. 120).
     1891---Nebraska (ch. 36, sanitary drainage only).
     1895---Washington (ch. 117).
     1896---Utah (ch. 132).
     1897---Michigan (No. 254).
     1900---Louisiana (No. 12).
     1904---Iowa (ch. 68).
     1905---Kansas (ch. 215), Montana (ch. 106) and Nebraska
            (ch. 161, for agricultural drainage.)
     1906---Mississippi (ch. 132) and Missouri (S.B. 238).
     1907---Texas (ch. 40).
     1908---Oklahoma (ch. 30).
     1909---Arkansas (No. 279), New York (Town Law of 1909),
            North Carolina (ch. 442) and Tennessee (ch. 185).
     1911---Colorado (ch. 124), Georgia (No. 265), Nevada (ch.
            134), South Carolina (No. 54) and Wyoming (ch. 95).
     1912---Arizona (ch. 38), Kentucky (ch. 132) and New Mexi-
            co (ch. 84).

1913---Florida (ch. 6458) and Idaho (ch. 16).
1915---Alabama (No. 167), Delaware (ch. 105), Indiana
        (ch. 98) and Oregon (ch. 340).
1917---Virginia (ch. 26) and West Virginia (ch. 26).
1919---Minnesota (ch. 13, Ex. Sess.) and Wisconsin (ch.
        557).
1920---South Carolina (No. 344) (a new law).

Some of these laws and their amendments and supplements
provide for only one form of drainage. For example, the 1891
law of Nebraska authorized only sanitary drainage and the
1905 law of the same state is applicable only to agricultural
drainage. The California law of 1903 (ch. 238, as amended by
Stats. 1949, ch. 418) applies only to agricultural lands other
than swamp and overflowed lands. In general, however, a drainage-district law envisages all kinds of drainage and permits
the construction of all drainage devices and works.

In a few states, there are two or more kinds of drainage
districts each governed by a separate law. For example, in
California there are the following sets of drainage-district
laws: (1) Stats. 1868, ch. 415, as amended by Stats. 1885, ch.
158; (2) Stats. 1903, ch. 238, as amended by Stats. 1949, ch.
418; (3) Stats. 1919, ch. 354, as last amended by Stats. 1947,
ch. 733; and (4) Stats. 1923, ch. 102. In Louisiana, there
are (1) the Drainage District Law of 1900 (No. 12), as amended by Act No. 159, etc. and generally revised by Act No. 85
of 1921, as further amended; and (2) the Gravity Drainage Law
of 1924 (No. 125), as last amended by Act No. 86 of 1934.
But the majority of states have only one drainage-district
law.

The constitutionality of drainage district laws was first
challenged in Hagar v. Reclamation District No. 108, 111 U. S.
701 (5 May 1884), in which the collection of assessments for
the support of the drainage districts was attacked as taking
property without due process of law. The Court, however, did
not pass upon the constitutionality of the establishment of
drainage district, but merely sustained the legality of special tax levy on the technical ground that it is not less
equitable than special benefit assessment. In Fallbrook Irrigation District v. Bradley, 164 U. S. 112 (1896) the following dictum was collaterally given (at 163):

> The case does not essentially differ from that of
> Hagar v. Reclamation District No. 108, 111 U. S.
> 701, where this Court held that the power of the
> legislature of California to prescribe a system
> for reclaiming swamp lands was not inconsistent
> with any provision of the Federal Constitution.
> The power does not rest simply upon the ground
> that the reclamation must be necessary for the pub-
> lic health. That indeed is one ground for inter-

position by the state, but not the only one.
Statutes authorizing drainage of swamp lands have
frequently been upheld independently of any effect
upon the public health, as reasonable regulations
for the general advantage of those who are treated
for this purpose as owners of a common property.
If it be essential or material for the property of
the community, and if the improvement be one in
which all the landowners have to a certain extent
a common interest, and the improvement cannot be
accomplished without the concurrence of all or
mearly all of such owners by reason of the peculiar natural condition of the tract sought to be
reclaimed, then such reclamation may be made and
the land rendered useful to all and at their joint
expense. In such case the absolute right of each
individual owner of land must yield to a certain
extent or be modified by corresponding rights on
the part of other owners for what is declared upon
the whole to be for the public benefit.

This upheld the constitutionality of the establishment of
drainage districts, in fact, of that of almost all kinds of
special districts.

Drainage districts are established in the following ways:

(1) By order of the local courts, after petition and
hearing (in 26 laws)---Except in Indiana, where drainage districts can be created only in a county having a city of 60,-
000-78,000 population, drainage districts can be formed either
in a single county or in two or more counties. If the district is located in a single county, the petition goes to and
the order of establishment is made by the county or district
court of the county concerned. If it covers two or more
counties, practices differ as to the court that is to approve
the petition. In Alabama, Delaware, Georgia, Kentucky (under
both act of 1912 and act of 1918), Minnesota, Mississippi,
Montana, New Mexico (ordinary drainage districts), North Carolina, South Carolina (under act of 1911), Tennessee, Virginia,
West Virginia, Wisconsin and Wyoming, the court of any of the
counties concerned may assume jurisdiction. In Arkansas,
Florida, Idaho, Illinois, Kansas, Missouri, Oregon and South
Carolina (law of 1920), the authority belongs to the court of
the county in which a greater portion of the district lies.[247]
As to the number of persons (who must be land owners) needed
to sign the petition, there is a high degree of diversity
among the provisions of the various laws, which fall under
the following categories:

> (1) Majority of land owners in the district who
>   own in the aggregate majority of the total
>   land area of the district: Tennessee and Vir-
>   ginia.

(2) Majority of land owners, <u>or</u> owners of majority of
     of total land area: Delaware, Florida, and South
     Carolina (both 1911 and 1920 laws, but under the
     1920 law the state budget and control board may
     also sign the petition).

(3) Majority of land owners: Indiana, Kansas and Nebraska.

(4) Owners of majority of land area: Missouri and Oregon.

(5) Majority of land owners, representing one-third of
     total land area <u>or</u> owners of majority of total land
     area: Montana, Wisconsin and Wyoming.

(6) Majority of land owners <u>or</u> owners of three-fifths of
     total land area: Georgia and North Carolina.

(7) Majority of land owners, owning in the aggregate one-
     third of total land area <u>or</u> one-third of land owners,
     owning in the aggregate majority of total land area:
     Alabama, Illinois, and Mississippi (under older law).

(8) Owners of one-third of total land area: Idaho.

(9) One-fourth of land owners <u>or</u> owners of one-fourth
     of total land area: Kentucky (under both 1912 and
     1918 laws).

(10) One-fourth of land owners: Minnesota and Mississippi
     (under 1912 law). In Minnesota, the governing board
     of the county, city or village concerned may also
     sign the petition.

(11) One-fourth of land owners, representing one-fourth
     of total land area: New Mexico.

(12) Three or more property owners: Arkansas and West
     Virginia.

In most state laws, the district is formed after a hearing on the petition, the main purpose of which is to determine the boundaries of the district or the lands to be benefited.[248] The court may ordinarily employ an engineer to
render the necessary technical assistance. In the laws of
Delaware, Georgia, Illinois, Kentucky (both law of 1912 and
law of 1918), North Carolina, South Carolina and Virginia,
provision is made for the appointment of a board of viewers,
usually composed of an engineer and two resident landowners,
for the conduct of investigation and survey. Court decree is
made only after a hearing on the report of this board. In
Delaware, Georgia and North Carolina, the board makes two surveys and reports, and hearing is given on each report before
the district is ordered established. In Virginia, the two
surveys and reports of the board are even more formalized,
in that an order of "preliminary establishment" is given after
hearing on the report of the preliminary survey, and then the
final order of establishment comes after hearing on the final
report. In North Carolina and South Carolina, after a district is established, the board of view proceed to classify
lands according to benefits receivable from the drainage works
and to make a final report thereon, which must be adjudicated
by the court. A strange provision is found in the 1920 act
of South Carolina, which stipulates that no drainage district

shall be formed without special election, although the establishment takes effect upon order of the court of common pleas.
Under Laws 1905, ch. 161, drainage districts in Nebraska are
required to be at least 160 acres in area. But in all other
laws the minimum area of a drainage district is not specified.
The courts, after hearing being given, have full discretion
to grant or withhold its decree of establishment of the district. However, under the Arkansas law, the order of establishment is compulsory if the petition is made by a majority of land owners or by owners of lands which represent a
majority of the total land are either in area of in value (the
regular minimum number of persons required to make the petition being three land owners).

(2) By order of the county administrative authorities
after petition and hearing (16 laws)---In all of the states
concerned the authorities refer to the governing board of
the county, except Michigan (for districts within one county),
where they refer to the county drainage commissioners. 249
The 1925 law of Kansas is peculiar in that it is complementary to a law of 1907, which provides for county drainage by
land owners upon petition to and approval by the county court
without forming a drainage district. The 125 law of Kansas
permits incorporation of lands to be drained under the 1907
law, which is to be effected by order of the county board of
commissioners upon petition of the drainage commissioners appointed by the court under provisions of the 1907 law, without any change in boundaries already decided upon by the
court. The laws of New York and Washington (for drainage improvement districts, (1913, as amended) and the above-mentioned 1925 law of Kansas, drainage districts are formed within
one county (or town in New York). In all other laws, inter-
county districts are permitted. In Louisiana (under both
law of 1900 and law of 1924, as amended), Michigan and Oklahoma, inter-county districts are established by joint county
authorities. With regard to drainage districts of Kansas
which are formed in valleys of natural water-courses, each of
the counties concerned takes its independent action. Whenever a majority of counties are in favor of the establishment,
the district is proclaimed established by the Governor of the
state. Under all other laws, inter-county districts are created by the authorities of the county in which a major portion
of the district is situated.

There is utter lack of uniformity on the number of petitioners. Under Stats. 1885, ch. 158, superseding Stats. 1868, ch.
415, of California, owners of two-thirds of land area make
the petition. Under Stats. 1919, ch. 354, as amended, of California, petition is made by 20 or more land owners, or by
owners of a majority of total land area in the district. 250
Under Stats. 1923, ch. 102, of California, the number of petitioners required is fifty or a majority of landowners representing a majority of total land area, or two-thirds of land-

owners owning in the aggregate one-third of total land area.
In Colorado, a majority of landowners representing a majority of total land area are required to sign the petition. Requirements in other states are as follows: Iowa and Illinois
(alternative method), owners of one-fourth of total land area;
Kansas (for districts in which three-fifths of land area are
owned by nonresidents), three fifths of landowners; Kansas
(for districts in counties of 85,000-130,000 population),
drainage commissioners appointed by court (Laws 1925, ch.
163); Kansas (for districts in valleys of natural watercourses, two-fifths of all land owners; Louisiana (under Act No.
12 of 1900, as amended and revised by Act No. 85 of 1921, as
amended) and New York, owners of a majority of total land
area; Louisiana (under Act No. 238 of 1924, as amended), owners of a majority of total land area, or 25 land owners if
the district area is more than 40 acres; Michigan (in a single
county), ten land owners; Michigan (inter-county), land owners
representing one-half of the assessed benefits of lands to be
benefited; Nevada, a majority of land owners representing
one-third of total land area, or one-third land owners representing a majority of total land area; Oklahoma, 50 percent
of land owners, or owners of 50 percent of total land area;
Utah, a majority of land owners representing one-third of total land area, or owners of a majority of total land area;
Washington (drainage districts, under Laws 1913, ch. 176, as
amended), four or more property owners.

Pre-hearing investigation is provided for in ch. 102 of
Stats. 1923 of California, and Oklahoma and Washington laws,
which is respectively conducted by an engineer appointed by
the county board and subsequently by the state engineer (California), by three viewers appointed by the county board (Oklahoma), and by an engineer appointed by the county board (or
city or town council as the case may be) or by the State Department of Conservation and Development if the district comprises 3,000 acres or more (Washington).

The authority of the county administrative authorities in
establishing the drainage districts under the above-mentioned
laws is administratively complete and conclusive in all cases
except two: (1) In Louisiana, under Act No. 12 of 1900, as
amended and revised, the order of the police jury or police
juries in establishing a drainage district must be approved
by the Board of State Engineers; (2) in Colorado, a special
election must be held if so requested by the original petitioners.

(3) By order of the county administrative authorities
after petition and hearing, followed by a special election or
referendum (8 laws)---Two laws, namely, the sanitary drainage
district law of Nebraska and the 1895 law of Washington, provide only for single-county districts.[251] In all other laws,
both intra-county and inter-county districts are provided for.
Under Laws 1909, ch. 225 (which, however, apply solely to in-

tercounty districts) of Washington, petition for the formation of inter-county districts must be addressed to the governing board of each of the counties concerned. Under all
other laws, petition for incorporation of an intercounty district is presented to the county board of the county in which
a majority of the lands of the proposed district is located.
The numbers of petitioners required under each of the laws
under discussion are given below:

Arizona---five land owners.
California (Stats. 1903, ch. 238, as amended)---fifty or
a majority of land owners.
Illinois---Majority of land owners representing one-third
of total land area, or one-third land owners representing a majority of total land area.
Nebraska---100 land owners (for sanitary drainage districts)
Nebraska---one-fourth of land owners, if entire land of
the district is owned by less than 20 persons; ten
land owners if entire land of the district is owned
by more than 20 persons (for agricultural drainage
districts).
New Mexico---majority of land owners representing one-
third of total land area (for districts for cooperation with U. S.)
Texas---25 taxpayers; or one third of taxpayers if their
number is less than 75.
Washington (1895 law)---owners of a majority of total
land area. A district must contain at least five
free-holders.
Washington (1909 law)---100 land owners, or a majority of
freeholders in area, in each of the counties concerned.

(4) By order of state water agency (1 law)---In the new
article 8 of the Conservation Law of New York, which was enacted in 1945 (ch. 889), a new type of drainage districts is
provided. In principle, each drainage district should include
all portions of a natural drainage basin. It is established
by order of the Water Power and Control Commission of the
State Department of Conservation upon petition by three or
more land owners, which is made prior to the conduct of preliminary investigation and first hearing and detailed survey
planning and benefit determination and final hearing. Districts may be formed by the said commission in its own initiative without petition if they are to be financed mainly
by federal grants. 252

In a number of laws, provision is made for the consolidation of drainage districts. Examples are laws of California (Stats. 1923, ch. 102), Florida, Illinois, Louisiana (Act
No. 12 of 1900, as amended and revised) and Washington (1913,
ch. 176, as amended). The procedure of consolidation is ana-

logous to, but different from, that of establishment of the
original drainage districts to be consolidated. For example,
in Flrodia, adjacent drainage districts may be consolidated
by popular vote at an election called by the board of supervisors of each of the districts involved (while the establishment of a drainage district is by order of the circuit court
of the county of major concern upon petition of State Board
of Drainage Commissioners or of a majority of land owners or
of owners of a majority of total land area without election).
In Illinois, two or more drainage districts may be consolidated by order of the county court of the county in which a major
portion of the consolidated is located, upon petition of one-
tenth of land owners representing one-fifth of total land
area in each of the constituent districts (while original
drainage districts are created by order of the county court
of the county of major concern upon petition of a majority of
land owners representing one-third of total land area or of
one-third land owners representing a majority of total land
area, or by county board of commissioners upon petition of
owners of one-fourth of total land area).

Most drainage district laws provide for the creation of
a governing board for a drainage district.[253] This governing
board is created in one of the following ways:[254]

(1)　Popularly elected (19 laws): Arizona, California
(Stats. 1903, ch. 238, as amended), Colorado, Florida, Kansas (for districts in valleys of natural watercourses and for districts organized by Laws 1911, ch.
168, as amended), Kentucky (under law of 1918), Missouri, Nebraska (all three kinds of districts), New
Mexico (both kinds of districts), Oregon, South Carolina, (all three kinds of districts) and West Virginia. In Florida, the law provides that if no majority of electors are present at the election, then
the state board of drainage commissioners shall appoint the vacant membership of the district governing board. Under the 1920 law of South Carolina, if
the district fails to elect its supervisor (one
elected each year) for any one year, appointment
shall be made by the state budget and control board.
In Kansas under L 1911, ch. 168, and in Nebraska
under the 1905 law, each acre of land represents one
vote. In all other cases, the land owners are equal
voters.

(2)　Appointed by the court (9 laws): Alabama, Arkansas,
Idaho, Illinois (under act of 29 May 1879), Minnesota, Mississippi (under L 1912, ch. 195), Tennessee,
Virginia, Wisconsin and Wyoming. In Minnesota, first
directors of the districts are named in the petition
for establishment, and their appointment is made ipso
facto upon order of establishment being given. In
Wyoming, the commissioners of a district should be

elected if owners of one-third of total land area of the district so petition the court.

(3) Appointed by the court after popular nomination (election) (4 laws): Delaware, Georgia, North Carolina and South Carolina (under 1911 act).

(4) Appointed by the county governing board (5 laws): California (Stats. 1885, ch. 158 and Stats. 1923, ch 102), Nevada, Texas and Utah. Under the 1885 law of California, first trustees of a district are named in the petition for establishment, and their appointment is automatically effected by the order of establishment. Under the 1923 law of California, one or more directors of a districts must be elected upon petition of 15 percent of land owners. In Texas, the board of drainage commissioners of a district should be elected by the land owners upon request of a majority of the land owners.

(5) Appointed by the county governing board upon recommendation of land owners (2 laws): Act No. 12 of 1900, as amended and revised, of Louisiana (appointed by the police jury or police juries upon recommendation of a majority of land owners or of owners of a majority of total land area) and Act no. 238 of 1924, as amended, of Louisiana (three of the five commissioners of a drainage district are appointed by the police jury of the parish concerned upon recommendation of owners of a majority of total land area and two of them are appointed by the governor of the state).

(6) First membership of the governing board of the drainage district appointed by the county court or governing board, but their successors are elected by land owners (3 laws): Kansas (districts in which three-fifths of total land area are owned by non-residents) (three directors. First directors are named in the petition for establishment and are automatically appointed by the county board in its order of establishing the district. Their successors are elected by the land owners), Kansas (under L' 1925, ch. 163), and Montana (District court appoints three commissioners for a drainage district to hold office until the first Tuesday of May following their appointment, when land owners elect their successors for overlapping terms of three years).

(7) A county ad-hoc board for all drainage districts organized within a county (3 laws): In Kentucky, under the 1912 law, there is a county board of drainage commissioners, of whom one is annually elected by each drainage district within the county or appointed by the county court failing such election in any drainage district. In Virginia, the circuit court of a county appoints a board of three commissioners at the time when the first drainage district of the county

is established, which shall be the governing board
of this district and all drainage districts to be
subsequently organized within the same county. In
Mississippi, under the older law, the board of county
supervisors appoints three drainage commissioners
for the county, who are in control of all drainage
districts of the county.

(8) No special governing board (7 laws): Under the 1945
law of New York, the water power and control commission of the state department of conservation is
the ex-officio governing board of all drainage districts of the state organized under the said law.
In Indiana, the governing board of any county or the
board of public works of any city which is included
in drainage district constitutes the ex-officio governing board of the district. Under the New York
Town Law of 1909, the town board is the ex-officio
governing board of all drainage districts organized
under that law within a town. In Michigan, drainage
districts are managed and administered by the county
drainage commissioner of each county concerned. Under Stats. 1919, ch. 354, of California, the county
surveyor is ex-officio engineer of construction of
a drainage district within the county jurisdiction.
In Iowa, the county board appoints a supervising engineer in charge of construction for a drainage district. In Oklahoma construction work is undertaken
by the county board of commissioners, which appoints
a drainage commissioner upon recommendation of 20
land owners to maintain the completed works. Drainage districts organized under the 1885 California
law may operate without a board of trustees if petitioners so indicate in their petition.

The governing boards provided in the drainage district
law of Tennessee (1909, ch. 185, as amended: Code, ch. 9, art.
4) and the 1913 law of Washington (ch. 176, as amended: Revised Code, ch. 85.08) are the only ones which has an ex-
officio member. In the former case, the judge or chairman
of the court is an ex-officio member of the board of directors, while the remaining two members are appointed by the
court. In the latter case, the district engineer (appointed
by the authority which establishes the district) is an ex-
officio supervisor, who, together with two other supervisors
elected by land owners, constitutes the governing board of
the district. In all other laws, all members of the governing board of a drainage district are officers specially selected for the job and are not in an ex-officio status. As for
membership of the governing board, it is five in the laws of
Louisiana (both laws), Missouri and Wisconsin, 1911 law of
Kansas and 1905 law of Nebraska; three or five in the law of
Arizona and the 1903 law of California; three to five in the
law of Minnesota and in Nebraska for districts organized by

vote of land owners; unknown in the law of Nevada and the
law of New Mexico with respect to districts organized not
for the purpose of cooperating with the Federal Government;
and variable with respect to Kansas districts formed in valleys of natural watercourses,[255] sanitary drainage districts
of Nebraska,[256] and districts of New Mexico organized for
the purpose of cooperating with the Federal Government.[257]
Under all other laws, the membership is three (28 laws).

The terms of office of the members of the governing
board are as follows:

3 years (14 laws)---California (1923 law), Florida,
    Idaho, Kansas (for districts in which three-fifths
    of total land area are in absentee ownership, and
    for districts in valleys of natural watercourses,
    and also for districts under 1911 law), Montana,
    Nevada, North Carolina, South Carolina (1920 law),
    Utah, and West Virginia.
2 years (6 laws)---Colorado, New Mexico (for districts
    cooperating with the Federal Government), Tennessee,
    Texas, Washington (law of 1913) and Wyoming.
4 years (6 laws)---Arizona, California (1903 law), Kan-
    sas (1925 law), Louisiana (1924 law), Minnesota
    and Nebraska (for sanitary drainage districts).
5 years (4 laws)---Louisiana (1900 law), Missouri, Nebras-
    ka (1905, ch. 161), and Wisconsin.
6 years (3 laws)---Alabama, Mississippi (1912 law).
Variable (1 law)---For drainage districts of Nebraska
    and Washington (as amended in 1953) formed by vote
    of land owners, the tenure of a director is equal
    to number of directors, so that one will be reelect-
    ed each year.
Unknown---(9 laws)---Arkansas, California (1885 law),
    Delaware, Georgia, Illinois (1895 law), Kentucky
    (1918 law), New Mexico (ordinary drainage districts),
    South Carolina (1911 law) and Virginia.

In a great majority of the laws it is provided that the terms
of the members of the governing board of a drainage district
are overlapping.

With the exception of some laws in which internal organization is not provided for, and of three laws which provide
for no president or chairman,[258] the governing board of a
drainage district elects a president (23 laws)[259] or a chairman (7 laws)[260] or a chairman and a vice-chairman (5 laws)[261]
or a president and vice-president (under 1924 law of Louisiana), and elects or appoints a secretary (or secretary or
clerk in Minnesota, and clerk for sanitary drainage districts
in municipalities in Nebraska).[262] Most laws also provide
for a district treasurer, who is elected by the governing
board (5 laws),[263] appointed by the board (in Florida and
under the 1920 law of South Carolina), or elected or appointed

by the board (in Minnesota and under the 1918 law of Kentucky), or who is the secretary of the board264 or the county
treasurer265 in his ex-officio capacity. A number of laws
provide for the employment of an engineer or a chief engineer or engineers.266 Some laws provide for the appointment
of a superintendent of construction,267 a drainage commissioner (Kansas under L. 1911, ch. 168 and Oklahoma) or a
superintendent of drainage (both 1912 and 1918 laws of Kentucky). The drainage districts may usually appoint an attorney and sometimes also other necessary personnel.

In a number of instances, the authority of the governing
body of a drainage district in the conduct of the drainage
enterprise is limited in a number of ways. In cases in which
drainage districts are established after preliminary and final
surveys and investigations being made by board of viewers,
limitation is already imposed upon the governing board before
it is organized. This limitation is an important one, inasmuch as the final survey usually covers the engineering lay-
out of the drainage works to be constructed as well as an
assessment of benefits accruing to lands. Similar pre-organ-
ization limitations to the authority of the governing board
may exist even when no surveys are required for the establishment of the district. For example, under the Tennessee law,
after a drainage district is already established by order of
the county court, the said court appoints an engineer to plan
and lay out the improvement works, then appoints three commissioners to classify lands and make preparations for the
assessment of benefits, and finally appoints the board of
directors whose function it is to contract for the construction of and maintain the drainage works already planned prior
to its existence.

There are also other forms of limitations to the authority of the governing board of a drainage district. For example, as provided in the laws of Alabama and Minnesota and
the 1895 law of Washington, all improvement works have to be
adjudicated by the county court of probate (Alabama), the
district court (Minnesota) or the superior court (Washington).
Under the 1885 law of California, the district board of trustees does not assess the lands and the benefits accruing
thereto, but the assessment is made by three commissioners
specially appointed by the county board of supervisors. Under
the 1923 law of California, special "advisory elections" may
be called on any administrative problem of a district. With
respect to the sanitary drainage districts in municipalities
in Nebraska, drainage works must first be approved by the
state department of roads and irrigation, and then by vote
of landowners at special elections called simultaneously by
all county courts concerned.268

With respect to taxation of the drainage districts, the
1924 law of Louisiana provides for either annual acreage tax

not more than 50 cents per acre or ad-valorem special tax
levy. For drainage districts of Kansas formed in valleys of
natural watercourses, a peculiar and complicated financial
system is adopted. It includes an annual special tax levy
for the redemption of bond principals and interests, and two
kinds of benefit assessments. One kind of benefit assessments
is called "general benefit assessments" and are levied on all
lands at a uniform rate. The other kind is the "special benefit assessments", which is not different from the special
benefit assessments adopted in all other laws, being proportionate to the amount of benefits accruing to each lot of
land. It is to be observed that the first kind of benefit
assessments is in substance a special ad-valorem tax levy.
For sanitary drainage districts in municipalities in Nebraska, authority is given for the collection of either special
tax levy or special benefit assessment or both. Special tax
levy prevails in Arizona, California (1903 law) (and also
1919 law, but for maintenance of works only) and Texas (not
to exceed 0.5 percent). In all other laws, special benefit
assessment is the legal tax for drainage districts. But
uniform acreage tax is authorized to defray preliminary expenses in addition to special benefit assessment for construction and maintenance drainage works in Florida (not to exceed
fifty cents per acre), Kentucky (under 1918 law, not to exceed fifty cents per acre), Oregon (not to exceed one dollar
per acre) and South Carolina (under 1920 law, not to exceed
fifty cents per acre). In Florida, Idaho, Illinois (1895 law),
Kentucky (1918 law), Missouri, North Carolina and South Carolina (1920 law), there are separate benefit assessments for
construction and for maintenance; but in all other cases assessments are levied for construction and maintenance costs
combined. Construction assessments cover all costs of construction and are as a rule collected in annual installments.
Except in Oregon, where the benefit assessments constitute a
lien upon the agricultural crops instead of the land itself,
all forms of drainage district taxes are a lien upon the lands
from which the taxes are to be drawn. With a few exceptions,269
all drainage district laws permit the issuance of bonds. Under the laws of Arkansas, Illinois (1895), Kentucky (1918),
Nebraska (for all three kinds of districts), South Carolina
(1920) and Wisconsin, the district may also make loans. Federal aid is anticipated with respect to New Mexico drainage
districts organized for the special purpose of cooperating
with the Federal Government, New York district under the 1945
law, and in other cases where a district is authorized or
permitted to cooperate with the Federal Government. Indiana
law allows the use of county loans in financing drainage districts. In the Colorado law, the sale of public lands is
authorized.

        In many instances, the financial power of the drainage
districts is under one form of limitation or another. Under
the 1903 and 1923 laws of California, bonds can be issued

only after popular approval in special referenda. Under the
1925 Kansas law, bonds must be approved at a special election
if their total amount is in excess of five percent of the
assessed valuation of all taxable property within the district.
Under the 1924 law of Louisiana, the adoption of acreage tax
must be made at a special election. In Utah, the issue of
bonds must be approved by county courts. In West Virginia
and Wisconsin as well as in Louisiana under the 1900 act,
court approval is necessary for the levy of special benefit
assessments. In Washington under the 1913 law similar approval is given by the county administrative authorities.
In Minnesota, special benefit assessments are collected by
the county, although the law provides for the selection of a
non-ex-officio district treasurer.[270]

Drainage districts can also be formed by special state
laws. Some examples may be given. An act of 1909 of California (ch. 680) created the Yolo Basin Drainage District.
The act specified the boundaries of the district, and stipulated that it was to be under the control of a board of five
trustees and that the county board of supervisors of Yolo
County should appraise the lands and benefits to accrue thereto. Except for these modifying provisions, the general law
of 1885 still applied to this district. By an act of 1943
(ch. 369), the Legislature of California created the Sacramento and San Joaquin Drainage District to furnish cooperation
with the California Debris Commission of the Federal Government and appropriated $17,700,000 for this purpose. This
District enforces on behalf of the state the joint Federal-
state plan for the erection, maintenance, and protection of
embankments and levees and channel rectification works in the
Sacramento and San Joaquin Valleys. It is governed by a Reclamation Board of seven members appointed by and serving at
the pleasure of the governor, with the State Director of Finance of the state as its executive officer. The board elects
a president, appoints a secretary, and may appoint a general
manager, a chief engineer, an assistant secretary and other
employees. Besides its principal function mentioned above,
the board may also cooperate with the Federal Government in
its flood control enterprise. In addition, it has the peculiar authority of granting permits to private persons, reclamation districts, drainage districts, cities, etc., to construct or repair levees within its jurisdiction. The District
levies special benefit assessments as its own source of revenue. It may also sell and lease lands, and, after a favorable vote at a special referendum, issue bonds. By an act of
1887 of Illinois (Laws 1887, p. 126: Revised Statutes, ch. 42,
sec. 354 et seq.), the city of Chicago was organized as a special drainage district having authority to build drainage works
on the Des Plaines River (cut-offs and diversion works) and
the Mud Lake (a dam) and to levy special benefit assessments
therefor. Under the Swamp and Overflowed Land Grant Act of
28 September 1850, "Florida received over 20,000,000 acres.

The Everglades, embracing some 2,800,000 acres, was the largest single unit of this land . . . .   Acts of the State Legislature in 1905, 1907, and 1913 created an agency known as
the Everglades drainage district, with power to tax and issue bonds . . . .   This district has carried on drainage operations in the Everglades up to the present time."   These
operations were started in 1906 with the dredging of canals,
which now consist of six major canals and a number of minor
canals and laterals, with an aggregate length of over 400
miles.   "It also provided spillway structures with navigation
locks in its major canals and a low levee around the southern
shore of Lake Okeechobee.   Practically all this work was com-
plated prior to 1928.   Expenditures by the Everglades drainage district have totaled over $18,000,000."   Some 96,000 ac-
res of the originally unproductive land are thus reclaimed.[271]

The following is a list showing the accomplishments of
drainage districts in 28 states as of 1950:[272]

State	Number of enterprises	Acreage
Alabama	3	35,936
Arizona	2	3,385
Arkansas	229	4,506,440
California	102	1,202,950
Colorado	39	255,753
Florida	98	5,416,739
Georgia	35	69,485
Idaho	37	135,172
Illinois	1,089	4,787,745
Kansas	82	352,589
Louisiana	404	2,143,670
Maryland(?)	90	319,482
Mississippi	249	2,772,485
Missouri	315	3,137,944
Montana	22	94,172
Nebraska	112	581,848
Nevada	4	125,595
New Jersey(?)	1	4,300
New Mexico	5	52,113
North Carolina	115	684,586
Oregon	44	161,286
South Carolina	14	167,994
Tennessee	62	5,155,647
Utah	25	130,003
Washington	126	257,853
Wisconsin	68	299,051
Wyoming	17	84,116
Total(28 states)	3,210	33,530,379

5. Water-supply districts---Special districts for the
single or primary purpose of providing domestic and municipal

water supply are organized by both general and special laws.

(1) By special laws: The first special district organized for the purpose of water supply was created by a special
law. It is the Metropolitan Water District of Massachusetts,
which was established by an act of 1895. It comprises twenty
cities of Boston, Arlington, Belmont, and so forth. Its governing body is the Metropolitan District Commission, which
was created by an act of 1889 and which controls and directs
not only the Metropolitan Water District, but also the Metropolitan Sewage District (18 cities in the North System and
14 cities in the South System) and the Metropolitan Park
District (comprising 37 cities), which were respectively
created by acts of 1889 and 1893. The Commission is composed of a commissioner and four associate commissioners appointed by the governor with the consent of the council for
a term of six years. The commission may appoint a secretary
and necessary number of engineers and other employees. The
commissioner, as the administrative head of the Commission,
may set up a necessary number of divisions, and appoint a
director for each division. All costs and expenses of the
Commission are shared by the member cities or towns in proportion to the services and water received. Water may also
be sold to towns, companies and special districts which are
not members of the Metropolitan District. The Commission may
issue bonds.273 When the Commission was first organized in
1895, it acquired the water supply works of the city of Boston, which were built from 1848 to 1895. Since 1895, the
Commission has constructed additional works. "The Water Supply at present is from four water sheds, namely, Swift River,
Ware River, Nashua River and Sudbury River, each delivering
water through a system of aqueducts." On the Sudbury River,
there is the Sudbury Reservoir with a capacity of 7 billion
gallons, which was built in 1875; on the Nashua River, the
Wachusett Reservoir with a capacity of 65 billion gallons,
which was built in 1898; and on the Swift River, the Quabbin
Reservoir with a capacity of 415 billion gallons, which was
built in 1933. ". . . The four water sheds have a combined
storage of 496,000,000,000 gallons of water, and a safe yield
of 340,000,000 gallons per day." The Commission now serve
23 cities and towns, of which 3 must be outside the Dis-
trict.274

In 1916, a law was passed by New Jersey (ch. 70) (amended
by Laws 1919, ch. 30) which divided the entire state into two
water supply districts, namely, (1) North Jersey Water Supply
District, comprising counties of Sussex, Warren, Hinterdon,
Passaic, Morris, Monmouth, Somerset, Bergen, Hudson, Essex,
Union and Middlesex, and (2) South Jersey Water Supply District, which includes all other counties. Each district is
governed by a bi-partisan Water Supply Commission of five members, who are appointed by the Governor with the consent of
the Senate upon petition of any city located within the dis-

trict for overlapping terms of four years. The commission
annually coopts a chairman. It appoints a secretary, engineers, counsel and other necessary personnel. Both districts
are public corporations, and cities are free to join them.
Special water-supply district laws have also been passed in
recent years in Rhode Island, Texas, New York, Louisiana, etc.

(2) By general laws: General laws authorizing the establishment of special districts for the conduct of water
supply enterprise have been enacted in a number of states.
The laws of the following states may serve as examples.

New York---New York laws provide for the creation of three
kinds of water supply districts; namely, water districts (Town
Law of 1909, art. 12, as amended), union water districts
(Conservation Law, sec. 530 et seq.: Laws 1913, ch. 233; as
amended), and county water districts (County Law, art. 5A:
Laws 1953, ch. 868). 275 A water district is created by the
town board of the town in which it is situated upon petition
by owners of at least one-half real property of the district,
and is governed by the town board. Its expenses are met by
special benefit assessments, in anticipation of which bonds
may perhaps be issued. The union water district is composed
of a number of municipalities, including water districts.
Any three municipalities may propose the creation of a union
water district and call a meeting of all municipalities concerned for this purpose. The district is established if (1)
ten municipalities join or if (2) so many municipalities
join which have an aggregate population of 25,000. After a
union water district, other cities may join by petitioning
the board of trustees of the former. The board of trustees,
the governing body of a union water district, consist of the
chief executives of all member municipalities. It must adopt
a plan of operation, which is to be approved by the water
power and control commission of the state department of conservation. Costs of construction are shared by the member
municipalities.

The county water district, whose function it is to provide and sell to cities and other districts within its boundaries, is formed by resolution of the county board of supervisors of the county concerned upon the petition of the chief
executive of a city or a water district, or by 25 owners of
real property and, if so petitioned by 100 real property owners or 5 percent of them, after a referendum, which resolution should be confirmed by the State Comptroller. Its gov-
ing body consists of an officer, a board or other body appointed or designated by the board of supervisors of the county concerned. Special benefit assessment is the only means
of finance of the district.

California---California has several kinds of special districts for water supply, such as county water districts, met-

ropolitan water districts, county waterworks districts, county
water authorities, storm water districts, and so forth. The
first two kinds will be discussed here. County water districts
are provided in a law of 1913 (ch. 592), as amended. They
are formed by popular vote at a special election called by
the board of supervisors of the county concerned, upon petition of ten percent of voters at the last gubernatorial election. They may cover both urban and rural areas. Their governing body is a board of five directors, popularly elected
for overlapping terms of four years. It elects a president,
and appoints a general manager, a secretary, and an auditor.
If reservoirs are constructed, recreational facilities may be
operated by the districts thereon. Besides water charges or
rentals, the districts may levy a special ad-valorem property
tax called "water tax". Bonds may be issued if approved by
two-thirds of voters at a special referendum. The metropolitan water districts are provided in a law of 1927 (ch. 429),
as amended, and comprise two or more municipalities. Any
municiaplity to be included in a proposed metropolitan water
district may pass a resolution making the proposal to form
the district and transmit copies of it to all other municipalities concerned, the governing councils of which may either
approve or reject the proposal. If the proposal is approved
by one of these other municiaplities, a district may be created. In this case, the legislative body of the initiating
municipality may call a special election in all of the municipalities which have consented to the formation of the district. The district is formed if majority of voters are in
favor of the formation. The metropolitan water district is
governed by a board of directors, consisting of at least one
director from each of the participating municipalities. The
board elects a chairman, a vice-chairman and a secretary.
All directors serve a term of two years. In the board, each
municipality is a voting unit. The metropolitan water districts may finance their works by a special tax levy not exceeding five mills on a dollar of property valuation and by
the issue of bonds.

The Metropolitan Water District of Southern California,
formed in 1928, is the largest metropolitan water district
in California. The original members of the District were
Los Angeles and twelve other municipalities. By 1950, the
number of members had been increased to 28. The principal
function of the District is to construct the Colorado River
Aqueduct to transport the Colorado River diverted at the
Parker Dam to the District, which was constructed with a bond
issue of $220 million.[276] "The Colorado River Aqueduct was
completed in 1941, and today carries water over mountain and
desert for 242 miles, through tunnels, conduits, canals, and
siphons to distribute it to homes and industries of southern
California. With a capacity of 1,500 cubic feet of water per
second or approximately a billion gallons daily, it is the
largest single domestic water supply system in the world."
Under a contract with the U. S. Bureau of Reclamation, the

District draws 1,212,000 acre-feet each years from the Colorado River through the Colorado River Aqueduct.277 Besides
the Colorado River Aqueduct, the District has other auxiliary
water supply works. For example, in 1935 it purchased from
the City of Pasadena the Morris Dam and Reservoir on the San
Gabriel Canyon, which the said city built in 1932 and completed in May 1934.278

Washington---In 1929 a law was passed providing for the creation of water districts (ch. 114, last amended by Laws 1953,
ch. 251). A water district may include one or more cities
or towns in any county. It is created by a majority vote at
a special election called by the county commissioners upon
petition of 25 percent of the electors of the district (after
a hearing of course). It is governed by a board of three
water commissioners popularly electeded for overlapping terms
of six years, who coopt a president and a secretary. The
board adopts a comprehensive plan, which, however, must be
approved by popular vote. With approval of three-fifths of
voters voting at a special election or referendum at which at
least 40 percent of all qualified voters must be present,
the board may incur indebtedness to carry out the said plan
to be redeemed by a special tax levy not exceeding two mills
on the dollar. Bonds may be issued for other uses after approval by ordinary majority vote at a special election. The
water district may also levy special benefit assessments.

Illinois ---On 25 July 1945, an act enacted authorizing the
creation of public water districts, which must include not
more than half a million population. A public water district
is formed at a special election called by the county judge
of the county in which the entire district or a major portion thereof is situated, upon petition by 100 voters (after
hearing of course). Its governing body is a board of five
trustees, which are appointed by the said judge for overlapping terms of five years. The board elects a chairman and a
vice-chairman, and appoints a secretary and a treasurer. It
may also appoint a general manager, an attorney, one or more
engineers, and other employees. Public water districts do
not have the authority to tax. They may issue revenue bonds,
but not other bonds. On 2 August 1951, an act was passed providing for the establishment of water authorities. They are
created in the same way as the public water districts, except
that the petition is made by 500 instead of 100 voters. Their
governing board consists of three trustees, appointed by the
county judge for overlapping terms of three years. It elects
a chairman and a secretary, and appoints a treasurer, an engineer, an attorney and other personnel. Its administrative
functions, which happen to be also the functions of the water
authority, are listed in the 1951 law as follows:

    1. To make inspections of wells, or other withdrawal
facilities, and to require information and data from the

owners or operators thereof concerning the supply, withdrawal and use of water.

2. To require the registration with them (i.e. the
board of trustees) of all wells or other withdrawal facilities in accordance with such form or forms as they deem
advisable.

3. To require permits from them for all additional
wells or withdrawal facilities or for the deepening, extending or enlarging existing wells or withdrawal facilities.

4. To require the plugging of abandoned wells or
the repair of any well or withdrawal facility to prevent
loss of water or contamination of supply.

5. To reasonably regulate the use of water and during any period of actual or threatened shortage to establish limits upon or priorities as to the use of water.

6. To supplement the existing water supply or provide additional water supply by such means as may be
practicable or feasible. They may acquire property or
property rights either within or without the boundaries
of the authority by purchase, lease, condemnation proceedings or otherwise, and they may construct, maintain
and operate wells, reservoirs, pumping stations . . . .
They shall have the right to sell water to municipalities
or public utilities operating water distribution systems
either within or without the authority.

It is interesting to note that functions 1 through 5 are in
the nature of ground water regulation and that only function
6 is concerned with water supply enterprise. Since special
districts are generally formed to undertake some enterprise
or enterprises, the regulatory function of Illinois water
authorities is worthy of our special attention. The water
authorities may issue bonds, and may also "levy and collect
a general tax on all of the taxable property within the corporate limits of the authority, the aggregate amount of which
for one year, exclusive of the amount levied for bonded indebtedness or interest thereon, shall not exceed 0.08 percent of the full fair cash value as equalized or assessed by
the Department of Revenue . . . ."

6. Electric power districts---In a number of states,
laws have been in force which allow the creation of districts
whose function it is to generate and/or distribute electric
energy (both hydro and fuel). Nebraska laws provide for the
organization of public power districts (Revised Statutes,
ch. 70, art. 6: Laws 1933, ch. 86, as amended).[279] They are
established by order of the State Department of Roads and
Irrigation upon petition of 15 percent of electors in each
proposed district (after hearing). Their governing body is
a board of 5-21 directors, who serve for overlapping terms
of six years. First directors are named in the petition for
establishment and are automatically appointed by the said

department when it issues the order of establishment. But
their successors are popularly elected. The board of directors elects a president and a vice-president, and appoints a
secretary, a treasurer, a general manager, and other employees. All public power districts have the power to borrow
money, but they do not possess the taxing power.

The Loup River Public Power District, formed in 1933, is
the only public power district engaged in hydroelectric power
development. With loans (about $10 million) and grants (a-
bout $5 million) of the Public Works Administration, the Dis-
trict constructed two hydroelectric plants, one at Monroe
and the other at Columbus, which have a combined generating
capacity of 48,150 kilowatts. It has also constructed transmitting sub-stations and lines. In 1939, the state-wide
Consumers Public Power District was created which, in 1942,
acquired all of the private electric utility companies (with
the exception of the Nebraska Power Company which serves
the City of Omaha and vicinity), thus exercising a virtual
monopoly of the business of selling electric energy in the
state of Nebraska. On 1 March 1946, the Consumers Public
Power District entered into an agreement with the Loup River
Public Power District and two Public Power and Irrigation Districts (to be discussed later), whereby the latter purchased
all of the former's major steam power plants and the former
agreed to purchase all of its power supply for its easter
system, that is, the area east of the North Platte River,
from the latter.[280] From these facts, it may be seen that
in Nebraska the business of both generating and selling commercial electric power, both hydro and fuel, is entirely in
the hands of the public.[281]

In Arizona, there are two kinds of power districts; namely, power districts (Code, ch. 75, art. 10: Laws 1919, ch.
173, as amended) and electrical districts (Code, ch. 75, art.
6: Laws 1923, ch. 7). The former are formed at a special
election called by the board of supervisors of the county in
which the proposed district or a larger portion thereof is
located, upon petition of five or more landowners concerned.
Their governing body is a board of five directors popularly
elected for terms of two years, which elects a president and
appoints a secretary and other employees. Power districts
are empowered to issue bonds and to collect a special ad-
valorem property tax. An electrical district is formed by
special election called by the board of supervisors of the
county in which the district or a major portion thereof is
situated, upon petition by one-third of all land owners or by
25 land owners in the district. It is governed by a board
of seven directors popularly elected for terms of three years.
By special election the number of the directors may be increased to 15 or reduced to 3. The board annually elects a chairman and a vice-chairman. It elects a treasurer, and elects
or appoints a secretary. With the approval of electors, the

board may issue bonds maturing in not more than 30 years.
Electrical districts may raise their "administration expenses" by special tax levy (uniform ad-valorem property tax)
and their "general burdens" by special acreage tax. The
Salt River Agricultural Improvement and Power District, one
of the power districts of Arizona, generates 71,350 kilowatts
of hydro, 30,000 kilowatts of steam and 10,000 kilowatts of
internal combustion electric energy. The Gila Valley Power
District, another power district of Arizona, does not generate electric energy, but transmits purchased energy.[282]

A Texas law of 1927 (Revised Civil Statutes, art. 7807d)
permits the formation of water power control districts. The
procedure is the same as that of water improvement districts
discussed before. Water power control districts are governed
by a board of directors, the number of whom is equal to that
of divisions into which a district may be divided, and who
are popularly elected to serve a term of two years, each
director representing one division. These districts may finance their expenses by special tax levy (ad-valorem property
tax) and borrowing. An example of these districts is the
Red Bluff Water Power Control District. Its enterprise consists primarily of a storage reservoir constructed on the
Pecos River, extending in Reeves and Loving Counties of Texas
and Eddy County of New Mexico. It is 300,000 acre-feet in
capacity and is used primarily for irrigation. As a subsidiary part of the enterprise, 780 horsepower of hydroelectric
power is developed.[283]

Besides the above-mentioned states, laws authorizing the
establishment of power districts have also been enacted by
Wyoming (1931), Alabama (1935), Nevada (1935), Tennessee (1935),
Mississippi (1936), and South Dakota (1950, replacing the
1935 law).

7. Sanitation districts---In many states special districts
may be formed for the purpose of sewage disposal, which is
the central work in water pollution control. There are also
special districts formed for mosquito control. The former
are designated as "sanitary districts", "sewer districts" or
"sewerage districts".[284] The Sanitary District Act of 29 May
1889 of Illinois is perhaps the first general sewerage disposal district law ever enacted by a state in the United
States. Under this act, as amended (Revised Statutes, ch. 42,
sec. 320 et seq.), a sanitary district is formed for the purpose of providing surface drainage and sewage disposal.[285]
Incidentally, docks facilitating navigation of and hydroelectric plants utilizing the waterpower inherent in drainage or
sewage-disposal canals may be constructed by the district.
But sanitary districts have no authority to construct navigation-improvement or power-development works on natural watercourses. A sanitary district is created by popular vote at
a special election called by the county judge of the county

in which the district is located upon petition of 5,000 voters. It is governed by a board of nine trustees, who are popularly elected for overlapping terms of six years. The board elects a president and a vice-president, and appoints a clerk, a treasurer, a chief engineer, a general superintendent and an attorney as its principal officers. The sanitary districts may borrow money and, after referendum, issue bonds; but the total indebtedness of a district at any time shall not exceed five percent of the total assessed valuation of all taxable property within the district. Improvements of the districts may be defrayed either by special benefit assessments or by special ad-valorem tax levy or by both combined.

The Chicago Sanitary District, which has undertaken the largest sewerage project,[286] was organized in 1890 under this act[287] for the sole purpose of preventing the discharge of sewage into Lake Michigan, in order to safeguard the public water supply."[288] The District comprises about 470 square miles, and serves 71 cities and villages having a total population of about 4,332,000.[289] The Chicago Sanitary and Ship Canal is the main sewage canal of the District. Its construction was commenced in 1892 and completed in 1900. It connects the Chicago River with the Des Plaines River, which flows southwest to the Illinois River and thence to the Mississippi River, and carries the sewage of the District into the Gulf of Mexico, while before the construction of the canal it was discharged into Lake Michigan, which is the source of the municipal water of the Chicago area, thus protecting Lake Michigan from being polluted by municipal sewage.[290] The Canal is 30 miles in length, and has a depth of 34 feet and a bottom width varying from 160 to 202 feet. Control works were constructed by the District at the mouth of the Chicago River under the authority of the River and Harbor Act (U. S.) of 3 March 1899, and are operated by the District under the direction of the Corps of Engineers of the U. S. Army.[291] The main Canal and its auxiliary canals total 58 miles, which receive sewage through more than 200 miles of intercepting sewers constructed by the District, which carry sewage and street drainage collected in sewers and drains built and operated by each of the 71 municipalities in the District. All sewage is treated in seven plants built and operated by the District before entering the canals. "A power plant was built at Lockport to recover energy from the canal as it drops to the level of the Des Plaines River. The District produces about 75,000,000 kilowatts-hours per year, about two-thirds of its requirements."[292] The Chicago Sanitary and Ship Canal, incidentally, too, is part of the Illinois Waterway, a navigation-improvement project of the Federal Government. It should finally be mentioned that the District owns nine wharves and partially owns six wharves, all of which are located on the Illinois Waterway.[293]

On 5 June 1911, another general law authorizing the creation of sanitary districts was passed by the Legislature of
Illinois. Under the provisions of this act, as amended (Revised Statutes, ch. 42, sec. 277 et seq.), a sanitary district
for the single purpose of sewage disposal is created by a
majority vote at a referendum called by the county judge upon
petition by 300 voters resident in two cities of a county.
It is governed by a board of five trustees appointed by the
county board of commissioners for overlapping terms of five
years, each trustee representing a ward. The board may levy
annual property taxes and may issue bonds, but the total indebtedness of the district must not exceed five percent of
all taxable property in the district at any time. The board
may not only construct and maintain sewage disposal works,
but it also has the regulatory authority to stop and prevent
pollution of all water sources.

Presumably under the authority of this law, "the East
Peoria sanitary district was created on December 30, 1927,
after the earlier flood of that year. It succeeded to the
right-of-way of the former Farm Creek drainage and levee
district and, except for the omission of certain areas in the
north and west parts of the city, its boundaries coincide
roughly with the city limits of East Peoria. An extensive
program of improvement (on the Farm Creek, Illinois) was
carried out in 1928-29, involving (a) straightening and enlarging the channel for three-quarters of a mile above the
work through East Peoria, completed in 1896; (b) a spillway
and relief channel with bottom width of 50 feet extending
north to the Illinois River; (c) widening and deepening the
main channel to a bottom width of 84 feet above the diversion
channel referred to above and a width of 70 feet downstream
from it, . . . together raising the levees to 15 feet above
bottom of channel; (d) channel improvements and levees on
small tributaries entering Farm Creek within the city; and
(e) bridge alterations and relocation of public utilities."[294]

Among the general laws authorizing the creation of special
district for the single purpose of sewage disposal of other
states, mention may be made of the sanitary district laws of
New York (Public Health Law, art. 5-A, sec. 90 et seq.: Laws
1932, ch. 132), Oregon (urban, Rev. Stats., sec. 450.305 et
seq.: L. 1917, ch. 293; rural, ibid., sec. 450.005 et seq.: L.
1935, ch. 385, as last amended by L. 1955, ch. 442) and West
Virginia (West Virginia Code, sec. 1408 (1) et seq., enacted
1933). In all these states, sanitary districts are created at
special elections called by local courts concerned upon petition of a certain number of voters (100 in New York, 10 in Oregon and 400 in West Virginia). In New York, a sanitary district
is governed by a commission composed of three commissioners appointed by the justice of the supreme court of the judicial
district concerned. "The sanitary district commission may
from time to time petition the board of supervisors, or the
several boards of supervisors where the whole or parts of

more than one county are included in the sanitary district,
to issue bonds in amounts to be set forth in said petition,
to pay for the construction of all or any part of a sewerage
system to serve the district . . . . The bonds shall be a
charge against the county . . ." Annual special tax levy,
by the name of "sewer tax", may be made after similar approval
by the county or counties concerned. Oregon rural sanitary
districts are governed by a board of three to five members
popularly elected for overlapping terms of three years, which
may issue bonds after special referenda and may collect taxes.
The governing board of West Virginia sanitary districts consists of three trustees appointed by the county court with
the consent of the governing body of the largest city in the
district for overlapping terms of three years. It may issue
bonds and collect a special annual ad-valorem property tax
not exceeding one third of one percent on assessed valuation
thereof.

      In California, Utah, Florida, Illinois, Virginia, Arkan-
sas and Montana, general laws have been enacted permitting
and providing for the organization of special districts for
the single purpose of mosquito control. Under the laws of
California (Health and Safety Code, Division 3, ch. 5: Statutes 1915, ch. 584, as amended), a mosquito abatement district, which must contain at least 100 persons, may be created by order of the board of supervisors of the county in
which the district or a larger portion thereof is situated,
upon petition by ten percent of all voters in the district
(according to next preceding gubernatorial election). It is
governed by a board of five trustees appointed by the county
and city governing bodies concerned for overlapping terms of
two years.295 It elects a president and a secretary. Special ad-valorem property tax may be collected by the county
authorities on behalf of the board of trustees to finance the
expenses of the district. If regular levy is insufficient,
the said authorities may collect additional taxes after approval by referendum called by the board of trustees. But the
board of trustees may borrow money. Utah mosquito abatement
districts, which also must contain 100 people (each district),
are created in exactly the same way as Califronia districts,
and are governed by a board of five trustees, of whom one is
appointed by each of the municipalities included and the rest
are appointed by the county governing board.296 The trustees
serve for overlapping terms of two years, and they elect a
president and a secretary, as the trustees of California districts.   The financial power is also the same as that of the
latter, except that Utah districts have no express borrowing
power.   Nevada mosquito abatement district law (as amended)
is substantially the same as that of Utah law, the only difference being that Nevada districts may borrow money but
cannot levy taxes while the reverse if true with Utah districts. Illinois mosquito abatement districts (1927, as
amended) must contain at least 300 people, and are created

by the county judge upon petition by five percent of voters
or by 25 voters. They are governed by a board of five trustees appointed by the said judge for a tenure of four years,
who annually elect a president, a secretary and a treasurer.
Illinois districts may levy a special ad-valorem property tax
not exceeding a rate of 0.25 percent, but they have no power
to borrow money.[297]

Florida laws provide for the organization of two kinds
of mosquito control districts; namely, mosquito-control districts (Statutes, ch. 389: Laws 1925, ch. 10178) and anti-
mosquito districts (Ibid., ch. 388: Laws 1929, ch. 13570).
The former are created by special election called by the
board of county commissioners upon petition by 15 percent of
land owners in the district. They are governed by a board of
five commissioners popularly elected for overlapping terms of
four years. The board elects a chairman, a vice-chairman and
a secretary-treasurer, and may employ a manager and other officers. Expenses of the districts are financed by special ad-
valorem property taxes not exceeding 1.5 mills on the dollar
of property valuation, which must be approved at biennial
elections. The borrowing power is not granted to them. Anti-
mosquito districts are coterminous with counties and are created by special election called by the county commissioners
upon petition by ten percent of land owners in a district.
Their governing body is a board of three commissioners appointed by the governor for a tenure of four years, whose successors, however, are to be popularly elected for the same tenure.
The state health officer or his delegate is an ex-officio
member of the governing boards of all anti-mosquito districts.
The board elects a chairman, a vice-chairman and a secretary-
treasurer. It annually adopts a plan of operation, which must
be approved by the state board of health. Anti-mosquito districts may incur indebtedness. They may also levy special
ad-valorem property taxes, the total amount of which shall
not exceed $10,000-25,000 in a county of 65,000 population or
less, $20,000-50,000 in a county of 65,000-265,000 population
and $20,000-100,000 in a county of 265,000 population or more.

Virginia mosquito control districts bear a close resemblance to Florida anti-mosquito districts in some administrative features. Instead of being co-terminous with one county,
they are made up of one or more counties, cities or towns, or
a county and a city, a county and a town or a city and a town,
and they are created entirely by administrative action of the
local unit or units concerned without election or petition.
They are governed by a mosquito-control commission of three
members, one member being a deputy of the state health commissioner, who shall also be the ex-officio chairman of the commission, and the other two to be designated by the governing
body or bodies of the local units concerned. The commission
is authorized to levy a special property tax not exceeding 25
cents per $100 of assessed property value, to be collected by
the governing body or bodies of the local units concerned.

Contributions may be made to a mosquito control district
which shall not exceed the amount of the taxes collected nor
exceed $5,000 in any year.

The mosquito abatement districts of Arkansas (1953) are
created by the county court concerned (which is both the county governing body and a court) upon petition by 15 percent
of the voters in a proposed district, and after two special
elections or referenda. One referendum is to decide upon
the question whether the district should be established and
the other is to determine whether a special tax may be levied,
which tax shall, however, not exceed seven mills per dollar
per year. The mosquito abatement district is governed by a
commission of five members appointed by the county court for
overlapping terms of five years, plus the state health officer as an _ex-officio_ non-voting "co-operating" member. The
commission elects a president and a secretary-treasurer, and
may employ a director and other necessary personnel All
working plans must be approved by the state health officer
(Acts 1953, No. 222).

Montana mosquito control districts (Laws 1953, ch. 183)
are established by the board of county commissioners concerned
upon petition by 25 percent of the residential freeholders
within a proposed district. The county board appoints a mosquito control board of 3-5 members for overlapping terms of
three years as the governing body of a mosquito control district. The board elects a chairman and a secretary and may
appoint other needed personnel. "The health officer having
jurisdiction in the proposed district, sanitarian or a member
of his staff, and the county extension agent, if the county
has any, or all such officer, shall be ex-officio members of
such board without vote." Mosquito control districts are
financed by a special tax levy not exceeding the annual rate
of 5 mills per dollar, the proceeds of which are to be deposited in the mosquito control fund established by the board
of county commissioners.

As of March 1951, there were in Florida three mosquito
control districts, five mosquito abatement districts and six
anti-mosquito districts; in Illinois, ten mosquito abatement
districts; and in Utah, four mosquito abatement districts.[298]
By September 1951, there were 48 mosquito abatement districts
in California.[299]

8. Park districts---Park districts are created under the
authority of either general or special state laws. In fact,
the first park district, the Metropolitan Park District of
Massachusetts, was created in 1893 by a special act of Massachusetts.[300] General laws providing for the formation of park
districts are in force in a number of states:

In Illinois, prior to 8 July 1947, there were four kinds

of park districts governed by different laws, to wit:

(1) Act of 19 June 1893: <u>Pleasure driveway and park districts</u>
(2) Act of 24 June 1895: <u>Submerged land park districts</u>
(3) Another act of 24 June 1895: <u>Park districts</u>
(4) Act of 29 May 1911: <u>Township park districts</u>

On 8 July 1947 a law was enacted consolidating all these laws but providing for only three kinds of park districts, namely, <u>pleasure driveway</u> and <u>park districts</u>, <u>submerged land park districts</u> and <u>township park districts</u>. All three kinds of districts are created at a special election or referendum called by the county judge upon petition by 100 voters. All of them may, after approval by referenda, issue bonds and levy taxes. The pleasure driveway and park districts are governed by a president and six trustees, who are popularly elected for a tenure of two years. The submerged land park districts are governed by five commissioners popularly elected for overlapping terms of six years. The governing body of the township park districts consists of three commissioners appointed by the county judge, the term of office of each of whom is to be fixed by the said judge.

North Dakota laws (<u>Code</u>, tit. 40, ch. 49: Laws 1905, ch. 143, as amended) provide for the organization of <u>park districts</u>, whose function it is to acquire, maintain and improve parks, boulevards and ways, and pleasure grounds. They are created by ordinance of a city or a village. A park district created by a city is governed by a board of five commissioners popularly elected for overlapping terms of six years, and a district created by a village is governed by a board of three commissioners popularly elected for overlapping terms of three years. The board of a park district elects a president and a vice-president, and may employ necessary personnel. But the city or village treasurer and engineer shall respectively be its <u>ex-officio</u> treasurer and engineer and surveyor. All park districts may levy either special benefit assessments or special <u>ad-valorem</u> property tax or both, and may issue bonds. But the <u>ad-valorem</u> tax shall not exceed 3 mills on the dollar of property valuation, excluding, however, levies for payment of debt principals and interests. The rate may be increased up to 10 mills on the dollar if authorized by a majority vote at any regular election.

In Washington there are <u>metropolitan park districts</u> (Revised Code, ch. 35.61: Laws 1907, ch. 98; as last amended by L. 1953, chs. 194 and 269), which are formed of a city of the first class and some contiguous area and are created by the ordinance of the city council either in its own initiative or upon petition by 15 percent of voters of the city, subject to the approval of a majority of voters at a special election

called for this pupose. Their governing body is board of
five park commissioners popularly elected for overlapping
terms of five years, who coopt a president and a clerk. The
function of the metropolitan park districts is to acquire
and improve lands either within or without the district for
parks, parkways, boulevards, playgrounds and aviation landings. The districts may levy a special ad-valorem property
tax at a rate not higher than 2 mills on the dollar and incur
indebtedness not exceeding 0.25 percent of all taxable property, which may be increased to 5 percent if authorized by
three-fifths of voters. Improvements of local nature may
be financed by special benefit assessments.

General park-district laws are also found in New York
(1909), Minnesota (1909), Ohio (1911), California (1939) and
Oregon (1941).

Park districts may also be created by special state laws.
The Metropolitan Parks District of Massachusetts was established by a special act of 1893. It comprises 37 cities, including Boston. Its governing authority is the Metropolitan
District Commission, which was discussed before. By an act
of 1895, the Metropolitan Parks District was authorized to
police the Charles River Basin with view to preserving its
recreational values. This constitutes perhaps the only case
in which a park district is intrusted with regulatory authority in addition to its enterprise functions. The expenses
of the District are apportioned among the member cities.

A law of Michigan of 1939 (Acts 1939, No. 147)[301] authorized the electorates of the Counties of Wayne, Washtenaw,
Livingston, Oakland and Macomb, or certain parts of these
counties to form the Huron-Clinton Metropolitan Authority for
the acquisition, construction and operation of parks, recreational grounds and/or limited access highways, either within or without the district.[302] The Authority is governed by
a board of commissioners, composed of two commissioners appointed by the governor of the state for terms of four years
and one commissioner elected by voters of each of the member
counties for a term of six years. The board is empowered to
levy a special ad-valorem property tax not exceeding 0.25
mills on the dollar of assessed property valuation, and to
issue bonds. The Huron-Clinton Metropolitan Authority was
established in 1940 by popular vote comprising all of the
above-mentioned five counties and covering the scenic valleys
of the Huron and Clinton Rivers. It consists of the following units: (1) St. Clair Metropolitan Beach (in Macomb County), (2) Marshbank Metropolitan Park (in Oakland County), (3)
Kensington Metropolitan Park (in Livingston and Oakland Counties), (4) Dexter-Huron Metropolitan Park (in Washtenaw County) and (5) Lower Huron Metropolitan Park (in Wayne County).
The St. Clari Beach is situated on Lake St. Clair and has an
area of 550 acres, being the largest controlled fresh-water

beach in the world. The beach itself is a stretch of 55
acres of fine sand with a length of about one mile. The
bathhouse has facilities for 6,000 people. The Marshbank
Park, 115 acres in area, is located in the famed lake region
of Oakland County, with a total of 2,800 front feet on two
of the largest lakes, Orchard and Cass. Kensington Park,
with an area of 4,000 acres, is the District's largest recreational unit. Recreational activities center around the
1,200-acre dam-impounded island-studded Kent Lake, and two
beaches, Martindale and Maple, which are respectively 1,000
feet and 600 feet long. Boating, fishing and picknicking
are available in all of the five units and camping and hiking
in most units.[303] Development work in none of the five units
of the District is complete but is merely underway. Except
the food service at the St. Clair Beach, which is handled by
a concessionaire, all recreational facilities are activities
are directly operated by the Authority itself.[304]

The State of New York has a number of park or parkway
authorities, which were all created by special state acts
during the 1930's and the early 1940's and which are governed
by boards consisting entirely of state or local officials
or officials of nearby state parks in an ex-officio capacity.
All these authorities have power to issue bonds, but they
have no taxing power.[305] However, these authorities appear
more like state agencies than special districts.

The Greenwood Recreation District, South Carolina, was
also established by a special act (Acts 1949, No. 338; as
last amended by Acts 1952, No. 875). It comprises the city
of Greenwood and its suburbs lying within school district
no. 18 as of 1 January 1952, and its functions are the construction and administration of parks and the conduct of recreational activities. It is governed by a commission of recreation, which is made up of the city manager of the city of
Greenwood, two members appointed by the governor for overlapping terms of three years upon the recommendation of the
said city and two members appointed in the same way for the
same terms upon the recommendation of the school district
no. 18. The district is authorized to levy a special annual
property tax not exceeding 2 mills per dollar.

The number of park districts in the United States, their
ages and numbers of parks included therein, as of 1950, are
given in the following table:[306]

State	Number of districts	Number of parks	Total acreage
California	14	36	4,252
Illinois	25	388	10,768
Massachusetts	1	36	13,128
Michigan	1	5	6,600
New York	1	8	218

North Dakota	1	6	200
Ohio	2	18	15,820
Oregon	1	2	20
Washington	2	53	1,763
Total	48	552	52,769

The Cleveland Metropolitan Park District, Ohio is the largest
park district in the United States. The Boston Metropolitan
Park District, Massachusetts, having an area of 13,128 acres,
is the second largest.[307]

9. Soil conservation districts---Soil conservation districts are established for the primary purpose of facilitating the administration of Federal technical and financial
assistance to private farmers as provided in the Act of 29
February 1936 (49 Stat. 1148), which is amendatory of the
Soil Conservation Act of 1935, as extended by subsequent
acts.[308] As a measure of promoting the organization of soil
conservation districts, the Department of Agriculture of the
United States, after consultation with representatives of
the several states, on 13 May 1936 published a "Standard Soil
Conservation Districts Act", as a model for legislation by the
several states and territories. This document calls for the
establishment in each state of a state soil conservation
committee. A soil conservation district is to be established by a majority vote of the farmers at a special election
called by this committee upon petition by at least 25 farmers and after hearing. It is governed by a board of five
supervisors of whom two are appointed by the state committee
and three elected by the farmers. All supervisors serve for
overlapping terms of three years. The board has the authority in all three fields of administration with respect to
soil conservation, namely, enterprise, regulation and assistance to private persons. The districts may receive Federal
and state monetary grants and "require money, services, etc.,
from land occupiers for benefits received" (i.e. special
benefit assessments), but they have no power to levy taxes
on property nor to incur indebtedness. Indiana, which enacted a soil conservation district act on 11 March 1937, was
the first state responding to this Federal action. By May
1947, all states and territories had enacted a soil conservation district act. All these state and territorial acts
follow closely the pattern of the "model act" above discussed, with only insubstantial changes or modifications.[309]
As of February 1952, "more than 2,400 soil conservation districts have been organized. They blanket 76 percent of the
country's agricultural land and includes more than 80 percent of all farms of the Nation."[310]

The principal work of the soil conservation districts is
to make soil survyes and investigations and to assist the
individual farmers or groups of farmers in formulating their

farm or soil conservation plans. As of 1 July 1950, surveys
made by the soil conservation districts in the whole nation
covered 334,770,000 acres of land, and 870,000 farm plans
had been made with their assistance and guidance.[311] The
soil conservation districts generally do not undertake any
soil conservation enterprise measures by themselves, except
that in some states the soil conservation districts operate
tree and shrub nurseries to furnish planting stock to private
farmers, with the technical assistance of the U. S. Soil Conservation Service.[312]

10. **Miscellaneous kinds of single-purpose special districts**---In California there are water conservation districts
organized for the conservation and storage of ground water
(1927, by Stats. 1949, ch. 846). A water conservation district
is created by popular vote at a special election called by
the board of supervisors of the county in which the proposed
district or a major portion thereof is situated, upon petition by landowners, and is governed by a board of three to
five directors popularly elected every two years. The board
is authorized to levy special taxes. The Santa Clara Valley
Water Conservation District, organized in 1929 and having an
area of 133,000 acres, is an outstanding example of such districts. It has constructed five storage reservoirs, ground
water spreading works consisting of low check dams on the
Alamitos Creek, the Guadalupe River and the Los Gatos Creek,
and a number of off-channel units through which water is diverted to canals over gravel areas where it is percolated
underground.[313] These works were constructed in 1935 and
1936. During the five years of their operation, the ground
water supply was augmented by nearly 80 percent.[314]

The Artesian Conservancy Districts of New Mexico (Statutes
ch. 77, art. 13: Laws 1931, ch. 97 and Laws 1941, ch. 98) are
of similar nature. As originally provided in the 1931 law,
their function is to conserve artesian waters. Other kinds
of ground water are added by the 1941 law. Each district
covers one or more aquifers. It is created by the district
court of the county in which the proposed district or a
larger portion thereof is situated, upon petition by owners
of more than one-third of all real property in district
either in acreage or in value. It is governed by a board of
six directors elected by land owners in six separate divisions for overlapping terms of six years. The board elects
a chairman, who is the president of the district, and elects
or appoints a secretary-treasurer. Each year the board adopts
a plan or program of water conservation, which may include
such measures as the plugging of leaking and abandoned wells.
The districts may levy special property taxes to be collected
by the respective county treasurers of the counties concerned,
and may raise funds by loans in anticipation of taxes. The
Pecos Valley Artesian Conservancy District is an example of
such districts. It was established in 1932. "The boundaries

. . . are approximately 12 miles in width and 60 miles in length." "The primary duty of the Conservancy District was to plug all leaking and abandoned artesian wells. A rotary rig was built for this job, then later another rig was built to keep up with plugging." "The Conservancy District today has plugged 850 artesian wells, included in the District was declared closed by the state engineer in 1932. Another work performed by the Pecos Valley District is concrete-lining of irrigation ditches, which was started March 1951. By 1 November 1951 approximately four miles of ditches had been lined.315

Texas laws provide for the organization of <u>water control and preservation districts</u> for the purpose of salinity control (<u>Revised Civil Statutes</u>, art. 7809 et seq., enacted 1918). A water control and preservation district is created by popular referendum called by the commissioners court or courts (in joint session) of the county or counties concerned upon petition by 25 tax-payers. It is governed by a board of three directors appointed by the county commissioners court. The board may levy taxes and, with popular approval issue bonds. Florida laws permit the organization of <u>erosion prevention districts</u> for the purpose of beach erosion prevention (<u>Statutes</u>, ch. 158: Laws 1941, ch. 20926). An erosion prevention district covers one or more election precincts of a county, and is created by a majority vote at a referendum called by the county commissioners upon petition by 20 percent of registered voters in each precinct concerned. Its governing body is a board of three commissioners appointed by the governor of the state for a tenure of four years. It shall adopt a plan of the construction of bulkheads, seawalls and other control works, and may employ an engineer, an attorney and clerks. The costs of the district are financed by Federal aids and special property taxes and bonds in anticipation thereof.

In 1933, the Oregon Legislature passed the Oregon Improvement District Act (ch. 439). The <u>improvement district</u> has the primary function of reforestation. It is established by the county court concerned upon petition by a majority of owners of logged-off or burned-over lands. It is under the government of a board of three directors to be elected by the land owners for overlapping terms of three years. The county treasurer serves as <u>ex-officio</u> treasurer of the district. The board classifies the lands, apply to the state agricultural college for the detail of soil experts and prepares and submits to the state relief committee a plan of improvement of the lands. The improvement districts are entitled to use county funds, and to issue bonds after popular approval. Under the laws of Massachusetts, "two or more cities or towns in any county, or two or more cities and towns of two or more contiguous counties, may in a city by vote of the city council thereof, and in a town by vote of the town,

with the permission of the Chief Moth Superintendent (of the
Division of Forestry) and upon approval of the Commissioner
(of the Department of Conservation), form a district for the
purpose of combining their efforts in the suppression of the
insect pests described as public nuisances, . . . and Dutch
elm disease, and may combine and pool and pay over to the
district treasurer . . . appropriations made for such purpose
and all payments made by the Commonwealth to such cities and
towns, together with any sums received from the Federal Government or any other source, for such suppression . . ."
"Persons engaged in such work shall be employees of the cities and towns in the district where they are domiciled and
not employees of the district . . ." (General Laws, ch. 132,
sec. 18A: Acts 1949, ch. 174; as amended by Acts 1952, ch.
489).

Texas wind erosion districts, which are co-terminous with
counties, are created by special election called by the county commissioners' court upon petition by 50 land owners. The
governing body consists of the county judge as chairman and
county commissioners. The county treasurer and county clerk
serve ex officio as district treasurer and district clerk
respectively. The districts may levy special benefit assessments, accept Federal aid, and borrow money. Montana is the
only state which permits the organization of grazing districts under state laws (Revised Codes, tit. 46, ch. 23:
Laws 1939, ch. 208, as amended). A grazing district is
created by the state grass conservation commission upon petition by three or more livestock operators. It may exist for
not more than 40 years. Its functions are to purchase or
market livestock and livestock products, to acquire grazing
lands, to make range improvements, and so forth. For any
or all of these purposes, money may be borrowed. No provision is made of the organization of the board of directors.
Since the objective of the enabling act is to provide cooperation as envisaged by the Federal Grazing Act of 1934, it
would seem that the provisions of the latter with respect to
the boards of directors of grazing districts (which are not
special districts as such), which will be discussed later,
will be applicable.316

11. Multiple-purpose districts---There are two kinds of
multiple-purpose districts: namely, districts engaged in
multiple-purpose enterprises, and districts engaged in several different single-purpose enterprises, although in many
instances the line of demarcation is obscure. The former
are river-conservancy or river-regulation districts or the
like; the latter include some of the metropolitan districts,
public utility districts, sanitary districts, and the like.
The two kinds of multiple-purpose districts are separately
discussed below.

(a) River-Conservancy or river-regulation districts

(1) Created by General laws---General laws permitting
the creation of districts for the undertaking of multiple-
purpose enterprises have been enacted in a number of states.
The major functions served by these districts are navigation
improvement, flood control, water conservation, irrigation
and hydroelectric power development. On 17 February 1914
the Ohio Legislature passed the Ohio Conservancy Act (Laws
1914, p. 13, House Bill No. 19) authorizing the establishment
of conservancy districts. This is probably the first state
law providing for multiple-purpose districts of the first
type. Under this act, as amended 19 July 1937 (Code, sec.
6828), "any area or areas in one or more counties may be organized as a conservancy district . . . for all or any[317]
of the following purposes: (a) of preventing floods; (b)
of regulating stream channels by changing, widening and deepening the same; (c) of reclaiming or of filling wet and overflowed lands; (d) of providing for irrigation where it may
be needed; (e) of regulating the flow of streams and conserving the waters thereof; (f) of diverting, or in whole or in
part eliminating water courses; (g) of providing a water supply for domestic, industrial and public use; (h) of providing for the collection and disposal of sewage and other liquid eastes produced within the district; (i) of arresting
erosion along the Ohio shore line of Lake Erie . . . ." A
conservancy district is established by the court of common
pleas of the county or any of the counties wherein the proposed district is situated, upon petition by 500 land owners
or a majority of land owners or owners of a majority of the
lands either in acreage or in value (and after hearing). It
is under the government of a board of three directors. The
first directors are appointed by the said court for the terms
of three, five and seven years respectively, and their successors are appointed by the same court for terms of five
years. The board elects a president and a vice-president and
employs a secretary. It may also employ a chief engineer, an
attorney and other personnel. Besides the functions above
listed, the board may also construct, maintain and operate
parks, forests and other recreational areas. Preliminary expenses of the district are financed by a special ad-valorem
property tax not exceeding the rate of three mills per dollar;
but the improvements are financed by special benefit assessments, in anticipation of which bonds may be issued.

Two examples may be given of the Ohio conservancy districts. The Miami River Conservancy District was formed in
1917. By 1923, five large retarding flood-control reservoirs
together with channel improvements had been constructed or
planned to protect Dayton, Hamilton and other municipalities
from flood damage.[318] The Muskingum Valley Conservancy District was created in 1933, and covers an area of 8,038 square
miles. Under the Federal Public Works program, a total of
fourteen reservoirs were constructed with an aggregate capacity of 1,539,200 acre-feet. Of these reservoirs, four are

single-purpose flood-control reservoirs without dead storage, and the remaining are single-purpose flood-control reservoirs with a dead storage varying from 420 to 3,550 acre-feet. More than 20,000 acres of hill lands adjoining these reservoirs have been reforested by the District.[319] As already discussed above, all of the fourteen reservoirs, which the U. S. Corps of Engineers built for the District, were taken over by the Corps in August 1939 under sec. 4 of the Flood Control Act of 1939. The District now only manages the recreational facilities on ten of these reservoirs which have a dead, conservation storage.[320]

New York laws provide for the establishment of river regulating districts (Laws 1915, ch. 662, as amended by Laws 1916, ch. 584). A river regulating district covers any watershed or an integral part thereof, and is created by order of a special commission composed ex-officio of the commissioner of conservation, the attorney-general and the state engineer upon petition by any person or corporation followed by a hearing. It is governed by a board of three members appointed by the governor of the state for overlapping terms of five years. The board elects a president, a secretary and a treasurer, and is required to prepare a general plan of improvement, which may include the construction of regulating dams and reservoirs and auxiliary hydroelectric power plants. Costs of the improvements are assessed separately against the benefited public corporations and private owners of real estate. The board may also collect charges for the maintenance and operation of the improvement works and issue bonds. By November 1953, only two river regulating districts had been established, namely, the Black River and the Hudson River Regulating Districts.[321] The Black River Regulating District was organized on 7 May 1919, and includes all lands drained by the Black River and its tributaries. The only improvement constructed by this district is the Stillwater Dam and Reservoir, which consists in the enlargement of the old Stillwater Reservoir to a capacity of 4.7 billion cubic feet by raising the dam 19 feet, and which was completed early in 1925. Besides, the district since 1920 has operated the Old Forge and Sixth Lake Reservoirs constructed by the State of New York in 1881 on the Moose River.[322] The operation of this reservoir results in a minimum of flow of about 1,000 cubic feet per second in the Black River at Watertown.[323] There is no power development at the Stillwater dam.[324]

The Hudson River Regulating District was established on 2 August 1922. The only work constructed by the district is the Sacandaga Reservoir, located at Conklingville, about six miles above the confluence of the Sacandaga and the Hudson Rivers, with a capacity of about 30 billion cubic feet.[325] "It was completed in 1930 . . . About 10 per cent of the capacity, in the upper part of the reservoir, is reserved solely for flood control, while the remaining 90 per cent is used

in the ordinary manner for regulating the flow of the Sacandaga and Hudson Rivers"[326] in the interests of power development, flood control, navigation improvement and sanitation.[327]
At the Conklingville Dam, there is a hydroelectric plant,
which, however, is owned and operated not by the district itself, but by a local electric company under a lease contract
with the district. This plant generates 25,000 kilowatts of
electric energy.[328] Boating, fishing, camping and other recreational facilities are available on and near the Sacandaga
Reservoir.[329]

The primary function of both the Stillwater and the
Sacandaga Reservoirs is downstream power development.[330] The
benefits of flood control seems to be secondary, and those
of navigation improvement, water pollution control, municipal
water supply and recreation are merely incidental. This is
evidenced by the burden of the construction costs of these
two reservoirs. With respect to the Stillwater Reservoir,
the entire cost of construction was borne by the water-power
properties benefited. That of the Sacandaga Reservoir "was
apportioned 4.66 per cent upon cities of Albany, Rensselaer,
Watervliet and Troy and the Village of Green Island for flood
abatement, and the remaining 95.34 per cent upon the water-
power properties of the Sacandaga and Hudson Rivers."[331]

In Colorado Statute (1922), provision is made for the organization of conservancy districts for the conduct of flood-
control and drainage enterprises either by themselves or in
cooperation with the Federal Government. A conservancy district is created by the decree of the district court of the
county concerned upon petition by 200 landowners or a majority
of landowners in the proposed district. It is governed by a
board of three directors appointed by the said court for overlapping terms of five years. The board elects a chairman,
who is to be the president of the district, and selects a
secretary. It may employ a treasurer (which position may be
held simultaneously by the secretary), a chief engineer, and
an attorney. Preliminary work of the conservancy district
is financed by the preliminary fund to be raised by a special
levy not exceeding 1 mill per dollar of assessed valuation on
the general property. The construction fund, used for construction purposes, is to be raised by special benefit assessments. Separate benefit assessments are to be collected for
purposes of operation and maintenance of the constructed works,
and are to be credited to the maintenance fund. Borrowing
is allowed.

The Pueblo Conservancy District was probably established
under the provisions of this legislation. This district in
1924-1925 constructed a retarding reservoir and a floodway
for flood control. "The retarding reservoir is located on
the main stem of the Arkansas River about 6.5 miles west of
Pueblo." "The total storage capacity of the reservoir including surcharge storage at maximum level is 28,400 acre-feet and

total discharge capacity at this level is 170,000 cubic feet
per second."   "The floodway portion of the flood protective
works . . . is approximately 10,000 feet in length and extends
through the city of Pueblo from the confluence of Dry Creek
and Arkansas River to a point just downstream from the Santa
Fe Avenue Bridge. The floodway consists of a concrete-faced
levee on the left bank and a natural bluff on the right bank
and was designed for a flow of 125,000 cubic feet per second."
"In the 23 years since floodway construction, discharges of
the Arkansas River have been of small magnitude." "The present general condition of the floodway is good."[332]

Colorado laws have also provided for the creation of
water conservancy district (Statutes, ch. 173B, art. 2: Laws
of 1937, p. 1309, as amended by Laws of 1951, p. 827). A
water conservancy district is created for the purposes of
domestic water supply, irrigation, hydroelectric power development and other beneficial uses by the decree of the county
court in which a prospective district is to be situated upon
petition by 1,500 owners of irrigated land in the district.
Its governing body is a board of not more than 15 directors,
to be appointed by the said court for a two-year term. Their
successors may be popularly elected if 15 percent of the electors in the district so petition the court. The board elects
a chairman, and selects a secretary. Besides revenues of operation, a water conservancy district may collect both special property tax not exceeding half a mill on the dollar and
special benefit assessments upon municipalities or irrigation
districts included in the district, or upon landowners. Power
to borrow money is not expressly mentioned. In New Mexico,
provisions for the establishment of conservancy districts are
contained in New Mexico Statutes Annotated, ch. 77, art. 27
(Laws 1923, ch. 140; as last amended by L. 1953, ch. 183).
The functions which these districts may serve are flood control, drainage, irrigation, hydroelectric power development
(incidental) and water supply (incidental). Cooperation with
the Federal Government is permitted. A conservancy district
is created by the decree of the district court of the county
concerned upon petition by owners of one-third of the real
property in the proposed district either in acreage or in value. It is governed by a board of five directors to be appointed by the said court for six years. The board elects a chairman, who is to be the president of the district, and selects
a secretary. It may employ a manager or chief engineer, an
attorney, and other officers. Conservancy districts raise
preliminary, construction and maintenance funds for the respective purposes of preliminary work, construction work and
maintenance of the constructed works, in the same manner as
the Colorado conservancy districts do, except that preliminary-
fund tax shall not exceed six mills on the dollar. As in the
case of Colorado conservancy districts, loans may be incurred
in anticipation of preliminary and maintenance revenues, and
conservancy bonds may be issued in anticipation of construction

assessments.

Presumably under the above-mentioned provisions, "the Middle Rio Grande Conservancy District was organized in 1925 to provide irrigation, drainage, and flood control for about 128,000 acres of land in Middle Valley. Its works, begun in 1930 and completed in 1935, consist of the following features: El Vado Dam and Reservoir, located on Rio Chama near Tierra Amarilla and having a capacity of approximately 200,000 acre-feet; four diversion dams and three headings on Rio Grande, in Middle Valley; about 630 miles of irrigation canals and laterals; about 340 miles of interior and river-side drainage ditches; and about 190 miles of levees along Rio Grande. The total original cost of construction (to 31 August 1935) was $9,130,143.33, which included $1,753,111.18 for El Vado Dam."333 However, by 1948 the district had found itself unable to maintain and rehabilitate its irrigation works.234 In the Flood Control Act of 30 June 1948 authority was given the Secretary of the Interior to purchase the bonded and other indebtedness of the District as a measure of Federal financial help (62 Stat. 1171, 1179). This Act also authorized the construction by the Bureau of Reclamation of the Middle Rio Grande project. It would thus seem that from 1948 the activities of the Middle Rio Grande Conservancy District have been reduced to the maintenance and operation of Federal-built irrigation and flood-control projects.

In Nebraska, <u>public power and irrigation districts</u> may be organized under the same laws which provide for the organization of <u>public power districts</u>.

By 1953, two public power and irrigation districts had been formed. These are the Platte Valley Public Power and Irrigation District and the Central Nebraska Public Power and Irrigation District, both of which were established in 1933. The former is engaged in diverting water of the North Platte River over the divide between the North and South Platte Rivers and across the South Platte River through a hydroelectric plant back into the Platte River. Then the water is further diverted to a number of irrigation districts for irrigation use. The hydroelectric plant has an ultimate capacity of 77,-500 horsepower and it generated 36,000 horsepower as of 30 June 1951. The Central Nebraska Public Power and Irrigation District has built a two-million-acre-foot reservoir together with its impounding dam, the Kingsley Dam (which is the second largest dirt-filled dam in the world) on the North Platte River to regulate the flows of the North Platte and the Platte Rivers. Water is diverted from the regulated Platte River through a 70-mile supply canal to return to the Platte River. On this canal are located three hydroelectric power plants with a rated capacity of 18,000 kilowatts each, which are respectively known as Jeffrey Canyon Plant, Johnson Canyon Plant No. 1 and Johnson Plant No. 2, Water spilled back from these plants into the Platte River is again diverted for irrigation. It is estimated that more than 200,000 acres of land may be irrigated. It should be mentioned that before water of the regulated Platte River is diverted through the supply canal for power development, there is diversion of water from the regulated North Platte River for use by the Platte Valley District. Water so diverted and utilized returns to the Platte River at a point above the intake of the above-mentioned supply canal. Both Districts have also constructed power transmission facilities.335

In 1947, a law was passed by Nebraska legislature providing for the organization of reclamation districts (Laws 1947, ch. 350; as last amended by L. 1953, ch. 108). They are established by the State Department of Roads and Irrigation "for conserving, developing and stabilizing supplies of water for domestic, irrigation, power, manufacturing and other beneficial uses" upon petition by owners of thirty per cent in area of rural lands which have a total assessed valuation of $2 million. Each reclamation district is governed by a board of 5-21 directors serving for overlapping terms of six years. First directors are to be appointed by the said Department, but their successors to be popularly elected. The board elects a chairman, who is also the president of the district, and a secretary, and may employ a chief engineer and other officers. In discharging its function, the district may seek cooperation from the Federal Government. Reclamation districts are entitled to the follow sources of income: (1) special general property surtax of a maximum rate of one mill per dollar, (2) special benefit assessments on urban properties, (3) special benefit assessments on lands in irrigation districts, and (4) special benefit assessments on lands receiving water service. Bonds may be issued in anticipation of these revenues.

Besides laws permitting the organization of water conservancy or similar districts have also been inacted in Minnesota (1919), Oklahoma (1923), Illinois (1925), Texas (1925), North Dakota (1935), Utah (1944) and Oregon 1947).

(2) Created by special laws---Under the authority of sec. 59 of article 16 of the State Constitution of Texas, a number of special acts have been enacted creating several types of special districts. The first of such districts is probably the Brazos River Conservation and Reclamation District, which was created by a special act of 1929 (41st legislature, second called session, ch. 13). Under this act, as amended, the Brazos District is created to undertake the enterprises of flood control, water conservation, irrigation and drainage in the Brazos River Basin. The act authorized the state board of water engineers and the state reclamation engineer to designate, subject to the approval of the governor, 21 persons to serve as a temporary board, whose function it is to prepare

a plan of improvement. After the plan was completed, this
temporary board called a special election at which 21 directors were elected, who constitute the governing board of the
District. The directors are popularly elected for overlapping
terms of six years. The District "shall not be authorized to
issue bonds nor to incur any form of continuing obligation or
indebtedness, . . . nor incur any indebtedness in the form of
a continuing charge upon lands or properties, . . . unless
. . . such proposition shall have been . . . approved by a
majority of such electors voting thereon" (sec. 10). At such
election any form of taxation, it would seem, may be authorized as a pledge of the bonds. The main structure of the
District is the Possum Kingdom Reservoir, which is a storage
reservoir of a capacity of 724,000 acre-feet, and which is
used for the multiple purposes of hydroelectric power development, flood control, and irrigation. "Water stored in this
reservoir is an important source of supply for the irrigation
of a large acreage of rice in the coastal area several miles
downstream. The Brazos River Conservation and Reclamation
District is planning three more dams downstream from Possum
Kingdom, which will be used for power."[336] The District plans
to develop hydroelectric power to the ultimate capacity of
47,250 horsepower. As of 30 June 1951, 31,500 horsepower was
actually generated.[337]

In 1934, the law creating the Lower Colorado River Authority was passed (Laws 1934, 43rd legislature, 4th called
session, ch. 7).[338] The District comprises the Counties of
Blancho, Burnet, Llano, Travis, Bastrop, Favette, Colorado,
Wharton, San Saba and Matagorda,[339] and is intrusted with the
enterprises of hydroelectric power development, irrigation,
flood control, water conservation and forest conservation and
watershed improvement. Its governing body is a board of nine
directors, of whom three are appointed by the governor, three
by the attorney general and three by the commissioner of the
general land office. All directors serve for overlapping
terms of six years. The board selects a secretary and appoints
a general manager and a treasurer. The District cannot borrow money, but revenue bonds may be issued which shall not exceed the total amount of $10 million outstanding at any time.
The act itself appropriated a sum of five thousand dollars
from the state treasury to the District to defray preliminary
expenses. This appropriation is in the nature of a loan, and
is required to be repaid by the District out of its operating
revenues.

The development of the Lower Colorado River Basin in Texas
is based on an investigation report of the Chief of Engineers
of the U. S. Army dated 30 June 1919, the investigation being
authorized by the River and Harbor Act of 27 July 1916 (39
Stat. 391, 408).[340] The principal benefit of the development
work, as pointed out in the report, is flood control, which
can be achieved either by the construction of levees or that

of reservoirs. Since the area to be protected from floods
was then primarily agricultural in character, it was recommended that the work should be left to state and local interests without Federal participation.341 On 1 April 1930
another report was made by the Chief of Engineers, pursuant
to the River and Harbor Acts of 31 May 1924 (43 Stat. 249)
and 12 February 1929 (45 Stat. 1164).342 The Colorado River
in Texas was still regarded as having no value of commercial
navigation, and even flood control, which was to be undertaken by state and local interests in all events, had only
benefits of such remote nature that "a more thorough examination" could be made only "at some future time". However,
"any survey to be undertaken should show the possibilities
of power development and irrigation."

Actual development of the basin dates back to 1893, when
the city of Austin completed the Austin Dam providing storage water for hydroelectric power, flood control and irrigation. "On April 7, 1900, a flood destroyed Austin Dam. Early in 1915 the dam was rebuilt, but in September of that
year a flood damaged the dam and power plant to such an extent
they were unusable. In June 1935, another flood further damaged the structure. Local interests undertook the construction of two other dams on the Colorado; the Alexamder Dam
near Marble Falls and the Hamilton Dam near Burnet. The Alex-
ander Dam was started prior to 1930, but due to financial
difficulties work was discontinued before the structure was
half completed. The Hamilton Dam was begun early in 1931,
but its construction was discontinued in April 1932 when the
dam was about 25 percent complete. On November 13, 1934,
the Texas State Legislature authorized the organization of
the Lower Colorado River Authority for the purpose of completing Hamilton Dam and constructing additional dams along
the river to provide irrigation, flood-control, and power benefits."343

"The newly organized Authority made application for Federal funds for the completion of Buchanan Dam and for the construction of other dams along the Colorado River. The proposed structures were designed for hydroelectric power, flood
control and storage of irrigation water. Under the terms of
the Emergency Appropriation Act of 1935, the President approved an allotment of $15,000,000 to the Public Works Admin-
istration for building the multiple-purpose project. The
President simultaneously allocated $5,000,000 to the United
States Bureau of Reclamation for the construction of the
project's flood control features. Subsequent to the allocation of funds, the Public Works Administration contracted
with the Lower Colorado River Authority for the purchase of
the Authority's revenue bonds not to exceed $10,500,000 and
for payment of a grant of 30 percent of the cost of labor and
materials. The grant was not to exceed $4,500,000. A con-
tract, executed in 1935 between the Secretary of the Interior

and the Lower Colorado River Authority, provided for the Bureau to prepare plans and construct flood control and irrigation features of the project. The Authority agreed to complete construction of Buchanan Dam and purchase the right-of-way for all project features. This contract was later amended to authorize the Bureau of Reclamation to complete construction of Buchanan Dam, including rehabilitation of the construction camp and equipment at Buchanan Dam site." Further amendment of this contract in 1936 returned to the Authority substantially the entire construction work of the Buchanan and Inks Dams, as well as the reconstruction of the Austin Dam. In the meantime, the Bureau of Reclamation constructed the Marshall Ford Dam, which was completed in May 1942.[344] In 1949, construction was started on two other dams, the Marble Falls and the Granite Shoals Dams, which are single-purpose power structures. "The construction of these two dams is being financed by the sale of bonds independently of any State or Federal aid."[345] A more detailed description of the various structures is given below:[346]

(1) Buchanan (Hamilton) Dam and power plant---"Storage behind the dam was initiated in May 1937." "The reservoir has an active storage capacity of 900,000 acre-feet and is used jointly for flood control and power purposes. Super storage of 115,000 acre-feet above the uncontrolled spillway crest is used for flood control." "The power plant contains two 12,500-kilovolt-ampere generating units. Provision has been made for the installation of a third unit, now on order and expected to be in operation late in 1949."

(2) Roy Inks Dam and power plant---"This dam, three miles downstream from Buchanan Dam, was constructed by the Lower Colorado River Authority for the development of an additional 64 feet of power head with water released from Buchanan Reservoir. Work on this structure, originally known as Arnold Dam, was completed in October 1938." The single power unit consists of a 12,500-kilovolt-ampere generator.

(3) Marshall Ford Dam and power plant---Although the Dam was constructed by the Bureau of Reclamation of the Federal Government, "the power plant was constructed by the Lower Colorado River Authority which took over operation and maintenance of the dam in 1945. The reservoir is operated by the Authority for flood control, power, and river regulation to augment the low water for irrigation purposes along the Colorado River below Austin." "The power plant consists of three 25,000-kilovolt-ampere generating units . . . ." "The reservoir inundates 44,448 acres and has a capacity of 3,223,-100 acre-feet with the reservoir at maximum water surface elevation of 748.8. Total controlled capacity is 1,951,400 acre-feet with the reservoir at the spillway crest (elevation 714)." "Dead storage capacity below the outlet works is 28,720 acre-feet. Of the controlled capacity, 780,300

acre-feet is allocated to flood control, 810,000 acre-feet
to power, and 361,000 acre-feet as a siltation reserve."

(4) Austin Dam and power plant---"Rehabilitation of the
Austin Dam at an estimated cost of $2,500,000 was begun by
the Lower Colorado River Authority in July 1938." "The
power plant, housing two 7,500-kilovolt-ampere generating
units, is located at the left downstream side of the dam."
"The dam and power plant are completed."

(5) Granite Shoals and Marble Falls Dams and power
plants---"These are primarily power dams but the two of
them will provide a combined storage of about 183,000 acre-
feet."347

The various hydroelectric power plants of the Lower Colorado River Authority have an aggregate generating capacity
of 239,000 kilowatts. Besides, it operates under lease a
steam power plant at New Braunfels with a generating capacity of 60,000 kilowatts.348 Power is sold wholesale to
11 rural cooperatives, 33 cities and 4 privately-owned utility companies.349 The effects of river regulation, which
are more or less incidental in character, are reflected in
the provision of dependable water supplies for Austin, a
city of 140,000 people, and for irrigation of 110,000 acres
of rice fields in the basin.350

The Lower Colorado River Authority also cooperates with
the Federal Government and private landowners in carrying
out a program of watershed soil and water conservation.
None of the activities of the Authority in this program,
however, is strictly enterprise in nature.351

Other districts of similar nature that have been created
by special state laws in Texas are the Sabine-Neches Conservation and Reclamation District (Laws 1935, ch. 97), Upper
Colorado River Authority (Laws 1935, ch. 126), Central Colorado River Authority (Laws 1935, ch. 338), Panhandle Water
Conservation Authority (Laws 1937, ch. 256, regular session),
and so forth.

In 1935, an act (ch. 70, art. 4) was passed in Oklahoma
"creating a Conservation and Reclamation District to be
known as Grand River Dam Authority in accordance with and by
authority set forth in sec. 31 of article 2 of the Constitution of the State of Oklahoma . . ."352 The area of the District comprises the seventeen counties of Adair, Cherokee,
Craig, etc. The Authority is invested with the functions of
(1) water conservation and supply, (2) hydroelectric power
development, (3) flood control, and (4) reforestation and
watershed protection. It is governed by a board of five directors appointed by the governor for overlapping terms of
six years. It selects a secretary, a general manager (chief
executive of the District) and a treasurer (who may hold the

office of the secretary). The Authority may issue revenue
bonds not exceeding in aggregate principal $25 million, of
which $10 million is used for the construction of Markham
Ferry and Fort Gibson Dams and transmission lines, and may
receive Federal grants. But it has no taxing power, nor can
it mortgage District property. In 1939, a similar act was
passed by Oklahoma legislature (ch. 70, art. 4) which created
the Fairfax-Law City Authority covering six counties of Washington , Kay, etc. and having the same functions with respect
to the Arkansas River Basin as the Grand River Dam Authority
with respect to the Grand River Basin. It is governed by a
board of three directors, appointed by the governor for overlapping terms of three years. The board also selects a secretary, a general manager, and a treasurer (who may hold the
office of the secretary). Its financial power is the same
as that of the Grand River Dam Authority, except that the
limit in the aggregate amount of the principal is $3 million.

In 1940 (?), the Grand River Dam Authority, under a license of the Federal Power Commission dated 26 July 1939, constructed a dam on the Grand (Neosho) River at the Pensacola
site for flood control and hydroelectric power development.352
In 1941 the construction work was taken over by the Federal
Works Agency in order to facilitate the construction and make
its power available to the defense plants.353 The Pensacola
Dam and Reservoir became a part of the Federal flood control
program for the Arkansas River Basin under provisions of the
Flood Control Act of 18 August 1941, which also provided for
the enlargement of its flood-control storage. Power phase
of the Pensacola project is now operated by the Department of
the Interior (through the Southwestern Power Administration).
The Grand River Dam Authority operates the flood-control storage of the Pensacola project as well as local protective works
at Wyandotte, under the direction of the Corps of Engineers.355
There is no information regarding the activities and performances of the Fairfax-Kaw City Authority.

The Colorado River Conservancy District of Colorado is
also established by a special state law (Statutes, ch. 138,
sec. 199(1) et seq.: Laws 1937, p. 997ff.). It comprises the
entire areas of Mesa, Garfield, Pitkin, Eagle, Delta, Gunni-
son and Summit Counties, and possesses the functions of water
conservation, irrigation and domestic and industrial supply.
The governing body of the district is a board of seven directors serving for overlapping terms of three years, to be appointed by the board of county commissioners of each of the
seven constituent counties. The board elects a president,
and appoints a secretary, a treasurer, engineers, attorneys,
and other personnel. Financial resources of the district consist of alternative revenues from either a special property
tax not exceeding two-tenths of one mill per dollar or special
benefit assessments, and bonds in anticipation thereof.

A number of special districts for multiple-purpose enterprises have been created by special laws in California. Two
examples may be given. The Mendocino County Flood Control
and Water Conservation District was created by an act of 1949
(Stats. 1949, ch. 995) for the control, conservation, diversion, storage and disposition of storm, flood and other surface waters in Mendocino County. It may construct all necessary works and hydroelectric power plants, and may cooperate
with the Federal Government in the construction work. The
board of supervisors of the County of Mendocino acts ex-officio as the board of directors of the District, which elects
a chairman, and principal county officers serve ex-officio
as District officers. The District may levy an annual special property tax of a maximum rate of two mills per dollar
of assessed property valuation, and may levy additional taxes
to pay debt-interest. Bonds may be issued after approval by
special referenda. The Alameda County Flood Control and Water
Conservation District was also created in 1949 (Stats. 1949,
ch. 1275). Its functions are ground water conservation storage, water pollution control, flood control, and the construction of parks and beaches. It may also cooperate with
the Federal Government in carrying out any of these functions.
The board of supervisors and other officers of the County of
Alameda, act ex-officio as the board of directors and other
officers of the District, respectively. The District board
of directors appoints an advisory commission of nine members,
and may appoint an engineer. The general administrative
costs of the District are raised through a special property
tax levy not exceeding one mill on the dollar of property valuation each year; but the costs of construction and maintenance of project works are raised by special benefit assessment. Issuance of bonds may be authorized by special referendum.

In 1953, the legislature of North Carolina established
the Neuse River Watershed Authority as a special district for
the purposes of flood control, irrigation, drainage, water
supply, sewerage and soil erosion control (Laws 1953, ch.
1115). The Authority is prohibited from undertaking hydroelectric power projects. Its jurisdiction covers the Counties of Durham, Wake, Johnston Wayne, Lenoir, Greene, Jones
and Craven. As a governing body, the Authority is composed
of two members appointed by the board of county commissioners
of each of the constituent counties for terms of three years.
A chairman, a vice-chairman and a secretary-treasurer are
elected from the membership. In addition, "two non-voting
advisory members may be appointed from each county within
the Neuse River Watershed area." They are appointed by the
county commissioners and the mayors of towns within the county in joint meeting. The Authority is required "to work out
and enter into agreements with the governing bodies of the
towns and the several counties within the Neuse River Watershed area for payment to the Authority of a sum reasonably

commensurate with any projects intended to conserve and develop the water resources of the Neuse River Watershed."
But the Authority has no independent financial power.

(b) Metopolitan, public utility and sanitary districts

Such districts may be created under general state laws in
many a state. Some examples may be given. Under an act of
11 July 1919 of Illinois (<u>Revised Statutes</u>, ch. 42, sec. 295),
sanitary districts with the single purpose of sewage disposal
may at the same time be water districts with the single purpose of water supply when one of its constituent cities of
towns owns a waterworks. Under the laws of California (<u>Gen-
eral Laws</u>, act 6393: Statutes 1921, ch. 218, as amended),
any number of public agencies may constitute a <u>municipal
utility district</u>, a public agency defined as a city, a county water district, a county sanitation district or sanitary
district. A municipal utility district is established by
popular vote at a special referendum called by the board of
supervisors of the county having the greatest number of electors in the district, upon petition by one half of the public agencies concerned, or by ten percent of the electors.
It is under the government of a board of five directors popularly elected for overlapping terms of four years. The board
elects a president and a vice-president, and appoints a general manager. It may appoint a secretary, a treasurer an
attorney, and other employees. Municipal utility districts
may be engaged in enterprises of water, light, heat, power,
transportation, telephone, and sewerage, some of which are
concerned with water resources. They are authorized to levy
special <u>ad-valorem</u> property taxes, to borrow money, and, after approval by a majority vote at a special referendum, issue
bonds.

In North Carolina (<u>General Statutes</u>, sec. 130-33 et seq.:
Laws 1927, ch. 357, as amended), <u>sanitary districts</u> are organized to embark upon the enterprises of sewerage, water
supply, mosquito control and fire prevention and to regulate
on sanitary matters. 51 percent of the resident freeholders
in a proposed sanitary district may petition the board of
county commissioners of the county in which the district or
a major portion thereof is situated to establish the district.
If after hearing the said board considers the proposal to be
feasible, it shall forward it to the state board of health
for final approval, which is given after another hearing. A
sanitary district is governed by a sanitary district board
of three members, who are elected by the board of county
commissioners of the county, or by the boards of county commissioners in joint meeting of the counties, in which the
district is located, and who serve for terms of two years.
The board may employ engineers, and may levy special <u>ad-valor-
em</u> property taxes and issue bonds and certificates of indebtedness.

The legislature of Ohio on 6 June 1919 enacted a law authorizing the organization of sanitary districts (Laws of 1919, p. 634) which may assume both enterprise and regulation duties in water pollution control and/or water supply. So far as the enterprise of water pollution control is concerned, a sanitary district may clean streams, or construct stream improvement works or works for the regulation of stream flow in the special interest of pollution control. By an amendment of 4 June 1941 (Laws of 1941, p. 581), the function of mosquito control is added to the list of functions which a sanitary district may perform. A sanitary district is created by order of the court of common pleas of the county in which the district is to be located, upon petition by 500 freeholders, or by a majority of freeholders within the proposed district, or by owners (either individuals, or public or private corporations) of a majority of total property in the proposed district either in acreage or in value. If the judges in the court are of even numbers, then the state supreme court may be requested to appoint a judge to preside at the said court for that purpose. In case the district is located in more than one county, the determination is to be made by a body consisting of one judge from the court of common pleas of each county. If the district is located in a single county, it is governed by a director appointed by the court of common pleas of that county for five years' term. If it is located in two or more counties, it is governed by a board of directors consisting of one director from each county appointed in the same way for the same tenure. The director or board of directors appoints a secretary and a treasurer, or a secretary and treasurer, and may employ a chief engineer and other officers. In case there is a board of directors, the board should elect a president. The director or board of directors prepares a plan of improvement, which must be approved by the state department of health. Preliminary fund of the sanitary districts are raised by ad-valorem special property tax; and construction and maintenance costs are separately raised by special benefit assessments. They may borrow money and issue bonds. The county or counties concerned may make loans to a sanitary district to defray its preliminary expenses.

An example of the Ohio sanitary districts is the Toledo Area Sanitary District, which is governed by a single director. It was organized in November 1945 for the sole purpose of mosquito control.356 "The District embraces approximately the eastern half of Lucas County, which lies at the western tip of Lake Erie." "This includes an area of 153.17 square miles, of which the municipalities of Toledo, Maumee and Sylvania comprise about 32.4 percent, or 49.82 square miles.357 "A detailed survey of mosquito breeding in and adjacent to the District was begun March 15, 1946 and completed December 17, 1946." "The control program was approved as submitted by the State Health Department on date of March 6, 1947 . . . .

The Mosquito Control Program was adopted by the Director of the District on April 30, 1947. Control operations . . . were actually begun on April 23rd."[358] The principal control measure is drainage, with the spraying of larvicides (which also kill adult mosquitoes) and the stocking of waters with mosquito-eating fishes as complementary measures.[359]

In Washington, the establishment of _public utility districts_ is authorized by an act enacted by vote of the people on 4 November 1930 and proclaimed effective on 3 December 1930 (Revised Code, tit. 54: Laws 1931, ch. 1; as last amended by L. 1951, chs. 207 and 209). The functions of a public utility district is to generate or purchase and transmit hydro or fuel electric power and to construct, operate and maintain works for irrigation and water supply. It may be observed that these purposes may be served, under certain conditions, by a multiple-purpose enterprise. A public utility district is established by popular vote at a special election ordered by the board of commissioners of the county in which the district is situated, upon petition of 10 percent of voters or in its own initiative. It is governed by a board of three commissioners, popularly elected for overlapping terms of three years. It may levy a special _ad-valorem_ property tax not exceeding two mills on the dollar each year, and may borrow money and issue bonds.[360] As of 1950, 29 public utility districts had been organized throughout the state, and 18 of these purchased electric power from the Bonneville Power Administration.[361] ". . . The Cowlitz Public Utility District . . . is engaged in the distribution of public utility services, including both power and domestic water." Part of the power is generated by the district itself, and part is purchased from the Bonneville Power Administration.[362] Public Utility District No. 1 of Chelan County and Public Utility District No. 1 of Okanogan County have constructed works for hydroelectric power generation, which have capacities of 1,960 kilowatts and 3,200 kilowatts respectively.[363] In February 1951, Public Utility District No. 1 of Pend Oreille County was granted by the Federal Power Commission a preliminary permit to investigate hydroelectric power development at the Box Canyon on the Pend Oreille River, which would involve the construction of a 260-foot dam and a power house containing four generators of 15,000 kilowatts each, at a cost then estimated to be $16 million.[364]

Special districts for a number of single-purpose enterprises may also be established by special laws. The Washington Suburban Sanitary District of Maryland is an outstanding example. Created by a law of 1918 (ch. 122), it is located in Montgomery and Prince George's Counties and has the functions of water supply, sewage disposal and drainage. Its governing body is a commission of three members, of whom one is appointed by the Governor and two are appointed by the two counties upon the recommendation of the State Board of Health.

The commission elects a chairman and appoints a secretary-
treasurer, a chief engineer, and other employees. It may
issue bonds to be redeemed by a special property surtax.
But the construction of sewage-disposal and water-supply works
is financed by special benefit assessments.

Article 4   Interstate Administration

Interstate administration is established by interstate
compacts, interstate agreements without Congressional consent, or interstate concurrent legislation.365 These are not
entirely distinct and disconnected processes. An interstate
compact is nothing but an interstate agreement plus the consent of Congress, and concurrent legislation is required to
provide the basis for or to give force and effect to interstate compacts and agreements. Instead of saying that interstate administration is established by three different
methods, it is perhaps more appropriate to say that it is
established with three different degrees of formality if
not of force. In general, the three processes may be shown
as follows:

> Interstate agreements---by administrative action of state
> agencies.
> Concurrent legislation---administrative action plus state
> legislative action.
> Interstate compacts---administrative action plus state
> legislative action plus Federal legislative action.

One remark should not be neglected. That is, although interstate administration is established by interstate compacts,
interstate agreements and concurrent legislation, not every
interstate compact, interstate agreement or every piece of
concurrent legislation provides for interstate administration. Any of these devices may create (1) interstate administration plus interstate organization, (2) interstate administration without interstate organization, (3) interstate organization without interstate administration, or (4) neither
interstate administration nor interstate organization.366 In
exceptional cases, interstate administration, especially at
local levels, may be created by unilateral state legislation
or by Federal legislation or by concurrent or joint action
of the local units of neighboring states concerned. Of all
the devices of establishing interstate administration (and/
or interstate organization), the interstate compact is of
primary importance.

The constitutionality of interstate administration was
recently challenged by West Virginia. In 1949, the State
Auditor of that state refused to issue a warrant for the dis-
bursement of funds to the Ohio River Valley Sanitation Commission already voted by the state legislature, believing
that it is unconstitutional to expend state funds to support

interstate activities. "The West Virginia Court of Appeals, in a three to two decision, sustained the auditor. This court interpreted the compact as: (1) Requiring the state to incur a financial obligation in violation of debt limitations imposed by the West Virginia constitution; and (2) resulting in a delegation of police power that is contrary to general principles of constitutional law. When this decision was taken to the Supreme Court of the United States for review, that body reversed the state court."[367] The latter sustained the constitutionality of interstate administration and perhaps all kinds of interstate instruments on the ground that it is a legitimate delegation of authority by a state legislature.[368]

It was ruled by the Supreme Court of the United States as early as 1823, in Green et al. v. Biddle, 8 Wheaton 1, that interstate compacts and agreements are contracts, and that the signatory states are prohibited by the Constitution of the United States to pass laws impairing such contracts[369] By inference, a participant state cannot by unilateral legislation abolish or interfere with interstate administration (or interstate organization) established by interstate compacts and agreements.

Interstate administration in the various fields of water resources management is discussed below.

1. Water conservation and development in general.---As early as 1771, the colonial provinces of New Jersey and Pennsylvania enacted concurrent legislation (Act of province of Pennsylvania being enacted on 9 March 1771 and that of province of New Jersey on 21 December 1771) providing for joint regulation of the flows of the Delaware River through both enterprise and regulatory acts, and for the appointment of a joint commission for that purpose. Immediately after the Revolution, the new States of New Jersey and Pennsylvania transformed this concurrent legislation into an interstate compact in 1783, which provided for interstate administration through concurrent legislation over particular objects. When the legislature of either state passed an act affecting the Delaware River, concurrence and consent of the legislature of the other must be secured. This compact, it is to be noted, was rendered obsolete if not abolished by the Code dispute occuring in 1815. In 1824, an attempt was made by the two states to enter into a new compact, but it was abortive. For all practical purposes, the year 1824, when the formality of concurrent legislation was last complied with (concerning the incorporation of the Delaware and Raritan Canal Company), may be regarded as the end of the interstate administration of the states of New Jersey and Pennsylvania over the Delaware River with respect to general matters of water conservation.[370]

In 1946, laws were concurrently enacted by the legislatures of New Hampshire (ch. 268) and Vermont (No. 16) providing for joint regulation of the waters of the Connecticut River bordering upon the two states. The laws require every person who undertakes to build dams, dikes, revetments and any other works or structures on the banks and bed of the Connecticut River which make it difficult to ascertain the location of the boundaries between the two states to apply for permits from the attorneys general of the two states before the construction of these works can be started. The permits are respectively issued by the two attorneys general after a joint inspection made by them or their representatives, at which the need of the erection of monuments to permanently mark the location of the boundary line will be determined. Although this is technically a measure of determining state boundaries, the attorney general of either state would incidentally exercise an affective control over the manipulation of the flow of the Connecticut River bordering upon the two states. This seems to be the only instance of interstate regulatory administration in the general field of water conservation and development.

With respect to enterprise, the River and Harbor Act of 8 August 1917 in sec. 5 (40 Stat. 250, 266) embodies the consent of the Congress to the conclusion of interstate agreement or agreements between Minnesota, North Dakota and South Dakota or any two of them to provide for navigation improvement and flood control on boundary waters, which are to be undertaken after the feasibility thereof is passed upon by the U. S. Department of the Army. Presumably under the authority of this provision, concurrent legislation has been in force in Minnesota (Laws 1939, ch. 60) and South Dakota (L. 1939, ch. 294) creating the South Dakota-Minnesota Boundary Water Commission to control and regulate the water levels of the boundary waters between the two states through both enterprise and regulation. It is reported that "this Commission has been active in making preliminary surveys and investigations for control works below the mouth of the Big Stone Lake for the purpose of regulating the level of the Lake in the interests of recreation and conservation in South Dakota and conservation, recreation and flood control in Minnesota. After considerable negotiations of the Commission between the two states and after completing rather extensive preliminary investigations, the two states are now agreed upon a preliminary plan and it is expected that the detailed plans and specifications leading up to the construction of the works will go forward during the next few years."[371]

In sec. 19 (first paragraph) of the Boulder Canyon Project Act of 21 December 1928 (45 Stat. 1057, 1065), the consent of the Congress is given to Arizona, California, Colorado, Nevada, New Mexico, Utah and Wyoming to negotiate and enter into compacts or agreements, supplemental to and in conformity with the Colorado River Compact and consistent with this act for a comprehensive plan for the development of the Colorado River and providing for the storage, diversion, and use of the waters of said river. Any such compact or agreement may provide for the construction of dams, headworks, and other diversion works or structures for flood control, reclamation, improvement of navigation, division of water, or other purposes and/or the construction of power houses or other structures for the purpose of the development of water power and the financing of the same; and for such purposes may authorize the creation of interstate commissions and/or the creation of corporations, authorities, or other instrumentalities." This is a general authorization of interstate multiple-purpose enterprises in the Colorado River Basin. This provision, however, has not yet taken advantage of by the Basin states, and the comprehensive development of the Colorado River Basin has in fact been an exclusive Federal enterprise.

In a special act of 8 June 1936 (49 Stat. 1490), the Congress gave its consent to "Maine, New York, New Hampshire, Vermont, Massachusetts, Rhode Island, Connecticut, Pennsylvania, West Virginia, Kentucky, Indiana, Illinois, Tennessee, and Ohio, or any two or more of them, to negotiate and enter into agreements or compacts for conserving and regulating the flow, lessening flood damage, removing sources of pollution of the waters thereof, or making other public improvements on any rivers or streams whose drainage basins lie within any two or more of the said states" (sec. 1). By June 1953, none of such compacts or agreements has come into existence.

In an act of 1949 of North Dakota (ch. 348), it is provided (in sec. 31) that a water conservation and flood control district of that state may "enter into contracts or other arrangements . . . with public corporations and state government of this or other states, with drainage, flood control, conservation, conservancy, or improvement districts, in this or other states, for cooperation and assistance in constructing, maintaining, using and operating" projects works, provided no connection should be made between boundary waters having different outlets. This is a unique provision which authorizes the establishment of interstate administration by local governmental units. There has been no report, however, regarding the operation of this provision.

At the initiative of the State Engineer of Nevada, under the special authority given him by an act of 1947 (ch. 173), coordinated surveys have been made by the State Engineers of Nevada and California (the latter acting under administrative authorization of the Director of the Department of Public Works) on the control and conservation of the waters of the interstate Lake Tahoe.372 It is possible that these coordinated (but not joint) investigations may lead to interstate enterprise and/or regulation of California and Nevada.

2. **Port and terminal facilities**---In 1921 an interstate
compact was entered into between New York and New Jersey
creating the Port of New York Authority.373 It authorized
the Authority to acquire, construct, lease and operate any
terminal or transportation facilities within the Port of New
York District, which it established. Additional duties may
be given the Authority by concurrent legislation of the two
states.374 A comprehensive plan for the Authority was adopted in a subsequent interstate compact in 1922,375 and the
enterprises of the Authority were begun in 1924.376 Terminal
facilities of the Authority consist of: (1) Inland Terminal
No. 1, which covers an entire Manhattan block, and which was
constructed by the Authority at a cost of $16,400,000 and
was completed in October 19 32. (2) Grain Terminal on the
Columbia Street in Brooklyn, which includes a grain elevator
and piers built by the State of New York in 1922 and acquired
by the Authority in 1944 and a new grain pier subsequently
built by the Authority. (3) La Guardia and New York International Airports leased in 1947 from the City of New York
for 50 years. (4) Port Newark and Newark Airport leased in
1947 from the City of Newark. (5) Two union truck terminals,
one in Manhattan and the other in Newark. (6) A bus terminal
in Manhattan, which was completed on 12 July 1950. It should
be remarked that all these terminal facilities constitute
but a small portion of the properties of the Authority, and
that about 90 percent of the Authority's income is derived
from toll charges on six interstate vehicular water crossings
(four bridges and two tunnels).377

The two other interstate enterprises similar to that of
the Port of New York Authority are the enterprises conducted
by the Delaware River Port Authority and the Missouri-Illinois Bi-State Development Agency. The former is the successor of the Delaware River Joint Commission of Pennsylvania
and New Jersey. In 1919, Pennsylvania created the Interstate
Bridge Commission (Act No. 338) and invested it with the function of constructing a bridge across the Delaware River connecting Philadelphia and Camden. In 1929, a similar commission was established by the laws of New Jersey (ch. 271).
After the said bridge was completed by the two states and
the City of Philadelphia jointly, an interstate agreement
was concluded by the two states in 1931 which created the
Delaware River Bridge Joint Commission replacing the two state
commissions. In addition to its primary function to maintain
and operate the Philadelphia-Camden bridge, the Commission
was given authority for "the promotion of the Delaware River
as a highway of commerce between Philadelphia and Camden and
the sea", "to study and make recommendations to the proper
authorities for the improvement of terminal, lighterage,
wharfage, warehouse and other facilities necessary for the
promotion of commerce on the Delaware River", and to investi-

gate additional means of communication between Philadelphia
and Camden and between these two cities and the sea by bridge,
canal, tunnel or otherwise.

The interstate agreement of 1931, to which Congress gave
its consent on 14 June 1932 (Joint Resolution, 47 Stat. 308),
was amended by a supplemental agreement of 1952 (Act of Congress of 17 July 1952: 66 Stat. 738). The Delaware River
Joint Commission was changed into the Delaware River Port
Authority, which has jurisdiction over the Delaware River
Port District, which comprises the Counties of Delaware and
Philadelphia in Pennsylvania and the Counties of Atlantic,
Burlington, Camden, Cape May, Cumberland, Gloucester, Ocean
and Dalem in New Jersey. The functions of the Authority are
(1) to operate and maintain the Philadelphia-Camden bridge,[378]
(2) to construct and operate terminal facilities at the end
of the bridge or any other bridge or tunnel owned or controlled by the Authority, (3) to improve and develop the Port
District for port purposes, etc.[379] It is not clear whether
the Authority has actually constructed any terminal or port
facilities.

The Missouri-Illinois Bi-State Metropolitan District and
its governing body, the Bi-State Development Agency, were
created by an interstate compact entered into between the
states of Missouri and Illinois, and approved by the Congress
in a Joint Resolution of 31 August 1950 (64 Stat. 568). The
District comprises the City of St. Louis and the Counties of
St. Louis, St. Charles, and Jefferson in Missouri and the
Counties of Madison, St. Clair, and Monroe in Illinois. The
only direct administrative function of the Bi-State Development Agency is "to plan, construct, maintain, own and operate
bridges, tunnels, airports and terminal facilities. . . "[380]
Additional functions may be conferred upon the Agency either
by concurrent legislation of the two states or by legislation
of the Congress.

The Metropolitan District has a total area of about 3,000
square miles and a population of about 1,750,000 people.[381]
The Bi-State Development Agency was organized and began to
function in the early part of 1950. As of July 1953, "the
only construction work the Agency has so far undertaken is
that of a harbor and wharf facility for the interchange of
freight between rail, truck and river barge. This harbor is
being built on the recently completed, Federally built, Chain
of Rocks Canal near Granite City, Illinois. The first unit
of construction contemplates a wharf of approximately 1,000
feet long at a cost of $1,500,000." ". . . The issuance of
revenue bonds . . . has been applied to the harbor project,
except that we have secured a temporary construction loan
from a large industry who later will become one of our important tenants."[382]

3. <u>Water pollution control</u>---In 1901, in the case of

Missouri v. Illinois, 180 U. S. 208, the Supreme Court decided that one state cannot pollute the waters of an interstate
stream to the detriment of other riparian states. This decision revealed the fact that water pollution can be of interstate concern.383

Interstate administration for the control of water pollution was first provided in the Tri-State Compact of 1935
(Joint Resolution of the Congress of 27 August 1935: 49 Stat.
932), which applies to the tidal and coastal waters of the
states of New York, New Jersey and Connecticut in an area
specified as the Interstate Sanitation District (arts. I and
II). The compact creates the Interstate Sanitation Commission as the interstate administrative agency of the three
signatory states (art. III). The compact classifies the waters of the District into Classes A and B. Class A waters
are those which are primarily used for recreation, shellfish
culture and fish life development, and Class B includes all
other waters (art. VI). Minimum standards of water quality
are established for each class (art. VII). In addition to
its advisory functions (art. XII), the Interstate Sanitation
Commission is authorized to prescribe by order, after investigation and hearing, "the reasonable date on or before
which each municipality or other entity discharging sewage
into the designated waters within the District shall be treating such sewage in accordance with the standards specified
in this Compact. Such orders may prescribe that certain
specific progress shall be made at certain definite times
prior to the final date fixed in such orders" (art. X, para.
1). Non-compliance with the Commission orders may be prosecuted by the Commission in the courts (art. XI, para.2).
The jurisdiction of the Commission does not extend to the
tributary waters, which are to be taken care of by the respective states separately (art. VIII). It should be remarked
that the interstate administration exercised by the Commission is not exclusive of state administration separately exercised by the three states, but that the two complement
each other (art. XI, para. 1). The Commission "has issued
orders upon municipalities which had not taken aggressive
steps toward establishing their own pollution abatement program. In general, these orders have provided not more than
a three-year period to complete the pollution abatement project."384 From 1937 when the Commission began to assume its
duties to 1950, pollution of the tidal and coastal waters of
the three Atlantic states had been reduced by about one-half,
as in 1950 fifty percent of the 1,600,000,000 gallons of
sewage discharged into these waters were treated. It is estimated that by 1959 all pollution will be ended.385

On 11 July 1940, the Congress by a special act (54 Stat.
752) approved the Ohio River Valley Sanitation Compact signed
by Illinois, Indiana, Kentucky, New York, Ohio, Pennsylvania,
Tennessee and West Virginia. The compact became effective
on 30 June 1948, when all of the eight signatory states had

ratified it.[386] A special district, designated as the Ohio
River Valley Water Sanitation District was created embracing
"all territory within the signatory states, the water in
which flows ultimately into the Ohio River, or its tributaries" (art. II). The compact also established the Ohio River
Valley Water Sanitation Commission to be the governing agency
of the said District (art. III). The compact provides minimum standard for the discharge of sewage into the interstate
waters,[387] which requires (1) complete removal of settleable
solids and (2) removal by 45 percent of total suspended solids. However, the Commission, when necessary, may prescribe
higher standards in specific instances after investigation
and hearing. No standards have been specified by the compact
for the treatment of industrial wastes: these are to be fixed
by the Commission entirely at its discretion. The jurisdiction of the Commission seemingly does not extend to tributaries of interstate waters which lie wholly within one
state. However, these waters are indirectly subject to the
authority of the Commission in the "all sewage or industrial
wastes discharged or permitted to flow into" these tributary
waters "shall be treated to that extent, if any, which may
be necessary to maintain such waters in a sanitary and satisfactory condition at least equal to the condition of the
waters of the interstate stream immediately above the confluence."[388] Higher-than-minimum standards have actually
been required by the Commission for a 22-mile stretch of the
Ohio River lying between navigation dams nos. 36 and 37, known
as the Cincinnati Pool. Special attention has also been paid
to waters in the Pittsburgh area and in the Hungtinton-Ash-
land-Ironton stretch of the river.[389]

Not only has the Commission the authority to set up minimum standards of disposition of the polluting substances,
but also it has the authority to execute them. "The Commission may from time to time, after investigation and after a
hearing, issue an order or orders upon any municipality, corporation, person, or other entity discharging sewage or industrial waste into the Ohio River or any other river, stream
or water, any part of which constitutes any part of the boundary line between any two or more of the signatory states,
or into any stream any part of which flows from any portion
of one signatory state through any portion of another signatory state" (art. IX, para. 1, first sentence, emphasis supplied).

On 31 July 1947, the New England Interstate Water Pollution Control Compact was approved by Congress (61 Stat. 682)
after it was signed by the states of Connecticut, Massachusetts and Rhode Island. Article XI, section 2 of the Compact
provides that "without further submission of the Compact, the
consent of Congress is given to the States of Maine, New Hampshire, and Vermont, and the State of New York pursuant to
Article X of the Compact, to enter into the Compact as a sig-

natory state and party thereto." New York, Vermont and New
Hampshire acceded to the Compact on 19 August 1949, 29 June
1951 and 30 July 1951, respectively.[390] It had not been
ratified by Maine by the end of June 1953.[391] "The area
embraced by the Compact (without Maine participating) includes 65,000 square miles with a population of about 9,200,-
000 and is the second most densely populated area in the
United States." ". . .There are over communities discharging untreated sewage directly into the waters of the Compact
area from a contributing population of over 6,600,000 (and)
. . . over 1,900 plants producing industrial wastes."[392]

An interstate agency is created by the Compact known as
the New England Interstate Water Pollution Control Commission
(art. II). It is provided in Article V of the Compact that
(second paragraph):

> The Commission shall establish reasonable
> physical, chemical and bacteriological standards
> of water quality staisfactory for various class-
> ifications of use. It is agreed that each of the
> signatory states through appropriate agencies
> will prepare a classification of its interstate
> waters in entirety or by portions according to
> present and proposed highest use and for this pur-
> pose technical experts employed by state depart-
> ments of health and water pollution control agen-
> cies are authorized to confer on questions relat-
> ing to classification of interstate waters affect-
> ing two or more states. Each state agrees to sub-
> mit its classification of its interstate waters
> to the Commission for approval. It is agreed that
> after such approval all signatory states through
> their appropriate state health departments and
> water pollution control agencies will work to es-
> tablish programs of treatment of sewage and indus-
> trial wastes, which will meet standards establish-
> ed by the Commission for classified waters. The
> Commission may from time to time make . . . chang-
> es in definitions of classification and in stan-
> dards . . . .

It may be seen from this provision that the Commission merely establishes minimum water quality standards and has no
authority to execute these standards by itself as does the
Ohio River Valley Water Sanitation Commission. "Tentative
standards were first adopted April 20, 1948 and later revised
under date of February 11, 1949. The standards were further
revised on recommendation of the Technical Advisory Board on
December 8, 1950 under the new title of Tentative Plan For
Classification of Waters. This revision defines the classes
of water according to (1) Suitability for Use and (2) Standards of Quality . . ."[393] This plan has not been amended

amended since 8 December 1950, and has been "used as the basis for the classifications being submitted to the Commission
for approval under Article V of the Compact."[394]

The Interstate Commission on the Delaware River Basin,
established by an Interstate agreement signed by Delaware,
New Jersey, New York and Pennsylvania in 1936, is not an
interstate <u>administrative</u> agency,[395] as the Interstate Commission on the Potomac River Basin, which is its replica.[396]
However, in its advisory capacity, the Interstate Commission
on the Delaware River Basin, shortly after its establishment,
prepared a draft interstate agreement for the control of pollution of the waters of the Delaware River system. This a-
greement divides the Delaware River and its West Branch into four zones, and establishes minimum requirements of treatment of sewage and industrial waste to be discharged into
each zone. It was signed by the health departments of all of
the basin states, namely, New York, New Jersey, Pennsylvania
and Delaware, and thus became effective at the administrative
level, in 1939. But the agreement has not created an interstate agency to execute these minimum requirements. This devolves upon the various state health departments which are its
signatories.[397] It may be said that this interstate agreement has instituted a form of interstate administration for
the Delaware River Basin with regard to water pollution control.[398] The abobe-mentioned agreement were subsequently approved by statute, and thus acquired statutory status, in New
Jersey (Laws 1939, ch. 146), New York (Laws 1939, ch. 600) and
Delaware (Laws 1941, ch. 93).[399]

The Interstate Commission on the Potomac River Basin, too,
has, among other functions, the function "to make and if need-
ful from time to time, revise and to recommend to the signatory bodies, reasonable minimum standards for the treatment of
sewage and industrial or other wastes, now discharged or to be
discharged in the future to the streams of the Conservancy
District (i.e. Potomac Valley Conservancy District created by
the Compact), and also, for cleanliness of the various streams
in the Conservancy District."[400] Such minimum standards, when
adopted by the signatory states (including the District of Columbia), or any number of them, statutorily or sub-statutorily, would likewise constitute a form of interstate administration.

Interstate sanitary administration can also be established by administrative agreements. For example, on 9 June 1928,
the departments of health of Minnesota, Wisconsin, Illinois,
Indiana, Michigan, Ohio, Pennsylvania and New York signed the
Great Lakes Drainage Basin Sanitation Agreement, in which they
pledged themselves

> to cooperate with each other and with the United
> States Public Health Service in carrying out a pol-
> icy for the improvement of the quality of the wa-

ters of these interstate lakes (i.e. Lakes Superior, Michigan, Huron, St. Clair, Erie and Ontario)
and their tributary streams wherever necessary in
these states, and the prevention or correction of
undue pollution thereof, to the end that the said
lakes and tributary streams may be maintained or
rendered suitable sources of public water supplies
as aforesaid.

A separate agreement was concluded by them on the same date
creating the Board of Engineers consisting of the sanitary
engineers of the signatory health departments whose functions
are to investigate as to the causes of water pollution and to
recommend interstate measures for its abatement and prevention. The chairman of the organization of the state health
officers of the signatory state departments acts _ex-officio_
as the chairman of such Board of Engineers.

On 24 November 1935, the Upper Mississippi River Drainage
Basin Sanitation Agreement, together with separate agreement
providing for an identical Board of Engineers was concluded
between Minnesota, Iowa, Wisconsin, Illinois and Missouri.
"Since shortly after the Upper Mississippi Board was created,
the boards of both of these agreements have met jointly each
year. At the meeting in 1953 it was voted to combine the two
engineering boards under the title of Great Lakes and Upper
Mississippi River Board of State Sanitary Engineers. The
Health Commissioners of the states signatory to these agreements do not attend meetings, but the chairman is designated
as Chairman of the Engineering Boards." "In recent years,
the boards have developed uniform standards for design of
sewage works and have spent considerable time on development
of similar standards for water works."[401]

On 15 July 1948, the Missouri River Basin Sanitation
Agreement was signed by the health departments of Montana,
Wyoming, North Dakota, South Dakota, Colorado, Nebraska, Kansas, Minnesota, Iowa, and Missouri for exactly the same purposes as are served by the above-mentioned Great Lakes and
Upper Mississippi Sanitation Agreements. This agreement established a permanent Missouri River Basin Health Council,
which is composed of the head and the sanitary engineer of
each of the signatory state health departments.[402] The Council has recorded "real progress in setting stream standards
and in developing uniform requirements for the construction
of structures for sewage and industrial waste treatment."[403]

4. _Marine fishery_---The following three interstate compacts are in force with regard to the preservation of marine,
shell and anadromous fishery resources:

(1) Atlantic States Marine Fisheries Compact of 1942
(Act of the Congress of 4 May 1942: 56 Stat. 267),[404] as amended in 1950 (Act of the Congress of 19 August 1950: 64 Stat.

467).405

(2) Pacific Marine Fisheries Compact of 1947 between
California, Oregon and Washington (Act of the Congress of 24
July 1947: 61 Stat. 419).

(3) Gulf States Marine Fisheries Compact of 1949, applicable to Florida, Alabama, Mississippi, Louisiana and Texas
(Act of the Congress of 19 May 1949: 63 Stat. 70).406

Each of these three compacts establishes an interstate
commission made up of representatives of the states parties
to the respective compacts. These commissions have two general functions: (1) To advise the signatory states as to the
conservation of marine, shell and anadromous fisheries at
both statutory and sub-statutory levels (i.e. to advise both
state legislatures and governors and state administrative
agencies concerned); and (2) to recommend to any two or more
of the signatory for joint stocking of waters with marine,
shell and anadromous fishes. In case of (1), should the recommendations and advices of a commission be accepted by the
signatory states concerned, some form of interstate administration is very likely to emerge, although the commission
need not be the executing agency thereof. Function (2) is
but a particular form of Function (1). But the compacts in
identical terms provide that ". . . when two or more states
party hereto shall jointly stock waters, the commission shall
act as the coordinating agency, for such stocking." The
term "coordinating agency" is not clearly defined. There is
no doubt that under certain circumstances, the commission
may be the interstate administrative agency for the execution
or prosecution of such joint stocking. Whether the commission
is charged with executory or administrative duties or not,
joint stocking is by itself always an interstate enterprise.

Article X of the Gulf States Marine Fisheries Compact
provides:

> It is agreed that any two or more states par-
> ty hereto may further amend this compact by acts
> of their respective legislatures subject to the
> approval of Congress . . . to designate the Gulf
> States Marine Fisheries Commission as a joint
> regulating authority for the joint regulation of
> specific fisheries affecting only such states as
> shall so compact, and at their joint expense.
> The representatives of such states shall consti-
> tute a separate section of the Gulf States Marine
> Fisheries Commission for the exercise of the add-
> itional powers so granted . . . (63 Stat. 70, 72).

This provides for a third form of interstate administration
in marine fisheries. Substantially the same provision is

found in the 1950 amendment of the Atlantic States Marine
Fisheries Compact, but it has not as yet been adopted by
the Pacific States. It may be noted that the term "regulation" is not here clearly defined, and that it may admit of
both regulation and enterprise.

Interstate marine fishery administration may also be established by interstate administrative agreements. For example, a law of North Carolina of 1953 (ch. 1086) authorized
the Department of Conservation and Development "to enter into reciprocal agreements with coastal states on the Atlantic
Seaboard with regard to fin fish, shrimp and other migrating
marine life." Such agreements may provide for measures of
interstate administration.

   5. Recreation---The Interstate Park of the Dalles of
the St. Croix River, Minnesota and Wisconsin, is the first
interstate park established in the United States. It was
established in 1895 by concurrent legislation of Minnesota
(ch. 169) and Wisconsin (ch. 315). This legislation designated the location of the park in the respective states, and
authorized the Governor of each state to confer and cooperate
with the Governor of the other with respect to the acquire-
ment of lands and park improvement and maintenance. "Interstate Park in Minnesota is under the administration of the
Minnesota Division of State Parks, Department of Conservation. The portion of the park in Wisconsin is under the direction of the Division of Forests and Parks of the Wisconsin Conservation Commission. There is no administering
board made up of members of each state as provided in the
original law." But "both states acquired the land with the
same objective in mind for the preservation of the scenic
dalles of the St. Croix River and the establishment of a
state park for public recreational opportunities."[407] There
is a marked similarity in the manner in which the respective
states administer the park lands under their respective jurisdictions. The relationship between the two states has been
most harmonious. In so far as practicable, regulations governing the taking of fish in the boundary waters have been
made uniform. For purposes of boating and other general
forms of recreation there is full reciprocity in so far as
the surface of the water is concerned."[408] The Minnesota
portion of the Park lies in Chisago County and is 167.5 acres
in area; and the Wisconsin portion lies in Polk County and is
581 acres in area.[409]

   In 1900 the States of New Jersey and New York, by concurrent legislation (N. J., ch. 87; N. Y., ch. 170), established the Palisades Interstate Park and provided for the
appointment of ten commissioners as its administering agency.[410] The identical laws of the two states designated the
area of jurisdiction of the commissioners, and authorized it
to acquire lands in such area and administer these lands as

the Palisades Interstate Park. These lands are situated in
the Palisades in the two states and in Rockland and Orange
Counties of New York. In 1937, the above concurrent legislation was formalized in an interstate compact (Joint Resolution of the Congress of 19 August 1937: 50 Stat. 719; Laws
of New York of 1937, ch. 170; Laws of New Jersey of 1937,
ch. 148).

From its inception in 1900, the Palisades Interstate
Park has gradually grown in area and activities.[411] As of
July 1953, the Palisades Interstate Park consisted of the
following sections, which totalled 49,864 acres:[412]

Tallman Mountain State Park	781	acres
Blauvelt State Park	536	"
Hook Mountain State Park	655	"
Nyack Beach State Park	61	"
Haverstraw Beach State Park	73	"
Storm King State Park	1,057	"
Bear Mountain State Park	4,490	"
Harriman State Park	39,837	"
Palisades (New York)	16	"
High Tor State Park	491	"
Stony Point Reservation	45	"
Palisades (New Jersey)	1,822	"

With the exception of the last-mentioned area, i.e., the New
Jersey portion of the Palisades Section (1,822 acres), all
of these areas lie in New York. Picnicking, hiking and fish-
ing are generally available in these areas, except that hiking is the only recreational opportunity provided in the
Blauvelt, Hook Mountain; High Tor and Storm King State Park.
Camping is provided for in the Bear Mountain and Harriman
State Parks only. Boating is available in the Bear Mountain
Park and in the Lakes Tiorati, Kanawauke and Sebago of the
Harriman Park. Beach-bathing is available in the Lakes Sebago and Tiorati of the Harriman Park. In the Bear Mountain
and Tallman Mountain Parks, swimming pools have been construt-
ed, the swimming pool in the former being formed by damming
the outlet of the Hessian Lake. Facilities for winter sports
have been provided in the Bear Mountain and Harriman Parks[413]

Since the end of the Second World War, the Palisades Interstate Park Commission has been engaged in the construction
of the 43-mile Palisades Interstate Parkway.[414] The entire
Parkway is expected to be completed in 1955.[415]

In an Act of 23 June 1936, the Congress gave its consent
"to any two or more states to negotiate and enter into compacts or agreements with one another with reference to planning, establishing, developing, improving, and maintaining
any park, parkway, or recreational area" (49 Stat. 1894,
1895). On 28 August 1937 it approved, by a special act (50

Stat. 865), the Interstate Compact between Ohio and Pennsylvania relating to the Pymatung Lake. As provided therein,
the Pymatung Lake, subject to the primary use by Pennsylvania
for regulating the flow of the Shenango and Beavers Rivers,
is devoted to recreational use by the citizens of both states.
No interstate agency is established, but the two states control the area under their respective laws, with concurrent
jurisdiction over the waters of the lake. The lake must be
kept free from pollution. Motor boats and hydroplanes are
prohibited from operating or landing on it. Licenses from
the respective states are required for the operation of sail
boats, row boats and canoes. Fishing is permitted, except
during the period from 10 December each to 13 June following,
which is the closed season. Creel limits and further regulations on open seasons are to be subsequently agreed upon by
the two states. Reciprocal rights to hunt migratory birds
over the lake and nearby areas are recognized.

On 27 July 1954, the Kentucky-Virginia Breaks Interstate
Park Compact was approved (68 Stat. 571). The park is "located along the Russell Fork of the Levisa Fork of the Big
Sandy River and on adjacent areas, . . ." which is under the
administration of the Breaks Interstate Park Commission composed of three commissioners from each state appointed by the
Governor for overlapping terms of four years.

6. Miscellaneous---In an Act of 25 June 1949 (63 Stat.
271), the Congress approved the Northeastern Interstate Forest Fire Protection Compact, which "shall become operative
immediately as to those states ratifying it whenever any two
or more of the states of Maine, New Hampshire, Vermont, Rhode
Island, Connecticut, New York and the Common wealth of Massachusetts have ratified it and the Congress has given its
consent" (art. II, first sentence, at 272). "Any state not
mentioned in this article which is contiguous with any member state may become a party to this compact" (art. II, 2nd
sent.). The Compact establishes the Northeastern Forest
Fire Protection Commission as the coordinating agency for the
participant states. The Commission was formally organized on
19 January 1950,[416] when all of the seven states listed in
the Compact except Rhode Island had ratified it.[417] The Compact does not create an interstate administration for its entire membership. The only form of interstate administration
directly derivable from it is that which is provided in Article V, which reads:

> Any two or more member states may designate
> the North-eastern Forest Fire Protection Commis-
> sion as a joint agency to maintain such common
> services as those states deem desirable for the
> prevention and control of forest fires. Except
> in those cases where all member states join in
> such designation for common services, the repre-

sentatives of any group of such designating states
in the Northeastern Forest Fire Protection Commission shall constitute a separate section of such
commission for the performance of the common service or services so designated provided that, if
any additional expense is involved, the states so
acting shall appropriate the necessary funds for
this purpose (1st and 2nd sentences).

The common services which the Commission performs on behalf
of any group of member states may well be those which are
recommended to them by the Commission in its capacity of advisory planning.

In the field of flood control, an act was passed by the
legislature of Arkansas in 1917 (Acts 1917, No. 83) which
consolidated certain existing levee districts into the Southeast Arkansas Levee District, and authorized the latter to
maintain existing levees in cooperation with the Mississippi
River Commission (Federal) and the Tensas Basin Levee District of Louisiana. The levees included in this consolidated
district consist of 64.7 miles of levees along the Arkansas
River and 75.6 miles on the Mississippi River, and are maintained jointly by the said district and the Tensas Basin
Levee District of Louisiana.[418]

In sec. 4 of the Flood Control Act of 22 June 1936 (49
Stat. 1570, 1571-1572), the consent of the Congress is given
"to any two or more states to enter into compacts or agreements in connection with any project or operation authorized
by this Act for flood control or the prevention of damage to
life or property by reason of floods upon any stream or streams
and their tributaries which lie in two or more such states,
for the purpose of providing in such manner and such proportion as may be agreed upon by such states and approved by
the Secretary of War (now the Secretary of the Army) funds
for construction and maintenance, for the payment of damages,
and for the purchase of rights-of-way, lands, and easements.
. ." (1st sent.). This provides for interstate administration
in connection with the maintenance and operation of Federal
flood-control projects. No such interstate compact or agreement seems to have been ever in existence.

Interstate local drainage enterprise is permitted in the
laws of Ohio, Missouri, South Dakota and Minnesota. Under
the laws of Ohio (Revised Code, sec. 6131.14 et seq.: Laws
1887, p. 236; as last amended by L. 1919, p. 969, sec. 95),
the authorities of the county or counties, upon the filing
of application by any landowner for the construction of drains
or dtiches, shall direct their engineer or engineers to make
a survey and investigation in collaboration with proper officials of the county or counties of an adjoining state. Thereafter, the authorities of the counties concerned of both

states shall constitute a joint board in which the Ohio county or counties shall have one-half of the votes to decide
upon the necessity of construction and the route of the drains
and ditches and to employ engineers to supervise the construction work. The costs of construction are to be apportioned between Ohio and the neighboring state.[419]

In South Dakota (Code, ch. 61.11: Laws 1917, ch. 209),
the drainage of lands bordering upon an interstate boundary
stream or lake requires first of all the establishment of a
drainage district. This is to be achieved by order of the
circuit court concerned upon petition by 50 freeholders or
by the board of county commissioners of any county included
in the proposed district. The district is governed by a
drainage commission of three member who are appointed by the
board of commissioners of the county or boards of commissioners of the counties included in the district. This commission may then enter into an agreement with the local governmental unit or units of the neighboring state or states concerned for the joint appointment of engineers to make investigations and conduct the construction work, if this is so
petitioned by 25 freeholders or by authorities of any county
or city within the district. The costs of construction are
to be apportioned between the district and the participating
neighboring state or states. Those apportioned to the district are to be raised by special benefit assessments.

As provided in the laws of Missouri, "any city which now
has or may hereafter contain more than one hundred thousand
inhabitants shall have power to contract with drainage districts or with other public corporations in this or any adjoining state for cooperation or joint action in building
sanitary and storm sewers, . . . and in constructing levees
along the banks of, or shortening, diverting, or otherwise
improving any natural watercourse to prevent its overflow .
. . (Statutes, sec. 70.330: Laws 1911, p. 334). In Minnesota,
the county of any county or a district court acting for two
or more counties may enter into a contract with similar local
authorities of an adjoining state for the construction and operation of drainage works (Statutes, sec. 106.551: Laws 1925,
ch. 415, sec. 88; as amended by L. 1947, ch. 143, sec. 55).

In 1935 a law (ch. 114) was passed by the legislature of
Wyoming giving force to the proposed interstate compact between Wyoming and South Dakota which provides for the creation of the Black Hills Power District. The District is to
embrace the Counties of Crook, Campbell, Weston, Johnson and
Sheridan in Wyoming and the Counties of Fall River, Custer,
Pennington, Meade, Lawrence and Butte in South Dakota, and
has the sole function of generating and distributing hydroelectric power either by itself or in cooperation with the
Federal Government. It is to be governed by the Black Hills
Joint Power Commission to be composed of five commissioners

from each state appointed by the governor for overlapping
terms of five years. The Commission may borrow money and
issue bonds but cannot levy taxes or assessments. However,
this proposed compact, up to June 1953, had not yet been approved by South Dakota, nor by the Congress of the United
States, and so had not come into effect.

7. Final remarks---Interstate administration practically
covers all aspects of water resources administration. However, constitutionally interstate administration has its
limits. Speaking of interstate compact, the most formal and
forceful instrument in which interstate administration may
be incorporated, the U. S. Supreme Court, as early as in
1856, in Pennsylvania v. Wheeling and Belmont Bridge Company,
18 How. 421, 59 U. S. 435, declared:

> The question here is, whether or not the Compact can op-
> erate as a restriction upon the powers of Congress among
> the several States. Clearly not. Otherwise Congress and
> two states would possess the power to modify and alter the
> Constitution itself (59 U. S. 435.438).

Thus, except for express authorization by the Congress itself,
interstate administration cannot touch upon matter which are
within the constitutional authority of the Congress. Such exceptional authorization has, in fact, been given by the Congress to some states in many instances which may be found in
the foregoing discussion.

In matters over which the states constitutionally have jurisdiction and for which special Congressional authorization is
not required, interstate administration may appear either in
the form of an interstate compact or in the form of some other
interstate instrument or even of unilateral state legislation.
This is also generally so with matters for which special Congressional permission is necessary, subject, in this case, to
any specifications which the Congress may make.

Article 5 International Administration

1. General administration over international boundary
waters[420]

(a) Boundary waters, United States and Canada---"The
International Boundary between Canada and the United States,
for a distance of some 2,055 miles or 54 percent of its entire length, passes through a series of lake and river waterways common to both counties."[421] In 1902, the Waterways
Commission was created by concurrent legislation of the United
States (12 June 1902: 32 Stat. 331) and Canada. "It was purely an investigatory body without any final jurisdiction. Its
powers were limited to investigating and reporting upon the
conditions and uses of waters adjacent to the boundary be-

tween the United States and Canada and making such recommendations for improvements and regulations as would best subserve the navigation of these waters. This Commission having
successfully discharged the limited jurisdiction that was
assigned to it, negotiations were entered into for the creation of a Commission having greater powers and a wider jurisdiction." These negotiations resulted in the conclusion of
a Treaty between the United States and Great Britain on 11
January 1909, which was ratified on 5 May 1910. An International Joint Commission was created, which replaced the
International Waterways Commission, which thus "passed out
of existence."422

International regulatory administration, which is intrusted to the International Joint Commission, is provided for in
Articles III and IV of the Treaty, which read as follows:
(all emphasis supplied):

Article III

It is agreed that, in addition to the uses,
obstructions, and diversions heretofore permitted
or hereafter provided for by special agreement between the Parties hereto, no further or other uses
or obstructions or diversions, whether temporary
or permanent, of boundary waters on either side
of the line, affecting the natural level or flow
of boundary waters on the other side of the line,
shall be made except by authority of the United
States or the Dominion of Canada within their respective jurisdictions and with the approval, . . .
of . . . the International Joint Commission.
The foregoing provisions are not intended to
limit or interfere with the existing rights of the
Government of the United States on the one side
and the Government of the Dominion of Canada on
the other, to undertake and carry on governmental
works in boundary waters for the deepening of channels, the construction of breakwaters, the improvement of harbors, and other governmental works for
the benefit of commerce and navigation, provided
that such works are wholly on its own side of the
line and do not materially affect the level or
flow of the boundary waters of the other, nor are
such provisions intended to interfere with the ordinary use of such waters for domestic and sanitary
purposes.

Article IV

The High Contracting Parties agree that, except
in cases provided by special agreement between
them, they will not permit the construction or main-

tenance on their respective sides of the boundary
of any remedial or protective works or any dams
or other obstructions in waters flowing from boundary waters or in waters at a lower level than the
boundary in rivers flowing across the boundary,
the effect of which is to raise the natural level
of waters on the other side of the boundary unless
the construction or maintenance thereof is approved by the aforesaid International Joint Commission.

It is further agreed that the waters herein
defined as boundary waters and waters flowing
across the boundary shall not be polluted on
either side to the injury of health or property
on the other

Two kinds of administration (regulatory) are created by
the above provisions:

(1) For boundary waters, i.e., waters which are themselves part of the international boundary, Article III establishes complementary administration[423] between the two governments on the one hand and the International Joint Commission on the other. So far as the United States is concerned,
it creates Federal-international complementary administration.
This administration deals, so far as subject matters are concerned, with the diversion of water from and the construction
of dams and other works which may change the flow or level of
the boundary waters.

(2) For tributaries of the boundary waters and for waters
which are not themselves part of the boundary but which run
across the boundary (e.g., the Columbia River), Article IV
establishes Federal-international composite administration[424]
over the construction of works on one side of the boundary
which raise the natural water level on the other side.

The Treaty also sets up the following guides to the above
two forms of administration:[425] (a) In approving diversions
of water[426] from boundary waters, the following order of precedence among the various uses of water should be observed:
first, domestic and sanitary uses; second, navigation; third,
hydroelectric power development and irrigation. (b) In all
other cases under both (1) and (2), "the Commission shall require . . . that suitable and adequate provision, approved by
it, be made for the protection and indemnity of all interests
on the other side of the line which may be injured thereby."
Both these guides are directed to the International Joint
Commission only.[427] So far as the diversion of the waters of
the Niagara River (a boundary river) for power purposes is
concerned, the Commission is further guided by the provisions
of the treaty of 27 February 1950 as discussed earlier in this
book.[428]

In connection with the international administration under Articles III and IV of the Treaty, "it has been the practice of the Commission at all times to grant a hearing on any application and that a Board of Engineer Advisers are then named by the Commission to make necessary surveys and technical investigations."[429] In issuing the orders, the Commission "has at times found it necessary to provide for the creation of International Boards of Control. These Boards in each case consist of two Engineer Members, one appointed by the Government of Canada and the other by the Government of the United States. The functions of the Boards are to ensure that the provisions of the Commission's orders of approval are observed. The Boards form the effective machinery in the field to ensure the observance of the international obligations which are embodied in the Commission's orders. The Boards report directly to the Commission, and in the event of disagreement between their members, the decision rests with the Commission."[430] The boards of control "report annually or oftener when required and in event of the failure of the applicants to carry out the orders of the Commission, in order that all interests of the United States and Canada are protected."[431]

(b) Boundary waters, United States and Mexico---International administration over the United States-Mexico boundary waters includes[432] both regulation and enterprise.

(1) Regulation: In Article III of a convention between the United States and Mexico dated 12 November 1884 (24 Stat. 1012-1013), it was provided that

> No artificial change in the navigable course of the river, by building jetties, piers, or obstructions which may tend to deflect the current or produce deposits of alluvium, or by dredging to deepen another than original channel under the Treaty when there is more than one channel, or cutting waterways to shorten the navigable distance, shall be permitted to affect or alter the dividing line; . . . but the protection of the banks on either side from erosion by revetments of stone or other material not unduly projecting into the current of the river shall not be deemed an artificial change.

This provision was in line with the Treaty of Guadalupe Hidaogo of 2 February 1848 which, in a provision, prohibited the construction by either the United States or Mexico of works that might impede or interrupt free navigation of the then boundary waters (first sentence, first para.: 9 Stat. 922, 928). But these provisions were administered by the governments of the individual contracting countries and did not constitute international regulation.

On 1 March 1889, a new convention was concluded between the United States and Mexico, which took effect on 26 December 1890 (26 Stat. 1512). This convention set up the International Boundary Commission (now International Boundary and Water Commission) (Art. II). Among other duties, this Commission was intrusted with the authority of administering the above-mentioned provisions of the treaties of 1848 and 1884 with respect to the present boundary waters of the two countries. As provided in Article V of the convention, whenever the local authorities of either country concerned shall think that works are being constructed in violation of the convention of 1884 or the treaty of 1848, they shall submit the matter to the Commission for examination. "The Commission may provisionally suspend the construction of the works in question pending the investigation of the matter, and if it shall fail to agree on this point, the works shall be suspended, at the instance of one of the two Commissioners." It seems that the Commission merely determines the permissibility of the works under examination, and that if the works should be found impermissible, they will be prohibited by competent domestic authorities. Strictly speaking, the regulation which the Commission exercises is part of international-domestic united administration.[433] The convention of 1889 was continued indefinitely by a convention of 21 November 1900, effective 24 December 1900 (30 Stat. 1936); and the International Boundary Commission was changed into the International Boundary and Water Commission by the Water Treaty of 1944 (to be discussed below).

(ii) Enterprise---By an exchange of notes between the two governments in 1932, the International Boundary Commission (since 1944 the International Boundary and Water Commission) was charged with the construction and maintenance of the Lower Rio Grande flood control project. "The original plan as developed by the Commission in 1932 contemplated the construction of levees along each bank of the river, set back a sufficient distance from the normal channel to create a floodway capable of carrying the anticipated flood discharges; openings through the levees leading to auxiliary floodways in each country though which flood waters in excess of the river floodway's capacities would be conveyed in artificial or natural channels to outlets in the Gulf of Mexico and two diversion dams for the diversion of the required flood waters into proposed auxiliary floodways leading from the river at those points." Construction of the floodways and river levees in accordance with the original plan was started in 1933 by both Sections of the Commission, while that of the proposed flood diversion structures was deferred pending an agreement for division of waters between the two countries.[434]

By a convention of 1 February 1933, effective 13 November 1933, the said Commission was authorized to construct and maintain the Rio Grande Rectification Project.[435] "The project extends from about the easterly limits of the cities of

El Paso and Ciudad Juarez downstream to the entrance to Quitman Canyon, and the works include 85.6 miles (137.8 kilometers) of rectified river channel, about 170 miles (273.6
kilometers) of levees, which together form a floodway; bridges, grade control structures and numberous small structures."
"The project, substantially completed during the period 1934-
1938, accomplished the shortening of this stretch of the river from 152.2 miles (244.9 kilometers) to 85.6 miles (137.8
kilometers), thereby eliminating a serious flood hazard to
the cities of El Paso and Ciudad Juarez, providing incidental irrigation, drainage and flood prevention benefits to
about 178,000 acres (72,000 hectares) of valley lands in the
two countries, and stabilizing international boundary."[436]

By an Act of 19 August 1935 (49 Stat. 660), the President
was authorized to construct on the Rio Grande below Fort
Quitman, Texas, flood control, water conservation, sanitation
and water pollution control, channel rectification and stabilization and other related works which might be recommended by the American Section of the International Boundary
Commission after investigation (sec. 2). Under the authority
of this provision, the Douglas-Agua Prieta and the Nogales
sanitation or water pollution control projects were respectively authorized by the State Department Appropriation Act
of 2 July 1942 (56 Stat. 468, 477) and the Departments of
State, Justice and Commerce and the Judiciary Appropriation
Act of 5 July 1946 (60 Stat. 446, 455), with provisoes that
both projects, when completed, are to be maintained and operated by city governments. "Construction of the Douglas-
Agua Prieta Sanitation Project was begun in July 1946 and
completed in the summer of 1947. The principal feature of
this project is the sewage treatment plant in Douglas, Arizona, which was constructed under contract awarded by this
Section of the Commission."[437] The Nogales project "consists
of an outfall sewer extending from a point in Mexico 1.5
miles south of the boundary to a point about 2 miles north
of the boundary, together with a disposal plant in the United
States at the northerly end of the outfall line." The date
of the commencement of construction is not known, but the
project was completed in May 1952, when the City of Nogales
took over the operation and maintenance of the American portion of the project.[438] By special Acts of 13 September 1950
(64 Stat. 846) and 27 July 1953 (67 Stat. 195), the Cities
of Douglas and Nogales were respectively released from the
obligation of operating and maintaining these two projects,
and the Secretary of State was directed, in both cases, to
enter into agreements with Mexico for the international operation and maintenance thereof.[439] The above-mentioned Act
of 13 September 1950 (sec. 301) in the same time authorized
the Secretary of State to negotiate and conclude with Mexico
an agreement "for the construction, operation and maintenance
by the International Boundary and Water Commission, United
States and Mexico, of a sanitation project for the cities of

Calexico, California, and Mexicali, Lower California, Mexico", and imposed upon the City of Calexico the obligation to contribute part of the construction, maintenance and operation costs.[440] Information is not available regarding the actual construction of this project.

A multiple-purpose enterprise program aiming at the comprehensive development of the boundary waters (including both limitrophe and non-limitrophe waters) was adopted by the Water Treaty of 3 February 1944, effective 8 November 1945 (Treaty Series 994; 59 Stat. 1219). The following enterprises are contained in this program and are authorized by this Treaty[441]

(A)   Enterprises of the International Boundary and Water Commission, United States and Mexico.

(1)   The construction (art. 5) and the maintenance and operation (arts 8 and 9) of storage and diversion dams on the Rio Grande main channel below El Paso, Texas. "One of the storage dams shall be constructed in the section between Santa Helena Canyon and the mouth of the Pecos River; one in the section between Eagle Pass and Laredo, Texas; and a third in the section between Laredo and Roma, Texas." However, "one or more of the stipulated dams may be omitted, and others than those enumerated added by the Commission subject to the approval of the two Governments." The first of these dams, the Falcon Dam, was constructed in December 1950. The Falcon Reservoir has a designed total capacity of 4,100,000 acre-feet, of which 300,000 acre-feet are allocated for hydroelectric power development, 2,100,000 acre-feet for water conservation in the interest of irrigation and other beneficial uses (1,230,000 acre-feet to the United States and 870,000 acre-feet to Mexico) and 1,700,000 for flood control. The water power head will be capable of generating about 63,000 kilowatts of electric power.[442] The Falcon Dam "is expected to be completed by September 1953."[443] The construction of other dams had not been started as of the end of 1953.

(2)   The operation and maintenance of hydroelectric plants to be built (by the two Sections of the Commission) at the international storage dams on the Rio Grande (art. 7). According to the provision of the Water Treaty of 1944, the construction of the plants is not a duty of the Commission, but that of its two Sections. However, in an Act of 5 October 1949 (63 Stat. 701), the Congress directed that negotiations be made with the Mexican Government "of an agreement . . . for the joint construction, operation and maintenance on a self-liquidating basis for the United States share, by the two Sections of the International Boundary and Water Commission, United States and Mexico, of facilities for generating hydroelectric energy at the Falcon Dam on the Rio Grande being constructed by the said Commission. . ." Thus the construction of the Falcon Dam Power Plant is to be undertaken by the Com-

mission.

(3) The maintenance and operation of a main diversion
structure on the limitrophe portions of the Colorado River,
which is to be built by Mexico under plans to be approved
by the Commission (art. 12). This work, which is the Morelos
Dam, was constructed in 1948 and completed in October 1950[444]

(4) Maintenance and operation of parts of works for
flood control to be constructed by the two Sections of the
Commission on the Lower Colorado River below the Imperial Dam
upon plans to be prepared by the Commission (art. 13). However, no such flood control works have as yet been constructed.[445]

(5) Maintenance and operation of parts of storage and
flood control works on the Tijuana River to be recommended
and planned by the Commission and constructed by the two Sections (art. 16). The Commission has made the necessary investigations and recommendations, but the construction work
has not as yet started.[446]

(B) The United States Section[447]

(1) Construction and operation of flood control works on
Rio Grande below Fort Quitman, Texas, upon recommendations
and plans of the Commission (art. 6). This is a continuation
and modification of the Lower Rio Grande flood control project originally adopted in 1932, which was already discussed
above. Recommendations for modification of the project, which
called for the substitution of the originally planned diversion dams by a single diversion dam at the Anzalduas site,
were made on 18 December 1950 and subsequently approved by
the two Governments. Congressional authorization is necessary for the construction of the recommended Anzalduas Dam,
which has not as yet been given.[448]

(2) Construction of hydroelectric plants at the international storage dams on Rio Grande (art. 7).[449]

(3) Construction, operation and maintenance, at the expense of Mexico, of levees and other flood protection works
to be recommended by the Commission to protect the United
States lands from flood and seepage damages resulting from
the construction by Mexico of the Morelos Dam (art. 12, para.
a). ". . . Agreements have been reached with respect to such
protective works. Levees upstream from the Morelos Diversion
Dam are being improved to provide protection against a design
flood of 140,000 second-feet. . ." These levees are divided
into two increments: "(a) that necessitated by the dam and
being performed at the expense of Mexico; and (b) the portion
which would have had to be performed even if the Morelos Diversion Dam had not been constructed, and which is being per-

formed at the expense of the United States." While the former is constructed by the United States Section, the latter
is under construction by the Bureau of Reclamation.[450] It
is not clear whether these works have been completed.

(4) Construction (or acquisition) and operation and
maintenance, at the expense of Mexico, of works to convey
part of the waters of the Colorado River allocated to Mexico
to the Morelos Dam (art. 12, para. b).

(5) Construction of additional flood control works on
the Colorado River below the Imperial Dam, and operation and
maintenance of parts of these works upon recommendations and
plans of the Commission (art. 13).

(6) Construction of storage and flood control works on
the Tijuana River, and operation and maintenance of parts of
these works upon recommendations and plans of the Commission
(art. 16).

The works described in (4) through (6) above have not as
yet been constructed.[451]

Under the Protocol signed 14 November 1944 and effective
8 November 1945, which is supplementary to the Water Treaty,
those works allocated to the United States Section which are
used only in part for international purposes are to be constructed by the Federal agencies concerned on behalf of the
Section. Only those works that are used exclusively for international purposes are to be constructed by the Section directly; and in constructing these works, the Section may
utilize the services of the Federal agencies concerned.[452]

Both the Commission and its two Sections, in the performance of their enterprise activities, are guided by the order
of priority among the different uses of the water as specified in Article 3 of the Water Treaty, in case of conflicts
between these uses. Such order is: (1) sanitation, (2) domestic and municipal water supply, (3) agriculture and stock-
raising, (4) hydroelectric power, (5) other industrial uses,
(6) navigation, (7) fishing and hunting, (8) any other beneficial uses to be determined by the Commission.

2. Fisheries---Two kinds of international fisheries administration are now in force: (a) the international regulation of Northern Pacific halibut fisheries and (b) the international regulation of Northern Pacific sockeye salmon fisheries.[453]

(a) Northern Pacific halibut fisheries---On 2 March 1923
a convention was signed by the United States and Great Britain
(on behalf of the Dominion of Canada), which went into effect
on 22 October 1924(43 Stat. 1841), providing for international

regulation of halibut fishing. The regulation was intrusted to the International Fisheries Commission, which was specifically created by the convention (art. II). The period from 16th of November to the 15th of the next February was made a closed season, in which no halibut fish could be taken by the nationals, inhabitants and fishing vessels of both the United States and Canada; but this closed season might be modified or suspended at any time after the expiration of the first such seasons by a special agreement between the two contracting parties upon recommendation of the said Commission (art. I). This convention was applicable to both territorial waters and high seas of the western coasts of the United States and Canada, including the Bering Sea (art. I).

On 9 May 1930 a new convention was signed, which became effective on 14 May 1931 (47 Stat. 1872), and which amended the above convention. The International Fisheries Commission was now given authority to modify or suspend the closed season for any part or all of the convention waters subject to the approval of the President of the United States and the Governor General of the Dominion of Canada (art. I, second para.). Subject to the same approval, the Commission was further authorized to (art. III, second para.):

(a) divide the convention waters into areas;
(b) limit the catch of halibut to be taken from each area;
(c) fix the size and character of halibut fishing appliances to be used therein;
(d) . . .
(e) close to all halibut fishing such portion or portions of an area or areas, as the International Fisheries Commission find to be populated by small immature halibut.

This convention was again replaced by another convention concluded 29 January 1937 and effective 4 August 1937 (50 Stat. 1351). In addition to its existing functions, the Commission was further authorized "to permit, limit, regulate and prohibit in any area or at any time when fishing for halibut is prohibited, the taking, retention and landing of halibut caught incidentally to fishing for other species of fish, and the possession during such fishing of halibut of any origin" (Art. II, second para.). The Commission may also "prohibit departure of vessels from any port or place, or from any receiving vessel or station, to any area for halibut fishing, after any date when in the judgment of the International Fisheries Commission the vessels which have departed for that area prior to that date or which are known to be fishing in that area shall suffice to catch the limit which have been set for that area. . . ." (art. III, second para., sub-para. (c)).

(b) Northern Pacific sockeye salmon fishing---This international administration extends to the territorial waters and high seas westward from the western coast of the United States and Canada, the Fraser River and the streams and lakes tributary thereto, and certain specified waters. It was established in a convention between the United States and Canada signed on 26 May 1930 and coming into force on 28 July 1937 (50 Stat. 1355). The convention created the International Pacific Salmon Fisheries Commission as the administrative agency (art. II). The administration consists of both enterprise and regulation. With respect to the former, the Commission is authorized and directed "to improve spawning grounds, construct and maintain hatcheries, rearing ponds, and other (fish-cultural) facilities, . . . and to stock any such waters with sockeye salmon . . ." (art. III, first para.). Lands needed for these purposes are to be furnished the Commission by the respective American and Canadian Governments (art.VIII, second para.). The Commission may also "recommend (emphasis added) to the Governments of the High Contracting Parties removing or otherwise overcoming obstructions to the ascent of sockeye salmon, that may now exist or may from time to time occur, in any of the waters covered by this Convention, where investigation may show such removal of or other action to overcome obstructions to be desirable. . ." (art. III, first para.). The mere recommendation of course does not constitute an administrative measure. However, such recommendation may very likely result in some international administrative measure or measures. For example, upon recommendation of the Commission dated 11 January 1944, notes were exchanged between the American and Canadian Governments on 21 July and 5 August 1944, which provided for the removal of rocks during railroad construction in a narrow gorge of the Fraser River known as the Hell's Gate Canyon and the construction at this site of a fish ladder (59 Stat. 1614). This project consists of two fishways, which were completed in 1945 and 1946, respecitively, at a total cost of less than one million dollars.[454]

With regard to regulation, the Commission is authorized to limit or prohibit the taking of sockeye salmon in any or all of the waters under its jurisdiction (art. IV, first para). "In order to secure a proper escapement of sockeye salmon during the spring or chinook salmon fishing season, the Commission may prescribe the size of the meshes in all fishing gear and appliances that may be operated during said season. . . . At all seasons of the year, the Commission may prescribe the size of the meshes in all salmon fishing gear and appliances that may be operated on the high seas. . ." (art. V, first para.). The regulatory authority of the Commission in all cases extends only to the nationals, inhabitants and vessels and boats of the United States and Canada. It should also be remarked that this international regulation is additional to "the requirements of the laws of the State of Wash-

ington or of the Dominion of Canada as to the procuring of a
license to fish in the waters on their respective sides of
the boundary, or in their respective territorial waters . .
." (art. IV, first para.).[455] "Regulation of the commercial
fishing was inaugurated in 1946 and has been undertaken yearly, particularly for the benefit of those races which are in
greatest need of rehabilitation."[456]

3. Miscellaneous---The River and Harbor Act of 25 June
1910 authorized the improvement of the St. Croix River, Maine.
To this authorization, the following proviso was attached:

> Provided, That the Secretary of State be, and he
> is hereby, authorized and directed to negotiate
> with the Government of Great Britain with a view
> to its cooperation in said improvement, and that
> the work shall be prosecuted on such terms as
> shall be mutually agreed upon by the two Govern-
> ments (36 Stat. 630, 631).

This provision evidently intimated that the work of the improvement of the St. Croix River should be an international
enterprise. As a matter of fact, however, it was conducted
by the Federal Government alone. Upon its completion in 1917,
the Government of Canada reimbursed the Federal Government
one-tenth of the cost of construction and maintenance, i.e.,
$19,891.65 out of $199,441.46.[457]

"Under an authorization by the Congress (Act of 2 May
1932: 47 Stat. 145; 16 U. S. C. 161a and 161b) and by the
Canadian Parliament, the Waterton Lakes National Park in Canada and Glacier National Park in the United States were established as the Waterton Glacier International Peace Park
in 1932. Negotiations have been under way for several years
with the Government of the Republic of Mexico for the establishment of a Mexican national park across the Rio Grande
from Big Bend National Park, with the idea that the two would
ultimately also become an international park."[458] On 18 August 1941 an act was passed (55 Stat. 630) looking forward to
the establishment by the United States and Mexico an international memorial designated as the Coronada International
Memorial. Such an attempt was, however, abandoned on 9 July
1952, when the said memorial became Coronado National Memorial (66 Stat. 510).

Concerned over the increasing diversion of water from the
Niagara River and Falls for hydroelectric power purposes, resulting in a lowering of the scenic water-head at the Falls,
the Governments of the United States and Canada, in 1925 and
1926, requested the Special International Board of Control
for the Niagara River (constituted in July 1923) to make an
investigation of the matter and recommendations for the construction of remedial works. Investigations were conducted

by the said Board and a report was presented to the two governments on 11 December 1929, which was printed as Senate Document No. 128, 71st Congress, second session. "The Board recommended the construction of certain remedial works as an initial program, consisting of excavations and weirs in the cascades to produce an unbroken crestline from shore to shore of the Horseshoe Falls and a submerged rock weir above the cascades to insure an adequate flow over the American Falls and between the Three Sister Islands."[459] ". . .The direct supervision over their construction should be made the responsibility of the permanent International Niagara Board of Control . . ."[460] Construction of the submerged rock weir was started in March 1942 under the supervision of the International Board of Control, and was completed on 7 January 1947, at a total cost of approximately $878,100. This weir has accomplished these two purposes: (1) "The rise in water level due to the construction of the weir has increased the power output of those plants on both sides of the river that have their intakes upstream from the weir and has reduced trouble from ice"; (2) "the weir has nearly doubled the flow over the American Falls and thereby has improved its appearance" and scenic value.[461] For works on the Horseshoe Falls, the United States and Canada agreed, in Niagara River Treaty of 10 October 1950 (Art. II),[462] to request the International Joint Commission, United States and Canada (to which the International Niagara Board of Control subordinate) to plan and recommend its construction, and to complete it within four years after the recommended plan is approved.[463]

In the Northeastern Interstate Forest Fire Protection Compact of 1949, it is provided (article II) that "subject to the consent of the Congress of the United States, any province of the Dominion of Canada which is contiguous with any member state may become a party to this Compact by taking such action as its laws and the laws of the Dominion of Canada may prescribe for ratification." This permits the establishment of international enterprise at the state level.

Article 6   Inter-Jurisdictional Administrative Coordination[464]

Administrative adjustments[465] may be needed in matters over which the Federal Government and the several states have co-jurisdiction or in matters over which two or more states, or the Federal Government and some foreign government or governments, have concurrent jurisdiction.[466] The making of administrative adjustments may be collectively designated as coordination. Coordination may be effected either by organizational means or by non-organizational means, or by both. The present discussion is confined to that part of non-organizational coordination known as administrative coordination. Inter-jurisdictional administrative coordination may be divided into (A) strong coordination, i.e., coordination which necessitates a merger of administration, and (B) weak coordination, in which there is no merger of administration.

(A) Strong Coordination

1. Joint administration[467]---By joint administration
it is meant the merger of administration of two or more administrative agencies of different jurisdictions, or in a
broader sense, of the same jurisdiction in such a way that
they share the task (not necessarily equally) of creating and
carrying out a certain administrative measure and the responsibility therefor. Such a collaboration usually entails a
pooling of personnel, material and finance, though the latter by itself does not produce a case of joint administration.

Although the word "joint" appears in a rather undefined
way quite frequently in both public and private publications
in connection with water resources administration, there are
relatively few instances of real inter-jurisdictional joint
administration in this field of public administration. A
typical case of Federal-state joint administration is found
in sec. 22 of the Federal Water Power Act of 1920 (41 Stat.
1063, 1074; 16 U. S. C. 815), under which contracts of service extending beyond the term of the license are to be approved jointly by the Federal Power Commission and the public
service commission of the state concerned (if there is such
an agency). In the field of forestry, there are cases in
which the Forest Service of the Federal Government and the
state forestry agencies join in fighting forest fires.[368]
In the memorandum of understanding between the Department of
Agriculture and the local interests of the Los Angeles Watershed dated 22 January 1941 (House Document 426, 77th Cong.)
regarding the improvement of this watershed, it was provided
that the Department, through the Forest Service, should join
the County of Los Angeles and City of Los Angeles, on a 50-
50 basis, in the installation but not maintenance of forest
fire control works on non-Federal, non-farm mountain lands
and join the County of Los Angeles on the same basis in the
construction but not maintenance of stream channel improvements, and, through the Soil Conservation Service, should
join the Los Angeles County Flood Control District, also on
50-50 basis, in the installation but not maintenance of debris basins and minor channel-improvement works on streams
in farm lands. It is not clear whether as has actually been
carried out this program incorporates a form of Federal-local
joint administration.[469]

The Cooperative Farm Forestry Act of 18 May 1937 (50
Stat. 188), which provided for the cooperation of the Federal
Government with the forestry and agricultural extension agencies of the several states in assisting farmers in the management and harvesting of farm forests, was actually administered as a joint Federal-state undertaking by 1 July 1948, when
it began to be administered by the states with Federal grants
in aid. During the period of joint administration, a great
number of "woodland marketing assistance", "farm forestry"

and "forest farming" projects were established.[470]

These cases may be said as examples of _full_ joint administration. Besides, there are examples of _partial_ joint administration, in which the collaboration of the administrative agencies concerned stops at the preliminary or preparatory phases or stages of administration, leaving both the management of the final phase or stage of administration and the responsibility for the entire administrative measure to one agency. On 28 October 1918, the Imperial Irrigation District entered into an agreement with the Department of the Interior for the joint survey in connection with the construction by the said District of a canal entirely within the territory of the United States to connect the Imperial Canal with the Laguna Dam on the Colorado River. A special board called the All-American Canal Board was named by the two contracting parties to actually conduct the survey.[471] "The initiation of the joint procedure among Federal, State and local agencies for the planning of the Columbia Basin Project of the Bureau of Reclamation is beginning to bear results; the first report appearing early in the fall of 1941. The technique of the joint investigation, as it has applied in the Columbia Basin, has met with such success that the Bureau is considering applying it to other projects."[472] In 1923, the State of California created the California Power Board represented by the Corps of Engineers, U. S. Army; Bureau of the Reclamation, U. S. Department of the Interior; U. S. Forest Service and the State Engineer of California to investigate the possibilities of hydroelectric power development on the Trinity, American and Stanislaus Rivers.[473] In these and possibly other similar instances, there is joint administration at the stage of _investigation_.

In sec. 1 of an Act of 7 June 1924 (43 Stat. 653), "the Secretary of Agriculture is authorized and directed, in cooperation with appropriate officials of the various states or other agencies, to recommend for each forest region of the United States such systems of forest-fire prevention and suppression as will adequately protect the timbered and cutover lands therein with a view to the protection of forest and water resources and the continuous production of timber on lands chiefly suitable therefor." This provision envisages a kind of joint Federal-state _planning_ for the benefit of state legislative bodies (not limited to state legislatures). In sec. 1 of the Cooperative Forest Management Act of 25 August 1950 (64 Stat. 473), which authorizes the Secretary of Agriculture to provide grants in aid to the states in providing technical services to private forest landowners, provides, among other things, that "all such technical services shall be provided in each State, Territory or possession in accordance with a plan agreed upon in advance between the Secretary and the State forester or equivalent official of the State, Territory, or possession" (second sentence). This is another instance of Federal-state joint administration in the stage of planning.

In subsections (a) and (b) of sec. 209 of the Federal Power Act of 1935 (49 Stat. 847, 853), provisions are respectively made for the examination by joint boards to be organized, and for the holding of joint hearings, by the Federal Power Commission and the state public service commission concerned in any case relating to the administration of that Act of the said Commission. In the investigation or examination of original costs of the utilities, the practice of the Commission has been to invite accountants and engineers of the state public service commissions to participate in the work without the organization of formal joint boards.[474] These devices are illustrative of Federal-state joint administration at a stage perhaps immediately preceding the final stage of decision.

Annex: Local Joint Enterprises

Local joint enterprise is permitted in many states for a number of purposes. It may be used as one of the alternatives to the establishment of special districts, the other alternatives being administrative extraterritoriality as discussed before and the authorization of special taxes and (or) bonds, which will be discussed later. Some examples of local joint enterprises are given below.

In the laws of New Jersey, it is provided that "whenever any one or more counties and municipalities shall have flowing through their respective boundaries and borders any inland waterways or navigable streams and it shall be deemed to the advantage of any two or more of said counties and municipalities to improve such inland waterways or streams by increasing their depth or width or both, they may, acting together, advertise for bids for the doing of such work, and enter into a joint contract therefor" (Statutes, sec. 40: 14-3: Laws 1921, ch. 178, sec. 1). In Indiana, "whenever two or more neighboring cities or towns . . . shall so desire, they may join for the purpose of establishing, owning, maintaining and controlling one or more parks. . . . The members of the park boards of such cities and towns shall become and be and constitute a joint park board, and all of the territory embraced in all of said towns and cities joining shall constitute a joint park district . . ." (Statutes, sec. 48-5804: Acts 1915, ch. 31, sec. 1; as amended by Acts 1919, ch. 80, sec. 1).

Under the provisions of a law of 1953 (ch. 871), two or more municipalities of the State of New York may enter into a contract providing for a common water-supply system, which may be developed and undertaken either by all contracting municipalities acting jointly or by one of them acting for all. In Wisconsin, any two adjoining municipalities may jointly construct, operate and maintain a joint sewerage system and appoint a joint sewerage commission for this purpose. This commission shall be a body corporate, and shall consist "of one member appointed by each of the governing bodies of such municipalities and a third member to be selected by the two members so appointed, or in lieu thereof . . . two members appointed by the governing body of each municipality and a fifth member to be selected by the four members so appointed." The members of the board serve for overlapping terms of six years, and the board may employ engineers and other personnel. After approval by the governing bodies of the parent municipalities, the board may issue bonds. Each municipality is required to pay its share of the expenses of the joint board (Statutes, sec. 144.07(4): Laws 1935, ch. 460; as last amended by L. 1949, ch. 262).

In Louisiana, a comprehensive enabling law for joint local enterprises was enacted in 1942. It provides that "any two or more parishes (equivalent to counties of other states), any two or more municipalities, or any one or more parishes and any one or more municipalities may engage jointly in the exercise of any power, the making of any improvement, or the promotion and maintenance of any undertaking which each of the participating authorities may exercise or undertake individually under any provision of general or special law" (Revised Statutes, tit. 33, sec. 1324: Acts 1942, No. 246, sec. 4) (1st sentence).

Some of the other provisions for local joint administration have already been discussed in the foregoing chapter, and will not be repeated.

2. Trust administration---Trust administration is a result of mutual agreement between two (or more) agencies or jurisdictions under which one (or more) of the parties undertake to administer a certain administrative measure on behalf of the other party or parties on terms mutually agreed upon. These terms may cover such matter as finance, personnel, administrative procedure and administrative responsibility. They confer on the administering or trustee party different degrees of administrative discretion.[475] The more discretion is given the trustee party (or parties), the more perfect is the trust administration.[476] In the following will be separately discussed:

(A) State or local trust administration---Trustee administration with state or local governments or agencies as trustees and the Federal Government as the truster exists in the following fields:

(a) Navigation There have been occasionally instances of such trust administration. For example, in the River and Harbor Act of 19 September 1890 (26 Stat. 426, 448) the City of Galena, Illinois, was given authority to accept Federal

trust, within five years from the passage of that act, "to
continue and complete the improvement and navigation of the
channel of Galena River from a point 800 feet below the Custom House in said city to the main channel of the Mississippi
River" and "to construct a dam . . . with a lock. . ." ". .
. The United States promise and agree to pay to the City of
Galena . . . the sum of $100,000, when a channel has been
opened and maintained for navigation . . ." "These improvements," it was further provided, "though managed and controlled by the City of Galena or her representatives shall
be held to belong to the United States, . . . and at the completion of the work, the improved channel with dam and lock
shall be turned over to the management, control, and ownership of the United States."[477] This improvement was for the
purpose of facilitating the movement of lead and farm products
and accepted for maintenance by the United States in March
1894. With the exhaustion of good-quality Galena ores, the
project was abandoned in 1922 in pursuance to the River and
Harbor Act of 22 September 1922, and the dam and lock was
demolished in 1926.[478] By the River and Harbor Act of 25
June 1910, the Township of Union, of Ocean County, New Jersey, was permitted and authorized, to maintain, on behalf of
the Federal Government, the Federal improvement work for
the Double Creek, New Jersey (36 Stat. 630, 637).[479] In the
River and Harbor Act of 17 May 1950, there is the following
proviso with respect to the improvement of Lake Worth Inlet,
Florida (64 Stat. 163, 165):

> Provided, That the Secretary of the Army is here-
> by authorized to reimburse local interests for
> such work as they may have done upon this project,
> subsequent to July 1, 1949, insofar as the same
> shall be approved by the Chief of Engineers and
> found to have been done in accordance with the
> project modification hereby adopted . . . .

Such local improvement work, it is manifest, is in the nature
of a Federal trust, although it is a retroactive trust.[480]

(b) Flood control---In the Mississippi and Sacramento
Flood Control Act of 1 March 1917, provisions were made to
the effect that all flood-control works (levees only) on the
Mississippi River when completed should be turned over to
the levee districts concerned for maintenance (sec. 1(d),
last para.: 39 Stat. 948, 949) and that flood-control works
on the Sacramento River when completed should be turned over
to the State of California for maintenance (sec. 2(c): 39
Stat. 948, 950). Thus in the Mississippi and Sacramento River Basins while the construction of flood-control works was
Federal enterprise, their maintenance (and operation, for
other works than levees, in the Sacramento River Basin)
was local or state trust administration. Similar provision
was found in sec. 3 of the Flood Control Act of 17 May 1928;[481]

and sec. 8a of the Flood Control Act of 15 June 1936.[482]
The provision in the latter was repeated in precisely the
same language in sec. 3 of the National Flood Control Act of
22 June 1936 (49 Stat. 1570, 1571). In the Flood Control Act
of 28 August 1937, it was provided that sec. 3 of the Flood
Control Act of 22 June 1936 applied to all flood control projects <u>except</u> as otherwise specifically provided by law (sec.
4: 50 Stat. 876, 877). Under this amendment, the Federal
Government, when so specifically authorized and directed by
law, might maintain and operate a flood-control project by
itself. In other words, exceptions to the general rule of
state or local trusteeship in the maintenance and operation
of Federally built flood-control works were possible. These
exceptions were concretely given in sec. 2 of the Flood Control Act of 28 June 1938 (52 Stat. 1215, 1216), which were
(1) dam and reservoir projects and (2) channel improvement
or rectification projects.

In the Flood Control Act of 22 December 1944, it was provided (sec. 3: 58 Stat. 887, 889)

> That section 3 of the Act approved June 22, 1936,
> as amended by section 2 of the Act approved June
> 28, 1938, shall apply to all works authorized in
> this Act, except that for any channel improvement
> or channel rectification project provisions . . .
> (c) of section 3 of said Act of June 22, 1936
> shall apply thereto and except as otherwise pro-
> vided by law: <u>Provided</u>, That the authorization for
> any flood-control project herein adopted requiring
> local cooperation shall expire five years from the
> date on which local interests are notified in writ-
> ing by the War Department (now Army Department) of
> the requirements of local cooperation unless said
> interests shall within said time furnish assurances
> satisfactory to the Secretary of War (now Secre-
> tary of the Army) that the required cooperation
> will be furnished.

This provision removed, so far as projects authorized by the
Act of 1944 were concerned, channel improvement and channel
rectification works from the exceptions to the general rule
of state or local trusteeship and, "in effect, provided that
. . . no local cooperation is required for dams and reservoirs solely for flood control, but that for local channel
improvement and levee projects the requirements for local
cooperation specified in 1936 Flood Control Act are applicable."[483] It also limited the time in which states or local
units could accept the Federal trust to five years. This
provision has been reenacted in all subsequent Flood Control
Acts, and is one of the guiding policies of the Federal Government with respect to flood control.[484]

Many states have responded to this Federal offer of trust by enacting special laws authorizing state agencies and/or local units to accept it,[485] in addition to similar enabling provisions in special districts laws in some states. State or local trust administration in this field is usually conducted under regulations of the Secretary of the Army and supplementary instructions of the district Army engineer.[486]

Another kind of state or local trust administration in flood control is permitted under sec. 3 of the Flood Control Act of 28 June 1938, which reads as follows (52 Stat. 1215, 1216):

> In any case where the construction of cost of levees or flood walls included in any authorized project can be substantially reduced by the evacuation of a portion or all of the area proposed to be protected and by the elimination of that portion or all of the area from the protection to be afforded by the project, the Chief of Engineers may modify the plan so as to eliminate said portion or all of the area: . . . And provided further, That the Chief of Engineers may, if he so desires, enter into agreement with states, local agencies, or the individuals concerned for the accomplishment by them, of such evacuation and rehabilitation and for their reimbursement from said sum for expenditures actually incurred by them for this purpose

It may be observed that there are practical difficulties in the application of this provision, since "as a general rule, people who live and earn a living near a waterway do so because of the proximity of the waterway, and they are unwilling to move to the hills where the facilities or fertility they desire do not exist."[487]

There is one more kind of state or local trust administration in connection with Federal flood control enterprise. According to sec. 9 of the Flood Control Act of 24 July 1946 (60 Stat. 641, 643), the relocation, restoration or protection of "any highway, railway, or utility" which "has been or is being damaged or destroyed by reason of the operation of any dam or reservoir project under the control of the War (the Army) Department" is the responsibility of the Chief of Engineers of the Army Department. However, as a matter of fact, in many an instance, such work was done by the state or local agency concerned in trust of the Chief of Engineers.[488]

(c) Irrigation---In the Reclamation Act of 17 June 1902, it is provided (sec. 6: 32 Stat. 388, 389):

That the Secretary of the Interior is hereby

> authorized and directed to use the reclamation
> fund for the operation amd maintenance of all res-
> ervoirs and irrigation works constructed under the
> provisions of this Act: _Provided_, That when the
> payments required by this Act are made for the
> major portion of the lands irrigated from the wa-
> ters of any of the works herein provided for, then
> the management and operation of such irrigation
> works shall pass to the owners of the lands irri-
> gated thereby, to be maintained at their expense
> under such form of organization and under such
> rules and regulations as may be acceptable to the
> Secretary of the Interior: _Provided_, That the title
> to and the management and operation of the reser-
> voirs and the works necessary for their protec-
> tion and operation shall remain in the Government
> until otherwise provided by Congress.

This provision has established the rule of operation and maintenance of _all_ Federal irrigation works by water users after
payment by them of the construction costs. When the water
users are not organized into irrigation districts, this rule
is the basis of _delegated_ administration, which is delegated
to the water users or associations thereof (who otherwise do
not possess governmental authority) by the Federal Government.

   The Reclamation Extension Act of 13 August 1914, in sec.
5 (38 Stat. 686, 687), provides

> That whenever any legally organized water users'
> association _or irrigation district_ (emphasis sup-
> plied) shall so request, the Secretary of the In-
> terior is hereby authorized, in his discretion, to
> **transfer** to such water users' association or irri-
> gation district the care, operation, and maintenance
> of all or any part of the project works, subject
> to such rules and regulations as he may prescribe.

This permits the above-mentioned delegated administration to
be transformed into local _trust_ administration, with an irrigation district organized by the water users as the trustee
agency. It should be remarked that under this provision, the
organization of a waters' association or an irrigation district
is a matter which theoretically the water users are to determine by themselves.

   In subsections F and G **of** sec. 4 of the Second Deficiency
Act of 5 December 1924 (sec. 4 being commonly called the "Fact
Finders' Act), it was provided that the work of the maintenance
and operation of a Federal irrigation project should be undertaken by a water users' association or an irrigation district
(43 Stat. 672, 702). When the work of maintenance and operation rests with an irrigation district or an organization of

the water users which partakes of the nature of a government
unit or an administrative agency, it is trust administration,
but otherwise it is delegated administration (private).[489]

In most cases, this work is done by irrigation districts.[490]
Thus it is essentially local trust administration. A number
of irrigation districts may join in the administration, constituting a case of joint trust administration. The maintenance and operation of the Boise Project, Idaho, is such an
example, the several irrigation districts concerned being
represented through their common agency, the Boise Project
Board of Control.[491]

No trust or delegated administration is possible with regard to the hydroelectric power and non-irrigation water supply features of Federal irrigation enterprise, since, according to sec. 9(c) of the Reclamation Project Act of 1939 (and
its forerunner provisions in the Boulder Canyon Project of
1928) (53 Stat. 1187,1193), they are subject to sale and lease
by the Secretary of the Interior, which are ordinary private
commercial transactions and not administrative measures, in
spite of the fact that they are run by the government. However, there is one exception. That is the operation of the
power plant at the Hoover Dam of Boulder Canyon Project, Colorado. This plant was originally leased to the City of Los
Angeles, the Southern California Edison Company, and the Metropolitan Water District of Southern California. But sec. 9
of the Boulder Canyon Project Adjustment Act of 19 July 1940
(54 Stat. 774, 777), terminated this lease, and re-designated
two of these former lessees as "operating agents", the City
of Los Angeles being the operating agent for all states and
municipalities, and the Southern California Edison Company
that for all private utility companies.[492] Consequently,
the operation of the Hoover Dam power plant becomes trust administration by the City of Los Angeles and delegated administration by the Southern California Edison Company.

All of the above discussion regarding the maintenance and
operation of Federal irrigation projects applies to normal
irrigation projects only, but not to "water conservation and
storage projects". These are in principle to be operated and
maintained by the Federal Government itself, as already discussed before.

Aside from the local trusteeship in the maintenance and
operation of Federal irrigation projects, local trust administration by an irrigation district (or private delegated administration by water users' association) is also possible
with respect to the rehabilitation and betterment of Federal
Irrigation projects, which is primarily construction work,
under provisions of an Act of 7 October 1949 (63 Stat. 724).
This local trust administration (or private delegated administration) is, however, alternative to Federal administration.

(d)   Recreation---As early as 1 October 1890, a joint resolution was passed by the Congress granting permission

> to the City of Chattanooga, in the State of Ten-
> nessee, through its mayor and aldermen, to improve
> and beautify that portion of the military reser-
> vation lying outside of the national cemetery in-
> closure, situated in and adjoining the city of
> Chattanooga, to make such improvements and fillings
> and erect and maintain such structures as the Sec-
> retary of War may, from time to time, approve:
> Provided, That this resolution shall not be con-
> strued to pass any title or claim in said land,
> but that the ownership and control of the said
> grounds shall remain in the United States, and
> shall be subject to such changes and uses for mil-
> itary or other purposes as the Secretary of War may
> direct (26 Stat. 685).

This is perhaps the first instance of local trust administration on behalf of the Federal Government in the field of recreation.

There have been occasionally other examples of similar nature. On 5 May 1926, an Act was enacted (44 Stat. 397; 16 U.
S. C. 405) by which a tract of Federal land, formerly a part
of the Coos Bay military wagon road grant, "are reserved and
set apart as public parks and campsites for recreational purposes and to preserve the rare groves of myrtle trees thereon,
such lands to be placed under the care, control, and management of the county court of Coos County, Oregon, in accordance
with such rules and regulations as the Secretary of the Interior may prescribe . . ." A special Act of 3 March 1931 (46
Stat. 1493) established trust administration by the then Commissioners of Lincoln Park, Illinois, a municipal corporation
(now Chicago Park District) over certain designated navigable
waters of Lake Michigan and a breakwater for the purposes of
shore protection, which included both construction and maintenance work.[493] The River and Harbor Act of 2 March 1945,
in sec. 4 (59 Stat. 10, 24), provided for the termination of
the trust, subject, however, to the consent of the Chicago
Park District.

The most extensive and significant application of the principle of state or local trusteeship over Federal properties
for the purposes of recreation is found in the management of
recreational facilities on Federally built reservoirs. The
Tennessee Valley Authority is the principal sponsor of this
principle and practice. It has developed a number of demonstration park areas on its reservoirs, and has made arrangements with the park agencies of the States of North Carolina,
Alabama, Tennessee and Kentucky under which the latter have
been intrusted with the responsibility of managing the recre-

ational facilities in these areas.[494] The same principle has
been in force with respect to the reservoirs constructed by
the Bureau of Reclamation since the memorandum of the Secretary of the Interior of 11 July 1947.[495] The recreational
facilities on some of the Bureau's reservoirs are under the
trust administration of state park or game agencies. The Al-
tus Reservoir in W. C. Austin project, Oklahoma; the Crane
Prairie and Wickiup Reservoirs in Deschutes project, Oregon;
etc. are examples.[496] In other cases, as with the Bocca Reservoir in Truckee River Storage project, California, Fruitgrowers Reservoir in Fruitgrowers project, Colorado, etc.,
the trust rests with irrigation or conservation districts.[497]

In exceptional cases, regular units of the National Park
System may be subject to state or local trust administration.
For instance, on 1 October 1948, the Department of State Parks
of Georgia took over the maintenance of the New Echota Marker
National Memorial (0.92 acres), which was established 28 May
1932, but "the National Park Service retains basic jurisdiction."[498]

State or local trust administration discussed above should
be distinguished from the grant of <u>easements</u> to state and
local agencies over Federal properties (e.g., national forests) for the construction and maintenance of recreational
facilities, which is part of Federal administration, and which
will be regarded by the courts as a measure of Federal land
management.

(e) <u>Forestry</u>---On 29 August 1935, an Act was enacted
which authorized the Secretary of Agriculture "to enter into
cooperative agreements with appropriate officials of any state
or states for acquiring in the name of the United states, by
purchase or otherwise, such forest lands within the cooperating state as in his judgement the state is adequately prepared to administer, develop,and manage as state forests. . ."
(sec. 1: 49 Stat. 963). After 30 June 1942, lands should not
be acquired "unless the state concerned has prior thereto provided by law for the reversion of title to the state or a
political unit thereof of tax-delinquent lands and for block-
ing into state or other public forests the areas which are
more suitable for public than private ownership and which in
the public interest should be devoted primarily to the production of timber crops and/or the maintenance of forests for
watershed protection . . ." (sec. 2(a)). The standards of
administration adopted by the states for the acquired areas
must be approved by the Secretary of Agriculture (sec. 2(f),
and the United States is entitled to one-half of the gross
proceeds derived therefrom (sec. 2(h)). "Upon the request
of the state concerned, any agreement made pursuant to this
Act may be terminated by the Secretary of Agriculture. The
Secretary of Agriculture may, with the consent and approval
of the National Forest Reservation Commission, after due no-

tice given the state and an opportunity for hearing by said
Commission, terminate any such agreement for violations of
its terms and/or the provisions of this Act. If such agreement is terminated, the United States shall reimburse the
state for so much of the state funds as have been expended in
the administration, development, and management of the lands
involved as the Secretary of Agriculture may decide to be fair
and equitable" (sec. 2(1)).

State and local agencies may be called into aid in sup-
pressing and fighting forest fires in Federal forested areas,
and are reimbursed by the Federal Government for their services. For example, in an Act of 30 October 1951 (65 Stat.
671) the Congress reimbursed the town of Mount Desert, Maine,
a sum of $26,986.60 for its services in combating a forest
fire in the Acadia National Park from 24 October 1947 to 1
November 1947.

(B) Federal trust administration---As a part of the "New
Deal" administration, with funds provided by the Emergency Relief legislation, the Federal Government, in the 1930's, assumed the trusts of state and local governments in rural rehabilitation and in a great number of public-works projects.

With regard to rural rehabilitation, in conformoty with
the directives of the Federal Emergency Relief Administration,
"rural rehabilitation corporations were created in 1933 or
1934 in every state for the purpose of resettlement and relief of drought-stricken farm families in so-called 'stranded
communities'."[499] Plans of these corporations were carried
out by the Rural Rehabilitation Division of the Federal Emergency Relief Administration, as successively succeeded by the
Resettlement Administration, the Farm Security Administration
and the Farmers Home Administration. In sec. 2 (f) of the
Farmers Home Administration Act of 14 August 1946, the Secretary of Agriculture was directed to "liquidate, as expeditious-
ly as possible, trusts under the transfer agreements with the
various State Rural Rehabilitation Corporations and . . . to
negotiate with responsible officials to that end" (60 Stat.
1062, 1064). By an Act of 3 May 1950 (64 Stat. 98), the Secretary of Agriculture was further directed to liquidate these
trusts in three years, and to return the trusted funds and
properties to the state rehabilitation corporations or their
successors upon request of the latter. However, this Act did
not terminate the trust administration, but only changed it to
another form; for after the return to the states of the trust
assets and funds the Secretary of Agriculture may continue to
administer them under new agreements with the states in accordance with the provisions of Titles I and II of the Bankhead-
Jones Farm Tenant Act of 22 July 1937.[500]

The New Deal Federal trust administration was mainly undertaken by the Works Progress Administration established by Executive Order 7034 of 6 May 1935, which was incorporated in the

Federal Works Agency and renamed as the Works Projects Administration by Re-organization Plan 1 effective 1 July 1939.
It was launched as a substitute for the grant system administered by the Federal Emergency Relief Administration. The
Works Progress (or Projects) Administration constructed project sponsored by a state or local agency, and after completion it was turned over to the sponsoring agency for operation and maintenance as the property of the latter. "Sponsors
shared in the program by paying a portion of the cost of the
project. No fixed minimum percentage was set up by the WPA
for the individual sponsor's contribution, the ERA (Emergency
Relief Appropriation Act) of 1939 contained a provision that
sponsors' contributions within a given state must aggregate
25 percent of the cost of all projects approved January 1,
1940." The program was liquidated on 30 June 1943, having a
life of eight years, and incurring a total expenditure of
$10,568,796,592 (sponsors' contributions totalling $2,837,-
713,000, or 21.9 percent of total funds). Expenditures on
water resources administration are as follows:

Type	By WPA	By Sponsors
Water conservation	$454,750,072	$ 79,262,146
Parks, etc.	987,717,455	153,202,089
Water supply and sewerage	1,303,063,708	322,277,922
Sanitation	236,233,331	51,644,158

Achievements of this program in the water resources administration field consisted of 1,021 new, 69 enlargement and 415
reconstruction projects of sewerage treatment; 276 new, 18 enlargement and 161 reconstruction projects of water treatment
3,985 new and 1,954 reconstructed wells; 16,117 miles of new
and 3,658 miles of reconstructed water delivery and distribution lines; 15,268 miles of new and 22,572 miles of mosquito-
control ditches and pipelines; 161 new, 135 enlarged and 159
reconstructed fish hatcheries; 6,337 miles of new and 914
miles of reconstructed firebreaks (forest-fire prevention);
the planting of 176,636,000 forest trees and 8,210,967 bushels
of oysters; 591 miles of new and 1,083 miles of reconstructed
levees and ditches; 1,820 miles of new and 135 miles of reconstructed revetments and retaining walls; 4,419 miles of
river bank improvements; 1,351 miles of new and 5,339 miles
of reconstructed irrigation flumes and pipelines; 193 miles
of new and 7 miles of reconstructed jetties and breakwaters;
169 miles of new and 135 miles of reconstructed bulkheads,
etc.

The Federal Government has also been engaged in important
trust activities in the special field of forestry. Under sec.
1 of an Act of 3 March 1925 (43 Stat. 1132), which provided
for the "contributions towards reforestation or for administration or protection of lands within or near the national

forests", the Federal Government, through the Forest Service, was able to assume the trust of state or local agencies (or Federal agencies other than Forest Service) or of private parties in extending the administrative services of the national forests to lands owned by these trusters. By an amendment adopted in sec. 5 of the Forest Service Act of 24 April 1950 (64 Stat. 82, 83), this practice has been formalized in the following language:

> Sec. 1(a) The Secretary of Agriculture is author-
> ized, where the public interest justifies, to co-
> operate with or assist public and private agencies,
> organizations, institutions, and persons in per-
> forming work on land in state, county, municipal
> or private ownership, situated within or near a
> national forest, for which the administering agen-
> cy, owner, or other interested party (i.e., the
> truster) deposits in one or more payments a suffi-
> cient sum to cover the total estimated cost of the
> work to be done for the benefit of the depositor,
> for the administration, improvement, reforestation,
> and such other kinds of work as the Forest Service
> is authorized to do on lands of the United States.
> . . .

Sometimes Federal trust administration in forestry is initiated by the states themselves. For example, in South Dakota, the Federal Forest Service has been requested by the state to issue permits for starting of fires in Black Hills Forest Fire Protection District as a measure of state forestry fire regulation (Code, ch. 20.05: Laws 1941, ch. 93; as amended by L. 1953, ch. 88).[501] Typical of the practices in some Western states, a Nevada law of 1947 (Stats. 1947, ch. 149, sec. 7) authorizes state forestry officers to enter into contracts with the Federal Government agencies "to provide for placing any or all portions of fire protection work under the direction of the agency concerned . . ." Under the Forest Cutting Practices Act of 1943 of Massachusetts, the Division of Forestry of the Department of Conservation may "authorize" employees of the U. S. Forest Service to administer the provisions of the Forest Cutting Practices Act of 1943 on its behalf. The Division of Forestry of the Department of Conservation and Development of Washington, with regard to the forest pest control in the southeastern part of the state, intrusted the actual control work to the U. S. Forest Service.[502]

As for Federal trust administration in other fields, it is provided in sec. 206(b) of the Federal Power Act of 26 August 1935 (49 Stat. 847, 852), that the Federal Power Commission may, either in its own initiative or upon the request of any state public service commission, without interfering with its regular duties, "investigate and determine the cost of the production or transmission of electric energy by means of facilities under the jurisdiction of the Commission in cases where the Commission has no authority to establish a rate governing the sale of such energy." These cases are within the jurisdiction of the state public service commissions and it is the latter which determine the sale rates. Under this provision, the Federal Power Commission undertakes to do the preliminary work in the administrative procedure of state rate regulation. This may be said as a case of _partial_ Federal trust administration, in which only certain stage or stages of a state or local administrative measure are under Federal trusteeship.

As will be discussed later, the River and Harbor Act of 1930 created the Beach Erosion Board in the Corps of Engineers, and authorized the Chief of Engineers, with the assistance of this Board, to make studies and investigations of beach erosion in cooperation with states. "Studies for shore protection and improvement are normally . . . initiated by the states or their political sub-divisions. When such a study is undertaken, the law requires this local political subdivision to participate with the United States in the cost of the study. By executive determination the amount of this local participation has been fixed at 50 percent of the estimated cost of the study and report."503 By 30 June 1951, a total of 76 studies had been launched and reports for 66 of them had been completed.504

3. Composite administration505---In the various River and Harbor Acts, there have been provisions making the construction of certain Federal improvement works conditional upon the construction by local governments of works without which the Federal works are unable to operate with full success. For example, in connection with the improvement of the harbor at South Haven, Michigan the River and Harbor Act of 3 March 1905 provided that construction should not be started "until proper dock lines shall have been established and suitable bulkheads shall have been built along these lines by the city of South Haven, or by the riparian owners . . ." (33 Stat. 1117, 1136). With respect to the improvement of the Cumberland River above Nashville, Tennessee, the River and Harbor Act of 25 June 1910 required that "local interests will provide a suitable landing place, convenient to the city of Burnside" (36 Stat. 630, 651). In authorizing the improvement of the Cumberland River, Tennessee and Kentucky, the River and Harbor Act of 2 March 1919 stipulated that "local interests will provide sufficient areas of water front and suitable water terminals at all towns or landings adequate for the traffic . . ." (40 Stat. 1275, 1282).

In an Act of 4 March 1929, it was provided that the establishment of the Badlands National Monument is conditioned upon the construction of a highway by South Dakota (45 Stat.

1553, 1555). In 1947 a program was initiated by the Tennessee
Valley Authority of distributing trees for reforestation purposes to land owners in the Tennessee Valley area of Alabama.
"The trees are furnished to all classes of landownership free
of cost. Applications from farmers are submitted to the Alabama Extension Service for approval while other applications
are approved by the Division of Forestry (of the Alabama Department of Conservation)."[506]

All these cases of composite administration existing between the Federal and state and local governments are related
to enterprise. As for composite regulatory administration,
sec. 9 of the River and Harbor Act of 3 March 1899 provides,
among other things, that dams, dikes, causeways and bridges
"may be built under authority of the legislature of a state
across rivers and other waterways the navigable portions of
which lie wholly within the limits of a single state, provided the location and plans thereof are submitted to and approved by the Chief of Engineers and by the Secretary of War (the
Army) before construction is commenced" (first proviso). Here
the state legislature is the principal regulatory authority
and the Department of the Army acting through the Corps of
Engineers is the auxiliary regulatory authority. In sec. 1
7(a) of the Regulations Relating to Migratory Birds and Certain Game Mammals, proclaimed by the President on 11 August
1944, as last amended on 29 July 1948 (13 F. R. 4411), it is
provided that

> Game mammals or parts or products thereof, taken
> in and transported from a state, territory, or the
> District of Columbia, may be transported to Mexi-
> co, if the importation thereof is not prohibited
> by law or regulation of that country, upon presen-
> tation to the collector of customs at the port of
> exit of the certificate of an official, warden, or
> other officer of the game department of such state,
> territory or District, that such game mammals, or
> parts thereof, which must be listed in the certi-
> ficate, were taken or acquired and are being trans-
> ported in compliance with the laws and regulations
> of such state, territory, or District.

In this case, the transportation of game mammals to Mexico
is within both Federal regulation and state regulation, which
are so merged that the latter may be regarded as a condition
of the former.[507]

4. Alternative administration---Alternative administration refers to cases of administrative coordination between
two or more jurisdictions or agencies in which all of them
have full administrative responsibility and authority over a
certain administrative act or measure, and any one of them
may perform it without the collaboration or assistance of the

others, but only one of them is to undertake it. In some
cases one of the jurisdictions or agencies concerned enjoys
a preferred status, and the alternative administration arising from this situation may be termed _preferred_ alternative
administration. Other cases of alternative administration
may collectively be called _free_ alternative administration.

Sec. 1 of an Act of 4 June 1897 cited above, is an instance of Federal-state alternative administration. Federal
administration is preferred for state administration would
be invoked apparently only in the absence of Federal administration. Under secs. 19 and 20 of the Federal Water Power
Act of 1920 (41 Stat. 1063, 1073-1074) the regulation of the
services and rates of licensees of the Federal Power Commission whose activities and business are of the nature of a public service corporation, rests with the state agencies, or,
in absence of a responsible agency in any state, with the
Federal Power Commission. This is Federal-state alternative
administration in which the state agencies enjoy a preferred
status. In the plan for the treatment of the Yazoo River Watershed in Mississippi, there was a provision for the retirement of some 730,000 acres of submarginal farm land. These
lands were to be acquired either by the Federal Government,
or by the state, or counties or other government units, but
purchase by the Federal Government was envisaged.508 Similar
proposal was made in regard to the purchase of 538,557 acres
of forest land in the plan of improvement of the Coosa River
Watershed, Georgia and Tennessee.509

It should be pointed out that alternative administration
refers to concrete cases in which the manner of alternative
administration is specified in definite terms. The mere possibility of alternative administration, which covers the entire area of Federal-state co-jurisdiction, is not alternative administration.510 While co-jurisdiction or possibility
of alternative administration is the source of inter-jurisdictional conflicts, alternative administration is a means to
avoid or eliminate these conflicts.

Discussed above are the main forms of strong inter-jurisdictional administrative coordination. Besides, there have
been occasionally other types of such coordination. For example, a case of Federal-state united administration was created by sec. 2 of the Weeks Act of 1 March 1911 (36 Stat.
961).511 Under this section the Secretary of Agriculture was
authorized "to stipulate or agree with any state or group of
states to co-operate in the organization and maintenance of a
system of fire protection on any private or state lands . . .
situated upon the watershed of a navigable river." A cooperating state must have provided by law a system of forest-fire
protection and must expend in any fiscal year a sum for this
purpose at least equal to Federal funds expended in that state.
As the program was actually carried out, Federal funds were

used exlusively in the employment of lookout-watchmen and patrolmen, which represented one aspect or integral part of the
whole task of forest-fire protection on non-Federal watershed
forest lands. The Federal Government expended these funds by
itself and the personnel paid with these funds are Federal em-
ployees.512 The program was terminated in 1924, when sec. 2
of the Weeks Act was superseded by the Clarke-McNary Act.
During the 14 years of operation, the number of cooperating
states increased from 11 to 28; the area protected from 61
million acres to 175 million acres; the yearly Federal expenditures from $53,000 to $400,000 and the yearly state expenditures from $350,000 to $1,900,000.513

(B) Weak coordination

1. Approval and recommendation---In some Federal administrative acts, particularly those involving the acquisition
of lands, state or local approval or consent is required.514
The purpose of this arrangement is twofold: first, to protect
state jurisdiction from possible encroachment by the Federal
Government, and secondly, to prevent losses in state and local
revenues derivable from property taxes (since Federal lands
are in general immune from state and local taxation). Only
the first purpose is related to administrative coordination.

In sec. 7 of the Weeks Act of 1 March 1911 (36 Stat. 961,
962), it is provided that purchases of forest lands by the
Federal Government under the provisions of that Act must be
consented to by the legislature of the state in which the
land lies. Under sec. 1 of an Act of 10 March 1934 the establishment of fish and game sanctuaries or refuges in national forests must be approved by the state legislatures of the
respective states in which the national forests concerned are
located (48 Stat. 400). In the Wildlife Coordination Act of
the same date (48 Stat. 401), it was provided, among other
things, that (sec. 5) the Federal Government might establish
game farms with the consent of the legislatures of the states
in which they were to be located. This provision, however,
was only in effect for a dozen years and was repealed by the
new Coordination Act of 14 August 1946 (60 Stat. 1080). As
already discussed above, under sec. 4 of the Rural Electrification Act of 20 May 1936 (49 Stat. 1363, 1366), Federal
loans for power-generation purposes cannot be made except
with the consent of the state agency "having jurisdiction in
the premises". In the Agriculture Department Appropriation
Act of 30 August 1951, it is provided in a proviso that no
part of the flood control funds appropriated "shall be used
for the purchase lands in the Yazoo and Little Tallahatchie
watersheds without specific approval of the county board of
supervisors of the county in which such lands are situated,
nor shall any part of such funds be used for the purchase of
lands in the counties of Adair, Cherokee and Sequoyah in the
State of Oklahoma without the specific approval of the board

of county commissioners of the county in which such lands are situated . . ." (65 Stat. 225, 235).

Next in importance and in force to approval and consent is advice and recommendation which, though having no binding force, is entitled to respect of the agency which seeks it. Under sec. 5 of an Act of 28 August 1937, the Secretary of the Interior is authorized, in formulating forest-practice rules and regulations in the administration of the revested Oregon and California Railroad grant and the reconveyed Coos Bay Wagon Road grant lands in the state of Oregon, "to consult with (i.e. to seek advice of) the Oregon State Board of Forestry, representatives of timber owners and operators on or contiguous to said revested and reconveyed lands, and other persons or agencies interested in the use of such lands" (50 Stat. 874, 875). Under sec. 209(c) of the Federal Water Power Act of 10 June 1920, as added 26 August 1935 (49 Stat. 853, 854), the Federal Power Commission is required to "make available to the several state commissions such information and reports as may be of assistance in state regulation of public utilities". The "information and reports" referred to in this provision is Federal advice to state agencies.

In the annual revision and promulgation of open seasons and hunting regulations by the Fish and Wildlife Service, "the individual state fish and game commissions are asked to make their pre-season recommendations within certain limitations, of dates which shall apply to the individual state."[515] The said Service has also entered into agreements with the state fishery agencies of a majority of states under which applications to the Service for fish for stocking streams and lakes are referred to them for review and recommendation. The recommendations of the state agencies are generally respected[516] In performing its duties under the Federal Water Power Act of 1920, the Federal Power Commission has adopted the practice "of notifying interested governors and state agencies, as well as county and city officials, regarding the receipt of applications for preliminary permits and licenses for major power projects, . . . and of giving them an opportunity to submit objections or comments." They are also invited to comment on applications for amendments of licenses which involve major changes.[517] Recently this practice has been extended to declarations of intention.[518]

In sec. 1 of the Flood Control Act of 22 December 1944, "the interests and rights of the states in determining the development of the watersheds within their borders and likewise their interests and rights in water utilization and control" is recognized (58 Stat. 887, 887-888). Under the guidance of this policy, the following provisions are made (among other things) (subsections (a) and (c), at 888-889):

(1) In connection with the initiation of navigation-im-

provement and flood-control projects, the Corps of Engineers
of the Department of the Army shall, during the stage of investigation, inform the affected state or states of the results of the investigation and provide them an opportunity
for consultation and cooperation. Before report is made by
the Corps of Engineer, through the Secretary of the Army, to
the Congress for approval, opportunity should be given the
affected state or states for review and the making of recommendations, which should be transmitted to the Congress together with the said report.

(2) The above procedure also applies to the authorization of irrigation projects by the Secretary of the Interior.[519] However, "in the event a submission of views and recommendations, made by an affected state, . . . sets forth objections to the plans or proposals covered by the report of
the Secretary of the Interior, the proposed projects shall not
be deemed authorized except upon approval by an Act of Congress; and subsection 9(a) of the Reclamation Project Act of
1939 (53 Stat. 1187, 1193) and subsection 3(a) of the Act of
August 11, 1939 (53 Stat. 1418), as amended, are hereby amended accordingly."

Under these provisions, the recommendations of the states
are entitled to the attention of the Congress. As a matter
of fact, projects of both the Departments of the Interior and
the Army that are more or less local in nature are proposed
by local interests. In these projects, basic harmony between
the Federal and the state and local government enterprises
can be taken for granted.

In sec. 2 of the new Wildlife Coordination Act of 12 August 1946 (60 Stat. 1080), it is provided that (1st para.)

> Whenever the waters of any stream or other body of
> water are authorized to be impounded, diverted, or
> otherwise controlled for any purpose whatever by
> any department or agency of the United States, or
> by any public or private agency under Federal per-
> mit, such department or agency first shall consult
> with the Fish and Wildlife Service and the head of
> the agency exercising administration over the wild-
> life resources of the state wherein the impound-
> ment, diversion, or other control facility is to
> be constructed with a view to preventing loss of
> and damage to wildlife resources, and the reports
> and recommendations of the Secretary of the In-
> terior and the head of the agency exercising ad-
> ministration over the wildlife resources of the
> state, for the purpose of determining the possi-
> ble damage to wildlife resources and the means
> and measures that should be adopted to prevent
> loss of and damage to wildlife resources, shall

be made an integral part of any report submitted
by any agency of the Federal Government for engineering survey and construction of such projects
(emphasis supplied).

This is an extension of the rule of the above-discussed sec.
1 of the Flood Control Act of 1944 to fish and wildlife management. The words "under Federal permit" refers to the licensing authority of the Federal Power Commission, and the
recommendations of the state game agencies as well as of the
U. S. Fish and Wildlife Service are made to the Federal Power
Commission and not to its licensees.[520]

2. Program coordination---Program coordination is an
arrangement between two or more agencies of the same jurisdiction or of different jurisdictions under which certain
kind or kinds of administrative acts performed by them are
united or pooled together so as to constitute a coherent program.

An excellent example of Federal-state-local program coordination is the recent program of flood control for the Brown's
Canyon in Scotts Bluff County of Nebraska (a tributary of the
North Platte River). The overall program calls for the construction of two dams, the lining of portions of the Fort
Laramie Canal, and channel improvements. "Since April 1953,
excellent progress has been made in constructing the major
features of the flood control plan. Dam No. 1, which will
hold approximately 300 acre-feet of water and is 62 feet high
and 260 feet long has been under construction by the Bureau
of Reclamation and is nearing completion. Dam No. 2, which
will hold approximately 185 acre-feet of water and is 760 feet
long and 45 feet high, is now under construction by the Nebraska Department of Roads and Irrigation. An underdrain on
the Mitchell Canal is under construction with good progress
being made. The Gering-Fort Laramie Irrigation District is
handling the construction of this feature. A tube and cul-
vert on the Lyman-Mitchell road has been re-placed by the
Scotts Bluff County and the Nebraska Department of Roads and
Irrigation. A bridge in the canyon has been raised 5 feet
to provide adequate capacity through Brown's Canyon Drain.
The Gering-Fort Laramie Irrigation District has made several
channel improvements by enlarging the channel and riprapping
bad curves. They are also replacing water crossings with
steel siphons and they are now completing the installation of
about 500 feet of canal lining on either side of the Fort
Laramie Canal siphon on Brown's Canyon." It was the United
States Soil Conservation Service that called together the
several parties concerned and brought the coordinated program
into being.[521] This is a case of program coordination because
there is no pooling of either funds or personnel but each of
the cooperating agencies performs its work independently. It
may incidentally be pointed out that the Bureau of Reclamation

undertook the construction of Dam No. 1 in order to protect
its irrigation works in the area and the dam itself is not
an irrigation project but a work designed as a "soil and moisture conservation" structure. When completed, this dam will
be maintained on behalf of the Bureau of Reclamation by the
Gering-Laramie Irrigation District.522

In sec. 2 of the Park, Parkway and Recreation Survey Act
of 23 June 1936 (49 Stat. 1894, 1894-1895), it is provided
that in order to develop "coordinated and adequate public
park, parkway and recreational facilities for the people of
the United States", the Secretary of the Interior, acting
through the National Park Service, may "aid the several states
and political subdivisions thereof in planning such areas
therein, and in cooperating with one another to accomplish
these ends." It is clear that in this provision program coordination between the Federal, state and local governments
is envisaged.523

In Pennsylvania, the Federal Government and the Common-
welath of Pennsylvania have since 1945 cooperated in carrying out the Schuylkill River Desilting Program. The Common-
welath, through the Water and Power Resources Board of the
Department of Forests and Waters, is responsible for "the
reclamation of the Schyulkill River along a seventy-five-mile
stretch from Hamburg to Norristown and the construction of
desilting dams as Kernsville on the main Schuylkill, Auburn
on the west branch and at Tamaqua on the east branch or Little
Schuylkill." The Federal Government, through the Corps of
Engineers of the Department of the Army is responsible for
"the portion of the Schyulkill River from below Norristown
to the tidewaters at Philadelphia by the construction of impounding basins on land provided by the Commonwealth."524
Such cooperation is also program coordination.

The establishment of sustained-yield units in Federal
forest lands in most cases involve program coordination between the Federal Government and the states and local units
or between the various Federal agencies having under their
jurisdictions forest lands or between the Federal Government
and private persons. In sec. 2 of "An Act relating to the
revested Oregon and California Railroad and reconveyed Coos
Bay Wagon Road grant lands situated in the State of Oregon",
approved 28 August 1937 (50 Stat. 874), which first introduced this practice into Federal forestry administration, it is
provided that

> The Secretary of the Interior is authorized, in
> his discretion, to make cooperative agreements with
> other Federal or state forest administrative agen-
> cies or with private forest owners or operators
> for the coordinated administration, with respect to
> time, rate, method of cutting, and sustained yield,

of forest units comprising parts of revested or
reconveyed lands, together with lands in private
ownership or under the administration of other public agencies . . . . (emphasis supplied).

Under sec. 4 of an Act of 29 March 1944 (58 Stat. 132, 133),
which extended the above practice to all Federally owned forest lands, each of the Secretaries of the Interior and Agriculture is authorized "to enter into cooperative agreements
with the other Secretary, or with any Federal agency having
jurisdiction over federally owned or administered forest land,
or with any state of local agency having jurisdiction over
publicly owned or administered forest land, providing for the
inclusion of such land in any coordinated plan of management
. . . . (emphasis added).[525] Such "coordinated" plans of
management must be plans of program coordination.[526]

In the latter half of 1949 the Territorial Government of
Puerto Rico and the Federal Government (through the Production
and Marketing Administration of the Department of Agriculture)
initiated an experimental program of coordinating the coffee
conservation program of the former and the agricultural conservation program of the latter. "Under this program the insular government furnishes financial aid for carrying out certain conservation practices and the Agricultural Conservation
Program furnishes financial aid for carrying out certain other
conservation practices. This approach is working out in a
satisfactory and effective way, and it eliminates duplica-
tions."[527] This is an example of program coordination in the
field of soil conservation.

The St. Lawrence Seaway Project is an example of international program coordination. The objective of the "Project"
is to secure a 27-foot depth for the accommodation of ocean-
going vessels throughout the 2,350-mile waterway from Duluth
at the western end of Lake Superior to the mouth of the St.
Lawrence River at Belle Isle near Newfoundland. This depth
is already available throughout the course of this great waterway except for the following short reaches:

> (1) St. Marys River, Michigan (connecting Lakes
> Superior and Huron), 63 miles, which, according to
> the latest authorized improvements as adopted by
> the River and Harbor Act of 1946, has a depth vary-
> ing from 20 to 27 feet.
> (2) St. Clari River, Michigan (connecting Lakes
> Huron and St. Clair), 40 miles, which, according
> to the latest authorized improvement adopted by
> the River and Harbor Act of 1946, has a depth vary-
> ing from 20 to 26 feet.
> (3) Detroit River, Michigan (connecting Lakes St.
> Clair and Erie), 31 miles, which, according to the
> latest authorized improvements adopted by the River

and Harbor Act of 1946, has a depth varying from 21 to 27 feet.

(4) The Welland Canal, which was constructed by the Canadian Government to bypass the Niagara Falls and which was completed in 1932. It has a depth of 25 feet.

(5) From the head of the St. Lawrence River to Chimney Point (Thousand Island Section), 67 miles, which is 25 feet in depth.

(6) The International Section, from Ogdensburg, New York and Prescott, Ontario to Montreal, 119 miles. Of these 119 miles 49 miles consist of **rapids** -- International Rapids, Soulanges Rapids and LaChine Rapids. These rapids are by-passed by canals built by Canadian Government in 1882-1901, which have a depth of between 14 and 16 feet.

The project (which should more properly be called a "program") will deepen the above bottlenecks to a minimum depth of 27 feet. Since the Great Lakes and the Saint Lawrence River, which form the Saint Lawrence Seaway, traverse the United States and Canada, concerted action between the two countries is necessary to carry out this program.[528] This is provided in an Agreement between the two **countries** concluded at Ottawa on 19 March 1941,[529] which was the result of more than two decades of negotiation.[530] This Agreement provides, in essence, (1) that bottlenecks entirely lying in the territory of Canada (including Soulange and LaChine Rapids) are to be deepened by the Government of Canada,[531] (2) that bottlenecks entirely lying in the territory of the United States are to be deepened by the Government of the United States and (3) that the work of increasing the depth of the International Rapids (i.e., that part of the International Section of the Saint Lawrence River which extends from Chimney Point to the **village** of St. Regis) is to be shared by the two Governments in accordance with a plan already agreed upon by them[532] and prosecuted under the supervision and coordination of the Great Lakes-Saint Lawrence Basin Commission, an international body specially created for this purpose. Power houses in the International Rapids Section may be constructed either simultaneously with the navigation works or later, but they need not be constructed by the national governments of the two countries.[533] It is to be noted that no part of the work is to be constructed by the two counties jointly as an international enterprise. The entire plan is one of international program coordination.

A Saint Lawrence Seaway Authority was created by Canada on 21 December 1951. On 13 May 1954, an Act was passed by the Congress of the United States (68 Stat. 92), which established the Saint Lawrence Seaway Development Corporation. These two agencies are special agencies for the navigation work in the International Rpaids Section, and are expected to complete the construction of the works assigned their respective governments as nearly concurrently as possible.[534]   Construction work of the United States Corporation was scheduled to commence in November 1954.[535]

3. Harmonious action (harmonization)---In order to bring about harmony between two or more jurisdictions or agencies, action may be taken by or is desired of one jurisdiction or agency to fit in with or to assimilate certain administrative act or acts of the other jurisdiction (jurisdictions) or agency (agencies). Such action may be called Harmonious action. For example, in the Sundry Civil Appropriation Act of 1 July 1916, it was provided that "no part of the appropriations herein for propagation of food fish shall be expended for hatching or planting fish or eggs in any state in which, in the judgment of the Secretary of Commerce (then supervising the Bureau of Fisheries), there are not adequate laws for the protection of the fishes . . ." (39 Stat. 262, 323). In this provision, harmonious action of the several states was called for to facilitate a Federal fishery measure. The uniform system of accounts promulgated by the Federal Power Commission on 16 June 1936 and taking effect on 1 January 1937[536] was similar to the utility accounting systems then in force in most of the states for the regulation of intra-state utilities.[537] Here a Federal administrative act is assimilated to existing state administration.

4. Administrative adoption---Administrative adoption is a form of administrative coordination in which certain administrative measure or measures of one jurisdiction or agency are adopted by another jurisdiction or agency, i.e., regarded by the latter as its own measure or measures. In the laws of Montana, for example, it is provided that "whenever state lands are located within the boundaries of federal irrigation projects, the land shall be sold in conformity with the classification of farm units as made by the United States . . ." (Revised Codes, sec. 81-906, enacted 1927). In this case, a measure of Federal land management is adopted by the State of Montana. In the Agricultural Department Appropriation Act of 4 March 1907, it is provided that ". . . hereafter officials of the Forest Service designated by the Secretary of Agriculture shall, in all ways that are practicable, aid in the enforcement of the laws of the states or territories with regard to stock, for the prevention and extinguishment of forest fires, and for the protection of fish and game" (34 Stat. 1256, 1269). In this provision, state and territorial forestry and fish and game administration is adopted and enforced by the Federal Government. The Federal Power Commission, acting through its regional office at Atlanta, in the exercise of its licensing authority in Georgia, Alabama, North Carolina, and Florida, keeps itself in contact with the health department of these states "with respect to compliance with the terms of FPC licenses in those states relating to mosquito

control", "the objective being to maintain through cooperative
efforts satisfactory health conditions at the licensed project reservoirs."[538] This seems to be the adoption by the
Federal Power Commission of state mosquito-control regulations
in the above-mentioned states.

Annex---Federal Inter-Agency Administrative Coor-

dination

1. Trust administration[539]---As already discussed before,
during 1886-1918, the Yellowstone, Sequoia, General Grant and
Yosemite National Parks were administered by the Department
of War on behalf of the Department of the Interior; and the
resident Army engineers in the Mount Rainier, Yellowstone and
Crater Lake National Parks constructed roads and trails in
these parks prior to 1916, 1918 and 1919 respectively. Many
major roads and approach roads in the National Park System
have been constructed by the Bureau of Public Roads. Many Indian irrigation projects were constructed by the Bureau of
Reclamation (and its predecessor, the Reclamation Service).
For example, the Blackfeet Indian Irrigation project was authorized by the Interior Department Appropriation Act of 1 March
1907 (34 Stat. 1015, 1035). On 28 June 1907, the Secretary of
the Interior instructed the Reclamation Service to construct
it.[540] In the Indian Appropriation Act of 18 May 1916, it was
provided, among other things, that "the work to be done with
the amounts herein appropriated for the completion of the Blackfeet, Flathead, and Fort Peck projects may be done by the Reclamation Service on plans and estimates furnished by that Service and approved by the Commissioner of Indian Affairs" (39
Stat. 123, 141). On 22 January 1908, the Secretary of the Interior entered into an agreement with the Secretary of Agriculture placing the forests in the Indian Reservations under
the administration of the Forest Service. This agreement,
however, was terminated in July 1909.[541]

"The Federal Power Commission requires licensees operating
hydroelectric porjects to measure the flow of streams used to
generate power." This work of the licensess is supervised by
the Geological Survey at the request of the Commission.[542]
As already mentioned above, forest lands of Federal agencies
other than the Forest Service in or near the national forests,
under sec. 1 of an Act of 1 March 1925, as amended by an Act
of 24 April 1950, may be placed under the administration of
the Forest Service. In sec. 5 of the Water Facilities Act of
28 August 1937 (50 Stat. 869, 870), it is provided that "the
Secretary of Agriculture, in administering the provisions of
this Act, . . . may . . . transfer to such other agencies of
the Federal Government as he may request to assist in carrying out any of the provisions of this Act, any funds available
for the purposes of this Act." Under this provision, trust
administration for the benefit of the Department of Agriculture

by other Federal agencies is possible.

The National Park Service under agreements with the Bureau of Reclamation and other Federal agencies, has assumed the administration of recreational facilities on lands and waters controlled by the latter. As discussed above, some Bureau of Reclamation reservoirs are administered by the National Park Service as National Recreational Areas. "Under a memorandum of understanding with the Bureau of Land Management, to which Angle Island, in San Francisco Bay, had been transferred for disposal, the National Park Service has undertaken temporary responsibility for its administration and protection."[543] Such trust administration of the National Park Service now tends to become an established practice, and, under an Act of 7 August 1946 (60 Stat. 885), appropriations of the Service may be allocated for such purpose. Recreational facilities on many other Bureau of Reclamation reservoirs are administered by other Federal agencies. In the following reservoirs, which are adjacent to national forests, recreational facilities are administered by the Forest Service: (1) Six reservoirs on the Salt River project, Arizona (under agreement with Salt River Valley Water Users Association, technically not trust administration), (2) Shasta Reservoir, Central Valley project, California; (3) Taylor Park Reservoir, Uncompahgre project, Colorado; (4) Island Park Reservoir, Minidoka project, Idaho; (5) Crane Prairie and Wickiup Reservoirs, Deschutes project, Oregon (in collaboration with Oregon Fish and Game Commission); (6) Deerfield Reservoir, Rapid Valley project, South Dakota; (7) Pine View Reservoir, Ogden River project, Utah (under agreement with the Bureau of Reclamation and Ogden River Water Users Association) and (8) Bumping Lake and five other reservoirs, Yakima project, Washington. Facilities for recreation on these following Bureau of Reclamation reservoirs are handled by the Fish and Wildlife Service: (1) Imperial Reservoir, All-American Canal project, Arizona-California; (2) Lake Huvasu, Parker Dam project, Arizona-California; (3) Lake Alice and Lake Minatare, North Platte project, Nebraska and (4) 5,000-6,000 acres of swamp land near Upper Klamath Lake, Klamath project, Oregon. Recreational facilities on the Bull Lake Reservoir, Riverton project, Wyoming, are managed by the Bureau of Indian Affairs.[544]

As for partial trust administration, the Geological Survey has accepted the trust of many other Federal agencies, such as the Corps of Engineers, the Bureau of Reclamation, the Fish and Wildlife Service, the Forest Service, and the Bonneville Power Administration, in the construction and operation of stream-gaging stations and water-resources investigation.[545] The same work is performed on behalf of the Department of State under the Mexican Water Treaty of 1944.[546]

2. <u>Approval and consent</u>---When the performance of a certain administrative act or measure of one agency concerns the

jurisdiction of another agency, the approval or consent of
the latter may be required. For example, in sec. 6 of an Act
of 9 April 1924, as added 31 January 1931 (46 Stat. 1054), it
is provided that whenever proposal is made of the construction of a national park approach road across or within any
national forest, "the Secretary of the Interior shall secure
the approval of the Secretary of Agriculture before construction shall begin." An Act of 7 August 1947 (61 Stat. 913)
authorizes the Secretary of the Interior to lease coal, phos-
phate, oil, oil shale, gas, sodium, potassium and sulphur deposits in Federal lands. However, "no mineral deposits . . .
shall be leased . . . except with the consent of the head of
the executive department, independent establishment, or instrumentality having jurisdiction over the lands containing
such deposits, or holding a mortgage or deed of trust secured by such lands which is unsatisfied of record, and subject
to such conditions as that official may prescribe to insure
the adequate utilization of the lands for the primary purposes for which they have been administered . . ." (sec. 3, 3rd
sentence).

     3. Administrative concentration---Administrative concen-
tration refers to cases in which similar activities of different agencies are brought under the control of the agency
that has primary responsibility over these activities. The
above-mentioned Act of 7 August 1947 authorizing the Secretary
of the Interior to lease mineral deposits in lands under the
control of other Federal agencies is a typical example of administrative concentration. Prior to the enactment of this
Act, each of these other Federal agencies would have to make
the leases by itself. Two important measures of administrative concentration have been made by the Flood Control Act of
22 December 1944. In the first place, hydroelectric power
generated at projects of the Department of the Army is, under
sec. 5 of the Act, to be disposed of by the Department of the
Interior. This has already been discussed before. Secondly,
sec. 7 (58 Stat. 887, 890-991) provides:

                    Hereafter, it shall be the duty of the Secretary
               of War (the Army) to prescribe regulations for the
               use of storage allocated for flood control or navi-
               gation at all reservoirs constructed or in part
               with Federal funds provided on the basis of such
               purposes, and the operation of any such projects
               shall be in accordance with such regulations: Pro-
               vided, That this section shall not apply to the Ten-
               nessee Valley Authority, except that in case of
               danger from floods on the Lower Ohio and Mississip-
               pi Rivers the Tennessee Valley Authority is di-
               rected to regulate the release of water from the
               Tennessee River into the Ohio River in accordance
               with such instructions as may be issued by the War
               (Army) Department.

Under this provision, there is administrative concentration
with regard to the operation of flood-control storages[547] of
reservoirs built by Federal agencies other than the Corps of
Engineers of the Department of the Army. Under the authority
of this provision, special regulations governing the operation of flood-control storages in particular reservoirs have
been issued by the Department of the Army.[548] The only Federal agency which has constructed dams that are provided with
navigation locks is the Tennessee Valley Authority. The locks,
lifts and all other facilities in aid of navigation in dams
of the Tennessee Valley Authority are operated and maintained
by the Corps of Engineers "in accordance with the general navigation laws placing control and supervision over navigable
waters in the Secretary of the Army."[549] Thus there is de-
facto administrative concentration with respect to the operation of navigation locks, lifts and similar facilities. As
mentioned above, under an Act of 1946, the National Park Service may expend its own funds in the administration of recreational facilities on reservoirs of other Federal agencies.
This may well be the beginning of a new field of administrative concentration.

There is also administrative concentration in the business
behavior of the sale of hydroelectric energy. The center of
concentration is the Federal Power Commission. There are two
aspects of this concentration:

(a) The Federal Power Commission determines the rates of
sale. This aspect has, however, been confined to multiple-
purpose projects constructed and controlled by the Corps of
Engineers of the Department of the Army. In sec. 6 (first
and second sentences) of the Bonneville Project Act of 20 August 1937 (50 Stat. 731, 735) it is provided that "schedules
of rates and charges for electric energy produced at the Bonneville project and sold to purchasers . . . shall be prepared
by the Administrator and become effective upon confirmation
and approval thereof by the Federal Power Commission. Subject
to confirmation and approval by the Federal Power Commission,
such rate schedules may be modified from time to time by the
Administrator, and shall be fixed and established with a view
to encouraging the widest possible diversified use of electric
energy." Identical provision is found in sec. 5 (first and
second sentences) of the Fort Peck Project Act of 18 May 1938
(62 Stat. 403, 405). By the Flood Control Act of 22 December
1944 (first sentence of sec. 5: 58 Stat. 887, 890), this rule
is extended to all other multiple-purpose projects constructed
by the Corps of Engineers.

This concentration practice does not prevail over (1) single-purpose projects constructed by the Corps of Engineers,
such as the St. Marys Falls project, Michigan (River and Harbor Act of 2 March 1945: 59 Stat. 10, 20); (2) projects controlled by the Tennessee Valley (TVA Act, sec. 14, para. 2,
last sentence: 49 Stat. 1075, 1077); and (3) irrigation and

multiple-purpose projects constructed by the Bureau of Reclamation, as a result of the provision in sec. 9(c), second sentence, of the Reclamation Project Act of 4 August 1939 (53 Stat. 1187, 1193).[550] But single-purpose hydroelectric power projects constructed by the Bureau of Reclamation are not within the purview of the said provision of the Reclamation Project Act of 1939. To these, the rate-determining authority of the Federal Power Commission may extend. The Eklutna project, Alaska, is the only single-purpose hydroelectric project ever constructed by the said Bureau; and, under sec. 2 (first sentence) of the Act authorizing this project (31 July 1950: 64 Stat. 382), the rate schedules of the sale of electric energy produced at this project are "to become effective upon confirmation and approval by the Federal Power Commission."[551]

(b) By sec. 14 of the Tennessee Valley Authority Act of 1933, ". . . the Federal Power Commission . . . is (hereby) empowered and directed to prescribe such uniform system of accounting, together with records of such other physical data and operating statistics of the Authority as may be helpful in determining the actual cost and value of services, and the practices, methods, facilities, equipment, appliances, and standards and sizes, types, location, and geographical and economic integration of plants and systems best suited to promote the public interest, efficiency, and the wider and more economical use of electric energy" (49 Stat. 1075, 1077). By sec. 213 of the Federal Power Act of 26 August 1935 (49 Stat. 847, 855), the Federal Power Commission is authorized to prescribe uniform systems of accounting (including depreciation accounts) for and to examine all accounts, books and records of "all agencies of the United States engaged in the generation and sale of electric energy for ultimate distribution to the public." "The Tennessee Valley Authority, Bonneville Power Administration, Southwestern Power Administration, Southeastern Power Administration, and the Bureau of Reclamation comply with these requirements so far as concerns their power operations. The Commission does not, however, audit the accounts."[552]

In some cases, it may be remarked, administrative concentration necessarily brings about complete or partial consolidation of the administrative agencies concerned. For example, if there should be any concentration with respect to the management of forest lands or of grazing lands, such concentration would require the consolidation between the Forest Service and the Bureau of Land Management, or between the Bureau of Land Management and the Soil Conservation Service and other agencies.

4. Advice and recommendation---It was reported in 1902 that the Secretary of War requested the technical advice of the Secretary of Agriculture regarding forest management in

eight military reservations embracing a total area of 117,468
acres.[553] Under the Administrative Regulations of the Department of Agriculture, the Soil Conservation Service, in administering the Water Facilities projects under the Case-Wheeler
Act of 1939, "shall advice and consult with the Farmers Home
Administration with respect to those phases which relate to
settlement arrangements, the location of persons on projects,
and farming practices", at the planning stage (Title I, ch.
7, sec. 4, para. 424). "Planning under the Water Facilities
Act has also made necessary a coordination of planning activities between the Department of Agriculture and the Department of the Interior." "Field representatives of the Department of Agriculture upon receipt of information that a specific proposal is to be prepared, inform representatives of
the Department of the Interior and invite their comments."
"Field representatives of the Department of the Interior forward their observations to the Washington office to enable
the Departmental officers to submit final comments to the
Water Facilities Board of the Department of Agriculture at
the time the area proposal is finally considered for planning."[554] These are some of the examples of Federal inter-
agency advice and recommendation at the administrative level.

At the statutory level, it is provided in sec. 1 of the
Flood Control Act of 22 December 1944, among other things,
that:

> (a) Plans, proposals, or reports of the Chief of
> Engineers, War Department, for any works of im-
> provement for navigation or flood control . . .
> shall be submitted to the Congress . . . . If such
> investigations in whole or part are concerned with
> the use or control of waters arising west of the
> ninety-seventh meridian, the Chief of Engineers
> shall give to the Secretary of the Interior, dur-
> ing the course of the investigations information
> developed by the investigations and also opportun-
> ity for consultation regarding plans and proposals,
> and to the extent deemed practicable by the Chief
> of Engineers, opportunity to cooperate in the in-
> vestigations . . . . The Secretary of War shall
> transmit to the Congress, with such comments and
> recommendations as he deems appropriate, the pro-
> posed report together with the submitted views and
> recommendations of . . . the Secretary of the In-
> terior . . .
>
>   . . . . .
>
> (c) The Secretary of the Interior, in making in-
> vestigations of and reports on works for irriga-
> tion and purposes incidental thereto shall, in re-
> lation to . . . the Secretary of War, be subject

> to the same provisions . . . as prescribed in par-
> agraph (a) of this section for the Chief of Engi-
> neers and the Secretary of War. In the event a
> submission of views and recommendations, made by
> . . . the Secretary of War, . . . sets forth ob-
> jections to the plans or proposals covered by the
> report of the Secretary of the Interior, the
> proposed works shall not be deemed authorized ex-
> cept upon approval by an Act of Congress . . . .

These provisions are self-explanatory.

Under sec. 2 of an Act of 12 August 1946, as cited above,
the Fish and Wildlife Service should be consulted regarding
the fish and wildlife aspects of water impoundments by such
Federal agencies as the Bureau of Reclamation, the Corps of
Engineers, the Tennessee Valley Authority, the Federal Power
Commission, and so forth.

5. Program coordination---The work assumed by the National Park Service and the Forest Service in 1939 of protecting
the Appalachian Trail, famous hiking way leading through the
eastern mountainous areas from Maine to Georgia, took the
form of program coordination between these agencies. They
"mutually agreed to promote the Appalachian Trailway as it
passed through national parkways and national forests, as
a distinct type of recreational area devoted particularly to
hiking and camping."[555]

The Water Facilities Program of the Soil Conservation
Service discussed before was also the result of program coordination between the said Service, which provided technical
assistance, and the Farm Security Administration (now Farmers
Home Administration), which furnished financial assistance to
private farmers. The success of this program led to the enactment on 19 October 1949 of an Act (63 Stat. 883) providing for the making of farm ownership and farm operation loans
and water facilities loans to persons who have made or make a
homestead entry on public land or who have contracted or contract for the purchase of other public land in a reclamation
project. In order to facilitate the administration of this
Act, "a memorandum of understanding was shortly concluded between the Departments of the Interior and Agriculture, "outlining the general procedure to be followed by the Farmers
Home Administration, the Bureau of Land Management, and the
Bureau of Reclamation when the former agency extends financial
assistance to settlers on public land . . . ."[556] This memorandum is the new instrument of program coordination regarding the Water Facilities Program of the Department of Agriculture.

It may finally be mentioned that the program of river-
basin development for the Missouri and Columbia River Basins
as discussed in Chapter 2, Section 12, above, co-relate the

activities of the Corps of Engineers and the Bureau of Reclamation by way of program coordination.[557]

Article 7   Popular Participation In Administration[558]

1.. Joint enterprise---Private persons or groups of private persons may join the Federal and/or state and local governments in enterprises activities.[559] At the Federal level, the Congress was the stockholder of many private canal companies during the early part of the nineteenth century. In the period 1825-1830, the Congress invested $100,000 in the Louisville and Portland Canal Company, $200,000 in the Chesapeake and Delaware Canal Company, $283,500 in the Dismal Swamp Canal Company and $1,000,000 in the Chesapeake and Ohio Canal Company.[560] In 1911, 1912 and 1913 (but not in other years) the Forest Service entered into agreements with a number of railroad companies and private forest-fire association providing for joint efforts in forest fire prevention, the costs of which were shared between the said Service and the private contracting parties in each case.[561] Federal-private enterprises are now rare.[562]

Private persons or organizations occasionally also join state, local or interstate agencies in undertaking enterprises. For example, the work of ground water spreading that started in 1911 in the Upper Santa Ana River Basin, California, was sponsored by the water conservation association, an organization financed by counties, municipalities and mutual water companies. In this joint undertaking, basins formed by 14 rock dikes of 1,500-5,000 feet in length and ditches totaling about 90,000 feet fed by a main canal of 33,000 feet were used.[563] The Palisades Interstate Park, New York and New Jersey, and the American Museum of Natural History "have jointly conducting an extensive museum and nature trail program for a number of years which handles over half a million participants."[564]

The "Tree Farm" and "Keep America Green" movements, two forestry mass-education programs, may be regarded as government-private joint enterprises at the state and local levels.[565] "A state Keep Green program is organized through a state-wide central committee headed by a leading public figure as chairman. This committee should consist of representatives from governmental, professional, civic and industrial groups with an evident interest in state welfare." The central theme of the program is forest fire prevention.[566] Tree Farms are established on private forest and wood lands with the primary objective of securing sound management practices.[567] The Tree Farm programs of the various states are sponsored and directed in the same manner as the Keep Green program.[568] In some states, such as Indiana, Minnesota, Oregon and Washington, the Keep Green committees have organized volunteer forest-fire fighting services.[569] In these states, the Keep Green program is more than a mere mass-education movement.

All of the instances discussed above belong to complete
joint enterprise. Partial public-private joint enterprise,
which occurs only at a certain stage or phase of an enterprise, is also possible. For example, partial joint enterprise at the operational level or stage, which may be called
"operational integration", found in the so-called "Fontana
agreement" between the Tennessee Valley Authority and the
Aluminum Company of America dated 14 August 1941.[570] Under
this agreement, the said Company "agrees that from and after
the date upon which the water in the Fontana reservoir first
reaches the minimum operating level, it will impound and release water at Company's plants.[571] (including water utilized
for the generation of power) in such manner, at such times,
and in such quantities as Authority (i.e. the Tennessee Valley
Authority) may from time to time direct, such directions if
verbal to be confirmed promptly in writing; provided, that
Authority may not require that water be released other than
through the turbines except for such amounts as cannot be
utilized through the turbines; provided, further, that Company
shall not be obligated to observe such direction if and to the
extent that in its judgment any operation required by any such
direction is not within the reasonable capacity of Company's
plants to generate power and to impound and release water .
. ." (Article II, para. 2). In exchange for this servitude
upon the Company's plants, the Authority agrees to allocate
certain amount of power generated at the Authority's plants
to the Company.[572] "Whenever the amount of water any of the
Santeetlah, Nantahala, or Glenville reservoirs above the minimum operating level exceeds 95 percent of the capacity between
the minimum operating level and the maximum operating level,
either (1) Authority shall direct the release of water from
said reservoir in preference to the release of water from any
of Authority's Norris, Hiwassee, Chatuge, Nottely or Cherokee
reservoirs at which the corresponding reservoir capacity is
proportionately less full and at which remaining storage space
is not, in the judgement of Authority, required for purposes
other than the generation of power, or (2) the amount of exchange power shall be increased by the amount by which such
exchange power would have been increased if Authority had directed the release of water as above provided" (Art. III, para.
3(b), first sentence).

The operation of the "power pools" constitutes cases of
operational integration of varying degrees. Complete operational integration is found in the "Hydro Grid System" of
Nebraska, or "Nebraska Public Power System", a power pool with
the three hydroelectric power districts (The Loup River Public Power District, the Platte Valley Public Power and Irrigation District and the Central Nebraska Public Power and
Irrigation District), which represents joint management of
these districts with revenues divided between them.[573] Only

no private utility participates in this pool. The Northwest
Power Pool is the best known electric power grid operating in
the United States in which Federal, local, private and foreign
plants participate.574 The Pool has a combined generating
capacity of nearly 5 million kilowatts of which about 90 percent is generated at hydro plants. The Bonneville Power Administration, the only Federal member, generates about one-
half of this amount. The operation of the Northwest Power
Pool has resulted in the addition of some of 600,000 kilowatts
of firm generating capacity together with savings and improvements in fuels and services. It is directed by an informal
"operating committee" made up of representatives of the 11
major members which meets bi-monthly, with the technical assistance of a corrdinating group of two engineers which prepares the annual operating schedules. This makes possible the
integrated operation of the various generating plants. But
there is no integration of the sale business. The Pool members buy and sell electric energy among themselves, and each
of them sells it to its own customers.575

2. Delegated administration---Private persons and organizations as such do not possess governmental authority and are
not in a position to embark upon any administrative activities.
However, the government may, by statute or sub-statutory instruments, delegate part of its authority to them, who are
thus embued with public character and enabled to perform administrative acts as if they were administrative agencies of
the government. As distinguished from administrative delegation between government jurisdictions or administrative agencies, which is as a rule compulsory, private delegated administration is normally contractual, for, unless such duty
is imposed on them by the constitution, private parties have
no duty to accept any mandate of administration from the government. Nevertheless, it is not to be confused with trust
administration, as private parties are generally conceived to
have no governmental authority.576 Any governmental authority
which a private party may possess must have been delegated to
him by the government, though in a contractual and not compulsory manner. Both enterprise and regulatory administration
may be delegated to private parties, although delegated enterprise is much more common.

(a) Delegated enterprise---An important kind of private
delegated enterprise is the operation and maintenance of Federal irrigation projects by water users' organizations (other
than irrigation districts), as discussed before. This is the
practice prevailing in the Ogden River project, Utah; Salt
River project, Arizona; Strawberry Valley project, Utah; etc.577
In the Sanpete project, Utah, the project works, built by the
Bureau of Reclamation, are operated and maintained by two private irrigation companies (Ephraim and Horseshoe).578 In
some projects, the water users' association also operates recreational facilities on Federal reservoirs, as in the Hyrum,

Moon Lake Newton, Strawberry, and Echo projects, Utah.[579] In
the Hoover Dam or Boulder Canyon project, as already mentioned before, the Southern California Edison Company is one of
the two operating agents of the Bureau of Reclamation in hydroelectric power development. Also as discussed above, the
Federal Government may delegate to the water users' organization of an irrigation project the work of rehabilitation and
betterment of the project.

Oftentimes, the Federal Government delegated to interested
private parties the authority to construct navigation-improvement or flood-control works which constituted part of Federal
navigation-improvement or flood-control programs and which,
after completion, were often acquired by the Federal Government. For example, the River and Harbor Act of 3 March 1881,
in authorizing the improvement of the Monongahela River, West
Virginia and Pennsylvania, stipulated that "the Monongahela
Navigation Company shall have undertaken in good faith the
building of lock and dam no. 7, at Jacob's Creek..." (21 Stat.
468, 471). In the River and Harbor Act of 11 August 1888,
the purhcase of this lock and dam by the Federal Government
was provided for (25 Stat. 400,411). A special Act of 26 August 1904 (33 Stat. 309) authorized the construction of the
Hales Bar Lock and Dam on the Tennessee River (33 miles below
Chattanooga) by the city of Chattanooga or a private company,
and provided that after completion the said Lock and Dam should
be transferred free of cost to the United States, in exchange
for which the constructing party was granted the right (called
"privilege" in the act) to use the water power for 99 years.
This work was actually constructed by the Chattanooga and
Tennessee River Power Company, and was completed and placed
in operation on 1 November 1913.[580] But it was purchased by
the Tennessee Valley Authority from the Tennessee Electric
Power Company in 1939.[581] In the River and Harbor Act of 27
February 1911, similar arrangement was made with respect to
the construction of Dam No. 4 on the Coosa River (36 Stat.
933, 939-941). The Secretary of War was authorized to enter
into a contract with the Ragland Water Power Company under
which the said Company undertook to complete, under his supervision, the said dam, which was already partially constructed
by the United States. Upon completion, the said works should
become Federal property, but the said Company was entitled to
use the water power for 50 years, with the obligation, however,
to pay for the use after 1925. The United States reserved the
right to construct the locks. The River and Harbor Act of 3
July 1930, in adopting the plans of the Corps of Engineers
for the improvement of the Green and Barren Rivers, Kentucky,
contained the following proviso:

> Provided, That under the provisions of the Federal
> Power Act, and before work is started on this pro-
> ject, a high dam with locks may be substituted near
> or below the site of Dam No. 4, and built by pri-

vate interests, municipalities, or the state:
Provided further, That in the event a high dam is
constructed, the United States shall contribute
to the cost of the substituted structure an amount
equal to the estimated cost of the works of navigation for which substitution is made (46 Stat.
918, 928).

"The only company interested in power development has stated
that it is unwilling to undertake construction of a power dam
under the conditions imposed."[582] This delegated enterprise
was therefore abortive.

In matter of forestry, sec. 2 of an Act of 27 June 1902
(32 Stat. 400, 404), which authorized the sale by the Secretary of the Interior of pine timber in the Chippewa Indian Reservation, Minnesot a, permitted the Secretary of the Interior
to "authorize the purchasers of timber . . . to build on rivers
and lakes on or within said ceded lands, under such rules and
regulations as he may deem proper, dams, coffer-dams, booms and
to make other river and lake improvements necessary to facilitate logging operations . . ." This should be taken as an example of private delegated enterprise. Under the administrative regulations of the Department of Agriculutre governing
the administration of the national forests (36 C.F. R. 211.1
et seq.: 16 F. R. 5952), permittees granted easements of occupancy in the national forests may organize, representative associations of advisory boards. These associations and advisory
boards may request the Forest Service for recognition. "Upon
receiving a request and recommendation of a majority of the
members of an association or from a majority of the permittees
of an area represented by an advisory board, the Forest Supervisor may authorize the operation by the association or advisory board of services or utilities of general character and
benefit which promote the protection and improvement of the
forest lands by the permittees." This is another provision for
private delegated enterprise relating to forestry.

The administration of the Agricultural Conservation Program of the Department of Agriculture is in the hands of locally elected farmer committees. "There is one of these farmer committees in every agricultural county and community in
the county." "Non-partisan elections are held each year for
the selection of these committeemen."[583] This is private delegated enterprise[584] in the field of soil conservation on a
national scale.

In Kansas there is the Water Storage Law (Laws 1909, ch.
108; as last amended by Laws 1941, ch. 400) providing for financial assistance (through tax reduction) for the construction
of dams and reservoirs on dry watercourses or small streams
by private landowners. Sec. 4 of the Law provides that:

Whenever during periods of drought, it is deemed
warranted in the judgment of a majority of the
board of county commissioners of any county in
this state, the commissioners may by resolution
duly adopted, declare a drought emergency to exist
and shall determine where surplus water supplies
exist and are available in reservoirs constructed
in that county under the provisions of this act
and may prescribe rules and regulations for obtaining such surplus waters. The owner of any land
on which such a water supply has been or may be
impounded, shall, upon being notified by the board
of county commissioners, permit entry upon his land
and access to the reservoir to all persons for the
purpose of obtaining water in accordance with the
rules and regulations prescribed by the board of
county commissioners.

This provision makes the construction of the above-mentioned
dams and reservoirs a private delegated enterprise.[585]

As already mentioned before, many facilities in the National Park System are operated by "concessionaires", i.e., private persons and corporations holding concessions or francises
from the National Park Service. The first such concession or
francise was granted on 1 September 1881, in which two concessionaries were given permission to occupy two tracts of
land in the Yellowstone National Park "upon which they agree
to build hotels of such design and dimensions, and at such
points as may be approved by the Department (of the Interior),
to run such lines of stages within the park as the travel may
render necessary, and to construct lines of telegraph from
the principal points in the park to connect it with the through
lines constructed near it. It is provided in the contract
that no greater charges shall be made for accommodations furnished and services rendered than those set forth in a schedule
to be approved by the Secretary of the Interior."[586] Now in
most national parks it is the concessionaires that run hotels,
lodges and eating places under the regulation of the National
Park Service as to seasons, rates, services, design of construction, and so forth. All concession contracts are limited
to 20 years, although most contracts are renewed at the expiration date. The contracts contain as a rule a clause for ultimate Government purchase of the facilities built by the
concessionaries.[587]

At the level of the state government, it may be mentioned
that the Royal Palm State Park of Florida, originally state
property, was ceded to and now owned and operated by the Florida Federation of Women's Clubs, a private organization, for
the benefit of the people (Statutes, sec. 258.11 et seq.: Laws
1915, ch. 6949; as amended by L. 1921, ch. 8577). Under the
laws of Kentucky, the Division of Parks of the Department of

Conservation may delegate the actual operation of any state
park to a corporation created for this special purpose (Revised Statutes, sec. 148.030, subdiv. (5): Acts 1948, ch. 227).

A number of examples may be given of private delegated
enterprise with respect to fish and wildlife conservation. In
sec. 1.71 of Title 50 of the Code of Federal Regulations, issued 1 May 1947 (12 F. R. 2975), it is provided that

> With respect to any lands which have been or may
> hereafter be acquired by the United States for fu-
> ture use as a migratory bird sanctuary or other
> wildlife refuge, subject to an outstanding posses-
> sory estate, the owner of such outstanding estate
> may, in accordance with a program for the develop-
> ment of the area and the limitation of shooting dur-
> ing such development period, approved by the Secre-
> tary of the Interior, take such measures as are cal-
> culated to maintain and increase the waterfowl pop-
> ulation of the area in question, and engage in the
> shooting of migratory birds within the limitations
> set forth in the approved program.

The development of the refuges (Federal) by the said owners
is Federal enterprise delegated to such owners, and it is
seemingly delegated as a condition of their right (sub-statutory right, or statutory privilege) of shooting.[588]

In 1947, the Game Commission of Washington was given the
authority (Laws 1947, ch. 275, sec. 65), to "enter into cooperative agreements with private landowners for the perpetuation, propagation . . . of beaver upon the land of such owners".
Such perpetuation work is apparently done by the owners, and
is in the nature of delegated enterprise.[589] The said Commission has also delegated to 4-H clubs authority to raise pheasants for release. Annually great numbers of pheasants eggs
and chicks are "turned over to 4-H Club Youngsters who, under
the joint supervision of their county agent and the Game Department, have set the eggs and will raise the pheasants up to
ten weeks of age. At that time they are turned back to the Department and are released in suitable habitat areas. The members are paid at the rate of $1.00 per bird."[590] "In addition
to the 4-H program the Department furnishes eggs to interested
clubs and individuals who wish to raise the birds as a hobby
and release them at no cost to the Department."[591]

In Wisconsin, private conservation clubs have recently been
delegated the state enterprise of removing roughfish. "These
clubs operate under a cooperative agreement with the Conservation Department. The department furnishes the necessary equipment and supervises the operations while the club supplies the
labor. All rough fish caught are the property of the club; however, if the fish are sold, any money received must be used
for conservation purposes."[592]

A very interesting type of private delegated enterprise is the establishment of state forests and state game refuges on private properties without giving the state any easements or interests thereon. They are state forests and game refuges in name, but in fact they are private areas. In North Carolina, for example, there are two kinds of state forests, namely, state forests which are owned and/or controlled by the state, and state forests which are private lands so designated. The latter are established or designated by the Governor upon application of the owners of wooded lands (General Statutes, sec. 113-45 et seq.: Laws 1908, ch. 89; as amended by L. 1925, ch. 122). The owners must abide by the plans approved by the State Department of Conservation and Development and pay to the county school fund a tax of 0.5 cents per acre per year; and the Governor shall appoint forest wardens to prevent the designated lands from forest fires.

In Pennsylvania, owners of forest lands may apply to the State Forestry Reservation Commission to designate their lands as state auxiliary forest reserves. If the application is approved by the Commission, it shall send a certificate to the county commissioners of the county where the lands are located whereupon it shall be the duty of the latter to care for and protect the forests until the trees are mature for commercial cutting. The owners are also entitled to a reduction in taxes, but they must obey the instructions and directions of the Commission with regard to forestry management. Should they fail to observe this requirement, the county commissioners may recover at suit the amount of taxes reduced (Statutes, tit. 32, ch. 2: Act of 5 June 1913).

In Alabama, the Department of Conservation, upon application of the owner, may designate private forest lands as auxiliary state forests, which shall be governed by a contract entered into between the governor and the owner. In that contract, it shall be agreed that the timber growing on such lands shall not be taxable until they are withdrawn as auxiliary state forests. But it shall also be agreed "that the owner of said lands will devote the same to forest culture and that no use shall be made of said land that will militate against the growth of the timber thereon; that the owner will use diligence in protecting the same against fire in accordance with rules established by the department of conservation and that the owner will not withdraw said lands as auxiliary state forests for a period of five years after the same are entered as such, and will not cut, turpentine, or otherwise utilize the timber thereon before the withdrawal of the same as auxiliary state forests, except in accordance with rules formulated by the department of conservation . . ." After the lands have been designated as auxiliary state forest for five years, the owner is entitled to withdraw the lands or any part thereof, or to harvest the timber growing thereon under the direction of the said Department. In either case, he is obliged to pay to the said Department (which shall equally share with the counties) a privilege tax equal to eight percent of the appraised value of the timber. An auxiliary state forest may also be terminated by the Governor when the landowner violates the terms of the contract. In this case, the privilege tax shall also become due and payable, but no penalty is to be imposed (Code, tit. 8, ch. 4, sec. 189 et seq.: Acts 1923, No. 486; as last amended by Acts 1951, No. 832). It may be noted that the state does not provide service for the auxiliary state forests, as is the practice in North Carolina and Pennsylvania. 593

Under the laws of Minnesota (Statutes, secs. 88.47 to 88.-53: Laws 1927, ch. 247; as last amended by L. 1953, ch. 246), wood lots of 5-10 acres may be designated by the county board concerned as auxiliary forests of the state upon petition of their respective owners or tenants for a maximum period of fifty years. A contract must be signed by the owner or tenant of an auxiliary forest and the Commissioner of Conservation prescribing the manner of forest management and tax collection.594

Private properties may also be designated as state game refuges. In Oregon, for example, the statute authorizes the State Game Commission "to enter into written contracts with the owner or owners of land or lands for a term of not to exceed 10 years in such localities in the different counties of the state of Oregon as may be then deemed appropriate, setting aside such lands as wild bird or game refuges" (Laws 1921, ch. 153, sec. 64, first sentence; as last amended by laws 1945, ch. 164, sec. 3).595 As of 30 April 1953, there were fifty such refuges (called contract refuges) with a total area of 55,000 acres. "Few of the contract refuges have provided benefits to wildlife that are commensurate with the cost of establishment and maintenance."596

Under the statute of Kansas, persons owning or controlling suitable lands 120-160 acres in area may petition the Director of the Forestry, Fish and Game Commission to set them apart as state game refuges to be administered in accordance with agreements concluded between them and the said director. Such refuges are closed to hunting, and the said Director "may furnish . . . such brood stock and game as he may deem advisable" (General Statutes, sec. 32-206 et seq.: 1921, ch. 197). Similar law is found in Wisconsin (Statutes, sec. 29.57: Laws 1917, ch. 668, sec. 3; as amended by Laws 1921, ch. 134; Laws 1927, ch. 196).

In Pennsylvania, as provided in an act of 3 June 1937, as amended 29 March 1945 (Statutes, sec. 1311.921 et seq.), the state Game Commission may create and maintain auxiliary state game refuges on lands of private persons or association or municipalities. One third of each of such refuges is to be

closed to hunting, but hunting and trapping is permitted in
the rest of the area. It is to be noted that these refuges
are to be "maintained" by the said Commission. In exchange
of this service, the owners open two-thirds of the acreage
to public hunting and make their lands a sort of public hunting grounds.

Michigan, too, has "a system of wildlife sanctuaries on
private lands. We are not entirely happy with the system,
for we doubt that it is very effective in increasing wildlife.
There are about 78 of these sanctuaries, in which no hunting
is allowed, and they total about 51,855 acres."[597] Minnesota, besides the state-owned game refuges, has "what is known
as a statutory game refuge system, whereby any lands, upon
public hearing, may if it is in the public interest and necessary to the preservation of any species of game life, be
closed as a game refuge -- or where all land owners sign a
petition, such an area may be closed without a public hearing.
All such types of (statutory) game refuges comprise 2,515,894
acres."[598] In North Dakota, in addition to 11 state-owned
refuges, which total about 12,990 acres, "there are approximately 65 areas containing approximately 58,635 acres of privately owned land in the state operated under an easement a-
greement with the State Game and Fish Department for refuge
purposes as of November 1, 1952. Because a state law requires,
that the land once accepted as a refuge remain as such for
ten years, this figure is constantly changing. The refuges
vary in size from 15 to approximately 3,000 acres. Twenty-
one refuges, containing approximately 13,151 acres were removed from refuge in 1951 and 1952."[599]

Another interesting example of private delegated enterprise, which is in the field of wildlife conservation, is the
control of predators through the grant of bounties, or the
"bounty system" of predation control. In this system, private
hunters are encouraged to kill the predatory animals and birds
designated by the state game laws. This being essentially
governmental enterprise, which is thus delegated to private
hunters, the latter are paid a bounty by the state game agency or by county government.[600] As discussed above, the bounty system now tends to be replaced by state enterprise. In
Washington, where the bounty system and state predation control enterprise exist side by side, the statute further authorizes the State Game Department, to "enter into cooperative
programs to control predators with sportsmen's groups, grang-
es, or others" (Laws 1947, ch. 275, sec. 80). This is a new
form of private delegated enterprise in predation control.[601]

(b) Delegated regulation---A few instances have been
found in which governmental regulatory administration is delegated to private parties. In the statute of Oregon (Laws
1919, ch. 264, sec. 104, as amended by Laws 1947, ch. 175),
it is provided that

Every person, company, municipal corporation, city,
town, water district, or agency thereof selling or
furnishing water to the public for drinking or
household purposes shall, when such water supply
is derived from surface sources, conduct an annual sanitary inspection of the watershed of said
of said source of water supply. In those cases
in which the water supply is taken from a stream
that has a minimum daily flow of 50 cubic feet
of water per second, said sanitary inspection
shall apply to 10 miles of watershed above the
water-works intake. The inspection . . . shall
include an examination of sewage and waste disposal facilities at houses, business establishments,
industries and buildings on the watershed, and
said sewage and waste disposal facilities shall be
constructed and operated in accordance with the
regulations of the state board of health and the
state sanitary authority, and whenever the person
or persons conducting a sanitary inspection . . .
shall determine that sewage disposal facilities
are not constructed and operated in conformance
with the said regulation, notice thereof in writing shall be given to the person or company responsible for the premises. Such notice shall outline
such defects in sewage or waste disposal facilities
and shall demand correction within a reasonable
length of time . . . Aditional sanitary inspections of a watershed may be required by the state
health officer whenever there is special reason
to believe that there may be new source of contamination of a public water supply. (Italics supplied).

That this provisions is an authorization of private delegated
regulation is self-explanatory. In Illinois, persons concerned may enter into a unanimous agreement with the owner or
owners of a dam for the equitable apportionment of the water
and water-power furnished by the dam to the use of which they
are entitled (Revised Statutes, ch. 92, sec. 12: L. 1877, p.
138). This is in effect delegated private regulation of water-use, and that part of it which is concerned with adjudication of water rights.

The laws of Connecticut provide that "as to any portion of
any railroad right of way and contiguous land that may be
found by the (state public utilities) commission to constitute a fire hazard, the (state forest) fire warden or the
owner or owners of any land adjoining such portion shall have
power, from time to time, to order the railroad company operating such railroad to furnish a patrol . . ." (General
Statutes, sec. 3485, op. cit., emphasis added). In Mississippi, the statute requires every person to control and extinguish a forest fire for the starting of which he is responsi-

ble; and if he fails to do so, "any organized agency recognized by the Mississippi Forestry Commission", which may be either public or private, may summarily abate the nuisance thus created and recover the costs of the operation from the former by civil action (Code, sec. 6046). In California, the Underwriters Laboratories, Inc., has been authorized to approve, on behalf of the state, the design of spark-arresters of engines and machines operating in forest, brush and grass areas during closed seasons (Public Resources Code, sec. 4167: Stats. 1945, ch. 777, sec. 17; as last amended by Stats. 1949, ch. 813, sec. 1).

It has already been discussed that municipalities of Maine have the authority to issue licenses for the construction on navigable waters wharves, fish weirs and fish traps. However, "in the case of islands not within the jurisdiction of any town, all powers of municipal officers to issue licenses to build weirs[602] are conferred upon the owner or owners of such islands" (Revised Statutes of 1954, ch. 98, sec. 7 2nd para., enacted by Revised Statutes of 1930).

The administration of the Lumber Code by the national and regional trade associations of the lumber industry under the authority of the National Industrial Recovery Act of 1933 was also an example of private delegated regulation. "The Lumber Code . . . contained an obligation on the part of the lumbermen to apply such practical forestry measures in connection with timber cutting as would be necessary to keep their timberlands continuously productive." "The Code forestry requirements became effective June 1, 1934, and terminated when all codes were abolished on May 27, 1935 -- a period of about one year."[603]

The delegation of governmental administration to private parties must be distinguished from voluntary organization and agreement among private parties themselves, which is purely a private affair, The organization of irrigation companies and associations is one of the many examples of this. The work of the Kings River Association in the administration of a schedule of water diversion among its members is a case of purely private service which may be confused with delegated private regulation.[604]

3. Public-private program coordination---The best example is the following provision in the laws of Maine (Revised Statutes, ch. 32, sec. 72-F: Laws 1949, ch. 355):

> The forestry department shall formulate emergency plans to establish manpower pools, equipment reserves, facilities for feeding, transportation and communication on forest fires. In preparing the plan other agencies and organizations having needed facilities should be contacted, such as fire

> chiefs, red cross, sheriffs, American Legion, nati-
> nal guard, state highway (sic), state fish and game
> department, state grange, colleges, civil air pa-
> trol and any other proective group so determined
> by the forest commissioner. Whenever or wherever
> a major forest fire occurs or threatens, the for-
> estry department shall be the coordinating agency
> until the governor of the state of Maine declares
> an emergency (emphasis added).

Public-private program coordination of this kind may operate
on a non-statutory basis in many other states.

The management of the Shelton Sustained Yield Unit by the
United States Forest Service in December 1946 is another example of program coordination between governmental agencies
and private persons. The unit includes 159,000 acres of lands
owned by the Simpson Logging Company and 111,000 acres of
national-forest lands, in the State of Washington. According
to the contract entered into between the Forest Service and
the Company, which lasts for 100 years, each parties agrees
to undertake certain responsibilities in the management of
the unit under a unified plan. It is reported that "cooperative relations have been most gratifying."[605]

NOTES

1. Constitutionality of this regulation has not yet been passed upon by the U. S. Supreme Court, although the constitutionality of municipal authority with respect to city zoning was sustained by the said Court
in Village of Euclid et al. v. Ambler Realty Co., 272 U. S. 365 (22 November 1926) more than a quarter of a century ago. The extension of the
ruling in this case to rural zoning is not possible as the Court expressly declared that "a regulatory zoning ordinance, which would be clearly
valid as applied to the great cities, might be clearly invalid as applied
to rural communicities" (at 387).

2. See U. S. Department of Agriculture, A Quarter Century of Land
Economics in the Department of Agriculture, 1919-1944 (mimeo.), October
1945, p. 25.

3. See Yearbook of Agriculture, 1938, p. 244 (by George S. Wehrwein
and Clarence I. Hendrickson); and House Document 426, 77th Cong., 1941,
p. 67. Also see S. C. Acts of 1942, no. 681, sec. 2.

4. U. S. Department of Agriculture, State Legislation For Better
Land Use, April 1941, p. 1.

5. Yearbook of Agriculture 1938, p. 242. But the original motive of
the 1929 Wisconsin amendment was not the regulation of land use as such.
See ibid., p. 243. Rural zoning (county regulation) as suggested "as a
means of preventing further encroachment in the flood plains of Cayuga,
Buffalo, and Cazenovia Creeks of Structures likely to be damaged by
floods" in the program of improvement of the Buffalo Creek Watershed,
N. Y. -- House Document 574, 78th Cong., 2nd sess., 1944, p. 25.

6. "In Idaho, even though the legislature has not passed an enabling
act, the constitution probably authorizes county zoning." -- State Legislation For Better Land Use, op. cit., p. 2. In Nebraska, the county
board may enact zoning resolutions necessary to implement zoning regulations of the State Zoning Agency. But the state zoning regulations are
made for the purpose of the construction of Federal forts, airports, manufacturing plants, arsenals, etc. -- Revised Statutes of Nebraaka, sec.
23-114 and secs. 81-830 et seq. Arkansas counties have zoning authority,
but only for school purposes. -- Acts 1949, no. 146, sec. 4. Under Acts
1946, no. 404 the Jefferson Parish of the State of Louisiana may establish residential, commercial and industrial zones, which is not rural
zoning.

7. It may be observed that this act was enacted at an earlier date
than the law providing for state regulation of timber cutting in any
other state.

8. In New Jersey, county navigation improvements may also be incidentally provided in connection with county highway administration, New-
Jersey Statutes, sec. 40: 23-8.3, being Laws 1942, ch. 198, sec. 1.

9. Information provided through the courtesy of Mr. R. E. Hunter
Chief, Technical Information Branch, Office of the District Engineer,
New Orleans District, U. S. Corps of Engineers, on 11 March 1952. Consult House Document 230 76th Cong., 1st sess., 1939, p. 12; Senate Document 190, 79th Cong., 2nd sess., 1946, pp. 5-7.

10. House Document 257, 76th Cong., 1st sess., 1939, p. 6.

11. House Document 237, 76th Cong., 1st sess., 1939, p. 7.

12.   House Document 106, 81st Cong., 1st sess., 1949, p. 8.

13.   House Document 173, 81st Cong., 1st sess., 1949, p. 19.

14.   House Document 256, 81st Cong., 1st sess., 1949, pp. 13-14.

15.   House Document 237, 76th Cong., 1st sess., 1939, p. 7.

16.   U. S. Corps of Engineers, Port and Terminal Facilities at the U. S. Ports on Lake Superior (mimeo.), 1945, p. 30.

17.   Rpt. Chief of E. 1952, p. 475.

18.   U. S. Corps of Engineers and U. S. Maritime Administration, Port Series No. 13, part 2, revised 1946, p. 124.

19.   U. S. Corps of Engineers, Lake Series No. 6 (mimeo.), revised 1949, p. 90.

20.   U. S. Corps of Engineers, Lake Series No. 9 (mimeo.), revised 1949, p. 61.

21.   House Document 686, 76th Cong., 3rd sess., 1940, p. 6.

22.   In 1819, by special legislation, Mississippi state legislature authorized Warren County to build levees against the Mississippi floods. Similar authority was subsequently given Counties of Tunica, DeSoto, Coahoma, Bolivar, Washington and Issaquena. -- Robert W. Harrison, "Flood Control in the Mississippi Valley", in unpublished manuscript form, made available to the author through the courtesy of Mr. B. R. Smith, Secretary-Manager, Delta Council (Stoneville, Mississippi), on 20 August 1951. Special legislation in other states has not been under study.

23.   Washington Department of Conservation and Development, 13th Biennial Report, October 1944-September 1946, p. 17.

24.   Letter to the author from Mr. Earle F. Bryant, Mayor, Town of Woodland, Washington, dated 19 September 1953.

25.   House Document 135, 81st Cong., 1st sess., 1949, p. 38.

26.   House Document 531, 81st Cong., 2nd sess., 1952, p. 1165.

27.   House Document 762, 77th Cong., 2nd sess., 1942, p. 31.

28.   House Document 889, 77th Cong., 2nd sess., 1942, p. 11.

29.   House Document 700, 77th Cong., 2nd sess., 1942, p. 9.

30.   House Document 621, 77th Cong., 2nd sess., 1942, p. 11.

31.   It seems that this act has not been affected by the Uniform Drainage Act of 1951 (L. 1951, ch. 151).

32.   In these states, it may be incidentally noted, the county drainage laws were enacted after 1940, and the county drains are not financed by special benefit assessments.

33.   Missouri laws provide that the drainage districts in county drainage enterprise are to be "established and incorporated" by the county governing body. However, the districts have no separate organization, no financial authority and no political or administrative entity.

34.   House Document 132, 81st Cong., 1st sess., 1949, pp. 15-16.

35. Letter to the author from Mr. Roy T. Sessums, Director, Louisiana Department of Public Works, dated 13 October 1953.

36. *Engineering News-Record*, 4 June 1953, p. 24.

37. U. S. Bureau of the Census, *1950 Census of Agriculture, Preliminary Release*, 30 October 1951.

38. *Recreation and Park Yearbook of 1950*, op. cit., p. 4.

39. *Ibid.*, pp. 22-66.

40. *Ibid.*, p. 13.

41. *House Document 442*, 80th Cong., 2nd sess., 1947, p. 38.

42. Special legislation is excluded from this discussion. It may also be pointed out that counties may own "forested" lands, but that these lands need not be officially designated and specifically administered as county forests. The authorization of county forests in New Jersey is indirect and is found in *New Jersey Statutes*, tit. 40, sec. 27-2 (Laws 1935, ch. 251, sec. 2).

43. Shirley Walter Allen, *An Introduction to American Forestry*, 2nd ed., 1950, p. 338.

44. Wisconsin Conservation Commission, *23rd Biennial Report*, p. 12.

45. South Carolina State Commission of Forestry, *Annual Report 1951*, p. 30.

46. Letter to the author from Mr. Don Young, Forester, Colorado State Board of Forestry, dated 17 March 1954.

47. For a typical example, see *Minnesota Statutes*, sec. 18.14 et seq. (Laws 1935, ch. 29).

48. U. S. National Park Service, *A Study of the Park and Recreational Problems of the United States*, 1941, pp. 135-271 (particularly p. 235).

49. *The Progressive Fish Culturist*, October 1949, p. 254 (by A. V. Tunison et al.).

50. California Fish and Game Department, *41st Biennial Report, 1948-1950*, p. 84; *42nd Biennial Report, 1951-1952*, p. 34.

51. It seems that (4) replaces (3), which replaced (2), which replaced (1); and that (4) is the present active law.

52. Governor's Water Committee of Kansas, *Report*, 2 August 1940, p.8.

53. D. A. Lane, "Artificial Storing of Groundwater By Spreading", *Journal of the American Water Works Association*, vol. 28, no. 9 (September 1936).

54. M. L. Brashears, Jr., "Artificial Recharge of Ground Water On Long Island, New York", 41 *Economic Geology* 503, 506 (August 1946).

55. *General Statutes of Kansas*, sec. 2-2004 (Laws 1937, ch. 189, sec. 4); *Oklahoma Statutes*, secs. 841 to 847 (Laws 1937, p. 250) and secs. 901 to 904 (Laws 1939, p. 244).

56. H. H. Stage, "Mosquito Control Agencies in the United States", 11 Mosquito News 8-22 (March 1951); and 13 Mosquito News 168 (June 1953). This list is not necessarily exhaustive. It may be noted that mosquito control work may be undertaken under the general authorization for the control of insect pests, or under the implied general authority of American counties to abate nuisances to public health.

57. 11 Mosquito News 170 (September 1951).

58. Harold E. Thomas, The Conservation of Ground Water, 1951, p.196.

59. Federal Power Commission, Statistics of Publicly Owned Electric Utilities, 1949.

60. Letter to the author from Mr. Robert C. Price, Regional Engineer, Federal Power Commission, Atlanta, Georgia, dated 21 June 1954. From the information of the Crisp County Power Commission, the Crisp County Power Project was completed on 1 August 1930. -- Your Crisp County Hydro-Electric Plant, Brief History, 1925-1954 (a folder). The assistance and advice of Messrs. W. Dan Sinclair, Manager, Crisp County Power Commission, Cordelle, Georgia, and Jno. B. Sloan, Chairman, Greenwood County Electric Power Commission, Greenwood, South Carolina, in their letters to the author dated respectively 28 June and 1 July 1954, is gratefully acknowledged.

61. Elwood Mead, Irrigation Institutions, 1903, pp. 234-235.

62. Municipal administration refers to administration by all local governmental units other than counties (in Louisiana parishes) and special districts. The word "municipal" or "municipality" does not admit of an accurate definition. If a municipality means an incorporated subdivision of the state, then every local governmental unit is a municipality. There seems to be no reason for exclusively identifying municipalities with cities. The word "municipal" is adopted in this Article for the lack of a more understandable and more popular term.

63. In some instances, beyond their respective jurisdictional limits.

64. House Document 223, 76th Cong., 1st sess., 1939, pp. 9-10.

65. Rpt. Chief of E. 1902, pp. 2575-2576.

66. House Document 231, 76th Cong., 1st sess., 1939, p. 18.

67. Rpt. Chief of E. 1902, p. 2568.

68. Ibid., p. 2585.

69. Ibid., p. 2584.

70. Ibid., pp. 2645; 2585; 2586; 2593.

71. House Document 256, 76th Cong., 1st sess., 1939, p. 11. Consult ibid., p. 6.

72. House Document 504, 79th Cong., 2nd sess., 1946, p. 17.

73. House Document 91, 79th Cong., 1st sess., 1946, pp. 13-14.

74. House Document 89, 82nd Cong., 1st sess., 1951, p. 13.

75. House Document 624, 77th Cong., 2nd sess., 1942, p. 7.

76. House Document 561, 79th Cong., 2nd sess., 1946, p. 15.

77. House Document 174, 81st Cong., 1st sess., 1949, p. 17.

78. House Document 664, 80th Cong., 2nd sess., 1948, p. 11.

79. When roads or highways are constructed on the shores of a non-navigable watercourse, the revetments constitute a flood-control measure. It may be noted that these revetments are part of the roads or highways. In addition, measures such as dredging and the removal of obstruction may be taken to protect roads and highways from floods. These measures belong to flood control and are not part of the work of the road or highway construction.

80. U. S. Corps of Engineers, Shore Control and Port Administration, 1923, pp. 99, 104; and "The Commission of Public Docks of the City of Portland, Oregon: Its Powers, Authority and Facilities" (mimeo), 10 November 1952, by the said Commission.

81. This is of course not a measure of navigation improvement. However, it is one of the non-consumptive uses of water.

82. Sherman Washburn, "Port of Portland, Chapter XIII" (mimeo.), broadcast on Noon Edition, KEX, at 12:15 p. m., 26 December 1951.

83. "The Commission of Public Docks of the City of Portland", op. cit.; "Facilities Report outlining facilities available for the interchange of Cargo at the Columbia River Ports of Portland, Oregon, etc." (mimeo.), 1 July 1952; and other material.

84. Rpt. Chief of E. 1951, p. 2214.

85. For cities on the Great Lakes, U. S. Corps of Engineers, Lake Series, Nos. 1-9, inclusive. Nos. 6 and 9, revised in 1949; Nos. 2, 3, 3 and 5, revised in 1950; Nos. 1, 7 and 8, revised in 1951. Also Rpt. Chief of E. 1951, pp. 1722; 1724; 1733; 1735. For the Delaware River, U. S. Corps of Engineers and U. S. Maritime Administration, Port Series No. 7 (mimeo.), Revised 1947, pp. 28; 205; 209; 210; Port Series No. 9 (mimeo.), revised 1947, pp. 33-34; 57-58; and Port Series No. 8 (mimeo.), revised 1947, pp. 24-25. For the rest, information made available to the author through the courtesy of Mr. W. A. C. Connelly, Chief, Statistical Division, U. S. Corps of Engineers, on 5 March 1953 and the Division and District Engineers concerned on other dates.

86. See U. S. Corps of Engineers and U. S. Maritime Administration, Port Series No. 22 (mimeo.), revised 1948, pp. 79-80; Port Series No. 15 (mimeo.), p. 15; etc.

87. See U. S. Corps of Engineers and U. S. Maritime Administration, Port Series No. 3 (mimeo.), revised 1946, pp. 44; 82; 85; 90; 92; 105; Port Series No. 10 (mimeo.), revised 1946, pp. 27-28; 164; 166-167; 267; Port Series No. 14 (mimeo.), revised 1946, p. 18; Port Series No. 30, revised 1951; Port Series No. 28 (mimeo.), revised 1946; Port Series No. 27 (mimeo.), p. 17; Port Series No. 12, revised 1939.

88. U. S. Corps of Engineers, Port and Terminal Facilities At the Port of New York (mimeo.), 1942, part 1, p. 60. In this publication are also discussed the terminal facilities owned by the cities of Jersey City, Newark, Bayonne and Elisabeth, New Jersey.

89. Port Series No. 7, op. cit.

90. See U. S. Corps of Engineers, Lake Series No. 8, op. cit., pp. 41; 49; 63-65; "Port of Milwaukee", World Ports Magazine, March 1953; and H. C. Brockel, "Milwaukee's Port Development Program Produces Large Divi-

dends For City", _Traffic World_, 30 May 1953. The assistance of Mr. H.
C. Brockel, Port Manager, City of Milwaukee, Wisconsin, given to the
author on 17 February 1954, is hereby gratefully acknowledged.

91. House Document 332, 81st Cong., 1st sess., 1949, p. 17.

92. House Document 560, 79th Cong., 2nd sess., 1946, p. 9.

93. Senate Document 104, 78th Cong., 1st sess., 1943, p. 16.

94. House Document 305, 81st Cong., 1st sess., 1949, pp. 15-16.

95. House Document 216, 81st Cong., 1st sess., 1949, pp. 44-45.

96. Charles S. Stevenson and Arthur E. Wall, "Portsmouth River Wall
Again Protects City", _Engineering News-Record_, 7 May 1936, pp. 669-671.

97. House Document 173, 81st Cong., 1st sess., 1949, p. 19.

98. Senate Document 245, 79th Cong., 2nd sess., 1946, pp. 18-19.

99. Texas State Board of Water Engineers, _Biennial Report_, November
1950, p. 46.

100. House Document 545, 78th Cong., 2nd sess., 1944, p. 23.

101. House Document 232, 81st Cong., 1st sess., 1949, pp. 18-19.

102. House Document 615, 78th Cong., 2nd sess., 1944, p. 25.

103. House Document 274, 80th Cong., 1st sess., 1947, pp. 16-17.

104. Evan E. Houk, _Irrigation Engineering_, vol. 1, 1951, p. 421.

105. See _Report_ of the Board of Water Commissioners of the City and
County of Denver, Colorado, for the year ending 31 December 1950. Also
consult Denver Water Department, _The Denver Municipal Works_, 1948, p. 25.

106. Elwood Mead, _Irrigation Institutions_, 1903, p. 237.

107. Letter to the author from Mr. D. F. Herrick, Executive Director, American Public Works Association, dated 1 August 1951. It may be
observed that in the prevailing laws of some states the words "wells"
and "cisterns" still appear. For example Nebraska cities of first class
are authorized "to establish, make and regulate public wells, cisterns,
aqueducts and reservoirs of water" (_Revised Statutes of Nebr._, sec. 15-
224, enacted 1901). In Tennessee, all cities have the authority "to dig
wells and erect cisterns, or provide for a water supply " (_Tenn. Code_,
sec. 3326, enacted 1915).

108. President's Water Resources Policy Commission, _Report_, vol. I,
p. 176; 180. Consult _Municipal Yearbook of 1950_, p. 347.

109. _Report_, vol. I, op. cit., p. 176.

110. A. G. Matthews, "Basic Water Problems in Florida", 40 _Journal
of American Water Works Association_ 441-442 (April 1948).

111. "Summary of Statistics---Chicago Water Works, Year Ending December 31, 1950" (mimeo.), sent to the author through the courtesy of Mr.
W. W. DeBerard, city engineer, department of public works, City of Chicago, on 23 November 1951.

112. The Saint Louis, Missouri, Municipal Water Works System, 39 pp. (quotation on p. 19).

113. City of Cincinnati Water Works System, 36 pp., sent to the author through the courtesy of City of Cincinnati Water Works on 19 November 1951. (Quotation on p. 15.)

114. Bureau of Water, Department of Public Utilities, City of Portland, Oregon, Map and Statistical Data, 1950, sent to the author through the courtesy of Mr. George A. Marshall, Superintendent of the Bureau of Water, on 19 November 1951.

115. "Information pertaining to the Memphis water system" (mimeo.), 24 April 1951, sent to the author through the courtesy of Mr. C. M. McCord, Director of water division, Memphis Light, Gas, and Water Division, on 20 November 1951.

116. Map and Statistics of Spokane Water System, 1 January 1933, sent to the author through the courtesy of Mr. Elmo James, Superintendent of Water, Department of Public Utilities, city of Spokane, on 19 November 1951, and revised as of that date. An "underground stream" as herein described should be distinguished from underflows.

117. U. S. Public Works Administration, America Builds, 1939, pp. 256-258.

118. 98 Cong. Rec. A830 (14 February 1952).

119. Letter to the author from Mr. William G. Myers, City Engineer, City of Harrisburg, Virginia, dated 24 September 1951.

120. Des Moines Water Works System (pamphlet), 1950, first three pages.

121. St. Paul Board of Water Commissioners, Beyond the Faucet, 3rd ed., 1945, pp. 11-12.

122. 1948 Report and Information Book of the Water Division of the Department of Public Utilities, City of Tacoma, Washington, pp. 6; 15; 18.

123. Compiled from Federal Power Commission, Statistics of Publicly Owned Electric Utilities, 1949; Annual Report of FPC 1951, pp. 152; 153; 155; FPC Opinions and Decisions; House Document 452, 77th Cong., 1st sess, 1941, p. 15 (city of Idaho Falls, Idaho); House Document 669, 76th Cong., 1940 (city of Rochester, Minnesota); Public Works Administration, America Builds, 1939, p. 277, table 7; and letter to the author from Mr. Lesher S. Wing, Regional Engineer at San Francisco, California, Federal Power Commission, dated 12 September 1952 (Monroe and Manti Cities, Utah). The list is not necessarily exhaustive. Enterprises of some cities may not be commercial in nature, in which they are strictly not enterprises. It is to be noted that the electric power enterprise, like the enterprises of water supply and sewerage, is a basic public service that is intrusted to the municipal government. This municipal enterprise exists in all of the 48 states.

124. Letter to the author from Mr. Leon M. Fuquay, Secretary, Federal Power Commission, dated 30 July 1951. It is to be noted that the Ross Dam power plant of the City of Seattle, Washington, having a generating capacity of 180,000 kilowatts as of May 1953, which is to be ultimately increased to 360,000 kilowatts, is now the largest municipal hydroelectric plant in the United States. It is also to be noted that as of May 1953, the Diablo and Gorge Plants of Seattle generated 132,000

and 110,000 kilowatts, respectively.

125. Carl L. Cooper, Seattle Post-Intelligencer, The Skagit Story (a pamphlet), 1951; Seattle Department of Lighting, 1951 Annual Report; Conference with Mr. Frank Pettit, Public Relations Division, Seattle Department of Lighting, on 5 May 1953 and telephone communication with Mr. W. D. Embuly, Statistics Division, Seattle Department of Lighting, on 6 May 1953.

126. The Cedar Falls plant is said to be the first municipal hydroelectric plant in the United States.

127. All information regarding hydroelectric power enterprise of Tacoma is, unless otherwise specifically indicated, obtained from the Division of Light, Department of Public Utilities of the City of Tacoma, Tacoma Municipal Power System and Tacoma City Light Hydro-Plants (undated pamphlets), and letter to the author from Mr. J. Frank Ward, Superintendent, Light Division, Tacoma Department of Public Utilities, dated 19 May 1953.

128. Federal Power Commission, Press Release No. 5752, 28 November 1951.

129. By the middle of 1954 the generating capacity of this steam plant will be increased to 45,000 kilowatts.

130. Letter to the author from Mr. Walker H. Graves, Director, Department of Electricity, Town of Martinsville, Virginia, dated 8 September 1951.

131. Letter to the author from Mr. L. A. Wootton, Manager, Heber Light and Power Plant, dated 5 September 1951.

132. Tacoma Municipal Power System, op. cit.

133. Federal Power Commission, Press Release, No. 5586, 16 August 1951.

134. The City and County of San Francisco and the two Irrigation Districts each embark upon their own enterprises to meet their respective needs without interdependence. However, they have entered into an agreement for the coordination of their enterprises. The following discussion of the San Francisco enterprise is based on San Francisco Public Utilities Commission, San Francisco Water and Power, June 1949, and "Cherry River Project" (mimeo.), September 1952; and letters to the author from Mr. R. V. Meikle, Chief Engineer, Turlock Irrigation District, dated 13 November 1952, Mr. C. E. Plummer, Chief Engineer, Modesto Irrigation District, dated 25 November 1952 and Mr. H. E. Lloyd, Manager and Chief Engineer, San Francisco Public Utilities Commission, dated 11 December 1952.

135. The primary interest of the two irrigation districts is irrigation and the primary interest of San Francisco is municipal water supply. However, both the city and the districts have attached hydroelectric power development to their respective enterprises; and, incidentally, the storage works of the three California local units provide partial storage for flood control. The effects of flood control are partly local and partly regional, and for this reason the Federal Government in the Flood Control Act of 22 December 1944, promised to pay part of the costs of construction of the new storage works, as will be discussed below.

136. The Eleanor Reservoir will then become a relay reservoir and will have no active primary storage.

137. Letter to the author from Mr. J. H. Jensen, Superintendent, Electric Power and Water, Ephraim City Corporation, Utah, dated 4 December 1952.

138. House Document 657, 78th Cong., 2nd sess., 1944, pp. 2; 20; and letter to the author from Mr. M. B. Cooper, Superintendent of Canal and Water Works, City of Augusta, Georgia, dated 2 October 1953.

139. 97 Cong. Rec. 8243 (12 July 1951). In the same fiscal year, by the Tennessee Valley Authority (that is, 42.5 percent) went to municipalities. -- Ibid., at 8242.

140. See Earle B. Phelps et al., Public Health Engineering, 1948, vol. 1, p. 380.

141. Incodel, Minutes of Clean Waters For American Conference, 16 January 1948, Section X, p. 1.

142. For examples in Connecticut River Basin, see President's Water Resources Policy Commission, Report, vo. II, p. 492.

143. See General Laws of Massachusetts, ch. 11, sec. 132 (Acts 1868, ch. 160, sec. 1); New Mexico Statutes, sec. 14-1810 (Laws 1884, ch. 39, sec. 14, subd. 12); etc.

144. Letter to the author from Mr. Joseph F. Pannone, Mosquito Control Supervisor, Rhode Island Department of Agriculture and Conservation, dated 16 March 1954; and the various annual reports of the said Department.

145. 116 Engineering News-Record 393 (12 March 1936).

146. Arthur H. Woody, "Mosquito Control Work in Portland, Oregon and Vicinity in 1950", 11 Mosquito News 158 (September 1951).

147. William B. Owen, "Important Species of Mosquitoes and Control Work in Wyoming", ibid., 163, 165-166.

148. William E. Bickley and George S. Langford, "Mosquito Control Work in Maryland in 1950", ibid., 170, 171.

149. H. H. Stage, "Mosquito Control Agencies in U. S.", 11 Mosquito News 8-22 (March 1951).

150. New Hampshire State Planning and Development Commission, New Hampshire Water, 1953, p. 37.

151. Report of the Chief of U. S. Forest Service for 1938, p. 25.

152. Richard T. Ely and George S. Wehrwein, Land Economics, 1940, p. 397.

153. Report of the Chief of U. S. Forest Service for 1950, p. 26. The word "community forests" as used in this publication may include county forests.

154. U. S. Dpt. of Agriculture, The Control of Reservoir Silting, Miscellaneous Publication No. 521 (by Carl B. Brown), 1944, p. 147.

155. Ibid., p. 148; Yearbook of Agriculture 1949, pp. 396-397; The American City, February 1952, p. 149.

156. The Control of Reservoir Silting, op. cit., p. 147.

157. Earle B. Phelps et al., _Public Health Engineering_, 1948, vol. I, p. 346.

158. _Report Cheif of U. S. Forest Service 1950_, p. 26.

159. Allen E. Thompson, "Forest Management on the Cedar River Watershed", 49 _Journal of Forestry_ 210-215 (March 1951).

160. _The American City_, January 1952, p. 154.

161. It may be noted that in many states municipalities may control and abate agricultural and horticultural pests.

162. Rhode Island laws specifically authorize cities and towns to appropriate moneys for this purpose (_General Laws_, ch. 229: Laws 1917, ch. 1540) (in sec. 5), but such authorization is not found in the statute books of other states.

163. Federal Inter-Agency Committee On Recreation, _Report on the Conservation and Development of Outdoor Recreation Resources_ (mimeo.), July 1950, p. A-8.

164. National Recreation Association, _Recreation and Park Yearbook of 1950_, 1951, p. 4.

165. Meyer and Brightbill, _State Recreation_, 1950, pp. 6; 65.

166. _Recreation and Park Yearbook of 1950_, op. cit., p. 26ff.

167. _Report on the Cons. and Deve. of Outdoor Recrea. Res._, op cit., p. A-12.

168. _Recreation and Park Yearbook of 1950_, op. cit., p. 9.

169. _Ibid._, p. 13.

170. _Rpt. on the Cons. and Deve. of Outdoor Recrea. Res._, op. cit., p. A-9.

171. Washington State Pollution Control Commission, _Clean Water and You_ (undated), p. 38.

172. _House Document 772_, 80th Cong., 2nd sess., 1948, p. 8.

173. _Ibid._, p. 16.

174. _Ibid._, p. 17.

175. _Ibid._, p. 31.

176. _House Document 350_, 82nd Cong., 2nd sess., 1952, p. 19.

177. _House Document 220_, 79th Cong., 1st sess., 1945, p. 10.

178. New Jersey Department of Conservation, _Annual Report_ for the fiscal year ending 30 June 1947, pp. 74-76.

179. Texas State Board of Water Engineers, _19th Biennial Report_, November 1950, p. 43.

180. _Port Series No. 10_, op. cit., p. 1.

181. The operation of ferries as such is not directly related to

the management of water resources. As for ferry docks, they are taken care of under "water terminals".

182. 43 Am. Jr. 86; 87.

183. Delegation of state police power over public utilities to municipalities is found in Missouri only. The regulatory authority given to first-class cities under the ordinary city-council form of government is comparable to that normally exercised by a state public service commission (Missouri Statutes, sec. 73.650 et seq.: Laws 1909, p. 138). The authority granted first-class cities under the commission form of government (ibid., secs. 74.123 and 74.127: Laws 1949, p. 383, secs. 8 and 10) and third-class cities (ibid., sec. 77.490: Laws 1893, p. 65; as last amended by L. 1905, p. 78) is limited primarily to the regulation of rates. It should be pointed out that in Missouri, as in all other states, all municipalities may grant franchises to public utilities and other private interests, and that therefore the above-mentioned special authority is quite unnecessary.

184. See Revised Civil Statutes of Texas, article 1119 (Laws 1907, p. 217, sec. 1; as amended by L. 1937, 45th Legislature, ch. 144, sec. 1); Wisconsin Statutes, sec. 196.58 (Laws 1907, ch. 499; as last amended by L. 1947, ch. 126); Illinois Revised Statutes, ch. 111-2/3, sec. 85 (act of 28 June 1921, sec. 85); Tennessee Code, sec. 3528, subsecs. (12) (13) (14) (Acts 1921, ch. 173, art. 2, sec. 2).

185. Railroads and other common carriers were regulated by the states even before 1900. It should also be remarked that the Federal Government assumed jurisdiction over the regulation of railroads and oil companies in 1987, of motor carriers and electric utilities (both hydro and fuel) in 1935, of aircraft carriers and natural gas companies in 1938, and of water carriers in 1940, although in none of these cases is the Federal regulation exclusive of state regulation.

186. Consult John Bauer, Standards For Modern Public Utility Franchises, 1930, pp. 7; 8; 12; 26; 28; The Public Utility Franchises, 1946, pp. 1; 2; 8; 9; 15.

187. Franchises in some states may also be granted by counties and the state. See New Mexico Statutes, sec. 72-103 (Laws 1909, ch. 141, sec. 3; as amended by L. 1949, ch. 8, sec. 1); Revised Code of Washington, sec. 80.32.010 (Laws 1903, ch. 173, sec. 1) and ch. 36.55 (L. 1937, ch. 187, sec. 38 et seq.; as amended by L. 1941, ch. 138, sec. 1); Compiled Laws of Michigan, sec. 460.551 (Acts 1909, No. 106, sec. 1); Iowa Code, sec. 489.1 (Acts 1909, ch. 94, sec. 1; as last amended by Acts 1937, ch. 205); Laws of Minnesota of 1951, ch. 261 (amending Minnesota Statutes, sec. 222.37). But state and county franchises are of much less importance than municipal franchises.

188. Fish weirs and traps are of course not water terminal facilities, but they are not separately discussed for the sake of convenience.

189. See Wisconsin Statutes, secs. 138.01 to 138.10 (Laws 1929, ch. 75; as amended by L. 1933, ch. 490).

190. See Iowa Code, secs. 137.13 (Acts 1866, ch. 107, secs. 1, 2; as last amended by Acts 1923-24, Ex. Sess., H. F. 260, sec. 49), and 420.175 and 420.176 (Acts 1882, ch. 168, sec. 6, 8); Ohio Revised Code, sec. 3707.10 et seq. (Laws 1869, p. 202, sec. 315); West Virginia Code, sec. 494 (Code of 1868, ch. 47, sec. 28; as last amended by Acts 1947, ch. 117).

191. The authority of Michigan cities extends to one-half of a mile beyond city limits, and that of Indiana cities extends to ten miles be-

yond city limits.

192. This authority extends to five miles beyond city limits.

193. America Land Co. v. City of Keene, 41 F (2d) 484 (4 June 1930);
New Hampshire State Planning and Development Commission, New Hampshire
Water, 1953, p. 5; letter to the author from Mrs. Margaret Arthur, Li-
brary, New Hampshire State Planning and Development Commission, dated 23
June 1954, forwarding a letter of Pillip A. Hazelton, Law Librarian, New
Hampshire State Library, of the same date; letter to the author from Mr.
Edward J. O'Brien, City Solicitor, City of Keene, New Hampshire, dated
13 August 1954.

194. See Illinois Revised Statutes, ch. 18, sec. 1 (Laws 1872, p.
210; as last amended by L. 1947, p. 330) (for towns) and ch. 24, sec.
23-93 (L. 1941, vol. 2, p. 177) (for cities and villages); Revised Codes
of Montana, sec. 11-985: Revised Code of 1921, sec. 5039 et seq.; as last
amended by L. 1927, ch. 20, sec. 1) (cities and towns), etc.

195. For the sake of convenience, the organization and finance of
the various kinds of special districts are discussed here instead of in
Chapters 5 and 6. Special districts, which are public corporations and
governmental units having specific corporate services and independent
governmental powers (primarily financial power), are to be distinguished
from administrative fields units of the state (or the county, city or
town) or an agency thereof, such as water districts formed for the purpose of administering state regulation on water rights, forest districts
and game districts formed for the purposes of administering state forest
and game laws, and the like. For interstate special districts, see Article 4, below.

196. In a broader sense, water terminal facilities include such harbor improvement works as seawall, mooring basins and turning basins,
bulkheads, jetties, etc.

197. First commissioners are appointed by the Governor of the state
and their successors elected by voters of the counties which they respectively represent. They serve staggering terms of 4 years.

198. For Oregon and Texas, see p. 705, below. Port districts of
Washington, Michigan and Idaho construct and maintain both terminal facilities (in their narrow sense) and harbor improvement works. The "port
authorities" of Arkansas (Arkansas Statutes, sec. 19-2720 et seq.: Acts
1947, No. 167) are not special districts but merely special agencies of
municipalities (like the Tennessee Valley Authority of the Federal Government).

199. Washington had 16 port districts as of 1951. See State of Washington 1951 Official List, published by Trick and Murray, Seattle.

200. Port of Seattle Commission, A Look At the Expanding Port of
Seattle (an undated and illustrated pamphlet), probably published in 1951.

201. Letters to the author from Mr. A. R. Wechner, auditor, Port of
Vancouver Commission, dated 18 November 1952, and Mr. Robert E. Mac-
Nannay, Office Manager, Port of Longview Commission, dated 21 November
1952.

202. Broadcast speech by Mr. Sherman Washburn on 2 January 1952 on
"Noon Edition", KEX, at 12:15 p. m.; and Commission of Public Docks of
the City of Portland, The Port of Portland, Oregon, undated pamphlet.

203. Albany Port District Commission, Annual Report 1950, pp.10-

11; 24.

204. U. S. Corps of Engineers and U. S. Maritime Administration, Port Series No. 7 (mimeo.), revised 1947, pp. 208; 364-366.

205. Information made available to the author through the courtesy of Mr. R. T. Spangler, Port Manager, Port Everglades, on 4 February 1953. Other port districts authorized by special state laws are Port of Calais Authority of Maine (Private and Local Laws of 1935, ch. 39; as amended by P. & L. L. 1945, ch. 15); North Haven Port District of Maine (P. & L. L. 1945, ch. 141; as amended by P. & L. L. 1947, ch. 168); Chicago Regional Port District of Illinois (act of 6 June 1951); Greater Baton Rouge Port Commission of Louisiana (Acts 1952, No. 10), etc.

206. "A Report of Waterfront Facilities and Freight Handling Equipment Available At Public and Private Terminals" (mimeo.), 1 October 1952; Annual Report of the District 1951 (mimeo.), p. 14; and The Port of Houston Today (undated pamphlet).

207. Annual Report 1951, op. cit., p. 10.

208. These structures have been also been built and maintained by drainage districts, which will be discussed below.

209. This tax is distinguished from the general property tax in that it is not ad valorem.

210. Robert W. Harrison, "Flood Control In the Mississippi Valley" (in manuscript form), made available to the author through the courtesy of Mr. B. F. Smith, Secretary-Manager, Delta Council, on 20 August 1951.

211. Since 1917, the expenditures of these districts consist of contributions to the Federal Government and costs of maintenance.

212. "Flood Control in the Mississippi Valley", op. cit.

213. Recent laws regarding the Mississippi Levee District are Laws 1918, ch. 152; 1922, ch. 167; 1926, ch. 245; 1930, chs. 85 and 110; 1932, ch. 154; 1934 chs. 139, 160 and 302; 1942, chs. 170 and 293; those regarding the Yazoo-Mississippi Levee District are Laws 1924, ch. 254; 1930, ch. 248; 1932, ch. 153; 1934, ch. 161; 1936, chs. 210 and 220; 1936, ex. sess., ch. 22; 1936, ex. sess., ch. 86.

214. See West's Louisiana Revised Statutes, 1951, tit. 38, ch. 4.

215. 19 State Government 239 (1946, by C. A. Nelson). It would seem that all these works were built prior to 1917, for since 1917 the Federal Government, through the Mississippi River Commission, has assumed flood control responsibilities in the alluvial valley of the Mississippi River, which includes the entire state of Louisiana.

216. U. S. Corps of Engineers and U. S. Maritime Administration, Port Series No. 20 (mimeo.), revised 1947, pp. 256-257.

217. Consult Rpt. Chief of E. 1902, p. 2600.

218. Also see Acts 1932, No. 88, sec. 1, as amended by Acts 1946, No. 204, sec. 2; and Acts 1938, No. 333, sec. 1.

219. Louisiana State Department of Public Works, Biennial Report, 1950-1951, p. 14.

220. Ibid., pp. 15-73. The Atchafalaya Basin Levee District has the largest, and the North Bossier Levee District the smallest, mile-

ages, namely, 385.2 miles and 3.6 miles respectively (pp. 28; 50).

221. For example, Act No. 93 of 1891; Act No. 14 of 1901; Acts Nos. 12, 20, 31, 71, 97 and 106 of 1905; Acts Nos. 41, 100, 415, and 441 of 1907; Acts Nos. 67, 120, and 229 of 1909; Act No. 83 of 1917; Act No. 58 of 1919, etc.

222. Iowa (1882, last amended 1947), Missouri (1887, last amended 1941), Kansas (1893), Indiana (1907, last amended 1947), Kentucky (1918), and Illinois (1937).

223. _Biennial Report of the State Reclamation Engineer (Tex.)_ (mimeo), 31 August 1936, p. 55. An example of Texas levee districts is given below. The levees built by this district are embanking and not protective levees. "Shortly after the flood of 1908, local interests at Fort Worth organized the Fort Worth Improvement District of Tarrant County for the purpose of constructing local protection works for the city. As a result, the Fort Worth floodway, protecting approximately 1,710 acres, was constructed in 1910 at a cost of $335,000. This floodway was formed by the construction of about 12.3 miles of levee, averaging 11 feet in height and having a 4-foot crown and 1 on 2.5 side slopes. Drainage through the levee was provided by gravity sluices. The original levee was overtopped and damaged to a considerable extent in 1922 after which emergency repairs were made. In 1936 a set-back levee approximately 1,200 feet in length was constructed as a WPA project on the Clear Fork . . . In addition, the levee system was raised and the floodway channel was snagged and cleared of roots, timber, and debris . . ." -- _House Document 242_, 81st Cong., 1st sess., 1949, p. 22. The levees built by the Dallas City and County Levee Improvement District (created in 1926, and reorganized as Dallas County Flood Control District in 1945) in 1928-1932 are also embanking levees. They are "parallel levees approximately 2,000 feet apart, located near the centerline of the Trinity River flood plain, with a new channel excavated between the levees forming the floodway." See _House Document 242_, 81st Cong., 1st sess., 1949, pp. 20-21.

242. Flood control districts in Pennsylvania are state administrative field units (_Pennsylvania Statutes_, tit. 32, sec. 654, 7 August 1936 and 10 March 1937) and flood districts in Utah and county administrative field units (_Utah Code_, tit. 17, ch. 7: Laws 1933, ch. 14). Oregon Flood Control District Law of 1935 (ch. 416) was repealed in 1949 (ch. 155).

225. Letter to the author from Mr. Charles E. Stricklin, Oregon State Engineer, dated 18 May 1953.

226. Letter to the author from Mr. Mark R. Kulp, Idaho State Reclamation Engineer, dated 18 May 1953.

227. Letter to the author from Mr. George R. Thompson, Assistant Director, Washington Dpt. of Conservation and Development, dated 19 May 1953.

228. Based on letter to the author from Mr. B. Loyal Smith, County Engineer, Walla Walla County, Washington, dated 22 May 1953, and _Rpt. Chief E. 1951_, pp. 2360-2361.

229. The principal amendments are made by Stats. 1921., ch. 749; Stats. 1925, ch. 448; Stats. 1927, ch. 332; Stats. 1931, ch. 639; Stats. 1947, ch. 142, sec. 14; Stats. 1947, ch. 1156 sec. 1; Stats. 1950, ch. 71.

230. _House Document 838_, 76th Cong., 3rd sess., 1940, p. 19.

231. ". . . No flood control works have been built on the Passaic River in New Jersey." "Flood control on the Passaic River has been studied by the Passaic Valley Flood Control Commission, the U. S. Army Engineers and other agencies, and although methods of solution have been recommended none have been undertaken. The difficulty seems to lie in the financing of such works." -- Letter to the author from Mr. Richard E. Bonyun, General Superintendent and Chief Engineer, Passaic Valley Water Commission, Clifton, N. J., dated 19 May 1953.

232. It replaces the Okeechobee Flood Control District, which was created by a special act of 1931 (ch. 14777) to furnish cooperation to the Federal Government with respect to the Callosahatchee River and Lake Okeechobee improvement authorized by the River and Harbor Act of 1930. Consult House Document 643, 80th Cong., 1949, p. 29.

233. Florida State Board of Conservation, Summary of the Central and Southern Flood Control Project, 31 August 1950, p. 5.

234. President's Water Resources Policy Commission, Report, vol. III, pp. 170-171.

235. In Texas, the districts are designated as "water improvement districts", which are not different except in name from the irrigation districts in other states.

236. County courts in Oregon, essentially judicial bodies, are at the same time county administrative authorities. A county court is composed of a judge and two commissioners.

237. Direct communication with state agencies concerned of these states in May-June 1953 (for Louisiana, the state bond and tax board; for all other states, state water agencies), except Colorado and Utah. For Colorado, letters to the author from Messrs. J. H. Knights, District Manager at Denver, Colorado, U. S. Bureau of Reclamation, and E. V. Lindseth, Assistant Director, Region 7, U. S. Bureau of Reclamation, dated respectively 19 and 23 March 1954. For Utah, letter to the author from Professor O. W. Israelsen, Utah State Agricultural College, dated 25 March 1954. The information for any of these states is not necessarily accurate.

238. Modesto Irrigation District, Modesto Irrigation District (Mimeo. pamphlet); and letters to the author from Mr. C. E. Plummer, chief engineer, Modesto Irrigation District, dated 25 November 1952, and Mr. R. V. Meikle, chief engineer, Turlock Irrigation District, dated 13 November 1952 and 26 May 1953.

239. Imperial Irrigation District, Statement Relating To Electric Revenue Bonds, 7 August 1951, pp. 27; 29; head of a letter to the author from Mr. Evan T. Hewes, President, Board of Directors, Imperial Irrigation District, dated 3 December 1951.

240. A. K. Lobeck, Geomorphology, 1939, pp. 237; 387.

241. Letter from Mr. Evan T. Hewes, op. cit. Statement Relating To Revenue Bonds, op. cit., p. 33.

242. Statement Relating to Electric Revenue Bonds, op. cit., pp. 11-12.

243. Letter to the author from Mr. Homer Moore, President, Talent Irrigation District, dated 27 May 1953, and accompanying informational material.

244. California State Department of Public Works, Report on Irrigation Districts in California, 1944-50, pp. 9-10.

245. It may be of interest to note that the Carden's Bottom Levee
District No. 2 of Yell County, Arkansas, organized by a special act of
1909 (No. 120), became a drainage district on 23 July 1927. -- House
Document 221, 80th Cong., 1st sess., 1947, p. 18. Many drainage districts
are commonly called "levee districts". See House Document 245, 80th
Cong., 1st sess., 1947, pp. 12-13; House Document 627, 80th Cong., 2nd
sess., 1948, p. 15; etc.

246. The following 14 states have no general statutes on drainage
districts: Connecticut, Maine, Maryland, Massachusetts, New Hampshire,
New Jersey, North Dakota, Ohio, Pennsylvania, Rhode Island, South Dakota
and Vermont. However, the drainage laws of Maine, Maryland and New Jersey resemble in many respects drainage-district laws of the listed 34
states. In Maine, a majority of land owners of any area may petition
the county court to undertake works in that area without forming a drainage district formally (Revised Statutes, ch. 84, sec. 160 et seq.). In
Maryland, 1/3 of the landowners or owners of 1/3 total land area of any
tract may petition counties to form Public Drainage Associations (Code,
art. 25, sec. 48 et seq.). In New Jersey, 100 freeholders of any area
may petition the supreme court judge for the county concerned to conduct
drainage enterprise (drainage only) for the area. The latter, on approving the petition, shall appoint a civil engineer and acommission of
three freeholders to supervise the enterprise (Laws 1881, ch. 210). These
provisions are of the same type as laws which were the predecessors of
many general drainage-district laws. The Virginia drainage districts
were changed into "drainage projects" by an act of 1954 (ch. 642), but
each drainage project is a drainage district in fact if not in name.

247. The county courts of Kentucky, Tennessee and West Virginia are
also the governing authorities of counties.

248.   See Fallbrook Irrigation District v. Bradley, op. cit., at
172-175.

249. For drainage improvement districts of Washington, it is the
governing body of the county if a district does not lie wholly within a
city or a town. For districts lying whooly within a city or a town, it
is the governing of the city or town concerned.

250. This is for districts which lie entirely within one county.
For inter-county districts, it is ten land owners or owners of a majority
of the total land area in the proposed district.

251. The Nebraska sanitary drainage districts are formed of a municipality or municipalities plus adjacent lands subject to overflows.

252. Drainage districts under this law are public corporations like
other drainage districts. It is improper to think of them as field units
of state administration.

253. Called board of directors in Arizona, California (1903 and
1923 laws), Colorado, Kansas (for districts in which three-fifths of
total land area are owned by absentees, for districts in valleys of natural water-courses, and for districts in counties of 85,000-130,000 population), Minnesota, Nebraska (for districts established by vote of land
owners) and New Mexico (for districts formed to cooperate with the Federal Government); board of supervisors in Florida, Kansas (1911, ch.
168), Missouri, Nebraska (1905, ch. 191), Nevada, Oregon, South Carolina
(1920 law), Utah, Washington (1913 law) and West Virginia; board of commissioners in Arkansas, Illinois (act of 29 May 1879), Louisiana (both

kinds of districts), Mississippi (1912 law), Montana, Washington (1895
and 1909 laws), Wisconsin and Wyoming; board of drainage commissioners
in Alabama, Delaware, Georgia, Idaho, New Mexico (ordinary districts),
North Carolina, South Carolina (1911 law) and Texas; board of trustees
in California (1885 law) and Nebraska (for sanitary districts); and
drainage board in Kentucky (1918 law).

254. The county courts of Arkansas and West Virginia are also the
governing boards of the counties.

255. One direct from each of the counties concerned. If the number is even, then an additional is to be elected at large.

256. Three if the district contains a city of 40,000 people. Otherwise, five.

257. Three if the total area of the district is 25,000 acres or
less; five if it is 25,000-50,000 acres; seven if it is 50,000-65,000
acres; nine if it is 75,000 acres or more.

258. Kentucky (1918), Louisiana (1900) and Wyoming.

259. Alabama, Arizona, California (1885, 1903 and 1923 laws), Colorado, Florida, Kansas (for districts in natural valleys), Kentucky(1912),
Minnesota, Mississippi (1912), Missouri, Nebraska (for districts under
law of 1905, districts organized by vote and sanitary districts in municipalities), New Mexico (both kinds), Oregon, South Carolina (1920), Utah,
West Virginia and Wisconsin.

260. Arkansas, Idaho, Illinois (1879), Indiana, Kansas (1911), Texas and Washington (1895).

261. Delaware, Georgia, North Carolina, South Carolina (1901) and
Virginia.

262. Under the following laws the secretary (or clerk) must be elected: California (1923), Idaho, Indiana, Kansas (for districts in natural
valleys), Kentucky (1918, there being no president of chairman), Louisiana (1924), Nebraska (all three kinds of drainage districts), Nevada, New
Mexico (both kinds of drainage districts), Oregon, Texas, Utah, Washington (1895), Wisconsin and Wyoming (there being no president or chairman).
Under the following laws, secretary must be appointed: Arizona, California (1903) and Colorado.

263. California (1923), Kansas (for district in natural valleys),
Nevada, Utah and Wisconsin.

264. Louisiana (1924), Oregon and West Virginia.

265. Colorado, Delaware, Georgia, Indiana, Kansas (1911, ch. 168),
Nebraska (1905, ch. 161), New Mexico (for districts cooperating with the
Federal Government), North Carolina, South Carolina (1911) and Texas.

266. Alabama, California (1885 and 1923), Florida, Kentucky (1912
and 1918), Louisiana (1900), Missouri, Nebraska (for sanitary drainage
in municipalities), South Carolina (1920), Texas, West Virginia and Wisconsin.

267. Delaware, Georgia, North Carolina, South Carolina (1911) and
Virginia.

268. Limitations on the financial power of the governing board will
be discussed below.

269. The 1885 law of California and the 1909 law of New York.

270. In states where common law is in force with respect to drainage, the owner of upper land is liable to benefit assessments for improvements on downstream lands which are made possible by artificial drainage of his own land. This rule is not effective in states adopting civil law of drainage. -- Bernard A. Etcheverry, Land Drainage and Flood Protection, 1931, p. 284.

271. House Document 643, 80th Cong., 1949, pp. 29-30.

272. U. S. Bureau of the Census, Preliminary Release of the 1950 Census of Agriculture, Drainage of Agricultural Lands, Released 30 October 1951. It may perhaps be observed that not all states having general drainage district laws have actually drainage districts, and that not every drainage district has reclaimed some lands. The drainage enterprises recorded for Maryland and New Jersey may have been undertaken by districts organized by special state laws, or in a manner short of the establishment of a drainage district. For Delaware "tax ditches" see Delaware Laws of 1951, ch. 151; for North Dakota "reclamation districts", see North Dakota Laws of 1953, ch. 348.

273. For all above, see General Laws of Massachusetts, chs. 28 and 92.

274. "Boston Water Supply" (mimeo.), made available to the author through the courtesy of Mr. Daniel M. Sullivan, Division Engineer, Public Works Department, City of Boston, on 19 November 1951. The dates of construction of the three reservoirs were supplied by Mr. Sullivan.

275. In addition, there are water supply districts and water supply authorities. The former do not construct water supply works but purchase water from a city or a water district or a private water company for fire-protection, sanitary or other purposes. Water supply authorities seem to be agencies of the county government. Water supply districts are governed by the same law as the water districts. Water supply authorities are governed by Laws of 1934, ch. 847.

276. Samuel B. Morris, "Water Works Management and Los Angeles Progress", 42 Journal of American Water Works Association 654-664 (July 1950).

277. U. S. Department of the Interior, The Story of Hoover Dam, 1950, p. 39.

278. Letter to the author from Mr. Morris S. Jones, Chief Engineer and General Manager, City of Pasadena Water Department, dated 13 November 1951. Pasadena is a member of the District and is dependent thereon for about two-thirds for its entire water supply.

279. Laws of 1915, ch. 206, as amended (Rev. Stats., ch. 70, art. 1) and Laws 1929, ch. 104, as amended (Ibid., ch. 70, art. 2) provided respectively for the organization of water power districts and hydroelectric power districts. But they were repealed by chs. 154 and 155 of the Laws of 1945, respectively. ". . .No Water Power Districts or Hydroelectric Power Districts were ever organized and operated under those Statutes." -- Letter to the author from Mr. Hugh W. Cargo, Chief Engineer, Nebraska State Railway Commission, dated 29 June 1953.

280. Clarence A. Davis, Nebraska's Public Power Explained, 1949, pp. 7-19.

281. U. S. Department of the Interior, Years of Progress, 1945-

<u>1952</u>, p. 22.

282. Federal Power Commission, <u>Statistics of Publicly Owned Electric Utilities</u>, 1949.

283. Federal Power Commission, <u>Annual Report for 1935</u>, pp. 69-70.

284. But not all districts so designated are single-purpose sewer-age-disposal districts.

285. Surface drainage and sewage disposal are so closely related to each other that for practical purposes they may be regarded as a combined single purpose.

286. U. S. Public Works Administration, <u>America Builds</u>, 1939, p.235.

287. <u>Enclyc. Bri</u>., 1951 ed., vol. 4, p. 449.

288. Information provided the author by the Engineering Department of the Sanitary District of Chicago in September 1951.

289. <u>Map of the Sanitary District of Chicago</u>, made available to the author through the courtesy of the Engineering Department of the District in September 1951.

290. <u>Enclyc. Bri</u>., 1951 ed., vol. 4, p. 449. According to the decree in <u>Wisconsin v. Illinois</u> 278 U. S. 399 (1929), the amount of waters of Lake Michigan which the District can divert to the Canal must not exceed 1,500 cubic feet per second (5,000 cubic feet per second prior to 21 December 1938 and 6,500 cubic feet per second prior to 31 December 1935).

291. Information furnished through the courtesy of Mr. Frederick Rex, Librarian, Chicago Municipal Reference Library, on 13 September 1951.

292. Information and map made available to the author through the courtesy of the Engineering Department of the Sanitary District of Chicago in September 1951.

293. <u>House Document 802</u>, 78th Cong., 2nd sess., 1944, p. 18.

294. U. S. Corps of Engineers, <u>Lake Series No. 7</u> (mimeo.), revised 1951, pp. 47-109. For further information regarding the Chicago Sanitary District, see <u>Senate Document 126</u>, 71st Cong., 2nd sess., 1930; and <u>House Public Works Committee Hearings on H. R. 3192, Etc</u>., 83rd Cong., 1st sess., July 1953, pp. 37; 60; 121; 147.

295. If the district is in one county and if there is no city within its boundaries, all five trustees are appointed by the board of supervisors of that county. If it is located in one county, and if it contains one or more cities, then each city, through its governing body, appoints one trustee, and the county board appoints all remaining trustees. If the district is located in two or more counties and contains no city, each of the counties appoints a trustee and the major county in addition appoints the remaining trustee or trustees if any. If two or more counties and a city are involved, then each unit appoints a trustee, with the remining trustee or trustees, if any, appointed by the largest county. The number of trustees may be increased or reduced by the county board upon request of the board of trustees.

296. If 75 percent of the lands of the district are located in one city or town, then all five trustees are appointed by the governing body of the said city or town.

297. <u>Revised Statutes</u>, ch. 11.5, sec. 74 et seq.: Act of 7 July 1927, as amended. Illinois sanitary districts, as provided in an act of 7 May 1907, as amended (<u>Revised Statutes</u>, ch. 42, sec. 247 et seq.), which are organized to drain overflows of natural waterways by the construction of levees and drains in the interest of public health, are in effect mosquito control districts.

298. H. H. Stage, "Mosquito Control Agencies in the United States", 11 <u>Mosquito News</u> 8-22 (March 1951).

299. 11 <u>Mosquito News</u> 169 (September 1951).

300. Consult National Recreation Association, <u>Recreation and Park Yearbook of 1950</u>, 1951, p. 4.

301. Effective 10 January 1942.

302. It is provided that the act should be ratified by the electorates of these five counties. All of the five counties has ratified it.

303. Based on informational material (folders and sheets) made availble to the author through the courtesy of Mr. P. K. McWethy, Secretary, The Huron-Clinton Metropolitan Authority on 11 June 1953.

304. Letter to the author from Mr. P. K. McWethy of the same date.

305. See <u>New York Public Authorities Law</u>, art. 2.

306. National Recreational Association, <u>Recreation and Park Yearbook of 1950</u>, 1951, pp. 22-66.

307. <u>Ibid</u>., p. 13.

308. Library of Congress, <u>Digest of Outstanding State Legislation on Agriculture</u>, 1935-1939, 1940, p. 27.

309. <u>Ibid</u>., pp. 28-31; U. S. Dept. of Agri., <u>State Legislation For Better Land Use</u>, April 1941, pp. 36-37; Ayres and Scoates, <u>Land Drainage and Reclamation</u>, 1939, pp. 214-217; <u>Report Chief of Soil Conservation Service for 1950</u>, pp. 12-13 (given dates of legislation in each state and territory).

310. 98 <u>Cong. Rec</u>. A2627 (25 April 1952).

311. 97 <u>Cong. Rec</u>. A6326 (2 October 1951). For accomplishments <u>by private farmers</u> under these plans, consult current annual report of the U. S. Soil Conservation Service.

312. <u>The Book of the States, 1950-51</u>, p. 407.

313. U. S. Department of Agriculture (by A. T. Nitchelson and D. C. Muckel), <u>Spreading Water For Storage Underground</u>, December 1937, pp.52-53.

314. Harold E. Thomas, <u>The Conservation of Ground Water</u>, 1951, p. 67.

315. Letter to the author from Mr. Russell Crawford, Superintendent, Pecos Valley Artesian Conservancy District, dated 1 November 1951.

316. For other kinds of single-purpose districts, see Laws of Maryland of 1950, ch. 65 (taxing and assessment districts for coast and bank erosion control); <u>Illinois Revised Statutes</u>, ch. 57.5 (Laws 1913, p. 395; as last amended by <u>L. 1953</u>, pp. 215 and 217) (forest preserve districts); <u>Nevada Compiled Laws</u>, sec. 31692 et seq. (Stats. 1949, ch. 248) (fire

protection districts, for forest fire control specifically); Laws of
Kansas of 1953, ch. 477 (watershed districts), etc.

317. The word "any" implies that the conservancy district is _poten-
tially_ a multiple-purpose district.

318. Barrows, _Floods_, 1948, pp. 233-234.

319. "A Review of Some of the Pertinent Considerations in River
Basin Development" (mimeo. paper), submitted by the American Watershed
Council to the President's Water Resources Policy Commission on 10 Aug-
ust 1950.

320. James B. Craig, "The Micracle of Muskingum", _American Forests_,
July 1949.

321. Letter to the author from Mr. Walter H. Wertime, Jr., Secretary and Treasurer, Hudson River Regulating District, dated 4 November
1953.

322. Black River Regulating District, _The Facts About the Panther
Mountain Reservoir_, 3rd ed., January 1953, pp. 19-21.

323. _Ibid._, p. 15.

324. _Ibid._, p. 10.

325. Letter from Mr. Wertime, _op. cit._; and Hudson River Regulating
District, _Sacandaga Reservoir_, 1950.

326. _The Facts About Panther Mountain Reservoir_, op. cit., p. 29.

327. _Sacandaga Reservoir_, op. cit.

328. Letter from Mr. Wertime, _op. cit._

329. _Sacanadaga Reservoir_, op. cit.; and _The Facts About Panther
Mtn., Res._, op. cit., p. 30.

330. See William P. Creager and Joel Justin, _Hydroelectric Handbook_,
2nd ed., 1950, p. 168.

331. _The Facts About Panther Mountain Reservoir_, op. cit., pp. 19;
29.

332. _House Document 327_, 81st Cong., 1st sess., 1949, pp. 22-24.

333. _House Document 243_, 81st Cong., 1st sess., 1949, p. 46.

334. _Ibid._, p. 59.

335. _Nebraska's Public Power Explained_, op. cit., pp. 8-11; Federal
Power Commission, _Annual Report for 1951_, p. 153.

336. Tex. Bd. of Water Engineers, _19th Annual Report_, November
1950, p. 59.

337. Federal Power Commission, _Annual Report for 1951_, p. 153.

338. The Act was amended by Laws 1935, ch. 405; Laws 1937, ch. 350
and Laws 1941, ch. 398.

339. These ten counties have a total area of 2,840 square miles.

340. For earlier authorization of investigation in the interest of navigation, see River and Harbor Act of 2 March 1907 (34 Stat. 1073, 1117).

341. See pp. 3; 4 and 11 of the Report. Possible damsites were given on p. 31.

342. This report was printed as House Document 361, 71st Cong., 2nd sess.

343. U. S. Bureau of Reclamation, Reclamation Project Data, p. 93 (1949 replacement).

344. U. S. Bureau of Reclamation, Region 5, "General Descriptive Statement: The Colorado River Project, Texas", June 1948. For Marshall Ford Dam, see pp. 385-386, above.

345. The Lower Colorado River Authority, op. cit.; Texas Board of Water Engineers, 19th Biennial Report, November 1950, p. 66.

346. "General Descriptive Statement: The Colorado River Project, Texas", op. cit.

347. Texas State Board of Water Engineers, Nineteenth Biennial Report, November 1950, p. 66.

348. The Lower Colorado River Authority, op. cit.

349. The Lower Colorado River Authority, "Soil Conservation Program" (undated, mimeographed article, sent to the author by Mr. John E. Babcock, Development Supervisor of the Authority on 8 August 1951), p. 2.

350. 38 Reclamation Era 287 (December 1952).

351. See "Soil Conservation Program", op. cit. For the Federal program of watershed treatment for the Colorado Valley in Texas, see p. 213, above.

352. Amended by Laws 1939, ch. 70, art. 2.

353. Rpt. Chief of E. 1951, p. 1142.

354. U. S. Dpt. of the Inter., Years of Progress, 1945-1952, p. 39.

355. Ibid., and Rpt. Chief of E. 1951, pp. 1142-1143.

356. Letter to the author from Mr. P. Bruce Brockway, Jr., Acting Superintendent, Toledo Area Sanitary District, dated 22 June 1953.

357. Toledo Area Sanitary District, Fifth Annual Report (mimeo.), 1951, p. 4.

358. Ibid., pp. 1-2.

359. Ibid., p. 14 ff.; and Sixth Annual Report, 1952, p. 4 ff.

360. The author gratefully acknowledges the help of Mrs. Virginia Barker, assistant secretary, Washington Public Service Commission, given in her letter of 21 November 1951.

361. 96 Cong. Rec. 12997.

362. House Public Lands Committee Hearings On Irrigation and Recla-

mation (U. S. Congress), February 1947, p. 527.

363. Federal Power Commission, Statistics of Publicly Owned Electric Utilities, 1949. In 1951, the Public Utility District No. 1 of Chelan County issued $33,600,000 of bonds for the construction of six generating units at the hydroelectric power development at Rock Island on the Columbia River which is owned by the Puget Sound Power and Light Company, under a lease agreement with the said Company. -- Puget Sound Power and Light Co., Interesting Facts About Rock Island Dam and Power Plant, undated pamphlet, first page.

364. Federal Power Commission, Press Release No. 5670, 12 October 1951.

365. For the distinction between interstate compacts or agreements with Congressional consent and interstate agreements without Congressional consent, see Virginia v. Tennessee, 147 U. S. 503, 518-520 (3 April 1893).

366. Water-apportionament instruments belong either to (3) or (4). Instruments for defining state boundaries belong to (4), as well as instruments which merely declare certain broad principles of administration or general rights and responsibilities of the state signatories.

367. Ohio River Valley Sanitation Commission, Third Annual Report, 15 November 1951, p. 6.

368. West Virginia v. Sims, 341 U. S. 22, 30-31 (9 April 1951). The decision was unanimous.

369. Article I, section 10, clause 1 of the U. S. Constitution: "No state shall . . . pass any . . . law impairing the obligation of contracts . . . ."

370. Rundle et at. v. The Delaware and Raritan Canal Co., 14 How. (U. S.) 80, 88-91 (1852).

371. Letter to the author from Mr. Dean W. Locks, South Dakota State Engineer, dated 9 November 1951. See Laws of South Dakota of 1953, ch. 114.

372. Biennial Report of the State Engineer of Nevada, July 1, 1948-June 30, 1950, 87-102.

373. Laws of New York of 1921, ch.154; Laws of New Jersey of 1921, ch. 151; Joint Resolution of Congress of 23 August 1921 (42 Stat. 174).

374. In 1947, the Authority was given authority to operate air terminals (Laws of New York of 1947, ch. 802; Laws of New Jersey of 1947, ch. 43).

375. Laws of New Jersey of 1922, ch. 9; Laws of New York of 1922, ch. 43; Joint Resolution of Congress of 1 July 1922 (42 Stat. 822).

376. See Frederick L. Bird, A Study of the Port of New York Authority, 1949, p. 13.

377. Ibid., pp. 14; 25-26; 31-32; 138; Annual Report of the Port of New York Authority for 1950, pp. 59; 115.

378. By another supplemental agreement of the same date (66 Stat. 747), the Authority was authorized to construct or acquire an additional tunnel or bridge for vehicular traffic between Philadelphia and Camden.

379. It may acquire the Tacony-Palmyra bridge, and construct or acquire other facilities or projects subject to the written consent of the governors of the two states.

380. Besides, the Agency acts as (1) a supervisory agency over the local governmental units with respect to sewerage and drainage; (2) planning agency for the same "for coordination of streets, highways, parkways, parking areas, terminals, water supply and sewage disposal works, recreational and conservation facilities and projects, land use pattern and other matters in which joint or coordinated action of the communities within the areas will be generally "beneficial"; and (3) an advisory body to the legislatures of the two states or to the Congress of the United States with respect to the improvement of transportation, terminal and other facilities in the Metropolitan District.

381. The Book of the States, 1952-53, pp. 38-39.

382. Letter to the author from Mr. Milton M. Kinsey, Chief Engineer, Bi-State Development Agency, Missouri-Illinois Metropolitan District, dated 7 July 1953.

383. But this decision did not necessitate interstate administration. Rather it presupposed that each of the riparian states took separate action to prevent and stop water pollution.

384. Interstate Commission on the Delaware River Basin, Minutes (mimeo.) of the Clean Waters For America Regional Confernece, held 16 January 1948, Section V, p. 2.

385. The New York Times, 28 August 1950.

386. Ohio River Valley Sanitation Commission, First Annual Report, p. 3. Article XI of the Compact provides that "this compact shall become effective upon ratification by the legislatures of a majority of the states located within the District and upon approval by the Congess of the United States; and shall become effective as to any additional states signing thereafter at the time of such signing" (54 Stat. 752, 756).

387. Interstate waters are defined as "those portions of the Ohio River and its tributaries which form boundaries between, or are contiguous to, two or more signatory states, or which flow from one signatory state into another signatory state."

388. All above, Article VI (54 Stat. 754).

389. Ohio R. Val. Water Sani. Comm., First Annual Report, p. 5.

390. New England Interstate Water Pollution Control Commission, Fifth Annual Report, for the fiscal year ending 30 June 1952, pp.30-31.

391. Implied in a letter to the author from Mr. Joseph C. Knox, Secretary, New England Interstate Water Pollution Control Commission, dated 29 June 1953.

392. Fifth Annual Report, op. cit., p. 5.

393. Ibid., p. 9.

394. Letter to the author from Mr. Joseph C. Knox, Secretary, New England Interstate Water Pollution Control Commission, dated 17 July 1953.

395. James H. Allen et al., "Development Plans For the Delaware Basin", 42 Journal of American Water Works Association 615, 616 (July 1950)

396. Consult U. S. Public Health Service, Report on Water Pollution Control, Potomac River Basin (mimeo.), 1951, p. 38.

397. Interstate Commission on the Delaware River Basin, Planned Progress in Pollution Control, January 1940, p. 5ff.

398. Unless interstate administration is strictly defined as administration by some interstate agency. Such a definition, however, is not adopted by the present author.

399. It had not been adopted by Pennsylvania legislature by 1951.

400. Interstate Compact for Potomac River Basin between the states of Maryland, Virginia, Pennsylvania and West Virginia and the District of Columbia, Joint Resolution of Congress of 11 July 1940, Art. II, para. (f). -- 54 Stat. 748, 750.

401. Letter to the author from Mr. F. L. Woodward, Director, Division of Environmental Sanitation, Minnesota Department of Health, dated 8 July 1953.

402. Copies of all of these agreements were made available to the author through the courtesy of Mr. F. L. Woodward on 8 July 1953.

403. Statement of Mr. Dwight F. Metzler, Secretary of the Council, also available to the author through the courtesy of Mr. Woodward.

404. This compact is applicable to Maine, New Hampshire, Massachusetts, Rhode Island, Connecticut, New York, New Jersey, Delaware, Maryland, Virginia, North Carolina, South Carolina, Georgia, and Florida. But up to 4 May 1942 only Maine, New Hampshire, Massachusetts, New York, New Jersey, Delaware, Maryland and Virginia had signed it.

405. As of 19 August 1950, this amendment (Amendment No. 1) was ratified by Maine, New Hampshire, Massachusetts, Rhode Island, Pennsylvania and North Carolina.

406. In (1) and (3), the right of accession is given to any state contiguous to any of the signatory states or riparian up waters which flow in waters under the jurisdiction of any of the signatory states and which are frequented by anadromous fishes.

407. Letter to the author from Mr. Lew E. Fiero, Director, Division of State Parks, Minnesota Department of Conservation, dated 25 June 1952.

408. Letter to the author from Mr. C. L. Harrington, Superintendent of the Forests and Parks Division, Wisconsin Conservation Commission, dated 11 July 1952.

409. Letters from Messrs. Fiero and Harrington, op. cit.; National Park Service, State Parks: Areas, Acreages and Accommodations, 31 December 1950, pp. 22; 42.

410. The five New Jersey commissioners constituted the New Jersey Commission, and the five New York commissioners the New York Commission. But there was a single executive director, assistant general manager for the entire interstate park. -- Commissioners of The Palisades Interstate Park, The Palisades Interstate Park, 1900-1929, p. 2. "From 1900 to 1937, the Commissioners of the Palisades Interstate Park had consisted of two separate bodies -- the New York and the New Jersey Commissions,

which, during the years of their existence, had, with one brief exception, identical personnel." -- Palisades Interstate Park Commission, The Palisades Interstate Park, 1929-1947, p. 14. So actually there were only five commissioners, each of whom received appointment from both New Jersey and New York.

411. See Commissioners of the Palisades Interstate Park, The Palisades Interstate Park, 1900-1929; and Palisades Interstate Park Commission, The Palisades Interstate Park, 1929-1947 (two pamphlets).

412. Letter to the author from Mr. Henry H. James, Assistant to General Manager, Palisades Interstate Park, N. Y. and N. J., dated 29 July 1953.

413. Mr. James' letter, op. cit.; Palisades Interstate Park, New York Section, Palisades Interstate Park, New Jersey Section; and Bear Mountain-Harriman Section of Palisades Interstate Park, Winter Sports, -- three folders (undated) published by the Palisades Interstate Park Commission and made available to the author through the courtesy of Mr. James on 13 July 1953; The Palisades Interstate Park, 1900-1929, op. cit. p. 15; The Palisades Interstate Park, 1929-1947, op. cit., pp. 18-21.

414. The Palisades Interstate Park, 1929-1947, op. cit., pp. 10-12; 30; The Book of The States, 1952-53, p. 36. Consult the accompanying map.

415. Letter of Mr. James, op. cit.

416. 23 State Government 42 (March 1950).

417. Ibid., and 23 State Government 1 (January 1950).

418. Louisiana Department of Public Works, Biennial Report 1950-1951, p. 15.

419. As an alternative to such interstate county enterprise, Ohio counties may construct drainage works outside of state limits without participation by the neighboring state if such privileges are specially granted them by the latter (Revised Code, sec. 6135.20). They may also ask county or counties of a lower neighboring state to construct or enlarge the outlets of their drainage works to take off water drained from Ohio (ibid., sec. 6135.23).

420. As will be shown in the discussion which follows, the administration actually extends beyond the boundary waters, waters that constitute a part of the international boundary or boundaries, or waters which divide the United States from Canada of Mexico.

421. Functions, Powers and Duties of the International Joint Commission and of the International Boards Operating Under Its Jurisdiction, published in Ottawa, Canada (official document), p. 3.

422. George Kyte, K. C., "Organization and Work of the International Joint Commission", a speech delivered over the coast-to-coast network of the Canadian Broadcasting Corporation at Sydney, N. S., on 5 January 1935.

423. Complementary administration is said to exist when two or more independent administrative authorities simultaneously but separately exercise administration over the same object or party about the same subject-matter in such a way that the administrative measures of these authorities in question complement each other or are conditional upon each other.

424. Composite administration is said to exist between two administrative authorities when they exercise administration over the object or
party about the same subject matter at the same time in such a way that
the administrative measure of one authority is a condition to the taking
effect of that of the other, in other words, that the former is absorbed
by the latter, or that the former is dependent on the latter. In this
instance, the international administration is a condition to, or is dependent upon, and is absorbed by, Federal administration.

425. Guides to administration must be distinguished from standards
of administration. While the latter are part of administration, the former are not part of administration, but are instructions to the administrative authority as to how administration is to be effected or carried
out. Administration is supplementary to standards; but guides are supplementary to administration.

426. It is to be remarked that the International Joint Commission,
under the abobe-cited Article IV of the Treaty of 1909, is not concerned
with diversions of water as such from waters tributary to boundary waters or from waters running across the international boundary.

427. These guides are contained in Article VIII of the Treaty.

428. For special rules applying to diversions of waters of the Lake
of the Woods, see Convention of Washington signed 24 February 1925, effective 17 July 1925 (44 Stat. 2108).

429. Letter to the author from Mr. Jesse B. Ellis, Secretary, U. S.
Section, International Joint Commission, dated 2 July 1953.

430. Functions, Power and Duties of the International Joint Commission, Etc., op. cit., p. 7. The boards of control must be distinguished
from the above-mentioned boards of engineer advisers.

431. Letter, op. cit.

432. The waters which form part of the boundary line between the
United States and Mexico consist of the Rio Grande from El Paso, Texas
to its mouth, covering a distance of 1,210 miles, and the 20-mile reach
of the Colorado River extending from Yuma to St. Luis, Arizona. -- International Boundary and Water Commission, United States and Mexico, In
The Field of Water Control and Utilization" (mimeo.), January 1952, p. 1;
and maps of the States of Texas and Arizona.

433. United administration is defined as the performance of an administrative act by two or more jurisdictions or agencies each of which
performs part of the administrative act. In this case, local authorities
make the preliminary examination, the International Boundary Commission
(now International Boundary and Water Commission) makes the final examination and determination, and there may be a Federal or state or local
agency which gives the order of permission or prohibition.

434.   "Activities of the International Boundary and Water Commission, U. S. and Mexico, In the field of Water Control and Utilization",
op. cit., pp. 7-9.

435. ". . . The prorotable cost of the works will be defrayed by
both governments in the proportion of 88 percent by the United States
of America and 12 percent by the United Mexican States" (art. II of the
convention).

436. "Activities of the International Boundary and Water Commission,
Etc.", op. cit., pp. 10-11.

437. Letter to the author from Mr. George H. Winters, Secretary, United States Section, International Boundary and Water Commission, United States and Mexico, dated 8 July 1953.

438. <u>Senate Report 595</u>, 83rd Cong., 1st sess., July 1953.

439. Cities of Douglas and Nogales were required to bear part of the costs of maintenance and operation.

440. Funds (not fixed) necessary for this purpose were appropriated by sec. 302 of the said Act. The plan of the project calls for the construction of an outfall pipe of about 3 miles long and a treatment plant to prevent the pollution of the New River, which empties into the Salton Sea. See <u>House Foreign Affairs Committee Hearings on Southwestern Border Projects</u>, 81st Cong., 2nd sess., June-July 1950, p. 7ff.

441. For the apportionment of waters of the Rio Grande system and the Colorado River between the two countries, as provided in Articles 4 and 10 of this Treaty, see p. 536a, above.

442. C. M. Ainsworth, "International Irrigation Developments Along Rio Grande Started", <u>Civil Engineering</u>, May 1951, pp. 38-41.

443. "Activities of the International Boundary and Water Commission, Etc.", <u>op. cit.</u>, p. 7. By an Act of 18 June 1954 (68 Stat. 255), the Department of the Interior is authorized to dispose of the electric energy generated at the Falcon Dam with view to amortizing the costs of production and transmission at rates to be approved by the Federal Power Commission.

444. <u>Ibid.</u>, p. 19.

445. <u>Ibid.</u>, p. 23.

446. <u>Ibid.</u>, p. 25.

447. The work of the United States Section is (unless otherwise specified) the same as the Mexican Section. It is to be noted that "the United States Section is not a part of the Department of State but is subject to the control of that Department in matters pertaining to policy. In most respects, it is administratively a quasi-independent agency." -- Letter to the author from Mr. L. M. Lawson, U. S. Commissioner, International Boundary and Water Commission, U. S. and Mexico, dated 7 August 1951.

448. "Activities of the International Boundary and Water Commission, Etc.", <u>op. cit.</u>, p. 9.

449. See (A) (2), above.

450. "Activities of the International Boundary and Water Commission, Etc.", <u>op. cit.</u>, p. 20.

451. <u>Ibid.</u>, pp. 22-25.

452. A memorandum of understanding was entered into between the Department of State (on behalf of the U. S. Section) and the Department of the Interior (for the Bureau of Reclamation) on 16 February 1945 to implement this Protocol.

453. It should be pointed out that not all fishery treaties provide for international administration. It is not constitutionally clear whether the several states can enter into agreements with equivalent local units of foreign countries creating international fishery administration. But the laws of Maine have authorized the State Commissioner of

cal units of foreign countries creating international fishery administration. But the laws of Maine have authorized the State Commissioner of
Inland Fisheries and Game (with approval of the advisory council) to
enter into agreement with Canadian authorities for the regulation of bag
limits, size limits, open or closed seasons and methods of taking game
and other fish from the inland boundary waters between the state of Maine
and Canada (Revised Statutes, ch. 33, sec. 2-A: Laws 1953, ch. 394, sec.
1). There is no information as to the actual operation of this provision.

454. Washington Department of Fisheries, 62nd Annual Report, February 1953, p. 2 (also p. 97).

455. The Convention provides that "each High Contracting Party
shall be responsible for the enforcement of the orders and regulations
adopted by the Commission . . ." (art. VIII, first para.). The enforcement law of the United States was passed by the Congress on 29 July 1947
(61 Stat. 511).

456. Washington Department of Fisheries, 1950 Annual Report, p. 73.

457. Rpt. Chief of E. 1917, p. 49; Rpt. Chief of E. 1918, p. 83.

458. National Park Service, The Development of the National Park
System and the National Park Service (mimeo.), January 1947, p. 7.

459. Senate and House Public Works Committees Joint Hearings on S.
689, Etc., 83rd Cong., 1st sess., May 1953, p. 11. The recommended plan
is outlined at p. 83 of Senate Document 128, 71st Cong., 2nd sess., 1931.

460. Senate Document 128, op. cit., p. 86.

461. International Niagara Board of Control, Final Progress Report
of the Construction Subcommittee, 1 September 1948, pp. 4-10.

462. Treaties and Other International Acts, No. 2130.

463. By February 1954, construction of this international project
had not been authorized by the two governments. -- Letter to the author
from Lt. Col. Holcombe, Executive Officer, Buffalo District Engineer's
Office U. S. Corps of Engineers, dated 18 February 1954. It is not
known whether the International Joint Commission (presumably through its
International Niagara Board of Control) has made, or when it made, the
recommendations regarding the construction of the Horseshoe project.

464. Coordination between state administration and local administration are omitted.

465. These adjustments constitute part of inter-jurisdictional relationships. There are other relationships between separate and distinct
jurisdictions which are based on their common administrative needs or
are motivated by other factors. Examples of the latter are the exchange
of information, loan of personnel, conferences unrelated to administrative adjustments, etc. Some relationships are purely financial in nature.

466. Concurrent jurisdiction is distinguished from co-jurisdiction
in that it exists between two or more constitutionally identical jurisdictions whereas co-jurisdiction is engendered by an overlapping of services between two or more constitutionally different jurisdictions, or,
in a broader sense, by an overlapping of functions between two or more
different administrative agencies. Thus there is con-current jurisdiction between one state and another state, or between the United States

and a foreign country; but there is co-jurisdiction between the Federal
Government and the several states collectively or separately, or between
the Department of the Interior and the Department of concurrent jurisdiction is in all cases territorial. (These definitions of co-jurisdiction and concurrent jurisdiction need not be the same as have been or may
be adopted in other publications.)

467. Interstate administration and international administration discussed before are technically two forms of joint administration.

468. Report of the Chief of Forest Service for 1951, p. 11.

469. It is always possible that there was only a sharing of costs
and no more.

470. U. S. Forest Service, Administrative Procedures For Cooperative
Forest Management Act of 1950 (mimeo.), 1951, p. 4; Report of the Chief
of Forest Service for 1948, p. 36. Compare, however, with Report of the
Chief of Forest Service for 1939, p. 14; Rpt. 1941, p. 24; Rpt. 1943, p.
28; Rpt. 1944, p. 7; Rpt. 1947, p. 21. Consult p. 1103, below.

471. U. S. Bureau of Reclamation, Boulder Canyon Project Final Report, Part I, Bulletin I, 1 December 1948, p. 42. The work was not undertaken for the Board recommended against it.

472. National Resources Planning Board, National Resources Development Report for 1942, 1942, p. 36.

473. R. D. Baum, Federal Power Commission and State Utility Regulation, 1942, p. 124.

474. Baum, op. cit., p. 163; and the various annual reports of the
Federal Power Commission.

475. The management of the public domain by the Federal Government
is said to be in "trust" of the people, and the entire Indian-affairs
administration to be in "trust" of the Indian tribes. However, neither
public-main and Indian-affairs administration is trust administration,
since both the people at large and the Indian tribes are not government
units or administrative agencies. Trust administration should further
be distinguished from delegated administration in that (1) the latter
is compulsorily imposed by a higher jurisdiction (or superior administrative agency) to a lower but constitutionally subordinate jurisdiction
(or inferior administrative agency), that (2) the government unit or
administrative agency to which a certain administrative measure is delegated need not, and generally does not, possess the jurisdiction or authority to perform it but for the delegation (i.e., it is not necessarily
within co-jurisdiction or con-current jurisdiction of the agencies concerned) and (3) delegation of administration is normally effected by
law. Administration may not only be delegated by law to a government
unit or an administrative agency, but also to private individuals or
groups of private individuals, who are thereby clothed with public authority. (Delegation of administration must in turn be distinguished from
delegation of rights and duties of a superior officer to an inferior
officer or of the head office to field offices of the same administrative
agency. Such delegation is purely a matter of internal organization or
of administrative procedure).

476. It may be observed that when there are two or more trustee
agencies, there is a joint trust administration, i.e., a combination of
joint administration and trust administration.

477. The present author regards the construction of project and its

maintenance and operation as separate administration acts or measures. Therefore trust administration covering either is regarded as _full_ and not _partial_ trust administration.

478. Rpt. Chief of E. 1906, p. 469; Rpt. Chief of E. 1922, p. 1243; House Document 669, 76th Cong., 1940, p. 23.

479. This is trust administration since the said Township was free to accept or reject the Federal offer.

480. Here, the Federal Government, acting through the Chief of Engineers of the Department of the Army, is to accept or reject the local offer.

481. "Except when authorized by the Secretary of War upon the recommendation of the Chief of Engineers, no money appropriated under authority of this Act shall be expended on the construction of any item of the project until the States or levee districts have given assurances satisfactory to the Secretary of War that they will (a) maintain all flood-control works after their competion, except controlling and regulating spillway structures, including special relief levees; maintenance includes normally such matter as cutting grass, removal of weeds, local drainage, and minor repairs of main river levee . . ." (45 Stat. 534, 535).

482. "That no money appropriated under authority of this Act shall be expended until States, political subdivisions thereof, or other responsible local agencies have given assurances satisfactory to the Secretary of War that they will . . . (c) maintain and operate all the works after completion in accordance with regulations prescribed by the Secretary of War . . ." (49 Stat. 1508, 1510).

483. Letter to the author from Brigadier General C. H. Chorpening, Assistant Chief of Engineers For Civil Works, Corps of Engineers, U. S. Army, dated 26 July 1951.

484. 60 Stat. 641; 62 Stat. 1171, 1175; 64 Stat. 163, 170.

485. For example, Laws of Louisiana of 1940, no. 240; Laws of Mississippi of 1940, ch. 211; Laws of New York of 1940, chs. 210 and 577; Laws of New Mexico of 1940, ch. 68; Laws of Pennsylvania of 1941, nos. 198, 199 and 200; Laws of Rhode Island of 1949, chs. 2263 and 2354.

486. See Missouri River Division, U. S. Corps of Engineers, The Development and Control of the Missouri River, December 1947, p. 12.

487. House Flood Control Committee Hearings, March 30 to April 9, 1938, p. 2 (statement of the Chief of Engineers, U. S. Army).

488. This conclusion is based on the reading of a number of public documents and reports.

489. It is to be noted that the above-mentioned provisions of the Acts of 1924 and 1939 are retroactive only upon request of the water users, organized or unorganized. Thus provisions of 1902, 1914, 1924 and 1939 are now all in force.

490. For each case separately, see U. S. Bureau of Reclamation, Reclamation Project Data, 1948.

491. Letter to the author from Mr. William H. Tuller, Regional Operation and Maintenance Supervisor, Region 1, U. S. Bureau of Reclamation, dated 17 August 1950.

492. Boulder Canyon Project Final Reports, Part I, Bulletin I, op. cit., p. 119.

493. It is trust and not delegated administration because it was effective only upon its acceptance by the said Commissioners (sec. 4).

494. The Book of the States, 1950-51, p. 425.

495. See p. 316, above.

496. Federal Inter-Agency Committee on Recreation, Report on the Conservation and Development of Outdoor Recreation Resources (mimeo.), July 1950, table following p. B-38; 38 Reclamation Era 7 (January 1952).

497. Table, op. cit.

498. National Park Service, Areas Administered By the National Park Service, 30 June 1950, p. 33.

499. Letter to the author from Mr. J. J. Walsh, Secretary and Chief Engineer of the North Dakota State Water Conservation Commission dated 9 November 1951.

500. The Act of 3 May 1950 also applies to assets of state rehabilitation corporations held in trust by other Federal agencies (sec. 3). See U. S. Farmers Home Administration, Annual Report for 1952, p. 26.

501. The author gratefully acknowledges the help of Mr. K. A. Taber, Acting Forest Supervisor, Black Hills National Forest, in his letter dated 12 January 1954.

502. Washington Department of Conservation and Development, 15th Biennial Report, 1950, 59. Consult pp.

503. Federal Inter-Agency Committee on Recreation, Report on the Conservation and Development of Outdoor Recreation Resources (mimeo.), July 1950, p. B-16.

504. Rpt. Chief of E. 1951, p. 2401.

505. For the definition of composite administration, see n. 424, above.

506. Alabama Department of Conservation, Annual Report for the fiscal year 1 October 1948 to 30 September 1949, p. 102. The said Division of Forestry also "delivers the seedlings by truck to the applicants" (ibid.). This part of the program should be regarded either as partial state trust administration or as state assistance to private persons.

507. The use of certificates and production thereof at the customs offices are purely matters of administrative technique having no substantial bearing upon the nature of the administration.

508. House Document 564, 78th Cong., 2nd sess., 1944, pp. 24; 26; 28; 28; 46.

509. House Document 236, 78th Cong., 1st sess., pp. 23; 41.

510. For example, the mere possibility that a certain irrigation project can be undertaken either by the Bureau of Reclamation or by a state doest not constitute alternative administration, even though both are ready for it.

511. United Administration is a form of inter-jurisdictional or inter-agency administrative coordination in which each jurisdiction or agency performs one aspect or part of an administrative measure or act.

512. Report of the Forest Service for 1911, pp. 62-63; Report for 1915, p. 21.

513. Report of the Forest Service for 1924, p. 14.

514. It is to be remarked that cases in which Federal approval is required of state and local administrative acts belong to Federal regulation.

515. Kansas Forestry, Fish and Game Commission, 13th Biennial Report, 30 June 1950, p. 23.

516. The Book of The States, 1948-49, p. 304; J. L. Carey, Game Conservation in Pennsylvania, 2nd ed., 1950, p. 82.

517. Federal Power Commission, Annual Report for 1949, pp. 137-138.

518. Federal Power Commission, Annual Report for 1950, p. 135; Annual Report for 1951, p. 129.

519. Irrigation projects are authorized by the Secretary of the Interior not by the Congress as in the case of navigation and flood control projects.

520. Federal Power Commission, Annual Report for 1951, p. 129.

521. Wesley K. Lundgreen, "They Could and They Did", 40 Reclamation Era 8-10 (February 1954).

522. Letter to the author from Mr. Wesley K. Lundgreen, Engineer, U. S. Bureau of Reclamation (at Torrington, Wyoming), dated 17 February 1954.

523. See Rpt. Sec. Inter. 1938, p. 35; Rpt. Sec. Inter. 1939, p.298.

524. Pennsylvania Department of Forests and Waters, Biennial Report for the biennium ending 31 May 1950, p. 18.

525. Program coordination between the Federal Government and private persons is provided in sec. 2 of the said Act (58 Stat. 132).

526. For the background of such device, see Problems and Programs of Forestry in the United States, 1947, pp. 19-20; 43.

527. U. S. Production and Marketing Administration, Annual Report for 1951, p. 67.

528. Rpt. Chief of E. 1951, pp. 1853-1871; U. S. Department of Commerce, The St. Lawrence Survey, Part II, 1941, pp. 2-3; Part VII, 1941, pp. 1-2.

529. The text of this Agreement may be found in House Document 153, 77th Cong., 1st sess.

530. See The Lawrence Survey, op. cit., Part I; Senate Documents 114 and 179, 67th Cong., 2nd sess.; River and Harbor Acts of 1917 and 1919 (40 Stat. 250 265; 1275, 1290); Second Deficiency Appropriation Act of 4 March 1925 (43 Stat. 1313, 1315-1316); Executive Agreement, U. S. and Canada, 13 and 31 October and 7 November 1940 (54 Stat. 2426).

531.   "The channels in the St. Lawrence River above Prescott are deeper than 27 feet now."   With respect to the Soulanges Rapids, "the major portion of the work has already been done in connection with the existing Beauharnois power development."   "The navigation work remaining to be done is little more than the installation of locks at the lower end of the power canal, for which provision has been made, and the dredging of connecting channels." -- 98 Cong. Rec. A465 (29 January 1952).

532.   The plan is embodied in the Annex to the Agreement of 1941. It calls for the construction of the following works: (1) a control dam in the vicinity of Iroquis Point, (2) a dam in the Long Sault Rapids at the head of Barnhart Island and two power houses, one on either side of the international boundary, at the foot of Barnhart Island, (3) a side canal with one lock on the United States mainland to carry navigation around the control dam and a side canal, with one guard gate and two locks, on the United States mainland south of Barnhart Island to carry navigation from abo e the main Long Sault Dam to the river south of Cornwall Island, (4) dykes where necessary on both the American and Canadian sides of the International boundary to retain the pool level above the Long Sault Dam and (5) certain channel enlargement works.

533.   About 2,200,000 horsepower of electric energy may be developed in the International Rapids Section.   This is to be developed by the State of New York of the United States and the Province of Ontario of Canada, each of which will put up about $230 million for the power installations. -- 98 Cong. Rec. A3291-A3292 (21 May 1952).   For the responsibility of the State of New York in developing hydroelectric power in this Section, see House Document 302, 79th Cong., 1st sess., 1945.

534.   The work of these two agencies is in turn to be synchrozined with that of the power agencies of the State of New York and the Province of Ontario.   See sec. 3(2) of the Act of 13 May 1954.

535.   Letter to the author from Mrs. Betsy P. Roscoe, Executive Secretary, American Association For Public Information, Education and Research, Washington, D. C., dated 10 September 1954.   It has been estimated that "the United States would contribute nearly $600,000,000 and Canada $251,000,000 to complete the waterway." -- 98 Cong. Rec. A2626 (April, 1952).The project is expected to be completed in six years. -- New York Times, 16 May 1954 (p. 66).

536.   Baum, Federal Power Commission and State Utility Regulation, 1942, pp. 153-155.

537.   14 George Washington Law Review 255 (by Rhyne).

538.   Federal Power Commission, Annual Report for 1949, p. 143.

539.   Joint administration, alternative administration, etc., have not singled out for special discussion.

540.   Reclamation Project Feasibilities and Authorizatbns, op. cit.. p. 47.

541.   Annual Report of the Forest Service for 1908, p. 28; Report for 1910, p. 46.

542.   Federal Power Commission, Annual Report for 1949, p. 191; Annual Report for 1950, p. 194.

543.   Rpt. Sec. Inter. 1951, p. 347.

544.   Federal Inter-Agency Committee On Recreation, Report on the

Conservation and Development of Outdoor Recreation Resources (mimeo.),
July 1950, table following p. B-38.

545. U. S. Geological Survey, "Cooperative Investigations of the
Water Resources of the United States" (mimeo.), 1929, made available to
the author through the courtesy of Mr. William E. Wrather, Director,
U. S. Geological Survey, on 1 October 1951; Oregon State Engineer, _Bi-
ennial Report_ for the biennium 1 July 1948-30 June 1950 (mimeo.), p. 28.

546. _Rpt. Sec. Inter. 1949_, p. 198; _Rpt. 1950_, p. 202.

547. It is to be observed that the flood storage of Tennessee Valley
Authority reservoirs is used chiefly to control floods of the Ohio and
Mississippi Rivers. The incidental flood-control effects of the non-
flood-control storages, it seems, are sufficient to prevent flood damages in the Tennessee River Basin. It should also be pointed out that
none of the Tennessee Valley Authority dams has a navigation storage,
but that navigation locks have been installed in a number of dams the
operation of which is under the supervision of the Corps of Engineers.

548. See 16 F. R. 454; 16 F. R. 11773, etc.

549. _Rpt. Chief of E. 1951_, p. 1466. Subsection (k) of sec. 5 of
the Tennessee Valley Authority Act of 18 May 1933 (48 Stat. 58, 62) provides that "upon the requisition of the Secretary of War, the Corporation
shall allot and deliver without charge to the War Department so much power as shall be necessary in the judgement of said Department for use in
operation of all locks, lifts, or other facilities in aid of navigation."
In this provision, the authority of the Department of the Army in the operation and maintenance of these facilities is implied and recognized.

550. And sec. 5, first paragraph, of the Boulder Canyon Project Act
of 21 December 1928 (45 Stat. 1057, 1059).

551. It may be noted that so far as multiple-purpose projects of
the Corps of Engineers are concerned, there is in the first place concentration at the Department of the Interior with respect to the authority of selling hydroelectric power and then there is further concentration at the Federal Power Commission with respect to the rates of sale.

552. Letter to the author from Mr. Bradford Ross, General Counsel,
Federal Power Commission, dated 4 March 1952. With respect to the Tennessee Valley Authority, the Federal Power Commission is, in addition,
authorized to approve proposed contracts made by the Tennessee Valley
Authority with states, counties, municipalities and non-profit organizations extending credit thereto for purposes of transmitting electric
energy generated by the Authority (TVA Act, sec. 15a, 9th sentence, as
added 31 August 1935: 49 Stat. 1075, 1078); sec. 15c, last para., 9th
sentence, as added 26 July 1939: 53 Stat. 1083).

553. _Rpt. Sec. Agri. 1902_, p. 118.

554. National Resources Planning Board, _National Resources Development Report for 1942_, January 1942, p. 36.

555. _Rpt. Sec. Inter. 1939_, p. 266.

556. _Rpt. Sec. Inter. 1950_, p. 36.

557. Private-governmental joint regulation is impossible because
private persons do not have governmental authority (unless delegated by
government).

558. For the device of the sustained-yield management of Federal forest lands as means of program coordination.

559. Relationships between the Government and private persons other than private participation in administration are omitted.

560. The Propeller Club of the U. S. (by Thomas A. Scott), _River and Harbor Improvements: How They Are Initiated, Authorized and Completed_, 1938, p. 8.

561. See the various annual reports of the Forest Service.

562. On 11 April 1924, a major license was issued by the Federal Power Commission to the State of Illinois, acting through its Department of Public Works, and Mr. Fred D. Breit, for a 5,300-horsepower hydroelectric power development on the Fox River. On 14 April 1924, it was transferred to the State of Illinois and the North Hydro Electric Company, whose president was then and is still now Br. Breit. On 20 March 1944, the State of Illinois was dropped from the license as a result of court decision. Although the State of Illinois was nominally co-owner of the Fox River hydroelectric power project for two decades, it "gave no assistance whatsoever in the promotion of this project." -- Letters to the author from Mr. Kenneth G. Tower, Regional Engineer, Chicago Regional Office, Federal Power Commission, dated 10 December 1952, and Mr. Fred D. Breit, dated 26 December 1952. Quotation is from Mr. Breit's letter. This of course cannot be regarded as an instance of Federal-private joint enterprise.

563. U. S. Dpt. of Agri. (by A. T. Mitchson and D. C. Muckel), _Spreading Water For Storage Underground_, Dec. 1937, pp. 16-18.

564. National Park Service, _A Study of the Park and Recreation Problem in the United States_, 1941, p. 17. However, there is likelihood that this work may not be a joint enterprise.

565. The Tree Farm program was initiated by the Weyerhaeuser Timber Company of Grays Harbor, Washington, in 1940, and in March 1943 the National Lumber Manufacturers' Association assumed the responsibility of sponsoring the program on a national scale. -- American Forest Products Industries, Inc., "History of Tree Farms" (mimeo.), made available to the author through the courtesy of Mr. J. C. McClellan, Chief Forester, American Forest Products Industries, Inc., on 5 November 1951. By the end of 1951, Tree Farm programs were adopted by 30 States. -- Ibid., As of 1 November 1951, a total of 3,372 tree farms aggregating 23,945,251 acres had been established in 29 states. -- Letter to the author from Mr. J. C. McClellan dated 5 November 1951. The Keep America Green (in the states, Keep Washington Green, Keep Oregon Green, etc.) program was officially inaugurated in the state of Washington on 15 April 1941, and had been followed by 29 other states by 1 July 1951. In 1944, the American Forest Products Industries, Inc., then a subsidiary of the National Lumber Manufacturers' Association, undertook to expand the program to all of the states. -- American Forest Products Industries, Inc., "History of Keep American Green" (mimeo.), made available to the author through the courtesy of Mr. J. C. McClellan on 16 November 1951. Since March 1946, the American Forest Industries, Inc., when it ceased to be a subsidiary of the National Lumber Manufacturers' Association, has been the national sponsor and coordinator of both programs. -- Letter to the author from Mr. McClellan, _op. cit._

566. American Forest Products Industries, Inc., _Keep Green in Action_ (undated and un-page-numbered), first page.

567. American Forest Proeucts Industries, Inc., _The American Tree_

Farm System (undated folder).

568. American Forest Products Industries, Inc., Tree Farm: Planning
A Program (undated and un-page-numbered pamphlet).

569. W. B. Greeley, "Keep Green Pays Off", American Forests, Octob-
ber 1949.

570. A copy of the Agreement was made available to the author
through the courtesy of Mr. B. J. Fletcher, Chief Hydraulic Engineer,
Aluminum Company of America, on 16 June 1952.

571. These following plants are included:
   (A) Owned by the Aluminum Company of America:
      1. Calderwood plant---A dam, 232 feet high, and a power
        house having a capacity of 168,000 horsepower, on the
        Little Tennessee River, about 43 miles above the mouth
        of the river.
   (B) Owned by the Carolina Aluminum Company of North Carolina,
      a wholly owned subsidiary of the Aluminum Company of Amer-
      ica:
      2. Cheoah plant---A dam of 225 feet and a power house of
        179,000 horsepower on the Little Tennessee River,
        about 52 miles above the mouth of the river.
      3. Santeetlah plant---A dam of 212 feet on the Cheoah Ri-
        ver about 9 miles from its conjunction with the Little
        Tennessee River; and a power house of 66,000 horse-
        power on the Little Tennessee River about 56 miles
        above the mouth of the river, connected with the Cheo-
        ah Reservoir by a conduit.
   (C) Owned by the Nantahala Power and Light Company of North
      Carolina, a wholly owned subsidiary of the Aluminum Com-
      pany of America:
      4. Glenville plant---A dam of 150 feet in height and a
        power house of 30,000 horsepower on the West Fork of
        the Tuckasegee River.
      5. Nantahala plant---A dam of 250 feet high and a power
        house of 60,000 horsepower on the Nantahala River. --
        From the Preamble of the Agreement of 1941 and "Gener-
        al Map and Profile, Power Developments, Little Tennes-
        see River" (a blueprint), made available to the author
        through the courtesy of Mr. Fletcher on 16 June 1952.

572. Tennessee Valley Authority, The Fontana Project, Tech, Rpt. No.
12, 1950, pp. 1-2. See Article III of the Agreement.

573. Clarence A. Davis, Nebraska's Public Power Explained, 1949, p.
13.

574. The pool consists of one Federal member, the Bonneville Power
Administration; two municipal members, the Seattle City Light and the
Tacoma City Light; one foreign member, the British Columbia Electric
Co.; seven major private utilities, namely, the Puget Sound Power and
Light Co., Washington Water Power Co., Pacific Power and Light Co., Port-
land General Electric Co., Montana Power Co., Idaho Power Co. and Utah
Power and Light Co. and a number of small private utilities. -- Rpt. Sec.
Inter. 1951, p. 141; E. N. Peterson, Northwest Power Pool; A Symposium,
22 July 1948. For the history of the Pool, see Ibid., and Walter C.
Heston, "Northwest Power Resources Pooled For War", Electrical World, 4
March 1944. The author gratefully acknowledges the assistance of Mr.
E. R. Hoffman, Superintendent of Lighting, City of Seattle Department
of Lighting, given in his letter of 17 October 1949, with respect to
that part of the Pool that concerns the Cities of Seattle and Tacoma,
Washington.

575. Wilbur D. Staats, "A Lesson In Democracy -- The Northwest Power Pool", 28 July 1950 (manuscript), kindly made available to the author by Mr. Staats during the author's visit to the Bonneville Power Administration on 11 August 1950.

576. It may be of interest to note that the United States Constitution provides, in the Tenth Amendment, that "the powers not delegated to the United States by the constitution, nor prohibited by it to the states, are reserved to the states respectively, or to the people." This may imply that constitutional rights which do not belong to the United States nor to the several states belong to the people or private persons. But constitutional rights of private persons are non-governmental. The non-compulsory character of private delegated administration is essential, for if it is compulsory, it becomes a measure of governmental regulation. See Federal Water Power Act of 10 June 1920, secs. 11 and 12 (41 Stat. 1063, 1070-1071).

577. Reclamation Project Data, pp. 195; 235; 259; 291; 299.

578. Ibid., p. 241.

579. Federal Inter-Agency Committee on Recreation, Report on the Conservation and Development of Outdoor Recreation Resources (mimeo.), July 1950, table following p. B-38.

580. Rpt. Chief of E. 1929, pp. 1202; 1204.

581. Tennessee Valley Authority, The Fort Loudoun Project (Tech. Rpt. No. 11), 1949, p. 1.

582. Rpt. Chief of E. 1931, p. 1403.

583. U. S. Production and Marketing Administration, Report for 1950, p. 67. For details, see 7 C.F.R. 713.1 et seq.

584. The Agricultural Conservation Program is Federal assistance to private persons. Here it is regarded as enterprise in a broad sense of the word.

585. The plan of construction must be approved by, and the construction is to be under the supervision of, the Chief engineer of the Division of Water Resources of the State Board of Agriculture. -- Secs. 2 and 3 of the said law.

586. Rpt. Sec. Inter. 1882, p. 47.

587. National Park Service, The Development of the National Park System and the National Park Service (mimeo.), January 1949, pp. 3-4; 17. The Federal Government collects from the concessionaries franchise fees. -- American Planning and Civic Manual, 1947, p. 24.

588. If they do not take measures to increase the population of the waterfowl, they cannot enjoy the right of shooting.

589. Consult O. L. Resner, "Washington's Beaver", Game Bulletin of Wash. State Game Dpt., January 1952.

590. Washington State Game Department, Game Bulletin, July 1951, p. 1.

591. Washington State Game Department, Game Bulletin, April 1950, p. 6.

592. Wisconsin Conservation Commission, 23rd Biennial Report for the biennium ending 30 June 1952, p. 82.

593. Missouri laws provide for the designation of private forest lands as "forest crop lands" (act of 6 July 1946). These lands, however, cannot be regarded as public administrative areas.

594. For tree bounties, see   n. 601, below.

595. The same refuges may be established on state lands. -- Revised Statutes, sec. 501.210 (L. 1921, ch. 153, sec. 63).

596. Letter to the author from Mr. John W. McKean, Chief of Game Operations, Oregon State Game Commission, dated 30 April 1953.

597. Letter to the author from Mr. D. W. Douglass, Game Division, Michigan Department of Conservation, dated 9 April 1953.

598. Letter to the author from Mr. Frank D. Blair, Director, Division of (State-owned game refuges total 1,211,730 acres).

599. "Refuges In North Dakota", a mimeographed sheet made available to the author through the courtesy of the North Dakota Game and Fish Department. The discussion of the inclusion of private property in governmental administration made in this section is not exhaustive.

600. In early bounty systems, bounties were generally paid by the county government. In recent years, this responsibility has been shifted to the state game agencies in most of the states having such systems. -- D. F. Switzenberg, "Examination of A State Fox Bounty", 15 Journal of Wildlife Management 288 (July 1951). Examples of bounty systems in which bounties are paid by the state are Arkansas, California, Colorado, Maine, Montana, North Dakota, Oregon, Pennsylvania, Vermont, Washington, West Virginia and Wisconsin. Examples of systems in which bounties are paid by counties or towns are Indiana, Kansas, Minnesota, Missouri, New Hampshire, New Jersey, New York, South Carolina, South Dakota and Virginia. In Oklahoma bounties are paid by counties out of the state game fund. In Connecticut the towns pay bounties for foxes, rattlesnakes, weasels, wild hares, porcupines, etc., and the state pays bounties for bobcats or lynxes. -- Bounty laws of these states.

601. For tree bounties, see North Dakota Revised Code, sec. 4-2101 et seq. (Laws 1905, ch. 187; as last amended by L. 1939, ch. 244) and Compiled Laws of Michigan, sec. 247.233: Acts 1919, No. 36, sec. 3).

602. But not wharves.

603. Annual Report of the Chief of Forest Service for 1935, pp. 4-5.

604. See 97 Cong. Rec. A5556 (21 August 1951).

605. Annual Report of the Chief of Forest Service for 1952, p. 20.

CHAPTER 5

ADMINISTRATIVE ORGANIZATION

Article 1   Federal Organization

Section 1   Federal Uncoordinated Organization[1]

1. The Department of the Army---The Department of the
Army, through the Corps of Engineers and other subordinate
agencies that are closely related to the Corps of Engineers,
is in charge of an important part of Federal water resources
administration.

(a) The Corps of Engineers---That the Department of the
Army, acting through the Corps of Engineers, is responsible
for Federal regulation with regard to the protection of navigable channels has already been explained before, and need not
be repeated. But the Corps is primarily an enterprise agency.
In the first three River and Harbor Acts, approved respectively 24 May 1824 (4 Stat. 32), 20 May 1826 (4 Stat. 174) and 2
March 1827 (4 Stat. 228), it was the President that was authorized by the Congress to direct the construction of all navigation improvement works. In the Act of 3 March 1827, which
authorized additional navigation improvement works on the
Ohio River, it was provided that the work should be done "under the supervision and direction of the Secretary of War" (4
Stat. 241-242). In the subsequent River and Harbor Acts, the
officer to direct the construction of the navigation improvement works was not designated. Then the River and Harbor Act
of 30 August 1852 prescribed that the construction work should
be prosecuted "under the superintendence of the Secretary of
War" (10 Stat. 56). Subsequent River and Harbor Acts designated the Secretary of War as the responsible officer for the
river and harbor work. Finally the River and Harbor Act of 13
July 1892 provided that works authorized thereby should be
constructed "under the direction of the Secretary of War and
the supervision of the Chief of Engineers" (27 Stat. 88).
This provision has been retained in all subsequent River and
Harbor Acts (except that the Secretary of War is now the Secretary of the Army). By the River and Harbor Act of 1894
(sec. 4, para. 1: 28 Stat. 338, 362), the Secretary of War
(now the Secretary of the Army) was vested with the duty "to
provide such rules and regulations for the use, administration,
and navigation of any or all canals and similar works of navigation that now are, or that hereafter may be, owned, operated, or maintained by the United States as in his judgment the
public necessity may require." But as a matter of fact, the
Corps of Engineers, ever since 1819, "has been entrusted with
the responsibility for investigating proposed river and har-

bor improvements, and it has been in charge of the construction and operation of most Federal navigation facilities after they have been authorized by Congress."[2]

As for flood control works, it is provided in the first National Flood Control Act of 22 June 1936 (sec. 2) that "hereafter Federal investigations and improvements of river and other waterways for flood control and allied purposes shall be under the jurisdiction of and shall be prosecuted by the War (now Army) Department under the direction of the Secretary of War (now of the Army) and supervision of the Chief of Engineers . . ." (49 Stat. 1570).

The Corps of Engineers maintains a number of Divisions, each headed by a division engineer, in the Continental United States.[3] With the exception of the New England Division, each Division is divided into from three to six Districts, each headed by a district engineer, there being no districts in the New England Division.[4] It is the district engineers (and in New England, the Division Engineer) that actually supervise and inspect the construction work of the Corps of Engineers and operate the Federal navigation improvement and flood control works under the control of the Army Department.[5] ". . . The Corps of Engineers . . . is much more decentralized than the Bureau of Reclamation . . . . At the present time its policy leaves large freedom to the district engineers within their respective areas." However, "the members of the Corps of Engineers, who direct the work, rotate from district to district in search of a variety of engineering experience. Rarely do they stay longer in one district than four years.[6]

It has already been mentioned before that the first Federal navigation-improvement project, which was authorized by the Congress in 1824, was the result of a survey authorized in 1820. In some of the earlier River and Harbor Acts, authorizations for improvements were casually intermixed with those for surveys and examinations.[7] Evidence of this practice was found in the River and Harbor Act of 20 May 1826 (4 Stat. 175, 176), 3 March 1837 (5 Stat. 187, 190), 30 August 1852 (10 Stat. 56, 59-60), etc. Beginning with the River and Harbor Act of 23 June 1866 (sec. 4: 14 Stat. 70), however, authorizations for surveys and examinations have been separated from those for improvement projects in all subsequent River and Harbor Acts.[8] In a Joint Resolution of 27 July 1868 (15 Stat. 262), the Congress required the Secretary of War (now the Army) to submit the reports of all surveys and examinations to the Congress, together with a statement in each report as to whether the project contained in the report "shall tend to subserve the general commercial and navigation interests of the United States." This policy has continued in effect to the present day and has been extended to all flood-control projects.

In the River and Harbor Acts of 5 August 1886 (sec. 7: 24 Stat. 310, 355), 11 August 1888 (sec. 14: 25 Stat. 400,

433), 19 September 1890 (sec. 18: 26 Stat. 426, 464-465) and
13 July 1892 (sec. 7: 27 Stat. 88, 115), a provision was
found reading as follows:

> . . . No survey shall be made of any harbors or
> rivers until the Chief of Engineers shall have
> directed a preliminary examination of the same by
> the local engineer in charge of the district, or
> an engineer detailed for the purpose, and such lo-
> cal or detailed engineer shall report to said Chief
> of Engineers, whether, in his opinion, said harbor
> or river is worthy of improvement, and shall state
> in such report fully and particularly the facts
> and reasons on which he bases such opinion, in-
> cluding the present and prospective demands of
> commerce; and it shall be the duty of the Chief of
> Engineers to direct the making of such survey if,
> in his opinion, the harbor or river proposed to be
> surveyed be worthy of improvement by the General
> Government; and he shall report to the Secretary
> of War the facts, and what public necessity or
> convenience may be subserved thereby, together
> with the full reports of the local engineer. Said
> reports of preliminary examinations and surveys
> shall be made to the House of Representatives, and
> are hereby ordered to be printed when so made.

This provision has not appeared in subsequent River and Harbor Acts, seemingly because that it has become such a well-
established practice that its reenactment is considered unnecessary.[9]

It has been a long practice that the Congress does not
authorize a navigation or flood control project until a report recommending its authorization is submitted to it by the
Chief of Engineers in the manner as stipulated in the above
provision.[9] This practice has been crystallized in a provision in the Flood Control Act of 24 July 1946 (sec. 2, 3rd
and 4th paras.: 60 Stat. 641, 642) and all subsequent Flood
Control Acts (62 Stat. 1171, 1175; 64 Stat. 163, 170).[10]

The River and Harbor Act of 13 June 1902, in sec. 3 (32
Stat. 331, 372), created in the office of the Chief of Engineers the Board of Engineers For Rivers and Harbors to be
composed of five engineers of the Corps, whose duty it was
to review all reports upon examinations and surveys.[11] By
an amendment in sec. 4 of the River and Harbor Act of 4 March
1913 (37 Stat. 801, 826-827), membership of the Board was
increased to seven senior engineers of the Corps (not lower
than the rank of lieutenant-colonel), and its duties were
broadened to cover reports on both general and special examinations and surveys authorized by the Congress. In addition,
". . . the said board shall also, on request by resolution of

the Committee on Commerce of the Senate or the Committee on Rivers and Harbors of the House of Representatives, submitted to the Chief of Engineers, examine and review the report of any examination or survey made pursuant to any Act or resolution of Congress, and report thereon through the Chief of Engineers, United States Army, who shall submit his conclusions as in other cases . . ." The Board "includes a chairman, generally Deputy Chief of Engineers, five officers, usually Division Engineers assigned to Board membership in addition to their other duties, and a resident member, permanently stationed with the Board."[13]

The actual procedure of the establishment of a navigation-improvement or flood-control project from preliminary examination by the district engineer of the Corps of Engineers to authorization by Congress, is briefly as follows:[14]

(1) Authorization of survey and examination by Congress at the proposal of the senator or congressman concerned made upon request of local industrial, navigational, commercial or other interests, after its review by the Public Works Committee of the Senate or the House of Representatives (formerly Commerce Committee of the Senate or the Committee on Rivers and Harbors of the House of Representatives).[15]

(2) Preliminary examination by district engineer, at which public and private interests are usually given a hearing or, as an alternative, an opportunity for presentment of views.

(3) District engineer's report to be reviewed in turn by the division engineer, the Board of Engineers for Rivers and Harbors and the Chief of Engineers.

(4) Comments by other Federal agencies concerned and governors of the affected states, to be asked for by the Chief of Engineers.

(5) Final decision by the Chief of Engineers. If this is unfavorable, he reports his conclusions to the Congress through the Secretary of the Army, and generally the matter is closed. If the Chief of Engineers thinks that the project is feasible, he shall not make a report to the Congress at this time, but order the district engineer to make a survey.

(6) Survey by the district, at which public hearing is again to be held and after which a definite project plan is to be formulated.

(7) Review and comment of the district engineer's survey report by the division engineer, the Board of Engineers for Rivers and Harbors, the Chief of Engineers, other Federal agencies interested and governors of affected states, in the case of the

preliminary examination report. However, public
hearing is generally held by both the division
engineer and the Board of Engineers for Rivers
and Harbors on the survey report of the district
engineer.

(8) Final decision by the Chief of Engineers,
which is generally favorable. Of course the division engineer, the Board and the Chief of Engineers
each may make modifications on the project plan.

(9) The Chief of Engineers submits his report
to the Secretary of the Army, who shall obtain the
advice of the Bureau of the Budget as to whether
the project is in harmony with the program of the
President and then transmit it to the Congress.

(10) Authorization of the project by the Congress (in a River and Harbor or a Flood Control
Act or in some special enactment). This is in
most cases a formality.

From a practical point of view there is some justification in
saying that navigation-improvement or flood-control projects
are sponsored by individual members of the Congress and approved by the Corps of Engineers.[16] It has been estimated that
about one-half of the projects initiated by the former are
rejected by the Corps of Engineers on the ground of economic
infeasibility.[17] Under the above-mentioned provision of the
River and Harbor of 1913, the House or Senate Public Works
Committee may direct the Chief of Engineers to review his
former reports on preliminary examinations or on project surveys. This provides a means by which projects rejected by
the Chief of Engineers may be subsequently revived and projects already approved brought up to date from time to time.[18]

The Corps of Engineers not only enjoys a high degree of
"autonomy" with regard to the authorization of projects, but
also has a free hand in their construction. In the field of
navigation improvement, it is provided (among other things)
in sec. 9 of the River and Harbor Act of 4 March 1913 (37
Stat. 801, 827) that channel dimensions given in any project
plan "shall be understood to admit of such increase at the
entrances, bends, sidings, and turning places as may be necessary to allow of the free movement of boats." Such technical matters are thus within the complete discretion of the
Corps of Engineers. Greater discretion is found in the flood
control enterprise. Almost all Congressional authorizations
for flood-control projects are couched in very flexible terms,
the actual wording being invariably, -- a certain project is
authorized "substantially in accordance with" the report of
the Chief of Engineers for that project. So a project need
not be constructed exactly in accordance with the project
plan of the Corps of Engineers as approved by the Congress:
modifications are always permissible.[19] However, the authority of the Corps in modifying a flood control or other pro-

ject is limited by a provision in sec. 2 (second and last sentences) of the Flood Control Act of 18 August 1941 (55 Stat. 638, 638-639), that modifications can only be made by way of reducing the sizes of the structures with prospects and possibilities of future enlargement and that the sites originally chosen for a structure cannot be changed unless, of course, there are special Congressional authorizations to the contrary. Under sec. 205 of the Flood Control Act of 30 June 1948 (62 Stat. 1171, 1182), small flood control projects may even be authorized by the Secretary of the Army without Congressional approval.

Prior to 1928, the Corps of Engineers was primarily concerned with single-purpose navigation-improvement projects. Flood-control work, which by that time was practically limited to the Mississippi Alluvial Valley, was intrusted to the Mississippi River Commission, which was until 1928 somewhat detached from the Corps of Engineers.[20]..Flood control work in other areas were minor in scope, and were regarded as part of the navigation-improvement enterprise. Since 1928, and particularly since the passage of the First National Flood Control Act in 1936, flood control has become a regular work of the Corps independent of and equal in importance to navigation improvement.

Prior to 1933, the Corps of Engineers was totally indifferent toward the development of hydroelectric power. A turn from this no-power policy was first made on 21 August 1933, when the Chief of Engineers submitted to the Congress its 308-report on the Bonneville dam project.[21] The Chief of Engineers not only approved of the views of the Board of Engineers For Rivers and Harbors that the Bonneville Dam should be constructed for the dual purpose of navigation improvement and power production, with an initial installation of 430,000 kilowatts, but also recommended that "the works should be designed so as to permit ready installation when desired of power up to five or six thousand kilowatts."

The interest of the Corps in power development was firmly established on 4 March 1938, when the Chief of Engineers made his reports on the flood-control surveys on the Dennison Reservoir in Texas and the Willamette River Basin in Oregon.[22] In the report on the Denison project, the Corps recommended that the dam and reservoir be constructed for both flood control and power development. In the other report, the seven reservoirs in the initial stage of development were to be built for flood control only, but provision was to be made for future raising of the dams for power development. In the flood-control survey report for the Grand (or Neosho) River Basin, made 4 January 1939,[23] the recommended plan called for the construction of three dams and reservoirs for the dual purpose of flood control and power development. The 308 report on the Etwah River, Georgia, dated 12 March 1940,[24] the flood-control survey report for the Susquehanna River system, New York, Pennsylvania and Maryland, dated 21 October 1941,[25] and the 308 report for the Youghiogheny River, Pennsylvania and Maryland, dated 31 January 1942,[26] all followed the line of the above-discussed reports in the recognition of power development as a legitimate Federal responsibility. Even the construction of single-purpose power dams was recommended. In subsequent flood-control survey and 308 reports, the view of the Corps of Engineers with respect to power is generally in favor of development by the Federal Government provided power benefits are substantial.[27] However, the Corps has not as yet committed itself to the commercial phase of power sale and disposition, which it has gladly yielded to the Department of the Interior.

Functional multiplication of the Corps of Engineers (civil works) is witnessed by and reflected in the changes in its internal organization. On 7 January 1947, separate offices of the Deputy Chief of Civil Works For Rivers and Harbors and the Deputy Chief of Civil Works For Flood Control were established, which are under the supervision of the Assistant Chief of Engineers For Civil Works. Prior to that date, the work of navigation improvement and that of flood control, each of which included hydroelectric power development as a subordinate or an incidental purpose, were not organizationally divided. On 16 February 1951, another office, that of the Deputy Chief of Civil Works For Power was branched out from the civil works program. On 24 October 1952, these offices were re-designated as Assistant Chiefs of Civil Works for Rivers and Harbors, Flood Control, and Power, respectively.[28] It is manifest that navigation improvement, flood control and hydroelectric power development are now three co-equal partners in the "civil works program" of the Corps of Engineers.

(b) <u>Mississippi River Commission</u>---[29] This agency was created by a special Act of 28 June 1879 (21 Stat. 37). According to this act, the Commission was to consist of seven members appointed by the President with the consent of the Senate. Of these seven members, three must be appointed from the Corps of Engineers, one from the Coast and Geodetic Survey, and three from civil life (of whom two must be civil engineers). The functions of the Commission were to complete the surveys which had already been stated by the Corps of Engineers of the Mississippi River between its mouth at the Head of the Passes and its headwaters, and to make additional surveys and investigations of the Mississippi and its tributaries, and to submit to the Congress, through the Secretary of War, plans for improvement works. The Secretary of War was required to detail an officer of the Corps of Engineers to serve as the Commission's secretary. It should be noted that "the office of the secretary . . . functioned separately from that of the president until 1928, when the two offices were combined."[30]

The primary duties of the Mississippi River Commission were the control of floods in the Mississippi Alluvial Valley.[31] Its main and immediate task, as provided in the Act of 1879, was as follows (sec. 4, proviso):

> That the Commission shall report in full upon the practicability, feasibility, and probable cost of the various plans known as the jetty system, the levee system, and the outlet system, as well as upon such others as they deem necessary.

These three "systems" were methods of flood control then known to the engineering world. The so-called "jetty system" is flood control through channel improvement works, primarily channel contraction (which is now a navigation improvement measure rather a flood control device); the "levee system" consisted of the construction of embanking levees (but not protective levees); and the "outlet system" of that of floodways. The report required by the above-cited provision was made by the Commission on 17 February 1880.[32] The Commission unanimously favored the "jetty system", conceding, however, that the "levee system" was " a desirable but not necessary adjunct" thereto. The "outlet system" was unanimously discarded as the bifurcation of channels tends to reduce the velocities of the water flows and thus give rise to aggradation. As conceived by the majority of the Commission, the "jetty system" excluded cut-offs, although the minority thought that cut-offs were useful means of channel improvement. The theoretical basis of the Commission in the adoption of the "jetty" or channel-improvement plan was that "this will result in a more easy and rapid discharge of the flowing water, and consequently in a lowering of the flood-surface," which "will ultimately render the maintenance of the levees as an aid to navigation practically needless above Red River." As initial stage of improvement, the Commission recommended the construction of contraction works at shoal places at New Madrid, Plum Point, Memphis, Helena, Choctaw Bend and Lake Providence having an aggregate length of about 200 miles, coupled with bank protection works. These works were designed to create a depth of the Mississippi below Cairo of 10 feet at extreme low-water stages. This plan was approved by Congress in the River and Harbor Act of 3 March 1881 (21 Stat. 468, 474). In addition, the act extended the coverage of the plan to "tributaries of the Mississippi River to the extent and no further, that may be necessary in the judgment of said commission to the perfection of the general and permanent improvement of said Mississippi River . . ." Although the Commission recommended that its duties be confined to planning and advice, the act directed the Commission to prosecute the works under the supervision of the Secretary of War. It is to be noted that the act expressly interdicted "the repair or construction of levees . . ."

Of the six places selected for initial contraction works, only two were actually placed under improvement in 1881. These were Plum Point and Lake Providence. The works constructed were dikes to contract the channel width at low water to 3,000 feet and bank revetments.[33]

The jurisdiction of the Commission was extended by the River and Harbor Act of 2 August 1882 to cover the Mississippi River from Cairo upstream to the mouth of the Des Moines Rapids (including Alton Harbor), the harbors of New Orleans, Natchez, Vicksburg, Memphis, a lock at the mouth of Bayou Plaquemine, Louisiana, and the rectification of the Red and the Atchafalya Rivers at the mouth of Red River (22 Stat. 191, 208). Furthermore, "the commission is authorized to repair and build levees if in its judgment it should be done as a part of their plan to afford ease safety to the navigation and commerce of the river and to deepen the channel. . ." As a matter of fact, the Commission started the construction and repair of levees in 1882.[34]

Although the act of 1882 extended the operations of the Commission to Des Moines Rapids, a special Act of 4 June 1906 (34 Stat. 208) defined the authority of the Commission in levee-construction as covering the main stem of the Mississippi River from the Head of the Passes to Cape Girardeau, Missouri. This authority was further extended by the River and Harbor Act of 4 March 1913 to Rock Island, Illinois, subject to the approval of the Chief of Engineers, U. S. Army. The same Act extended the jurisdiction of the Commission in other respects to the mouth of the Yazoo River and the harbor at Vicksburg, Mississippi. The general jurisdiction of the Commission was further extended by the River and Harbor Act of 27 July 1916 to cover the Ohio River from Cairo to the mouth of the Cache River (39 Stat. 391, 402). However, this extension excluded the construction of locks and dams, which are definitely devices for navigation improvement and only have indirect effect upon flood control. The Commission was, in addition, authorized to make surveys for the Atchafalaya River and the lower Arkansas River. The authority of the Commission over the tributaries of the Mississippi River was re-defined and clarified by sec. 13 of the River and Harbor Act of 22 September 1922 (42 Stat. 1038, 1947),[35] as covering "for the purposes of levee protection and bank protection,"[36] "the tributaries and outlets of the Mississippi River between Cairo, Illinois, and the Head of the Passes, in so far as these tributaries and outlets are affected by the flood waters of the Mississippi River." The authority of the Commission over both the main stem and the tributaries of the Mississippi River was finally summarized in the Second Flood Control Act of 4 March 1923 (42 Stat. 1505, 1506).[37]

The dikes constructed by the Commission in Plum Point and Lake Providence happen to be the only structures of the kind

ever constructed by the Commission. These dikes were completed before 1890.[38] In 1893, a stone closure dam was built at
Elmot Bar. This is the third and last contraction work ever
undertaken by the Commission.[39] In 1896, the Commission considered it as well settled that contraction could at most supplement bank protection works in its flood-control program,
and could be used "only in minority of cases." The Commission
flatly conceded that "for several years past the amount expended on such works have been relatively small."[40] "The project
of the Commission adopted in January 1896 contemplated the
building of levees, the annual dredging of channels through
shoal places, and such minor bank work as may be necessary for
the prevention of cut-off, and the protection of harbor and
threatened levee lines of exceptional importance."[41] It is
evident that levee-construction was the principal means of
flood control adopted in this program.[42] This was the policy
of the Commission up to its complete subordination to the Corps
of Engineers in 1928.[43] This is the reason why the Federal
flood-control program for the Lower Mississippi River in the
period 1881 (actually 1882)-1928 has been commonly described
as one of "levee only."

The "levee above all others" policy seemingly held the
Commission in a semi-autonomous position up to 1928; for to
the Corps of Engineers the construction of levees[44] was and
still is primarily a local responsibility. In the 1920's the
embanking levees proved inadequate to control the floods of
the Lower Mississippi River. On 17 April 1926 a special Act
was enacted by Congress (44 Stat. 300) directing the Secretary
of War, through the Corps of Engineers, "to cause a survey to
be made, and estimates of the costs, of such controlled and
regulated spillway or spillways as may be necessary for the
diversion and control of a sufficient volume of the excess
flood waters of the Mississippi River between Point Breeze and
Fort Jackson in Louisiana," . . . and to "cause the Mississippi River Commission to transmit to him all engineering records,
data, field notes and such other information as he may deem
desirable and useful in carrying out the purposes of this act."
The results of the survey were embodied in a report of the
Chief of Engineers dated 1 December 1927.[45] The spillway or
floodway plan, i.e., the "Outlet system" that had been con-
demned by the Mississippi River Commission, was recommended.
In the same report, it was pointed out that

> At present the Chief of Engineers and the Secretary
> of War have veto power over the Mississippi River
> Commission, but not initiative control. It is rec-
> ommended that under the direction of the Secretary
> of War the Chief of Engineers be given authority
> to plan and direct the work on the Mississippi Ri-
> ver, with the president of Commission reporting
> direct to him. The Commission as at present con-
> stituted can be continued as an advisory, but not

as an executive, commission . . . . The president
of the commission, . . . to be eligible for such
assignment, have the qualifications now prescribed
by law for the Assistant Chief of Engineers (at
pp. 33-34).

All of the recommendations of the Chief of Engineers in this
report were approved by the Congress in the Mississippi River
Flood Control Act of 15 May 1928 (45 Stat. 534). The works
recommended by the Chief of Engineers were to be prosecuted
by the Commission "under the direction of the Secretary of
War and supervision of the Chief of Engineers", and the president of the Commission was made its "executive officer" (sec.
8, at 537). By administrative action in 1929, the headquarters of the Commission were moved from St. Louis, Missouri, to
Vicksburg, Mississippi, and the president of the Commission
was to assume simultaneously the duties and office of the
division engineer of the Lower Mississippi Valley Division of
the Corps of Engineers. Similar personnel union has prevailed of the three district engineers of the Commission and the
three district engineers of the Division.[46] It should be remarked that the authority and jurisdiction of Commission has
remained unchanged. What has changed is its internal organization and its status.

Annex: Missouri River Commission---This special agency
was created by the River and Harbor Act of 5 July 1884 (23
Stat. 133, 144-145). It consisted of five members appointed
by the President with Senate consent, of whom three were to
be officers of the Corps of Engineers and two civil engineers.
Plans and reports of the Commission were to be transmitted to
the Congress through the Chief of Engineers, U. S. Army. So,
unlike the Mississippi River Commission in 1879-1928, the
Missouri River Commission was strictly subordinate to the
Corps of Engineers. The duties of the Commission, as provided in this act, were "to superintend and direct such improvement" of the Missouri River "and to carry into execution such
plans for the improvement of the navigation of said river
from its mouth to its headwaters . . ." By the River and
Harbor Act of 13 July 1892, its jurisdiction was extended to
the harbors and localities on the Missouri River from its
mouth to Sioux City, Iowa (27 Stat. 88, 108); and by the River and Harbor Act of 18 August 1894, it was further extended
to cover the improvement of the Gasconade and Osage Rivers,
Missouri (28 Stat. 338, 358). The Commission was abolished
by the River and Harbor Act of 13 June 1902 (32 Stat. 331,
367-368), and its work was transferred to the Corps of Engineers. In contrast to the Mississippi River Commission, which
has been a flood-control agency, the Missouri River Commission
confined itself to navigation-improvement work. The work it
performed, though limited in scope,[47] consisted of snagging,
dredging, revetment, contraction and canalization, all of
which are primarily measures of navigation improvement.[48]

The original status of the Missouri River Commission of complete subordination to the Corps of Engineers and its final abolition in 1902 certified to the fact that Federal enterprise of navigation improvement belongs exclusively to the Corps of Engineers and is not to be shared by other agencies.[49]

(c) **California Debris Commission**[50]---This Commission was established by an Act of 1 March 1893 (27 Stat. 507). It consists of three members appointed by the President with the consent and advice of the Senate from among the officers of the Corps of Engineers, and is under the supervision of the Secretary of the Army and the Chief of Engineers (sec. 1). One member is designated as the president, and one as the secretary of the Commission. The latter "has immediate supervision of the work of the Commission."[51] The jurisdiction and functions of the Commission were already discussed before.

(d) **Beach Erosion Board**---This Board was created by the last paragraph of sec. 2 of the River and Harbor Act of 3 July 1930 (46 Stat. 918, 945-946), which authorized the Chief of Engineers of the Department of War (the Army) to make studies and investigations and devise means of control and prevention of the erosion of the shores of the ocean and Great-Lake coasts in cooperation with agencies of the states concerned. The duty of this Board is to assist and advise the Chief of Engineers in performing this function. It is made up of seven members, "of whom four shall be officers of the Corps of Engineers and three shall be selected with regard to their special fitness by the Chief of Engineers from among the state agencies cooperating with the War (Army) Department." Investigations of beach erosion without state participation are authorized by an Act of 31 July 1945 (59 Stat. 508). Investigations under the authority of the former provision are generally made upon application by the state or local agencies concerned to the Chief of Engineers. "After approval by the Chief of Engineers, the local District Engineers make the studies and prepare the reports. The Beach Erosion Board furnishes consultant technical service to the District Engineers and reviews the completed reports." Investigations without state and local participation are authorized by Congress and seemingly conducted in the same manner.[52]

2. **The Department of the Interior**---The activities of the Department of the Interior in the fields of irrigation, drainage, land and soil management, hydroelectric power development, fish and wildlife, recreation and water resources investigations, performed through the Bureau of Reclamation, Bureau of Land Management, the various subordinate power agencies, Fish and Wildlife Service, National Park Service, Bureau of Indian Affairs and Geological Survey, have already been discussed in the foregoing Chapters. But a few more comments will be made here in connection with the work of the Bureau of Reclamation.

According to sec. 9(a) of the Reclamation Project Act of

4 August 1939 (53 Stat. 1187, 1193), regular Federal irrigation projects which are self-liquidating are authorized by
the Secretary of the Interior; and according to sec. 1 of the
Water Conservation and Utilization Act of 11 August 1940 (53
Stat. 1418), the Secretary of the Interior may undertake any
water conservation and utilization project. As a matter of
fact, initiation of a project is as a rule assumed by the
local land interests concerned. " . . . No project can be
built without a community's clamoring for it . . ."[53] The
Bureau maintain a number of Regional Offices, each headed by
a Regional Director, in the 17 Western states which are under
its jurisdiction. Its planning, construction and operation
activities are actually performed at the regional level.[54]

It is needless to say that the jurisdiction of the Bureau
of Reclamation does not extend east of the 98th meridian.
Even in the West, the Bureau shares with the Corps of Engineers the task of planning and prosecuting the main phases
of river-basin development in all cases except in the Colorado River Basin. "In the case of the Colorado River Basin,
the Bureau of Reclamation has principal responsibility for
preparing a 'comprehensive plan' for water resources development."[55] Here the watercourses are all practically non-navigable, and the Corps is inactive. In this area, the Bureau
goes beyond the work of irrigation, and has undertaken, in
addition, works that normally and nationally fall within the
jurisdiction of the Corps of Engineers. For example, the Bureau builds and operates the Colorado River project, which is
a single-purpose flood control project authorized by the River and Harbor Act of 26 August 1937 (50 Stat. 850).[56]

The Bureau of Reclamation is extremely ardent in the development of hydroelectric power as a supplementary means of
financing the irrigation projects. "Of the West's estimated
potential 50,000,000 kilowatts of hydroelectric power that
might be developed, some 8,700,000 kilowatts have now been
harnessed. Approximately 4,300,000 (i.e. approximately one-
half) kilowatts of this power have been developed on Reclamation projects, with some 700,000 kilowatts on other Federal
projects, and the remainder on local and private projects."[57]
Thus the Bureau is the greatest producer of hydroelectric
power in the entire West.[58]

3. The Department of Agriculture---The services of the
Department of Agriculture in water resources administration,
performed through the Forest Service, the Soil Conservation
Service, the Rural Electrification Administration, the Farmers Home Administration and the Agricultural Conservation
Program Service, have already been discussed in Chapters 1
and 2, and will not be repeated here.[59] Those services which
are of the nature of Federal assistance to private persons
uniquely identify the Department in its role in Federal water
resources administration and bear no close resemblance to the

activities of any other Federal agency. Its enterprise services, however, are so closely related to the activities of the Department of the Interior and the Army Corps of Engineers that interdepartmental boundaries are hard to draw.

The Bureau of Land Management and the United States Forest Service practically duplicate their efforts in the management of Federal grazing or pasture lands. The Revested Oregon and California Railroad Grant and the Reconveyed Coos Bay Wagon Road Grant Lands (i.e., the so-called "O & C lands") under the jurisdiction of the Bureau of Land Management is virtually a "petit national forest". The recreational facilities of a national forest may be comparable to those found in a national or a state park. A National park may compete with a national forest in the conservation and protection of forests. Most national forests have been made wildlife management areas. From the point of view of wildlife administration, differences are at most shadowy between a Federal upland game or a big game wildlife refuge and a national forest. To common people unfamiliar with the administrative and legal technicalities of these areas, it may well appear that the Federal Government chooses to manage its non-farm lands through two land departments instead of one.

As a matter of fact, the measures of soil protection are the same for Federal lands under the jurisdiction of both the Department of the Interior and the Department of Agriculture. This is why prior to the Reorganization Plan No. 4 of 30 June 1940 the Soil Conservation Service was responsible for the application of these measure on lands controlled by both departments.

In the several states, the state game agency is in control of both the protection of wildlife in its "wild" state and artificial propagation of wildlife. The latter is in a certain sense the domestication of wildlife and is done in the game farms. It is a good question whether this aspect of wildlife management belongs properly to wildlife management and whether or not it should be taken care of by the agriculture agency. At the Federal level this is a jurisdictional question affecting the Fish and Wildlife Service of the Department of the Interior on the one side and the Department of Agriculture on the other.[60] On 30 April 1946 an Act was passed by Congress (60 Stat. 127) transferring "all the functions of the Secretary of the Interior and the Fish and Wildlife Service of the Department of the Interior, which affect the breeding, raising, producing, marketing, or any other phase of the production of domestically raised fur-bearing animals, or products thereof" to the Department of Agriculture.

It is needless to say that both the Bureau of Reclamation and the Soil Conservation Service have the statutory authority to build and operate water-conservation facilities and struc-

tures in the Great Plains area, although funds have never
been appropriated by the Congress to the latter for such purpose, and that irrigation enterprise, the most important enterprise that has been intrusted to the Department of the Interior, is in essence an agricultural measure, especially
when the lands to be irrigated are non-Federal lands.

From the above discussion it may be seen that the entire
body of Federal enterprise activities which are administered
by the Department of Agriculture and the Department of the
Interior are intermixed in such a way that any clear-cut distinction between the enterprise jurisdictions of these two
Departments cannot but be arbitrary.

One aspect of the enterprise or assistance jurisdiction
of the Department of Agriculture is interlocked with the activities of the Corps of Engineers. Under sec. 2 of the Flood
Control Act of 22 June 1936 (49 Stat. 1570), as amended (33
U. S. C. 701b), the latter is in charge of the work of flood
control while the former is responsible for "investigations
of watersheds" and for the prosecution of "measures of runoff and waterflow retardation and soil-erosion prevention
on watersheds." The term "watershed"has never been clearly
defined. Probably it means the "upland" of the drainage basin of a watercourse. That is to say, while the Department
of Agriculture controls the upland, the Corps of Engineers
works in the valley, of a drainage basin. But since most watercourses are tributaries to other watercourses, many upland
areas or "watersheds" must be at the same time valleys. As
a matter of fact, the Corps of Engineers have investigated
and recommended works for very small streams, the drainage
basins of which may very likely be commonly regarded as "watershed" areas of a certain region.[61] The overlapping of the
functions of the two agencies is unavoidable unless there is
a clear definition of the word "watershed".[62]

4. <u>The Department of Commerce</u>---The most important contribution of this Department to water resources administration is perhaps the flood-forecasting services conducted by
the Weather Bureau. The general activities of this Bureau
in climatological observations and research are also of in-
valuable help to irrigation and conservation enterprises,
both governmental and private. This Bureau and the Geological Survey of the Department of the Interior indeed constitute
the "brain" of Federal (and also non-Federal) water resources
administration. Another subordinate agency of the Department
of Commerce which renders indispensable services to the management of water resources of the nation is the Coast and
Geodetic Survey, which surveys and charts coastal and inland
waters in aid of navigation. The Bureau of Public Roads constructs roads in national parks and national forests. In
planning and supervising the construction of the Federal-aid
state highways and parkways, it also exercises some indirect

control over that part of the state recreation enterprise which consists of the construction and maintenance of waysides and parkways.[63]

5. <u>Federal Power Commission</u>---The Federal Power Commission is the most important Federal regulatory agency in the field of water resources administration.[64] The Commission was established in 1920 by the Federal Water Power Act. Under sec. 1 of this act, the Commission was to be "composed of the Secretary of War, the Secretary of the Interior, and the Secretary of Agriculture." Of the three <u>ex-officio</u> members, one was to be designated by the President to be the chairman of the Commission. "The Commission shall appoint an executive secretary, . . . and may request the President of the United States to detail an officer from the United States Engineer Corps to serve the Commission as engineer officer . . ." (sec. 2, first para.). But no other personnel were provided for: "the work of the Commission shall be performed by and through the Departments of War, Interior, and Agriculture and their engineering, technical, clerical, and other personnel . . ." (sec. 2, second para.). However, in 1928, the Commission was granted authority to employ its own personnel, although its staff was not greatly expanded until 1935.[65]

A general reorganization of the Commission was effected by an Act of 23 June 1930 (46 Stat. 797), by which it was changed from an agency with <u>ex-officio</u> membership and staff into an independent agency. The Commission now consists of five commissioners appointed by the President with the consent and approval of the Senate. Under the Act of 1930, the Commission elected among its membership a chairman and a vice-chairman. This arrangement was changed by the President's Reorganization Plan No. 9 of 24 May 1950 (15 F. R. 3175), under which the chairman is to be designated by the President and exercises, on behalf of the Commission, "the executive and administrative functions of the Commission, including functions of the Commission with respect to (1) the appointment and supervision of personnel employed under the Commission, (2) the distribution of business among such personnel and among administrative units of the Commission, and (3) the use and expenditure of funds." Thus the Commission as such passes upon policies and budgetary matters while its chairman actually performs the regulatory and other duties of the Commission[66]

6. <u>U. S. Public Health Service of the Department of Health, Education and Welfare</u>---This agency is in charge of Federal activities concerning water pollution, although part of these activities are instructed to the Corps of Engineers. The services of the Public Health Service in matters regarding water pollution and mosquito control and the administration of the Water Pollution Control Act of 1948 (to be discussed later).[67]

7. Tennessee Valley Authority---The organization and functions of the Tennessee Valley Authority are stipulated in the Tennessee Valley Authority Act of 1933, as amended (16 U. S. C. 831 et seq.). Technically speaking, the Authority is occupied with two primary or basic functions; namely, (1) the manufacturing of nitrogen and nitrogen products for defense and agricultural purposes, and (2) the production and disposition of electric power (sec. 5 of the Tennessee Valley Authority Act: 16 U. S. C. 831d). Electric power is produced at the multiple-purpose dams (sec. 9a, as added in 1935: 16 U. S. C. 831h-1); and technically only "surplus power" is to be sold (sec. 10: 16 U. S. C. 831i). All other activities of the Authority center around these two primary or basic duties, which are themselves closely associated with each other.[68] This is a purely technical analysis. In a practical sense, it would seem that the Authority has only one basic or principal responsibility; namely, to produce electric energy at multiple-purpose dams. A small part of the electric energy produced is used for the manufacture of nitrogen and nitrogen products. The remaining part of the energy produced, which is designated as "surplus power", is to be sold on a commercial basis. Attendant upon the construction and operation of dams and reservoirs, which serve power as well as other purposes, are activities such as the operation and leasing of recreational facilities, mosquito control, the forestry and soil conservation programs on project lands, and so forth, activities that are common to all Federal and non-Federal multiple-purpose projects of comparable sizes.

The Tennessee Valley Authority, with its head office located in Knoxville, Tennessee, is a regional agency in the sense that its primary operational activities are confined to the Tennessee River System and its drainage basin. It is a regional agency also in the sense that it is the only Federal agency responsible for the construction and operation of multiple-purpose, power-dominant dams and reservoirs in the Tennessee River Basin, an enterprise which elsewhere in the country is intrusted to, or rather absorbed in, the enterprise of the Corps of Engineers or the Bureau of Reclamation. But it should be remarked that in the Tennessee River Basin the Authority replaces none of the Federal agencies having national jurisdiction over water resources administration. It is not authorized to construct single-purpose navigation-improvement or flood-control projects in or along the Tennessee River or any of its tributaries: These belong to the jurisdiction of the Corps of Engineers. Even the operation of the navigation locks constructed by the Authority in its multiple-purpose dams is controlled by the Corps of Engineers, like that of the locks constructed at private and other non-Federal power dams.[69] Except in reviewing the license applications to the Federal Power Commission, it has no regulatory authority whatever. It does not administer any national park or national forest or national wildlife refuge located in the Tennessee River

Basin. Nor has it driven the Public Health Service, the Soil
Conservation Service or the Farmers Home Administration out
of this region.[70]

However, the Tennessee Valley Authority maintains certain
statutory (sec. 12 of the organic act, as added in 1935: 16
U. S. C. 831k-1) and extra-statutory relationships with the
Tennessee-valley states and their local units. But all these
relationships are voluntary and none of them encroach upon
the constitutional rights of the states. The only ground of
fear for people concerned with states' rights is the fact
that in the Tennessee Valley water-power is developed by the
Tennessee Valley Authority, a special Federal agency, and not
by the states. That this is unwarranted by sound logic needs
only a moment of reflection. The Tennessee River Basin hap-
pens to be the only instance in which water-power is developed
by an agency independent of the Corps of Engineers or the Bureau of Reclamation. In all other river basins the same job
is performed by the Corps and/or the Bureau. The conception
that the Federal Government must create a Valley Authority
before it can constitutionally develop the nation's water-power will startle all constitutional lawyers.[71]

The establishment of the Tennessee Valley Authority is an
administrative experiment. It is an experiment, however, not
of the use of an "authority" but rather of the development of
water-power on a river-basin basis. It is a continuation and
expansion of the experiment of the Boulder Canyon project established in 1928, which successfully proved the feasibility
and necessity of the construction of large-scale hydroelectric
power projects by the Federal Government. The Tennessee Valley experiment, the second and last experiment of the Federal
Government in hydroelectric power enterprise, being again successful, the Federal Government, immediately after the Second
World War, gave national application to the results of this
experiment. But an "authority" was no longer necessary, for
the Corps of Engineers and the Bureau of Reclamation are better equipped than, and as willing as, the Tennessee Valley Authority, in regional water-power development. The Corps and
the Bureau are better equipped not only because of their longer and richer technical experience in the construction and operation of dams and reservoirs, but also of their special statutory advantages in taking care of such non-power purposes as
navigation improvement, flood control, irrigation, and water
conservation. In the Tennessee River Basin efforts have to be
made to coordinate the activities of the Tennessee Valley Authority and the Corps of Engineers with respect to the operation of the dams (including locks) and reservoirs. Additional
coordination has to be made between the Authority and the Bureau of Reclamation should the Tennessee Valley fall within the
jurisdiction of the Bureau. But when the same dams and reservoirs are constructed and operated and maintained by the Corps
or the Bureau, such coordination arrangement, which necessari-

ly involves certain administrative friction, will be avoided.[72] There is no question that the Tennessee Valley Authority has done a splendid job in the development of water resources in the Tennessee River Basin. This does not necessarily dictate the use of a special corporate agency in multiple-purpose river-basin development for other regions of the country. After all, one should not ignore the equally successful work of the Corps of Engineers and the Bureau of Reclamation. The transplanation of the "authority" set-up to other regions than the Tennessee Valley (where a special regional agency was set up because of the experimental nature of the enterprise) can only be justified by reasons alien to the principles of public administration. This seems to have been the view of the Congress, as it has consistently rejected proposals leading to such administrative anomaly.[73]

Section 2   Federal Coordinated Organization

Subsection 1   Supervisory Coordination[74]

1. The Congress---The Congress keeps itself informed of the activities of the several Federal administrative agencies (through written and oral reports and through hearings), and in exercising supervision over a particular agency is in a position of taking into consideration duties and rights of other agencies, thus indirectly but authoritatively bringing needed coordination among the various agencies.[75] The supervision likely to effect such coordination is exercised either by the Congress at large or by its standing and ad-hoc committees. The Congress at large, in exercising such supervision, is advised, as a rule, by the standing and ad-hoc committees or by ad-hoc commissions consisting of persons other than members of the Congress. The standing and ad-hoc committees usually may be advised by their sub-committees, but ordinarily they are supposed to be sufficiently informed at all times as to render unnecessary any organized advice. Each standing committee usually works with a particular administrative agency or a particular group of administrative agencies. For this reason, coordination to be expected of Congressional committees can be nothing but purely theoretical and legalistic.

The most common form of supervision of the Congress over water resources administration, exercised by the Congress at large, is the authorization of projects. As has already been mentioned, all national park, navigation improvement, hydroelectric power, major flood control and most national forest projects are authorized by the Congress in statutory enactments.[76] In the case of projects of the Corps of Engineers, even examinations and surveys are authorized by the Congress (or Congressional committees).[77] In general, the initiation of irrigation projects does not require Congressional authorization. However, those projects which, in the opinion of the Secretary of the Interior are not self-liquidating must be authorized by Congress in the form of ordinary legislation (Reclamation Project Act of 1939, sec. 9(a)). Additional irrigation works to be constructed by the Department of the Interior on flood control projects of the Corps of Engineers must be authorized by Acts of Congress, too (Flood Control Act of 1944, sec. 8: 58 Stat. 891). In recent appropriation, Congress has required that the construction of the Glendo Unit, Missouri River "project", and the Moorhead Dam and Reservoir, Montana, and the reclamation works in the Chief Joseph Project, Washington, must not be started until their project plans are approved by the Congress.[78] In at least one instance, an irrigation project was directly authorized by Congress in a procedure similar to the authorization of a river and harbor or a flood control project, without following the regular procedure provided in sec. 9(a) of the Reclamation Project Act of 1939.[79] As for Indian irrigation projects, it is provided in the Indian Office Appropriation Act of 4 April 1910 that ". . . no new project to cost in the aggregate to exceed $35,000 shall be undertaken on any Indian reservation or allotment without specific authority of Congress . . ." (36 Stat. 269, 270).

Another control exercised by the Congress over water resources projects is appropriation of funds for construction and maintenance. Authorized projects cannot be constructed without this additional process of Congressional control. Regarding the authorized units of the Ohio River Basin flood control program, the author is informed of the following practice, which may very likely be the general practice of all flood control and river basin development programs:[80]

> Before units are programmed for definite construction, detailed studies and estimates are made as a basis for appropriation requests. As a result of such studies, it is found from time to time that some of the units are not economically feasible under conditions current at the time of detailed studies, and under such circumstances those units are omitted from the immediate construction program.

For a flood control project in the Yellowstone River Basin, that was authorized by the Flood Control Act of 1936, construction did not become available until as late as 1948.[81] Authorization and appropriation thus constitute a double brake upon the construction of water resources projects. Appropriation is by far the stronger part of the entire mechanism. Even though ordinary irrigation projects do not require Congressional authorization, Congressional control over these projects is practically the same over navigation improvement or flood control projects.[82]

It may finally be mentioned that the Congress may directly perform certain purely administrative acts which, from the

point of view of the Government, are <u>self</u>-executing.[83] These
consist of special acts or special provisions in general acts
permitting certain non-Federal parties to construct certain
water resources projects and similar acts. Such acts should
be performed by administrative agencies as Federal regulatory
measures either according to existing general statutory provisions or by the nature of these acts. Mention should also
be made of sec. 7(c) of the Reclamation Project Act of 1939,
which provides for the approval by Congress of water contracts.
Such approval is also purely administrative, although it is
not a self-executing act of the Congress. Supervision of this
kind goes into the very heart of administration.

The most important role played by the standing committees
is the authorization of preliminary examinations and surveys,
a task which they equally share with their mother body. For
the fifty years beginning 1902, there had been a total of 7,-
700 authorizations for preliminary surveys and examinations
for navigation improvement and flood control. Of this number,
2,700, or 35 percent, were made by Congressional committees.[84]
These authorizations are of no less force or influence than
those made by the Congress at large. Indeed, all leading
multiple-purpose river-basin-development surveys have been authorized by Congressional committees as "review examinations".
The Congress itself has authorized surveys for a wide area only in a few cases. However, surveys authorized by the Congress in statutory enactments are all basic ones and are of
greater importance than committee-authorized surveys.[85]

The standing committees, like the Congress itself, may
perform certain purely administrative acts (i.e. acts which
should ordinarily be performed by administrative agencies, considering that the Congress itself is not an administrative
agency). At present, there is only one instance of such practice, which is provided by an Act of 7 October 1949 (63 Stat.
724-725). Under this act, repayment contracts for the construction of irrigation rehabilitation and betterment works should
be laid before the Senate Committee on Interior and Insular
Affairs and the House Committee on Public Lands for sixty days
before they can come into force, unless they are approved by
the said committees at an earlier time. When the Congress is
not in session, the said contracts may become effective upon
approval by the chairman and the ranking minority member of
each of the said committees.

The above discussion refers to the ways in which the Congress exercises special supervision over Federal water resources administration (assuming that general legislation is not
a part of administration). These supervisory practices may
or may not produce effects of coordination among the various
administrative agencies (assuming that the Congress itself is
not an administrative agency). This is contingent upon (1)
the degree of cohesion in the internal organization of the Con-

gress itself and (2) the degree to which the Congress is informed of inter-relationships of the several agencies in particular cases.

Among the standing committees of the Congress, the following are concerned with water resources administration:[86]

(A) Senate
(1) Committee on Agriculture and Forestry (for all functions of the Department of Agriculture, except national forests which are not part of the public domain)
(2) Committee on Interstate and Foreign Commerce (navigation; all functions of the Department of Commerce with respect to water resources administration; fish and wildlife; probably also regulation by Federal Power Commission of interstate power transmission)
(3) Committee on Interior and Insular Affairs (on Public Lands) (all functions of the Department of the Interior except fish and wildlife; national forests created out of the public domain)
(4) Committee on Public Works (among other duties, navigation improvement; flood control; multiple-purpose projects of the Corps of Engineers; licensing of water-power projects by the Federal Power Commission)
(5) Committee on Labor and Welfare (among other duties, public health)
(6) Committee on Foreign Relations (among other duties, international boundary waters)
(B) The House of Representatives
(1) Committee on Agriculture (same as Senate Committee on Agriculture and Forestry)
(2) Committee on Interstate and Foreign Commerce (among other duties, functions of the Inland Waterways Corporation and the Weather Bureau; public health; interstate power transmission)
(3) Committee on Merchant Marine and Fisheries (among other duties, functions of the Geodetic Survey; navigation regulation; fish and wildlife)
(4) Committee on Public Lands (same as Senate Committee on Interior and Insular Affairs)
(5) Committee on Public Works (same as Senate Committee on Public Works)
(6) Committee on Foregin Affairs (same as Senate Committee on Foreign Relations)

Among these committees, the Committee on Public Lands of the House of Representatives and the Committee on Interior and Insular Affairs of the Senate control all aspects of Federal land management except wildlife and certainly have considerable coordination potentiality. Enterprises dealing with the control and conservation of water are sadly divided under the land-management committees and the Public Works Committees. Coordination for these enterprises will be nearly perfect if

the construction of irrigation projects now under the control
of the land-management committees and matters of fishery now
under the control of the Senate Interstate and Foreign Commerce Committee and the House Merchant Marine and Fisheries
Committee be transferred to the Public Works Committees. The
Public Works Committees and land-management committees in proper cooperation (through joint meetings or otherwise) will
achieve a reasonably good coordination for entire Federal enterprise administration. And it is the field of enterprise
that coordination is most needed.

2. The President---Supervision of the President likely
to produce effects of coordination is formally[87] exercised in
three general ways.[88]

(a) Approval and authorization of certain administrative
acts: The prominent example of this practice has been found
in the irrigation enterprise. An Act of 25 June 1910 (36 Stat.
835) appropriated $20 million to the Department of the Inter-
ior for the completion of irrigation projects already started.
The same act provided that expenditure on any project could
not be made until the engineering feasibility of the project
was approved by the President. In the Second Deficiency Appropriation Act of 5 December 1924, it was provided that no
irrigation project could be constructed with funds appropriated thereby unless the President approved its agricultural and
engineering feasibility and practicability (43 Stat. 672, 685).
Under the Water Conservation and Utilization Act of 14 October 1940 (54 Stat. 1119), all water conservation and utilization projects are to be authorized by the President (sec. 3
(a)).[89] Under the emergency legislation of the 1930's, some
water-resources-management projects were approved or authorized by the President. However, in the fields of navigation
improvement and flood control, very few projects were authorized by the President: most projects constructed with emergency funds were those already authorized by Congress.[90]

(b) Performance or prosecution of certain administrative
acts in the name of the President: As mentioned above, navigation-improvement works authorized in the first three River
and Harbor Acts were stipulated to be constructed by the President. Under sec. 9 of the Act of 7 June 1924 (43 Stat. 653,
655), national forests in public domain are established by
the President. Under sec. 1 of the Act of 25 June 1910 (36
Stat. 847), the President makes temporary reservations of public lands. As provided in sec. 203(2) (1) of the National Industrial Recovery Act of 16 June 1933 (48 Stat. 195, 202), all
public work projects authorized under the authority thereof
were to be constructed by the President through the Federal
Emergency Administration of Public Works or other agencies
which he might designate. The construction of water conservation and other projects provided for in an Act of 19 August
1935 (49 Stat. 660) was also intrusted to the President. It

may also be mentioned that the Parker Dam project on the Colorado River and the Grand Coulee project on the Columbia River as first authorized in the River and Harbor Act of 30 August 1935 (49 Stat. 1028, 1039) were constructed by "the President, acting through such agents as he may designate." Under the Act of 28 May 1940 (54 Stat. 224), the President, acting upon recommendations of the Departments of Agriculture and the Interior, makes and revokes reservations of national-forest lands for protection of municipal water supplies. It may finally be mentioned that by an Act of 19 August 1935, the President was authorized "to construct, operate, and maintain on the Rio Grande River below Fort Quitman, Texas, any and all works or projects which are recommended to the President" by the International Boundary Commission, United States and Mexico, or under provisions of treaties between the United States and Mexico (49 Stat. 660).

(c) Special measures of coordination: One instance is found in sec. 13 of the Taylor Grazing Act of 1934 (48 Stat. 1269, 1274), under which the President may transfer lands situated in national forests but suitable for grazing to the Bureau of Land Management to be put to such use, and lands under the jurisdiction of the latter to the Department of Agriculture to be included in national forests. There has been much complaint on the part of students of public administration about the lack of coordination between the Corps of Engineers and the Bureau of Reclamation, particularly at the Presidential level.[91] This situation has been to some degree alleviated since 1940, as a result of the enactment of two Executive Orders. In the first Order, dated 26 June 1940 (5 F. R. 2420), it was provided, inter alia, that

> Each construction agency, in submitting any report to the Congress or to any committee or member thereof on the results of any examination, survey, investigation, or research directed toward the preparation of any reports, plans, programs, or estimates of construction costs for any project to be constructed and financed in whole or in part by the Federal Government, shall include therein a statement as to the relationship of such report to the program of the President. Such reports shall be submitted to the Bureau of the Budget before the agency submits them to the Congress or to any committee or member thereof, and the Bureau of the Budget shall advise the agency as to the relationship of such report to the program of the President.

This Order was superseded by the second one, which was issued on 4 October 1943 (8 F. R. 13782-13783). Under this Order, each executive agency shall formulate and keep up to date an advance program for the agency, and the Bureau of the Budget shall prepare an overall advance program for the entire Fed-

eral Government. "Before any department or establishment
shall submit to the Congress, or to any committee or member
thereof, a report relating to, or affecting in whole or in
part, its advance program, or the public works and improvement projects comprising such programs, or the results of any
plan prepared for such programs or projects, such report shall
be submitted to the Bureau for advice as to its relationship
to the program of the President. When such report is thereafter submitted to the Congress, or to any committee or member thereof, it shall include a statement of the advice received from the Bureau."

These Orders evidently have special application to the
Corps of Engineers. "From 1941 to 1951 the Budget cleared
1,221 reports referred to it by the Corps. Of these, 625
reports recommended against Federal improvement and were
cleared by the Budget without objection." Of the rest, 49
reports, or 8 percent, were found to be not in accord with
the program of the President and 82 reports, or 14 percent,
were returned with special reservations or comments. It
should be pointed out that whether a report is in accord with
Presidential program or not, it is submitted to the Congress
all the same. However, "there have been cases where the Budget Bureau specifically requested certain changes and they have
been made."[92]

    3. The Department Heads---Discussion under this topic is
confined (1) to the Departments of Agriculture and the Interior, each of which has a relatively great number of special
subordinate water resources administrative agencies, and (2)
to formal supervision and coordination, that is, supervision
and coordination by the Secretaries of Agriculture and the
Interior through respective specialized staffs.

    (a) The Department of the Interior---By an Departmental
Order of 18 May 1938, a Director of Forests was created in the
Office of the Secretary with duties of coordinating the activities of the various agencies of the Department with respect
to forestry.[93] This was the first time that a staff office
was created for the special purpose of assisting the Secretary of the Interior in bringing about supervisory coordination among the subordinate agencies in matters concerning
water resources administration. On 15 April 1940, by another
Departmental Order, this office was expanded into the Office
of Land Utilization, whose head was known by the name of the
Assistant to the Secretary in charge of Land Utilization and
whose duties it was to coordinate the activities of all subordinate agencies of the Department having general and special
jurisdiction over the public lands, with special emphasis on
soil and moisture conservation on lands controlled thereby.[94]
It was the counterpart of the Office of Land Use Coordination
in the Department of Agriculture (to be discussed below), and
was supposed to be in close cooperation with it.

On 18 April 1941, the Secretary ordered the establishment "in the office of the Secretary a Division of Power which shall have supervision over all the functions in connection with electric power matters in the Department of the Interior, the study of power problems, and the coordination of power policies and activities within the Department and with other agencies dealing with power."[95]

Another arm of the Secretary in his supervision over the Departmental functions in water resources administration, the Water Resources Committee, was established on 2 May 1944. This Committee coordinated the Department's programs and activities relating to the development and conservation of water resources.[96] The Committee also reviewed project reports of the Corps of Engineers and applications to the Federal Power Commission for power permits and licenses which were referred to the Department for review and comment as required by law. As a matter of fact, this function, together with the examination of the project reports of the Bureau of Reclamation, constituted the principal work of the Committee.[97] "The Assistant to the Secretary in charge of Land Utilization is chairman of the Department's Water Resources Committee and cooperates with the Executive Officer of that Committee in the coordination of the water development programs of the Department."[98] Thus the Water Resources Committee was virtually a part of the Office of Land Utilization, and later became referred to (rather inofficially) as the Water Resources Sub-Committee in the annual reports of the Secretary of the Interior.

On 1 December 1950, the above-mentioned three offices were regrouped into the following offices: (1) the Division of Water and Power, which took over the duties of the former Division of Power and the Water Resources Committee,[99] and (2) the Division of Land Utilization, which replaced the former Office of Land Utilization,[100] each being headed by a director and each being under the immediate supervision of an Assistant Secretary (Assistant Secretary for Water and Power Development and Assistant Secretary for Public Land Management). The Secretary of the Interior, aided by the Assistant Secretary for Water and Power Development, through the Division of Water and Power, supervised and coordinated the Bureau of Reclamation, the Bonneville Power Administration, the Southwestern Power Administration, and the Southeastern Power Administration. The Secretary, aided by the Assistant Secretary for Public Land Management, through the Division of Land Utilization, supervised and coordinated the Bureau of Land Management, the Fish and Wildlife Service, the National Park Service and the Bureau of Indian Affairs (as well as the Office of Territories).[101]

It should be remarked that the Division of Public Land Management and the Division of Water and Power Development

(as the Division of Minerals and Fuels) directly advised and
assisted the several Assistant Secretaries instead of the Secretary himself, although the Assistant Secretaries are part
of the Office of the Secretary. On 16 December 1947, a staff
unit by the name of "Program Staff" was established by order
(No. 2394) of the Secretary to serve as the Secretary's immediate staff on matters relating to general policies of the Department.[102] This unit was not limited to water and land resources matters. It was not a specialized[103] staff, but the
Secretary's "general staff". The Program Staff was "headed
by a Director who reports to the Secretary." It was "responsible for assisting the Secretary to exercise supervision
over the formulation and execution of the department-wide programs and policies on a regional and national basis."[104]

The Program Staff was not affected by the departmental
re-organization of 1950, and so it existed side by side with
the three specialized staffs of the Assistant Secretaries.
In May 1953, both the Program Staff and the Divisions of Public Land Management and Water and Power Development (and Minerals and Fuels) were abolished. In their place the Technical Review Staff was created.[105] However, the offices of the
Assistant Secretaries for Public Land Management and Water and
Power Development (and Mineral Resources) have continued to
assist the Secretary (and the Under Secretary) in bringing
about coordination among the various subordinate agencies of
the Department.[106] The Technical Review Staff, headed by a
Director, began operation on 24 June 1953. It is concerned
with matters requiring coordination between the various subordinate agencies of the Department of the Interior and between the Department of the Interior and other Federal agencies. "The staff specialists on the Technical Review Staff
are avilable to the Office of the Secretary and the bureaus
on policy and program matters on which advice and assistance
is considered desirable."[107]

(b) The Department of Agriculture[108]---The Department of
Agriculture was ahead of the Department of the Interior in
providing for special assistants to the Secretary in his supervision and coordination over the Department's activities
in water resources administration. The Office of Land Use
Coordination, headed by the Coordinator of Land Use Planning
or Land Use Coordinator, was established on 12 July 1937 by
the Secretary's Memorandum No. 725, to assist the Secretary
in coordinating the policies and activities of the Department
in land and soil conservation. However, this Office operated
as a subordinate unit of the Department rather than part of
the Secretary's staff.

In accordance with the agreement between the Soil Conservation Service, the Farm Security Administration, the Bureau
of Agricultural Economics on the Water Facilities Program,
approved by the Secretary of Agriculture on 1 July 1938, a

Water Facilities Board was established in the Office of Land Use Coordination consisting of representatives of the four signatory agencies, with a chairman (who was also the board's executive officer) appointed by the Coordinator of Land Use Planning. This board coordinated the functions of these four agencies in connection with the administration of the Water Facilities Program, of which the Soil Conservation Service and the Farm Security Administration, which were responsible for the enterprise (i.e. construction of projects by the Department itself) and the loan aspects of the Program, were the principal ones. Among its specific duties, the board might recommend the allotment of funds, approve area plans and priorities and pass on loans of a certain amount. It may be noted that although attached to the Office of Land Use Coordination, the Water Facilities Board was purely an inter-agency board, and one of the concentric type.

To insure coordination between the agencies concerned in the Department's Flood Control Program (i.e., duties assigned the Department by the various Flood Control Acts), Memorandum No. 890 was issued on 27 February 1941 (effective 15 March 1941) designating a member of the staff of the Office of Land Use Coordination as the Department's officer in charge of flood control, who was to be "responsible for interdepartmental and inter-bureau coordination." This officer was assisted by two advisory bodies: (1) an "advisory committee" (for policy matters) made up of one representative from the Bureau of Agricultural Economics, one from the Soil Conservation Service and one from the Forest Service; and (2) a "technical review board" (for technical matters) composed of a forester, a soil conservationist, a hydrologist, and an economist. These two advisory bodies were eccentric in form but were concentric inter-agency coordination bodies so far as the agencies to be coordinated were concerned. It may be seen that this set-up was a considerable improvement over the somewhat anomalous arrangement of subordinating a concentric inter-agency Water Facilities Board to the Land Use Coordinator.

On 12 January 1942, the Secretary of Agriculture issued Memorandum No. 969, ordering that "effective July 1, 1942, the Water Facilities Board of the Office of Land Use Coordination is abolished, and the Land Use Coordinator or his representative shall be responsible for relating the water facilities program to other programs of this Department and the land and water programs of the Department of the Interior." This measure was taken, however, not because of the organizational defect of the said Board, but because of the fact that the same Memorandum cancelled the enterprise aspect of the Water Facilities Program and made it a pure loan program to be administered by the Farm Security Administration alone.

It may be noted that up to 29 April 1943 the Office of Land Use Coordination was a subordinate agency in status. By Memorandum 1087 of this date, it was made "a staff unit in the

Office of the Secretary". By General Departmental Circular No. 21 of 1 January 1944, the "Office" of Land Use Coordination itself was abolished, and the Land Use Coordinator was to become "a member of the Secretary's staff", assisting the Secretary "on matters with respect to which it is desirable that the land use policies and programs of the Department be properly related to one another and to the work of other Federal or state agencies."

On 10 November 1944, by administrative action of the Administrator, the Office of Water Utilization was set up in the War Food Administration,[109] headed by a director, who "shall exercise general supervision over and shall coordinate the functions and responsibilities of the agencies of the War Food Administration with respect to all phases of water development, use and disposal."[110] He was also directed to keep close contact with the Land Use Coordinator on policy matters.[111] Since such agencies as the Soil Conservation Service, Farm Security Administration, Extension Service, etc. were placed in the War Food Administration, the functions performed by the Office of Water Utilization were complementary to those of Land Use Coordinator of the Department of Agriculture.

Departmental Memorandum No. 1120, dated 21 August 1945 (effective the next day), abolished both the position of the Land Use Coordinator and the Office of Water Utilization, and transferred their duties and functions to the Assistant Secretary of Agriculture. However, what was abolished were only the two head officers of coordination, but not their subordinates, for the Memorandum provided (in article 4) that

> The personnel of the Office of Water Utilization is hereby transferred to the staff of the Secretary's Office, and together with the present personnel of the Secretary's Office now concerned with any phases of the land and water resources activities of the Department are hereby placed under the direction of the Assistant Secretary for the aforesaid purposes, and the Assistant Secretary is instructed to coordinate and direct the activities of said personnel under the general supervision of the Secretary. (Emphasis added).

It is clear that there was a group of specialized assistants in the office of the Secretary who were under the immediate supervision of the Assistant Secretary and whose duties were to furnish necessary informational and other services to the Secretary to activate his role as the supervisor and coordinator of the Department's activities in water and land resources administration. This groups was known as the "Land and Water Resources Staff", headed by an Administrator.[112]

In March 1946 the Secretary appointed a Special Representative (temporary) to represent the Department in the Columbia Basin Inter-Agency Committee and at the same time to coordinate the activities of the various subordinate agencies of the Department in that region. On 1 July 1946 this officer was succeeded by a Secretary's Representative.[113] This measure was an experimental one, and it gave rise to the appointment of the following permanent Field Representatives of the Secretary of Agriculture:[114]

(1) Field Representative in the Missouri River Basin, created by Memorandum No. 1176 of 17 October 1946.

(2) Field Representative for the Pacific Northwest, created by Memorandum No. 1236 of 27 July 1949.

(3) Field Representative for Pacific Southwest, created by Memorandum No. 1250 of 3 February 1950.

(4) Field Representative for Arkansas, White and Red River Basins, created by Memorandum No. 1261 of 17 July 1950.

(5) Field Representative for New England-New York Region, created by Memorandum No. 1297 of 14 June 1951.

(6) Field Representative for Cumberland River Basin, created by Memorandum No. 1315 of 23 July 1952.

These field representatives served as the Department's representatives in the respective Federal Inter-Agency River Basin Committees and at the same time the coordinating officer among the various field units of the subordinate agencies of the Department having duties in the respective regions. It should be noted that all field representatives were officially members of the Land and Water Resources Staff discussed above.[115] Thus the Land and Water Resources Staff was the nerve center of the Department of Agriculture through which coordination among the various subordinate agencies of Department was brought about both at the national capital and in the field.

On 1 April 1953, Memorandum No. 1325 was issued, which abolished both the Land and Water Resources Staff and the various Field Representatives, and transferred their functions to the Soil Conservation Service. "Representatives of the Soil Conservation Service were appointed to report, through the Soil Conservation Service, to the Secretary, regarding activities in the river basins" (except the Cumberland River Basin, in which the Department's work in this respect was discontinued).[116] These representatives were the seven regional directors of the Soil Conservation Service. In the re-organization of 2 November 1953 (Memorandum No. 1320, Supplement 4),[117] all of the regional offices of the Soil Conservation Service were abolished, although the Soil Conservation Service itself "will continue as the Department's technical service agency in the field of soil and water conservation and flood prevention."

On 4 June 1953 a general re-organization (Presidential)
of the entire Department of Agriculture took place,[118] which
increased the number of Assistant Secretaries of Agriculture
from one to three (excluding the newly created Administrative
Assistant Secretary of Agriculture), and grouped the various
subordinate agencies of the Department into four main categories in the following manner:

(1) Under the supervision of the Assistant Secretary of
Agriculture for Research, Extension and Land Use---
Agricultural Conservation Program,
Agricultural Research Administration,
Bureau of Agricultural Economics,
Forest Service,
Soil Conservation.

(2) Under the supervision of the Assistant Secretary of
Agriculture for Commodity Marketing and Adjustment--
Commodity Credit Corporation,
Commodity Exchange Authority,
Federal Crop Insurance Corporation,
Production and Marketing Administration.

(3) Under the supervision of the Assistant Secretary of
Agriculture for Foreign Agricultural Service---
Foreign Agricultural Service.

(4) Under the supervision of the Director of Agricultural
Credit Services--
Farm Credit Administration,
Farmers Home Administration,
Rural Electrification Administration.

In the above-mentioned reorganization plan of 2 November 1953
(Departmental), the above plan was further revised as follows:[119]

Group (1), agencies concerning Federal-States Relations,
under the supervision of an Assistant Secretary:
Agricultural Research Service
Forest Service
Soil Conservation Service
Federal Extension Service
Agricultural Conservation Program Service
Farmer Cooperative Service
Group (2), agencies concerning Marketing and Foreign Ag-
riculture, under the supervision of an Assistant Sec-
retary:
Agricultural Marketing Service
Foreign Agricultural Service
Commodity Exchange Authority
Group (3), agencies concerning Agricultural Stabilization,
under the supervision of an Assistant Secretary:
Commodity Stabilization Service
Community, County and State Committees
Federal Crop Insurance Corporation
Group (4), agencies administering Agricultural Credit,

under the supervision of an Assistant to the Secretary:
Farmers Home Administration
Rural Electrification Administration

This general Departmental reorganization has brought new
coordination among the various subordinate agencies having
jurisdiction in matters of the management and administration
of land and water resources, and has automatically deprived
the Soil Conservation Service of the functions which it in-
herited from the Land and Water Resources Staff and the Department's Field Representatives under the provisions of Memorandum No. 1325 of 1 April 1953.

(c) Concluding remarks---Secretarial supervisory coordination over the water-resources agencies in both the Department of the Interior and the Department of Agriculture has
passed from the type of specialized staffs, which strengthens
the position of the Secretary as a supervisor and coordinator, to the type of functional assistant secretaries, which
reduces the burden of the Secretary in this capacity (through
the delegation of authority).[120] The Department of Agriculture was in advance of the Department of the Interior in the
introduction of the first method of coordination, while the
Department of the Interior took the lead in the use of the
second method.

All of the above discussion is about the coordinating role
of the Department Heads within the respective Departments.
As a member of the Executive Cabinet, a Department Head or a
deputy thereof may supervise and coordinates independent establishments on behalf of the President. An example of this
is found in the Saint Lawrence Seaway Development Corporation
Organic Act of 13 May 1954 (68 Stat. 92). It provides that
the said Corporation, an agency not subordinate to any Department, shall be under the supervision of the President or such
agency as he may designate. After the Corporation was organized in June 1954, the President designated the Deputy Secretary of Defense to supervise the said Corporation.[121] This
officer, doubtless, is in a position to coordinate the activities of the said Corporation with those of the Corps of Engineers of the Department of the Army.

Subsection 2 Cooperative Coordination

(A) Formal Coordination[122]

(1) Concentric Coordination: Inter-Agency Committees or
Commissions---This type of coordination, as particularly ap-
lied to water resources administration in particular, is found
in the following cases:

(a) Statutory Inter-Agency Bodies---In sec. 4 of the Weeks

Act of 1 March 1911 (36 Stat. 961, 962), provision is made for
the establishment of the National Forest Reservation Commission, which is to consist of the Secretary of the Interior,
the Secretary of Agriculture, the Secretary of the Army, two
members of the Senate to be selected by the President of the
Senate and two members of the House of Representatives to be
selected by the Speaker of the House, and whose function it
is to consider and approve purchases by the Federal Government
of forest lands as authorized by the said Act. The function
of this Commission is more accurately defined in sec. 8 of
the Act of 7 June 1924 (43 Stat. 653,655), which provides
that all national-forest land purchases are to be initiated
by the Secretary of Agriculture after examination by him in
cooperation with the Geological Survey of the Department of
the Interior. Under sec. 6 of the same Act, (43 Stat. 654),
the said Commission also passes upon the inclusion of public-
domain lands in the national forests, upon determination of
the Secretary of Agriculture as to the appropriateness of such
inclusion.

Another statutory inter-agency body is the Migratory Bird
Conservation Commission, created by sec. 2 of the Migratory
Bird Treaty Act of 18 February 1929 (45 Stat. 1222).[123] Composed of the Secretary of the Interior, as chairman, the Secretaries of Commerce and Agriculture and two members each of
the Senate and the House of Representatives to be selected by
the President of the Senate and the Speaker of the House respectively, the Commission is authorized to consider and pass
upon any area of land, water, or land and water that may be
recommended by the Secretary of the Interior for the purchase
or rental as Federal migratory bird refuges, and to fix the
prices or rentals in each case.

These two Commissions are permanent bodies whose functions
are primarily of the nature of coordination. Ad-hoc inter-
agency bodies of a temporary nature may also be created by
statute. One such example may be given. In sec. 1 of the
Mississippi River Flood Control Act of 17 May 1928 (45 Stat.
534), provision was made for the creation of a special board
consisting of the Chief of Engineers of the U. S. Army, the
president of the Mississippi River Commission, and a civil engineer appointed from civil life by the President of the United States with Senate approval, whose duties it was to consider and conciliate the differences between the project plan
of the Mississippi River Commission in its report of 28 November 1927 (which was not adopted by the Congress) and that of
the Corps of Engineers as adopted by the said Act (for the control of floods of the Mississippi River). Recommendations of
this board were to be approved by the President, and were to
be conclusive when so approved.[124]

(b) Non-statutory Inter-Agency Bodies---On 29 December
1943, by an agreement between the Departments of the Army (then

War), the Interior, and Agriculture and the Federal Power Commission, the Federal Inter-Agency River Basin Committee was formed in order to facilitate the preparation of reports on multiple-purpose projects and programs. On 27 September 1946 and 27 July 1950, the Departments of Commerce and of Health, Education, and Welfare (then Federal Security Agency) respectively acceded to this agreement. The Committee met regularly each month, with its chairmanship rotating annually among its six member-agencies. An employee of the Bureau of Power of the Federal Power Commission served _ex-officio_ as its secretary.[125]

In December 1947, an additional agreement was adopted by the various member agencies specifying the procedure of coordination to be followed by the Committee in preparing and submitting their reports to the Congress. Such coordination, however, was to be achieved outside of the Committee. For the study of special subjects, the Subcommittees on Benefits and Costs, Hydrology and Sedimentation, and Energy-Conversion Procedures were established; and ad-hoc sub-committees were set up from time to time to consider problems of temporary nature.[126] There were also established the following regional committees:

(1) Missouri Basin Inter-Agency Committee, 29 March 1945.
(2) Columbia Basin Inter-Agency Committee, February 1946.
(3) Arkansas-White-Red Basins Inter-Agency Committee, June 1950.
(4) New England-New York Inter-Agency Committee, 27 October 1950.

Each of these committees was composed of one member from each of the six member agencies of the mother Committee.[127] The Missouri Basin and the Columbia Basin Committees annually elected a chairman from among their respective memberships; but the chairmanships of the other two committees were held by the Department of the Army. The cooperation of the states with each of these regional committees was secured by the participation of the Governors of all the states concerned without vote.[128] Each regional committee met about once a month, at different places in the basin.

Besides these four regional committees, there was a Pacific Southwest Federal Inter-Agency Technical Committee, which was set up in July 1948 for the exchange and coordination of technical data among the several Federal agencies in the Colorado River Basin, the Great Basin and in southern California. Its chairmanship rotated annually among its members; but it had no state representatives. It met at least once every two months, at locations designated by the chairman.[129]

On 26 March 1954, the President approved an agreement between the Departments of the Interior, Agriculture, Commerce,

Health, Education and Welfare and the Army and the Federal
Power Commission abolishing the Federal Inter-Agency River
Basin Committee and in its place establishing the Inter-Agency
Committee on Water Resources.130 This Committee is composed
of the six signatory agencies as full members and the Department of Labor as an associate member. Each member agencies
is represented by a "principal policy official", that is,
the Secretary, Under-secretary or an assistant secretary, or,
with respect to the Department of the Army, the Chief of Engineers, or, with respect to the Federal Power Commission,
its chairman or a member. The chairmanship rotates annually
among the member agencies. It meets at least once every two
months. Where necessary, other Federal agencies may be requested to participate in the Committee meetings. It maintains a staff, consisting of a secretary, to be provided by
the chairman agency, and a principal staff assistant to be
detailed by each of the other member agencies. In general
terms, the responsibility of the Committee is "to establish
means and procedures to promote coordination of the water and
related land resources activities of the member agencies; to
undertake resolution of inter-agency differences to the extent
possible under existing law and administration policy; and to
suggest to the President changes in existing law or administration policy which would promote coordination and eliminate
or reduce inter-agency differences." It may be noted that
the functions of the former Inter-Agency River Basin Committee
were primarily connected with the preparation of multiple-purpose river-basin development programs. As these programs had
by 1954 already been completed or well advanced toward completion, the duties of the new Committee on Water Resources would
be to facilitate the execution of these programs. The agreement also provides for the reconstitution of the above mentioned regional committees of the former Inter-Agency River
Basin Committee and for the revision of their "charters".

Another inter-departmental body similar in character to
the Inter-Agency Committee on Water Resources is the Federal
Inter-Agency Committee on Recreation. It was organized in
the fall of 1946, and consists of the following member-agencies: Corps of Engineers of the Department of the Army; the
National Park Service, the Fish and Wildlife Service, the Bureau of Reclamation and the Bureau of Land Management of the
Department of the Interior; the Extension Service and the For-
est Service of the Department of Agriculture; and the Office
of Education and the Children's Bureau of the Federal Security
Agency (now the Department of Health, Education, and Welfare).[131]
The Committee coordinates the work of its member agencies in
the field of recreation. "The Committee meets monthly and
Sub-Committees have been set up to work on special projects.
Since its inception, the Committee has had the services of an
Executive Secretary and office assistance."132

The device of the inter-agency committee has been adopted
by the Departments of Agriculture and the Interior in securing

coordination in the field among their subordinate agencies having a share in Federal water resources administration. As a matter of fact, this was motivated by the necessity of assuring departmental cohesion at the meetings of the various river-basin branches of the Federal Inter-Agency River Basin Committee. The Field Committees of the Department of the Interior will be discussed first. "On May 31, 1946, by order of the Secretary of the Interior, the Interior Missouri Basin Field Committee was established. Its purpose as described in the order was to achieve successful coordination of the Department's program for the development of the land and water resources of the Missouri River Basin and to facilitate cooperation with appropriate Federal agencies and with State and public agencies. The Committee is composed of one representative from the Geological Survey, Fish and Wildlife Service, National Park Service, Bureau of Indian Affairs, Bureau of Mines, Bureau of Land Management, and two representatives from the Bureau of Reclamation. The Chairman of the Interior Missouri Basin Field Committee was designated as Interior's representative on the Missouri Basin Inter-Agency Committee."[133] On 17 July of the same year, the creation of the Portland Temporary Field Committee was directed by the Secretary of the Interior, consisting of Bonneville Power Administrator as chairman and one representative each of the Fish and Wildlife Service, Bureau of Land Management, Office of Indian Affairs, National Park Service, Bureau of Reclamation, Geological Survey and Bureau of Mines, which served to coordinate the activities of the various member agencies in the Pacific Northwest.[134] By Departmental Order No. 2257 dated 26 September 1946, this temporary committee was replaced by a Pacific Northwest Coordination Committee with the same membership, which functioned "with respect to the States of Washington, Oregon, and Idaho, in connection with the water, power, and mineral programs in the area of Montana west of the Continental Divide." The Committee elected its own chairman. "In order to implement its program and to provide continuity in its operations, the committee shall have a small permanent full-time staff headed by an Executive Director."[135] In July 1948, the Alaska Field Staff and the Alaska Field Committee were established, the director of the former being _ex-officio_ chairman of the latter. This Committee was made up of the heads of the regional offices of the Department's subordinate agencies operating in the Territory of Alaska.[136]

The establishment of these more or less temporary regional coordination bodies having proved somewhat successful, the Departmental Order No. 2465 was issued on 25 August 1948 which divided the whole country into seven "Field Committee Regions" entitled respectively as Alaska (Region 1), Pacific Northwest (Region 2), Pacific Central (Region 3), Colorado River-Great Basin (Region 4), Missouri River Basin (Region 5), Southwest (Region 6) and Eastern (Region 7). Each Field Committee was to be composed of "(a) a chairman who shall be selected by and represent the Secretary of the Interior", (b) a member from

each agency of the Department which engages in field operations in the region", and "(c) a full-time staff . . ."   "For
each of these agencies which has a field official with full
administrative authority over all functions of his agency in
all of, or a greater part of the area, such official shall
be the committee member representing that agency. Each such
member also may designate an alternate. The head of each
agency not so organized administratively shall designate the
field officials to serve as member and alternate on the committee."   Among their various coordination activities, the
Field Committees assisted and advised the Department "in the
preparation of annual appropriation estimates and annual allocations of funds in order to achieve a balanced program
for the Department as a whole in the region."

The chairman of each Field Committee was in a sense the
executive officer of the committee. The committee, through
the chairman, reported to the Secretary of the Interior
through the Director of the Program Staff or through the
Chairman of the Program Committee with respect to program
recommendations. "On matters of common departmental interest
in the region . . . he shall represent the Department as a
whole in relationships with other Federal agencies, state and
local agencies, and other public and private groups or persons."   In fact, the very raison d'etre of the Field Committee seemed to be the substantiation of the representativeness
of their chairmen, who served as the representatives of the
Department of the Interior in the corresponding regional
branches of the Federal Inter-Agency River Basin Committees.
The Field Committees met generally once a month at times and
places to be designated by the chairman.[137]

The Order prescribed that the Alaska and the Missouri River Basin Field Committees (which were established prior to
the issuance of this Order) should begin to function immediately, that the Pacific Northwest Field Committee (which was
to replace the Pacific Northwest Coordination Committee) should
begin to function on 1 October 1948, and that the Southwest
Field Committee should be established on 1 October 1948. The
dates for the establishment of other Field Committees were
to be designated by the Secretary of the Interior. "The Colorado River-Great Basin Field Committee began operations .
. . in August 1950, but it never had an independent Chairman
and staff. . ."[138] The Pacific Central Field Committee was
set up in about October 1948 with similar status.[139] "The
Eastern Field Committee began operations in November 1949,
with a chairman appointed from the Department's Program Staff.
It functioned until October 1950, when it became inactive."
When the New England-New York Inter-Agency Committee was organized in October 1950, "the Department appointed a special
representative to this Committee with offices in Boston, Massachusetts, and established a small Northeast Field Staff to
assist him. This representative acted as Chairman of an in-

formal committee of representatives of the four Interior De-
partment bureaus operating in the region (Geological Survey,
Bureau of Mines, National Park Service, and Fish and Wildlife
Service)."[138]

There were some deviations from the terms of the order of
25 August 1948. For example, the Missouri River Basin Field
Committee continued to be, as it was before, financed by the
Bureau of Reclamation instead of by the Office of the Secretary.[138] The Colorado River-Great Basin Field Committee was
composed of two representatives each from the Bureau of Reclamation, the Fish and Wildlife Service and the Bureau of Indian Affairs and one representative each from the Bureau of
Land Management, the Bureau of Mines, the Geological Survey
and the National Park Service.[140] The temporary nature of
this and the Pacific Central Field Committees was also outside of the provisions of the order.

It should be noted that "by memorandum dated May 6, 1953
signed by Under Secretary of the Interior, . . . all of the
Field Committees as established under Order 2465 (of 25 August 1948) were abolished."[141] However, "field committees
which operate in the major river basins will be reconstituted
with the designation of operating field representatives of
bureaus, generally within the same geographic areas as existing committees." "For the eastern United States a field
staff was also stationed at Boston assigned to study New England resource problems."[142] Thus the institution of the Field
Committees has been continued, although the instrument which
founded it is no longer in force.

On 2 June 1953, the following changes in the chairman-
ships of the Field Committees and the representatives of the
Department of the Interior in the Inter-Agency River Basin
Committees:[143]

Chairman of Field Committees:

    Alaska---Governor of Alaska
    Pacific Northwest---Regional representative of the Geolo-
        gical Survey at Portland, Oregon.
    Pacific Southwest---Regional director of the Bureau of
        Reclamation at Salt Lake City, Utah.
    Missouri River Basin---Field representative of the Secre-
        tary of the Interior.
    Southwest---Regional director of the Bureau of Mines at
        Amarillo, Texas.

Representatives of the Department in River Basin Committees:

    Columbia River Basin---Regional director of the Bureau of
        Reclamation at Boise, Idaho. (Besides, the Bonne-
        ville Power Administrator, representing, however,

not the Department but the Bonneville Power Admin-
istration)
Missouri River Basin---Chairman of the Department Field
Committee.
Arkansas-White-Red River Basins---Chairman of the Depart-
ment Field Committee.
Pacific Southwest Inter-Agency Technical Committee---Re-
gional director of the Bureau of Reclamation at
Boise, Idaho.
New England-New York---Regional director of the Fish and
Wildlife Service at Boston, Massachusetts.

From the above list, it may be noted that of all Field Committee chairmanships, only that of Missouri River Basin was a
special representative of the Secretary of the Interior. Of
the representatives in the Federal Inter-Agency River Basin
Committees, only those for the Missouri River Basin and the
Arkansas-White-Red River Basin Area were chairmen of the corresponding Field Committees.[144] "The offices of the new
Field Committees and departmental representatives on inter-
agency committees received no financing from the Office of
the Secretary, although the Arkansas-White-Red Office and
Northeast Staff continue to receive some financing from this
source."[145]

Within each Field Committee, sub-committees are as a rule
established to expedite the work of the Committee. For example, the Pacific Northwest Field Committees has sub-committees
on (1) basic data, (2) land, (3) water and energy, (4) minerals, (5) fish and wildlife, (6) recreation, (7) industrial
and economic development, (8) program review and (9) service
study, each of which are composed entirely of the Committee
members.[146] The program review sub-committee met once or
twice a year to review the Committee's reports; but other
sub-committees usually met about three times a year.[147] Within the Colorado River-Great Basin Field Committee, there were
the sub-committee on topographic mapping, the Lower Colorado
River Land Use Committee, and the Interior Little Colorado
River Conservation Committee, which were established in June
1950, September 1950 and April 1952, respectively. All these
sub-committees were made up of member agencies of the mother
Field Committee, except that in the Lower Colorado River Land
Use Committee there were representatives of the fish and game
agencies of the States of California, Nevada and Arizona.[148]

It has been reported that the chairmen of the various
Field Committees meet when necessary to discuss problems of
mutual interest, and that "joint meetings of full Field Committees are often arranged."[149] It is not clear whether this
has become an established practice.

At first, the various Field Committees were coordinated
by the Program Staff. By Order No. 2421 of the Secretary,

dated 14 April 1948, a Program Committee was set up in the
Office of the Secretary, with the Director of the Program
Staff as its chairmen and with the heads of the following subordinate agencies, most dealing directly with land and water
resources administration, as members: Bureau of Reclamation,
Bureau of Indian Affairs, Geological Survey, Bureau of Mines,
National Park Service, Fish and Wildlife Service, Bureau of
Land Management, Bonneville Power Administration, Southwestern Power Administration and the Division of Budget and Administrative Management. "Directors of other staff offices
of the Secretary are ex-officio members of the Program Staff,
was the sole channel through which the Secretary of the Interior and the various Field Committees communicated with
each other. It may be said that by this Order, the Program
Committee, acting through its Chairman, was the body which
coordinated the various Field Committees.[150] The Program
Committee has not as yet been formally abolished; "but its
activities lapsed at the time the Program Staff was abolished
and the Technical Review Staff was established."[151] It is apparent that the Technical Review Staff has taken the place of
the Program Committee in coordinating the various regional
Field Committees.

Inter-agencies committees were also used by the Department of Agriculture to achieve coordination among its various
subordinate agencies in the field. Memorandum No. 1176 of 17
October 1946, which established the first Field Representative of the Department of Agriculture, that for the Missouri
River Basin, permitted the organization of an advisory committee to the Field Representative, to be composed of the
heads of the field units of the agencies which the Field Representative was authorized to coordinate. This advisory committee was set up as so permitted. On 9 July 1948, Memorandum No. 1220 was issued which established a Departmental Working Group consisting of representatives of the above-mentioned field units, and a representative of the Field Representative as its chairman. This Group replaced the advisory committee, and was formally charged with the function of assisting in preparing a multiple-purpose agricultural plan for the
Missouri River Basin. By Memorandum No. 1248 of 12 January
1950, this body was transformed into the Field Committee for
the Missouri River Basin. This was the first Field Committee
of the Department of Agriculture. It was followed by the establishment of the following Field Committees:

   Field Committee for the Columbia River Basin---Memoran-
         dum No. 1257 of 9 May 1950
   Field Committee for the Arkansas, White, and Red River
         Basins---Memorandum No. 1261 of 17 July 1950
   Field Committee for the New England-New York Region---
         Memorandum No. 1297 of 14 June 1951

The functions of all the four Field Committees were the same:

the preparation of a basin-wide multiple-purpose agricultural development plan. Each Field Committee was chaired by the respective Field Representative of the Secretary of Agriculture, and included as its members a representative from each of these nine agencies, -- Agricultural Research Administration, Bureau of Agricultural Economics, Farm Credit Administration, Farmers Home Administration, Forest Service, Production and Marketing Administration, Rural Electrification Administration, Soil Conservation Service, and Agricultural Extension Service. Since the Field Committees were primarily concerned with the preparation of a river-basin agricultural plan, they would cease to exist when such plans were completed. In fact, with respect to the Field Committees for the Arkansas, White and Red River Basins and the New England-New York Region, it was expressly provided that "the Committee will be continued in existence throughout the period of development of a Comprehensive Agricultural Plan and as long thereafter as the Secretary deems advisable." It is this temporary nature of the Field Committees of the Department of Agriculture that distinguished them from their counterparts of the Department of the Interior.

Memorandum No. 1315 of 23 July 1952 called for the preparation of a comprehensive agricultural plan for the Cumberland River Basin by the Secretary's Field Representative for this region with the assistance of "responsible Department agency people in the area or their designated representatives." A Field Committee was not provided for. The same arrangement prevailed in the Pacific Southwest Region.[152]

As mentioned before, the various Field Representatives of the Secretary of Agriculture were abolished on 1 April 1953, when the Soil Conservation Service was made the Department's representative in all matters on soil conservation and flood control. With this, the various Field Committees were automatically deactivated.[153]

During the Second World War, "war boards" were set up in each state and each county to provide inter-agency coordination at the state and county levels. By Memorandum No. 1132 of 26 October 1945, these war boards were transformed into State and County U. S. D. A. Councils (U. S. D. A. being abbreviation for United States Department of Agriculture). They were composed principally of the heads of state or county offices of the various subordinate agencies of the Department of Agriculture,[154] and their sole function and responsibility was "to help the agencies of the Department to coordinate their respective activities." But on 22 December 1953 (Memorandum 1343), these state and county U. S. A. councils were abolished.[155]

To solve problems of mutual interest to two or more agencies, ad-hoc inter-agency bodies may be set up from time to time. For example, in the fiscal year 1939, an Inter-Departmental Committee was established jointly by the Department of the Interior and the Department of Agriculture which was made up of two members from each Department, -- one representative of the Secretary of the Interior, one representative of the Secretary of Agriculture, one representative of the National Park Service and one representative of the Forest Service. "Through this interdepartmental committee agreement was reached during the year with respect to reports made to the Congress by the Bureau of the Budget on more than 30 separate legislative proposals. Agreement was also reached on proposals to transfer certain national-forest areas to (1) the Rocky Mountain National Park in Colorado and (2) the Glacier Bay National Monument in Alaska."[156] In the next fiscal year, "the Interdepartmental Committee considered a number of proposals involving transfer of jurisdiction of certain lands between the Departments of Agriculture and (the) Interior and various other interdepartmental matters. Many were disposed of satisfactorily. In other instances arrangements were made for joint studies."[157] On 15 August 1935, the President requested the Secretary of War, the Secretary of the Interior and the chairman of the Federal Power Commission each to name a representative to constitute a special board to investigate the feasibility of the construction of the Clark Hill Dam project on the Savannah River. The report of this special board, which favored the construction of this project, was submitted to the President through their superiors on 29 February 1936[158] and was adopted by the Congress in the Flood Control Act of 28 June 1938 (52 Stat. 1215, 1217).

(2) Eccentric Coordination: Advisory Boards or Councils---The Advisory Board of the Bonneville Power Administration is a typical example. Its creation was authorized by the Bonneville Project Act of 20 August 1937, which provides (in sec. 2) that the Bonneville Power Administrator "shall act in consultation with an advisory board composed of a representative designated by the Secretary of War (the Army), a representative designated by the Secretary of the Interior, a representative designated by the Federal Power Commission, and a representative designated by the Secretary of Agriculture" (50 Stat. 731, 732). "In accordance with these provisions, the Bonneville Advisory Board was established and held its first meeting in Washington (D. C.) on August 18, 1939. The Board met periodically, usually in Washington (D. C.), in response to a summons by the BPA administrator. There was one meeting in 1939, one in 1940, one in 1942, three in 1943, one in 1945 and two in 1946. The last meeting was on September 24-25, 1946. The Board dealt with Pacific Northwest power problems as they related to the problems of the other government agencies represented. In March 1946, membership of the BAB (Bonneville Advisory Board) was changed from Washington, D. C. officials to regional officials of the agencies named in the Bonneville Act. The War Department designated the

Division Engineer (of the Portland District) (at Portland);[159]
the Department of the Interior the regional director of the
Bureau of Reclamation; the FPC (Federal Power Commission) the
regional director (i.e., the regional engineer), San Francisco; the Department of Agriculture a representative of the
Office of the Secretary in Portland. After the Columbia Basin Interagency Committee (CBIAC) was created in February,
1946, consisting of the same federal officials as were on the
Advisory Board (with the addition of the governors of the
seven Northwest states or their representatives), agreement
was reached that the BPA administrator would take up with the
CBIAC such matters as he wished to discuss with them as an
advisory board. The Administrator has each year reminded the
Federal CBIAC members that they were doubling as BAB members
and that he purposely makes his monthly report to the CBIAC
as complete as possible in order to keep them fully informed
on BPA matters. There have been no separate meetings of the
BAB since 1946, and the Board in effect has been merged with
the CBIAC."[160]

In the Public Works Administration, there was a Special
Board for Public Works consisting of the Secretary of the Interior (chairman), the Secretary of War, the Attorney General,
the Secretary of Agriculture, the Secretary of Commerce, the
Secretary of Labor, the Director of the Budget, a representative of the Department of Treasury and a representative of
the Public Works Administration itself. This Board had the
following functions: "(a) To advise the President upon all
major matters of policy arising in connection with the administration and interpretation of those portions of the National
Industrial Recovery Act that relate to public works; (b) to
advise and confer with the Administrator on major appointments
in the Public Works Administration; and (c) to pass upon all
recommendations for allotments to applicants of Public Works
funds, either as loans or grants. The actual allotments are
made by the President of the United States upon the recommendation of the Special Board . . ."[161] The Civilian Conservation Corps had an Advisory Council, although in the last years
of the Corps this body was often bypassed on important policy
matters.[162]

These advisory bodies advise on policy matters. There is
another category of advisory bodies which merely deal with
technical matters. An example of this type of advisory bodies
was the Board of Consultants on Malaria of the Tennessee Valley Authority, which was established by the said Authority in
February 1935. The original membership of the Board consisted
of three representatives of the U. S. Public Health Service,
a representative of the Bureau of Entomology and Plant Quarantine of the Department of Agriculture, and a representative of
the Rockfeller Foundation (private). In 1938, a representative each of the Department of Entomology of Cornell University
(in private capacity), the U. S. Department of Navy and the

State Health Department of Alabama were added. The next year
a representative of the Department of the Army and an additional representative of the U. S. Public Health Service were
added. The Board gave advice to the Tennessee Valley Authority with regard to the planning and review of mosquito-control operations. "Annual conference with the Board were held
each year through 1940." The Board has not since been activated.[163] It should be noted that the Board was primarily a
Federal inter-agency coordination body in so far as the Tennessee Valley Authority, the Bureau of Entomology and Plant
Quarantine and the U. S. Public Health Service were concerned.

In the administration of the Agricultural Conservation
Program of the Department of Agriculture at the state level,
there is in each state a State Technical Committee. It is
composed of local representatives of agricultural agencies
and groups concerned, including the Forest Service and the
Soil Conservation Service. It makes recommendations to the
State Committee of the Department of Agriculture as to the
conservation practices to be authorized each year. The state
technical committees were originally established by the Agricultural Adjustment Agency in May 1944, and have been continued without material changes.[164]

(B) Informal Coordination

One type of informal coordination is the union of personnel. As discussed before, the president of the Mississippi
River Commission is at the same time the division engineer
of the Lower Mississippi Valley Division, Corps of Engineers;
and the three district engineers of the said Commission are
simultaneously the three district engineers of the said Division. The Public Works Administration was established by the
President on 16 June 1933. On 8 July 1933 the Secretary of
the Interior was appointed the Federal Emergency Administration
of Public Works.[165] At one time, officers of the Public
Health Service and the Indian Office were appointed as superintendents of national parks.

Conference or discussions between the agencies concerned
provide another form of informal coordination. In the agreement between the Chief of Engineers, U. S. Corps of Engineers,
the Commissioner of the Bureau of Reclamation, the Land Use
Coordinator of the Department of Agriculture and the chairman
of the Federal Power Commission signed 29 December 1943 with
regard to the preparation of reports on multiple-purpose dam
projects, conferences between these officers and between their
local agents constitute the principal method in achieving the
necessary coordination between them. In the fiscal year 1951,
conferences were held between the Soil Conservation Service
and the Fish and Wildlife Service on the management of marshes
in soil conservation districts.[166] There were discussions between the district engineer of the Corps of Engineers at Omaha,

Nebraska, and the regional representatives of the Bureau of Reclamation on the proposed plan of improvement for the Elkhorn River Basin, when such plan was in preparation by the said district engineer.[167]

As was already discussed before, the Act of 1 March 1917 provided for the examinations and surveys of watersheds of rivers and streams in connection with the prevention of floods. It was expressly provided in this Act that "the heads of the several departments of the Government may, in their discretion, and shall upon the request of the Secretary of War, detail representatives from their respective departments to assist the Engineers of the Army in the study and examination of such watersheds, to the end that duplication of work may be avoided and the various services of the Government economically coordinated therein . . ." (39 Stat. 948, 950). This is certainly an important form of informal coordination. In Memorandum No. 1278 of 15 February 1951 of the Secretary of Agriculture, it was provided, among other things, that the personnel of the Soil Conservation Service and those of the then Production and Marketing Administration (with special to Agricultural Conservation Branch), in each state and each county should be housed in the same office building. This measure, like other measures adopted in that Memorandum, was directed at "the unified and coordinated leadership, service and action needed to meet to the fullest possible extent Department of Agriculture responsibilities regarding soil, water, range, and forest conservation." But conferences between the personnel of these two agencies at both state and county levels were also provided for in that instrument. It is doubtless that such conferences will be greatly facilitated if the conferees are in the same office building.

Article 2   State Organization[168]

Section 1   State Uncoordinated Organization[169]

(1) Regulatory Water Agencies

(a) Water-use agencies---In the Western states of Oklahoma and Washington and the Eastern states of Minnesota, New Jersey, New York, North Carolina and Pennsylvania, the state agency in charge of the regulation of water use or water rights is the department of conservation[170] and in Wisconsin it is the public service commission. These two agencies will be discussed later. The water-agencies of other states which have them (all Western) may be distinguished as follows:[171]

(A) Specialized Agencies (that is, agencies whose sole or primary function is the regulation of water use)
        1. Single-headed (a state engineer)
              (a) Independent state engineers-Colorado;
                   Idaho (state reclamation engineer); Nebras-

ka (state engineer being head of the Department of Roads and Irrigation, and his
functions regarding water-use regulation
being delegated to the chief of the Bureau of Irrigation); Nevada; South Dakota;
Utah.

(b) Affiliated state engineers
North Dakota (the state engineer being
appointed by the state water conservation
commission which itself has no authority
over water-use regulation);
Oregon (the state engineer being appointed
by the governor with the approval of the
state reclamation commission, which commission has no statutory authority to regulate water use).

(c) Mixed type---Montana (where the state engineer is appointed by the governor with
senate confirmation and has independent
authority over water-use regulation; but
he is subject to the supervision and control of the state board of land commissioners and the Carey land act board with respect to the state enterprise -- not activated -- of irrigation).

2. Plural-headed---Texas (Board of Water Engineers)

3. Mixed type ---Wyoming (State Engineer with
State Board of Control---the former issues water-use permits and supervises actual distribution of water; the latter adjudicates water
rights and hears appeals from orders of the
former) (The state engineer is the president
of the Board of Control).

(B) A unit in other state departments

1. Arizona (state land department)

2. California (division of water resources, headed
by the state engineer, of the department of
public works)

3. Kansas (division of water resources, headed by
a chief engineer, of the state board of agriculture).

The appointment of the State Engineer in North Dakota,
Oregon and Montana is already mentioned above. In Colorado,
Idaho and Nevada, this officer is appointed by the Governor;
in New Mexico, South Dakota, Utah and Wyoming, by the Governor
with the consent of the Senate; and in Nebraska, by the Governor subject to the confirmation of the unicameral state legislature.   The term of office is two years in Colorado and
New Mexico; four years in Montana, Nevada, Oregon, South Dakota and Utah; six years in Idaho and Wyoming; and coterminous
with the term of office of the Governor in Nebraska.   The

State Engineer of North Dakota serves for a term to be determined by the Conservation Commission. The Board of Water Engineers of Texas consists of three members appointed by the
Governor with the consent of the Senate from the three water
divisions of the state for terms of six years. The Governor
designates one of the members as its chairman, who is also
its chief administrative officer. It employs a chief engineer, a secretary and other necessary personnel. The Board
of Control of Wyoming is composed of the State Engineer as
president and the superintendents of the four water divisions
of the state who are appointed by the Governor with the consent of the Senate for terms of four years (Compiled Statutes,
Sec. 71-102: Laws 1890-91, ch. 8, sec. 13; as last amended by
L. 1941, ch. 118, sec. 1).

The State Engineers in all these states except Colorado
and Nebraska and the Water Engineers of the state of Texas
are statutorily required to be experienced and competent engineers. The same requirement must have been implied in the
laws of Colorado and Nebraska. The authority to appoint administrative assistants is conferred on the State Engineers
of Colorado (a Deputy State Engineer and deputies), Nevada
(Assistant State Engineer, Deputy State Engineer, etc.), New
Mexico, Oregon, South Dakota, Utah (chief deputy, etc.) and
Wyoming (Deputy State Engineer and first and second Assistant
Engineers).[172] Administrative assistants of the State Engineer of Nebraska are appointed by the Governor.

In Arizona, the State Land Commissioner is the officer
in charge of water-use regulation. The State Engineer of California, who heads the Division of Water Resources of the Department of Public Works, is appointed by the Director of Public Works. Both the chief engineer and other officers of the
Division of Water Resources of the Kansas State Board of Agriculture are employed by the said Board.[173]

In the various Western states, the distribution of water
among the approved water users is usually under the supervision of water commissioners or water masters, each of whom
is in charge of a certain area, watercourse, or ditch. In
Arizona the water commissioners and in Idaho the water masters are appointed by the courts (in Idaho, upon petition by
the water users concerned).[174] No provision is made of the
appointment of such officers in Kansas and Montana, but it
would seem that the courts can always appoint them in properly instituted proceedings. Court-appointed water commissioners or masters are necessarily temporary officers. In Texas,
the state is divided into three water divisions[175] but it is
not clear whether they are established for the purpose of appointing the members of the Board of Water Engineers or for
both this purpose and water distribution. In the remaining
Western states, the statutes provide for the administrative
appointment of regular water commissioners or water masters
to be in charge of the several water districts of the state.[176]

The water districts are established by statute in Colorado. In Wyoming, they are established by the Board of Control. In California, Nebraska, Nevada, New Mexico, Oregon, and Washington,[177] it is the State Engineer who divides the state into a number of water districts. Each water district generally represents the drainage basin of a watercourse or a part thereof or the drainage basins of a number of watercourses. Water commissioners or water masters are appointed by the State Engineer upon the request of water users concerned in California, New Mexico and Washington; by the State Engineer in his own initiative in Nebraska, Oregon, South Dakota and Utah; by the Governor in Colorado (upon the recommendation of the county authorities concerned), Nevada (upon the recommendation of the State Engineer) and Wyoming (upon the recommendation of the superintendent of the water division and with the approval of the county authorities concerned). For each water district, there may be one or more water commissioners or water masters. In case there is only one such officer, there may be one or more deputies working on a temporary basis. In all cases, the salaries and expenses of the water commissioners and water masters and their deputies, however appointed, are paid by the water users concerned.

In Colorado, Nebraska and Wyoming, there are, above the water districts, water divisions (called "irrigation divisions" in Colorado), the purpose of which is to coordinate the work of the various water districts. There is a division engineer for each irrigation division in Colorado, who is appointed by the State Engineer or the Governor as the law may provide in each particular case. The state of Nebraska is divided into two water divisions, headed by division engineers appointed by the State Engineer. There are four water divisions in Wyoming, each under the jurisdiction of a superintendent as mentioned before. The State Engineer, the division engineers or superintendents, and the water commissioners or water masters constitute a hierarchy in the distribution of water among persons having rights to the use of water.[178]

(b) <u>Agencies regulating the construction of dams and other water-utilization or control works</u>---As already mentioned before, the agency entrusted with the authority to regulate the construction of dams and reservoirs (for any purpose) is the water-use-regulation agency discussed above in California, Kansas, Colorado, Montana, Oregon, Utah and Washington (which, in Washington, is the "department of conservation"). In North Dakota, it is the Water Conservation Commission (<u>Revised Code</u>, sec. 61-0220), which will be discussed below. It is the Department of Public Works in California,[179] Massachusetts, New Jersey, New York and Rhode Island; the "department of conservation" in Kentucky, Minnesota and Ohio; and the "public service commission"[180] in Vermont, West Virginia and Wisconsin. The agency regulating the construction of dams in New Hampshire and Iowa are respectively the Water Resources Board and Natural

Resources council, which will be discussed below.[181]

Connecticut is the only state which has a special agency for the regulation of dams, dikes, reservoirs and similar structures. That agency is a state board (without an official designation) consisting of the Director of the State Water Commission as chairman and five members trained in engineering appointed by the Governor for terms of five years. The board annually elects a secretary and may employ necessary consultants and assistants (General Statutes, sec. 4728 et seq.: Acts 1878, ch. 131; as last amended in 1939).

As to agencies responsible for the regulation of works of a particular nature, the "department of conservation" regulates the construction of hydroelectric power works in New York and Pennsylvania, and the same function devolves upon the "public service commission" in New Hampshire, Virginia and Wisconsin. Oregon is the only state which has organized a special agency for this purpose. It is the Hydroelectric Commission, which is made up of the State Engineer ex-officio and two other members appointed by the Governor for indefinite terms. The Commission elects a chairman and a vice-chairman, and the State Engineer serves as its secretary ex officio (Laws 1931, ch. 67). The state regulatory agency in the field of flood control is the "department of conservation" in Washington (which is also the regulatory agency for water use), Iowa and Kentucky, the water-use regulatory agency in Kansas, and the public service commission in Wisconsin. New York seems to be the only state which regulates drainage, the agency in charge of which is the Department of Conservation. The regulation of water terminals is a function of the "department of conservation in Iowa, Minnesota, New Jersey and New York, of the "department of Public Works" in Illinois, Massachusetts and Rhode Island, and of the "public service commission" in Montana (officially designated as "Montana Railroad Commission).

The "department of conservation" and the "public service commission" will be discussed below. The "department of public works" will not be discussed, as it is not an agency primarily concerned with water-resources administration.

(2)   Water Enterprise Agencies

(a)   Water Terminals---The "department of public works"[182] constructs or acquires and operates and maintains water terminal facilities in Rhode Island (General Laws, ch. 112, secs. 28, 28 and 33: Acts 1910, ch. 568; 1912, ch. 810; 1915, ch. 1223, as amended 1925, ch. 574) (also Acts 1939, ch. 660, sec. 107), Illinois (Revised Statutes, sec. 19-146 et seq.: Act of 13 July 1933, as amended by act of 9 July 1939), Tennessee (Code, sec. 3260.1 et seq.: Acts 1935, ch. 36) and Massachusetts (General Laws, ch. 91, sec. 9A: Acts 1938, ch. 407, sec. 2). In Florida, this function is exercised by the "public

service commission" (officially known as the State Railroad
and Public Utilities Commission) (Laws 1915, ch. 6977, sec.
1). The same function is vested in Michigan in the State
Waterways Commission, which will be discussed below.

The following states have a special water-terminal agency:

> Connecticut---Commissioners of Steamship Terminals, five
> members appointed by the Governor with Senate con-
> sent for a six-year term. Their jurisdiction is
> limited to the city of New London and the towns of
> Waterford and Groton (General Statutes, ch. 243:
> Acts 1911, ch. 105; as amended in 1939).

> Delaware---Delaware Waterfront Commission, a bi-partisan
> commission of three members appointed by the Gov-
> ernor for six years, one member from each of the
> three counties of the state. The commission an-
> nually elects a chairman and a secretary (Code, tit.
> 23, sec. 301 et seq.: Laws 1927, ch. 65).

> Alabama---Department of State Docks and Terminals, headed
> by a Director, who is appointed by the Governor
> to serve during his pleasure, and who is assisted
> by an advisory board consisting of the Governor as
> chairman, the Director himself and three members
> appointed by the Governor for six years. The Di-
> rector may appoint a secretary-treasurer, archi-
> tects, engineers and other employees (Code, tit.
> 38, sec. 2: Acts 1939, No. 12). The Department
> superseded the State Docks Commission, which was
> created for the same function by sec. 93 of the
> State Constitution (adopted November 1922) and Acts
> 1923, No. 303, and which replaced the State Harbor
> Commission established by Acts 1915, No. 628 for
> harbor improvement.

> South Carolina, North Carolina and Virginia---State Ports
> Authority (corporate).

The South Carolina Ports Authority is governed by a board
of five members appointed by the Governor with Senate approval for seven years. It elects a chairman, a vice-chairman,
a treasurer, and a secretary (Code of Laws, secs. 54-1, to 54-
4, 54-11 and 54-14: 1942, No. 626, secs. 1-3). North Carolina State Ports Authority is managed by a board of seven members appointed by the Governor for four years. It elects a
chairman and a vice-chairman, and elects or employs a secretary and a treasurer. It appoints an executive director and
other necessary employees (General Statutes, sec. 143-216 et
seq.: Laws 1945, ch. 1097; as last amended by L. 1953, ch.
191). Virginia State Ports Authority was created by an act
of 1952 (Acts 1952, ch. 61), which abolished the Division of
Ports of the Department of Conservation and Development. It
is headed by a board of seven members appointed by the Governor

for six years. The board elects a chairman, a vice-chairman
and a secretary, and appoints a director of ports as its chief
executive officer.

The World Trade Corporation of New York may, among its
other functions, construct and operate piers and warehouses
and other terminal facilities on behalf municipalities which
sponsor the construction of such structures. The Corporation
was created in 1939 and was to be "in existence for five years
and thereafter until all of its liabilities have been discharged. Upon its ceasing to exist, all its rights and properties shall pass to the sponsor" (Laws 1939, ch. 870; as
amended by L. 1947, ch. 738).

In each of the following ports, there is a state agency
which administers all state-owned terminal facilities located
therein:

> San Francisco, California---Board of State Harbor Commis-
>   sioners consisting of three commissioners appointed
>   by the Governor for four years. The board elects
>   a president and a secretary, and appoints a port
>   manager, a secretary, an administrative assistant
>   and other employees. The Governor and the mayor
>   of the City and County of San Francisco serve as
>   additional ex-officio members of the board for cer-
>   tain special purposes (Harbors and Navigation Code,
>   sec. 1700 et seq.: Stats. 1875, ch. 104, as amend-
>   ed).
> San Diego, California---Board of State Harbor Commission-
>   ers, consisting of three commissioners appointed
>   by the Governor for four years, with the Governor
>   and the mayors of San Diego and National City as
>   additional ex-officio members. The board elects
>   president, secretary and assistant secretary (ibid.,
>   sec. 3500 et seq.: Stats. 1889, ch. 211; as last
>   amended by Stats. 1937, ch. 373).
> Humbolt Bay (Eureka), California---Board of State Harbor
>   Commissioners, consisting of three members appoint-
>   ed by the Governor with Senate consent for four
>   years. The Governor designates one members as sur-
>   veyor of the port and secretary of the board (ibid.,
>   sec. 3800 et seq.: Stats. 1945, ch. 179). Before
>   1945, the port of Eureka was directly administered
>   by the State Department of Public Works (Stats.
>   1927, ch. 516, as amended).
> Boston, Massachusetts---The Port of Boston Authority, con-
>   sisting of a bi-partisan board of five members ap-
>   pointed by the Governor with the consent of the
>   Council for five years. Not more than two members
>   shall be residents of the city of Boston. The Gov-
>   ernor designates one member as chairman. The Auth-
>   ority may appoint a director and necessary experts,

counsel, clerks, engineers, assistants and employees. With the approval of the Governor and the
Council, the Authority may ask the state Treasurer
to issue bonds to finance its projects (Acts 1945,
ch. 619: General Laws, chs. 6 and 91A). The Port
of Boston Authority is the successor of the former
Boston Port Authority, which was created by Acts
of 1929, ch. 229, to replace the Board of Directors
of the Port of Boston, created by Acts of 1911,
ch. 748.

Portland, Maine---Port of Portland Authority (corporate),
governed by a board of four directors appointed by
the Governor with the consent of the Council for
four years and one director appointed by the city
council of the city of Portland. The board elects
a president and a treasurer and may select other
officers (Laws 1919, chs. 84 and 123; as last amended by L. 1947, ch. 99).

(b) The "Department of Conservation"---This department is
capable of undertaking, at least potentially, a variety of
projects in a number of states, as will be discussed later.

(c) Agencies in charge of one enterprise---The State Engineer of Montana with the approval of the State Land Board,
may initiate irrigation projects (Revised Codes, sec. 81-2007,
op. cit.). In Colorado, the State Board of Land Commissioners
has the authority to improve and irrigate state-owned lands
(Statutes, ch. 134, sec. 92: Laws 1913, ch. 160, sec. 1). The
State Engineer of South Dakota "shall have charge of irrigation
with the state by means of artesian wells, dams, reservoirs,
basins, or other methods. . . (and) recommend to the legislature . . . the enactment of such measures as he may deem necessary to perfect a system of irrigation" (Code, sec. 55-1912,
1st para., 1st sent.: Revised Code of 1919, sec. 8204). The
Division of Water Resources of the State Board of Agriculture
of Kansas is vested with the function to operate (by leasing
to private parties) state-owned irrigation works (General Statutes, sec. 74-506b, op. cit.; and Laws 1919, ch. 218).

The State Waterways Commission of Michigan may construct
and maintain not only water terminal facilities but all river
and harbor improvement works. It is made up of five members
appointed by the Governor with the consent of the Senate for
unspecified terms. It elects a chairman and a vice-chairman and
appoints a director, who is its administrative officer. The
director may employ necessary assistants with the approval of
commission (Acts 1947, No. 320). This is the only state agency specialized in navigation improvement. The Massachusetts
Department of Public Works, acting through its Division of
Waterways, also possesses the authority to undertake projects
of river and harbor improvement (General Laws, ch. 91, sec. 11:
Acts 1909, ch. 481, secs. 1, 2; as last amended by Acts 1950,

ch. 516). The said Division is under the management of a
director appointed by the Commissioner of Public Works with
the approval of the Governor (ibid., ch. 16, sec. 5A: Acts
1938, ch. 407, sec. 1; as amended by Acts 1946, ch. 591, sec.
20). The same authority is enjoyed by the Department of Public Works of Rhode Island (Acts 1939, ch. 660, sec. 107).

The State Land Board of Utah has been authorized to construct flood-control works (Code, sec. 65-1-75: Laws 1925,
ch. 37, sec. 1). But the Iowa Natural Resources Council is
the only special state agency for flood control administration in the United States. The Council is made up of seven
members appointed by the Governor with the approval of two-
thirds of the entire membership of the Senate for terms of
six years. It annually elects a chairman and is authorized
to employ a director on merit basis. The latter, with the
approval of the Council, may appoint necessary assistants and
technicians (Code, ch. 455A: Acts 1949, ch. 203). The jurisdiction of Council covers both enterprise and regulation.

The New York State Power Authority, the Arizona Power
Authority and the Washington State Power Commission are the
three special state agencies for hydroelectric enterprise
that now exist in the United States. The Arizona agency is
managed by a commission of five members qualified by administrative and business experience, who are appointed by the Governor with the approval of the Senate for terms of six years.
It biennially elects a chairman and vice-chairman, and is authorized to determine its own internal organization and administrative procedure (Code, ch. 75, art. 19: Laws 1944, 2nd
S. S., ch. 32). As a matter of fact, "the management and
direction of the Authority is under an Administrator, who reports directly to the Commission. Under the Administrator is
a staff of engineers, attorneys, accountants, secretaries,
clerks and stenographers to handle the business of the Authority in accordance with the policies established by the Commission."[183]

The Washington State Power Commission also consists of
five members, who are appointed by the Governor for a six-
year term, and of whom three are appointed from lists of nom-
inees submitted respectively by the public utility districts,
the city council of the city owning and operating the largest
electric generating facilities (Seattle) and city or cities
generating more than 250,000 kilowatts of electricity, and
two from the state at large. It elects a chairman. With the
approval of the Commission, any two or more cities or public
utility districts may form an "operating agency" of the Commission either in the generation or in the transmission of
electricity (Revised Code, ch. 43.52: Laws 1953, ch. 281).

As the Arizona and Washington agencies have jurisdiction
over the entire state, the New York Power Authority is in

charge of the development of the water-power of the Saint
Lawrence River System only. Its governing body consists of
five full-time trustees appointed by the Governor with the
consent of the Senate for terms of five years. It elects a
chairman and a vice-chairman, and employs necessary engineering, administrative, legal and clerical personnel (Public Authorities Law, art. 5, tit. 1: Laws 1931, ch. 772; as last
amended by L. 1954, ch. 311, sec. 20).

It may be noted that as the Washington and New York agencies are primarily concerned with the generation of electric
power, the Arizona agency emphasizes transmission of Federally
and locally generated electric power. All three power agencies are corporate in form, and have the authority to issue
revenue bonds.

(d) Multi-functional agencies other than the "Department
of Conservation"[184]---Included in this group are the "departments of public works" of Illinois and Louisiana. The Illinois Department of Public Works and Buildings was first given
authority to manage and control the Illinois and Michigan Canal (Revised Statutes, ch. 19, sec. 8: Act of 27 March 1874,
as last amended by act of 16 July 1941) and the Illinois Waterway (sec. 84: Laws 1919, p. 977, sec. 6). In 1939, it was authorized to have jurisdiction over all the rivers and lakes of
the state, and to improve them in the interests of the public
(ibid., secs. 52 and 63: Laws 1939, p. 308, secs. 5 and 15;
as amended by L. 1943, p. 259). Finally, in 1945, it obtained the authority to undertake flood-control projects (ibid.,
sec. 126b: Laws 1945, p. 376, sec. 2). The Louisiana Department of Public Works was created by an act of 1942 (No. 2),
to supersede the Louisiana Flood Control and Water Conservation
Commission and six other agencies. Among other functions, the
Department may construct, operate and maintain "levees, canals,
dams,[185] locks, spillways, reservoirs,[185] drainage systems,
irrigation systems, . . . (and) inland navigation projects,
flood control and river improvement programs." These functions, it may be noticed, originally belonged to the Louisiana Flood Control and Water Conservation Commission (Act No.
74 of 1936). By a number of special acts,[186] the Department
has also been authorized to construct water-manipulation works
for the protection and preservation of fish and wildlife.

Special multi-functional water agencies have been set up
in four states. They are:

Montana State Water Conservation Board---Irrigation, hydro-
    electric power, and water-supply for stock, domes-
    tic, industrial, fire-protection and other public
    purposes (Laws 1933, ch. 35; as amended by L. 1935,
    ch. 95).
New Hampshire Water Resources Board---Reservoirs, dams,
    diversion and distribution canals, lateral ditches,
    pumping units, mains, pipelines and water-works

systems (<u>Revised Laws</u>, ch. 266: Laws 1935, ch. 121;
as augmented by L. 1950, Sp. Sess., ch. 5, part
12, sec. 2).

North Dakota Water Conservation Commission---Water conservation, flood control, navigation improvement,
water pollution control, irrigation, recreation,
drainage, domestic and stock water supply, hydroelectric power development and wildlife conservation (<u>Revised Code</u>, sec. 61-0204 et seq.: 1937,
ch. 255; as last amended by L. 1949, ch. 344).

Utah Power and Power Board---Water conservation, hydroelectric power development, and possibly flood control, irrigation, and water supply (<u>Code</u>, sec. 73-
10-1 et seq.: Laws 1947, ch. 141; as amended by L.
1953, ch. 133).

All these agencies are public corporations and are thus enabled to make contracts, to dispose of their property and to sue
and be sued in their own names.

The Montana State Water Conservation Board is composed of
the Governor (chairman) and State Engineer <u>ex-officio</u>, and
three members appointed by the Governor for terms of six years.
The Board elects a vice-chairman, who also acts as its secretary and treasurer. The New Hampshire Water Resources Board
consists of five members appointed by the Governor with the
consent of the Council for terms of five years, one of whom
is desiganted as chairman. The Water Conservation Commission
of North Dakota includes the Governor as chairman, the Commissioner of Agriculture and Labor, and five members appointed
by the Governor for a six-year term. It elects a vice chairman and the State Engineer serves <u>ex-officio</u> as its secretary
and chief engineer. The Water and Power Board of Utah has a
membership of fifteen, including the <u>ex-officio</u> State Engineer,
of whom two (one from each party) are appointed by the president of the Senate, two (one from each party) by the speaker
of the House of Representatives, and ten (five from each party) by the Governor.[187] The Board elects a chairman and one
or more vice-chairmen and may appoint an executive secretary
and other engineering and administrative personnel.[188]

All of these four agencies have the financial power to
issue revenue bonds.

Special agencies organized for multiple-purpose state river-basin development enterprise, analogous to the Tennessee
Valley Authority of the Federal Government, have been found
in California and South Carolina, In California, there is the
State Water Project Authority, which is supposedly responsible for the construction and operation of the Central Valley
Project, which the state authorities have always thought should
be constructed and maintained and operated by the state instead of the Federal Government and which they have proposed
to purchase from the latter. It is composed of the Director

of Public Works (chairman), the Attorney General, the State
Controller, the State Treasurer, and the Director of Finance
as members, with the State Engineer as its executive officer
(Water Code, sec. 11100 et seq.: Stats. 1933, ch. 1042; as
amended by Stats. 1943, ch. 370). For the development of the
water resources of the basins of the Cooper, Santee and Congaree rivers, South Carolina has created the South Carolina
Public Service Authority. It is governed by a board of seven
directors appointed by the Governor, one from each congressional district and one from the state at large, who is the
chairman. All members serve for a term of seven years. The
Governor, the Attorney General, the State Treasurer, the Comptroller General and the Secretary of the State constitute ex-
officio an advisory board, through which the board of directors reports to the state legislature and which has the authority to remove a director from office for cause (Code of
Laws, sec. 59-1 et seq.: Acts 1934, No. 887; as amended by
Acts 1944, No. 517-B). Both these Authorities are public
corporations and may issue revenue bonds to raise necessary
capital funds.

(e) Agencies in charge of interstate streams---In New
Mexico and Arizona there are permanent state agencies which
are in charge of the waters of interstate streams.[189] Both
are entitled the "Interstate Stream Commission". The New Mexico Interstate Stream Commission is composed of the State Engineer, ex-officio, and six members appointed by the Governor
for terms of six years. It elects a chairman. It is authorized to make investigations and undertake projects leading to
the conservation and development of water resources of interstate streams and to represent the state in all suits and negotiations of interstate compacts regarding the rights of the
state to the waters of such streams (Statutes, sec. 77-3301 et
seq.: Laws 1935, ch. 25; as last amended by L. 1943, ch. 26).
The Arizona Interstate Stream Commission, which is corporate,
has the same organization and functions as its New Mexico pro-
totype, except that all of the seven members are appointed by
the Governor with the consent of the Senate and that a chairman and a vice-chairman are elected every two years (Code, sec.
75-2201 et seq.: Laws 1945, 1st S. S., ch. 4; as last amended
by L. 1948, 3rd S. S., ch. 4).

(3) Water Sanitation Agencies (Pollution Control Only)[190]
---The "State Health Department" (used generically) is responsible for all or part of state regulation over water pollution
in all of the forty-eight states.[191] The organization of this
agency will be analyzed later. But in some thirty states,
where there is comprehensive state regulation over water pollution, the "state health department" as such has yielded to
some other agency in the exercise of such comprehensive regulation, although it has otherwise retained its jurisdiction
in the general field of water-pollution control.[192] The agencies responsible for comprehensive regulation over water pollu-

tion in these states may be grouped as follows:[193]

(a) Existing agencies
     Mississippi---Mississippi Game and Fish Commission
     Kansas---Department of Health, with the approval
     of the State Forestry, Fish and Game Commission
     Vermont---State Water Conservation Board.
     (All these agencies will be discussed later.)
     North Dakota---State Water Conservation Commission
     (discussed above), with the approval of the State
     Department of Health.
(b) Special water-pollution-control agencies within the
     "state health department"---Pennsylvania, Oregon,
     North Carolina, Arkansas, New York, South Carolina
     and Kentucky.
(c) Independent special water-pollution-control agencies
     ---Connecticut, Michigan, West Virginia, Wisconsin,
     South Dakota, Louisiana, Maine, Indiana, Minnesota,
     Tennessee, Washington, Virginia, Alabama, Delaware,
     Maryland, New Hampshire, California, Illinois and
     Ohio.

The various special water-pollution-control agencies,
whether they are within or independent of the "state health
department", are all closely associated with the latter, the
State Water Commission of Connecticut and the State Water Control Board of Virginia being the only exceptions. The Connecticut commission is composed of three members appointed by the
Governor with the consent of the Senate for terms of six years.
It elects a chairman, and may employ a director, a deputy director and other assistants. The State Water Control Board of
Virginia consists of five members appointed by the Governor
with the approval of the General Assembly for terms of four
years. The board elects a chairman, and may employ an executive secretary.

Of the agencies of the remaining states, the following are
made up entirely of ex-officio members:

Wisconsin, Committee On Water Pollution---The State Chief
          Engineer, a member or employee of the Public Service
          Commission, a member or employee of the Conservation
          Commission, the State Health Officer or a member of
          the Board of Health, and the state sanitary engineer
          or some other engineer designated by the Board of
          Health.
South Dakota, Committee On Water Pollution---Superintendent
          of the State Board of Health (chairman), State En-
          gineer and Director of Game and Fish.
Louisiana, Stream Control Commission---Commissioner of
          Wildlife and Fisheries (chairman), President of the
          State Board of Health, Commissioner of Agriculture
          and Immigration, Commissioner of Conservation, Execu-

tive Director of Department of Commerce and Industry and the Attorney General.

Washington, Pollution Control Commission---Director of
Conservation and Development, Director of Fisheries, Director of Game, Director of Health and Director of Agriculture.

New York, Water Pollution Control Board---Commissioner of
Health (chairman), Commissioner of Conservation,
Commissioner of Agriculture and Markets, Commission-
er of Commerce, and Superintendent of Public Works.
The Board appoints an executive secretary.

The other agencies include both <u>ex-officio</u> and <u>ad-hoc</u> members.[194] The names of these agencies and their <u>ex-officio</u>
members are given below:

Pennsylvania, Sanitary Water Board---Secretary of Health,
Secretary of Forests and Waters, and Commissioner
of Fisheries.

Michigan, Water Resources Commission (before 1949, stream
Control Commission)---Director of Conservation,
Commissioner of Health, Director of Agriculture,
and Highways Commissioner.

West Virginia, State Water Commission---Commissioner of
Health and the Chairman of Game and Fish Commission.

Oregon, State Sanitary Authority---State Health Officer,
State Engineer, and Chairman of State Fish commission.

Maine, Water Improvement Commission---Commissioner of
Health and Welfare only.

Indiana, Stream Pollution Control Board---Secretary of
State Board of Health, Director of Conservation,
and the Lieutenant Governor.

Minnesota, Water Pollution Commission---Secretary of State
Board of Health, Commissioner of Conservation,
Commissioner of Agriculture, Dairy and Food, and
Secretary of State Livestock Sanitary Board.

North Carolina, Stream Sanitation Committee--Chief Engineer of State Board of Health, and chief engineer
of Water Resources and Engineering Division of Department of Conservation and Development.

Tennessee, Stream Pollution Control Board---Commissioner
of Public Health, Commissioner of Conservation,
and Executive Director of State Planning Commission.

Alabama, Water Improvement Advisory Commission (not advisory since 1949)---State Health Officer, Director
of Conservation, Commissioner of Agriculture and
Industries, and State Geologist.

Delaware, Water Pollution Commission---President of Game
and Fish Commission, President of Commission of
Shell Fisheries, chief engineer of Wilmington Water
Department New Castle County engineer, chief engineer of State Highway Department, Executive Secre-

tary of State Board of Health, and director of
Division of Sanitation of State Board of Health.

Maryland, Water Pollution Commission---Director of Health,
chairman of Board of Natural Resources, State Game
Warden, and the Director of Research and Education.

New Hampshire, Water Pollution Commission---State Health
Officer, Director of Fish and Game Department,
director of Division of Recreation of the Department of Forestry and recreation, Executive Director
of State Planning and Development Commission, a
member of Public Service Commission, and Chairman
of Water Resources Board.

Arkansas, Water Pollution Control Commission---One representative each from State Board of Health, Game
and Fish Commission, Oil and Gas Commission, Resources and Development Commission, and State Forestry and Parks Commission.

California, Water Pollution Control Board---Director of
Public Health, State Engineer, Director of Natural
Resources, Director of Agriculture, and Director
of Fish and Game.

Kentucky, Water Pollution Control Commission---Commission-
er of Health, Commissioner of Conservation, Attorney General and Director of Division of Game and
Fish.

South Carolina, Water Pollution Control Authority---The
State Health Officer, and two members of the Executive Committee of the State Board of Health.

Illinois, Sanitary Water Board---Director of Public Health,
Director of Agriculture, Director of Conservation,
and Director of Public Works and Buildings.

Ohio, Water Pollution Control Board---Director of Health,
Director of Natural Resources, and Director of
Commerce.

The size of the ad-hoc membership varies as follows: Three
for Pennsylvania, Michigan, West Virginia, Oregon, Minnesota,
Delaware, Maryland and Arkansas; two for Ohio (bi-partisan),
Tennessee, Kentucky and Illinois; four for Indiana(bi-partisan)
and New Hampshire; six for Maine and North Carolina; seven for
South Carolina; nine for California and eleven for Alabama.
The ad-hoc members are appointed by the Governor in Oregon,
Indiana, Tennessee, Maryland, California, Kentucky, South
Carolina and Illinois; by the Governor with the approval of
the Council in Maine and New Hampshire; and by the Governor
with the consent of the Senate in Michigan, West Virginia,
Minnesota, North Carolina, Delaware, Arkansas and Ohio. Their
tenure is four years in Oregon, Indiana, Tennessee, California,
Kentucky, South Carolina, Illinois and Ohio; six years in West
Virginia, Minnesota, Alabama, Maryland, New Hampshire; three
years in Michigan, Maine and Delaware; two years in North Caro-
line, and unspecified in Pennsylvania. They are representative
entirely of special interests, which consist in general of

waste-producing industries and sewage-producing municipalities, in Michigan, North Carolina, Tennessee, Alabama, New Hampshire, Delaware, Arkansas, California, Kentucky, South Carolina, Illinois and Ohio;[195] entirely representative of the general public in Oregon; and representative of both in Maine and Minnesota. Alabama is the only case in which there are members chosen presumably because of their knowledge.[196] In all of the states except Delaware, the ad-hoc members are selected from the state at large; but in Delaware the three members are equally distributed among the three counties of that state.[197]

With regard to the internal organization of the various special agencies of water-pollution control, a chairman is provided for in most cases. The chairmanship is held ex-officio by the head of the "state health department" in Pennsylvania, South Dakota, Tennessee, Alabama (with the Director of Conservation as ex-officio vice-chairman), South Carolina and Ohio.[198] The chairman is designated by the Governor from among the ad-hoc members in Maryland and New Hampshire. This officer is elected by the agency-membership in Maine (annually), Indiana, Minnesota (annually, and also a vice-chairman), North Carolina, Washington, Arkansas (annually, and also a vice-chairman), California, Kentucky (annually, and also a vice-chairman) and Illinois. As mentioned before, the Commissioner of Wildlife and Fisheries is the ex-officio chairman of the Lousiana Stream Control Commission.[199]

The agencies generally have an executive officer. He is:

(i) The Commissioner of Wildlife and Fisheries (who is also chairman) in Louisiana.

(ii) Appointed by the Governor upon the recommendation of the agency in Washington (director).[200]

(iii) Elected by the agency in Maine (secretary).

(iv) Employed by the agency in North Carolina (executive secretary), Maryland (director), California (executive officer) and South Carolina (executive director).

(v) Employed by the agency in North Carolina (executive secretary), Maryland (director), California (executive officer) and South Carolina (executive director).

(vi) The director of the Division of Sanitary Engineering or the chief sanitary engineer (in Washington, "Chief Public Health Engineer") of the "State Health Department", who serves ex-officio as the technical secretary of the agency, in South Carolina, Indiana, Tennessee, Washington, New Hampshire, Alabama, Arkansas and Illinois.

(vii) The secretary of the agency, who is a sanitary engineer appointed and paid by the State Board of Health in Ore-

member of the agency) in Minnesota, one of the two representatives (Executive Secretary of the State Board of Health and the Director of the Division of Sanitation of the said Board) of the State Board of Health in the membership of the agency in Delaware, and the Commissioner of Health in Kentucky.[201]

(viii) There are no executive officers as such in the Pennsylvania, West Virginia and Ohio agencies. However, the Director of the Division of Sanitary Engineering of the State Health Department of West Virginia is required to perform such services for the State Water Commission as may be requested by the said Commission; and the Director of Health of Ohio issues orders, permits, rules and regulations in the name of the Water Pollution Control Board. In Pennsylvania, the Department of Health is the "enforcement agent" of the Sanitary Water Board.[202]

It may further be noted that the various agencies are generally discouraged from employing a full-fledged staff of administrative assistants, but instead are required to utilize the technical services and facilities of the "state department of health" and other existing agencies as far as possible.

The regular meetings of the various agencies are held semiannually in Wisconsin, North Carolina, Delaware, Alabama, Maine (at least), Tennessee and California; quarterly in Ohio, Maryland, Minnesota, New Hampshire and Arkansas; bi-monthly in Kentucky, Washington (at least) and Indiana, and monthly in Louisiana and Michigan. Regular meetings are to be determined by agency itself in West Virginia, South Carolina and Illinois. The Committee on Water Pollution of South Dakota do not hold regular meetings. Special meetings are called by:[203]

The chairman or two members in Illinois, Indiana, Minnesota, North Carolina, Tennessee, Arkansas, California and Kentucky.
The chairman or three members in Delaware and Maryland.
The chairman or four members (i.e. two-fifths of membership) in New Hampshire.
The chairman or five members (i.e. one-third of membership) in Alabama.
The chairman only in West Virginia and South Dakota.
The State Board of Health or the State Health Officer or three members in Wisconsin.

Special meetings are determined by the agency itself in Maine, Washington and South Carolina, and there are no statutory provisions for the calling of special meetings in Michigan and Louisiana.[204] In Pennsylvania and Oregon, there are statutory provisions for either regular or special meetings.

California is the only state in which under the state water-pollution-control agency there are regional water-pollution

agencies. By an act of 1949 (last amended 1953), the state
of California is divided into nine regions, for each of which
there is set up a Regional Water Pollution Control Board.
Each Regional Board is composed of five members (representative respectively of domestic and municipal water supply business, irrigation farming, industries, cities and counties)
appointed by the Governor for a four-year term. It elects a
chairman annually, and appoints an executive officer and necessary assistants. Regular meetings of the several regional
boards are held quarterly, and special meetings may be called by the chairman or any two members. The regional boards
assist the State Water Pollution Control Board in its state-
wide regulation of water pollution, and have the authority to
issue orders for the correction of water pollution in their
respective regions (Water Code, sec. 13040 et seq.: Stats.
1949, ch. 1549, sec. 1; as last amended by Stats. 1953, ch.
1297).

There is no comprehensive water-pollution regulation and
therefore no need for the establishment of special water-pollution-control agencies in states other than those mentioned
above. However, in Texas and Wyoming, there have been established advisory agencies of water-pollution control. The advisory agency in Wyoming is a council which consists of the
Director of the Department of Public Health, the Game and Fish
Commissioner, the State Engineer, and the State Commissioner
of Agriculture, and five other members (of whom one represents
industries and one represents municipal government) appointed
by the Governor for terms of four years. "The primary duty
of the council shall be to advise the state department of public health in developing a comprehensive program for the prevention, control and abatement of new or existing pollution
of the waters of the state" (Compiled Statutes, sec. 63-201:
Laws 1923, ch. 92, sec. 1; as amended by L. 1951, ch. 42).

The Water Pollution Advisory Council of Texas was created
in 1953. It is composed of the State Health Officer, the Executive Secretary of the State Game and Fish Commission, the
Chairman of the State Board of Water Engineers, the Chairman
of the Railroad Commission, and the Attorney General, ex-officio.
It conducts studies and disseminates information relating to
water pollution and its control and prevention, and advises
other state agencies and groups and industries concerned in
solving the problems of water pollution (Revised Civil Statutes, art. 7621a: Laws 1953, ch. 353).

(4) Forestry Agencies[205]---Forestry agencies have been
established in all of the forty-eight states except Arizona
and Wyoming. These agencies fell under the following general
categories:[206]

(A) A unit or sub-unit of the "Department of Conservation"
---Alabama, California, Illinois, Indiana, Iowa, Kentucky,

Massachusetts, Michigan, Minnesota, Missouri, New
Jersey, New York, North Carolina, Ohio, Oklahoma,
Pennsylvania, Rhode Island, Tennessee, Virginia,
Washington, West Virginia and Wisconsin (22 States).
(B) A part of the combined forestry, parks and fish and
wildlife agencies---Arkansas, Connecticut, Kansas,
Maryland, Nebraska, New Hampshire, South Dakota,
and Vermont (8 States).
(C) A special forestry board or commission---Colorado,
Delaware, Florida, Georgia, Idaho, Louisiana,
Mississippi, Montana, Oregon, South Carolina and
Utah (11 States).
(D) Single-headed special forestry agencies (either ad-
hoc or ex-officio)---Maine, Nevada, New Mexico,
North Dakota and Texas (5 States).

(A) and (B) will be discussed later. Only (C) and (D) will
be discussed here.

(a) Forestry boards and commissions[207]---There is a State
Cooperative Board of Forestry in Idaho; a State Board of Forestry in Oregon, Florida, Colorado and Montana; a State Board
of Forestry and Fire Control in Utah; a State Forestry Commission in Mississippi, Delaware, Louisiana and Georgia, and a
Commission of Forestry in South Carolina.[208] All these agencies, except those of Florida, Georgia and Colorado, are made
up of both ex-officio and special members. The Florida and
Georgia agencies consist entirely of special members, while
the State Board of Forestry of Colorado is nothing but the
State Board of Land Commissioners acting in an ex-officio capacity. With the exception of the State Board of Forestry and
Fire Control of Utah, which is within the State Department of
Agriculture, all of these agencies are independent establishments. The ex-officio members of the various agencies are as
follows:

Idaho---Governor, Attorney General, Secretary of State,
State Auditor, State Superintendent of Public In-
struction, State Land Commissioner, dean of the
School of Forestry of the University of Idaho, and
State Commissioner of Reclamation.
Oregon---Governor and head of Forestry School of Oregon
Agricultural College.
Mississippi---Governor, Commissioner of Agriculture and
State Land Commissioner.
Delaware---Governor.
South Carolina---President of Clemson Agricultural College.
Utah---A member of the State Department of Agriculture, a
member of "state departments representing the de-
partment of finance and the state land board", a
member of the faculty of the School of Forestry of
Utah State Agricultural College and a member of
Fish and Game Department.

Montana---Governor, a member of State Water Conservation
          Board, and a faculty member of Montana School of
          Forestry.
Louisiana---Head of Department of Forestry of Louisiana
          State University and Agricultural and Mechanical
          College, and Commissioner of Wild Life and Fisher-
          ies.

The numbers of the special members are as follows: Four,
in Idaho, Delaware (bi-partisan) and South Carolina; five, in
Florida, Montana, Louisiana and Georgia; six, in Mississippi
and Utah; and eight in Oregon.[209] The special members are
representative of special interest groups in Idaho, Oregon,
Utah, Montana, Louisiana and Georgia[210] and are partly representative of special interests and partly of the general public in South Carolina. In Mississippi and seemingly in Delaware and Florida the special members are all chosen from the
general public. The special members are appointed by the Governor in all of these states except Georgia, where they are
appointed by the Governor with the consent of the Senate.
Their term of office is four years in Mississippi, Florida and
Montana; five years in Louisiana; six years in South Carolina;
seven years in Georgia; eight years in Delaware; and unspecified in Idaho, Oregon and Utah.

In Montana, the Governor serves ex-officio as the Chairman
of the agency. The Florida agency annually elects a President
and a Vice-President. In Delaware, South Carolina, Utah, Louisiana and Georgia, the agency elects a chairman.[211] There
is no statutory provision for a chairman or president of the
agency in Idaho, Oregon and Mississippi. Regular meetings of
the agency are held semiannually in Idaho and Montana; annually in Florida; quarterly in Oregon and Louisiana and as determined by the agency in Mississippi and Georgia. The agencies
of South Carolina and Utah do not hold regular meetings. Special meetings are called by the Governor or the secretary of
the agency in Idaho and Oregon; by the Governor of three members in Mississippi; by the President or a majority of members
in Florida; by the Chairman or a majority of members in Georgia; by the Chairman, Chief Forester-Fire Warden, Governor or
three members in Utah; by the Chairman or four members in
Louisiana. In Montana, the agency is authorized to prescribe
the manner in which special meetings may be held. The laws of
Delaware make no mention of either regular or special meetings
of the agency.

The agencies of Florida and Louisiana are corporate bodies, and as such may sue and be sued.

All of the state forestry boards and commissions are merely
deliberative bodies. Their functions are generally the determination of policies, the enactment of rules and regulations,
and the authorization of expenditures. But the actual admin-

istration of the forestry laws passed by the state legislature
and the rules and regulations promulgated by the board or commission is in each state entrusted to an administrative officer[212] who is entitled "Director" in Georgia, "Chief Forester-
Fire Warden" in Utah, and "State Forester" in all other states.
Such officer, who is invariably a forestry expert, is appointed by the State Board of Land Commissioners upon the nomination of the agency in Idaho; by the Governor with the consent
of the Senate in Montana; and by the agency in Oregon, Mississippi, Delaware, Florida, South Carolina, Colorado, Utah
(upon the nomination of the dean of the School of Forestry of
the State Agricultural College, the nominee to be a faculty
member thereof) and Georgia (with the approval of the Governor). He serves for a term of four years in Mississippi and
Montana and for an indefinite term in all other states. He
acts as the secretary of the agency in all of these states except Colorado, Florida and Mississippi.[213]

The State Forester or like officer generally has one or
more assistants,[214] who are employed in the following manner:

Idaho---The State Board of Land Commissioners appoints a
        Deputy State Forester upon the recommendation of
        the State Forester.
Oregon---The State Forester, with the approval of the agen-
        cy, appoints a Deputy State Forester and one or
        more Assistant State Foresters (and fire wardens).
Delaware---The State Forester employs necessary assistants
        with the approval of the agency.
Florida---The agency employs all necessary personnel.
Utah---The Chief Forester-Fire Warden, with the approval
        of the agency, employs one or more deputies. He em-
        ploys other assistants(and fire wardens) without such
        approval.
Montana---The State Forester, with the approval of the
        State Board of Land Commissioners, appoints neces-
        sary assistants.
Louisiana---The State Forester employs necessary assistants.

(b) Single-headed forestry agencies---In Maine, the Governor, with the consent of the Senate, appoints an expert Forest Commissioner for a term of four years to administer the
forestry laws of that state and manage all state-owned forest
lands. The said Commissioner appoints a clerk, who is also
the Deputy Forest Commissioner to serve at his pleasure and
district foresters and other personnel on a merit basis (Revised Statutes, ch. 32, sec. 1 et seq.: Laws 1823, p. 323;
as last amended by L. 1949, ch. 437). In Nevada, the State
Surveyor serves ex-officio as the State Forester Fire Warden,
who is assisted and guided, with respect to forest fire control, by the State Board of Fire Control. The said Board is
composed of the Governor (chairman), director of agricultural
extension of the University of Nevada and the State Forester-

Fire Warden, with the approval of the Board, appoints an expert Assistant Forester Fire Warden (Compiled Laws, sec. 3169
et seq.: Stats. 1945, ch. 149). The latter office may be held
by the extension forester of the agricultural extension service on a part-time basis (Stats. 1953, ch. 149).

The State Forester of Texas is appointed by and under the
supervision of the Board of Directors of the State Agricultural
and Mechanical College. He may employ necessary assistants,
subject to the confirmation of the said board (Revised Civil
Statutes, art. 2613, sec. 10, being Laws 1915, p. 220, as amended by L. 1951, ch. 201, sec. 1; and ibid., sec. 10a, being L.
1941, ch. 530, sec. 1). In North Dakota, the president of the
State School of Forestry is the State Forester ex-officio (Revised Code, sec. 4-1901: Laws 1913, ch. 170, sec. 1). There
is no forestry officer or agency as such in New Mexico. However, the State Commissioner of Public Lands is charged with
the duty of administering logging and timber laws of the state
(Statutes, sec. 64-104: Laws 1939, ch. 141, sec. 4).

For reasons of administrative convenience and expediency,
that part of the state forestry administration which deals
with the control of forest pests and diseases is in many cases
shared between the state forestry agency and the "state department of agriculture" (generically). For example, in Iowa the
Department of Agriculture, the Conservation Commission and the
State Agricultural Experiment Station have cooperated in the
state white pine blister control program, with primary authority
given to the State Entomologist of the Department of Agriculture.[215] In Virginia, while the authority of assisting landowners in forest pest control rests with the state forestry agency, quarantine operations are under the jurisdiction of the Department of Agriculture and Immigration (Code, sec. 10-90.3: Acts
1952, ch. 657). In Minnesota, a law of 1953 (ch. 711) transferred all duties of the Division of Forestry of the Department of
Conservation relating to the control of white pine blister rust
to the Department of Agriculture, Dairy and Food.

(5) Fish and Wildlife Agencies---The fish and wildlife
(or game) agencies of the several states are of the following
different patterns:

(A) One or two divisions in the "State Department of Con-
     servation"---Alabama, Illinois, Indiana, Iowa, Mas-
     sachusetts, Michigan, Minnesota, Missouri, New Jer-
     sey, New York, Ohio, Rhode Island, Tennessee, West
     Virginia and Wisconsin. (In the North Carolina de-
     partment, a Division of Commercial Fisheries) (15
     states)
(B) A part of combined forestry, fish and wildlife and
     parks agencies---Kansas, Nebraska and South Dakota.
     (3 states)
(C) Special plural-headed agency

(a) Consolidated---Arizona, Arkansas, California,
Colorado, Georgia, Idaho, Kentucky, Mississippi,
Montana, Nevada, New Hampshire, New Mexico, Oklahoma, South Carolina, Texas, Utah, Vermont and Wyoming. (18 states)
(b) With a separate agency in charge of commercial
fisheries---North Carolina, Oregon, Pennsylvania
and Washington. (4 states)
(c) With a separate agency in charge of shell-
fisheries---Connecticut, Delaware, Florida, Maryland and Virginia. (5 states)
(D) Special single-headed agency
(a) Consolidated---Louisiana and North Dakota (2
states).
(b) With a separate agency in charge of marine fish-
eries---Maine (1 state).

Since (A) and (B) will be discussed in Section 2 below, only
(C) and (D) are discussed in this section.

(a) <u>Special plural-headed agencies</u>---These include all
agencies under (C) (a) and the main agencies under (C) (b) and
(C) (c) above.[216]

These agencies have the following different official designations:

"Game and Fish Commission"---Arizona, Mississippi, Color-
ado, Wyoming. Georgia, Oklahoma and Texas.
"Fish and Game Commission"---New Hampshire, Montana, Utah,
Arkansas, Idaho and California.
"Game Commission"---New Mexico, Oregon, Pennsylvania and
Washington.
"Commission of Fish and Game"---Vermont.
"Wildlife Resources Commission"---North Carolina and
South Carolina.
Other designations---Nevada "Board of Fish and Game Com-
missioners"; Delaware "Board of Game and Fish Com-
missioners"; Connecticut "Board of Fisheries and
Game"; Florida "Game and Fresh-Water Fish Commis-
sion"; Virginia "Commission of Game and Inland
Fisheries"; Maryland "Game and Inland Fish Commis-
sion"; and Kentucky "Department of Fish and Wild
Life Resources Commission".

With the only exception of the Colorado agency, in which
the Governor is an <u>ex-officio</u> member, all of these agencies
are made up of special members.[217] The agency-membership is
five in New Hampshire, Vermont, Montana, New Mexico, Utah,
Arizona, Mississippi, Idaho, California, Oregon, Connecticut,
Florida and Maryland; seven in Arkansas, Wyoming and South
Carolina; eight in Colorado (excluding the Governor), Oklahoma
and Pennsylvania; nine in Kentucky, Texas, North Carolina and

Virginia;[218] three in Delaware; six in Washington; fifteen in Georgia;[219] and seventeen in Nevada. In all of these states, the members of the agency all represent the general public, although they are generally selected on a district basis[220] and required to be well informed about the problems of fish and wildlife.[221] The members are appointed by the Governor in Montana, Mississippi, Colorado, Arkansas, Idaho, Nevada, Texas, Oregon, Washington, North Carolina, Delaware, Connecticut, Maryland and Kentucky; by the Governor with the consent of the Senate in Vermont, New Mexico, Utah, Arizona, Wyoming, Georgia, California, Oklahoma, South Carolina, Pennsylvania (two-thirds of entire senate membership) and Florida; by the Governor with the consent of the Council in New Hampshire; and by the Governor with the consent of the state legislature (the bi-cameral General Assembly) in Virginia. They serve for a term of six years in Vermont, Utah, Colorado, Idaho, California, Texas, South Carolina, Washington, North Carolina, Delaware and Virginia; for a term of five years in New Hampshire, New Mexico, Arizona, Oregon, Connecticut and Maryland; a term of four years in Montana, Mississippi, Wyoming, Nevada and Kentucky; a term of seven years in Arkansas and Georgia; and a term of eight years in Oklahoma and Pennsylvania.[222]

The agency is presided over by a Chairman or President.[223] This officer (as well as the vice-chairman or the vice-president) is (a) the member at large in South Carolina; (b) designated by the Governor in Vermont (for two years) and Mississippi; and (c) elected by the agency in all other states except Nevada.[224] Apparently because of the comparatively large size of the Nevada agency, the Nevada laws uniquely provide for the organization of an Executive Board of five members, who are elected by the agency, as an operating nucleus of the agency. The said board elects a chairman and a secretary, who are also respectively the Chairman and secretary of the agency. The agencies of New Hampshire, Colorado, Idaho and Oklahoma also elect a secretary, at the time when the presiding officer is elected. But in the remaining states, the administrative officer (to be discussed below) of the agency serves as its secretary ex-officio or by implication.[225]

The agency holds its regular meetings quarterly in New Hampshire, Montana, Utah, Arizona, Mississippi, Colorado, Idaho, Texas, Oregon, Washington, Florida, Virginia and Kentucky; semi-annually in Wyoming, Nevada, California, Pennsylvania, North Carolina and Maryland; annually in New Mexico; monthly in Oklahoma; and as determined by the agency in Georgia. Special meetings may be called by the presiding officer or a majority of the members in Montana, Arizona, Colorado, Idaho, Georgia, Washington (two-thirds' majority) and Oklahoma; by the chairman or three members in Wyoming and North Carolina; by the chairman in Mississippi; by the chairman or the director (to be discussed below) in Maryland; by the Governor or a majority of the members in New Mexico; by the Chairman or the Governor in Oregon; and by the director (to be discussed below) or three members in Florida. In New Hampshire, Nevada and Pennsylvania and probably also in Virginia, California and Kentucky, the calling of special meetings is to be prescribed by the agency itself.[226]

The various state fish and wildlife commissions and boards are concerned only with matters pertaining to policies and expenditures and with the making of rules and regulations. They also proclaim open and closed fishing and hunting seasons and make similar decisions where the state legislsture has refrained from such decisions and proclamations.[227] But they are not engaged in other acts or activities regarding the executions of either the laws or the rules, regulations and decisions made by themselves. There is an administrative officer who is responsible for these acts and activities. Such officer is known as director[228] in New Hampshire, Colorado, Idaho, Georgia, South Carolina, Oregon, Pennsylvania, Washington, North Carolina, Florida, Virginia, Maryland, California, Vermont, Utah, Nevada, and Mississippi; as state fish and game warden in Montana; as state game and fish warden in New Mexico; as chief game and fish warden in Delaware; as executive secretary in Arkansas and Texas; as superintendent of fisheries and game in Connecticut; as state game and fish commissioner in Wyoming; and as commissioner in Kentucky. The administrative officer is appointed by the Governor in California; by the agency with the approval of the Governor in Vermont and Utah; and by the agency in all other states.[229] Except in Wyoming, where such officer may be a member of the agency, he is not a member of the agency.[230] The administrative officers of the agencies of Vermont, Arizona and Utah serve for terms of six, five and four years respectively. In Kentucky, he is a permanent officer, subject to removal for cause only. In all other states, the administrative officer serves at the pleasure of the agency (or, in Washington and California, the Governor).

Under the administrative officer, there are a number of administrative assistants. They are employed by the agency in New Mexico, Colorado, Arkansas, Wyoming, Georgia, Nevada, Pennsylvania, Delaware, Virginia, Idaho (the fish culturist only) and Texas (the assistant executive secretary only); by the administrative officer with the approval of the agency in Vermont, Montana, Arizona, Mississippi, Oklahoma, North Carolina, Connecticut and Maryland; and by the administrative officer in New Hampshire, Utah, Idaho (except the fish culturist), California, Texas (except the assistant executive secretary), Washington, Oregon, Florida, and Kentucky (in Kentucky, examinations for each position being held by the agency).

It should be pointed out that in Georgia general administrative officer has no direct authority over coastal fisheries (primarily shell fisheries), which are placed under the immediate care of a Supervisor of Coastal Fisheries, who is appoint-

ed by the agency to serve at its pleasure, although it would
seem that this officer is under the supervision of the administrative officer. In South Carolina, the director of the
Division of Game is not concerned with commercial fisheries
(including shell fisheries) at all. There is within the agency a separate Division of Commercial Fisheries headed by a
director, who is appointed in the same way as the director of
the Division of Game and who has the same authority of employing assistants as the latter. The Director of Commercial
Fisheries is advised by a Commercial Fisheries Advisory Board,
which is composed of three members, all representing special
professional and territorial interests, appointed by the Governor for terms of three years.[231]

(b) Special agencies auxiliary to (a)[232]---These include
the Fish Commissions of Oregon and Pennsylvania and the Department of Fisheries of Washington, which control and regulate commercial fisheries (including shell fisheries);[233] the
Delaware Commission of Shell Fisheries, the Connecticut Shellfish Commission, the Florida Board of Conservation, the Commission of Fisheries of Virginia, and the Department of Tidewater Fisheries of Maryland, which are all agencies for marine and shell fisheries; and the Utah State Board of Big
Game.[234]

The Oregon Fish Commission consists of three members appointed by the Governor for four years. It elects a chairman
and holds monthly meetings. It appoints a Master Fish Warden
as its executive or administrative officer. The latter employs certain assistants. Its Pennsylvania counterpart consists of eight members appointed by the Governor with the
consent of two-thirds of the members of the Senate for terms
of eight years. It holds regular semiannual meetings, elects
a president and a vice-president and employs an executive director. The Washington Department of Fisheries is headed by
a Director appointed by the Governor to serve at his pleasure.
The Director employs all personnel of the Department.

The Delaware shell-fish agency is a bi-partisan body of
five members (representative of special interests) appointed
by the Governor for three years. It elects a President and
a secretary. The agency controls and regulates the shellfish
industry, and may lease certain areas in the Indian River and
Rehoboth Bays to local residents for oyster planting. But it
is the collector of oyster revenues, a financial officer outside of the agency, who issues shell-fishing licenses. The
Connecticut Shellfish Commission is composed of five shellfish commissioners appointed by the Governor with the consent
of the Senate for four years. It appoints a clerk and an engineer for shell-fisheries. The Board of Conservation of Florida is made up of the Governor, the Secretary of State, the
Attorney General, the Comptroller, the State Treasurer, the
Superintendent of Public Instruction, and the Commissioner of

State, the Attorney General, the Comptroller, the State Treasurer, the Superintendent of Public Instruction, and the Commissioner of Agriculture, ex officiis. It both regulates marine and shell fisheries and is responsible for the lease of river and coastal beds. The Governor appoints a Director as the administrative officer of the Board and other personnel. The Director, with the approval of the Board, may establish divisions and other units within the Board.

The Commission of Fisheries of Virginia consists of five members appointed by the Governor with the consent of the General Assembly to serve at his pleasure. One member is designated by the Governor as Chairman, who is also the Commissioner of Fisheries. The Commission meets only upon the call of the Chairman (i.e. the Commissioner). The Commissioner of Fisheries is the administrative officer of the Commission and appoints all necessary personnel. The Department of Tidewater Fisheries of Maryland is administered by a Commission of Tidewater Fisheries, which consists of three members appointed by the Governor with the consent of the Senate for six years. The Chairman of the Commission is designated by the Governor. The Commission employs a secretary, a commander of the fishery force, and other personnel.

The State Board of Big Game of Utah consists of the State Fish and Game Director as chairman and four members appointed by the Governor upon the recommendation of certain professional organizations for terms of two years. The Board determines the open and closed seasons for big-game hunting and establishes policies for the protection and regulation of big-game animals (Laws 1927, ch. 31, sec. 2; as last amended by Laws 1953, ch. 39, Fish and Game Code, ch. 4). It may be noted that the policy and other decisions of the Board are, like those of the State Fish and Game Commission, are administered by the Fish and Game Director, and that both the Commission and the Board are within the "State Fish and Game Department".

(c) Special single-headed agencies---The Department of Wildlife and Fisheries of Louisiana is "directed and controlled by a Commissioner of Wildlife and Fisheries, to be appointed by the Governor, by and with the consent of the Senate, for the term of four years." He employs all departmental personnel, and may sue and be sued (Revised Statutes, sec. 56:1 et seq.: Constitution, art. VI, sec. 1, adopted 7 November 1944; last amended by Acts 1950, No. 60). North Dakota Game and Fish Department is under the direction of the State Game and Fish Commissioner, who is appointed by the Governor for a term of two years. He appoints a Deputy Commissioner, a Chief Game Warden and other assistants (Revised Code, sec. 20-0201 et seq.: Laws 1909, ch. 128; as last amended by L. 1953, ch. 159).

In Maine, wildlife and fresh-water fishes are under the
jurisdiction of the Department of Inland Fisheries and Game,
and marine fisheries are controlled by the Commissioner of
Sea and Shore Fisheries. The latter is appointed by the Governor with the approval of the Council to serve for a maximum
term of four years. He employs one or more clerks, and is advised by an advisory council of five members appointed by the
Governor with the consent of the Council for terms of three
years (Revised Statutes, ch. 34, sec. 1 et seq.: Laws 1909,
ch. 204; as last amended by L. 1953, ch. 372, sec. 2). The
Department of Inland Fisheries and Game is headed by a Commissioner of Inland Fisheries and Game, who is assisted by a
Deputy Commissioner. Both the Commissioner and the Deputy
Commissioner are appointed by the Governor with the approval
of the Council, the latter to be appointed upon the recommendation of the Commissioner. The Commissioner serves for a
term of three years, and the Deputy Commissioner serves at the
pleasure of the Commissioner. The Commissioner is advised by
an advisory board of seven members appointed by the Governor
with the approval of the Council for six year (ibid., ch. 33:
L. 1919, ch. 201; as amended by L. 1929, chs. 331 and 332).

The above-mentioned agencies are the regular fish and
wildlife agencies of the several states. In exceptional cases, part of the state fish and wildlife administration is placed under the jurisdiction of other state agencies. For example, in some states, the control of predators and rodents is
undertaken by the "department of Agriculture" (generic).[235]
In Florida, the State Board of Parks and Historic Memorials
administers two wildlife refuges.[236]

(6)   State Parks Agencies[237]---Agencies in charge of the
administration of state parks and other recreational areas are
found in all states except Arizona. These agencies may be
divided into the following groups:

(A)   A division or unit in the "Department of Conserva-
        tion"---Alabama, California, Illinois, Indiana,
        Iowa, Kentucky, Massachusetts, Michigan, Minnesota,
        New Jersey, New York, North Carolina, Ohio, Okla-
        homa, Pennsylvania, Tennessee, Virginia, West Vir-
        ginia and Wisconsin (19 states).
(B)   A part of combined forestry, fish and game and parks
        agency---Arkansas, Connecticut, Maryland, Nebraska,
        New Hampshire, South Dakota and Vermont (7 states).
(C)   Special agencies---Colorado, Delaware, Florida, Lou-
        isiana, Maine, Mississippi, Missouri, Nevada, New
        Mexico, Texas, Washington, Wyoming (all these states
        plural-headed) and Georgia (single-headed) (13
        states).
(D)   Other state agencies---Idaho, Kansas, Montana, North
        Dakota, Oregon, Rhode Island, South Carolina and
        Utah (8 states).

As (A) and (B) will be discussed in the next Section, only (C) and (D) will be discussed here.

(a)   Special state parks agencies[238]---The agencies of twelve states which are plural-headed are called by the following different names:[239]

> "State Parks and Recreation Commission"---Washington and
>   Louisiana.
> "State Park Commission"--- Maine, Nevada and Delaware.
> "State Parks Commission"---New Mexico and Wyoming.
> "State Park Board"---Colorado and Missouri.
> Other names---Texas, "State Parks Board"; Mississippi,
>   "State Board of Park Supervisors"; Florida, "Flori-
>   da Board of Parks and Historic Memorials".

The agencies of Mississippi and Colorado are made up entirely of ex-officio members: the Mississippi agency consists of three members of the State Forestry Commission selected and designated by the Governor and the Colorado agency consists of three trustees who are the three members of the State Board of Land Commissioners. The agencies of Louisiana, Maine, New Mexico and Wyoming are composed partly of ex-officio members and partly of special members, although the ex-officio members of the Wyoming agency have no voting right. The ex-officio members of these agencies are as follows:[240]

> Louisiana---Governor; registrar of State Land Office.
> Maine---Commissioner of Inland Fisheries and Game; Forest
>   Commissioner.
> New Mexico---State Highway Engineer.
> Wyoming (non-voting)---State Game and Fish Commissioner;
>   State Engineer.

The size of the special membership varies in the following order: Nine in Louisiana; seven in Washington; six in Texas and Missouri; five in Nevada, Delaware and Florida; four in New Mexico; and three in Maine and Wyoming.[241] They are appointed by the Governor in Texas, Louisiana, Nevada, New Mexico, Delaware, and Florida; by the Governor with the approval of the Council in Maine; and by the Governor with the consent of the Senate in Washington, Missouri and Wyoming. Their tenure is four years in New Mexico, Mississippi, Missouri, and Florida; six years in Washington, Texas and Louisiana; five years in Nevada and Delaware; and three years in Maine and Wyoming. The five members of the Florida agency are selected from and representative of five specially designated park regions; but in all other states the special members are chosen from the state at large.

The agency elects a Chairman in Texas (probably), Louisiana (annually, and also a vice-chairman), Delaware, Missouri, and Florida (annually, and also a vice-chairman) and a President in Wyoming (probably). In the other states, the laws have not provided for a chairman or president. In addition to this officer, the Delaware and Florida agencies elect, and the Maine agency employs, a secretary, and the Colorado agency, may employ a clerk. With the exception of the Texas agency, which acts by a two-thirds vote of the entire membership, other agencies pass their resolutions in the normal procedure of a plural-headed agency. Meetings of the agency are provided for only in the laws of Texas, Missouri, Wyoming and Florida. In Florida, the agency meets semi-annually; in the other three states, quarterly. Special meetings may be called by the Governor or Chairman or a majority of members in Texas, by the Chairman or a majority of members in Missouri, and by the President or a majority of members in Wyoming. There is no mention of special meetings in Florida laws.

There is a statutory provision for an administrative officer of the agency in all these states except Texas, Delaware, Maine and Mississippi.[242] This officer is called <u>director</u> in Washington, Louisiana, Colorado, Missouri, Wyoming and Florida, and <u>superintendent</u> in Nevada and New Mexico. He is employed by the agency in Washington, Louisiana (removable only a two-thirds vote of entire agency membership), Missouri, Wyoming and Florida, and by the agency with the approval of the Governor in Colorado. In Nevada the superintendent of state parks is the State Highway Engineer acting <u>ex-officio</u>. New Mexico superintendent of state parks is the "member initially appointed for four years". It may be noted that the agencies of Delaware, Maine, Mississippi and Georgia are authorized to employ necessary personnel, and that a director has been employed by the agencies of Maine, Mississippi and Georgia. A director has also been employed by the Texas agency, although it has no express authority for this. The administrative officer of the Delaware agency seems to be its secretary.[243]

Besides the administrative officer (or the chief administrative officer), the Washington agency, upon the recommendation of the former, may employ a supervisor of recreation and other necessary personnel. The administrative officer of the Louisiana agency, with the approval of the agency, may appoint an assistant director. The agencies of Maine, Mississippi, Delaware, Missouri, Wyoming and Florida and the administrative officer of the New Mexico agency are authorized to employ necessary personnel. As the State Highway Engineer is the <u>ex-officio</u> superintendent of state parks in Nevada, it would seem that all administrative duties of the Nevada parks agency are carried out by the State Highway Department. The agencies of Texas and Colorado would be able to employ administrative assistants if so authorized by proper appropriation laws.

Advisory recreational committees to the agency, regional or state-wide, may be appointed by the Governor in Louisiana and by the agency itself in Colorado.

The state parks agency of Georgia is the Department of State Parks, Historic Sites and Monuments, which is headed by a director appointed by the Governor with the consent of the Senate for a term of four years.[244]

(b) Other state parks agencies---In Idaho, the administration of the state parks and other recreational areas is intrusted to the State Board of Land Commissioners (Code, sec. 58-501: Laws 1937, ch. 201, sec. 1). In Kansas, it is a function of the State Forestry, Fish and Game Commission, although its statutory basis is somewhat obscure.[245] It would seem that the position of this agency is that of coordination, for each state park or other recreational area is under the management of a separate board of trustees appointed by the governor.[246] In South Carolina, the State Commission of Forestry has been given the control and supervision over the state park system (Code of Laws, sec. 51-1: Acts 1934, No. 900). To discharge this function, a Division of State Parks, headed by a director, has been established within that Commission. In Rhode Island, a Division of Parks and Recreation was established within the Department of Public Works in 1952 (Acts 1952, ch. 2973), which is headed by a chief appointed by the Director of Public Works.[247]

In Oregon, it is the State Parks Division of the State Highway Commission that administers the state park system. The said Division is headed by a state parks superintendent and staffed with engineers, architects and other personnel employed by the said Commission (Revised Statutes, secs. 366.175 and 366.180: Laws 1947, ch. 184). The state park system of Montana was originally under the management of an independent State Parks Commission of three special members appointed by the Governor with the State Forester as the ex-officio state park director (1929, ch. 111, sec. 2; L. 1939, ch. 48; L. 1949, ch. 161). In 1953, this organizational set-up was abolished, and all of its functions and duties were transferred to the State Highway Commission (L. 1953, ch. 178). On 1 July 1953, the said Commission set up a Park Division to administer the state park system. This Division is headed by a State Park Director appointed by the Commission, and staffed with personnel employed by this officer.[248]

In North Dakota, the State Historical Society (a state agency)[249] is the state agency for the administration of state parks and other recreational areas. For the exercise of this function, the board of directors of this Society, with the approval of the Governor, may create a State Park Committee of five persons, who are members of the said board or other qualified persons (Revised Code, sec. 55-0201 et seq.: Laws 1935, ch. 216). In Utah, the State Historical Society (a state agency)[250] is in charge of two historical monuments (Camp Floyd and Old State House at Fillmore), while "This Is The Place" Monument and all other state parks and recreational areas which

may be acquired and established by the state of Utah are under the jurisdiction of the State Engineering Commission (Code,
sec. 63-11-3 et seq.: Laws 1951, ch. 75).[251]

(c) Auxiliary state park agencies---The state park agencies of the 47 states mentioned in this Subsection are general
state park agencies. Most of these agencies possess exclusive
or nearly exclusive jurisdiction over the entire state park
system in their respective states. However, in some states
certain state parks and memorials are excluded from their
jurisdiction and are administered either by independently ad-
hoc agencies or by other state agencies.

In Texas, the State Parks Board has no jurisdiction whatever over historic sites and memorials (unless they are designated as "state parks"), which are under the administration
of the State Historical Board. This Board consists of five
members appointed by the Governor for four years. It elects
a chairman and a secretary (Revised Civil Statutes, art. 6145:
Laws 1923, 2nd C. S., p. 62). Moreover, the following state
parks are under the management of the State Board of Control
with the assistance in each case of three commissioners appointed by the Governor: (1) San Jacinto State Park, (2)
Gonzales State Park and (3) King's Memorial State Park. The
following units are each administered by an ad-hoc commission
of three members appointed by the Governor: (1) Golliad State
Park, (2) Fannin State Park and (3) Governor James Stephen
Hoggs Memorial Shrine. The Battleship "Texas" Memorial is
placed under the management of an ad-hoc "commission of control" consisting of nine members appoint4d by the Governor
(ibid., arts. 6071 et seq., 6145-1 and 6145-2).

In North Carolina, there was established in 1953 (L. 1953,
ch. 1197) the Historic Sites Commission, which consists of
the Director of Archives and History (who also serves as its
secretary) and five members appointed by the Governor for a
term of five years. The functions of the Commission are to
examine and acquire historic sites. However, the sites which
have been acquired by the Commission must be transferred to
the State Parks Division of the Department of Conservation
and Development for maintenance and operation.

The Florida State Board of Parks and Historic Memorials
had, by 1953, jurisdiction over only two units, namely, the
Rauscher Park and the St. Michael's Cemetery Park,[252] in addition to whatever parks and memorials which the said park may
acquire and establish after 1953. The Dade Memorial, the
Stephen Foster Memorial, and the Constitution Monument Park
are each managed by a special commission.[253] As mentioned before, the Royal Palm State Park is the property and under the
control of the Florida Federation of Women's Clubs.

In Idaho, the Lava Hot Springs is administered by an ad-hoc agency by the name of the Lava Hot Springs Foundation, which consists of three members appointed by the Governor for six-year terms. It employs a superintendent and other necessary personnel, and meets annually to transact its duties (<u>Code</u>, sec. 67-4401 et seq.: Laws 1919, ch. 30; as last amended by L. 1949, ch. 137). In Maine, the Baxter State Park is administered jointly by the State Forest Commissioner, the Commissioner of Inland Fisheries and Game and the Attorney-General who, since 1949 (Laws 1949, ch. 78), have been constituted for this purpose as the Baxter State Park Authority (<u>Revised Statutes</u>, ch. 32, secs. 31, 31-A to 31-D, and 32: Laws 1933, ch. 281; as first amended by L. 1939, ch. 6 and last amended by L. 1949, chs. 70 and 78). The Delaware State Park Commission does not administer the Indian River Inlet Park, which is placed under the control of the State Highway Department.254

The Division of State Parks of Oklahoma Planning and Resources Board is the statutory general agency for all state parks. However, in 1953, the State Game and Fish Commission was given authority, by special legislation, to construct and administer two dam-and-reservoir state parks on the Mountain Fork Creek and the Gates Creek, in Haskell and Choctaw Counties, respectively (Laws 1953, p. 118, S. B. 384, and p. 120, H. B. 691).255

The above-mentioned agencies are those which perform functions that normally belong to the general state park agencies. It should be noted that general state parks generally do not engage themselves in beach erosion control or beach protection work, unless beaches are part of state parks. Such work (found only in a few states) is assigned to other agencies or units. For example, in New Jersey, while the Division of Forestry, Geology, Parks and Historic Sites of the Department of Conservation is in charge of the state park system, the Division of Navigation is given responsibilities over beach erosion control. In Massachusetts, there is a Division of Public Beaches in the Department of Public Works which is specialized in this enterprise (<u>General Laws</u>, ch. 16, sec. 5B: Acts 1953, ch. 666, sec. 1).256 As discussed before, in many states the "State Highway Department" (generically) instead of the general state park agency has been charged with duties relating to waysides or wayside (or roadside) parks. The same Department, in some states, has been authorized or requested to construct, maintain or repair roads and bridges in the state parks.257

(7) The "<u>Department of Health</u>"---This agency, which has exclusive jurisdiction over water supply in most states and complete or partial jurisdiction over water pollution control in all of the 48 states, is found in all of the 48 states. It is also responsible for mosquito control in a number of states. Though not an exclusive water-resources agency, it

is an important agency in state water-resources administration. In a majority of states, this department is plural-headed; in other states, it is single-headed.[258]

(a) <u>Plural-headed "Departments of Health"</u>---They are found in Alabama, Arizona, Arkansas, Colorado, Connecticut, Delaware, Florida, Georgia, Kansas, Kentucky, Louisiana, Maryland, Massachusetts, Minnesota, Montana, Nebraska, Nevada, New Hampshire, New Jersey, New Mexico, North Carolina, North Dakota, Ohio, Oklahoma, Oregon, South Carolina, Tennessee, Texas, Utah, Vermont, Virginia, West Virginia, Wisconsin and Wyoming.[259] The controlling body (hereafter abbreviated as "board") is a "Public Health Council in Connecticut, Massachusetts, New Jersey, Ohio and Tennessee; a "Board of Public Health" in Georgia and New Mexico; a "Health Council" in North Dakota; a "Health Commission" in Vermont, and a "State Board of Health" in all other (26) states.[260] In its general outlook, the board is composed entirely of special members. But full or advisory <u>ex-officio</u> members are found in the following states:

Connecticut, Mississippi, Massachusetts, Oregon and Texas
      ---The administrative officer (in Texas, advisory)
Arizona and Georgia---The Governor.
Maryland---The administrative officer; the commissioner
      of health of the City of Baltimore.
Nevada---The Governor; the Secretary of State.
New Hampshire---The Attorney-General.
South Carolina---The Attorney-General; the Comptroller-
      General.
North Carolina---The administrative officer; the Attorney-
      General; the State Superintendent of Public In-
      struction; the Chairman of the Board of Administra-
      tion; the State Fire Marshall; the Executive Sec-
      retary of the State Board of Nurse Examiners; the
      Executive Director of the State Board of Public
      Welfare; and such other persons as the Governor may
      designate (all advisory).

With regard to special members, their number is nine in Arkansas, Colorado, Minnesota, Mississippi, North Carolina, North Dakota, Oklahoma, Tennessee, Texas and West Virginia; seven in Montana, Nebraska, New Jersey, Ohio, Utah, Vermont, Virginia and Wisconsin; five in Arizona, Florida, New Mexico and Wyoming; six in Connecticut, Maryland, Massachusetts and New Hampshire, Wyoming, Delaware, Kentucky, Louisiana and Oregon; ten in Kansas; three in Nevada and fourteen in Georgia. In Alabama and South Carolina, the entire membership of the State Medical Association constitute the board; and in Mississippi, although there is a state board of health, the Department of Public Health is made up of the entire memberships of the State Medical Association and all other state, district or county medical organizations.

The special members are appointed by the Governor in Arkansas, Georgia, Kansas, Kentucky, Louisiana, Maryland, Minnesota (except one member, who is to be elected by the State Medical Association), Montana, Nevada, North Dakota, Ohio, Tennessee, Virginia and Wyoming; by the Governor with the consent of the Council in Massachusetts and New Hampshire; by the Governor with the consent of the Senate in Arizona, Colorado, Connecticut, Delaware, Florida, Mississippi, New Jersey, New Mexico, North Carolina (except four members, who are to be elected by the State Medical Association), Oklahoma, Oregon, South Carolina (Executive Committee of the State Board of Health), Texas, Utah, Vermont, West Virginia and Wisconsin; and by the Governor with the consent of the majority of the membership of the unicameral state legislature in Nebraska. They serve for a term of six years in Colorado, Connecticut, Georgia, Maryland, Massachusetts, Mississippi, New Hampshire, New Mexico, Texas, Vermont and Wyoming; four years in Arkansas, Delaware, Flrodia, Kentucky, Louisiana, Nevada, North Carolina and Oregon; seven years in Montana, New Jersey, Ohio, South Carolina (Executive Committee), Utah, Virginia and Wisconsin; three years in Kansas, Minnesota, Nebraska, North Dakota and Tennessee; nine years in Oklahoma and West Virginia; and five years in Arizona.

In Alabama, Georgia, Kansas, Kentucky, Louisiana, Maryland, Minnesota, Mississippi, Nevada, New Jersey, New Mexico, Oregon, South Carolina, Texas and Utah, the entire special membership of the board are required to be experts, i.e., men with training in and knowledge of the medical sciences, who are usually appointed upon the nomination of the professional groups to which they belong. A majority of the special members of the board must be such experts in Arizona, Arkansas, Delaware, Florida, Massachusetts (one half), Montana, Nebraska, New Hampshire, North Carolina, North Dakota, Ohio, Oklahoma, Tennessee, Vermont, West Virginia and Wyoming. In North Carolina and Virginia, only a minority of the special members are professional medical men. Wisconsin and Colorado are the only states which have no rigid, statutory requirement as to the professional training of the members of the board. Special interests (other than the medical profession) are represented only in North Carolina, where a member is to be a dairyman, and Tennessee, where one of the special members represents the Tennessee Congress of Parents and Teachers and the Tennessee Federation of Women's Clubs jointly. In the following states, the members or a majority of them are appointed on a territorial basis:

Arkansas, Colorado, Georgia, Louisiana, Mississippi, Ohio and West Virginia (by Congressional districts)
Kansas, North Dakota, Tennessee and Virginia (by grand divisions)
Delaware (by counties)

In Delaware, West Virginia and Wyoming, the bi-partisan principle governs the appointment of the special members.

The officers of the board consists of a presiding officer,
known in most states as the President, and a secretary. In
Louisiana and Vermont, the President is designated by the Governor; in Nevada the Governor and in Connecticut the administrative officer of the board is the President ex-officio.
In all other states (except Massachusetts and Oklahoma, where
there is no statutory provision for the presiding officer)
the President (and in Colorado, Montana, Tennessee and Wyoming also a vice-president; in Louisiana vice-president only) or Chairman (Arizona, Georgia, New Jersey, New Mexico,
North Dakota, Ohio, South Carolina, Texas and West Virginia;
and a vice-chairman in Arizona, Georgia, New Mexico and Texas)
is elected by the board.261 The secretary (or the secretary-
treasurer in North Carolina and Louisiana) is employed by the
board in Arizona, Delaware, Georgia, Kansas, Louisiana, Minnesota (may be a member of the board), New Mexico, North Carolina (with the approval of the Governor and for a term of
four years), Oregon and Wisconsin, and also in Colorado, Montana and Wyoming if the board chooses not to have the administrative officer to act as its secretary. In Ohio and Virginia, the administrative officer and in Nevada the Governor
desigantes an employee to be the board's secretary. In all
other states (except Connecituct, where there is no statutory
provision for a secretary) the administrative officer acts or
may be authorized to act as the board's secretary.

The board holds its regular meetings quarterly in Arizona,
Arkansas, Colorado, Connecticut, Kansas, Louisiana, Maryland,
Minnesota, Nebraska, New Hampshire, Ohio, Texas, Utah and
Wyoming; semi-annually in Kentucky, Nevada, North Dakota, Ok-
lahoma and Tennessee; annually in Flrodia, North Carolina,
Oregon and Virginia; monthly in Delaware, Massachusetts, New
Jersey and Wisconsin and bi-monthly in Montana.262 Special
meetings of the board may be called by:263

(1)   The presiding officer or the administrative or a ma-
      jority of the members in Arizona, Colorado, Mon-
      tana, and Wyoming;
(ii) The presiding officer or a majority of the members
      in Arkansas, New Mexico and Tennessee;
(iii) The administrative officer or a majority of the
      members in Connecituct, Massachusetts and Ohio;
(iv) The presiding officer in Mississippi, Nevada and
      North Carolina;
(v)   The administrative officer or two members in Minne-
      sota and Texas;
(vi) The presiding officer or three members in Louisiana
      and Nebraska;
(vii) The presiding officer or the governor in Florida,
      the presiding officer or the governor or three

members in Vermont, the presiding officer or as
otherwise prescribed by the board in Wisconsin;

(viii)   As prescribed by the board in Delaware, Kansas,
Kentucky, Maryland, New Jersey, North Dakota, Oklahoma, Oregon, Virginia and West Virginia.

The board, being a deliberative body, needs an administrative officer. This officer is known as the "state health
officer" in Alabama, Arkansas, Delaware, Florida, Louisiana,
Nevada, New Hampshire, North Carolina, North Dakota, Oregon,
South Carolina, Texas and Wisconsin; "commissioner" in Arizona, Connecticut, Kentucky, Massachusetts, New Jersey, Oklahoma, Tennessee, Utah, Vermont and Virginia; "director" in
Colorado, Georgia, Maryland, Nevraska, New Mexico, Ohio, West
Virginia and Wyoming; "executive officer" in Minnesota, Mississippi and Montana; and "executive secretary" in Kansas.
He is appointed (1) by the board in Alabama (term to be fixed
by the board), Arizona (maximum 5 years), Colorado, Georgia
(6 years), Kentucky (4 years; may be a member of the board);
Maryland (removable only for cause), Mississippi, Montana
(maximum 10 years), Nebraska (removable only by a majority
of the members of the board and only for cause), New Hampshire,
New Mexico, Oklahoma, Texas (by a majority of the members;
and removable by a majority of members for cause), West Virginia and Wyoming; (2) by the board with the approval of the
Governor (for 4 years) in Nevada and Vermont; (3) by the Governor upon the recommendation of the board in South Carolina
(to serve at the pleasure of the board) and Tennessee; (4)
by the Governor with the consent of the Senate upon recommendation of the board in Utah (to serve at the pleasure of the
board); (5) by the Governor in Connecticut (6 years), Florida
(4 years), North Dakota and Virginia (4 years); and (6) by
the Governor with the consent of the Senate in Massachusetts,
New Jersey and Ohio. In Arkansas, Delaware, Kansas, Minnesota, North Carolina, Oregon and Wisconsin the secretary of the
board and in Louisiana the President is the administrative
officer ex-officio.[264]

Other administrative personnel of the department, who are
subordinates of the administrative officer, are appointed by
the administrative officer in Arizona, Arkansas, Colorado,
Georgia, Kentucky, New Jersey, North Dakota, Ohio, Oklahoma,
Oregon, Tennessee, Texas and Wyoming; by the administrative
officer with the approval of the board in Connecticut, Delaware (field personnel), Louisiana, Massachusetts (both departmental and field personnel), Montana, Nevada, Utah, Vermont
and Virginia (except sanitary engineers); and by the board in
Florida, Maryland, (field personnel), Minnesota, Mississippi
(field personnel), New Hampshire, New Mexico, North Carolina,
South Carolina (field personnel), Virginia (sanitary engineers
only), West Virginia and Wisconsin (both departmental and
field personnel).

In states such as Colorado, Connecticut and Tennessee,
the law designates the divisions and bureaus to be established within the department. In states such as New Hampshire,
Ohio and Wisconsin, the divisions and bureaus of the department are created by the board. In other states, such as Arizona, New Jersey, Texas and Vermont, such units are established by the administrative officer with the approval of
the board. In Kentucky, the divisions are established by
law, but they may be re-grouped by the administrative officer. In Nevada and West Virginia, the law sets up the basic
divisions, leaving necessary additional division or divisions
to be set up by the administrative officer with the approval
of the board in the former and by the board in the latter.

(b) Single-headed "Departments of Health"---These are
found in California, Idaho, Illinois, Indiana, Iowa, Maine,
Michigan, Missouri, New York, Pennsylvania, Rhode Island,
South Dakota and Washington.[265] The head of the department
is a "director" in California, Illinois, Indiana, Missouri,
Rhode Island and Washington; a "commissioner" in Idaho, Iowa,
Maine, Michigan and New York; "secretary" in Pennsylvania and
the "state health officer" in South Dakota. He is appointed
by the Governor with the consent of the Senate in Illinois,
Iowa, Michigan, Mississippi, New York, Pennsylvania and Washington; by the Governor in California, Indiana and Rhode Island; by the Governor with the approval of the Council in
Maine; and by the Governor with the approval of the advisory
council of the department in South Dakota. He serves for a
term of four years in California, Indiana, Iowa, Michigan,
Mississippi and Pennsylvania, a term of two years in Illinois,
a term of three years in Maine and for a term expiring with
the term of the Governor in New York, and at the pleasure of
the Governor in Rhode Island, South Dakota and Washington.
Idaho department is of a unique organizational pattern in
that the Governor is the ex-officio commissioner, who appoints
a Director of Public Health as the administrative officer of
the department.

Administrative assistants of the head of the department
are appointed by the latter in all of these states except
Missouri and Indiana.[266] In Missouri, the Governor, with
the consent of the Senate, appoints the directors of divisions;
and the director of each division, with the approval of the
director of the department, appoints his own subordinate officials. In the Indiana department, there is a division of
health and preventive medicine, which is in charge of the
functions that are related to water resources administration.
The said division is composed of the State Board of Health,
the State Health Commissioner and the Stream Pollution Control Board, which are equivalent to a department of health
in most other states. The board consists of nine members,
all professional medical men except one, who are appointed by
the Governor for a term of four years. With the approval of

the Governor, the board appoints a secretary, who is its executive or administrative officer and is known as the State
Health Commissioner. The latter employs all necessary subordinate personnel and, with the approval of the board, establishes (and abolishes) divisions and sub-divisions of the
board. The board elects a Chairman every two years, and meets
at least once every two months (Statutes, tit. 35, ch. 1:
Acts 1945, ch. 352; as amended by Acts 1949, ch. 157).

Divisions of the department are created by law in states
such as Indiana, Maine and Missouri, and by the head of the
department in such states as California (with the approval of
the Governor), New York and South Dakota.

In all of these states with the only exception of Idaho
there is within the department an advisory body which advises
the head on policy matters.[267] It is known by various names[268]
and are appointed by the Governor (in Maine, with the consent
of the council) or by the Governor or with the consent of the
Senate for terms varying from two to six years. It may be
noted that all of these advisory bodies are the degeneration
of the State Board of Health that was originally created as a
plural-headed independent agency.[269]

(8) "The Public Service Commission"---This agency exists
in all of the forty-eight states, and in most states it is
the successor of the old "Railroad Commission".[270] As discussed in Chapter 3 above, the "Public Service Commission"
(generic) has jurisdiction over one or more aspects of water
resources administration in all of the forty-eight states except Minnesota, Mississippi, South Dakota and Texas.[271] It
regulates the construction and operation of dams and other
water structures in Wisconsin, Vermont and West Virginia; of
hydroelectric power projects in Wisconsin, Virginia and New
Hampshire, and of water terminals in Montana. The Wisconsin
Public Service Commission is also given authority over flood
control and water use.

The agency is officially called "Public Utilities Commission" in California, Colorado, Connecituct, Idaho, Maine,
Massachusetts, New Hampshire, Ohio and South Dakota; "Corporation Commission" in Arizona, Kansas, Oklahoma and Virginia;
"Commerce Commission" in Illinois and Iowa; "Railroad and Public Utilities Commission" in Florida and Tennessee; "Utilities
Commission" in North Carolina; "Board of Public Utility Commissioners" in New Jersey; "Public Utility Commission" in Pennsylvania; "Railroad and Warehouse Commission" in Minnesota;
"Railway Commission" in Nebraska; "Railroad Commission" in
Texas; and the "Public Service Commission" in all other states
except Oregon and Rhode Island. It may be noted that in the
last-mentioned two states, the agency is single-headed, and
known as the "Public Utility Hearing Board besides the Administrator.[272] The agency is created by the state constitution in

Arizona, California, Louisiana, Nebraska, North Dakota, Oklahoma and Virginia, but by statute in all other states.

The Public Service Commission distinguishes itself from other plural-headed state agencies in that it is a full-fledged administrative agency. It combines the functions of the commission or board and those of the administrative or executive officer of an ordinary plural-headed agency. This is in part caused by the relative scarcity of routine work and the complete lack of enterprise activities. But it largely results from the fact that both the general policies and the governing rules of state public-utility administration are in general set forth in detail by statute,[273] which leaves little room for that sort of administrative action that is the main concern of the commission or board of an ordinary plural-headed state agency. There is relatively little need of the implemention of the statutory provisions by administrative regulations; but all that is needed is the execution of statutory provisions by administrative orders. With an ordinary plural-headed agency of the state government, these two broad types of administrative action are divided between the commission or board and the administrative or executive officer. With the lack of regulations on the one hand and of routine business on the other, the public service commissions become occupied with the making of orders, in the same way as the courts are occupied with the making of decrees. Since in American public administration (which in broad sense includes both non-judicial and judicial administration) both administrative orders and judicial decrees are made after public hearings, the work of the State Public Service Commission takes on a judicial appearance.[274]

The above facts have produced a chain reaction on the organizational pattern of the Commission, which is reflected on the following characteristics:

1.   The Commission does not have an administrative or executive officer.
2.   The members of the Commission, unlike those of other plural-headed state agencies discussed in this Book, receive a salary.
3.   With the exception of Nebraska, Montana, Utah and Wyoming, the Commission is composed entirely of special members. In Nebraska, the State Engineer is a non-voting ex-officio member. The Board of Railroad Commissioners of Montana, the Commission of Business Regulation of Utah and the State Board of Equalization of Wyoming are the Public Service Commissions ex-officio in these states.
4.   The members of the Commission do not represent special interest groups or professional organizations.

The number of members of the Commission is seven in South

Carolina; five in California, Georgia, Illinois,[275] Massachusetts, Missouri, New York,[276] North Carolina and Pennsylvania; and three in all other states. In Idaho, Illinois, Indiana, Kansas, Massachusetts, Nevada, New Jersey, Ohio, Rhode
Island, Washington and Wyoming, the membership is required to
be bi-partisan.

The members are appointed:

1. By the Governor in California, Delaware (one from
   each county), Indiana, Maryland, Nevada, Oregon and
   Rhode Island.
2. By the Governor with the consent of the Council in
   Maine, Massachusetts and New Hampshire; and
3. By the Governor with the consent of the Senate in
   Arkansas, Colorado, Idaho, Illinois, Kansas, Kentucky,
   Michigan, Missouri, New Jersey, New Mexico, New York,
   North Carolina, Ohio, Pennsylvania, Vermont, Washington, West Virginia, Wisconsin, Utah and Wyoming.
   They are elected:
4. By the people at large in Alabama, Arizona, Georgia,
   Florida, Iowa, Minnesota, Montana, Nebraska, Oklahoma, South Dakota and Texas;
5. By the people on a district basis in Louisiana, Mississippi, South Carolina and Tennessee;
6. By the General Assembly in Virginia; and
7. By the General Assembly upon the nomination of the
   Governor in Connecticut.

The members of the Commission serve for a term of seven
years in Maine; ten years in New York and Pennsylvania; two
years in North Dakota and South Carolina; five years in Illinois and Massachusetts; four years in Alabama, Florida, Idaho, Indiana, Iowa, Knasas, Kentucky, Mississippi, Nevada and
Oregon (the Commissioner); and six years in all other states.
The Public Utility Administrator of Rhode Island is appointed
by the Director of Business Regulation with the approval of
the Governor to serve for an indefinite term of office.

The members are removable for cause (and after a hearing):[277]

1. By the Governor with the consent of the Council in
   Maine, New Hampshire and Massachusetts;
2. By the Governor with the consent of the Senate in
   Pennsylvania (two-thirds of the Senate membership)
   and Delaware;
3. By the state legislature in California, Missouri (also 5), Louisiana (in all of these three states, two-
   thirds of entire membership of each house) and Georgia;
4. By the courts in Connectitcut (superior court), Washington (a special court consisting of three judges
   named by the chief justice of the supreme court), Ten-

nessee (for acceptance of gift or favor only) and
Iowa; and
5. By the Governor in all other states (including Missouri).

In other states, the members of the State Public Service Commission can only be impeached.[278]

The Commission is presided over by a President in Alabama,
California, **Idaho**, New Jersey and North Dakota, and by a
Chairman in all other states.[279] The Chairman or President
is:

1. Designated by the Governor in Alabama, Arkansas, Colorado, Delaware, Illinois, Kansas (first chairman only), Kentucky, Maine, Maryland, Massachusetts, Michigan, Missouri, Nevada, New Hampshire, New Jersey, New York, North Carolina, Ohio, Pennsylvania, Utah, Vermont (annually), Washington, West Virginia (annually) and Wisconsin (biennially);
2. Elected by the members in Arizona, California, Georgia (biennially), Idaho, Iowa (annually), Kansas (except the first chairman), Montana, Nebraska, North Dakota, Oklahoma, Rhode Island, South Carolina, Tennessee (biennially), Texas and Wyoming (biennially); and
3. In New Mexico, the commissioner who is in longest continuous service.

Each Commission also has a secretary or clerk,[280] who is appointed by the Commission in a great majority of states.[281]
With a few exceptions, the Commission in general may also employ other necessary clerical and technical assistants. In
Colorado, Kansas and Utah, all personnel are employed by the
Commission with the approval of the Governor. In Maryland,
the Governor appoints a general counsel upon the recommendation of the Commission. In Pennsylvania, the Attorney General appoints a counsel to the Commission with the approval of
the Governor. In West Virginia, the Governor appoints a counsel; and in Indiana the Governor may appoint a public counselor.

(9) **The Land Management Agencies**---They are grouped under
the following categories:[282]

(a) A single-headed independent special **agency**---Arizona,
Arkansas, Louisiana, Maryland, Mississippi, South
Dakota and Texas.
(b) A plural-headed independent special agency---Colorado, Idaho (entirely _ex-officio_), Montana (entirely
ex-officio), New Mexico (partly _ex-officio_), North
Dakota (entirely _ex-officio_), Oklahoma (entirely _ex-officio_), Oregon (entirely _ex-officio_), Washington

(partly ex-officio), West Virginia (entirely ex-officio), Wisconsin (entirely ex-officio) and Wyoming (entirely ex-officio).

(c) A plural-headed special agency within other state agencies---California (an entirely ex-officio body within the Department of Finance) and New York (similar body within the Department of State).

(d) Other state agencies acting ex-officio as land agencies---Florida (Department of Agriculture), Iowa and Kentucky (Secretary of State), Kansas (State Auditor), Nevada (State Surveyor General), Pennsylvania (Department of Internal Affairs), Utah (Department of Finance) and Virginia (State Librarian).

(e) "The Department of Conservation"---Alabama (but the Department of Finance is in charge of land sales), Michigan, Minnesota, and Ohio (lands administered by that department).

(f) Other state agencies---Connecituct (State Treasurer), Delaware (State Highway Department), Indiana (State Auditor), Maine (Forest Commissioner), Massachusetts (Department of Public Works), Ohio (Department of Public Works, but the State Auditor keeps land records), South Carolina (State Budget and Control Board) and Tennessee (State Property Administration).

(g) No state land agencies, but the Secretary of State keeps land records---Georgia, Missouri and North Carolina.

(h) No state land agencies---Illinois (but the Director of Revenue keeps records of land sales made by county authorities), New Hampshire, New Jersey (but the Department of Conservation administers submerged lands) and Vermont.

(10) State Soil Conservation Agencies---The state soil conservation agency, unlike other state agencies discussed in this Section, is not in charge of some state administration, but is created for the purpose of approving the organization of and coordinating and assisting the soil conservation districts. The only exception is New Hampshire, where the entire state constitue a soil conservation district, and the state soil conservation agency is an administering agency for this district and is authorized to undertake all soil conservation measures.

Soil conservation agencies are found in all of the forty-eight states, and may be divided into the following types:[283]

(a) A unit of other state agencies---Alabama (The Extension Service of the Alabama Polytechnic Institute), Arkansas (Resources and Development Commission), Arizona (Division of Soil Conservation of the State Land Department), Connecticut (Commissioner of Farms and

Markets, with the advice of the State Soil Conserva-
tion Advisory Committee) and Illinois (Department of
Agriculture, assisted by the State Soil Conservation
Districts Advisory Board).

(b) A Soil Conservation Committee (in California, Commission) within the "Department of Conservation"---Cal-
ifornia, Kentucky and Rhode Island.

(c) A Soil Conservation Committee within other state agen-
cies---Maryland (State Board of Agriculture and the
Regents of the University of Maryland), Massachusetts
(department of Agriculture and New York (New York
State College of Agriculture).

(d) An independent Soil Conservation Committee (or Board
in Colorado, Florida, Oklahoma and Texas, or Commission in Idaho and Missouri) in all other states.

The agencies in the last-mentioned three groups and the
advisory bodies of Connecticut and Illinois are, in their general pattern, composed partly of _ex-officio_ and partly of
special members.[284] Ex-officio members usually include the
directors of the state agricultural experiment station and
the state extension service and the head of the "state department of agriculture" (generic); and special members, number-
ing from one to seven (mostly three or five), are generally
appointed by the governor (in Maine and New Hampshire, with
the consent of the council) or by the governor with the consent of the senate[285] for a term varying from two to six (mostly four) years. They are farmers representative of soil
conservation districts. The agency elects a chairman, and,
with a few exceptions, is authorized to employ an administrative officer and necessary technical and other assistants.

(11) _Miscellaneous State Agencies_---Several groups of
such agencies may be mentioned:

(a) Agencies to seek or accept cooperation with the Federal Government in flood control, navigation improvement and
other enterprise---In Connecticut, there is the bi-partisan
State Flood Control and Water Policy Commission, composed of
a Director and four other members, whose functions it is to
cooperate with the Federal Government in flood control, navigation improvement and water pollution control projects (_Gen-
eral Statutes_, ch. 166: Enacted in 1939;; amended 1943).
Oregon has created the Willamette River Commission (_Revised
Statutes_, sec. 542.110 et seq.: Laws 1939, ch. 110), to acquire lands needed and render other assistance for the construction by the Federal Government of the comprehensive multiple-purpose flood-control program authorized by Congress on
28 June 1938 (52 Stat. 1222). The State Water Conservation
Board of Vermont, created by an act of 1947 (No. 83), is now
an agency primarily concerned with cooperation with the Federal Government with respect to flood control and navigation
improvement projects (_Statutes_, sec. 6299 et seq.).

(b) Agencies having jurisdiction only over special districts---Under the laws of Oregon, the Governor, the State Treasurer, and the Secretary of State are constituted as a State Reclamation Commission, with the Governor as chairman and the state engineer as secretary. Its functions are to make investigations and studies regarding the operations of the irrigation and drainage districts and formulate plans for necessary improvements. However, it has no authority of control over such districts. The Water Conservation Board of Colorado is a special agency for the organization, supervision and assistance of water conservancy districts. It consists of the Governor, the Attorney General, the State Engineer, the Director of the State Planning Commission, its own director and nine members appointed by the Governor for a term of three years. The Governor is its chairman, and it elects a vice-chairman and a secretary. The latter is the director of the Board, who serves at the pleasure of the Board (Statutes, ch. 173B, sec. 1 et seq.: Laws 1937, ch. 265; as last amended by L. 1947, ch. 332). In Wisconsin, a Water Regulatory Board was established in 1937 (ch. 379), consisting of a representative of the College of Agriculture of the University of Wisconsin, a representative of the Conservation Commission, and a representative of the Public Service Commission. It may elect a Chairman and employ an engineer as its administrative agent. Its functions are to supervise the operation, repair and maintenance of the dams, dikes and other works of drainage districts. The Water Resources Commission of Michigan, while primarily a state water pollution regulatory agency, has been also authorized to assist and advise the flood control districts (Acts 1949, No. 117, sec. 2).

(c) Planning and investigation agencies---The Columbia Basin Commission of Washington is an outstanding example of such agencies. It consists of the director of the Department of Conservation and Development as chairman, one representative each from three designated irrigation districts of the Columbia River Basin in Washington, and three members appointed by the Governor to serve at his pleasure. Its duties are to study and promote the comprehensive multiple-purpose development of the water and allied resources in that part of the Columbia River Basin which lies in the State of Washington. The three members representing and selected by the three irrigation districts constitute the Reclamation Section, and the three appointive members constitute the Resources Section. Both these Sections are presided over by the Director of the Department of Conservation and Development. They are in effect sub-committees of the Commission (Revised Code, ch. 43.49: Laws 1943, ch. 283).

The San Luis Rey Water Authority of California and the Upper Columbia River Basin Commission of Oregon are of the same nature as the Columbia Basin Commission of Washington. The former consists of seven members appointed by the Governor for a term of four years, all representing local interests, and their reports are filed with the State Engineer and the authorities of San Diego County (Water Code, sec. 1200 et seq.: Stats. 1939, ch. 420). The latter is organized in the same fashion; but the Attorney General, the State Engineer and the Director of the State Department of Geology and Mineral Industries are its legal adviser, engineer and geologist respectively (Revised Statutes, sec. 542.310 et seq.: L. 1951, ch. 522; as amended by L. 1953, ch. 622). In 1953, an act was enacted in Oregon (L. 1953, ch. 658), which created the State Water Resources Committee. This agency differs from the above-mentioned agencies in that it is intrusted with duties to study the multiple-purpose utilization of the water resources of the whole state. The Committee is composed of seven members appointed by the Governor, and has an existence of only two years. In the same year a Water Resources Committee was created by the legislature of Texas (L. 1953, ch. 359), which has the same duties. The Texas Committee consists of three members appointed by the Governor, three senators and three members of the house of representatives, all of whom serve for a term of two years. It will be terminated in 1957.

Investigation and planning bodies may also be established for certain particular aspect of water resources administration. The Forest Lands Advisory Commission of Montana (L. 1943, ch. 176), the Commission on Forest Resources of Virginia (Joint Resolution No. 22 of the General Assembly of 1954), the National Park, Parkway and Forests Development Commission of North Carolina (L. 1947, ch. 422), the Columbia River Gorge Commission of Oregon (L. 1953, ch. 475) and the Underground Water Commission of Arizona (L. 1952, ch. 49) are examples.

It may be noted that state investigation and planning agencies are ordinarily temporary in nature. While supposedly investigating and planning for the state, these agencies may actually lay foundation for Federal or local administration.

The Wyoming Natural Resources Board is a mixed investigatory and administrative agency. It was created in 1951 (Laws 1951, ch. 73; as amended by L. 1953, ch. 187) with both functions of investigation and planning and the authority to make loans to state and local agencies and private parties for the construction of small projects of water development and utilization. It consists of nine members, distributed evenly between the two major political parties, appointed by the Governor with the consent of the Senate for terms of six years, with the Governor, the State Highway Superintendent, the State Engineer, the State Game and Fish Commissioner, the President of the University of Wyoming and the Commissioner of Agriculture sitting as ex-officio non-voting members. The Board elects a president and a vice-president and employs a secretary. With the approval of the Governor, the Board appoints a director, who may be the State Engineer or his deputy ex-officio, and who employs necessary assistants with the approval of the Board.

Section 2   State Coordinated Organization

1. Organizational Consolidation

(a) The "Department of Conservation"---This department, which combined the functions of two or more agencies discussed in Section 1 above, is found in the twenty-three states of Alabama, Arkansas, California, Illinois, Indiana, Iowa, Kentucky, Massashusetts, Michigan, Minnesota, Missouri, New Jersey, New York, North Carolina, Ohio, Oklahoma, Pennsylvania, Rhode Island, Tennessee, Virginia, Washington, West Virginia and Wisconsin.[286] It is officially designated by the following titles:

1. "Department of Conservation" or "Conservation Department"---Alabama (director), Illinois (director), Indiana (a commission of four), Kentucky (commissioner), New Jersey (commissioner), New York (commissioner) and Tennessee (commissioner and an advisory conservation commission of nine).
2. "Conservation Commission"---Iowa, Missouri, West Virginia (commission being advisory to the director) and Wisconsin.
3. "Department of Conservation and Development"---North Carolina (a board of 15 and a director as its administrative officer), Virginia (director and an advisory board) and Washington.
4. "Department of Natural Resources"---California (director and an advisory commission), Massachusetts (board of five) and Ohio (director).
5. Other designations---Department of Agriculture and Conservation of Rhode Island; Resources and Development Commission of Arkansas; Planning and Resources Board of Oklahoma; and Department of Florests and Waters of Pennsylvania (headed by a secretary).

It may be noted that the agency is single-headed in Alabama, California, Illinois, Kentucky, Minnesota, New Jersey, New York, Pennsylvania, Rhode Island, Tennessee, Virginia, Washington and West Virginia; and plural-headed in Arkansas, Indiana, Iowa, Massachusetts, Michigan, Missouri, North Carolina, Oklahoma and Wisconsin.

The functions of the Department of Conservation with respect to water resources administration vary[287] from one state to another. For the sake of brevity, they are listed in the following table:[288]

State	I	II	III	IV	V	VI	VII
Alabama		x	x	x		x	
Arkansas	x						x
California		x		x			x
Illinois		x	x	x			
Indiana	x	x	x	x			
Iowa		x	x	x			
Kentucky	x	x		x	x		x
Massachusetts		x	x	x	x		
Michigan		x	x	x		x	
Minnesota	x	x	x	x		x	
Missouri		x	x				
New Jersey	x	x	x	x	x		
New York	x	x	x	x			
North Carolina	x	x	x	x			
Ohio	x	x	x	x		x	x
Oklahoma	x	x		x	x		
Pennsylvania	x	x		x			
Rhode Island		x	x				x
Tennessee		x	x	x	x		
Virginia	x	x		x			
Washington	x	x					
West Virginia		x	x	x			
Wisconsin		x	x	x	x		

23 (100%)	12	22	16	19	6	4	5
	(52%)	(96%)	(70%)	(83%)	(26%)	(17%)	(22%)

The Directors or Commissioners of the single-headed "Departments of Conservation" are appointed by the Governor in Alabama, California, Kentucky, Rhode Island and Tennessee; by the Governor with the approval of the General Assembly in Virginia; and by the Governor with the consent of the Senate in Illinois, Minnesota, New Jersey, New York, Ohio (also with the approval of the Natural Resources Commission), Pennsylvania (two-thirds of entire Senate membership), Washington and West Virginia. They serve for a term of four years in Kentucky and Pennsylvania, for a term of six years in Minnesota and Ohio, for a term of two years in Illinois and at the pleasure of the Governor in the remaining states. In general, the Director or Commissioner employs necessary subordinate administrative personnel. In six states, there is an advisory body which advices him on policy matters. These advisory bodies are as follows:[289]

      Alabama---Advisory Board of Conservation, consisting of
                the Governor, the Commissioner of Agriculture
                and Industries, the Director of Agricultural
                Extension Service, and 8 members appointed by
                the Governor for 6 years.
      Ohio------Natural Resources Commission, composed of the
                dean of the College of Agriculture of Ohio
                State University and 7 members appointed by the

Governor with the consent of the Senate for 7
years. The Commission is bi-partisan.

Rhode Island---Advisory Council, bi-partisan, consisting
of 7 members appointed by the Governor for 5
years.

Tennessee---State Conservation Commission, consisting
of the Governor, the Commissioner of Conservation, and nine members appointed by the Governor for 6 years.

Virginia---Board of Conservation and Development, composed of 13 members appointed by the Governor
for 4 years.

West Virginia---The Conservation Commission itself,
which consists of 6 members appointed by the
Governor with the consent of the Senate for
6 years.

The plural-headed Departments are all made up of special
members, Oklahoma being the only exception. The membership
is seven in Arkansas, Iowa and Michigan; four in Indiana and
Missouri; five in Massachusetts; six in Wisconsin; eleven in
Oklahoma (including the Governor, the Director of the Department of Highways, the Director of the Game and Fish Commission and the President of the Department of Agriculture); and
fifteen in North Carolina, Geographical distribution of the
members is taken into consideration in Massachusetts, and the
bi-partisanship is required of the membership in Iowa, Indiana
and Missouri. The members are appointed by the Governor with
the consent of the Senate in Arkansas, Iowa (two-thirds of
senators), Michigan and Wisconsin; by the Governor in Missouri, North Carolina and Oklahoma (except the four ex-officio
members); by the Governor with the approval of the Council
in Massachusetts and by an appointing board consisting of the
Governor, the Lieutenant Governor and the State Treasurer in
Indiana. Members serve for a term of six years in Iowa, Michigan, Missouri and Wisconsin; for a term of seven years in
Arkansas and Oklahoma (the four ex-officio members excepted);
for a term of four years in Indiana and North Carolina, and
for a term of five years in Massachusetts.

For the plural Departmental head, the Governor appoints
a Chairman in Arkansas and a Chairman and a vice-chairman in
Oklahoma. The plural body elects a Chairman in Wisconsin and
elects a Vice-Chairman in Arkansas. It annually elects a
Chairman in Iowa, Massachusetts and Michigan. In Oklahoma,
the Governor appoints a secretary of the plural body; in Iowa
the secretary of the Executive Council acts ex-officio as the
secretary of Conservation Commission. In Arkansas and Wisconsin the plural body elects and in Massachusetts it annually
elects a secretary. The Commission of Conservation of Michigan either elects or employs a secretary.[290] Regular meetings
of the body are held quarterly in Iowa and North Carolina and
monthly in Michigan. The frequency of regular meetings is to

be determined by the body itself in Arkansas. Wisconsin Conservation Commission seemingly does not hold regular meetings.
Special meetings may be called by the Chairman or a majority
of members in Arkansas and Michigan and by the Chairman or two
members in Iowa and Wisconsin. The manner of holding special
meetings is to be prescribed by the body itself in North Carolina.[291]

        Each of the plural Departmental heads has an administra-
tive officer. In Oklahoma the Chairman is the administrative
officer, but a separate person is selected to assume this position in all remaining states. The administrative officer,
who assumes various official names, is appointed by the Governor in Indiana (director) and North Carolina (director of conservation and development). He is appointed by the plural Departmental head with the approval of the Governor in Arkansas
(Executive Director). He is employed by the plural body in
the remaining states.[292] He serves for a term of four years
in Indiana and for a term of two years in Arkansas. In all
other states, he serves at the pleasure of the appointing authority. Subordinate officers (unless otherwise specially provided by law) are appointed by the plural Departmental head in
Oklahoma. In Massachusetts, the administrative officer with
the approval of the plural head, appoints the division directors and assistants for general administration, but the director of each division, with the same approval, employs his own
assistants. In all other states, subordinate personnel are
employed by the administrative officer with the approval of
the plural Departmental head.

        Since the Department of Conservation is established to
consolidate the originally independent agencies, the divisions
and other units of the Department are generally specified by
law. These divisions and units, in functional groups, are discussed below.[293]

        (1) Water Conservation and Development Units---Two gen-
eral types of organizational patterns may be observed. The
first type of organization is found in Arkansas, Minnesota,
New York, North Carolina, Oklahoma, Pennsylvania and Virginia,
where there is only one division or unit in the Department in
charge of all aspects of water conservation and development.
The names of the various divisions or units under this type
are as follows:

        Arkansas---Division of Flood Control, Water and Soil Con-
                servation (also in charge of soil conservation),
                headed by a Director.
        Minnesota---Division of Waters, headed by a Director.
        New York---Division of Water Power and Control (headed
                by the Water Power and Control Commission).
        North Carolina---Water Resources and Engineering Division
                consisting of three principal engineers and one

associate engineer (functions being primarily
investigatory).
Oklahoma---Division of Water Resources, headed by a Director.
Pennsylvania---Water and Power Resources Board.
Virginia---Division of Water Resources, headed by a Commissioner, who may be assisted by an advisory
committee on water resources to be composed of
five members appointed by the governor.

The Pennsylvania Water and Power Resources Board is the
successor of the former independent Water Supply Commission
(created by an act of 1905). It consists of the Secretary of
Forests and Waters (chairman), the Secretary of Health, the
Executive Director of Pennsylvania Fish Commission, a member
of the Public Utility Commission designated by the Governor,
and an engineer appointed by the Governor. The acts of the
Board are not subject to the approval or disapproval of the
Department or the Secretary of Forests and Waters. Within
the Department, however, there is a Deputy Secretary of Waters,
under whose supervision are a chief engineer and Divisions of
Encroachments, Dams, Flood Control and Hydrography. The latter make the studies and prepare the technical work for the
information and guidance of the Water and Power Resources
Board."[294] In 1947 (Laws 1947, No. 252), a Flood Control Commission was established as a subordinate agency of the Water
and Power Resources Board, whose function it is to make investigations and studies on problems on flood control for the
consideration of the said Board. The Commission is composed
of the Secretary of Forests and Waters (chairman), four members appointed by the President pro tempore of the Senate
from the Senate membership, four members appointed by the
Speaker of the House of Representatives from the House membership and four members appointed by the Governor. It may appoint a secretary and necessary personnel.

The Water Power and Control Commission of New York is
made up of three ex-officio officers, namely, the Conservation
Commissioner (chairman), the Superintendent of Public Works
and the Attorney. Not only each of these three members is not
responsible to the Department, but it expressly provided that
the Department cannot be a party to any suit with respect to
any act of the Water Power and Control Commission but that
the latter will be a party in such suit. It is clear that
the Division of Water Power and Control, while nominally a
unit of the Department, is actually outside the control thereof.

Under the second type of organization, there are a general division concerned with water conservation and development, and, in addition, one or two special divisions having
responsibilities over certain particular aspects of water conservation and development. This form obtains in the following
states:

Indiana---(a) Division of Water Resources (general), (b) Division of Engineering (assisting levee and drainage districts) and (c) Division of Parks, Lands and Waters (in charge, *inter alia*, of navigable waters and their beds, each headed by a Chief.

Kentucky---(a) Division of Soil and Water Resources (general), headed by a Director; and (b) Flood Control and Water Usage Board (in charge of flood control and water supply particularly flood control regulation).

New Jersey---(a) Division of Water Policy and Supply (general, and also particularly water supply) and Division of Navigation, each headed by a Council of nine members.

Ohio---(1) Division of Water (general), headed by a Water Resources Board; and (2) Division of Shore Erosion (beach and bank erosion control, and harbor improvement), headed by a Chief.

Washington---(a) Division of Water Resources (general), (b) Division of Flood Control (flood control only), and (c) Division of Reclamation (administering the Reclamation Revolving Fund, used to make loans to reclamation districts), each headed by a Supervisor.

All of the single-headed divisions are units of the Department in its full sense. The plural-headed divisions, however, are only loosely attached to the Department.[295]

(2) Forestry Units---There is a "Division of Forestry" or "Forestry Division" in the Departments of Alabama, California, Illinois, Indiana, Kentucky, Michigan, Minnesota, Missouri, North Carolina, Ohio, Oklahoma, Rhode Island, Tennessee, Virginia, Washington and West Virginia. In New York, there is a "Division of Forests and Lands." These uni-functional forestry divisions are headed by a State Forester in Alabama, Illinois, Indiana, North Carolina, Ohio, Tennessee, Virginia and West Virginia; by a Director in Kentucky, Minnesota and Oklahoma; by a Chief in Michigan, Missouri and Rhode Island; by a Superintendent in New York, and by a Supervisor in Washington. The heads of the units of Rhode Island and Virginia are each advised and assisted by an advisory body of five members.[296] The California unit is under the care of a State Board of Forestry of seven members, who represent special interest groups and who are appointed by the Governor with the consent of the Senate for a term of four years. Its administrative officer is the State Forester, who is appointed by the Director of Natural Resources upon the recommendation of the Board.

In Pennsylvania, an independent State Forestry Commission was established by an act of 1919, which consisted of a Commissioner of Forestry and four other members appointed by the Gov-

ernor with the consent of the Senate to serve for terms of
four years. When the Department of Forests and Waters was established on 7 June 1923, this Commission was retained, but
the Commissioner of Forestry was replaced by the Secretary of
Forests and Waters, who also serves as its chairman. The Department administers all forestry laws of the state. However,
on important matters such as the acquisition and management
of state forests and the making of rules and regulations, the
approval of the Commission is required. The Commission also
advises the Department, in a general way, in its work on forestry and parks. The Secretary of Forests and Waters, in matters of forestry (and parks), is assisted by a Deputy Secretary for Forests, under whose immediate supervision there are
Divisions of Administration, Protection, Nurseries, Research
and Recreation.

In Iowa, Massachusetts, New Jersey and Wisconsin, the
forestry functions of the Department are intrusted to a combined forestry and parks Division, known by the following
names:[297]

>Iowa---Division of Lands and Waters (Chief). Within this
>   Division, there is a Superintendent of Forestry,
>   also known as the State Forester.
>Massachusetts---Division of Forests and Parks (Director).
>   Within this Division, there are Bureaus of In-
>   sect Pest Control, Forest Fire Control and For-
>   est Development.
>New Jersey---Division of Forestry, Geology, Parks and His-
>   toric Sites, headed by a Council of nine mem-
>   bers organized in the same way as the Councils
>   of the Divisions of Water Policy and Supply
>   and of Navigation discussed above.
>Wisconsin---Division of Forests and Parks (Superintendent).
>   In addition, there are a Forest Protection Di-
>   vision (Chief Ranger) and a Cooperative Fores-
>   try Division (Superintendent).

With the exception of New Jersey, the forestry unit or units
are well merged into the Department of Conservation in all of
the states discussed. The position of the California State
Forester may need further clarification, for he is under the
supervision of both the Director of Natural Resources and the
Board of Forestry, which are independent of each other.

(3) Fish and Wildlife Units---There is a combined fish
and wildlife unit in the Departments of Alabama, Indiana,
Iowa, Massachusetts, Minnesota, Missouri, New Jersey, Ohio,
Rhode Island and Tennessee. It is officially designated as
the Division of Fish and Game in Indiana, Iowa, Missouri, New
Jersey and Rhode Island; the Division of Game and Fish in Alabama and Minnesota; the Division of Fisheries and Game in Massachusetts; the Division of Wildlife in Ohio, and the Game and

Fish Commission (before 1949, a Division of Game and Fish headed by a Director) in Tennessee. These units are headed by a
Chief in Alabama, Iowa, Missouri, Ohio and Rhode Island; by a
Director in Minnesota, and by a Superintendent in Indiana.
The head of the Illinois unit is advised by a Board of Fish and
Game Conservation Advisors, which is composed of five persons
appointed by the Governor with the consent of the Senate for a
term of two years; the head of the Rhode Island unit is likewise advised by an Advisory Council on Fish and Game, consisting of seven members appointed by the Governor for five years.
The Chief of the Ohio Division of Wildlife is but the nominal
head of the Division which is actually headed by a Wildlife
Council, of which the Chief, an appointee of the Director of
Natural Resources, is the secretary ex-officio, and which consists of the Director of Natural Resources, and eight members
(bi-partisan) appointed by the Governor with the consent of
the Senate for a term of eight years. The New Jersey unit is
headed by a Council of nine members appointed in the same way
and having the same organizational authority as the Councils
of other divisions.

    The Tennessee Game and Fish Commission is composed of the
Governor, the Commissioner of Conservation, and nine members
appointed by the Governor for a term of six years on a district
basis. It annually elects a chairman and a vice-chairman, and
annually selects a secretary, who may be either a member of
the Commission or an outside person. It holds regular meetings bi-monthly; and special meetings may be called by the
chairman. It employs a State Director of Game and Fish to
serve at its pleasure, who is its chief administrative officer.
It may also appoint local conservation officers. It should be
remarked that this Commission is practically an independent
agency and that its acts and decisions are not controlled by
the Commissioner of the Department of Conservation.[298]

    It is even more interesting to note that the laws of Mass-
achusetts have expressly provided that the Division of Fisheries and Game, although it is within the Department of Natural
Resources, is not controlled by that Department. That is to
say, while it appears as a unit of the Department in the organizational chart, it is legally an independent agency. The
Massachusetts Division is administered by a Fish and Game Board,
which is made up of five members (bi-partisan) appointed by the
Governor with the approval of the Council for a five-year term
on a territorial basis. It employs a Director as its administrative officer.

    It may be noted that the Alabama and New Jersey Divisions
have no jurisdiction over marine fisheries, which are under
the control of the Division of Seafoods (Chief) and the Division of Shell Fisheries (a Council of nine members, as other
Divisions), respectively.

    In the following states, there are separate fish and game

divisions:

    Illinois---Division of Fisheries, Division of Game Mana-
            gement, and Division of Game Protection (each head-
            ed by a Superintendent).
    Michigan---Division of Fish and Fisheries and Division of
            Game (each headed by a Chief).
    West Virginia---Division of Fish Management and Division
            of Game Management (each headed by a Chief).
    Wisconsin---Fish Management Division and Game Management
            Division (each headed by a Superintendent).

    It may be noted that the North Carolina Department of Con-
servation and Development has jurisdiction over commercial
fisheries only but no jurisdiction over wildlife and sport or
game fishing. The Division of Commercial Fisheries (under a
Commissioner) is in charge of commercial fisheries.

    (4) Parks and Recreation Units---They fall under three
general groups as follows:

(A) A combined parks and forestry division:
    Iowa---Division of Lands and Waters (Chief). (Within
            this Division, there is a Superintendent of Parks).
    Massachusetts---Division of Forests and Parks (Director).
            (Within this Division, there is a Chief of Recrea-
            tion.)
    New Jersey---Division of Forestry, Geology, Parks and His-
            toric Sites (Council of nine).
    Wisconsin---Division of Forests and Parks (Superintendent).

(B) A combined parks and recreation division:
    Michigan---Division of Parks and Recreation (Chief).
    Oklahoma---Division of Recreation and State Parks (Direct-
            or).
    Pennsylvania---Division of Recreation (one of the five
            Divisions under the supervision of the Deputy Sec-
            retary for Forests).
    Tennessee---Division of State Parks and Recreation (Direct-
            or).

(C) A parks division:
    Alabama---Division of Parks, Monuments and Historical
            sites (Chief).
    California---Division of Beaches and Parks (Chief, and
            State Park Commission).
    Illinois---Division of Parks and Memorials (Superinten-
            dent). (The law provides for the appointment of a
            Board of Park Advisers of five members by the Gov-
            ernor with the consent of Senate, to serve for
            terms of two years).
    Indiana---Division of Parks, Lands and Waters (Superin-
            tendent). (This Division is also in charge of
            navigable streams and their beds).
    Kentucky---Division of Parks (Director).

Minnesota---Division of State Parks (Director).
New York---Division of Parks (Executive Officer and State
          Council of Parks).
North Carolina---Division of State Parks (Superintendent).
Ohio---Division of Parks (Chief).
Virginia---Division of Parks (Commissioner).
West Virginia---Division of State Parks (Chief).

The California and New York Divisions are worth special
notice. The California Division is actually managed by the
State Parks Commission, with the Chief of the Division as its
administrative agent. The Commission consists of five members appointed by the Governor with the consent of the Senate
for a four-year term. It has the authority to employ all administrative personnel of the Division other than the Chief,
who is appointed by the Director of Natural Resources upon
the nomination of the Commission. It may be observed that
the Chief is controlled by both the Director and the Commission but that between the Director and the Commission there
is no direct line of association.

The New York set-up is an improvement over its California
counterpart. The Executive Officer is appointed by the Conservation Commissioner and acts as the secretary of the State
Council of Parks. The Council, which, like the California
Commission, is the head of the Division, is composed of the
Superintendent of Lands and Forests of the Conservation Department, the president or a member of the Palisades Interstate Park Commission, and the presiding officers of the administering bodies of eight state parks, all of whom are subordinates of the Conservation Commissioner. The control of
the Department over the Division is made more complete by the
provision that all acts and decisions of the Council are to
be approved by the Conservation Commissioner.

(5) Units of Land Management and Soil Conservation---The
Soil Conservation Committees of California, Kentucky and Rhode
Island, as mentioned before, are within the Departments of
Conservation. In fact, however, they are fully independent
agencies. There is no Soil Conservation Committee in Arkansas, and functions that usually belong to such Committees in
other states have been assigned to the above-mentioned Division of Flood Control, Water and Soil Conservation. In Alabama, Michigan and Minnesota, there are respectively a State
Land Division (Chief, who is the State Land Clerk of Agent),
a Division of Lands (Chief) and a Division of Lands and Minerals (Director), all of which perform functions of state land
management. There is a Division of Lands and Soil (Chief) in
the Ohio Department, which manages lands that are under the
jurisdiction of the Department, but not other state lands.
The management of such lands mainly consists of measures of
soil and moisture conservation.

The existence in the Departments of Conservation of some states of units which are actually independent agencies and which are "within" the Departments only in organizational charts is peculiar to the organizational pattern of such Departments. These units are bound to be temporary. Ultimately they will either become fully integrated units or part with the Departments.

In certain cases, the Department of Conservation itself has proved to be fluid in its internal organization. There are always forces of integration and disintegration at work against each other within the Department. While in many states the Department of Conservation was established and has grown in a process of integration, there is no lack of instances in which the Department has suffered from bruises of disintegration. For example, a Department of Conservation and Development was created in Vermont in 1935 (Laws 1935, No. 17), which included a Fish and Game Service, a Forest Service and a Publicity Service. In 1943, this Department was changed into the Department of Natural Resources comprising the three above-mentioned Services and the State Geologist (L. 1943, No. 9). The Department was headed by a State Conservation Board. In 1947, Department was entirely disintegrated owing to the establishment of the independent Commission of Fish and Game and Board of Forests and Forest Parks. However, the State Conservation Board still exists as a state agency. In 1937, a Department of Natural Resources was established in **Georgia** (L. 1937, No. 103), which included a Division of Forestry, a Division of Wildlife, a Division of Mines, Mining and Geology and a Division of State Parks, Historic Sites and Monuments. But the 1943, this Department was abolished outright. (L. 1943, No. 125).

In 1912 the Conservation Commission of Louisiana, set up in 1908 (Acts 1908, No. 144), was re-organized as the Department of Conservation (Acts 1912, No. 127, and Constitution, art. 6, sec. 1), which had jurisdiction over forestry, fish and wildlife and mineral resources. By an act of 7 November 1944, independent Department of Wildlife and Fisheries and Forestry Commission were created, making the Department of Conservation a special agency for oil and gas conservation only. The Department of Conservation and Development of North Carolina was originally invested with authority over the entire field of fish and wildlife. However, the creation in 1947 of the Wildlife Resources Commission has left with the Department only functions relating to commercial fisheries. Fish and game administration and beach erosion control both used to be functions of the California Department of Natural Resources, but were divorced from it as a result of the creation of the independent Fish and Game Department and the transfer of beach erosion control operations to the Department of Public Works, in 1951 (Stats. 1951, ch. 715) and 1953 (Stats.

1953, ch. 1859), respectively. The Arkansas Resources and
Development Commission was deprived of functions on forestry
and parks in 1953, when its Division of Forestry and Parks
became the independent State Forestry and Parks Commission
(Acts 1953, No. 42). In Iowa the creation of the Natural Resources Council in 1949 has resulted in the loss of the functions of the Iowa Conservation Commission in the field of
flood control, particularly flood control regulation.

No study has been made by this author of the factors
which have caused the fission or fictitiousness of the Department. Considerations over the size of the Department (especially in comparison with that of an average Department),
the disposition of funds, the wishes and influence of the
special interest groups and administrative traditions may be
brought into play at one time or another and have varying degrees of justifiableness. There is also the possibility that
sheer political or personal influences struggle for a show-
down with the administrative planners, who surrender in a
state of despondency and helplessmess. On the whole, the
State Department of Conservation seems to be an experiment
in American public administration. Its general success has
been fully attested by the fact that it is now a regular state
Department in one-half of the states (including Louisiana).

(b) Combined Forestry, Fish and Wildlife and Parks and
Recreation Agencies---In the following states, there is a combined forestry and parks and recreation agency:299

Maryland---Department of Forests and Parks (Commission).
New Hampshire---Forestry and Recreation Commission.
Connecticut---State Park and Forest Commission.
Vermont---State Board of Forests and Forest Parks.
Arkansas---State Forestry and Parks Commission.

The Department or Commission of Forests and Parks of
Maryland is composed of five members appointed by the Governor
for a term of five years, partly representing special forestry
interests and partly representing people interested in parks
and recreation. The Commission elects a chairman and employs
all necessary personnel. New Hampshire Forestry and Recreation Commission consists of three members appointed by the
Governor with the consent of the Council for a term of three
years. It appoints as its administrative officer the State
Forester to serve at its pleasure. The latter employs all
office and field assistants. Prior to the Reorganization Act
of 1950, the Commission had no jurisdiction over the beaches
as such, which were under the administration of a separate a-
gency named the Shore and Beach Preservation Development Commission. But the act of 1950 abolished the latter and transferred its functions to the Forestry and Recreation Commission.

The State Park and Forest Commission of Connecticut con-

sists of six members appointed by the Governor with the consent of the Senate for a term of six years. It annually elects
a Chairman and appoints a Director to serve at its pleasure.
The latter is its administrative officer and secretary. The
Commission may appoint patrolmen for the various districts.
The Director appoints a State Forester to serve at his pleasure. The latter, in turn, "may employ such field and office
assistants as in the judgment of the director may be necessary . . ." In its actual operation, the Commission has divided itself into two divisions -- Forestry Division, headed
by the State Forester, and the State Park Division, headed by
a Superintendent of State Parks.300 The State Board of Forests and Forest Parks of Vermont consists of six members appointed by the Governor with the consent of the Senate for
a term of six years. The Governor biennially designates a
member as chairman. The Board, with the approval of the Governor, appoints a State Forester as its executive secretary,
who shall serve for a term of six years. The State Forestry
and Parks Commission of Arkansas is composed of nine members
appointed by the Governor with the consent of the Senate on a
district basis for a term of nine years. It elects a Chairman and a Vice-Chairman, and employs a State Forester as its
secretary and administrative officer. The latter employs all
necessary assistants and subordinates with the approval of
the Commission. The Commission holds quarterly regular meetings, and special meetings may be called by the Chairman or a
majority of the members.

Prior to 1949, there was a Board of Forestry and Parks in
Florida, but in 1949 it was split into separate forestry and
parks agencies (L. 1949, chs. 25324 and 25353). In Montana,
when the office of the State Park Director was created in
1929 (L. 1929, ch. 111, sec. 2), it was held by the State Forester ex-officio, and when the State Park Commission was established in 1939 (L. 1939, ch. 48), the State Forester, too,
was designated to be its ex-officio secretary. It may be also noted that at least in the period of 1949-1951, the State
Forester of the State Forestry Commission and the State Park
Director of the State Board of Park Supervisors of Mississippi
were the same person,301 although there is no statutory provision to that effect.302

In the following states, there is a combined forestry, fish
and wildlife and parks and recreation agency:303

Kansas---Forestry, Fish and Game Commission.
Nebraska---Game, Forestation and Parks Commission.
South Dakota---Game, Fish and Parks Commission.

The Kansas Commission is composed of six members appointed by the Governor with the consent of the Senate for a term
of four years, one from each of the six special districts.
The Governor serves as its chairman ex-officio. The Commis-

sion employs a director as its administrative officer and ex-officio secretary. The director, with the approval of the Commission, appoints necessary assistants.[304] The Nebraska Commission is made up of five members appointed by the Governor with the consent of a majority of the members of the state legislature (unicameral). It annually elects a chairman, and appoints a secretary to serve for a term of six years. The latter appoints deputy conservation officers and agents.[305] The South Dakota Commission is a bi-partisan body of eight embers appointed by the Governor with the consent of the Senate for six years. It elects a chairman and a vice-chairman each year. It may employ a director of game and fish as its administrative officer, and a superintendent of fisheries, a chief game warden, and a number of game wardens. Forestry affairs are under the care of a Division of Forestry, headed by a State Forester, who is appointed by the Commission with the approval of the Commissioner of School and Public Lands. Assistants of the State Forester are employed by the Commission upon the recommendation of the state forester.[306]

It is interesting to note that the laws of Connecticut provide for the existence of a Commission on Forests and Wild life (General Statutes, sec. 3468 et seq.: Acts 1925, ch. 8; as last amended in 1939), which is nothing but the State Park and Forest Commission and the State Board of Fisheries and Game constituted jointly. Its functions are to accept donations of lands and to acquire Federal lands either by purchase or by lease, and to construct and repair dams. The Commission annually elects a president, a vice-president and a secretary. It meets quarterly, and special meetings may be called by the president or three members.

Since the several Departments of Conservation primarily deal with matters of forestry, parks and recreation and fish and wildlife, it may be concluded that the coordination of state water-resources agencies through consolidation mainly operates in these three fields.

2. Inter-Agency Bodies

(a) General Inter-Agency Bodies---Such agencies have been established in a number of states to coordinate the activities of practically all agencies of water resources administration. In Ohio, a law of 1941 set up a State Natural Resources Coordinating Board which consists of the Chairman of the Conservation Committee of the House of Representatives, the State Geologist, the State Forester, and the Directors of Natural Resources, Archaelogical and Historical Society, Agricultural Experiment Station, Highways, Public Works, Education, and Health, and whose function is to coordinate work of the agencies represented. It employs an executive secretary. In Illinois, a State Water Resources and Flood Control Board was created in 1945, consisting of the Director of Public Works and Buildings, the Director of Conservation, the Director of Agriculture, the Director of Registration and Education, and the Director of Health, one of whom is to be designated by the Governor as chairman. The Department of Public Works and Buildings may detail an employee to be its technical secretary. The Board investigates and coordinates the various beneficial uses of water. A Council on Resources and Development was established in New Hampshire by the Reorganization Act of 1950. It consists of delegates from the Fish and Game Commission, the Planning and Development Commission, the Water Pollution Commission, the Forestry and Recreation Commission and the Water Resources Board, with chairmanship rotated among these members. "The council shall meet at least once every quarter to advise and consult upon common problems in the field of natural resources and their development; to make such reports and recommendations as may be desirable to the governor and council; and . . . to effectively coordinate the work of the agencies enumerated . . ."

The Wisconsin Natural Resources Committee (Statutes, sec. 23.26: L. 1951, ch. 203; as amended by L. 1953, chs. 61 and 441) and the Montana Council on Natural Resources and Development (L. 1953, ch. 95) are organized on the same pattern, and have similar functions. The former includes in its membership the Governor (chairman), two members of the Joint Legislative Council appointed by its chairman, two representatives of the Conservation Commission, two representatives of the University of Wisconsin, two representatives of the Public Service Commission, two representatives of the Department of Agriculture, one representative of the Department of Health, one representative of the State Planning Division, one representative of the Attorney General, one representative of the Department of Taxation, one representative of the State Highway Commission, and one representative of the State Soil Conservation Committee. It elects a secretary. The latter is made up of the Commissioner of State Lands and Investments, the State Game Warden, the State Forester, the Secretary of Grass Conservation Commission, the State Engineer, the Executive Secretary of the Oil Conservation Board, the Director of the State Bureau of Mines and Geology, and the State Highway Engineer. It elects a chairman, a secretary and other necessary officers.

In Missouri there is an unofficial committee which examines on behalf of the state Federal flood control or irrigation projects proposed to be constructed in that state. "The membership of this committee is made up of representatives from the Division of Resources and Development (of the Department of Business and Administration), the State Agricultural College, the Conservation Commission, the State Highway Commission, the Department of Agriculture, the Division of Public Health, the Public Service Commission, the State Park Board, the Soil Conservation (Districts) Commission, and the Division of Geological Survey and Water Resources (of the Department of Business

and Administration)."[307] What is peculiar to this committee
is that it coordinates the several state agencies not on state
but on Federal administration. However, it seems that the unofficial and unstatutory manner in which it was created and
operates may be applied to state administration as well and to
other states.

The Board of Natural Resources of Maryland differs from
the above discussed bodies in that it is more than a mere inter-agency coordinating body. It is composed of the heads or
administrative officers of the Commission of Tidewater Fisheries (chairman of the Board), the Game and Inland Fish Commission, the Department of Forests and Parks, the Department
of Geology and the Department of Research and Education, and
eight special members appointed by the Governor on a district
basis for terms of six years. Besides coordinating the several agencies represented with respect to both state and Federal administration, the Board is authorized to "deal with such
matters, complaints, suggestions or proposals as can be handled more satisfactorily by the Board than by the several departments represented on the Board, and review the work of each
such department . . ." So the Maryland Board has not only elements of independent and corporeal existence as visible in
the presence of the special members but also functions which
transcend those of the departments under coordination.

(b) Ad-Hoc Inter-Agency Bodies---Inter-agency committees
on recreation have been set up in recent years in a number of
states (e.g. Alabama, California, Florida, Minnesota, Ohio,
Tennessee and Washington)[308] which includes in their memberships representatives of state parks, forestry, highways, fish
and wildlife and water conservation and utilization as well
as those of other state agencies concerned with recreation.
These committees would be able to achieve a coordinated program of using the state parks and other recreational areas
under the jurisdiction of the state parks agency and lands under the jurisdiction of other state agencies for purposes of
recreation.

Ad-hoc inter-agency bodies are however, almost absent in
other fields of water resources administration.

3. Implied coordination

It is of interest to note that of most plural-headed uni-
functional agencies the plural body at the head of the agency
is composed in whole or in part of heads or administrative officers of other agencies, a practice peculiar to American state
government and administration. This practice, although it necessarily creates some confusion in organization and administrative responsibilities, may produce some effects of coordination.[309]

Article 3   Interstate and International Organization

Section 1   Interstate Organization

Two types of interstate agencies will be discussed: (a)
Administrative agencies, whose functions are to carry out some
interstate administration; and (b) non-administrative agencies, which do not have administrative functions and duties
of their own, but which advise and assist the governments of
the signatory states (or the signatory state agencies) either
in a general way or with respect to some particular program,
with view to coordinating their activities. An administrative agency may be invested with non-administrative functions.
However, non-administrative agencies are so defined that they
will not perform any administrative function.[310]

(a)   Administrative Agencies---Interstate compacts providing for the allocation among signatory states of waters of interstate watercourses usually do not provide for the establishment of an interstate administrative agency, for they are
generally "executed" and not "executory". However, some such
compacts contain certain executory provisions, which may
necessitate the creation of an interstate administrative agency. For example, a Costilla Creek Compact Commission is created by the said Compact, to which Colorado and New Mexico are
parties (11 June 1946: 60 Stat. 246), which consists of the
State Engineers of these two states. The Commission not only collects hydraulic data and operates gaging stations, but
also determines certain factual problems instrumental to water distribution such as the existence and amount of surplus
water and the "safe yield" of the Costilla Reservoir system.
The latter is an administrative function in its strict sense,
for it involves administrative discretion not allowable to
non-administrative agencies. Furthermore, "when it appears
to the Commission that any part of the water allocated to
one state for use in a particular year will not be used by
that state, the Commission may permit its use by the other
state during that year . . ." That this is an administrative
function should leave us no doubt.

The Canadian River Commission, created by the Canadian
River Compact of 17 May 1952 between Oklahoma, Texas and New
Mexico (66 Stat. 74), is of the same status. Besides operating gaging stations for the collection of hydraulic data, the
Commission is authorized to permit New Mexico and Texas to
impound more water than is prescribed by the Compact for a
maximum period of twelve months, provided that there is enough
surplus water. The Commission is made up of one commissioner
appointed or designated by each signatory state, and a fourth
commissioner designated by the President of the United States,
who is the Commission's presiding officer without vote. All
acts of the Commission are to be taken by unanimous vote.

In the Yellowstone River Compact of 30 October 1951 (65 Stat. 663), it is admitted that "no Commission or administrative body is necessary to administer this Compact or divide the waters of the Yellowstone River Basin as between the States of Montana and North Dakota." However, the said Compact, "as between the States of Wyoming and Montana, shall be administered by a Commission composed of one representative from the State of Wyoming and one representative from the State of Montana, to be selected by the governors of said States, . . . and one representative . . . of the United States Geological Survey . . . who shall . . . act as chairman . . . without vote . . ." The Commission is authorized to make and amend rules and regulations in the administration of the Compact. It is also granted the status of a public corporation.

Administrative agencies are also found in other fields of inter-state administration. In the Tri-State Compact of 27 August 1935 between New York, New Jersey and Connecticut (49 Stat. 932), provision is made for the organization of a corporate Interstate Sanitation Commission, which consist of five commissioners appointed by the government of each signatory state. The Commission elects a chairman and a vice chairman, and appoints necessary administrative personnel. A majority of the commissioners of each state constitute a quorum, and no action can be taken unless concurrence is obtained of three commissioners of each state.[311] The Ohio River Valley Water Sanitation Commission (also corporate) is the administrative agency created by the Ohio River Valley Water Sanitation Compact of 11 July 1940 (54 Stat. 752). It consists of three commissioners appointed by the United States. It elects a chairman and a vice-chairman, and may appoint necessary administrative assistants. "One or more commissioners from a majority of the member states shall constitute a quorum for the transaction of business." There is no provision as to the number of votes necessary for the passage of a resolution. However, orders of the Commission are issued with the concurrence of a majority of commissioners from each of the majority of the member states, including the state in which an order is to take effect. The Commission is a "body corporate" and has the right to sue and to be sued in civil actions. Moreover, it has the authority to institute equity actions to enforce its orders.

In 1939, a Boundary Waters Commission was established by concurrent legislation of South Dakota and Minnesota for the regulation of the levels of the Big Stone Lake. It consists of the Director of the Game and Fish Commission of South Dakota and the Commissioner of Conservation of Minnesota, and an engineer appointed by the mutual consent of the Governors of the two states.[312] The Commission has the authority to make both rules and regulations and orders, for the enforcement of which it may seek injunction decrees from courts of either state.

The Port of New York Authority (New York and New Jersey),
the Delaware River Port Authority (Pennsylvania and New Jersey), the Bi-State Development Agency of Illinois and Missouri, and the Palisades Inter-state Park Commission (New York
and New Jersey) all have administrative authority. They are
also public corporations, with the right to judicial action.[313]
The Port of New York Authority consists of six, the Delaware
River Port Authority eight, and the Bi-State Agency and the
Palisades Commission consist of five commissioners from each
constituent state. In all these agencies, unanimity among
the states is required for every action to be taken, although
a majority of the members of each state is sufficient to represent the state within the agency. The first three agencies
elect a chairman and a vice chairman, and the Palisades Commission elects a president and a vice president. All of them
may employ administrative officers.[314] The acts of the Port
of New York Authority and the Bi-State Agency may be vetoed
by the Governors of their constituent states, although it
would seem clear that this gubernatorial brake is to be exercised only in extremely exceptional cases.[315]

The Northeastern Forest Fire Protection Commission is a
non-administrative agency. But when it is authorized by its
constituent states or any number of them for the performance
of common services on their behalf, it becomes an administrative agency for this purpose.

(b) Non-Administrative Agencies---By an interstate compact between Maryland, West Virginia, Virginia, Pennsylvania
and the District of Columbia of 11 July 1940 (54 Stat. 748),
the Interstate Commission on the Potomac River Basin was established, with the function of advising these states and coordinating their activities with respect to the control of
pollution of the waters of the Potomac River and its tributaries. It consists of three members from each signatory
state or District, and three members appointed by the President of the United States, serving for terms to be prescribed
by the respective appointing authorities. It elects a chairman
and a vice-chairman, and appoints necessary technical and
clerical personnel. A majority of the members of the Commission constitutes a quorum; but "no action of the Commission
relating to policy shall be binding on any one of the signatory bodies unless at least two of the commissioners from such
signatory body shall vote in favor thereof." The Commission
may determine minimum standards for sewage and waste treatment
to be submitted to the signatory bodies for adoption and approval. The New England Interstate Water Pollution Control Commission, created by a compact entered into between the six New
England States (Maine, Massachusetts, Connecticut, New Hampshire, Rhode Island and Vermont) and New York on 31 July 1947
(61 Stat. 682),[316] has the same functions and organization as
the Potomac Commission, except that there are five instead of
three commissioner from each member state, that there is no
Federal representation, and that the chairman and vice-chair-

man are elected annually.[317]

The counterparts of these two interstate bodies in the field of fisheries are the Atlantic States Marine Fisheries Commission, the Pacific Marine Fisheries Commission (California, Oregon and Washington) and the Gulf States Marine Fisheries Commission (Alabama, Florida, Louisiana, Mississippi and Texas), created respectively by compacts of 4 May 1942 (56 Stat. 267), 24 July 1947 (61 Stat. 419) and 19 May 1949 (63 Stat. 70). The Pacific Commission is composed of one or more representatives appointed by each member state for four years. The Atlantic and Gulf Commissions consist of three members from each member state, one of whom is the chief fishery administrative officer, one a legislator and one a person appointed by the Governor. All three Commissions elect a chairman and a vice-chairman, and employs necessary personnel. In all three Commissions, action is taken by the affirmative vote of a majority of member-states, including a majority of the states interested. All three Commissions may appoint an advisory committee representing special interest groups. The Pacific Commission conducts research through the several state research agencies, Atlantic and Gulf Commissions through the United States Fish and Wildlife Service (representatives of which may attend the meetings of the Commission without vote) with the assistance of the several state research agencies.[318]

The Northeastern Interstate Forest Fire Protection Compact of 25 June 1949 (63 Stat. 271) established the Northeastern Forest Fire Protection Commission (Maine, New Hampshire, Vermont, Rhode Island, Connecticut, New York and Massachusetts), which is also a non-administrative body. It is organized in the same fashion as the Gulf States Marine Fisheries Commission, except that a chairman and a vice-chairman are elected annually. Like the latter Commission, it may also appoint an advisory committee of special interest groups. "A majority of the members of the Commission representing a majority of the signatory states shall constitute a quorum for the transaction of its general business, but no action of the Commission imposing any obligation on any signatory state shall be binding unless a majority of the members from such signatory state shall have voted in favor thereof."

Other non-administrative interstate agencies in field of water resources administration have been formed on an informal basis without the sanction of either interstate compacts or agreements or concurrent state legislation. One outstanding example of this type of interstate organization is the Interstate Commission on the Delaware River Basin, which was created by the Commissions on Interstate Cooperation of the States of New York, New Jersey, Pennsylvania and Delaware in 1936, for the purpose of coordinating the activities of these states in matters of water and soil conservation, water pollution control and forest conservation. It is composed of five members from each member state who are the four members of the Commission on Interstate Cooperation[319] and a member selected by that Commission. The Commission has employed an executive secretary, a chief engineer, an agronomist and a forester to carry on research and investigation activities.[320]

On 10 January 1949, the water pollution control agencies of Alaska, Washington, Oregon, Montana, Utah, Nevada and the Province of British Columbia of Canada and the regional officer of the U. S. Public Health Service entered into an agreement setting up the Pacific Northwest Pollution Control Council, in order "to develop a comprehensive plan for water pollution control in the Pacific Northwest Basin." It promotes coordination among the member agencies by recommending to them uniform standards of sewage and waste treatment and stream cleanliness.[321] On 29 October 1948, the game and fish agencies of California and Oregon and the supervisors of the Modoc and Fremont National Forests concluded an agreement entitled the Interstate Winter Deer Range Management Plan. An agency called the Interstate Deer Herd Committee was established consisting of representatives of the above-mentioned parties. It studies the composition and the interstate movement of the winter deer herd and the conditions of the range, and formulates a coordinated management plan for approval and adoption by the party-agencies.[322]

(c) Internal organization of interstate agencies: the committee system---There are generally committees in an interstate agency (administrative or non-administrative, formal or informal), which advise the agency on special technical problems. They are equivalent to the divisions of a state agency. For example, the Upper Colorado River Commission has three standing committees, namely, the Engineering Committee, the Legal Committee and the Budget Committee. "Members of committees may or may not be members of the Commission. The number of members of each committee shall be determined from time to time by the Commission. Each member of the Commission shall designate the member or members on each committee representing his government. In all committee action the vote shall be taken by governments with each government having one vote." The chairman and secretary of the Commission are ex-officio members of all committees. Besides the three standing committees, "the Commission may from time to time create special committees, composed of such members and others and assigned such tasks as the Commission may determine."[323] In the Arkansas River Compact Administration, there are also three standing committees, namely, the Administrative and Legal Committee, the Engineering Committee and the Operations Committee, each of which is made up of the chairman and two members of the Administration. The chairman of each committee is designated by the Administration. All committees vote by states. Special committees consisting of members of the Administration and other persons may be set up by the Administration as needs arise.[324] The By-Laws of the Bi-State Development Agency of

Missouri and Illinois also provide for the organization of
standing or temporary committees, which are appointed by the
Board of Commissioners from time to time from its own members.
In addition, the Board may set up an Executive Committee.

The Ohio River Valley Sanitation Commission has an executive committee, which consists of (for the year ending 30 June
1954) the chairman, the past chairman, one the three members
of each of the eight member states and one of the three Federal members; and committees on engineering, audit, by-laws,
finance, policy, public agencies, public relations, pension
plan, personnel, soil erosion and interstate relations, consisting of from three to eleven members.[325] In the Interstate
Commission on the Potomac River Basin, "there has been created
a number of advisory committees. These include a Technical
Committee, an Industrial Committee, a Land Committee, a Local
Governments Committee and a Wildlife and Recreation Committee.
Members of these committees are appointed by the Chairman of
the Commission annually and may or may not be members of the
Commission, . . . the Technical Committee being composed of
members of the state planning agencies and of the state water
pollution control agencies, the Industrial Committee of industrial representatives, the Land Committee of state and Federal agencies interested in soil and forest conservation, the
Local Governments Committee of officials of municipalities
throughout the basins and the Wildlife and Recreation Committee of state and Federal agencies interested in this phase,
together with persons of prominence throughout the basin who
have an interest in this work."[326] The Interstate Commission
on the Delaware River Basin has an executive committee and
committees on stream pollution, water supply, finance, planning, conservation and legal work.[327]

The Atlantic States Marine Fisheries Commission has, in
pursuance of the Compact, an Executive Committee consisting
of the chairman and vice-chairman of the Commission and the
chairmen of the delegations of the several member-states, and
an Advisory Committee. As the Commission has a relatively
large number of member-states, it is divided into the following sections: the North Atlantic Section (Maine, New Hampshire, Massachusetts, Rhode Island and Connecticut), the Middle Atlantic Section (New York, New Jersey, Pennsylvania, and
Delaware), the Chesapeake Bay Section (Maryland and Virginia)
and the South Atlantic Section (North Carolina, South Carolina,
Georgia and Florida).[328] These Sections may be regarded as
special territorial committees of the Commission. They are
presumably made up of delegations of the states concerned.
It may be noted that the Advisory Committee has proved unpract-
ical and "has been broken down by states and the members of
the Advisory Committee in each state are nominated by the Commissioners in that state and consulted by them with respect to
legislative program in such state."[329]

Section 2   International Organization

The most important international agencies are the International Joint Commission of the United States and Canada and the International Boundary and Water Commission of the United States and Mexico, created by treaties of 1909 and 1944, respectively. The former is "composed of six commissioners, three on the part of the United States appointed by the President thereof, and three on the part of the United Kingdom appointed by His Majesty on the recommendation of the Governor in Council of the Dominion of Canada" (art. VII). "The United States and Canadian sections of the Commission may each appoint a secretary, and these shall act joint secretaries of the Commission at its joint sessions, and the Commission may employ engineers and clerical assistants from time to time as it may deem advisable" (art. XII, 2nd para., 1st sent.), it being understood that the three commissioners from the United States and the three commissioners from Canada constitute respectively the United States and the Canadian Sections. "The majority of the Commissioners shall have power to render a decision. In case the Commission is evenly divided upon any question or matter presented to it for decision, separate reports shall be made by the Commissioners on each side to their own Government. The High Contracting Parties shall thereupon endeavor to agree upon an adjustment of the question or matter of difference, and if an agreement is reached between them, it shall be reduced to writing in the form of a protocol, and shall be communicated to the Commissioners, who shall take such further proceedings as may be necessary to carry out such agreement" (art. VIII, last para.). With respect to questions or matters over which the two governments are originally unable to come to an agreement and which are referred to the Commission for a decision, if the Commission, too, fails to make a decision, then the two governments shall refer the question or matter to an umpire chosen in accordance with the Hague Convention of 1907 (art. X). Each Section elects a chairman. "Regular sessions of the Commission shall be held annually at Washington beginning on the first Tuesday of April and at Ottawa beginning on the first Tuesday of October. Special meetings may be held at such times and places in the United States and the Dominion of Canada as the chairmen of the two sections may determine." The chairman of the United States and Canadian Sections preside at all meetings held respectively in the United States and Canada.330

Both Sections of the Commission are kept in close association with the water-resources administrative agencies of the two governments. As of 1951, two of the three commissioners of the United States Section are engineers of the Federal Power Commission. "The advice of officers of the Bureau of Reclamation and of the Corps of Engineers has been obtained by the United States Section . . . in connection with projects to which it is giving consideration." Furthermore, the Commission establishes Joint International Engineering Boards, whose memberships include employees of agencies such as the Corps of Engineers and the Bureau of Reclamation and their Canadian counterparts.[331]

The International Boundary and Water Commission of the United States and Mexico is also composed of a United States Section and a foreign section (the Mexican Section), each of which consists of an Engineer Commissioner, who is its head, two principal engineers and a secretary, appointed by the respective governments. "The Commission or either of its two Sections may employ such assistants and engineering and legal advisers as it may deem necessary" (art. II of the Treaty of 1944). As has already been discussed before, the Commission in most cases acts through its two Sections, and in the few instances where duties fall directly upon the Commission, it acts by the concurrence or joint action of the Commissioners of the two Sections.[332]

The only other international agencies intrusted with duties in water resources administration are the International Fisheries Commission and the International Pacific Salmon Fisheries Commission, established by bi-lateral instruments between the United States and Canada of 1924 and 1937 respectively. The former consists of four members, two to be appointed by each of the two governments. It would seem that action of the Commission is taken by the unanimous consent of all four commissioners. The latter is composed of three members from each government. Action is taken by the Commission by an affirmative vote of at least two members of each government, and is enforced by the proper authorities of the two governments.[333]

Article 4   Popular Participation In Administrative Organization

Private citizens or citizen-groups have participated in governmental agencies of all levels either by virtue of their status as common citizens or of their special knowledge and training. Participation of common citizens in administrative agencies is political in nature and that of experts and specialists non-political. Common citizens participate in administrative agencies either as members of the general public or as members of some special profession, and their participation may be designated as professional or non-professional accordingly. Private participants in administrative agencies may be either organized or unorganized.

(a) Unorganized Popular Participation---Private citizens, while retaining their private status or their association with their professional groups, may individually join administrative agencies as consultants (experts) or even as employees (experts or common citizens). The latter groups consists pri-

marily of volunteers. But other types of participation than
volunteering are also possible. For example, until at least
1950, the Executive Secretary of the Federal Inter-Agency
Committee on Recreation was a member of the staff of the National Recreation Association [334] Under the laws of Colorado,
all hunters of predatory animals employed under the joint
Federal-state predator-control program are employed upon the
recommendation of local county livestock growers' associations
(Laws 1935, ch. 177, sec. 5).[335]

(b) Organized Popular Participation---Private citizens,[336]
either exclusively or together with ex-officio governmental
employees, may form administrative agencies (political) and
advisory agencies of the governments of all levels. The former include almost all plural-headed state agencies except
the public service commissions and most interstate agencies.
In the same category are bodies or agencies responsible for
joint government-private administration or for government-private program coordination, although such bodies or agencies
are always required. An example of such bodies or agencies
is the Predator Control Board of Montana. It "is composed of
the Montana Fish and Game Department, the U. S. Fish and Wildlife Service, the Wool Growers and the Livestock Association.
Each contributes a portion of the cost of controlling predators
since benefits are shared equally." This Board, it seems, only determines problems of policy. "Control operations are
actually conducted by employees of the Predator Control Division of the U. S. Fish and Wildlife Service and costs are
paid from the cooperative fund."[337]

Advisory agencies made up in whole or in part of private
citizens are of two types: namely, purely advisory agencies
(political or non-political) and advisory agencies which act
on behalf of their principal agencies (i.e., agencies to which
the advisory agencies are advisory) at certain stage of the
administrative procedure (political). Examples of the latter
will be given first.

In February 1935, the Secretary of the Interior called a
meeting of the special interest groups concerned at Denver,
Colorado, on the administration of the Taylor Grazing Act of
1934. At the meeting the Secretary proposed election of advisory committees of stockmen in all grazing districts. After
the meeting, Circular No. 1 was issued on 23 April 1935, providing for the election of such committees.[338] On 14 July 1939,
sec. 17 was added to the Taylor Grazing Act (53 Stat. 1002),
which endorsed the experiment initiated by the said Circular.
Under the provisions of this section, an advisory board of advisers is to be set up in each grazing district, which consists
of a wildlife representative appointed by the Secretary of the
Interior and from five to twelve stockmen.[339] The functions
of such advisory boards are to "offer advice and make a recommendation on each application for (such) a grazing permit with-

in its district, provided that in no case shall any grazing district adviser participate in any advice or recommendation concerning a permit or an application therefor in which he is directly or indirectly interested"; and to advise on the making of rules and regulations, the establishment of grazing districts and the change of their boundaries, the seasons of use and carrying capacity of the range, and like matters.[340] The boards meet at least once each year, at times and places to be prescribed by the Secretary of the Interior. Each grazing district board of advisers elects two members and two alternates to form a state advisory board; and each state advisory board elects a representative and an alternate to the national advisory board council (43 C. F. R. 161.12 (j) and (k)). However, the national advisory board council and the state advisory boards are purely advisory bodies and are functionally distinct from district boards (ibid., (1)).

Similar advisory boards have been organized in national-forest ranges. By order of the Secretary of Agriculture dated 31 March 1906, livestock associations in some Western national-forest ranges were recognized as official advisory bodies to forest officers on matters of grazing. In 1909, there were 46 such advisory associations in national-forest areas.[341] The practice was given statutory status by the act of 24 April 1950 (in sec. 18: 64 Stat. 82, 87). Under the provisions of this act, "a local advisory board shall be constituted and elected . . . for each national forest or administrative subdivision thereof whenever a majority of the grazing permittees of such national forest or administrative subdivision so petitions the Secretary of Agriculture . . ." Each such board is made up of from three to twelve members elected by the grazing permittees in the area and a wildlife representative appointed by the state wildlife agency concerned. Regular meetings are held annually, and special meetings may be called by the chairman or the Secretary of Agriculture or as otherwise determined by the board. "Upon the request of any party affected thereby, the Secretary of Agriculture, or his duly authorized representative, shall refer to the appropriate local advisory board for its advice and recommendations any matter pertaining to (1) the modification of the terms, or the denial of a renewal of, or a reduction in, a grazing permit, or (2) the establishment or modification of an individual or community allotment." A local advisory board also advises the Department of Agriculture on the making of rules and regulations on national-forest grazing which are applicable to or affect its area.

In the administration of lands benefited by Water Conservation and Utilization projects of the Bureau of Reclamation, such lands are sold by the Soil Conservation Service to farm settlers to be selected by local advisory boards.[342] These boards, known as the Family Selection Committees, are composed of seven residents of the community or county in which a project is located (7 C. F. R. 600.6(d)). Similar procedure is

adopted for the disposition of lands in Reclamation projects
(that is, projects governed by the Reclamation Act of 1902
and its amendments). Homesteaders on such project lands are
selected by local Boards of Examiners. Each such board consists of not less than two citizens residing in the area appointed by the Commissioner of the Bureau of Reclamation, and an
official of the Bureau, who shall be the secretary of the Board
(43 C. F. R. 401.6; 16 F. R. 10894).

In the administration of the Agricultural Conservation
Program of the Department of Agriculture, all preliminary decisions are made by the Agricultural Stabilization and Conservation County Committees in the counties of the country (which
also have similar functions in connection with the price support, crop insurance and sugar programs), which are assisted
by Agricultural Stabilization and Conservation Community Committees. Each county and community committee is composed of
three members (including a chairman and a vice-chairman) and
two alternates. The members of a community committees are
annually elected by qualified farmers of the area, and those
of a county committee annually elected at a convention attended by a delegate and an alternate of each community committee
in the county. The county agricultural extension agent is the
secretary of the county committee _ex-officio_. Each county
committee may employ an office manager, and presumably other
personnel (7 C. F. R. 7.1 et seq.).

The loans authorized by an act of 14 July 1953 are approved by "special committee appointed by the Secretary (of Agriculture) to serve for the particular area as determined by
the Secretary" when they do not exceed $5,000. "The Committee
shall consist of at least three members . . . from local persons having recognized knowledge of the livestock industry .
The Committee shall perform such additional functions, . . .
including general direction of the servicing of the loans,
as the Secretary may prescribe."

The states have made much less use of this kind of advisory bodies than the Federal Government. An example of such
advisory bodies at the state level is found in the provisions
of an act of Georgia of 1943 (Laws 1943, No. 31). Under this
act, the Governor appoints an advisory committee of five citizens in each county in which there is a state park. Such advisory committees receive complaints regarding the operation
of the state parks, and submit them to the Governor and the
Director of Parks.

As for purely advisory bodies, those which advise state and
interstate agencies have already been discussed and will not
be repeated. Our discussion will be confined to Federal Administration. In sec. 3 of Historic Sites Act of 21 August 1935
(49 Stat. 666, 667), provisions is made for the establishment
of an Advisory Board on National Parks, Historic Sites, Buildings, and Monuments, "to be composed of not to exceed eleven

persons, . . . to include representatives competent in the
fields of history, archaeology, architecture, and human geo-
graphy, who shall be appointed by the Secretary (of the Interior) and serve at his pleasure." The Board advises the
Secretary of the Interior on the administration of the National Park System. The equivalent of this Board for the National
Forests is the National Forest Advisory Council, which is composed of three citizens appointed by the Secretary of Agriculture on the basis of personal competence. "It meets at the
call of the Secretary, whenever a question arises on which
its disinterested consideration is desirable. It also makes
field studies of special problems at the request of the Secretary." The Council was first set up in 1948 by the name of
the National Forest Board of Review, and was changed to the
present name in 1950.343 In the Bonneville Power Administration, there is an unofficial Regional Advisory Council, which
was established in the early 1930's and which consists of
local utility officials, grange and labor leaders, college and
university officials, industrialists and businessmen interested in power development.344 In the Organic Act of the
Saint Lawrence Seaway Development Corporation, enacted 13 May
1954 (68 Stat. 92), provision is made for the appointment by
the President with the consent of the Senate of a bi-partisan
five-member Advisory Board, which advises the Administrator
of the Corporation on and reviews general policies of the Corporation (sec. 2).

These Federal advisory bodies and the state and interstate
advisory bodies previously discussed all advise an administrative agency on general policies and activities of the agency.
Besides, there are those purely advisory bodies, permanent or
temporary, which advise an administrative agency on a certain
particular administrative program or even on a certain particular administrative measure or project. The State Forestry
Committee of the Department of Natural Resources of Massachusetts, authorized by an act of 1943 (Acts 1943, ch. 539), is
an advisory body to the said Department with respect to its
administrative program on forestry practices. It consists of
four members representative of special interest groups (three
members) and the general public (one member) appointed by the
governor with the consent of the Council for terms of four
years, with the Director of the Division of Forestry of the
Department as an ex-officio member. The members elect a chairman. The Committee prepares and amends practices of forest
management and guides for timber cutting, and submits them to
the Commissioner of the Department for approval and adoption.
The district forest practice boards provided in the New York
Forest Practice Act of 1946 (Laws 1946, ch. 52; as amended in
1947 and 1949) are of the same type and have the same functions
as this Committee. Each such board is composed of three members appointed by the authorities of each county included in
the district, of whom two members represent the public and
serve for a term of three years and one represents the county
government and serves for a term of two years. It elects a

chairman and a secretary. The recommendations of these boards
are to be approved and adopted by the Conservation Commissioner, through the State Board (consisting of one representative
from each district board and three ex-officio members).

The Bureau of Land Management of the Department of the
Interior has a special Advisory Board to advise it in the administration of the O. and C. land, which is one of the programs of the Bureau. It was first set up by a memorandum of
the Acting Assistant Commissioner of the General Land Office
dated 5 July 1938, as approved by the Secretary of the Interior on 9 July 1938 and reconstituted by an order of the Secretary dated 27 July 1948. It consists of persons representative of special interest groups appointed by the Secretary of
the Interior for one-year terms, with the Director of the
Bureau of Land Management or his representative as an ex-
officio member. The Board elects a chairman, and the Director of the Bureau designates an employee to be its secretary.
Regular meetings of the Board are held quarterly, and special
meetings may be called by the said Director. Besides the general Advisory Board for the whole area, there is a District
Advisory Board for each district of the area, the members of
which are appointed by the regional administrator of the Bureau with the approval of the Director for a term of one year,
with the district forester or his representative as an ex-
officio member. The latter, or some other official of the
Bureau, serves as the secretary of the district board. The
general and district advisory boards advise the Director or
the regional administrator and the district forester with respect to the management of the O and C lands as a whole and
such lands in the various districts, respectively. It may be
noted, however, that so far as the regional administrator and
particularly as the district foresters are concerned, such
boards are advisory boards on general policies and not on particular programs.

As for advisory boards on particular administrative measures or projects, the Secretary of the Interior in 1923 appointed a special committee of seven disinterested (i.e., non-
professional) citizens of national prominence having a knowledge of irrigation matters to make an exclusive study and analysis of the problem of the repayment of the costs of construction. The committee completed its work next year and a report
was forwarded to the President.[345] On 29 May 1928, a Joint
Resolution was passed by the Congress (45 Stat. 1011), which
authorized and directed the Secretary of the Interior to appoint a special board of five engineers and geologists to examine a damsite for the then proposed boulder Dam project. Both
bodies were temporary. Although examples may be multiplied,
there is no information as to the total number of such advisory
bodies which have been established by the Federal Government
and the several states. It may perhaps be presumed that a considerable proportion of them must have been established in an
unofficial and informal manner.

NOTES

1. This refers to the existing agencies of the Federal Government that have direct responsibilities in water resources administration.

2. House Document 159, 79th Cong., Sept. 1944, p. 329. For a brief history of the Corps of Engineers, see Rpt. Chief of E. 1951, Part I, vol. 3, p. 3. For navigation works the construction and operation of which has not been undertaken by the Corps of Engineers, see (b) and (c), below.

3. Besides, there is an Alaska District, a Honolulu District and a Panama District, each headed by a district engineer who directly communicates with the Chief of Engineers.

4. See the table of contents of the current annual report of the Chief of Engineers, U. S. Army.

5. The Engineer School, Civil Works Administration: Initiation of Projects (mimeo.), 1950, p. 10; 96 Cong. Rec. A2787 (6 April 1950), for one instance; and the various annual reports of the Chief of Engineers. "Only one regional schedule, that of the Engineer Department's river and harbor divisions and districts, completely ignores state lines -- the boundary in this case being drawn along the watersheds of the country." -- National Resources Planning Committee, Regional Factors in National Planning, 1935, p. 76.

6. National Resources Planning Committee, Regional Planning, Part I, 1936, p. 185.

7. It may also be mentioned that by a special Act of 30 April 1824 (4 Stat. 22) the President was authorized to make surveys and plans of roads and canals of national importance.

8. As in the case of improvement projects, examinations and surveys have occasionally been authorized by special Congressional enactments. See joint resolutions of 11 April 1898 (30 Stat. 738) and 10 January 1899 (30 Stat. 1386).

9. Based on the reading of a vast number of House Documents dealing with navigation and flood control matters.

10. In all authorizations of a river and harbor project, it is provided that the project is authorized "in accordance with House (or Senate) Document No. ---" This practice seems to have been first established by the River and Harbor Act of 2 March 1907 (34 Stat. 1073), such phrase appearing only occasionally in previous River and Harbor Acts.

11. Occasionally ad-hoc boards of engineers were organized to conduct surveys of certain important projects. See, for example, River and Harbor Acts of 10 June 1872 (17 Stat. 370, 372), 23 June 1874 (18 Stat. 237, 244), 3 June 1896 (29 Stat. 202, 217), 3 March 1905 (33 Stat. 1117, 1135 and 1143) and 2 March 1907 (34 Stat. 1073, 1104).

12. Now Senate and House Committees on Public Works.

13. Interstate Commission on The Potomac River Basin, News-Letter, vol. 8, no. 7, October 1952.

14. U. S. Corps of Engineers, South Pacific Division, Civil Works By The Corps of Engineers in California (mimeo.), March 1952, pp. 3-5; National Resources Planning Board, Transportation and National Policy, May 1942, p. 431; and a reading of a great number of public documents.

15. Authorization is usually given in a River and Harbor or Flood
Control Act. It may be noted that the proposal may be killed either by
the Committee or by the Congress.

16. Consult Arthur A. Maass, "Congress and Water Resources", 44
American Political Science Review 576 (September 1950).

17. 96 Cong. Rec. A5058.

18. Action by the Chief of Engineers on such requests varies from
case to case. Instead of assigning the work to the district engineer as
in the case of ordinary examinations and surveys authorized by the Congress, he may assign a review request either to the Board of Engineers
for Rivers and Harbors or to the division engineer or to the district engineer, according to the nature and scope of the review. -- Based on the
reading of a great number of public documents.

19. See House Flood Control Committee Hearings on Flood Control Bill
of 1946, p. 9 (statement of the Chief of Engineers). For a particular
form of modification as provided in sec. 3 of the Flood Control Act of
28 June 1938, see p. 1042, above.

20. See 1126ff, below. It may be remarked that the establishment of
the Mississippi River Commission in 1879 was not substantially different
from that of the Tennessee Valley Authority in 1933.

21. Senate Committee Print, 73rd Cong., 2nd sess.

22. House Documents 541 and 544, 75th Cong., 3rd sess.

23. House Document 107, 76th Cong., 1st sess.

24. House Document 674, 76th Cong., 3rd sess.

25. House Document 702, 77th Cong., 2nd sess.

26. House Document 644, 78th Cong., 2nd sess.

27. Consult pp. 487, 492, 516-517, above.

28. These dates were made available to the author through the courtesy of Colonel John P. McWhorter, Chief, Engineer Historical Division,
U. S. Corps of Engineers, on 25 September 1953.

29. The office of the Commission was, until 1928, located in St.
Louis, Missouri. In 1928, it was moved to Vicksburg, Mississippi. -- Let-
ter to the author from Mr. Roy D. McCarty, Secretary, Mississippi River
Commission, dated 3 June 1952.

30. Letter from Mr. MaCarty, op. cit.

31. Arthur DeWitt Frank, The Development of the Federal Program of
Flood Control on the Mississippi River, 1930, pp. 42-44. For the historical background of the Commission, see ibid., pp. 28-42.

32. House Executive Document No. 58, 46th Congress, 2nd session.
This report also appeared in Annual Report of the Chief of Engineers for
1881, p. 2720 ff.

33. Rpt. Chief of E. 1882, p. 2748.

34. D. O. Elliot, The Improvement of the Lower Mississippi River For
Flood Control and Navigation, May 1932, p. 16.

35. Consult a provision of the First Flood Control Act of 1 March 1917 (39 Stat. 948, 949).

36. It is to be noted that these were principal means of flood control adopted by the Commission prior to 1928.

37. The jurisdiction of the Commission over the main stem from the Head of Passes to Rock Island is exclusive, and measures of flood control undertaken for the main stem (dredging and revetment in particular) are at the same time measures of navigation improvement. Jurisdiction of the Lower Mississippi Valley Division of the Corps of Engineers does not extend to the main Head of the Passes (Baton Rouge, Louisiana). -- Letter from Mr. Roy D. McCarty, op. cit.; also see the current annual report of the Chief of Engineers, U. S. Army.

38. Rpt. Chief of E. 1891, p. 3393ff; Rpt. Chief of E. 1893, p. 3545ff; and later reports of the Commission.

39. Rpt. Chief of E. 1896, p. 3406; and later reports of the Commission.

40. Rpt. Chief of E. 1896, p. 3419.

41. Rpt. Chief of E. 1899, p. 616. Consult Rpt. Chief of E. 1928, p. 1894.

42. Bank protection work, in preventing bank erosion, also protects the levees.

43. Consult Rpt. Chief of E. 1918, pp. 3460-3461; and later reports of the Commission.

44. However, no distinction has been made between embanking levees and local-protection levees. The benefits of the former are not limited to any particular localities.

45. House Document 90, 70th Congress, 1st session.

46. Letter from Mr. Roy D. McCarty, op. cit. Such personnel union began in 1925. See Official Register of the United States, editions of 1925-1952 inclusive.

47. U. S. Corps of Engineers, Missouri River Division, The Development and Control of the Missouri River, December 1947, p. 1.

48. See the various annual reports of the Commission, which appeared as Appendixes to the annual reports of the Corps of Engineers.

49. The Federal enterprise of flood control in the 17 Western states except for the construction of levees and channel-improvement works, is, in a practical though not fully legal sense, shared by the Bureau of Reclamation. In the production (but not disposition) of hydroelectric power, the Corps shares responsibility with the Bureau of Reclamation in the 17 Western states, and yields its responsibilities in the Tennessee River Basin to the Tennessee Valley Authority. Now that the Corps is as interested in power development as in navigation improvement and flood control, the creation of agencies similar to the Tennessee Valley Authority is sure to meet strong opposition of the Corps.

50. The office of the Commission is in San Francisco, California.

51. Rpt. Chief of E. 1951, p. 24-5.

52. Federal Inter-Agency Committee on Recreation, Report on the Conservation and Development of Outdoor Recreation Resources (mimeo.), July 1950, p. B-15.

53. 38 Reclamation Era 277 (December 1952).

54. See Rpt. Sec. Inter. 1949, pp. 85-102.

55. President's Water Resources Policy Commission, Report, vol I, p. 299.

56. U. S. Dpt. of the Inter., How Reclamation Pays, 1947, p. 59. Also see Reclamation Project Data, pp. 89; 93 and 345.

57. Bureau of Reclamation, Reclamation Anniversary Facts (mimeo.), 1952, p. 5.

58. For the history, functions (summary) and the internal organization of the various subordinate agencies of the Department of the Interior, see the current editions of the United States Government Organization Manual and the Official Register of the United States.

59. For the history, function (summary) and the internal organization of these agencies, see the current editions of the United States Government Organization Manual and the Official Register of the United States For the history of the Forest Service in particular, see Fifty Years of Forestry in the U. S. A., 1950, pp. 165-170 (by Lyle F. Watts). It may be observed that the services and activities of the last three agencies consist entirely of assistance to private persons and that those of the first two consist partly of assistance to private persons and partly of enterprise.

60. It should be remarked that artificial propagation of wildlife at the Federal level is still in experimental stage, and that the Federal Government does not operate any game farm.

61. In ordinary usage, any heavily forested area is a watershed area.

62. For possible conflicts between the Department of Agriculture and the Corps of Engineers, see House Document 530, 82nd Cong., 2nd sess., 1952, p. 13. For an extended discussion of this point, see Luna B. Leopold and Thomas Maddock, The Flood Control Controversy, 1954, 278 pp.

63. For the history, internal organization and a summary of their functions of these agencies, see current editions of the United States Government Organization Manual and the Official Register of the United States.

64. For its activities and authority, reference should be made to the foregoing chapters. It may be remarked that as the navigation improvement and flood control tend to be exclusively Federal enterprises, the regulatory authority of the Corps of Engineers is of less importance than that of the Federal Power Commission.

65. Baum, Federal Power Commission and State Utility Regulation, 1942, p. 149.

66. For other details concerning the internal organization and functions of the Commission, see current editions of the United States Government Organization Manual and the Official Register of the United States. For administrative procedure of the Commission, see Baum, op. cit., pp. 17; 32; 90-91; 116.

67. For the functions, history and internal organization of the Service, see current editions of the <u>United States Government Organization Manual</u> and the <u>Official Register of the United States</u>.

68. The first duty serves as a constitutional basis for the second duty. The multiple-purpose nature of the dams is another constitutional basis for the productionand sale of hydroelectric power.

69. See <u>Rpt. Chief of E. 1951</u>, pp. 1463-1466; 1491-1493 (particularly p. 1466).

70. But the loan program of the Authority is alternative to the activities of the Rural Electrification Administration so far as the transmission facilities of the Authority's power distributors are concerned.

71. However, the argument of the state-rightists with respect to power development is naturally associated with the Tennessee Valley Authority, as the enterprise of the Authority is the <u>first</u> Federal enterprise of water-power development of regional scope.

72. Of course, there is the problem of coordination between the Corps and the Bureau in the 17 states in the West (but not elsewhere in the country). It is evident the creation of an additional agency by the name of "authority" will not eliminate this problem.

73. For the internal organization of the Tennessee Valley Authority, see "Organization of the Tennessee Valley Authority", approved by the Board of Directors of the Authority on 1 June 1951 (16 F. R. 5663-5664). Also see the TVA Act, for the organization and duties of the Board. For the historical background of the Authority, consult existing publications on TVA.

74. Discussion here is confined to cases and practices which have special application to water-resources administrative agencies.

75. The enactment of acts which establish the various administrative services is not regarded as part of this supervision.

76. For authorization of TVA projects, see 16 U. S. C. 831h-2. For the authority of the Congress in authorizing land withdrawals, see 43 U. S. C. 150. Some navigation improvement, flood control and hydroelectric power projects were authorized by the President in the 1930's under emergency legislation.

77. See (in addition to previous discussion) <u>Senate Public Works Committee Hearings on H. R. 5472</u>, Part I, July 1949, p. 20.

78. Government Appropriation Act of 6 September 1950 (64 Stat. 685, 686), Interior Department Appropriation Acts of 31 August 1951 (65 Stat. 248, 255), 9 July 1952 (66 Stat. 445, 451), and 31 July 1953 (67 Stat. 261, 266-267); Act of 17 July 1952 (66 Stat. 753).

79. "Determined to save their community, the people of Colfax appealed to their leaders in Congress. The Congress requested the Bureau of Reclamation to find out what, if any, help the farmers could get in the way of repairing the irrigation works, under the reclamation law. Bureau of Reclamation engineers made an investigation of conditions in the area and submitted their report to the Congress. The Congress in turn authorized the Vermejo project by the act of September 27, 1950, as amended by the act of March 5, 1952." -- 39 <u>Reclamation Era 117</u> (June 1953).

80. Letter to the author from Col. Paschal N. Strong, Division En-

gineer, U. S. Corps of Engineers, Ohio River Division, dated 2 May 1952.

81. House Document 216, 91st Cong., 1st sess., 1949, p. 4.

82. The approval of long-range plans for the development of a river or river system (as distinguished from the authorization of particular projects embodied in such plans) has no practical significance, and is therefore omitted from the present discussion.

83. Actually, these acts are executed by the Congress itself.

84. Rpt. Chief of E. 1951 part I, vol. 3, p. 15.

85. The aboge statements are based upon the reading of a vast number of documents.

86. Legislative Re-Organization Act of 2 August 1946 (60 Stat. 812). The Senate Committee on Public Lands has been known since January 1949 (the beginning of the 81st Congress) as Senate Committee on Interior and Insular Affairs (95 Cong. Rec. 498-499, 24 January 1949).

87. Informal supervision is omitted because of lack of information.

88. The establishment of an administrative service through Presidential action (e.g., the establishment of "Presidential permits", p. 494, above) is not supervision.

89. These projects concern the jurisdictions of both the Department of the Interior and the Department of Agriculture.

90. House Document 159, 79th Cong., Sept. 1944, p. 328.

91. See, for example, Arthur A. Maass, "Congress and Water Resources", 44 American Political Science Review 576, 585-586 (September 1950).

92. Rpt. Chief of E. 1951, part I, vol. 3, pp. 10-11. It is to be remarked that the Budget Bureau, in commenting thereupon, ordinarily states specifically that it will raise "no objection to the submission of the report to Congress."

93. Rpt. Sec. Inter. 1939, p. 303.

94. Rpt. Sec. Inter. 1941, p. 265.

95. The text of this order appears in Rpt. Sec. Inter. 1941, at p.77.

96. Rpt. Sec. Inter. 1944, pp. 167-168.

97. See the various reports of the Secretary of the Interior.

98. 43 CFR pl. 21(c), as amended on 10 March 1947 (12 F. R. 1774), 2nd sent.

99. Rpt. Sec. Inter. 1951, pp. 123-124. The staff of the Water Resources Committee was transferred from the Office of Land Utilization to the office of the Assistant Secretary for Water and Power on 17 July 1950 -- Ibid., p. 244.

100. Ibid., p. 241.

101. See U. S. Government Organization Manual, 1952-1953, p. 197; and U. S. Department of the Interior, Years of Progress, 1945-1952, p. 177.

102. Order No. 2394 of 16 December 1947 was amended by Order No. 2603 of 1 December 1950.

103. In the sense that it was not specialized in any part of the duties and responsibilities of the Department. The members of this staff would still be "specialists" in the skills of administrative coordination, as compared with the Secretary, the Under Secretary and the Assistant Secretaries, who may all be amateurs in public administration.

104. Order 2603 of L December 1950. For further information on the nature and work of the Program Staff, consult Norman Wengert and John C. Honey, "Program Planning in the U. S. Department of the Interior, 1946-53", 14 Public Administration Review 193 (August 1954).

105. U. S. Department of the Interior, Press Release, 13 May 1953.

106. Rpt. Sec. Inter. 1953, p. XI.

107. Memorandum of the Under Secretary to head of bureaus and offices, dated 25 June 1953.

108. The author gratefully acknowledges the help granted by Mr. J. Earl Coke, Assistant Secretary, U. S. Department of Agriculture, on 12 and 29 October 1953, and Mr. John Thurston, Administrative Officer, Office of the Secretary, U. S. Department of Agriculture, on 21 June 1954.

109. For the history, organization and abolition of the War Food Administration, see United States Government Organization Manual, 1953-54, pp. 638-639.

110. Memorandum of the Administrator, War Food Administration, No. 27, Supplement 11, dated 10 November 1944.

111. Revision 1 to the above Memorandum, dated 13 December 1944.

112. Official Register of the United States, 1952 edition, p. 292. It is to be noted that the Department of Agriculture had only one Under Secretary and one Assistant Secretary at this time.

113. Information obtained through an interview with Mr. Herbert M. Peet, Secretary's Representative of the Department of Agriculture in the Columbia River Basin, on 11 August 1950.

114. The author gratefully acknowledges the help given by Mr. J. Earl Coke, Assistant Secretary, U. S. Department of Agriculture, on 14 October 1953.

115. See the various editions of the Official Register of the United States. For the position of the Secretary's Field Representatives as chairman of the various Field Committees, see p. 1160, below.

116. Letter to the author from Mr. J. Earl Coke, Assistant Secretary, U. S. Department of Agriculture, dated 14 October 1953.

117. Formally promulgated by a Departmental Order of 24 December 1953 (19 F. R. 74ff).

118. Reorganization Plan No. 2 of 1953, effective 4 June 1953 (18 F. R. 3219).

119. Consult advance notice of this plan released 13 October 1953. Italicized agencies are those concerned with water resources administration.

120. It should be remarked that both the specialized staffs and the functional assistant secretaries are auxiliary officers of the Secretary and constitute part of the office of the Secretary. Neither the specialized staffs nor the functional assistant secretaries have independent duties and responsibilities of their own; they all work on behalf and in the name of the Secretary. It should also be remarked that these two different methods of re-inforcing Secretarial supervision and coordination need not be mutually exclusive. As a matter of fact, in the Department of the Interior the functional Assistant Secretaries have existed alongside the program Staff and its successors, the Technical Review Staff.

121. Letter to the author from Mrs. Betsy P. Roscoe, Executive Secretary, American Association For Public Information, Education and Research, dated 10 September 1954. The said Corporation, as provided in the said Organic Act, is administered by an Administrator, who is assisted by a Deputy Administrator. Both these officers are appointed by the President with the consent of the Senate. For the functions of the Corporation, see Act of 13 May 1954 (68 Stat. 92).

122. Formal coordination is characterized by the existence of some coordinating body.

123. Chairmanship was originally assigned to the Secretary of Agriculture. As a result of the Re-Organization Plan No. II of 1939 (4 F. R. 2731; 53 Stat. 1433), the Secretary of the Interior has become the chairman of the Commission

124. For the text of the report of this board, see Rpt. Chief of E. 1929, p. 1927ff.

125. This bore witness to the fact that the central theme of the Committee was electric power.

126. Rpt. F. P. C. 1951, pp. 136-137.

127. In the New England-New York Committee, a representative of the Department of State served as a consultant to the Committee without vote. This is seemingly necessitated by the international nature of the Great Lakes-St. Lawrence Seaway program.

128. For the Missouri Basin Committee, the ten basin states were represented by four Governors until 1947, by five Governors until January 1952, and by all ten Governors since January 1952. -- Missouri Basin Inter-Agency Committee and the Missouri River States Committee, The Missouri River Basin Development Program, June 1952, p. 11. In this Committee, " the votes of state members have been recognized as having equal validity with those of the Federal members." -- 96 Cong. Rec. A1374. In the New England-New York Committee, the states were represented by representatives designated by the Governors.

129. Letter to the author from Mr. Frank L. Weaver, Chief of the Division of River Basin, Bureau of Power, Federal Power Commission and Federal Power Commission member to the New England-New York Committee, dated 3 August 1951; Rpt. F. P C. 1951, pp. 138-141.

130. The author is indebted to Col. A. C. Welling, Executive, U. S. Corps of Engineers, for his courtesy in making available to him a copy of the agreement of 1954.

131. The original members were the Corps of Engineers, the National Park Service, the Fish and Wildlife Service, the Extension Service, the Forest Service, the Office of Education and the Public Housing Authority (of the Housing and Home Finance Agency). -- Federal Inter-Agency Committee On Recreation, The Role of the Federal Government In The Field of Pub-

lic Recreation (mimeo.), June 1949, p. 7.

132. All information in this paragraph, a mimeographed sheet entitled "Federal Inter-Agency Committee On Recreation", made available to
the author through the courtesy of Mr. George E. Dickie, Executive Secretary, Federal Inter-Agency Committee on Recreation, on 6 November 1951.

133. U. S. Dpt. of the Interior, Missouri Basin Field Committee, "
Re-Statement of the Program of the Interior Department in the Missouri
Basin" (mimeo.), 1949, p. 89.

134. U. S. Department of the Interior, Pacific Northwest Coordination Committee, Annual Report to the Secretary (mimeo.), 7 January 1948.

135. Text of the Order. By Order No. 2429 of 18 May 1948, the Pacific Northwest Coordination Committee was directed to "function with respect to the States of Washington, Oregon and Idaho; and also, to those
parts of the Columbia River Basin which extend into Montana, Wyoming,
Utah, and Nevada" (sec. 2). The Committee, acting through the Chairman,
reported to the Secretary of the Interior through the Chairman of the
Program Committee. The Chairman was assisted by a full-time staff headed by an executive director. -- ibid., (secs. 6 to 8).

136. U. S. Department of the Interior, Press Release, 15 July 1948.

137. The Alaska Field Committee was chaired by the Director of the
Alaska Field Staff, who was the ex-officio Commissioner of Alaska, and
had the following additional members: Governor of Alaska and a representative of the Alaska Railroad and of the Alaska Road Commission. It met
at least once every three months. There has been no Federal Inter-Agency
River-Basin Committee in Alaska. However, the Director of the Alaska
Field Staff and Chairman of the Alaska Field Committee had once a year a
meeting with the heads of the regional offices of all other Federal agencies in Alaska. -- Letter to the author from Dr. Kenneth J. Kadow, Director of the Alaska Field Staff, dated 26 June 1950.

138. Letter to the author from Mr. John G. Marr, Director Technical
Review Staff, U. S. Department of the Interior, dated 20 October 1953.

139. Letter to the author from Mr. L. T. Hoffman, Regional Administrator, Bureau of Land Management, U. S. Department of the Interior, San
Francisoo, California, dated 16 October 1953.

140. Letter to the author from Mr. Noris Benge, Staff Assistant,
Pacific Southwest Field Committee, U. S. Department of the Interior, dated 20 November 1953.

141. Letter from Mr. L. T. Hoffman, op. cit.

142. U. S. Department of the Interior, Press Release, 13 May 1953.

143. Memorandum from Mr. John G. Marr, Special Assistant to the Un-
der Secretary, to heads of Bureaus and Offices. The Pacific Central
Field Committee and the Colorado River-Great Basin Field Committee were
merged into the Pacific Southwest Field Committee on 1 October 1953. --
Letter from Mr. John G. Marr, op. cit. The offices of the various Field
Committees are as follows: Pacific Northwest, Portland, Oregon; Pacific
Southwest, San Francisco, California; Missouri, Billings, Montana, Southwest, Albuquerque, New Mexico; Eastern Washington, D. C. (not activated
by October 1953). -- Interior Department Press Release, 13 May 1953; a
map showing "Field Committee Regions", made available to the author
through the courtesy of Mr. Marr; and letter from Mr. L. T. Hoffman, op.
cit.

144. By Memorandum of the Secretary of the Interior dated 27 May 1953, the chairman of the Pacific Northwest Field Committee was designated as the alternate of the Department's representative in the Columbia River Basin Inter-Agency Committee.

145. Letter from Mr. John G. Marr, op. cit.

146. U. S. Department of the Interior, Pacific Northwest Field Committee, Annual Report for 1949 (mimeo.), pp. 9-10.

147. Interview with Mr. Arthur M. Piper, Staff Scientist, U. S. Geological Survey, at Portland, Oregon, on 15 December 1953. Mr. Piper was the last chairman of the Pacific Northwest Field Committee at that time. Mr. Piper told the author that these sub-committees had not been active for nearly a year and that it was unlikely that they would be reactivated in the near future.

148. Letter from Mr. Noris Benge, op. cit.

149. Letter to the author from Mr. W. G. Sloan, Chairman, Missouri River Basin Field Committee, U. S. Department of the Interior, dated 23 June 1950.

150. The predecessor of the Program Committee seems to be the Coordination Committee, which was established by Order No. 2205 of 4 June 1946. It consisted of the Under Secretary as chairman, an assistant secretary as vice-chairman and all other assistant secretaries and heads of all subordinate agencies and independent units of the Department as members. The chairman appointed a steering committee as the nucleus of the Committee. This Committee should have been automatically inactivated by the establishment of the Program Committee. However, this Committee was never given the duty of coordinating the various subordinate agencies at the regional level. As discussed above, so far as this function was concerned, the Program Staff was the predecessor of the Program committee.

151. Letter from Mr. John G. Marr, op. cit.

152. Letter to the author from Mr. Carl B. Brown, Assistant Chief of Operations, U. S. Soil Conservation Service, dated 13 November 1953.

153. A circular of the Chief of the Soil Conservation Service to heads of eight other subordinate agencies of the Department of Agriculture concerned dated 15 May 1953. It should be pointed out that the Comprehensive Agricultural Plan for the Missouri River Basin was completed in August 1949, and was submitted to the House of Representatives by the Secretary of Agriculture on 29 September 1949. It was printed as House Document 373 of the first session of the 81st Congress. "Investigations in the Cumberland River area are to be closed down on or before June 30, 1953, Development of a comprehensive agricultural program for the Colorado River area, to complement the main river developments proposed by the Department of the Interior, is not to be initiated at this time." -- the above-cited Circular.

154. "Membership in the State Council shall be extended to the Director of the State Extension Service and to the Director of the State Experiment Station. Membership may also be extended by the council to the head of any interested State agricultural agency." Membership in a County Council "shall be extended to the heads of the Production Credit Association the National Farm Loan Association, the Rural Electrification Administration Cooperative in the county, the County Agent, the County Home Demonstration Agent, and the County FSA (Farm Security Administration) Home Supervisor."

155. Each State or County Council annually elected a chairman and a secretary, and met at least once a month.

156. *Annual Report of the U. S. Forest Service for 1939*, p. 32.

157. *Annual Report of the U. S. Forest Service for 1940*, p. 8. This inter-departmental committees was not mentioned in later reports.

158. *House Document 657*, 78th Cong., 2nd sess. p. 12.

159. The original "of the Portland District" should be changed into "at Portland".

160. Letter to the author from Mr. Wilbur D. Staats, Chief, Information Service Section, Bonneville Power Administration, dated 16 June 1954.

161. *Senate Document 167*, 73rd Cong., 2nd sess., 1934, p. 5. It should be remarked that the Secretary of the Interior was *ex-officio* Administrator, Federal Emergency Administration of Public Works (i.e., Public Works Administration). In this quotation, the President, the Administrator and the Secretary of the Interior actually referred to the same person.

162. Conrad L. Wirth, *Civilian Conservation Corps Program of the United States Department of the Interior* (a report to the Secretary), January 1944, p. 4.

163. Letter to the author from Mr. F. E. Gartrell, Assistant Director of Health, Tennessee Valley Authority, dated 24 October 1951.

164. U. S. Department of Agriculture, Agricultural Conservation Program Memorandum 56, 16 October 1947; interview with Mr. James A. Johnston, Agricultural Extension Agent, King County, State of Washington, on 16 June 1954.

165. *Senate Document 167*, 73rd Cong., 2nd sess., 1934, p. 5.

166. *Annual Report of the Chief of the Soil Conservation Service for 1951*, p. 25.

167. *House Document 215*, 81st Cong., 1949, p. 58. Ordinarily the engineers of the Corps of Engineers correspond with other agencies concerned.

168. In general, when a state agency is in the form of a commission or board the terms of the members of the commission or board are staggered. This will be understood throughout the discussion in this Article.

169. An agency made up in whole or in part of the head or heads of other agency or agencies *ex-officio* is not *prima facie* an instance of organizational coordination, and is regarded as an uncoordinated agency.

170. The term "department of conservation" is used in this Section *generically*. It may be officially known as Department of Conservation or it may have some other official designation.

171. *Arizona Code*, sec. 75-103 (Laws 1919, ch. 164, sec. 2; as amended by L. 1943, ch. 28, sec. 5); *California Water Code of 1943*, secs. 200 201, 202 and 1050.5 (as amended by Stats. 1945, ch. 831); *Colorado Statutes*, ch. 90, secs. 201, 203, 207(1), 208 and 209 (Laws 1889, p. 371; as amended by L. 1943, ch. 125, sec. 1); *Idaho Code*, sec. 67-2404 (Laws 1919, ch. 8, sec. 4; as last amended by L. 1947, ch. 238, sec. 2) and

secs. 42-1801 to 42-1805 (L. 1943, ch. 58, secs. 6-10); General Statutes of Kansas, sec. 74-506a et seq. (Laws 1927 ch. 293; as last amended by L. 1937, ch. 329, sec. 12); Revised Codes of Montana, sec. 81-2006 et seq. (Laws 1903, ch. 114, sec. 6 et seq.; as last amended by L. 1911, ch. 128, sec. 1); Revised Statutes of Nebraska, secs. 81-102 (Laws 1929, ch. 51, sec. s; as last amended by L. 1953, ch. 335, sec. 1), 81-107 (L. 1919, ch. 190, sec. 5; as last amended by L. 1951, ch. 311, sec. 6), 81-109 (L. 1919, ch. 190, sec. 8; as last amended by L. 1953, ch. 335, sec. 4) and 46-208 and 46-209 (L. 1919, ch. 190, tit. VII, art. V, division 2, secs. 1 and 14); organizational charts appearing in the 1949-1950 biennial report of the Nebraska Department of Roads and Irrigation; Nevada Compiled Laws, secs. 7390 and 7391 (Stats. 1919, ch. 108; as last amended by Stats. 1949, ch. 208); New Mexico Statutes, secs. 77-201 and 77-202 (Laws 1907, ch. 49, secs. 4 and 5; as last amended by L. 1947, ch. 142, sec. 1); North Dakota Revised Code, sec. 61-0301 (Laws 1905, ch. 34, sec. 5; as last amended by L. 1941, ch. 228, sec. 1); Oregon Revised Statutes, secs. 536.010 (Laws 1927, ch. 434, sec. 3; as amended by L. 1945, ch. 339, sec. 1) and 536.060 (L. 1909, ch. 216, sec. 5; as amended by L. 1923, ch. 208, sec. 3); South Dakota Code, secs. 55.1801 (Revised Code of 1919, sec. 8183; as amended by L. 1920, S. S., ch. 86, sec. 1) and 55-1802 (Revised Code of 1919, sec. 8184; as last amended by L. 1949, ch. 217, sec. 1); Revised Civil Statutes of Texas, art. 7477 (L. 1913, ch. 171, sec. 7; as last amended by L. 1953, ch. 357, sec. 1); Utah Code, secs. 73-2-1 (Laws 1919, ch. 67, sec. 7; as last amended by L. 1941, ch. 96, sec. 1) and 73-2-4 (L. 1919, ch. 67, sec. 58; as last amended by L. 1949, ch. 97, sec. 1); Constitution of Wyoming, art. 8, secs. 2 and 5; Wyoming Compiled Statutes, secs. 18-1104 (Laws 1890-91, ch. 8, sec. 9) and 18-1105 (ibid., sec. 10; as last amended by L. 1953, ch. 188, sec.3).

172. The deputy state engineer acts ex-officio as the secretary of the state board of control. -- Wyoming Compiled Statutes, sec. 71-202 (Laws 1899, ch. 59, sec. 1; as last amended by L. 1933, ch. 86, sec. 1).

173. There is no state regulation of water use in Maryland. However, "the control, as far as is practicable, of the appropriation or use of surface and underground waters of the state" is entrusted to the state department of geology, mines and water resources. -- Code, Art. 66C, secs. 15 to 17 (Laws 1941, ch. 508, sec. 12A et seq.).

174. Idaho Code, sec. 42-901 (Laws 1899, p. 380, sec. 17; as amended by L. 1909, p. 104, sec. 1). In Idaho the water users apply to the courts for the appointment of water masters only when they appoint one themselves.

175. Revised Statutes, art. 7475 (Laws 1913, ch. 171, sec. 6; as amended by L. 1917, ch. 88, sec. 8).

176. In California, these districts are called "watermaster service areas"; in Colorado, "irrigation districts" (which, however should be distinguished from special districts organized for irrigation projects and enterprises which have the same designation); in all other states, "water districts". But there are water districts in Nevada, South Dakota, and Utah; water commissioners are appointed for the various streams. The officers are called "water mas ters" in California, New Mexico, Oregon and Washington, and "water commissioners" in all other states.

177. In Nevada, the water districts are not service areas of the water commissioners, but for each water district, the State Engineer appoints an advisory board of representative citizens.

178. For this and the foregoing paragraphs: Water Code of California, secs. 4025 (Stats. 1913, ch. 586, sec. 37, 1st sentence; as last amended by Stats. 1931, ch. 804, sec. 1) and 4050 (Stats. 1921, ch. 365, sec. 2;

as amended by Stats. 1931, ch. 804, sec. 2); Colorado Statutes, ch. 90, sec. 224 et seq. (Laws 1879, p. 99, sec. 17; and L. 1911, ch. 165, as last amended by L. 1945, chs. 72 and 156); Revised Statutes of Nebraska, sec. 46-215 et seq. (Laws 1895, ch. 69; as last amended by L. 1953, ch. 157); Nevada Compiled Laws, sec. 7937 et seq. (Stats. 1913, ch. 140, secs. 52, 53; as last amended by Stats. 1947, ch. 159); New Mexico Statutes,,sec. 77-301 et seq. (Laws 1907, ch. 49, sec. 13 et seq.; as amended by L. 1919, ch. 131, sec. 2); Oregon Revised Statutes, sec. 540.010 et seq. (Laws 1909, ch. 216, sec. 37 et seq.; as last amended by L. 1953, ch. 395, sec. 3); South Dakota Code, sec. 61.0121 (added by 1939 Code as a new section); Utah Code, sec. 73-5-1 (Laws 1919, ch. 67, sec. 62; as last amended by L. 1941, ch. 96, sec. 1); Revised Code of Washington, sec. 90.08.010 et seq. (Laws 1917, ch. 117, secs. 9, 10, as amended by L. 1947, ch. 123, sec. 2; and L. 1925, Ex. S., ch. 162); Wyoming Compiled Statutes, secs. 71-101 to 71-103 (Laws 1890-91, ch. 8; as last amended by L. 1941, ch. 118) and 71-301 to 71-308 (L. 1890-91, ch. 8; as last amended by L. 1953, ch. 33).

179. Which is also the water-use-regulation agency.

180. Terms in quotation marks are used generically.

181. The government of the state of Maryland does not regulate dams and reservoirs. However, the Department of Geology, Mines and Water Resources is charged with the "control of the construction and repairs of reservoirs, dams and waterway obstructions" (Code, art. 66C, secs.15 to 17: Laws 1941, ch. 508, sec. 12A et seq.).

182. This term is here used generically. It is Department of Public Works in Massachusetts and Rhode Island, the Department of Public Works and Buildings in Illinois and the Department of Highways and Public Works in Tennessee.

183. Letter to the author from Mr. K. S. Wingfield, Administrator, Arizona Power Authority, dated 19 August 1953.

184. These agencies are defined as agencies capable of undertaking single-purpose projects of two or more kinds and multiple-purpose projects.

185. Dams and reservoirs and other works for municipal and domestic water supply are included. -- Letter from Mr. Roy T. Sessums, Director, Louisiana Department of Public Works, dated 13 October 1953.

186. See Acts of 1934, No. 139; 1940, No. 39; 1948, No. 277; 1950, No. 222; 1952, Nos. 248, 320 and 489, etc. It would seem that the Department of Public Works constructs these works as the engineering agent of the state fish and wildlife agency, for its administrative jurisdiction does not extend to this field.

187. Seven of the ten appointees of the governor are appointed upon the recommendation of the Utah Water Users' Association, one from each of seven defined districts. The Association recommends two names in each district.

188. The Washington State Power Commission , though a unifunctional power agency, may maintain and operate incidental navigation, reclamation, flood control and fishery works. The Florida State Improvement Commission, which is not a water agency as such, may construct, maintain and operate "water control and conservation facilities and works." -- Florida Statutes, ch. 420 (Laws 1933, ch. 22821; as last amended by L. 1951, ch. 26851). (This commission may also issue revenue bonds).

189. The author gratefully acknowledges the assistance given by Mr. Dan S. Jones, Jr., Chief, Bureau of Irrigation, Water Power and Drainage, Nebraska State Department of Roads and Irrigation, in his letter dated 25 September 1952.

190. Mosquito-control agencies and agencies in charge of special water-pollution-control regulation are omitted.

191. In Rhode Island and Iowa, the state health department is in charge of comprehensive general water-pollution regulation.

192. It is proper to remark again that Rhode Island and Iowa are the only two states in which the state health department is the agency for comprehensive water-pollution regulation.

193. Alabama Acts 1947, No. 523, as amended by Acts 1949, No. 460; General Statutes of Connecticut, sec. 4041 (Acts 1925, ch. 143, sec. 2, as last amended in 1943); Revised Statutes of Maine, ch. 72, sec. 1 (Laws 1945, ch. 345, sec. 1, which superseded L. 1941, ch. 209 and which was last amended by L. 1953, ch. 403, sec. 1); General Statutes of North Carolina, sec. 143-213 (Laws 1945, ch. 1010, as last amended by L. 1953, ch. 1295); Pennsylvania Statutes, tit. 71, sec. 12 (enacted 1923, amended 1929); Wisconsin Statutes, sec. 144.52 (Laws 1931, ch. 184, as amended by L. 1933, ch. 159, sec. 27); California Stats. 1953, ch. 1067, amending Water Code, sec. 13011. For other statutory citations, see pp. 698-700, above.

194. It may be observed that in Oregon and Pennsylvania the ex-officio members equal the ad-hoc members, that in Michigan, Minnesota, Tennessee, Delaware, Maryland, New Hampshire, Arkansas, Kentucky, Illinois and Ohio the ex-officio members out-number the ad-hoc members, and that in West Virginia, Maine, Indiana, North Carolina, Alabama, California and South Carolina the ad-hoc members are preponderant over the ex-officio members. The Delaware commission is the only agency in which there are representatives of local government; and the South Carolina Water Pollution Control Authority is the only agency which ex-officio members are selected exclusively from the state health department.

195. This would seem to be justifiable by the fact that all of the ex-officio members are supposedly representative of the general public.

196. There is a member each from the Alabama Polytechnic Institute and the University of Alabama. Expert members may be assumed as one of the two general types of the representatives of the general public, the other being laymen. Cf. West Virginia Code, sec. 1402. The representative nature of the members of the agencies of Pennsylvania, West Virginia, Indiana and Maryland is not statutorily specified.

197. In California, the nine appointive members should, as far as possible, be evenly distributed among the nine water-pollution-control regions of the state.

198. It may be noted that in Wisconsin the State Board of Health or the State Health Officer has the authority of calling special meetings of the Committee On Water Pollution, a privilege ordinarily accorded to the presiding officer of a plural-headed agency.

199. There is no statutory provision for the selection of chairman (or president) in Michigan, Wisconsin, Oregon and Delaware, although a "chairman" is mentioned in the laws of Delaware.

200. For technical secretary, see discussion below.

201. The Commissioner of Health of Kentucky may appoint an **executive director** for the agency.

202. There is no statutory provision for administrative officers in Michigan. However, the Water Resources Commission has employed an Executive Secretary, engineers and other personnel. -- An organizational chart made available to the author through the courtesy of Mr. Milton P. Adams, Executive Secretary, Michigan Water Resources Commission, on 25 March 1954.

203. In Delaware, special meetings may also be called by the "executive secretary". However, there is no statutory provision for the appointment or selection of such an officer.

204. It may be remarked that in these two states regular meetings are held **monthly**.

205. For a brief history of the state forestry agencies, see Fifty Years of Forestry in the U. S. A., 1950, chapter 1 (by Robert K. Winter); The Book of the States, 1948-49, p. 308; R. R. Renne, 23 State Government 136 (1950).

206. It may be noted that in a majority of the 46 states, the head of executive officer of the agency or unit or sub-unit of forestry is entitled the "state forester". This is presumably in compliance with provisions of sec. 2(b) of an Act of Congress of 29 August 1935 (49 Stat. 963, 964), which stipulates that each cooperative state "shall provide for the employment of a state forester, who shall be a trained forester of recognized standing." The extension service of each state, which has some duties in forestry extension, is omitted.

207. Idaho Code, sec. 38-101 et seq. (Laws 1925, ch. 150; as last amended by L. 1945, ch. 105); Oregon Revised Statutes, ch. 526 (Laws 1925, ch. 281; as last amended by L. 1953, ch. 68); Mississippi Code, sec. 6022 et seq. (Laws 1926, ch. 161; as amended by L. 1950, ch. 224); Delaware Code, tit. 7, part III, ch. 29 (Laws 1927, ch. 50; as last amended by L. 1953, ch. 108); Florida Statutes, sec. 589.01 (Laws 1927, ch. 122383; as last amended by L. 1949, chs. 25118 and 25324); Code of Laws of South Carolina, sec. 29-1 et seq. (Acts 1927, No. 201; as last amended by Acts 1953, No. 122); Colorado Statutes Annotated, ch. 134, sec. 131(1) et seq. (Laws 1937, ch. 211); Utah Code, sec. 24-1-1 (Laws 1937, ch. 24, sec. 1; as last amended by L. 1945, ch. 33, sec. 1); Revised Codes of Montana, sec. 28-101 (Laws 1939, ch. 128, sec. 1; as amended by L. 1941, ch. 141, sec. 1), sec. 81-1403 (L. 1925, ch. 179, sec. 3; as amended by L. 1949, ch. 151, sec. 1) and sec. 81-201 (L. 1927, ch. 60, sec. 5); Louisiana Revised Statutes, tit. 56, sec. 1471 et seq. (Constitution, art. 4, sec. 1, as amended 7 November 1944; Acts 1944, No. 328); Code of Georgia, sec. 43-209 et seq. (Laws 1949, No. 248).

208. The Commission of Forestry of South Carolina is also in charge of state parks. However, the Commission is not regarded in this treatise as a combined forestry and parks agency.

209. Including a nominee of the United States Forest Service in Idaho, Oregon and Montana and a nominee each of the United States Forest Service and the United States Bureau of Land Management in Utah. All these Federal-nominated members serve in an advisory capacity, except in Montana, where the member representing the Forest Service presumably has full membership rights.

210. The Federal Government as the owner of the national forests may be regarded as a special interest group.

211. The Louisiana agency also elects a Vice-Chairman.

212. It may be of interest to notice the varying shades of the organizational relationships between the agency and its administrative
officer. Four general types of such relationships may be distinguished.
First, the administrative officer is appointed by the agency; second,
he is appointed by the agency with the approval of an extraneous authority; third, he is appointed by an extraneous authority upon the recommendation of the agency; and fourth, he is appointed by an extraneous
authority. (In the last three cases, further distinctions can be made
by the criterion whether the officer is removable by the agency). From
a purely organizational point of view, a dual system may be said to exist when the administrative officer is appointed by an extraneous authority and is thus organizationally beyond the control of the agency.
However, from the standpoint of administrative procedure, the administrative officer is under the guidance and direction of the agency in all
cases.
     The above statement also applies to other state agencies.

213. In Florida the agency elects its secretary. The Colorado agency is the State Board of Land Commissioners ex-officio. There is no
statutory provision for a secretary of the agency in Mississippi.

214. There is no statutory provision for the employment of such assistants in Mississippi, South Carolina and Colorado.

215. Iowa State Conservation Commission, Biennial Report, 1950-52,
p. 120.

216. Revised Laws of New Hampshire, tit. 20, ch. 240 (Laws 1869, ch.
45; as last amended by the Reorganization Act of 17 May 1950, part 24);
Vermont Statutes, sec. 6312 et seq. (Laws 1904, No. 118; as last amended
by L. 1953, No. 259); Revised Codes of Montana, sec. 26-101 et seq. (Laws
1907, ch. 176; as last amended by L. 1951, ch. 133); New Mexico Statutes,
sec. 43-101 et seq. (Laws 1921, ch. 35; as last amended by L. 1945, ch.
26); Utah Code, sec. 23-1-1 et seq. (Laws 1923, ch. 36; as last amended
by L. 1953, ch. 39); Arizona Code, sec. 57-102 (Laws 1929, ch. 84; as
last amended by L. 1953, ch. 31); Mississippi Code, sec. 5841 (Laws 1932,
ch. 123; as last amended by L. 1952, ch. 186); Colorado Statutes, ch. 73,
sec. 4 (Revised Statutes of 1908, sec. 2728; as last amended by L. 1943,
ch. 108, sec. 2), sec. 3 (L. 1899, ch. 98, sec. 3; as last amended by
L. 1943, ch. 108, sec. 1) and sec. 238 et seq. (L. 1937, ch. 153; as last
amended by L. 1951, ch. 184); Arkansas Statutes, sec. 47-101 et seq.
(Constitutional Amendment No. 35, and Acts 1939, No. 347, sec. 13); Idaho Code, sec. 36-101 et seq. (Laws 1939, Init, Meas.; as last amended by
L. 1953, ch. 269); Wyoming Compiled Statutes, sec. 47-101 et seq. (Laws
1939, ch. 65; as last amended by L. 1953, ch. 139, sec. 16 et seq.);
Code of Georgia, sec. 2-2801a (Constitutional Amendment adopted 3 August
1943), and sec. 45-136 et seq. (Laws 1943, No. 30; as last amended by L.
1950, No. 528); Nevada Compiled Laws, sec. 3035.09 et seq. (Stats. 1947,
ch. 101, sec. 9 et seq.; as amended by Stats. 1949, ch. 146); California Fish and Game Code, sec. 10 et seq. (Stats. 1927, ch. 128; as last
amended by L. 1953, ch. 1678, sec. 1.5); Oklahoma Statutes, tit. 29, ch.
1 (Laws 1909, ch. 10, art. 6; as last amended by L. 1951, p. 69); Penal
Code of Texas, art. 978f-3 (Laws 1951, ch. 476); South Carolina Reorganization Plan No. 8 of 30 January 1952 (Acts 1952, p. 2890); Oregon Revised Statutes, sec. 496.105 et seq. (Laws 1941, ch. 275; as last amended by L. 1949, ch. 242); Pennsylvania Statutes, tit. 34, sec. 1311.201
et seq. (Act of 3 June 1937, art. II); Revised Code of Washington, sec.
77.04.020 et seq. (Laws 1947, ch. 275; as amended by L. 1949, ch. 205,
sec. 1); General Statutes of North Carolina, sec. 143-237 et seq. (Laws
1947, ch. 263); Delaware Code, tit. 7, ch. 1 (Laws 1911, ch. 162; as
last amended by L. 1949, ch. 148); General Statutes of Connecticut, sec.
4847 (Acts 1923, ch. 259; as last amended by Acts 1953, No. 513); Florida Statutes, sec. 372.01 et seq. (Laws 1929, ch. 13644; as last amended
by L. 1951, ch. 26766); Code of Virginia, sec. 29-3 et seq. (Acts 1930,
ch. 247; as last amended by Acts 1944, ch. 361); Code of Maryland, art.

by L. 1951, ch. 26766); <u>Code of Virginia</u>, sec. 29-3 et seq. (Acts 1930, ch. 247; as last amended by Acts 1944, ch. 361); <u>Code of Maryland</u>, art. 66C, sec. 114 et seq. (Laws 1939, ch. 354; as last amended by L. 1949, ch. 198); <u>Kentucky Revised Statutes</u>, ch. 150 (Acts 1952, ch. 200, which superseded Acts 1942, ch. 68, as last amended by Acts 1948, ch. 78).

217. The Arkansas agency includes an ex-officio non-voting "asso-ciate member", who is the head of the Department of Zoology of the Uni-versity of Arkansas.

218. "Not more than one member from each congressional district." There are at present nine Congressional districts in Virginia.

219. "One member from each congressional district in this state, and one additional member from one of the following named counties, to wit: Chatham, Bryan, Liberty, McIntosh, Glynn or Camden." There are at pre-sent ten Congressional districts in Georgia.

220. One member from a specially designated district in Montana, Utah, Mississippi, Colorado, Idaho, California (not mandatory), Oklaho-ma, Arkansas, Pennsylvania, Kentucky, and North Carolina; one member from each county in New Hampshire, Arizona, Nevada, Delaware and partly in Georgia (five members); one member from each Congressional district in South Carolina (with a member chosen from the state at large), Flori-da, Virginia and partly in Georgia (ten members); otherwise geographi-cally distributed in New Mexico, Wyoming, Texas, Oregon (with one member chosen from the state at large) and Maryland. The memberships of the agencies of New Hampshire, New Mexico, Utah, Arizona, Colorado, Wyoming and Kentucky are required to be bi-partisan. The special districts form-ed for this purpose are designated by statute in all states except Ken-tucky, where they are designated administratively.

221. This requirement may limit the agency-membership to those who are actually engaged in hunting and fishing, who form a special interest group by themselves. It may be noted that in Kentucky it is expressly provided that the members are appointed upon the recommendation of the meetings of sportsmen (i.e. hunters and fishmen) in the respective Wild Life Districts.

222. The term of office of the members of the Florida agency is not specified.

223. It is president in Colorado, California, Pennsylvania and Del-aware, and chairman in all other states. There is a vice-chairman in Oklahoma, North Carolina and Maryland, a vice-president in Colorado, Pen-nsylvania and Delaware, Delaware president and vice-president (and also secretary) do not appear in law, but it seems to be a practice that the three members of the agency in that state elect themselves to these of-fices. See Delaware State Board of Game and Fish Commissioners, <u>Annual Report 1952</u>, pp. 2, 4. In Kentucky it seems that the administrative of-ficer is the agency's presiding officer.

224. Elected annually in Montana, Colorado, Arkansas, Idaho, Wyoming, Georgia, Oregon and North Carolina; elected biennially in Arizona and Washington. In Texas, the chairman is elected by two-thirds of the en-tire membership of the agency.

225. However, the secretary of the Wyoming agency is its Chief Clerk, who is appointed by the agency.

226. The executive board of the Nevada agency "shall meet at such times and places as may be deemed necessary and proper."

227. In states where the fish and wildlife agency is the "Department of Conservation", such authority is generally delegated to the head of that department. In New Hampshire, the Director makes and promulgates rules and regulations with the approval of the commission.

228. In Pennsylvania, North Carolina and Virginia, "Executive Director"; in South Carolina, the director of the division of game; in Washington, the director of game; in Utah, fish and game director; in Arizona, state game and fish director; in Oklahoma, director of game and fish; in Nevada and Vermont, director of fish and game; in Mississippi, director of conservation.

229. In Washington, the director is appointed by two-thirds of entire membership of the agency.

230. In Arkansas it is constitutionally provided that "the Commission shall elect (emphasis added) an Executive Secretary . . . and other executive officers, supervisors, personnel, office assistants, wardens, game refuge keepers, and hatchery employees. . ." The word "elect" evidently means "employ".

231. In South Carolina, prior to the re-organization of 1952, there were a state game and fish commission in charge of wildlife and game fish and a state board of fisheries in charge of commercial fisheries. Cf. Laws of Washington of 1921, ch. 7 and Laws of 1933, ch. 3 (secs. 5, 7).

232. It should be noted that (b) are of no less importance than (a).

233. The Division of Commercial Fisheries of the Department of Conservation and Development of North Carolina will be discussed later.

234. Oregon Revised Statutes, sec. 506.105 et seq. (Laws 1921, ch. 2; as amended by L. 1945, ch. 441); Pennsylvania Statutes, tit. 71, sec. 102 (Act of 9 April 1929, as superseded by act of 25 April 1949); Revised Code of Washington, sec. 43.25.010 et seq. (Laws 1949, ch. 112); General Statutes of Connecticut, sec. 5021 et seq. (Acts 1881, ch. 160; as last amended by Acts 1929, ch. 142); Florida Statutes, sec. 370.01 et seq. (Laws 1953, ch. 28145); Virginia Code, sec. 28-11 et seq. (Acts 1898, ch. 225; as last amended by Acts 1944, ch. 361); Code of Maryland, art. 66C, sec. 6 et seq. (Laws 1941, ch. 508, sec. 5 et seq.; as amended by L. 1947, ch. 860); Delaware Code, tit. 7, ch. 19 (Laws 1943, ch. 151; as last amended by L. 1949, ch. 271) and ch. 21 (L. 1893, ch. 653, sec. 36 et seq.; as last amended by L. 1951, ch. 150, sec. 1).

235. Oregon Revised Statutes, sec. 610.005 et seq. (Laws 1919, ch. 366; as last amended by L. 1953, ch. 606); Laws of North Dakota of 1953, ch. 20, sec. 3, subdivision 12b; Laws of Wyoming of 1953, ch. 77.

236. National Park Service, State Parks: Areas, Acreages, and Accommodations, 31 December 1950 (mimeo.), p. 13. (These two refuges may be state parks designated as game refuges.)

237. Agencies in charge of recreational activities and not of recreational areas are omitted.

238. Revised Code of Washington, ch. 43.51 (L. 1921, ch. 149; as last amended by L. 1947, ch. 271); Revised Civil Statutes of Texas, art. 6067 et seq. (L. 1923, 38th Legis., 2nd C. S., ch. 25; as amended by L. 1937, ch. 345); Louisiana Revised Statutes, tit. 56, sec. 1681 et seq. (Acts 1934,, No. 91; as last amended by Acts 1952, No. 390); Revised Statutes of Maine, ch. 32, sec. 23 (L. 1935, 144; as last amended by L. 1947, ch. 2); Nevada Compiled Statutes, sec. 5585.01 et seq. (Stats.

1935, ch. 86; as last amended by Stats. 1939, ch. 150); New Mexico Statutes, sec. 4-101 et seq. (L. 1935, ch. 57; as amended by L. 1953, ch. 11); Mississippi Code, sec. 5957 et seq. (L. 1936, ch. 194; as last amended by L. 1946, ch. 408); Colorado Statutes, ch. 156A, sec. 1 et seq. (L. 1937, ch. 204); Delaware Code, tit. 7, ch. 47 (L. 1937, ch. 259); Missouri Statutes, sec. 253.010 et seq. (L. 1937, p. 520; as amended by L. 1953, Nos. 8 and 32); Wyoming Compiled Statutes, sec. 18-2001 et seq. (L. 1937, ch. 103; as amended by L. 1953, ch. 99); Florida Statutes, ch. 592 (L. 1949, ch. 25353); Laws of Georgia of 1943, No. 125 and letter to the author from Mr. L. A. Hargreaves, Jr., Assistant to the Director, Georgia Forestry Commission, dated 18 August 1954.

239. As their names denote, the agencies of Washington and Louisiana are in charge of both state parks and the coordination of recreational programs of all public and private agencies and institutions in the state. The agencies of Louisiana and Colorado are public corporations.

240. In Washington, three of the seven members of the agency "may be elected officials and shall be appointed by the governor and serve during the terms for which they were elected."

241. Bi-partisan in Maine, Delaware and Missouri.

242. However, in Georgia the term "director of state parks" first appeared in Laws of 1943, No. 31. For the relationship between the administrative officer and the agency, consult n. 212, above.

243. Maine State Park Commission, Annual Report for 1950, p. 6; Mississippi Forestry and Park Services, Biennial Report 1949-1951, p. 30; National Park Service, List of Agencies Administering State Parks and Related Recreation Areas (mimeo.), June 1951

244. For the incompleteness of the jurisdiction of the state parks agencies of certain states, see (c), below.

245. General Statutes of Kansas, sec. 32-214 (L. 1927, ch. 221, sec. 8) and sec. 32-221 (L. 1931, ch. 190, sec. 1). This Commission is not regarded as a combined forestry, fish and game and parks agency.

246. See ibid., ch. 76, art. 20.

247. Prior to this law, there was a Division of Forests, Parks and Parkways in the Department of Agriculture and Conservation.

248. Letter to the author from Mr. Ashley C. Roberts, State Park Director, Montana State Highway Commission, dated 1 July 1954.

249. See North Dakota Revised Code, sec. 55-0101 (Revised Code of 1895, sec. 152; as last amended by Laws 1915, ch. 169).

250. See Utah Code, sec. 64-5-1 et seq. (Laws 1917, ch. 71; as last amended by L. 1951, ch. 110).

251. For the organization of the State Engineering Commission, see Utah Code, sec. 63-1-2 (Laws 1941, 1st S. S., ch. 9, sec. 2).

252. Florida Statutes, secs. 258.09 and 258.·0 (Laws 1939, ch. 193-45) and sec. 258.15 (L. 1949, ch. 25464).

253. Ibid., sec. 258.01 et seq. (L. 1921, ch. 8503; as last amended by L. 1941, ch. 20677); sec. 265.13 et seq. (L. 1931, ch. 15028; as last amended by L. 1945, ch. 22858, sec. 7); secs. 265.07 and 265.08 (L. 1937 ch. 17799; as last amended by L. 1945, ch. 22858, sec. 7).

254. Information made available to the author through the courtesy of the Delaware State Park Commission on 18 May 1953.

255. In Georgia, there are a State Park Authority, which constructs self-liquidating state park and recreational projects (L. 1941, No.278); a Jekyll Island State Park Authority, which administers the Jekyll Island State Park (L. 1950, No. 630; as amended by L. 1953, No. 306); and a Harts Creek Park Authority, which administers the Harts Creek State Park (L. 1953, No. 473). The relation of these authorities with the Department of State Parks, Historic Sites and Monuments is not clear.

256. Consult p. 1168, above.

257. See Wisconsin Statutes, secs. 20.49(6) and 84.28 (Laws 1923, ch. 320, sec. 3; as last amended by L. 1953, ch. 318); California Streets and Highways Code, sec. 122 (Stats. 1933, ch. 909, sec. 3); Code of Georgia, sec. 43-126 (L. 1937, No. 103, sec. 9, a paragraph at p. 278); Louisiana Revised Statutes, tit. 48, sec. 215 (Acts 1942, No. 4, sec. 47; as last amended by Acts 1948, No. 26, sec. 1); Revised Code of Washington, sec. 43.27.040 (L. 1943, ch. 253, sec. 1); Virginia Acts of 1944, ch. 7; Florida Statutes, sec. 592.09 (L. 1949, ch. 25353, sec. 9); Code of Laws of South Carolina, sec. 33-74 (Acts 1951, No. 329, sec. 18); Iowa Conservation Commission, Biennial Report for 1951-1952, p. 41 (not necessarily exhaustive).

258. Code of Alabama, tit. 22, sec. 1 et seq. (Acts 1903, No. 542; as last amended by Acts 1949, No. 182); Arizona Code, sec. 68-107 et seq. (L. 1941, ch. 105; as last amended by L. 1954, ch. 140); Arkansas Statutes, sec. 82-101 et seq. (Acts 1913, No. 96; as last amended by Acts 1949 No. 302); Colorado Statutes, ch. 78, sec. 21(1) et seq. (L. 1947, ch. 208); General Statutes of Connecticut, sec. 3797 et seq. (Acts 1878, ch. 140; as last amended in 1941); Delaware Code, tit. 16, sec. 102 et seq. (L. 1893, ch. 642; as last amended by L. 1941, ch. 91); Florida Statutes, ch. 381 (L. 1889, ch. 3839; as last amended by L. 1949, ch. 24070); Code of Georgia, sec. 88-101 et seq. (L. 1933, No. 318; as amended by L. 1947, No. 312) (superseding L. 1903, p. 72; as amended by L. 1931, No. 298); General Statutes of Kansas, sec. 74-901 et seq. (L. 1885, ch. 129; as last amended by L. 1951, ch. 435); Revised Statutes of Kentucky, ch. 211 (Acts 1893, ch. 185; as last amended by Acts 1954, ch. 157); Louisiana Revised Statutes, tit. 40, sec. 1 et seq. (Acts 1898, No. 192; as last amended by Acts 1952, No. 297); Code of Maryland, art. 41, sec. 178 (L. 1922, ch. 29) and art. 43, sec. 1 et seq. (L. 1874, ch. 200; as last amended by L. 1941, ch. 7); General Laws of Massachusetts, ch. 17, sec. 1 et seq. (Acts 1869, ch. 420; as last amended by Acts 1950, ch. 794) and ch. 111, sec. 2 et seq. (Acts 1969, ch. 420; as last amended by Acts 1946, ch. 152); Mississippi Code, sec. 7016 et seq. (Code of 1892, sec. 2267 et seq.; as last amended by L. 1948, ch. 395); Revised Codes of Montana, sec. 69-101 et seq. (L. 1907, ch. 110; as last amended by L. 1953, ch. 181); Revised Statutes of Nebraska, sec. 81-101 et seq. (L. 1919, ch. 190; as last amended by L. 1953, ch. 355); Nevada Compiled Laws, sec. 5235 et seq. (Stats. 1911, ch. 199; as last amended by Stats. 1947, ch. 235); New Hampshire Laws 1943, ch. 15, as last amended by the Reorganization Act of 17 May 1950; New Jersey Statutes, tit. 26, art. 1A (L. 1915, ch. 288; as last amended by L. 1953, ch. 165); New Mexico Statutes, sec. 81-101 et seq. (L. 1937, ch. 39; as last amended by L. 1947, ch. 136); General Statutes of North Carolina, sec. 130-1 et seq. (L. 1879, ch. 117; as last amended by L. 1945, chs. 281 and 1095); North Dakota Revised Code, sec. 23-0101 et seq. (L. 1885, ch. 63; as last amended by L. 1947, ch. 200); Ohio Revised Code, sec. 3701.01 et seq. (L. 1908, p. 492; as last amended by L. 1945, p. 3); Oklahoma Statutes, tit. 63, sec. 1 et seq. (L. 1945, p. 224; as amended by L. 1949, p. 421) (repealing former laws); Oregon Revised Statutes, sec. 431.010 et seq. (L.

1903, p. 82, sec. 1 and L. 1919, ch. 264; as last amended by L. 1939, ch. 371); <u>Code of Laws of South Carolina</u>, sec. 32-1 et seq. (Acts 1878, No. 610; as last amended by Acts 1949, No. 263); <u>Code of Tennessee</u>, sec. 255.65 et seq.; sec. 325 et seq. and title 13 (Acts 1877, ch. 98; Acts 1923, ch. 7; Acts 1935, ch. 2; Acts 1937, ch. 33; Acts 1939, ch. 102; etc.); <u>Revised Civil Statutes of Texas</u>, art. 4415a et seq. (L. 1927, 1st C. S., ch. 42; as amended by L. 1931, ch. 266); <u>Utah Code</u>, sec. 26-1-1 (L. 1941, ch. 30; as last amended by L. 1951, ch. 46); Vermont Laws of 1949, No. 184; <u>Code of Virginia</u>, sec. 32-1 et seq. (Acts 1871, ch. 91; as last amended by Acts 1946, ch. 398); <u>West Virginia Code</u>, sec. 1265 et seq. (L. 1949, ch. 101); <u>Wisconsin Statutes</u>, sec. 140.01 et seq. (L. 1876, ch. 366; as last amended by L. 1953, ch. 61); <u>Wyoming Compiled Statutes</u>, sec. 63-144 et seq. (L. 1947, ch. 67).

259. The department is officially known as "**Department of Public Health**" in California, Colorado, Georgia, Idaho, Illinois, Massachusetts, Mississippi, New Mexico, Tennessee and Wyoming; as "Department of Health and Welfare" in Maine and Missouri; and as the "Department of Health" or "State Board of Health" in all other states.

260. The board of Wisconsin is corporate.

261. Annually in New Jersey, North Dakota, Ohio and Tennessee and biennially in Texas and West Virginia.

262. Regular meetings are prescribed by the board in Mississippi and West Virginia; there are statutory provisions for regular meetings in Alabama, Georgia, New Mexico, South Carolina and Vermont.

263. There are no statutory provisions for special meetings in Georgia, New Hampshire, South Carolina and Utah.

264. The boards of Alabama, North Carolina and South Carolina have an Executive Committee. The Executive Committee of Alabama is the board of censors of the state medical association; that of North Carolina is made up of the president and two members elected by the board. The Executive Committee of South Carolina has already been discussed above. It may be noted that the Executive Committee is also a deliberative body.

265. <u>California Health Safety Code</u>, sec. 100 et seq. (Stats. 1927, ch. 49; as last amended by Stats. 1953, ch. 1884); <u>Idaho Code</u>, sec. 67-2401 et seq. (L. 1919, ch. 8; as last amended by L. 1947, ch. 238); <u>Illinois Revised Code</u>, ch. 127, sec. 3 et seq. (L. 1917, p. 2; as last amended by L. 1951, H. B. 994); <u>Indiana Statutes</u>, sec. 60-2003 et seq. (Acts 1953, ch. 197); <u>Iowa Code</u>, sec. 135.2 et seq. (Acts 1880, ch. 151; as last amended by Acts 1923-24, Ex. Sess., H. F. 260, sec. 6) and sec. (Acts 1880, ch. 151; as last amended by Acts 1923-24, Ex. Sess., H. F. 260, sec. 27 et seq.); <u>Revised Statutes of Maine</u>, ch. 22, sec. 1 et seq. (L. 1931, ch. 216, art. I; as last amended by L. 1939, ch. 299); <u>Compiled Laws of Michigan</u>, sec. 325.1 et seq. (Acts 1873, No. 81; as last amended by Acts 1933, No. 69); <u>Missouri Statutes</u>, sec. 191.010 et seq. (L. 1945, p. 945, in pursuance of Constitution, art. IV, sec. 37); <u>New York Public Health Law of 1954</u>, various sections (L. 1893, ch. 661; as first amended by L. 1913, ch. 559 and last amended by L. 1952, ch. 318); <u>Pennsylvania Statutes</u>, tit. 71, sec. 1401 et seq. (acts of 27 April 1905 and 17 March 9 April 1929, sec. 448, as last amended by act of 24 August 1951, se. 3); <u>General Laws of Rhode Island</u>, ch. 255, sec. 1 et seq.(first enacted by Acts 1929, ch. 1432), as amended by Acts 1939, ch. 660; <u>South Dakota Code</u>, sec. 27.0101 et seq. (L. 1895, ch. 96; as last amended by L. 1951, ch. 134); <u>Revised Code of Washington</u>, sec. 43.20.010 et seq. (L. 1891, ch. 98; as last amended by L. 1953, ch. 174, sec. 2).

266. It may also be noted that in Iowa the governor appoints the

five health officers and that in Maine the bureau chiefs are appointed
by the head of the department with the approval of the governor and the
council.

267. In Pennsylvania, such body also makes rules and regulations.
In Washington, it makes rules and regulations on prevention of diseases
and on local matters, as well as quarantine orders.

268. In California, Iowa and Washington, "state board of health";
in Illinois, "board of public health advisors"; in Indiana, health and
welfare"; in Michigan, "state council of health"; in Missouri, "state
advisory council"; in New York, "public health council"; in Pennsylvania, "advisory health board"; in Rhode Island, "advisory council"; in
South Dakota, "public health advisory council".

269. There never has been a state board of health in Idaho. The
present Idaho Department of Public Health was formerly the Department
of Public Welfare a single-headed agency. See the old codes of the
various states concerned.

270. U. S. Chamber of Commerce, National Aspects of Water Power Development, September 1930, p. 66.

271. The discussion in this subsection will include the agencies of
these four states, in spite of this. There is a possibility that the law-
makers of these states may some day find it necessary or expedient to in-
vest such agencies with regulatory authority over some aspect or aspects
of water resources administration.

272. For the sake of convenience, this Board is discussed together
with the Commissions of other states.

273. This is perhaps based on the consideration that in this administrative measure substantial private property rights are involved.

274. Consult James W. Fesler, The Independence of State Regulatory
Agencies, 1942, p. 16. However, there is little point in designating
the State Public Service Commission as a "semi-" or "quasi-judicial"
body or agency, for the use of the device of public hearing is as characteristic of non-judicial as of judicial administration (in the United
States). It may be noted that the North Carolina Utilities Commission
is constituted as a court of record and that the Oklahoma Corporation
Commission and the Vermont Public Service Commission have the authority
and standing of a court of record.

275. Besides, the governor may appoint five assistant commissioners.

276. The Governor may increase it to seven.

277. Codes of Utah, sec. 67-1-3; Vermont, sec. 448; Wisconsin, sec.
17.07(3); Wyoming, sec. 18-104; Massachusetts, ch. 30, sec. 9; Iowa, sec.
66.1.

278. This is expressly provided in the Public Utilities laws of Alabama.

279. For Connecticut, Florida, Indiana, Louisiana, Minnesota, Mississippi, South Dakota and Virginia, in which there is no statutory provision for such an officer, see the Membership List of the National Association of Railroad and Utilities Commissioners, 10 May 1949.

280. In Maine, Vermont and Virginia, a Clerk; in North Carolina, a
Chief Clerk; in South Carolina a Secretary or a Clerk; in all other

states, a Secretary. The secretary or clerk in Alabama, Arkansas, Georgia, Massachusetts, New Hampshire, North Carolina, Rhode Island and Virginia does not appear in statute.

281. In Ohio, the Director of Commerce appoints the secretary of the Commission, but the Commission may appoint an additional secretary. In South Dakota, the secretary is elected by the Commission. The secretary is appointed by the Commission with the approval of the governor in Kansas and Utah, and with the approval of the senate in Mississippi.

282. References to state laws are omitted.

283. References to state laws are omitted.

284. Agencies of Massachusetts, Louisiana, Mississippi, Nevada, New Jersey and Wyoming consist entirely of ex-officio and those of Idaho, Oklahoma and Texas entirely of special, members. In New York and Georgia, the ex-officio members have no voting rights.

285. In North Dakota and Tennessee, appointed by the Soil Conservation Committee itself; in Texas, elected by the people; in Maryland, appointed by the state board of Agriculture, in Colorado, elected on an area basis by the supervisors of the soil conservation districts; in Nebraska, elected by such supervisors at their annual conference; in North Carolina, the three special members are the president, first president and immediately past president of the state association of soil-conservation-district supervisors.

286. Code of Alabama, tit. 8, sec. 1 et seq. (Acts 1939, No. 162; as last amended by Acts 1951, No. 476); Arkansas Statutes, sec. 9-101 et seq. (Acts 1945, No. 138; as last amended by Acts 1953, No. 401); California Public Resources Code, sec. 501 et seq. (Stats. 1927, ch. 128, sec. 1; as last amended by Stats. 1953, ch. 1859, sec. 1); Revised Statutes of Illinois, ch. 127 (L. 1917, p. 2; as last amended in 1951); Indiana Statutes, sec. 60-701 et seq. (Acts 1919, ch. 60; as last amended by Acts 1945, ch. 353); Iowa Code, ch. 107 (Acts 1935, ch. 13; as last amended by Acts 1953, ch. 76); Revised Statutes of Kentucky, sec. 12.040 and ch. 146 (Acts 1944, ch. 6; as last amended by Acts 1952, ch. 202) and sec. 104.390 et seq. (Acts 1948, ch. 229; as last amended by Acts 1952, ch. 201); General Laws of Massachusetts, ch. 21 (Acts 1953, ch. 631, superseding Acts 1919, ch. 350, as last amended by Acts 1948, ch. 651); Compiled Laws of Michigan, ch. 299 (Acts 1921, No. 17; as last amended by Acts 1952, No. 215); Minnesota Statutes, sec. 84.025 et seq. (L. 1931, ch. 186; as last amended by L. 1951, ch. 713, sec. 11); Constitution of Missouri, art. IV, sec. 40 et seq., adopted 27 February 1945; New Jersey Statutes, tit. 13, sec. 1A (L. 1945, ch. 22, superseding previous laws) and sec. 23: 2-4 (L. 1895, ch. 209, sec. 2; as last amended by L. 1953, ch. 335, sec. 1); New York Conservation Law (L. 1911, ch. 647; as last amended by L. 1954, ch. 311); General Statutes of North Carolina, ch. 113 (L. 1925, ch. 122; as last amended by L. 1953, ch. 808); Ohio Revised Code, chs. 1501, 1503, 1507, 1511 and 1541 (L. 1949, p. 84); Oklahoma Statutes, tit. 74, sec. 344.9 et seq. (L. 1947, p. 602; as last amended 1953); Pennsylvania Statutes, tit. 71, secs. 51 to 732 (Administrative Code of 1923, as last amended by Acts 1953, No. 291); General Laws of Rhode Island, ch. 223 (Acts 1935, ch. 2188; as last amended by Acts 1952 ch. 2973); Acts of Tennessee of 1937, ch. 33; as last amended by Acts 1953, ch. 248; Code of Virginia, sec. 10-1 et seq. (Acts 1926, ch. 169; as last amended by Acts 1954, ch. 487); Revised Code of Washington, sec. 43.17.010 et seq. (L. 1921, ch. 7; as last amended by L. 1953, ch. 174) and ch. 43.21 (L. 1921, ch. 7, sec. 61 et seq.; as last amended by L. 1951, ch. 57); West Virginia Code, ch. 20, arts. 1 and 1A (L. 1933, Ex.

Sess., ch. 55; as last amended by L. 1951, chs. 96 and 97); Wisconsin
Statutes, sec. 23.09 (L. 1923, ch. 118; as last amended by L. 1953, ch.
219). The Department of Conservation of Louisiana has no jurisdiction
in water resources administration.

287. In some states, the functions of this agency are not limited
to water resources administration. For example, the agencies of Arkansas, California, Indiana, Michigan, Minnesota, New Jersey, North Carolina, Ohio, Tennessee,Virginia and Washington are also concerned with
mineral resources.

288. I, water conservation and development (including water conservation, navigation improvement, flood control, irrigation, water supply,
drainage, hydroelectric power development or the like); II, forestry;
III, fish and wildlife; IV, parks and other recreational areas; V, recreation; VI, land management; and VII, soil conservation.

289. In the Minnesota Department of Conservation, there is an unofficial advisory committee of citizens appointed by the governor. -- Letter of Mr. Chester S. Wilson, Commissioner, Minnesota Department of Conservation, to Professor William F. Schulz, Jr. of the School of Law,
University of Pittsubrgh, dated 26 October 1951, copy made available to
the author through the courtesy of Mr. E. V. Willard, Deputy Commissioner, Minnesota Department of Conservation, on 5 December 1951.

290. There are no statutory provisions for a chairman or a secretary
in Indiana, Missouri and North Carolina.

291. In the laws of Indiana, Massachusetts, Missouri and Oklahoma,
there is no mention of either regular or special meetings.

292. Iowa, State Conservation Director; Massachusetts, Commissioner;
Michigan and Missouri, Director of Conservation; Wisconsin, Conservation
Director.

293. Information additional to statutory provisions: Alabama Depart-
ment of Conservation, Report 1949; Alabama Forestry Laws, State Lands
Laws and State Parks Laws and Regulations, 1951; Illinois Department of
Conservation, Outdoors in Illinois, Spring-Summer 1954; Indiana Depart-
ment of Conservation, Report 1952; Iowa Conservation Commission, Biennial
Report 1950-1952; Michigan Department of Conservation; Its Organization
and Functions, March 1948; North Carolina Department of Conservation and
Development, Two Years of Progress, 1950; Pennsylvania Department of For-
ests and Waters, Biennial Report, 1948-1950; Organizational Chart of 13
January 1954; Rhode Island Department of Agriculture and Conservation,
Report 1951; Washington Department of Conservation and Development,
Biennial Report 1950-1952; West Virginia Conservation Commission, Report
1952; Wisconsin Conservation Commission, Organization Chart, made avail-
albe to the author (with revisions) through the courtesy of Mr. W. R.
Scott, Administrative Assistant, Wisconsin Conservation Commission, on
29 August 1951; Biennial Report 1951-1952; and letters to the author from
Miss Bettye Hornbuckle, Administrative Assistant to the Director, Missouri Conservation Commission, dated 27 August and 28 November 1951; and
Messrs. John J. Patton, Chief Engineer, Alabama Department of Conservation, dated 4 October 1951; E. E. Nuuttila, State Forester, Illinois Department of Conservation, dated 1 April 1954; Lewis E. Martin, Assistant Director, Illinois Department of Conservation, dated 24 August 1954;
R. J. Gillis, Deputy Secretary, Pennsylvania Department of Forests and
Waters, dated 25 August 1954; Buford W. McRae, Executive Assistant, Tennessee Department of Conservation, dated 28 August 1951.

294. Letter from Mr. Gillis, op. cit.

295. The Flood Control and Water Usage Board of Kentucky is composed of nine members (bi-partisan) appointed by the governor on a district basis for four years, with the commissioners of highways, the commissioner of health, the director of the division of game and fish and the president of the University of Kentucky as advisors or consultants. The Councils of the above-mentioned two divisions of New Jersey are each composed of nine members appointed by the governor with the consent of the senate for nine years. Each Council elects its own chairman and employs its own administrative personnel. The Ohio Water Resources Board consists of the director of natural resources (chairman), the director of commerce, the director of health, the director of public works, the dean of the college of engineering of the Ohio State University and the chief of the Division of geological survey (of the Department of Natural Resources), all acting ex-officio. The Board employs a Chief of the division of water, a secretary and all other administrative personnel. With the Board, there is an advisory committee consisting of six members (bi-partisan) appointed by the governor for five years, who represent different special interest groups, together with an appointee of each of the two houses of the state legislature. There is no statutory provision, with respect to any of these agencies, to the effect that their official acts can be changed or vetoed by their respective Departments of Conservation.

296. The Rhode Island Advisory Council consists of five persons representative of special interests concerned appointed by the governor for five years. The Virginia Advisory Committee is composed of five members appointed by the governor.

297. It may be noted that in Pennsylvania the Deputy Secretary for Forests is in charge of both forestry and parks and that the State Forestry, Commission advises the Department on both forestry and parks. However, at the division level, forestry and park administration are separated.

298. There are only two ways in which the Commission is subordinately connected with the Department: first, the Commissioner of Conservation may require the Commission to render assistance to the various Divisions of the Department (Acts 1949, ch. 50, sec. 19); and secondly, the Commissioner of Conservation and the Director of Game and Fish divide each of the three grand divisions of the state into three districts from each of which a member of the Commission is to be appointed. (Acts 1953, ch. 254). It is not clear whether the Commissioner of Conservation can settle controversies arising between the Commission and any of the Divisions of the Department. However, from the provisions of sec. 19 of Acts 1949, ch. 50, op. cit., there seems to be no doubt that the Commission is a unit of the Department. The author was informed to this effect by Mr. McRae in his letter cited above. But it is merely a factitious unit of the Department and is not subject to the supervision of the latter. To solve the dilemma, it is provided in law that the Conservation Commission may hold joint meetings with the Game and Fish Commission.

299. Code of Maryland, art. 66C, sec. 340 et seq. (Laws 1906, ch. 294; as last amended by L. 1951, ch. 623); Revised Laws of New Hampshire, ch. 233, sec. 1 et seq. (L. 1909, ch. 128; as last amended by L. 1935, ch. 126); General Statutes of Connecticut, sec. 3428 et seq. (Acts 1913, ch. 230; as last amended in 1953); Vermont Statutes, sec. 7033 et seq. (L. 1947, No. 112; L. 1951, No. 167); Acts of Arkansas of 1953, No. 42.

300. Organization chart made available to the author through the courtesy of Mr. Donald C. Mathews, Director, Connecticut State Park and Forest Commission, on 6 December 1951; Digest of Connecticut Administrative Reports to the Governor, 1951-1952, pages on "Park and Forest Commission".

301. Mississippi Forestry and Park Services, <u>Biennial Report 1949-1951</u>, pp. 1-2; 30.

302. It may also be mentioned that the South Carolina State Commission of Forestry administers state parks.

303. <u>General Statutes of Kansas</u>, sec. 74-3301 et seq. (L. 1925, ch. 257; as last amended by L. 1949, ch. 414); Laws of Nebraska of 1929, ch. 133; as amended by L. 1935, ch. 174; <u>South Dakota Code</u>, ch. 25.01 (L. 1945, ch. 91; as last amended by L. 1951, ch. 116). The Kansas Commission was given authority over parks by special legislation (L. 1927, ch. 221, sec. 8; L. 1931, ch. 190, sec. 1).

304. The Commission had the following divisions as of 1950: Fisheries, Game, State Parks and State Lakes, Law Enforcement, Federal Aid to Wildlife Restoration Projects, and Public Relations. But there was no division on forestry. -- <u>Biennial Report</u>, 30 June 1950.

305. The Commission had the following divisions as of 1952: Fishery, Game, Land Management (state parks and other lands administered by the Commission), Education and Information, Law Enforcement, Construction and Engineering, and Legal Counsel. -- <u>Annual Report 1952</u>.

306. <u>South Dakota Code</u>, ch. 25.13 (L. 1945, ch. 90).

307. Letter to the author from Mr. Edward L. Clark, State Geologist, Division of Geological Survey and Water Resources, Missouri Department of Business and Administration, dated 7 December 1951.

308. See Federal Inter-Agency Committee On Recreation, "Resume Of Recreation Service of State Agencies To Communities" (mimeo.), 6 July 1949 and "Summary Of Recreation Services of State Agencies to Communities and to Rural Areas" (mimeo.), 12 July 1950; 44 <u>Recreation</u> 118-119 (June 1950).

309. Other forms of implied coordination are omitted.

310. Both administrative and non-administrative agencies may undertake investigations and research as their preliminary work.

311. There is a unanimity among the states, though not among the membership.

312. "The State Engineer of South Dakota has been this third member during the last five years and is serving on his second four-year appointment." -- Letter to the author from Mr. Dean W. Loucks, State Engineer of South Dakota, dated 9 November 1951.

313. It may be noted that since these agencies are enterprise and not regulatory agencies, the right or capacity to sue and to be sued is all that is needed for their activities. This right is equivalent to the right to seek judicial injunctions of the above-mentioned Boundary Waters Commission, Minnesota and South Dakota.

314. The Port of New York employs an executive director as its chief administrative officer. -- Frederick L. Bird, <u>A Study of the Port of New York Authority</u>, 1949, pp. 34-35.

315. See <u>ibid.</u>, p. 38.

316. See President's Water Resources Policy Commission, <u>Report</u>, Vol. II, p. 490..

317.. The New England Commission is a "body corporate and politic".
The Potomac Commission has a special district called the Potomac Valley
Conservancy District, and has the right to make by-laws and to adopt a
seal: all this would amount to the same status. Among the five commissioners from each state-member of the New England Commission, one is an
officer of the state health department, one an officer of the state water pollution control agency, one a representative of industries, one a
representative of municipalities and one an officer of the state fishery agency.

318. The Gulf States Commission is a body corporate, The Atlantic
States Marine Fisheries Compact was signed by New Hampshire, Massachu-
setts, Rhode Island, New York, New Jersey, Delaware, Maryland and Vir-
ginia, and has been ratified by Pennsylvania, South Carolina, Georgia,
Connecticut, Florida and North Carolina as assessories. See Rules and
Regulations, sec. 1.

319. One of the members is a state senator, one a member of the
house of representatives, one a member of the governor's cabinet and
one the chairman or director of the state planning board.

320. Interstate Commission on the Delaware River Basin, Annual Report 1944, p. 19. The Commission has a chairman and three vice-chairmen. -- Annual Report 1948, Roster of members.

321. Letter to the author (with a copy of the agreement) from Mr.
Robert R. Harris, Senior Sanitary Engineer, Officer in Charge, Regional
Office at Portland, U. S. Public Health Service, dated 24 September 1951.

322. Letter to the author from Mr. John E. McDonald, Forest Supervisor, Fremont National Forest (Oregon), dated 18 July 1952. For the Colorado River Basin States Committee and the Missouri Basin States Committees and similar organizations, see 19 State Government 236 (1946, by C.
H. Stone); 233 (by M. Q. Sharpe); 237 (by Aiken and Strickland); 23 State
Government 89 (1950, by R. R. Renne).

323. By-Laws amended on 19 March 1951 (appearing in the Second Annual Report).

324. By-Laws, adopted 14 November 1949.

325. First Annual Report, p. 15; Fifth Annual Report, p. 20.

326. Letter to the author from Mr. Edwin R. Cotton, Director, Interstate Commission on the Potomac River Basin, dated 16 July 1951.

327. Organizational chart, appearing in The Delaware River Basin Water Project, published by the Commission in January 1951.

328. Rules and Regulations, adopted 5 June 1942, as last amended 30
September 1949.

329. Letter to the author from Mr. Wayne D. Heydecker, Secretary-
Treasurer, Atlantic States Marine Fisheries Commission, dated 19 July
1951.

330. Rules of Procedure, adopted 2 February 1912, as last amended 6
April 1926.

331. Letter to the author from Mr. William R. Vallance, Counsel with
the United States, dated 11 August 1951. It may be noted that the International Joint Commission is the successor of the former Waterways Commission, created by concurrent legislation of the two countries in 1902.

The three commissioners of this Commission were statutorily required to be an officer of the Corps of Engineers, a civil engineer versed in the hydraulics of the Great Lakes, and a lawyer experienced in international and riparian law (22 U. S. C. 267(b)). -- Letter to the author from Mr. Jesse B. Ellis, Secretary, United States Section, dated 11 September 1951.

332. It is worthy of notice that both Sections are single-headed.

333. There are no provisions as to the organization of these two Commissions.

334. The said Committee, Report on the Conservation and Development of Outdoor Recreation Resources (mimeo.), July 1950, Forward.

335. Contractors are not regarded as private citizens joining administrative agencies.

336. They do not receive salaries from the government. But if they receive a salary, they will not be regarded as private citizens.

337. Montana Fish and Game Commission, Biennial Report 1950-52, p. 23.

338. U. S. Department of the Interior, Forest Conservation on Lands Administered by the Department of the Interior (mimeo.), January 1940, pp. 255-256; Rpt. Sec. Inter. 1935, pp. 15-16.

339. They are first elected by the stockmen of each district on a precinct baxis, and then appointed by the Secretary of the Interior. They serve for overlapping terms of three years. -- 43 C. F. R. 161.12.

340. It is reported that these advisory boards have in effect become administrative committees. See American Planning and Civic Manual, 1947, p. 44.

341. Report of the Forester for 1906, p. 18; Rpt. Sec. Agri. 1909, p. 23.

342. U. S. Department of Agriculture, Budget Justifications For Fiscal Year 1953 (mimeo.), p. 421.

343. U. S. Department of Agriculture, Our National Forests, 1951, p. 5.

344. Letter to the author from Mr. Wilbur D. Staats, Chief, Information Services Section, Bonneville Power Administration, dated 16 June 1954.

345. Rpt. Sec. Inter. 1923, p. 2; Rpt. 1924, pp. 6-7.

CHAPTER 6

FINANCE

Section 1   Federal Finance

Funds needed for the performance of Federal water resources administration largely come from <u>appropriation</u> from the general funds in the Treasury, which are raised by the Federal Government from all sources of revenues, including all taxes and indebtedness, and which are not specifically earmarked for water resources or any other administration. Appropriation from revenues specifically assigned to water resources administration is limited to irrigation enterprise only, and they are negligible in amount. This principal means of financial support of Federal water resources administration is supplemented by (1) <u>self-finance</u> (i.e., finance by the receipts derived from water resources administration itself)[1] and (2) <u>contributions</u> (made by states and their local units and private persons).

It may be noted that in general Federal self-finance is not accompanied by financial autonomy. In all Federal water resources administrative programs having self-finance, all the revenues earned by the programs are covered into the Treasury, although they are usually kept in special funds or accounts (if there are no such special funds or accounts, then they are credited to "Miscellaneous Receipts", which constitute by themselves a special fund or account.) It should also be pointed out that all funds to be expended for self-financing programs are, not unlike those for non-self-financing ones, <u>appropriated</u> by the Congress, the appropriation being made either from special funds or the general fund.

1. <u>Appropriation</u>---There are <u>regular</u> and <u>emergency</u> appropriations, for both self-financing and non-self-financing programs. Regular appropriations consist of appropriations made by (1) the regular annual appropriation acts of the various departments and agencies and (2) special annual appropriation acts such as the deficiency appropriation acts and the supplemental appropriation acts. Both these kinds of regular appropriations are made in normal times. Emergency appropriations are made only in times of emergency. Outstanding examples of emergency appropriations are those made or authorized by the National Industrial Recovery Act of 16 June 1933 (48 Stat. 1955), the several Emergency Relief Appropriation Acts passed since 1935,[2] and other emergency appropriation acts enacted in the 1930's.[3] Regular appropriations will be discussed first.

Regular appropriations for all Federal water resources ad-

ministrative programs are now generally made by programs under
the various responsible agencies in lump-sums devoted to such
programs.[4] With the exception of the irrigation enterprise,
these appropriations are as a rule made from the general fund
of the Treasury. Expenses for irrigation projects are appropriated from both the general fund and some special funds, the
most important of which is the Reclamation Fund.

Prior to 1949, appropriations for the Indian irrigation
projects consisted of both itemized and lump-sum appropriations.[5] The first itemized appropriation was made by the Indian Office Appropriation Act of 27 July 1868 (15 Stat. 198),
in which $50,000 was set aside "for completing the construction
of irrigating canal on the Colorado (River) reservation in Arizona . . ." (222).[6] There has since been, however, no other
itemized appropriations until the Indian Office Appropriation
Act of 3 March 1893 (27 Stat. 612) appropriated $40,000 for
the construction of irrigation works in Navajo Reservation,
Arizona (627-628). The first lump-sum appropriation for Indian irrigation enterprise appeared in the Indian Office Appropriation Act of 4 July 1884 (23 Stat. 76), which authorized
the expenditure of $50,000 "for the purpose of constructing ir-
rigating ditches on Indian reservations and instructing Indians
in farming in connection therewith" (94).[7] This was followed
by a lump-sum appropriation in the Indian Appropriation Act of
3 March 1891 of $30,000 "for the construction, purchase, and
use of irrigating machinery and appliances in Arizona, Montana,
and Nevada for the uses of Indian reservations, in the discretion of the Secretary of the Interior and subject to his control . . ." (26 Stat. 989, 1011). Since this appropriation,
there was a lump-sum appropriation for Indian irrigation projects on all Indian reservations in each of the annual appropriations to the Bureau of Indian Affairs passed between 1892
and 1949 (inclusive of both years). It may be noted that the
larger Indian projects were as a rule first financed by itemized appropriations. Beginning with the Interior Department
Appropriation Act of 6 September 1950 (64 Stat. 595, 679), Indian irrigation projects have been grouped together with other
Indian development projects for lump-sum appropriation under
the two topics "Resources Management" and "Construction".

The regular irrigation projects, i.e., projects governed
by the Reclamation Act of 1902 and the Reclamation Project Act
of 1939, received itemized appropriations prior to 1949. Since
1950, appropriations for these projects have been made in lump-
sums segregated under costs of construction, costs of operation
and maintenance, and costs of investigations. It should be remarked, however, this practice of segregation was first clearly
established in the Interior Department Appropriation Act of 12
January 1927 (44 Stat. 935, 957). The Water Conservation and
Utilization projects are always financed by lump-sum appropriations.

Appropriations for the Indian irrigation projects have been made from both the general fund and the various Indian tribal funds; those for the Water Conservation and Utilization projects, always from the general fund; and those for the regular irrigation projects, from (1) the Reclamation Fund, (2) the general fund, (3) the Colorado River Dam Fund and (4) the Colorado River Development Fund.

In the past, appropriations for navigation-improvement and flood-control projects were partly made in the War Department Appropriation Acts and partly incorporated in the River and Harbor Acts, and were in general itemized.[8] The River and Harbor Act of 2 March 1919 (40 Stat. 1275) was the last of such acts.[9] From 1920 to 1936, appropriations for these projects appeared in the War Department Appropriation Acts. Since 1937, they have been embodied in the Army (War) Department Civil Functions Appropriation Acts, the first of such acts being the act of 19 July 1937 (50 Stat. 515). These appropriations have since 1920 never been itemized. Lump sums are appropriated under two general headings "Rivers and Harbors" (for navigation-improvement projects) and "Flood Control". However, appropriations for the Mississippi River Basin and the Sacramento River flood-control programs have always been singled out from the general "Flood-Control" appropriations. A few other flood-control projects have also been occasionally itemized in the same way.[10] It may be noted that although there is no itemization in appropriations for navigation-improvement and flood-control projects, the estimated amounts of the costs of construction are usually set down in the Flood Control Acts for the flood-control projects and in the project plans approved by the River and Harbor Acts for the navigation-improvement projects. Prior to the Civil Functions Appropriation Act of 27 July 1953 (67 Stat. 197), there was no segregation between "construction", "operation and maintenance" and "examinations and investigations". In this act, such segregation was first adopted, and it was followed in the Civil Functions Appropriation Act of 20 June 1954 (68 Stat. 330).

The absence or abolition of itemization of appropriations in the various enterprises of Federal water resources administration may be taken as an important attribute of modern professionalized administration. But this practice is subject to special Congressional control over the allotment of funds by the administrative agencies. This control consists in the designation of the maximum sum of money which may be expended for a certain project or program. The specified sum is the ceiling of allotment for such project or program. The project-ceilings are mostly made by way of the addition of provisoes to the appropriations on an ad-hoc basis. But the program-ceilings are contained in special enactments of the Congress and are permanent in nature.

Under a provision in sec. 1 of the River and Harbor Act of

25 June 1912 (37 Stat. 201, 222), as last amended by sec. 3 of the River and Harbor Act of 2 March 1945 (59 Stat. 10), the allotment for the program of snagging is set at a maximum of $300,000 for any one fiscal year. Under sec. 5 of the Flood Control Act of 18 August 1941 (55 Stat. 638,650), as last a-mended by sec. 206 of the Flood Control Act of 30 June 1948 (62 Stat. 1171, 1182), annual allotment for the maintenance, repair, restoration or rescue work must not exceed $2,000,000. As provided in sec. 15 of the Flood Control Act of 22 December 1944 (58 Stat. 887, 907), as amended by sec. 216 of the Flood Control Act of 17 May 1950 (64 Stat. 163, 184), funds allotted to emergency run-off-retardation and soil-erosion-prevention work performed by the Department of Agriculture were limited to $300,000 for each fiscal year. According to sec. 204 of the Flood Control Act of 30 June 1948 (62 Stat. 1171, 1182), as amended by sec. 212 of the Flood Control Act of 1950 (64 Stat. 163, 183), the maximum annual allotment to small flood-control projects not specifically authorized by Congress is $3,000,000. These are outstanding examples of program-ceilings.

Perhaps the only important project-ceiling that is not made on a case-to-case basis is that for the water conservation and utilization projects of the Department of the Interior. The maximum sums of money allowable for expenditure on the construc-tion of any such project are $2,000,000 on dams and reservoirs allocated to irrigation and $500,000 for project features de-voted to flood control, or to non-irrigation water supply or to hydroelectric power development.[11]

The ceilings for program-allotments must be distinguished from appropriation-authorizations, which frequently appear in Flood Control Acts, acts authorizing other administrative pro-grams and some special acts,[12] and which are promises made by the Congress, and limitations, if they be, which the Congress sets upon itself.

The nature and extent of emergency appropriations to Fed-eral water resources administrative programs is best illustrat-ed by the emergency appropriations made in the period 1930-1942. Funds of these appropriations were made available to the Federal Government itself for expenditures in Federal water re-sources administration in two ways: (1) direct appropriation to the various Federal water resources administrative agencies, and (2) allocation to these agencies by the several emergency finance agencies. The following are direct appropriations:

By the Emergency Construction Appropriation Act of 20 December 1930:

1. For the general improvement of the national forests, $3,000,000.
2. For the construction and improvement of highways with-in the national forests, $3,000,000.
3. For the National Park System, $1,500,000.
4. For navigation improvement, $22,500,000.

5. For flood control, Mississippi River System, $3,000,000.

By the Emergency Relief and Construction Act of 21 July 1932, Title II:

1. For national-forest highways, $5,000,000.
2. For national-forest improvement, $5,000,000.
3. For the National Park System, $3,000,000.
4. For roads in Indian reservations, $1,000,000.
5. For roads in other public lands, $1,000,000.
6. For navigation improvement, $30,000,000.
7. For flood control, $15,500,000.
8. For Hoover Dam, $10,000,000.

By the Fourth Deficiency Appropriation Act of 16 June 1933, under the authority of the Unemployment Relief Act of 31 March 1933 and the National Industrial Recovery Act of 16 June 1933:

1. To the Tennessee Valley Authority, $50,000,000.

By the Emergency Appropriation Act of 19 June 1934:

1. For loans to disaster-stricken areas, $525,000,000.
2. For national-forest roads and trails, $10,000,000.
3. For roads in public domain: $2,500,000.
4. For roads in Indian reservations, $2,000,000.
5. For the National Park System, $5,000,000.

By the Emergency Relief Appropriation Act of 30 June 1939:

To the Bureau of Indian Affairs, $1,350,000.

By the Emergency Relief Appropriation Act of 26 June 1940:

To the Bureau of Indian Affairs $1,700,000.

As for allocations from emergency finance institutions, a total of $181,704,377, of which $56,867,996 was allocated to the several water resources administrative agencies,[13] was allocated to the regular Federal agencies by the Work Projects Administration[14] and a total of $1,921,338,286, of which $501,153,936 was allotted for projects in the water resources field,[15] was allocated to the regular Federal agencies by the Public Works Administration.[16] The total allocation by these two agencies[17] to regular Federal agencies was approximately $2,103 million, of which approximately $558 million was used in the field of water resources administration.

The total amount of emergency funds (including funds directly appropriated by the Congress and funds allocated by the emergency finance agencies) received by the Corps of Engineers for expenditure on water resources projects is $517,720,122.17 (including $381,286,041.77 for navigation improvements, $128,267,009.48 for flood control and $8,167,070.92 for miscellaneous

projects).[18] Although this is perhaps the largest item of
emergency funds in the field of water resources administration,
it is negligible in comparison with the regular appropriations
to the Civil Works program of the Corps of Engineers.[19]   In
the field of irrigation, emergency funds made available to the
Bureau of Reclamation totalled $192,478,530, which is approxi-
mately 7.7 percent of the total appropriations made to the said
Bureau for its irrigation enterprise up to 30 June 1951 ($2,496,-
447,901).[20] As for Indian irrigation projects, a total of $121,-
379,303.88 had been made available to the Bureau of Indian Affairs for such projects by 30 June 1950. Of this amount, $10,-
856,416.85, or approximately 9 percent, came from emergency
funds.[21]

2. Self-finance---Self-finance is said to exist with respect to a certain administrative program when the costs of
the program are derived from its proceeds or otherwise repaid
by its beneficiaries. Self-finance is complete or incomplete
in according as the proceeds equal or are short of the costs.
A program with complete or incomplete self-finance may be designated as a self-liquidating or partially self-liquidating
program. If the proceeds of a program exceed its costs, it may
further be distinguished from other self-financed programs as
a revenue-making program. The various self-financed programs
of Federal water resources administration are separately discussed below.

(a) Irrigation---All costs incurred by the Federal Government in both the construction and the operation and maintenance
of irrigation projects are in principle to be repaid by the water users.[22] Different procedures have prevailed for different
types of construction work in the repayment of the costs of construction, but the costs of operation and maintenance are generally repaid under the same procedure for all types of irrigation projects. The repayment of costs of construction will be
discussed first.

(1) Costs of Construction of Regular Works[23]

(i) Regular Irrigation Projects[24]---The history of the repayment of the costs of construction, so far as the normal procedure is concerned, may be divided into two stages, with the
enactment of the Reclamation Project Act on 4 August 1939 as
the dividing line. The first stage, which covers the period
from the enactment of the Reclamation Act on 17 June 1902 to 4
August 1939, was governed by the Reclamation Act of 1902. In
the second stage, the Reclamation Project Act has been the controlling law of the construction-cost repayment.

First Stage:

The principle and manner of repayment of the costs of construction were both provided in sec. 4 of the Reclamation Act
of 1902, which reads as follows (emphasis supplied):

Upon the determination by the Secretary of the Interior that any irrigation project is <u>practicable</u>,
he may cause to be let contracts for the construction of the same, in such portions and sections as
it may be practicable to construct and complete as
parts of the whole project, providing the necessary
funds for such portions or sections are available
in the reclamation fund, and thereupon he shall
give public notice of the lands irrigable under the
project; . . . also of the <u>charges</u> which shall be
made <u>per acre</u> upon said entries, and upon lands in
private ownership which may be irrigated by the waters of the said irrigation project, and the number of <u>annual installments, not exceeding ten</u>, in
which such charges shall be paid and the time when
such payments shall commence. The said charges
shall be determined with a view of returning to
the reclamation fund the <u>estimated cost of construc-
tion</u> of the project, and shall be <u>apportioned equit-
ably</u> . . . (32 Stat. 388, 389).

No provision was made regarding the organization of the water
users, and the repayments were therefore to be made between the
Department of the Interior and the individual water users.

The maximum number of annual installments, which was ten in
the above provision, was increased by the Reclamation Extension
Act of 13 August 1914 (38 Stat. 686) as follows: (1) For old
projects, the costs of construction or that thereof which remained unpaid on 13 August 1914 were to be repaid in twenty annual installments, with an interest on unpaid costs of 4 percent per year on the first four and 6 percent on the remaining
installments (sec. 2); (2) for new projects, an initial installment equivalent to 5 percent of total construction cost was to
be paid at the time of homestead entry or water-right application, and the balance in fifteen annual installments (sec. 1).
However, the repayment contracts were still to be concluded with
the individual water users.

On 15 May 1922, an Act was passed (42 Stat. 541) which authorized the Secretary of the Interior to enter into repayment
contracts with irrigation districts. In such contracts, the
number of annual or other periodic installments was indefinite,
and was to be such as would "best conform to the district and
taxation laws of the respective states." The period of repayment actually agreed upon in each particular case might be longer (or shorter) than was allowed under the Reclamation Extension Act of 1914.

This enactment did not apply to individual water users, to
whom the Reclamation Extension Act of 1914 was applicable. However, an Act was passed on 31 March 1922 (42 Stat. 489) which
permitted an individual water user who was unable to pay charges
due in 1922 to <u>defer</u> the payment for one year, or to pay them
during 1923. But an irrigation district or other water users'

during 1923. But an irrigation district or other water users' organization might also take advantage of this act. By an amendment of 28 February 1923 (42 Stat. 1324), the deferment was increased from one year to two years. It should be remarked that a deferment is not an extension of the period of repayment, and that the deferment provided for by the abovementioned legislation was subject to a penalty-interest charge of 6 percent per year.

The 1922-23 deferment was continued by an Act of 9 May 1924 (43 Stat. 116), under which all water charges accrued prior to 2 March 1924 might be deferred to as late as 1 March 1927, subject to an annual interest of 5 percent. However, if a water user or a water users' organization represented to the Secretary of the Interior before 1 January 1925 that even this deferment could not relieve his or its difficulties in repayment the Secretary might permit the total amount of the charges due as of 1 March 1925 to be paid in twenty annual installments (equal or graduated) beginning with this date, together with an interest of 5 percent per year on the unpaid charges.

The general inability of the water users to meet their repayment obligations led to the enactment of sec. 4 of the Second Deficiency Appropriation Act of 5 December 1924 (43 Stat. 672, 702), which section (a "rider") was commonly designated as the Fact Finders' Act.[25] Under the Reclamation Act of 1902, an irrigation project could be authorized and constructed as far as it was physically "practicable" and no consideration need be given of whether the project would be economically feasible. It was discovered that "dams and canals has been constructed on some projects for the irrigation of lands having inadequate water supply and were either not capable of development or had soil inherently too poor to support a family."[26] No repayment could be expected of these projects. To correct this defect, the Fact Finders' Act stipulated that (Subsec. B)

> No new project or division of a project shall be approved for construction or estimates submitted therefor by the Secretary (of the Interior) until information in detail shall be secured by him concerning the water supply, the engineering features, the cost of construction, land prices, and the probable cost of development, and he shall have made a finding in writing that it is feasible, that it is adaptable for actual settlement and farm homes, and that it will probably return the cost thereof to the United States.

It further provided for a system of repayment in the manner of special benefit assessment (assessments being proportionate to land values) in place of the previous uniform acreage charge (irrespective of diversity in land productivity) (Subsec. D). It even went to such length as to provide (Subsec. F) that "hereafter all project construction charges (whether on old or new projects) shall be made payable in annual installments (variable) based on the productive power of the land." "The installment of the construction charge per irrigable acre payable each year shall be 5 p er centum of the average gross annual per acre income for the ten calendar years first preceding, or for all years of record if fewer than ten years are available, of the area in cultivation, . . . as found by the Secretary annually." "These annual installments shall continue until the total construction charge against each unit is paid." But the time was not yet ripe for such a delicate method, and this provision was repealed by an Act of 25 May 1926 (in sec. 47: 44 Stat. 636, 650).

Aside from these general remedies, the Fact Finders' Act authorized the Secretary of the Interior to make an actual survey of each existing irrigation project and to report (and recommend relief) to the Congress as to any case in which a greater construction charge had been imposed upon the water users than the land productivity could justify (Sub-sec. K). In consequence, the Omnibus Adjustment Act was passed on 25 May 1926 (44 Stat. 636), which provided for the deduction of the construction charges and suspension of payments on a great number of irrigation projects (secs. 1 to 40, inclusive).[27] As a general measure of rectification, all unproductive lands were removed from the assessment lists (secs. 41 to 43, inclusive).[28] As for valid repayment obligations, an extension was granted in the repayment period.[29] The Secretary of the Interior was, on this account, authorized "in his discretion, upon request of the individual water users or districts . . . to amend any existing water-right contract to provide for increase in time for payment of construction charges, which have not then accrued, . . . subject to the limitation that there shall be allowed for repayment not more than forty years from the date the first payment matured under the original contract, . . . and to contract for the payment of the construction charges then due and unpaid within such terms of years as the Secretary may find to be necessary, with interest payable annually at the rate of 6 per centum per annum until paid" (sec. 45, para. 2). For new projects, all construction costs were to be repaid within a maximum period of forty years (sec. 46), and were not necessarily to be repaid in annual installments.

These modifications in repayment were generous enough. But only a few years afterwards came the general economic depression of the country, which so aggravated the misery of the irrigation farmers that nothing could be derived from their crops to enable them to discharge their lawful obligations to the Government, however small they might be. Under such circumstances an Act was enacted on 1 April 1932 (47 Stat. 75), which deferred the payment by all water users of all unpaid construction and operation and maintenance charges (together with penalties or interests) for all years up to and including the calendar year

1930, regular construction charges due the calendar year 1931 and one-half of the construction charges due 1932. This deferment was successively extended down to **and including the calendar year 1943** by a series of amendatory enactments.[30]

In addition to the **above**-mentioned measures of relief of general application, there were provisions for extension of the repayment period applicable to certain particular projects. For the Milk River project, Montana, for example, it was provided in the Interior Department Appropriation Act of 24 January 1923 that "repayment of the construction cost of the project may be made through a division by the Secretary of the Interior of such cost into a primary construction and a supplemental construction charge (emphasis added), of approximate equality, the former payable according to sec. 2 and the latter payable according to sec. 4 of the Extension Act of August 13, 1914" (42 Stat. 1174, 1206). For the Sun River, Owyhee, Vale and Baker projects, repayment periods as long as 40 years were allowed by the Interior Department Appropriation Act of 10 May 1926 (44 Stat. 453, 479). With respect to the construction cost of the Marshall Ford Dam of the Colorado River project, Texas, the Secretary of the Interior was authorized to require its reimbursement "to the extent and in the manner determined by him" (Interior Department Appropriation Act of 10 May 1939: 53 Stat. 685, 714).[31]

It may be noted that the first period of irrigation cost repayment was characterized almost entirely by extensions, deferments and cancellations of water users' obligations.

Second Stage:

The second stage was inaugurated by the Reclamation Project Act of 4 August 1939 (53 Stat. 1187) which, with the benefit of the experiments made in the first stage, sought to establish a stable and lasting system of repayment. The Reclamation Project Act, in the first place, takes full cognizance of the possible multiple-purpose use of an irrigation project (which will be discussed later), and limits the water users' payments to that part of the cost of construction that is allocated to the strict function of irrigation. As every irrigation project is likely to produce some incidental effects on flood control and navigation improvement (by way of flow regulation), the operation of this multiple-purpose principle serves as a ballast against the practical limitations of the water users' ability of repayment. The reimbursable cost, thus curtailed, is to be repaid, as provided in section 5 and subsections (d) and (e) of section 9 of the Act, in the following manner:

(A) For the irrigation feature or function of the general multiple-purpose water-supply works (i.e., storage reservoirs and their impounding dams), the Secretary of the Interior may either (a) enter into service con-

<u>tracts</u> with either individual water users or water
users' organizations, of periods not exceeding 40
years, providing for the payment of water rentals or
charges (presumably in terms of the number of acre-
feet or other volumes of water furnished, or in terms
of the acreages of the lands serviced) each year,
which will produce revenues sufficient to cover the
allocated irrigation cost or (b) enter into <u>repayment
contracts</u> with the water users' organizations only.

(B) For single-purpose irrigation works, whether for the
storage or the distribution of water, the Secretary
should only enter into <u>repayment contracts</u> with the
water users' organizations (and not with individual
water users).

Each <u>repayment contract</u> may provide for (1) a <u>development per-
iod</u> of not more than ten years, in which water charges are to
be paid each year, at rates fixed by the Secretary of the Interior "per annum per acre-foot" or on some other basis, in advance of the delivery of water, in addition to (2) repayment
period proper, which may run to as long as 40 years, during
which the entire irrigation construction cost is to be repaid
by the organization in annual or semiannual installments.   The
development period is the time required for the gradual development of the <u>irrigable</u> lands to a degree of full cultivation
and production. It should be noted that no part of the constuc-
tion cost is to be paid during this period and that for this
reason the designation of such a period simply means deferment
of construction-cost repayment. While charges during the development period are paid at per-acre-foot or other <u>uniform</u>
rates, the water-users-organizations, in collecting the construction charges on behalf of the Federal Government "may
vary its distribution of construction charges in a manner that
takes into account the productivity of the various classes of
lands and the benefits accruing to the lands by reason of the
construction . . ." In other words, construction charges may
be collected in the form of special benefit assessments.

Each repayment contract governs an <u>irrigation block</u>, which
is defined as "an area of arid or semi-arid lands in a project
in which, in the judgment of the Secretary, the irrigable lands
should be reclaimed and put under irrigation at substantially
the same time. . ." (sec. 2(k)). Each project may consist of
one or more irrigation blocks. No water can be delivered to
any irrigation block until the execution of a repayment contract. This provision protects the Federal Government and the
water users alike. The former is protected, as can easily be
seen, through the assurance of the payment. The latter are protected in that they need not committ themselves to the payments
when water is not yet available for delivery. When an irrigation block consists largely of non-Federal lands, the repayment
contract should include both the development period and the repayment period proper. But when an irrigation block consists

largely of Federal lands, the development period may not be included in the repayment contract, and therefore the water users
need not bind themselves to such contract until their lands are
fully cultivated.

The above-discussed procedure applies not only to projects
to be authorized after 4 August 1939, but also, in as far as
is allowable, to those projects which were authorized prior to
but not yet completed on this date (sec. 7(b)).[32]

Liberal and flexible though it is, this new irrigation repayment arrangement is further mellowed by the following modifications:

(I) Deferment---As provided in sec. 5, para. 2 of the Reclamation Project Act, "the Secretary (of the Interior) may provide such deferments of construction charges as in his judgment
are necessary to prevent said requirements from resulting in
inequitable pyramiding of payments of said charges."

(II) Extension---Although there is no general provision
in the Reclamation Project Act itself providing for the extension of the period of repayment, such extensions have been effected for a number of projects by special enactments. By the
end of 1954, the following extensions had been authorized:[33]

Act of 31 July 1946 (60 Stat. 717) extended the repayment
period of the Lewiston Orchards project, Idaho to not
more than 50 years.
Act of 25 June 1947 (61 Stat. 181) extended the repayment
period of the Paonia project, Colorado, to a maximum
of 68 years.
Act of 15 June 1948 (62 Stat. 442) extended the repayment
period of the Preston Bench project, Idaho, to a maximum of 74 years.
Flood Control Act of 30 June 1948 (62 Stat. 1171, 1179)
permitted the extension of the repayment period of
the Middle Rio Grande project, New Mexico, beyond 40
years.
Act of 27 September 1950 (64 Stat. 1072) extended the repayment period of the Vermejo project, New Mexico, to
an indefinite period of time.
Act of 27 July 1954 (68 Stat. 568) extended the repayment
period of the Foster Creek Division of the Chief Joseph
Dam project, Washington, to 50 years.
Act of 28 July 1954 (68 Stat. 575) permitted the extension
of the repayment period of the De Luz Dam project, California, to 56 years and that of the development period of the same project to 17 years.
Act of 20 August 1954 (68 Stat. 752) extended the repayment
period of the Rouge River Basin project, Talent Division, Oregon, to not more than 60 years.

In order to clear the ground for the effectuation of the new

system, the Reclamation Project Act further carries measures
granting relief to water users who were already under repayment
obligation to the United States on 4 August 1939. The types
of relief available to those water users are as follows:

(I) Extension---In the first place, the Secretary of the
Interior may extend the period of repayment originally established to a maximum of 40 years in such a manner that the number of the annual installments remaining unpaid should in no
case be doubled (sec. 3). Secondly, when individual water users in an existing irrigation project organize themselves into
an association or irrigation district, the Secretary, upon representation of such association or district, may consolidate
all charges due from its members in a general repayment contract, under which all charges remaining unpaid are to be paid
in a number of annual installments to be determined on the basis of adjustable "weighted average gross crop return per acre,"
five percent of such return being normally the measure of each
installment (sec. 4, as amended on 24 April 1945, 59 Stat. 75).
For obligations to which neither of the above two arrangements
may justifiably apply, the Secretary is given discretion to negotiate and, upon approval of the Congress, execute, contracts
"which, in his judgment, both would provide fair and equitable
treatment of the repayment problems involved and would be in
keeping with the general purpose of this Act" (sec. 7, as amended on 24 April 1945, 59 Stat. 75). All these extensions, it
may be noted, are temporary and will expire on 31 December
1954.[34]

(II) Deferment--- The Secretary may defer any charges that
may fall due at any time, even though an extension of period is
granted (25 April 1945 amendment of sec. 17(b)): 59 Stat. 75,
76).[35]

The above-discussed repayment procedures, which are provided for in the Reclamation Act of 1902 and the Reclamation Project Act of 1939, and their modifications, are all normal procedures. Besides, there have been special repayment arrangements
authorized by special statutory enactments. Under these special
arrangements, reimbursable project costs are not repaid by the
water users or water users' organizations directly, as is the
case of the normal repayment procedures. Such special arrangements have prevailed in cases where Indian lands (either tribal
or allotted) are incidentally benefited by projects built by
the Bureau of Reclamation under the Reclamation Laws. Indian
lands which were first included in such projects were those of
the Yuma and Colorado River Indian Reservations in California
and Arizona, and the Pyramid Lake Indian Reservation in Nevada.
The irrigation of these lands with water to be supplied by the
Bureau of Reclamation was authorized by secs. 25 and 26 of the
Indian Office Appropriation Act of 21 April 1904 (33 Stat. 189,
224-225). Under this provision, the lands of these two Indian
Reservations that were irrigable in this way were to be taken

out of Indian ownership and sold as homesteads to non-Indians
for their fair market value, except that five acres (increased
to ten acres by the Indian Office Appropriation Act of 3 March
1911, 36 Stat. 1058, 1063) were reserved and allotted to each
of the Indians of these two Reservations. The proceeds of the
land-sales were placed to the credit of the two Reservations.
As for the reimbursable project construction costs, the non-
Indian homesteaders were required to repay that part of such
costs which were apportioned to the originally Indian lands
now sold to them, according to normal repayment procedure.
Costs due the allotted lands retained by the Indians were to be
repaid out of the proceeds of the land-sales, or, with respect
to the Yuma and Colorado River Reservations, "from any other
funds that may become available for such purpose" (Indian Appropriation Act of 3 March 1911, 36 Stat. 1058, 1063).

In the Indian Office Appropriation Act of 30 April 1908,
permission was given the Secretary of the Interior to irrigate
Indian allotments (but not tribal lands) in Nevada with water
made available from irrigation projects of the Bureau of Reclamation, and provision was made to the effect that no construction or operation and maintenance charges should be collected
from Indians owning allotments so irrigated but that they were
to be repaid out of the Departmental appropriations (35 Stat.
70, 85).

In the Indian Office Appropriation Act of 1 August 1914 (38
Stat. 582), provision was made for the delivery of 720 cubic
feet of water from the storage works of the Yakima irrigation
project, Washington, of the Bureau of Reclamation to the Yakima
Indian Reservation, for the irrigation of more than 100,000 acres of Indian allotted lands,[36] and for the repayment of costs
due out of Departmental appropriations in annual installments
(at 60¢). The quantity of water to be delivered has been successively increased, but the manner of repayment remains unchanged.[37] The principle of having the United States itself
bear the reimbursable irrigation costs against benefited Indian
lands has been applied to all other cases in which Indian lands
are incidentally irrigated by regular irrigation projects of
the Bureau of Reclamation.[38]

Up to 30 June 1946, the Bureau of Indian Affairs had paid
to the Bureau of Reclamation (Reclamation Fund), for the irrigation of Indian lands, a total of $2,977,830 (in comparison
with a total repayment of $67,163,000 by ordinary water users).[39]

In the American-Mexican Water Treaty of 1944 (effective 8
November 1945), the Republic of Mexico is required to repay the
proportionate share of that part of the construction and operation and maintenance costs of the Imperial Dam and the Imperial
Dam-Pilot Knob Section of the All-American Canal which are not
to be amortized by the revenues of hydroelectric power generated at Pilot Knob power plant (art. 14). No repayment, however,

had been made by Mexico up to July 1953, as "under the option
provided in Article 15(G) of the Water Treaty, Mexico has thus
far taken delivery in the limitrophe section of the Colorado
River of all of the waters of that river allotted to Mexico by
the Treaty, and no deliveries have been made through the All-
American Canal."[40]

Another interesting special repayment arrangement is found
in the Interior Department Appropriation Act of 18 June 1940,
which provided that all expenditures for the construction of
the Modoc Unit of the Klamath project, Oregon-California,"shall
be reimbursed from net revenues hereafter received from the
lease of grazing and farming lands within the Tule Lake Division . . ." (54 Stat. 406, 436).[41]

(ii) Water Conservation and Utilization Projects---In the
Water Conservation and Utilization Act (original) of 11 August
1939 (53 Stat. 1418), passed after a few days after the passage
of the Reclamation Project Act, it was merely provided that all
moneys expended on the construction of water conservation and
utilization projects "shall be repaid to the United States by
the water users in not to exceed forty annual installments"
(sec. 2, 1st sent.). In the 14 October 1940 amendment of this
Act (54 Stat. 1119), a detailed repayment procedure is provided
for, which is substantially the same as that adopted by the Reclamation Project Act with the exceptions (1) that no allocation
of costs is to be made to navigation improvement, (2) that repayment contracts may be concluded either with water users' organizations or with individual water users, although the former
are preferred, and (3) that there is no authorization for the
water-service contracts as substitutes for repayment contracts
or for semiannual installments.[42]

(iii) Indian Irrigation Projects---Early Indian irrigation
works were mostly financed by tribal funds of the Indians themselves.[43] Small sums of moneys were from time to time made
available from the general or special appropriations to the Office of Indian Affairs for the construction of such works.[44]
In the report of the Commissioner of Indian Affairs to the Secretary of the Interior for 1898, the Indians of the Fort Peck
Reservation, Montana, who "had no funds of their own", were reported as being "desirous of ceding a portion of their reservation so as to obtain funds for irrigation." Thus the third
way of financing Indian irrigation works, namely, the sale of
Indian lands,[45] was for the first time brought under consideration. The action was recommended as feasible, but it was thought
that Congressional authorization was necessary.[46] That was given by the Congress in sec. 14 of the Act of 23 April 1904 (33
Stat. 302, 305). The same financial method was adopted by the
Indian Office Appropriation Act of 21 April 1904 (33 Stat. 189),
in connection with the irrigation of the lands of the Yuma and
Colorado River Reservations in California and Arizona (sec. 25,
at 224) and the Pyramid Lake Reservation in Nevada (sec. 26, at

225), although the irrigation works were to be constructed by the Reclamation Service (predecessor of the Bureau of Reclamation) under the Reclamation Act of 1902.

Since the major Indian irrigation works were directly financed by the funds and lands of the Indians themselves, no problem could arise of cost-repayment, which refers only to expenses incurred by the Federal Government out of Federal funds. As for the relatively small appropriations from Federal funds made for the early irrigation works, no provision was made for reimbursement. In the report of the Commissioner of Indian Affairs to the Secretary of the Interior dated 5 September 1890, it was first suggested that Federal appropriations for Indian irrigation projects should be reimbursed, and that "either from funds now belonging to the Indians or from the sale of their surplus lands" (p. CXLI). However, this idea was not actualized until 1905,[47] when the sale of Indian tribal lands was adopted as the method for the reimbursement of Federal appropriations.

In sec. 10 of the Indian Office Appropriation Act of 3 March 1905 (33 Stat. 1048, 1081), which appropriated $50,000 for the irrigation of the lands of the Pima Indians in Arizona, it was provided that "when said irrigation system is in successful operation and the Indians have become self-supporting the cost of operating the said system shall be equitably apportioned upon the lands irrigated and to the annual charge shall be added an amount sufficient to pay back into the Treasury the cost of the work within thirty years, _suitable deduction being made for the disposal of lands which now form a part of the said reservation_" (italics added).[48] Provisions of identical terminology were found in the Indian Office Appropriation Acts of 21 June 1906 (34 Stat. 325, 375-376, irrigating the lands of the Uncompahgre, Uintah and White River Utes in Utah) and 1 March 1907 (34 Stat. 1015, 1035-1036, Blackfeet Indian Reservation, Montana).[49]

In the appropriation for the "extension of the irrigation system on lands allotted to Yakima Indians in Washington", which was incorporated in the Indian Office Appropriation Act of 1 March 1907, _op. cit._ (at 1050) all pleonasms were dropped, and straightforward stipulation was adopted that the cost of construction should be "reimbursable from the proceeds of the sale of surplus lands". Reproductions of this type of provision were made in subsequent Indian Office Appropriation Acts with respect to a number of Indian irrigation projects.[50]

The use of Indian tribal funds to reimburse Federal appropriated funds began with the Milk River project on the Fort Peck Reservation in Montana under the Indian Office Appropriation Act of 4 April 1910 (36 Stat. 269, 277). Subsequent Federal appropriations reimbursable in the same way were those for the Yuma and Colorado River Reservations in California and Arizona and the Milk River project on the Fort Belknap Reservation in Montana in the Indian Office Appropriation Act of 3 March 1911 (36

Stat. 1058, 1063 and 1066),[51] for the Gila River Reservation
in Arizona in the Act of 24 April 1912 (37 Stat. 518, 522),
for the Moapa River Reservation in Nevada in the Act of 3 March
1921 (41 Stat. 1225, 1228), for the San Xavier Reservation in
Arizona in the Act of 24 May 1922 (42 Stat. 552, 566), for the
Pyramid Lake Reservation in Nevada in the Act of 24 January
1923 (42 Stat. 1174, 1193), and for the Fort Apache Reservation
in Arizona in the Act of 5 June 1924 (43 Stat. 390, 402).

Besides the reimbursement from tribal funds and the proceeds of the sale of tribal lands, a new method was developed
of reimbursing Federal funds, which consisted in the levying
of construction costs against the lands benefited and the actual payment of such costs by non-Indian landowners only. It
may be regarded as a transformation of reimbursement from the
sale of Indian lands. In the Indian Office Appropriation Act
of 1 March 1907, it was provided, with respect to the irrigation system for the Fort Hall Indian Reservation in Idaho (34
Stat. 1015, 1024-1025), that the non-Indian beneficiaries of
the system should pay to the United States, in five annual installments, charges at $6 per acre, which supposedly covered
all construction costs of the project and the cost of operation
and maintenance during the repayment period, and should assume
the operation and maintenance of the project after the said
repayment period. The Indian water users were to be supplied
with irrigation water free of both construction and operation
and maintenance charges. But if the **Indians** should lease their
lands to non-Indians to a period longer than three years, the
lessees must pay the operation and maintenance costs chargeable
to the lands in lease.

A modification of this method was that in theory and in law
both Indians and non-Indians must repay the Government for costs
of construction (and operation and maintenance) but that in
practice only the latter were required to pay. Liens were
placed on the Indian lands for the reimbursable construction
charges, but they were not enforceable as long as the lands re-
mained in Indian ownership. If the Indians sold their lands to
non-Indians, the non-Indian (but not other Indians) purchasers
were obligated to pay to the United States all accumulated charges on such lands. By 1928, this method had been adopted in the
following systems or projects:

> Yuma Reservation in California and Colorado River Res-
> ervation in Arizona---Indian Office Appropriation Act
> of 3 March 1911 (36 Stat. 1058, 1063);
> Gila River Indian Reservation in Arizona---Indian Of-
> fice Appropriation Act of 24 August 1912 (37 Stat. 518,
> 522);
> Irrigation systems in the Blackfeet, Flathead and Fort
> Peck Reservations in Montana and the Wapato distribu-
> tion project on the Yakima Reservation in Washington--
> Indian Office Appropriation Act of 18 May 1916 (39

Stat. 123, 141 and 154);
Crow Reservation in Montana---Special Act of 4 June
1920 (41 Stat. 751, 753-754, sec. 8);
Fort Hall Reservation in Idaho---Interior Department
Appropriation Act of 24 May 1922 (42 Stat. 552, 568);
San Carlos project on the Gila River Reservation in
Arizona---Special Act of 7 June 1924 (43 Stat. 475);

This new procedure gained such a momentum that a provision
of general application was inserted in the Interior Department
Appropriation Act of 7 March 1928 (45 Stat. 200,210),[52] which
read:

> The costs of irrigation projects and of operating and
> maintaining such projects where reimbursement thereof
> is required by law shall be apportioned on a per acre
> basis against the lands under the respective projects
> and shall be collected by the Secretary of the Interior
> as required by such law, and any unpaid charges out-
> standing against such lands shall constitute a first
> lien thereon, which shall be recited in any patent or
> instrument issued for such lands.

But this provision did not expressly stipulate that the liens
for construction charges on Indian lands were not enforceable.
This omission was soon rectified by a special Act enacted on 1
July 1932, commonly called the Levitt Act (47 Stat. 564), which
provided, among other things, that "the collection of all construction costs against any Indian owned lands within any government irrigation project is hereby deferred, and no assessments shall be made on behalf of such charges against such lands
until the Indian title thereto shall have been extinguished, and
construction assessments heretofore levied against such lands
. . . and uncollected are hereby cancelled. . ." The 1928 provision as supplemented by the 1932 provision, has remained in
force to the present time. It did not replace the above-mentioned special provisions, but it extended them to all other Indian irrigation systems and projects financed by Federal appropriations, with the single exception of the irrigation system
on the Belknap Indian Reservation, Montana, to which the provisions in the Act of 4 April 1910 (36 Stat. 269, 277) (reimbursement from tribal funds) have continued to apply.[53]

So the law has been established that although the Indian Reservations in their collective capacities have borne the repayment obligations (with respect to Federal funds) with their tribal funds and tribal lands, the individual Indians are not required to repay the Federal Government for irrigation costs, if
any repayment is required by special statutory enactment in any
given case.[54] Actual repay ment, however, did not begin until
1920. In the Indian Office Appropriation Act of 14 February
1920 (41 Stat. 408), the following measure was adopted aiming at
the collection of the construction charges:

The Secretary of the Interior is hereby authorized and
directed to require the owners of irrigable land under
any irrigation system heretofore or hereafter constructed for the benefit of Indians and to which water for
irrigation purposes can be delivered to begin partial
reimbursement of the construction charges, where reimbursement is required by law, at such times and in such
amounts as he may deem best; all payments hereunder to
be credited on a per acre basis in favor of the land
in behalf of which such payments shall have been made
and to be deducted from the total per acre charge as-
sessable against said land. . .(409).

"In accordance with the provisions of the act appropriate
regulations were issued whereby the owners of land within the
various Indian irrigation projects were to pay 5 percent of
the per-acre construction cost of the respective projects each
year, the payments to begin on November 14, 1920, and continue,
over a period of 20 years. Subsequently, during the year 1927,
the regulations . . . were modified so as to spread the annual
installments for reimbursement of the construction costs over
an additional period of time so that 2.5 percent of the total
unpaid balance at that time should be payable on November 15
of each year instead of the larger amount theretofore required.
The explanation given for spreading the payments . . . was that
considerable difficulty had been experienced in collecting the
charges owing to the fact that many of the landowners were financially unable to meet their payments."[55] The regulations
applied to Indian allotments (i.e. lands of Indian individuals)
and non-Indian-owned lands, but did not apply to Indian tribal
or unallotted lands, which do not bear construction charges.

Exempted from these regulations are the San Carlos project
on the Gila River Reservation in Arizona, the Wapato (distribution) project on the Yakima Reservation in Washington, and the
irrigation systems on the Blackfeet, Fort Peck, Flathead and
Crow Reservations in Montana and the Fort Hall Reservation in
Idaho, which have continued to be governed by the special statutory provisions mentioned above.[56] These special provisions
provide for different annual installments, the first installment being as a rule to be paid after the irrigation water became or becomes available. In the Act of 7 June 1924, which is
on the San Carlos project, the non-Indian landowners are required to organize themselves into an irrigation district and
to enter into a repayment agreement contract with the Secretary
of the Interior in the name of such district (sec. 4). This
provision was adopted by the 1926 amendment to the Flathead Reservation and the 1946 supplement to the Crow Reservation law,
and represents a tendency of assimilation between the regular
and Indian irrigation projects.

All of the above discussion is concerned with the reimbursement of Federal appropriations. As reimbursement began to be
required of Federal funds, a need was felt to reimburse the tri-

bal funds belonging to the whole reservations, "only a certain
portion of the Indians have received any benefit from the irrigation systems."57 The first requirement for the reimbursement
of tribal funds advanced for the construction of irrigation projects appeared in the Indian Office Appropriation Act of 25 May
1917, with respect to the Big Horn Canal project on the Crow
Indian Reservation in Montana (40 Stat. 561, 574). The sum of
$200,000 to be withdrawn from the tribal funds of the said re-
servation was required "to be reimbursed to the tribe under such
rules and regulations as may be prescribed by the Secretary of
the Interior." Similar provisions were found in the Indian Office or Interior Department Appropriation Acts of 14 February
1920 in connection with the San Carlos project in Arizona (41
Stat. 408, 416), 5 June 1924 in connection with the Fort Apache
Reservation in Arizona (43 Stat. 390, 402), 14 May 1930 in connection with certain irrigation works on the Klamath Reservation in Oregon, and so forth. In the Indian Office Appropriation Act of 1 August 1914, a general provision was made which
required all Indians to repay tribal funds expended on irrigation projects when they are able to do so (38 Stat. 582, 583).58

It may be observed that the reimbursement of Indian tribal
funds is entirely at the discretion of the Secretary of the Interior and that no statutory provisions are available concerning the procedure of repayment. It is not known whether any
tribal funds have been repaid to the several Indian reservations up to the present time.59

The obligations of the water users (non-Indian) of Indian
irrigation projects may be extended and deferred. By a series
of acts such obligations were suspended during the period 1930-
1943, inclusive, the same privilege as enjoyed by the water users of regular irrigation projects.60 Some extensions and deferments of repayment obligations have also been made by special statutory enactments.61

Besides extension and deferment, another type of relief is
cancellation of the charges. In the afore-mentioned Act of 1
July 1932 (47 Stat. 564), the Secretary of the Interior was
"authorized and directed to adjust or eliminate reimbursable
charges . . . against individual Indians or tribes of Indians62
in such a way as shall be equitable and just in consideration
of all the circumstances under which such charges were made .
. ." Under this Act, about $12 million of the accumulated char-
ges were written off either because of the infeasibility of the
project or the inability of the Indians to pay.63 The Act of
28 June 1946 on the irrigation system on the Crow Reservation
in Montana (60 Stat. 333) authorized the Secretary of the Interior to declare as temporarily non-irrigable any land (whether
Indian-owned or non-Indian-owned) potentially irrigable under
the system for any period of time, and cancelled all construction charges against such lands during such period (sec. 1,
subsec. (3)).

All above discussion concerns the reimbursement of costs
of projects constructed by the Bureau of Indian Affairs. With
regard to the moneys paid by the Federal Government directly
into the Reclamation Fund on behalf of Indian lands benefited
by the regular irrigation projects constructed by the Bureau
of Reclamation, it seems that they are not to be reimbursed by
the individual Indians or Indians tribes benefited, for there
has not been any statutory provision requiring such reimbursement. But the funds paid by the Federal Government to state
and local agencies in payment of water services furnished by
them to Indian lands through projects constructed or operated
by them have been required by law to be returned to the Federal
Government by the Indian beneficiaries.[64]

(2) <u>Other Construction Costs</u>---Under the (Warren) Act of
21 February 1911 (36 Stat. 925), all construction costs of
works for the storage and delivery of supplemental water to
lands irrigated under non-Federal irrigation projects must be
repaid to the United States by the owners of such projects.
In the Act of 3 July 1930 (46 Stat. 852), which authorized the
appropriation of $750,000 for the rehabilitation (largely fi-
nancial) of the Bitter Root project, Montana, it was provided
that the appropriated sum should be "repaid to the United States
within a period . . . of not more than 40 years, with interest
at the rate of 4 percentum per annum . . ." On 7 October 1949,
a general law was enacted (63 Stat. 724) stipulating that "expenditures of funds hereafter specifically appropriated for rehabilitation and betterment of irrigation systems on projects
governed by the Federal reclamation laws shall be made only
after the organization concerned shall have obligated themselves
for the return thereof in installments fixed in accordance with
their ability to pay . . ." (sec. 1). Finally, under sec. 5(a)
of the Water Conservation and Utilization Act of 1940, the costs
of land development are to be reimbursed by the settlers in annual or semiannual installments over a maximum period of 50
years beginning from the first date settlement.

The costs of operation and maintenance are reimbursable,
too. In the Reclamation Act of 1902, provision was made for
the expenditures of the Reclamation Funds for the operation and
maintenance of Federal irrigation project by the Federal Government itself pending the transfer of such task to the water users
(sec. 6), but the act was silent as to whether such expenditures
are reimbursable. The Federal Government insisted on their repayment, which was upheld by the Supreme Court in <u>Swigert v.
Baker</u>, 229 U. S. 187, 193 (1913). In the Reclamation Extension
Act of 13 August 1914 (sec. 5), the Second Deficiency Appropriation Act of 5 December 1924 (sec. 4, subsec. N) and the Reclamation Project Act of 4 August 1939 (sec. 6), the repayment of
costs of operation and maintenance advanced by the Federal Government is expressed stipulated. It is to be provided for in
each construction-cost repayment contract, and the cost of operation and maintenance for each year are to be paid in advance.[65] The same principle and procedure of the repayment of

costs of operation and maintenance are also required by the
Water Conservation and Utilization Act of 14 October 1940 (sec.
4(c)(2)) and the (Warden) Act of 21 February 1911 (sec. 1).

With regard to the Indian irrigation projects, provision
for the repayment of costs of operation and maintenance was
first made in sec. 9 of the Act of 29 May 1908 (35 Stat. 444,
450) for the irrigation system on the Flathead Reservation in
Montana. However, as reported in 1913, "on a majority of the
reservations no provision is made for the repayment of this expense."[66] In the Indian Office Appropriation Act of 1 August
1914, a general rule was enacted which authorized the Secretary
of the Interior to fix the costs of the operation and maintenance of any Indian irrigation project and to require the repayment thereof (38 Stat. 582, 583). This general provision
was reiterated in the Interior Department Appropriation Act of
7 March 1928 (45 Stat. 200, 210).[67] According to the Act of
1914, only those Indians are required to pay such costs who
are financially able to pay.[68] This provision, coupled with
the provision in the 1928 Act that such costs constitute a
first lien upon the lands benefited, is tantamount to a provision to the effect that only non-Indians are to pay such costs.
The only difference between the repayment of construction costs
and that of costs of operation and maintenance is that while
in the former case repayment obligations fall only upon non-
Indian landowners but not the non-Indian lessees of Indian-
owned lands, in the latter case both categories of non-Indian
persons are obligated to pay.[69] It may also be noted that costs
incurred for the repair of damages to Indian irrigation works
caused by floods are always non-reimbursable.[70]

The repayment of operation and maintenance costs is also
subject to the various types of relief. For example, by a provision (sec. 45, 2nd para.) in the Omnibus Adjustment Act of
25 May 1926 (44 Stat. 636, 648), the Secretary of the Interior
has been authorized to extend such repayment for any project
or division of project for a maximum period of five years, with
charges so extended bearing an annual penalty interest of 6
percent. By an Act of 1 August 1942 (56 Stat. 732), operation
and maintenance charges levied against the Bridgeport irrigation district, in the North Platte irrigation project, Nebraska
and Wyoming, for the years 1926 to 1942, inclusive, which fell
delinquent, were cancelled. The deferment of repayment for
both regular and Indian irrigation projects for the years 1930
through 1943 as discussed above applied not only to construction costs but also to costs of operation and maintenance.

Maintenance would include minor repairs. If substantial
repairs are required, such works would not be treated as those
of routine maintenance. They may either be regarded as works
of rehabilitation and betterment or works of new construction
according to the directions of the authorizing authorities.
Should they be still considered works of maintenance, some special procedure of repayment of costs would be necessitated.[71]

Federal irrigation enterprise is not meant to be merely
partially self-financing. Nevertheless, Federal policies on
irrigation cost repayment have not as yet been designed on the
basis of commercially complete self-liquidation. In order to
confine the reimbursable costs to the lowest possible amount,
the following measures have been adopted by the Federal Government:

One---Ever since the enactment of the Reclamation Act on
17 June 1902, no interest has ever been required of any reimbursable charges;[72] except in cases where interests are charged as a penalty for delinquency in payments (as discussed before). It has been reported that interest charges would amount
to more than half of the cost of a project.[73]

Two---The costs of administration are non-reimbursable.
This was first provided in sec. 4, subsec. 0 of the Second Deficiency Appropriation Act of 5 December 1924 (43 Stat. 672,
704), and was reiterated and amplified in sec. 4(a) the Water
Conservation and Utilization Act of 14 October 1940 (54 Stat.
1119, 1121) and a special Act of 19 April 1945 (59 Stat. 54,
ch. 80).[74]

Three---As far as practicable, revenue-making functions are
to be attached to each irrigation project, and the net revenues
earned are to be used to reimburse the costs of pure irrigation
works, thus relieving the water users of part of their burdens![75]

Four---"No increase in the construction charges shall hereafter be made, after the same have been fixed by public notice,
except by agreement between the Secretary of the Interior and
a majority of water right applicants and entrymen to be effected by such increase . . ."[76] This provision is a great favor
to the water users, as the costs of construction estimated at
the time of the construction or completion of a project may
rise considerably after the project is operation for some time.[77]

These four measures to reduce the amount of reimbursement
are but one of the attempts of the Federal Government at the
prevention of repayment delinquency. In many special statutory
repayment arrangements, provisions have been made to the effect
that repayment contracts should be concluded before the construction of the project is started, and that an irrigation district
or districts should be organized representing all water users.[78]
The first part of the requirement is at once an assurance to the
Federal Government and a favor to the water users (for the cost
estimates at the time of planning of a project are the lowest
that can be obtained.) But the second part is a solid guarantee
of repayment. Not only an irrigation district normally has the
power to tax the lands, but also the area of lands taxable may
exceed the area of lands to be irrigated.[79] The security con-
tai ned in this requirement is, however, a relative one, for in
1949 more than 20 irrigation districts were themselves in financial straits.[80]

Another guarantee against repayment delinquency is in the following provision in the Interior Department Appropriation Act of 9 July 1952 (66 Stat. 445, 451).[81]

> No part of this or any other appropriation shall be available for the initiation of construction under the terms of reclamation law of any dam or reservoir or water supply, or any tunnel, canal, or conduit for water, or water-distribution system related to such dam or reservoir until the Secretary (of the Interior) shall certify to the Congress that an adequate soil survey and land classification has been made and that the lands to be irrigated are susceptible to the production of agricultural crops by means of irrigation.

This provision is to assure that sufficient crops will be raised from each acre of the irrigated land to provide money for the payment of water charges.

As of 30 June 1952, total Federal investment in irrigation projects of the Bureau of Reclamation (including both regular irrigation projects and Water Conservation and Utilization projects) was $2,174,633,749 and the total value of repayment contracts was $628,299,427 (or less than 20 percent). Of the latter sum, $234,500,000 was actually repaid to the Federal Treasury.[82] Charges on Indian irrigation projects have been made since 1920.[83] As of 30 June 1950 their repayment situation is as follows (covering both construction and operation and maintenance costs):[84]

Total costs reimbursable	$121,379,203.88
Collections for Construction	2,800,204.85
Operation and Maintenance	23,956,657.06
Cancellations	12,348,058.06
Unpaid	72,274,283.91

(b) Multiple-Purpose Dam and Reservoir Projects---For the purpose of this Subsection, multiple-purpose dam and reservoir projects, of which the development and sale of hydroelectric power is always the principal paying element, may be separated into: (1) projects under the jurisdiction of the Corps of Engineers, in which power development is merely self-liquidating;[85] and (2) projects under the jurisdiction of the Tennessee Valley Authority and the Bureau of Reclamation, in which power development is revenue-making. The projects of the Tennessee Valley Authority are further distinguished from those of the Bureau of Reclamation in that the power element therein is purely revenue-making[86] while in the latter power is produced primarily to provide subsidies to irrigation.[87] While a multiple-purpose project of the Corps of Engineers can never be self-liquidating (within the amoritzation period of power), a multiple-purpose project of the Tennessee Valley Authority or of the Bureau of Reclamation can be self-liquidating or even revenue-making.

The multiple-purpose dam and reservoir (and other multiple-purpose) projects of the Bureau of Reclamation (and Indian irrigation projects with multiple-purpose features) are of unique importance and deserve detailed discussion. The introduction of non-irrigation purposes into a project of the Bureau of Reclamation or the Bureau of Indian Affairs is solely financial. As will be discussed later, such purposes are either "reimbursable" or "non-reimbursable". The admission of every "reimbursable" purpose or function means a subsidy to, and that of every "non-reimbursable" purpose or function a reduction of, the reimbursable costs of irrigation. Thus both the reimbursable and the non-reimbursable non-irrigation purposes or functions operate to facilitate the repayment of irrigation costs.

According to the Reclamation Project Act of 1939, the non-reimbursable non-irrigation functions are (a) navigation improvement and (b) flood control,[88] and the reimbursable non-irrigation functions are (a) hydroelectric power development and (b) non-irrigation water supply (sec. 9 (a) and (b)). Among these four functions, it may be noted, navigation improvement, flood control and non-irrigation water supply are all purely incidental,[89] and for this reason they share with the irrigation function only costs of construction but not costs of operation and maintenance. So far as the costs of operation and maintenance are concerned, they are only to be divided between irrigation and power development, as power development is the only non-irrigation function which may possibly require a way of operation and maintenance of the project different from that required by irrigation.[90]

The rentals of non-irrigation water supply of a project must be sufficient to cover that part of the cost of construction of the project which the Secretary of the Interior thinks should be allocated to such purpose or function, with an interest ranging from zero to 3.5 percent per year. The proceeds of the sale of commercial or non-irrigation electric power[91] are to be used to return the costs of construction allocated to power development, the costs of operation and maintenance allocated to power development, costs of construction allocated to irrigation but assigned to power development for repayment, and interest at 3 percent per year on the construction costs allocated to power development.[92] The maximum period of amortization is 40 years for both of these functions, although it may be prolonged by special statutory provisions.[93] Since non-irrigation water supply is normally incidental to irrigation, any income which may be derived from this function is a subsidy to irrigation. Power revenues constitute a subsidy to irrigation to the extent that they pay for irrigation. When they are used merely to reimburse the costs of construction and operation and maintenance, though with interest, the power function can only be regarded as commercially self-liquidating.

To the four non-irrigation functions provided in the Recla-

mation Project Act of 1939, another function, fish and wildlife
conservation, which is non-reimbursable (so far as cost of construction is concerned?), was added by sec. 2 (2nd para.) of
the Fish and Wildlife Conservation Act of 14 August 1946 (60
Stat. 1080, 1081). Other reimbursable and non-reimbursable
non-irrigation purposes may be added from time to time by special enactments for any particular projects.[94] Of all non-
irrigation functions, only power development is to be allocated
costs of operation and maintenance. For any other such function, such allocation cannot be made except when specifically
authorized by the Congress.[95]

The sale of surplus water under the (Warren) Act of 21 February 1911 (36 Stat. 925), although part of the irrigation function, is a function or use of the project that is wholly seperate and distinct from the project function of irrigation, and
is not materially different from the sale of non-irrigation water.[96] However, the sale of water under this Act is mainly
aimed at the amortization of the costs of construction of necessarily additional storage and distribution works, and is unproductive of a substantial net profit.

Under an Act of 20 May 1920 (41 Stat. 605), unneeded irrigation project lands may be sold in public sales and the proceeds
therefrom are to be "covered into the reclamation fund and be
placed to the credit of the project for which such lands had
been withdrawn." The sale of project lands can hardly be considered as a function of a project. However, financially it
is no less a subsidy to irrigation than a reimbursable non-irrigation function discussed above. This Act was amplified by sec.
10 of the Reclamation Project Act of 1939, which authorizes the
sale of sand, gravel and other building materials on irrigation
project lands and the grant of leases, licenses (other than
those for hydroelectric power projects, which are granted by
the Federal Power Commission), easements or rights-of-way, for
maximum periods of fifty years, on or affecting such lands.
There seems to be no doubt that revenues from such transactions
will also go to the credit of the projects concerned.

All of the subsidies to irrigation enterprise discussed
with the exception of power revenues have always been subsidies
to individual projects and not to the whole enterprise.[97] With
regard to power revenues, they were subsidies to individual projects in all general and special statutory provisions enacted
prior to 1929.[98] In the Interior Department Appropriation Act
of 4 March 1929 (45 Stat. 1562), power revenues from the Boise
and Shoshone projects (in Idaho and Wyoming respectively, 1590
and 1592)[99] were to be credited not to these two projects (respectively) but to the "reclamation fund", which represents the
entire irrigation enterprise. However, this tendency of making
power revenues from some projects subsidize the entire irrigation enterprise was soon arrested by the Congress in a provision in the Interior Department Appropriation Act of 9 May 1938
(52 Stat. 291, 318), which directs that all residual power revenues or receipts of power sales after payment of all costs al-

located and assigned to power development from any and all irrigation projects should "be transferred to and covered into the
General Treasury as 'miscellaneous receipts' . . ." As of the
end of 1954, there were only two projects of the Bureau of Reclamation in which power revenues are allowed (and required) to
subsidize not only the projects in which power is produced but
also other projects. One is the Boulder Canyon or Hoover Dam
project in California and Arizona (which was excepted by the
above-mentioned provision of 1938), the power revenues from
which are partly used to subscribe to the Colorado River Fund
Development (to be discussed later) for the financing of the
investigation and construction of irrigation projects in the
Colorado River Basin. The other exception is provided in an
Act of 28 June 1949, under which the costs of construction of
the irrigation features of the Eden project, Wyoming, are to be
repaid by "net revenues derived from the sale of power generated at the hydroelectric plants of the Colorado River storage project in the Upper Basin . . . when such plants are constructed"
(63 Stat. 277).

The multiple-purpose **nature** of the Water Conservation and
Utilization projects is provided in secs. 3 and 10 of the Act
of 14 October 1940 (54 Stat. 1119, 1120 and 1124). There is
only one non-reimbursable function, which is flood control.
The reimbursable functions, other than project irrigation, are
(1) power development, (2) non-irrigation water supply and (3)
irrigation of Indian lands. It should be noted, however, that
the irrigation of Indian lands, though nominally reimbursable
or reimbursable from the point of view of the Bureau of Reclamation, is actually non-reimbursable as the costs allocated
thereto are usually paid by the Federal Government itself without their being further reimbursed by water users. With regard
to power development and non-irrigation water supply, it is expressly provided that both the costs of construction and those
of operation and maintenance are reimbursable. Interest, not
fixed by law, may be imposed by the Secretary of the Interior
on the reimbursable charges allocated to both of these functions. As to Indian irrigation, both costs of construction and
costs of operation and maintenance should be reimbursable, in
the practice and spirit of both the reclamation laws and the
Indian irrigation provisions. Flood control, however, in the
absence of special enactments, would be confined to costs of
construction.[100]

As of 30 June 1952, the allocations of costs of construction made by the Bureau of Reclamation of all projects under
its jurisdiction are as follows:[101]

		Percent
Total estimated cost	$6,883,489,746	100.00
Irrigation	4,512,641,014	65.56
Commercial power development	1,366,313,349	19.85
Non-irrigation water **supply**	106,526,714	1.55
Flood control	496,234,567	7.21

Fish and wildlife conservation	4,357,700	0.06
Recreation	8,508,000	0.12
Downstream benefits (navigation improvement)	41,720,780	0.61
Unallotted	301,248,798	4.38
Special contributions	12,636,284	0.18
Columbia Basin programs	16,126,000	0.23
Serving Mexican treaties	11,415,128	0.17
Highway construction (a trust function)	872,645	0.01
Non-reimbursable power development	4,888,767	0.07

Commercial power development is the largest paying factor. It will repay not only the $1,366,313,349 allocated to commercial power development as such, but also (1) $2,502,718,668 of irrigation (which is 55.4 percent of entire cost allocated to irrigation), (2) $25,000,000 of flood control in the Boulder Canyon project, (3) $41,720,780 of downstream power benefits in Columbia Basin project and Kendrick division, (4) $10,398,-078 serving Mexican treaties and (5) $5,528,000 of the costs allocated to recreation and fish and wildlife conservation, or a grand total of $3,951,678,875, or some 57.4 percent of the total estimated cost of construction of all projects.

Indian irrigation projects are, unlike projects of the Bureau of Reclamation, not inherently multiple-purpose in nature. However, certain revenue-making activities have been recognized and fully taken advantage of. Power development on Indian irrigation projects was first authorized by the Interior Department Appropriation Act of 10 May 1926, which authorized the construction of a power plant on the irrigation system of the Flathead Reservation in Montana (44 Stat. 453, 466). The net power revenues were to be used, -- "first, to liquidate the cost of the power development; second, to liquidate payment of the deferred obligation on the Camas Division; third, to liquidate construction cost on an equal per acre basis on each acre of irrigable land within the entire project, and fourth, to liquidate operation and maintenance costs within the entire project." The Interior Department Appropriation Act of 7 March 1928 authorized power development on the Coolidge Dam of the San Carlos project in Arizona and stipulated that the net receipts therefrom should be devoted, first to the reimbursement of the costs of such power development, second, to that of the cost of construction of the entire San Carlos irrigation project, and third, to that of the cost of operation and maintenance of the same project (45 Stat. 200, 212). In the Act of 7 August 1946 (60 Stat. 895), a general provision was made (sec. 3) to the effect that the revenues from power development at any Indian irrigation project should be applied to the following purposes: "(1) payment of the expenses of operating and maintaining the power system; (a) . . . making repairs and replacements . . . of the Power system; . . . (3) amortization . . . of construction costs allocated to be returned from power revenues; and (4) payment of other expenses and obligations chargeable to power revenues. . . ."

In the above-mentioned Interior Department Appropriation
Act of 7 March 1928, provision was also made for the sale of
surplus water of the San Carlos project in Arizona to the State
of Arizona and its political subdivisions, presumably to obtain additional revenues for the repayment of the costs of the
project. In an Act of 4 April 1938 (52 Stat. 193), the Secretary of the Interior was authorized to lease unneeded project
lands of the San Carlos , Fort Hall, Flathead and Western Shoshone irrigation projects for agricultural, grazing and other
uses for maximum terms of ten years, and provided that the rentals of such leases "shall be available for expenditure in accordance with the existing laws in the operation and maintenance of the irrigation projects with which they are connected."

It should be remarked that the utilization of non-irrigation revenues in Indian irrigation projects, as in regular irrigation projects, is project-wise, and that the revenues from
one project cannot be applied to another. It may also be noted
that unlike regular irrigation projects, Indian irrigation projects are basically single-purpose and that no allocation of
costs to non-reimbursable purposes is allowed.

The repayment of the costs (of construction and operation
and maintenance) of a multiple-purpose project resolves itself
into the repayment or non-repayment of the costs incurred on
each of the purposes served. The essence of this problem is
therefore the allocation of the costs of the entire project
among the various purposes of the project. There is no question that the costs expended on all single-purposes features
(e. g., irrigation canals and laterals, hydroelectric power
plant and transmission facilities, navigation locks, fish ladders and screens, etc), go with the respective purposes concerned. But with regard to the multiple-purpose part of the project (i.e., features serving two or more purposes, mainly the
storage reservoir and its impounding dam),[102] several methods
or theories of allocation are in theory applicable. The following methods have received the consideration of the Federal Government:[103]

(1) Benefit theory---The joint costs of a multiple-purpose
facility or structure of a multiple-purpose project are apportioned among the various purposes served in the proportion of
benefits (usually expressed monetary units) derived from each
of these purposes. In their single-purpose projects, both the
Bureau of Reclamation and the Corps of Engineers have relied
on this theory in considering the feasibility of the individual
projects.[104] The measure of benefits is generally the increase
in commerce for navigation improvement, the amount properties
and the number of human lives rendered safe from flood for
flood control, and the increase in crop production for irrigation. It would seem that in cases where only these purposes

are involved the benefit theory will be the natural method for the allocation of joint costs.

(2) The theory of alternative justifiable expenditure---This is said to be a "variant of the benefits theory". The joint costs are divided among the various purposes served "in proportion to the alternative investment for the respective purposes in single-use projects." "It is recognized that in many instances this theory probably provides the most reliable method of approach in determining ceilings. Its principal weakness lies in the fact that it is not possible in every instance to obtain an alternative method of providing the service, the cost of which would not exceed the benefits. In such cases, the capitalized benefits are used as the alternative justifiable expenditure.

(3) The theory of the use of facilities---The joint costs are divided among the several purposes served on the basis of the use of the facility or structure for each purpose. For a multiple-purpose dam and reservoir, the use of the structure for each purpose is usually measured in terms of the volume of storage devoted thereto. To be accurate, the factor of time should be added, so that the final unit of measure would be something like the acre-foot-day.

(4) The vendibility theory---This theory is derived from the theory of price determination under conditions of joint supply, e. g., mutton and wool, cotton fiber and cotton seed, lead and zinc from common ores, etc. "Under conditions of effective competition, joint products, produced for an open market, will tend to be sold at prices which in total will equal their joint cost of production plus a competitive profit; but the apportionment of the total receipts between them will depend upon the relative demands for each." "If one of the joint products is of minor importance as to income yield, or if it has only recently attained commercial significance having formerly been a waste, it is known as a by-product." This theory is applicable to purposes which are commercially marketable, primarily hydroelectric power and non-irrigation water supply.

(5) The specific cost theory---The costs of multiple-purpose parts of the project are apportioned among the purposes included in proportion to the expenditures for these purposes in single-purpose parts of the project. This theory is inapplicable in cases in which one or more of the purposes served by the multiple-purpose parts are not served by single-purpose structures.

(6) The theory of equal apportionment---". . . The joint costs are divided equally among the principal purposes served." This theory, as well as the specific cost theory, is to be used only for the sake of convenience.

Different methods or combinations of methods have been employed by the Federal Government in allocating the joint costs
of the multiple-purpose parts of the various multiple-purpose
projects. The method of joint-cost allocation which has been
employed by the Tennessee Valley Authority is that based on
the alternative justifiable expenditure.[105] Allocations **are
made** each year for the entire system operated by the said Authority instead of each individual project. Although the Tennessee Valley Authority Act (sec. 14) directs that the Authority's
investment should be allocated to the five purposes of flood
control, navigation improvement, hydroelectric power development, fertilizer manufacture and national defense, no allocations have as yet been made to the last two purposes. All costs
assigned to navigation improvement and flood control are included in joint costs, although there are single-purpose navigation-
improvement facilities, namely, the navigation locks. Part of
the costs for power is included in the joint costs, the rest
being for single-purpose power structures, namely, power plants
and transmission facilities.[106] The allocations made for the
fiscal year 1953 are as follows:[107]

Purpose	Joint Costs	Separate Costs	Total Costs
Navigation improvement	156,580,240	--------	156,580,240
Flood control	182,405,217	--------	182,405,217
Power development	379,766,001	544,747,489	924,513,490
Total	718,751,458	544,747,489	1,263,498,947

The alternative justifiable expenditure theory was adopted
in the allocation of costs of the Columbia Basin or Grand Coulee Dam project of the Department of the Interior, which is as
follows:[108]

Purpose	Joint Costs	Separate Costs	Total Costs
Navigation improvement and flood control	1,000,000	--------	1,000,000
Irrigation	55,155,760	286,774,234	341,929,994
Power at the site	39,925,249	73,901,994	113,927,243
Benefits to power at the Bonneville Dam	30,272,991	---------	30,272,991
Total	126,354,000	360,676,228	487,030,228

In the Central Valley project, two methods were used, namely the alternative justifiable expenditure and the use of facilities theories, and the final allocation to each purpose was
obtained by taking the mean of the figures derived from these
two different theories. The actual allocation is as follows:[109]

Purpose	Theory (1)	Theory (2)	Final
Navigation improvement	18,083,000	18,083,000	18,083,000

Flood Control	31,444,000	31,444,000	31,444,000
Irrigation (including salinity control)	187,587,200	211,735,000	199,661,100
Contra Costa distribution system	3,074,600	3,074,600	3,074,600
Canal capacity for future water	18,815,900	18,815,900	18,815,900
Municipal water supply	14,431,000	3,752,600	9,091,800
Commercial power	110,878,300	97,408,900	104,143,600
Total	384,314,000	384,314,000	384,314,000

In the Grand Valley or Palisades Dam and Reservoir project (in Idaho, Bureau of Reclamation), compromise was made between the benefit theory and the use of facilities theory. While according to the former theory the joint costs would be allocated in the proportion of 39.1 percent to flood control, 41.2 percent to irrigation and 19.7 percent to power, the final allocations made of such costs were $7,431,000 (41 percent) to flood control, $7,794,000 (43 percent) to irrigation and $2,900,000 (16 percent) to power. With separate single-purpose cost allocations, the final project allocation was $8,165,000 for flood control, $7,794,000 for irrigation and $5,711,000 for power.[110]

With respect to the Bonneville project of the Corps of Engineers, the Federal Power Commission felt that since power feature of the project was technically purely incidental to navigation improvement there might be no allocation of costs to it and that if an allocation was to be made it could not be more than half of the joint costs of power and navigation. But the final allocation made of the joint costs was 50 percent each to power and navigation.[111] It may be seen that the theory applied here is the equal apportionment theory.

In an attempt toward the unification of the practices of the Federal Government in cost allocation in multiple-purpose projects, the Federal Inter-Agency River Basin Committee in 1946 appointed a Subcommittee on Benefits and Costs for the study of this problem. The Subcommittee reported its recommendations to the parent Committee on 15 May 1950, which were adopted by the latter on 25 May 1950.[112] The method recommended for the allocation of the joint costs of a multiple-purpose project was a mixture of the benefit theory and the theory of alternative justiable expenditure. The traditional method for the calculation of the costs of single-purpose features was also slightly modified. The costs for the several purposes served by single-purpose features are called separable costs. "The separable cost for each project purpose is the difference between the cost of the multiple-purpose project and the cost of the project with the purpose omitted. Separable costs include more than the direct or specific costs of physically identifiable facilities serving only one purpose, such as irrigation distribution system. They also include all added costs of increased

size of structures and changes in design for a particular purpose over that required for all other purposes, such as the
cost of increasing reservoir storage capacity." The total
costs of the project as a whole deducted by the total of all
separable costs give the joint costs, which are divided among
the purposes included in proportion to the "remaining benefits!
of each of these purposes. The remaining benefits for each
purpose are the estimated benefits derivable therefrom (under
the benefit theory) or the alternative justiable cost of this
purpose (under the alternative justifiable expenditure theory),
whichever is smaller, minus the separable cost of this purpose
(which may be zero). The following is an illustration of the
recommended method:

Allocation of Costs by Separable Costs-Remaining Benefits Method

GENERAL CASE

[In thousands of dollars]

Item	Flood control	Power	Irriga-tion	Navi-gation	Total
1. Benefits	500	1,500	350	100	2,450
2. Alternate cost	400	1,000	600	80	2,080
3. Benefits limited by alternate cost (lesser of items 1 and 2)	400	1,000	350	80	1,830
4. Separate costs	380	600	150	50	1,180
5. Remaining benefits (items 3—4)	20	400	200	30	650
6. Allocated joint cost [1]	18	360	180	27	585
7. Total allocation (items 4+6)	398	960	330	77	1,765

[1] In this example, the total joint costs to be allocated ($585,000 in line 6) are 90 percent of total remaining benefits ($650,000 in line 5). Therefore each purpose is charged with joint costs equal to 90 percent of its remaining benefits. The same results will be obtained by using distribution ratios (percent of each item in line 5 to their total).

Although this method has been approved by the Inter-Agency
River Basin Committee, it has not yet been formally adopted
as the only applicable method by any of the Federal agencies
concerned.[113]

In the various multiple-purpose projects, hydroelectric
power is as a rule the main paying component. In the Bonneville navigation and power project, the capital investment for
power amounted, as of 30 June 1953, to $59,824,785.32 (com-
prising $59,561,589.76 of construction costs allocated to pow-
er, $196,293.73 of replacements and $66,901.83 of miscellaneous items). By that date, $20,343,163.00 of this sum had
been repaid. Besides this repayment of capital investment,
power revenues had left no arrears in the payment of $17,070,-
745.16 of accrued interest and $8,061,614.68 of maintenance
and operation costs.[114] As for the electric power transmission system, which costed a total of about $133 million as of
January 1950, $27.4 million has been paid back by that time.
The rate of repayment has been higher than was originally expected.[115] With respect to the Columbia Basin or Grand Coulee project, $36.7 million of the $218.4 million investment had
been reimbursed by 30 June 1952, which also testifies to the
tremendous earning ability of power.[116] Although the Tennessee Valley Authority system has been in a continuous process
of development, with investment added each year, by 30 June
1953 the said Authority had earned a net income (all from

power) of nearly $226 million, as against some $1,785 million of Congressional appropriations. It is true that only $50 million of the $226 million income were paid into the Federal Treasury toward the amortization of the Congressional appropriations.[117] However, there need not be any doubt but that with its rate of earning it will not find it difficult to amortize all Congressional appropriations with the 40-year periods, especially so as it is not required to pay interest thereon.[118]

Because of its high rate of return, power has been able to subsidize other purposes of water resources administration, particularly irrigation, which is required by law to be self-liquidating. In the Colorado River-Big Thompson project, Colorado, for example, the costs allocated to irrigation and power are respectively $99,356,000 and $63,224,000. However, power, besides repaying its own share of $63,224,000, is responsible for the repayment of $70,467,000 of the $99,356,000 allocated to irrigation.[119] In the Eden project, Wyoming, although the entire cost of construction, amounting to $6,152,-000, has been allocated to irrigation, only $1,500,000 is required to be repaid by the irrigation water users, while the balance, $4,652,000, is to be paid from the proposed Colorado River Storage Project power revenues.[120] In the combined Parker Dam and Davis Dam project (combined for the purpose of repayment)[121] in Arizona, California and Nevada, the combined reimbursable cost is $129,958,450, of which $106,014,361 is allocated to power, $13,646,011 to irrigation and $10,398,078 to Mexican Treaty service. It should be noted that all these allocations are to be repaid by power alone! [122] If in an average multiple-purpose project power is the main source of revenue, irrigation repayment is limited to the actual ability of the water users to pay and no reimbursement is required of the costs for navigation improvement and flood control, then it would seem that the whole process of cost allocation serves no other practical purpose than the determination of the rate of sale of power.

(c) Other Fields---The management of public lands by the Bureau of Land Management is a revenue-making enterprise. The sale of lands has been of course the largest item of the revenues, although this activity is hardly a productive undertaking. But even after the land sales have been practically brought to an end as a result of the passage of the Grazing Act in 1934, the enterprise of land management (by the said Bureau) has still been revenue-making. This is witnessed by the following table, in which are listed the total amounts of receipts of and appropriations to the Bureau of Land Management in each of the fiscal years 1941-1950, inclusive:[123]

Year	Receipts	Appropriations
1941	$ 8,654,796.56	$2,962,841
1942	9,914,134.99	2,983,958
1943	10,543,207.25	2,983,958

1944	15,168,693.69	3,526,818
1945	14,147,035.24	3,636,241
1946	13,840,333.83	4,124,622
1947	21,012,154.34	4,398,804
1948	33,286,434.23	4,540,677
1949	37,149,433.89	4,917,500
1950	36,177,349.42	5,939,187

The largest item of the receipts is the revenues derived from the Mineral Leasing Act of 25 February 1920, principally oil and gas rentals and royalties. This is shown by the following table:[124]

(Unit: $1,000)

Fiscal Year	Total Receipts	From Mineral Leases
1950	36,177	26,971
1951	49,082	34,951
1952	64,518	41,884
1953	66,846	43,532

At the hearings on public lands policy before the House of Representatives of the 80th Congress in April-May 1947, it was felt that the amount of grazing fees charged under the Grazing Act of 1934 should be limited to those costs for works and activities which directly or primarily benefit stockmen and should not include costs incurred for works and activities which primarily or directly benefit the general public, and that a careful analysis and allocation of costs was needed.[125] In the Interior Department Appropriation Act of 6 September 1950, there appeared the following appropriation (64 Stat. 595, 682):

> For construction, purchase and maintenance of range improvements pursuant to the provisions of sections 3 and 10 of the Act of June 28, 1934, as amended (43 U. S. C. 315), sums equal to the aggregate of all moneys received as range improvement fees under section 3 of said Act and of 25 percent of all moneys received under section 15 of said Act during the current and prior fiscal years but not yet appropriated, to remain available until expended.

Substantially the same provision has been incorporated in all subsequent Interior Department Appropriation Acts. Thus the management of grazing lands by the Bureau of Land Management has since the fiscal year 1949 been essentially a self-liquidating but not revenue-making undertaking.

The management of national forests is also productive of some sizable returns. The three main sources of income are timber selling, grazing and the grant of special-use permits. Total receipts from the national forests for some selective years are given below:[126]

Source	1910	1920	1930	1940	1950	1953
Timber sale	1,011	2,044	4,390	3,943	29,379	69,252
Grazing	970	2,486	1,943	1,463	3,385	4,416
Special permits	60	263	419	453	831	1,064
Total	2,041	4,793	6,752	5,859	33,595	74,732

"Many national forests more than pay their own way--that is, cash income exceeds operating costs, and, in several, both operating and investments." However, "areas above timber line and such non-commercial forest lands as, for example, the chaparran forests of southern California are largely of non-revenue producing character." Taken the various national forests as a whole, the costs have been higher than revenues,[127] although the tendency clearly points to the eventual reversal of this situation. The total amounts of the receipts from and expenditures on the national forests for the fiscal years 1944 to 1953, inclusive, are given in the following table:[128]

Year	Receipts	Expenditures
1944	$15,616,940	$59,866,675
1945	16,047,935	27,262,156
1946	13,875,091	32,624,609
1947	18,372,799	46,462,951
1948	24,956,254	45,105,793
1949	31,992,033	44,989,703
1950	33,594,614	50,043,610
1951	56,147,342	54,955,490
1952	69,720,198 (a)	59,235,758
1953	74,732,468 (b)	64,540,364

(a) Failing of self-liquidation due to payments to states ($17,490,091).

(b) Failing of self-liquidation due to payments to states ($18,783,086).

As provided by statute, "all revenues of the national parks shall be covered into the Treasury to the credit of miscellaneous receipts, . . . and the Secretary of the Interior is directed to submit, annually, estimates of the amounts required for the care, maintenance, and development of the said parks" (16 U. S. C. 452: Acts of 12 June 1917, sec. 1, 40 Stat. 153, and 24 May 1922, 42 Stat. 590). From the tone of this enactment, the National Park System is supposed to earn its own support. "There are four sources of revenues in a national park: 1. Taxes on concessions, which may be (a) a fixed portion of the authorized rate for service; (b) a reasonable arbitrary tax based on the number of guests accommodated during the season; (c) a stipulated annual fee fixed after careful analyzation of the concessioners' gross revenue, operating expenses, net profits and other elements; (d) a percentage of the gross receipts of the season's business; or (e) a fair share of the net profits of an enterprise. . . 2. Public utilities, such as water systems, electric power plants, telephone service, etc. 3. Natural resources . . . derived from the sale of dead timber, stone, hides of predatory animals, etc. 4. Automobile and motorcycle permits."[129] Among these, the last item (which may roughly be measured by the number of visitors) creates the lion's share of the total revenues of the National Park System.[130] The total amounts of Congressional appropriations to and revenues of the National Park Service, together with the total number of visitors, for the fiscal years 1941 to 1953, inclusive, are shown in the following table,[131] which clearly indicates that the degree of self-finance of the National Park System is relatively low. It is hardly able to support itself, even with the further help of contributions (to be discussed later).

NATIONAL PARK SERVICE

Summary of appropriations, revenues, and visitors

Year	Appropria- tions	Revenues	Visitors
1941	9,370,030	2,179,119	21,236,947
1942	14,609,775	2,080,702	9,370,969
1943	5,487,365	1,061,992	6,828,420
1944	4,563,560	807,601	8,339,775
1945	4,740,810	824,078	11,713,852
1946	5,487,375	1,592,947	21,752,315
1947	26,027,955	2,923,587	25,534,188
1948	10,628,055	3,303,328	29,858,828
1949	14,047,649	3,467,606	31,736,402
1950	30,104,850	3,527,607	33,252,589
1951	33,975,700[1]	3,534,372	37,106,440
1952	28,248,564	3,568,094	42,299,836
1953	33,162,330[1]	4,190,643	46,224,794[2]
1954	33,853,850	4,200,000[2]	47,500,000[2]
1955	28,468,000[2]	4,600,000[2]	50,000,000[2]

[1] Net appropriations after reductions pursuant to law.
[2] Estimated.

Among other self-financing programs may be mentioned the water-pollution-control projects of the California Debris Commission of the Department of the Army. According to sec. 23 of its Organic Act of 1 March 1893 (27 Stat. 507, 510), as last amended by an Act of 25 June 1938 (52 Stat. 1040; 33 U. S. C. 683), the beneficiaries of each of these projects should annually pay to the said Commission, "for each cubic yard mined from the natural bank, a tax equal to the total capital cost of the dam, reservoir, and rights-of-way divided by the total capacity of the reservoir for the restraint of debris . . ." In addition the Secretary of the Army (but not the said Commission) may "supply storage of water and use of outlet facilities from debris storage reservoirs for domestic, irrigation and power purposes", to further help in the self-finance of the respective projects. The self-finance covers both the costs of construction and the costs of maintenance. The Commission has constructed the Englebright and the North Fork Dams,[132] at a cost of $3,-924,675 and $738,400.[133] As of January 1955, total receipts of the debris taxes were estimated to be $60,000 for the Englebright Dam and Reservoir and $13,000 for the North Fork Dam and Reservoir. Receipts from the storage of water and use of outlet facilities were, as of the same date, $198,100 for the former and $1,500 for the latter.[134] It may be noted that there is no requirement for the payment of interest on the capital investment.

In the field of fish and wildlife, an Act was enacted on 16 March 1934 (48 Stat. 451), under which every person wishing to hunt migratory game birds should each year buy from a post office a Federal migratory-bird hunting stamp, the price of which is one dollar. The receipts from the sale of these stamps are used to help in the establishment and maintenance of Federal migratory-bird refuges.[135] However, since hunting and fishing in general are under state regulation, there are as a rule no charges for hunting and fishing in Federally owned or controlled areas in addition to license fees charged by state game and fish agencies. The only exception is the Elgin Field Reservation of the Department of Air Force, where, under an Act of 11 October 1949 (63 Stat. 759) paid permits are required for hunting or fishing for the purpose of making it self-liquidating. The management of the retired submarginal lands by the Forest Service (formerly by the Soil Conservation Service) also produces some revenues. In the following table are given revenues earned for the calendar years 1945-1952, inclusive:[136]

Year	Revenues
1945	$ 550,000
1946	728,341
1947	833,756
1948	995,793
1949	925,820
1950	1,021,430
1951	1,187,267
1952	1,752,455

Beginning with 1948, the revenues have exceeded all costs of operation and maintenance. Since 1951, the revenues have been able to cover both operation and maintenance costs and construction costs. In 1952, the revenues struck a fair balance against all expenditures on the retired lands (i.e., costs of operation amd maintenance and costs of construction) plus payments (25 percent of all revenues) to the several states, and established a record of net profits.

Navigation improvement (exclusive of terminal facilities)

is the only enterprise in Federal water resources administration which is capable of self-finance but in which self-finance is ruled out. Under sec. 4 of the River and Harbor Act of 4 July 1884 (23 Stat. 133, 147), as amended by sec. 6 of the River and Harbor Act of 3 March 1909 (35 Stat. 815, 818), no tolls or other charges can be collected by the Federal Government for the use of waterways constructed or improved by the Federal Government.[137] This prohibition, however, does not apply to the Panama Canal and the St. Lawrence Seaway, which are required by law to be at least self-liquidating.[138]

In the Federal licensing regulation of hydroelectric power development, there is found not only self-finance of this regulation, but that of the Federal water resources administration as a whole. For, according to sec. 17 of the Federal Power Act of 10 June 1920 (41 Stat. 1063, 1072), as amended by sec. 208 of the Act of 26 August 1935 (49 Stat. 803, 845), the license fees collected by the Federal Power Commission are to be in the following manner:

1. "All proceeds from any Indian reservation shall be placed to the credit of the Indians of such reservation."
2. Of the receipts collected from areas other Indian reservations, enough sum is to be used to reimburse the United States for the costs of the licensing administration.
3. The remainder of the receipts are to be distributed as follows:
    (a) 50 percent of the fees charges for the occupancy and use of public lands and national forests are to be paid into the Reclamation Fund to help in the finance of the irrigation projects of the Bureau of Reclamation.
    (b) 37.5 percent of the fees charged for the occupancy and use of public lands and national forests within the boundaries of any state are to be paid to the state.
    (c) 50 percent of the fees charged for the use of the waters of navigable watercourses and of water power in Federal owned structures are covered into a special fund in the Treasury of the United States to be expended by the Department of the Army "in the maintenance and operation of dams and other navigation structures owned by the United States or in the construction, maintenance, or operation of headwater or other improvements of navigable waters of the United States."

From 11 June 1920 to 30 December 1952, receipts from the licensing fees totalled $23,520,684.41, which were made in the following manner:[139]

(a) For use of Indian lands: $ 2,802,593.05
(b) For use of public lands and
     national forests: 2,170,396.98
(c) For use of navigable waters and
     Federal-owned dams: 7,074,698.23
(d) Administrative fees: 12,072,996.15

The receipts were distributed as follows:[139]

(a) For reimbursement of costs of administration (begin-
     ning with the calendar year 1935): $9,446,780.50
(b) For payment to the Indian funds: 2,802,593.05
(c) For payment to the Reclamation Fund: 1,329,244.45
(d) For payment to a special fund under the
     control of the Secretary of the Army: 4,453,639.81
(e) For payment to the several states: 996,933.21
(f) Balance, covered into the Treasury: 4,638,722.16

In some of the self-financing programs, there are specific
statutory stipulations as to the use of the revenues (besides
requirements for payments to states and their administrative
subdivisions). As mentioned above, all receipts from grazing
fees collected under the Grazing Act of 1934 must be used for
the improvement of the ranges. In the Agriculture Department
Appropriation Act of 4 March 1913 (37 Stat. 828), it is provided that "ten percentum of all moneys received from the national forests during each fiscal year shall be available at
the end thereof, to be expended by the Secretary of **Agriculture**
for the construction and maintenance of roads and trails within the national forests in the states where such proceeds are
derived . . ." (at 843: 16 U. S. C. 501, 1st sentence). These
and similar provisions and arrangements are limitations on the
fiscal authority of the Congress, and concessions which the
latter made either to the interested groups or to the Federal
administrative agencies concerned.

Self-finance does not in itself infer fiscal autonomy, which
must be granted by special statutory enactment, if by fiscal
autonomy it is meant the dispensing of Congressional appropriations. Among all self-financing agencies or programs of the
Federal Government, only the Tennessee Valley Authority has complete latitude in the disposal of its revenues. According to
sec. 26 of the its Organic Act (48 Stat. 71, 49 Stat. 1079; 16
U. S. C. 831y), the said Authority may hold for its own disposition without forwarding them to the Congress such part of its
earnings "as in the opinion of the Board shall be necessary for
the Corporation in the operation of dams and reservoirs, in conducting its business in generating, transmitting and distributing electric energy and in manufacturing, selling and distributing fertilizer and fertilizer ingredients", in addition to a
continuing fund of $1,000,000 for emergency uses. From the be-
ginning of its operation in 1933 to 30 June 1953, the Tennessee
Valley Authority earned a net income of some $226 million. Of
this, only $81 million was paid back to the Federal Treasury,

the remaining being disposed of by the Authority itself in re-
investment in electric power facilities.[140] The Bonneville
Power Administration, which represents certain multiple-purpose
hydroelectric power projects of the Corps of Engineers and the
Bureau of Reclamation, has financial freedom only over the
$500,000 continuing fund.[141] In all other cases all revenues
of the Federal Government from its self-financing programs
must be delivered to the Federal Treasury and deposited either
in the general fund or in the various special funds, which cannot be touched except by Congressional appropriation.

3. Contributions---Contributions may be made to the Federal Government either by private individuals or groups or by
states or their local units. Contributions are made voluntarily. In some cases, however, the contribution of funds by a
non-Federal party or parties is statutorily stipulated to be
a condition for the initiation of a Federal administrative program or project. In such cases, the said party or parties are
actually compelled to make the constributions, although the
contributions so made are still voluntary (because they are on
a contractual basis) and not compulsory.

Contributions have existed in many enterprises of Federal
water resources administration. In the field of navigation improvement and flood control, the statute has authorized the
Secretary of the Army "to receive from private parties such
funds as may be contributed by them to be expended in connection with funds appropriated by the United States for any authorized work of public improvement of rivers and harbors, whenever such work and expenditure may be considered by the Chief
of Engineers as advantageous to the interests of navigation."[142]
Under this provision, the amount of the contributions required
of the private parties benefited in each project would be determined by the Chief of Engineers of the Department of the
Army. When contributions are made in excess of the prescribed
amount, "then such excess contributions may, with the approval
of the Secretary of War (the Army), be returned to the proper
representatives of the contributing interests", in the absence
of contrary statutory provisions.[143] With respect to flood
control particularly, local contributions to Federal flood-control projects have been provided for in flood control laws for
the Mississippi and Sacramento Rivers. In the Act of 1 March
1917 (39 Stat. 948), it was provided that at least one half of
the moneys required for the construction and repair of levees
on the Mississippi River and its tributaries should be contributed by the local interests benefited (948) and that the State
of California should contribute annually for the control of
floods, the removal of debris and the general improvement of
the Sacramento River a sum equal to the sum of funds appropriated by the United States for the same purposes (949). In the
Act of 17 May 1928, the state or the levee districts concerned
were required to contribute one-third of the costs of the construction of flood-control works on the Mississippi River be-

tween Rock Island, Illinois, and Cape Girardeau, Missouri and
on such outlets and tributaries of the Mississippi River between Rock Island and the Head of Passes as were affected by
the backwaters of the Mississippi River (45 Stat. 534, 536).

Some contributions to flood-control and navigation-improvement works were made in exchange for certain specific and concrete rights or benefits, in the fashion of commercial transactions. In the second and third paragraphs of sec. 5 of the
Flood Control Act of 22 June 1936, as added by the War Department Civil Functions Appropriation Act of 19 July 1937 (50
Stat. 515, 518), authority is given the Secretary of the Army
to receive, upon the recommendation of the Chief of Engineers,
contributions from states or local units to any dam and reservoir flood-control project and to provide additional storage
for domestic water supply or other conservation storage for the
benefit of the contributors. For example, by March 1952, the
City of Fargo, North Dakota, had contributed about $160,000 to-
wards the cost of the Bald Hill Dam on the Sheyenne River "for
the privilege of diverting a portion of the flow from the Sheyenne River into the Red River in time of need."[144] In the River and Harbor Act of 30 June 1948, the navigation-improvement
project of the Neches and Angelina Rivers of Texas was modified
and permission was given local interests to withdraw from the
pool of Dam B not to exceed 2,000 cubic feet of water per second for municipal use at the payment of a contribution of $5
million (62 Stat. 1174).

In the enterprise of irrigation, contributions are accepta-
ble under sec. 2 of the Water Conservation and Utilization Act
of 14 October 1940 (54 Stat. 1119). With respect to regular
irrigation projects, contributions for construction work are
usually limited to distribution works of certain particular projects. For example, the distribution system of the Upper Snake
River Storage of the Minidoka project in Idaho was built with
private funds.[145] In the Deschutes project, Oregon, "the Pacific Power and Light Company, by June 30, 1946, paid for work
performed by the Bureau in improving its facilities. The City
of Prineville is obligated to pay for a concrete siphon built
by the Bureau of Reclamation."[146] However, as the costs of construction of the Federal irrigation projects are to be returned through reimbursement by the water users, the costs of investigation of such projects are to be partly reimbursed by contributions from states or local units or private parties concerned. In the Joint Resolution of 7 June 1924 (43 Stat. 668),
it was provided that at least one-half of the costs of investigation and planning of the proposed Casper-Alcova project in
Wyoming, the Deschutes project in Oregon and the Southern Las-
sen project in California should be "advanced by the states in
which the project is located, or by parties interested." In
the Second Deficiency Appropriation Act of 5 December 1924, a
general provision was incorporated which authorizes the Secretary of the Interior "to receive moneys from any state, municipality, irrigation district, individual, or other interest,

public or private, expend the same in connection with moneys
appropriated by the United States for any such cooperative investigation, and return to the contributors any moneys so con-
tributed in excess of the actual cost of that portion of the
work properly chargeable to the contributors" (43 Stat. 672,
685). In the Interior Department Appropriation Act of 1 July
1946, it was provided that at least 50 percent of all costs
of investigations of a project of the Bureau of Reclamation[147]
should be contributed by the state, local unit or special interests which requested the investigations (60 Stat. 348, 365).
This provision has been reiterated in all subsequent Interior
Department Appropriation Acts.[148]

In the administration of the national forests, "under the
provisions of the Act of June 30, 1914 (38 Stat. 430; 16 U. S.
C. 498), contributions may be accepted by the Forest Service
for such cooperative projects as access roads and trails; camp-
ground construction and maintenance; fencing; stream, lake and
range improvements; and similar improvements to facilitate
wildlife management on, and related protection of the national
forests."[149] Under the provisions of sec. 3 of an Act of 9
June 1930 (46 St t. 527), "the Secretary of Agriculture may,
when in his judgment such action will be in the public interest, require any purchaser of national-forest timber to make
deposits of money, in addition to the payments for the timber,
to cover the cost to the United States of (1) planting (including the production or purchase of young trees), (2) sowing with
tree seeds (including the collection or purchase of such seeds),
or (3) cutting, destroying, or otherwise removing undesirable
trees or other growth, on the national-forest land cut over by
the purchaser, in order to improve the future stand of timber:
Provided, That the total amount so required to be deposited by
any purchaser shall not exceed, on an acreage basis, the average cost of planting (including the production or purchase of
young trees) other comparable national-forest lands during the
previous three years" (first sentence). On 27 March 1946 (11
F. R. 3245), regulations were issued[150] by the Secretary of Agriculture under the authority of sec. 18 of the Federal Highway
Act of 9 November 1921 (42 Stat. 212, 216, which is rather vague)
which authorized the Chief of Forest Service to enter into cooperative agreements with interested parties providing for
their contributions toward the investigation, construction and
maintenance of forest development roads and trails in national
forests.[151]

In the program of the control of white-pine blister rust
as authorized by the Act of 26 **April** 1940 (54 Stat. 168), the
Secretary of Agriculture, under the provisions of the same law,
may require non-Federal parties to make contributions toward
the control work performed on their lands, except where such
lands are inseparably intermingled with Federal lands.

In the program of predator and rodent control of the Fish

and Wildlife Service, the major part of the funds expended has
come from non-Federal contributions, as is shown by the following chart:[152]

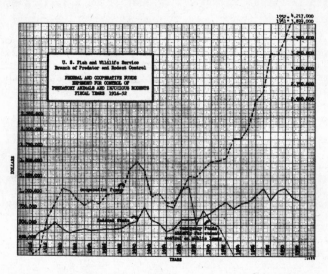

Under the Grazing Act of 1934 (sec. 9), the Secretary of
the Interior may accept contributions for the administration
and management of lands within the various grazing districts.
The program of watershed protection and improvement administered by the **U. S. Forest** Service is in many instances insus-
ceptible of an accurate administrative analysis. But there can
be no doubt that certain types of work under this program may
be performed by the Federal Government with the help of non-
Federal contributions.

Under the authority of an Act of 27 February 1925 (43 Stat.
1011), the Geological Survey may enter into cooperative agreements with states or local units for the making of topographic
and hydrographic surveys, the expenses of which are shared between the Federal Government and such non-Federal parties. In
the Interior Department Appropriation Act of 7 March 1928, it
was provided that Federal expenditure in such surveys should in
no case exceed one-half of the total expenses incurred. This
requirement has been reiterated in all subsequent Interior Department Appropriation Acts. Contributions have been made by
every state for such surveys.[153]

In all these cases, contributions are _imposed_ upon the non-
Federal parties by the Federal Government, which also stipulates the amounts of the contributions. The non-Federal parties in these cases have only the choice of making the required
contributions or suffering the denial of the desired Federal
services. The administration of the national park system is

perhaps the only enterprise of Federal water resources administration in which contributions are made by way of donation by
the general public instead of special interest groups without
the expectation of corporeal benefits. The donations may be
either accepted by the Secretary of the Interior, under the
provisions of sec. 1 of an Act of 5 June 1920 (41 Stat. 917)
and sec. 4 of an Act of 10 July 1935 (49 Stat. 477, 478), or by
the National Park Trust Fund Board under the authority of sec.
2 of the latter Act.

    4. Borrowing---Borrowing has been resorted to by the Fed-
eral Government as a financial device in the various enterprises of water resources administration only in very exceptional
cases. On 25 June 1910, an Act was enacted (36 Stat. 835) which
authorized the Secretary of the Treasury to advance to the Secretary of the Interior for the construction of irrigation projects a maximum sum of $20 million and to issue certificates of
indebtedness bearing a maximum annual interest of 3 percent for
this purpose. As a matter of fact, such certificates (which
were in the nature of bonds) were not issued, and $20 million
were taken out from the general fund of the Treasury.[154] This
Act originally provided (sec. 3) that beginning five years after the date of the first advnace, fifty percent of the annual
receipts of the reclamation fund should be paid into the general fund to repay the advances; but by an amendment adopted
on 12 June 1917 (40 Stat. 149) the Secretary of the Interior
was directed to pay into the general fund $1 million from the
reclamation fund each year beginning 1 July 1930. By a series
of enactments, the beginning date was extended to 1 July 1938.[155]
On 3 March 1931, an Act was passed (46 Stat. 1507) which authorized the Secretary of the Treasury, with the approval of the
President, to make another loan to the Secretary of the Interior for the same purpose in the sum of $5 million, the reimburse-
ment of which was to be made "by transfer annually of the sum
of $1,000,000 from the reclamation fund to the general funds
in the Treasury beginning July 1, 1933." But the reimbursement
date was also extended to 1 July 1938.[155] These two loans totalled $25 million, of which $10 million had been repaid by 9
may 1938. On that date, the Interior Department Appropriation
Act for the fiscal year 1939 was passed, in which there was a
provision providing for the transfer (a grant) to the credit
of the reclamation fund 52.5 percent of all moneys which accrued
to the United States from lands within the naval petroleum reserves, except those in Alaska, from 25 February 1920 to 30
June 1938 and for the deduction therefrom of $15 million for
the liquidation of the loans (52 Stat. 291, 322-323).[156] These
two loans were thus completely repaid.

    In sec. 37 of the Agricultural Adjustment Act of 12 May (48
Stat. 31, 50), "the Reconstruction Finance Corporation, upon
request of the Secretary of the Interior, is authorized and empowered to advance . . . to the reclamation fund . . . such sum
or sums as the Secretary of the Interior may deem necessary,

not exceeding $5,000,000, for the completion of projects or divisions of projects now under construction or projects approved and authorized. Funds so advanced shall be repaid out of any receipts and accretions accruing to the reclamation fund within such time as may be fixed by the Reconstruction Finance Corporation, not exceeding five years from the date of advance, with interest at the rate of 4 percentum per annum." This provision however, was not taken advantage of by the Secretary of the Interior, because of the passage of the National Industrial Recovery Act shortly afterwards.[157]

The Tennessee Valley Authority, under sec. 15 of its Organic Act of 18 May 1933 (48 Stat. 66), was authorized to issue bonds aggregating a maximum sum of $50 million maturing within a maximum period of fifty years and bearing a maximum interest of 3.5 percent per annum, for the construction of electric facilities. Under sec. 15a of the same Act, which was added on 31 August 1935 (49 Stat. 1078), the Authority was authorized to issue up to $50 million bonds for the purpose of making loans to states, municipalities and non-profit organizations. On 26 July 1939, sec. 15c of the said Act was enacted (53 Stat. 1083) which granted authority to the Tennessee Valley Authority to issue bonds in the maximum amount of $61,500,000 for the same purpose as well as for the acquisition and construction of electric facilities. Under these provisions, the following bond issues have been made:[158]

Under sec. 15 of the T. V. A. Act:

1. 1 September 1938, $2,000,000, for the acquisition of certain properties of the Tennessee Public Service Company.
2. 23 December 1938, $1,000,000, for the acquisition of certain properties of the Kentucky-Tennessee Light and Power Company and the West Tennessee Power and Light Company, and for the construction of interconnections.
3. 22 June 1939, $5,300,000, for the acquisition of certain properties of the Memphis Power and Light Company and the construction of interconnections.

    The above three issues, totalling $8,300,000, were sold at par to the reconstruction Finance Corporation and bore an annual interest rate of 2.5 percent.

Under sec. 15a of the same Act: 9 January 1939, $272,500, bearing an interest rate of 2.8 percent, sold to the U. S. Treasury.

Under sec. 15c of the same Act: 15 August 1939, $56,500,000, bearing an interest rate varying from 1.75 to 2.5 percent per year, sold to the U. S. Treasury for the acquisition and rehabilitation of properties of the Tennessee Electric Power Company, and for related purposes.

The total amount of all these bond-issues was $65,072,500.
As of 30 June 1953, $31,072,500 of this amount had been retired,
with $34,000,000 outstanding.159

The Saint Lawrence Seaway Development Corporation, under
sec. 5 of its Organic Act of 13 May 1954 (68 Stat. 92), may
from time to time issue revenue bonds to the United States Treasury, which shall in no time aggregate more than $105 million.
Information is not as yet available as to whether any revenue
bonds have actually been so issued by the said Corporation.

It may be noted that all the borrowings discussed so far
were credit extended to some Federal agency by another Federal
agency, and that they do not constitute indebtedness of the
Federal Government in any manner whatsoever.160

Under an Act of 15 October 1940 (54 Stat. 1176), advances
may be made to the Secretary of the Army by a state or local
unit for the construction of a duly adopted and authorized flood-
control project, such advances to be repaid by the said Secretary without interest from subsequent Congressional appropriations. These advances are nothing but short-terms loans, although it should be **remarked** that unlike ordinary loans, these
loans are not made to meet shortage of funds on the part of the
Federal Government, which is the borrower, but are made rather
voluntarily by the "creditors" in order to hurry the construction of certain Federal projects to their own benefit.

It may be concluded that there is no Federal borrowing in
the customary meaning of the term in water resources administration, with the only exception of the Panama Canal, the discussion of which is omitted.

5. Special Funds---Special funds are funds established by
special statutory enactments in the United States Treasury
which are separate and distinct from the general fund and which
are devoted to special administrative programs or projects.
The establishment of each special fund, which is to be expended-
for certain specified purpose or purposes, is an act of self-
limitation on the part of the Congress. A special fund is characterized either by a fixed amount of money or by a specially
designated source or sources of revenue or both. Some special
funds are trust funds, which are derived from sources to which
the Federal Government is not legally entitled, and which are
held by the Federal Government in its capacity of a trustee.
The establishment of a special fund does not in itself carry
financial autonomy. But financial autonomy can be attached to
a special fund as a result of special Congressional authoriza-
tion.161

Special funds may be distinguished into (1) "enterprise
funds", which are established for the primary purpose of financing a certain program or project, and (2) "fiscal funds", which

are created not so much to facilitate the administration of administrative programs or projects as to prevent certain revenues from deviation to undesired uses. The former may be further divided into "complete enterprise funds", which are used or supposed to finance all the expenses incurred in the administration of a certain administrative program or project (including investigation, planning, construction, acquisition, operation and maintenance), and "operating funds", which are merely used to keep a completed program or project going. Even a complete enterprise fund may not be self-sufficient, for at times it may be necessary to augment it with allocations from the general fund. The various kinds of special funds which exist in water resources administration are separately discussed below.

(a) Complete Enterprise Funds---The most important of these is no doubt the Reclamation Fund. This special was established by sec. 1 of the Reclamation Act of 17 June 1902 (32 Stat. 388) for the examination, construction and maintenance of irrigation projects in the seventeen Western states.[162] The initial moneys of this fund, as provided in the same provision, consisted of the proceeds from the sale, lease and other forms of disposal of public lands in these seventeen states, beginning with the fiscal year 1 July 1900-30 June 1901, "including the surplus of fees and commissions in excess of allowances to registers and receivers, and excepting the five percentum of the proceeds of the sales of public lands in the above states set aside by law for educational and other purposes . . ." Accruals to the Reclamation are derived from the following categories of sources:

1. Incomes from the irrigation projects themselves:
    (i)   Water charges --- Under sec. 5 of the Reclamation Act of 1902 (4th sentence).
    (ii) Proceeds from the sale of surplus water for non-irrigation uses---Under Act of 25 February 1920 (41 Stat. 451).
    (iii) Receipts from the Warren Act---Under sec. 3 of the said Act (36 Stat. 925, 926).
    (iv) All other receipts, including that part of the power revenues which is used to repay construction costs allocated to power---Under the Interior Department Appropriation Act of 9 May 1938 (52 Stat. 291, 322-323).
2. Accruals related to the construction and operation of irrigation projects:
    (i)   Proceeds from the sale, lease and other forms of disposition of project lands and properties---Under the following acts: Acts of 3 March 1905, sec. 1 (33 Stat. 1032, sale of material and property, and refunding of moneys in connection with the operation of the projects); 16 Aptil 1906, sec. 2 (34 Stat. 116, sale of project lands as town sites); 27 June 1906, sec. 3 (34 Stat. 519, sale of town

sites established on lands in or near projects);
11 June 1910 (36 Stat. 466, same); 2 February 1911
(36 Stat. 895, sale of project lands); 19 July 1919
(41 Stat. 202, lease of project and sale of products therefrom); 20 May 1920 (41 Stat. 605, sale
of project lands); 16 May 1930 (46 Stat. 367, sale
of unproductive project lands and contiguous small
tracts to homesteaders and resident farmers); 27
September 1944 (58 Stat. 745, sale of sand, stone,
gravel, vegetation and timber and other forest
products on project lands); 31 March 1950 (64 Stat.
39, sale of small tracts of project lands to resident farmers and entrymen).

- (ii) Contributions for surveys, construction or development work---Under the Interior Department Appropriation Act of 4 March 1921 (41 Stat. 1367, 1404).
- (iii) Moneys collected from defaulting contractors or
their sureties---Under an Act of 6 June 1930 (46
Stat. 522).

3. Extraneous sources:
- (i) Royalties and rentals of the lease of potassium
deposits on public lands---Act of 2 October 1917,
sec. 10 (40 Stat. 297, 300).
- (ii) Bonuses, royalties and other receipts of mineral
leases---Act of 25 February 1920 (Mineral Leasing
Act), sec. 35 (41 Stat. 437, 450).
- (iii) Fifty percent of licensing fees collected by the
Federal Power Commission for the occupancy and
use of public lands, national monuments, national
forests and national parks---Federal Water Power
Act of 10 June 1920, sec. 17 (41 Stat. 1063, 1072).
4. Borrowings---See p. 1311, above.
5. Special Congressional appropriations---Only one such
appropriation, which, as mentioned before, was made by
the Interior Department Appropriation Act of 9 May
1938 (52 Stat. 291, 318). It should be noted that
this appropriation was made of funds derived a
special source of Federal revenue.

It may be noted that receipts under categories 1 and 2 are
in general deposited to the credit of the particular project
concerned in each case, but not to the Reclamation Fund as a
whole. Receipts from categroeis 3, 4 and 5 are, however, accruals to the whole Fund.

An Act of 25 January 1917 (39 Stat. 868) authorized the
Yuma Mesa project in Arizona as an auxiliary reclamation project (sec. 1). All moneys received from the sale of project
irrigable lands and water rights of this project were not to
be covered into the Reclamation Fund, but into a seperate fund
called the auxiliary reclamation fund of the Yuma project, Arizona (sec. 3). But by a provision in the Interior Department

Appropriation Act of 9 May 1935 (49 Stat. 176, 198) this special fund was abolished and consolidated with the Reclamation Fund.

As of 30 June 1952, total receipts into the Reclamation Fund amounted to $753,582,747.18, which were distributed among the various sources as follows:[163]

Water charges and rentals:	$234,532,183.48
Leases and sales of public lands:	119,111,436.71
Mineral leases:	197,797,130.25
Royalties, rentals, rights-of-way and licenses:	6,879,455.33
Power sales:	191,434,736.17
Other sources:	3,827,805.24
Total:	$753,582,747.18

Prior to 1 July 1915, funds were expended from the Reclamation Fund by allotments authorized by the Secretary of the Interior.[164] In this period, there was thus financial autonomy in the administration of the Reclamation Fund. In sec. 16 of the Reclamation Ext4nsion Act of 13 August 1914 (38 Stat. 686, 690), it was provided that "from and after July 1, 1915, expenditures shall not be made for carrying out the purposes of the Reclamation law except out of appropriations made annually by Congress therefor . . . out of the Reclamation Fund . . ." This brought to an end the financial autonomy of the Secretary of the Interior over the Reclamation Fund. The first Congressional appropriation of the Reclamation Fund was made in the Sundry Civil Appropriation Act of 3 March 1915 (38 Stat. 822, 859). By 30 June 1952, a total of $685,547,208 was appropriated from the Reclamation Fund.[165]

Although the Reclamation Fund was orignally designed to finance the construction and operation of all regular irrigation projects, it has as a matter of fact failed of this objective. "The construction funds are allocated between the general fund and the reclamation fund on the basis of their legislative history. The larger multiple-purpose projects[166] are financed from the general fund. The smaller irrigation developments are financed from the reclamation fund. Prior to the fiscal year 1951, work under the Boulder Canyon Act was financed by advances to the Colorado River Dam Fund from the general fund, but is now financed directly from the general fund."[167] All the water conservation and utilization projects are financed by the general fund. Up to 30 June 1953, expenditures on the irrigation projects of the Bureau of Reclamation had totalled $2,940,162,042, of which $1,884,816,294 came from the general fund, $758,492,-658 from the Reclamation Fund, $192,478,530 from emergency appropriations (part of the general fund), $77,511,780 from permanent appropriations (part of the general fund) and $26,862,-780 from the Colorado River Dam Fund.[168]

The Colorado River Dam Fund is another complete enterprise fund.[169] It was created by sec. 2 of the Boulder Canyon Project Act of 21 December 1928 (45 Stat. 1057). It is a complete enterprise fund because "all revenues received in carrying out the provisions of this Act (i.e., in the operation of the Boulder Canyon or Hoover Dam and appurtenant power facilities and the All-American Canal) shall be paid into and expenditures (i.e., expenditures in the construction and operation and maintenance of these works) shall be made out of the fund, under the direction of the Secretary of the Interior" (sec. 2(a), 2nd sentence).

So far as its financial nature is concerned, "that fund is set up for dual purposes. It was to be the recipient of the advances from the General Treasury, and it was to be the source of payments for construction. That was the first purpose . . . The other purpose was that the same fund is to function in the reverse order. It is to receive the revenues from the electric energy and from water."[170] Only in its first function of receiving the advances made by the United States Treasury is the fund **strictly** an enterprise fund. Such advances are of two kinds, namely, original advances and re-advances. The former are provided for by sec. 2(b) of the Boulder Canyon Project Act, which stipulates, among other things, that "the Secretary of the Treasury is authorized to advance to the fund from time to time and within appropriations therefor, such amounts as the Secretary of the Interior deems necessary for carrying out the provisions of this Act, except that the aggregate amount of such advances shall not exceed the sum of $165,000,000" (1st sentence). The original advances are "available only for expenditures for construction and the payment of interest during construction upon the amounts so advanced" and "no expenditures out of the fund shall be made for operation and maintenance except from appropriations therefor" (sec. 2(c)). The sum of $165,000,000 represents the estimated construction of the entire Boulder Canyon Project, including the Hoover Dam, power facilities and the All-American Canal system, plus interest accrued during the construction period.[171] This estimated cost of construction was, however, too conservative, for the construction cost of the Hoover Dam and the power facilities (without the All-American Canal system) at the beginning of 1954 was estimated to be $172,660,000.[172]

The re-advances are provided for by sec. 5 of the Boulder Canyon Project Adjustment of 19 July (54 Stat. 774, 777), which reads:

> If at any time there shall be insufficient sums in the Colorado River Dam Fund to meet the cost of replacements, however necessited, in addition to meeting the other requirements of this Act (to be discussed later), or of regulations authorized hereby and promulgated by the Secretary (of the Interior),

the Secretary of the Treasury, upon request of the
Secretary of the Interior, shall readvance to the
said fund, in amounts not exceeding, in the aggregate, moneys repaid to the Treasury pursuant to
sec. 2(b) hereof (to be discussed later), the amount
required for replacements, however necessitated, in
excess of the amount currently available therefor
in the Colorado River Dam Fund . . . All such re-
advances shall bear interest.

It may thus be seen the re-advances are purely transient in nature and are used only to make replacements. They do not add
to the total indebtedness which the Fund owes to the United
States Treasury. They are not additions to the original advances, though they necessarily postpone the repayment. thereof.
It may be noted that while the original advances are made in
the form of Congressional appropriations, the re-advances are
made by the administrative action of the Secretary of the Treasury.

That the entire Colorado River Dam Fund is a debt to the
United States Treasury distinguishes itself from the Reclamation Fund which, though reimbursable, is not considered as a
loan of the general fund. It is probably in the light of this
difference that while the general reclamation laws "simply require that repayment contracts be obtained before water is delivered", the Boulder Canyon Project Act has "required that revenue contracts adequate to liquidate the investment (i.e., the
original advances), both in the dam and All-American Canal, be
obtained in advance of construction and indeed in advance of
appropriations (sec. 4(b))."[173]

It may be noted that expenditures for the construction of
the Boulder Canyon Project (including both the Hoover Dam and
the All-American Canal and their appurtenant works) "were made
from the Colorado River Dam Fund created by advances from the
General Treasury on appropriation by Congress through fiscal
year 1950.[174] Thereafter expenditures have been made from appropriations for construction and rehabilitation, Bureau of Reclamation."[175] Thus beginning with the fiscal year 1951, the
Colorado River Dam Fund as an enterprise fund has been out of
existence. "Advances made by the Secretary of the Treasury for
construction of the dam, power plant, and appurtenant works a-
mounted to $158,099,940.62, as of May 31, 1952, of which $25,-
000,000 has been allocated by law to flood control benefits."
As of the same date, "a total of $70,456,302.41 has been return-
ed to the Treasury, of which $54,041,467.47 was in payment of
interest at 3 percent and $16,414,834.94 was in repayment of ad-
vances."[176]

The Colorado River Dam Fund, like the Reclamation Fund, has
failed of being a complete enterprise fund, as the sum of $165,-
000,000 is not sufficient to cover the actual construction cost

of the Boulder Canyon Project.

In the above discussion, the Colorado River Dam Fund is regarded as a "deficit" fund. But in one capacity it is not a deficit fund but rather a "credit" fund, expenditures from which, like those from the Reclamation Fund, are to be reimbursed.[177] In the above-cited sec. 2(c) of the Boulder Canyon Project Act of 1928, it is provided, inter alia, that "no expenditures out of the fund shall be made for operation and maintenance except from appropriations therefor" (2nd sentence). According to this provision, and also sec. 2(a) of the Boulder Canyon Project Adjustment Act of 1940, appropriation may be made from the Colorado River Dam Fund, which is thus looked upon as a credit fund, to defray the costs of operation and maintenance of the Boulder Canyon project, which are reimbursable (secs. 4 and 14 of the Project Act). Since all original advances are to be used only for construction, they cannot be re-appropriated for operation and maintenance. Thus only the receipts and not the advances into the fund are available for the latter purpose. This is clearly provided in sec.2(a) of the Adjustment Act. But it is with reference to its receipts that the Colorado River Dam Fund is a credit fund.

Appropriations from the Colorado River Dam began with the fiscal year 1937, and, up to 30 June 1953, had reached the total of $26,862,780.[178] All these appropriations were used in the operation and maintenance of the project.[179]

As the costs of operation and maintenance (including replacements) are financed only by appropriations from the receipts of the Colorado River Dam Fund and re-advances (for replacements only) made to the Fund by the Secretary of the Treasury, the Colorado River Dam Fund is a complete enterprise fund so far as the operation and maintenance of the Boulder Canyon project is concerned.

In sec. 15 of the Project Act, it is provided that

The Secretary of the Interior is authorized and directed to make investigation and public reports of the feasibility of projects for irrigation, generation of electric power, and other purposes in the states of Arizona, Nevada, Colorado, New Mexico, Utah and Wyoming for the purpose of making such information, available to such states and to the Congress, and of formulating a comprehensive scheme of control and the improvement and utilization of the water of the Colorado River and its tributaries. The sum of $250,000 is hereby authorized to be appropriated from said Colorado River Dam Fund . . . (45 Stat. 1057, 1065, emphasis added).

In the strict terminology of this provision, the Colorado River Dam Fund as a credit fund would have served another purpose, namely, the payment of $250,000 for the conduct of investiga-

tions of irrigation and other projects in the above-listed
states. As a matter of fact, however, moneys needed for this
purpose were made, prior to 1940, a part of the original advances, and thus statutorily were considered as part of the
construction cost of the Boulder Canyon project. Under the Adjustment Act of 1940, a separate fund called the Colorado River
Development Fund (to be discussed below) was established which
has been made the above-cited sec. 15 of the Project Act in-
operative.[180]

The Colorado River Development Fund, created by sec. 2(d)
of the Boulder Canyon Project Adjustment of 19 July 1940 (54
Stat. 774, 775-776), is a complete enterprise fund, which is,
however, inadequate to cover all the costs of the enterprise
to which it is devoted. This fund is made up of transfers from
the Colorado River Dam Fund "of the sum of $500,000 for the
year of operation ending May 31, 1938, and the like sum of
$500,000 for each year of operation thereafter, until and in-
cluding the year of operation ending May 31, 1987". "Receipts
of the Colorado River Development Fund for the years of operation ending in 1938, 1939 and 1940 are authorized to be appropriated only for the continuation and extension, under the dis-
credtion of the Secretary (of the Interior), of studies and investigations by the Bureau of Reclamation for the formulation
of a comprehensive plan for the utilization of waters of the
Colorado River system for irrigation, electrical power and other
purposes, in the states of the upper division and the states of
the lower division . . .[181] The next such receipts up to and
including the receipts for the year of operation ending in 1955
are authorized to be apportioned only for the investigation and
construction of projects for such utilization in and equitably
distributed among the four states of the upper division." "Such
receipts for the years of operation ending in 1956 to 1987, inclusive, are authorized to be apportioned for the investigation
and construction of projects for such utilization in and equitably distributed among the states of the upper division and the
states of the lower division."[182]

According to this provision, the Colorado River Development
Fund has, since 1941, been available either for investigation
or construction. However, up to 1954, no appropriations from
this fund have been used for construction purposes.

The Colorado River Development Fund has the potentiality of
financing the construction and operation of all water-utilization projects in the Colorado River Basin subsequent to the
Boulder Canyon project.[183] But this potentiality cannot be re-
alized unless the fund is augmented with additional sources.[184]
As a matter of fact, all costs of construction and operation
and maintenance of other projects of the Bureau of Reclamation
(Parker Dam, Davis Dam, Paonia and Eden projects) than the Boulder Canyon project have been appropriated from the general fund
and the Reclamation Fund. The plan of the proposed Upper Colorado River Storage Project even calls for the establishment of

a separate **enterprise** fund.[185] In sec. 2 of the Act of 1 June
1948 (62 Stat. 274, 285), it is made clear that the Colorado
River Development Fund is not the only fund available for the
construction of new projects of water utilization in the Colorado River Basin. This provision clarifies the nature and
function of the Colorado River Development Fund, but it cannot
settle the confusion created by the co-existence of several
funds earmarked for the same purpose.[186]

It may be noted that all of the enterprise funds discussed
above are connected with the enterprise of the Bureau of Reclamation and that none of them is accompanied by financial autonomy on the part of the said Bureau or the Department of the
Interior.

(b) Operating Funds---In the Tennessee Valley Authority
Act of 18 May 1933 (sec. 26: 48 Stat. 58, 71), "a continuing
fund or $1,000,000" is established which is used "to defray
emergency expenses and to insure continuous operation " of the
works of the said Authority. In the Bonneville Project Act of
20 August 1937, there is provision (sec. 11: 50 Stat. 731, 736)
for the creation of a continuing fund of $500,000, for similar
purposes. Identical provision is found in the Fort Peck Project of 18 May 1938 (52 Stat. 403, 406-407). Continuing funds
have also been established for the Southwestern Power Administration[187] and the Southeastern Power Administration.[188]

In an Act of 26 June 1948 (62 Stat. 1052), the Congress
created an Emergency Fund (out of the Reclamation Fund) for the
Bureau of Reclamation to be "available for defraying expenses
which the Commissioner of Reclamation determines are required
to be incurred because of unusual or emergency conditions."[189]
This fund was established by the First Deficiency Appropriation
Act of 24 May 1949, with an appropriation of $1,000,000 (63
Stat. 76, 86). Subsequent appropriations to the fund **consist**
of one of $400,000 made by each of the Interior Department Ap-
propriation Acts of 31 August 1951 (65 Stat. 248, 256), 9 July
1952 (66 Stat. 445, 452) and 31 July 1953 (67 Stat. 261, 267)
and one of $200,000 **contained** in the Interior Department Appro-
priation Act of 1 July 1954 (68 Stat. 361, 367). In the Flood
Control Act of 18 August 1941 (sec. 5: 55 Stat. 638, 650), the
Secretary of War (now the Army) was authorized to set aside
$1,000,000 for any one fiscal year from funds appropriated to
the War (now Army) Department for emergency rescue work and for
emergency repair of flood-control works. This sum was doubled
by the Flood Control Act of 24 July 1946 (60 Stat. 641, 652),
and was finally raised to $15,000,000 by the Flood Control Act
of 17 May 1950 (64 Stat. 170, 183). The Act of 1950 designated
the fund as Emergency Fund (for flood control), and requires
that both the initial sum and the replenishments must be appropriated by the Congress.

All these operating funds were established by Congressional

appropriations, the _continuing fund_ of the Tennessee Valley
Authority, which consists of moneys retained by the said Authority out of its own revenues, being the only exception. Expenditures from these funds do not require Congressional appropriation. That is to say, all these funds are characterized by
financial autonomy. However, with respect to the continuing
fund of the Southwestern Power Administration (in the amount of
$300,000), it is provided in the Interior Department Appropriation Act of 1951, _op. cit_., that "expenditures from this fund
to cover (such) costs in connection with the purchase of electric power and energy and rentals for the use of facilities
are to be made only in such amounts as may be approved annually
in appropriation acts . . ." Thus there is only a limited financial autonomy in this fund.[190]

(c) _Fiscal Funds_---So far as the deposit of the water charges, power revenues and other project receipts are concerned,
the Reclamation Fund is at the same time a fiscal fund; for to
cover these revenues into the Reclamation Fund is to make sure
that they are to be used for the repayment of project costs and
for no other purposes. In the same token, the Colorado River
Dam Fund serves to train and channel the various receipts of the
Boulder Canyon project. As an enterprise fund, the Colorado
River Dam Fund includes both the Hoover Dam and appurtenant power facilities and the All-American Canal system. As for its
capacity as a fiscal fund, it is provided in sec. 1 of the Boulder Canyon Project Act that the expenditures for the All-American Canal system should be reimbursed "as provided in the reclamation law", and should "not be paid out of revenues derived
from the sale or disposal of water power or electric energy at
the dam authorized to be constructed at said Black Canyon or
Boulder Canyon, or for water for potable purposes outside of
the Imperial and Coachella Valleys . . ." Thus the Colorado
River Dam Fund as a fiscal fund applies only to the Hoover Dam
project (including power facilities).[191] The power revenues are
of course the principal revenue, in addition to which there are
(1) receipts from the sale of project lands as farm units (sec.
9 of the Project Act) and (2) receipts from the lease of lands
within the exterior boundaries of the Boulder City, Nevada (Interior Department Appropriation Act of 18 June 1940: 54 Stat.
405, 437).

As provided in sec. 2 of the Boulder Canyon Project Adjustment Act of 1940, the receipts of the Boulder Canyon Project
(without the All-American Canal) are to be used for the following purposes: (1) annual appropriations for operation and maintenance, including emergency operations, (2) payments into the
Colorado River Development Fund, (3) payments to the States of
Arizona and Nevada as provided in the last paragraph of sec.
4(b) of the Project Act, and (4) the repayment of all original
advances made by the Congress to the Fund with interest[192] within an amortization period of 50 years (costs allocated to flood
control to be repaid thereafter.[193]

Among the purely fiscal funds, mention should first be made of the Debris Fund and the Columbia Basin Land Development Account, created respectively by sec. 23 of the California Debris Commission Organic Act of 1 March 1893 (27 Stat. 507, 510-511), as last amended by an Act of 25 June 1938 (52 Stat. 1040) and sec. 6 of the Columbia Basin Project Act of 10 March 1943 (57 Stat. 14, 19-20). The former is used to receive debris taxes collected by the said Commission "for the repayment of any funds advanced by the Federal Government or other agency for the construction of restraining works and settling reservoirs, and for the maintenance" of same. The latter is the receptacle of the receipts of the sale and lease of improved project lands, with which to reimburse costs incurred by the Federal Government in acquiring and/or developing these lands, with an annual interest of 3 percent, and, in the event of a surplus, to help in the liquidation of the cost of construction of irrigation works.

In an Act of 1 February 1905 (sec. 5: 33 Stat. 628), it was provided that "all moneys received from the sale of any land or resources of said forest reserves (i.e. the national forests) shall be covered into the Treasury of the United States, and for a period of five years from the passage of this Act shall constitute a special fund available . . . for the protection, administration, improvement, and extension of Federal forest reserves." This special fund was a typical fiscal fund, for its sole function was to insure that all receipts of the national forests should be used for the improvement of the national forests for a period of five years. In an Act of 9 June 1930 (46 Stat. 527), the Secretary of Agriculture, in the sale of timber of the national forests, is authorized to require the purchasers to pay additional charges to defray the cost of reforestation and the removal of undesirable vegetation. In order to protect the purchasers against the diversion of such additional charges to other uses, the same Act provides that they should constitute a special fund. In the Hunting Stamp Act of 16 May 1934 (48 Stat. 452), all proceeds from the sales of the hunting stamps are to be deposited in a special fund called the Migratory Bird Conservation Fund, which is used for the protection and preservation of migratory birds (sec. 4, as last amended on 20 October 1951:65 Stat. 451).[194]

In some of the Acts discussed before providing for the reception of non-Federal contributions, provision is made to the effect that the contributions should be kept in a special fund. By sec. 20 of the Permanent Appropriation Repeal Act of 26 June 1934 (48 Stat. 1224, 1235), all these kinds of non-Federal contributions are required to be placed in special trust funds, where they are to be disbursed only in compliance with the respective trusts. All such trust funds are evidently fiscal funds.[195]

Section 2   State and Local Finance

1. Financial Sources[196]

Funds supporting state and local water resources administration are derived from the following sources:

(1) Appropriation From General Funds---The use of the general funds in state and local water resources administration
is practically limited to navigation improvement, flood control,
forestry and recreation, and is generally found at the state
level only. Since navigation improvement and flood control
have in general ceased to be active state enterprises, recreation and forestry are now the only active state enterprises
that draw upon the general funds of the state treasuries for
their finance.[197] The appropriations from the general funds
for parks and recreation are generally made for capital improvements, including repairs. For example, the legislature
of Iowa in 1947 appropriated $2,713,100 for the improvement of
state parks and other recreational areas (including recreational facilities in state forests) (Laws 1947, ch. 29). In 1949,
the legislature of Tennessee appropriated $1,500,000 to be ex-
pended by the Department of Conservation in its program of the
expansion and enlargement of the state parks (Acts 1949, ch.
231). A law of Oklahoma of 1951 (No. 302) appropriated $215,-
000 for the improvement of the state parks in general and in
addition funds devoted to each of the eight state parks and
recreational areas aggregating $244,000. The Department of
Public Works of Illinois in 1951 received an appropriation of
$50,000 to make improvements in Kickapoo State Park alone (Act
of 4 August 1951). In a law of 1951 (ch. 75) the legislature
of Utah authorized the Engineering Commission to condemn certain lands for state park purposes and appropriated, out both
the general and the emergency relief funds (the latter being
also part of the general funds) whatever amount of money is
needed for such purposes. Occasionally, general funds are used
for the maintenance and operation of state parks too. For example, a law of 1939 of North Carolina (ch. 334) carried an
appropriation of $70,000 for the biennium 1939-1941 "for the
purpose of administration, operation, development and maintenance of state-owned parks."

For the fiscal year 1952, funds available for expenditure
by the South Carolina State Commission of Forestry totalled
$1,224,152, of which $865,950 came from general-fund appropriation.[198] The corresponding figures for the Forestry Division
of the Missouri Conservation were $792,813 and $225,000.[199]
The same figures for Vermont Forest Service for the calendar
year 1952 were $317,276 and $185,584.[200] The regular annual
or biennial state budget usually contains items on forestry.
For example, for the biennium beginning 1 July 1953, $2,276,000
was earmarked for forestry in Florida (L. 1953, ch. 2811, sec.
1), and $1,761,933 (in four items) was set aside for forestry
in Washington (L. 1953, ch. 288, sec. 2, at p. 784). For the
fiscal year 1954, the Division of Forestry of Massachusetts Department of Conservation was appropriated $621,018 (excluding

expenses for pest control) (Acts 1953, ch. 489).[201] Besides, there are special appropriations, to meet the expenses of special projects or activities. In Oregon, a total of 457,000 was appropriated to finance costs of projects undertaken by the Civilian Conservation Corps (L. 1935, ch. 373; L. 1937, ch. 144; L. 1939, ch. 423). A Pennsylvania law of 1949 (No. 556) appropriated $170,000 for the acquisition of certain lands for a state forest. In a law of Wisconsin of 1951 (ch. 359), a special appropriation of $182,116 from the general fund was made to be pooled with an appropriation from the conservation fund for the acquisition of lands in the Flambeau River State Forest. In 1953, Florida made two special appropriations, which are of the sums of $20,000 and $30,000 respectively, for forestry research purposes (L. 1953, chs. 28304 and 28310). As will be discussed later forestry expenses in South Dakota are paid out of the game and fish fund. However, when this method of finance proves inadequate, special appropriations (to defray either general or special expenses) may be made to supplement it. One such appropriation was made in 1951 (ch. 329).

General funds are sometimes also used to finance commercial fisheries administration (which, however, generally has full self-finance, its revenues being paid into the general fund), the planning and investigation of water and land resources, certain regulatory activities such as water sanitation, certain programs which provide assistance to private individuals, and so forth.

(2) Special Taxation---Special taxation as a means of financing water resources administration occurs primarily at the local level. It is employed by the state government for the same purpose only in exceptional cases. Special taxes are of two general kinds; namely, the uniform special taxes and the proportionate special-benefit assessments. These two forms of special taxation are constitutionally interchangeable at the discretion of the taxing authorities.[202] Uniform special taxes are further distinguishable into two kinds: the surtax, which is generally expressed in terms of certain mills per dollar of land value and which is in the nature of an addendum to the general property tax; and the acreage tax, which is levied on the basis of land area. Both the surtax and the acreage tax can be used (in theory) as the basis of special-benefit assessments, although the former in practice prevails.

Special taxation by special districts has already been discussed, and there is no need to repeat it. It should only be added that in the majority of cases special districts are created for the primary purpose of special taxation (or the issue of revenue bonds). With the regular local units, such as counties and cities, special taxation is also an important though not necessarily exclusive means of water-resources financing. Under certain state programs, this form of finance is sometimes also used.

All the county drainage systems[203] are financed by special-benefit assessments with respect to both construction and maintenance and operation, with the exception of: (1) Kansas, where county commissioners may levy a surtax for the purpose of operation and maintenance; (2) North Carolina, where a surtax of 2 mills per dollar is levied for both construction and maintenance; (3) Louisiana, where construction is financed by both surtax and county general funds and maintenance is financed by surtax alone;[204] and (4) New Jersey, where county general funds are used for both construction and maintenance.

With regard to county flood control enterprise, it is financed by surtaxes in Kansas, Louisiana (levees) and Texas; by special-benefit assessments in Ohio and Nebraska; by general funds in Indiana; and by both general funds and surtax in Arizona. In New Mexico, county flood-control enterprise is financed by a 1.5-mill surtax which **is, however, levied not on all** taxable property of the county as under the surtax system but only on the taxable property located within five miles of the two banks of the watercourse concerned. This system may be regarded as a combination of surtax and special-benefit assessments.

With respect to municipal flood control and drainage enterprises, they are financed by special-benefit assessments in such states as Idaho and Kentucky and by surtaxes in such states as Louisiana and Texas. In Kansas, construction work is financed by special-benefit assessments and the work of maintenance and repair is financed by surtax. In Illinois, both surtax and special-benefit **assessments are allowed in financing municipal drainage works**.

County parks are financed (in addition to the collection of charges) by special-benefit assessments in Wisconsin only. In other states, county parks are financed (in addition to the collection of charges) in the following different ways:[205]

Surtax with maximum rate unspecified in statute---Ohio, Wyoming, North Carolina, Arizona (as an alternative to the appropriation of the general funds), Indiana (**with** petition) and Georgia (with petition and referendum).

Surtax, with maximum rate specified by statute---California (Government Code, sec. 50400: Stats. 1887, ch. 41, Secs. 1 and 2; as last amended by Stats. 1953, ch. 1121), Pennsylvania (Statutes, sec. 1617: Act of 8 July 1919, sec. 7; as last amended by an Act of 24 March 1927, sec. 7), Utah, Missouri (for maintenance only; but in first-class counties, both construction and maintenance---Statutes, sec. 64.320: L. 1927, S. B. 345; as last amended 1953), and Kansas (General Statutes, sec. 19-2803: L. 1929, ch. 158, sec. 3). Also Mississippi, in acquiring lands to be conveyed to the state for state parks and for-

ests (Code, sec. 6037: enacted 1934, as amended
1935). With approval by referendum: Texas (Civil
Statutes, art. 6078: L. 1941, ch. 270) and North
Dakota (for a higher rate than the maximum authorized one) (L. 1953, ch. 116, sec. 6). With both
petition and referendum: Virginia and South Carolina (Acts 1935, No. 92, secs. 8-10).
Approrpations from general funds, without amount ceilings-
--Colorado, Arkansas (Acts 1949, No. 333), Washington (L. 1949, ch. 94, sec. 7), West Virginia (Acts
1951, ch. 52, sec. 4), Kentucky (Acts 1952, ch. 54,
sec. 4), New York (L. 1952, ch. 834, sec. 501, subsec. 1), Oregon, Missouri (for land acquisition
only---Statutes, sec. 64.320, op. cit.) and Texas
(counties owning and maintaining parks prior to
1941 and having a population of 50,000 to 78,000-
--Civil Statutes, art. 6079b: L. 1945, ch. 365, sec.
1).
Approprations from general funds, with maximum sum limited
---Michigan (Acts 1913, No. 90, sec. 4), Montana
(Revised Codes, sec. 62-102: L. 1929, ch. 51, sec.
2; as last amended by L. 1945, ch. 115, sec. 1),
Mississippi (for installment of recreational facilities only---L. 1950, ch. 296, sec. 2), South Dakota (amount equivalent to certain millage of general property tax---Code, sec. 12.2404: L. 1935, ch.
76, sec. 7), New Jersey (same as South Dakota---L.
1940, ch. 33, sec. 4), and Nevada (county authorities may "fix a yearly rate as a part of the county budget"; applicable only to counties of at least
10,000 inhabitants; only for acquisition of land-
---Stats. 1945, ch. 206).

Forest-fire control, which is largely a state enterprise,
is, in general, supported by (1) Federal grants, which will be
discussed below, (2) state and/or county appropriations and (3)
levies on private landowners. Only (3) is discussed here. In
states such as North Carolina, Pennsylvania, West Virginia, New
Mexico and Utah, the funds provided by private landowners take
the form of "contributions". As to how these contributions are
made, notice may be made of the statute of Missouri, under
which "any owner may make application to the (Conservation)
Commission for special attention in forest fire control . . .
by subscribing a payment of not less than three cents per acre per year for such added protection as the Commission may
deem advisable and desirable." Contributions of this nature
differ from an acreage tax only by technical construction of
the statute. In Oregon, Washington, Alabama (Acts 1939, No.
562, sec. 1), Montana (L. 1939, ch. 128, sec. 9), Mississippi
and probably some other states, an acreage tax is imposed on
the landowners benefited. In Mississippi, however this levy
is made only upon the petition of 20 percent of the lectors of
the lands affected and after a referendum (L. 1944, ch. 238,
sec. 4), In Louisiana and Kentucky, the acreage tax is alter-

native or supplementary to county appropriations.[206] In states such as Minnesota (Statutes, sec. 88.04: L. 1925, ch. 407, sec. 11; as amended by L. 1949, ch. 676, sec. 1), Maine, Colorado (Statutes, ch. 45, sec. 103: L. 1945, ch. 107) and California Government Code, sec. 25210.1 et seq.: Stats. 1953, ch. 858) a millage-surtax is authorized to support state or county enterprise in forest-fire control. While the millage-surtax is collected from all property owners of the state or county or municipality, the burdens of both voluntary contributions and the acreage tax fall only on the land-owners benefited. It is this fact which makes the latter resemble special-benefit assessments.[207]

Special taxation is also used in other aspects of state and local water resources administration. For example, under the laws of California (Harbors and Navigation Code, sec. 4130 et seq.: Stats. 1945, ch. 1500, sec. 1), counties may, for purposes of harbor improvement, levy a special tax for construction purposes upon approval by a two-thirds vote at a general or special election, and annually levy a maintenance tax of a minimum rate of 15 cents per $100. They may also levy special taxes for the improvement of non-navigable waters (Water Code, sec. 8129; as amended by Stats. 1953, ch. 320). The municipal mosquito-control enterprise in Minnesota is also financed by millage surtaxes. Under a law of 1953 (ch. 298), the City of Chestertown of the State of Maryland is authorized to levy special taxes for the acquisition and construction of a water-supply system.

Special taxation may also be used to raise funds as state and local contributions to Federal programs. In Washington, for example, each county or any group of counties jointly may, upon the petition of at least 100 qualified freeholders, levy special-benefit assessments to assist in the financing of Federal river or harbor improvements (Revised Code, ch. 88.32: L. 1907, ch. 236). In Kansas, the counties may levy a 0.8-mill surtax for predator control (L. 1949, ch. 203, sec. 7), which is primarily a Federal activity.[208] For the same activity in Colorado, "there shall be levied for the year 1949 and for each year thereafter, a tax of six mills on each dollar of assessed valuation . . ." (Game and Fish Laws, sec. 1611, effective 3 May 1949). Many types of special districts, notably irrigation districts and flood-control districts, are created for the sole purpose of operating and maintaining Federal projects, and the special taxes collected by them are expended on these projects instead of projects of their own.

(3) Self finance (Operating Revenues)---The state and local water-supply and hydroelectric power projects are generally entirely self-financed. Navigation improvements can also be self-financed, as in the case of the New York State Barge Canal and the Illinois and Michigan Canal. Special taxation used to prevail in municipal sewerage projects, but it is being gradually replaced by service charges.[209] The operating revenues

of parks greatly help in park maintenance, but are far from
adequate for the acquisition of properties and the construction of facilities. The degree of self-finance of state park
enterprise is shown in the following table: [210]

Year	General fund	Other funds	Revenues	Total expenditure
1946	$15,775,064	$3,402,651	$3,918,178	$13,930,731
1947	23,489,109	9,536,744	4,294,927	22,817,886
1948	26,632,163	10,923,423	5,215,439	28,184,843
1949	28,104,261	12,797,905	5,540,833	29,037,932
1950	27,043,434	22,197,400	6,243,543	34,122,311

Local parks are even less self-financing, as may be seen
in the following table: [211]

Source of financial support	Amount($)	Percentage	Number of parks
Appropriations	237,967,585	90	1,658
Self-finance	16,330,554	6	645
Contributions	9,305,457	4	630
Total	263,603,596	100	1,776

(Total expenditure was $268,911,957 in 1,848 parks, of
which $86,966,727 was for capital investment in 1,232
parks.)

The management of state forests also produces some revenues,
which are chiefly derived from the sale of timber and other
forest products. In general, these revenues can be used to finance at most the cost of maintenance and minor repairs and improvements, and are not expected to bear any part of the cost
of land acquisition. In reforestation programs, some income
is possible through the sale (generally at cost) of planting
stock which, too, can meet only a fraction of the total program cost. The reforestation program of Tennessee, for example,
costs about $40,000 per year. "The source of these funds is
$9,500 from the Federal Government, $15,000 sale of seedlings
and the balance State appropriations."[212] In South Dakota, the
same program "is self-liquidating except for $2,000 which is
transferred annually from the Game Fund . . . and approximately
$8,000 which is received annually through the Clarke-McNary co-
operation (i.e., Federal grant)."[213] For the fiscal year 1952,
the expenditures of the State Forest Nursery of South Carolina
amounted to $59,290, while its revenues totalled only $31,230.[214]
For the same period, the corresponding figures of the reforestation program of Vermont were $36,976 and $6,414.[215] In the
state service of forest-fire-fighting, the persons causing or
otherwise responsible for the setting of the fire may be required to pay all or part of the costs of such service.[216]

Many regulatory activities are completely self-financing
or nearly so or even revenue-making. These include state fish
and wildlife regulation, state public-utility regulation, state

hydroelectric power regulation, state water-use regulation, state and county dam regulation, and practically all other regulatory activities involving the issuance of licenses or permits or certificates, for which an administrative fee is normally charged.

(4) <u>Transferred Revenues</u>---Part of the revenues from non-water-resources-administrative activities may be transferred to the various aspects of water-resources administration, or part of the revenues from one aspect of water-resources administration to some other aspect or aspects of water-resources administration. For example, in Washington, "approximately 25 percent of the monies received from the State Highway Code Laws and 40 percent or $1.20 of each $3.00 Drivers License Fee from the Drivers License Law are allocated to the Parks and Parkways Fund."[217] This is representative of state park finance in general," since a large proportion of travel is for recreation and state parks are the destination of a considerable number of automobiles."[218] In the same state, a law was passed in 1939 (ch. 209), which appropriated all receipts from hydroelectric power licensing to the Reclamation Revolving Fund. In South Dakota, "any civil township or county not divided into civil townships may use one-half of the general road fund to help defray the expense of making fireguards (against prairie fires). . . ." (<u>Revised Code</u>, sec. 6131: L. 1893, ch. 191, sec. 4; as amended by L. 1905, ch. 111). In California, "the 1947 Legislature diverted $9,000,000 due the State from horse racing operations from the general fund to the Wildlife Restoration Fund. . ."[219] As mentioned above (p. 1094), $2,000 is diverted annually from the game fund to finance the reforestation program in South Dakota. A 1953 law of Alabama (Acts 1953, No. 737) diverted all of the net revenues derived from the sale of sand and gravel from the submerged lands of the state which are not under the control of any state agency into the State Park Fund of the Department of Conservation, to be used in the administration of state parks.

In many cases, two or more administrative programs are combined in a unified administration, whereby the revenues from one program automatically subsidizes the other program or programs without the explicit transfer of funds. This may be called "administrative grafting" from the financial point of view.[220] For example, under the laws of South Dakota, the game and fish finances not only fish and game administration but also its forestry and park programs, all these activities being managed by the same agency (<u>Code</u>, sec. 25.0115: L. 1945, ch. 36, sec. 11). In Ohio, where the Department of Natural Resources has jurisdiction over both fish and wildlife and forestry, considerable sums of money from the deer license funds have recently been used for the purchase of state-forest lands.[221] "In a few States where State parks are under the jurisdiction of an agency which also has responsibility for fish and game, a certain proportion of fish and game fees has been allocated for State

parks. Until recently the total budget for State parks in Nebraska and Missouri came from this source, and at present this
is the only source of State park funds in Kansas." "In Oregon,
where the State Highway Department administers the parks, they
are financed from State highway funds. . ."[222] In 1951, an
act was passed by the Washington state legislature which appropriated $150,000 from the motor vehicle fund to the Department
of Highways for the biennium ending 31 March 1953 for the maintenance and construction of roads within state parks. Such
roads, it may be noted, may fall under the jursidiction of either the state parks agency or the said Department. In this act,
they are made subject to the jurisdiction of the latter merely
as a measure of financial grafting. As discussed before, this
is prevailing practice in state park administration. As already discussed before, many state and local works of flood control and navigation improvement are built as an incident to road
construction. In one sense, this is also an instance of financial grafting.

(5) Sale of Property---As discussed before, the Federal
Government used to grant public lands to states and local units,
which the latter would sell and use the proceeds therefrom to
finance reclamation and river-improvement works and the construction of canals as well as other construction or non-construction
projects. At the present time, although the sale of property
is permitted in the statutes of most states, it is negligible
as a source of finance in the field of water resources administration.

(6) Grants In Aid---There are many types of Federal grants
in aid to the states in water resources administration. Some
states sometimes extend similar assistance to their local units.
For the country as a whole, the expenditures of the states (at
the state level) on "natural resources" constitute never more
than 4 percent of their total expenditures.[223] Of the expenditures on "natural resources", about one-half are those on agriculture.[224] Thus not more than 2 percent of the states' financial resources go to water resources administration. The need
of Federal assistance is evident.

Some of the Federal grants to the states are general in
scope. One of these is the five percent of the proceeds from
the sale of public lands in certain public-land states granted
to them on their admission to the Union for "roads and internal
improvements" or for "internal improvements."[225] All other general grants were made on an emergency basis.

On 21 July 1932, the Emergency Relief and Construction Act
was passed which, among their things, authorized the Reconstruction Finance Corporation to make loans to states and local units
for relief construction uses, and appropriated $300 million for
this purpose. Of this sum, "the RFC actually disbursed $299,-
984,999 to 42 states and to Hawaii and Puerto Rico. A comparatively small part of this amount ($19,624,581) was loaned to

cities or counties." These loans were turned into grants by
sec. 14 of an Act of 18 June 1934 (48 Stat. 993, 996), when
$17,159,232 had already been repaid by some states.[226]

The First Emergency Relief Appropriation Act of 12 May 1933
set up the Federal Emergency Relief Administration whose principal function it was to make grants to the several states for
emergency needs. In 1935, the Works Progress Administration
was created (Executive Order 7034 of 6 May 1935) to replace
the Federal Emergency Relief Administration, and the Federal
policy of making grants to the states was changed to one of
Federal trust administration.[227] Appropriations available for
grants totalled, by 30 June 1941, $3,256,405,045.36, of which
$3,067,694,752 was granted to the several states.[228] "Of the
total amount granted to the states by the FERA, obligations
amounting to $2,767,361,699 were incurred for the general re-
lief and special emergency relief programs and an additional
$324,114,105 was used for certain special relief programs" (em-
phasis added). One of the general relief programs was the emergency work relief program, on which a total of $1,288,532,813
was expended from April 1934 till the liquidation of the Federal Emergency Relief Administration on 241,281 projects. Of
which these projects, those in the field of water resources
administration are as follows:[229]

Type	Number	Expenditure
Parks	4,643	$103,680,387
Roadside improvement	2,980	13,181,348
Forestation	642	3,891,268
Soil conservation	774	4,396,360
Flood control, irrigation and water conservation	4,968	44,517,652
Other conservation projects	3,438	10,148,220
Water supply	6,849	36,880,857
Sewerage	8,255	70,272,176
Hydroelectric power	Unknown	Unknown
Total (except hydroelectric power)	32,549	286,968,268
Percentage of all general relief programs	13.4%	22.3%

Of the special emergency relief programs, the rural rehabilitation program and the cattle and drought contracts program
were in the water resources field, which entailed an expenditure of $58,213,000 and $41,877,231, respectively. The self-
help cooperatives program, also an emergency relief program,
on which $3,775,977 was expended, also had some bearing on
water resources management. Of the special relief programs,
the civil works program might have included some projects of
water resources administration (possibly parks and recreation).
The total expenditure on this program was $35,742,022.[230]

The National Industrial Recovery Act of 17 June 1933 created the Federal Emergency Administration of Public Works (48
Stat. 195, 200), and authorized the President to make grants
to states and local units, up to 30 percent of the cost of
labor and materials of each project, for the construction, repair or repair of public-works projects (48 Stat. 195, 200),
and authorized the President to make grants to states and local units, up to 30 percent of the cost of labor and materials
of each project, for the construction, repair or repair of public-works projects (48 Stat. 202)[231] "The agency was authorized, with Presidential approval, to provide 45 percent[232] of
the cost of approved projects as direct Federal grants, to
make loans towards the 55 percent to be borne by the sponsors,
and to make allotments to various Federal agencies."[233] By 30
June 1942, grants totalling $1,511,946,857 had been made on
16,637 projects, with an aggregate construction cost of $4,207,-
419,105. The numbers of those categories of projects which
are in water resources field are as follows:[234]

Category	Number	Construction Cost
Sewerage	1,522	$453,859,651
Water Supply	2,415	311,920,652
Sewerage and water supply	196	23,809,208
Flood control, water power and reclamation	128	193,364,197
Navigation improvement	8	4,540,319
Water terminals	53	28,333,813
Recreatinn	134	23,753,097
Total	4,456	1,039,580,937

Normal-time Federal grants to the several states are made
in the following special fields:

(i) Forestry---The first area of Federal assistance is
state forest-fire control enterprise, which is provided under
1 March 1911 (36 Stat. 961), as magnified by secs. 1-3 of the
(Clarke-McNary) Act of 7 June 1924, as last amended by an Act
of 26 October 1949 (63 Stat. 909).[235] Assistance under the
act of 1911 was limited to those forest lands which are watersheds of navigable streams. The act of 1924 extended to other
forested lands, and an amendment of 1925 further extended it to
non-forested lands which are watersheds of waters for domestic
or irrigation use. The 1924 law authorized an annual appropriation of $2,500,000, which was increased by the 1949 amendment
to $11 million for the fiscal year 1950, $13 million for the
fiscal year 1951, $15 million for the fiscal year 1952, $17 million for the fiscal year 1953, $19 million for the fiscal year
1954, and $20 million for each subsequent fiscal year, with per-
mission for additional expenditure in case of unusual need.
Under both the 1911 and the 1924 acts, Federal grants to any
state cannot exceed the total non-Federal expenditure in that
state. However, no matching expenditure need be made by the
state or other non-Federal parties on preliminary investigatians

(under 1924 law). As of March 1952, all of the forty-eight states, excdpt Arizona, Kansas, Nebraska, North Dakota and Wyoming, had taken advantage of this Federal grant program.[236] Federal grants and matching state and other non-Federal expenditures (in $1,000) for the fiscal years 1925 to 1951 are as follows:[237]

Fiscal Year	Federal	State	Private
1925	361	1,844	
1926	585	1,875	
1927	607	2,537	
1928	868	3,073	
1929	1,069	3,042	
1930	1,252	4,118	
1931	1,537	5,011	
1932	1,573	4,370	
1933	1,452	3,142	
1934	1,468	3,795	
1935	1,457	4,131	
1936	1,427	3,795	
1937	1,473	5,379	
1938	1,463	5,448	
1939	1,793	6,617	
1940	1,988	7,200	
1941	1,979	7,299	
1942	2,703	6,272	2,193
1943	4,624	6,714	2,405
1944	5,870	6,351	1,739
1945	5,925	6,562	2,114
1946	7,012	7,498	2,389
1947	7,890	9,477	2,236
1948	8,604	12,831	2,065
1949	8,572	17,201	2,102
1950	8,551	18,121	2,262
1951	8,996	21,885	2,279

It may be seen that "the Federal contribution (i.e., grants) has never matched state and private funds."[238]

Federal grants to states (and local units) for reforestation are authorized by sec. 4 of the Act of 7 June 1924 (43 Stat. 653, 654). The ceiling of annual expenditure by the Federal Government for this purpose was originally fixed at $100,000. By an amendment of 26 October 1949 (63 Stat. 909), it has been increased to $1 million for the fiscal year 1950, $1.5 million for the fiscal year 1951 $2 million for the fiscal year 1952, and $2.5 million for each subsequent fiscal year. Grants for the same purpose were also available under the Cooperative Farm Forestry Act of 1937 to be discussed below. Grants under the Act of 1924 in any one state for any fiscal year should not exceed the sum total of all state expenditures for the same purpose. The grants made and corresponding state expenditures (in $1,000) for fiscal years 1926-1951 are given below:[239]

Fiscal year	Grants	State funds
1926	$ 45	$223
1930	81	322
1935	55	151
1937	71	251
1938	70	295
1939	97	301
1940	140	384
1941	113	413
1942	115	412
1943	115	333
1944	119	344
1945	114	458
1946	113	524
1947	117	769
1948	113	1,065
1949	113	1,293
1950	189	1,314
1951	377	2,644

Under sec. 5 of the Act of 7 June 1924 (43 Stat. 653, 654), Federal grants are available for educational programs of state forestry or other agencies of assisting farmers in forest or woodlot management, particularly reforestation and the **harvest**ing and marketing forest and wood products, Federal funds expended in cooperation with (i.e., in assistance to) any state agency not to exceed the latter's expenditures for the same purpose for any fiscal year, except on preliminary investigations (as provided in 1949 amendment). Federal expenditure for this grant program was originally limited to $100,000 a year, but was increased to $500,000 a year by an amendment of 26 October 1949 (63 Stat. 909, 910). Federal grants made for the fiscal years 1926-1953 are as follows:[240]

Fiscal Year	Grants (in $)
1926	32,021
1927	43,252
1928	50,665
1929	51,688
1930	55,218
1931	59,552
1932	60,444
1933	60,371
1934	44,754
1935	43,982
1936	48,324
1937	49,702
1938	50,105
1939	68,429

1940	68,429
1941	57,578
1942	56,215
1943	53,182
1944	47,710
1945	49,416
1946	53,342
1947	79,888
1948	85,325
1949	85,261
1950	86,665
1951	86,740
1952	83,647

As mentioned before, in July 1948 the Federal Government began to make grants to the states, without requiring matching expenditures by the latter, under the provision of the Cooperative Farm Forestry Act of 18 May 1937 (50 Stat. 188). On 25 August 1950, it was repealed and replaced by the Cooperative Forest Management Act (64 Stat. 473). The latter applies to both woodlands and potential woodlands,[241] to both farmers and processors of primary forest products, to both private landowners and managers, land supervisors and operators of privately owned land acting as the landowners' agents, and is thus much broader in scope than the previous legislation. Only the state forestry agencies, but not other agencies, are eligible for the grants. Only their technical services are to be subsidized. Federal grants to any state (or territory or possession) for any fiscal year must at least **be equalled by expenditures of the** latter during the same fiscal year for the same purpose. An annual appropriation of $2.5 million is authorized for the making of the grants. As of 30 June 1952, 36 States were recipients of these grants. The total amounts of Federal grants and matching state expenditures for the fiscal years 1949-1952 are shown below:[242]

Fiscal Year	Federal Grants	State Funds
1949	353,179	467,129
1950	349,117	573,882
1951	538,812	726,973
1952	548,608	886,250

(ii) Fish and Wildlife---Under the (Pittman-Robertson) Federal Aid to Wildlife Restoration Act of 2 September 1937 (50 Stat. 917), as last amended on 24 July 1946 (60 Stat. 656), Federal grants may be made to state **and territorial** game agencies on their "wildlife restoration projects", which include projects of land acquisition, habitat improvement and investigation and research regarding the protection and propagation of wildlife, in an amount not exceeding 75 percent of the total cost of each project. In principle, grants for habitat improvement work are to be used only for planning and construction; and not more than

25 percent of the total of grants made to any state can be expended on maintenance work. The moneys available for the making of such grants consist of all receipts from the Federal excise tax on firearms, shells and cartridges. These receipts are to be placed in a special fund called the "Federal aid to wildlife restoration fund" in order to prevent their diversion into other uses. Up to 8 percent of the revenues from this source for any fiscal year may be used for the administration of the grants and the administration of the Migratory Bird Conservation program. The remainder is to be apportioned to the several states (as ceilings of grants) one-half on the basis of the state area of and one-half on the basis of the number of game license holders in each state. But no state "shall receive less than one-half of one percentum nor more than five percentum of the total amount apportioned to all the states." It may be noted that not all the moneys available for **appropriation and** authorized to be **appropriated for this purpose in each fiscal** year are actually so appropriated by Congress and that not all the moneys so appropriated and apportioned by the Secretary of the Interior among the several states (and territories) are actually granted away. The total amount of the receipts of the above-mentioned fund, the amount appropriated therefrom and the total amount of the grant for each of the fiscal years 1939-1953 are listed below:[243]

Fiscal Year	Receipts($)	Appropriated($)	Grants($)
1939	2,976,020	1,000,000	890,000
1940	3,707,844	1,500,000	451,299
1941	5,535,773	2,500,000	1,844,359
1942	5,072,588	2,750,000	1,882,880
1943	1,149,333	1,250,000	1,695,375
1944	1,061,045	1,000,0000	1,033,547
1945	3,132,402	900,000	1,306,450
1946	5,232,465	1,000,000	1,191,795
1947	8,423,216	2,500,000	2,211,628
1948	12,134,601	9,031,273	2,520,975
1949		11,276,687	8,894,844
1950		10,378,538	11,624,486
1951	17,846,424	9,351,614	7,823,628
1952	10,679,059	17,846,424	9,585,031
1953	12,147,554	10,679,059	12,474,131

On 9 August 1950 (effective 1 July 1950), the (Dingell-Johnson) Federal Aid to Fisheries Act was enacted (64 Stat. 430) making similar Federal grants to state fish and game agencies on their game-fish restoration and improvement projects. The features of this Act are identical with those of the Federal **Aid** to Wildlife Act discussed above except for the following: (1) The moneys authorized to be appropriated consist of all receipts from the Federal tax on sport fishing tackle. (2) The annual Congressional appropriation, after deducting up to 8 percent

thereof for the administration of the grants and interstate
administration, is apportioned in such a manner that "40 percentum in the ratio which the area of each state including
coastal and Great Lakes waters (as determined by the Secretary
of the Interior) bears to the total area of all the states and
60 percentum in the ratio which the number of persons holding
paid licenses to fish for sport or recreation in the state in
the second fiscal year preceding the fiscal year for which
such apportionment is made . . . bears to the number of such
persons in all the states . . ." (3) "No state shall receive
less than 1 percentum nor more than 5 percentum of the total
amount apportioned to all of the states;" nor shall a state
receive less than $4,500. (4) No Federal special fund is es-
tablished. Grants made for the fiscal years 1951 and 1952 are
shown in the following table:[244]

Fiscal year	Receipts($)	Appropriated($)	Grants($)
1951	2,929,251	--------	1,499,863
1952	2,857,094	2,929,250	2,628,527

(iii) Other Fields---In Louisiana Admission Act of 20 February 1811, it is provided that five percent of the proceeds
from the sale of public lands in that state should be granted
to the state for the construction of roads and levees (2 Stat.
641, 643). Similar grants have appeared in the Admission Acts of
Indiana (19 April 1816: 3 Stat. 289, 290), Mississippi (1 March
1817: 3 Stat. 348, 349),[245] Missouri (6 March 1820: 3 Stat.
545, 547), Wisconsin (6 August 1846: 9 Stat. 56, 58), Arkansas
(23 June 1836: 5 Stat. 58), Michigan (same date: 5 Stat. 59,
60) and Iowa (3 March 1845: 5 Stat. 789, 790); but the funds
are used for the construction of roads and canals. In Alabama
Admission Act of 2 March 1819, the same grant was authorized
for the construction of roads and canals and the improvement
of rivers (3 Stat. 489, 491). In the Admission Acts of Nevada
and Colorado, both dated 21 March 1864, five percentum of the
proceeds of public-land sales in the respective states were
granted to them for roads, ditches and canals to effect a general system of irrigation (13 Stat. 30, 32 and 32, 34).[246] As
for irrigation, it may be noted that Federal grants to states
and local units are possible under sec. 2(3) of the Water Facilities Act of 28 August 1937 (50 Stat. 869); but as a matter of
fact no such grants have ever been made.

Under sec. 1 of the Soil Conservation and Domestic Allotment Act of 27 April 1935 (49 Stat. 163), and sec. 7(b) of the
same act as added on 29 February 1936 (49 Stat. 1148), the Federal Government, through the Secretary of Agriculture, may make
grants to states and local units on their soil-conservation projects. Again no such Federal grants have actually been made.
In the Watershed Protection and Flood Prevention Act of 4 August 1954 (68 Stat. 666), Federal grants to states and local
units are also provided for to assist them in the construction

or installation of watershed-improvement works.

Under the National Defense Public Works Act of 28 June 1941
(55 Stat. 361), the President may make loans or grants or both
to public or private agencies for the construction of water
supply, sewerage, recreational and other public works in localities where Federal defense installments are located. By 30
June 1949, grants made under this act (to both public and private agencies) totalled $171,014,473.[247]

In sec. 304 of the Defense Housing and Community Facilities
and Services Act of 1 September 1951 (65 Stat. 293, 305), the
Housing and Home Finance Agency is authorized to make "loans
or grants, or other payments, to public and non-profit agencies
for the provision, or for the maintenance," of facilities for
health, refuse disposal, sewage treatment, recreation, water
purification, day-care centers and fire protection.[248] By 31
December 1953, "100 projects with an estimated construction
cost of $47.5 million had been approved under this program.
The cost would be met through Federal grants of $21.3 million,
Federal loans of $3.7 million, and applicants' funds of $22.5
million. Of the 100 projects approved, 67 were under construction, 13 were completed, and 20 had not yet reached the construction stage. Of the 80 projects completed or under construction, 28 were for water facilities, 31 for sewer facilities, 10 for water and sewer, and 11 for other types of facilities."[249] It is not known, however, what percentages of the
above figures are allocable to state and local agencies.

By an Act of 13 August 1946 (60 Stat. 1056),[250] the Chief
of Engineers of the Department of the Army may make a grant
to a state or local agency for the construction, but not maintenance, of a beach-protection project which may amount up to
one-third of the total cost of the project. The plan of the
project must be prepared by the Beach Erosion Board of the
Corps of Engineers on behalf of the state or local agency concerned, and approved by the Congress. It would seem that no
grants had been made under this provision by 30 June 1953.[251]

Two types of Federal grants are provided in the Water Pollution Control Act of 30 June 1948 (62 Stat. 1155), as amended
bn 17 July 1952 (66 Stat. 755), and both **lasted** until 30 June
1956.[252] Under sec. 8(a), grants may be made "to the states
for expenditure by or under the direction of their respective
state water pollution agencies, and to interstate agencies for
expenditure by them, for the conduct of investigations, research, surveys, and studies related to the prevention and control of water pollution caused by industrial waters" (emphasis
added). Grants made under this provision up to 30 June 1953
consisted of $995,000 for the fiscal year 1950, $866,853 for
the fiscal year 1951, $835,572 for the fiscal year 1952 and
$20,223 for the fiscal year 1953.[253] Under sec. 8(c), the Fed-
eral Government may "make grants to states, municipalities, or

interstate agencies to aid in financing the cost of engineering, architectural, and economic investigations and studies,
surveys, designs, plans, working drawings, specifications,
procedure and other action preliminary to the construction of
projects approved by the appropriate state water pollution
agency or agencies and by the Surgeon General" (emphasis added). By 30 June 1953, no grants had been for this purpose.[254]
It may be noted that no Federal financial aid is available for
either the construction or the maintenance and operation of
water pollution control works.

The payments to states and local units in lieu of property
taxes in connection with certain aspects of Federal water resources administration are not grants to states and local units.
However, if the recipient parties select to expend such funds
to state water resources administration, they become de-facto
grants. Federal payments out of the public-land grazing fees
have been reportedly become such grants.[255]

As for grants of the state governments to local units some
examples may be given. As discussed before, the Department of
Agriculture and Conservation of Rhode Island has, since 1934,
made grants to towns and cities for the construction and maintenance of mosquito-control works. In Florida, a law of 1953
(ch. 28131) authorized the Health Department to grant to any
county or mosquito-control district which has set up a special
item in its annual budget for the control of mosquitoes and
other arthropods funds up to 75 percent of the county or dis-
truct appropriation for that item. In 1953, the legislature
of California appropriated a sum of $300,000 for the fiscal
year 1953-54 for the making of subsidies to local districts
and other public agencies for the control of mosquitoes and
gnats (Stats. 1953, ch. 1763).

In 1925, an act was passed by the legislature of Texas (ch.
35) granted to the County of Cameron the revenues from the part
of the general property tax collected in the county which is in
excess of ten cents on the hundred dollars valuation of the taxable property in the 25-year period beginning 1 January 1926
for the construction of flood-control works. Under a law of
1951 (ch. 240), the State of Washington may grant to any local
unit or special district, for the maintenance and operation of
(but not construction) a flood-control project (which is in all
probability a Federal project) by the latter, up to one-half of
the cost of maintenance and operation of the project. As mentioned before, the Department of Public Works of Louisiana, under the County Drainage Act of 1946, has made grants to parishes for the administration of their drainage programs. In 1953,
a law was enacted in North Dakota (ch. 59) which appropriated
$140,000 to the State Water Conservation Commission for the
making of grants to irrigation districts on a matching basis to
assist them in the construction and repair of irrigation and
drainage works for the fiscal years 1954-1957.

In Iowa, an act of 1951 (ch. 13) appropriated $350,000 for
assistance in the construction of sewerage facilities by the
Great Lakes Sanitary District of Dickinson County. In 1953,
$843,000 was appropriated to the State Conservation Commission
"for the treatment of waters or emergency work to maintain
state-owned lakes and waters" (ch. 16). Of this sum, $500,000
was allocated by the said Commission for assistance in the construction of a sewer system around Clear Lake in Cerro Gordo
County by the Clear Lake Sanitary District.[256] In New York,
the state may reimburse any county up to one-half, but in no
case more than $5,000, of the cost which the county government
incurs in any one year in the administration of the county forest or forests (County Law, sec. 219, subsec. 3: L. 1929, ch.
194; as last amended by L. 1953, ch. 553). "The Michigan State
Legislature, in its Special Session of 1944, appropriated one
million dollars to the Huron-Clinton Metropolitan Authority
for the purchase of land within its district, provided that
the Authority match this amount with its own funds." "The Authority started its Land Acquisition Program in 1944, and since
that time has acquired by purchase and gifts approximately 7,-
500 acres of land . . . (as of 1951)."[257]

**In general it may perhaps be said that state grants do not
constitute a regular and reliable item in the water resources
administration budget of a local unit.**

7. Contributions---The state governments may accept contributions from the local units and private persons. For example, one-third of the costs of beach-protection works in Avon Lake, Lakeview and Century State Parks of Ohio was contributed by the local units concerned, as mentioned before. In
May 1951-December 1952, Iowa State Conservation Commission built
a recreational reservoir at a total cost of $532,250, of which
$125,000 was contributed by the Southwestern Federated Power
Cooperative and $100,000 by the City of Creston, in return for
certain privileges to the use of water impounded therein.[258]
Under the laws of Iowa (Code, sec. 111.28: Acts 1925, ch. 121,
sec. 1; as amended by Acts 1933-34, Ex. Sess., ch. 22, sec. 1),
"any one or more cities or towns may . . . expend money to aid
in the purchase of land within the county for state parks which,
when purchased, shall be the property of the State of Iowa . . ."
In Massachusetts, when the State Forester assumes the work of
fighting forest fires in a town which are beyond the control
of the local forest warden, one-half of the cost is to be paid
by the town government (General Laws, ch. 48, sec. 24: Acts
1927, ch. 280, sec. 3). The same financial arrangement obtains when upon request of a town the State forester undertakes
forest-fire patrol in the town (ibid., sec. 28A: Acts 1929, ch.
284; as last amended by Acts 1953, ch. 496). The funds for
state forest pest control enterprise in Vermont in 1951 and
1952 (in $) were composed of:

	1951	1952
Federal contributions	28,483	25,463
State funds	5,021	4,682
Town contributions	6,900	6,500

As mentioned before, private land owners concerned contributed a sum which is equal to the state appropriation in the state forest insect control program of 1945-1953.

In many cases, the Federal Government makes contributions to states and local units. Contributions differ from grants mainly in that while the latter are made on activities which distinctively belong to state jurisdiction, contributions are payments for parts or **portions** of state and local projects or programs for which the Federal Government has certain responsibilities or for benefits accruable to the Federal Government. For example, in the War (now Army) Department Appropriation Act of 15 May 1936, the Secretary of War (now of the Army) was authorized to expend, on the recommendation of the Chief of Engineers and the Board of Engineers for Rivers and Harbors, necessary amount of money "for the maintenance of harbor channels provided by a state, municipality or other public agency outside of harbor lines and serving essential needs of general commerce and navigation . . ." (49 Stat. 1278, 1306-1307). Expenditures of this type should be classified as Federal contributions. This provision was reiterated in all subsequent annual appropriation legislation for the navigation-improvement enterprise of the Corps of Engineers up to and including that of 24 October 1951 (65 Stat. 616, 618). Under the above-mentioned National Defense Public Works Act of 1941, the Federal Government, besides making grants (and loans) to non-Federal parties in the construction or installment of water-supply, sewerage, recreational and other public works, may also make contributions to them for the maintenance and operation thereof (sec. 202(c)). Under an authority contained in the Flood Control Act of 1944, the Secretary of the Army entered into an agreement with the City and County of San Francisco and the Turlock and Modesto Irrigation Districts on 26 September 1949 which obligated the Federal Government to contribute a sum of $12 million to the latter toward the prosecution of their multiple-purpose development program for the Tuolumne River, in return for the flood-control benefits received by the Federal Government therefrom.[259] Similarly, in the Act of 6 July 1954 (68 Stat. 450), authorization was made (sec. 3) for the appropriation of $6,500,000 "as a monetary contribution by the United States for flood-control storage in the Markham Ferry project" authorized to be constructed by the Grand River Dam Authority of Oklahoma. In the various watershed-treatment programs of the Department of Agriculture, there are many provisions for Federal payments to states and local units for the initiation of prescribed treatment measures.[260] These payments should be regarded as contributions rather than grants.

2. Financial Administration

(1) Borrowing---Moneys are borrowed by states and local units, as by private persons, by way of either the procurement of loans or the issuance of bonds. The bonds issued by the states and local units in the field of water resources admin- istration are generally of the following three kinds: (1) the revenue bonds,which are to be redeemed by the revenues from the operation of the self-financing state or local enterprise concerned and which are not different from the bonds issued by private business concerns; (2) the tax-anticipation bonds, which are to be redeemed by the regular taxes; and (3) what may be called the "absolute bonds", which are to be redeemed by ad-hoc taxes levied for the special purpose of redeeming the principal and interests of the bonds.

With regard to state and local hydroelectric power enter- prise, "their capitalization usually consists initially entire- ly of bonds, which may be and frequently is larger than the first cost of their properties."[261] Such bonds are almost en- tirely revenue bonds.[262] In general, statutes authorizing state and local hydroelectric enterprises only allow the is- suance of revenue bonds. In the field of water supply, both original acquisition and construction and major replacemtnts are "almost 100-percent debt-financed." "Types of financing most frequently used: general obligation bonds or revenue bonds, with a distinct tendency toward revenue bonds.[263] The issuance of revenue bonds is also the usual method of financing the initial cost of improvement of municipal and county parks,[264] although it would seem that appropriations from the general funds are generally relied upon for the acquisition of lands. In recent years, revenue bonds have been authorized in some states for state park administration, too.[265] Debt secured by operating revenues is also a common method of financing capital outlays in state and local water-terminal projects.[266] In a few states standing authority is given state agencies concerned to issue revenue bonds to finance projects of irrigation, flood control, navigation improvement and the like.[267]

Tax-anticipation bonds include general-obligation bonds and bonds in anticipation of special taxes, secured respectively by the general revenues (i.e., revenues from all taxes) and special taxes.[268] Bonds issued by counties in financing the various enterprises in water resources administration are gen- erally special-tax-anticipation bonds, as municipal and state bonds are mostly revenue and general-obligation bonds.[269] "Ab- solute bonds" differ from bonds in anticipation of taxes only procedurally. In most cases, these two types of bonds are iden- tical in substance, for the funds to be raised under either pro- cedure are no more and no less than what area actually required for the administration of the projects concerned. Absolute bonds are issued by both county and city governments,[270] as well as by special districts. Sometimes a county or city is given option between two or three different types of bonds.[271]

As discussed above, municipalities generally may issue bonds for the construction or acquisition of water-supply, electric and water-terminal enterprises. These bonds are usually revenue bonds. In many states, municipalities are also authorized to issue sewerage bonds, which are mostly revenue bonds,[272] or revenues bonds and other types of bonds alternatively,[273] and in a few states non-revenue bonds.[274]

In a number of states, general authority has been given municipalities to issue bonds for the construction and acquisition of public utilities or public improvements.[275] In the majority of cases, the municipalities are authorized to issue revenue bonds.[276] In states such as Nebraska and Ohio, they are authorized to issue general-obligation bonds; and in states such as Montana, Colorado and Pennsylvania they may issue either revenue or general-obligation bonds. In Missouri and Louisiana, municipal bonds issued for this purpose are special-tax-anticipation bonds and absolute bonds respectively. In Pennsylvania, water supply is the only public utility in water-resources field for which bonds may be issued. In Ohio bonds are issued for any permanent improvement authorized by law. In Maine and Oregon, the authority applies to "any revenue producing public improvement"and to any revenue-producing work or project, respectively. But in other states, the authority covers two or more of the municipal enterprises (those not in the field of water resources administration **have** been omitted) of water supply, electric-power, sewerage, water terminals, parks and recreation, flood control and drainage.

Besides the state revenue bonds discussed above, state forestry bonds have been authorized in Washington, South Carolina and Oregon. In Washington, the State Forestry Board may issue "state forest utility bonds" for the acquisition and improvement of lands for state forests, the principal and interest of which are to be paid from a special fund called the "forest development fund", which consists of all revenues from the management of the state forests, after deducting advances, if any, from tne state reclamation revolving fund (Revised Code, sec. 76.-12.090 et seq.: L. 1923, ch. 154, sec. 5 et seq.; as last amended by L. 1953, ch. 21, sec. 1). The State Commission of Forestry of South Carolina may issue revenue bonds from time to time to carry out its programs, which may not exceed $500,000 in the aggregate (Code of Laws, secs. 29-24 and 29-25: Acts 1933, No. 360, secs. 2 and 3). Under the laws of Oregon, the State Board of Forestry "may sell . . . Oregon forest development revenue bonds in an amount not exceeding $500,000" for the development of state forests (Revised Statutes, sec. 530.100 et seq.: L. 1945, ch. 154, sec. 7 et seq., as amended by L. 1951, ch. 51, sec. 1). It may also issue bonds in the amount of $750,000 each year "for the rehabilitation, management and development of state-owned forest lands and the acquisition of lands for

said purposes." These bonds are to redeemed partly by revenues from the forest lands on which funds raised by the bonds
are expended and partly by a special tax levy (Ibid., sec.
530.220 et seq.: L. 1949, ch. 102, sec. 2 et seq.). In Kentucky, under an act of 1946 (ch. 126), any state agency as well
as any local unit may issue revenue bonds for any "public project" (which covers all aspects of water resources administration).[277]

Statutes authorizing issuance of state and local bonds
usually contain certain limitations upon the issuing authorities. In general, those on state bond issues consist of stipulations as to the amount of the issue, the interest rate, the
maturity and the security. For local non-revenue bonds, these
are usually left to the discretion of local governing bodies,
which issue the bonds, but the issuance of bonds is to be approved by a popular vote of at least simple majority at a referendum.[278] The statute may also specify the amount of the
bonds to be either in monetary figures or in terms of percentage of taxable property.[279] Local revenue bonds are in general exempt from these limitations, but the enabling legislation
may provide for interest rates and lengths of maturity.

State legislation enabling state agencies and local units
to borrow moneys usually provide for the issuance of bonds only. However, under Federal legislation the Federal Government
has been authorized to make loans to the several states and
their local units for many types of activities in water resources administration. As discussed before, the Reconstruction
Finance Corporation, under the authority of the Emergency Relief and Construction Act of 1932,[280] made some loans to states
and local units for the construction of self-liquidating projects. By sec. 36 of the Agricultural Adjustment Act of 12
May 1933 (48 Stat. 31, 48), as last amended on 22 June 1936
(49 Stat. 1818), the said Corporation was authorized to make
loans in a maximum aggregate amount of $125 million to drainage,
levee, drainage and similar districts (including private associations) and to regular local units in connection with their
irrigation and drainage enterprises, to enable them to reduce
and redeem their outstanding indebtedness. This Federal loan
program was terminated in 1947. Under an amendment to an Act
of 13 April 1934 (48 Stat. 589), adopted 17 April 1936 (49 Stat.
1232), the same Corporation made "disaster loans" to local units
and special districts for the repair, construction, reconstruction and rehabilitation of irrigation, drainage, electric, navigation, water supply and sewer works and facilities. The total
amount of these loans is, however, unknown. By an amendment to
sec. 4(a)(3) of its Organic Act adopted 13 April 1938 (52 Stat.
212), as amended 25 May 1948 (62 Stat. 261, 263), the same Corporation was authorized to make loans (aggregating not more than
$290 million at any time) to state agencies and local units for
the financing of self-liquidating projects. Loans made under
this provision totalled about $1.5 billion.[281] As mentioned be-

fore, the Reconstruction Finance Corporation was abolished and all of its loan programs liquidated by an Act of 30 July 1953 (67 Stat. 230).[282]

The former Public Works Administration had the authority "to provide 45 percent of the cost of approved projects (of states and local units) as direct Federal grants (and) to make loans toward the 55 percent to be borne by the sponsors . . ."[283] As of 30 June 1942, such loans totalled $819,876,637.[284]

By title V of the War Mobilization and Reconversion Act of 3 October 1944 (58 Stat. 785, 791), the former Federal Works Agency was authorized to make interest-free loans to states and local units for the financing of preliminary costs of public works projects. This Federal loan program was liquidated by the Independent Offices Appropriation Act of 30 July 1947 (61 Stat. 585, 597). Its emphasis was on water supply and water sanitation.[285] By 31 December 1952, a total of 6,552 such loans had been made **aggregating** about $47 million.[286] On 13 October 1949, an Act was passed (63 Stat. 841) which revived the above loan program for a period of two years. This second program was liquidated in 1951, as directed by the legislation.[287] Loans made under the second program are as follows (as of 31 December 1952):[288]

Type of projects	Number of projects	Loans ($)	%
All types	1,283	21,656,000	100.0
Sewerage	506	8,617,000	39.8
Water supply	186	2,744,000	12.7
Parks and recreation	27	205,000	0.9
Other (Unrelated to water resources)		(Omitted)	

At the present time, the following Federal loan programs are **available** to states and local units:

As discussed before, the rural electrification loans provided by the Act of 20 May 1936 (49 Stat. 1363) and the T. V. A. loans are available to states and local units. Of the millions of dollars loaned by the T. V. A. to its distributors, it may be noted, only $352,548 were loaned to municipalities.[289] Rural electrification loans under the act of 1936 made to state and municipal agencies up to 28 February 1955 are as follows.[290]

Type of loans	Public power districts(47)	Other public bodies (26)
Distribution	$99,078,542	$20,072,049
Generation and transmission	24,128,186	2,699,290
Consumer facilities	450,199	None
Total	$123,656,927	$22,771,339

These loans were less than five percent of the total amount of
such loans made during the same period (which was $2,961,450,
024).

Under the above-mentioned **National** Defense Public Works
Act of 28 June 1941 (55 Stat. 361) and Defense Housing and
Community Facilities and Services Act of 1 September 1951 (65
Stat. 293), loans are available to state agencies and local
governments (as well as to private parties) for the construction of water-supply, sewerage, recreation and other public
facilities needed in Federal defense-services concentrations.
Federal loans made under the former act totaled $8,115,116 as
of 30 June 1949.[291] As of 31 December 1953, a total of $3.7
million of Federal loans had been approved under the second
act.[292] It would seem that these loans were largely extended
to municipalities and other non-Federal public parties.[293]

Under sec. 5 of the Water Pollution Control Act of 30 June
1948 (62 Stat. 1155, 1158), the Public Health Service may "make
loans to any state, municipality, or interstate agency for the
construction of necessary treatment works to prevent the discharge by such state or municipality of untreated or inadequate-
ly treated sewage or other waste into interstate waters or into a tributary of such waters, and for the preparation of engineering reports, plans, and specifications in connection
therewith." Any such loan is limited to one-third of the total
estimated cost of the project concerned, but it shall in no
case exceed $250,000. These loans bear an annual interest of
2 percent. As of 30 June 1953, no such loans had actually been
made.[294]

On 4 June 1936, an Act was enacted (49 Stat. 1461) which
authorized the Farm Credit Administration and the various farm
credit agencies under its supervision to make secured loans to
irrigation, drainage and conservancy districts. As of April
1955, no loans had been made under this provision.[295]

Under sec. 201 of the Act of 28 February 1920 (41 Stat.
456, 458), as amended by an Act of 4 March 1921 (41 Stat. 1392),
the Inland Waterways Corporation, in the name of the Secretary
of Commerce, "is authorized to make loans to states, municipalities, and transportation companies that will contribute to the
improvement of transportation facilities (i.e., water terminal
facilities) along the inland waterways. As of June 30 , 1949,
there was one **loan** outstanding of $105,568 to the City of New
Orleans."[296] As of 30 June 1953, there had been no report of a
new loan or loans. As the said Corporation is now nearing liquidation, it would seem that this provision has become obsolete.[297]

Federal loans may also be authorized by the Congress to a
particular state or state agency or local unit on an individual
or ad-hoc basis. For example, by sec. 4 of an Act of 31 August

1954 (68 Stat. 1045, 1046), the Secretary of the Interior was authorized to lend $500,000 to the Palo Verde Irrigation District of California for necessary modification of its existing irrigation works.

In general, the states are not capable of making loans to local units. But sometimes exceptions can be found. For example, the Washington Department of Conservation and Development may make loans out of a reclamation fund raised by a special surtax of 0.5 mill to irrigation and drainage districts to help finance their works (Revised Code, ch. 89.16: L. 1919, ch. 158; as last amended by L. 1943, ch. 279). As of 30 September 1952, the reclamation loans made by the said Department totaled about $2,300,000.[298] The Wyoming Farm Loan Board may make loans of a maximum sum of $200,000 to a local unit or a special district for the construction of small irrigation projects (Compiled Statutes, sec. 21-401: L. 1951, ch. 132, sec. 1). The State Bond Commission of Oregon (L. 1949, ch. 500; as last amended by L. 1953, ch. 287), the State Water Pollution Control Board of California (Water Code, sec. 13100 et seq.: Stats. 1953, ch. 221) and the Governor and Council of New Hampshire (Revised Laws, ch. 166-A, sec. 4-s: L. 1953, ch. 247, sec. 2) may make loans to local units for the construction of sewerage works.

Federal loans to states and local units and state loans to local units often go hand in hand with the bond issues of the debtor states and local units, and the former are in many instances secured by the latter.

(2) Special Funds---The use of special funds has a prominent place in state finance.[299] They are used extensively in the fields of fish and wildlife, forestry, and parks and recreation.

(a) Fish and Wildlife ---First, there is the general fish and wildlife fund, which exist in almost every state and which is known by various names.[300] This fund is both a fiscal fund and a complete enterprise fund, as it consists of all receipts of the state fish and game agency and pays all of its expenditures. As a fiscal fund, it is established under the influence of the above-mentioned Federal Aid in Wildlife Restoration Act of 1937, which requires every recepient to pass laws prohibiting the diversion of fish and game license fees into uses other than fish and game administration (in sec. 1). In states such as California, Idaho, Kansas, Kentucky, Minnesota, Oklahoma, Oregon, Pennsylvania and Wyoming, this fund is accompanied by financial autonomy. That is to say, the state fish and game agency in these states may expend this fund without appropriatioh by the state legislature. But in states such as Alabama, Colorado, Illinois, Louisiana, Massachusetts, Ohio, Tennessee, Texas, Virginia, Washington and Wisconsin, there is no such financial autonomy and the fund cannot be expended unless appropriated by

the state legislature. In Alabama and Kentucky, the laws specifically provide that the unexpended amount in each year of
the general fish and game fund should be covered into the general fund, and so the fund is not allowed to accumulate.[301]
But in all other states, this fund is a continuing fund. It
may be also be remarked that this fund does not include the
receipts nor does it defray the expenses of commercial fisheries.

Besides this general fish and game fund, there are in some
states special funds covering only a part of the state fish
and game enterprise. For example, in Florida there is the autonomous "conservation fund" for commercial fishery (Statutes,
sec. 370.6(10): L. 1953, ch. 28145, sec. 2, subsec. 6, subdiv.
(10)) and in Alabama the non-autonomous "seafoods fund" (Acts
1951, No. 476). In New Jersey, "sixty cents of every resident
hunting 'license fee, and twenty-five cents of every resident
fishing fee . . . shall be placed to the credit of a fund to
be known as the public shooting and fishing grounds fund, which
FUND shall be used exclusively for the acquisition . . . and
the development, maintenance and stocking of game, birds, animals and fish . . . for use as public hunting and fishing
grounds and game refuges . . ." (Revised Statutes, sec. 23-3-11:
L. 1914, ch. 152, sec. 5; as last amended by L. 1953, ch. 334).
In Oregon, three percent of the state game fund, but not exceeding $30,000 in any one calendar year, is segregated from
the said fund and established as the predatory animal control
fund to be used for predatory animal control in cooperation
with the Federal Government (Revised Statutes, sec. 610.020:
L. 1937, ch. 105, sec. 1; as amended by L. 1951, ch. 452, sec.
1). Under an act of 1951 of California (Stats. 1951, ch. 1401),
the Wildlife Restoration Fund is established as a necessarily
autonomous complete enterprise to carry out the provisions of
the Wildlife Conservation Act of 1947 (ch. 1325), the said fund
consisting of all appropriations for the same purpose.

(b) Forestry Funds---Forestry funds have been established
in many a state. In the majority of cases, the (general) forestry fund consists of only the receipts and is used for the
maintenance of state forests and other state-owned forest lands.[302]
In Delaware (Code, tit. 7, sec. 2906: L. 1927, ch. 50, sec. 14)
and Tennessee (Code, sec. 630.16: et seq.: Acts 1937, ch. 280,
sec. 11 et seq.), it is made up of appropriations from the general fund, revenues and fines of the state forestry agency and
Federal grants-in-aid, and is a complete enterprise fund. In
Alabama (Code, tit. 8, sec. 202: Acts 1923, No. 486, sec. 13;
as amended by Acts 1945, No. 227), Indiana (Statutes, tit. 32,
ch. 4: Acts 1945, ch. 187; as last amended by Acts 1947, ch.
320), Oklahoma (Statutes, tit. 74, sec. 353.11: L. 1945, p. 391,
sec. 11), etc., it comprises state appropriations to and receipts
(including fines) of the state forestry agency, and is also a
complete enterprise fund. In Mississippi (Code, sec. 6027 et
seq.: L. 1926, ch. 161) and Colorado (Statutes, ch. 134, sec.

131(10): L. 1943, ch. 150, sec. 2), it covers only Federal grants-in-aid and is purely a fiscal fund.303

In some states, special forestry funds have been establish-ed. For example, all funds supporting the reforestation pro-gram of South Dakota are deposited in a fiscal fund called the "tree fund".304 In Michigan, all receipts of the Department of Conservation from the sale of forest products on tax-revert-ed lands are credited to the reforestation fund to be used for the reforestation of lands in certain counties of the state (Acts 1945, No. 268; as amended by Acts 1947, No. 105). In Washington, there is the forest insect and disease control fund (Revised Code, sec. 76.06.100: L. 1951, ch. 233, sec. 8); and in Oregon there are forest development fund, revolving fund for fire protection, forest fire emergency fund, forest insect fund, and Oregon forest rehabilitation fund.

(c) Parks and Recreation Funds---General park funds exist in a majority of states. In most cases, the general state park fund is an operation fund consisting of revenues from the state park system, as in Texas (Revised Civil Statutes, art. 6070a: L. 1931, ch. 168; as amended by L. 1941, ch. 431), Louisiana (Revised Statutes, tit. 56, sec. 1688: Acts 1934, No. 91, sec. 5; as last amended by Acts 1940, No. 110, sec. 3), Maine (Re-vised Statutes, ch. 32, sec. 25: L. 1935, ch. 144, sec. 2, para. (k)), Mississippi (Code, sec. 5961: L. 1936, ch. 194), Minneso-ta (Statutes, sec. 85.22: L. 1951, ch. 460), etc. In a few states, such as New Mexico (Statutes, sec. 4-116: L. 1935, ch. 57, sec. 16) and Florida (Statutes, sec. 592.11: L. 1949, ch. 25353, sec. 11), it consists of revenues of the state parks, donations and contributions, and state appropriations (from other funds), and is therefore a complete enterprise fund. In states such as Montana (Revised Codes, sec. 62-305: L. 1939, ch. 48, sec. 5), Oklahoma (Statutes, tit. 74, sec. 351k: L. 1937, ch. 24, art. 27, sec. 17), and Missouri (Revised Statutes, ch. 253: L. 1953, p. 37), it is made up of revenues of the state park system and donations and contributions, and is in the na-ture of a fiscal fund, the purpose of which is to prevent the diversion of these moneys to extraneous uses. This fund is in general an autonomous305 continuing fund.306

In some states, special funds have been established either for a particular state park or recreational area or for a par-ticular aspect of the state park and recreation enterprise. For example, in Texas there is the "Jim Hogg State Park Build-ing Fund", which is made up of the proceeds from the sale of timber in the said park and which is used for the improvement thereof (Revised Civil Statutes, art. 6077h-1: L. 1951, ch. 82). In Oregon, all moneys received by the Columbia River Gorge Com-mission for the recreational development of the Columbia River Gorge are placed in an autonomous continuing fiscal fund. (Re-vised Statutes, secs. 358.615 and 358.630: L. 1953, ch. 475, secs. 2 and 5). In California there is the State Beach Fund, which is a complete enterprise fund used for the construction and acquisition (non-autonomous) and the improvement and maintenance (autonomous) of the state beaches. It includes a certain percentage of the proceeds from the sale of school lands, and certain funds originally earmarked for the acquisition and maintenance of state beaches (Public Resources Code, sec. 5014: Stats. 1941, ch. 619, sec. 2; as last amended by Stats. 1944, Ex. Sess. ch. 8, sec. 1).

(d) Combined Forestry and Park Fund---This exists in Maryland (Code, art. 66C, sec. 354: L. 1914, ch. 824), New Hampshire (Revised Laws, ch. 234, sec. 14: L. 1927, ch. 130, sec. 1; as last amended by L. 1949, ch. 295, sec. 3) and Arkansas (Acts 1953, No. 42, sec. 8 et seq.). The Arkansas fund is a complete enterprise fund comprising state appropriations (from other sources), revenues of the state forests and parks, donations and contributions and Federal grants. The Maryland and New Hampshire funds are operation funds made up of operational revenues only.

(e) Other Special Funds---In California, for example, all moneys appropriated by the state for the construction, improvement, maintenance, operation or planning and investigation of any project of navigation improvement, irrigation, flood control, hydroelectric power development or the like are placed in a continuing fund called the Water Resources Fund (Political Code, sec. 363: Stats. 1939, ch. 667, sec. 3, 1st para.).[307] Similar to this fund is the Revolving Fund for the Oklahoma Planning and Resources Board, which is used for the construction of farm ponds, levees, irrigation ditches and other water utilization and conservation projects, and which is composed of all moneys appropriated by the state for and receipts from this enterprise (Statutes, tit. 74, sec. 352.1 et seq.: L. 1941, p. 456).[308] The Utah Water and Power Board Construction Fund belongs to the same category (Code, sec. 73-10-8: L. 1947, ch. 14, sec. 8; as amended by L. 1953, ch. 133, sec. 3). The reclamation fund of Washington, which was discussed before, is used to finance a state loan program. In California, a law of 1946 (Stats. 1946, ch. 142) created the State Flood Control Fund, and appropriated $32,250,000 to constitute it. The fund is used to pay state's contributions to the construction and maintenance and operation of Federal flood-control projects.[309]

Section 3   Interstate Finance

In general, the problem of interstate finance arises only when there is an interstate agency.[310] In cases where an interstate agency has no operational revenues of its own, its expenses (other than the compensation of the representatives of the state-members) are borne by the member states either equally,[311] when the benefits derived by each member-state are equal or approximately equal to those derived by the other member-state or states from the interstate administration or arrangement, or in proportion to the benefits accorded them. There seems to have been no fixed standards in assessing the varying benefits of the member-states in the allocation between them of the costs of an interstate agency. In the Arkansas River Compact of 31 May 1949, 60 percent of such costs is borne by Colorado and 40 percent by Kansas (63 Stat. 145, 150). These percentages are not the same as those in which the waters of the river are apportioned. In the Ohio River Valley Water Sanitation Compact of 11 July 1940, one-half of the costs of the agency set up thereby are "to be pro-rated among the several states in proportion of their population within the (Sanitation) District at the last preceding federal census, the other half to be prorated in proportion to their land area within the District" (54 Stat. 752, 755-756). In the Upper Colorado River Compact of 6 April 1949, the expenses of the interstate agency are borne by its member-states "according to the percentage of consumptive use apportioned to each . . ." (63 Stat. 31, 35). With respect to the Pacific Marine **Fisheries** Commission set up by the compact of 24 July 1947, its expenses are borne by the three member-states "in proportion to the primary market value of the products of their fisheries as recorded in the latest published reports (five year average), provided no state shall contribute less than $2,000 per annum . . ." (61 Stat. 419, 422). In the case of the Connecticut River Flood Control Commission, which was set up by a compact of 6 June 1953, the moneys to be paid by each member each year have been fixed to be $7,500 for Massachusetts, $6,500 for Connecticut, and $1,000 each for New Hampshire and Vermont (67 Stat. 45, 52).

In most interstate compacts providing for interstate finance, possibilities of Federal contributions are taken into account. It would seem that services performed by the United States on behalf of the interstate agencies are generally done at the expenses of the former. "Contributions by federal and state agencies" to the Port of New York Authority up to 31 December 1947 "in aid of construction amounted to $10,860,412 . . ."[312] Contributions may also be received from private sources. For example, the Palisades Interstate Park received in 1909, 1917, 1919 and 1925 private contributions totalling $1,625,000, $1,921,594, $666,000 and $200,000 respectively.[313]

In revenue-producing interstate enterprises, authority is usually given agencies operating these enterprises to issue revenue bonds.[314] As mentioned above, Federal water-pollution-control grants and loans are available to interstate agencies.

(Chapter 6 was originally entitled "Administrative Powers", and included, besides finance, personnel, acquisition and enforcement. Discussions on these three powers are omitted due to consideration of space. By administrative powers it is meant means by which administrative services are carried out.)

NOTES

1. Not all such receipts are necessarily to be used in self-finance, which is here defined in its narrow sense. For example, if revenues from fish and wildlife were used for flood control, it does not constitute self-finance. It will be regarded as appropriation from special revenues.

2. Emergency Relief Appropriation Act of 8 April 1935 (49 Stat. 115); Emergency Relief Appropriation Act of 22 June 1936 (49 Stat. 1608); Emergency Relief Appropriation Act of 29 June 1937 (50 Stat. 352); Emergency Relief Appropriation Act of 30 June 1939 (53 Stat. 927); Emergency Relief Appropriation Act of 26 June 1940 (54 Stat. 611); Emergency Relief Appropriation Acts of 1 July 1941 (55 Stat. 396) and 2 July 1942 (56 Stat. 634). For additional emergency relief appropriations, see 50 Stat. 8, 10; 52 Stat. 83; and 55 Stat. 14, 15.

3. Emergency Construction Appropriation Act of 20 December 1930 (46 Stat. 1030); Fourth Deficiency Appropriation Act of 16 June 1933, emergency appropriations (48 Stat. 274, 275); Additional Emergency Appropriation Act of 15 February 1934 (48 Stat. 351); Emergency Appropriation Act of 19 June 1934 (48 Stat. 1021) (these last three appropriations were authorized by the National Industrial Recovery Act of 1933, op. cit., the Unemployment Relief Act of 31 March 1933, 48 Stat. 22, and the Federal Emergency Relief Act of 12 May 1933, 48 Stat. 55); Work Relief and Public Works Appropriation Act of 21 June 1938 (52 Stat. 809).

4. From the point of view of the whole appropriation act these special lump-sum appropriations for irrigation are itemized appropriations.

5. An Indian irrigation project might be first financed by an itemized appropriation but subsequently supported by lump-sum appropriations, or vice versa, or by the two types of appropriations alternatively.

6. In the Indian Office Appropriation Act of 2 March 1867, there was a sum of $5,000 to defray the "expense of collecting and locating the Colorado River Indians in Arizona, . . . including the expense of constructing a canal for irrigating said reservation" (14 Stat. 492, 514).

7. Many early Indian irrigation works were financed (or partly financed) from general appropriations to the Indian Office, which were separated by states and which did not contain special items for irrigation.

8. For occasional lump-sum appropriations made prior to 1920, see River and Harbor Acts of 28 June 1864 (13 Stat. 200), 10 August 1869 (16 Stat. 44), 3 March 1910 (35 Stat. 815) and 5 June 1920 (41 Stat. 1009).

9. The River and Harbor Act of 5 June 1920 did not authorize any new projects.

10. See 49 Stat. 120, 146; 50 Stat. 515, 519; 52 Stat. 667, 671; 60 Stat. 160, 163.

11. Act of 14 October 1940, sec. 1 (54 Stat. 1119), as last amended by Act of 16 July 1943, sec. 1 (57 Stat. 566), and Act of 14 October 1940, sec. 9 (54 Stat. 1124). There is no limit on the expenditures on canals and laterals for irrigation.

12. For example, an Act of 12 July 1943 (57 Stat. 521), authorizing an "emergency fund" of $10,000,000 for the repair and strengthening of

levees destroyed or threatened by recent floods; the Joint Resolution of
11 October 1949 (63 Stat. 763), authorizing appropriations for reforestation and revegetation work of the Forest Service, etc.).

13. The Forest Service, $18,186,613; the National Park Service, $17,-
946,029; the Soil Conservation Service, $14,457,428; the Corps of Engi-
neers, $2,238,823; the Fish and Wildlife Service, $3,449,964; the Rural
Electrification Administration, $362,219; the General Land Office (now
Bureau of Land Management), $105,737; the Bureau of Indian Affairs, $91,-
848; the Bureau of Reclamation, $29,235.

14. Federal Works Agency, Final Report on the WPA Program, 1935-
1943, 1946, pp. 10; 99; 119. All of the funds of the Work Projects Administration (originally Works Progress Administration) were appropriated
by the Emergency Relief Appropriation Acts. The President allocated to
other Federal agencies funds appropriated by the acts of 1935, 1936 and
1937, but the Administration allocated to them funds appropriated by subsequent acts.

15. Sewer systems, water system, sewer and water systems, flood control, navigation improvement, reclamation, water power, parks and recreation, and fish and wildlife. See Federal Works Agency, Annual Report for
1942, p. 132.

16. Federal Works Agency, Annual Report for 1942, p. 130; and Annual
Report for 1943, p. 65.

17. They were the only two Federal emergency finance agencies which
made allotments of emergency funds to regular Federal agencies.

18. Rpt. Chief of E. 1949, p. 17.

19. As of 30 June 1953, the appropriations for navigation improvement and flood control totalled $4,430,403,908.92 and $4,267,015,581.22
respectively. -- Rpt. Chief of E. 1953, p. 21.

20. Rpt. Sec. Inter. 1951, p. 86.

21. U. S. Bureau of Indian Affairs, Annual Statement of Costs, Cancellations, and Miscellaneous Irrigation Data of Indian Irrigation Projects, Fiscal Year 1950, p. 1. "Emergency funds" as used in this paragraph means emergency appropriations (direct and indirect).

22. A water user is a homestead-entryman if he settles upon vacant
Federal land benefited by an irrigation project under the Reclamation
and the Homestead Laws, or a water-right applicant (i.e., an applicant
to the Department of the Interior for the right to the use of the irrigation water made available by an irrigation project, which right is not
complete until repayment obligations are fully discharged) in case he is
a private land owner and a beneficiary of the irrigation project.

23. That is, works which serve the project lands only. The project
lands are public and private lands which an irrigation project is originally planned to irrigate.

24. That is, projects which are governed by the Reclamation Act of
17 June 1902 (32 Stat. 388) and acts amendatory thereof or supplementary
thereto, including the Reclamation Project Act of 4 August 1939 (53 Stat.
1187).

25. For the origin of this Act, see Senate Document No. 92, 68th

Congress, 1st session, April 1924.

26. <u>Rpt. Sec. Inter. 1925</u>, p. 8.

27. These adjustments were completed by the acts of 3 July 1930 (46 Stat. 1010) and 27 June 1934 (48 Stat. 1266).

28. Sec. 43 was slightly amended by an Act of 23 April 1930 (46 Stat. 249).

29. This was already granted by the Interior Appropriation Act of 10 May 1926 (44 Stat. 453, 479), enacted only two weeks before the passage of the Omnibus Adjustment Act.

30. Acts of 3 March 1933 (47 Stat. 1427); 27 March 1934 (48 Stat. 500); 13 June 1935 (49 Stat. 337); 14 April 1936 (49 Stat. 1206), sec. 3; and 21 August 1937 (50 Stat. 737), and sec. 17(b) of the Reclamation Project Act of 4 August 1939 (53 Stat. 1187, 1198). The terms of the enactments of 1937 and 1939 applied only to those water users who were actually unable to pay.

31. "The contract which provides for operation of the dam and reservoir by the Lower Colorado River Authority of Texas contains provisions for repayment of the reimbursable cost in no more than 35 annual installments, commencing after completion of payments on bonds issued by the Authority, but not later than June 1, 1975." -- <u>Reclamation Project Data</u>, op. cit., p. 94.

32. Details of sec. 7(b) are omitted. For special enactments providing for the inclusion of a development period in repayments concluded prior to 4 August 1939, see, as an examp,e, Act of 31 July 1953 (67 Stat. 243).

33. For actual repayment periods, see U. S. Bureau of Reclamation, <u>Repayment Histories and Payout Schedules---1952</u>, 1953.

34. Sec. 17(a); as last amended by Act of 6 March 1952 (66 Stat. 16).

35. An Act of 31 July 1953 (67 Stat. 241) cancelled $297,752 obligation of the Greenfields Irrigation district, Montana, which represents the reimbursable cost of the abandoned part of the main canal of the Sun River project, situated between station 0 and station 278 (5.26 miles). -- <u>House Report 554</u>, 83rd Cong., 1st sess., 15 June 1953. Such cancellation, however, was not a measure of relief (and was not based on any provision of the Reclamation Project Act).

36. See U. S. Bureau of Reclamation, <u>Project Feasibilities and Authorizations</u>, 1949, p. 570.

37. See Act of 1 July 1940 (54 Stat. 707), and <u>House Report 2477</u>, 76th Cong., 3rd sess., 7 June 1940.

38. See Indian Office Appropriation Act of 18 May 1916 (39 Stat. 123, 130) (for Salt River Indian allotments in Arizona, and Act of 27 June 1930 (46 Stat. 820) (both for Piute Indian lands in Nevada).

39. <u>House Public Lands Committee Hearings on Irrigation and Reclamation</u>, 80th Cong., 1st sess., February 1947, pp. 5-6.

40. Letter to the author from Mr. George H. Winters, Secretary, U. S. Section, International Boundary and Water Commission, United States

and Mexico, dated 8 July 1953. It may be noted that under the convention between the United States and Mexico proclaimed 16 January 1907 (34 Stat. 2953, part III) the Mexican Government was not obliged to repay the United States for the storage and delivery of water (60,000 acre-feet annually), which was imposed upon the United States in return of Mexico's waiver of all claims to the waters of the Rio Grande. In the Sundry Civil Appropriation Act of 4 March 1907, authority was given the Secretary of the Interior for the construction of the Elephant Butte Dam and Reservoir and provision made to the effect that $1,000,000 be non-reimbursable on account of allocation of water to Mexico in accordance with the said convention (34 Stat. 1295, 1357). See Reclamation Project Data, op. cit., p. 369.

41. For the auxiliary reclamation fund in the Yuma project, see p. , below.

42. Secs. 3, 4 and 9, as slightly amended on 16 July 1943 (57 Stat. 566).

43. House Executive Document No. 5, 59th Cong., 2nd sess., 1907 (Rpt. Sec. Inter. 1906), p. 82.

44. See p. 1268, above, and the annual reports of the Commissioner of Indian Affairs during the period 1870-1905.

45. It may be noted that a substantial part of the tribal of the various Indian reservations was the proceeds of the sale of their lands and payments by the United States in the settlement of the claims of the Indians to the ownership or occupancy of public lands.

46. Report of the Commissioner of Indian Affairs for 1898, p. 50. For the motive of this action, see House Public Lands Committee Hearings on Flathead Indian Project, Montana, 80th Cong., 2nd sess., February-March 1948, p. 69.

47. The impact of the Reclamation Act of 1902 was preceptible.

48. Consult House Executive Document 5, 59th Cong., 1st sess., 1906 (Rpt. sec. Inter. 1905), Part I, pp. 74-75.

49. The repayment plan for the Blackfeet Project was abandoned in 1919, as no lands had been sold. -- U. S. Bureau of Indian Affairs, Area Office at Billings, Montana, Report No. 140 (mimeo.), March 1954, Introduction.

50. See Indian Office Appropriation Acts of 30 April 1908 (35 Stat. 70, 83-84, Flathead Reservation, Montana), 4 April 1910 (36 Stat. 269, 273, a pumping plant and canals in the Colorado River Reservation, Arizona), 3 March 1911 (36 Stat. 1058, 1063 and 1071, Yuma Reservation in California and Klamath Reservation in Oregon) (for the Modoc Point project on the Klamath Reservation, funds reimbursable "from the proceeds from the sale of timber or lands . . .").

51. For the Milk River irrigation system on the Fort Belknap Reservation, also see the Act of 3 March 1909 (35 Stat. 781, 795).

52. This provision was re-iterated in all subsequent Interior Department Appropriation Acts down to and including the Act of 3 July 1945 (59 Stat. 318, 328).

53. See 25 C. F. R. 151.1. Also consult 45 Stat. 212, 1574.

54. A few appropriations are not reimbursable. See Acts of 21 June 1906 (34 Stat. 325, 371, wells on the Yankton Reservation in South Dakota), 1 March 1907 (34 Stat. 1015, 1035, the Tongue River Reservation in Montana), 30 April 1908 (35 Stat. 70, 76-77, Indians in California), 3 March 1925 (43 Stat. 1141, 1153, San Juan Pueblo project, New Mexico), etc. It is not known whether there are any npn-Indian lands within these projects.

55. House Report 2369, 74th Cong., 2nd sess., 3 April 1936, p. 2. The 1927 regulations appear in the Code of Federal Regulations as sec. 141.1 to 141.6, inclusive, of tit. 25.

56. The provision for the Flathead Reservation was amended by the Interior Department Appropriation Act of 10 May 1926 (44 Stat. 453, 466), that for the Wapato (distribution) project in Washington was last amended by a special Act of 24 February 1938 (52 Stat. 80), and that for the Crow Reservation was supplemented by a special Act of 28 June 1946 (50 Stat. 333, in secs. 4, 5 and 6).

57. Report of the Commissioner of Indian Affairs for 1933, p. 5.

58. See Senate Report 519, 63rd Cong., 2nd sess., 15 May 1914.

59. Neither is it known whether these funds are to be repaid by the Indians alone or by both Indians and non-Indians.

60. Acts of 26 January 1933 (47 Stat. 776), 3 March 1933 (ch. 201: 47 Stat. 1427), 13 June 1935, sec. 2 (49 Stat. 337), 14 April 1936, sec. 3 (49 Stat. 1206, 1207), 21 August 1937 (50 Stat. 737), 31 May 1939 (53 Stat. 792), 4 August 1939, sec. 17(b) (53 Stat. 1187, 1198).

61. See Acts of 25 May 1922 (42 Stat. 595, 596), 9 May 1935 (49 Stat. 176, 187-188), 24 February 1938, sec. 2 (52 Stat. 80).

62. But not non-Indians.

63. House Appropriations Committee Supplemental Hearings on Interior Department Appropriation Bill For 1937, 74th Cong., 2nd sess., 1936, p. 168.

64. See Acts of 13 March 1928 (45 Stat. 312), 27 June 1930 (46 Stat. 820), and 11 August 1939 (53 Stat. 1411).

65. Not later than 1st of March each year. -- Omnibus Adjustment Act of 25 May 1926, sec. 46 (44 Stat. 636, 650), (43 U. S. C. 423e), proviso.

66. Report of the Commissioner of Indian Affairs for 1913, p. 18.

67. Requirements for the repayment of costs of operation and maintenance have also been repeated in all special statutory provisions concerning Indian irrigation enterprise enacted since 1916.

68. Consult U. S. Department of the Interior (by Felix S. Cohen), Handbbok of Federal Indian Law, 1941 (4th printing in 1945), p. 250.

69. Report of the Commissioner of Indian Affairs for 1932, pp.18-19; House Hearings on Interior Department Appropriations for 1955, 83rd Cong., 2nd sess., 1954, p. 590.

70. See all appropriations for such costs.

71. For example, Act of 22 April 1940 (54 Stat. 155).

72. See House Irrigation and Reclamation Committee Hearings On H. R. 5124, 79th Cong., 2nd sess., February-March 1946, p. 64.

73. 3 Western Political Quarterly 435-436 (1950, by Taylor).

74. For actual practice, see House Public Lands Committee Hearings on Irrigation and Reclamation, 80th Cong., 1st sess., February 1947, p. 55.

75. This will be discussed in the following Section.

76. Sec. 4 of the Reclamation Extension Act of 13 August 1914 (38 Stat. 686, 687; 43 U. S. C. 469).

77. See Acts of 3 March 1925 (Interior Department Appropriation, 43 Stat. 1141, 1167ff), 10 May 1926 (Interior Department Appropriation, 44 Stat. 453, 479ff), 18 June 1926 (44 Stat. 753), 12 January 1927 (Interior Department Appropriation, 44 Stat. 934, 958), 21 December 1928 (45 Stat. 1057, in sec. 4(b), para. 2, at 1059), 9 August 1937 (Interior Department Appropriation, 60 Stat. 564, 592), 2 August 1937 (50 Stat. 557, as amended on 9 April 1938, 52 Stat. 211), 28 June 1941 (Interior Department Appropriation, 55 Stat. 303, 331), 10 March 1943 (57 Stat. 14, in sec. 2(a)), 29 August 1949 (63 Stat. 677), 27 September 1950 (64 Stat. 1072, as slightly amended on 5 March 1952, 66 Stat. 13). For certain Indian irrigation projects, see p. 1037, above. Consult Reclamation Project Act of 4 August 1939, sec. 9(d) (53 Stat. 1187, 1195).

78. See 96 Cong. Rec. 10739 (19 July 1950); 97 Cong. Rec. 8230 (12 July 1951).

79. See Shoshone Irrigation District v. Lincoln Land Co., 51 F(2d) 128 (1930) and Saylor v. Gray, 20 P(2d) 441 (1933).

80. House Public Lands Committee Hearings on H. R. 830, 81st Cong., 1st sess., March 1949, p. 73.

81. Consult Reclamation Project Act of 4 August 1939, sec. 8 (53 Stat. 1187, 1192-1193).

82. U. S. Bureau of Reclamation, Fifty Years of Reclamation, 1952, pp. 5; 32.

83. Report of the Commissioner of Indian Affairs for 1931, p. 18.

84. U. S. Bureau of Indian Affairs, Annual Statement of Costs, Cancellations, and Miscellaneous Irrigation Data of Indian Irrigation Projects For Fiscal Year 1950, p. 1. In his letter of 1 December 1954, Mr. Glenn L. Emmons, Commissioner of the U. S. Bureau of Indian Affairs, advised the author of the following figures: (1) Total construction cost of all Indian irrigation projects as of 30 June 1953, $91,517,616; (2) total construction cost reimbursable as of the same date, $87,369,777; and (3) total construction cost repaid as of the same date, $4,147,839. It should be noted that these figures do not include costs of operation and maintenance. It also seems that costs cancelled are left out.

85. See Bonneville Project Act of 20 August 1937 (50 Stat. 731), Fort Peck Project Act of 18 May 1938 (52 Stat. 403) and sec. 5 of the Flood Control Act of 22 December 1944 (58 Stat. 887, 890).

86. Tennessee Valley Authority Act of 18 May 1933, sec. 14, as a-mended 31 August 1935 (16 U. S. C. 831m): ". . . The surplus power will be sold at rates which . . . will produce gross revenues in excess of the cost of production . . ." (last para., last sent.). It may be noted that since navigation improvement and flood control have never been self-liquidating, any subsidies which power development may give to these pur-poses should be disregarded.

87. The projects of the Bureau of Reclamation here include the irri-gation projects of Bureau of Indian Affairs. It may be noted in projects of the Corps of Engineers which contain both the element of power devel-opment and the element of irrigation, power development still remains to be self-liquidating and will not subsidize irrigation.

88. Under the Boulder Fanyon Project Act of 21 December 1928 (45 Stat. 1057, sec. 2(b)), flood control is reimbursable. This is the only case in the entire Federal water resources administration in which flood control is reimbursable.

89. That navigation improvement and flood control are purely inciden-tal is clear from the provisions of the Reclamation Project Act of 1939. For the incidental nature of non-irrigation water supply, see Act of 25 February 1920 (41 Stat. 451; 43 U. S. C. 521).

90. Consult House Public Lands Committee Hearings on H. R. 830, Etc. 81st Cong., 1st sess., March 1949, p. 51.

91. The generation of hydroelectric power for the exclusive use of irrigation is considered part of irrigation and not a separate function or purpose. See Act of 5 June 1924 (43 Stat. 390, 416).

92. See House Document 172, 79th Cong., 1st sess., a letter of the Secretary of the Interior to the President dated 27 March 1945.

93. For example, Acts of 31 July 1946 (60 Stat. 717), 20 August 1954 (68 Stat. 752).

94. For example, Acts of 29 August 1949 (63 Stat. 677, Weber Basin project, Utah, recreation non-reimbursable) and 29 December 1950 (64 Stat. 1124, Canadian River project, Texas, recreation and silt control, reim-bursable.)

95. For example, in the Act of 29 December 1950, op. cit., flood control and fish and wildlife propagation are to be allocated cost of op-eration and maintenance.

96. See Second Deficiency Appropriation Act of 5 December 1924, sec. 4, subsec. J (43 Stat. 672, 703; 43 U. S. C. 526).

97. For increments to the whole enterprise, see "Reclamation Fund", below. But these increments are not subsidies, but mere advances to the fund.

98. Acts of 16 April 1906, sec. 5 (34 Stat. 116, 117), 18 September 1922 (42 Stat. 847), and 5 December 1924, sec. 4, sebsec. (43 Stat. 672, 703).

99. For the latter project, also see Act of 9 April 1938 (52 Stat. 210).

100. The above-mentioned provision of the Act of 14 August 1946 mak-

ing the preservation and propagation of fish and wildlife a non-reimbursable function does not apply to these projects.

101. U. S. Bureau of Reclamation, Repayment Histories and Repayment Schedules---1952, 1953, p. 3. For highway construction, see Highway Bridge Act of 29 July 1946 (60 Stat. 709).

102. It should always be remarked that a certain facility may be regarded as single-purpose according to one standard or definition, but as multiple-purpose according to another. By the same token, the number of purposes to be included in a multiple-purpose facility varies under different considerations of policy.

103. Federal Power Commission, Opinions and Decisions, vol. 4, p. 970; House Document 709, 75th Cong., 3rd sess., June 1938, pp. 8-20; U. S. Bureau of Reclamation, Central Valley Project Studies, Problems 8-9, 1947, pp. 33-34.

104. The author's own knowledge and observation.

105. House Document 709, 75th Cong., 3rd sess., p. 7.

106. See the various annual reports of the Tennessee Valley Authority.

107. Rpt. T. V. A. 1953, pp. A88; A89.

108. House Document 172, 79th Cong., 1st sess., 1945, pp. 7-22.

109. House Document 146, 80th Cong., 1st sess., 1947, p. 15. Theories (1) and (2) are respectively the alternative justifiable expenditures and the use of facilities theories.

110. House Document 452, 77th Cong., 1st sess., 1941, pp. 22-23. The storages for flood control, irrigation and power are respectively 500,000 acre-feet, 800,000 acre-feet and 120,000 acre-feet, which represent the respective proportions of the use of joint facilities.

111. Federal Power Commission, Opinions and Decisons, vol. 4, pp. 970-972.

112. The report was published by the U. S. Government Printing Office under the title "Proposed Practices For Economic Analysis of River Basin Projects", 85 pp. The recommended method appears on p. 53ff.

113. For the Tennessee River Authority projects, the Board of Directors of the Authority with the approval of the President (Tennessee River Authority Act of 18 May 1933, sec. 14, para. 1: 48 Stat. 58, 66); for projects constructed by the Bureau of Reclamation, the Secretary of the Interior (Boulder Canyon Project Act of 21 December 1928, secs 2(b) and 5: 45 Stat. 1057, 1058) (Reclamation Project Act of 4 August 1939, sec. 9(a) and (b): 53 Stat. 1187, 1194) (subject to consultation with the Chief of Engineers and the Secretary of the Army with respect to flood control and navigation improvement purposes); projects of the Corps of Engineers, the Federal Power Commission (Bonneville Project Act of 20 August 1937, sec. 7: 50 Stat. 731, 735) (Fort Peck Project Act of 18 May 1938, sec. 6: 52 Stat. 403, 405) (Flood Control Act of 22 December 1944, sec. 5: 58 Stat. 887, 890, by implication).

114. Rpt. Chief of E. 1953, pp. 1833-1834.

115. 96 Cong. Rec. A419. Also see Rpt. Sec. Inter. 1951, p. 129.

116. U. S. Department of the Interior, Years of Progress, 1945-1952, p. 36.

117. Rpt. T. V. A. 1953, pp. 24; A7; A10.

118. But the Authority pays low-rate interests on its borrowings from the U. S. Treasury and the Reconstruction Finance Corporation. See House Document 172, 80th Cong., 1st sess., 1947, p. 22

119. Repayment Histories and Payment Schedules - 1952, op. cit., p. 44.

120. Ibid., p. 53.

121. See Act of 28 May 1954 (68 Stat. 143).

122. Repayment Histories and Payment Schedules-1952, op. cit., p. 145.

123. U. S. Department of the Interior, Land of the Free, 1951, p. 4.

124. Statis. Abs. U. S. 1954, pp. 180; 183. For details, see the Statistical Appendixes of the various annual reports of the Bureau of Land Management.

125. See House Hearings on Public Lands Policy, 80th Cong., 1st sess., April-May 1947, p. 16ff.

126. Statis. Abs. U. S. 1954, p. 721.

127. Our National Forests, op. cit., p. 27.

128. From the various annual reports of the Chief of the Forest Service of the U. S. Department of Agriculture.

129. Rpt. Sec. Inter. 1917, p. 804. Consult 16 U. S. C. 3 (Act of 25 August 1916, sec. 3, 39 Stat. 535, as amended).

130. See Rpt. Sec. Inter. 1950, p. 336; House Hearings on Interior Department Appropriations, 83rd Cong., 2nd sess., Part 1, p. 368.

131. House Hearings on Interior Department Appropriations, op. cit., p. 368.

132. Rpt. Chief of E. 1953, p. 2012.

133. Letter to the author from Colonel William J. Ely, Secretary, California Debris Commission, dated 14 January 1955. The cost of operation and maintenance were estimated to be $243,594 for the Englebright and $120,000 for the North Fork project (as of 30 June 1953). -- Ibid.

134. Ibid. Col. Ely advised that the first payment of the debris tax was probably made during 1942. These reservoirs have not been in operation since 1946. See the various annual reports of the Chief of Engineers, U. S. Department of the Army.

135. Slightly amended by an Act of 15 June 1935 (49 Stat. 378). Strictly or narrowly speaking, this is not self-finance, as the income does not originate from the administration of the migratory-bird refuges.

136. From the various annual reports of the Chief of the Soil Con-

servation Service of the U. S. Department of Agriculture.

137. For the recommendation of the Federal Coordinator of Transportation in 1939 for the charge of tolls for new navigation-improvement projects, see Daring and Owen, National Transportation Policy, 1949, pp. 88-89.

138. For the Panama Canal, see Act of 24 August 1912, sec. 5 (37 Stat. 560, 562), as last amended by an Act of 24 August 1937 (50 Stat. 750), and House Hearings on Army Department Civil Functions Appropriations, 83rd Cong., 1st sess., Part 1, pp. 76-77. For the St. Lawrence Seaway, see Act of 13 May 1954, sec. 5 (68 Stat. 92).

139. Rpt. F. P. C. 1953, pp. 202-203.

140. Rpt. T. V. A. 1953, p. 24.

141. Bonneville Project Act of 1937, sec. 11 (50 Stat. 731, 736).

142. River and Harbor Act of 4 March 1913, sec. 8 (37 Stat. 801, 827). For examples of pr4vious special statutory provisions, see River and Harbor Acts of 3 March 1905 (33 Stat. 1117, 1142), 25 June 1910 (36 Stat. 630, 637, 661 and 664) and 4 March 1913 (37 Stat. 801, 812), etc.

143. River and Harbor Act of 4 March 1915, sec. 4 (38 Stat. 1049, 1053).

144. Letter to the author from Mr. H. H. Behlmer, Superintendent, Water Department, City of Fargo, North Dakota, dated 7 March 1952. Consult Rpt. Chief of E. 1952, p. 1225.

145. U. S. Department of the Interior, How Reclamation Pays, 1947, p. 157.

146. U. S. Department of the Interior, Reclamation Data, op. cit., p. 117.

147. Whether a regular irrigation project or a water conservation and utilization project.

148. Acts of 25 July 1947 (61 Stat. 460, 473); 29 June 1948 (62 Stat. 1112, 1126); 12 October 1949 (63 Stat. 765, 779); 6 September 1950 (64 Stat. 679, 685); 31 August 1951 (65 Stat. 248, 255); 9 July 1952 (66 Stat. 445, 450); 31 July 1953 (67 Stat. 261, 265).

149. U. S. Forest Service, National Forest Manual (tentative), 1952, title 9, sec. 202.1. For fish and wildlife management, special regulations were issued by the Secretary of Agriculture on 15 April 1941 (6 F. R. 1988; 34 C. F. R. 241.3(b)).

150. Last amended on 17 February 1950 (15 F. R. 983; 36 C. F. R. 212.4).

151. Such roads and trails are distinct from access roads and trails to national forests.

152. Courtesy of the U. S. Fish and Wildlife Service.

153. See the various annual reports of the Secretary of the Interior. The author gratefully acknowledges the help kindly extended by Mr. William E. Wrather, Director, U. S. Geological Survey, in his letter dat-

ed 1 October 1951.

154. U. S. Department of the Interior, Reclamation Laws, 1943, p. 128.

155. First Deficiency Appropriation Act of 6 February 1931 (46 Stat. 1064, 1069); Act of 1 April 1932, sec. 10 (47 Stat. 75, 78); Act of 3 March 1933, sec. 2 (47 Stat. 1427); Interior Department Appropriation Act of 22 June 1936 (49 Stat. 1757, 1784).

156. See Rpt. Sec. Inter. 1938, p. 59.

157. Rpt. Sec. Inter. 1933, pp. 9-10.

158. Rpt. T. V. A. 1939, p. 129; Rpt. 1940, p. 42; Rpt. 1942, p. 36.

159. Rpt. T. V. A. 1953, p. A4.

160. The Panama Canal bonds, issued by the Department of the Treasury (31 U. S. C. 744-745), are omitted.

161. By financial autonomy it is here meant that moneys can be expended without Congressional appropriation.

162. The water conservation and utilization projects are not financed by the Reclamation Fund.

163. U. S. Department of the Interior, Fifty Years of Reclamation, 1952, p. 32.

164. Consult secs. 1, 2 and 6 of the Reclamation Act of 1902.

165. Fifty Years of Reclamation, op. cit., p. 32.

166. For example, the Grand Coulee, Hungry Horse, Central Valley, Missouri River Basin and the Colorado River (Texas) projects.

167. House Hearings on Interior Department Appropriations For 1953, January 1952, p. 745.

168. Rpt. Sec. Inter. 1953, p. 199.

169. See House Committee On Irrigation and Reclamation Hearings on H. R. 6629, 76th Cong., 1st sess., July 1939, pp. 56-57.

170. Ibid., p. 56. Revenue from the electric energy are derived from the Hoover Dam power plant; and revenues from water are derived from the All-American Canal system.

171. U. S. Department of the Interior, Boulder Canyon Project Final Reports, Part I, Bulletin 1, 1948, p. 57.

172. House Hearings on Interior Department Appropriations For 1955, Part 2, February 1954, p. 926.

173. House Document 717, 80th Cong., 2nd sess. (The Hoover Dam Documents), 1948, p. 47.

174. See the Interior Department Appropriation Act of 6 September 1 1950 (64 Stat. 679, 687).

175. U. S. Department of the Interior, Repayment Histories and Payout Schedules---1952, 1953, p. 29.

176. U. S. Bureau of Reclamation, Eleventh Annual Report, Boulder Canyon Project, 1952, pp. 63-64. That part of the Colorado River Dam Fund advances which are used in the construction of the All-American Canal system is to be repaid by the Imperial Irrigation District, the Coachella Valley County Water District and the City of San Diego, California, under and in accordance with contracts dated respectively 1 December 1932, 15 October 1934 and 2 October 1934. The total value represented by these repayment contracts is $52 million. -- Repayment Histories and Payout Schedules-1952, op. cit., p. 28. It may be noted that $4.5 million of the cost of the All-American Canal system has been allocated to flood control and is non-reimbursable. -- Reclamation Project Data, op. cit., p. 4.

177. These expenditures are of the nature of loans from the fund.

178. Rpt. Sec. Inter. 1953, p. 199.

179. Including expenditures for the education of the dependents of the Federal employees on the project. See the various Interior Department Appropriation Acts.

180. Appropriations for this section are as follows: $100,000, by the Second Deficiency Appropriation Act of 3 July 1930 (46 Stat. 860, 877); $50,000, by the Interior Department Appropriation Act of 14 February 1931 (46 Stat. 1115, 1146); $50,000, by the Interior Department Appropriation Act of 17 February 1933 (47 Stat. 820, 845); and $35,000, by the Second Deficiency Appropriation Act of 12 August 1935 (49 Stat. 571, 598), which totals $235,000.

181. The states of the upper division are Arizona, Colorado, New Mexico, Utah and Wyoming as lie above the Lee Ferry; and the states of the lower division are Arizona, California, Nevada, New Mexico and Utah as lie below the Lee Ferry. -- Colorado River Compact, art. II.

182. Adjustment Act of 1940, sec. 2(d), as amended by Act of 1 June 1948, sec. 1 (62 Stat. 284).

183. See House Report 2328, 76th Cong., 3rd sess., 28 May 1940. p.11.

184. The construction cost of the initial works of the Upper Colorado River Basin project is estimated to be $2,331,939,800 (comprising $848,671,800 for the fifteen participating projects, the former being in general revenue-making and capable of subsidizing the latter). -- Senate Report 1983, 83rd Cong., 2nd sess., 26 July 1954.

185. Senate Report 1983, 83rd Cong., op. cit.; House Document 364, 83rd Cong., 2nd sess., April 1954, pp. 1, 75-76, 174-175.

186. The author favors (1) the enlargement of the Colorado River Development Fund, or (2) its splitting into an Upper Colorado River Development Fund and a Lower Colorado River Development Fund, or (3) its merger with the Reclamation Fund.

187. First Supplemental National Defense Appropriation Act of 23 December 1944 (57 Stat. 611, 621); as amended by the Interior Department Appropriation Acts of 12 October 1949 (63 Stat. 765, 767) and 31 August 1951 (65 Stat. 248, 249). The amount of this fund is $300,000.

188. Interior Department Appropriation Act of 31 August 1951 (65 Stat. 248, 249). The amount of the fund is $50,000.

189. No emergency fund has been created out of the Colorado River Dam Fund, but the said Fund has the combined functions of both an enterprise and an emergency fund. (In theory, no separate emergency fund need be created out of a complete enterprise fund.)

190. The Army Department Civil Functions Appropriation Act of 27 July 1953 created the Corps of Engineers' Civil Functions Revolving Fund in the amount of $140 million (67 Stat. 197, 199). But this fund is not used for direct water resources administration.

191. According to sec. 7 of the Project Act, the net proceeds from any power development that may be made on the All-American Canal should be covered into the Colorado River Dam Fund, but they are to be credited to the parties, which are responsible for the repayment of the costs of the All-American Canal system in accordance with the reclamation laws.

192. According to the Project Act, the interest was at the rate of 4 percent per year. It was reduced by the Adjustment Act (sec. 6) to 3 percent per year. But interest is not to be charged on the $25,000,000 allocated to flood control. The Interior Department Appropriation Act of 29 June 1948 designated all costs incurred for the construction, acquisition and maintenance of facilities in the Boulder City, Nevada other than school facilities as "non-project costs" (62 Stat. 1112, 1130). However, "there has been no reduction granted by the United States Treasury to the project in the amounts required for the payment of interest on advances used to construct non-project works." -- Eleventh Annual Report, Boulder Canyon Project, op. cit., p. 6.

193. 1937-1987.

194. Compare the fund set up by an Act of 2 September 1937 (50 Stat. 917), which is not used to finance Federal Administration.

195. Since the enactment of this Act, some of listed trust funds have been abolished (only one of which was abolished by a special Act -- see Act of 15 June 1943, 57 Stat. 152) and some combined. -- Letter to th3 author from Mr. Gilbert L, Cake, Acting Commissioner, Bureau of Accounts, U. S. Department of the Treasury, dated 12 November 1954.

196. Payments to states and local units by the Federal Government in lieu of property taxes in Federal water resources administration are omitted, because they do not constitute a specific financial source of state and local water resources administration. The Federal Government pays to each public-land state five percent of the proceeds of the sales of public land and materials thereon within its boundaries (to be used for education, road construction and other public improvements). For other Federal payments in lieu of taxes, see Act of 23 May 1908 (35 Stat. 251, 260) as last amended by Act of 21 September 1944, sec. 212 (58 Stat. 734, 737); Act of 1 March 1911, sec. 13 (961,963) and Act of 20 June 1910, secs. 6 and 24 (36 Stat. 557, 561 and 573) (national forests); the Mineral Leasing Act of 25 February 1920, sec. 35 (41 Stat. 437, 450); the Federal Water Power Act of 10 June 1920, sec. 17(a) (41 Stat. 1063, 1072); Act of 13 July 1926 (44 Stat. 915) (O and C lands); the Tennessee Valley Authority Act of 18 May 1933, sec. 13 (48 Stat. 58, 66), as amended by the Joint Resolution of 26 June 1940, sec. 39 (54 Stat. 611, 626); the Grazing Act of 28 June 1934, sec. 10 (48 Stat. 1269, 1273), as amended by an Act of 26 June 1936, sec. 4 (49 Stat. 1976, 1978); Act of 15 June 1935, sec. 401 (49 Stat. 378, 383) (Federal wildlife refuges); the Farm Tenant

Act of 22 June 1937, sec. 33 (50 Stat. 522, 526) (retirement of submarginal lands). Seventy-five percent of the revenues from the leases of recreational facilities on reservoirs controlled by the Department of the Army are paid to counties concerned for expenditure on county schools and roads. See House Hearings on Civil Functions Appropriations for 1953, January 1952, pp. 237-238.

197. Based on a great number of laws and reports.

198. South Carolina State Commission of Forestry, Annual Report 1952, p. 119.

199. Missouri Conservation Commission, Annual Report 1952, p. 59.

200. Vermont Forest Service, Biennial Report 1951-1952, p. 49. The figure $185,583.84 is obtained by subtracting $131,692.15 from $317,275.-99.

201. Under Massachusetts law, all receipts of the Division of Forestry should be paid into the general fund (General Laws, ch. 132, sec. 34A: Acts 1923, ch. 288, sec. 3; as last amended by Acts 1947, ch. 366). It is presumed that these receipts cannot meet all the expenses of the Division.

202. Fallbrook Irrigation District v. Bradley, 164 U. S. 112, 176-177 (1896).

203. Including the Public Drainage Associations of Maryland. -- Code, Art. 25, secs. 77 (L. 1941, ch. 261, sec. 67) and 78 (L. 1949, ch. 71, sec. 67A).

204. Consult State Constitution of 1921, art. 10, sec. 10, para. 1 (as last amended 1950).

205. In Oregon only tax-delinquent lands are to be designated as county parks or county forests and the statute has not provided any means of financing county parks in addition to the collection of charges. Surtaxes are usually supplementary to appropriations from the general funds.

206. County appropriations are in the nature of contributions to the state government.

207. Consult the Opinions of the Attorney General of the State of Mississippi for 1931-1933, p. 122.

208. However, of the 0.8 mills, 0.125 mills are to be used for the payment of bounties, which is a county activity. -- L. 1951, ch. 482, sec. 1.

209. The Municipal Yearbook of 1950, pp. 329-335.

210. National Park Service, State Park Statistics, July 1951, p. 3. The statistics covers less than 40 states.

211. National Recreation Association, Recreation and Park Yearbook of 1950, 1951, p. 22. The figures are for 1950 and cover county and city parks and park districts.

212. Letter from Mr. Carl I. Peterson, State Forester, Tennessee Department of Conservation, dated 29 March 1954.

213. South Dakota Department of Game, **Fish** and Parks, <u>Annual Report</u> <u>1953</u>, page 85 (emphasis added).

214. South Carolina State Commission of Forestry, <u>Annual Report</u> <u>1952</u>, pp. 119-120.

215. Vermont Forest Service, <u>Biennial Report 1951-1952</u>, p. 49.

216. See, for example, Revised Laws of New Hampshire, ch. 233, sec. 31 (L. 1909, ch. 128, sec. 10; as last amended by L. 1953, ch. 187); <u>Georgia Code</u>, sec. 43-249 (Acts 1937, No. 103, sec. 9, subsec. 1, subdivision (b)); and <u>General Statutes of Connecticut</u>, sec. 3495 (1943).

217. Washington State Parks and Recreation Commission, <u>Annual Report</u> <u>1950</u>, p. 16. See Laws 1937, chs. 53, 187 and 189; and L. 1949, ch. 52.

218. National Park Service, <u>A Study of the Park and Recreation Problems in the United States</u>, 1941, p. 95.

219. <u>California Fish and Game Program</u>, 15 May 1950, <u>op. cit.</u>, Forward, 1st sentence.

220. Multiple-purpose projects are not regarded as examples of administrative grafting, even one purpose of a project subsidizes the other purpose or purposes; for the various purposes are technically "inseparable".

221. Ohio Department of Natural Resources, <u>Annual Report 1953</u>, p.28. It may be noted that the Federal Aid to Wildlife Restoration Act of 2 September 1937 (50 Stat. 917) expressly requires (sec. 1) the states which accept the aid to pass laws prohibiting the diversion of hunting-license fees (but not fishing license fees and other revenues of the state game and fish agencies) for any other purpose than the administration of fish and game resources. For instances in which moneys from the general fund are appropriated to the fish and game agency for projects or activities not directly related to fish and game administration, see Laws of Delaware of 1953, ch. 336; Laws of Oklahoma of 1953, p. 120.

222. <u>A Study of the Park and Recreation Problems in the United States</u>, op. cit., p. 95. Under a law of 1953 (ch. 28340), "the boards of county commissioners in all counties in Florida having a population of not more than 18,600 or less than 18,300 . . . are authorized to expend county road and bridge fund for the acquisition, construction and maintenance of county public parks."

223. See <u>Hist. Statis. U. S., 1949</u>, p. 316; <u>Statis. Abs. U. S. 1952</u>, pp. 368; 997. The figures may include some Federal grants.

224. See U. S. Bureau of the Census, <u>Compendium of State Government Finances in 1948</u>, p. 6; <u>Compendium of State Government Finances in 1950</u>, p. 6.

225. See, for example, Acts of 26 February 1857 (11 Stat. 166, 167, for Minnesota); 14 February 1859 (11 Stat. 383, 384, for Oregon); 29 January 1861 (12 Stat. 126, 127, for Kansas); 3 March 1875 (18 Stat. 474, 476, for Colorado).

226. Federal Works Agency, <u>Final Statistical Report of the Federal Emergency Administration</u>, 1942, pp. 3-4.

227. Federal Works Agency, <u>Final Report of the WPA Program, 1935-</u>

-1943, 1946, pp. 7-8.

228. Final Statistical Report of the Federal Emergency Relief Administration, op. cit., pp. 101; 103.

229. Ibid., pp. 53-54; 104.

230. Ibid., pp. 79; 104. For the Civil Works Program, consult Final Report of the WPA, op. cit., pp. 3-4.

231. For the history of the agency, see U. S. Government Organization Manual 1954-55, p. 618; Act of 30 June 1944 (58 Stat. 169, 180) and the Report of the Federal Works Administration for 1944, p. 33.

232. See Public Works Administration Appropriation Act of 1938 (being Title II of the Joint Resolution of 21 June 1938), sec. 201(d) (52 Stat. 816).

233. Annual Report of the Federal Works Agency for 1940 (Rpt. FWA 1940), p. 132.

234. Rpt. FWA 1942, 128; 131. No grants were made after 30 June 1942.

235. Grants were also possible under sec. 2 of the (Weeks) Act of 1 March 1911 (36 Stat. 961). However, as a matter of fact, Federal funds provided by this provision were actually used in the employment of watchmen and patrolmen by the Federal Government itself.

236. Letter to the author from Mr. A. R. Spillers, Chief, Division of Cooperative Forest Management, U. S. Forest Service, dated 13 March 1952.

237. Statis. Abs. U. S. 1952, p. 668; His. Statis. U. S., p. 127.

238. Rpt. Chief Forest Service 1951, p. 13.

239. Statis. Abs. U. S. 1952, p. 665.

240. U. S. Department of Agriculture, Report of Cooperative Extension Work for 1929, p. 122; Rpt. 1934, p. 73; Rpt. 1941, p. 60; Rpt. 1947, p. 42; Rpt. 1953, pp. 44-45.

241. Administrative Procedures For Cooperative Forest Management Act of 1950, op. cit., p. 5.

242. Agricultural Statistics 1953, p. 704. The Cooperative Forest Management Act began to take effect on 1 July 1951. -- Report of the Chief of Forest Service for 1951, p. 54.

243. The various annual reports of the Secretary of the Interior; House Hearings on Interior Department Appropriation Bills for fiscal year 1955; and the various annual reports of the Secretary of the Treasury.

244. Annual reports of the Secretary of the Interior for 1951-1953; House Hearings on Interior Department Appropriations for 1955, January 1954, p. 206.

245. Amended by an Act of 14 March 1826 (4 Stat. 149), to the effect that three-fifths of the grant may be used for the improvement of navigable rivers and bays.

246. The Colorado admission legislation was amended by an Act of 3 March 1875 (18 Stat. 474, 476), which provided that the grant was to be used for internal improvements.

247. Federal works Agency, Report for 1949 (mimeo.), p. 113. It is not known whether these grants include contributions. Special figures for water supply, sewerage and recreational facilities are not available. Also unknown are data for fiscal year 1950 and subsequent fiscal years.

248. Consult Executive Order No. 10296 dated 2 October 1951.

249. Housing and Home Finance Agency, Annual Report for 1953, pp. 48-49.

250. Consult the Act of 26 June 1936 (49 Stat. 1982), as discussed before.

251. See the various annual reports of the Chief of Engineers, U. S. Army.

252. See Reorganization Plan No. 16 of 24 May 1950 (64 Stat. 1268) for change of administrative agencies.

253. Annual reports of the Secretary of the Treasury for the fiscal years 1951-1953. Also consult the annual reports of the U. S. Public Health Service for the fiscal years 1949-1953. The figures given here are subject to possible correction.

254. Ibid. The $1,093,193 expended in the fiscal year 1953 for grants to states and local units "for the construction of community facil-ities" were seemingly made under the above-mentioned sec. 304 of the De-fense Housing and Community Facilities and Services Act of 1951.

255. House Hearings on Public Lands Policy, 80th Cong., 1st sess., April-May 1947, pp. 36-37.

256. Letter to the author from Mr. Wilbur A. Rush, Chief, Division of Lands and Waters, Iowa State Conservation Commission, dated 27 April 1954.

257. Huron-Clinton Metropolitan Authority, Fifth Biennial Report, 1950-1951, p. 48.

258. Letter to the author from Mr. J. A. Wymore, Assistant Engineer, Iowa State Conservation Commission, dated 4 May 1954. Also see Iowa State Conservation Commission, Biennial Report for the biennium ending 30 June 1952, p. 30.

259. U. S. Corps of Engineers, South Pacific Division, Civil Works By The Corps of Engineers in California (mimeo.), March 1952, p. 34; House Public Works Committee Hearings on H. R. 183, Etc., 83rd Cong., 1st Sess., April-July 1953, p. 28ff.

260. See, for example, House Document 426, 77th Cong.; House Docu-ment 892, 77th Cong., p. 33; House Document 563, 78th Cong., p. 39.

261. 96 Cong. Rec. 13000.

262. Based on the reading of a vast amount of informational material.

263. Letter to the author from Mr. D. F. Herrick, Executive Director,

American Public Works Association, dated 1 August 1951.

264. National Recreation Association, Recreation and Park Yearbook of 1950, 1951, p. 22.

265. See Virginia Acts of 1946, ch. 387; Kentucky Acts of 1948, ch. 227; Arkansas Acts of 1953, No. 42, sec. 5(h); West Virginia Laws of 1953, ch. 110, etc.

266. See South Carolina Acts of 1942, No. 626; Georgia Laws of 1945, No. 422 (as amended by L. 1949, No. 174); North Carolina Laws of 1945, ch. 1097 (as last amended by L. 1953, ch. 191); Alabama Acts of 1947, No. 211; and laws cited at p. 665, above.

267. See Montana Laws of 1935, ch. 96, sec. 8 (Water Conservation Board); Ohio Laws of 1940, p. 98 (Division of Water, Department of Natural Resources); California Water Code, secs. 11553, 11700 (1943; as amended by Stats. 1951, ch. 144, sec. 3) (Water Project Authority).

268. Tax-anticipation bonds of a special district are general-obligation bonds of the district but they are bonds in anticipation of special taxes from the standpoint of the tax-payers.

269. Statutory citations, which appear in the discussion of the county and municipal enterprises, are not reiterated. (A nearly complete discussion is made in this Section of state and **municipal bonds**).

270. See New Jersey Statutes, tit. 40, sec. 179-21 et seq. (L. 1905, ch. 244); Revised Civil Statutes of Texas, arts. 803 (L. 1923, ch. 128) and 6830 (L. 1901, 1st S. S., p. 23; as last amended by L. 1925, ch. 96); Constitution of Georgia, art. 7, sec. 7, para. 1 (2 November 1926); Code of Tennessee, tit. IX, ch. 4A (Acts 1935, ch. 32); Laws of Delaware of 1949, chs. 38 and 39; Laws of Mississippi of 1952, ch. 214 (consulting Laws 1924, ch. 319); General Statutes of North Carolina, sec. 153-77 (L. 1927, ch. 81, sec. 8(g)); North Dakota Revised Code, secs. 61-1237 and 61-1244 (L. 1919, ch. 116, secs. 22 and 23, as amended by L. 1935, ch. 160, sec. 5) (interest only, principal being in anticipation of special benefit assessments), etc.

271. See Code of Virginia, sec. 15-609 (Acts 1940, ch. 386); Kentucky Revised Statutes, secs. 104.090 and 104.100 (Acts 1946, ch. 226, secs. 8 and 9), etc.

272. See Compiled Laws of Michigan, secs. 123.201 (Acts 1931, No. 316, sec. 1) and 123.241 et seq. (Acts 1927, No. 320); General Statutes of Connecticut, sec. 4048 (1939); Colorado Statutes, ch. 163, sec. 27(3) (L. 1949, ch. 244, sec. 3); General Statutes of North Carolina, ch. 160, art. 34A (L. 1949, ch. 1213; as amended by L. 1951, ch. 941); etc.

273. See Florida Statutes, sec. 184.03 (L. 1951, ch. 26919, sec. 3); Revised Statutes of Nebraska, sec. 18-501 et seq. (L. 1933, ch. 146; as last amended by L. 1951, ch. 19); North Dakota Revised Code, ch. 40-34 (L. 1933, ch. 179; as amended by L. 1935, ch. 202); Acts of Virginia of 1950, ch. 593, etc.

274. See Ohio Revised Code, sec. 729.40 (L. 1904, p. 51; as amended by L. 1933, p. 151), in anticipation of special taxes; Idaho Code, sec. 50-3222 et seq. (L. 1905, p. 334, sec. 12), etc.

275. See, for example, Wisconsin Statutes, sec. 66.066 (L. 1895, ch. 182; as last amended by L. 1947, ch. 362); Revised Statutes of Nebraska, sec. 16-601 et seq. (L. 1901, ch. 18, sec. 50 et seq.; as last amended

by L. 1951, ch. 26); <u>Arizona Code</u>, sec. 16-602 (L. 1921, ch. 31; as a-
mended by L. 1933, ch. 77, sec. 1); <u>Revised Statutes of Louisiana</u>, tit.
39, sec. 553 et seq. (Acts 1921, Ex. Sess., No. 46, sec. 7 et seq.; as
last amended by Acts 1928, No. 239, sec. 1); <u>Revised Codes of Montana</u>,
sec. 11-966 (<u>Revised Code of 1921</u>, sec. 5039, subsec. 64; as last amended by L. 1953, ch. 152, sec. 1); <u>Colorado Statutes</u>, ch. 137, secs. 37 (L.
1927, ch. 192, secs. 1-2) and 3 (L. 1913, ch. 127, sec. 3; as amended by
L. 1947, ch. 253, sec. 1); <u>Ohio Revised Code</u>, sec. 133.24 (L. 1927, p.
365; as amended by L. 1933, p. 52); <u>South Carolina Code of Laws</u>, sec. 59-
361 et seq. (Acts 1933, No. 299; as last amended by Acts 1951, No. 124);
<u>Mississippi Code</u>, sec. 3538 et seq. (L. 1934, ch. 317; as last amended
by L. 1942, ch. 231); <u>Florida Statutes</u>, secs. 180.6 and 180.8 (L. 1935,
ch. 17118, secs. 3 and 5); <u>New York General Municipal Law</u>, sec. 400 et
seq. (L. 1935, ch. 525; as last amended by L. 1945, ch. 838, sec. 35);
<u>West Virginia Code</u>, sec. 510(1) et seq. (L. 1935, ch. 68; as amended by
L. 1945, ch. 90); <u>North Dakota Revised Code</u>, ch. 40-35 (L. 1937, ch. 104);
<u>Oregon Revised Statutes</u>, sec. 287.302 et seq. (L. 1937, ch. 443); <u>General
Statutes of North Carolina</u>, ch. 160, art. 34 (L. 1938, Ex. Sess., ch. 2;
as last amended by L. 1953, ch. 922); <u>Pennsylvania Statutes</u> tit. 53, sec.
2011.601 (L. 1941, No. 87, sec. 601); <u>Missouri Statutes</u>, sec. 74.400 (L.
1949, p. 482, sec. 239); <u>Revised Statutes of Maine</u>, ch. sec. 153 et seq.
(1. 1953, ch. 421).

276. Wisconsin, South Carolina, Mississippi, Florida, New York, West
Virginia, North Dakota, Oregon, North Carolina, Maine. Oregon municipal
bonds are re-financing bonds.

277. It may be noted that while at the local level only the governing bodies may issue bonds state bonds in the various fields of water resources administration are issued by the responsible state agencies concerned. Bonds of special districts have already been discussed and are
not repeated.

178. In Louisiana, under a law of 1944 (Acts 1944, No. 286), all local bond issues must be approved by the State Bond and Tax Board, which
is composed of the governor (chairman), the secretary of state, the attorney general, the supervisor of public funds and an appointee of the governor (secretary). Such additional limitation may be considered an exception.

279. In Washington, the maximum indebtedness of an irrigation district "shall not exceed one dollar per acre of the total irrigable area
within the district" (<u>Revised Code</u>, sec. 87.01.220: L. 1921, ch. 129, sec.
25; as superseded by L. 1953, ch. 108) (in para. 3).

280. Said authority to make loans was terminated by sec. 301 of the
National Industrial Recovery Act of 16 June 1933 (48 Stat. 195, 210).

281. See Reconstruction Finance Corporation, <u>Annual Report and Financial Statements For 1951</u>, p. 14; <u>Rpt. 1952</u>, p. 12; <u>Rpt. 1953</u>, p. 10.

282. The present Small Business Administration does not make any
loans to public agencies. -- Letter to the author from Mr. Norbert Engles,
deputy Administrator, Small Business Administration, dated 25 April 1955.

283. Federal Works Agency, <u>Annual Report for 1940</u>, p. 132.

284. Federal Works Agency, <u>Annual Report for 1942</u>, p. 128. No such
loans have been made since that date.

285. General Services Administration, Report July-December 1949, p. 50.

286. General Services Administration, Report for 1952, p. 101.

287. General Services Administration, Report for 1951, p. 98.

288. General Services Administration, Report for 1952, p. 103.

289. Rpt. T. V. A. 1945, p. 67.

290. U. S. Rural Electrification Administration Monthly Statistical Bulletin, No. 166, February 1955.

291. Federal Works Agency, Annual Report For 1949 (mimeo.), p. 113.

292. Federal Housing and Home Finance Agency, Annual Report for 1953, pp. 48-49.

293. The amounts of loans in the field of water resources administration are unknown.

294. See the various annual reports of the Federal Works Agency, General Services Administration and Public Health Service.

295. Letter to the author from Mr. J. E. Pitts, Jr., Comptroller, U. S. Farm Credit Administration, dated 20 April 1955.

296. U. S. Budget For 1950-1951, p. 597.

297. Compare this loan program with the above-mentioned electric transmission loan program of the Tennessee Valley Authority. Both operate on a regional basis.

298. Washington Department of Conservation and Development, 16th Biennial Report, p. 11 (table 2).

299. Special funds at the local level are omitted.

300. For example, "state game fund" in Florida (Statutes, sec. 372.-09: L. 1929, ch. 13644, sec. 13; as last amended by L. 1951, ch. 26766, sec. 5); "State Game and Fish Commission Fund" in Georgia (Code, sec. 45-144: Acts 1943, No. 30, sec. 1); "Inland Fisheries and Game Fund" in Massachusetts (General Laws, ch. 131, sec. 3A: Acts 1945, ch. 548, sec.1), etc. No special name in Delaware and Missouri.

301. Kentucky Revised Statutes sec. 150.150 (Acts 1942, ch. 68, s sec. 15); Alabama Code, tit. 8, sec. 20 (Acts 1939, No.523).

302. For examples, see Wisconsin Statutes, sec. 25.30 (L. 1925, ch. 129; as last amended by L. 1953, ch. 425, sec. 1); California Public Resources Code, sec. 4382 (Stats. 1939, ch. 100, sec. 1); Revised Laws of Nebraska, ch. 234, sec. 14 (L. 1911, ch. 166, sec. 1; as amended by L. 1937, ch. 151, sec. 8); Illinois Statutes, ch. 57.5, sec. 27a (L. 1939, p. 674; as amended by L. 1943, vol. 1, p. 791); General Statutes of North Carolina, sec. 113-36 (L. 1915, ch. 253, sec. 2; as amended by L. 1925, ch. 122, sec. 22, no special name); Vermont Statutes, sec. 7053 (L. 1937, No. 96, sec. 2), etc.

303. The "forest fund" of Minnesota is also a fiscal fund. It is

made up of the receipts of the state forests. One-half of the fund is distributed among the counties in which the state forests are situated, and one-half covered into the general fund. -- _Statutes_, sec. 89.035 et seq. (L. 1943, ch. 171, sec. 6 et seq.).

304. South Dakota Department of Game, Fish and Parks, _Annual Report For 1953_, p. 85.

305. Missouri is an exception.

306. Minnesota is an exception ("Annually, . . . the unencumbered balance in excess of $30,000 shall be cancelled into the general revenue fund").

307. This fund is necessarily autonomous, since the moneys have already been appropriated by the state legislature

308. Compare Laws of Montana of 1951, ch. 148.

309. Sinking funds for the redemption of bonds are not regarded as special funds as defined in this Subsection.

310. It should be pointed, however, that an interstate agency is not necessarily necessitated by interstate administration, and that interstate administration does not necessarily require interstate organization.

311. For examples, see the Rio Grande Compact of 31 May 1939 (53 Stat. 785, 791), the Pecos River Compact of 9 June 1949 (63 Stat. 159, 162), the Yellowstone River Compact of 30 October 1951 (65 Stat. 665), and the Canadian River Compact of 17 May 1952 (66 Stat. 74). All these compacts have adopted complicated formulae for the apportionment of interstate rivers among the member-states.

312. Frederick L. Bird, _A Study of the Port of New York Authority, 1949_, p. 69.

313. Commissioners of the Palisades Interstate Park, _The Palisades Interstate Park, 1900-1929_, pp. 28-32.

314. See, for example, Port of New York Authority Compact of 1921, art. IV; Missouri-Illinois Bi-State Development Agency Compact of 31 August 1950, Art. III, para. 4 (64 Stat. 568, 569); New Jersey-Pennsylvania Supplemental Compact Concerning the Delaware River Port Authority of 17 July 1952, art. IV, para.(j) (66 Stat. 738, 741; also see agreement of 1931, art. IV); the Breaks Interstate Park Compact (Kentucky and Virginia) of 27 July 1954, art. VI (68 Stat. 571, 572).